INTERNATIONAL HUMAN RIGHTS

Text and Materials

PHILIP ALSTON

*John Norton Pomeroy Professor of Law at
New York University School of Law*

1

Citation. Philip Alston, *International Human Rights* (New York, NYU Law, 2024).

ISBN. 9798335680240 (Part II Sections D, E &F)
Imprint. Independently published.

www.humanrightstextbook.org

PREFACE

This is a substantially revised edition of a human rights textbook newly-designed to be accessible to all, both in whole, or in its various parts, everywhere in the world. It is presented free of charge for all users, including students, teachers, activists and practitioners, and will be updated on an annual basis. It is also available in a hard copy, print-on-demand format priced at cost, to ensure affordability. The author aims to update the materials annually to ensure that they are timely and reflect key current developments.

This book is a successor to previous volumes entitled *International Human Rights in Context* (1996, 2000 and 2008) and *International Human Rights: Text and Materials* (2013). All four volumes were published by Oxford University Press. After lengthy discussions, the Press generously agreed to revert all rights to the author in order to enable this Open Access publication.

While I was a co-author for all of these editions, the lead author for the first three was Professor Henry Steiner, who founded Harvard Law School's Human Rights Program in 1984 and directed it until 2005. Henry was the driving force behind those three volumes, and they stand as a tribute to his depth of understanding, his endlessly probing intellect and his vision of how human rights should be taught. The 2008 and 2013 editions were also jointly authored with Professor Ryan Goodman whose major contributions continue to be reflected in this new edition. I am deeply grateful to both Henry and Ryan for their expertise, insights, friendship, and support.

Basic purposes

Almost eight decades after the human rights regime began to emerge out of the disasters of the Second World War, human rights norms and institutions deeply inform the rhetoric, practice and theory of international law and politics, as well as the internal constitutional structures of many states. Although the frailties and shortcomings of human rights as an ideal, an ideology or practice are all too evident today, the concept of human rights has become a part of modern consciousness, a lens through which to see the world and a universal if inevitably contested discourse. The course book uses the term 'human rights regime' to include post-1945 governmental, intergovernmental and nongovernmental institutions and practices in both national and international contexts in the recognition and protection of human rights.

Although the human rights regime now forms an indelible part of our legal, political and moral landscape, and indeed perhaps precisely because of that status, recent years have witnessed some of the deepest challenges to the foundations upon which the regime has been built, its aspirations to universality, and its claims of growing success in spreading and realizing its message. In response to these challenges, the book seeks to examine the regime's failures as well as triumphs and dilemmas in seeking to achieve human rights ideals across the world's many histories and cultures.

The book aims to enable readers to see the 'big picture', to understand the history, doctrine and institutional structures of the regime, and above all, to think critically about the subject. The book seeks to describe, analyze, criticize and propose, by drawing from a diverse range of political, cultural, moral and geopolitical perspectives. It tries not to impose any single dogma, direction or method for thinking about the history or the future of human rights.

Principal features of the book

The conceptual framework for the book consists, in sequence, of the historical development and character of human rights discourse and basic norms; the dilemmas of rights and duties, and of universalism and cultural relativism; the architecture of international institutions as well as their functions, powers and interplay with norms; and the interaction of states with international law and organizations as well as with each other. Certain major themes run through the different parts of the book — for example, the colonial and imperial objectives often pursued in the name of human rights, evolving notions of autonomy and sovereignty, the changing configuration of the public-private divide in human rights ordering, the escalating tensions between international human rights and national security, and the striking evolution of ideas about the nature and purposes of the regime itself.

The book emphasizes the *international dimensions* of the human rights system, while also exploring the vital relationships between that system and states' internal orders. It provides more than a doctrinal understanding of human rights, particularly by including materials from a range of disciplines other than law. For those who do not have any background knowledge of international law, the first two or three chapters provide an introduction to basic concepts, sources, processes and norms of that field.

Practical details on materials

Most of the materials have been sharply edited in order to make them as compact as possible. Omissions (except for footnotes) are indicated by the conventional use of ellipses. Retained footnotes are renumbered within the consecutive footnote numbering of each chapter. When a final page number is not available for a publication, these materials list it as 000. The book uses British rather than American spelling, primarily because previous editions were published in the United Kingdom.

The choice of materials, and particularly the length of excerpts, is significantly dependent on the willingness of publishers to grant permission. Some publishers refuse to participate in any Open Access work available free online, others require exorbitant fees which cannot be accommodated in an enterprise that generates no royalties.

Acknowledgements

Many people have helped to shape this book. In addition to Henry Steiner and Ryan Goodman, successive generations of students have been sharp and discerning critics. Various research assistants have made invaluable contributions over the years to the course from which the book draws. For assistance in the preparation of this edition, I am especially grateful to Lucy Forbes, Katarina Sydow, Jackson Gandour, Brianne Cuffe, Matthew Scarfo, and Youssef Farhat. Among my academic colleagues, Hélène Tigroudja was extraordinarily generous and wise with her advice, and Fionnuala Ní Aoláin, Steven Ratner and César Rodriguez-Garavito provided very helpful comments. Sally Engle Merry offered important guidance. Gráinne de Búrca was a constant and indispensable source of advice, inspiration and support.

Philip Alston
New York University School of Law, July 2024

Table of Contents

PART D: INTERNATIONAL AND REGIONAL HUMAN RIGHTS ORGANIZATIONS

Chapter 8. The United Nations Human Rights System

This chapter explores the complex and often confusing set of institutional arrangements that make up the United Nations human rights system. It places particular emphasis on the role played by the UN Human Rights Council, set up in 2006 as the direct successor to the UN Commission on Human Rights which first met in 1946. Other UN organs of major importance include the Security Council and the General Assembly. Individual office-holders, such as the UN Secretary-General and the UN High Commissioner for Human Rights, also play central roles.

The chapter starts with a brief overview of the different UN organs, before considering how the Human Rights Council performs its principal functions: responding to violations, setting human rights standards, dealing with complaints against states, and monitoring states' compliance with their obligations. It then looks at the roles played by the High Commissioner and the Security Council.

In considering the work of these institutions, it is necessary to keep in mind two crucial sets of issues that are implicated, in different ways, at almost every turn. The doctrinal issues concern the relationship between notions of state sovereignty and human rights, and the closely related challenge of determining the extent of a state's domestic jurisdiction. The policy-related issues concern the extent to which we would like to see the international community 'enforcing' human rights in concrete situations.

SOVEREIGNTY AND DOMESTIC JURISDICTION

The complex and unresolved relationship between the sovereignty of states and their obligations to respect human rights is nowhere better exemplified than in the UN Charter. Article 1(3) lists one of the purposes of the UN as being 'to achieve international cooperation ... in promoting and encouraging respect for human rights'. And Article 55(c) tasks the UN with promoting 'universal respect for, and observance of, human rights'. Article 2(7), on the other hand, reassures governments that nothing in the Charter 'shall authorize the United Nations to intervene in matters which are essentially within the domestic jurisdiction of any State', with the sole exception of binding measures prescribed by the Security Council. While the two sets of provisions are not directly contradictory, they clearly raise and leave unresolved the question of how far the UN and other states can go in insisting upon respect for human rights, while respecting sovereignty and not interfering in the internal affairs of a state.

The past three decades have seen dramatic changes in the weight attached to sovereignty by governments. In 1991, at the end of the Cold War, 35 states from eastern and western Europe as well as North America, adopted a statement in which they 'categorically and irrevocably declare[d] that the commitments undertaken [in relation to human rights, democracy and the rule of law] are matters of direct and legitimate concern to all participating States and do not belong exclusively to the internal affairs of the State concerned.'[275] This was followed by efforts in the early 2000s to promote the doctrine of the 'responsibility to protect' (R2P) which is discussed in Sec. D, below.

But, in recent years, the pendulum has swung in the opposite direction with major states proclaiming the centrality of sovereignty. On 25 June 2016, Russia and China adopted a joint Declaration on the Promotion of International Law stating that 'the principle of sovereign equality is crucial' and affirming their full support for 'the principle of non-intervention in the internal or external affairs of States'. And when foreign governments criticized China's suppression of the Hong Kong democracy movement in March 2021, the Chinese Ambassador in Geneva characterized their approach as a 'plot', 'in the name of human rights ... to interfere in China's internal affairs'. U.S. President, Donald Trump, told the UN General Assembly on 25 September 2019:

> If you want freedom, take pride in your country. If you want democracy, hold on to your sovereignty. And if you want peace, love your nation. Wise leaders always put the good of their own people and their own country first. The future does not belong to globalists. The future belongs to patriots. The future belongs to sovereign and independent nations

---

[275] 30 *Int'l Leg. Mat.* (1991) 1670, at 1672.

who protect their citizens, respect their neighbors, and honor the differences that make each country special and unique.

These issues arise throughout the book. The introduction to international law considered the clash between international regulation and national governments' internal control of their polity — cases *like Chattin or Minority Schools in Albania*, for example. States' arguments based on sovereignty provided a counterpoint in Chapter 3 to the description of the growth of the human rights regime. States' claims based on notions of cultural relativism in Chapters 6 and 7 often spoke the language of autonomy and sovereign independence. And subsequent chapters, whether addressing the limits of the reach of the European Court of Human Rights, or the international community's response to massive tragedies, also raise the same themes.

Consider at the outset brief comments of several scholars about the meaning of this notion in contemporary international law and argument. James Crawford considers the category of domestic jurisdiction to be primarily 'a source of confusion'.[276] Similarly, Martti Koskenniemi[277] observes that it is 'notoriously difficult to pin down the meaning of sovereignty', but that nonetheless the literature characteristically starts with a definition. Usually the concept is connected with ideas of independence (external sovereignty) and self-determination (internal sovereignty). He quotes a classic definition in an arbitral decision to the effect that sovereignty 'in the relations between States signifies independence: independence in regard to a portion of the globe is the right to exercise therein, to the exclusion of any other States, the functions of a State.' Sovereignty thus implies freedom of action by a state.

If, argues Koskenniemi, this or any agreed-on definition of sovereignty had a clear, ascertainable meaning, then 'whether an act falls within the State's legitimate sphere of action could always be solved by simply applying [that definition] to the case'. But '[t]here simply is no fixed meaning, no natural extent to sovereignty at all'. Thus in disputes between two states, each may base its argument on its own sovereignty.

Some see sovereignty as particularly important for Global South states. Margaret Keck and Kathryn Sikkink, observed in *Activists Beyond Borders: Advocacy Networks in International Politics* (1998), at 215 that for many Global South actors, sovereignty and non-intervention are 'the main line of defense against foreign efforts to limit domestic and international choices that third world states (and their citizens) can make.' Similarly, Benedict Kingsbury has warned that 'discarding sovereignty in favour of a functional approach will intensify inequality, weakening restraints on coercive intervention, diminishing critical roles of the state as a locus of identity and an autonomous zone of politics and re-dividing the world into zones.'[278]

Others see it differently. Consider Lukas Schmid, in 'Saving Migrants' Basic Human Rights from Sovereign Rule', 116 *Am. Pol. Sci. Rev.* (2022) 954:

> "Sovereignty" is a discursive construction laden with difficult histories and prone to functional appropriation by all sorts of political projects. In political theory, it is most prominently known to have developed both in association with the social contract theories and as a quasi-theological notion of total dominion in, among others, Bodin and Schmitt. In political practice and international law, we commonly understand sovereignty as a state's "supreme authority within a territory," a bulwark against external encroachment. However, … the narrative of absolute authority has become largely fictitious in a globalized post-World War II order of multidimensional realignments of powers and jurisdictions. What is less often foregrounded is that the legal and political practice of state sovereignty developed (also) as an instrument of colonial subordination, granting inviolability of territory and peoplehood only to racially defined "civilized" populations, and thereby enabled rather than precluded imperial impositions in the colonial era. … "Sovereignty," … is a concept in flux, with its manifold meanings and purposes constructed in response to concrete political practice and social struggles. …

---

[276] J. Crawford, *Brownlie's Principles of Public International Law* (9th edn., 2019), at 437.
[277] M. Koskenniemi, *From Apology to Utopia: The Structure of International Legal Argument* (1989), Ch. 4.
[278] B. Kingsbury, 'Sovereignty and Inequality', 9 *Eur. J. Int'l. L.* 599 (1998).

> ... [O]ngoing, postcolonial power differentials between states [let] some states enjoy not only unquestionable sovereignty over their own development but also dominance over many of the resources that other states require to fulfil their sovereign aspirations. In practice, sovereign power is unevenly distributed, with some states enjoying supersovereignty, and others left unable to translate formal sovereignty into meaningful self-determination. Nevertheless, the understanding of state sovereignty as the universal prerogative of states to (largely) self-determine matters of territory and population without imposed external interference remains hegemonic in international law and politics, exerting "normative dominance" over the ways in which state entitlements are constructed and state behavior is judged. ...

Indeed, some philosophers, such as John Rawls and Joseph Raz, have suggested that one possible criterion for something being a human right is that its violation can be seen as warranting armed intervention by another state or an international organization in order to remedy the situation. Few, however, go that far.[279] And while legal doctrines such as the responsibility to protect might raise these concerns, most commentators do not see human rights obligations *per se* as posing any serious challenge to sovereignty. James Crawford notes that while the human rights movement has clearly eroded the domestic domain, sovereignty 'is not exhausted by the concession or recognition of rights'. 'Human rights standards qualify, but do not displace, the sovereignty of states. Indeed in subtle ways they reinforce it: the more we look to the state for human rights compliance, the more we seem to concede to a state domain.'[280]

Within the UN context, these theoretical debates about the status of sovereignty and its relationship to the human rights agenda have played out largely in relation to Article 2(7) of the Charter, which safeguards the 'domestic jurisdiction' of states. The main questions are what constitutes a domestic matter for this purpose and who decides. Most commentators consider that (1) the General Assembly must have the power to interpret its own mandate, including the implications of Article 2(7); (2) a teleological approach should be applied in interpreting Article 2(7) in light of the (developing) purposes of the Organization (Art. 1); (3) the resolutions of the UN and other bodies have made clear that a narrow interpretation is to be given to Article 2(7); and (4) as legitimate matters of international concern, human rights cannot reasonably be characterized as being exclusively an internal matter.

Since the 1940s, UN organs have systematically reduced the scope claimed for the domestic jurisdiction 'defence'. The early case of South Africa was critical. A special Commission on the Racial Situation in the Union of South Africa appointed by the General Assembly in 1952 concluded that Article 2(7) prohibited only 'dictatorial interference', a phrase interpreted as implying 'a peremptory demand for positive conduct or abstention — a demand which, if not complied with, involves a threat of or recourse to compulsion ... .' Article 2(7) referred 'only to direct intervention in the domestic economy, social structure, or cultural arrangements of the State concerned but does not in any way preclude recommendations, or even inquiries conducted outside the territory of such State.'[281] The Commission's report gave rise to extensive debate, in which South Africa took the position that the General Assembly could not even discuss the subject of race relations in that country. Only rarely today does one hear even distant echoes of that extreme position. The domestic jurisdiction defence continues to be regularly invoked, but it rarely prevails. J. Samuel Barkin concludes in his book *The Sovereignty Cartel* (2021) at 182, that sovereignty is 'a claim that needs to be continually maintained through political action. Looking at this political action, at how these claims are made and reinforced, rather than arguing about what sovereignty might mean in the abstract, is how the concept of sovereignty can be of most use to us in understanding contemporary international relations.'

An insightful metaphor for sovereignty in today's world is provided by Eyal Benvenisti, in 'Sovereigns as Trustees of Humanity: On the Accountability of States to Foreign Stakeholders', 107 *Am. J. Int'l. L.* (2013) 295. He suggests that past conceptions envisaged it as being 'akin to owning a large estate separated from other properties by rivers or deserts.' But today, the 'reality is more analogous to owning a small apartment in one densely packed high-rise that is home to two hundred separate families. The sense of interdependency is heightened when we recognize the absence of any alternative to this shared home, of any exit from this global

---

[279] J. Waldron, 'Human Rights: A Critique of the Raz/Rawls Approach', in A. Etinson (ed.), *Human Rights: Moral or Political?* (2018) 117.
[280] J. Crawford, 'Sovereignty as a Legal Value', in J. Crawford & M. Koskenniemi (eds.), *The Cambridge Companion to International Law* (2012) 117, at 122.
[281] UN Doc. A/2505 (1953), 16–22.

high-rise. The privilege of bygone days of opting out, of retreating into splendid isolation, of adopting mercantilist policies or erecting iron curtains is no longer realistically available.'

CONCEPTIONS OF ENFORCEMENT

Many observers would assume that the effectiveness of the UN human rights system should generally be judged by its ability to 'enforce' respect for the legal norms that originated within it. But, for most governments, the very concept of international 'enforcement' is controversial, leading some to oppose it overtly, and others to invoke more subtle arguments to preclude or undermine such measures. It is therefore not surprising that the UN's efforts have focused mostly on setting and monitoring human rights standards and trying to mobilize pressure on states to comply, rather than seeking to secure enforcement.

Evaluating the UN's performance will largely depend on the observer's starting point or perspective on world order. For example:

(1) Do we assume that the 'globalization' of issues such as human rights is desirable, even unavoidable, so that a nation's treatment of its own nationals is a legitimate concern of all others (an *erga omnes* approach)? Or do we hold to a more traditional image of the sovereign state that emphasizes the inviolability of national boundaries for at least some human rights issues as well as many other purposes?

(2) Even if the former, do we envisage a world in which an effective multilateral organization such as the UN should be able to act against the will of the government(s) concerned to enforce universal norms? Or do we believe that despite the pressures towards harmonization of international standards, the actual implementation by individual governments of human rights norms, each in its own way, remains the most effective, desirable or realistic approach?

(3) Are we prepared to accept that the measures that we would happily support against another country might, in a different context, be applied against our own? Do we assume that international enforcement actions must be applied equally to powerful nations and to smaller states, so that we should only adopt policies that can be applied across the board, consistently? Or are there legitimate differences in the ways in which the international community should respond to human rights violations in different types of states (democratic/non-democratic, large/small, developed/developing, etc.)?

The answers to such questions depend partly on the definition of enforcement. Should it be defined only to include peacekeeping, policing or military action that involves the presence in a state of UN or other foreign forces? The only use of the term 'enforcement' in the UN Charter is in Chapter VII relating to the powers of the Security Council (Article 45). This has led some international lawyers to equate enforcement with the use of, or threat to use, economic or other sanctions or armed force. Although most dictionary definitions of enforcement include an element of coercion, it is nonetheless true that coercion may be moral as well as physical. It is also true that the use of force for human rights purposes has won some support in recent years in response to mass atrocities, but this is surely not what is meant by calls for the UN to 'enforce', routinely, universal human rights norms.

At the other extreme from the use of sanctions or armed force, enforcement has been defined as 'comprising all measures intended and proper to induce respect for human rights'.[282] That definition could encompass even the softest forms of UN action such as debates or recommendatory resolutions of the Human Rights Council or the General Assembly. But such a definition is so open-ended that it provides no criteria against which to evaluate the UN's performance. It puts the emphasis on intentions rather than on results achieved, and suggests that 'enforcement' measures might be confined to the adoption of resolutions and other such hortatory activities of the UN.

---

[282] R. Bernhardt, 'General Report', in R. Bernhardt and J. A. Jolowicz (eds.), *International Enforcement of Human Rights* (1985), at 5.

> ## QUESTION
>
> Is the term 'enforcement' the right term to use to describe what you would like the UN to be able to do in response to a finding that major human rights violations, or perhaps mass atrocities, have occurred, or seem likely to? Are there other powers, stopping short of this sense of 'enforcement', that you would wish to vest in the UN or any other international organization to respond to gross violations?

A. OVERVIEW OF THE UN HUMAN RIGHTS MACHINERY

The UN's human rights regime reflects a 'two-track' approach:

(1) *UN Charter-based bodies* including those
   a. whose creation is directly mandated by the UN Charter, such as the General Assembly and the Human Rights Council (as the successor to the Commission on Human Rights),
   b. subsidiary bodies created by one of the principal organs, such as the Commission on the Status of Women or the Human Rights Council Advisory Committee, and
   c. groups or individuals accorded specific mandates by those organs to monitor, draft standards or for other purposes.
(2) *Treaty-based bodies* such as the Human Rights Committee established under the ICCPR, to monitor compliance by states with their obligations under those treaties. Such treaty bodies include the CEDAW Committee (dealt with in Chapter 3), the ESCR Committee (Chapter 4) and the ICCPR Committee (Chapter 9).

The focus of this Chapter is on Charter-based bodies. While the Human Rights Council is of particular importance, other UN organs also play significant roles. The UN Charter of 1945 establishes several 'principal organs': the Security Council, the General Assembly, the Economic and Social Council, the Trusteeship Council, the Secretariat and the International Court of Justice. One of these organs is now virtually defunct — the highly successful postwar decolonization processes overseen by the UN rendered the *Trusteeship Council* superfluous and it suspended its work in 1994. Although the *Economic and Social Council* (ECOSOC) once played a major role as an intermediary between the Assembly and the Commission on Human Rights, and still has a theoretically important role of coordination within an increasingly disparate UN system, its substantive contributions to the human rights debate since the 1970s have been extremely limited and its coordination efforts have had little practical impact. One of the aims of creating the Human Rights Council in 2006 was to bypass ECOSOC and enable the new Council to report directly to the General Assembly. As a result, the main human rights-relevant role played today by ECOSOC concerns the granting of 'consultative status' with the UN to nongovernmental organizations (see Ch. 14C, below).

We turn now to the organs whose work is examined in this Chapter. Until the mid-1990s, the *Security Council* was reluctant to become involved in human rights matters. Since that time, its role in the field has varied considerably (see Sec. D, below). Similarly, the *International Court of Justice* (ICJ) exerted a relatively marginal influence over the understanding and interpretation of international human rights law until the mid-1990s, despite its consideration of a handful of important cases focusing on issues such as self-determination and genocide. Over the past two decades, however, the ICJ has adopted a series of judgments of major importance in terms of their contribution to an understanding of aspects of the international human rights regime.

The *Secretariat* is led by the *Secretary-General*, who is appointed for five years by the General Assembly on the recommendation of the Security Council. A nominee may thus be vetoed by any of the five permanent members of the Council (China, France, Russia, the United Kingdom and the United States). The Secretary-General is the chief administrative officer of the UN and also exerts important moral authority within the wider international system. For decades, successive Secretaries-General were very reluctant to embrace human rights concerns actively for fear of offending governments and jeopardizing their wider role in the promotion of international peace and security. Two examples illustrate this reluctance. In the 1950s, Dag Hammarskjöld (Sweden) was said to have directed that the UN human rights programme should cruise at no more than 'minimum flying speed'. In 1993, the proposal that led to the creation of the post of High Commissioner for Human Rights in December 1993 was strongly opposed by then Secretary-General Boutros Boutros-Ghali (Egypt). In contrast, Kofi Annan (Ghana), Secretary-General from 1997 to 2006, took a much more active human rights stance than any of his predecessors and appointed a series of strong High Commissioners. He also oversaw a process of 'mainstreaming' human rights throughout the organization, which meant that bodies dealing with issues such as development, peacekeeping and environment were encouraged to address systematically the human rights dimensions of their work. His successor, from 2007 to 2016, was Ban Ki-moon (South Korea). He generally favoured 'quiet diplomacy' and engaged only minimally with human rights, although he took a strong stand on issues such as sexual orientation, and the Responsibility to Protect. The notion that the UN and its staff should 'take a principled stance' and 'act with moral courage' in the face of serious and large-scale human rights violations (the Human Rights Up Front policy) was adopted on his watch, but effectively mothballed by his successor, António Guterres (Portugal, 2017-2026). He too has generally avoided engaging directly with controversial human rights challenges.

Under the Secretary-General, the *High Commissioner for Human Rights* (HCHR) is the UN official with principal responsibility for human rights. In formal terms the HCHR is subject to the direction and authority of the Secretary-General and acts within the mandate given by the policy organs. In practice the HCHR and the Office (the OHCHR) are now viewed as central players in their own right (see Sec. C, below).

The *General Assembly* is empowered by the UN Charter to 'discuss any questions or any matters within the scope of the . . . Charter' (Art. 10) and to 'initiate studies and make recommendations for the purpose of . . . [*inter alia*] assisting in the realization of human rights' (Art. 13). The Assembly's principal significance derives from the fact that it is composed of all UN member states, each of which has one vote regardless of population, wealth or other factors. While most issues are decided by a simple majority vote, decisions on important questions, such as those on peace and security, admission of new members and budgetary matters, require a two-thirds majority. Nevertheless, much of its work is carried out on a consensus basis, thus avoiding the need for a vote. The Assembly meets intensively from September to December each year and at other times as required. Its resolutions are not *per se* legally binding but they are an important reflection of the will of the world community. Much of the debate and drafting occurs in six Main Committees, three of which are of particular relevance to human rights: the Third (Social, Humanitarian and Cultural issues); the Fifth (Administrative and Budgetary issues); and the Sixth (Legal issues).

In 2006, the *Human Rights Council* replaced the *Commission on Human Rights* which had functioned since 1946. We examine these two bodies in some depth in Section B below.

The *Commission on the Status of Women* was established in 1946 and reports to ECOSOC in relation to policies to promote women's rights in the political, economic, civil, social and educational fields. It consists of 45 governmental representatives, and meets for only ten days each year. It drafted many of the key treaties dealing with women's rights ranging from the 1952 Convention on the Political Rights of Women to the 1979 Convention on the Elimination of All Forms of Discrimination against Women. Its mandate includes follow-up to the four UN Women's Conferences held since 1975, and especially that held in Beijing in 1995. Its importance has been enhanced by the creation in 2010 of the UN Entity for Gender Equality and the Empowerment of Women, known as 'UN Women', one of whose roles is to assist the Commission in formulating relevant policies, global standards and norms.

In contrast with the treaty-based bodies discussed earlier, most of the Charter-based bodies are political organs, which have a much broader mandate to promote awareness, to foster respect and to respond to violations. They derive their legitimacy and their mandate, in the broadest sense, from the human rights provisions of the Charter. Consider the following contrasts between the two types of organs.

Treaty-based organs are distinguished by: a limited clientele consisting only of states parties to the treaty in question; a limited mandate reflecting the terms of the treaty; a limited range of procedural options for responding to violations; consensus-based decision-making as far as possible; a preference for a non-adversarial relationship with states parties (particularly with respect to state reports) based on the concept of a 'constructive dialogue'; and a particular concern with addressing issues in ways that contribute to developing the normative understanding of the relevant rights.

By contrast, the political organs such as the General Assembly and the Human Rights Council generally: focus on a diverse range of issues; insist that every state is an actual or potential client (or respondent), regardless of its specific treaty obligations; work on the basis of a flexible and expanding mandate designed to respond to crises as they emerge; engage, as a last resort, in adversarial actions vis-à-vis states; rely more heavily upon NGO inputs and public opinion generally to ensure the effectiveness of their work; take decisions by often strongly contested majority voting; pay less attention to normative issues *per se*; and are very wary about establishing specific procedural frameworks within which to work, preferring a more *ad hoc* approach in most situations.

B. THE UN HUMAN RIGHTS COUNCIL[283]

Rather than including an international bill of rights in the UN Charter in 1945, it was agreed instead to create a Commission on Human Rights whose primary function would be to draft such a bill. In late 1945, the UN appointed a Preparatory Commission to make provisional arrangements for institutional competences. It envisaged a Commission directed towards: a) formulation of an international bill of rights; b) formulation of recommendations for an international declaration or convention on such matters as civil liberties, status of women, freedom of information; c) protection of minorities; d) prevention of discrimination on grounds of race, sex, language, or religion; and e) any matters within the field of human rights considered likely to impair the general welfare or friendly relations among nations.[284]

The Commission was, however, set up as a subsidiary body of ECOSOC. The Council deleted paragraph (e) from the terms of reference it gave to the so-called Nuclear Commission, which was to make detailed suggestions for the shape of the new Commission. The Nuclear Commission's nine members, chaired by Eleanor Roosevelt, proposed a body consisting solely of independent experts with an open-ended mandate including the role of aiding 'the Security Council in the task entrusted to it by Article 39 of the Charter, by pointing to cases where a violation of human rights committed in one country may, by its gravity, its frequency, or its systematic nature, constitute a threat to the peace' (E/38/Rev.1 (1946), p. 7). But this conception was rejected by ECOSOC which insisted that the Commission would be an intergovernmental rather than an expert body and would focus primarily on standards, studies and recommendations. It did, however, insert a new paragraph (e), giving the Commission a role with respect to 'any other matter concerning human rights not covered by items (a) (b) (c) and (d)'. In its later years, the Commission was able to build upon this open-ended provision to expand its range of activities.

For the first 20 years of its existence, the Commission devoted itself largely to standard-setting, and particularly to the drafting of the UDHR and the two Covenants. Meanwhile, the Cold War and the decolonization movement dominated much of the action in the General Assembly and the Security Council, and most of the 'real' action on human rights took place in the Assembly.

The Commission's response to violations went through three distinct phases. The first (1946–1966) began with a statement that the Commission had 'no power to take any action in regard to any complaints concerning human rights' (ESC Res. 75 (V) (1947)). UN officials warned at the time that this approach would 'lower the prestige and the authority' of both the Commission and the UN as a whole. Hersch Lauterpacht called it an 'extraordinary . . . abdication' of the UN's proper functions. During a second phase (1967–1978) the Commission's composition was changed dramatically as a result of decolonization and the new members demanded responses to the problems associated with racism and colonialism. New procedures were adopted (the so-called 1235 and 1503 Procedures, named after ECOSOC's authorizing resolutions) and strong measures were taken against apartheid in particular. At the same time, it failed to act in response to horrendous violations in Pol Pot's Democratic Kampuchea (Cambodia), Amin's Uganda, Bokassa's Central African Empire, Macias's Equatorial Guinea, the military's Argentina and Uruguay and several other situations. As the human rights

---

[283] See generally, B. Ramcharan, *The Protection Role and Jurisprudence of the United Nations Human Rights Council* (2022); E. Tistounet, *The UN Human Rights Council: A Practical Anatomy* (2020); J. Pace, *The United Nations Commission on Human Rights: 'A Very Great Enterprise'* (2020); and R. Freedman, 'The Human Rights Council', in F. Mégret and P. Alston (eds.), *The United Nations and Human Rights: A Critical Appraisal* (2nd. ed., 2020) 181.
[284] Report of the Preparatory Commission of the United Nations (1945), PC/20, Ch. III, Sec. 4, paras. 14–16.

movement grew, public opinion began to assert itself, and the Carter Administration became more engaged, the Commission entered a third phase (1979–2005) in which it evolved more effective procedures and tackled a growing range of state violators. All of these procedures were passed on to the new Council in 2006.

While the Commission's achievements were actually considerable, its demise resulted from the disenchantment of all of its key constituencies, often for directly contradictory reasons. The United States was mostly frustrated in its efforts to condemn China's violations in the wake of the Tiananmen Square uprising of 1989, and irked by the active role of Cuba, Libya, Sudan and others. Its failure to win re-election in 2001 was the last straw. China, on the other hand, led a large number of developing countries in criticizing the Commission as a forum in which the North put countries of the South in the dock. They called instead for dialogue and consensus. And human rights NGOs considered the Commission to be unresponsive on key issues. By the end, all groups were accusing it of being 'politicized', albeit in very different ways. The resolution creating its successor body was a compromise among strongly competing visions.

GENERAL ASSEMBLY RESOLUTION 60/251
(2006)

The General Assembly,

...

Reaffirming further that all human rights are universal, indivisible, interrelated, interdependent and mutually reinforcing, and that all human rights must be treated in a fair and equal manner, on the same footing and with the same emphasis,

Reaffirming that, while the significance of national and regional particularities and various historical, cultural and religious backgrounds must be borne in mind, all States, regardless of their political, economic and cultural systems, have the duty to promote and protect all human rights and fundamental freedoms,

...

Affirming the need for all States to continue international efforts to enhance dialogue and broaden understanding among civilizations, cultures and religions, ...

...

1. *Decides* to establish the Human Rights Council ... as a subsidiary organ of the General Assembly ...;

2. *Decides* that the Council shall be responsible for promoting universal respect for the protection of all human rights and fundamental freedoms for all, without distinction of any kind and in a fair and equal manner;

3. *Decides also* that the Council should address situations of violations of human rights, including gross and systematic violations, and make recommendations thereon. It should also promote the effective coordination and the mainstreaming of human rights within the United Nations system;

4. *Decides further* that the work of the Council shall be guided by the principles of universality, impartiality, objectivity and non-selectivity, constructive international dialogue and cooperation ...;

5. *Decides* that the Council shall, inter alia:

> (a) Promote human rights education and learning as well as advisory services, technical assistance and capacity-building ...;

> (b) Serve as a forum for dialogue on thematic issues on all human rights;

> (c) Make recommendations to the General Assembly for the further development of international law in the field of human rights;

> (d) Promote the full implementation of human rights obligations undertaken by States ...;

> (e) Undertake a universal periodic review ...;

(f) Contribute, through dialogue and cooperation, towards the prevention of human rights violations and respond promptly to human rights emergencies;

(g) Assume the role and responsibilities of the Commission on Human Rights relating to the work of the [OHCHR];

(h) Work in close cooperation ... with Governments, regional organizations, national human rights institutions and civil society;

(i) Make recommendations with regard to the promotion and protection of human rights;

(j) Submit an annual report to the General Assembly;

...

12. *Decides also* that the methods of work of the Council shall be transparent, fair and impartial and shall enable genuine dialogue, be results oriented, allow for subsequent follow-up discussions to recommendations and their implementation and also allow for substantive interaction with special procedures and mechanisms;
...

1. Structure

Membership: Where the Commission on Human Rights (CHR) had 54 members, the Council has 47. General Assembly Resolution 60/251 diluted the proportion of European states and maintained the strong emphasis on regional blocs that had dogged the Commission. The Council thus consists of 13 states from Africa, 13 from Asia, six from Eastern Europe, eight from Latin American and the Caribbean, and seven from Western Europe and Other states (which includes the United States, Australia, Canada, New Zealand and Israel).

GA Res. 60/251 (2006), para. 8, authorizes the General Assembly, by a two-thirds majority of the members present and voting, to suspend the membership rights of a country 'that commits gross and systematic violations of human rights.' In 2011, Libya was suspended after a violent government crackdown on unarmed protesters. In 2022, Russia was suspended (by a vote of 93-24-58) in response to its aggression against Ukraine.

In 2018, the United States withdrew from Council membership, criticizing entrenched bias against Israel, and arguing that because it had not addressed 'the massive abuses in Venezuela and Iran' but had welcomed the Democratic Republic of Congo as a new member, it had 'cease[d] to be worthy of its name' (Ambassador Haley). Secretary of State Pompeo called it 'a hypocritical and self-serving organization that makes a mockery of human rights'. Under the Biden administration, the U.S. was re-elected in October 2021.

Term: States are elected for three-year terms and are not eligible for immediate re-election after two consecutive terms. The big powers, such as the United States and the USSR/Russia, had served almost continuously on the CHR.

Elections: One of the major issues that led to the disbanding of the Commission was the criticism that its members included governments which were major violators of human rights. As the U.S. Ambassador put it in 2005, the members of the Commission 'must be the firefighters of the world, not the arsonists'. The United States had previously urged that only democratic and human rights-respecting states should be elected to the Commission. In 2003, Human Rights Watch put forward a much modified set of criteria proposing that potential members 'should have ratified core human rights treaties, complied with their reporting obligations, issued open invitations to U.N. human rights experts and not have been condemned recently by the Commission for human rights violations.' But all too few states, the United States included, could meet such criteria.[285] The innovation in relation to the Council was to urge that those voting for states 'shall take into account the contribution of candidates to the promotion and protection of human rights and their voluntary pledges and commitments'. Once elected a state 'shall uphold the highest [human rights] standards'. In the first round of elections many states took the pledge seriously; few have done so subsequently. Civil society campaigns

---

[285] P. Alston, 'Promoting the Accountability of Members of the New UN Human Rights Council', 15 *J. Transnat'l L. & Pol'y.* (2005) 49.

have, however, succeeded in dissuading some states from nominating, and have contributed to the defeat of some candidacies.

Sessions: The CHR met for a single six-week annual session, with very occasional special (emergency sessions). The Council's *regular* sessions are held for four weeks in March, three in June and three in September. *Special* sessions 'to address human rights violations and emergencies' can be convened upon the request of one-third of the Council's members. Recent special sessions have addressed the human rights situation in: Sudan (may 2023); Iran (November 2022), Ukraine (May 2022); Ethiopia (December 2021); the Sudan (November 2021); Afghanistan (August 2021); the Occupied Palestinian Territory (May 2021); and Myanmar (February 2021).

Presidency: The Council's presidency rotates annually among the regional groups, but the office is considerably more powerful than was the case under the CHR. The President has a full-time personal staff to provide 'support ... and to enhance efficiency and institutional memory'.

Apart from states – both members and non-members – the main actors in the Council are the High Commissioner and the OHCHR, independent experts, NGOs and national human rights institutions (NHRIs).

OHCHR: We consider the role of the High Commissioner (HC) in Sec. C, below. One of the HC's principal roles is to direct the OHCHR, which provides the secretariat to the Council and is charged with implementing the great majority of the Council's decisions. In the formal institutional hierarchy, however, the HC is answerable to the General Assembly rather than the Council. It is the Assembly's Fifth Committee that exercises direct oversight of the Office's budget and administration. In 2010, Cuba and allied states proposed that the HC would answer first to the Council, but this was strongly resisted by the HC and the majority of states. The compromise (PRST 18/2 of 30 Sept. 2011) was to 'invite' the HC to include a detailed budgetary breakdown in an annual report to the Council.

Experts: The Commission and the Council have both accorded important and diverse roles to 'independent experts', although their efforts remain almost entirely advisory rather than determinative. The most important group are those holding specific 'mandates' under the Special Procedures system, which we examine below. In addition, a range of other expert bodies report regularly to the Council. The largest, and the one with the deepest roots in the system, is the *Human Rights Council Advisory Committee*. Consisting of 18 independent experts, it is officially described as the Council's 'think-tank' and 'work[s] at its direction' rather than on its own initiative. It generates studies and 'research-based advice' and meets in two sessions for a total of ten days per year. It replaced the *Sub-Commission on the Promotion and Protection of Human Rights* that advised the Commission on Human Rights from 1947 to 2006 and produced some 73 studies, starting in 1956, on issues such as the rights of indigenous populations, contemporary forms of slavery, minorities, transnational corporations, the administration of justice and the right to food. Whereas the Sub-Commission adopted resolutions on a wide range of issues, including violations in specific countries, the Advisory Committee is prohibited from doing so and must limit itself to providing 'advice' on thematic issues.

Other expert bodies include the *Expert Mechanism on the Rights of Indigenous Peoples* (established in 2007) which consists of five experts who meet annually and undertakes studies relating to the rights of indigenous peoples. It is separate from the Council's Special Rapporteur on the rights of indigenous peoples and ECOSOC's *Permanent Forum on Indigenous Issues* (established in 2000). The latter consists of 16 independent experts, half of whom are nominated by governments and half by indigenous organizations. It meets annually in New York for two weeks.

The *Forum on Minority Issues* (2007) meets for two days and bring together experts to advise the Council's Independent Expert on minority issues in relation to national, ethnic, religious and linguistic minorities. The *Social Forum* (2002) meets for two or three days annually and brings together civil society, experts and governments to discuss pressing social issues. The most recent additions are the *Forum on Human Rights, Democracy and the Rule of Law* (2015) and the *Permanent Forum on People of African Descent* (2021).

NGOs and NHRIs: NGOs and the representatives of those NHRIs that are accredited by the International Coordinating Committee of National Institutions for the Promotion and Protection of Human Rights (ICC) are entitled to attend Council meetings, to submit written statements and to speak in debates. The 'space' that is in fact made available to these groups is a matter of significant contention, with many governments being more committed in theory than in practice to supporting such participation.

QUESTIONS

1. A major debate in establishing the Council concerned its optimum size. The Commission had 53 members and the United States proposed that the Council should have only 20, or a maximum of 30. After an examination of the issue, a High-Level Panel reporting to the UN Secretary-General in 2004 (UN Doc. A/59/565 (2004), 282) concluded that efforts to identify membership criteria would have little chance of changing the negative dynamics in the Commission and only risked 'further politicizing the issue'. It advocated membership for all UN member states. This was rejected and the compromise chosen was 47. What are the arguments for and against a universal or a very selective membership for the Council?

2. UN Watch, an NGO that describes its role as 'combating racism, antisemitism, and anti-Israel prejudice at the UN' has consistently argued that states with poor human rights records should not be elected to the Council. In October 2020, its Executive Director argued that electing 'dictatorships' such as China, Cuba, Russia, Saudi Arabia, Pakistan and Uzbekistan to the Council was 'like making a gang of arsonists into the fire brigade'. Do you agree?

---

2. The Council at Work

The work of the Council and its offshoots appears in many different contexts throughout this book, including sections dealing with violence against women, fact-finding, business and human rights, counter-terrorism, and climate change. In the materials that follow, consideration is first given to two case studies showing the Council at work, then to its Special Procedures system, and then to its Universal Periodic Review. The picture that emerges is one of a body that performs a wide range of functions, albeit with varying degrees of effectiveness.

For all of the reliance on arduously negotiated procedures and the routine invocation of legal norms, political considerations are almost always uppermost in the minds of states. Virtually every issue is viewed, at least partly and too often entirely, through the lens of national interests. This is especially obvious in the case of the largest states such as China, India, the United States, and Russia, but it applies across the board. Consider the case of Indonesia, the fourth most populous and the largest Muslim-majority country in the world. Moch Faisal Karim, in 'The Limits of Global Human Rights Promotion: Indonesia's Ambivalent Roles in the UN Human Rights Council', 26 *Contemp. Pol.* (2020) 351, asks why, given its ready embrace of the UN's normative regime, and its strong promotion of human rights at the sub-regional level within ASEAN, Indonesia has been 'reluctant to play a constructive role in strengthening global human rights mechanisms.' He concludes that the key considerations are its 'historical memory' of the criticism it faced over human rights abuses in East Timor, and its concern not to expose itself to more scrutiny in relation to its response to the ongoing separatist movement in Papua.

When Australia votes, it is mindful of its history of abuses relating to its indigenous population and asylum-seekers. When India votes, the contested status of Kashmir and the plight of the Dalits are never irrelevant. When the United States votes, its history of racial segregation and its global economic and security interests are foremost. When China votes, it thinks of criticism directed at the situations in Tibet, Hong Kong, and Xinjiang, its historical memories of humiliation at the hands of Western imperialism, and its newfound global economic interests through its Belt and Road Initiative. And so on, for every country. But the system works, nonetheless, because these pre-occupations are sometimes trumped by other factors, such as geopolitical interests and rivalries, a reluctance to be shamed, domestic pressures to support progressive initiatives, and aspirations to show international 'leadership'.

The Council's functions include acting as a forum which brings states together and facilitates consultation on a vast array of human rights issues within and among the different geopolitical and other groupings. It also provides a setting in which co-operative solutions to problems can be sought, despite the fact that the public perception of its role is dominated by its grappling with intractable issues. It provides a focus and a gathering place for civil society actors seeking to ensure that issues of deep concern that are not being resolved elsewhere can become the focus of concerted attention. It can act as a catalyst to action by various actors, whether because they are asked to submit their views, to respond to requests, or challenged to provide explanations. It is a source of empowerment for experts and groups that act in its name and with a mandate from it. It can be a protector of rights when it mobilizes media attention, puts pressure on governments, and reinforces the legitimacy of a cause. It can also, of course, fall short of all of these aspirations, both in general and in particular cases, and it can be the conduit for backsliding.

Two other functions involve the consideration of complaints and the drafting of standards.

Complaints
Ever since the Magna Carta, a right to petition has been an important aspect of human rights, although it was not included in the UDHR. As noted earlier, the Commission was deprived almost from the outset of the ability to examine the many petitions that poured in from all over the world. This changed only in 1970, when ECOSOC Resolution 1503 (XLVIII) established a confidential process for examining communications which appeared 'to reveal a consistent pattern of gross and reliably attested violations of human rights'. It involved a cumbersome procedure and yielded very few known results. It nevertheless had its supporters among those who felt that any procedure that put governments under pressure to account must be a step forward.

When the Council replaced the Commission, it effectively 'inherited' the 1503 procedure. HRC Res. 5/1 of 18 June 2007 established two bodies to manage the procedure. The Working Group on Communications (WGC) consists of five independent expert members of the Council's Advisory Committee. It determines whether complaints are admissible and forwards those, along with its recommendations, to the Council's Working Group on Situations (WGS) which consists of one state representative designated by each of the five regional groups. The latter makes recommendations to the Council, which may or may not decide to take any action. Because the procedure is confidential, almost nothing is known about its impact.

Standard-setting
In historical terms it might well be considered that the single most important contribution made by the Charter-based bodies, and especially by the Commission and now the Council, has been the elaboration of an ever-growing body of standards designed to flesh out the meaning and implications of the relatively barebones norms enunciated in the UDHR. Although the Commission's 1946 terms of reference included a general mandate to address any human rights matter, it spent most of its first 20 years engaged almost exclusively in standard-setting. This included the preparation of the first draft of the UDHR and the two Covenants, as well as a range of other instruments.

Since the entry into force of the two Covenants in 1976, the need for additional standards has often been questioned. Even when new treaties on discrimination against women, or torture, or the rights of the child, or the rights of people with disabilities, were first mooted there were those who observed that the issues were already dealt with in the Covenants and who urged that the focus should instead be on better implementing existing standards and developing their content through interpretation. Such suggestions, as we know, proved unpersuasive. When the Human Rights Council was created, there were again suggestions that new standards were not a high priority. Diverse reasons have been suggested: new standards are often duplicative; the process is too time-consuming; priority should go to implementing existing standards; and states are already over-burdened with reporting and other obligations.[286] It has also been suggested that formal standard-setting processes disadvantage delegations from the Global South, because they lack the capacity and resources to engage fully.[287]

---

[286] International Council on Human Rights Policy, *Human Rights Standards: Learning from Experience* (2006).
[287] M. Mutua, 'Standard Setting in Human Rights: Critique and Prognosis', 29 *Hum. Rts. Q.* (2007) 547, at 606.

In fact, the Council has continued to draft new standards at a steady pace, including the International Convention for the Protection of All Persons from Enforced Disappearances, the Declaration on the Rights of Indigenous Peoples, and optional complaints protocols for the ICESCR and the CRC. It has also adopted declarations on the Right to Peace (GA Res. 71/189 (2016) and the Rights of Peasants (GA Res 73/165 (2018), as well as recognizing 'the right to a clean, healthy and sustainable environment as a human right' (Ch. 15A, below). Various other standard-setting activities relating to racism, an instrument on private security companies, a draft treaty on the right to development, and a draft treaty on business and human rights are all ongoing as of 2024.

Impact

For various reasons, systematically evaluating the Council's impact is an almost impossible task. It consists of a great many different bodies and mechanisms and their impact varies greatly. In addition, governments will almost never acknowledge the extent to which Council-generated pressures to change course have had any influence, even when they end up doing precisely what was requested. But some formal indicia are relevant, including the extent of competition to be elected to the Council, the level of participation in its activities by heads of state, foreign ministers, and other prominent figures, the amount of effort invested by civil society in trying to influence governments, and making elaborate proposals, and the intensity of governmental lobbying designed to influence the outcome of Council deliberations.

Racism Case Study

The following materials provide an overview of the Council's engagement with racism. The goal is to shed light on the issue itself, but also to provide insights into the strengths and weaknesses of its action in response to an issue of central and enduring importance.

Recent scholarship has drawn attention to two very different perspectives on efforts within the human rights regime to fight racism. On the one side is the prohibition of racial discrimination in the UN Charter and the UDHR, along with an impressive history of initiatives to abolish slavery and the slave trade, to condemn racial discrimination, to vanquish apartheid, and to establish mechanisms such as a treaty body, a Special Rapporteur, a Working Group, a Forum, a Group of Independent Eminent Experts, and other bodies described below. On the other side is a growing volume of critical literature calling attention to deep underlying racism within the regime itself and exposing the denial or downplaying of the links between imperialism/colonialism and racism. Critics also point to determined efforts by states to avoid confronting racist structures or the political economy underpinning them, and the refusal to take reparations claims seriously.

The human rights field is, of course, not alone. Antony Anghie concluded in his path-breaking study, *Imperialism, Sovereignty and the Making of International Law* (2005) at 312, that 'international law continuously disempowers the non-European world, even while sanctioning intervention within it'. Building on such analyses, and as detailed below, the Third World Approaches to International Law (TWAIL) group of scholars has developed an extensive critique of international law in general,[288] and other studies have exposed the corrosive effects of racism in relation to international humanitarian law,[289] international refugee law,[290] international criminal law,[291] and international relations in general.[292]

The materials that follow focus extensively, although not exclusively, on the United States. Amitav Acharya, in 'Race and Racism in the Founding of the Modern World Order', 98 *Int'l Aff.* (2022) 22, after surveying the role of race as a topic in the academic discipline of International Relations (IR), argues that 'as the United States became both the leading world power and the centre of gravity for IR as a field of study after 1945, race was

---

[288] A. Anghie, 'Rethinking International Law: A TWAIL Retrospective', 34 *Eur. J. Int'l L.* (2023) 7; and J.T. Gathii, 'The Promise of International Law: A Third World View', 36 *Am. U. L. Rev.* (2021) 377

[289] For an overview, see B. van Dijk, 'What Is IHL History Now?', 104 *Int'l Rev. Red Cross* (2022) 1621; and F. Mégret, 'From "Savages" to "Unlawful Combatants": A Postcolonial Look at International Humanitarian Law's "Other"', in A. Orford (ed.), *International Law and Its 'Others'* (2006) 265.

[290] M. Jackson Sow, 'Ukrainian Refugees, Race, and International Law's Choice Between Order and Justice', 116 *Am. J. Int'l L.* (2022) 698; and T. Achiume, 'Migration as Decolonization', 71 *Stan. L. Rev.* (2019) 1509.

[291] R. DeFalco and F. Mégret, 'The Invisibility of Race at the ICC: Lessons from the US Criminal Justice System', 7 *London Rev. Int'l L.* (2019) 55.

[292] B. Freeman, D. Kim and D. Lake, 'Race in International Relations: Beyond the "Norm Against Noticing"', 25 *Ann. Rev. Pol. Sci.* (2022) 175.

(and continues to be) swept under the carpet, and racism even legitimized, by mainstream scholarship and policy discourses about international affairs and world order.'

It should also be acknowledged that the materials present a critical perspective that could be faulted for not giving equal attention to the many positive UN contributions towards the elimination of racial discrimination. Some of those are documented by John Pace, in *The United Nations Commission on Human Rights: 'A Very Great Enterprise'* (2020) 57, and include:

- a series of important studies on discrimination carried out by the Human Rights Sub-Commission;
- a long-running focus on apartheid in southern Africa that involved the establishment of several important committees and working groups as well as various forms of Security Council-imposed sanctions;
- the proclamation of Decades to Combat Racism and Racial Discrimination (1973, 1983, 1993, and 2003) followed by an International Decade for People of African Descent 2015-2024;
- the holding of World Conferences to Combat Racism and Racial Discrimination (1973, 1983, and 2001);[293] and
- the adoption of the Convention on the Elimination of All Forms of Racial Discrimination, leading to the creation of the CERD Committee and the generation of an extensive jurisprudence documented in Patrick Thornberry, *The International Convention on the Elimination of All Forms of Racial Discrimination: A Commentary* (2016).

But perhaps the most important part of the story is the extent to which all of these initiatives were heavily contested, watered down, poorly implemented, and systematically underfunded. The following snapshots of the engagement of various United States actors provide both a historical overview and a picture of the current state of the art.

A. THE 1920S

Perhaps surprisingly, African Americans and their supporters in the U.S. have viewed the international stage as a vitally important one for airing their grievances since at least the early twentieth century.

UNIVERSAL NEGRO IMPROVEMENT ASSOCIATION (UNIA), DECLARATION OF THE RIGHTS OF THE NEGRO PEOPLES OF THE WORLD, 1920[294]

Be It Resolved, That the Negro people of the world, through their chosen representatives in convention assembled in Liberty Hall [in New York City, in August 2020] protest against the wrongs and injustices they are suffering at the hands of their white brethren ... .

... [W]e demand and insist on the following Declaration of Rights:
...
3. That we believe the Negro, like any other race, should be governed by the ethics of civilization, and therefore should not be deprived of any of those rights or privileges common to other human beings.

4. We declare that Negroes, wheresoever they form a community among themselves should be given the right to elect their own representatives to represent them in Legislatures, courts of law, or such institutions as may exercise control over that particular community.

5. We assert that the Negro is entitled to even-handed justice before all courts of law ... .
...
7. We believe that any law or practice that tends to deprive any African of his land or the privileges of free citizenship within his country is unjust and immoral, and no native should respect any such law or practice.

---

[293] D. Petrova, "'Smoke and Mirrors": The Durban Review Conference and Human Rights Politics at the United Nations', 10 *Hum. Rts. L. Rev.* (2010) 129.
[294] Reprinted in J. Dixon et al. (eds.) *The Marcus Garvey and Universal Negro Improvement Association Papers,* (Vol XII, 2014) 32.

8. We declare taxation without representation unjust and tyran[n]ous, and there should be no obligation on the part of the Negro to obey the levy of a tax by any law-making body from which he is excluded and denied representation on account of his race and color.

9. We believe that any law especially directed against the Negro to his detriment and singling him out because of his race or color is unfair and immoral, and should not be respected.
…
15. We strongly condemn the cupidity of those nations of the world who, by open aggression or secret schemes, have seized the territories and inexhaustible natural wealth of Africa … .
…
18. We protest against the atrocious crime of whipping, flogging and overworking of the native tribes of Africa and Negroes everywhere. These are methods that should be abolished and all means should be taken to prevent a continuance of such brutal practices.
…

Outcome

The Declaration consisted of 54 demands in total. In 1922, it formed the basis of a petition by the UNIA to the League of Nations. Arnulf Becker Lorca, in 'Petitioning the International: A 'Pre-history' of Self-determination', 25 *Eur. J. Int'l L.* (2014) 497, recounts how the Secretary-General of the League rebuffed efforts to hold a hearing on the petition, and declined to meet with its drafters in Geneva. Eventually, the Iranian ambassador agreed to submit the petition, but nothing came of the efforts.

B. THE LATE 1940S AND EARLY 1950S

1947: AN APPEAL TO THE WORLD: A STATEMENT ON THE DENIAL OF HUMAN RIGHTS TO MINORITIES IN THE CASE OF CITIZENS OF NEGRO DESCENT IN THE UNITED STATES OF AMERICA AND AN APPEAL TO THE UNITED NATIONS FOR REDRESS (NATIONAL ASSOCIATION FOR THE ADVANCEMENT OF COLORED PEOPLE)

Introduction by W. E. Burghardt Du Bois

There were in the United States of America, 1940, 12,865,518 citizens and residents, something less than a tenth of the nation, who form largely a segregated caste, with restricted legal rights, and many illegal disabilities. They are descendants of the Africans brought to America … and reduced to slave labor. This group has no complete biological unity, but varies in color from white to black, and comprises a great variety of physical characteristics
… …
The so-called American Negro group, therefore, while it is in no sense absolutely set off physically from its fellow American, has nevertheless a strong, hereditary cultural unity, born of slavery, of common suffering, prolonged proscription and curtailment of political and civil rights; and especially because of economic and social disabilities.
…
… Poverty, ignorance, disease and crime have been forced on these unfortunate victims of greed to an extent far beyond any social necessity; and a great nation, which today ought to be in the forefront of the march toward peace and democracy, finds itself continuously making common cause with race-hate, prejudiced exploitation and oppression of the common man. Its high and noble words are turned against it, because they are contradicted in every syllable by the treatment of the American Negro for [368 years].

Slavery in America is a strange and contradictory story. It … evidently was a matter of economics, a question of income and labor, rather than a problem of right and wrong, or of the physical differences in men. Once slavery began to be the source of vast income for men and nations, there followed frantic search for moral and racial justifications. Such excuses were found and men did not inquire too carefully into either their logic or truth.
…

… [D]iscrimination practiced in the United States against her own citizens and to a large extent a contravention of her own laws, cannot be persisted in, without infringing upon the rights of the peoples of the world and especially upon the ideals and the work of the United Nations.

This question then, which is without doubt primarily an internal and national question, becomes inevitably an international question …; it is therefore, fitting and proper that the thirteen million American citizens of Negro descent should appeal to the United Nations and ask that organization in the proper way to take cognizance of a situation which deprives this group of their rights as men and citizens … .

1951: CIVIL RIGHTS CONGRESS, WE CHARGE GENOCIDE: THE HISTORIC PETITION TO THE UNITED NATIONS FOR RELIEF FROM A CRIME OF THE UNITED STATES GOVERNMENT AGAINST THE NEGRO PEOPLE[295]

Out of the inhuman black ghettos of American cities, out of the cotton plantations of the South, comes this record of mass slayings on the basis of race, of lives deliberately warped and distorted by the willful creation of conditions making for premature death, poverty and disease., …

…

… [T]he oppressed Negro citizens of the United States, segregated, discriminated against and long the target of violence, suffer from genocide as the result of the consistent, conscious, unified policies of every branch of government.

The Civil Rights Congress has prepared and submits this petition to the General Assembly of the United Nations on behalf of the Negro people in the interest of peace and democracy, charging the Government of the United States of America with violation of the Charter of the United Nations and the Convention on the Prevention and Punishment of the Crime of Genocide.

…

According to international law, and according to our own law, the Genocide Convention, as well as the provisions of the United Nations Charter, supersedes, negates and displaces all discriminatory racist law on the books of the United States and the several states.

…

We, Negro petitioners whose communities have been laid waste, whose homes have been burned and looted, whose children have been killed, whose women have been raped, have noted with peculiar horror that the genocidal doctrines and actions of the American white supremacists have already been exported to the colored peoples of Asia. We solemnly warn that a nation which practices genocide against its own nationals may not be long deterred, if it has the power, from genocide elsewhere. White supremacy at home makes for colored massacres abroad. …

Outcome

The immediate response to the 1947 petition was for the UN's Economic and Social Council, with full U.S. support, to declare that the Commission on Human Rights had 'no power to take any action in regard to any complaints concerning human rights' (ESC Res. 75(V) 1947). That move quickly put an end to the consideration of the NAACP petition, or any other such complaint. The Chair of the Commission during this period was Eleanor Roosevelt. Carol Anderson, in *Eyes Off the Prize: The United Nations and the African American Struggle for Human Rights, 1944–1955* (2003), at 2, describes how the NAACP formed alliances with President Harry Truman and Eleanor Roosevelt in an effort to secure support for a helpful response from the United Nations. But she quotes Truman as saying that 'Negroes want justice, not social equality.' As for Roosevelt:

> … in her role as chair of the UN Commission on Human Rights, although she
> sympathized with the plight of the African Americans, she was even more responsive to
> the public relations exigencies of the Cold War, which called for sanitizing and
> camouflaging the reality of America's Jim Crow democracy. She, therefore, joined with
> Texas Senator Tom Connally and others in an attempt to thwart a complaint to the UN
> charging South Africa with racial discrimination and systematic human rights violations.

---

[295] Presented to the UN General Assembly in Paris by William Patterson and to the UN Secretariat in New York by Paul Robeson. See J. Pope, 'El-Hajj Malik El-Shabazz: The Continuity and Legacy of a Critical Africana Human Rights Consciousness', 24 *J. Afr. Stud.* (2020) 357.

Roosevelt, Connally, and the other members of the U.S. delegation voiced strong concerns that, if the complaint succeeded, it would set a dangerous precedent that could ultimately lead to the United Nations investigating the condition of "negroes in Alabama."

Roosevelt also used her chairmanship and influence to manipulate the human rights treaties in ways that would shield the United States from UN scrutiny and assuage the powerful Southern Democrats, who "were afraid" that the UN's treaties just "might affect the Colored question." After all, the senators from Georgia and Texas railed, those treaties were nothing more than a "back-door method of enacting federal anti-lynching legislation." Mrs. Roosevelt, therefore, fought for the insertion of a clause in the Covenant on Human Rights that would allow states that were in a federal system, such as Georgia, to disregard the treaty completely. … In essence [she] had just assured the Dixiecrats [a pro-segregation political party named the States' Rights Democratic Party] that the sacred troika of lynching, Southern Justice, and Jim Crow schools would remain untouched, even with an international treaty to safeguard human rights. Obviously, then, although the United States was willing to use the rhetoric of human rights to bludgeon the Soviet Union and play the politics of moral outrage that the Holocaust engendered, the federal government, even the liberals, steadfastly refused to make human rights a viable force in the United States or in international practice.

Indeed, the President of the American Bar Association, Frank Holman, waged war against the UDHR before its final adoption in December 1948. Motivated primarily by a concern to uphold states' rights, especially to maintain racial segregation and to avoid the imposition of 'world-wide socialism, he warned 'the American people [of] the revolutionary nature of the proposals and the dangerous implications with respect to our form of government.'[296] While Holman was unable to prevent the adoption of the UDHR, he played a crucial behind the scenes role in supporting Senator Bricker, whose unsuccessful efforts to secure a constitutional amendment nevertheless provoked the U.S. to undertake not to submit the Genocide Convention (Holman had warned that a White driver who accidentally ran over a Black child could be charged with genocide under the Convention) or the draft Covenants to the Senate for its advice and consent. In 1956, the Supreme Court held in *Reid v. Covert* (354 U.S. 1) that no treaty could confer powers on the federal government 'free from the restraints of the Constitution', thus assuaging concerns that domestic race policies might be jeopardized.[297]

Starting in 1950, the U.S. and its allies launched a process to review the operations of the ECOSOC and its commissions. Steven L. B. Jensen, in 'Inequality and Post-War International Organization: Discrimination, the World Social Situation and the United Nations, 1948–1957', in C. Christiansen and S. Jensen (eds.), *Histories of Global Inequality* (2019) at 131 observes that '[t]he process … became a concerted attempt by major Western countries to close down key UN Commissions and Committees that were focusing on social and humanitarian issues, including human rights. … [T]his attempt at closures by the United States and the United Kingdom was about sanitizing the normative and political food chain of UN diplomacy in the field of human rights and anti-discrimination. It thereby represented a battle over the type of international organization that the UN should be. Should it focus solely on security politics and technically oriented economic development or should it also include various dimensions of "the social" and human rights?' The effort failed in the end, but a clear message had been sent. Similarly, Jensen notes that the UN's first World Social Situation Report, issued in 1952, 'highlighted economic inequality within and between countries, inequalities in income distribution between people as well as global and national inequalities in food and nutrition, mortality rates, inequalities in access to and quality of primary and secondary education, in land ownership, in the impact of taxation (progressive vs. regressive).' The follow up report, published five years later made no substantive mention of inequality. In this instance, the message had been received.

---

[296] F. Holman, 'Human Rights on Pink Paper', *American Affairs* (January 1949) 18, at 24.
[297] See generally, E. Borgwardt, *A New Deal for the World: America's Vision for Human Rights* (2005).

C. THE 1960S: MALCOLM X AND MARTIN LUTHER KING, JR.

In a speech at the Founding Rally of his Organization of Afro-American Unity, in Washington Heights, New York, on 28 June 1964, (available at www.blackpast.org) Malcolm X, an American Muslim minister and civil rights activist who was assassinated in 1965, proclaimed that his new organization would 'work with every leader and other organization in this country interested in a program designed to bring your and my problem before the United Nations.' Since the U.S. government was not 'capable of even hearing our problem', the solution was to 'internationalize' the issue, take advantage of the UN and its UDHR, and bring US racism 'into the UN before a world body wherein we can indict Uncle Sam for the continued criminal injustices that our people experience in this government.'

Malcolm X also attended a meeting of the Organization of African Unity (OAU) in Cairo in July 1964, where he was given 'observer' status. The *New York Times* ('Malcolm X Seeks U.N. Negro Debate; He Asks African States to Cite U.S. Over Rights', (13 August 1964)) reported that he told the OAU that 'The American Government is either unable or unwilling to protect the lives and property of your 22 million African-American brothers and sisters. We stand defenseless, at the mercy of American racists who murder us at will for no reason other than we are black and of African descent.' He told the African leaders that 'Your problems will never be fully solved until and unless ours are solved. You will never be fully respected until and unless we are also respected.'

Malcolm X frequently compared the situation in the United States with that in countries which were being discussed at the United Nations. The *New York Times* article reported him as saying that 'If [U.S.] Supreme Court Justice Arthur Goldberg [then U.S. Ambassador to the UN] ... could find legal grounds to threaten to bring Russia before the United Nations and charge her with violating the human rights of less than three million Russian Jews—what makes our African brothers hesitate to bring the United States Government before the United Nations and charge her with violating the human rights of 22 million African-Americans?'

A recent biography by Les Payne and Tamara Payne, *The Dead Are Arising: The Life of Malcolm X* (2020), at 449, suggests a different analogy, quoting him as saying: 'South Africa is like a vicious wolf, openly hostile towards black humanity. But America is cunning like a fox, friendly and smiling, but even more vicious and deadly than the wolf. And if South African racism is not a domestic issue, then American racism also is not a *domestic* issue.'

While Martin Luther King, Jr., did not petition or appear before the United Nations human rights bodies, 'his transnational advocacy helped elevate the Black American Civil Rights Movement and globalized the international human rights movement against racism, apartheid, colonization, and war. In fact, as Henry J. Richardson III observes,[298] King was the first "modern black leader, subsequent to DuBois to most prominently embody" the unity of the civil rights and international human rights discourses and movements.'[299] On 10 December 1962, King joined the African National Congress leader, Chief Albert J. Lutuli, in a 'Call for an International Boycott of *Apartheid* South Africa':

> ... In South Africa today, all opposition to white supremacy is condemned as
> communism, and in its name, due process is destroyed; a medieval segregation is
> organized with twentieth century efficiency and drive; a sophisticated form of slavery is
> imposed by a minority upon a majority which is kept in grinding poverty; the dignity of
> human personality is defiled; and world opinion is arrogantly defied.

> ...

> ... [When the United States concluded] that our interests were threatened in the
> Dominican Republic [we] inundated that small nation with overwhelming force, shocking
> the world with our zealousness and naked power. With respect to South Africa, however,
> our protest is so muted and peripheral it merely mildly disturbs the sensibilities of the

---

[298] H.J. Richardson III, 'Dr. Martin Luther King, Jr. as an International Human Rights Leader', 52 *Villanova L. Rev.* (2007) 471.
[299] J. I. Levitt, 'Beloved Pan-Africanism: Martin Luther King's Stride Toward Africa, International Human Rights, and the Black International Tradition', in Z. Yihdego et al. (eds.), *Ethiopian Yearbook of International Law* 2019, 163.

segregationists, while our trade and investments substantially stimulate their economy to greater heights. …

Outcome

Advocacy by U.S. civil rights leaders vis-à-vis the UN contributed to the ferment that was generated by the emergence from colonial status to independence of dozens of new states in the 1950s and early 1960s. The result was a decision by the UN General Assembly in 1963 to develop an anti-racism treaty.[300] Archival research by H. Timothy Lovelace, Jr., in 'Civil Rights as Human Rights', 71 *Duke L. J.* (2022) 1850 has revealed an important part of the U.S. response. The UN's human rights Sub-Commission was requested to draft what would become the Convention on the Elimination of All Forms of Racial Discrimination:

> The Sub-Commission was well-positioned to [do so because, as a body of independent experts, it] … was designed to advance the idea that human rights were to be above politics, neutral, and universal in application. The [UN] hoped the arrangement would minimize power politics and … provide … global solutions … . [But, in practice, many experts] operated as state agents. …
>
> …
>
> Thus, … the Sub-Commission often transformed into a forum where foreign officials shamed the body's U.S. members for proclaiming the United States' commitment to democracy abroad while denying Black Americans democracy at home. Such outward criticism harmed U.S. foreign policy interests because U.S. policymakers understood the United States' position in the Cold War increasingly depended upon its ability to influence decolonizing and newly independent countries. The persistence of U.S. racism thus proved to be a liability in the international arena. …
>
> However, when the U.N. General Assembly requested that the Sub-Commission draft the Convention, State Department officials saw an opportunity and seized the moment. Those officials charged two of the United States' foremost civil rights lawyers, Morris Abram and Clyde Ferguson, to help develop a U.S. draft of the Convention for the Sub-Commission's debates. …

These two were celebrated civil rights advocates. Abram, born in Georgia, was the son of a Jewish immigrant, who served with distinction in World War II, became a staff lawyer at the Nuremburg Trial, and was later an attorney for Martin Luther King, Jr. Ferguson, an African-American from North Carolina, also had a very distinguished service record, graduated from Harvard Law School, became prominent in both the civil rights and human rights fields, and Dean of Howard Law School in 1963. Lovelace describes the task assigned to them:

> … [T]he State Department['s] drafting instructions for Abram and Ferguson … were resoundingly clear: "… the approach should be along [the] lines of the 'equal protection' concept in our 14th Amendment." For the State Department, incorporating U.S. constitutional principles into the U.N. Convention presented many benefits. First, if the Convention mirrored the principles in constitutional law, the United States could credibly argue that it was at the vanguard of racial progress. Second, State Department officials hoped to persuade newly independent countries and the Sub-Commission to embrace U.S. constitutional values more broadly. Moreover, the closer the Convention's language was to the Constitution, the fewer conflicting obligations the United States would encounter if it were to adopt the Convention. …
>
> However, for Abram and Ferguson, the goal of transplanting U.S. law into the Convention created a paradox. Abram and Ferguson were cold warriors and firmly believed in America's democratic potential. Yet, exporting U.S. democracy abroad would also mean exporting American problems. Despite the Fourteenth Amendment's great promise, if Abram and Ferguson were successful in grafting the Equal Protection Clause

---

[300] See generally H. T. Lovelace, *The World is on Our Side: America and the Race for Human Rights under Law* (2023).

onto the Convention, they would also saddle the Convention with the state action doctrine. That doctrine limited the application of the clause only to government entities and, in turn, put private discrimination beyond constitutional reach. The doctrine had long stymied racial progress in the United States. ...

The two experts subsequently submitted to the Sub-Commission a draft of the treaty that had emerged from consultations within the State Department. It formed the basis of the UN negotiations. The key issue was whether private discrimination, which was rampant in the United States, the United Kingdom and other Western countries, would also be prohibited. In the final version of the treaty, the definition of racial discrimination applies to 'the political, economic, social, cultural or any other field of public life.' Proponents of a comprehensive approach, especially those from Eastern Europe, believed that this covered both the public and private sphere but Western governments consistently made clear during the drafting that they believed that the word 'public' was synonymous with the U.S. notion of 'state action'. Lovelace observes that 'Abram and Ferguson's strategy worked brilliantly'.

The U.S. then doubled down on that interpretation by lodging a reservation to its ratification of the CERD Convention, which happened on 21 October 1994, almost 30 years after the treaty's adoption:

> ... The United States understands that the identification of the rights protected under the Convention by reference in article 1 to fields of `public life' reflects a ... distinction between spheres of public conduct that are customarily the subject of governmental regulation, and spheres of private conduct that are not. To the extent, however, that the Convention calls for a broader regulation of private conduct, the United States does not accept any obligation under this Convention to enact legislation or take other measures
> ... .

In 2021, reporting on a country that had undergone relentless privatization of previously public functions since the 1980s, the U.S. government reported to the CERD Committee that it still considers it has no obligation to 'prohibit and punish purely private conduct' (UN Doc. CERD/C/USA/10-12, para. 11). In response, the Committee plaintively reiterated 'its recommendation that the State party consider withdrawing or narrowing the scope of its reservation to article 2 of the Convention and broaden the protection afforded by law against all discriminatory acts perpetrated by private individuals, groups or organizations' (UN Doc. CERD/C/USA/CO/10-12 (2022), para. 7).

D. THE 2020S

On 25 May 2020, as the COVID-19 pandemic raged, George Floyd was brutally murdered by officers of the Minneapolis Police Department, setting off large-scale riots, initially in the United States, and soon worldwide, against police brutality, especially directed at people of African descent. On 8 June 2020, the American Civil Liberties Union, on behalf of the family members of four recent victims of police violence in the U.S. (George Floyd, Breonna Taylor, Philando Castile, and Michael Brown) and 660 human rights organizations worldwide, petitioned the Council 'to urgently convene a Special Session on the situation of human rights in the United States in order to respond to the unfolding grave human rights crisis borne out of the repression of nationwide protests.' The petition noted, inter alia, that:

> [P]olice departments across the United States, backed by federal government agencies ...,
> are escalating the situation with further militarization and excessive use of force against
> protesters. We note with particular concern the deployment of at least 62,000 National
> Guard soldiers in two dozen states, the encouragement of the use of violence and mass
> arrests by President Donald Trump on social media, and his labeling of the protesters as
> "terrorists." Several cities around the country have imposed sweeping night curfews ... .

On 15 June 2020, the Group of African States requested the Council to convene an 'urgent debate on racially inspired human rights violations, systemic racism, police brutality and violence against peaceful protest.' In this context, the Group, along with other sponsors, submitted a draft resolution for the consideration of Council members in the following terms:

[The Human Rights Council]

> 1.   Strongly condemns the continuing racially discriminatory and violent practices perpetrated by law enforcement agencies against Africans and people of African descent, and the structural racism endemic to the criminal justice system in the United States of America and other parts of the world recently affected;
>
> 2.   Expresses alarm at the recent incidents of police brutality against peaceful demonstrators defending the rights of Africans and of people of African descent;
>
> 3.   Decides to establish an independent international commission of inquiry ... to establish the facts and circumstances relating to the systemic racism, alleged violations of international human rights law and abuses against Africans and people of African descent in the United States of America and other parts of the world ...;
>
> ...

Many speakers addressed the Council over two days on 16-17 June 2020, including the following:

Philonise Floyd

> [In the widely-watched video of George Floyd's murder] [y]ou watched my brother die. That could have been me. I am my brother's keeper. You in the United Nations are your brothers and sisters' keepers in America, and you have the power to help us get justice for my brother George Floyd. I am asking you to help him. I am asking you to help me. I am asking you to help us - Black people in America. ...

Michelle Bachelet, UN High Commissioner for Human Rights

> ...
>
> Today's protests are the culmination of many generations of pain, and long struggles for equality. Too little has changed, over too many years. We owe it to those who have gone before, as well as those to come, to seize the moment – at long last – to demand fundamental change and insist upon it.
>
> As 20 of my fellow senior UN leaders, each of African origin or descent, jointly wrote this week, "to merely condemn expressions and acts of racism is not enough. We must go beyond and do more."
>
> ...
>
> Black lives matter. Indigenous lives matter. The lives of people of colour matter. All human beings are born equal in dignity and rights: that is what this Council, like my Office, stands for. I thank the African Group of States for initiating this debate, and this Council for holding it. I trust it will be followed by swift and decisive reforms.

Representative of Australia

> ... Australia supports all efforts to address and eliminate racial discrimination in all its forms, wherever it occurs. ...
>
> We deplore the tragic death of George Floyd. And we support the United States' recent steps to address racism, police brutality and violent responses to peaceful demonstrations. We note, for example, the charging of officers over George Floyd's death, the removal of others responsible for excessive force, as well as moves towards police reform.
>
> The United States is an open, liberal democracy, governed by the rule of law and we have confidence in their transparent justice system to address these issues appropriately. ...

On behalf of the European Union, Ambassador of Croatia, Vesna Batistić Kos

...

The European Union expresses its deepest sympathy ...

...

The EU supports the African Group and the calls from civil society and relatives of victims for the need to discuss these matters at the Human Rights Council. Incidents of racially motivated violence and hatred take place in all regions of the world, and we need to look into our own souls. ...

...

All societies must remain vigilant against the excessive use of force and ensure that all such situations are addressed safely, effectively and in full respect for the rule of law and human rights. The EU will continue calling on all States to uphold the rights to participate in public affairs, freedom of peaceful assembly and association, including for human rights defenders and peaceful protesters, as well as freedom of opinion and expression online and offline with particular emphasis on the safety of journalists, bloggers and other media workers.

...

Tendayi Achiume, Special Rapporteur on [Racism]

...

For people of African descent in the United States, the domestic legal system has utterly failed to acknowledge and confront racial injustice and discrimination. ...

... The situation in the United States requires an international response that can help ensure that people of African descent in that country are no longer subject to the routine but egregious violations that prompted this Urgent Debate in the first place. It is for this reason that any resolution adopted by the Council at the conclusion of this debate must provide for an international commission of inquiry with the necessary authority to investigate systemic racism in law enforcement in the United States. Failure to do so would be to deny people of African descent in the United States the opportunity to draw on the global human rights system to challenge entrenched racial injustice. Failure to establish an international commission of inquiry would signal that Black lives do not matter, or that if they do, they do not matter enough to mobilize the Human Rights Council to intervene where it should. People of all racial and ethnic groups have been taking to the streets, risking their lives day after day to protest systemic racism in the face of global health pandemic.

...

The truth is that there has been a steady erosion within the United Nations of commitment to the anti-racism human rights framework ... .

...

We are aware that some member states have argued that a Commission of Inquiry should be reserved for more serious human rights violations. We disagree. If the national and global uprisings we are witnessing are not sufficient evidence of the gravity of the issues before you, it is difficult to imagine ... what might convince you to demonstrate the equal worth of people of African descent. ...

American Civil Liberties Union (on behalf of a group of NGOs)

> ... The protesters in the streets across the United States and around the world are demanding radical change; now is the time for accountability, for reimagining public safety and the role of police in a democratic society. It's time to dismantle structural racism and invest in people and communities of color. We urge the Council to respond rapidly and effectively, and mandate an independent investigation into U.S. racist policing practices and suppression of peaceful protests. We cannot remain complicit in the oppression of Black Americans and must take immediate action to end this legacy of state-sanctioned violence.

Outcome

The result was Human Rights Council Resolution 43/1, of 19 June 2020, which was adopted unanimously.

> The Human Rights Council,
>
> ...
>
> 1. Strongly condemns the continuing racially discriminatory and violent practices perpetrated by law enforcement agencies against Africans and people of African descent, in particular which led to the death of George Floyd on 25 May 2020 in Minnesota ... and the deaths of other people of African descent, and also condemns the structural racism in the criminal justice system;
>
>
> 2. Deplores the recent incidents of excessive use of force and other human rights violations by law enforcement officers against peaceful demonstrators defending the rights of Africans and of people of African descent;
>
> 3. Requests the United Nations High Commissioner for Human Rights ... to prepare a report on systemic racism, violations of international human rights law against Africans and people of African descent by law enforcement agencies, especially those incidents that resulted in the death of George Floyd and other Africans and people of African descent, to contribute to accountability and redress for victims;
>
> ...

An insight into the process that led to this outcome is provided by Sejal Parmar, in 'The Internationalisation of Black Lives Matter at the Human Rights Council', *EJIL: Talk!* (26 June 2020):

> ... The reason for the weakened text was behind-the-scenes influence, 'extreme pressure', and even 'bullying' of Council member states – particularly from many members of the Western [Group] ... towards ensuring that the outcome resolution was generic rather than focused upon the US, and did not provide for a commission of inquiry. The US, which had memorably withdrawn from the Council exactly two years previously, was thus able to rely on others to ensure that the resolution was diluted, even though its ambassador had stated that his country 'was not above scrutiny' on the very day of the debate.
>
> In various ways, through their public rhetoric during the debate, the majority of states displayed a worrying aversion to ensuring global human rights accountability for the US. First, the reality of the ultimate, shocking trigger for the urgent debate seemed often hidden, even denied, in states' comments. Whilst many states referred to the killing of George Floyd, it was almost always as a 'tragedy' or 'tragic death', as if it were an accident or misfortune. Similarly, the outrage and calls for action of protestors globally were reduced to passive expressions of 'sadness' by the diplomats of their states (e.g. Croatia on behalf of the EU). Second, the US seemed to be the elephant in the Assembly Hall for much of the debate, with the vast majority of states managing to avoid any direct mention

of the US at all. When the US was cited by [Western] states, it was often with approval, to indicate 'confidence' in the US ... and only exceptionally to express '[concern] ...' (Switzerland). The strongest statements for the original draft resolution came from South Africa, Botswana, and Namibia, and also, predictably, Cuba, Venezuela, the Democratic People's Republic of Korea, Iran, and Russia, states marked by serious human rights records. Third, many states argued that, since racism is a 'global scourge' or 'problem' (e.g. UK, Brazil, Germany), 'no country should be singled out' (e.g. Brazil, Australia), and that a 'collaborative' and 'constructive' approach (e.g. UK, Japan) that is unifying rather than divisive ought to be embraced – a claim that justified the deflection of the Council's attention away from the US.

The official response, by US Secretary of State Michael R. Pompeo, was entitled 'On the Hypocrisy of UN Human Rights Council' (20 June 2020):

> The United Nations Human Rights Council, now comprised of Venezuela and recently, Cuba and China, has long been and remains a haven for dictators and democracies that indulge them. It is a grave disappointment to those genuinely seeking to advance human dignity. Even so, the Council's decision to vote yesterday on a resolution focusing on policing and race in the United States marks a new low.

> The ongoing civic discourse about the tragic death of George Floyd in the United States is a sign of our democracy's strength and maturity. Americans work through difficult societal problems openly, knowing their freedoms are protected by the Constitution and a strong rule of law. ...

> Unfortunately, the Council has once again reaffirmed the wisdom of our decision to withdraw in 2018. If the Council were serious about protecting human rights, there are plenty of legitimate needs for its attention, such as the systemic racial disparities in places like Cuba, China, and Iran. If the Council were honest, it would recognize the strengths of American democracy and urge authoritarian regimes around the world to model American democracy and to hold their nations to the same high standards of accountability and transparency that we Americans apply to ourselves.

The High Commissioner engaged in wide-ranging consultations in preparing the report requested by the Council. She observed in introducing the report (UN Doc. A/HRC/47/53 (2021) para. 10) that:

> [P]eople of African descent face interconnected, intersectional and compounded forms of racial discrimination, marginalization and exclusion that are shaped by historical legacies and mutually reinforced through cycles of structural inequalities that have lasted for generations, affecting the enjoyment of human rights in every part of life. Systemic racism persists, in large part, due to misconceptions that the abolition of slavery, the end of the transatlantic trade in enslaved Africans and colonialism, and measures taken by States to date, have removed the racially discriminatory structures built by those practices and created equal societies.

The report concluded with a detailed 'Four-point Agenda Towards Transformative Change for Racial Justice and Equality', summed up in these terms in the longer version of the report (UN Doc. A/HRC/47/CRP/1 (2021), para. 313):

> (a) Reverse the cultures of denial, dismantle systemic racism and accelerate the pace of action;

> (b) End impunity for human rights violations by law enforcement officials and close trust deficits;

(c) Ensure that the voices of people of African descent and those who stand up against racism are heard and that their concerns are acted upon;

(d) Confront legacies, including through accountability and redress.

In some respects, the most revealing sentence in the report came in paragraph 314, in which the High Commissioner 'calls upon all States to translate the agenda into action plans and concrete measures developed through national dialogues.' In other words, while the UN itself could document the extent of systemic racism, help to galvanize and perhaps add legitimacy and credibility to local efforts, and undertake ongoing monitoring, real redress could only happen at the national level. But the enormity of that challenge was confirmed in a follow-up report one year later (UN Doc. A/HRC/51/53 (2022)) which surveyed states' responses to the report and concluded that 'for the most part these initiatives fall short of comprehensive evidence-based approaches … that address systemic racism … .'

The other part of the Council's response was to establish an International Independent Expert Mechanism to Advance Racial Justice and Equality in Law Enforcement (Res. 47/21 (2021)). It was instructed to function in close collaboration with other existing actors such as the Working Group of Experts on People of African Descent and the Special Rapporteur on racism. The Expert Mechanism's mandate called for it:

11. … to advance racial justice and equality in the context of law enforcement in all parts of the world by …;

(a) Examining systemic racism, including as it relates to structural and institutional racism …;

(b) Examining the root causes of systemic racism in law enforcement and the criminal justice system …;

(c) Making recommendations regarding how domestic legal regimes on the use of force by law enforcement officials can be brought into line with the applicable human rights standards …;

(d) Making recommendations on the collection and publication of data … to drive and assess responses to systemic racism;

…

Structural Approaches

The Expert Mechanism's first report (UN Doc. A/HRC/51/55 (2022)) focused on 'the collection, publication and analysis of data disaggregated by race or ethnic origin with regard to interactions of Africans and people of African descent with law enforcement authorities and the criminal justice system'. While it is essential to establish a firm foundation for its work, the challenge ahead will be whether to focus narrowly on the criminal justice system or to expand to consider the structural and systemic dimensions emphasized in the report of the High Commissioner.

An example of such an approach is provided by a report by the Working Group of Experts on People of African Descent on an official visit to Portugal in late 2021 (UN Doc. A/HRC/51/54/Add.2 (2022)). The Group begins by recognizing the significance of the government's adoption of a National Plan to Combat Racism and Discrimination 2021–2025, making it the first European Union member to do so. For the Group, it constitutes 'political recognition that there is racism in Portugal, in both interpersonal and structural dimensions, which results from historical processes and perpetuates structural discrimination models [para. 9].' But a brief excerpt of its focus indicates the potential relevance of wider structural issues:

24. Language is an important reflection and expression of culture. Portuguese is proudly claimed as the fifth most spoken language in the world, but an insistence on maintaining the purity of the European dialect does reflect hierarchy and operates as a de facto limit

to the human rights of people of African descent. The Working Group was consistently informed that the Portuguese language is a site of persistent racial profiling, with serious impacts on people of African descent in terms of education and employment, as a result of ongoing linguistic supremacy as a pervasive form of white supremacy, whereby European-inflected Portuguese created access and African-inflected Portuguese created barriers in a hierarchy that could be defined precisely by region or nation. Language variety was reported as a basis for filtering students, downgrading performance and prejudging intellectual aptitude.

25. ... [C]hildren of African descent who are native speakers of Portuguese are categorized as "Portuguese second language speakers", depriving such children of appropriate intellectual education and classmates if their Portuguese contained markers of Brazil or Portuguese-speaking African countries. ... [W]hite Portuguese children, whose speech was influenced by Brazilian media content, faced corrective or remedial speech interventions to regain the purity of their language. ... Portuguese speakers of African descent faced barriers to accessing health services and other public services because their Portuguese did not sound European.

We conclude this case study of the Council's response to racism by exploring the implications of some of the strongest critiques by scholars focused on structural approaches.

E. TENDAYI ACHIUME AND DEVON CARBADO, CRITICAL RACE THEORY MEETS THIRD WORLD APPROACHES TO INTERNATIONAL LAW
67 UCLA L. REV. (2021) 1462

Introduction
This Article articulates six important parallel thematic developments in Critical Race Theory (CRT) and Third World Approaches to International Law (TWAIL). ... [W]e are interested in both the critical moves through which CRT and TWAIL are articulated and the resistance, obfuscation, or delegitimization of those moves, especially in scholarly arenas. For simplicity, we frame international law as the site of concern for TWAIL scholars and constitutional law as the site of concern for Critical Race Theorists.

... [T]his Article is a critique of neither CRT nor TWAIL. One might, for example, reasonably ask the colonization question vis-à-vis CRT (why are the problems of empire, imperialism, and colonization largely absent from CRT?). In a similar vein, one might reasonably ask the racialization question vis-à-vis TWAIL (why are problems of racialization--particularly of nations, global power, and international law and relations--not a more central part of TWAIL?). ...

...

I. Parallel Moments of Inequality and Interventions

A. Moment I: Foundational Racial Capitalism

The first moment we describe implicates what Cedric Robinson calls "racial capitalism." Which is to say, here, both international law, on the TWAIL side, and constitutional law, on the CRT side, operate as regimes of power and violence that implicate racism, capitalism, and colonialism. ... [In] Moment I, there are social meaning attributions to nations and peoples (and nations of peoples) that facilitate, legitimize, and entrench global and domestic orderings of white supremacy, whose entailments have included conquest, expansionism, militarism, economic extraction, slavery, and genocide. ...

...

TWAIL's racial critique of sovereignty specifically and the international legal order more generally pays particularly close attention to positivism, the methodological means through which the racialization of sovereignty was achieved. ... TWAIL scholars have long argued that non-European nations did not, a priori, lack sovereignty. Positivist jurisprudence produced that "lack" through ostensibly objective facts about racially inferior people, uncivilized cultures, and dysfunctional and backward governments. ... By effectively defining

sovereignty as Europeanness, international law underwrote a white-dominated global order in which European nations exploited, dominated, and, in some instances, facilitated the genocide of Third World people.
...

B. Moment II: Formal Equality and Racial Inclusion

In Moment II, CRT and TWAIL foreground the problem of racial inclusion, albeit at different scales. ... TWAIL scholars focus on the formal inclusion of nonwhite peoples into the international society of sovereign nation states (under First World and white dominated international terms and norms) and CRT scholars focus on the formal inclusion of nonwhite peoples into citizenship (under white dominated domestic terms and norms). ... [These] acts of inclusion ... are not a fundamental reconfiguration of power but rather a particular technology through which to maintain, manage, and legitimize the prior hierarchical domestic and global racial orderings. ...

...

... [TWAIL sees] formal decolonization of the Third World ... as inclusion on terms that have ultimately ensured neocolonial domination, not substantive sovereignty for the former colonial nations. ... [T]he former colonial powers ... [promoted] international law and policy doctrines that were designed to maintain not only the subordinate status of Third World nations, but also the control First World nations had over the international legal system. The former colonies organized in various attempts to disrupt this reassertion of colonial power. But their efforts largely failed. ...

... [T]he postcolonial world was not a departure from the racial hierarchy on which colonialism was based but rather a rearticulation of that hierarchy on neocolonial terms. Antony Anghie and Siba N'zatioula Grovogui's scholarship have advanced a version of this claim, extending the analysis of neocolonial scholars, such as Kwame Nkrumah and Walter Rodney, to demonstrate how, following formal decolonization, First World nations deployed multiple dimensions of the international system, including sovereignty doctrine and international institutional arrangements, to reproduce the economic and political domination of the First World over the Third. ...

The story we are telling about the inclusion of Third World nations into sovereignty on racially hierarchical terms transcends the boundaries of formal sovereignty doctrines. Neocolonial assertions of the international legal system implicate development doctrines, international economic law, international humanitarian law, and domestic legal regimes. ...

...

C. Moment III: Colorblindness

In Moment III, CRT and TWAIL expose and contest various iterations of colorblindness, including the idea that race no longer matters in structuring society and lived experience. In this moment, the analytical and normative fight is about both the speakability of race and racism and whether the real and pressing issues of inequality are somewhere (anywhere) beyond the boundaries of race and racism--think class, think religion, think nationalism, think culture. ...

...

... TWAIL scholars have analyzed ... the reliance of international legal doctrine on purported cultural differences that Europeans used to establish themselves as morally and legally superior to non-European peoples they colonized, exploited, and exterminated, cloaking imperial projects of racial subordination in the language of distinctions between the "civilized" and the "uncivilized."

... [S]ome scholars in the field have been unwilling to name and confront the ways in which race has operated on the international landscape. Other scholars insufficiently distinguish between (and sometimes conflate) racial and cultural difference in ways that obfuscates how race has structured the global order and the treatment of nations and peoples within it. Still other scholars "in effect, minimize the role that race plays in international law," elide the "sociopolitical system of Global White Supremacy," and reduce their conceptualization of racism to the individual prejudices of a small number of aberrant international law scholars and practitioners. Each of the preceding scholarly approaches reflects a particular technique of colorblindness in the sense of avoiding or marginalizing concerns about race and racism or disappearing them altogether.

...

D. Moment IV: Social Responsibility and Agency

In Moment IV, CRT and TWAIL scholars engage and repudiate neoliberal claims about social responsibility and agency. Often expressed in the form of rhetorical questions, those claims look something like this: What's wrong with Africa? What's wrong with Black people? Why are Black people always rioting in their own communities? Why are they always killing themselves? Why are African nations always at war? Why are they so corrupt? Why are they so violent? Fundamentally, these questions are ... ways of rearticulating concerns about Black people's fitness for citizenship and non-white nations' fitness for sovereignty, to wit: Why can't Black people properly manage the citizenship they have been given (by white people) and why can't non-white nations properly manage the sovereignty they have been given (by white nations)?

Against the background normality, legitimacy, and ubiquity of questions of the foregoing sort, it is no wonder that the interventionary table for both civil rights and international law is set largely with ideas about foreign aid, antidiscrimination, and "racial preferences," rather than ideas about reparations, redistribution, unjust enrichment, and disgorgement. ...

...

TWAIL scholars, too, have surfaced how international law and its implementations have racialized the Third World and its peoples as "proper" subjects of First World receivership. For example, Makau Mutua contends that, as a historical matter, international law routinely depicted the Third World as culturally aberrant savages-- corrupt, despotic, and violent -- and the populations of those states as "powerless, helpless innocent[s] whose naturalist attributes have been negated by the primitive and offensive actions of the [Third World] state. . . . "

...

...

E. Moment V: Quasi and Second-Class Scholarship

... Moment V ... [focuses on] an epistemological legitimacy problem. ... CRT and TWAIL are always already under pressure to signal and supply intellectual credibility and to assimilate into, dare we say, the "civilized" conventions of constitutional law and international law, respectively. The perception that both literatures exist outside the boundaries of the presumptively neutral scholarly conventions of constitutional law and international law has engendered either criticism or willful disattention and nonengagement. ...

...

F. Moment VI: Reconstruction and Transformation

Moment VI speaks to CRT's and TWAIL's reconstructive interventions. In neither CRT nor TWAIL is this interventionary sensibility predicated on the view that law, standing alone, can produce a racially emancipatory world. The point is rather that law as a site of power should not be ceded but rather mobilized progressively to move the social justice needle. ...

...

... While the critique of international law is a fundamental part of TWAIL's intellectual identity, the theory also reflects a commitment to rearticulate international law to achieve less subordinating and more liberatory ends. ... [To] borrow from Luis Eslava and Sundhya Pahuja, ... "[r]esistance and reform ... come together in TWAIL to form a single process of destabilisation and renewal of international law's history and operation. Rather than replacement, TWAIL scholarship is more interested in overcoming international law's problems while still remaining committed to the idea of an international normative regime ... ."[301] For many within TWAIL, international law retains transformative potential, and law remains a means of constraining power, notwithstanding the indeterminacy that inheres in international law and in law generally. Thus, even while TWAIL scholars remain determined to confront and critique the imperial and colonial nature of international law, they view the abandonment of international law as a site of struggle, and potential emancipatory gains as a luxury that many Third World peoples cannot afford. ...

...

---

[301] L. Eslava and S. Pahuja, 'Beyond the (Post)Colonial: TWAIL and the Everyday Life of International Law,' 45 *Verfassung Und Recht In Übersee* (2012) 195, at 204.

QUESTIONS

1. What conclusions might be drawn from the century-long history of engagement by both U.S. civil society groups and the U.S. Government in international debates over racism?

2. Consider the feasibility of the Council's global approach to anti-racism in light of the following analysis by Kevin Davis, in 'Legal Responses to Black Subordination, Global Perspectives', 134 *Harv. L. Rev.* (2021) 359:

[A] global perspective need not and should not presume that there is either a universal Black experience, a universal definition of Blackness, or a universally effective set of legal responses to Black subordination. ... ['Legal universalist'] projects founder whenever either (a) the people in the relevant jurisdictions face different problems or (b) the relevant legal response can be expected to have different effects in different environments. Both these factors ... are likely to limit the value of comparative analysis as a way of identifying legal responses to the problems that Black people face. Afro-descendants in different countries have different histories and do not necessarily have the same ideals and aspirations.

3. Does it matter if the focus of international anti-racism efforts is on 'racism' as opposed to 'racial discrimination'? Anna Spain Bradley, in 'Human Rights Racism', 32 *Harv. Hum. Rts. J* (2019) 1, at 58, suggests that UN efforts have stopped short of tackling racism per se. She argues that it is essential to 'acknowledge the deeper problems embedded in racism, including the use of race as a means for categorizing humans, racial ideology that promotes racial supremacy, and racial bias.'

4. Critical Race Theory, with its emphasis on the need for intersectional and structural approaches to ending racism, has drawn a backlash in the United States. In March 2022, former President Trump said: 'Getting critical race theory out of our schools is not just a matter of values, it's also a matter of national survival. ... If we allow the Marxists and Communists and Socialists to teach our children to hate America, there will be no one left to defend ... its freedom' [Newsweek, 13 March 2022]'. On 22 April 2022, Florida Governor Ron de Santis signed House Bill 7 on Individual Freedom (the 'Stop Woke Act') to confront 'both corporate wokeness and Critical Race Theory in schools'. 'Schools are required to teach factual information on topics including African American history and the Holocaust instead of subjective indoctrination that pushes collective guilt."[302] Discuss in light of the materials above.

Israel

The situation in the Palestinian territories occupied by Israel since 1967 has long been among the most controversial and divisive of issues both on the global agenda and on that of the UN Human Rights Council. The United States vetoed 57 Security Council resolutions critical of Israel between 1972 and 2024.[303] One consequence was to move such debates to other UN organs. In 1975, the General Assembly (Res. 3379) notoriously declared that 'Zionism is a form of racism'. The vote was 72 in favour, 35 against, and 32 abstentions. That resolution was revoked in 1991 (Res. 46/86).

The Human Rights Council's Agenda has long been divided into ten different 'items'. Under item 4 – 'human rights situations that require the Council's attention' – violations anywhere in the world can be debated. A separate item 7 concerns the 'human rights situation in Palestine and other occupied Arab territories'. No other country situation is accorded a separate item. The Organization of Islamic Cooperation and other blocs within the Council argue that this is justified because the situation is different by virtue of the ongoing occupation.

---

[302] 'Governor Ron DeSantis Signs Legislation to Protect Floridians from Discrimination and Woke Indoctrination' (22 April 2022) at www.flgov.com
[303] https://www.un.org/depts/dhl/resguide/scact_veto_table_en.htm

The Western Group and others consider the separate item to be discriminatory and evidence of a double standard that singles out Israel and downplays other situations of grave concern. In December 2006, the UN Secretary-General expressed his concern at the Council's 'disproportionate focus on violations by Israel.' He added: 'Not that Israel should be given a free pass. Absolutely not. But the Council should give the same attention to grave violations committed by other states as well.'

In 1993, the Council appointed a Special Rapporteur on the situation of human rights in the Palestinian territories occupied since 1967, who reports annually to the Human Rights Council and the General Assembly. The Council has also launched a series of high-profile inquiries. One of the most controversial was the so-called Goldstone Report, named after Richard Goldstone, the chairman of the Fact Finding Mission on the Gaza Conflict. The 452-page report (UN Doc. A/HRC/12/48 (2009)) concluded that grave violations of international human rights and humanitarian law and possible war crimes and crimes against humanity had been committed by both the Israel Defence Forces and the Palestinian armed groups. It called for action by the Council, as well as the Security Council and the General Assembly. The Gaza authorities facilitated a visit by the Commission, but Israel refused cooperation.

The report proved to be the start of a new round of ongoing and continuing controversy. It was powerfully criticized by Israel, the United States, and some other Western governments, and led to a severe backlash against human rights organizations in Israel,[304] culminating in six leading Palestinian NGOs being designated by Israel as 'terrorist organizations' in 2021, and raids on their offices in August 2022 leading to their closure under Article 319 of the Emergency Regulations of 1945. The representative of Human Rights Watch had already been expelled from Israel in 2019.

Since the Goldstone Report, the Council has continued to appoint various inquiries to examine the situation but Israel has consistently refused to cooperate and has rejected the relevant reports. On 19 June 2018, the Trump administration withdrew the United States from membership of the Council. U.S. Ambassador Nikki Haley condemned the Council as 'a protector of human rights abusers and a cesspool of political bias.' She especially singled out:

> [T]he chronic bias against Israel. Last year, the United States made it clear that we would not accept the continued existence of agenda item seven, which singles out Israel in a way that no other country is singled out. Earlier this year, as it has in previous years, the Human Rights Council passed five resolutions against Israel – more than the number passed against North Korea, Iran, and Syria combined. This disproportionate focus and unending hostility towards Israel is clear proof that the council is motivated by political bias, not by human rights.

Israeli Prime Minister Benjamin Netanyahu was reported to have thanked 'Trump and Haley for their "courageous decision against the hypocrisy and the lies of the so-called UN Human Rights Council".'[305]

In May 2021, the Council convened a Special Session in response to an outbreak of violence that, according to the Special Rapporteur, led to the deaths of at least 12 civilians in Israel and 240 Palestinians, including 63 children, in Gaza. In response, the Council (Res. S-30/1, adopted by 24 votes in favour, nine against, and 14 abstentions) created 'an ongoing independent, international commission of inquiry' with a mandate 'to investigate in the Occupied Palestinian Territory, including East Jerusalem, and in Israel all alleged violations of international humanitarian law and all alleged violations and abuses of international human rights law leading up to and since 13 April 2021, and all underlying root causes of recurrent tensions, instability and protraction of conflict, including systematic discrimination and repression based on national, ethnic, racial or religious identity'.

The following is a UN summary of the debate in the Third Committee of the General Assembly on 27 October 2022 (UN Doc. GA/SHC/4360) when the Commission's first report was presented:

---

[304] H. Khoury-Bisharat, 'The Unintended Consequences of the Goldstone Commission of Inquiry on Human Rights Organizations in Israel', 30 *Eur. J. Int'l L.* (2019) 877.

[305] 'US leaving UN Human Rights Council – "a cesspool of political bias"', CNN (20 June 2018).

NAVANETHEM PILLAY, Chairperson of the Commission …, presenting her report (UN Doc. A/77/328), highlighted the responsibility of Member States to ensure a just solution for the situation in Israel and Palestine that protects the human rights of all. Israel is treating the occupation as permanent, she said, annexing parts of the West Bank while hiding behind a fiction of temporariness. This permanence and annexation, including the purported de jure annexation of East Jerusalem and the Golan Heights, have led the Commission to conclude that Israel's occupation is now unlawful, she added. Actions of the Israeli Government may constitute the war crime of transferring – directly or indirectly – part of one's own civilian population as well as deportation or forcible transfer.

… Noting Israel's security-based justifications for some of its actions, the Commission found that many actions in the West Bank are often used as a pretext to justify territorial expansion and that it could not identify efforts to end the occupation. Instead, statements made by officials indicate that the State intends for the occupation to be permanent. Citing coercive treatment of Palestinians, including destruction of properties and homes, mass incarceration and limitations on access to livelihoods, she said this environment is meant to force Palestinians to leave their homes to make room for more Israeli settlements. The report suggests that Israel has no intention of ending the occupation, and the conflict, if left unaddressed by the international community, will continue interminably, she said. The General Assembly should address the fact that Palestine is occupied due to the persistent refusal of successive Israeli governments to abide by international law. Next month, it will be 55 years since the Security Council adopted resolution 242, calling for Israel to withdraw from territories it occupied in the 1967 war, and yet Israel remains in occupation without any consequence, she said. …

In the ensuing interactive dialogue, the *representative of Israel* recounted the death of five-year-old Ido Avigal by Hamas rocket shrapnel that penetrated a bomb shelter in Lod during a strike. He said that his story, like those of all Israeli victims of terror, is omitted from the hate-filled Commissioners' report, as it deliberately omits Hamas rockets in lieu of placing blame on the law-abiding democracy of Israel. Pointing to Ido Avigal's parents in the conference room, he asked Commission members to explain why they ignored their son's murder, calling them heartless and dismissing the report as illegitimate. He said that, although it is no longer politically correct today to be antisemitic, the world now burns the Jewish State, as it once burned Jews at the stake, and decried the Human Rights Council's disproportionate targeting of his country. The Council has adopted more resolutions condemning Israel than condemning Syria, the Democratic People's Republic of Korea and Iran combined, he said. Adding that this inquisition of the Commission of Inquiry is led by countries like Libya, Venezuela and China, he cited the United States and United Kingdom's opposition to Ms. Pillay's open-ended mandate, calling her and her colleagues antisemitic and non-objective.

The *observer for the State of Palestine* said that Israel has no sovereignty over the Occupied Palestinian Territory, including East Jerusalem. This is guaranteed by law and not an opinion, she stressed. She condemned Israel's refusal to allow the Special Rapporteur and Commission of Inquiry entry, as well as its obstructing Security Council visits to the Territories, stating that this is evidence of Israel's efforts to hide its colonial and apartheid regime. … Israel's refusal to implement [various UN] resolutions and the continued lack of action or accountability from the international community will only result in more arbitrary detentions, land theft, maimings and killings. She asked what third party obligations are regarding impunity in the context of occupation.

The *representative of the European Union* … said that his delegation did not support the creation of this Commission of Inquiry because of concerns over its broad mandate. He expressed great concern over the occupation that began in 1967, calling on Israel to significantly improve the lives of the Palestinian people.

...

> Responding to delegates, Ms. PILLAY said: "I am 81 years old, and this is the first time I
> have been accused of antisemitism." Expressing astonishment at antisemitic labels for the
> report, she stressed that it is based on law and that Israel is bound by international law,
> just like all countries. Addressing criticism of the mandate itself, she said it is open-ended
> and will allow time to address issues raised, such as armed Palestinian groups and the
> implications of the conflict on children. She said that the Commission condemns all
> violence and expressed condolences to the mother of Ido Avigal, adding that, if Israel will
> allow her Commission access to the country, she will express her sympathies personally to
> all victims. ...

On 7 October 2023, heavily-armed Hamas forces launched a wave of attacks on Israel from Gaza, targeting and killing some 1,200 people - overwhelmingly civilians - in Israel, and taking 240 hostages, including children and elderly people. The Government of Israel responded that it was at war and within ten weeks over 20,000 people in Gaza (70 per cent of whom were women and children) were said to have been killed by Israeli bombing.[306] On 14 June 2024 the UN reported that at least 37,266 Palestinians had been killed and 85,102 injured.[307]

Within three days of the Hamas attacks, the UN COI pointed to clear evidence of war crimes on both sides and on 27 October 2023 it accused 'all parties to the conflict' of having 'shown reckless disregard for civilian life' and called for them to 'comply with international law to prevent atrocities from continuing'.

While some partisans on each side suggested that the blame lay entirely with the other side, the UN Secretary-General, António Guterres, told the Security Council on 24 October 2023:

> I have condemned unequivocally the horrifying and unprecedented 7 October acts of
> terror by Hamas in Israel. Nothing can justify the deliberate killing, injuring and
> kidnapping of civilians – or the launching of rockets against civilian targets. All hostages
> must be treated humanely and released immediately and without conditions. ...

> It is important to also recognize the attacks by Hamas did not happen in a vacuum. The
> Palestinian people have been subjected to 56 years of suffocating occupation. They have
> seen their land steadily devoured by settlements and plagued by violence; their economy
> stifled; their people displaced and their homes demolished. Their hopes for a political
> solution to their plight have been vanishing.

In response, Israeli ambassador Gilad Erdan accused Guterres of expressing 'an understanding for terrorism and murder'. Israel called for Guterres's immediate resignation and refused visas to UN humanitarian officials.

After various draft resolutions were vetoed by different states in the Security Council, the General Assembly, by a vote of 120-14-45 called for a 'humanitarian truce' and urged all parties to comply with IHRL and IHL. Ambassador Erdan responded that "the UN is committed to ensuring further atrocity. According to the family of nations, Israel has no right to defend itself.'

In June 2024, the COI presented two reports to the Human Rights Council. The first was a 59-page report on Hamas's attacks in Israel (UN Doc. A/HRC/56/CRP.3) and the second a 126-page report on Israel's assault on Gaza (UN Doc. A/HRC/56/CRP.4). In summarizing its findings (UN Doc. A/HRC/56/26) the COI found that a range of war crimes had been committed both by Hamas and Israeli forces. But by this time the main focus of the international community was on the announcement by the Prosecutor of the International Criminal Court that he had sought arrest warrants against three leaders of Hamas and the Prime Minister and Defense Minister of Israel (see Ch. 16B, below).

---

[306] '20,000 Dead and Counting: The Battle Over Verifying Gaza's Death Toll', *Haaretz*, 26 December 2023.
[307] https://www.ochaopt.org/content/humanitarian-situation-update-179-gaza-strip

On 29 December 2023, South Africa instituted proceedings against Israel before the International Court of Justice (ICJ)[308] claiming that 'the conduct of Israel — through its State organs, State agents, and other persons and entities acting on its instructions or under its direction, control or influence — in relation to Palestinians in Gaza, is in violation of its obligations under the Genocide Convention'. It sought provisional measures, some of which were included in an Order delivered by the Court on 26 January 2024. By a vote of 15-2 (with Judge Sebutinde and Judge ad hoc Barak dissenting) the Court ordered Israel, in relation to Palestinians in Gaza, to:

> ... take all measures within its power to prevent the commission of all acts within the scope of Article II of this Convention, in particular:
>
> > (a) killing members of the group;
> >
> > (b) causing serious bodily or mental harm to members of the group;
> >
> > (c) deliberately inflicting on the group conditions of life calculated to bring about its physical destruction in whole or in part; and
> >
> > (d) imposing measures intended to prevent births within the group;

In addition, Israel was ordered to: 'ensure with immediate effect that its military does not commit any' of those acts; 'take all measures within its power to prevent and punish the direct and public incitement to commit genocide in relation to members of the Palestinian group in the Gaza Strip'; 'take immediate and effective measures to enable the provision of urgently needed basic services and humanitarian assistance to address the adverse conditions of life faced by Palestinians in the Gaza Strip; and to report to the Court within a month on the measures taken to give effect to its Order. On 28 March 2024, the Court indicated additional measures.

On 24 May 2024 further measures were ordered in response to what the Court characterized as a 'disastrous' humanitarian situation in Rafah, the last remaining part of Gaza that had not been devastated and to which over one million Palestinians had fled. Rafah was then being targeted by a major military ground offensive. It concluded that the exacerbated crisis constituted a change in the situation that warranted new measures. The Court (by 13 votes to 2) ordered Israel to:

> Immediately halt its military offensive, and any other action in the Rafah Governorate, which may inflict on the Palestinian group in Gaza conditions of life that could bring about its physical destruction in whole or in part; ...
>
> Maintain open the Rafah crossing for unhindered provision at scale of urgently needed basic services and humanitarian assistance; ...
>
> Take effective measures to ensure the unimpeded access to the Gaza Strip of any commission of inquiry, fact-finding mission or other investigative body mandated by competent organs of the United Nations to investigate allegations of genocide; ...

QUESTION

The United States has consistently argued that the issues that have arisen in the complex and contested relationship between Israel and Palestine could only be resolved through a political settlement. Where do the various elements described above fit within such an approach?

---

[308] *Application of the Convention on the Prevention and Punishment of the Crime of Genocide in the Gaza Strip (South Africa v. Israel).*

3. The Special Procedures System

In 2006, former UN Secretary-General Kofi Annan described the special procedures as 'the crown jewel of the [UN human rights] system'. Those procedures consist of mandates focused solely on a specific country and a range of 'thematic procedures' devoted to a theme rather than a state or region and thus with a potentially global scope. The first such mechanism was the Working Group on Disappearances, established by the Commission in 1980. Its origins lay in efforts to respond to the massive 'disappearances' that took place during the 1970s in Argentina's 'dirty war' against leftist and other forces opposed to the military government. The government's strategy was effective in avoiding condemnation by international human rights fora until 1978, when the Inter-American Commission on Human Rights issued a damning indictment. Despite this precedent, within the UN context many governments were reluctant to 'name' Argentina, for a variety of reasons ranging from trade interests to fear that they themselves might be next on the list.

To get around this opposition, the UN Commission opted to avoid a country-specific inquiry and instead established the first 'thematic' mechanism. Argentina hoped that the thematic approach would not single out any one country, would demonstrate that it was only one of many countries that had problems and would give a significant number of governments a strong incentive to ensure that the new mechanism would be kept under careful political control and thus remain ineffectual. But in the first few years of its existence, the Disappearances Working Group played an important role in developing techniques which were subsequently to serve as a model for a growing range of mechanisms dealing with other themes.

Number and Scope

Rapporteurs focused on specific countries are dealt with in Sec. B3, below. While the number of country rapporteurs has remained relatively stable, the thematic mechanisms have grown almost exponentially. In 1985, there were three, there were six in 1990, 14 in 1995, 21 in 2000, 28 in 2007, and by 2024 there were 46. Of these, six were working groups: on disappearances, arbitrary detention, mercenaries, people of African descent, discrimination against women, business, and peasants' rights. In 2023, by way of example, these mechanisms submitted 174 reports to the Council or the Assembly, including 56 country visit reports. The same year, 723 communications were sent to 126 governments and 163 non-state actors. In only about 43% of cases did governments reply. 484 press releases or other media notices were issued, and these often drew more of a response from the government concerned.[309]

The 46 mandates deal with: (1) disappearances; (2) extrajudicial executions; (3) torture; (4) freedom of religion or belief; (5) the sale of children, child prostitution and child pornography; (6) arbitrary detention; (7) freedom of opinion and expression; (8) contemporary forms of racism; (9) independence of judges and lawyers; (10) violence against women; (11) hazardous substances and waste; (12) extreme poverty; (13) migrants; (14) foreign debt; (15) the right to education; (16) the right to food; (17) the right to housing; (18) human rights defenders; (19) indigenous peoples; (20) people of African descent; (21) the right to health; (22) internally displaced persons; (23) trafficking in persons; (24) mercenaries; (25) terrorism; (26) international solidarity; (27) business; (28) minority issues; (29) contemporary forms of slavery; (30) right to water and sanitation; (31) cultural rights; (32) freedom of assembly and association; (33) discrimination against women; (34) a democratic and equitable international order; (35) truth and justice; (36) environment; (37) older persons; (38) persons with disabilities; (39) unilateral coercive measures; (40) privacy; (41) persons with albinism; (42) sexual orientation and gender identity; (43) right to development; (44) persons affected by leprosy; (45) climate change; and (46) peasants' rights. Thus, in the years since the creation of the first mechanism in 1980, more than one new mechanism has been created on average every year.

The terminology used for the different mechanisms is confusing — 'Working Group', 'Special Rapporteur', 'Independent Expert', 'Representative' or 'Special Representative' of the Secretary-General — but relatively little significance attaches to it in practice. A few are appointed by the Secretary-General or the HCHR but most are appointed by the Chairperson of the Council who is expected to 'consult' with the regional groups before making an appointment. Those selected are generally prominent personalities from human rights-related

---

[309] Facts and figures with regard to the special procedures in 2023, UN Doc. A/HRC/55/69/Add.1 (2024).

backgrounds, including academics, lawyers, economists and NGO leaders. The first female expert was not appointed until 1994, but by 2023 mandate-holders were 58% female. The experts receive no financial reward for their work, although their expenses are covered. They rely upon the OHCHR for secretariat services, but they have long complained of the gross inadequacy of the assistance available to them as a result of chronic financial and staff shortages within that Office. Some of them receive considerable financial support from governments or foundations, but others do not.

Mandate-holders self-nominate through a transparent nomination process. A Consultative Group, consisting of five government representatives who consult with all stakeholders, then makes ranked recommendations to the President of the Council. If the latter does not follow the group's recommendations, reasons must be provided for the divergence. 'Individuals holding decision-making positions in governments or in any other organization or entity which could represent a conflict of interest with the responsibilities arising from the mandate' are not eligible. A mandate-holder may be renewed once for a total of two three-year terms. The resolution establishing the Council envisaged that the Council might 'streamline, merge or eventually dismantle' some mandates. While some country mandates have been terminated, no thematic mandate has been.

Functions

The functions undertaken by the Special Procedures (with variations according to whether it is a country or a thematic mandate, and the nature of the issues involved) include the following: (i) responding to allegations of violations brought to their attention, usually through correspondence with the government and sometimes by issuing public statements; (ii) visiting a country to assess the situation and make recommendations to the government and the Council; (iii) undertaking 'thematic' studies that enhance the understanding of an issue perhaps contributing to the process of developing jurisprudence; and (iv) reporting annually to the Council and, in many cases, also the General Assembly.

We turn now to consider each of the principal functions of the Council, in which the Special Procedures play an important part: standard-setting, country reporting, examining complaints, and carrying out the Universal Periodic Review.

Standard-Setting

The work of many of the Special Procedures has led to the elaboration of many new sets of guidelines, codes, recommendations and such like.[310] Among the more prominent examples of the latter are the Guiding Principles on Business and Human Rights (2011) and the Guiding Principles on Internal Displacement (1998),[311] both of which originated from the work of experts reporting to the Council. A more recent example are the Méndez Principles on Effective Interviewing for Investigations and Information Gathering (2021), which emerged from the work of the former Special Rapporteur on torture, Juan Méndez.

QUESTIONS

In 1986, the General Assembly (Res. 41/120) adopted 'guidelines' for future human rights standard-setting. It suggested that proposed instruments should, inter alia:

(a) be consistent with the existing body of international human rights law;
(b) be of fundamental character and derive from the inherent dignity and worth of the human person;
(c) be sufficiently precise to give rise to identifiable and practicable rights and obligations;
(d) provide, where appropriate, realistic and effective implementation machinery, including reporting systems;
(e) attract broad international support.

---

[310] See generally J. Alvarez, 'Standard-Setting in UN System Organizations', in J. Klabbers (ed.), *The Cambridge Companion to International Organizations Law* (2022) 120.
[311] 'Twenty Years of the Guiding Principles on Internal Displacement', 59 *Forced Migration Rev.* (2018) 4-51.

Are these guidelines likely to exclude very many proposals? What factors do you consider might be the most crucial in deciding whether to embark upon a new standard-setting exercise?

Country Reports

Reporting on the human rights situation in individual countries constitutes an important part of the work of the Council, although it remains controversial and contested. Country reports are prepared by country rapporteurs, thematic rapporteurs and ad hoc commissions of inquiry. It bears emphasizing that the focus on violations is only one part of the Council's overall work.

A. COUNTRY RAPPORTEURS

As of 2024, the following 14 country situations were being examined under separate 'country mandates' by the Human Rights Council: Afghanistan, Belarus, Burundi, Cambodia, Central African Republic, Democratic People's Republic of Korea, Eritrea, Islamic Republic of Iran, Mali, Myanmar, Palestinian territories occupied since 1967, Russia, Somalia, and the Syrian Arab Republic. The establishment of a separate country mandate is considered to be a 'badge of dishonour' by concerned states and such decisions are always hotly contested. Over the past decade, however, the Council has been much more likely to establish a commission of inquiry rather than seek to create a new country mandate. The latter generally have three commissioners, a sizeable staff, and a broad mandate. For now, we consider the functions that are served by a country rapporteur and the ways in which they might make a difference. The following report on Iran provides an example. Note that this reporting takes place parallel to examinations by treaty bodies of the reports submitted by States Parties to each treaty.[312] The Council first appointed a Special Rapporteur on Iran in 1984. The position finished in 2002 but was reinstated in 2011.

JAVAID REHMAN, REPORT OF THE SPECIAL RAPPORTEUR ON THE SITUATION OF HUMAN RIGHTS IN THE ISLAMIC REPUBLIC OF IRAN UN DOC. A/HRC/49/75 (2022)

Introduction

...

2. The Special Rapporteur would again like to highlight that, despite repeated requests, he has not yet been granted access to the Islamic Republic of Iran. ...

3. The Special Rapporteur was able to engage with victims, their families and members of civil society and collect information, most notably through submissions and interviews. ...

4. The high risk of reprisals that individuals and organizations face for engaging with international human rights mechanisms represents in itself a serious human rights concern, but is equally a distressing sign of how the authorities view international human rights mechanisms and the individuals engaging with them. ...

II. Overview of the situation of human rights in the Islamic Republic of Iran

A. Arbitrary deprivation of life

5. Between 1 January and 1 December 2021, at least 275 people were executed, including at least 2 child offenders and 10 women, for charges involving murder, drug crimes, moharebeh (taking up arms to take lives or property or to create fear in the public), efsad-e fil-arz (spreading corruption on earth), baghy (armed rebellion) and rape. ...

...

---

[312] For example, see the concluding observations of the Human Rights Committee on Iran (UN Doc. CCPR/C/IRN/CO/4 (2023).

Excessive use of force

9. The use of unlawful force by security, law enforcement and other State agents continued at an alarming scale in the context of peaceful assemblies, against border couriers and in places of detention, without subsequent investigations or accountability. The atmosphere of impunity surrounding arbitrary deprivation of life by State agents sends an affirmation that there will be no consequences for such illegal acts.

10. One of the most egregious examples in the context of peaceful protests during 2021 was the use of lethal force against participants in a series of protests that erupted in mid-July 2021 in over 20 cities in Khuzestan Province, subsequently extending to other areas [and] referred to as the "Uprising of the Thirsty". Testimonies, photographs and video footage show widespread use of unlawful force against protesters, many of whom belong to the Arab minority. …

…

Prison conditions

16. The Special Rapporteur regrets the continued ill-treatment by prison guards, overcrowding, and hygiene deficiencies in prison, as detailed in previous reports. Leaked videos from closed-circuit television cameras in the public wards of Evin prison, hacked by the group Edalat-e Ali, show prison guards beating or otherwise ill-treating prisoners, overcrowded prison cells, and a solitary cell with inhuman conditions. On 24 August 2021, the head of the Prisons Organization apologized and promised to investigate abuses and prevent further violations. …

…

B. Arbitrary detention

Situation of human rights lawyers and defenders

22. The Special Rapporteur remains dismayed at the continued arbitrary detention of human rights defenders and lawyers following unfair trials, and their long prison sentences and harsh bail conditions as they face vaguely worded charges of "acting against national security" and using "propaganda against the regime". They operate in an increasingly unpredictable and repressive environment for merely exercising the right to freedom of expression, association or assembly. …

…

C. Rights to freedom of expression, association and peaceful assembly

28. In November 2021, the Press Supervisory Board of the Ministry of Culture and Islamic Guidance revoked the operating licence of the State-run newspaper Kelid, forcing it to stop publishing … days after Kelid published an article with a headline that translates to "Millions of Iranians living under the poverty line".

29. The authorities continued to unduly restrict freedom of expression online, including through the imposition of localized Internet shutdowns during protests or sensitive periods … .

…

D. Adequate standard of living

34. … [A]bout 20 per cent of the population with the highest income holds 47 per cent of the wealth, while the 20 per cent with the lowest income holds 0.5 per cent of the wealth. High food and living costs, combined with low wages, continued to push people below the poverty line and increase the inequality gap. Over 30 per cent of the population was estimated to live below the poverty line as of August 2021, while some lawmakers estimate the number to be 60 per cent. At least 25 million people are in absolute poverty, unable to meet their most basic needs, such as food, water, housing and education. …

…

F. Situation of women and girls

40. In November 2021, the Guardian Council ratified the law on young people and protection of the family. The Special Rapporteur has previously raised grave concerns about the damaging consequences of the law in terms of the right of women and girls to sexual and reproductive health. The law is aimed at increasing

population growth by imposing severe restrictions and prohibitions on abortion, voluntary sterilization and access to modern contraceptive goods, services and information. ...

41. The 2021 law also provides direct and indirect incentives to increase early marriage, without providing an age restriction. The legal age of marriage for girls remains 13, and girls at a younger age can also enter into a marriage contract with the consent of their father and the permission of a competent court, in violation of international law. ...

42. The Special Rapporteur notes with regret that there has been no development in the adoption of the bill on preserving the dignity of women and protecting them against violence. The Special Rapporteur continued to receive reports of "honour" killings, where perpetrators are exonerated or their punishments reduced due to particular exemptions from criminal liability in law or the families' reluctance to pursue the prosecution of a family member.

...

III. Accountability for human rights violations

...

49. The fundamental challenge to accountability in the Islamic Republic of Iran is presented by the institutional legal and political apparatus, which in itself is not compliant with the State's obligations under international law. The exercise of power, the basis for governance, including the relationship between those in power and those subject to that power, is based on the Constitution of 1979, which entrenches an Islamic political ideology as both the foundation for and the aim of governance. The form of government, known as *velayat-e faqih*, consolidates executive, legislative and judicial authority in the position of the Supreme Leader, which is not a popularly elected position. The Assembly of Experts, an 88-member clerical body, is authorized to appoint, monitor and dismiss the Supreme Leader, but has never questioned the Supreme Leader in practice. As such, and as elaborated in the Constitution, there is no meaningful separation of power within this system of governance. The Constitution further establishes a system of governance bodies that are either not subject to popular elections, for example the Guardian Council and the Expediency Council, or that are subject to elections based on strict criteria for candidates who are vetted by the Guardian Council, such as the parliament, the Assembly of Experts and the President. The ideology of the State features as a precondition for any form of political participation, is foundational for the policies of the State and its various bodies, and is further used for the interpretation of individual rights. It is clear that this system of governance establishes a particular relationship between individuals and the State, where the maintenance of the system of governance and the political ideology takes precedence over protecting and respecting the rights of individuals. ... The Government stressed the right of each nation to choose its form of government and ... noted the complete independence of the judiciary ... .

...

IV. Recommendations

A. Accountability for human rights violations

67. The Special Rapporteur recommends that the Islamic Republic of Iran:

(a) Undertake fundamental reforms towards the establishment of a system of accountability in line with international law, including constitutional, legislative and administrative reforms to ensure separation of powers, political pluralism and democratic participation in governance and decision-making;

(b) Undertake reforms to ensure the complete independence of the judiciary, including through the dissolution of the revolutionary courts, and reforms to ensure transparency in judicial appointments, which should be made based on merit and in the absence of any discriminatory conditions;

...

B. Death penalty

68. The Special Rapporteur calls on the authorities to immediately abolish, through legislation, the death penalty for all offences. ...

...

70. The Special Rapporteur urges States imposing sanctions on the Islamic Republic of Iran to ensure that measures such as humanitarian exemptions are given broad and practical effect and are promptly and effectively implemented to minimize the adverse consequences of sanctions on human rights, especially during the COVID-19 pandemic.

71. The Special Rapporteur urges the international community to call for accountability with respect to long-standing emblematic events that have been met with persistent impunity, including the enforced disappearances and summary and arbitrary executions of 1988 and the November 2019 protests.

* * *

Also in 2022, another Special Rapporteur, whose mandate focuses on 'the negative impact of unilateral coercive measures on the enjoyment of human rights", undertook an official country visit to Iran. Her report concluded that sanctions against Iran have had 'a serious negative impact on the country's economy, leading to serious violations of human rights and humanitarian challenges.' She recommended that the sanctions be lifted and called 'on international community and humanitarian actors to assist the Government' to mitigate their impact. (UN Doc. A/HRC/51/33/Add.1 (2022)).

QUESTION

How far should a Special Rapporteur go in challenging the basic system of government in a country? What considerations might be relevant?

B. COUNTRY REPORTS BY THEMATIC SPECIAL RAPPORTEURS

Thematic mandate-holders generally undertake two or three country missions annually. The purpose of these missions is explained below in the Manual prepared by the mandate-holders to guide their own activities. We then examine a critical report concerning a mission to China, and the government's response.

MANUAL OF OPERATIONS OF THE SPECIAL PROCEDURES OF THE HUMAN RIGHTS COUNCIL
(11 AUGUST 2008)

...

52. Country visits are an essential means to obtain direct and first-hand information on human rights violations. They allow for direct observation of the human rights situation and facilitate an intensive dialogue with all relevant state authorities, including those in the executive, legislative and judicial branches. They also allow for contact with and information gathering from victims, relatives of victims, witnesses, national human rights institutions, international and local NGOs and other members of civil society, the academic community, and officials of international agencies present in the country concerned.

53. Country visits generally last between one and two weeks but can be shorter or longer if the circumstances so require. The visit occurs at the invitation of a State … .

54. Country visits ... enhance awareness ... of the specific problems ... inter alia, through meetings, briefings, press coverage of the visit and dissemination of the report.

...

56. When a State does not respond to requests for an invitation to visit, it is appropriate for a mandate-holder to remind the Government concerned, to draw the attention of the Council to the outstanding request, and to take other appropriate measures … .

57. Considerations which might lead a mandate-holder to request to visit a country include, inter alia, human rights developments at the national level (whether positive or negative), the availability of reliable information regarding human rights violations falling within the mandate, or a wish to pursue a particular thematic interest. Other factors ... might include considerations of geographical balance, the expected impact of the visit and the willingness of national actors to cooperate with the mandate-holder, the likelihood of follow-up on any recommendations made, the recent adoption by one or more treaty bodies of relevant concluding observations, the upcoming examination of the situation by one or more treaty bodies, recent or proposed visits by other Special Procedure mandate-holders, the list of countries scheduled for consideration under the Council's Universal Periodic Review (UPR) mechanism, follow up to the recommendations and conclusions of the UPR mechanism, and the priorities reflected in OHCHR's country engagement strategy.

REVISED TERMS OF REFERENCE FOR COUNTRY VISITS BY SPECIAL PROCEDURE MANDATE HOLDERS
UN DOC. A/HRC/34/34/ADD.1 (2017) 51

During country visits, special procedures mandate holders of the United Nations Human Rights Council, as well as United Nations staff accompanying them, should be given the following guarantees and facilities by the Government that invited them to visit its country:

(a) Freedom of movement in any part of the country, including facilitation of transport, particularly to restricted areas;

(b) Freedom of inquiry, in particular as regards:

    (iii)   Contacts with central and local authorities of all branches of government;

    (iv)   Private contacts with representatives of civil society, including non-governmental organizations, other private institutions and the media;

    (v)   Confidential and unsupervised contact with witnesses and other private persons, including persons deprived of their liberty, considered necessary to fulfil the mandate of the mandate holder;

    (vi)   Access to all prisons, detention centres and places of interrogation as considered necessary by the mandate holder to fulfil his or her mandate; and

    (vii)   Full access to all documentary materials relevant to the mandate;

(c) Assurance by the Government that no person or group of persons, whether acting in their official or individual capacities, who cooperate, seek to cooperate, or have cooperated with the mandate holder in relation to the mandate, will for this reason suffer intimidation, threats, harassment or punishment, be subjected to judicial proceedings or to any other kind of reprisals by any means whatsoever; assurance that any measures that could deter such cooperation or be perceived as such, will be avoided. These assurances should apply before, during and after the conduct of country visits.

(d) Appropriate security arrangements without, however, restricting the freedom of movement and inquiry referred to above;

(e) Extension of the same guarantees and facilities mentioned above to the appropriate United Nations staff who will assist the special procedures mandate holder before, during and after the visit.

PHILIP ALSTON, REPORT OF THE SPECIAL RAPPORTEUR ON EXTREME POVERTY AND HUMAN RIGHTS ON HIS MISSION TO CHINA UN DOC. A/HRC/35/26/ADD.2, (28 MARCH 2017)

...

Government cooperation

5. ... Between 1997 and 2015, six mandate holders visited [China]: on arbitrary detention (1997 and 2004); torture (2005); the right to education (2003); the right to food (2010); discrimination against women in law and in practice (2013); and foreign debt (2015). ...

6. The Special Rapporteur commends the Government for inviting him to China, but would also wish to draw attention to some difficulties that arose in the course of the mission:

(a) The Government's view that it was fully responsible for determining every detail of the agenda of the visit reflects a misunderstanding of the role of special rapporteurs as independent experts;

(b) The Government advised the Special Rapporteur not to make direct contact with civil society organizations to arrange meetings, and requested full details of any private meetings held. However, in conformity with established procedures, he notified the Government only when requested to do so by the civil society actor concerned;

(c) The Special Rapporteur was regularly followed by security officers posing as private citizens, thus making it virtually impossible to meet privately with civil society organizations and individuals;

(d) The Government warned the Special Rapporteur not to meet with individuals it considered "sensitive", and those individuals were warned not to meet with the Special Rapporteur; in one case, a person with whom the Special Rapporteur was supposed to meet was taken into custody for a couple of hours, thus preventing the meeting from happening;

(e) As a result of these combined measures, the Special Rapporteur was unable to meet with the great majority of civil society actors with any degree of freedom or confidentiality;

(f) The Yunnan visit was organized by the Government in a way that ignored the Special Rapporteur's stated preferences and ensured that most of the meetings and other activities were formalities;

(g) Both during and after the mission, certain individuals with whom the Special Rapporteur met or was supposed to meet were subjected to what appear to be acts of intimidation and reprisal. ... [Particular concern was expressed about] the disappearance on 21 November 2016 of human rights lawyer Jiang Tianyong, whom the Special Rapporteur had met in Beijing.

7. The ability of the special procedure mandate holders to carry out their tasks of promoting and protecting human rights depends on their being able to engage in free and unsupervised communication with civil society and private individuals, before, during and after country visits. This applies as much to visits to China as to any other country.

8. A mandate holder's programme is organized in consultation with the Government, but this does not mean that the Government is entitled to determine and control every aspect of the agenda or to insist that, apart from government officials, meetings can only be held with "approved" non-governmental actors. A mission conducted on that basis would not enable a special rapporteur to discharge his or her obligation to establish the facts impartially and independently. The resulting report would rightly be criticized for providing only an incomplete and distorted picture.

9. The basis on which United Nations human rights fact-finding missions are undertaken by special procedure mandate holders reflects long-standing practice spanning many decades — including initial sets of standards adopted in the 1950s and 1960s, the terms of reference adopted for the 1978 mission to Chile, and follow-up work by the Commission on Human Rights and the Economic and Social Council.

10. The procedural arrangements that were agreed in the late 1970s have been followed ever since, and were reflected in the 1998 terms of reference for fact-finding missions by special rapporteurs/representatives of the Commission on Human Rights and in the 1999 special procedures' manual of operations. ...

11. Both the 2007 code of conduct and 2008 revised manual of operations, which the Council noted are to be read "in consonance" with one another, emphasize the importance of experts acting "in an independent

capacity", having the "freedom to assess" situations, establishing "facts, based on objective, reliable information", preserving "the confidentiality of sources", establishing a dialogue not only with government authorities but also "with all other stakeholders" and having their security protected "without prejudice to the privacy and confidentiality that mandate holders require to fulfil their mandate". The position expressed by the Government is clearly not compatible with these long-established principles.

OFFICIAL RESPONSE BY THE GOVERNMENT OF CHINA
(22 MARCH 2017)

...

XI. Visit Arrangement (paragraph 6, 72)

The Chinese side carefully prepared the visit to China by the Special Rapporteur, made utmost efforts to meet the requests of the Special Rapporteur, and arranged rich field visit activities. The Chinese side would like to carry out constructive dialogue and cooperation with the Special Rapporteur. At the same time, the Chinese side hopes that the Special Rapporteur could value the good faith of the Chinese side, strictly abide by its mandate, and refrain from dealing with questions irrelevant to poverty alleviation.

HUMAN RIGHTS WATCH, THE COSTS OF INTERNATIONAL ADVOCACY:
CHINA'S INTERFERENCE IN UNITED NATIONS HUMAN RIGHTS MECHANISMS
(5 SEPTEMBER 2017)

...

As a UN member state and party to several international human rights treaties, China engages with the UN human rights system. It is a member of the Human Rights Council (the "Council"), participates in reviews of its treaty compliance, allows some UN independent human rights experts to visit China, and joins in assessments of its human rights record and those of other countries as part of the Council's Universal Periodic Review (UPR) process.

Even as it engages with UN human rights institutions, however, China has worked consistently and often aggressively to silence criticism of its human rights record before UN bodies and has taken actions aimed at weakening some of the central mechanisms available in those institutions to advance rights. Because of China's growing international influence, the stakes of such interventions go beyond how China's own human rights record is addressed at the UN and pose a longer-term challenge to the integrity of the system as a whole.

Chinese officials have harassed activists, primarily those from China, by photographing and filming them on UN premises in violation of UN rules, and restricting their travel to Geneva. China has used its membership on the Economic and Social Council's (ECOSOC) NGO Committee to block NGOs critical of China from being granted UN accreditation, and it has sought to blacklist accredited activists to bar their attendance. Behind the scenes, Chinese diplomats, in violation of UN rules, have contacted UN staff and experts on treaty bodies and special procedures (independent experts focusing on specific human rights issues), including behavior that at times has amounted to harassment and intimidation.

In a particularly egregious case in 2013, authorities in China detained activist Cao Shunli after she urged the Chinese government to consult with civil society in drafting China's second Universal Periodic Review, and tried to travel to Geneva to participate in trainings on the Human Rights Council. After Cao became gravely ill in detention and died, the Chinese delegation in Geneva in March 2014 blocked a moment of silence called for by NGOs at the Council.

China has also repeatedly sought to block or weaken UN resolutions on civil society, human rights defenders, and peaceful protests, including when they do not directly concern policy and practice in China. And it has pushed back against efforts to strengthen some of the key mechanisms available at the UN to advance human rights, notably country-specific resolutions on grave situations like North Korea and Syria, and efforts to strengthen treaty body reviews.

...

While UN officials have at times pushed back against improper Chinese pressure or steadfastly ignored it, in other instances, they have capitulated, as illustrated by the Dolkun Isa case, or have soft-pedaled their concerns, presumably to avoid confrontation with China.

China is not alone in playing a negative human rights role at the UN but, as with all other countries, it should be expected to cooperate and constructively engage with UN institutions. When its actions are in bad faith, it should publicly be held to account.
...

DAVID KAYE, A REJOINDER TO CHINA'S RESPONSE TO UN HUMAN RIGHTS EXPERTS JUST SECURITY (27 JUNE 2020)

On [26 June 2020], fifty independent United Nations human rights experts published a statement expressing "alarm regarding the repression of fundamental freedoms in China." The statement calls for the implementation of immediate and decisive measures to protect against human rights abuses in the country. ... [T]he statement notes a range of concerns and urges China to permit independent experts access to the country to conduct independent human rights monitoring missions and calls on the UN Human Rights Council to consider mechanisms to monitor Chinese human rights behavior.

The Government of China was quick to respond. As a drafter and signer of the statement, I wanted to [reply].
...

Statements and Actions on China

For the last several years, the UN Human Rights Council has observed increasing repression of human rights in China. It is, of course, a complicated and remarkable country, with a history and culture as rich as any on earth and a massive potential to influence the development of international law and institutions. ... China regularly highlights the strides it has made in development terms, elements of which are certainly praiseworthy
... .

Nonetheless, it is impossible to avoid the very serious ongoing allegations ... .

We, as independent UN monitors, have regularly highlighted our concerns with the Government. ... [C]ommunications ... have addressed concerns about repression of the Uyghur population in Xinjiang, the attacks on autonomy and protest in Hong Kong, the role of censorship in the country, the detention of lawyers and activists in Tibet and across the country, and many other issues of extremely serious concern. However, despite these communications, and regular rejection of our concerns by the Government, the Government ... has not invited an expert focused on civil and political rights since 2005 ... .

The call for such measures is not all that unusual. In fact, we took the same approach the previous day, calling for an investigation into the widespread threats in the Philippines. Such calls are a regular part of our work. Such monitoring is not an interference with the sovereignty of any State but an example of robust implementation of the mandates the Human Rights Council has assigned us. If we avoided this kind of monitoring, we would be abandoning our mandated responsibilities.

The same day we issued our statement, China quickly objected. Saying that the Government "categorically rejects and strongly condemns" the UN experts' statement China called the statement an interference with its internal affairs. It also stated the following:

> In recent years some Special Procedures "experts" have repeatedly abused their mandates out of ulterior motives and made press release based on unverified information to interfere with the sovereignty and internal affairs of States, to the extent of hijacking the work of the inter-governmental organization consisting of sovereign States. These acts have gravely breached the Charter of the United Nations, seriously undermined the credibility of the Special Procedures and aroused concerns from more and more States. The Human Rights Council must hold misconducts of "experts" accountable to ensure

that the Special Procedures truly facilitate and contribute to the international human
rights cause, instead of becoming obstacles to or undoers of human rights the world over.

A Brief Reply by the Special Procedures Mandate-Holders

It is entirely fair and even important for China to object and to identify any statements or allegations made in
error. Experts on China, for their part, may wish to weigh in on the specifics of our statement and China's
response. But we make our assessments in good faith, and ... we call out all sorts of government behavior,
whether from democratic or authoritarian States. Indeed, many democratic governments wonder why we call
them out when there are such serious examples of repression worldwide.

... [T]he last line should be of particular concern ... – the threat to hold rapporteurs "accountable" for some
kind of vague breach of standards. It's true that the Council adopted a Code of Conduct in 2007 to guide Special
Procedures, but there is nothing in that document that precludes the kind of statement we issued yesterday.

... Monitoring human rights is not some interference with state sovereignty or an "external intervention in
China's domestic affairs." Monitoring human rights is the international community's way to ensure that States
meet their obligations to all people within their jurisdictions.

That oversight is obviously uncomfortable for many States, but it is the nature of the human rights system that
the commitment to human rights means accepting that those obligations are international, owed to other States
and to those subject to their jurisdiction. Human rights monitoring by its nature involves investigating the
"internal affairs" of States. There is no magic wand of sovereignty that can wave that away.

* * *

Rana Siu Inboden concludes in 'China, Power and the United Nations Special Procedures', 15 *Global Policy*
(2024) Suppl. 2, 74 at 81 that China's 'impact on this part of the UN remains modest overall since the
functioning and independence of the [Special Procedures] remains intact.' In Sec. C, below, dealing with the
High Commissioner, further consideration is given to China's engagement with UN human rights bodies.

C. THEMATIC REPORTS BY SPECIAL RAPPORTEURS

MARY LAWLOR, STATES IN DENIAL:
THE LONG-TERM DETENTION OF HUMAN RIGHTS DEFENDERS –
REPORT OF THE SPECIAL RAPPORTEUR ON THE SITUATION OF HUMAN RIGHTS
DEFENDERS
UN DOC. A/76/143 (2021)

I. Introduction

1. In December 2015, woman human rights defender Lodkham Thammavong was 1 of some 30 people who
protested outside the Lao Embassy in Bangkok to express their concern over the Lao Government's alleged
human rights violations.

2. Three months later, when she returned to the Lao People's Democratic Republic, she and two other human
rights defenders, Soukane Chaithad and Somphone Phimmasone, were arrested by Lao police.

3. The Special Rapporteur has received credible information that they were not informed of the charges against
them and no arrest warrants were presented at the time of arrest or afterward. Ms. Thammavong and the others
were reportedly forced to make false confessions, paraded on national television to apologize for being traitors
and denied their rights to legal representation.

4. A year later, in March 2017, after an unfair trial, Ms. Thammavong was found guilty of "treason to the nation,
propaganda against the State, and gatherings tied at causing social disorder". She was sentenced to 12 years in

prison. Mr. Chaithad and Mr. Phimmasone were also convicted on the same charges, and given 16 and 20 years, respectively.

5. At the time of writing, Ms. Thammavong is currently being held in Tan Piao Prison, located around 60 km from Vientiane, making family visits difficult. She is said to be lacking access to water and still has had no access to legal counsel.

6. Unfortunately, such attacks on human rights defenders are not rare. Hundreds of human rights defenders across the world are serving long prison sentences after being convicted on fabricated charges following unfair trials. ...

7. The Special Rapporteur has monitored numerous cases of defenders serving more than 10 years in prison ...
.

8. Many are held in harsh conditions, and/or have been forced to confess to crimes they did not commit. Some suffer from ill health and are deprived of adequate medical attention. Some are also denied regular access to their families. Some are at risk of being sentenced to death, and some have died in jail while serving long sentences.
...
10. The full extent of this problem is not known. Human rights defenders are serving long terms in detention on every continent, but there are very likely many more cases than those featured in the present report that have not been brought to the Special Rapporteur's attention.

11. The cases included here are only those where consent has been obtained directly from the defenders themselves, or from their families or representatives. ...

12. There is a wide range of defenders serving long terms in detention. Some are labour leaders, some are lawyers, others are journalists. Some are jailed for defending article 21 of the [UDHR], which outlines the right for people to vote in elections. Others are targeted for peacefully advocating for democratic reform, or for exposing deficiencies in governance. The Special Rapporteur reiterates that peacefully defending these and other rights that States have promised to safeguard is never a crime.

13. Some defenders have been targeted and jailed in reprisal for their engagement, or intended engagement, with United Nations mechanisms. ...

14. Some defenders have been convicted in mass trials and some have been sentenced in absentia. Some defenders sentenced to long terms in jail are living in exile, unable to return to their country for fear of arrest. Others are kept in long periods of pretrial detention, not knowing if or when they will face charges that could send them to prison for long terms.

15. Other defenders are seized and nothing is heard from or about them for many years. Not all are held by Governments. ...

16. Other human rights defenders sentenced to long terms in jail die in custody. ...

17. The Special Rapporteur notes there is often a flurry of attention and activity around a case when a human rights defender is arrested or convicted, sometimes accompanied by intense international media coverage and advocacy from foreign governments and United Nations mechanisms. But even with the most prominent defenders, attention typically fades over the years as fresh cases demand the attention and resources of non-governmental organizations (NGOs), independent United Nations experts and interested Governments.

18. Many defenders serving long sentences feel forgotten or abandoned.

19. The effect of the long-term detention of defenders can be devastating – to themselves, to their families, to their communities and to the civil societies to which they belong. Just fighting a legal case can exhaust a

defenders' resources, and that of their NGO. Indeed, this damage to them and their work is often the motivation for their being targeted.

…

25. States … enable themselves to jail human rights defenders by passing vague laws, often in the name of national security or countering terrorism, by staging sham trials that fail meet international standards, by torturing defenders into making false confessions and by lying about the work of human rights defenders.

26. Some States contest that those jailed are not defenders but subversives, traitors or terrorists. The Special Rapporteur knows the difference … .

…

31. [In a 2021 report] (A/HRC/46/35), the Special Rapporteur focused on the killing of human rights defenders. She identified a lack of political will from Member States to hold the perpetrators accountable as a key driver of the murders. In the case of long-term detention of defenders, it is less the absence of political will to prevent this abuse, but rather the active presence of a political will in States to target defenders.

32. Some representatives of Member States have told the Special Rapporteur, in response to her raising the case of an unfair trial, that they cannot interfere in their countries' independent judicial process. While the Special Rapporteur respects the principle of judicial independence, she cannot be silent when a criminal justice system falls short of international standards and is used to unjustly jail human rights defenders.

…

A. Data and methodology

37. [Between 1 January 2020 and 30 June 2021], the Special Rapporteur sent 28 communications to 22 Member States on the long-term detention of 148 human rights defenders … .

38. Of these 148 defenders, 40 were lawyers working on human rights cases, 15 worked on women's human rights, 9 worked on the defence of the environment and indigenous peoples' rights and 7 worked on providing humanitarian aid. …

39. Of the total number of defenders … [f]ifty-four have been charged with crimes related to national security, 53 charged with crimes under anti-terrorism laws, 30 with violations of both national security and anti-terrorism laws and 11 with other crimes, such as murder, robbery, extortion, kidnapping and blasphemy, among others.

…

43. The present report is based on discussions the Special Rapporteur has had with hundreds of human rights defenders around the world since the beginning of her mandate in May 2020, and on information she continuously receives on trends on human rights defenders in long-term detention.

…

C. Trends related to the long-term detention of human rights defenders

1. Evidence of the widespread misuse of counter-terrorism and related legislation

66. The Special Rapporteur conducted a study of 61 cases in 13 countries across the Americas, Asia-Pacific, Europe and Central Asia, the Middle East and North Africa and sub-Saharan Africa in which a human rights defender had been sentenced to 10 years or more and was either still serving their sentence or had died in prison, or had never been sentenced in the first place but had remained in State custody for a lengthy period of time, suggesting worrying patterns.

67. Of the cases studied, 77 per cent involved the human rights defender being convicted under counter-terror or national security legislation. At least 46 per cent of the jailed defenders alleged ill-treatment or torture during their arrest or while in detention. Four human rights defenders died while in prison or after having been released to a hospital immediately prior. And 11 per cent of the cases related to a reprisal for having cooperated with United Nations human rights mechanisms … .

68. The Special Rapporteur notes further commonalities across the cases of those accused, or convicted, of crimes that carry heavy sentences.

...

71. For example, in Turkey, article 314 of the Turkish Penal Code and article 7 of the Anti-Terror Law have both been used extensively to silence human rights defenders and categorize them as members of terrorist organizations. In March 2020, woman human rights defender Sevda Özbingöl Çelik was arrested ... .

...

73. [In China, the] concepts of "ringleader", "major crime" and "serious circumstances" in the Criminal Code are broad and vague. The lack of an upper limit on the length of imprisonment in articles 105 (2) and 120 (a) does not meet the principle of legal certainty and allows for the imposition of long sentences. ...

74. In Egypt, accusations commonly made against human rights defenders include the joining of an unspecified terrorist group (punishable under art. 12 of the Anti-Terrorism Law and/or art. 86 bis of the Penal Code), and/or publishing false news and supplying international institutions with false information (art. 80 D and/or arts. 102 bis and 188 of the Penal Code).

...

76. In the United Arab Emirates, human rights defenders are liable to be sentenced to 10 years in prison or more under the under various laws, including Federal Law No. 7 of 2014 on combating terrorism offences. The law is vague, fails to define terrorism, and includes phrases such as "contradicting the basic principles of underlying State governance", "opposing the country", and "prejudicing national unity" to define terrorism without further elaboration.

...

II. Conclusions and recommendations

A. Conclusions

155. Many Governments are failing in their legal and moral obligations by sentencing human rights defenders to long terms in prison, and then denying that they have done so.

156. This is due primarily to the presence of a political will to silence those who peacefully defend the rights of others, and the negligible international consequences for States that commit these violations. ...

157. Targeting human rights defenders with long jail terms destroys lives, families and communities. States should end this unjustifiable, indefensible and contemptible practice immediately and forever.

B. Recommendations

158. States should:

    (a) Desist from jailing human rights defenders for their legitimate human rights work, and stop subjecting them to long terms in detention;

    (b) Immediately and unconditionally release all human rights defenders currently held in detention;
    ...
    (k) Permit representatives of the United Nations, other international and regional organizations, NGOs and diplomats of other Governments access to visit defenders in detention;
    ...

159. [Foreign] Governments carrying out advocacy efforts should:

    (a) With the defenders' consent, regularly and publicly call for the release of defenders held in detention;

    (b) Raise with other States the cases of human rights defenders in long- term detention;

    (c) Request that their officials be allowed to visit human rights defenders in detention;

    (d) State publicly if a trial of a human rights defender their representative has observed met international legal standards.

    ...

* * *

In a 2022 report, the Special Rapporteur focused on defenders working on the rights of refugees, migrants and asylum-seekers (UN Doc. A/77/178 (2022)), making the following observations:

38.   The Special Rapporteur notes that some laws enable the prosecution and criminalization of defenders advocating for the rights of migrants. Defenders are brought before courts for protecting the rights of others as solidarity is criminalized and often conflated with people smuggling. A number of these domestic laws stem from the European Union Facilitation Directive.

39.   … [T]he organization Research Social Platform on Migration and Asylum (ReSOMA) … criticizes the Directive for "the 'vague and ambiguous' definition of facilitation-related crimes and offences and lack of fundamental rights standards within the Facilitation Directive. It opens the gates for misinterpretations and misuses". In 2020, … ReSOMA detailed cases of 171 individuals in 13 European Union member States [thus] criminalized … .

40.   … [Another] study notes that many European Union countries "continue to criminalize not-for-profit behaviour, like giving free food, shelter or a lift with a car for undocumented migrants" despite the directive containing an optional "humanitarian exemption clause", and suggests that these "so called 'criminalization of solidarity' cases, entail serious chilling effects for civil society, in particular, the freedom of association and freedom of speech". …

41.   Defenders are vulnerable to attack partly because of the lack of protections at the national and regional levels. A study commissioned by the European Parliament and published in October 2020 noted that while many "migrant rights' defenders were subject to smear campaigns, verbal and physical attacks, administrative fines and even criminal prosecutions … no regional mechanism is developed to protect human rights defenders in Europe".

D. RESPONDING TO COMPLAINTS

The great majority of special procedures mandates envisage a process of 'communicating' with governments about alleged human rights violations either through 'allegation letters' seeking an official response to alleged violations or through 'urgent action' letters which allege imminent harm unless a government acts immediately. This system seeks to: raise international awareness of allegedly significant violations; give states an opportunity to set the record straight and justify their actions; generate a record of abuses alleged against states over time; enable the mandate-holder to offer an interpretation of the applicable law; and provide an incentive for governments to act to rectify any violations.

The most sophisticated of the Special Procedures communications processes is that developed by the five-member Working Group on Arbitrary Detention, established in 1991. The Group receives cases from any relevant source, transmits the allegations to governments with a request for a reply within 90 days and then adopts an 'opinion' on the case. It was previously termed a 'decision', but this characterization was resisted by governments.

The following are examples of 'communications' issued by Special Procedures to different actors.

COMMUNICATION SENT TO THE GOVERNMENT OF ITALY, BY SPECIAL PROCEDURES MANDATE HOLDERS DEALING WITH: HUMAN RIGHTS DEFENDERS; INTERNATIONAL SOLIDARITY; THE HUMAN RIGHTS OF MIGRANTS; AND TRAFFICKING IN PERSONS (19 MAY 2022)

… [W]e would like to bring to the attention of your Excellency's Government information we have received concerning the criminal prosecution of three human rights defenders for providing assistance to migrants and asylum seekers.

…

According to the information received:

On 14 March 2016, Messers. Gebremedhn, Ghebrehiwet and Mebrahtom, along with three other Eritrean men, were arrested on suspicion of being members of an international people smuggling organisation. They were charged with criminal conspiracy to facilitate illegal immigration under article 416 of the Italian Criminal Code and article 12 of the Consolidated Immigration Act, 1998. The accusations against these men stemmed from acts of assistance towards other Eritreans, which they had performed between May 2014 and October 2015. These acts included giving advice on how to use public transport, helping the migrants and asylum seekers buy tickets for buses or trains, buying them clothes, food, phones and sim cards, as well as hosting recently arrived migrants and asylum seekers and helping them find places to stay. …

… The case was opened following an investigation involving the Italian Anti-Mafia Directorate in Rome and the Italian Coastguard into an alleged international organisation of people smugglers claimed to be involved in organising the journeys of people from Eritrea to Europe, via Italy. Proposed evidence against the accused men was collected through surveillance conducted in the course of this investigation, including by means of wiretapping.

In the first instance, [the three, along with others], were convicted by the Rome Criminal Court of the charge of aiding and abetting illegal immigration … and sentenced to between 2 and 4 years imprisonment, along with fines of up to €125,000. … The decision was based on the Court's interpretation of the acts performed by the men as having been aimed at aiding the migrants and asylum seekers to cross Italy's borders into another State, an offence punishable under the Consolidated Immigration Act without a requisite profit motive. The Court dismissed the charge that the men had been involved in a criminal conspiracy [and the] charges relating to the illicit transfer of money [for lack of evidence].

The decision in the first instance was appealed by the defence to the Court of Appeal of Rome, … [and subsequently] to the Court of Cassation … .

…

Without wishing to prejudge the accuracy of the above-detailed allegations, we wish to underline our concern at the prosecution of [the three men], whose pursuit by the State would appear to represent the criminalisation of acts of solidarity and assistance towards migrants and asylum seekers through the misapplication of elements of the national legal framework designed, in principle, to regulate migration and combat trafficking in persons. … We fear that this investigatory approach has contributed to the conflation of humanitarian acts of solidarity aimed at defending, promoting and enabling the fulfilment of the human rights of migrants, including the right to seek asylum, with criminal activity. We further state our concern that the result of this approach has been to repress the legitimate work of human rights defenders and to deter individuals from engaging in acts of solidarity with migrants and asylum seekers.

In this regard, we wish to stress the crucial role played by human rights defenders undertaking humanitarian action aimed at preventing and alleviating suffering of migrants … .

…

… [W]e would be grateful for your observations on the following matters:

1. Please provide any additional information and comment(s) [on these allegations].

2. Please provide detailed information to clarify the legal and factual basis for the prosecution[s] … .

3. Please provide detailed information as to the legal basis for the pre-trial detention of [the three men], along with information as to the assessments taken to evaluate the necessity of such detention and information concerning the reasons for its extended duration.

4. Please provide information on any measures to ensure that criminal justice laws are not misused to punish migration-related humanitarian acts or to harass human rights defenders or civil society organizations that work with migrants.

This communication and any response received from your Excellency's Government will be made public via the communications reporting website within 60 days. They will also subsequently be made available in the usual report to be presented to the Human Rights Council.

We may publicly express our concerns in the near future as, in our view, the information upon which the press release will be based is sufficiently reliable to indicate a matter warranting immediate attention. We also believe that the wider public should be alerted to the potential implications of the above-mentioned allegations. The press release will indicate that we have been in contact with your Excellency's Government's to clarify the issue/s in question.

COMMUNICATION SENT TO THE GOVERNMENT OF ERITREA, BY SPECIAL PROCEDURES MANDATE HOLDERS
DEALING WITH: TRAFFICKING IN PERSONS; DISABILITIES; ERITREA; THE RIGHT TO HEALTH; INTERNALLY DISPLACED PERSONS; SALE AND SEXUAL EXPLOITATION OF CHILDREN; AND CONTEMPORARY FORMS OF SLAVERY
(11 MAY 2022)

… [We] have received [information] which indicates the occurrence of trafficking in persons, especially women and girls, for purposes of sexual exploitation, including sexual slavery, by members of the Ethiopian National Defense Force, the Eritrean Defense Forces, the Amhara Regional/Special Forces, Tigrayan forces, and militia groups, in the context of the armed conflict in the Tigray region of Ethiopia since November 2020, and later in neighbouring Ahmara and Afar regions.

According to the information received:

Sexual violence against women and girls in the Tigray, Afar, and Amhara regions of Ethiopia, has reportedly included abductions of women and girls, who have been arbitrarily detained, held in captivity for short periods (several days) and long periods of time (one or two months), and subjected to sexual exploitation including sexual slavery.

Women and girls have been held captive, and subjected to sexual exploitation, including sexual slavery, in military camps, in houses and in remote locations in rural areas. It is alleged that the acts of trafficking include the transfer and harbouring of women and girls, by means such as the use of force, abduction, coercion or abuse of a position of vulnerability, for purposes of sexual exploitation including sexual slavery.

There is a lack of effective action by the State to prevent such trafficking in persons for purposes of sexual exploitation, or to assist and protect victims of trafficking and persons at risk of trafficking.
…
Refugee women and girls in [five named camps] camps may have been trafficked for purposes of sexual exploitation by armed groups and armed forces. …

Information received indicates that children, particularly in the Tigray region, may have been victims of trafficking for purposes of sexual exploitation by armed groups and armed forces. Further it is alleged that the high number of separated and unaccompanied children may be at particular risk of trafficking and have been provided with limited support or assistance to ensure a protective environment. … The continuing lack of humanitarian access heightens risks … .

It is reported that victims of trafficking for purposes of sexual exploitation, who are pregnant as a result of being trafficked and raped, are not receiving specialized and adequate assistance or protection.

…

Men and boys may have also been victims … . …

It is further alleged that commanders of armed forces, or other superiors knew or ought to have known that such violations of international human rights law, international humanitarian law and international criminal law, were being or were about to be committed, and failed to take all necessary and reasonable measures to prevent or punish these acts.

There are reportedly no effective investigations into [these] allegations … .

Without pre-judging the allegations raised, we express our grave concerns … .

… [We] would be grateful for your observations on the following matters:

1.   Please provide any additional information and/or comment(s) you may have on [these] allegations … .

2.   Please provide information on any policies in place and/or the orders given to armed and security forces prohibiting sexual and gender-based violence, including trafficking ….

3.   Please provide details, and where available the results, of any investigations, prosecution or criminal charges, and other inquiries carried out in relation to the allegations … .

4.   Please provide information on what measures are being taken to ensure prompt identification of and assistance of victims of trafficking … .

…

E. THE UNIVERSAL PERIODIC REVIEW

The Universal Periodic Review (UPR), established in 2006, requires all UN member states to report to the Council once every 4½ years on their human rights record. This mechanism ensures that every state, rather than only those accused of serious violations, must account to the Council. It is a peer mechanism in the sense that the review is undertaken by states, rather than experts, and the reporting state retains significant control over the outcome.

The review is carried out by all 47 Council members acting as a Working Group. Three states, chosen by lottery (the 'troika'), act as Rapporteurs in the review of a given state's report. In addition to the National Report, there is (1) a 'Compilation' by the OHCHR of information from treaty bodies, special procedures and other UN sources; and (2) a 'Stakeholder Summary' of information submitted by civil society, researchers, national human rights institutions and others.

The 'constructive dialogue' between the 'State under Review' and the Working Group lasts for 3.5 hours. NGOs may observe but not pose questions. The troika then prepares a review of issues raised and the government concerned indicates which recommendations it accepts or rejects. The final outcome of the review is adopted by consensus. At the next cycle, the state is expected to report on the recommendations it has implemented in the intervening 4-5 years. The fourth round of the UPR began in 2022.[313]

---

[313] See generally, D. Etone et al. (eds), *Human Rights and the UN Universal Periodic Review Mechanism: A Research Companion* (2024); and S. Molloy, 'The Universal Periodic Review and Peace Agreement Implementation: Conceptualising Connections, Challenges, and Ways Forward, 12 *London Rev. Int'l L.* (2024) 95.

HILARY CHARLESWORTH AND EMMA LARKING (EDS.), HUMAN RIGHTS AND THE UNIVERSAL PERIODIC REVIEW: RITUALS AND RITUALISM
(2015) 1

...

We understand rituals as ceremonies or formalities that, through repetition, entrench the understandings and the power relationships that they embody. Rituals are a means of enacting a social consensus – or at least of demonstrating the efficacy of the mode of power they internalise. They can be markers of success, indicating that a way of thinking or of being has achieved some degree of permanence and importance: enshrining a practice as ritual reduces contestation. An example is rituals of transitional justice and of apology that mark a break between the old and the new, and signal a society's recognition of certain wrongs, as well as its determination to leave these wrongs behind. Although they seek to inaugurate a new order, such rituals are signs of success in the sense that they embody a new consensus about how a society now relates to its past and also intends to move beyond it. In doing so, rituals can help to establish and entrench that consensus. Rituals can also be understood as a more prosaic form of human engagement, helping make sense of incoherence in our social and political lives. On this account, rituals are concerned with 'the endless work of building, refining, and rebuilding webs of relationships in an otherwise fragmented world'. They may contribute to 'a world that, for brief moments, creates pockets of order, pockets of joy, pockets of inspiration'.

To engage in a ritual is to take part in an embodied performance. As such, participants' focus is often on the requirements of the performance rather than on its regulatory significance. Our aim here is, first, to highlight the presence of ritual in the UPR process. The cyclical nature of this process, and its carefully managed calendar of events, contributes to its ritualistic character. The process itself is also intricately managed and highly formalised. All parties must conform to the requirements of the process in order to secure their participation.
...

Observers of the UPR, whether sitting in the spectacular Salle XX of the Palais des Nations in Geneva where the Council meets, watching webcasts of proceedings, or ploughing through the summary records, are spectators to the elaborate rituals embedded in the process. These include the extended formal introductions, the courtly congratulations, the rigorously observed time constraints … and the formulaic structure and style of UPR documents. Observers may register these rituals as entertaining, foreign, intimidating, bizarre, or perhaps just enervating, but they may be less likely to understand them as forms of social control and instances of regulatory power.

REPORT OF THE WORKING GROUP ON THE UNIVERSAL PERIODIC REVIEW: UNITED STATES OF AMERICA
UN DOC. A/HRC/46/15 (15 DECEMBER 2020)[314]

Introduction
1. … The review of the United States of America was held … on 9 November 2020. The delegation [included the U.S. Ambassador to the UN in Geneva, the Assistant Secretary, Bureau of Democracy, Human Rights and Labor, and the Acting Legal Adviser, both from the State Department].
2. [The troika] to facilitate the review [consisted of]: the Bahamas, Germany and Pakistan.
4. A list of questions prepared in advance by [12 States] … was transmitted to the [U.S.] … .

I. Summary of the proceedings of the review process

A. Presentation by the State under review

5. The Permanent Representative of the [U.S.] began by underscoring the pride of the [U.S.] in its human rights record. The [U.S.] advocated strongly for the universal freedoms of religion or belief and expression, including for members of the press, and for the rights of individuals to assemble peaceably and to petition their government for redress for grievances. In 2020, the United States had launched the International Religious

---

[314] Note that a Presidential election took place in the U.S. on 3 November 2020. As a result, the U.S. report was presented by the outgoing Trump administration, while the official response was provided in March 2021 by the incoming Biden administration.

Freedom or Belief Alliance ... [and] also joined 32 countries in signing the Geneva Consensus Declaration on Promoting Women's Health and Strengthening the Family ... .

6. The Assistant Secretary, ... Department of State, said that promoting human rights was a foreign policy priority for the [U.S.] ... . [It] was also firmly committed to finding meaningful remedies for claims of injustice at home. The demonstrations over the tragic death of George Floyd had shown the world that the citizens of the [U.S.] understood that they had the inherent right to raise their voices, individually and collectively, to demand that their government address their grievances.

7. A representative of the [U.S.] Department of Justice added that the [Minnesota] government ... had filed strong charges against four police officers for the death of Mr. Floyd. While the vast majority of police officers in the [U.S.] did their job bravely and righteously, some officers did not live up to their responsibilities, leading some individuals, particularly in the black community, to lose confidence in the [U.S.] criminal justice system. ... Between 1994 and January 2020, the Department of Justice had opened 70 civil investigations into police departments ... . On 16 June 2020, the President, Donald J. Trump, had signed an Executive Order entitled "Safe policing for safe communities" to develop and incentivize critical policing reforms.

8. The representative noted that the federal Government and most states in the United States had hate crime laws ... . The [U.S.] did not criminalize speech, ... even when such ideas were found by some to be extremely offensive or harmful. The authorities did, however, act forcefully when hateful expressions turned into discrimination or violence, threats of violence or solicitations to commit violence.

B. Interactive dialogue and responses by the State under review

9. During the interactive dialogue, 116 delegations made statements. ...

...

11. The Acting [State Department] Legal Adviser ..., noted that the United States was a party to many human rights treaties and took those obligations very seriously. The reasons for not ratifying all treaties varied from treaty to treaty. ... In many cases, such as in respect of the Convention on the Rights of Persons with Disabilities, United States domestic protections were even stronger than those of international treaties. ...

12. The Attorney General for the State of Utah underscored state-level efforts to promote human rights. ...

13. A representative of the .... Department of Homeland Security said that the Department took seriously its role in ensuring proper implementation of immigration laws to protect the rights of citizens and non-citizens ... . The Trump Administration had taken decisive action to strengthen the country's border system, address the unintended consequences of laws and judicial rulings and work with neighbouring countries ... .

...

17. A representative of the ... Department of Defense said that the [U.S.] had no plans to close its facilities at Guantanamo Bay ... .

18. The representative said that the [U.S.] military took scrupulous care to ensure that military and counter-terrorism operations were conducted in accordance with all applicable domestic and international laws, in particular the law of war. ...

19. The representative of the [U.S.] Department of Justice said that the Federal Bureau of Prisons met its constitutional and statutory mandates by confining inmates in prisons and community-based facilities that were safe, humane and appropriately secure. The Constitution prohibited the use of solitary confinement in a manner that constituted cruel and unusual punishment. ...

...

25. The Permanent Representative of the United States thanked States for their constructive recommendations and reaffirmed the commitment of the United States to creating a more perfect union.

II. Conclusions and/or recommendations

26. The following recommendations will be examined by the United States ... .

[347 separate recommendations are recorded in the report. The list below is illustrative, and the response subsequently given by the U.S. is noted in italics in square brackets, and is taken from UN Doc. A/HRC/46/15/Add.1 (4 March 2021).]

26.1 Consider ratifying all remaining human rights conventions (Somalia); [other states suggested ratification of CEDAW, CRC, CRPD, ICESCR, the Migrant Workers Convention, various optional protocols, the ICC Statute, the American Convention, and certain ILO Conventions]. [*Response: support recommendations to ratify CEDAW, CRPD, ILO Convention 111, and CRC.*]

...

26.65 Take immediate steps to overturn the executive branch decision to withdraw from the Paris Agreement (Fiji); *[Response: already done.]*

26.66 ... [L]ift sanctions against the International Criminal Court and constructively collaborate in investigations aimed at preventing impunity for international crimes (Switzerland); *Response: 'We continue to have concerns about the ICC's activities related to the Afghanistan and Palestinian situations. ... There may be exceptional cases where we consider cooperating with the court as we sometimes have in the past. ...]*

...

26.76 Recommit to multilateral human rights institutions (Poland); *[Response: support.]*

...

26.95 Consider establishing a national human rights institution in accordance with the Paris Principles (India); *[Response: do not support.]*

...

26.105 Stop interfering in the internal affairs of sovereign States (Russian Federation); *[Response: do not support.]*

26.106 Stop interfering, for political purposes, in other countries' internal affairs under the pretext of human rights (China); *[Response: do not support.]*

26.107 Put an immediate end to the blockade against Cuba, which seriously violates the human rights of the Cuban people (Cuba); *[Response: do not support.]*

...

26.109 Respect the peoples of the world in their freedoms and in the democratic development of their own constitutional electoral processes (Nicaragua); *[Response: support.]*

...

26.112 Take effective measures to review policies at the federal, state and local levels with a view to preventing , racial discrimination, xenophobia and related intolerance (Slovakia); *[Response: 'share the ideals'.]*

...

26.123 Enhance laws and legislation based on the abolition of all forms of discrimination, racism and hatred (Saudi Arabia); *[Response: 'share the ideals'.]*

...

26.141 Take necessary measures to end systemic racism against minorities, including African-Americans (Islamic Republic of Iran); *[Response: support.]*

...

26.145 Address issues of racism, xenophobia and bullying among children at schools (Myanmar); *[Response: we share the ideals.]*

26.146 Take all possible steps at the state and federal levels to prohibit discrimination based on sexual orientation or gender identity in credit, education, employment, housing, jury service, public accommodation and taxpayer-funded programmes (Belgium); *[Response: support.]*

...

26.164 Prohibit torture in detention and ensure detainees have access to fair trials and full redress (Malaysia); *[Response: support in part.]*

...

26.167 Hold United States political and military personnel to account for war crimes committed by the United States military forces in the Syrian Arab Republic ... (Syrian Arab Republic); *[Response: do not support.]*

...

26.173 Stop the use of torture in antiterrorism operations, halt military intervention in other countries and stop killing civilians in military operations (China); *[Response: do not support.]*

...

26.180 Repeal the decision to resume federal capital punishment and take steps to promote federal- and state-level moratoriums on executions with a view to permanently abolishing the death penalty (Norway); *[Response: do not support.]*

...

26.215 Take necessary measures to reduce gun violence, concerned at the large number of gun-related deaths and injuries, which disproportionately affect members of racial and ethnic minorities (Iceland); *[Response: support.]*

...

26.228 Take urgent action to end systemic racism in police work and bring those responsible for racially motivated violence to justice (Belarus); *[Response: support.]*

...

26.240 Address further the issue of sexual violence in the military (Israel); *[Response: support.]*

...

26.242 Take further action to prevent overcrowding of jails and prisons, especially during the current pandemic; eliminating or reducing mandatory minimum sentences would be crucial to this effect (Portugal); [*Response: we share the ideals.*]

26.243 Take legal and practical measures to end deep-rooted racism and racial discrimination, police brutality, killings by guns and torture in national detention facilities (Democratic People's Republic of Korea); [*Response: support.*]

...

26.255 Continue to reduce the role of policing as a response to societal problems largely related to poverty, while investing in direct solutions to those problems that do not involve criminalization (Malta); [*Response: support.*]

...

26.261 Address the growing influence of extremist groups, such as white supremacists, within law enforcement agencies and start comprehensive training mechanisms focused on human rights and fundamental freedoms for law enforcement members (Turkey); [*Response: support in part, although do not agree with some premises.*]

26.262 Redouble efforts in addressing issues of racial disparities in the criminal justice system (South Sudan); [*Response: support.*]

...

26.266 Combat the increasingly severe religious intolerance and xenophobic violence (China); [*Response: support in part, although do not agree with some premises.*]

...

26.268 Adopt new measures to guarantee freedom of expression on the Internet (Haiti); [*Response: support in part.*]

...

26.271 Investigate any allegations of the excessive use of force by law enforcement officials against protesters and investigate any allegations of torture and reduce restrictions on the right to peaceful assembly (Egypt); [*Response: support.*]

...

26.275 Ensure the exercise of the right to vote, including by demanding that states refrain from using voter identification requirements that can have a discriminatory impact on voters (Germany); [*Response: support in part.*]

...

26.285 Introduce reforms to reverse the high rates of poverty and inequality and recognize economic, social and cultural rights internally (Cuba); [*Response: support in part; The U.S. is not a party to the ICESCR, and we understand that the rights therein are to be realized progressively. … [W]e support the policy goals of reducing poverty and inequality.*]

...

26.293 Ensure access to health care, drugs and treatment to all segments of society (Iraq); [*Response: support.*]

...

26.299 Lift funding restrictions on United States foreign assistance to promote women's full access to sexual and reproductive health and rights (Norway); [*Response: support.*]

26.300 Clarify its approach to ensuring access to comprehensive sexual and reproductive health services (United Kingdom …); [*Response: support.*]

...

26.318 Encourage further private employers to strengthen equality and to offer paid maternity leave (Israel); [*Response: support.*]

...

26.337 Seek alternatives to the present immigration detention system and improve conditions of confinement to meet basic human rights standards (Zambia); [*Response: support.*]

...

26.345 Include in legislation the ban on the separation of families in the context of migration (Luxembourg); [*Response: support.*]

....

* * *

The format and language used by states in responding to UPR recommendations varies considerably. While the U.S. indicated explicitly its non-support for various recommendations, other states merely 'take note' of recommendations with which they do not agree. Some also situate their response in light of a general policy statement. Consider Singapore, for example:[315]

> 2.   … Singapore takes a practical and outcomes-based approach to implementing our human rights obligations. This involves the careful balancing of competing rights according to our national priorities and unique circumstances. Singapore's approach to human rights is premised on two tenets. First, human rights do not exist in a vacuum and must take into account a country's specific circumstances including cultural, social, economic, and historical contexts. Second, the rule of law is an essential pre-condition for the promotion and protection of human rights.
>
> …
>
> 4.   For many of the recommendations we have noted, Singapore already has legislation and policies that address the underlying objectives in ways that best suit our unique social and cultural context. Singapore has not supported recommendations which are predicated on unfounded assertions, inaccurate assumptions, or erroneous information. We also cannot implement recommendations that are not appropriate in our national context.

COMMENTARY ON THE UPR

The UN has emphasized the importance of the UPR process for country-level advocacy. It notes that 'UPR recommendations accepted by a State – publicly in front of all its peers and other stakeholders - present an important entry point for positive engagement and advocacy on many issues within the mandate of [the UN Country Teams] and peace operations'.[316] A review of experience with the UPR concluded that the process has been characterized by an unusually 'collaborative spirit' among stakeholders, and points to the enhanced involvement of national parliaments, NHRIs, UN agencies, and a broad array of civil society groups.[317] This is, of course, not always the case, as illustrated by Guatemala in 2023, when the Government 'noted' 40 per cent of the 207 recommendations received (UN Doc. A/HRC/53/9/Add.1), thereby effectively rejecting them.

ROCHELLE TERMAN AND ERIK VOETEN, THE RELATIONAL POLITICS OF SHAME: EVIDENCE FROM THE UNIVERSAL PERIODIC REVIEW
13 REV. INT'L ORG. (2018) 1

…

The informative value of politicized peer-review

Theoretical argument

We propose that governments are sensitive to symbolic political assessments, even when those assessments are neither independent nor impartial. …

… [O]ur explanation for shaming in the UPR emphasizes the political relationship between source and target. Because states behave primarily to further their material interests, they strive to avoid alienating other states on which those interests depend. Goodliffe and Hawkins call this set of partners a "dependence network": those with whom a state "regularly engages in exchanges of valued goods, where those exchanges would be costly to break". These goods can be economic, security, or political in nature, including humanitarian aid, foreign policy support, and military alliance. States exchange such goods in the context of a strategic partnership, where each party cooperates as a means to further their own interests. Insofar as states value these relationships, they will strive to maintain them by anticipating potential reactions from their partners. As Goodliffe and Hawkins note, these reactions need not involve explicit rewards or punishments contingent on the behavior in question.

[315] UN Doc. A/HRC/48/16/Add.1 (10 September 2021).
[316] OHCHR, *Maximizing the use of the Universal Periodic Review at country level: Practical Guidance* (2020).
[317] M. Kothari, *Study on emerging Good Practices from the Universal Periodic Review* (UPR) (OHCHR, 2021). See also M. Lane, 'The Universal Periodic Review: A Catalyst for Domestic Mobilisation', 40 *Nordic J. Hum. Rts.* (2022) 507.

Rather, states merely anticipate the *potential* costs (or benefits) to a valued relationship, and factor these into their decision calculus. All else equal, states would rather avoid provoking a negative judgment from their strategic partners.

How does this insight pertain to interstate interactions in the UPR? We propose that peer-review is mediated by strategic relations between reviewer and target, affecting the behavior of each party. This involves two distinct yet interrelated mechanisms. First, we expect governments to vary their evaluations depending on their political ties to the SuR [state under review]. Although delegations are mandated to be objective in their reviews, the reality is that recommendations vary widely in tone, ranging from disparaging to congratulatory. On average, states will condemn their strategic partners less harshly so as to signal their commitment to a valued relationship. In general, states do not take well to accusations of human rights abuse. When evaluating a partner, delegations on average mute their criticisms so as to avoid this negative reaction.

At the same time, some states genuinely do care about human rights. This concern may originate in domestic societal pressure (e.g., an outraged public demanding condemnation of an abuse abroad) or the normative beliefs of government officials. In some cases, these preferences are strong enough to warrant a tough stance and risk alienating an otherwise beneficial partnership. When a state publicly shames its strategic partner, it serves as a credible signal reflecting the shamer's preferences vis-à-vis human rights, and the target will take such criticism seriously in order to maintain the relationship.

…

When deciding whether or not to accept a recommendation, states must factor in political context, because recommendations reveal very different signals depending on the source. In a politicized environment, governments interpret criticism by their enemies as a cynical attempt to sully their country's reputation. Not only are there few incentives to comply in such cases, doing so may confer costs on the part of the SuR if they are seen as "kowtowing" to the enemy. On the other hand, recommendations mean something very different when coming from a state that shares strong political, economic, or security ties with the target. Since there are few *strategic* incentives to criticize friends, shaming in this case serves as a credible signal reflecting the critic's preferences on a particular norm. In this context, the SuR is more likely to accept the recommendation in order to avoid damaging a valuable partnership.

…

KAROLINA M. MILEWICZ AND ROBERT E. GOODIN, DELIBERATIVE CAPACITY BUILDING THROUGH INTERNATIONAL ORGANIZATIONS: THE CASE OF THE UNIVERSAL PERIODIC REVIEW OF HUMAN RIGHTS
48 BRIT. J. POL. S. (2016) 513

Pinning any great hopes on international organizations has, since the failure of the League of Nations, generally been thought to be the province of dewy-eyed idealists. Hard-headed realists know that international organizations are simply the products of deals struck by nation states for their own purposes. They are creatures of states, at the service of states; states can enter reservations and derogations upon joining them and, by and large, states can leave them whenever they want with due notice. Realists have trouble seeing how such organizations could ever transcend the narrow purposes of the states that created them. It is hard for them to see how such organizations can get states to do anything they seriously do not want to do.

Organizational sociologists, however, know all is not quite as it seems to the self-styled realists. International organizations 'bring people together'. They 'convene'; they 'orchestrate'. Once created, international organizations – like all organizations – take on a life of their own. They acquire purposes and missions, proud histories and follow-on aspirations, all of which infuse the lives of those working in them and with them. Maybe they make only soft, unenforceable law in the first instance. But that takes on increasingly hard forms over time, as actors in and around the organizations increasingly invest their outputs with normative force.

Realists may scoff, saying that demands that are ultimately unenforceable are practically irrelevant. But norms developed within and around international organizations can increasingly come to constrain even powerful players. …

…

Assessing the UPR's Contribution to the Deliberative System

...

A threshold question is whether the UPR process really involves much deliberation. Its centerpiece is a highly public moment of state-to-state discursive accountability, during the Interactive Dialogue in the grand Salle XX of the Palais des Nations in Geneva. That is a hugely important event, at which national governments are questioned on their human rights performance by other states, with NGOs in the room and many of their citizens back home watching the live or archived webcast. The live webcasts of their countries' Interactive Dialogues was watched by some 5,000 people in China, 6,000 in Malaysia and an astonishing 7,000 in tiny Vanuatu (almost 3 per cent of its population). In some cases, citizens were seeing their rulers publicly account for their human rights practices for the first time; the Saudi delegation seems to have felt this particularly, coming to its first UPR with an exceptionally large, senior and well-prepared delegation.

...

While the proceedings on the day itself may fall short of the highest deliberative ideal, the requirement that states present themselves for questioning induces a great deal of high-quality deliberation in the run-up to (and the backwash of) the open session. There are protracted discussions within the government of the SuR – and with and among stakeholders – about formulating the national report to be submitted to the UPR and anticipating challenges that might arise during it. There are protracted discussions within the UNOHCHR, and between them and stakeholders, in preparing the stakeholder report, and within the UNOHCHR in preparing its own submission to the UPR. The troika passes questions from other states to the SuR in anticipation of the Interactive Dialogue, and facilitates discussion among states over their recommendations afterwards. While the SuR does not have time to respond to all the interventions and recommendations on the day, it is expected to give a written response to each recommendation within a few months of its Interactive Dialogue. Furthermore – crucially – each country will be subject to another Interactive Dialogue in four-and-a-half years. So responding to the last Interactive Dialogue blends into preparing for the next, as part of an ongoing dialogic process.

In short, the UPR as a whole is a protracted deliberative process, with a moment of highly public state-to-state accountability at its heart. ...

We now assess the quality of the deliberation involved in terms of the elements introduced above. The first element of a high-quality deliberative system is inclusiveness. The UPR is insistently open and inclusive, certainly with respect to all UN member states and to all internationally recognized human rights organizations. It is specifically designed to 'ensure universal coverage and equal treatment of all States' and to 'promote the universality, interdependence, indivisibility and interrelatedness of all human rights'.

Universality is not merely UPR's aspiration: it is its hallmark. Every state took part in its first UPR and, so far, every state has taken part in its second. ...

Looking beyond member states, the UPR also mandates the participation of all relevant stakeholders, 'guided by the principles of universality, impartiality, objectivity and non-selectivity'. This de-monopolizes states as suppliers of information. NGOs provide independent information and transparency, especially where the states fail to report fully or reliably. Taken as a whole, NGOs introduce a diversity and range of views that would be missing under standard practices of monitoring and reporting. They also play a leading role on the ground, gathering together different segments of their society in UPR-related events prior to the review, disseminating information and providing training to less experienced NGOs.

...

Why It Works: Deliberative Capacity in Action

The case of the HRC's UPR reveals 'what it takes' for deliberation to 'have effect' in the international setting. Three features of the deliberation seem highly useful in that connection.

One crucial source of the UPR's deliberative capacity is the fact that it is a repeated game among the same players. Repeat play can evoke more co-operative behavior, simply because players will have an opportunity to reward or punish one another in subsequent rounds of the game, depending on how they behave in this round; as a consequence, the shadow of the future makes players better behaved in the current round. This is one plausible interpretation of how international law constrains states' behavior in general.

...

A second, related source of the UPR's deliberative success is peer-to-peer accountability. It matters greatly that the UPR is a system of peers reviewing one another's performance, because peers care about each others' opinions. ... States can dismiss experts and NGOs, but not other states.

Among some states, particularly of the Global South, it is a point of pride to boast of the large percentage of UPR recommendations that they accepted. ...

But the peer pressure is felt equally keenly by the most powerful states in the world. Members of the G20, and especially the P5, are under special scrutiny in the UPR precisely because they are ordinarily immune. They particularly feel the obligation to 'look good' – or as good as they can – at their UPR in order to vindicate their position of international leadership.

The third crucial element of the UPR process is discursive entrapment. This is a particular instance of a more general process by which recalcitrant states are socialized into international norms, including human rights norms: 'Norm-violating governments accepted the norms rhetorically in order to decrease the international and domestic pressures against them.' But after making what started as a purely tactical rhetorical concession, states are increasingly held responsible (by themselves as well as others) for acting on it. This leads to increasingly co-operative joint action toward increasingly convergent goals. Parties have simply 'talked themselves into a corner', as a result of 'rhetorical coercion', 'persuasion' or 'socialization'.

An analogous cycle of self-entrapment seems to be at work in the UPR. In one cycle, the SuR receives a raft of recommendations. As a tactical concession to placate critics (at least in the short term), an SuR that is under heavy pressure over its human rights record might 'accept' some of the recommendations. But at its next UPR, it will have to account for its follow-through on the recommendations it accepted.
...

Conclusion

The UPR of human rights is, at face value, a toothless mechanism. Realists would scoff at its absence of any serious sanctions. But under some conditions, seemingly toothless mechanisms can have a real impact. Peer-to-peer accountability – universal in scope and repeated in form – engages states in co-operative dialogue that leads, for example, to their ratifying human rights treaties that they had failed to ratify before. Furthermore, the deliberative engagement is not only with other states but also with civil society, and the dialogue is continuous in form – occurring not only in anticipation of moments of peer-to-peer accountability but also because of it. In this way, the UPR mechanism induces a much more co-operative, deliberative culture across the system as a whole.
...

QUESTION

Cowan has argued that the UPR process 'deflects attention away from human rights harm caused by parties beyond the state, including the actions of states that are acting as monitors.' She cites the example of the 2016 review of Greece in which only Iceland acknowledged that there was an element of collective responsibility on the part of other European states and the International Monetary Fund in the austerity policies that had caused so many problems in the country.318 To what extent does the UPR decontextualize problems and serve to ignore the responsibility of actors other than the State?

---

[318] J. K. Cowan, 'Modes of Acting Virtuously at the Universal Periodic Review', in G. Vasconcelos Vilaça and M. Varaki (eds.), *Ethical Leadership in International Organizations: Concepts, Narratives, Judgment, and Assessment* (2021) 176, at 201.

C. THE HIGH COMMISSIONER FOR HUMAN RIGHTS

The first UN High Commissioner for Human Rights (HC) took office on 5 April 1994. The following day, the aircraft carrying the Rwandan President, a Hutu, was shot down, and a wave of genocidal killing ensued in Rwanda. The HC was plunged immediately into having to deal with an epochal human rights crisis with a mere handful of staff. Over the following three decades, the HC has been at the heart of many of the most intractable challenges in the field, as well as being responsible for managing a rapidly growing office that today has over 1,800 staff from 154 nationalities, half of whom are located in Geneva and New York, with the other half in 101 'field offices' around the world.

Proposals to create such a post emerged in 1947. The Soviet Union and its allies were strongly opposed, most developing countries were very wary, and even the West was ambivalent. The breakthrough came at the Vienna World Conference on Human Rights in 1993. A combination of factors were at play: the demise of the Socialist bloc, post-Cold War optimism, and a new (Clinton) administration in the United States. Boutros Boutros-Ghali, then UN Secretary-General, opposed the initiative. He subsequently did all he could to limit the potential of the office.

General Assembly Resolution 48/141 (1993) decided that the HC was to be appointed by the Secretary-General, with the approval of the General Assembly (which, in practice, has been a formality). The HC can serve a maximum of two four-year terms, although not one of the office-holders has so far served for the full eight years. The likelihood of earning the enmity of powers great and small seems too great. In principle, there should be 'geographical rotation' in terms of the nationalities and regions from which the appointee comes.

Resolution 48/141 described the HC as the UN 'official with principal responsibility for [UN] human rights activities under the direction and authority of the Secretary-General; within the framework of the overall competence, authority and decisions of the General Assembly, the Economic and Social Council and the Commission on Human Rights'. The HC's responsibilities are:

> (a) To promote and protect the effective enjoyment by all of all civil, cultural, economic, political and social rights;

> (b) To carry out the tasks assigned to him/her by the competent bodies of the United Nations system in the field of human rights and to make recommendations to them with a view to improving the promotion and protection of all human rights;

> ...

> (e) To coordinate relevant United Nations education and public information programmes in the field of human rights;

> (f) To play an active role in removing the current obstacles and in meeting the challenges to the full realization of all human rights and in preventing the continuation of human rights violations throughout the world, as reflected in the Vienna Declaration and Programme of Action;

> (g) To engage in a dialogue with all Governments in the implementation of his/her mandate with a view to securing respect for all human rights;

> ...

> (j) To rationalize, adapt, strengthen and streamline the United Nations machinery in the field of human rights with a view to improving its efficiency and effectiveness;

> ...

The following individuals have served as HC:

o   1994-1997: José Ayala-Lasso, previously Foreign Minister of Ecuador;
o   1997-2002: Mary Robinson, previously a human rights lawyer and President of Ireland;
o   2002-2003: Sergio Vieira de Mello, a UN humanitarian specialist from Brazil, killed in a bombing in Baghdad;[319]
o   2003-2004: B. G. Ramcharan, a senior UN official from Guyana, who served as acting-HC;
o   2004-2008: Louise Arbour, previously a judge of the Supreme Court of Canada, and ICTY Prosecutor;
o   2008-2014: Navanethem Pillay, former South African High Court judge, and President of the ICTR;
o   2014-2018: Zeid Ra'ad Al Hussein, former Jordanian Ambassador to the UN;
o   2018-2022: Michelle Bachelet Jeria, former President of Chile; and
o   2022---   : Volker Türk, previously a senior official in the UN and the Office of the UN High Commissioner for Refugees.

The HC plays many roles, including being the main UN spokesperson on human rights issues, the principal human rights interlocutor with governments at the foreign minister and presidential levels as well as with all levels of civil society, CEO of the Office of the HC, and human rights envoy to other UN and international organizations. The complexity of the job was highlighted by HC Zeid Ra'ad Al Hussein in his farewell speech to the Council on 18 June 2018:

> … [T]he UN is symptomatic of the wider global picture. It is only as great or as pathetic as the prevailing state of the international scene at the time. …
>
> There is a dangerous remove and superficiality to so many of our discussions, so much so that the deepest, core issue seems to have been lost on many.
>
> …
>
> Those of us in the UN Secretariat … work collaboratively and we do not answer to any State. In contrast, too many governments represented at the UN will often pull in the opposing direction: feigning a commitment to the common effort, yet fighting for nothing more than their thinly-thought interests … . The more pronounced their sense of self-importance – the more they glory in nationalism – the more unvarnished is the assault by these governments on the overall common good: on universal rights, on universal law and universal institutions, such as this one.
>
> And as the attack on the multilateral system and its rules, including most especially international human rights law, intensifies, so too will the risk increase of further mischief on a grander scale. The UN's collective voice must therefore be principled and strong; not weak and whining, obsessed with endless wrangling over process, the small things, as it is the case today.

The HC is also chief fund-raiser for the Office, a role made more difficult by chronic under-funding, which is often intentional on the part of governments. In 2022, OHCHR's total budget was $374 million. Only $152m was effectively guaranteed because it came from the UN's regular budget (see UN Doc. A/77/6 (Sect. 24) (2022)). An additional $222m was raised through voluntary contributions, including by: the European Commission ($30m), Sweden ($29m), USA ($28m), Norway ($19m), Netherlands ($15m), Germany ($13m), Switzerland ($10m), UNDP ($9m), Finland ($9m), Belgium ($6m), Denmark ($5), UK ($5m), Canada, France and Ireland (each $4m). In total, these voluntary contributions, which depend on the goodwill of states from year to year, accounted for almost 60 percent of the total budget, and two-thirds of those contributions were 'earmarked', or donated for specific purposes.[320]

---

[319] S. Power, *Chasing the Flame: One Man's Fight to Save the World* (2008).
[320] OHCHR, *United Nations Human Rights Appeal 2023*, at 6.

1. Reporting from Field Offices

Among the many functions played by the HC, we briefly consider the Office's in-country presences, and its external monitoring and reporting role, which is its most contentious activity. The OHCHR's field offices include 19 Country/Stand-alone Offices/Human Rights Missions, 12 Regional Offices/Centres, 11 Human rights components, of UN Peace/Political Missions, 50 Human Rights Advisers deployed under the framework of the UN Sustainable Development Goals, and 9 other types of field presences.[321]

Andrew Clapham, in 'The High Commissioner for Human Rights', in Frédéric Mégret and Philip Alston (eds.), *The United Nations and Human Rights: A Critical Appraisal* (2nd. Ed., 2020) 667 reflects on the dilemmas that arise if criticism of a country's record has to be muted in the hope that the government will agree to permit the establishment of a field office.

> … [W]hen the prospects of obtaining a foothold [such as a field office] are weak, denunciation rather than just the threat of it should be considered a definite option. Indeed, even after an agreement is successfully concluded allowing the High Commissioner to establish such a field presence, the tension is likely to remain as the government can terminate its consent and demand that the mission leave the country ([as in] Rwanda). Given this dynamic, two questions arise. First, is it worth remaining mute in the hope of obtaining a presence? Second, is it worth negotiating a presence which will have no power to monitor human rights violations and will merely legitimize the government's claim that it is doing everything possible to cooperate on human rights with the United Nations?

This is a tension that lies at the heart of contemporary international human rights work more generally. All organizations that seek to engage with governments in a constructive way are faced with the difficulty of knowing how and when to complain about violations and denounce non-cooperation or obstruction. It is acknowledged that the most effective fieldwork tends to combine assistance and reporting. In the words of one experienced field worker:

> Some local officials refused outright to allow HROs [human rights officers] to interview refugees during investigations into alleged human rights violations. They regarded us with suspicion, unsure of our motives or how we would use the information we gathered. In such situations, we would invest time in implementing the assistance aspects of our mandate: human rights training for officials, making local human rights broadcasts. Only after developing a relationship of mutual trust with local authorities could we implement our monitoring and investigating roles. Without the assistance aspect of our mandate— important in and of itself—we would never have succeeded in seeking accountability for violations.[322]

A related problem, but one for which OHCHR is not responsible, occurs when the main United Nations office in a country is unwilling to broach human rights issues with the government, or even inhibits or prevents others from doing so.[323]

a. Colombia

One of the longest standing, best resourced, and probably most effective field offices was established in Colombia in 1997. The Government agreed to it largely in order to avoid the perceived stigma of the appointment of a country rapporteur. An in-depth evaluation of the first 15 years of the mission concluded that it had made an important contribution to reducing extrajudicial killings, and that it did so through combining intensive on the ground monitoring, continuing dialogue with the government including in relation to specific

---

[321] *Ibid,* 32.
[322] B. Majekodunmi, 'United Nations Human Rights Field Officers' in Y. Danieli (ed.), *Sharing the Front Line and the Back Hills* (2002) 137.
[323] See, in relation to Laos, UN Doc. A/HRC/41/39/Add.2 (2019), para. 80; and in relation to Myanmar, *How the UN is Failing Myanmar* (Special Advisory Council for Myanmar, October 2023) 54.

cases, an active public media presence, and regular reporting to the Council.[324] In 2022, the Office submitted a detailed analysis reporting on and condemning violence carried out by 'non-state armed groups and criminal organizations'. But it was also critical of the government's role in response:

> 7. Despite the efforts of the State, the predominantly military response to combat these groups has not been able to stop their expansion and the violence they generate. In addition, the weakness of the rule of law and development alternatives in the territories affected by violence have exacerbated the situation.

> 8. The affected communities denounce State abandonment and the absence or limited presence of civil State authorities to deal with this situation. In various territories, mistrust in the State is growing and in some cases acts of collusion between authorities and non-State armed actors have been denounced.[325]

The Government published a 30-page response, expressing appreciation of the report, outlining all that has already been done, and the future steps it proposes to take.[326]

b. Ukraine

In 2014, after the Russian annexation of the Crimean Peninsula, OHCHR established the UN Human Rights Monitoring Mission in Ukraine (HRMMU). As a result, after the Russian invasion of Ukraine in February 2022, the OHCHR was well placed to provide in-depth reporting. The following is an example of its regularly updated reports to the Council (UN Doc. A/HRC/52/CRP.1 (December, 2022)):

> 3. As at 31 October 2022, OHCHR – through the … HRMMU – had documented summary executions and attacks on individual civilians in 102 villages and towns of the [Kyiv, Chernihiv and Sumy] regions between 24 February and 6 April 2022. The acts in question were committed by Russian armed forces in control of these areas and led to the deaths of 441 civilians (341 men, 72 women, 20 boys and 8 girls). One hundred of those killings are analysed in this report and its annex, as illustrative examples of the suffering borne by civilians in these areas.

> 4. … [The actual numbers are likely to be] considerably higher.

> 5. OHCHR found that the killings of civilians were not confined to specific locations, although some areas were more affected than others. [Statistics follow.]

> 6. … In most cases, victims of killings in places of detention were found with their hands cuffed or bound by duct-tape, and with injuries suggesting torture or other ill-treatment before being killed. In at least one case, the body of one of the victims showed signs consistent with sexual violence. The circumstances of the summary executions provide strong indications that these killings may amount to the war crime of wilful killing, a grave breach of the Geneva Conventions.

> 10. This report is based on information gathered during OHCHR field visits to those areas, including through interviews with victims and witnesses, as well as other relevant material. The information obtained through interviews was further cross-checked and corroborated by other sources, including official records, open-source documents, audio and photo materials, forensic reports, criminal investigation materials, court documents, and other relevant sources assessed as credible and reliable in line with established methodology.

---

[324] C. Salazar Volkmann, 'Evaluating the Impact of Human Rights Work: The Office of the [UNHCHR] and the Reduction of Extrajudicial Executions in Colombia', 4 *J. Hum. Rts. Prac.* (2012) 396.
[325] OHCHR in Colombia, *Territorial Violence in Colombia: Recommendations for the New Government* (2022) (machine translation from Spanish).
[326] Ministerio de Relaciones Exteriores de Colombia, 'Observaciones' (2 July 2022), at https://www.ohchr.org/es/documents/country-reports/violencia-territorial-en-colombia

11. Findings are included in the report where they meet the "reasonable grounds to believe" standard … … …

…

13. … In accordance with regular practice, OHCHR shared the draft report with the concerned States for factual comments.

2. Reporting on the Basis of Limited or No Access

When the OHCHR was first created, the likelihood that it would evolve into an organization that could actively monitor ongoing situations with little or no cooperation from the government concerned, and report on them to the Council, seemed slight. But through a series of precedent-setting initiatives by successive HCs, and especially in the aftermath of the Arab Spring in 2011, the Office has firmly established its role in this regard. In principle, it seeks an invitation to visit, but if this is not forthcoming, it must rely on other sources. We consider two examples. The first is Nicaragua, which has refused to cooperate with the Office. The second is China, which involved a prolonged and complex set of negotiations, resulting in a very brief and highly controversial visit by the HC.

a. Nicaragua

On 15 December 2022, the Council held an 'Interactive Dialogue on the Periodic Update of Nicaragua'.

Oral update by HC Volker Türk:

> The number of people arbitrarily detained for expressing their political views or for being perceived as critics of the Government went up from 195 in September to 225 today … .
> … [T]heir conditions of detention are precarious. … With humiliating and degrading treatment of family members visiting prisoners, such as elderly women subjected to strip-searching. … Over 3,000 national and international NGOs were shut down … . Muzzling of the media, with 26 national outlets and three international outlets closed by the Government. And a new law adopted in October requiring registration and Government authorization for the production, filming and exhibition of any audio-visual material in the country.
>
> …
>
> Human rights defenders, journalists, clergy or those perceived to be political opponents, are arrested, harassed, intimidated. Some are prosecuted for the offences of conspiracy to undermine national integrity or for "false news". All part of a systematised effort to stifle opposition and dissent.
>
> The lead up to and holding of the November municipal elections had the trappings of an exercise in autocracy. With a wave of arrests and dismissals of political opponents in the months leading up to the elections.
>
> …
>
> The effects of this crisis continue rippling beyond its borders. Between January and October 2022, Costa Rica received 70,000 new asylum applications from Nicaraguans. Over 147,000 Nicaraguans ended up at the borders of the United States of America.
>
> What can be done. … My Office is ready to work with the authorities in these areas, and I request access to the country for my staff.

Speech by the Delegation of Nicaragua (machine translation)

The legitimate Government of Reconciliation and National Unity of Nicaragua will not tire of repeating with dignity, loudly and irrefutably, our TOTAL REJECTION of this type of mechanism, which "updates its Human Rights reports", in a unilateral and biased manner; acting as an "instrument of pressure and interference" by using arguments that are far from the reality of our homeland, with the sole purpose of keeping us underdeveloped and undermining our achievements, to keep us submerged in the guidelines of foreign powers.

…

We reaffirm that with these Update Reports [the OHCHR] continues to be infamous towards us, discrediting and denigrating our authorities and national institutions. Despite this, we maintain our dignity, our sovereignty and our progress in all areas … .

… [We denounce the OHCHR for 'not pronouncing itself, for example, on the arbitrary, aggressive and illegal sanctions that some countries have imposed on us, which really directly attack the essential Human Rights of our people and that constitute a true crime against humanity.

We are aware that the developments achieved in our country do not please those who have lived at the expense of other peoples: looting, attacking and intervening, in order to hoard all the wealth for themselves; however, we are convinced, -as we have already stated-, that without the democratization of wealth, real Human Rights could never exist.
…

b. China

Prior to the brutal suppression of protests in Tiananmen Square, in Beijing, on 4 June 1989, China's profile in the UN human rights system was low. Sustained criticism by the US and its allies thereafter prompted deep engagement, initially to defend itself, and subsequently to seek to influence the shape of the overall regime, in both normative and institutional terms.[327]

In terms of engagement with UN procedures, China has ratified most of the major treaties, but not the ICCPR. It has reported reliably to the treaty bodies, but has been reluctant to facilitate visits to the country. Between 1997 and 2023, eight Special Procedures have made official visits (arbitrary detention (1997 and 2004); education (2003); torture (2005); food (2010); discrimination against women (2013); foreign debt (2015); poverty (2016); and older persons (2019)). Successive HCs have also sought to visit. In 2005, Louise Arbour (UN Press Release, 2 September 2005) visited for one week. In trying to capture the tenor of her approach she stated that: "In a spirit of cooperation and constructiveness we can sometimes be critical. … I leave China encouraged about taking this work forward, energized by the prospect of helping the country face daunting challenges, and guardedly optimistic about the enormous potential for positive change." But her main achievement was to sign a memorandum of understanding with the Government providing for future cooperation. Little was to come of the MOU in substantive terms. Not until 2022 was agreement reached to enable Michelle Bachelet to visit.

While many issues could have been on Bachelet's agenda, including Hong Kong and Tibet, the situation in the Xinjiang Uyghur Autonomous Region (XUAR) was the most pressing. With a population of some 25 million, it is China's only majority Muslim region and, in 2014, in response to civil unrest, China had responded with a 'Strike Hard Against Violent Extremism' campaign. In 2017, civil society groups began sending allegations to the OHCHR of systematic human rights violations. In 2018, the UN Working Group on Enforced or Involuntary Disappearances reported a dramatic increase in cases of disappearances, and a range of other UN expert groups and NGOs claimed that torture and other ill-treatment, including sexual violence, and forced labour, were common in the XUAR. In 2021, Human Rights Watch reported, for example, that:

---

[327] See generally: E. Pils, 'Autocratic Challenges to International Human Rights Law: A Chinese Case Study', 75 *Current Legal Problems* (2022) 189; Yu-Jie Chen, 'The United States, China and the European Union at the UN Human Rights Council', in Chien-Huei Wu et al. (eds.), *Multilateralism in Peril: The Uneasy Triangle of the US, China and the EU* (2022) 36; and R. Siu Inboden, *China and the International Human Rights Regime* (2021).

As many as a million people have been arbitrarily detained in 300 to 400 facilities, which include "political education" camps, pretrial detention centers, and prisons. Courts have handed down harsh prison sentences without due process, sentencing Turkic Muslims to years in prison merely for sending an Islamic religious recording to a family member or downloading e-books in Uyghur. Detainees and prisoners are subjected to torture and other ill-treatment, cultural and political indoctrination, and forced labor. ... [O]utside the detention facilities ... the Chinese authorities impose on Turkic Muslims a pervasive system of mass surveillance, controls on movement, arbitrary arrest and enforced disappearance, cultural and religious erasure, and family separation.

The United States State Department and the parliaments of Belgium, Canada, and the Netherlands have determined that China's conduct also constitutes genocide under international law. Human Rights Watch has not documented the existence of the necessary genocidal intent at this time. ...[328]

In September 2018, the HC requested access to the XUAR and her Office began preparing an 'assessment of available information ... with a view to making it public'. Delays ensued, COVID-19 struck, and only in March 2022 was agreement reached, although the assessment remained unpublished at that time. In October 2021, 43 mainly Western countries, led by France, made a public statement to the Council demanding that the HC be given immediate, meaningful and unfettered access. In response, Cuba made a counter-statement on behalf of 62 countries insisting that the XUAR was part of China's internal affairs and dismissing the allegations as being based on 'political motivation' and 'disinformation'. Days before her visit, Human Rights Watch and other groups warned that the HC's credibility was at stake and that her 'legacy [as HC] will be measured by her willingness to hold a powerful state accountable for crimes against humanity.'[329] Amnesty International warned that 'the UN must avoid becoming complicit'.

The HC's six-day visit took her only to Guangzhou and the two largest cities in the XUAR. China insisted that pandemic-related restrictions required her visit to be conducted in a 'closed loop', and they characterized it as 'a private visit to enhance exchanges and cooperation'. She met with President Xi Jinping by videolink, and the Foreign Minister in person. On 28 May 2022, she held a press conference to report the results of her visit. Before announcing various forms of follow up between her Office and the Chinese Government, she clarified the goals of the visit:

> This visit was not an investigation – official visits by a High Commissioner are by their nature high-profile and simply not conducive to the kind of detailed, methodical, discreet work of an investigative nature. The visit was an opportunity to hold direct discussions – with China's most senior leaders – on human rights ... .
>
> ...
>
> To those who have sent me appeals, asking me to raise issues or cases with the authorities - I have heard you. Your advocacy matters and my visit was an opportunity to raise a number of specific situations and issues of concern with the Government. I will continue to follow up on such issues and instances of concern on a sustained basis.

Reporting on the outcome, one journalist wrote that '[c]ritics had expected Bachelet to lambast Beijing on its heavy-handed way of dealing with the Uyghurs – which some call "genocidal", and which Beijing denies – during that press conference, but Bachelet did not do that.' He added that she 'was right, however, to remind her audience of the importance of engaging China at a time of increased global challenges ...'.[330]

Amnesty International said that Bachelet's 'visit has been characterized by photo opportunities with senior government officials and manipulation of her statements by Chinese state media, leaving an impression that she has walked straight into a highly predictable propaganda exercise for the Chinese government.' Amnesty called for the release of 'the long-awaited report on Xinjiang'.

---

[328] Human Rights Watch, *'Break Their Lineage, Break Their Roots': China's Crimes against Humanity Targeting Uyghurs and Other Turkic Muslims* (2021) 2.

[329] *Ibid*, 'UN: Rights Chief's Credibility at Stake in China Visit' (22 May 2022).

[330] V. Ni, 'Bachelet's Xinjiang visit is emblematic of the growing divide between China and the west', *The Guardian* (30 May 2022).

In the months that followed there was considerable speculation as to the HC's intention, especially as her term of office was to expire on 31 August 2022, unless she sought and was given a new term. Minutes before midnight on her last day, the Office released a 45-page report, which concluded that:

> 143. Serious human rights violations have been committed in XUAR in the context of the Government's application of counter-terrorism and counter-"extremism" strategies. The implementation of these strategies, and associated policies in XUAR has led to interlocking patterns of severe and undue restrictions on a wide range of human rights. These patterns of restrictions are characterized by a discriminatory component, as the underlying acts often directly or indirectly affect Uyghur and other predominantly Muslim communities.
>
> …
>
> 148. … The extent of arbitrary and discriminatory detention of members of Uyghur and other predominantly Muslim groups, pursuant to law and policy, in context of restrictions and deprivation more generally of fundamental rights enjoyed individually and collectively, may constitute international crimes, in particular crimes against humanity.

The report did not, however, address the hotly contested issue of whether the crimes might have qualified as genocide. In a statement on the same day, China released a lengthy rebuttal:

> … Based on the disinformation and lies fabricated by anti-China forces and out of presumption of guilt, the so-called 'assessment' distorts China's laws and policies, wantonly smears and slanders China, and interferes in China's internal affairs, which violates principles including dialogue and cooperation, and non-politicization in the field of human rights, and also undermines the credibility of the OHCHR.

Soon after leaving China, Michelle Bachelet announced that she had informed the Secretary-General several months earlier that she did not wish to be re-appointed as HC. The Secretary-General subsequently nominated a long-time UN and UN High Commissioner for Refugees official, Volker Türk, as HC. The former Executive Director of Human Rights Watch, Kenneth Roth, (in 'The U.N. Gave a Quiet Diplomat the Wrong Job', *Foreign Policy*, September 16, 2022) harshly criticized the choice on the grounds that 'by virtue of temperament and experience, [Türk] seems poorly suited for the U.N.'s top human rights post'. His reasoning was that:

> … [T]he U.N. human rights chief['s] … only ability to move governments is by generating pressure through his investigations and public reporting of human rights violations and his public condemnation of misconduct.
>
> Such public reporting and commentary can be shameful, tarnishing the reputation for respecting human rights that most government seek to cultivate, however disingenuously. That shaming, if done well, can change the cost-benefit calculation behind repression, leading to positive change. But Türk has no history of publicly criticizing particular governments. Like his boss [the Secretary-General], he seems to prefer to work behind the scenes while speaking publicly in only broad generalities.

On 6 October 2022, the Human Rights Council considered a Western-sponsored resolution to 'take note with interest' of the HC's report and to hold a debate on the situation in Xinjiang at the following session in March 2023. Intense lobbying on both sides led to the defeat of the resolution, with 17 states in favor, 19 against, and 11 abstaining.

QUESTIONS

1. How would you assess the fact that the OHCHR relies, for two-thirds of its funding, on voluntary contributions, mostly from governments?

2. What do you make of the virulent denunciations of the Office by countries under scrutiny?

3. Is public condemnation ('naming and shaming') the only responsible approach for a HC to take in situations such as that existing in China? Are there alternative, and legitimate, conceptions of the role of a HC in response to serious violations?

4. When reading about China and the UN[331] consider the assessment of Malin Oud, in 'Powers of Persuasion? China's Struggle for Human Rights Discourse Power at the UN', 15 Global Policy (2024) Suppl. 2, 85, at 92

… China has always advocated for a state-centric 'development-based approach to human rights' and defended its oppressive policies on grounds of national security and economic development. However, in the last decade … China has abandoned its previous foreign policy of 'keeping a low profile and biding one's time' and instead become an active international norm entrepreneur that does not shy away from mobilising compulsory power means. …

China's strategic narratives on human rights and development have traction because they speak to real grievances about Western hypocrisy and global inequalities in many parts of the world. …

… In essence, China seeks to reshape international norms so that human rights become each member state's 'internal affairs' rather than a legitimate concern of the international community.

D. THE SECURITY COUNCIL AND THE RESPONSIBILITY TO PROTECT

For more than four decades, the Security Council exercised a remarkably limited role in human rights matters. With the end of the Cold War, however, that role expanded significantly and many of the issues coming before it over the past 35 years have had human rights dimensions. Most notably, the Council played the central role in establishing the ad hoc criminal tribunals in relation to the former Yugoslavia and Rwanda, thus paving the way for the International Criminal Court (see Ch. 16A, below). It has ensured the inclusion of human rights provisions in peace agreements, and engaged in efforts to eliminate the use of child soldiers and ostracize groups that violate that ban. We consider some of its key roles elsewhere in this book, including in relation to counter-terrorism, the imposition of sanctions, and the Women, Peace and Security Agenda. Its biggest challenge, however, has involved the authorization of forcible measures, including military intervention, to stop massive human rights violations in member states.

The Security Council consists of 15 members, five of which are permanent — China, France, Russia, the United Kingdom and the United States.[332] Ten others are elected by the General Assembly for two-year terms. Each member has one vote. Substantive decisions require nine votes out of the 15, and must include the concurring votes (defined by the Council to include abstentions) of all five permanent members. This is the so-called 'veto' power. The Council is able to be convened at any time and non-members may be invited to participate, but without a vote, when their interests are affected.

---

[331] See also J. Neagli, 'Bend, Don't Break: China's Approach to the International Human Rights Order', 64 *Harv. Int'l L. J.* (2023) 489.

[332] See generally M. Wood and E. Sthoeger, *The UN Security Council and International Law* (2022).

The Council is given 'primary responsibility' for the maintenance of international peace and security under the collective security system provided for in the UN Charter (Art. 24), and member states are obligated to carry out its decisions (Art. 25). It can act under *Chapter VI* of the Charter (Arts. 33–8) to achieve the pacific settlement of 'any dispute, the continuance of which is likely to endanger the maintenance of international peace and security'. It is empowered to investigate any such dispute and to recommend 'appropriate procedures or methods of adjustment'. It can act under *Chapter VII* (Arts. 39–51) whenever it determines 'the existence of any threat to the peace, breach of the peace, or act of aggression'. In such situations, the Council can call on states to apply sanctions of various kinds (Art. 41) or to take such military action 'as may be necessary to restore international peace and security' (Art. 42). Since all states are obligated by Article 2(4) of the Charter to 'refrain in their international relations from the threat or use of force against the territorial integrity or political independence of any state', except in the exercise of the right of self-defence against an armed attack (Art. 51), the Council enjoys a legal monopoly over the use of force in all other circumstances. This monopoly extends to Article 53(1) which authorizes the Council to make use of 'regional arrangements or agencies for enforcement action under its authority'. But the latter are not permitted to act without the Council's authorization.

Precedents Set in the Struggle Against Apartheid

Many procedures and techniques which were eventually developed by the General Assembly and the Security Council to deal with human rights were hammered out on the anvil of the South African apartheid system. The issue was first brought to the Assembly in 1946 by India, which complained of the discriminatory treatment of persons of Indian origin. Very early on, India suggested that such conduct could be seen as a threat to international peace and thus as requiring the attention of the Council. South Africa replied that most of those concerned were its nationals and that, in any event, the issue was exclusively a domestic affair.

The battle lines were thus set for a struggle continuing until today to clarify two key issues: (1) the relationship between the human rights provisions of the UN Charter and the domestic jurisdiction clause in Article 2(7) of the Charter (considered in Ch. 3A, above); and (2) the circumstances under which gross human rights violations can be considered to threaten international peace and security and thus warrant Security Council measures under Chapter VII. While South Africa was the main focus of these debates, the situations in Southern Rhodesia (Zimbabwe) and the Portuguese colonies in southern Africa (Angola and Mozambique) also figured.

With the influx of newly independent states into the United Nations from the late 1950s onwards, the South African case pitted a Security Council, dominated by Western governments that were reluctant to act, against a General Assembly which was increasingly frustrated at the intransigence of the racist governments in southern Africa and the failure of the Assembly's barrage of resolutions to make any difference. In 1962, the Assembly tested the limits of its division of labour with the Security Council by itself calling upon member states to break off diplomatic relations with South Africa, to refuse entry to its ships and aircraft, to boycott its goods and to impose an arms embargo. In 1963, the Council characterized the South African situation as 'seriously disturbing international peace and security' and called for, but did not mandatorily impose, an arms embargo. The Assembly raised the stakes again in 1966 by condemning apartheid as 'a crime against humanity', an approach which was taken further by its adoption in 1973 of the Convention on the Suppression and Punishment of the Crime of Apartheid (GA Res. 3068 (XXVIII)). Three years later, the Assembly concluded that 'the continued brutal repression, including indiscriminate mass killings' by the apartheid regime left 'no alternative to the oppressed people of South Africa but to resort to armed struggle to achieve their legitimate rights', thus giving its imprimatur to the national liberation struggle.

It was not until 1977 that the Council (Res. 418) imposed a mandatory arms embargo under Chapter VII. In 1984, the Council rejected a new constitution that had been adopted by an exclusively white electorate as contrary to UN principles and thus 'null and void'. With the end of apartheid and the transition to democracy, the Council terminated the arms embargo and all other restrictions in May 1994.

From Humanitarian Intervention to the 'Responsibility to Protect'

It has long been claimed that, despite the prohibition on the use of force contained in Article 2(4) of the UN Charter, there is a humanitarian exception of some sort, which would justify the use of force by a state to protect individuals in another state from egregious violations of human rights. With the end of the Cold War, the 1990s brought a distinctly greater willingness on the part of some states, including the United States, to intervene for such reasons. Somalia, Haiti and the former Yugoslavia were key examples. But the failure to intervene in the face of genocide in Rwanda and to stop a genocidal massacre in Bosnia traumatized the UN and other actors and led to extensive soul-searching as to the nature of any principle of intervention for humanitarian reasons. A UN-commissioned report on Rwanda characterized the 1994 genocide in which 800,000 people were killed in about 100 days as 'one of the most abhorrent events of the twentieth century'. It condemned the failure to 'prevent, and subsequently, to stop the genocide in Rwanda' as a failure by the UN system as a whole. 'The fundamental failure was the lack of resources and political commitment devoted to developments in Rwanda and to the United Nations presence there. There was a persistent lack of political will by Member States to act, or to act with enough assertiveness … .' It called upon the 'Security Council and troop contributing countries ... to act to prevent acts of genocide or gross violations of human rights wherever they may take place.'[333] The UN also published a report criticizing its failure to stop massacres in Bosnia.

In the same year as the UN published these strongly self-critical reviews a crisis erupted in Kosovo, then a province of Serbia. Since 1993, reports to the UN Commission on Human Rights had documented serious human rights abuses by Serbia against the Kosovo Albanians who made up 90 per cent of the province's population. In 1998, the Security Council, acting under Chapter VII, imposed an arms embargo (Res. 1160) and subsequently determined that there was 'a threat to peace and security in the region' (Res. 1199). Russia and China, however, made clear that they would veto any Council resolution authorizing the use of force. After a grave deterioration of the situation, and the failure of talks among the relevant parties held in Rambouillet (France), the North Atlantic Treaty Organization (NATO) launched military action against Serbia for non-compliance with the Council resolutions and in the name of 'humanitarian intervention'. It was estimated that 90 per cent of the Kosovo Albanian population — some 1.45 million people — had been displaced by the conflict by the time it ended.[334]

The challenge of framing a new 'doctrine' that would enable effective action to prevent or terminate atrocities was encouraged by the UN Secretary-General, given conceptual form by an independent commission organized by Canada, promoted by some states within the UN, and given a degree of institutional recognition through the UN Secretary-General's appointment of a Special Adviser on the Prevention of Genocide (in 2004) and a Special Adviser on the Responsibility to Protect (in 2007). The two now work together in a 'Joint Office' at the UN (https://www.un.org/en/genocideprevention/).

KOFI ANNAN, IMPLICATIONS OF INTERNATIONAL RESPONSE TO EVENTS IN RWANDA, KOSOVO EXAMINED BY SECRETARY-GENERAL
UN PRESS RELEASE GA/9595 (20 SEPTEMBER 1999)

[Report of a speech by UN Secretary-General, Kofi Annan]

'While the genocide in Rwanda will define for our generation the consequences of inaction in the face of mass murder, the more recent conflict in Kosovo had prompted important questions about the consequences of action in the absence of unity on the part of the international community', he said. In the case of Kosovo, the inability of that community to reconcile the question of the legitimacy of an action taken by a regional organization without a United Nations mandate, on one side, and the universally accepted imperative of effectively halting gross and systematic violations of human rights, on the other, could only be viewed as a tragedy. It had revealed the core challenge to the Security Council and the United Nations in the next century:

---

[333] Report of the Independent Inquiry into the Actions of the United Nations During the 1994 Genocide in Rwanda, UN Doc. S/1999. On Bosnia, see 'The Fall of Srebrenica', UN Doc. A/54/549 (1999).

[334] See generally A. Hehir, 'Kosovo 1999: The False Dawn of Humanitarian Intervention', 38 *Comparative Strategy* (2019) 454.

To forge unity behind the principle that massive, systematic violations of human rights — wherever they might take place — should not be allowed to stand.

He said that, to those for whom the greatest threat to the future of international order was the use of force in the absence of a Council mandate, one might ask — not in the context of Kosovo, but in the context of Rwanda — if a coalition of States had been prepared to act in defence of the Tutsi population, but had not received prompt Council authorization, should such a coalition have stood aside and allowed the horror to unfold? To those for whom the Kosovo action heralded a new era when States and groups of States could take military action outside the established mechanisms for enforcing international law, one might ask: Was there not a danger of such intervention undermining the imperfect, yet resilient, security system created after the Second World War, and of setting dangerous precedents for future interventions?

...

... [I]n the Charter's own words, 'armed force shall not be used, save in the common interest'. ...

...

... In [Rwanda and Kosovo] Member States of the United Nations should have been able to find common ground in upholding the principles of the Charter, and acting in defence of 'our common heritage'. The Charter required the Council to be the defender of the 'common interest'. Unless it was seen to be so, there was a danger that others could seek to take its place.

ICISS, THE RESPONSIBILITY TO PROTECT
(2001)

In order to address systematically the policy issues emerging from situations such as Rwanda and Kosovo the Canadian Government established an International Commission on Intervention and State Sovereignty (ICISS) which reported in 2001. Its report, entitled *The Responsibility to Protect* put forward a series of 'core principles' premised on the argument that while the notion of state sovereignty could not be brushed aside in the name of intervention, it should be interpreted as implying that 'the primary responsibility for the protection of its people lies with the state itself'. But where a state is 'unwilling or unable' to halt or avert serious harm to its own population, 'the principle of non-intervention yields to the international responsibility to protect'. A similar approach was subsequently endorsed by a 'High-Level Panel' appointed by the UN Secretary-General.

A MORE SECURE WORLD: OUR SHARED RESPONSIBILITY, REPORT OF THE HIGH-LEVEL PANEL ON THREATS, CHALLENGES AND CHANGE
(2004)

201. The successive humanitarian disasters in Somalia, Bosnia and Herzegovina, Rwanda, Kosovo and now Darfur, Sudan, have concentrated attention not on the immunities of sovereign Governments but their responsibilities, both to their own people and to the wider international community. There is a growing recognition that the issue is not the "right to intervene" of any State, but the "responsibility to protect" of *every* State when it comes to people suffering from avoidable catastrophe — mass murder and rape, ethnic cleansing by forcible expulsion and terror, and deliberate starvation and exposure to disease. And there is a growing acceptance that while sovereign Governments have the primary responsibility to protect their own citizens from such catastrophes, when they are unable or unwilling to do so that responsibility should be taken up by the wider international community — with it spanning a continuum involving prevention, response to violence, if necessary, and rebuilding shattered societies. The primary focus should be on assisting the cessation of violence through mediation and other tools and the protection of people through such measures as the dispatch of humanitarian, human rights and police missions. Force, if it needs to be used, should be deployed as a last resort.

202. The Security Council so far has been neither very consistent nor very effective in dealing with these cases, very often acting too late, too hesitantly or not at all. But step by step, the Council and the wider international community have come to accept that, under Chapter VII and in pursuit of the emerging norm of a collective international responsibility to protect, it can always authorize military action to redress catastrophic internal

wrongs if it is prepared to declare that the situation is a "threat to international peace and security", not especially difficult when breaches of international law are involved.

203. We endorse the emerging norm that there is a collective international responsibility to protect, exercisable by the Security Council authorizing military intervention as a last resort, in the event of genocide and other large-scale killing, ethnic cleansing or serious violations of international humanitarian law which sovereign Governments have proved powerless or unwilling to prevent.

B. The question of legitimacy

…

207. In considering whether to authorize or endorse the use of military force, the Security Council should always address — whatever other considerations it may take into account — at least the following five basic criteria of legitimacy:

(a) *Seriousness of threat*. Is the threatened harm to State or human security of a kind, and sufficiently clear and serious, to justify *prima facie* the use of military force? In the case of internal threats, does it involve genocide and other large-scale killing, ethnic cleansing or serious violations of international humanitarian law, actual or imminently apprehended?

(b) *Proper purpose*. Is it clear that the primary purpose of the proposed military action is to halt or avert the threat in question, whatever other purposes or motives may be involved?

(c) *Last resort*. Has every non-military option for meeting the threat in question been explored, with reasonable grounds for believing that other measures will not succeed?

(d) *Proportional means*. Are the scale, duration and intensity of the proposed military action the minimum necessary to meet the threat in question?

(e) *Balance of consequences*. Is there a reasonable chance of the military action being successful in meeting the threat in question, with the consequences of action not likely to be worse than the consequences of inaction?

2005 WORLD SUMMIT OUTCOME
GENERAL ASSEMBLY RES. 60/1

138. Each individual State has the responsibility to protect its populations from genocide, war crimes, ethnic cleansing and crimes against humanity. This responsibility entails the prevention of such crimes, including their incitement, through appropriate and necessary means. We accept that responsibility and will act in accordance with it. The international community should, as appropriate, encourage and help States to exercise this responsibility and support the United Nations in establishing an early warning capability.

139. The international community, through the United Nations, also has the responsibility to use appropriate diplomatic, humanitarian and other peaceful means, in accordance with Chapters VI and VIII of the Charter, to help to protect populations from genocide, war crimes, ethnic cleansing and crimes against humanity. In this context, we are prepared to take collective action, in a timely and decisive manner, through the Security Council, in accordance with the Charter, including Chapter VII, on a case-by-case basis and in cooperation with relevant regional organizations as appropriate, should peaceful means be inadequate and national authorities are manifestly failing to protect their populations from genocide, war crimes, ethnic cleansing and crimes against humanity. We stress the need for the General Assembly to continue consideration of the responsibility to protect populations from genocide, war crimes, ethnic cleansing and crimes against humanity and its implications, bearing in mind the principles of the Charter and international law. We also intend to commit ourselves, as necessary and appropriate, to helping States build capacity to protect their populations from genocide, war crimes, ethnic cleansing and crimes against humanity and to assisting those which are under stress before crises and conflicts break out.

UN SECRETARY-GENERAL, IMPLEMENTING THE RESPONSIBILITY TO PROTECT (2009)

This report [UN Doc. A/63/677] introduced a three-pillar strategy for implementing R2P:

> Pillar 1: Every state has the Responsibility to Protect its populations from the four mass atrocity crimes.

> Pillar 2: The wider international community has the responsibility to encourage and assist individual states in meeting that responsibility.

> Pillar 3: If a state is manifestly failing to protect its populations, the international community must be prepared to take appropriate collective action in a timely and decisive manner and in accordance with the UN Charter.

Differing Views on R2P

Whatever its practical impact, R2P has succeeded in generating a vibrant scholarly debate. Consider the following examples.

Robert Kolb, *Peremptory International Law – Jus Cogens: A General Inventory* (2015) 121:

> Simply stated, the antinomy here is between the non-use of force rule, which knows of no exception for human rights, and the active protection of the most fundamental rights of human persons, for example against the commission of genocide or massacres, if necessary by using a proportionate amount of force. Conflicts between these two norms may occur in different settings. Either the nonuse of force rule is a binding prohibition and the human protection rule is a mere legal faculty, which can but must not be exercised by States; or alternatively the norm on human protection is also framed as an internationally recognised duty to act, possibly imbued with peremptory status. In this latter case, a duty to act would directly conflict with a duty to abstain. In reality, there is much doubt as to the existence of a rule allowing for the use of force in such situations; even more doubtful is the existence of a rule requiring the use of force. Conversely, if the rule on human protection is negated in the sense that it does not encompass a licence or a duty to use force, the antinomy disappears. If we assume for the sake of our argument that some rule on human protection exists in such extreme contexts, either as a faculty or as a duty, how is the antinomy to be solved?

> … The balancing process is as follows. First, the overwhelming majority of States… have emphatically rejected the idea that one State or a self-proclaimed coalition of States can intervene militarily in another State without the latter's consent, even if massacres are being perpetrated there. There are many arguments in favour of this position, in particular the fact that in view of the chronic instability of many States and the open-ended spectrum of possible triggering situations, a power to intervene militarily would destabilise the international system and open the gates to subjective, pretexted and power-policy interventions. Second, the same overwhelming majority of States accept the recent Chapter VII … interpretation which gives the Security Council the power (and morally the duty) to take collective measures in order to prevent, to halt and to remedy such gross human rights violations (today under the banner of the ' Responsibility to Protect '). In other words, the faculty or duty to act is transferred from the plane of States taken individually to the plane of the organised community acting through [the Security Council]. … The two imperatives are taken into account and harmonised through an interpretation which upholds the non-use of force rule and acknowledges at the same time the necessity to act. The solution is found along the lines of differentiating the actors called to deal with the humanitarian urgency. …

Ilia Siatitsa, *Serious Violations of Human Rights: On the Emergence of a New Special Regime* (2022) 141:

> The responsibility to protect threshold was from the very beginning set too high. In … 2005 …, states opted [to enumerate] four international crimes: genocide, war crimes, crimes against humanity, and ethnic cleansing. … The suggestion that massive human rights violations be included was overlooked, on the understanding that the crimes were more specific.
>
> The chosen terminology was still unfortunate. The states chose to use individual criminal responsibility terminology to deal with state responsibility matters. The reference to crimes instead of human rights violations points towards individuals (as perpetrators or victims) rather than states. In addition, international crimes have strict definitions, as prescribed by the principle of legality in criminal justice. As a result, their invocation in the context of mobilising the international community outside a judicial framework either makes the threshold unnecessarily rigid, or jeopardises the deliberation of criminal justice.
>
> …
>
> The concept of responsibility to protect has undergone considerable transformations since its inception, and in more than one direction, to the point where it is materially impossible to pin down exactly what it describes— whose responsibility and to do what. …
>
> … [R2P] does not address the question of the possible direct responsibility of a state for these crimes; it only underlines the primary responsibility to protect the populations from such acts, and the residual responsibility of the international community, including international organisations and states, to help protect them. Protection in that sense includes the criminal prosecution of the individuals responsible for these crimes, overshadowing the responsibility of the state itself for the commission of such crimes. …
>
> …
>
> The ICISS relied heavily on the idea that changing the permissive authority (a possibility) to an affirmative obligation (a duty) would challenge the status quo, establishing a duty of the Security Council to react and to legitimise unilateral action in the event that the former was blocked. However, the simple change of terminology was not sufficient to shift the legal order already in place. States embraced an abstract responsibility to protect without any solid commitments and specific considerations regarding the content of this so-called responsibility.
>
> … [E]ven as a framework that reinforces the normative power of existing legal rules and principles, [R2P] is significant. It facilitated the mobilisation of political pressure on the United Nations to take action in extreme circumstances. It did not generate legal obligations. …

Anastasia Prokhorova, 'The Special Adviser on the Responsibility to Protect: Performing Norm Leadership', 14 *Global Responsibility to Protect* (2022) 281:

> [The Special Adviser on R2P drafts the Secretary-General's annual report on R2P], which lays the ground for and stirs the discussion of the principle in the General Assembly held either as an informal dialogue (2010–17) or as a recently resumed formal debate (2009, 2018–21). The performativity of the Special Adviser in the Assembly meetings manifests not only in 'setting the scene' with the annual report but also in a strategic debate with the member states. Its participants display their competing interpretations of the norm, which can be roughly grouped in three categories: (category i) R2P does not generally apply to their domestic politics but shapes their foreign policy (Canada, Germany, Switzerland, United Arab Emirates, United States); (category ii) R2P is degraded, exploited, and misused by some states to justify military interventions and undermine the sovereignty of

others (the Philippines, Russia, Syrian Arab Republic, Ukraine, Venezuela); (category iii) R2P amplifies 'sovereignty as responsibility', which can and should be implemented primarily through domestic or (sub)regional, consensual, and preventive means (UN Secretariat, European Union, the Group of Friends of R2P). Following the reiteration and enaction of these clashing meanings of R2P in the Assembly over the last decade, the mainstreaming of R2P in foreign policy agendas (category i) has been criticised by the 'watchdogs' of sovereignty (category ii) but also by the Special Advisers, and eventually subsided to the vision that R2P and atrocity prevention 'start at home' and should focus on building up local, state, and regional capacities to withstand crises (category iii).

...

[The author concludes that successive Special Advisers have engaged in 'performative leadership', thereby contributing] to protection against atrocities by 'framing' certain situations as at risk of mass violence to incentivise action; shaping states' experience with norm use; reinterpreting the mandate given the needs at a specific time and context; strategically using language and rhetorical tools to navigate R2P through contestation and to support norm implementation. ...

QUESTIONS

1. Are the criteria identified by the High-Level Panel likely to be very helpful in resolving a concrete situation that comes before the Security Council? If not, why not?

2. In light of the materials above, how would you assess the following critiques by Philip Cunliffe: (1) R2P inverts the burden of justification for intervention; (2) R2P usurps self-determination in favour of paternalism; (3) victims' rights provide license for powerful states to further abuse their power; (4) the doctrine imposes imperfect duties; and (5) R2P diffuses post-conflict responsibilities.[335]

The Women, Peace and Security Agenda[336]

In Chapter 3 we traced the evolution of the concept of violence against women and its central role in much human rights advocacy over the past thirty years or more. An important exception to the Security Council's aversion to engaging with human rights issues has come in the form of a series of resolutions since 2000 linking women to issues of peace and security. The so-called Women, Peace and Security (WPS) Agenda rests on four pillars: (i) the role of women in conflict prevention; (ii) women's participation in peacemaking and peacebuilding; (iii) the protection of women's rights during and after conflict; and (iv) women's specific needs during repatriation, resettlement, rehabilitation, reintegration and post-conflict reconstruction.

The foundation stone was this resolution:

SECURITY COUNCIL RESOLUTION 1325
(2000)

The Security Council,

...

---

[335] P. Cunliffe, 'From ISIS to ICISS: A Critical Return to the Responsibility to Protect Report', 51 *Cooperation and Conflict* (2016) 233; see also *ibid., Cosmopolitan Dystopia: International Intervention and the Failure of the West* (2020).
[336] C. Chinkin, *Women, Peace and Security and International Law* (2022).

1. Urges Member States to ensure increased representation of women at all decision-making levels in national, regional and international institutions and mechanisms for the prevention, management, and resolution of conflict;

…

5. Expresses its willingness to incorporate a gender perspective into peacekeeping operations, and urges the Secretary-General to ensure that, where appropriate, field operations include a gender component;

6. Requests the Secretary-General to provide to Member States training guidelines and materials on the protection, rights and the particular needs of women, as well as on the importance of involving women in all peacekeeping and peace- building measures …;

…

8. Calls on all actors involved, when negotiating and implementing peace agreements, to adopt a gender perspective, including, inter alia:

> (a) The special needs of women and girls during repatriation and resettlement and for rehabilitation, reintegration and post-conflict reconstruction;

> (b) Measures that support local women's peace initiatives and indigenous processes for conflict resolution, and that involve women in all of the implementation mechanisms of the peace agreements;

> (c) Measures that ensure the protection of and respect for human rights of women and girls, particularly as they relate to the constitution, the electoral system, the police and the judiciary;

9. Calls upon all parties to armed conflict to respect fully international law applicable to the rights and protection of women and girls, especially as civilians …;

10. Calls on all parties to armed conflict to take special measures to protect women and girls from gender-based violence, particularly rape and other forms of sexual abuse, and all other forms of violence in situations of armed conflict;

11. Emphasizes the responsibility of all States to put an end to impunity and to prosecute those responsible for genocide, crimes against humanity, and war crimes including those relating to sexual and other violence against women and girls, and in this regard stresses the need to exclude these crimes, where feasible from amnesty provisions;

Up until January 2024 there have been nine additional resolutions. Some have focused especially on enhanced participation by women: Resolutions 1889 (2013), 2122 (2013), 2242 (2015) and 2493 (2019). Others have focused mainly on conflict-related sexual violence (CRSV): Resolutions 1820 (2008), 1888 (2009), 1960 (2010), 2106 (2013), and 2467 (2019).

* * *

Karen Engle, Vasuki Nesiah, and Dianne Otto, in 'Feminist Approaches to International Law', in Jeffrey Dunoff and Mark Pollack (eds.), *International Legal Theory: Foundations and Frontiers* (2022) 174 explain the background to Resolution 1325:

> … SCR 1325 was a bold initiative, seeking the admission of at least some feminist ideas into the inner sanctum of the Security Council … . At the same time, many feminist antiwar goals, especially those directed towards achieving "positive peace," were glaringly absent.

> [Its adoption] can be understood as a crisis measure in at least two senses. First, … antiwar feminists rode the global wave of panic about the high rates of sexual violence in

armed conflict … . This panic helped focus attention – even in SCR 1325 – on a specific set of women's experiences during armed conflict and in its wake, neglecting feminist concerns about other war time experiences such as racism and xenophobia, forced displacement, erosion of the space for dissent, and increased precarity of basic livelihood. Second, SCR 1325 was adopted during a period of heightened anxiety about the legitimacy of the superpower-dominated Security Council … . [The resolution reassured] the global community of the Security Council's commitment to a social agenda that includes providing for the safety of civilians – paradigmatically Third World women – during armed conflict and in its wake.

… [But] sexual violence came to dominate in the resolutions, even though the primary original impetus for feminist support for SCR 1325 was the promise of increased women's participation in conflict-related decisionmaking – a move away from the ubiquitous representation of women as always vulnerable and in need of masculine/military protection. SCR 1820, for example, even proposes that women "under imminent threat of sexual violence" be given priority in evacuation plans, presumably jumping other queues of those who are seriously injured or threatened with death.

… [M]ost of the sexual violence resolutions can be read to justify the lawful use of force by using language often found in Chapter VII resolutions, expressing the "readiness" of the Security Council, "where necessary," to take steps to address widespread or systematic sexual violence in situations on its agenda. As we see below, in 2015, SCR 2242 brought the Security Council's counterterrorism tools to bear on sexual violence. It also calls for targeted sanctions to respond to sexual violence, and increases the range of possible justifications for the use of force in the name of protecting women. …

CHRISTINE CHINKIN, 'WOMEN, PEACE, AND SECURITY: A HUMAN RIGHTS AGENDA?' GRÁINNE DE BÚRCA (ED.) LEGAL MOBILIZATION FOR HUMAN RIGHTS (2022) 30

Is Resolution 1325 an instrument for advancing women's human rights in conflict settings as wished for by many of those who mobilized for its adoption? On the one hand, the resolution reaffirms the need to implement human rights law and states are explicitly reminded of relevant human rights instruments, CEDAW and CRC. On the other hand, concepts and obligations that were already part of human rights law are either unacknowledged or weakened. There is no provision for a monitoring body such as is provided for within the UN human rights treaties. Difficult questions of human rights law are evaded; for instance, the Council does not explore the human rights obligations of non-state actors but merely assumes the applicability of international law to them. But if Resolution 1325 is ambiguous as a human rights treaty the same is true of it as a feminist peace agenda … … . [It] makes no mention of disarmament …, reduction of military expenditure, or of any connection between promotion of women's human rights and peace, or between eradication of gender-based violence and sustainable peace.

…

[Resolution 1820 (2008) emphasized sexual violence in armed conflict.] Under human rights law, all people are entitled to be free from sexual violence, not just civilians and not just women and girls. The attention paid to sexual violence including rape as a tactic of war is limiting for women and girls within the civilian population at whom it is directed. It discounts the many other reasons for conflict-related sexual violence and that it is committed by the state as well as by a range of non-state actors. Nor does it take account of the additional vulnerabilities to gender-based discrimination and violence caused by factors such as displacement, collapse of social norms and structures, poverty, and unemployment. These contribute to further human rights violations against women and girls including the unavailability of appropriate healthcare following sexual violence and denial of their sexual and reproductive rights, harassment, lack of access to education, the destruction of shelter, livelihoods, and food for women who are the primary carers within their families and communities. It has the potential to create a hierarchy of rights and of victims, contrary to the universalism of human rights. There is no direct reference to the Global South as the location of wartime sexual violence against civilians, but this is the tenor of the resolutions … . For WPS 'champions' such as the US and UK, 'rapacious violence' happens in foreign territories, not at home.

Human rights law has a lower explicit profile in Resolution 1820 than in Resolution 1325. ... Resolution 1820 assumes sexual violence committed by (male) military personnel and women's security as both transgressed and upheld through military means. In the Security Council's militarized and masculinized view of the world this inevitably involves the securitization of rights, transforming people into objects of the security apparatus to be protected in the interests of international peace and security rather than as individual and collective rights bearers.

...

... [By 2019] the political climate had harshened with respect to women's rights with backlash against progress, opposition to women's and girls' equal rights, rising violent misogyny, and a growing number of brutal attacks on those challenging social gender norms including women in politics, and women human rights defenders. ...

... [In negotiating WPS resolutions in 2019, two] issues were especially contentious ... . Sexual and reproductive rights had explicitly entered the WPS agenda in [2013]. [The preamble, but not the operative part of Resolution 2122 (2013)] notes 'the need for access to the full range of sexual and reproductive health services, including regarding pregnancies resulting from rape, without discrimination' ... . [It] was adopted on the same day as the CEDAW Committee's General Recommendation No. 30 that directly upholds women's right to safe abortion services. Neither Resolution 2467 nor 2493 refer directly to sexual and reproductive rights. ... [T]he US delegate stated that it could not 'accept references to "sexual and reproductive health", nor any references to "safe termination of pregnancy" or language that would promote abortion or suggest a right to abortion'. ...

With respect to ... the word 'gender'— the Security Council has never offered any definition and uses it in practice to mean 'women'. The WPS resolutions make minimal references to men and boys and none to persons who reject the gender binary. Nevertheless, some delegations feared its use would incorporate the rights of trans persons or uphold gay rights. ...

...

6. Conclusions

So where are we? Women human rights and peace activists mobilized in the 1990s to secure the adoption of Resolution 1325 but was it a strategic decision to engage the world's most powerful actors for advancement of women's rights in conflict? Or was it a misjudgement to rely on the Security Council thereby making human rights a hostage to geopolitical imperatives? Was it absurd to think that the Council—a state-centric body that considers military intervention as the norm and with the world's leading arms dealers as members—could ever be committed to human rights, especially those of women in armed conflict? Can proponents of human rights take language found in one instrument—a Security Council resolution—and tie it back to a human rights context to reinforce state obligations, or does the institutional divide prevent this consistency? And any such attempt is made harder by fluctuating language in the WPS resolutions; it cannot be assumed that good wording in one resolution that civil society can mobilize around will be repeated in subsequent resolutions.

I don't have the answers. What we have is an international system based in militarized security that is prioritized over a human security approach that might be progressed through human rights, a system trapped in hierarchical power structures, and a civil society not quite ready to reframe the discussion for fear of this issue being 'downgraded' to human rights, and an overall failure to commit resources.

...

* * *

Karen Engle, in *The Grip of Sexual Violence in Conflict: Feminist Interventions in International Law* (2020) 176 argues that the pre-occupation with sexual violence in the WPS and related contexts has:

> ... narrowed and distorted the lens through which feminists understand, represent, and address issues of gender, sex, ethnicity, and armed conflict. Through power they often deny, many feminists—including women's rights advocates and women's peace advocates—have facilitated, if not deployed, stereotyped images of victims and their communities to support militarized or criminalized responses to sexual violence in conflict. Those responses have had distributive effects. Not only have they failed to make a significant dent in incidences of sexual violence in conflict, but they have displaced

attention to imperialism, economic distribution, and—relatedly—the causes of the very armed conflicts in which they aim to intervene. Also, somewhat ironically, they have sidelined attention to a great deal of gender inequality. Further, whether or not military interventions and counterterrorism measures have women at the helm or are done in the name of protecting women, they have had devastating effects on uncountable lives, mostly in the global South, and have perpetuated both political and economic global inequality.

… [F]eminist successes in bringing international institutional attention to sexual violence—whether through military intervention, criminal law, or the [WPS agenda]— have cemented and even amplified some of the very imaginaries about rape and sexual violence that nearly all feminists originally hoped to dispel. … [F]eminists, however unwittingly, have participated in the continuation of the common-sense view that rape is a fate worse than death. Relatedly, their efforts have led to … the "hypervisibility" of wartime rape, which elides not only other issues but also other aspects of victims' lives.

The Security Council in the 2020s

Before reading an overall assessment of the Council's role in relation to human rights, consider some diverse case studies.

a. The Democratic People's Republic of Korea (the DPRK, or North Korea)

The UN Human Rights Council has used every technique available to it in response to human rights violations in the DPRK. There has been a country Special Rapporteur since 2004 (UN Doc. A/77/522 (2022)). Following a damning report by a Commission of Inquiry, which concluded that crimes against humanity had been committed (UN Doc. A/HRC/25/63 (2013), a field office was established in Seoul to monitor human rights in the DPRK in 2015, a group of experts on accountability was created (UN Doc. A/HRC/34/66/Add.1 (2017)), the Security Council held annual debates on the subject from 2014 to 2017, and the Secretary-General presents an annual report (UN Doc. A/78/212 (2023)). A more institutionally sustained case for Security Council action would be difficult to imagine. But between 2018 and 2022, requests for an open meeting of the Council to discuss the situation were rejected. As noted in December 2022:

> … [M]embers hold differing views as to whether human rights violations in the DPRK constitute a threat to international peace and security. China has argued that the Security Council is not a forum for discussing human rights issues, that such issues should not be politicised and that discussion of human rights in the DPRK jeopardises the denuclearisation of the Korean peninsula. Russia, together with some elected members, has adopted a similar position.[337]

In August 2023, the Council held an open meeting on the DPRK, at which the High Commissioner spoke.

b. Climate change

Consider the following Research Report by Security Council Report, 'The UN Security Council and Climate Change: Tracking the Agenda after the 2021 Veto' (30 December 2022)

> On 13 December 2021, the Security Council voted on a draft resolution on the security implications of climate change, proposed by Ireland and Niger. The draft emphasised the need for "a comprehensive, whole of UN approach to address climate change and its effects". It requested the Secretary-General to "… [report to the Council] … on how climate-related security risks can be addressed". And it encouraged relevant UN

---

[337] Security Council Report, 'DPRK: Meeting on the Human Rights Situation under "Any Other Business"' (8 December 2022).

peacekeeping operations and special political missions to deploy dedicated capacity, as appropriate, on climate security.

[This] represented the first time a thematic resolution on climate change and security had been tabled for a vote in the Council. But the idea for such a resolution was years in the making. Germany had proposed a similar, albeit more ambitious, draft in July 2020, but ultimately aborted the effort because the US, which was in the final year of the Trump presidency, informed Germany that it would block any thematic outcome on climate change and security. The Irish-Nigerien draft resolution had the support of 12 Council members and was co-sponsored by 113 member states, but China, India, and Russia expressed strong reservations from the outset of the negotiations.

…

While 12 members voted in favour of the draft resolution, Russia vetoed it. India also voted against the draft, while China abstained. …

c. Responding to Coups

Consider the following analysis by the International Crisis Group, 'Why the UN Security Council Stumbles in Responding to Coups' (24 January 2022):

> [The UN Security Council has a poor record in terms of meaningful responses to coup d'états involving the military ouster of governments.]
>
> … [T]he Council did not address coups at all until the Cold War ended and has taken only a "highly selective" approach to them since. It has responded to fewer than a quarter of the coups that have taken place in this period, ignoring military takeovers in cases including Pakistan (1999), Thailand (2006 and 2014) and Egypt (2013). Although it has acted forcefully on rare occasions – including mandating a U.S. military intervention in Haiti to restore the democratically elected President Jean-Bertrand Aristide to power in 1994 – it more often confines itself to making statements of ['serious concern'].
>
> **A Record of Inaction**
>
> There is no consensus among Council members about how far the body should go in responding to coups. Some, including China and Russia, argue that the Council should stay out of UN member states' internal politics altogether and often aim to rein in Council comments on coups. Beijing and Moscow are generally suspicious of UN sanctions in principle and oppose applying such measures to coup plotters. … But non-Western Council members counter that Western countries display double standards in response to military takeovers. …
>
> **Reasons to Hit the Brakes**
>
> Beyond fundamental disagreements about the Council's remit in countries' internal affairs, there are three recurrent considerations that appear to contribute to its stuttering response to this type of crisis: confusion, geopolitics and the Council's lack of leverage in the countries concerned.
>
> First, the element of confusion tends to be especially important in the early stages of the Council's response to a coup. In the aftermath of a military takeover, Council members often lack good information about what is happening on the ground. They may also have no clear instructions from their capitals. …
>
> Secondly, as the initial diplomatic confusion following a military takeover dissipates, the geopolitical interests of the Council's five veto-wielding permanent members are liable to hamper its long-term response. While Beijing was surprised and displeased by events in Myanmar, where it had developed close ties with the civilian government, China grew somewhat closer to the junta over the course of 2021. … Russia was even quicker to

show support for the Myanmar junta – which is a limited but growing purchaser of Russian arms … .

Finally, … Council members … leverage is limited. … [F]ew diplomats in New York, whatever their national stances on coups, believe the body has the will or capabilities to take drastic action to reverse military takeovers.

…

Evaluation

Consider the following assessment by Frédéric Mégret, in 'The Security Council', in Frédéric Mégret and Philip Alston (eds.), *The United Nations and Human Rights: A Critical Appraisal* (2nd ed., 2020) 39:

The Council's impact on human rights appears at the same time potentially formidable and problematic in practice. …

…

… The creation and support of international criminal tribunals … stands as a remarkable example of the diversification of the Council's activities, as does the increasing mainstreaming of human rights within peacekeeping operations.

Together, these developments suggest, in the best of cases, an approach in which ends and means are increasingly seen as inseparable: human rights are the means to a lasting peace that has respect for human rights as one of its foundations. In the most utopian of scenarios, the Council might be seen as gradually pulling itself up by the boot- straps: its actions in favour of human rights today will provide the standards to which it can be held tomorrow … . … By the same token, at least four, not necessarily compatible, major concerns arise in relation to the Council's increased interest in human rights, which potentially cast a long shadow over its role.

First, … the Council is (still) not doing enough. … [T]he Darfur and the Rohingya crises are a reminder that for all its rhetoric, the Council continues to have tremendous difficulty in transcending its divides and in taking resolute action where it would be most needed. … [T]he tension between the demands of human rights and respect for sovereignty, even though it has been powerfully mediated by 'international peace and security', remains a particularly resilient one.

…

A second [is inconsistency.] … For each circumstance where human rights have been taken into account by the Council, there are many if not more when it was not, even though a strong argument existed that it should. Whereas restoring democracy, for example, was a major ground for intervention in Haiti, this Council precedent has not been matched by similar action in any other context and in fact the Kovoso intervention may have been deeply undemocratic; although the Security Council created the ICTY and the ICTR and usefully referred the Darfur situation to the ICC, it has at the first opportunity used its referral power vis- à- vis the ICC to block prosecutions of peacekeepers of non-state parties … .

At the heart of these dilemmas is a tension between a vision of the Council increasingly bound by its precedents and acting as a law enforcer, and a vision of the Council as merely a decision- making mechanism endlessly tied to the contingent interests of its members. …

A third concern is that the Council is interested in human rights in certain areas of its activities, but has often failed to see the negative human rights impact that it has in other areas, especially as it takes on more and more governance responsibilities. In quantitative terms, no type of measure has done more harm to the Council's claims that it cares about human rights than embargoes, in Iraq and beyond. The behaviour of peacekeepers or troops more generally under Council mandate and the risk of rights violations arising out of the regime set up to deal with terrorism are also significant concerns. ...

...

A fourth ... concern is that the Council may already be ... doing too much. The oft-heard clamour for the Council to intervene (for example, in Syria) may be a case of 'beware what you wish for' on the part of the human rights community. ... There is certainly consensus that at the very least the Council should not violate or otherwise negatively affect human rights through its actions, a sort of 'do- no- harm' minimalist line. What is more contentious is the issue of the Council more proactively seeing itself as a defender of human rights. Indeed, it remains to be seen whether, even were the Security Council to adopt a higher human rights profile, this is something that should be welcomed as an unmitigated blessing and whether regular encroachments on the sovereignty of states guided by human rights concerns, might not end up weakening rights.

QUESTION

What are the principal arguments for and against the Security Council taking an active, even a leading, role in promoting human rights? Consider, in this context, the following critique of UN peacekeeping operations:

During the transformative era of decolonisation in the mid-twentieth century, UN peacekeeping staff orchestrated a reinvention of sovereignty and a remaking of colonial-era hierarchies for Global South populations on the front lines of post-colonial statehood. Peacekeeping missions perpetuated colonial structures, imaginaries, and staffing into newly independent or politically transitional spaces. Using a humanitarian guise, the organisation set host populations and international community expectations of the rights-based motivations and interests protected by peacekeeping staff.
...
... Cold War-era peacekeeping missions and staff played an integral role in perpetuating racial hierarchies, international interference, and technocratic supremacy within conflict contexts.[338]

---

[338] M. Tudor, *Blue Helmet Bureaucrats: United Nations Peacekeeping and the Reinvention of Colonialism, 1945–1971* (2023) 1.

Chapter 9. Treaty Bodies: The ICCPR Human Rights Committee

This chapter continues the inquiry into the structure, roles, functions and processes of international human rights bodies. We continue to emphasize the relationships among human rights norms, institutions and processes, as well as the reasons and techniques for 'institutionalization' of norms.

The Human Rights Council, created under the UN Charter (thus a 'Charter organ'), which was examined in Chapter 8, remains the most complex and politically charged of the specifically human rights organs with universal reach. It differs markedly in organization, functions and powers, as well as public prominence, from the ten 'treaty bodies' established to monitor implementation of the key UN treaties (dealing respectively with civil and political rights, economic, social and cultural rights, racial discrimination, gender discrimination, torture (a committee and a separate sub-committee), children's rights, migrant workers' rights, persons with disabilities and enforced disappearances. Each of the treaty bodies is distinctive in some respects; each has functions only in relation to the treaty creating it; each such treaty regime is now to some extent 'monitored' or 'implemented' or 'developed' by that body.

Chapter 9 provides a systematic study of one such treaty body, the Human Rights Committee, created by and functioning within one of the UN's two umbrella human rights treaties, the International Covenant on Civil and Political Rights. In 2024, 174 states are party to the ICCPR. We refer to it as the 'ICCPR Committee' to distinguish it from the 'Human Rights Council', with which it shares the same acronym ('HRC').

In reading the materials, keep in mind the extent to which the ICCPR Committee is distinct from or very much a part of the broad international human rights regime, and also the extent to which the different functions performed by the Committee interact with and ideally complement one another.

A. POWERS, FUNCTIONS AND PERFORMANCE OF THE ICCPR COMMITTEE[339]

1. Introduction

Based on Articles 40 and 41 of the Covenant, and on the first Optional Protocol to the ICCPR, the Committee has four main functions: (1) the consideration of states' reports; (2) the adoption of 'General Comments'; (3) the examination of 'communications' (i.e. complaints) from individuals claiming to be victims of violations by states parties of the Covenant; and (4) an interstate complaints procedure (Art. 21). While the latter was considered to be potentially important when the Covenant was drafted, it has never been used by states, although comparable procedures under other treaties, such as the ECHR and the Convention on the Elimination of All Forms of Racial Discrimination (three complaints as of January 2024), have been addressed.

Before considering the first three of these functions we consider the organizational arrangements reflected in the ICCPR.

<u>Article 28</u>

1. There shall be established a Human Rights Committee ... . It shall consist of eighteen members and shall carry out the functions hereinafter provided.

2. The Committee shall be composed of nationals of the States Parties to the present Covenant who shall be persons of high moral character and recognized competence in the field of human rights, consideration being given to the usefulness of the participation of some persons having legal experience.

---

[339] For a detailed bibliography on the ICCPR see P. Taylor, *A Commentary on the International Covenant on Civil and Political Rights* (2020) 824-841. For analysis, see W. Schabas, UN *International Covenant on Civil and Political Rights: Nowak's CCPR Commentary* (3rd. ed. 2019); L. Hennebel, 'The Human Rights Committee', in F. Mégret and P. Alston (eds.), *The United Nations and Human Rights: A Critical Appraisal* (2nd. ed., 2020) 339; and I. Jelić and L. Mührel, 'The Human Rights Committee: Challenges and Prospects for Enhanced Effectiveness and Integration', 14 *J. Hum. Rts. Prac.* (2022) 17.

3. The members of the Committee shall be elected and shall serve in their personal capacity.

...

Article 31

1. The Committee may not include more than one national of the same State.

2. In the election of the Committee, consideration shall be given to equitable geographical distribution of membership and to the representation of the different forms of civilization and of the principal legal systems.

...

Article 38

Every member of the Committee shall, before taking up his duties, make a solemn declaration in open committee that he will perform his functions impartially and conscientiously.

...

Article 39

... (2)(b) Decisions of the Committee shall be made by a majority vote of the members present.

The professional background of Committee members has varied considerably and includes judges, prosecutors, university teachers, public interest lawyers, former diplomats and former government officials. In general, members have demonstrated a high level of competence. Because Article 31(2) does not actually set regional quotas, the group of experts elected to the Committee has not always reflected the 'equitable geographical' balance called for.

Gender balance has improved significantly over the years. From 1977 to 1983, there were no female members. In 1999 there were four, in 2001 there were two, and in 2023-24 there were seven, making up just under 40 per cent. Since 1987, the Committee has elected a new Chair every two years, each time from a different region, but not necessarily in strict rotation. There are also three vice-Chairs and a Rapporteur.

Under Article 28(3), all members are to be 'elected and shall serve in their personal capacity'. The UN term for such members is 'experts', as opposed to the 'representatives' of states who sit on the UN Human Rights Council. The inference is that Committee members are to act independently of the governments of their states.

Generally, this aspiration appears to have been realized, but in many contexts 'independence' in the sense identified has been a relative rather than absolute concept. Since Committee membership is a part-time activity, a minority of members have continued to hold government (diplomatic and other) posts, thus qualifying the degree of possible independence from their governments' positions on given issues. But even determinedly independent individuals have to be in sufficiently good standing with their own governments in order to gain nomination in the first place. Consider the following 'Guidelines' (UN Doc. A/67/222 (2012), Annex 1) applicable to all treaty bodies, and to the ICCPR Committee according to Rule 15 of its Rules of Procedure (2021):

> 2. ... Treaty body members shall not only be independent and impartial, but shall also be seen by a reasonable observer to be so.

> 3. ... [A] treaty body member shall not be considered to have a real or perceived conflict of interest as a consequence of his or her race, ethnicity, religion, gender, disability, colour, descent ... .

> ...

> 5. The principle of independence requires that members not be removable during their term of office ... ... [They] are accountable only to their own conscience and the relevant treaty body and not to their State or any other State.

> ...

8. A member shall not participate or influence in any way the consideration of a State party report by the treaty body, or … [in procedures] such as follow-up, early warning or urgent action … .

…

10. A member shall not participate in, be present during, or influence in any way the examination of a communication … .

…

12. The independence and impartiality of treaty body members is compromised by the political nature of their affiliation with the executive branch of the State. Members of treaty bodies shall consequently avoid functions or activities which are, or are seen by a reasonable observer to be, incompatible with the obligations and responsibilities of independent experts under the relevant treaties.

…

16. Observance of the above guidelines falls first and foremost within the individual responsibility of each treaty body member and his or her own conscience. … Ultimately, the relevant committee as a whole shall take any measures deemed necessary to safeguard the requirements of independence and impartiality of its members.

The Committee meets in Geneva for three sessions annually, for a total of 13 weeks. There is some inter-sessional work by individual members in the context of working groups, which meet for one week prior to the start of each session. Living and travel expenses are paid by the UN but in 2002 an annual honorarium of $3,000 paid to members was reduced to a token $1, in order to save money. The work is part time, members hold 'regular', often full-time, jobs, and must fit the Committee's work into already busy schedules. Most meetings (other than those considering 'communications' under the Optional Protocol) are public. Public attendance is usually rather limited, but public meetings have been webcast live since 2012 (available at https://webtv.un.org/en) and in 2020-21, in response to the Covid-19 pandemic, most Committee sessions took place online.

Decisions of the Committee are, in theory, by majority vote pursuant to Article 39(2). In practice, all decisions relating to concluding observations or the text of a General Comment, have been taken by consensus. This is also generally the case in relation to communications, even though individual concurring or dissenting opinions are now common. In general, working by consensus puts a premium on cooperation, avoids polarization, enables trade-offs over time and generates positions endorsed by the Committee as a whole. By the same token, it privileges compromise, interrupts the flow of consistent reasoning, and rules out bolder steps.

Historical Evolution

As with the Council, the ICCPR Committee has witnessed vast changes in global politics since it first met in 1977. The disputes and compromises over the Committee's basic structure and functions that marked the drafting of the Covenant and the Optional Protocol have left a strong imprint on the Committee today. Consider the following brief summaries by two authors of the nature of the earlier disputes and their continuing influence. The first is taken from Dominic McGoldrick, *The Human Rights Committee* (1994), at 13–14:

1.18 There was general agreement during the drafting that the primary obligation under the ICCPR would be implementation at the national level by States. There was continuing disagreement, however, on the question whether there should also be international measures of implementation. A minority of States, principally the Soviet bloc, insisted that there should be provisions to ensure implementation but that there should be no international measures of implementation. It was argued that such measures were a system of international pressure intended to force States to take particular steps connected with the execution of obligations under the Covenant. They were, therefore, contrary to the principle of domestic jurisdiction in article 2(7) of the United Nations Charter, would undermine the sovereignty and independence of States and would upset the balance of powers established by the UN Charter. Moreover, the establishment of petitions systems would transform complaints into international disputes with consequent effects upon peaceful international relations.

1.19 Against these views it was argued that the undertaking of international measures of implementation was an exercise of domestic jurisdiction and not an interference with it. International measures were essential to the effective observance of human rights, which were matters of international concern. However, even within those States that agreed that international measures were essential, there were significant differences of opinion as to the appropriate types of measures. The proposals included an International Court of Human Rights empowered to settle disputes concerning the Covenant; settlement by diplomatic negotiation and, in default, by *ad hoc* fact-finding Committees; the establishment of an Office of High Commissioner (or Attorney-General) for Human Rights; the establishment of reporting procedures covering some or all of the provisions in the Covenant; empowering the proposed Human Rights Committee to collect information on all matters relevant to the observance and enforcement of human rights and to initiate an inquiry if it thought one necessary.

...

1.21 The lengthy drafting process of the ICCPR largely coincided with the depths of cold war confrontation, the explosive development of notions of self-determination and independence, the accompanying political tensions of large scale decolonization, and the consequential effects of a rapidly altering balance of diplomatic power within the United Nations. In retrospect then it must be acknowledged that it was much more difficult to agree on the text of a Covenant containing binding legal obligations and limited measures of international implementation than it had been to agree upon the statement of political principles in the Universal Declaration in 1948 ... .

The second summary is by Torkel Opsahl, 'The Human Rights Committee', in Philip Alston (ed.), *The United Nations and Human Rights* (1992), at 371:

... The draft Covenant prepared in 1954 by the Commission envisioned a quasi-judicial Human Rights Committee quite different in its powers and functions from that which actually came into existence. It was another twelve years before the General Assembly's Third Committee debated the proposed implementation provisions, at which time they were drastically altered. The majority was opposed to making obligatory the procedure for interstate communications ... .

All of the various positions, except that of dispensing with the Committee altogether, were taken into account by a formula worked out by the Afro-Asian group. According to this version, the Committee's only compulsory role would be to study and comment generally upon the reports of States Parties, a function originally intended for the Commission on Human Rights. Many of the details of this proposal were amended, which later caused doubts and disagreements about the proper role of the Committee in the reporting system. The functions relating to communications were made entirely optional, and arrangements providing for the consideration of individual complaints of violations were separated from the Covenant and put in the Optional Protocol. In other words, the result was a compromise between those States which favoured strong international measures and those which emphasized the primacy of national sovereignty and responsibility. As is inevitably the case with such compromises, many specific issues were left unresolved, perhaps intentionally. As a result the subsequent evolution of the arrangements has had to be shaped by a continuing give-and-take within the Committee over many years.

2. State Reporting

A requirement that States Parties submit reports to a human rights treaty body about their implementation of that treaty is now the norm. Prior to the adoption of the Covenant, it would have seemed nearly inconceivable that most of the world's states would periodically submit a report to an international body about their internal matters involving many politically sensitive aspects of relations between government and citizens, and then participate in a discussion about that report with members of that body drawn from all over the world.

The relevant provision is Article 40:

> 1. The States Parties to the present Covenant undertake to submit reports on the measures they have adopted which give effect to the rights recognized herein and on the progress made in the enjoyment of those rights:
>
>> (a) Within one year of the entry into force of the present Covenant for the States Parties concerned;
>>
>> (b) Thereafter whenever the Committee so requests.
>
> 2. ... Reports shall indicate the factors and difficulties, if any, affecting the implementation of the present Covenant.
>
> ...
>
> 4. The Committee shall study the reports ... [and shall submit them], and such general comments as it may consider appropriate, to the States Parties ... .
>
> 5. The States Parties to the present Covenant may submit to the Committee observations on any comments that may be made in accordance with paragraph 4 of this article.

The Covenant makes no provision about the form of reports, and the system has evolved considerably over the past decade or so. An initial report is due within one year after the Covenant enters into force for that state. But where once both the initial and subsequent 'periodic' reports were comprehensive in scope, almost all reporting today follows the LOIPR procedure ('list of issues prior to reporting') which involves the Secretariat preparing a comprehensive 'country file', containing all relevant data about that country, on the basis of which the Committee draws up a list of issues on which the state is required to report. Since 2020, the Committee has followed a 'predictable review cycle' of eight years between required reports.[340]

Neuman describes the value of the reporting process in these terms:

> The activity of generating the report should focus the attention of State organs on their ICCPR obligations and on the needs expressed by civil society; the constructive dialogue between the State and the HRC gives the State the opportunity to educate the Committee and the world at large on its efforts to comply, and to receive legal guidance and advice

---

[340] UN Doc. A/74/256 (2019), Annex III.

from the HRC; the transparency of the dialogue, especially if webcast, offers the State's populace a different perspective on their government; the HRC's welcoming and use of NGOs' information can bolster the legitimacy of their activities and their issues; the HRC's concluding observations offer a form of public accountability for human rights violations; the concluding observations give the HRC an opportunity to indicate its interpretation of the ICCPR; and the follow-up activities create a further forum for civil society engagement.[341]

Diverse and accurate information is essential to the Committee's work. For its first decade or so the Committee was pressured by a majority of its members not to rely upon any information other than that presented by states. Information from intergovernmental organizations, let alone from NGOs, was strongly contested. In the course of the 1990s these self-imposed restrictions gradually evaporated and the Committee now receives regular briefings from key stakeholders. The submission of 'shadow reports' by civil society groups (both domestic and international) is an integral part of the process and these reports are available on the OHCHR website. NGOs also brief the Committee in public for one to two hours prior to the examination of a State report, and can provide additional information in private sessions with Committee members held over the lunch break without interpretation. UN agencies also meet with the Committee in private, and sometimes submit confidential reports.

The formal procedure for examining reports consists of several steps. The first is the appointment of a 'country report task force' of five members. They have the main responsibility for the conduct of the debate on the report. One of these members will also be designated as the 'country rapporteur'. He or she takes the lead in preparing a list of issues to be sent to the state party which is requested to provide written replies. The identity of the task force members is confidential.

During the 'constructive dialogue' with the representatives of the state party, which lasts for six hours in total, the country rapporteur and other task force members take the lead in posing questions, and other members may participate if time permits. The task force then drafts the concluding observations, which are debated in private, adopted and usually released at the end of the relevant session. The Committee normally deals with no more than five to six reports at each session.

The concluding observations generally highlight up to three 'urgent recommendations' in relation to which the Committee requests follow-up information to be provided within three years, or sometimes more speedily. The relevant issues are chosen because of the gravity and/or urgency of the situation. Concise and focused responses are sought and the Committee has a Special Rapporteur (and Deputy) on follow-up who assess the information received and report to the Committee. All stakeholders are invited to submit information during this process and the responses are then 'graded' on the following scale: A - Information/action largely satisfactory; B - Information/action partially satisfactory; C - Information/action not satisfactory; D - No cooperation with the Committee; E – The information or measures taken are contrary to or reflect rejection of the recommendation (UN Doc. CCPR/C/5 (2021)).

By way of example, the Committee considered the report of New Zealand in 2016. Its concluding observations (UN Doc. CCPR/C/NZL/CO/6) recommended that '[t]he State party should strengthen efforts to combat domestic and all forms of gender-based violence, including sexual violence, particularly in relation to Māori and Pasifika women and girls, as well as women and girls with disabilities' and identified specific issues in that regard. In response to a request for 'follow up' information, the Government noted the work undertaken by a Ministerial Group on Family Violence and Sexual Violence, the allocation of additional budget funding, new legislation designed to strengthen the justice sector response to family violence and to develop a better integrated system, and a range of initiatives undertaken by the police to deliver better responses to domestic and gender-based violence, including sexual violence. The Committee welcomed the various measures, sought additional information, and graded the response as an 'A'.

The third issue highlighted by the Committee was a recommendation for revised legislation to ensure 'respect of the customary rights of Māori on their land and resources, and their cultural development.' The Government

---

[341] G. Neuman, 'Giving Meaning and Effect to Human Rights: The Contributions of Human Rights Committee Members' in D. Moeckli, H. Keller, and C. Heri (eds.), *The Human Rights Covenants at 50: Their Past, Present, and Future* (2018) 31.

replied that it had no plans to revise the relevant legislation, leading the Committee to award a 'C' and to reiterate its original recommendation (UN Doc. CCPR/C/132/2/Add.3 (2021)).

The Committee also has a procedure for examining the situation in states that have either not reported or are interminably late in doing so. If necessary, this is done in the absence of a report or even a delegation from the country concerned. In November 2022, the Committee adopted a set of concluding observations (UN Doc. CCPR/C/RUS/CO/8) on the report of the Russian Federation, after the government had twice postponed scheduled appearances before the Committee. The same procedure was also applied to Nicaragua, at the same session.

Case Studies

Below are case studies relating to the Democratic People's Republic of Korea (the DPRK, or North Korea), Kenya, and the United States. The latter two are 'concluding observations' adopted by the Committee. The document below is a LOIPR ('list of issues prior to reporting') for the DPRK, which ratified the Covenant in 1981. Previous reports by the DPRK had been considered by the Committee in 1984 and 2001. In-between time, the Government had sought to withdraw from the Covenant in 1997 after its record was criticized by another UN human rights body. Because the Covenant contains no provision for withdrawal, the Secretary-General replied that it would only be possible if all States Parties to the Covenant agreed.[342] In 2021, some 15 years after its third report was due, the Committee proceeded to schedule consideration of the situation. The LOIPR is the starting point in that process. Ten different groups of civil society organizations submitted information to facilitate the Committee's consideration, and the DPRK had also submitted an updated 'Common Core document', designed to provide general background for all treaty body reporting by the relevant state. In describing the country's political structure, it notes:

> 12.   The Korean people won the Fatherland Liberation War (1950-1953) against the US and its satellite countries … . They … established a socialist system free from exploitation and oppression of man by man.
>
> 13.   The DPRK … made the people's power and the socialist system invincible by relying on the single-minded unity and patriotic efforts of the people who are the masters of the State and the society … . …
>
> …
>
> 15.   Today, the Korean people, led by Comrade Kim Jong Un, … who realizes the politics of prioritizing, respecting and loving people, are channeling all their efforts into economic construction, making a vigorous onward march towards a prosperous and powerful socialist country in which people's ideal and desire will become a reality. (HRI/CORE/PRK/2019 (2019))

HUMAN RIGHTS COMMITTEE, LIST OF ISSUES PRIOR TO THE SUBMISSION OF THE THIRD PERIODIC REPORT OF THE DEMOCRATIC PEOPLE'S REPUBLIC OF KOREA UN DOC. CCPR/C/PRK/QPR/3 (22 JUNE 2021)

…

B. Specific information on the implementation of articles 1 to 27 of the Covenant, including with regard to the previous recommendations of the Committee

…

Anti-corruption measures (arts. 2 and 25)

4. Please respond to reports that corruption is endemic within the State party, including among Government officials and police officers, and discuss any steps taken to prevent and address such practices. In this regard,

---

[342] UN memo C.N.467.1997.TREATIES-10 (12 November 1997).

please include information about: (a) reports that individuals are required to pay bribes to public officials, including police officers, in order to exercise their fundamental rights, including to liberty and freedom of movement; (b) whether there are any independent mechanisms in place within the State party to investigate and prosecute cases of corruption; and (c) the extent to which information relating to the functioning of the Government is made publicly available in order to ensure transparency and accountability, including any legislation in place to ensure freedom of information.

Derogations (arts. 4, 9, 12 and 21–22)

5. Please provide information about the measures taken by the State party to address the coronavirus disease (COVID-19) pandemic. Please discuss whether any measures taken to address the COVID-19 pandemic derogate from the State party's obligations under the Covenant, including with respect to freedom of assembly, freedom of movement, liberty and due process. If they do, please specify whether the measures were strictly required by and proportional to the exigencies of the situation and limited in duration, geographical coverage and material scope, as outlined by the Committee … .

Non-discrimination (arts. 2, 19–20 and 26)

6. Please describe the legislative and other measures taken during the reporting period to combat discriminatory laws and social practices based on discriminatory grounds, in particular family background (*songbun*), sexual orientation, gender, religion and disability. …

…

Violence against women, including domestic violence (arts. 2–3, 6–7 and 26)

8. … Please: (a) respond to allegations of violence and of cruel and degrading treatment of women in detention facilities, including reports of sexual violence and women being forced to undergo abortions or witness the infanticide of their newborn babies; (b) discuss the legal provisions in place to criminalize all forms of rape, including marital rape, and clarify the criminal penalties for all related offences and the support services in place for women; and (c) outline the steps taken to address high levels of domestic violence … .

Right to life (art. 6)

9. … Please: (a) detail which crimes are eligible for the death penalty, according to the Criminal Code, and provide information on how it is ensured that the punishment is only used in cases of the most serious crimes, as outlined in article 6 (2) of the Covenant; (b) provide data on the number of executions that have taken place within the reporting period, including information about the crimes for which the death penalty was applied and the age and gender of the individuals subjected to the punishment; and (c) describe the degree of judicial oversight of death penalty cases and respond to reports that extrajudicial executions have taken place in detention facilities. Please also respond to reports that public executions have taken place within the reporting period.

…

11. Please respond to reports that shoot-to-kill orders have been issued to prevent those suspected of having COVID-19 from entering the State party's territory, in contravention to the non-derogable character of the right to life. …

12. Bearing in mind paragraph 66 of the Committee's general comment No. 36, please describe the steps taken within the reporting period to stop the proliferation of weapons of mass destruction, including measures: to prevent their acquisition by non-State actors; to refrain from developing, producing, testing, acquiring, stockpiling, selling, transferring and using them; to destroy existing stockpiles; to take adequate measures of protection against accidental use; and to negotiate in order to achieve nuclear disarmament. Please also discuss the environmental impact of nuclear test sites, including responding to reports that groundwater sources have become contaminated and have exposed people in affected areas to radiation.

13. Recalling the previous recommendation of the Committee (para. 12), please provide information about the steps taken within the reporting period to improve access to food, reduce infant mortality and improve life expectancy ... .

...

Prohibition of torture ... (arts. 6–7)

14. In the light of the Committee's previous recommendation (para. 15), please respond to reports of the widespread use of torture and other cruel, inhuman or degrading treatment or punishment, including violence by State officials, forced confessions, sexual harassment and violence, and deliberate withholding of food, in detention facilities within the State party. ...

Liberty and security of persons and the treatment of persons deprived of their liberty (arts. 9–10)

15. Please respond to reports of widespread arbitrary detention within the State party. ...

...

Elimination of slavery, servitude and trafficking in persons (arts. 2, 7–8 and 26)

18. ... Please also respond to reports that forced labour is widespread within the State party, in particular within political prison camps and labour reform camps, where prisoners, including children, are subjected to long hours of physically demanding, unpaid labour with limited access to food, water and basic sanitation.

...

Right to privacy (art. 17)

24. Please discuss reports of large-scale surveillance activities within the State party and comment on their compatibility with article 17 of the Covenant. Please include information about: (a) the activities of the neighbourhood watch units (*inminban*) and Group 109, including reports that they search private homes without a warrant or notice; (b) reports of State monitoring of the written and telephone communications of individuals, and of surveillance of 3G technology usage among mobile telephone owners; and (c) the legal basis for such surveillance activities, and the processes for judicial oversight of their application.

...

HUMAN RIGHTS COMMITTEE, CONCLUDING OBSERVATIONS ON THE FOURTH PERIODIC REPORT OF KENYA[343]
UN DOC. CCPR/C/KEN/CO/4 (11 MAY 2021)

1. The Committee considered the fourth periodic report of Kenya (CCPR/C/KEN/4) [during three sessions from 9-11 March 2021]. The meetings were held virtually, owing to the coronavirus disease (COVID-19) pandemic. ...

...

C. Principal matters of concern and recommendations

Domestic implementation and dissemination of the Covenant

4. ... While noting that the Covenant and other international legal provisions have direct applicability in domestic law following ratification, the Committee is also concerned that the Constitution and its interpretation are not in full conformity with the Covenant. ...

---

[343] Note that specific issues are dealt with in paired paragraphs. The first expresses the Committee's 'concerns', while the second, in bold, contain its recommendations.

5. The State party should:

(a) Continue evaluating and revising, where necessary, domestic legal provisions, including the Constitution, to ensure harmonization with the rights guaranteed in the Covenant and ensure that domestic laws are interpreted and applied in conformity with its provisions;

...

(d) Expedite the process of ratification of the first Optional Protocol ...;

(e) Accelerate the process of appointing new commissioners to the Kenya National Commission on Human Rights.

Corruption

6. The Committee notes the development of draft legislation, including the Anti-Corruption Laws (Amendment) Bill of 2021 and the Whistleblower Protection Bill of 2021. It is concerned, however, about the lack of information about when the draft provisions are likely to be enacted into law and about the low overall number of convictions for corruption. ...

7. The State party should continue and strengthen its efforts ... to combat corruption and promote good governance, transparency and accountability. It should also expedite the passing into law of [the two Bills] ... . The State party should step up efforts to investigate and prosecute corruption and, if a person is convicted, apply penalties commensurate with the seriousness of the offence and ensure asset recovery, where appropriate. ...

Fight against impunity and past human rights violations

8. The Committee is concerned by the limited progress made in providing full redress for the gross human rights violations that occurred between 1963 and 2008. It is also concerned that Public Finance Management (Reparations for Historical Injustices Fund) Regulations of 2017, which were designed to operationalize the Restorative Justice Fund, remain at the consultative stage; therefore, victims cannot yet access reparations. It also notes with concern a lack of information about how the Government will ensure the implementation of all the recommendations of the Truth, Justice and Reconciliation Commission [which reported in 2011]. ...

9. The State party should:

(a) Intensify efforts to ensure the full and effective implementation of all the recommendations of the ... Commission ...;

(b) Step up efforts to provide access to remedies for victims of post-election violence in 2017 ...;

...

Non-discrimination

10. The Committee is concerned about the lack of comprehensive anti-discrimination legislation, in line with article 27 of the Constitution and the provisions of the Covenant ... .

11. The State party should:

(a) Adopt comprehensive legislation prohibiting discrimination, including multiple, direct and indirect discrimination, in all spheres, in both the public and the private sectors, on all the grounds prohibited under the Covenant, including sex, sexual orientation, gender identity, religion, disability, albinism, socioeconomic status, HIV/AIDS status, ethnic and political affiliation or other status;

(b) Guarantee effective remedies for victims of discrimination in judicial and administrative proceedings;

(c) Take concrete steps, such as comprehensive awareness-raising campaigns and sensitization activities, to address stigma and discriminatory attitudes and promote sensitivity and respect for diversity among the general public.

Sexual orientation, gender identity and intersexuality

12. The Committee is concerned about:

(a) Sections 162 and 165 of the Penal Code criminalizing same-sex relations, and the High Court ruling in 2019 that declared those provisions to be constitutional;

(b) The State party reporting that that prohibition is based upon same-sex relations being unacceptable to Kenyan culture and values but not providing information about any measures taken to address discriminatory attitudes and stigma among the general public;

(c) Reports of lesbian, gay, bisexual, transgender and intersex individuals experiencing harassment, discrimination and violence, including violations perpetrated by law enforcement officers and vigilante groups, and facing barriers to access justice and remedies;

(d) Incidences of children being expelled from schools on the basis of actual or suspected sexual orientation and/or gender identity;

(e) Cases of non-urgent, irreversible surgical procedures, infanticide and abandonment among intersex children … .

13. The State party should take appropriate steps to:

(a) Amend all relevant laws … to decriminalize consensual sexual relations between adults of the same sex;

(b) Address discriminatory attitudes and stigma towards [LGBTI persons] …, including through comprehensive awareness-raising and sensitization activities;

…

(d) Take immediate action to address the expulsion of children from schools on the basis of their actual or suspected sexual orientation and/or gender identity;

(e) Strengthen measures to end the performance of irreversible medical acts, especially surgical operations, on intersex children who are not yet capable of giving their full, free and informed consent, except in cases where such interventions are absolutely necessary for medical reasons. Access to effective remedies for victims of such interventions should also be ensured.

Gender equality

14. The Committee remains concerned that constitutional provisions requiring not more than two thirds of elective and appointive positions to be persons of the same gender have not been implemented. It notes with concern that women's representation in both the National Assembly and Senate remains below one third of the

membership of those bodies and that multiple attempts to ensure the implementation of the constitutional provisions have not been effective. ...

15. The State party should intensify efforts to implement [the relevant] constitutional provisions ... .

Counter-terrorism measures

16. While acknowledging the terrorist threat faced by the State party, the Committee remains concerned that the legal framework governing counter-terrorism efforts does not clearly set out that human rights must be respected in the fight against terrorism. The Committee is concerned that the Prevention of Terrorism Act (... 2012) contains a definition of terrorism that is vague, overly broad and has been used to oppress those critical of the Government. ... The Committee is also concerned about reports of arbitrary arrests, harassment, extortion, forcible relocation, extrajudicial killings, refoulement and enforced disappearances being perpetrated by State officials in the context of counter-terrorism operations ... .

17. The State party should undergo a process of legal review and reform to ensure respect for human rights in the fight against terrorism ... . It should also take steps to ensure counter-terrorism legislation is not used to limit any rights enshrined in the Covenant ... .

Violence against women

18. The Committee is concerned about:

(a) Continuing female genital mutilation ... ;

(b) Reports of other harmful traditional practices in the State party, including wife inheritance, ritual cleansing and child marriage;

(c) Sexual offences, including gang rape, being perpetrated against women in the period surrounding the 2017 elections, and a lack of access to protection and remedies among victims;

(d) High levels of domestic violence ... weaknesses in the legal and institutional response, ..., and a failure to criminalize marital rape;

(e) Safe spaces for women who have been subjected to violence not being available to women in all parts of the State party's territory;

...

19. The State party should:
[Take steps to address each of these concerns]

Voluntary termination of pregnancy and sexual and reproductive rights

20. The Committee is concerned that while article 26 of the Constitution allows for voluntary termination of pregnancy in limited circumstances, ... the Penal Code criminalize[s] acts relating to the provision of abortion services. ...

21. Bearing in mind paragraph 8 of the Committee's general comment No. 36 (2018) on the right to life, the State party should take steps to ensure clear and harmonized laws, policies and guidelines to govern access to safe and legal termination of pregnancy, as permitted under article 26 of the Constitution, including in cases of pregnancy resulting from sexual violence. ... It should also consider widening access to safe and legal termination of pregnancy.

Death penalty

22. While welcoming the steps taken by the State party to implement the judgment in the 2017 Supreme Court case of [*Muruatetu*, Ch. 1B, above, concerning the mandatory death penalty]… the Committee is concerned about the lack of information about when the process of legal reform to enact that judgment and the resentencing of eligible death row inmates will likely conclude. The Committee is concerned that the State party has yet to take concrete steps to implement the recommendation of the Task Force on the Implementation of the Supreme Court Ruling on the Death Penalty to abolish the death penalty, as well as to accede to the Second Optional Protocol to the Covenant, aiming at the abolition of the death penalty … .

…

Enforced disappearances, extrajudicial killings …

…

25. The State party should:

> (a) Step up efforts to ensure timely investigations, prosecutions and punishments of all reported cases of enforced disappearances, extrajudicial killings and other unlawful uses of force …;

> (b) Revise the legal framework to ensure that all forms of enforced disappearance are clearly defined in criminal law with associated penalties that are proportionate to the severity of the offence;

> (c) Ensure that the training of police officers is extended to all relevant State officers … .

Climate change and environmental degradation

…

27. The State party should continue and expand its efforts to develop its resilience to climate change through adaptation and mitigation measures. All [related] projects … should be developed with the meaningful and informed participation of the affected population, including indigenous peoples. …

Prohibition of torture …

28. The Committee is concerned about reports of torture and ill-treatment, including in the context of policing activities and places of detention, and about the low number of convictions and punishments for such crimes.

…

…

Prison conditions

…

31. The State party should continue and intensify its efforts to improve conditions and reduce overcrowding in places of deprivation of liberty, in particular by increasing the use of alternatives to detention … .

Liberty and security of person

32. The Committee is concerned about reports of the use of arbitrary arrest and detention, including among human rights defenders, journalists, civil society representatives and lesbian, gay, bisexual, transgender and intersex individuals. It is also concerned about the compatibility of provisions in the Prevention of Terrorism Act (… 2012), which allows suspects to be held in pretrial detention for up to 90 days, with article 50 of the Constitution and the provisions of the Covenant. …

…

Internally displaced persons

…

39. The State party should intensify its efforts to expedite durable solutions for internally displaced persons in accordance with relevant international standards, including the Covenant and the Guiding Principles on Internal

Displacement. The State party should also operationalize the National Consultative Coordination Committee for Internally Displaced Persons as a matter of priority.

Forced evictions

40. The Committee is concerned about continued reports of forced, and sometimes violent, evictions, including among indigenous populations in forest areas … .

41. The State party should ensure that all evictions are carried out in accordance with national and international standards, including by:

> (a) Putting in place a sustainable system of equitable land tenure to prevent forced evictions;

> (b) When there is no alternative to forced evictions, taking all necessary measures to implement effective protections, including the need for adequate notice and prior and meaningful consultation with and the provision of adequate compensation and/or resettlement of those affected. …;

> (c) Strictly upholding the moratorium declared during the COVID-19 pandemic and all judicial decisions on evictions;

> (d) Improving compensation and resettlement among those affected by evictions …;

> (e) Ensuring the investigation, prosecution, conviction and punishment of all individuals who breach the law during evictions.

Freedom of expression

42. The Committee is concerned about the lack of harmonization of the legal standards in the State party, including sections … of the Penal Code, the Computer Misuse and Cybercrimes Act (… 2018), the Prevention of Terrorism Act (… 2012), the Kenya Information and Communications (Amendment) Act (… 2013) and the Security Laws (Amendment) Act (… 2014), with articles 33 and 34 of the Constitution and articles 19 and 20 of the Covenant. The Committee is also concerned that national legal provisions have been used to limit online expression, repress lesbian, gay, bisexual, transgender and intersex individuals, and quell criticism of the Government … .

43. … The State party should ensure that any restrictions on the exercise of freedom of expression, including online expression, comply with the strict requirements of article 19 (3) of the Covenant. They should also take concrete steps to prevent any interference with the free press during the 2022 elections and protect journalists and media workers from all forms of harassment and violence.

Right of peaceful assembly

44. The Committee welcomes that the Public Order (Amendment Bill) of 2019, and provisions therein creating criminal and civil liability for harms and losses during assemblies, has been deemed unconstitutional and rejected by the parliament. It is concerned, however, about reports that the requirements in the Public Order Act (… 1950) to notify the police of all assemblies are being used in practice to deny authorization for peaceful assemblies. The Committee is also concerned about reports of the excessive use of force to disperse protests and of the arbitrary detention and arrest of human rights defenders for exercising their right to peaceful assembly … .

…

Rights of the child

…

47. The State party should expedite the enactment of the Children (Amendment) Bill 2018 into law, harmonize all national provisions to reflect 12 years as the minimum age of criminal responsibility and ensure the consistent application of the best interests of the child principle in all incidences of children in conflict with the law.

Participation in public affairs

48. The Committee is concerned that continued impunity for the grave human rights violations that occurred in the context of the 2017 elections … could undermine the electoral process in 2022. It is also concerned that the root causes of violence in 2017, including inter alia multiple violations of electoral regulations, voting irregularities, failure to effectively decentralize the electoral process and challenges faced by the Independent Electoral and Boundaries Commission in effectively and independently implementing their mandate, have not been adequately addressed. … .

49. The State party should intensify efforts to provide remedies to all victims of violence in the context of the 2017 elections, including guarantees of non-repetition. The State party should also take all necessary steps ahead of the 2022 elections to prevent violence and ensure the effective and independent functioning of the Independent Electoral and Boundaries Commission. In addition, it should adopt all measures necessary to ensure transparency in voting and in vote-counting procedures.

Indigenous peoples

…

51. The State party should:

> (a) Develop and enact dedicated legislation to expand specific protection for indigenous peoples;

> (b) Step up safeguards against forced evictions of indigenous peoples and ensure the consistent and effective application of the principle of free, informed and prior consent before any developmental or other activities take place on lands traditionally used, occupied or owned by indigenous communities;

> …

> (d) Publish without delay the recommendations of the task force to advise the Government on the implementation of the decision of the African Court on Human and Peoples' Rights in respect of the rights of the Ogiek community of Mau and enhancing the participation of indigenous communities in the sustainable management of forests, and comply with the decision of the Court;

> (e) Ensure that specific measures are in place to promote and protect the rights of indigenous women.

D. Dissemination and follow-up

52. The State party should widely disseminate the Covenant, its two Optional Protocols, its fourth periodic report and the present concluding observations with a view to raising awareness of the rights enshrined in the Covenant among the judicial, legislative and administrative authorities, civil society and non-governmental organizations operating in the country, and the general public. The [State report and these concluding observations should be] translated into the official languages of the State party.

53. … [T]he State party is requested to provide, by 26 March 2023, information on the implementation of the recommendations made by the Committee in paragraphs 19 (violence against women), 41 (forced evictions) and 49 (participation in public affairs) above.

…

HUMAN RIGHTS COMMITTEE, CONCLUDING OBSERVATIONS ON THE FIFTH PERIODIC REPORT OF THE UNITED STATES OF AMERICA UN DOC. CCPR/C/USA/CO/5 (3 NOVEMBER 2023)

[Selected excerpts from the diagnosis rather than the resulting recommendations follow:]

4. The Committee remains concerned at the lack of measures to effectively incorporate the Covenant in the domestic legal order. …

10. … the Committee is concerned about the persistence of hate crimes, including mass shootings, and hate speech against people of African descent, Indigenous Peoples, persons of Hispanic/Latino origin, persons of Asian descent, members of Muslim and Jewish communities, migrants, asylum seekers and against persons based on their real or perceived sexual orientation and gender identity, including by politicians and high-level officials, as well as in the media and on social media platforms. It is also concerned at the underreporting of hate crimes by law enforcement agencies to the Federal Bureau of Investigation (FBI) due to the voluntary nature of such reporting, which has led to a lack of statistical data on hate speech.

14. … [T]he Committee continues to be concerned that persons belonging to racial and ethnic minorities, in particular people of African descent, Indigenous Peoples and persons of Hispanic/Latino origin, are overrepresented in the criminal justice system, are disproportionately placed and held in pre-trial detention and affected by parole and probation sentences, and are more often subject to prison labour and harsher sentences

26. … [T]he Committee is deeply concerned at the increase of maternal mortality and morbidity in the State party, which has the highest rate of maternal mortality among developed countries, and particularly affects women from vulnerable and minority groups. …

32. The Committee remains seriously concerned at the continuing practice of the State party of killings in extraterritorial counter-terrorism operations using armed drones, the lack of full and continuous transparency regarding the legal and policy criteria for drone strikes, the alleged possibility of variations through classified plans, as well as the lack of accountability for the loss of life and for other serious harm caused, particularly to civilians. The Committee notes that the State party maintains its position that extraterritorial counter-terrorism operations, including drones strikes, are conducted in the course of its armed conflict with Al-Qaida and associated forces in accordance with its inherent right of national self-defence, and that they are governed by international humanitarian law as well as by the current Presidential Policy Memorandum that establishes standards and procedures that govern the use of lethal force outside of various active hostilities. However, it reiterates its concern about the State party's broad approach to the definition of "armed conflict", including an overbroad geographical and temporal scope. While noting the adoption of the Civilian Harm Mitigation and Response Action Plan (CHMR-AP), the Committee is seriously concerned that it only applies to lethal strikes carried out by the Department of Defence and not by other agencies such as the Central Intelligence Agency (CIA). It is further concerned at the very limited use of ex gratia payments to affected civilians and their families in recent years.

34. … [T]he Committee is gravely concerned at the increase in gun-related deaths and injuries, which disproportionately affects racial and ethnic minorities as well as women and children.
…
36. The Committee remains deeply concerned at police brutality and the excessive and deadly use of force by law enforcement officials, including by Customs and Border Protection (CBP) officers, which has a disparate impact on people of African descent, Indigenous peoples, persons of Hispanic/Latino origin, migrants and asylum seekers. It is also concerned at reports of the lack of accountability in the majority of cases of excessive and deadly use for force by law enforcement officials.
…
40. The Committee is concerned about reports of an increase of state and local laws criminalizing homelessness, of violence against homeless persons as well as at the higher risk of premature death that they experience due to homelessness. …

42. ... the Committee is seriously concerned that the specific offence of torture has not yet been introduced at the federal level.

44. ... [T]he Committee is concerned at reports of the extensive use of solitary confinement in the State party, including prolonged and even indefinite confinement, and of its use with respect to juveniles and persons with mental disabilities and health needs.

64. ... [T]he Committee is concerned at the increase of legislative initiatives and practices at the state level that limit the exercise of the right to vote, inter alia, partisan gerrymandering, restrictions on voting by mail and on ballot collection, and burdensome voter identification requirements. It is also concerned about the disproportionate impact of these measures on low-income voters, persons with disabilities, and racial and ethnic minorities as well as at reports of increasing harassment and attacks against election officials. ...

...

* * *

Impact

Questions inevitably arise as to the impact of the treaty bodies' 'dialogues' with states and the value of the concluding observations. Cosette Creamer and Beth Simmons, in 'The Proof is in the Process: Self-Reporting Under International Human Rights Treaties', 114 *Am. J. Int'l L.* (2020) 1, have undertaken in-depth analyses around these questions:[344]

> ... [S]tate self-reporting [to treaty bodies] can lead to positive consequences [through elite] socialization, learning and capacity development, domestic political mobilization, and law development ... . [This analysis shows] that improved human rights practices on the ground are theoretically and evidentiarily connected to the report-and-review process.
> ...

> ...

> A finding that self-reporting "works"—even when states have an incentive to shirk and prevaricate—will strike some observers as hopelessly naïve. Critics look at the proliferation of treaty obligations and assert that the reporting system is breaking under its own unwieldy weight. "Reporting fatigue" is a common diagnosis of the problem and a major reason for reporting delinquency. But evidence of serious reporting fatigue is weak. Failure to report is best explained by a lack of state capacity ... .

> ...

> Perhaps a more insidious critique is that reporting may become a bureaucratized end in itself. ... ...

> The self-reporting process is evolutionary, not revolutionary, and is certainly one part of a wider ecosystem of human rights accountability. But research demonstrates that repeat participation in the process sometimes results in important improvements. Moreover, the proof—the why and the how—is in the process: engagement quality is improving, not declining. Ritualism may be a risk, but even actors who think they are engaged in ritual may be socialized into meaningful dialogue. ... [E]ager publics and alert press reporters have not permitted the process to become meaninglessly performative across the board.

Policy Recommendations

> ...

---

[344] See also C. Creamer and B. Simmons, 'Do Self-Reporting Regimes Matter? Evidence from the Convention Against Torture', 63 *Int'l Stud. Q.* (2019) 1051.

First, treaty bodies should increase efforts to encourage states to participate, especially to submit their first report, since doing so familiarizes governments with the process. ...

Second, as socialization research makes clear, the nature of the dialogue with treaty bodies is central to successful internalization of rights norms. Committee members' language and tone matter. Many governments have suggested the dialogue should follow a more "positive" and "constructive" narrative geared toward a "positive impact on the ground through implementation," which would facilitate socialization and learning. Despite an increasing turn to grades and rankings at the international level, we discourage the use of performance "grades" by the treaty bodies. Persuasion is potentially undermined by a superficial scramble to avoid low marks.

Expertise is also central to the process of persuasion, suggesting that the independence and professional qualifications of the treaty body members should be a focus of reform efforts. ...

Third, the composition of delegations sent to Geneva—and particularly the representatives' connectedness to domestic policy implementation—improves the chances for relevant lessons to seep into policy discussions back home. ...

Fourth, successful learning and capacity development depend on interactive dialogue, geared toward problem-solving and resulting in a limited set of priority recommendations that are targeted and actionable. ...

Fifth, we support "bring[ing] the treaty body system closer to the people on the ground," by holding some committee meetings away from Geneva and within the region of the countries under review. ...

...

Over time, governments develop some capacity and expertise to collect and analyze information, detect violations, and deal with them in their domestic settings. Civil society organizations offer additional and sometimes contradictory information, mobilize around the reporting process, and articulate demands for change. Regional courts have increasingly looked to the expert committees' concluding observations to support their judgments. The reporting system therefore has the potential to reverberate in domestic and regional politics, policy, and law and thereby improve the realization of human rights on the ground.

QUESTIONS

1. Does the Committee cover too much ground in its concluding observations? Should it limit their scope in some way?

2. How would you assess the Committee's concluding observations in terms of their specificity, robustness, and potential to make a difference? What alternative styles or approaches might be envisaged?

3. Responding to the perceived inefficacy of the Committee's concluding observations, Tomuschat has argued that these analyses 'should be relied upon by the entire international community, States and international organizations alike, when making policy determinations vis-à-vis a State whose compliance with the obligations under the ICCPR is seriously defective.' Are these documents formulated in such a way as to fulfill that function effectively?

4. On 3 March 2022, one week after Russia's invasion of Ukraine, the Committee adopted a statement (UN Doc. CCPR/C/134/2) expressing 'its extreme concern at the ongoing military invasion … conducted in breach of the fundamental principles of the United Nations, including the prohibition on the threat or use of force'. Is this a constructive precedent, and if so, under what circumstances should the Committee make such statements in the future?

3. General Comments

The text of the ICCPR is characteristically terse and ambiguous about what is intended by 'general comments'. Article 40, after setting forth the undertaking of states to submit periodic reports to the Committee, provides in paragraph 4 that the Committee 'shall study the reports' submitted by states and 'shall transmit its reports, and such *general comments* as it may consider appropriate' to the states (emphasis added). Under paragraph 5, states 'may submit to the Committee observations on any [such] comments'.

The adoption of the phrase in 1966 followed extensive debate over whether any comments resulting from the Committee's examination of reports should be general or specific in nature, and a deliberate failure to resolve the issue. It was thus left to the Committee to decide. Western European members of the Committee wanted country-specific and violations-focused comments to emerge from the reporting process, but the Eastern Europeans rejected both specificity and appraisal. In their view, since the Covenant was not a 'control mechanism', general comments should be directed to all states parties rather than one. Under a 1980 compromise, the committee decided that such comments would be designed to 'promote co-operation' and 'stimulate activities' by states and would focus on procedural issues as well as 'questions related to the application and the content of individual articles of the Covenant'. They thus evolved from a concept of unclear and contested meaning to a tool of fundamental importance in the armoury of those seeking to promote greater clarity and interpretative detail in international human rights law.[345]

Evolution of General Comments[346]

Between 1981 and January 2024 the ICCPR Committee adopted 37 General Comments. While most are devoted to specific rights or articles, there are also a number of wide-ranging General Comments which deal with broader issues such as reservations, emergencies, gender equality and states' obligations in general.[347]

A close reading of these Comments and of the evolution in style and substance reflected therein reveals that the Committee's record might usefully be understood by distinguishing four somewhat, but not entirely, separate phases in its approach to General Comments. They are: (1) consolidation of procedures — 1981–1983; (2) tentative first substantive steps — 1984–1988; (3) the post-Cold War period in which agreement could be reached on expansive interpretations of key substantive rights; and (4) since 2000 when the Committee has adopted an important set of umbrella comments designed to consolidate its understanding of the system as a whole.

---

[345] P. Alston, 'The Historical Origins of the Concept of "General Comments" in Human Rights Law', in L. Boisson de Chazournes and V. Gowlland-Debbas (eds.), *The International Legal System in Quest of Equity and Universality: Liber Amicorum Georges Abi-Saab* (2001), at 763.

[346] See H. Keller and L. Grover, 'General Comments of the Human Rights Committee and their Legitimacy', in H. Keller and G. Ulfstein (eds.), U.N. *Human Rights Treaty Bodies: Law and Legitimacy* (2012) 116.

[347] The subjects and dates of adoption are as follows: No. 1 Reporting obligations (1981); No. 2 Reporting guidelines (1981); No. 3 Implementation at the national level (1981); No. 4 Equal right of men and women (1981); No. 5 Derogations; No. 6 Right to life (1982); No. 7. Prohibition of torture or cruel, inhuman or degrading treatment or punishment (1982); No. 8. Right to liberty and security of persons (1982); No. 9. Article 10 (Humane treatment of persons deprived of their liberty (1982); No. 10 Freedom of opinion (1983); No. 11 Article 20 (propaganda for war and advocacy of hatred) (1983); No. 12 Right to self-determination (1984); No. 13 Administration of justice (1984); No. 14 Right to life (1984); No. 15 The position of aliens under the Covenant (1986); No. 16 Right to privacy (1998); No. 17 Rights of the child (1989); No. 18 Non-discrimination (1989); No. 19 The family (1990); No. 20 Prohibition of torture, or other cruel, inhuman or degrading treatment or punishment (1992); No. 21 Humane treatment of persons deprived of their liberty (1992); No. 22 Freedom of thought, conscience religion (1993); No. 23 Rights of minorities (1994); No. 24 Reservations (1994); No. 25. Participation in public affairs and the right to vote (1996); No. 26 Continuity of obligations (1997); No. 27 Freedom of movement (1999); No. 28 The equality of rights between men and women (2000); No. 29 Derogations during a state of emergency (2001); No. 30 Reporting obligations (2002); No. 31 The nature of the general legal obligation imposed on States Parties to the Covenant (2004); No. 32 Right to a fair trial (2007); No. 33 Obligations of States Parties under the Optional Protocol (2008); No. 34 Freedom of opinion and expression (2011); No. 35 Liberty and security of person (2014); No. 36 Right to life (2018); and No. 37 Right of peaceful assembly (2020).

The output in the first of these phases has been described as 'laconic', 'hesitant', 'bland and uninspiring'.[348] Judged by today's standards this is fair, but in fact the General Comments adopted during this phase played a very important role in consolidating various procedural and organizational innovations in the Committee's working methods which, up until that point, might have been reversible. The caution of this phase was also justified by the need to ensure that states would acquiesce in the development of the notion of General Comments.

The second phase saw the adoption of only three Comments but they were considerably longer, more detailed and reflected more sophisticated legal analysis. The constraints imposed by political factors were nevertheless evident, both in the Comments that were adopted and those that were not (e.g., a long-term effort to adopt a draft on the rights of minorities had to be abandoned)[349] and the jurisprudential innovations were rather limited.

The third phase, after 1989, showed a Committee which had freed itself from most of the limitations that flowed from competing socialist and liberal perceptions of the nature of human rights and of the appropriate role of treaty bodies and from the constraints that flowed from the early understandings of the limited functions of General Comments. It adopted expansive Comments on the rights of the child, non-discrimination and the family, and it marked a definitive break with the past by adopting revised Comments on Articles 7 and 10 which replaced the very tentative efforts it had made during the first phase with much longer and more assertive texts. The end of the influence of the Cold War was also strongly underlined by the range of topics on which detailed and progressive Comments were adopted after 1992. In particular, the Comments on freedom of expression (1993), minorities (1994), the right to vote and take part in government (1996) and freedom of movement (1999) could never have been agreed during the earlier phases and each contains very important jurisprudential elements.

The fourth phase, since 2000, has seen the Committee consolidate its views on the system as a whole with detailed and expansive statements on gender equality, rights in emergency contexts, reporting obligations, the legal nature of states' obligations, freedom of expression and assembly, and the right to life.

Illustrations of General Comments

In reading the sampling of General Comments (GCs) that follows you should re-read the relevant articles of the Covenant.[350] Consider: the functions played by GCs, what their evolution reflects in terms of the changing roles of the Covenant and of the Committee, what they reveal about the Committee's understanding of the Covenant, the significance of GCs in expanding the interpretive reach of the Covenant and its norms and the relevance of GCs in relation to the human rights regime in general.

A. PHASE 1 (1981–1983)

> The purpose of [the Committee's] general comments is to make this experience available
> for the benefit of all States parties in order to promote their further implementation of
> the Covenant; to draw their attention to insufficiencies disclosed by a large number of
> reports; to suggest improvements in the reporting procedure and to stimulate the
> activities of these States and international organizations in the promotion and protection
> of human rights … .[351]

GC No. 2, 'Reporting Guidelines' (1981):

---

[348] T. Buergenthal, 'The Human Rights Committee', 5 *Max Planck Y.B. of U. N. Law* 341 (2001), at 387.

[349] For the record of debates over an aborted draft, see UN Docs. CCPR/C/SR 590, 607, 618, 633 (1985).

[350] In addition to those excerpted below, other GCs feature elsewhere in the book. See e.g.: (1) GC No. 26 at 165, above, on a state's withdrawal from the Covenant; (2) GC No. 22 at 604, above, on freedom of religion; (3) GC No. 24 at 1097, above, on reservations to the ICCPR; (4) GC No. 29 at 397, above, on states of emergency; and (5) GC No. 32 at 470, above, on the right to a fair trial.

[351] UN Doc. HRI/GEN/1/Rev.8 (2006).

3. The Committee considers that the reporting obligation embraces not only the relevant laws and other norms relating to the obligations under the Covenant but also the practices and decisions of courts and other organs of the State party ... .

GC No. 3, 'Implementation at the National Level' (1981):

1. The Committee notes that article 2 of the Covenant generally leaves it to the States parties concerned to choose their method of implementation in their territories within the framework set out in that article. It recognizes, in particular, that the implementation does not depend solely on constitutional or legislative enactments, which in themselves are often not per se sufficient. ... [T]he obligation under the Covenant is not confined to the respect of human rights, but that States parties have also undertaken to ensure the enjoyment of these rights to all individuals under their jurisdiction. This aspect calls for specific activities by the States parties to enable individuals to enjoy their rights. [I]n principle this undertaking relates to all rights set forth in the Covenant.

...

B. PHASE 2 (1984–1988)

GC No. 14, 'Article 6' (1984) builds on GC No. 6, 'Article 6' (1982). Both address the right to life, and their orientation reflects the revived influence of Cold War concerns, as well as efforts to explore how the ICCPR Covenant might relate to economic and social rights-type concerns. These GCs were subsequently superseded by GC No. 36. Consider the following excerpt from GC No. 6:

...

5. Moreover, the Committee has noted that the right to life has been too often narrowly interpreted. The expression 'inherent right to life' cannot properly be understood in a restrictive manner, and the protection of this right requires that States adopt positive measures. In this connection, the Committee considers that it would be desirable for States parties to take all possible measures to reduce infant mortality and to increase life expectancy, especially in adopting measures to eliminate malnutrition and epidemics.

Compare these provisions from the earlier GC with *GC No. 14*, two years later:

3. While remaining deeply concerned by the toll of human life taken by conventional weapons in armed conflicts, the Committee has noted that, during successive sessions of the General Assembly, representatives from all geographical regions have expressed their growing concern at the development and proliferation of increasingly awesome weapons of mass destruction, which not only threaten human life but also absorb resources that could otherwise be used for vital economic and social purposes, particularly for the benefit of developing countries, and thereby for promoting and securing the enjoyment of human rights for all.

4. The Committee associates itself with this concern. It is evident that the designing, testing, manufacture, possession and deployment of nuclear weapons are among the greatest threats to the right to life which confront mankind today. This threat is compounded by the danger that the actual use of such weapons may be brought about, not only in the event of war, but even through human or mechanical error or failure.

...

6. The production, testing, possession, deployment and use of nuclear weapons should be prohibited and recognized as crimes against humanity.

7. The Committee accordingly, in the interest of mankind, calls upon all States, whether Parties to the Covenant or not, to take urgent steps, unilaterally and by agreement, to rid the world of this menace.

GC No. 16, 'Article 17' (1988) (at 21) elaborates the article's reference to interference with privacy. The following excerpt illustrates the Committee's preparedness to go into substantive issues in more depth and to read more into the terms of the Covenant than it had been prepared to do at the outset:

> 10. The gathering and holding of personal information on computers, databanks and other devices, whether by public authorities or private individuals or bodies, must be regulated by law. Effective measures have to be taken by States to ensure that information concerning a person's private life does not reach the hands of persons who are not authorized by law to receive, process and use it, and is never used for purposes incompatible with the Covenant. In order to have the most effective protection of his private life, every individual should have the right to ascertain in an intelligible form, whether, and if so, what personal data is stored in automatic data files, and for what purposes. Every individual should also be able to ascertain which public authorities or private individuals or bodies control or may control their files. If such files contain incorrect personal data or have been collected or processed contrary to the provisions of the law, every individual should have the right to request rectification or elimination.

C. PHASE 3 (1989–1999)

GC No. 18, 'Non-discrimination' (1989) deals with several provisions of the Covenant — Articles 2, 3 and 26 among others — that state the principle of non-discrimination. Compare it with GC No. 28 on equality, adopted during the fourth phase.

> 7. ... [T]he Committee believes that the term 'discrimination' as used in the Covenant should be understood to imply any distinction, exclusion, restriction or preference which is based on any ground such as race, colour, sex, language, religion, political or other opinion, national or social origin, property, birth or other status, and which has the purpose or effect of nullifying or impairing the recognition, enjoyment or exercise by all persons, on an equal footing, of all rights and freedoms.
>
> ...
>
> 10. The Committee also wishes to point out that the principle of equality sometimes requires States parties to take affirmative action in order to diminish or eliminate conditions which cause or help to perpetuate discrimination prohibited by the Covenant. ... [A]s long as such action is needed to correct discrimination in fact, it is a case of legitimate differentiation under the Covenant. ...
>
> ...
>
> 12. ... [A]rticle 26 does not merely duplicate the guarantee already provided for in article 2 but provides in itself an autonomous right ... . [T]he application of the principle of non-discrimination contained in article 26 is not limited to those rights which are provided for in the Covenant.
>
> 13. [N]ot every differentiation of treatment will constitute discrimination, if the criteria for such differentiation are reasonable and objective and if the aim is to achieve a purpose which is legitimate under the Covenant.

GC No. 20, 'Article 7' (1992) concerns torture and cruel or degrading treatment or punishment. Note the detail in the following provisions that bear on implementation:

> 11. ... To guarantee the effective protection of detained persons, provisions should be made for detainees to be held in places officially recognized as places of detention and for their names and places of detention, as well as for the names of persons responsible for their detention, to be kept in registers readily available and accessible to those concerned, including relatives and friends. To the same effect, the time and place of all interrogations

should be recorded, together with the names of all those present and this information should also be available for purposes of judicial or administrative proceedings. Provisions should also be made against incommunicado detention. In that connection, States parties should ensure that any places of detention be free from any equipment liable to be used for inflicting torture or ill-treatment. The protection of the detainee also requires that prompt and regular access be given to doctors and lawyers and, under appropriate supervision when the investigation so requires, to family members.

12. It is important for the discouragement of violations under article 7 that the law must prohibit the use of admissibility in judicial proceedings of statements or confessions obtained through torture or other prohibited treatment.

…

15. The Committee has noted that some States have granted amnesty in respect of acts of torture. Amnesties are generally incompatible with the duty of States to investigate such acts; to guarantee freedom from such acts within their jurisdiction; and to ensure that they do not occur in the future. States may not deprive individuals of the right to an effective remedy, including compensation and such full rehabilitation as may be possible.

D. PHASE 4 (2000–PRESENT)

Today, the process for adopting a GC is much more complicated than it once was. For the Committee member who serves as rapporteur on a new GC it represents 'a huge time commitment, both during and between sessions. The rapporteur produces the initial draft, and shepherds the evolving text through the stages of discussion. The procedure … has become highly consultative, and the HRC receives very useful suggestions from States and other stakeholders, … and each paragraph of the text is adopted by consensus.'[352] Thus, for example, in drafting GC No. 36 (below) 23 states (all except Brazil, Egypt, and Namibia, from the global North), a UN agency, a UN treaty body, three Special Procedures mandates, two national human rights institutions, 33 academics, and 108 civil society groups made submissions. Another important innovation in this phase is the inclusion of footnote references to establish or reinforce many of the propositions put forward. GC No. 36, for example, is more than 15,000 words and has 281 footnotes. The drafting process began in July 2015 and was completed in October 2018.

GC No. 28, 'Equality of rights between men and women' (2000):

3. The obligation to ensure to all individuals the rights recognized in the Covenant, established in articles 2 and 3 of the Covenant, requires that States parties take all necessary steps to enable every person to enjoy those rights. These steps include the removal of obstacles to the equal enjoyment of such rights, the education of the population and of State officials in human rights, and the adjustment of domestic legislation so as to give effect to the undertakings set forth in the Covenant. The State party must not only adopt measures of protection, but also positive measures in all areas so as to achieve the effective and equal empowerment of women. …

4. States parties are responsible for ensuring the equal enjoyment of rights without any discrimination. Articles 2 and 3 mandate States parties to take all steps necessary, including the prohibition of discrimination on the ground of sex, to put an end to discriminatory actions, both in the public and the private sector, which impair the equal enjoyment of rights.

5. Inequality in the enjoyment of rights by women throughout the world is deeply embedded in tradition, history and culture, including religious attitudes. The subordinate role of women in some countries is illustrated by the high incidence of prenatal sex

[352] Neuman, n. 3 above, 39.

selection and abortion of female foetuses. States parties should ensure that traditional, historical, religious or cultural attitudes are not used to justify violations of women's right to equality before the law and to equal enjoyment of all Covenant rights. ...

GC No. 31, 'Nature of the General Legal Obligation' (2004):

> 2. While article 2 is couched in terms of the obligations of State parties towards individuals as the right-holders under the Covenant, every State party has a legal interest in the performance by every other State party of its obligations. This follows from the fact that the "rules concerning the basic rights of the human person" are *erga omnes* obligations. ... [The Committee then urges States parties to make use of the so far moribund interstate complaints procedure provided for in Article 41.] To draw attention to possible breaches of Covenant obligations by other States parties and to call on them to comply with their Covenant obligations should, far from being regarded as an unfriendly act, be considered as a reflection of legitimate community interest.
>
> ...
>
> 4. The obligations of the Covenant in general and article 2 in particular are binding on every State party as a whole. All branches of government (executive, legislative and judicial), and other public or governmental authorities, at whatever level (national, regional or local) are in a position to engage the responsibility of the State party. The executive branch that usually represents the State party internationally, including before the Committee, may not point to the fact that an action incompatible with the provisions of the Covenant was carried out by another branch of government as a means of seeking to relieve the State party from responsibility for the action and consequent incompatibility ... .
>
> ...
>
> 14. The requirement under article 2, paragraph 2, to take steps to give effect to the Covenant rights is unqualified and of immediate effect. A failure to comply with this obligation cannot be justified by reference to political, social, cultural or economic considerations within the State.
>
> 15. Article 2, paragraph 3, requires that in addition to effective protection of Covenant rights States parties must ensure that individuals also have accessible and effective remedies to vindicate those rights. Such remedies should be appropriately adapted so as to take account of the special vulnerability of certain categories of person, including in particular children. ...
>
> 16. Article 2, paragraph 3, requires that States parties make reparation to individuals whose Covenant rights have been violated. ... [T]he Covenant generally entails appropriate compensation. The Committee notes that, where appropriate, reparation can involve restitution, rehabilitation and measures of satisfaction, such as public apologies, public memorials, guarantees of non-repetition and changes in relevant laws and practices, as well as bringing to justice the perpetrators of human rights violations.
>
> 17. In general, the purposes of the Covenant would be defeated without an obligation integral to article 2 to take measures to prevent a recurrence of a violation of the Covenant ... .
>
> 18.... [W]here public officials or State agents have committed violations of the Covenant rights referred to in [Articles 6, 7 or 9], the States parties concerned may not relieve perpetrators from personal responsibility, as has occurred with certain amnesties (see general comment No. 20 (44)) and prior legal immunities and indemnities. Furthermore, no official status justifies persons who may be accused of responsibility for such violations being held immune from legal responsibility. ...

...

GC No. 34, 'Article 19: Freedoms of opinion and expression' (2011):

...

Freedom of expression

11. Paragraph 2 requires States parties to guarantee the right to freedom of expression, including the right to seek, receive and impart information and ideas of all kinds regardless of frontiers. This right includes the expression and receipt of communications of every form of idea and opinion capable of transmission to others, subject to the provisions in article 19, paragraph 3, and article 20. It includes political discourse, commentary on one's own and on public affairs, canvassing, discussion of human rights, journalism, cultural and artistic expression, teaching, and religious discourse. It may also include commercial advertising. The scope of paragraph 2 embraces even expression that may be regarded as deeply offensive, although such expression may be restricted in accordance with the provisions of article 19, paragraph 3 and article 20.

12. Paragraph 2 protects all forms of expression and the means of their dissemination. Such forms include spoken, written and sign language and such non-verbal expression as images and objects of art. Means of expression include books, newspapers, pamphlets, posters, banners, dress and legal submissions. They include all forms of audio-visual as well as electronic and internet-based modes of expression.

Freedom of expression and the media

13. A free, uncensored and unhindered press or other media is essential in any society to ensure freedom of opinion and expression and the enjoyment of other Covenant rights. It constitutes one of the cornerstones of a democratic society. ...

...

Right of access to information

18. Article 19, paragraph 2 embraces a right of access to information held by public bodies. Such information includes records held by a public body, regardless of the form in which the information is stored, its source and the date of production. ...

...

Limitative scope of restrictions on freedom of expression in certain specific areas

...

38. ... [T]he mere fact that forms of expression are considered to be insulting to a public figure is not sufficient to justify the imposition of penalties, albeit public figures may also benefit from the provisions of the Covenant. Moreover, all public figures, including those exercising the highest political authority such as heads of state and government, are legitimately subject to criticism and political opposition. Accordingly, the Committee expresses concern regarding laws on such matters as, *lese majeste, desacato*, disrespect for authority, disrespect for flags and symbols, defamation of the head of state and the protection of the honour of public officials, and laws should not provide for more severe penalties solely on the basis of the identity of the person that may have been impugned. States parties should not prohibit criticism of institutions, such as the army or the administration.

...

48. Prohibitions of displays of lack of respect for a religion or other belief system, including blasphemy laws, are incompatible with the Covenant, except in the specific circumstances envisaged in article 20, paragraph 2, of the Covenant. Such prohibitions must also comply with the strict requirements of article 19, paragraph 3, as well as such articles as 2, 5, 17, 18 and 26. Thus, for instance, it would be impermissible for any such laws to discriminate in favour of or against one or certain religions or belief systems, or their adherents over another, or religious believers over non-believers. Nor would it be permissible for such prohibitions to be used to prevent or punish criticism of religious leaders or commentary on religious doctrine and tenets of faith.

...

GC No. 36, Article 6: right to life (2018):

I. General remarks

1. This general comment replaces general comments [No. 6 (1982) and No. 14 (1984)].

2. Article 6 of the [ICCPR] recognizes and protects the right to life of all human beings. The right to life is the supreme right from which no derogation is permitted, even in situations of armed conflict and other public emergencies that threaten the life of the nation. ...

3. The right to life is a right that should not be interpreted narrowly. It concerns the entitlement of individuals to be free from acts and omissions that are intended or may be expected to cause their unnatural or premature death, as well as to enjoy a life with dignity. ...

...

6. Deprivation of life involves intentional or otherwise foreseeable and preventable life-terminating harm or injury, caused by an act or omission. It goes beyond injury to bodily or mental integrity or a threat thereto.

7. States parties must respect the right to life. This entails the duty to refrain from engaging in conduct resulting in arbitrary deprivation of life. States parties must also ensure the right to life and exercise due diligence to protect the lives of individuals against deprivations caused by persons or entities whose conduct is not attributable to the State. The obligation of States parties to respect and ensure the right to life extends to reasonably foreseeable threats and life-threatening situations that can result in loss of life. States parties may be in violation of article 6 even if such threats and situations do not result in loss of life.

8. [For excerpts from para. 8, see above.]

9. While acknowledging the central importance to human dignity of personal autonomy, States should take adequate measures, without violating their other Covenant obligations, to prevent suicides, especially among individuals in particularly vulnerable situations, including individuals deprived of their liberty. ...

...

II. Prohibition against arbitrary deprivation of life

...

11. The second sentence of article 6 (1) requires that the right to life be protected by law, while the third sentence requires that no one be arbitrarily deprived of life. The two requirements partly overlap in that a deprivation of life that lacks a legal basis or is

otherwise inconsistent with life-protecting laws and procedures is, as a rule, arbitrary in nature. ...

12. Deprivation of life is, as a rule, arbitrary if it is inconsistent with international law or domestic law. A deprivation of life may, nevertheless, be authorized by domestic law and still be arbitrary. The notion of "arbitrariness" is not to be fully equated with "against the law", but must be interpreted more broadly to include elements of inappropriateness, injustice, lack of predictability and due process of law, as well as elements of reasonableness, necessity and proportionality. ...

...

14. While preferable to more lethal weapons, States parties should ensure that less-lethal weapons are subject to strict independent testing and evaluate and monitor the impact on the right to life of weapons such as electro-muscular disruption devices (Tasers), rubber or foam bullets, and other attenuating energy projectiles, which are designed for use or are actually used by law enforcement officials, including soldiers charged with law enforcement missions. ... [L]ess-lethal weapons must be employed only subject to strict requirements of necessity and proportionality, in situations in which other less harmful measures have proven to be or clearly are ineffective to address the threat. States parties should not resort to less-lethal weapons in situations of crowd control that can be addressed through less harmful means, especially situations involving the exercise of the right to peaceful assembly.

...

III. Duty to protect life

18. The second sentence of article 6 (1) provides that the right to life "shall be protected by law". This implies that States parties must establish a legal framework to ensure the full enjoyment of the right to life by all individuals as may be necessary to give effect to the right to life. The duty to protect the right to life by law also includes an obligation for States parties to adopt any appropriate laws or other measures in order to protect life from all reasonably foreseeable threats, including from threats emanating from private persons and entities.

...

20. States parties must enact a protective legal framework that includes effective criminal prohibitions on all manifestations of violence or incitement to violence that are likely to result in deprivation of life, such as intentional and negligent homicide, unnecessary or disproportionate use of firearms, infanticide, "honour" killings, lynching, violent hate crimes, blood feuds, ritual killings, death threats and terrorist attacks. The criminal sanctions attached to these crimes must be commensurate with their gravity, while remaining compatible with all the provisions of the Covenant.

[For excerpts from paras. 21 and 22, see above.]

23. The duty to protect the right to life requires States parties to take special measures of protection towards persons in vulnerable situations whose lives have been placed at particular risk because of specific threats or pre-existing patterns of violence. Such persons include human rights defenders (see also para. 53 below), officials fighting corruption and organized crime, humanitarian workers, journalists, prominent public figures, witnesses to crime and victims of domestic and gender-based violence and human trafficking. They may also include children, especially children in street situations, unaccompanied migrant children and children in situations of armed conflict, members of ethnic and religious minorities, indigenous peoples, lesbian, gay, bisexual, transgender and intersex persons, persons with albinism, alleged witches, displaced persons, asylum

seekers, refugees and stateless persons. States parties must respond urgently and effectively in order to protect individuals who find themselves under a specific threat, by adopting special measures such as the assignment of around-the-clock police protection, the issuance of protection and restraining orders against potential aggressors and, in exceptional cases, and only with the free and informed consent of the threatened individual, protective custody.

24. Persons with disabilities, including psychosocial or intellectual disabilities, are also entitled to specific measures of protection so as to ensure their effective enjoyment of the right to life on an equal basis with others. Such measures of protection must include the provision of reasonable accommodation when necessary to ensure the right to life, such as ensuring access of persons with disabilities to essential facilities and services, and specific measures designed to prevent unwarranted use of force by law enforcement agents against persons with disabilities.

…

26. [For excerpts from para. 26, see below.]

…

30. The duty to respect and ensure the right to life requires States parties to refrain from deporting, extraditing or otherwise transferring individuals to countries in which there are substantial grounds for believing that a real risk exists that their right to life under article 6 of the Covenant would be violated. Such a risk must be personal in nature and cannot derive merely from the general conditions in the receiving State, except in the most extreme cases. For example, as explained in paragraph 34 below, it would be contrary to article 6 to extradite an individual from a country that had abolished the death penalty to a country in which he or she might face the death penalty. Similarly, it would be inconsistent with article 6 to deport an individual to a country in which a fatwa had been issued against him or her by local religious authorities, without verifying that the fatwa was not likely to be followed; or to deport an individual to an extremely violent country in which he or she had never lived, had no social or family contacts and could not speak the local language. …

…

IV. Imposition of the death penalty
[For excerpts from Section IV, see above.]

V. Relationship of article 6 with other articles of the Covenant and other legal regimes

…

59. A particular connection exists between article 6 and article 20, which prohibits any propaganda for war and certain forms of advocacy constituting incitement to discrimination, hostility or violence. Failure to comply with these obligations under article 20 may also constitute a failure to take the necessary measures to protect the right to life under article 6.

60. Article 24 (1) of the Covenant entitles every child to such measures of protection as are required by his or her status as a minor, on the part of his or her family, society and the State. This article requires adoption of special measures designed to protect the life of every child, in addition to the general measures required by article 6 for protecting the lives of all individuals. When taking special measures of protection, States parties should be guided by the best interests of the child, and by the need to ensure all children's survival, development and well-being.

61. The right to life must be respected and ensured without distinction of any kind, such as race, colour, sex, language, religion, political or other opinion, national or social origin, property, birth, or any other status, including caste, ethnicity, membership of an indigenous group, sexual orientation or gender identity, disability, socioeconomic status, albinism and age. Legal protections for the right to life must apply equally to all individuals and provide them with effective guarantees against all forms of discrimination, including multiple and intersectional forms of discrimination. Any deprivation of life based on discrimination in law or in fact is ipso facto arbitrary in nature. Femicide, which constitutes an extreme form of gender-based violence that is directed against girls and women, is a particularly grave form of assault on the right to life.

62. [For excerpts from para. 62, see below.]

63. [Para. 63 is excerpted below.]

64. Like the rest of the Covenant, article 6 continues to apply also in situations of armed conflict to which the rules of international humanitarian law are applicable, including to the conduct of hostilities. While rules of international humanitarian law may be relevant for the interpretation and application of article 6 when the situation calls for their application, both spheres of law are complementary, not mutually exclusive. Use of lethal force consistent with international humanitarian law and other applicable international law norms is, in general, not arbitrary. By contrast, practices inconsistent with international humanitarian law, entailing a risk to the lives of civilians and other persons protected by international humanitarian law, including the targeting of civilians, civilian objects and objects indispensable to the survival of the civilian population, indiscriminate attacks, failure to apply the principles of precaution and proportionality, and the use of human shields would also violate article 6 of the Covenant. States parties should, in general, disclose the criteria for attacking with lethal force individuals or objects whose targeting is expected to result in deprivation of life, including the legal basis for specific attacks, the process of identification of military targets and combatants or persons taking a direct part in hostilities, the circumstances in which relevant means and methods of warfare have been used, and whether less harmful alternatives were considered. They must also investigate alleged or suspected violations of article 6 in situations of armed conflict in accordance with the relevant international standards (see paras. 27–28 above).

65. [For excerpts from para. 65, see above.]

66. [For excerpts from para. 66, see below.]

70. States parties engaged in acts of aggression as defined in international law, resulting in deprivation of life, violate ipso facto article 6 of the Covenant. At the same time, all States are reminded of their responsibility as members of the international community to protect lives and to oppose widespread or systematic attacks on the right to life, including acts of aggression, international terrorism, genocide, crimes against humanity and war crimes, while respecting all of their obligations under international law. States parties that fail to take all reasonable measures to settle their international disputes by peaceful means might fall short of complying with their positive obligation to ensure the right to life.

Some Controversies Addressed in GCs

In some important instances GCs have been the Committee's chosen vehicle for propounding far-reaching and often controversial, interpretations of the Covenant. Consider the following examples relating to reservations, succession, jurisdiction, and nuclear weapons.

A. RESERVATIONS: GC NO. 24 (1994)[353]

8. ... [P]rovisions in the Covenant that represent customary international law (and a fortiori when they have the character of peremptory norms) may not be the subject of reservations. Accordingly, a State may not reserve the right to engage in slavery, to torture, to subject persons to cruel, inhuman or degrading treatment or punishment, to arbitrarily deprive persons of their lives, to arbitrarily arrest and detain persons, to deny freedom of thought, conscience and religion, to presume a person guilty unless he proves his innocence, to execute pregnant women or children, to permit the advocacy of national, racial or religious hatred, to deny to persons of marriageable age the right to marry, or to deny to minorities the right to enjoy their own culture, profess their own religion, or use their own language. And while reservations to particular clauses of article 14 may be acceptable, a general reservation to the right to a fair trial would not be.

...

18. It necessarily falls to the Committee to determine whether a specific reservation is compatible with the object and purpose of the Covenant. This is in part because, as indicated above, it is an inappropriate task for States parties in relation to human rights treaties, and in part because it is a task that the Committee cannot avoid in the performance of its functions. In order to know the scope of its duty to examine a State's compliance under article 40 or a communication under the first Optional Protocol, the Committee has necessarily to take a view on the compatibility of a reservation with the object and purpose of the Covenant and with general international law. Because of the special character of a human rights treaty, the compatibility of a reservation with the object and purpose of the Covenant must be established objectively, by reference to legal principles, and the Committee is particularly well placed to perform this task ... .

Nowak notes that, prior to the adoption of GC No. 24, several members of the Committee had expressed the view that it was not authorized to review the validity of reservations. He notes that several governments — in particular France, the United States, and the United Kingdom — expressly objected to some of the conclusions reached in the GC, and that some academic commentators have also been critical.[354] Nowak characterizes GC No. 24 as 'one of the most important legal documents ever adopted on the controversial question of reservations to human rights treaties'. While supportive of the Committee's conclusions as to its own competence, he questions the broad range of reasons given to justify the incompatibility:

> First of all, the Committee made no clear distinction between customary international law and peremptory norms (ius cogens) ... . Secondly, the list of provisions regarded as representing customary law seems far too broad ... . [Since rights relating to self-determination, marriage, minorities and incitement to hatred] have in fact been the subject of reservations by a considerable number of States, it is not surprising that Governments objected to this comprehensive list which, according to the Committee, may not be the subject of reservations.[355]

In written comments, submitted in 1995, France rejected the 'entire analysis' contained in paragraph 18 and stated that:

> As for the opinion that the Committee is particularly well placed to take decisions on the compatibility of a reservation with the object and purpose of the Covenant, France points out that the Committee, like any other treaty body or similar body established by agreement, owes its existence exclusively to the treaty and has no powers other than those conferred on it by the States parties; it is therefore for the latter, and for them alone,

---

[353] Note that more detailed excerpts from this GC appear below.
[354] Nowak, UN *Covenant on Civil and Political Rights: ICCPR Commentary* (2nd edn. 2005), xxxi–xxxiii.
[355] Ibid.

unless the treaty states otherwise, to decide whether a reservation is incompatible with the object and purpose of the treaty.[356]

B. SUCCESSION AND DENUNCIATION: GC NO. 26 (1997)

Two very important issues in relation to treaty law concern whether: (1) a successor state is automatically bound by the international human rights treaty obligations of its predecessor; and (2) whether a state which is a party to the ICCPR can denounce it, and is thus no longer bound by its provisions. The text of the Covenant is silent on both issues, although Article 12 of the First Optional Protocol to the ICCPR explicitly provides for a state to denounce the Protocol.

GC No. 26, Continuity of obligations (1997):

> 1. [The Committee observes that the issue is governed by customary law as reflected in the Vienna Convention on the Law of Treaties]. On this basis, the Covenant is not subject to denunciation or withdrawal unless it is established that the parties intended to admit the possibility of denunciation or withdrawal or a right to do so is implied from the nature of the treaty.

> 2. [The Committee notes that denunciation is specifically provided for in relation to (i) the interstate procedure under Article 41(2); (ii) the First Optional Protocol to the ICCPR; and (iii) the International Convention on the Elimination of All Forms of Racial Discrimination, adopted before the ICCPR.] It can therefore be concluded that the drafters of the Covenant deliberately intended to exclude the possibility of denunciation. The same conclusion applies to the Second Optional Protocol in the drafting of which a denunciation clause was deliberately omitted.

> 3. Furthermore, it is clear that the Covenant is not the type of treaty which, by its nature, implies a right of denunciation. Together with the simultaneously prepared and adopted [ICESCR], the Covenant codifies in treaty form the universal human rights enshrined in the [UDHR], the three instruments together often being referred to as the "International Bill of Human Rights". As such, the Covenant does not have a temporary character typical of treaties where a right of denunciation is deemed to be admitted, notwithstanding the absence of a specific provision to that effect.

> 4. The rights enshrined in the Covenant belong to the people living in the territory of the State party. The Human Rights Committee has consistently taken the view, as evidenced by its long-standing practice, that once the people are accorded the protection of the rights under the Covenant, such protection devolves with territory and continues to belong to them, notwithstanding change in government of the State party, including dismemberment in more than one State or State succession or any subsequent action of the State party designed to divest them of the rights guaranteed by the Covenant.

> 5. The Committee is therefore firmly of the view that international law does not permit a State which has ratified or acceded or succeeded to the Covenant to denounce it or withdraw from it.

The succession issue arose in relation to some of the successor states to the former Soviet Union and Hong Kong and Macau. While most of the former group accepted the continuing applicability of the ICCPR obligations, they nonetheless deposited instruments of succession, rather than assuming the automaticity of the process.[357] Kazakhstan was the exception, but the Committee continued to treat it as a state party and requested reports. Eventually, in 2006, Kazakhstan ratified the Covenant. When China resumed its control of Hong Kong and Macau in 1997 it also agreed to succeed to the pertinent ICCPR obligations of the United Kingdom (in

---

[356] UN Doc. A/51/40 (1995), Annex VI, para. 14.
[357] One Committee member subsequently indicated in remarks under an Optional Protocol case that he agreed with para. 4 of GC No. 26 'as a matter of policy, but I cannot agree with it as a statement of a rule of customary international law' (Mr Ando in *Kuok Koi v. Portugal*, No. 925/00).

relation to Hong Kong) and Portugal (Macau), and has since presented a report to the ICCPR Committee on compliance with the Covenant in those two territories.

Denunciation was more complex. The GC was adopted in October 1997 in direct response to North Korea's purported denunciation of the ICCPR, lodged with the UN in August 1997. North Korea did not pursue it plans, and subsequently presented a report to the Committee. But other states had also previously contemplated denunciation. Thus, for example, the Netherlands considered withdrawal after decisions of the ICCPR Committee on non-discrimination in relation to social security law which had major financial implications.[358]

C. JURISDICTION

ICCPR Article 2 (1) states: "Each State Party to the present Covenant undertakes to respect and to ensure to all individuals within its territory and subject to its jurisdiction the rights recognized …'. Consider the Committee's analysis of this issue in para. 63 of GC No. 36, above.

In observations submitted after the adoption of the GC, France stated that the text relating to extraterritoriality is 'too broad and does not conform to the letter or the spirit of the Covenant or to the jurisprudence of the European Court of Human Rights. The vague and imprecise criteria used are a source of legal uncertainty.'[359]

The United States has regularly objected to the Committee's interpretation of the Covenant's jurisdictional provision. In 2008, in response to GC No 31, the U.S. submitted these observations (https://2001-2009.state.gov/s/l/2007/112674.htm):

> 4. This interpretation [of Article 2 (1)], which dispenses with the well-established rules of treaty interpretation, is inconsistent with the plain text of the Covenant as well as its negotiating history. … Without any analysis or reasoning to support its view, the Committee's interpretation would have the effect of transforming the "and" in Article 2(1) into an "or."
>
> 5. … It is lamentable that the General Comment treats this provision in such a cavalier and inconsistent manner … . [The GC's] demonstrated indifference to the precise wording of this carefully negotiated text is unfortunate and serves to undermine the Committee's persuasive authority.
>
> …
>
> 9. … [T]he United States considers this interpretation wholly incorrect as a matter of international law on the interpretation of treaties.

Five years later, under the Obama administration, the United States took a marginally more conciliatory approach. It recalled its earlier position, but also acknowledged its awareness 'of the jurisprudence of the International Court of Justice, which has found the ICCPR '"applicable in respect of acts done by a State in the exercise of its jurisdiction outside its own territory," as well as positions taken by other States Parties.' (Fourth Periodic Report, United States of America, UN Doc. CCPR/C/USA/4 (2012), para. 505.)

But days before the Committee adopted GC No. 36 in 2018, the United States reiterated its earlier position and added:

> 14. We likewise do not agree that an individual on State-Party-registered ships located beyond that State Party's territorial sea, or on State Party-registered aircraft flying in international airspace (or in another State's airspace), would be located within the territory of that State Party for purposes of application of ICCPR rights. Merely being on a ship or aircraft registered in a State (and thereby being generally subject to its exclusive jurisdiction on the high seas, for example) does not constitute being in a State's territory. And with respect to individuals in distress, search and rescue regions are expressly distinct

---

[358] See *Broeks v. The Netherlands,* No. 172/1984; and generally Nowak, n. 16, above, xxxvi.

[359] 'France', at https://www.ohchr.org/en/hrbodies/ccpr/pages/gc36-article6righttolife.aspx

from questions of jurisdiction and control. Even the reliance on the concept that there are "areas of the high seas over which particular States Parties have assumed de facto responsibility" is at odds with fundamental law of the sea principles. We therefore urge deletion of these assertions.

15. Although some States Parties may have accepted somewhat broader jurisdictional obligations as parties to regional human rights conventions, or because doing so might correspond with their domestic laws, the United States has not done so. To the extent that there are differing views among States Parties, the Committee has no mandate to resolve them or to interpret authoritatively the Convention's terms. ...[360]

Ryan Goodman has pointed out that despite its position in relation to the ICCPR, the United States has long accepted the existence of such obligations as a matter of customary international law. He cites the position taken by the U.S. in relation to the Soviet Union's conduct in Afghanistan, Iran's and Russia's in Syria, and Iraq's in Kuwait. In addition, the U.S. military's 2018 *Operational Law Handbook* states that '[i]n contrast to much of human rights treaty law, fundamental customary [international human rights law] binds a State's forces during all operations, both inside and outside the State's territory.'[361]

Consider the following defence of the Committee's position by Nowak:

When States parties ... take *actions on foreign territory* that violate the rights of persons subject to their sovereign authority, it would be contrary to the purpose of the Covenant if they could not be held responsible. It is irrelevant whether these actions are permissible under general international law (e.g., sovereign act by diplomatic or consular representatives, or in border traffic or by border officials in customs-free zones; actions by occupation forces in accordance with the rules of the law of war) or constitute illegal interference, such as the kidnapping of persons by secret service agents.

Departing from earlier views in the literature, which had adhered to a literal reading of Art. 2(1), the Committee has sought to correct the wording of this provision by developing case law oriented along the object and purpose of the Covenant and affording increased legal protection. In the first place, it has made it clear that persons who have fled abroad are not prevented by Art. 2(1) from submitting individual communications. Second, in the so-called *Passport cases* concerning Uruguay, it held that States parties are also responsible for violations of the Covenant (at least of Art. 12) by foreign diplomatic representatives. Third, it has considered communications by persons who had been kidnapped by Uruguayan agents in neighbouring States to be admissible, reasoning that States parties are responsible for the actions of their agents on foreign territory.[362]

D. NUCLEAR WEAPONS

The Committee first raised its concerns about nuclear weapons in GC No. 14 (1984). But despite being virtually silent in the interim years, it returned to the issue in GC No. 36 in 2018:

66. The threat or use of weapons of mass destruction, in particular nuclear weapons, which are indiscriminate in effect and are of a nature to cause destruction of human life on a catastrophic scale, is incompatible with respect for the right to life and may amount to a crime under international law. States parties must take all necessary measures to stop the proliferation of weapons of mass destruction, including measures to prevent their acquisition by non-State actors, to refrain from developing, producing, testing, acquiring, stockpiling, selling, transferring and using them, to destroy existing stockpiles, and to take adequate measures of protection against accidental use, all in accordance with their

---

[360] 'United States of America', at https://www.ohchr.org/en/hrbodies/ccpr/pages/gc36-article6righttolife.aspx Note this position was reiterated by the United States in its fifth periodic report to the Committee, in 2021 (UN Doc. CCPR/C/USA/5, para. 14).
[361] R. Goodman, 'Human Rights Law and U.S. Military Operations in Foreign Countries: The Prohibition on Arbitrary Deprivation of Life', *Just Security*, 19 February 2019.
[362] Nowak, n. 16 above, at 43–4.

international obligations. They must also respect their international obligations to pursue in good faith negotiations in order to achieve the aim of nuclear disarmament under strict and effective international control, and to afford adequate reparation to victims whose right to life has been or is being adversely affected by the testing or use of weapons of mass destruction, in accordance with principles of international responsibility.

...

Roger S. Clark, in 'The Human Rights Committee, the Right to Life and Nuclear Weapons: The Committee's General Comment No 36 on Article 6 of the Covenant on Civil and Political Rights', 16 *New Zealand Y.B. Int'l L.* (2018) 263, provides a detailed analysis of the international standards that underpin each of the propositions in the foregoing paragraph:

> When ... the HRC was preparing its first reading version of *GC 36*, the word "threat" was seating itself in the *Treaty on the Prohibition of Nuclear Weapons* ("*tpnw*"). The HRC placed "threat" in brackets at that point and several subsequent submissions supported the removal of those brackets, now having the *tpnw* to rely on. The use of the term "indiscriminate effect" is a reference to the laws of armed conflict. The phrase "of a nature to cause destruction of human life on a catastrophic scale" is also an echo of the similar notion in the 1899 *Hague Convention* ("of a nature to cause superfluous injury"). The phrase "respect for the right to life" combines the content of article 6 of the *iccpr* with article 2's reference to respecting and ensuring the rights contained in the *iccpr*. The use of the word "incompatible" is a stronger statement than the [International Court of Justice's] proposition that nuclear weapons are "scarcely reconcilable" with the laws of armed conflict. The assertion that the threat or use "may amount to a crime under international law" is both tentative and ambiguous. Unlike, for example, the General Assembly resolution in 1946 that asserted bluntly that "genocide *is* a crime under international law", the critical word here is "may". Does "may" mean that some cases are crimes and some are not? Or, is it an acknowledgement that the law is not quite there yet? And, is this a reference to individual criminal responsibility or to some notion of state criminal responsibility? Note, in this respect, that it had not been possible to include a prohibition of the employment of nuclear weapons in the *Rome Statute*.

> The second sentence begins by addressing the non-proliferation of all weapons of mass destruction, not only nuclear ones, and the measures which all parties to the *iccpr* "*must take*". The footnote refers to the 1968 *Treaty on the Non-Proliferation of Nuclear Weapons* ("*npt*"), the *Comprehensive Nuclear-Test-Ban Treaty*, the *tpnw* and the biological and chemical weapons conventions. The phrase "including measures to prevent their acquisition by non-state actors" is a direct use of the term "non-state actors", which is probably a blunter version of the *tpnw*'s wording of "transfer to any recipient whatsoever". The obligation to refrain from developing, producing, testing, and the like is essentially the list of prohibitions in the *tpnw*. The obligation to "destroy existing stockpiles" goes beyond what the nuclear powers have accepted, and is a bone of contention for them. The reference to taking "adequate measures of protection against accidental use" sits a little strangely with an obligation to destroy existing stockpiles, as does the phrase "all in accordance with their international obligations". Is this a reference to customary obligations being enshrined in the *GC 36*? Or, do different parties to the *iccpr* have different obligations, depending on which weapons treaties they have ratified?

> The third sentence contains two notions. One is that parties "must also respect their international obligations to pursue in good faith negotiations in order to achieve the aim of nuclear disarmament under strict and effective international control". I take this as a reference both to the treaty obligation under art VI of the *npt* and to the corresponding customary law obligation to the same effect, which is asserted in the [ICJ's] *Nuclear Weapons Advisory Opinion*. The nuclear powers have failed dismally in fulfilling that obligation, and the effort by the Marshall Islands to enforce it in the ICJ was rejected by a

bare majority of the court on procedural grounds, based on jurisprudence that is frankly incoherent.

The other is the obligation "to afford adequate reparation to victims whose right to life has been or is being adversely affected by the testing or use of weapons of mass destruction, in accordance with principles of international responsibility". Victim assistance and environmental remediation is an important aspect of the *tpnw*, but this is not where the footnote to this sentence refers. Rather, it cites the HRC's 2015 *Concluding Observations* concerning France. The relevant section in these observations notes that some 98.3% of claims relating to damage suffered during the French tests in Moruroa and Fangataufa between 1966 and 1996 were rejected, and urges something more effective. Article 6 of the *tpnw* speaks of "assistance" to those under a state party's jurisdiction who are affected by the use or testing of nuclear weapons. This is exactly the situation in which the inhabitants of French Polynesia found themselves. The *GC 36*'s reference to "reparation" is perhaps a little stronger than the *tpnw*'s mention of "assistance", and the word "victims" would surely include people in neighbouring states or those involved militarily in testing activities.

France and the United States, both nuclear powers, objected to the Committee's formulation. The United States stated that:

19. … [T]he International Court of Justice (ICJ) acknowledged in its advisory opinion on the Legality of the Threat or Use of Nuclear Weapons that "[t]here is in neither customary nor conventional international law any comprehensive and universal prohibition of the threat or use" of nuclear weapons as such. The Committee provides no legal support for its speculation; to the contrary, and moreover, these views go far beyond the Committee's mandate under the ICCPR. The [relevant questions are] governed by IHL … . The Committee should not seek to opine on issues related to IHL with respect to the study, development, acquisition, adoption, or use of various types of weapons, including non-lethal weapons, nor on the nature of obligations of parties to treaties other than the ICCPR, such as the Treaty on the Non-Proliferation of Nuclear Weapons.

Brazil, in contrast, informed the Committee that it 'considers that weapons of mass destruction, nuclear weapons chief among them, are incompatible with the right to life. Nuclear weapons are, by their very nature, abhorrent to the principle of humanity and to the dictates of the public conscience.' It added that the ICJ had stated 'in its 1996 Advisory Opinion, that the use and threat of use of nuclear weapons are generally contrary to international law. The illegality of these weapons has been further reinforced by the adoption, on 7th of July [2017], of the Treaty on the Prohibition of Nuclear Weapons, with the support of two thirds of the United Nations membership.'

QUESTIONS

1. In paragraph 14 of GC No. 31, the Committee says the requirement in Article 2(2) to 'take the necessary steps … to adopt such legislative or other measures as may be necessary to give effect to the rights' is 'unqualified and of immediate effect'. It goes on to state that 'failure to comply with this obligation cannot be justified by reference to … economic considerations within the State'. What do you think this means in practice? The prevention of torture as a technique of policing, for example, usually requires careful training of law enforcement personnel, the creation of effective monitoring and complaints mechanisms and the existence of a vigilant and independent judiciary. How do Sweden's obligations differ from Swaziland's?

2. The then Executive Director of Human Rights Watch stated in 2004 that, in its work on prison conditions, his organization 'routinely avoids recommending large infrastructure investments' and instead 'focus[es] on improvements in the treatment of prisoners that would involve relatively

inexpensive policy changes. Similarly, our advocacy of due process in places such as Rwanda with weak and impoverished judicial systems implicitly takes account of the practical limitations facing the country leading us to be more tolerant of prosecutorial compromises such as *gacaca* courts than we would be in a richer country.'363 Is this approach consistent with GC No. 31?

3. What characteristics make the ICCPR the type of treaty which is not susceptible to denunciation? How potentially far-reaching are the implications of the Committee's reasoning, especially in paragraph 3 of GC No. 26?

4. How would you respond to the following criticisms of GC No. 36, made by Australia and Canada?

Australia

[C]onduct or measures will only engage the right to life in Article 6 where they constitute arbitrary deprivation of life or a failure to protect the right to life by law. ...

... [Some] statements do not reflect the current state of international law, for example:
• 'The right to life is a right which should not be interpreted narrowly' [para. 3]
• 'States should take adequate measures, without violating their other Covenant obligations, to prevent suicides, especially among individuals in particularly vulnerable situations' [para. 9]
• 'States parties should take appropriate measures to address the general conditions in society that may eventually give rise to direct threats to life or prevent individuals from enjoying their right to life with dignity' [para. 26]

... [N]ot all human rights violations are connected to the right to life. Rather, each provision of the Covenant should be interpreted and applied independently.

Many paragraphs of the draft General Comment relate to obligations that are the subject of a separate, specific treaty or a specific area of international law. ... [T]hese matters. For example,

[R]ights or obligations which arise under: the [ICESCR], international humanitarian law, and international environmental law [should be dealt with in the context of those treaties and those areas of international law, and not in this GC].

... Australia does not agree with the characterisation of Article 6 as 'the supreme right'. ...

Canada

Article 6 does not provide the authority for the Committee to expand the scope of measures required by the Covenant to prevent violations of the right to life. It is appropriate for the Committee to recommend effective measures and "best practices". The Committee should refrain from intimating that these measures are legally required to be adopted by States Parties pursuant to Article 6. ...

[The GC] raises issues that fall more squarely within other bodies' mandates, particularly [CAT and CESCR]. Canada urges this Committee to focus on its core mandate.

... Canada regrets that the Committee has described Article 6 as encompassing many protections already protected under the rubric of other civil, political, economic, social and cultural rights. Its approach ... is too expansive and does not provide helpful guidance to States ... . Canada urges the Committee to restrict its comments to the substantive and procedural obligations under the Covenant, rather than what is required under other branches of international law, such as refugee law.

---

363 K. Roth, 'Defending Economic, Social and Cultural Rights: Practical Issues Faced by an International Human Rights Organization', 26 *Hum. Rts. Q.* (2004) 63.

Canada disagrees with the Committee's assertion that the right to life includes a right to a life with dignity to the extent that this could be read to encompass certain socio-economic entitlements. … [T]he ICESCR imposes a different standard of implementation of States Parties' obligations, which is progressive realization … .

4. Individual Communications[364]

In 2024, 116 of the 174 states parties to the ICCPR were also parties to the First Optional Protocol. The Protocol allows for individuals to submit 'communications' (complaints). Note some of its critical provisions. The communications must be 'from individuals … who claim to be victims of a violation' by a state party to the Protocol 'of any of the rights set forth in the Covenant'. After being notified of the communication, the state party shall 'submit to the Committee written explanations or statements clarifying the matter …'. The Committee considers communications 'in the light of all written information made available to it by the individual and by the State Party concerned.' It will not consider a communication before ascertaining that the matter is 'not being examined under another procedure of international investigation or settlement'. Examination of the communications takes place at 'closed meetings'. The Committee is to forward 'its views' to the individual and state concerned. The goals of the procedure are to: (1) enable the Committee to identify steps that States should take to comply with their international legal obligations in the context of concrete individual situations; (2) to offer individual relief to victims of human rights violations; and (3) to stimulate general legal, policy and programme change.

The historical background to the adoption of the Optional Protocol highlights two aspects: (1) the deep disagreement over whether such a procedure was appropriate; and (2) the extremely vague understanding of how such a procedure should work which emerged from the hurried drafting process. A decision in principle was taken by the General Assembly in 1950 to include a petition procedure in the Covenant, but various draft proposals were unsuccessful and the draft adopted in 1954 contained no such provision.

> Twelve years passed before the [General Assembly] once again took up this issue. In 1966 the Netherlands [proposed] an optional right of communication on the part of individuals and groups; in a supplementary motion, Jamaica even sought to make this procedure obligatory … . But opposition persisted from a variety of States, particularly Socialist countries, all of whom viewed the individual communication as a violation of State sovereignty, a threat to international relations and a departure from the principle that individuals are not subjects of international law. On account of this, France introduced a compromise that sought to limit the function of the Committee to the mere acknowledgement of and confidential reply to communications by individuals and groups. The three drafts were ultimately withdrawn in favour of a proposal introduced by 10 States from all geopolitical regions with the exception of Eastern Europe. …
>
> … The text finally adopted is based on a Nigerian proposal, which was clearly oriented along the "10 State Draft" … . The time pressure under which these provisions were drafted led to a rather rudimentary description of the procedure, to systematic absurdities and to lack of clarity at points. It is thus not incorrect to assume that the Committee had been provided with quite wide discretion … to work out the details of the procedure … .[365]

The resulting provisions led to the adoption of a rather barebones procedure. Note the following characteristics:

1. The proceedings are not a continuation of, or appeal from, judicial proceedings in the state in which the dispute originated. They are fresh, distinct proceedings that may involve the same two parties to prior proceedings, or different parties.

---

[364] All of the main UN human rights treaties provide for communications procedures, but the ICCPR Committee's system is the oldest of them and has received and examined far more complaints than the others put together.

[365] Nowak, 'Historical Background to the OP', in *UN Covenant on Civil and Political Rights: ICCPR Commentary* (2nd ed. 2005), at 821.

2. Unlike some other international procedures, the complaint need not allege that the violation complained of is systemic — that is, involves a consistent pattern of violations reaching a certain level of gravity. Thus, an isolated, atypical violation can suffice to found a communication.

3. Only once has an oral hearing taken place, although the Committee has in place a set of guidelines to enable use of this option (UN Doc. CCPR/C/159/Rev.1 (2019)). The system essentially involves exchanges of written submissions, and there is no provision for independent fact-finding (such as examination of the parties or witnesses or independent experts, or on-site visits) by the Committee.

4. There are no public hearings or open debates by the Committee about how to deal with a particular communication.

5. There is no formally agreed statement of the precise legal effect of Views, nor are there any particular consequences for a State that rejects the Views out of hand.

The procedures have evolved significantly through the practice of the Committee. This sets the scene for the main challenge in evaluating the Committee's work under the Optional Protocol: how to reconcile the paucity of powers and resources given to the Committee in consequence of the determinedly modest original vision of the drafters, with the substantial subsequent evolution of the aspirations of the Committee and the overall human rights regime in relation to such procedures. The questions to focus upon in reading the following materials are: (1) the extent to which the ICCPR Committee is using rather primitive tools to achieve increasingly sophisticated goals; and (2) whether such an approach is optimal given the need to balance continuing concerns about state sovereignty with the Committee's goals of holding states to some account, ensuring remedies for violations, and developing a more sophisticated jurisprudence.

The Committee's Caseload

Between 1977 and 2021 the Committee registered 3,727 communications concerning 94 states parties. Of those, 1,737 led to the adoption of Views, including 1,289 in which violations of the Covenant were found. There were 791 declared inadmissible, 527 which were discontinued or withdrawn and 1,990 were pending. Given the speed at which it works (in 2020 it adopted views on 119 communications), this is an immense backlog. In its 2021 annual report (UN Doc. A/76/40, par-a. 35), the Committee observes that its ability to move faster is 'seriously compromised' by a lack of staff, which in turn has 'a serious impact on victims' rights.'

The Committee's Working Methods

Complaints alleging a violation of the ICCPR by a state party to the Optional Protocol are considered first by the Committee's Special Rapporteur on new communications and interim measures, who decides whether to register them and send them on to states for a response, and where appropriate to request interim measures (see below). The Working Group on Communications can itself declare some communications to be inadmissible. While the Protocol envisages separate admissibility and merits stages in the examination of a communication, the two are now generally considered together. The bulk of the Committee's work on any particular communication is carried out by the Special Rapporteur and the Working Group, and the Committee as a whole generally only examines a communication once in light of the Working Group's recommendations.

The Committee's substantive analysis is often terse and sometimes almost peremptory. Ludovic Hennebel has noted that its views 'are occasionally rather poor on the fundamentals' and follow 'a syllogistic formal reasoning' which 'is sometimes difficult to identify and apprehend'.[366] The growing frequency of dissenting views that expose the vulnerabilities of the majority, and of concurrences that either provide additional argumentation to supplement the majority view or provide a different justification, enriches the Committee's overall output. As Neuman notes:

> Separate opinions bring internal debates into the open, which may prompt wider
> discussion, and they record arguments that may prove influential when a related issue

---

[366] Hennebel, above, 365.

arises in a later case. The individualized style of many separate opinions has potential to persuade a variety of audiences that the concise institutional style of HRC majority opinions may lack.[367]

Findings of Fact

One of the biggest challenges for the Committee is its inability to undertake independent fact-finding when confronted with contradictory evidence offered by a complainant and a state party, or when a state essentially refuses to cooperate. The Committee very often defers to the state when issues relating to a fair trial or the situation in a destination country in deportation proceedings are raised. As it noted in response to a claim that an individual on death row in Guyana had been tortured:

> 5.2 The Committee maintains its position that it is generally not in the position to evaluate facts and evidence presented before a domestic court. In the current case, however, the Committee takes the view that the instructions to the jury raise an issue under article 14 of the Covenant, as the defendant had managed to present prima facie evidence of being mistreated, and the Court did not alert the jury that the prosecution must prove that the confession was made without duress. This error constituted a violation of Mr. Deolall's right to a fair trial ... .[368]

The Committee has long been criticized for its approach to evidentiary matters:

> The HRC appears to rely frequently on circumstantial evidence, including evidence of a consistent pattern of conduct ... . The use of inference can be highly prejudicial to a state party as it is a very small shift in logic to conclude from the existence of a general pattern that this person, the author, suffered from the alleged violation. It therefore becomes particularly important that the HRC identify the circumstantial evidence, such as patterns of conduct, that it is using to raise an inference or a rebuttable presumption.

The same author advocates the use of oral proceedings and rejects the argument that the Committee lacks the competence to initiate such an approach. She also calls for increased fact-finding:

> This would not necessarily entail embarking on on-site missions or extensive research in every case. In some cases, the HRC could simply charge its Secretariat with using material obtained through other treaty or U.N. bodies that would confirm the author's allegations. In addition, there are many NGOs that could be invited to provide evidence in support of allegations, such as corroborative testimony or relevant statistics.
>
> The HRC is in no way barred from sending missions to a state party where that state party has consented ... .369

In 2020, the Committee amended its Rules of Procedure to provide that 'the Committee or its special rapporteur may accept information and documentation submitted by third parties which may be relevant for the proper determination of the case.' (UN Doc. CCPR/C/3/Rev.12 (2021), Rule 96(1)). This has opened up important new sources of information and legal analysis, although the Committee's very out of date listing of registered cases makes it difficult for outside groups to learn of the opportunity in a particular case. Under Rule 111 petitioners of the State party can make public their submissions, unless otherwise requested by the Committee.

Case Studies

The Views adopted by the Committee feature prominently in various chapters of this book. Most of the Views that it generates could be considered routine and unremarkable in terms of the jurisprudence and the outcome. Compliance will depend on many different factors,[370] and is generally difficult to assess, especially if the only

---

[367] Neuman, above, 39.
[368] *Deolall v. Guyana*, Communication No. 912/2000, UN Doc. CCPR/C/82/D/912/2000 (28 January 2005).
[369] K. A. Young, *The Law and Process of the U.N. Human Rights Committee* (2002), at 299–300.
[370] A. Ullmann and A. von Staden, 'A Room Full of 'Views': Introducing a New Dataset to Explore Compliance with the Decisions of the UN Human Rights Treaty Bodies' Individual Complaints Procedures', 68 *J. Confl. Resolut.* (2024) 534.

criterion is an explicit reversal of government policy. But there are many other ways in which this process can generate more positive human rights outcomes. The two principal case studies below, from Italy and the Netherlands, are not routine, partly because of the challenging nature of the issues addressed, and partly because of the diversity of opinions reflected in the Committee's Views. Before examining those cases, it is instructive to consider how the communications procedure has functioned in the context of a particular country.

AUSTRALIA: A CASE STUDY

Australia ratified the Optional Protocol in 1991 and has since been engaged extensively with this procedure. The first case lodged and one of the best known was *Toonen v. Australia* (UN Doc. CCPR/C/50/D/488/1992, Views adopted 31 March 1994).

In 1867, Tasmania was the last Australian state to carry out the death penalty for sodomy, and it continued to prosecute the offence vigorously over the next century. The author of this communication was a leading member of the Tasmanian Gay Law Reform Group. He challenged two provisions of the Tasmanian Criminal Code which criminalized 'various forms of sexual conduct between men, including all forms of sexual contacts between consenting adult homosexual men in private'. The Tasmanian police had not charged anyone with violations of these statutes, such as 'intercourse against nature', but there remained a threat of enforcement. Moreover, the author alleged that the criminalization of homosexuality had nourished prejudice and 'created the conditions for discrimination in employment, constant stigmatization, vilification, threats of physical violence and the violation of basic democratic rights.'

...

6.5 The state party does not accept the argument of the Tasmanian authorities that the retention of the challenged provisions is partly motivated by a concern to protect Tasmania from the spread of HIV/AIDS, and that the laws are justified on public health and moral grounds. This assessment in fact goes against the Australian Government's National HIV/AIDS Strategy, which emphasizes that laws criminalizing homosexual activity obstruct public health programmes promoting safer sex. ...

6.6 Nonetheless, the State party cautions that the formulation of article 17 allows for *some* infringement of the right to privacy if there are reasonable grounds, and that domestic social mores may be relevant to the reasonableness of an interference with privacy. The State party observes that while laws penalizing homosexual activity existed in the past in other Australian states, they have since been repealed with the exception of Tasmania. ... The Federal Government has declared sexual preference to be a ground of discrimination that may be invoked under ILO Convention No. 111 (Discrimination in Employment or Occupation Convention) ... .

6.7 ... [T]he State party contends that there is now a general Australian acceptance that no individual should be disadvantaged on the basis of his or her sexual orientation. Given the legal and social situation in all of Australia except Tasmania, the State party acknowledges that a complete prohibition on sexual activity between men is unnecessary to sustain the moral fabric of Australian society. On balance, the State party 'does not seek to claim that the challenged laws are based on reasonable and objective criteria'.

...

Examination of the merits:

...

8.2 Inasmuch as article 17 is concerned, it is undisputed that adult consensual sexual activity in private is covered by the concept of 'privacy', and that Mr. Toonen is actually and currently affected by the continued existence of the Tasmanian laws.

...

8.3 The prohibition against private homosexual behaviour is provided for by law ... . As to whether it may be deemed arbitrary, the Committee ... interprets the requirement of reasonableness to imply that any interference with privacy must be proportional to the end sought and be necessary in the circumstances of any given case.

...

8.5 ... [T]he Committee notes that the criminalization of homosexual practices cannot be considered a reasonable means or proportionate measure to achieve the aim of preventing the spread of AIDS/HIV ... .

8.6 The Committee cannot accept either that for the purposes of article 17 of the Covenant, moral issues are exclusively a matter of domestic concern, as this would open the door to withdrawing from the Committee's scrutiny a potentially large number of statutes interfering with privacy. It further notes that with the exception of Tasmania, all laws criminalizing homosexuality have been repealed throughout Australia and that, even in Tasmania, ... there is no consensus ... . Considering further that these provisions are not currently enforced, which implies that they are not deemed essential to the protection of morals in Tasmania, the Committee concludes that the provisions do not meet the 'reasonableness' test in the circumstances of the case, and that they arbitrarily interfere with Mr. Toonen's right under article 17, paragraph 1.

8.7 The State party has sought the Committee's guidance as to whether sexual orientation may be considered an 'other status' for the purposes of article 26. The same issue could arise under article 2, paragraph 1, of the Covenant. The Committee confines itself to noting, however, that in its view the reference to 'sex' in articles 2, paragraph 1, and 26 is to be taken as including sexual orientation.

9. The [Committee] is of the view that the facts before it reveal a violation of articles [17(1) and 2(1)].

10. ... In the opinion of the Committee, an effective remedy would be the repeal of Sections 122 (a), (c) and 123 of the Tasmanian Criminal Code.

...

Malcolm Langford and Cosette Creamer, in 'The Toonen Decision: Domestic and International Impact', in Siri Gloppen and Malcolm Langford (eds.), *International Sexual and Reproductive Rights Lawfare* (2024) 000 conclude that the case 'had a partly transformative effect on LGBT politics in Australia, helped spark increased reporting by states on the theme, was cited by judges in some key decisions around the world and legitimized the advocacy of LGBT rights by international agencies.'

Compare that assessment with the following comment by Alfred de Zayas, in 'Review of W.A. Schabas, Nowak's CCPR Commentary, 3rd rev. ed.', 67 *Neths. Int'l L. Rev.* (2020) 553:

... [A]t the time of the adoption of the Covenant in 1966 and its entry into force in 1976, marriage meant only and exclusively the union of a man and a woman and was not understood as encompassing a civil union between same-sex couples. ... [R]edefining terms to meet subsequent aspirations does not constitute good faith interpretation under [the Vienna Convention on the Law of Treaties (VCLT)]. [The author then notes arguments by some states and NGOs of the incompatibility of LGBT rights with States' obligation] to protect the family as 'the natural and fundamental group unit of society' ... and 'to found a family' [Article 23 of the ICCPR] ..., by which it was meant the husband, the wife and the children that may emanate from this union. ... The credibility of the Committee—and the predictability of international law in general—depends on its rigorous application of the Covenant and its 'judicial restraint'. ...

Besides opening a 'Pandora's box', the quasi-judicial reinterpretation of Article 23 would entail changing the substantive content of a Covenant provision without the agreement of the States parties. Moreover, an obvious conflict would arise with the application of Article 18 of the Covenant which guarantees the 'freedom to have or to adopt a religion' and the prohibition on States to interfere with these beliefs, which for billions of human beings are sacred and very much part of their identities. Bearing in mind that same-sex relations are considered wrong or even 'sinful' in many societies, a universal treaty like the ICCPR cannot be instrumentalized to impose 'Western' approaches on the rest of humanity.

In June 2023, there were 26 applications from Australia awaiting the Committee's consideration. Between 2000 and 2022, the Committee adopted Views on some 50 communications from Australia. They addressed a range of issues, including climate change-related claims (see *Daniel Billy et al. v. Australia* (2022), in Ch. 15B, below). Immigration and asylum claims were especially prominent. In 2021-22, for example, six cases were decided. One concerned a Chinese national, deported back to China. Her claim that much of her personal data had been inadvertently published on a government website was upheld, leading to a finding that Article 17 had been violated *(J.S. v. Australia*, UN Doc. CCPR/C/135/2804/2016 (2022)). In *A.K. et al. v. Australia* (UN Doc. CCPR/C/132/D/2365/2014 (2022)), the Committee held that placing several unaccompanied minor asylum-seekers from Afghanistan in immigration detention was arbitrary and violated Articles 9(1) and 24 of the Covenant. In *Thileepan Gnaneswaran v. Australia* (UN Doc. CCPR/C/133/D/3212/2018 (2022)), it held that deporting a husband/father to Sri Lanka had taken place without consideration of important changes in his circumstances and violated Article 17 of the Covenant. In *O.H.D., O.A.D, and B.O.M. v. Australia* (UN Doc. CCPR/C/134/D/3023/2017 (2022)) it found that sending three Nigerian nationals back to Nigeria did not violate the right to non-refoulement. And in *Graham Cayzer v. Australia* (UN Doc. CCPR/C/135/D/2981/2017 (2022)) it held that the deportation of a man who had lived in Australia since 1965 to the United Kingdom following his conviction of a sex crime did not violate the Covenant.

Finally, two important cases involving indigenous peoples were *A.S. v. Australia* (UN Doc. CCPR/C/132/D/2900/2016 (2021)), in which the Committee found that the detention and treatment of an indigenous Australian within the criminal justice of the Northern Territory violated five different provisions of the Covenant; and *Roy v. Australia* (UN Doc. CCPR/C/137/D/3585/2019 (2023)) involving a violation of the right to a fair hearing (Article 14(1)) in relation to a contested land rights claim. It reasoned that because 'human rights treaties are living instruments that must be interpreted and applied taking into account contemporary circumstances, States are bound to adopt measures to guarantee and give legal certainty to indigenous peoples' rights in relation to ownership of their traditional territories, through the establishment of such mechanisms and procedures for delimitation, demarcation, and titling in accordance with their customary law, values and customs.'

What is instructive about these examples is that they address issues in relation to which the Australian justice system has long been found wanting, and in areas where political actors have generally resisted complying with international human rights standards. In addition, domestic remedies are often inadequate, either because there is no federal Bill of Rights, or because Parliament has legislated to minimize judicial review.[371] While government Ministers have, on occasion, been dismissive of the relevance of the Committee's Views, the government generally provides a detailed public response on the website of the Attorney-General's Department. When it disagrees, it might challenge the Committee's interpretation of the law or the Covenant, accuse it of misconceiving or misconstruing the facts, or simply state its disagreement. On occasion, however, it is clear that the Committee's Views have prevailed. Thus in 2017, it advised the Committee that legislation had been adopted to permit same sex couples to marry and divorce in Australia. This was in response to the finding of a violation in that regard in *C. v. Australia* (UN Doc. CCPR/C/119/D/2216/2012 (2017)).

---

[371] 'Australia has a patchwork legal framework of human rights protection. The rights that are protected are located in scattered pieces of legislation, the Constitution and the common law. It is incomplete and piecemeal.' Australian Human Rights Commission, *Free and Equal: A Human Rights Act for Australia* (2022) 11. In support of that Commission's call for the adoption of an Australian Human Rights Act, see Parliamentary Joint Committee on Human Rights, *Inquiry into Australia's Human Rights Framework* (May 2024).

A.S., D.I., O.I. AND G.D. V. ITALY
UN DOC. CCPR/C/130/D/3042/2017 (2021), VIEWS ADOPTED 4 NOVEMBER 2020

[*Note*: This communication was submitted on 19 May 2017, and decided on 4 November 2020. It was submitted at the same time as a companion case, *A.S. et al v. Malta* (Communication No. 3043/2017, UN Doc. CCPR/C/128/D/3043/2017 (27 January 2021)). The facts were essentially the same, but the Committee found the complaint against Malta to be inadmissible because of the applicants' failure to have exhausted domestic remedies.]

1.1 The authors of the communication are A.S. a national of Palestine, born in 1958, and D.I., O.I. and G.D., nationals of the Syrian Arab Republic, born in 1983, 1988 and 1977, respectively. They are submitting the communication on their own behalf and on behalf of 13 of their relatives who, on 11 October 2013, were on board a vessel that shipwrecked in the Mediterranean Sea, 113 km south of Lampedusa, Italy and 218 km from Malta, causing the estimated death of more than 200 people. …

1.2 The authors allege that the State party authorities failed to take appropriate measures to render assistance to their relatives, who were in distress at sea, in violation of their relatives' rights under article 6 of the Covenant. …

The facts as presented by the authors

2.1 The authors … relatives attempted to escape from the serious threats to their lives that they and their children were facing in Syria. On 10 October 2013, [they] arrived in Libya and were transported … to a fishing vessel anchored outside the port of Zuwarah, which set out to sea the following day at around 1.00 a.m. The vessel was reported to have carried over 400 people. A few hours after the vessel had set off, it was shot at by a boat flying a Berber flag. Large quantities of water were entering the vessel and one person on the vessel, M.J., called the Italian number for emergencies at sea around 11.00 a.m., explaining that the vessel was going to sink and also informing the emergency operator that there were children on board the vessel. M.J. also forwarded the geographical coordinates of the vessel … .

2.2 The first call was followed by several others [12.26 p.m., 12.39 p.m. and 12.56 p.m. In a call at 1.17 p.m.] the operator explained that their vessel was in the Maltese search and rescue zone and gave them the phone number of the Rescue Coordination Centre of Malta (RCC Malta).

2.3 Several calls were made from the vessel to the Armed Forces of Malta (AFM Malta) between 1 p.m. and 3 p.m., as well as calls made to the MRCC at 2.22 p.m. and 3.37 p.m.. The persons on board the vessel were finally told that their vessel had been identified and that rescue units would arrive within 45 minutes. [In a subsequent] press statement … AFM Malta stated that the vessel was not detected until 4.00 p.m., and that the first rescue boat, an AFM patrol boat, did not reach the site of the shipwreck until 5.50 p.m., with an Italian navy ship ITS Libra reaching the location at around 6 p.m. The authors claim that AFM Malta did not contact MRCC Rome for assistance until after the vessel had capsized. …
…

State party's observations on admissibility and the merits
…
4.5 The State party submits that as the alleged violation of the duty to protect the lives of the alleged victims took place outside Italian territorial waters and outside its SAR area, the facts under review do not fall within its jurisdiction under article 2 of the Covenant and article 1 of the Optional Protocol. … [In Italy's view] it cannot be argued that Italy would have *de facto* responsibility over the area concerned merely due to the fact that Italian authorities organize rescue interventions, in an autonomous and non-obligatory manner, in the Maltese SAR area. The State party argues that by establishing its own SAR area, Malta has assumed the power and responsibility to fulfil its own obligations in its own area and it submits that the vessel carrying the migrants was not under the jurisdiction, understood as power and control, of Italy. The State party further notes that the Maltese authorities had made a formal undertaking of coordinating the rescue operation. Malta had also sent, although informed by MRCC Rome that there was an Italian Navy ship in the area, rescue assets to intercept

the vessel in distress. The State party argues that Malta had therefore formalized its intention to exercise its jurisdiction of the rescue operation and had in fact exercised it. ...

...

Issues and proceedings before the Committee

Consideration of admissibility

...

7.3 The Committee notes the State party's submission that the communication is inadmissible under article 1 of the Optional Protocol for lack of jurisdiction as the events occurred outside the territorial waters of the State party. It notes the authors' submission that the complaint falls under the State party's jurisdiction as State party authorities were exercising *de facto* control over the Maltese search and rescue area; were in continuous contact with the vessel in distress; and had activated rescue procedures, thus exercising control over the persons in distress.

7.4 The committee ... has competency to receive and consider communications from individuals subject to the jurisdiction of States parties. [It recalls its general comments No. 31 (2004) and No. 15 (1986)]. ...

7.5 The Committee further recalls paragraph 63 of its general comment No. 36 (2019) on the right to life, in which it observed that: "In light of article 2, paragraph 1, of the Covenant, a State party has an obligation to respect and to ensure the rights under article 6 of all persons who are within its territory and all persons subject to its jurisdiction, that is, all persons over whose enjoyment of the right to life it exercises power or effective control. This includes persons located outside any territory effectively controlled by the State, whose right to life is nonetheless impacted by its military or other activities in a direct and reasonably foreseeable manner. States parties must respect and protect the lives of individuals located in places that are under their effective control, such as occupied territories, and in territories over which they have assumed an international obligation to apply the Covenant. States parties are also required to respect and protect the lives of all individuals located on marine vessels and aircraft registered by them or flying their flag, and of those individuals who find themselves in a situation of distress at sea, in accordance with their international obligations on rescue at sea."

...

7.6 The Committee further notes that according to article **98** of the 1982 United Nations Convention on the Law of the Sea, each State shall require the master of a ship flying its flag "to proceed with all possible speed to the rescue of persons in distress, if informed of their need of assistance, in so far as such action may reasonably be expected of him" ... . In addition, it notes that specific arrangements concerning the provision and coordination of search and rescue services are found in the 1979 International Convention on Maritime Search and Rescue and in the Regulations adopted pursuant to the 1974 International Convention for the Safety of Life at Sea (SOLAS), including on coordination of search and rescue operations of ships from different States by the regional coordination center, and the duty of states to cooperate in search and rescue activities upon receiving information on situations of distress at sea.

7.7 In the present case, the Committee notes that it is undisputed between the parties that the shipwreck occurred outside the State party's territory, and that none of the alleged violations occurred when the authors' relatives were on board a vessel hoisting an Italian flag. The question before the Committee is therefore whether the alleged victims could be considered to have been within the power or effective control of the State party, even though the incident took place outside its territory. ...

7.8 The Committee considers that in the particular circumstances of the case, a special relationship of dependency had been established between the individuals on the vessel in distress and Italy. This relationship comprised of factual elements – in particular, the initial contact made by the vessel in distress with the MRCC, the close proximity of ITS Libra to the vessel in distress and the ongoing involvement of the MRCC in the rescue operation and – as well as relevant legal obligations incurred by Italy under the international law of the sea, including a duty to respond in a reasonable manner to calls of distress pursuant to SOLAS Regulations and a duty to appropriately cooperate with other states undertaking rescue operations pursuant to the International Convention on Maritime Search and Rescue. As a result, the Committee considers that the individuals on the vessel in distress were directly affected by the decisions taken by the Italian authorities in a manner that was reasonably foreseeable in light of the relevant legal obligations of Italy, and that they were thus subject to Italy's jurisdiction for the purposes of the Covenant … . … Consequently, the Committee finds that it is not precluded by article 1 of the Optional Protocol from considering the present communication.

…

Consideration of the merits

8.3. The Committee notes that the right to life includes an obligation for States parties to adopt any appropriate laws or other measures in order to protect life from all reasonably foreseeable threats. It also notes that such due diligence require taking reasonable, positive measures that do not impose disproportionate burdens on States parties in response to reasonably foreseeable threats to life. [*Ed.: omitted footnotes refer to General Comment No. 36, paras. 18 and 21.*]

8.4 In the present case, the authors maintain that the Italian authorities have failed to respond promptly to the initial distress call, and have greatly delayed the dispatch of ITS Libra towards the vessel in distress. They further claim that the naval ship was ordered to move further away from the vessel in distress as, had it been identified by Maltese patrol boats, the latter would have avoided taking charge of the rescue operation. …

8.5 The Committee notes that the principal responsibility for the rescue operation lies with Malta, since the capsizing occurred in its search and rescue area, and since it undertook in writing responsibility for the search and rescue operation. The Committee however considers that the State party has not provided a clear explanation for what appears to be a failure to promptly respond to the distress call, prior to the assumption of responsibility for the search and rescue operation by the Maltese authorities. It also notes that the State party has not provided any information about measures taken by State party authorities to ascertain that the RCC Malta was informed of the exact location of the vessel in distress and that it was effectively responding to the incident, despite the information about the deteriorating situation and the need for Italian assistance. In addition, the State party failed to explain the delay in dispatching the ITS Libra, which was located only one hour away from the vessel in distress, towards it, even after being formally requested to do so by RCC Malta. Finally, the Committee notes that the State party has not clearly explained or refuted the authors' claim that intercepted phone calls indicate that the ITS Libra was ordered to sail away from the vessel in distress. In light of these facts, the Committee considers that Italy has failed to show that it has met its due diligence obligations under article 6 (1) of the Covenant.

…

9. The [Committee] … is of the view that the facts before it disclose a violation of article 6, read alone and in conjunction with article 2 (3).

10. Pursuant to article 2 (3) (a) of the Covenant, the State party is under an obligation to provide the author with an effective remedy. This requires it to make full reparation to individuals whose Covenant's rights have been violated, bearing in mind the potential responsibility of other States for the same incident. Accordingly, the State party is obligated, inter alia, to proceed with an independent and effective investigation in a prompt manner and, if found necessary, to prosecute and try those who are responsible for the death and disappearance of the authors' relatives. The State party is also under an obligation to take all steps necessary to prevent similar violations from occurring in the future.

…

ANNEX: 1: INDIVIDUAL OPINION OF YUVAL SHANY, CHRISTOF HEYNS AND PHOTINI PAZARTZIS (DISSENTING)

1. We do not agree with the majority's decision … .

2. Paragraph 7.8 of the Views explains that a "a special relationship of dependency" had been established between the victims found on the vessel in distress and Italy … . … We are of the opinion that the majority Views fails to distinguish between situations in which states have the *potential* to place under their effective control individuals who are found outside their territory or areas already subject to their effective control, and

situations involving the *actual* placement of individuals under effective state control. Only the latter situations establish jurisdiction for the purposes of the Covenant and the Optional Protocol.

...

4. Although initial contact was made between the vessel in distress and the MRCC in Rome, this fact alone ... is not sufficient to conclude that the State actually exercised jurisdiction over the individuals on board the vessel from that moment onwards or was legally obliged to do so. In particular, it is significant that Italy did not actually coordinate the search and rescue operation, but rather referred the distress call to the competent authorities in Malta, and that the latter confirmed in writing Malta's coordinating role ... . [T]he vessel in distress did not become under the effective control of an Italian Navy party before 6:30 pm on the day of the sinking (more than an hour after it had capsized), at which time ITS Libra arrived at the scene and became the on-site coordinator of the rescue operation.

5. While there may have been critical failures in the response of the MRCC in Rome and the Italian Navy to the distress calls and to the Maltese requests for assistance that contributed to the tragic loss of life of large numbers of victims, such failures do not establish in and of themselves effective control by Italy over the individuals on the vessels in distress, regardless of whether or not such failures entail criminal responsibility under Italian law or a violation of Italy's law of the sea obligations vis-a-vis Malta and other states, This is especially the case in circumstances where the said individuals are located in an area for which another state has assumed legal responsibility – and by implication, jurisdiction - under the law of the sea for search and rescue operations. Since Malta, and not Italy, was responsible *de jure* or *de facto* for the overall conduct of the operation, we do not consider it appropriate to hold Italy accountable under the Covenant for failing to deploy more quickly Italian vessels which would enable it to assume earlier *de facto* responsibility over the search and rescue operation.

6. We further consider that the approach taken by the majority of collapsing the ability to engage in a maritime operation in search and rescue areas for which another state is internationally responsible with the notion of jurisdiction over the individuals on vessels in distress might disrupt the legal order which the SOLAS and SAR Conventions attempted to introduce, with a view to minimizing the "tragedy of the global commons", generated by the lack of a clear division of labor between coastal states over search and rescue operations. ...

7. As a result, ... the Committee should not have concluded that that the victims on board of the capsized vessel fell before, or at the time of capsizing, under the jurisdiction of Italy for the purposes of the Covenant .... .

ANNEX: 2: INDIVIDUAL OPINION OF ANDREAS ZIMMERMANN (DISSENTING)

1. ... [T]he mere fact that a person did find him- or herself in a SAR zone administered by a given State party of the Covenant does not bring that person within the jurisdiction of such State party for purposes of Art. 2 (1) ... .

2. [I]taly, by refusing to have its naval ship ITS Libra undertake a rescue operation to save the lives of the persons in distress at sea, was violating its obligations under applicable rules of the law of the sea. Yet, this was neither the question that was before the Committee nor what the Committee had to decide ... .

...

4. Finally, the Committee attempts to limit its holding when stating "that *in the particular circumstances of the case*, a special relationship of dependency had been established between the individuals on the vessel in distress and Italy" which then triggered, in the majority's view, the applicability of the Covenant. It is however safe to assume that the outcome of both cases, i.e. the Maltese and the Italian case, when read together, will be perceived as providing for a general applicability of the Covenant as far as persons are concerned that find themselves in distress at sea either in the SAR zone of a State party or close to a ship flying the flag of a State party. This might ... eventually have the very unfortunate effect of States parties of the Covenant no longer be willing to undertake such obligations, respectively might even try to avoid coming close to boats in distress so as to avoid any impressions of a 'special relationship of dependency' having been created.

ANNEX: INDIVIDUAL OPINION OF DAVID MOORE (DISSENTING)

...

4. The Committee's decision to find jurisdiction outside [Italy's SAR] region in this tragic case reflects noble intent, particularly given Italy's questionable actions. Yet I fear the decision adds a layer of uncertainty, and even apprehension, regarding responsibility on the high seas that may hinder, rather than sharpen, the response to future emergencies. I would find the communication inadmissible.

…

ANNEX: 5: INDIVIDUAL OPINION OF JOSÉ SANTOS-PAIS (CONCURRING)

1. I agree with the decision … .

2. … [T]he main question is whether victims were within the power or effective control of Italy, even though the incident took place outside its territory (para 7.7). Also, whether, under relevant international instruments, Italy failed to provide assistance to rescue of persons in distress at sea.

…

10. [N]ot only did Italian naval authorities refuse to act when they were still the First RCC responsible for coordinating the case and issued the first navigational warning, they consistently omitted valuable information to Maltese authorities and kept deliberately Libra, the closest ship, away from intervening in rescue operations until after the shipwreck.

11. I therefore consider individuals on the vessel in distress were under Italy's jurisdiction for the purposes of the Covenant (paras 7.5-7.8). Furthermore, there was a failure by Italian authorities to explain convincingly motives for not providing timely assistance under such pressing circumstances, thus affecting lives of so many people (para 8.5).

…

ANNEX: 7: INDIVIDUAL OPINION OF HÉLÈNE TIGROUDJA (CONCURRING)

1. I fully support the solution reached by the majority. The views are a first contribution of this Committee aiming at addressing some "Maritime Legal Black Holes." They may provide some substance to a new "right to be rescued at sea". … I am not fully convinced by the way the majority solved the question [of the *extraterritorial jurisdiction* exercised by Italy] (para. 7.8). There is a mix up between substantive obligations and the existence of a jurisdictional link with Italy. More importantly, the grounds for establishing this jurisdictional link are unclear … .

D. Z. V. THE NETHERLANDS
UN DOC. CCPR/C/130/D/2918/2016 (2021), VIEWS ADOPTED ON 19 OCTOBER 2020

1. The author of the communication is D.Z., born on 18 February 2010 without a recognized nationality. He claims that, by his nationality being registered by authorities of the State party as "unknown" since his birth, and by leaving him with no prospect of acquiring a nationality, the State party has violated his rights under article 24, read alone and in conjunction with article 2 (2) and (3), of the Covenant. …

Facts as submitted by the author

2.1 The author's mother was born in China in 1989, but her birth was not registered in the civil records in that country. … After her brother was born a few years later, her parents abandoned her.

2.2 As the author's mother was not registered in the civil registry in China she was unable to obtain proof of Chinese citizenship. She holds no documentation proving her identity. In 2004, at the age of 15, she was trafficked to the Netherlands but was able to escape upon her arrival at Schiphol airport in Amsterdam. [An asylum application was rejected.] In 2006, she was forced into prostitution. She eventually managed to escape and on 20 March 2008 she reported to the Netherlands police that she was a victim of human trafficking. [After 14 months] … the investigation was closed as the police could not identify or locate her traffickers. [Her] temporary residence permit … was revoked … and she is currently classified as an "illegal alien", as is the author. The author's father is not in contact with him or with his mother and has not recognized paternity.

2.3 The author was born on 18 February 2010 in Utrecht and was registered in the Municipal Personal Records Database with the annotation "unknown nationality", as his mother had provided no proof of his nationality.
...

2.4 For this reason, and despite years of efforts, the author's mother has been unable to change the author's nationality entry in the civil registry to "stateless" so that he can enjoy the international protections afforded to stateless children, including the right to acquire the nationality of the State in which he was born – the Netherlands. It is impossible to correct the author's registration, due to the strict proof required under domestic rules applicable to the registration process, and the lack of an appropriate statelessness status determination procedure. ... As at September 2016, the total number of "unknown" nationality entries [in the Netherlands] was 74,055, which included 13,169 children under 10 years of age.

2.5 ... On 17 September 2012, the [Utrecht] municipality rejected [a request for civil registration], on the ground that there was no proof that the author lacked a nationality. [Since it had not been] established, with official legal or State-issued documents, that the author was stateless, [the presumption was that he was a Chinese national.]

2.6 [Appeals subsequently reached] ... the Council of State, the highest appeal court in the country, [which] ruled that the municipality was correct when it decided that the author had not adequately demonstrated that he was stateless. The Council of State ... found that it was not up to the authorities to conduct inquiries and determine statelessness status. The Council of State did, however, acknowledge that the lack of a status determination procedure meant that individuals entitled to protection, including children, were falling through a gap in legislation. However, the Council of State concluded that it was for the legislature to provide a remedy
.... .

2.7 The author notes that without being registered as stateless he cannot acquire Dutch nationality. Furthermore, even if he were to be successful in changing his registration from "unknown nationality" to stateless, he would still have no clear means of acquiring Dutch nationality, as the State party requires that children born stateless in the country hold a lawful residence permit for at least three years before they are eligible to apply for Dutch nationality. He notes that this position contravenes the obligations of the Netherlands as a party to the 1961 Convention on the Reduction of Statelessness, under which States may only impose habitual residence requirements. He notes that the State party has acknowledged that its law is not in line with the 1961 Convention.

2.8 ... [Further appeals all led to the same outcome.]

2.9 The author lives with his mother in a restricted freedom centre for failed asylum seekers with young children. He has nearly no contact with Dutch society and lives under permanent threat of deportation. His mother is not eligible for any social benefits besides a small weekly allowance. ... He notes that this system has been severely criticized by children's rights groups as especially damaging and traumatic for children. Residents cannot leave the municipal area to which they are assigned, and have strict daily reporting requirements on all days except Sundays, enforced by threat of criminal detention. Children experience constant fear, health problems, family tensions and social exclusion, due to living under such restrictions in the centres.
...

Issues and proceedings before the Committee
...

Consideration of the merits
...

8.2 The Committee recalls that, under article 24, every child has a right to special measures of protection because of her or his status as a minor. ... The Committee recalls its general comment No. 17 (1989), in which it ... notes that "States are required to adopt every appropriate measure, both internally and in cooperation with other States, to ensure that every child has a nationality when he is born. In this connection, no discrimination with regard to the acquisition of nationality should be admissible under internal law as between legitimate children and children born out of wedlock or of stateless parents or based on the nationality status of one or both of the parents".

8.3 The Committee notes that in the UNHCR Guidelines on Statelessness No. 4 [reflecting the 1961 Convention on the Reduction of Statelessness] – a Convention to which the Netherlands is a party – it is stated that "a contracting State must accept that a person is not a national of a particular State if the authorities of that State refuse to recognize that person as a national. ...". [The Guidelines also state that] the burden of proof must be shared between the claimant and the authorities of the contracting State to obtain evidence and to establish the facts as to whether an individual would otherwise be stateless. [Under the Guidelines, the determination period should not exceed five years.]

...

8.5 [T]he Human Rights Committee notes that the author's mother has contacted Chinese authorities several times to confirm whether they consider the author a Chinese national, without success. ... It also notes that in their decisions the domestic authorities [in the Netherlands] did not outline any further steps that the author's mother could have taken to obtain official documents from Chinese authorities ... [and] the domestic authorities made no inquiries of their own in order to attempt to confirm the author's nationality status, or lack thereof. It notes that the Council of State, in its decision of 21 May 2014, acknowledged that the lack of a status determination procedure in the State party meant that individuals entitled to protection, including children, were falling through a gap in legislation. The Committee notes the State party's declaration that having examined the author's complaint, it has concluded and acknowledged that the author is currently unable to effectively enjoy his right as a minor to acquire a nationality. Accordingly, the Committee concludes that the facts before it disclose a violation of the author's rights under article 24 (3) of the Covenant. The Committee also considers that the failure to provide the author with an effective remedy amounts to a violation of the author's rights under article 24 (3) read in conjunction with article 2 (3) of the Covenant.

...

10. In accordance with article 2 (3) (a) of the Covenant, the State party is under an obligation to provide the author with an effective remedy. This requires it to make full reparation to individuals whose Covenant rights have been violated. Accordingly, the State party is obligated, inter alia, to provide the author with adequate compensation. The State party is also required to review its decision on the author's application to be registered as stateless in the civil registry of the State party, as well as its decision on the author's application to be recognized as a Dutch citizen, taking into account the Committee's findings in the present Views; the State party is also requested to review the author's living circumstances and residence permit, taking into account the principle of the best interests of the child and the Committee's findings in the present Views. Additionally, the State party is under an obligation to take all steps necessary to avoid similar violations in the future ... .

...

INDIVIDUAL OPINION OF COMMITTEE MEMBER YADH BEN ACHOUR (CONCURRING)

1. I fully agree with the Committee's finding of a violation ... under article 24 (3) of the Covenant.

2. [The member contests the Committee's decision not to also find a violation of articles 2 (2).]

3. ... I disagree with the two general rules laid down by the Committee in [its caselaw.]. The first rule states that the provisions of article 2 of the Covenant set forth a general obligation for States parties and cannot give rise, when invoked separately, to a claim in a communication under the Optional Protocol. The second rule states that article 2 cannot be invoked in conjunction with other articles of the Covenant, unless it can be proven that the State party's failure to observe its obligations under article 2 is the proximate cause of a distinct violation of the Covenant directly affecting the victim.

4. The first rule ... is based on the notion that the provisions of article 2 of the Covenant are of a secondary or "ancillary" nature and do not have a substantive impact on the individual rights that are enshrined in the Covenant. Since these rights are not set out until part III of the Covenant, the preamble and articles 1 to 5 cannot be directly invoked in a communication submitted under the Optional Protocol ... . This interpretation ... seems questionable for a number of reasons, particularly because it contradicts the rules of interpretation established in article 31 of the Vienna Convention on the Law of Treaties and because it is hard to understand

why such an obligation may be invoked ... in the Committee's concluding observations ... but ... not ... in a communication submitted under the Optional Protocol. ...

...

6. ... [The second] rule is perfectly applicable in precisely the present case. The lack of diligence on the part of the legislature of the Netherlands ... was the direct and sole cause of the great harm suffered by the author. ...

7. The State party's behaviour in the present case is of such gravity as to fall within the scope of article 16 of the Covenant, for it amounts almost to denial of recognition as a person before the law. ...

8. Consequently ... the State party's failure to observe its obligations under article 2 (2) of the Covenant is the direct and proximate cause of a distinct violation of the Covenant. ...

...

INDIVIDUAL OPINION OF COMMITTEE MEMBER HÉLÈNE TIGROUDJA (CONCURRING)

1. I fully share the conclusion [as] to the violation of article 24 (3) ... .

2. However, ... I regret that the majority did not elaborate on the other breaches of the Covenant ... .

...

4. Indeed, as recently affirmed by the African Court on Human and Peoples' Rights, "the right to nationality is a fundamental aspect of the dignity of the human person". In the same vein, the jurisprudence of the Inter-American Court of Human Rights – whose persuasive authority in this field is recognized in the UNHCR Guidelines on Statelessness No. 5 adopted in May 2020 – affirms that nationality is "an inherent right of all human beings", as well as "the basic requirement for the exercise of political rights" and a key element for "the individual's legal capacity". More critically, the Inter-American Court of Human Rights pointed out in the *Yean and Bosico Girls* case that while persons without nationality are in a situation of extreme vulnerability, children are in an even more vulnerable situation. ...

5. This is exactly the situation described by the author ... . Therefore, his situation of statelessness does not only constitute a violation of his right to a nationality (art. 24 (3) of the Covenant). It should also have been analysed by the majority as a violation of the right to be recognized by the law as a legal person (art. 16) and the right to be treated with humanity and dignity (art. 7).

Political Cases

The Committee has also issued Final Views in several high-profile and politically-charged cases. In *Garzón v. Spain* (UN Doc. CCPR/C/132/D/2844/2016), decided in July 2021, a very prominent judge of the Spanish National Court, Baltasar Garzón, alleged that prosecutions against him for abuse of authority in two high-profile cases had violated his human rights. In the *Franco* case, he assumed jurisdiction under the Spanish Historical Memory Act to investigate enforced disappearances that occurred during the Civil War and subsequent dictatorship of General Francisco Franco, as crimes against humanity. In 2010 he was suspended from office and faced criminal charges, although he was ultimately acquitted by the Supreme Court in 2012. In the *Gürtel* case, he authorized wiretapping of conversations between the accused and their lawyers in a case involving alleged illegal financing of the Spanish center-right political party, the Partido Popular. He was convicted of abuse of power and disbarred from office for 11 years in 2012.

The Committee held both prosecutions to have been arbitrary. His actions in the *Franco* case 'were at least a plausible legal interpretation, the appropriateness of which was reviewed on appeal, without it being concluded that such decisions constituted misconduct or incompetence that could justify his inability to perform his duties'. In the *Gürtel* case, the Committee noted that Garzón's interpretation had been shared by other judges and the Public Prosecutor and that even if it had been erroneous, as argued by the State, it 'did not constitute serious misconduct or incompetence that could justify his criminal conviction'. It concluded that any judicial error should have been corrected in proceedings before a higher court, rather than through a criminal prosecution. In addition, his right to be tried by an impartial tribunal was violated because some Supreme Court judges had participated in both cases, the trials were conducted simultaneously, and the judgements were issued 18 days apart.

The Committee concluded that the State Party should provide Garzón with an effective remedy, including expunging his criminal record, providing adequate compensation for the harm suffered and taking measures to prevent similar violations in the future. The importance of the Committee's views in this case is suggested by the fact that 97% of cases claiming the protection of fundamental rights taken to the Spanish Constitutional Court between 2007 and 2020 were held inadmissible, and a similar result prevailed at the European Court of Human Rights in such cases from Spain.[372]

Luiz Inácio Lula da Silva v. Brazil (UN Doc. CCPR/C/134/2841/2016) involved a complaint submitted in 2016 by the former President of Brazil (2003-2010)). The Committee published it Final Views in March 2022. Lula had been investigated in 2016 for alleged involvement in 'Operation Car Wash', which involved corruption between the State-owned oil company, Petrobrás, several construction companies, and Brazilian politicians. to obtain secret campaign funds. Federal Criminal Court Judge Sergio Moro approved a request by the prosecutor to tap the telephones of Lula, his family, and his lawyer. Moro then released the recordings to the media even before charges had been filed. He also leaked the details of a warrant to detain Lula for questioning, leading to media photos of Lula making it look as if he were under arrest. Lula was sentenced to nine years in prison, subsequently increased to 12 years. That in turn led to the rejection of his candidacy for the Presidential Elections which he had been widely favoured to win. In 2021, the Supreme Federal Court quashed the sentence, on the grounds that Moro had lacked jurisdiction, and that he had not acted impartially. In 2022, he was again elected as President.

The Committee found violations of Lula's right to personal liberty, right to privacy, right to be tried by an impartial tribunal, right to presumption of innocence, and his right to run for office:

> 8.8 ... [T]he Committee notes that the Supreme Federal Court characterized all disclosures ... as "manipulatively selective", and considered that the tapping of the [lawyers'] telephones was conducted "in order to monitor and anticipate defence strategies" in "flagrant violation of [the author's] constitutional right to a full defence". The Committee therefore considers that the timing and manner of [the wiretapping and the] disclosures reveal ulterior purposes that are "unauthorized by law" ... and thus arbitrary ... [and] in violation of article 17 of the Covenant.

> 8.9 With regards to [the right to an impartial tribunal] the Committee recalls its longstanding jurisprudence according to which the right to be tried by an independent and impartial tribunal is an absolute right that ... has a subjective and an objective element. According to the first one, judges must not allow their judgement to be influenced by personal bias or prejudice, nor harbour preconceptions about the particular case before them, nor act in ways that improperly promote the interests of one of the parties to the detriment of the other. According to the second one, the tribunal must also appear to a reasonable observer to be impartial. That is, judges must not only be impartial, they must also be seen to be impartial, and there are ascertainable objective facts which may raise doubts as to their impartiality. ...

> 8.10 In [Lula's] case, the Committee notes that the Supreme Federal Court found seven facts that showed that Judge Moro was subjectively partial. ... The Committee observes that a timely decision on the matter would have avoided the harm caused to the author, which included a conviction, the confirmation of the conviction, being debarred from running for president, and 580 days of wrongful imprisonment....

> ...

> 10 ... [T]he State party is obligated, inter alia, to ensure that the criminal proceedings against the author comply with all the due process guarantees set out in article 14 of the

---

[372] I. de la Rasilla, 'The Trials of Judge Garzón and the Enforceability of Decisions by Human Rights Treaty Bodies in Spain', 28 *Int'l J. Hum. Rts.* (2024) 759.

Covenant. The State party is also under an obligation to take all steps necessary to prevent similar violations from occurring in the future.

...

Finally, the case of Belarus is instructive. The state is not a party to the European Convention on Human Rights, but acceded to the Optional Protocol in 1992. Since 2000 the Committee has received over 175 complaints from Belarus, many of which related to religious freedom. In November 2021 the Committee found that 'by convicting and fining [an individual] for creating and leading a religious organisation without State registration and by restricting [his] right to peacefully manifest his religious beliefs in community with others', the State party violated article 18 (1) on the freedom of religion (UN Doc. CCPR/C/131/D/2695/2015 (2021)). In response, Belarus withdrew from the Optional Protocol, effective in February 2023. The Deputy Foreign Minister attributed the decision to the 'arbitrary expansion of the powers of the Human Rights Committee, creating additional unreasonable obligations for the state, which it did not accept when joining' the treaty.[373]

QUESTIONS

1. How would you respond to de Zayas's argument that the Committee has failed to show good faith by 'redefining' the terms of the Covenant to cover issues of sexual orientation?

2. *A.S. et al v Italy* addresses a 'maritime legal black hole', a feature of what Benhabib has called practices that 'create deterritorialized zones of lawlessness at border crossing, airports, and maritime ports and encourage the excision of territories as well as the building of outsourced camps on the territories of failed states'.[374] What contribution could a set of Views by the ICCPR Committee make by way of a response to such a set of practices? Achiume argues that 'achieving an ideal form of global migration governance would ... require remedying the fatally flawed conception of state sovereignty at the heart of international law and which nation States are strongly incentivized to protect.'[375] Is there a risk that the work of the Committee ends up reinforcing such a system of sovereignty?

Communications Procedures

A. EVIDENCE

A former Committee member, Christian Tomuschat, argues in 'Human Rights Committee', in R. Wolfrum and A. Peters (eds), *Max Planck Encyclopaedia of Public International Law* (2019, online ed.), para. 33 that:

> '[t]he appraisal of evidence placed before the [Committee] remains highly unsatisfactory. ... [W]here there are clear contradictions between the allegations of the petitioner and the defence of the respondent government, the [Committee] has evolved the rule of thumb that governments are under a duty to respond specifically and in detail to factual contentions which have every appearance of seriousness. If the government concerned does not launch an investigation [or] abstains from presenting the results thereof, the Committee proceeds from the assumption that the allegations of the petitioner must be given due weight as long as they are sufficiently substantiated, thus making a 'default finding'. Blanket denials of the respondent government are not enough. In cases where

---

[373] O. Glace, 'Belarus: Closing "one of the last remaining opportunities to seek justice"', *Forum 18*, 2 September 2022.
[374] S. Benhabib, 'The End of the 1951 Refugee Convention? Dilemmas of Sovereignty, Territoriality, and Human Rights', 2 *Jus Cogens* (2020) 75, at 96.
[375] E. T. Achiume, 'The Fatal Flaw in International Law for Migration', 56 *Colum. J. Trans'l L.* (2018) 257, at 262.

both sides have advanced substantiated contentions, it is almost impossible for the HRC to disentangle the factual situation.

One possibility would be oral hearings, a technique only used once, in *Muller and Carrol v. New Zealand* (UN Doc. CCPR/C/121/D/2502/2014 (2017). The procedure was apparently not considered to have worked well. In Tomuschat's view, 'the practical difficulties entailed by oral hearings would be insurmountable at world level. Granting a fair hearing to everyone, irrespective of his/her place of residence, including his/her presence at the proceedings, cannot be arranged in practical logistical terms. Additionally, if transformed into a trial body, the HRC would have to sit permanently because of the increased time requirements.'

B. REMEDIES[376]

In its early years the Committee was reluctant to recommend specific remedies and instead relied upon the standard phrase, still used at the end of every set of Views, that calls upon the state party to adopt 'measures . . . to give effect to the Committee's Views'. But, over time, the Committee has become increasingly specific as to the measures it believes states should take. In 2016 it adopted 'Guidelines on measures of reparation under the Optional Protocol'(UN Doc. CCPR/C/158):

Restitution

6.   The Committee requests that States parties provide for measures of restitution with a view to restoring rights that have been violated. ...

7.   In cases of deprivation of liberty the Committee may, as appropriate, request the person's release, [review of the case or re-trial]. ...

Rehabilitation

8.   ... [If appropriate] the Committee indicates that the State party is to provide the victim or his or her family, as appropriate, with medical or psychological treatment, or the funds to pay for such treatment.

Compensation

9.   As a general rule, the Committee does not specify sums of money.

...

Measures of satisfaction

11.   When specifying measures of satisfaction, the Committee takes into consideration, inter alia, the following elements:

(a)   When appropriate, the Committee may indicate that the fact that its Views declare that a violation of the Covenant has occurred constitutes in and of itself a form of reparation. That will not prevent the Committee from indicating additional measures of reparation;

(b)   In many cases, the Committee requests that the State party conduct investigations ... ;

(c)   When appropriate, the Committee requests that States parties take measures to commute, reduce or not enforce a sentence;

...

---

[376] See generally K. Roach, *Remedies for Human Rights Violations: A Two Track Approach to Supra-National and National Law* (2021).

(e)   The Committee may request that States parties issue a public apology, particularly in cases of grave or systematic violations where the injury cannot be fully redressed by restitution or compensation only. ...;

(f)   ... [O]ther measures of satisfaction [might include] the possibility of having a monument built, putting up a commemorative plaque or changing the name of a street or other public place ...;

Guarantees of non-repetition

...

13.   The following are examples ...:

(a)   When laws or regulations in the State party are found to be at variance with Covenant obligations, the Committee should request their repeal or amendment ... .;

(b)   Improvements in conditions in places of detention, in accordance with international standards;

(c)   Changes in official procedures and practices. When identifying such measures, the Committee should be as specific as possible;

(d)   Where applicable, the Committee should consider recommending measures for training and raising the awareness ... .

In practice, the Committee has been less ambitious than those Guidelines might suggest. Dinah Shelton, in *Remedies in International Human Rights Law* (3rd. ed., 2015) 198 lists the type of remedies used by the Committee: (a) public investigation to establish the facts; (b) bringing to justice the perpetrators; (c) compensation; (d) ensuring non-repetition of the violation; (e) amending the law; (f) providing restitution of liberty, employment, property, and human remains; (g) rehabilitation, including medical care and treatment; (h) permitting the victim to leave the country; and (i) enjoining an imminent violation.

C. FOLLOW-UP AND COMPLIANCE

The Committee appoints a Special Rapporteur for Follow-up on Views. This UN Press Release (21 March 2022) illustrates the sort of results achieved:

> ... [The] communication concerning Canada concerned the refusal of a First Nations individual's application for social services, and preferential treatment of Indian men over Indian women born prior to 1985 regarding social service registration. The Committee commended the State party for allowing the person involved to register, reforming the Indian Act to remove barriers to registration, and for taking steps to address residual discrimination within First Nations groups. It called on the State party to continue discussions with the person involved and First Nations groups and to work on implementing the legislative changes.
>
> Regarding Cameroon, the communication concerned the wrongful imprisonment of an individual. [T]here had been no response received from the State party to the Committee's call to immediately release the individual pending trial, to conduct the trial without delay, and provide compensation to the author. The Committee noted the State party's unsatisfactory response, and proposed to follow-up on the case in the State party's next periodic report.
>
> On Colombia, the communication concerned the conviction of two former officials, with the State party offering no possibility of review of the cases. The Committee repeated its calls for compensation to be provided to the persons concerned, and for measures to be

implemented to prevent repetition of similar incidents. The Committee planned to continue dialogue with the State party on the issue.

Regarding Lithuania, the communication concerned a violation of the rights of an individual in court proceedings, especially when it came to the use of handcuffs and metal cages in court rooms. The Committee closed the dialogue on the communication, noting that although the State party had not yet paid compensation ..., it had provided an avenue for the person involved to obtain adequate compensation [and had] taken measures to eliminate the use of handcuffs and metal cages in court rooms.

As for *D.Z. v The Netherlands* [see above] ... the compensation which had been provided by the Netherlands to the person involved was inadequate, and [the Committee] criticised the State party for not reviewing the author's application to be recognised as a citizen of the Netherlands. The Committee further faulted Netherlands for not reviewing the living circumstances of the person involved, and not implementing measures to review legislation on determining statelessness and eligibility for citizenship applications.

Regarding the Russian Federation, the communication concerned the arrest without record of an individual, and the failure of the State to provide adequate health care to the individual while in detention. The ... State party had not provided compensation [nor] taken measures to prevent repetition of similar incidents. ...

Concerning Tajikistan, the communication related to the torture and death of an individual in police custody. The Committee said that the State party had not sufficiently prosecuted and punished the perpetrators in the case, noting its lack of communication with the author of the communication regarding the progress of the investigation, and not providing the author with adequate compensation. The Committee resolved to close the case with a note of unsatisfactory implementation of the Committee's views.

An earlier implementation survey by the UN Secretariat suggested the following reasons to explain States failure to implement the Views:

> a lack of understanding by States parties of their obligations under the respective treaties; unwillingness, on the part of certain States parties to abide by their obligations; the 'non-legally binding' nature of decisions; the divergent views between States and the Committees on the interpretation of treaty provisions; weak decisions often resulting from consensus decision-making; insufficient follow-up by the Committees themselves; lack of political support (unlike ECHR — where implementation is monitored by the Council of Ministers, i.e. the States themselves); lack of expertise within States parties and lack of assistance to them on how to better implement; and failure to adopt enabling legislation.[377]

Based on an empirical analysis, Vera Shikhelman, in 'Implementing Decisions of International Human Rights Institutions: Evidence from the United Nations Human Rights Committee', 30 *Eur. J. Int'l L.* (2019) 753 suggests that the following factors influence the willingness of states to implement the Committee's Final Views: (i) the level of democracy and human rights protection in the state; (ii) internal capacity; (iii) strength of civil society; (iv) type of remedy; (v) representation on the HRC; (6) subject matter of the communication. Other relevant factors included the state's internal capacity and whether it is a member of the Human Rights Council.

D. THE LEGAL STATUS OF VIEWS

The legal status of the Committee's Views is important. If they are legally binding, then their relative neglect by many states is deeply problematic. If they are merely advisory, it would hardly be surprising if states downplayed their significance. The views of commentators vary.

---

[377] 'Follow-up procedures on individual complaints', UN Doc. HRI/ICM/WGFU/2011/3 (16 Dec. 2010), at 5.

Manfred Nowak argues that the Committee 'cannot be termed a court in the strict sense of the word' because of 'the relatively brief term of office of its members and the lack of internationally binding effect of its decisions', as well as its designation as a 'Committee'. He concludes that it is a 'quasi-judicial organ', and has suggested that the Views enjoy a 'quasi-binding nature'.[378]

A former member of the Committee, Martin Scheinin, argues that its Views are, in effect, binding:

> ... They are the end result of a quasi-judicial adversarial international body established ...
> for the purpose of interpreting the provisions of the Covenant and monitoring
> compliance with them. ... If a state wishes to question the correctness of a legal
> interpretation by the Committee, it should at least resort to some other procedure before
> an international court or independent expert body. As this is not likely to happen in
> practice, the presumption should be that the Committee's views in Optional Protocol
> cases are treated as the authoritative interpretation of the Covenant under international
> law.[379]

In contrast, Walter Kälin, also a former Committee member, considers the Views to be 'legally non-binding', but adds that they 'possess considerable authority because they stem from a body entrusted and empowered by states parties to determine authoritatively whether human rights have been violated in specific cases. Thus, the principle of good faith ... requires that states at least weigh the reasons why they are not ready to implement a finding of a violation.'[380] Christian Tomuschat says 'States Parties cannot simply ignore [the Views], but have to consider them in good faith. [But] they are not debarred from dismissing them, after careful consideration ... . Not to react at all ... however, would appear to amount to a violation of the obligations under the ICCPR.' An even more tentative formulation is suggested by Leonardo Borlini and Luigi Crema, in 'The Legal Status of Decisions by Human Rights Treaty Bodies: Authoritative Interpretations or *Mission Éducatrice?'*, *Global Community Yb. Int'l L. & Juris. 2019* (2020) 129 who conclude that 'the authoritativeness of [treay bodies'] pronouncements lies in the quality of their reasoning, their methodological rigour and the persuasiveness of the views expressed. And, when these qualities emerge, it is appropriate for domestic courts to consider their pronouncements attentively.'

In its General Comment No. 33 (2008) the Committee observed that its Views 'exhibit some important characteristics of a judicial decision. They are arrived at in a judicial spirit, including the impartiality and independence of Committee members, the considered interpretation of the language of the Covenant, and the determinative character of the decisions' (para. 11). It added that they 'represent an authoritative determination by the organ established under the Covenant itself charged with the interpretation of that instrument' (para. 13), and that States Parties have a 'duty to cooperate with the Committee [arising] from an application of the principle of good faith to the observance of all treaty obligations' (para. 15). It concluded that even where the state has clearly rejected the Views, 'the Committee regards dialogue between the Committee and the State party as ongoing with a view to implementation' (para. 18).

The Committee's current approach is reflected in a provision that is included near the end of its Views in cases where it has found a violation. It states:

> Pursuant to article 2 (3) (a) of the Covenant, the State party is under an obligation to
> provide the author with an effective remedy. This requires it to make full reparation to
> individuals whose Covenant rights have been violated. Accordingly, the State party is
> obligated, inter alia, to take appropriate steps to provide adequate compensation to the
> author for the violation suffered. The State party is also under an obligation to take all
> steps necessary to prevent similar violations from occurring in the future.[381]

---

[378] M. Nowak and E. McArthur, *The United Nations Convention against Torture: A Commentary* (2008), at 77-8.

[379] R. Hanski & M. Scheinin (eds.), *Leading Cases of the Human Rights Committee* (2003), at 22.

[380] W. Kälin and J. Künzli, *The Law of International Human Rights Protection* (2nd. ed., 2019), at 218.

[381] From *J. S. v. Australia*, UN Doc. CCPR/C/135/2804/2016 (2022) para. 10.

E. SITUATING THE COMMITTEE IN THE BROADER REGIME

Consider the comments by a former Chair of the Committee comparing it with the European Court of Human Rights (Yuval Shany, 'Can Strasbourg be Replicated at a Global Level? A View from Geneva', in Helmut Aust and Esra Demir-Gürsel (eds.), *The European Court of Human Rights* (2021) 71, at 82):

> In *Yaker v France* (2018) the HRCttee found the French criminal ban on wearing full-facial veils to violate the ICCPR, deviating from the position of the ECtHR, which found in *S.A.S. v France* (2014) such a ban to fall within France's margin of appreciation. In *Mellet v Ireland* (2016), the Committee held that Ireland's broad ban on abortion violates the ICCPR, effectively rejecting the approach taken by the ECtHR in *A, B and C v Ireland* (2010), in which the Court found the conditions of the Irish ban on abortion to fall within that state's margin of appreciation. [I]n 2018 Ireland held a referendum leading to a change of its constitution, paving the way for the passage of new legislation on abortion which conforms with the formally non-binding Views of the Committee.

He then asks how one might explain the Committee's comparatively more demanding approach.

> … [O]ne possibility is that the Committee's lack of binding legal authority actually serves as a liberating factor, which allows it to adopt progressive interpretations of the law without assuming full responsibility for the consequences of following its Views. According to this hypothesis, … the Committee is less concerned than the ECtHR with the question of whether or not states would comply with them. As a result, it can be less timid in its decisions than its regional judicial counterpart, which expects its decisions to be regularly followed by the member states and would suffer a set-back if they were not. … [T]he HRCttee … may … have less to lose than the ECtHR by confronting 'high-reputation' states like France or Ireland, or by adopting interpretations of the law not likely to be followed.

> … [But the Committee is not] agnostic about compliance with its decisions. To the contrary, it invests considerable efforts in monitoring compliance with them … . [This] is likely to serve as a constraint against normative overreach in its decisions. Furthermore, the lack of formally binding authority compels the Committee to rely not on *ipse dixit* [simple assertions], but rather on persuasion as a central compliance-inducing strategy. This, in turn, is expected to incentivize the HRCttee to exercise incrementalism in norm-development and to base new decisions on persuasive past precedents.

Finally, he addresses the consequences of the Committee's universal constituency:

> [I]n some areas of activity, the HRCttee did indeed adopt a minimalist approach to the interpretation of the Covenant, arguably in view of the diversity of its membership. While not invoking the margin of appreciation doctrine, which the Committee considers to conflict, in principle, with the notion of universality of human rights law, it has often settled for a 'thin' construction of the rights provided in the Covenant and exercised 'light review' of the justifications provided by state parties for limiting rights. Arguably, awareness of a global audience, which at times explains the Committee's preference for restricting state discretion regarding the manner of implementing the Covenant, explains, at other times, a modest reading of Covenant rights and a flexible reading of justifications for restricting them. The fundamental nature of the right in question and the risk of abuse of discretion in light of actual state practice may help to distinguish between these two modes of operation by the Committee.

> …

> [Unlike the Court, the Committee] is not involved in a political, legal or economic integration project and does not serve a community of predominantly democratic or secular-liberal states (but rather a very diverse group of states). As a result, it draws much of its legitimacy from the intrinsic moral value of human rights as universal norms. This

means that it must consider the implications of its decisions for protection of rights in both democratic and non-democratic countries – that is, develop rights as a barrier against both authoritarian regimes and tyranny of the majority in democracy.

Furthermore, the Committee operates in an institutional framework – the UN – that involves only a limited level of inter-state cooperation and works at great distance from the member states. The Committee itself is comprised of members coming from only a small percentage of the state parties (18 out of 174). As a result, the Committee as a whole is less exposed than the ECtHR to the political expectations of the state parties and is less influenced by the overarching international framework in which it operates.

Lacking an enforcement machinery, and facing states with chronic compliance problems, the Committee positions itself primarily as a norm-supporting and not a regime-supporting institution. Hence, it sees its role as an external monitoring body, whose principal loyalty is to the norms it seeks to uphold and to the beneficiaries of the said norms: once it deems a specific interpretation of a human rights norm fit for universal application, it should identify violations of the norm whenever it sees them and provide as much as possible concrete contents to such human rights, even if prospects for compliance with its decisions remain low.

F. RECONCILING COMPETING TREATY BODY INTERPRETATIONS

One of the problems that inevitably arises as a result of the proliferation of treaty bodies with overlapping competences is the risk of divergent or dissonant interpretations of the same or similar norms in different contexts. Cora True-Frost, in 'Listening to Dissonance at the Intersections of International Human Rights Law', 43 *Mich. J. Int'l L.* (2022) 361 provides examples arising out of the work of the CRPD, the HRC and the CRC. She observes that in its General Comment No. 35 on liberty and security 'the HRC disagreed with the CRPD Committee "regarding whether involuntary hospitalization [by the state] is ever permitted."' [Another] example pertains to the CRC and the CRPD Committees' continuing debate about the right to live in a family, and the related issue of the permissibility of placing children with disabilities in group homes. The CRC Committee holds that such placement by the state may be necessary, even as the CRPD Committee maintains that institutional living for children with disabilities should not be an option for state parties.'

But True-Frost resists calls for harmonization or normative hierarchies on the grounds that minority-sensitive perspectives would inevitably lose out:

> … People with specialized, compounded, or intersectional rights claims within and across race, gender, and disability, may have more opportunities to have their rights violations acknowledged and addressed through varying, un-harmonized, and sometimes even dissonant interpretations. … [Dissonance, at least] in the short-term … may benefit historically marginalized people by moving toward new conceptualizations of time-honored legal doctrine. … [But this also] leaves treaty bodies, human rights claimants, and states frustratingly vulnerable to indeterminacy and power differentials.

> … The quest for a "coherent system" should not destroy the potential to develop overlapping and intersectional norms for minority groups such as female children with physical disabilities; poor pregnant women who are religious minorities; or Deaf Blackmen. …

> In the near term, dissonance may be modulated by design modifications, including deepening consultation between treaty bodies, encouraging joint General Comments regarding the intersectionality of rights, and strengthening treaty bodies' capacity to develop the scientific and policy records that apply to persistent conflicts. … [For example, acknowledging conflicting interpretations] would promote transparency and credibility for the treaty bodies and possibly create more urgency for working toward substantive resolution of the conflict.

While it is also important to acknowledge that despite the clear risks associated with fragmentation, it is increasingly common for treaty bodies to explicitly engage with and endorse the findings of other such bodies. [382]

QUESTIONS

1. Do you consider states to be 'bound' by the Views? If so, on the basis of what theory of obligation? Is it desirable for the communications procedure to have a binding outcome? What techniques do you think the Committee should use to promote compliance with its Views?

2. Some members of the Committee have suggested that 'the most meaningful approach to interpretation of the Covenant as a global human rights treaty is one that is dynamic, conscious of the evolving nature of this subject, and attentive to the developments occurring in other international bodies.'[383] What are the legal and practical implications of such an approach?

3. 'Each of the Committee's three functions can be found inadequate from different perspectives. But if we look at the Committee as a totality, and examine these functions not discretely but as complementary approaches, we reach a far more favourable judgment about the significance of the Committee's contribution to the human rights regime.' Do you agree?

B. REFORMING THE OVERALL UN HUMAN RIGHTS TREATY BODY SYSTEM

While this chapter has focused on the ICCPR, many of the techniques used are followed by the other treaty bodies operating within the UN human rights regime. Since 2011, there have been ten so-called 'core' treaties in force, each with its own monitoring body. They are: (1) ICCPR: Human Rights Committee; (2) ICESCR: Committee on Economic, Social and Cultural Rights; (3) CERD: Committee on the Elimination of Racial Discrimination; (4) CEDAW: Committee on the Elimination of Discrimination against Women; (5) CAT: Committee against Torture; (6) OPCAT: the Subcommittee on Prevention of Torture; (7) CRC: Committee on the Rights of the Child; (8) CMW: Committee on Migrant Workers; (Convention on the Protection of All Migrant Workers and Members of Their Families); (9) CRPD: Committee on the Rights of Persons with Disabilities; and (10) CED: Committee on Enforced Disappearances. The accompanying Table provides some relevant details about each.

This final section takes note of various proposals made over the years to improve the functioning of the treaty body system as a whole. As early as the late 1980s a range of shortcomings had been identified which led to concerns about the sustainability of a system which is fragmented, complex and under-resourced. The problems included widespread non-reporting and late reporting by states, superficial reports, a lack of domestic debate around the reports, insufficient expertise among committee members and limited independence of some, excessively general concluding observations, and inadequate follow-up in general.

The ups and downs of the 'reform' process that began in 1988 and is still going is described by Suzanne Egan, in 'Transforming the UN Human Rights Treaty System: A Realistic Appraisal', 42 *Hum. Rts. Q.* (2020) 762. She describes several sets of reform initiatives. The first consisted of three reports, presented between 1988 and 1997 by Philip Alston, in his capacity as an Independent Expert appointed by the UN Secretary-General.[384]

---

[382] See, for example, Wahaj Ali, Imran Ali and Bakhtaware Ali v. Norway, Views of the Human Rights Committee concerning communication No. 2926/2017, UN Doc. CCPR/C/135/D/2926/2017 (2023).

[383] *Eugénie Chakupewa et al. v. Democratic Republic of Congo*, UN Doc. CCPR/C/131/D/2835/2016 (2021), concurring opinion of A. Bulkan and H. Tigroudja.

[384] P. Alston, 'Final Report on Enhancing the Long-Term Effectiveness of the United Nations Human Rights Treaty System', UN Doc. E/CN.4/1997/74. Earlier reports were published as UN Doc. A/44/668 (1989) and UN Doc. A/CONF.157/PC/62/Add.11/ Rev.1 (1993).

Alston's recommendations … comprised a broad swathe of measures including the extension of meeting times …; the development of concerted practices and procedures to deal with persistent non-reporting states; as well as various methods of reducing the overall burden of reporting requirements. … [H]is final report set out a range of [longer-term] options … [including] a single consolidated report for all of the treaty bodies, based on issues identified in advance by the treaty bodies … . As further "food for thought", he mooted the possibility of consolidating the existing network of treaty bodies, potentially into an entirely new "super-committee" or possibly two such committees … . [But he] warned that the idea … would require "a sustained exchange of views in order that the advantages and disadvantages can be adequately articulated."

[S]ome of the less far-reaching measures advocated by Alston were gradually introduced … . [In 2006, High Commissioner Louise Arbour presented] a detailed proposal for a Unified Standing Treaty Body . … [T]his proposal … was an abject failure … . Objections raised included a fear that the focus on specific issues in particular treaties would be lost in a unified treaty body; that the creation of such a body would raise complex legal and political problems; and that … there was insufficient evidence that a unified treaty body would necessarily mark an improvement in human rights protection or [solve systemic problems]. … [The proposal was presented] without advance consultation, … [and] was widely perceived as [a] "top-down" exercise that failed to generate buy-in from the key stakeholders. …

The third major initiative … was spearheaded by [High Commissioner] Navanethem Pillay [who] championed a consultative process from 2009 to 2011 involving most of the key stakeholders … . [The resulting] recommendations … focused largely on ways and means of streamlining and harmonizing treaty body working methods. …

[These] proposals eventually formed the basis for … an intergovernmental process … [which] culminated in General Assembly Res. 68/268 (2014). [The resolution endorsed additional meeting time but also adopted … various cost-saving measures mooted in Pillay's report … . While no mention was made of [Pillay's] idea of national reporting and coordinating mechanisms, the text encouraged the treaty bodies to harmonize their working methods including with respect to a streamlined SRP [simplified reporting procedure], the conduct of the constructive dialogue, and an aligned consultation process for General Comments. It also endorsed the notion of an enhanced role for the [annual meeting of the Chairpersons of all of the treaty bodies] in steering harmonization.

Many have criticized the proposal for a single unified treaty body. Tomuschat (para. 36) argues that:

[There would be] a fierce competition for the few posts … . Smaller countries would no longer have a chance to be represented … . Moreover, some of the human rights treaties require special expertise … . … Lastly, the experts on a permanent body would have to serve full time. It is the advantage of the current system, in contrast, that the experts maintain their ties with their countries of origin. They do not become part of a bureaucratic elite.'

In Res. 68/268 the General Assembly also promised additional staff resources for the treaty body system, but this did not eventuate. COVID-19 hit the system hard and exacerbated existing backlogs. While online meetings were introduced, they too were assessed to have suffered from '(a) poor communication systems; (b) a lack of reliable data systems; (c) the need for online platforms to be tailored to meet the special needs of people with disabilities; (d) insufficient interpretation services; and (e) concern regarding lack of compensation to help experts to offset the costs associated with online meetings', Report of the Office of Internal Oversight Services, UN Doc. A/76/197 (2021).

As the system has continued to expand, most problems have been exacerbated. Between 2013 and 2021, the total number of ratifications increased by 13%. By 2021, there were some 1,800 communications awaiting processing and the staff-time available to undertake this work was diminishing. Only 14% of states had no overdue reports, and 441 reports were awaiting consideration (UN Doc. A/77/279 (2022)). Despite a series of requests by the treaty bodies and by the Secretary-General, states have maintained the existing severe underfunding of the system.[385]

The principal locus for reform is the annual meeting of the Chairpersons of all of the treaty bodies. Although it has produced important blueprints (e. g. UN Doc. A/78/354 (2023), Egan (above, 788) is critical of the 'conflicting strategic agendas' of the key stakeholders, a leadership vacuum which implicates both the OHCHR and the chairpersons, and the overall failure to envision treaty body reform within the overall context of the UN human rights system.

An important dimension of future endeavours will be what the chairpersons have called the 'digital uplift' of the system (UN Doc. A/77/228 (2022) para. 55), although these will also require adequate financial resources to be provided by states:

> (a) While State party reviews should always be held in person, there are areas of treaty body work that could benefit from using advanced, integrated digital platforms, including hybrid meetings with States parties in exceptional circumstances. ... ;

> (b) A digital case file management system for individual communications ... must be completed to allow for uploading communications and tracking the process, including the status of the case. The submission process is to be streamlined, and allow the option of videoconferencing, oral evidence and States parties' responses in real time. ... ;

> (c) The digital option could also be offered to those small island developing States and least developed countries that request it either as a cost-saving measure ... or as a result of temporary exceptional circumstances ...;

> (d) Greater engagement with civil society organizations and other non-State actors would be enhanced by the undertaking of ... online outreach activities ... .

QUESTION

What do you see as the principal disadvantages of a unified treaty body? Could these be overcome through creative arrangements in establishing the new body, or would too much of the appeal of the existing system be lost?

A World Court for Human Rights?

As early as 1947, Australia called for the creation of an international human rights court, and the United Kingdom responded by suggesting that the International Court of Justice could be authorized to give advisory opinions on human rights. Neither proposal was successful, but the idea has continued to surface periodically. In recent years, several NGO-led, but government-supported, initiatives have put forward elaborate proposals for such a world human rights court. Note that the International Criminal Court already has jurisdiction over crimes against humanity, thus enabling it to adjudicate on a significant range of human rights violations. The most developed proposal for a new court has been put forward by Julia Kozma, Manfred Nowak and Martin Scheinin in *A World Court of Human Rights: Consolidated Statute and Commentary* (2010). Nowak summarizes the proposal in 'A World Court of Human Rights', in Gerd Oberleitner (ed.), *International Human Rights Institutions, Tribunals, and Courts* (2018) 271:

---

[385] See T. Kleinlein and D. Steiger, 'The State of the International Human Rights System—Normativity and Compliance: Introduction', 14 J. *Hum. Rts. Prac.* (2022) 1; and G. Zyberi and I. Salama, 'The Influence of Politics on the Work of the UN Human Rights Treaty Bodies', in B. Andreassen (ed.), *Research Handbook on the Politics of Human Rights Law* (2023) 310.

… The [draft] Statute proposes a permanent court with international legal personality, based in Geneva with the power to decide in a legally binding manner on all complaints about alleged human rights violations brought before it in accordance with this Statute. The court should have 21 judges to be elected by the States parties to the Statute, sitting as a plenary court, in chambers of seven and committees of three judges, similar to the European Court of Human Rights (European Court of Human Rights). The Court shall render binding judgments on individual complaints, declare complaints inadmissible, facilitate friendly settlements, order interim measures, or strike out complaints, similar to other human rights courts. It shall also be entrusted with the power to provide advisory opinions upon request of States, the UN Secretary General, and the UN High Commissioner for Human Rights, similar to the Inter-American Court of Human Rights. Final judgments of the court are binding under international law. Their implementation by States shall be supervised by the UN High Commissioner for Human Rights, who may seize the Human Rights Council or, in exceptional cases through the UN Secretary General, the Security Council, with a request to take the necessary measures that will bring about the enforcement of the judgment (Article 18).

The Statute does not create any new substantive human rights obligations for States parties. As applicable law, Article 5 defines a total of 21 existing human rights treaties of the United Nations. Of course, the provisions of these treaties are only applicable if the State concerned is also a party to the respective treaty in addition to having ratified the Statute of the WCHR. In addition, Article 50 contains an opting out clause which provides any State party to the WCHR with the right to declare that it does not recognize the jurisdiction of the Court in relation to certain human rights treaties or certain provisions thereof. …

For "Entities," which are defined in Article 4 as "any inter-governmental organization or non-State actor, including any business corporation, which has recognized the jurisdiction of the Court in accordance with Article 51," the Statute envisages a special "opting in" clause. Such "Entities" cannot usually become parties to any international human rights treaty. … Under the draft Statute …, such Entities are invited to voluntarily declare under Article 51 that they recognize the competence of the WCHR to "receive and examine complaints from any person, non-governmental organization or group of individuals claiming to be the victim of a violation by the respective Entity of any human right provided for in any human rights treaty listed in Article 5(1)." When making such a declaration, the "Entity" may specify under Article 51(2) which human rights treaties and which provisions thereof shall be subject to the jurisdiction of the Court. …

Finally, there is no hierarchy between the proposed WCHR and regional human rights courts. As other similar treaties, the draft Statute requires as admissibility criteria the exhaustion of domestic remedies (Article 9) and various other criteria, including in Article 19(1)(b) the pre-condition that the same matter has not "already been examined in substance by the Court or by any other procedure of international investigation and settlement, including before a regional human rights court." In other words, applicants must make up their minds whether they prefer to lodge a complaint … with the WCHR or with a regional human rights court, if applicable. Consequently, there will be no review of a judgment of a regional court by the WCHR if it concerns the same matter.

After reviewing the history of such proposals, Ignacio de la Rasilla, concludes in 'The World Court of Human Rights: Rise, Fall and Revival?', 19 *Hum. Rts. L. Rev.* (2019) 585 that the idea of a World Court is 'a useful heuristic' for appraising the challenges involved in global human rights protection. He recalls Isaiah Berlin's comment that 'Utopias have their value as nothing so wonderfully expands the imaginative horizons of human potentialities.' Olivier de Frouville generally supports the project in his book *Cosmopolitanism to Human Rights* (2021) 215. Others have been more critical. See Philip Alston, 'Against a World Court of Human Rights', 28 *Ethics & Int'l Aff.* (2014) 197.

QUESTION

What arguments do you see for and against the creation of a World Court as proposed above? Writing in 2004, Stefan Trechsel noted: 'If one imagines an ideal world, certainly a WCHR is desirable. . . . If one looks at the world today, one will have very serious doubts. The conflicts which we read about every day are not of a kind that could be solved by judicial proceedings.' He concluded that such a Court is 'neither desirable, nor necessary, nor probable'.

Chapter 10. International Human Rights Fact-Finding

Fact-finding is at the core of most human rights advocacy. In recent years there has been a huge increase in the number and variety of fact-finding missions undertaken by intergovernmental bodies, international NGOs and a range of other actors. There is, however, no clear definition of the term 'fact-finding'. Indeed, on its face, the notion that an investigator will simply find the 'facts' of a complex and contested situation or incident is problematic at various levels. Nevertheless, fact-finding has become a term of art in the human rights field. It might involve: (1) seeking to ascertain the facts about alleged human rights abuses, ideally through on-site visits, (2) determining state and group responsibility and perhaps also individual responsibility for violations of human rights, and (3) making recommendations as to reforms and reparations. Such functions clearly go beyond the necessary implications of the term 'fact-finding'.

International law has long made use of the technique of establishing fact-finding mechanisms in the form of commissions of inquiry (COI) in order to resolve disputes among states. The 1899 Hague Convention for the Pacific Settlement of International Disputes contained an entire chapter on such international inquiries. States unable to resolve a dispute diplomatically were urged to institute a COI 'to facilitate a solution of [their] differences by elucidating the facts by means of an impartial and conscientious investigation.' Important protections were, however, built in. The provisions did not apply to disputes involving 'honor [or] vital interests', and reports were 'limited to a statement of facts', thus leaving 'the conflicting Powers entire freedom as to the effect to be given to this statement'. Subsequently both the League of Nations Covenant of 1919 (Article 12) and the UN Charter (Article 33(1)) called for the use of international inquiries as one of the measures that should be considered in seeking to resolve disputes endangering international peace and security.[386]

In the human rights area, the 1919 Constitution of the International Labour Organization (Article 26) provided for the creation of a COI in cases of persistent violations of labour rights. Although only used 14 times — most recently in relation to Myanmar (1998, and 2023), Belarus (2004), Zimbabwe (2010), and Venezuela (2015) — the procedure was developed in a systematic and relatively rigorous manner, making it an important reference point.

By far the largest volume of fact-finding undertaken in the human rights area is carried out by nongovernmental organizations. Amnesty International began country missions in 1962, and Human Rights Watch (HRW, then Helsinki Watch) in the early 1980s. HRW's later approach to reporting has been widely imitated. Many other groups, such as the International Commission of Jurists, the Center for Economic and Social Rights, the International Crisis Group, the International Federation of Human Rights, and diverse specialist groups now generate hundreds of fact-finding reports every year. There is also much national level reporting by local NGOs, national human rights institutions, or sector-specific groups. While the focus of the present chapter is primarily on fact-finding by intergovernmental organizations such as the UN, the principles discussed are broadly applicable to these other actors as well.

The international dimension of fact-finding is increasingly central. Given that human rights violations usually imply governmental wrongdoing, the governments in question are often unlikely to undertake meaningful domestic investigations. International involvement thus becomes a means to break through the domestic stalemate. Today, serious human rights violations are increasingly likely to attract sustained international attention and lead to insistent calls for some form of international monitoring or other involvement. The result is often the establishment of an international fact-finding mechanism, generally but not always labeled as a COI. This became especially common after the 'Arab Spring' uprisings in 2011, with major UN Human Rights Council-mandated investigations in relation to Libya and Syria, an independent COI on Bahrain, and reports by the OHCHR on countries such as Egypt, Libya, Tunisia and Yemen.

The most appropriate and potentially effective fact-finding can usually be done at the domestic level,[387] but this is probably only viable or likely after a change of government or some other major upheaval. Otherwise,

---

[386] For a historical overview, see M. Becker, 'Challenging Some Baseline Assumptions about the Evolution of International Commissions of Inquiry', 55 *Vand. J. Transnat'l L.* (2022) 559.

[387] This chapter is not concerned with questions relating to judicial modes of human rights fact finding. See T. Stirner, *The Procedural Law Governing Facts and Evidence in International Human Rights Proceedings* (2021).

governments are more likely to seek to head off international involvement by authorizing a fresh investigation into previously rejected allegations, urging a re-trial in a controversial case, permitting scrutiny of the police and the judiciary's performance by an independent actor or perhaps even creating a national commission of inquiry with a fact-finding mandate. But most such initiatives can be effectively captured, diverted or muzzled if the government concerned chooses to do so. International involvement in fact-finding thus becomes a way to transcend obstacles that might otherwise seem insurmountable.

Some of this fact-finding activity has become relatively routinized, such as the monitoring and reporting carried out by a large number of UN Special Rapporteurs, the Council of Europe's Human Rights Commissioner, and the Inter-American Commission on Human Rights. But a great deal of fact-finding is relatively *ad hoc*. It takes the form of diverse types of inquiries established by a range of intergovernmental bodies, both international and regional. Such inquiries are set-up on a one-time only basis in response to a particularly serious or politicized incident or pattern of abuses. These fact-finding bodies are differently composed, are given varying mandates, use widely differing methodologies, and tend to serve a broad range of objectives.

As a general matter, reports from intergovernmental organizations carry more weight internationally than those of even the most credible NGOs. That influence comes from the special legitimacy and credibility they enjoy as emanating from an organization of which the target state is a member. In addition, COI members and staff must be independent of any state. As a result, the state's argument that the report is biased, or a product of another state's foreign policy agenda, is less likely to be accepted by audiences both inside and outside the state.

Unsurprisingly, and indeed perhaps appropriately, some of the more routinized fact-finding has proven to be very controversial, and there has been extensive criticism by governments of such activities. But it is the *ad hoc*, or one-time only, inquiries that have often proven to be the most contentious.

This proliferation of major inquiries across a wide range of situations challenges the common wisdom, which portrays the emergence of the various international and mixed criminal courts and tribunals over the past three decades as the most significant development in the human rights field. The explosion of international fact-finding activities has been a development of comparable significance, but while the criminal courts and tribunals have generated a veritable industry and a vast literature, fact-finding has been relatively under-researched.

At its best, fact-finding is comparatively cost-effective, flexible in design, able to be mobilized rapidly, can transform public and governmental understanding of a situation, and has the potential to promote wide-ranging political or institutional reform. It can also play a crucial role in attributing criminal responsibility and laying the groundwork for subsequent prosecutions. But many COIs fall well short of this ideal.

Before looking at specific fact-finding exercises, it is important to ponder the broader philosophical and other implications of the field's heavy reliance on fact-finding.

FRÉDÉRIC MÉGRET, DO FACTS EXIST, CAN THEY BE 'FOUND,' AND DOES IT MATTER?
P. ALSTON AND S. KNUCKEY (EDS.), THE TRANSFORMATION OF HUMAN RIGHTS FACT-FINDING (2016) 27

We live in an era that has banished certainty, but in which certainty has lost nothing of its allure. It may therefore come as no surprise that fact-finding as a particular institution of international law is witnessing a new popularity … . The idea behind rights violations, after all, is that they are concrete, identifiable, and knowable, and not simply subjective political claims. …

In this context, fact-finding commissions, fact-finding by NGOs, indicators, and benchmarks, all seem to be part of a "turn to the factual," one characterized by an increased attention to the ways in which facts are and ought to be produced and generated. The drivers of this … include, in addition to the appeal of certainty, the need for actionable, real-time information. Who after all can wait for a trial to determine that genocide has occurred? Long before judicial fact-finding can occur, there is a need for a sort of instant, rapid-fire fact-finding that is the basic building block of decision-making. Fact-finding can be an alternative to improbable and/or lengthy adjudication. ...

...

But we may also have reason to be skeptical of a range of practices that appear under this "turn to the factual." ... [T]here is an evident politics of describing certain things as facts. To be able to claim that something is a fact is generally a way of insulating it from debate, or at least from the inevitable politics of value or legal judgment. ... "Facts" are part and parcel of discursive strategies. This does not tell us anything about whether facts exist in some essential way, but it does tell us something about the existence of a background politics of fact designation, and an inevitable tendency to compete for "facts."

... The central question is: What gets described as a fact in the human rights context? ... One could say fact-finding is a form of power. Facts are all-important in justifying international action ... . The failure to produce facts may paralyze action, as when international inaction is justified by the failure to establish that genocide is ongoing (Rwanda, Darfur).

...

I. Fact-Finding: The Conventional View

...

A. Do Facts Exist?

The question as to whether facts exist is really another way of asking what facts are. Here, it is important to distinguish between conversational, philosophical, and legal uses of the term that may not be all the same. ... In actuality, there is almost no limit to what one might describe as a fact conventionally ... ,

...

1. Facts as Opposed to Opinion

... The idea of facts is that they are incontrovertible, certain, highly conducive to truth ... . The traditional Enlightenment criterion to distinguish the two is that facts are provable, whereas opinions are not. Yet in practice the distinction between fact and opinion has often proved challenging to uphold consistently, at least in ways that do not involve some arbitrary convention.

Perhaps the most reliable tools in this respect are those of scientific knowledge ... . Fact-finding strives to be, essentially, an empirical science. For evident reasons, human rights violations are not a phenomenon that can be replicated in a laboratory, but some human rights violations (for example, those that involve attacks on the right to life) leave traces susceptible to scientific analysis. Scientific, notably forensic, evidence is therefore a part and perhaps an increasingly important one of human rights fact-finding, all the more so that more and more grave and systematic human rights violations are considered to qualify as crimes. New methods based on the analysis of big data or various forms of technological surveillance may also open a sort of brave new world of scientific human rights surveillance. But scientific fact-finding can only ever be a part of human rights fact-finding. It may be particularly strong when establishing certain outcomes (people were killed, people were tortured) but relatively weak when it comes to some issues of attribution within complex organizations, not to mention a range of rights violations (freedom of expression, freedom of association, discrimination, etc.) that clearly do not lend themselves to forensic analysis. Short of scientifically produced evidence, facts typically seem constructed on the basis of at least three theories of facts, all of which at least raise some puzzling questions in the context of human rights about the extent to which they can be distinguished from opinion.

First, facts emerge from a process of exploration directed by triers of facts who are themselves supposed to have certain qualities, notably of impartiality, neutrality, and objectivity. This is the one thing that human rights fact-finding has in common with judicial fact-finding. It underscores the significance of having fact-finders who are beyond allegations of bias. The choice is one of relying on "persons whose psychological makeup, independence, training and reputation for perspicacity is such that their fact determinations (while not necessarily true in the objective—and irrelevant—sense) will carry a respectable warrant of credibility." One expects fact-finders, at any rate, to have an ability to, as it were, "step out of their own shoes," and distance themselves as much as possible from their own privately held opinions in order to endorse a purely public function. This has occasionally been problematic in the human rights context, because of a tendency of human rights fact-finders ... to have a track record in terms of denouncing certain human rights violations and being known for certain substantive stances. ...

Second, facts are also understood in terms of the impact that a certain demonstration has on its intended audience. ... The law, it should be noted, already incorporates some trade-offs between certainty and practicality. The plausibility of allegations and the relative weight of parties will shift the burden of proof in ways that maximize the ability to determine what really happened. On the one hand, this construction of facts relativizes the distinction between fact and opinion, making facts into a form of confidently held opinion, perhaps merely what a majority happens to decide happened. This adaptation to the difficulty or impossibility of certainty does something to reinforce facts' status by at least not holding them to an impossible standard. On the other hand, it is not clear who needs to be convinced in human rights fact-finding, and on the basis of what threshold. ...

Third and most importantly, facts are derived from certain recognized methods of constructing them. Even a perfectly impartial fact-finder would be suspicious if he failed to follow such a method. Opinion is not necessarily without method, but facts adhere to some presumably exacting and recognized procedure. ... [But, human rights] fact-finding missions are more likely to happen without a systematic contradictory procedure and honest confrontation (with the exception of subsequent disparagement of a fact-finding exercise's quality). The default of one party (e.g., a state) although it may superficially make things easier for the mission, ultimately risks undermining its authority. At any rate, human rights fact-finding is in a sense all fact-finding and very little procedure, even though various sides to a story may ultimately risk considerably in at least the court of international opinion. There is neither adversarial debate nor representation, although it is becoming increasingly customary to confront various parties to allegations made against them, and this provides at least an after-the-facts option to voice disapproval. Evidence is not introduced but "found," and issues of probative value trump any issue of admissibility. Again, this risks relativizing the distinction between opinion-making and fact-finding.

In practice, human rights fact-finding is part art and part science, and this is probably inescapable. What counts as a fact, then, is something quite complicated. It is typically a reconstruction based on some source and a particular theory of why that source makes it plausible, perhaps very highly plausible, that a certain thing occurred or is. For example, conventionally we may say that if a hundred people saw a shooting and testify to it in consistent terms and in a context where there is no reason to think that they would lie, then it is a fact that this shooting occurred. It is unlikely, until proof to the contrary, that they were all the victims of a collective illusion. The fact is that "a shooting occurred," but it might as well be that "a hundred people saw a shooting occur and testified to it in identical terms." Fact-finding often involves various types of facts (contextual, background facts; individual facts; facts concerning victims, concerning causation, or concerning state of mind) for which different types of evidence is required. Moreover, these facts rely on very different types of evidence (forensic, indicators, statistics) and, most importantly, a number of mental operations that tie them together (presumptions, deductions, inferences, extrapolations).

Of course, not even a solid method is a guarantee that what is obtained is more than an educated guess. If it has been suggested that as many as half of the testimonies before international criminal tribunals (made under oath in a context of thorough cross-examination and strict rules about admissibility of statements) are unreliable, then what are we to make of witness testimonies before fact-finding bodies, at times when passions will often run high and polarization be extreme? Even testimonies that are made in good faith may be wrong as witnesses confuse their perceptions and facts, or are betrayed by their memory, or allow their worldview to color their rendition of facts. In addition, one must consider that human rights fact-finding may concern facts whose scope and complexity is potentially far greater than the facts that are normally investigated by the judicial system (e.g., a single act of murder).
...

2. Facts as Opposed to Law

The second typical dichotomy involved in the constitution of facts is facts as opposed to norms, particularly legal norms. ...

Yet this dichotomy between fact and law is always at risk of collapsing. ...

...

The tendency for fact-finding to become engaged quite deeply in forms of legal assessment is inevitable but potentially problematic. Fact-finding will be vulnerable to the accusation that it is a form of adjudication without adjudication, or "adjudication lite." Legal issues will not be discussed in any detail and reduced to simple containers for facts that conveniently help label them and accelerate their delivery. For example, while judgments of international criminal tribunals include page after page of discussions of what constitutes a "generalized and systematic attack" for crimes against humanity, or "intention" and "civilians" when it comes to "intentionally targeting civilians," fact-finding exercises may omit such discussions, making them seem less important than they ought to be. This will then beg the question of why these complex substantive legal discussions are deemed essential to adjudication but can be taken lightly in the fact-finding context. The same thing applies to the absence of a formal procedure, and the existence of an opportunity for all parties to defend their point of view according to equitable rules.

B. Can They Be Found?

The idea of "fact-finding" tends to suggest an image of "fact finders" busily visiting various sites to find facts. This is potentially confusing. The idea of facts being "found" suggests quite literally that facts are, as it were, lying around waiting to be found. The suggestion seems to be that facts exist independently of our structures of thought, and that they can therefore be "found," almost literally. ...

The better view is that one does not find facts, as much as, potentially, clues that lead one to conclude that certain things are worthy of the label "factual." "Facts," as Jerome Frank put it, "do not walk into court." They are better seen as a category of understanding rather than a thing in itself. ...

Moreover, what gets apposed the label "fact" is contentious not only in relation to a fact's verifiability but also in relation to what one might describe as facts' enduring "unit of analysis" problem. The world is arguably made of endlessly embedded facts, each smaller fact nested into bigger facts, each bigger fact only deriving its fact-ness as a result of the fact-ness of its constituent units. The question therefore is not only what facts are but how they are strung together or, on the contrary, seen as independent. How one relates a series of smaller facts, for example, to the overall "fact" that Israel or Sri Lanka in certain circumstances engaged in campaigns to terrorize or target civilian populations or, on the contrary, defended themselves from terrorist attacks, is bound to be a complex process.

...

Ultimately, facts are constructed by our sense of what are socially relevant and salient facts. There is no fact-finding that is not a deliberate search for some preexisting fact that one speculates ought to be there, or whose absence would be notable. Every exercise in fact-finding is one that has been authorized at least at some level and that is saturated with the presuppositions that went into this particular search being made socially relevant. In that respect, human rights fact-finding is not just fact-finding for its own sake but fact-finding informed by a particular logic. ...

Allowing for such caveats, facts can no doubt still be constructed. But it is also important to remember that there are all kinds of prisms and filters that may hamper that construction. ...

II. Fact-Finding as Strategic Exercise

Even as fact-finding is an increasingly popular exercise in international human rights, it encounters significant resistance. ... There is, in fact, a certain imperviousness to facts, and simply labeling them as such will not necessarily help much. Holocaust denialism is a well-known example but there are others, such as 9/11 conspiracy theories. The Internet has if anything made facts both less and more accessible, and ensured that every "fact" is immediately in competition with a variety of "counter-facts." ...

...

... Ultimately, for the purposes of political action, questions about the "reality" of facts may matter less than the question of what it takes to make facts credible in the social world. ... The goal ... is not only to uncover facts but to produce credible ones. ... I focus on three ways in which it may be useful to move beyond a supposedly uncontested notion of facts-as-outcome to a focus on taking the process of fact-finding in new directions, by looking at practices that are not typically thought of as central in the current model of fact-finding.

A. Legitimizing

Rather than simply thinking in terms of the sheer potency of "facts," it may be useful to think of the legitimacy of various fact-finding exercises, and the ways that legitimacy can be forcefully enhanced by a constant attention to what might otherwise weaken it. In the same way that it is often said that "justice should not only be done but be seen to be done," fact-finding should also "appear to be done." ...
...

B. Communicating

Second, fact-finding also crucially involves a degree of communicating the facts to potential audiences. One may think that the production of facts is also a constant process of persuasion and indeed of education about facts. In this context, it seems to matter less whether something is a fact or not than whether it is believed in or not. ...
...
[T]hinking of fact-finding as a form of communication also means that fact-finding can be imagined as a form of a dialogue. Communication is not one-way but a dialogical process, in which upon learning of the conclusions of a fact-finding exercise relevant constituencies may have new evidence to bring to the table. This also has implications for the temporality of fact-finding. ...
...

C. Strategizing

Finally, fact production can be seen as vulnerable to a series of tensions that create a variety of strategic dilemmas. First, we can think of facts as having two purposes, notably in the UN context: facts are needed for action, and they are needed for adjudication. The facts needed for each, however, are not the same. Facts necessary for action are merely quasi-facts, facts as they can best be ascertained in the circumstances; there is a recognition that time is of the essence, that decision cannot afford to wait for certainty. Facts as needed for adjudication are more in the manner of incontrovertible, demonstrable, or highly probable truth because of the way the negative consequences they portend for persons or institutions and because one does not have, unlike political action, the excuse that time is pressing. Human rights fact-finding, and therein lies some of its challenges, now more often than not occupies a dual space: providing facts both for the political decision-maker and potentially for the adjudicator. But there are evident tensions between the needs for urgency and certainty, especially in a context of lack of resources and in perilous environments.
...

III. Conclusion

... [F]acts can be rescued from relativism precisely by safeguarding their relativity. It is when one claims too much in the name of facts that one exposes the practice of fact-finding to brutal reversals. ...

... This chapter has sought to propose a modest approach focused on fact-finding as a practice, one that is broader ultimately than its name suggests and includes the ability to legitimize, communicate, and strategize about facts. In the end, though, we are left with nothing but the struggle over facts, a struggle that should be appreciated at its just value as certainly not doomed but evidently fraught with ambiguities.
...
... [T]here is also an ethical dimension to facts. Refusing to believe what one has no way of disproving, asking for perfection in fact-finding, excluding facts that provoke narrative dissonance, always assuming the worse in others, engaging in conspiracy theories: all such behavior that presents itself as based on a critique of knowledge

may in the end merely reveal moral ineptitude. The Holocaust denier in this perspective is perhaps less a flawed scientist/historian than he is someone who has distanced himself from the ability to listen to witnesses, hear sad stories of pain and grief, and, fundamentally, empathize with humanity. This inability to hear the obvious is perhaps a characteristic of many of the campaigns of denigration that have been launched against certain fact-finding exercises, which are never as weak as when they seem to entirely and callously distance themselves from the lived experience of pain of victims, complicated and constructed as it may be. The moral stance, on the contrary, may be to cautiously believe in the best attempts at producing facts, for to not do so on the basis that there is always a possibility that they may not be true—that there is some stone left to be unturned— may not be to defend facts but to be their enemy.

A. UN COMMISSIONS OF INQUIRY: CASE STUDIES

As of January 2024, there were active Human Rights Council-created COIs focused on Sudan (established in 2023), Nicaragua (2022), Ukraine (2022), the Occupied Palestinian Territories and Israel (2021), Libya (2020), Venezuela (2019), Myanmar (2018), the Democratic Republic of the Congo (2018), and Syria (2011). A UN *Research Guide on International Commissions of Inquiry, Fact-finding Missions: Chronological list* identifies 93 UN COIs created between 1963 and 2022, 75 of which were established after 2000. UN fact-finding panels can be set up by institutions other than the Human Rights Council, such as the Secretary-General, and the Security Council.

An evaluation of whether these COIs make a difference depends both on the criteria that are used to define success and on complex issues relating to causality. Michael Becker and Sarah Nouwen, in 'International Commissions of Inquiry: What Difference Do They Make? Taking an Empirical Approach', 30 *Eur. J. Int'l L.* (2019) 819, suggest a typology of the differences that a COI could make. They begin by noting that COIs might facilitate or encourage either action or inaction:

> A COI is inherently a response to a particular situation. International attention may begin a process of agenda setting and marshalling political will to take other action, or it may provide the impetus (or 'cover') for a government to undertake domestic reforms or engage in negotiations aimed at resolving the underlying problem. The fact that an inquiry body was set up to investigate a situation may in itself have (legal) significance. ...

> However, the creation of a COI may also accommodate inaction. It may forestall more destabilizing actions (such as states or non-state actors seeking recourse through the use of force) by giving parties a 'cooling-off' period that can help to prevent decisions being taken in a fog of disputed facts or in the heat of the moment. But it may also (or instead) be a stand-in for other action – a means to signal 'concern without commitment'. Establishing a COI may placate (at least temporarily) concerned parties or function as the best alternative to other potential responses that decision-makers cannot agree upon (for instance, military intervention, peacekeeping or sanctions). ... A COI may also be created to pre-empt or obstruct other forms of intervention (inquiry or otherwise) that are viewed as hostile or more intrusive. For example, in response to the outbreak of violence in South Sudan in December 2013, the African Union created a COI, almost overnight, to avoid a referral of the situation by the UNSC to the ICC. And, ... Bahrain's creation of its Bahrain Independent Commission of Inquiry (BICI) largely extinguished international support for a UN-led inquiry body.

Becker and Nouwen note that COIs might serve to justify other forms of international action, either before or after they report. They also identify a number of other binaries that help us to think about the impact of COIs. Thus, they might (i) foster a shared narrative or harden competing narratives; (ii) legitimize some groups and delegitimize others; (iii) enhance political dialogue or intensify division; (iv) mobilize or demobilize certain constituencies or cause a backlash; and (v) spur reform or encourage more of the same.

We turn now to two in-depth case studies of UN COIs, relating first to Venezuela and then to Myanmar.

Venezuela Case Study

We begin with the mandate given to the COI by the Council and then consider the Mission's 2022 report on crimes against humanity committed in Venezuela. The focus is on the methodology used to build the report, the standard of proof used, and the approach to naming individuals considered to be responsible for crimes.

HUMAN RIGHTS COUNCIL, RESOLUTION 42/25 (2019) ON THE SITUATION OF HUMAN RIGHTS IN THE BOLIVARIAN REPUBLIC OF VENEZUELA

[Adopted by a vote of 19-7-21. States voting against were Cameroon, China, Cuba, Egypt, Eritrea, Philippines, Saudi Arabia.]

The Human Rights Council,
...
Expressing grave concern at the alarming situation of human rights in [Venezuela], which includes patterns of violations directly and indirectly affecting all human rights – civil, political, economic, social and cultural – in the context of the ongoing political, economic, social and humanitarian crisis, as stated in the reports of the [UN HCHR] and of other international organizations,
...
Expressing deep concern for the more than 4 million people compelled to leave [Venezuela] ... because of, inter alia, violations of the rights to food and health, violence and insecurity, the collapse of basic services, the deterioration of the education system, lack of access to pre- and post-natal care, and insufficient mechanisms for protection from violence and persecution on political grounds,
...
Welcoming the mission of the [OHCHR in March 2019] to prepare the visit of the High Commissioner ... from 19 to 21 June 2019, and the resulting commitments, including with regard to the establishment of a permanent presence of the [OHCHR] in the country ...,

Welcoming also the ongoing dialogue between the High Commissioner and the Venezuelan authorities ... ,
...
Mindful that the Prosecutor of the International Criminal Court has decided to open a preliminary examination of the situation ... to analyse crimes allegedly committed in this State Party since at least April 2017 ...,
...
2. Strongly condemns all violations and abuses of international human rights law in [Venezuela] ...;

3. Also strongly condemns the widespread targeted repression and persecution on political grounds ... including the excessive use of force against peaceful protests, the excessive use of force during security operations, arbitrary detention, torture, ill-treatment, extrajudicial executions and enforced disappearances by security forces ...;
...
5. Deplores the ... erosion of the rule of law and of democratic institutions ...;
...
22. Requests the High Commissioner to continue to monitor and report on the situation ...;
...
24. Decides to establish, for a period of one year, an independent international fact- finding mission, to be appointed by the President of the Human Rights Council, and to dispatch that mission urgently to [Venezuela] to investigate extrajudicial executions, enforced disappearances, arbitrary detentions and torture and other cruel, inhumane or degrading treatment since 2014 with a view to ensuring full accountability for perpetrators and justice for victims ...;

25. Urges the Venezuelan authorities to cooperate fully with the fact-finding mission, to grant it immediate, full and unfettered access to and throughout the country, including to victims and places of detention, and to provide it with all the information necessary to fulfil its mandate;
...

DETAILED FINDINGS OF THE INDEPENDENT INTERNATIONAL FACT-FINDING MISSION ON THE BOLIVARIAN REPUBLIC OF VENEZUELA UN DOC. A/HRC/51/CRP.3 (2022)

Crimes against humanity committed through the State's intelligence services: structures and individuals involved in the implementation of the plan to repress opposition to the Government

[The report focuses largely on SEBIN, which is the Bolivarian National Intelligence Service, and DGCIM, which is the General Directorate of Military Counter-Intelligence.]

…

B.   Methodology

13. [T]he Mission followed established methodologies and best practices for human rights fact-finding, as developed by the United Nations. [It] conducted its work in accordance with the principles of independence, impartiality, objectivity, transparency and integrity.

14. The Mission continued to base its information gathering on the investigation of cases … . [This] report is based on 471 interviews conducted by the Mission: [125 with victims; 40 with family members; 65 with legal representatives; 53 with former government employees; and 188 with intermediaries, journalists, NGO representatives and others].

15. The Mission has decided to focus the present investigation on deepening its understanding of the chains of command and responsibilities for violations and crimes within two detention centres, SEBIN's El Helicoide and DGCIM's Boleíta. This is due to the especially high number of violations and crimes occurring within these detention centres between 2014 and present, and the availability of information. …

16. The Mission was able to collect information primarily through …: (1) confidential interviews, both in-person and via secure telephone or video connections; (2) confidential documents obtained from individuals and organizations, including legal case files; and (3) review of open source information.

17. The factual findings on material facts made in the present report are based on at least one credible source of direct information, which was independently corroborated by at least one other credible source of information. Where the report describes patterns of conduct, these are based on the common elements established by the cases investigated, corroborated by other credible information collected.

18. The Mission considered the following to be sources of direct information, where the sources were reliable and credible:

> Interviews with victims and other witnesses with direct knowledge of incidents

> Interviews with family members and lawyers of victims with direct knowledge of certain aspects of cases/incidents

> Legal case files and other verified confidential documents

> Interviews with former Government, intelligence and military officials and others with direct knowledge of specific cases or of the internal workings of certain institutions (insiders)

>> • Publicly available statements or information regarding relevant facts provided by Government institutions and representatives (including televised statements or statements posted on social media)

>> • Laws, policies, directives and other legal documents of the Government of Venezuela

19. The Mission devoted throughout its investigations specific attention to gendered issues and impacts of violations and strove to implement a gender approach, using gender-sensitive methodologies and tools for collecting, organizing, analysing and reflecting information … .

20. The Mission ensured it had the informed consent from each person it interviewed before using any information provided. It has anonymized the identities of sources, witnesses and victims, where revealing these could place the individual and/or his/her family members at risk of reprisals. While preserving the confidentiality of the interaction of victims and other witnesses with the Mission, it maintains a full database of information and evidence upon which it bases the analysis and conclusions contained in the present report. The information is stored on safe platforms, with strict and controlled access, applying best practices in terms of digital security and permanent control. Access will only be granted to the extent that witnesses or the originators of other sources of information have given their informed consent, and protection concerns have been addressed.

21. … The Mission regrets that three years into its mandate, the Government of Venezuela still has not permitted its members or its Secretariat staff to visit Venezuela in order to undertake in-country fact-finding.

C. Standard of proof

22. [T]he Mission used "reasonable grounds to believe" as its standard of proof. [This] standard is met when factual information has been collected, which would satisfy an objective and ordinarily prudent observer that the incident has occurred as described with a reasonable degree of certainty.

23. The Mission applied the standard of proof to determinations as to whether: (a) the violation or crime occurred, and (b) the individual identified was responsible. This standard of proof is lower than that required in criminal proceedings for a criminal conviction (certainty beyond a reasonable doubt) as well as that required to sustain an indictment. It is also lower than the balance of probability test in civil matters (meaning that something is more likely than not to have happened). However, it is sufficiently high to indicate that further investigations are warranted.

…

[Before reading the next excerpt from the Mission's report, consider OHCHR's 'summary of key guidance' to COIs on attributing individual responsibility:[388]

- Investigative bodies may attribute responsibility to individuals for crimes or violations … [of] international human rights law, international humanitarian law and international criminal law;
- Individuals can be identified as "responsible" for violations and crimes, whether in the criminal legal sense in [sic] or the administrative, civil, moral or political sense;
- For international human rights law findings, the individual identified must have been in a position to invoke the State's responsibility under international law (i.e., must be a State agent); while for de facto authorities and NSAs, the individual must be similarly situated;
- Even in the absence of explicit language in an applicable international human rights law treaty, the conduct of superiors and accomplices who may be indirectly involved can and should be captured by the investigation;

…

- The personal security of interviewees is never more important than when the topic concerns specific individuals and their responsibility for crimes and violations. Staff must pay maximum attention to witness protection, consent, and information security protocols.]

D. Naming of individuals in the present report

25. The Mission has concluded, on reasonable grounds to believe, that certain individuals addressed in the present report may be responsible for crimes and violations and should therefore be investigated. The Mission reiterates that it is an investigative but not a judicial body, and in essence any determination of criminal

---

[388] OHCHR, *Who's Responsible? Attributing Individual Responsibility for Violations of International Human Rights and Humanitarian Law in United Nations Commissions of Inquiry, Fact-Finding Missions and Other Investigations* (2018), at 68

responsibility with respect to the individuals mentioned in this report must be made by the appropriate judicial authorities acting with full respect for due process guarantees and fair trial standards. The Mission has chosen to publicly name some of the individuals whose contributions to crimes and violations it investigated. ...

26. The Mission considers that this approach upholds the value of the publicity of the work of fact-finding bodies and carries the potential to act as a deterrent to further violations. The Mission has carefully considered all possible implications and conducted risk-assessments. In light of particular security concerns, including the risk of reprisals against victims, family members, and others, the Mission has decided to anonymize certain individuals whose contributions to crimes and violations it investigated. ...

27. The Mission ... has actively sought to gather the views of the implicated individuals and to provide them with a right to reply to the allegations made against them. In parallel, the Mission publicly invited interested individuals, groups and organizations to submit information ... . [It] made available an online form and invited interested individuals to submit any "exculpatory information" they may possess.
...
29. The Mission regrets not having received any response or additional information from the relevant individuals, nor from the Government ... . Its factual determinations are therefore based on a rigorous analysis of the information it was able to gather ... [T]hese determinations should prompt thorough criminal investigations ... .

D. Determinations

457. ... [I]t has been established on reasonable grounds to believe that individuals who operated within SEBIN and DGCIM were involved in the commission of crimes and violations ... .

458. Information gathered by the Mission, both from present and previous investigations, supports that the President, seconded by other high-level State officials, put in place a policy/plan that included acts aimed at silencing, discouraging and quashing opposition to the Government, by targeting opponents, persons perceived as such and their relatives or friends. This conduct included the commission of violations and crimes through individuals serving in DGCIM's Boleíta and SEBIN's Helicoide.

459. SEBIN and DGCIM operate as hierarchical and organized institutions under the control of the President, seconded by other high-level State officials. To ensure compliance with orders, SEBIN and DGCIM maintain a sufficient pool of available individuals, recruited amongst those prone to commit arbitrary detentions and acts of torture and other cruel, inhuman or degrading treatment, including sexual and gender-based violence. The selection takes into account the manner they react to violent practices, they are often very young and belonged to vulnerable communities. In addition, a system of rewards (promotions and financial benefit) and punishments (retaliation against them and their families) is maintained to ensure compliance. ...

460. ... The Mission finds, with reasonable grounds to believe, that the President and the high-level State officials that [supported] him should be subjected to judicial investigations for their responsibility with regard to the crimes and violations committed through DGCIM and SEBIN officials ... .
...

* * *

The Mission recommended, inter alia, that Venezuela investigate those named in its report and it called upon other States to 'consider initiating legal actions' against the same individuals 'in accordance with their relevant domestic legislation and applicable international principles.' It also drew its report and its focus on the specific individuals to the attention of the International Criminal Court.

In response to the Mission's reporting, Venezuela told the Council (UN Press Release, 26 September 2022) that:

[T]he so-called fact-finding Mission had surpassed itself, creating a fiction about the country, aiming to please the international media circus, whose vultures just wanted to feed, and not reflect what was really happening.

Everything was invented - millions of phantom migrants, so-called terrorist camps, and even a parallel President, whose existence was improbable. They had struck low, but had failed in the criminal aim of regime change, as desired by the United States. The report submitted and the statements made therein were a sad proof of how banal international law had become. It was a perverse media alliance, making such unsubstantiated allegations, bandied about without any proof; a laboratory report, beggaring belief, and aiming to incriminate the President. The Mission used anonymous sources which could not be proved, and were unreliable. This was a testament of fake news. These tactics were often used against countries of the South.

Venezuela was moving forward with freedom and determination, despite its persecution from all these quarters ... . Venezuela protected human rights and did not recognise these parallel mechanisms which sought to destabilise the country, but would always fail. These hegemonic agendas did not foster dialogue nor human rights. Venezuela would take the relevant diplomatic measures if this interventionist mandate continued.'

In October 2022, the Council renewed the Mission's mandate for two more years.

QUESTIONS

1. In the Venezuela COI report, an important focus is on criminal accountability, even though no resolution of the situation is in sight. How would you reconcile this with the analysis of Steven Ratner in 'After Atrocity: Optimizing UN Action Toward Accountability for Human Rights Abuses', 36 *Mich. J. Int'l L* (2015) 541, at 553. Ratner played a key role in COIs on Cambodia, Sri Lanka, and Ethiopia. He argues that, in general, focusing on criminal accountability is 'extremely short-sighted ... . First, in situations where atrocities are ongoing, termination is more important than accountability. ... In rare cases, criminal accountability can serve as a means to end ongoing violations ... but most of the time, the UN should make ending the abuses the priority.' He adds that 'accountability is a gradual process, and a consensus must be built for it; one cannot simply move directly to putting a state's leaders or former leaders in the dock, and certainly not at the ICC. A demand by the UN for immediate trials of named individuals when a state has no willingness to do so will merely allow opponents of accountability to accuse the UN of undermining its sovereignty and wanting nothing more than the heads of governmental leaders.'

2. What is the role of politics in relation to COIs? Ratner's view is that a priority goal 'must be to gain domestic support for accountability' He notes this 'does not mean ignoring a state's legal obligations and international standards' but the report should be 'sensitive to the politics of the country. ... Politics does and should affect the interpretation of a commission's mandate, the tone of the report, and the recommendations. Fact-finding, then, demands political expertise and awareness among those undertaking it ... .' How should a COI balance the need to state the facts or allegations clearly with the need to adopt a tone that will promote political support for its report both within the state and internationally?

3. Could the focus on individual criminal accountability be seen as a 'distraction or decoy drawing attention away from addressing the role of States in perpetrating atrocity crimes and in maintaining structures that may threaten peace'?[389]

---

[389] L. Fletcher, 'A Wolf in Sheep's Clothing: Transitional Justice and the Effacement of State Accountability for International Crimes', 39 *Fordham Int'l L. J.* (2016) 447, at 517.

Myanmar Case Study

In 1948 Myanmar, then Burma, gained independence from British colonial rule. From 1948 to 1962, it was a parliamentary democracy but, in 1962, General Ne Win took power in a military coup. One-party rule ensued, until massive demonstrations forced his resignation in 1988. The military retained power in the guise of the State Law and Order Restoration Council (SLORC). The head of the National League for Democracy (NLD), Daw Aung San Suu Kyi, was placed under house arrest in 1989. Elections were held in 1990 and, although the NLD won 81% of the seats, the military refused to relinquish power. Since independence, the military has been in constant conflict with ethnic and other minorities and, in 1992, this led to a mass exodus of Myanmar Muslims from Rakhine State into neighboring Bangladesh.

A new Constitution was adopted in 2008 but it was carefully designed to ensure the military's continuing dominance of politics and the economy. In 2010, the Government undertook wide-ranging reforms, but without amending the Constitution. Sanctions were lifted and foreign investment welcomed. The NLD took office in 2016 after an overwhelming electoral victory but the Tatmadaw, the Myanmar military, retained the upper hand. Violent attacks against the Rohingyas and other minorities continued on a large-scale, even under the government led by Aung San Suu Kyi. In February 2021, a military coup overthrew the civilian government, leading to sustained resistance and ever greater repression.

In the face of international pressure, the government has regularly created its own COIs to investigate allegations, but none has ever led to meaningful change or prosecutions. The UN Commission on Human Rights appointed a Country Rapporteur in 1992 and, as of 2023, there have been six different Rapporteurs. In 2017, the Human Rights Council established a three member COI called the International Fact-Finding Mission on Myanmar (FFM, or FFMM). It produced several major reports, including a 444-page report in September 2018 and a follow-up report in September 2019. In that year, it handed over its accumulated records to a new Independent Investigative Mechanism for Myanmar (IIIM) established by the Council with a mandate to collect, consolidate, preserve and analyse evidence of the most serious international crimes and violations of international law committed in Myanmar since 2011, and to prepare files in order to facilitate and expedite fair and independent criminal proceedings, in accordance with international law standards, in national, regional or international courts or tribunals. In 2020, the Council called for the Mechanism to cooperate closely with the ICJ and the ICC. In 2023, the Mechanism reported (UN Doc. A/HRC/54/19) that its repository contained over 23 million information items, including interview statements, documentation, videos, photographs, geospatial imagery and social media material.

The COI's findings featured prominently in argument in *The Gambia v. Myanmar* before the International Court of Justice since 2019 (Ch. 2D, above). The Court had discussed the weight to be accorded to such reports in an earlier case, *Armed Activities on the Territory of the Congo (Dem. Rep. Congo v. Uganda)*, 2005 I.C.J. 168, in which it noted that it would 'treat with caution evidentiary materials … emanating from a single source. It will prefer contemporaneous evidence from persons with direct knowledge. … [It will also] give weight to evidence that has not … been challenged by impartial persons for the correctness of what it contains' (para. 61) Ultimately, the Court found 'the coincidence of reports from credible sources [including from a country Special Rapporteur] sufficient to convince it that massive human rights violations and grave breaches of international humanitarian law were committed' (para. 207).[390]

In 2018, the UN Secretary-General appointed a senior Guatemalan diplomat, Gert Rosenthal, to assess the UN's own role in Myanmar between 2010 and 2018. The organization was widely accused of standing by and doing little in response to the ever-mounting evidence of atrocities commitment by the government, with which it continued to work closely. On the basis of a desk review and no on-site visit, he concluded that there had been systematic failures and that the UN's performance had been 'obvious[ly] dysfunctional'.[391]

A major challenge in fact-finding, including in Myanmar, is how to respond to sexual and gender-based violence (SGBV), which is a major element in the vast majority of conflict situations. Thus, the Council of Europe's

---

[390] For a critique of this approach, see S. Halink, 'All Things Considered: How the International Court of Justice Delegated its Fact-Assessment to the United Nations in the Armed Activities Case', 40 *NYU J. Intl. L. & Pol.* (2008) 13.
[391] For the UN's own response, see UN Doc. A/HRC/49/73 (2022).

Commissioner for Human Rights reported in a 'Memorandum on the human rights consequences of the war in Ukraine' (Doc. CommDH (2022)18), that she had ' received from many sources numerous reports of war-related sexual violence, including rape, gang rape, threats of sexual violence, or coercion to watch an act of sexual violence committed against a partner or a child, allegedly committed by Russian troop members at various locations under their control in Ukraine' (para. 29). For many years, the specificities of the issues raised by SGBV were largely unrecognized. As awareness has grown, especially since the early 1990s, there have been many efforts to ensure that a nuanced, tailored and sensitive approach is adopted by fact-finders and other human rights missions.[392] In the Ukraine case, the Commissioner observed that:

> [V]ictims and witnesses of sexual violence may be reluctant to speak about their ordeal or to file complaints out of fear or because of trauma or the social stigma associated with sexual violence. Notwithstanding the importance that all allegations of war-related sexual violence are investigated without delay, the Commissioner highlights that the creation of safe conditions for victims to come forward and cooperate with law enforcement, including by preserving their privacy and avoiding re-traumatisation, must be prioritised. Survivors of war-related sexual violence must have effective access to redress for the harm suffered, including medical rehabilitation and psychosocial support, as well as access to justice. … [T]hey should be treated individually in terms of the type of response needed and their wishes in this regard should be always respected (para. 31).

The excerpts below give a flavor of the approach adopted by the Myanmar COI. The first report focuses on the situation of the Rohingya ethnic group, and the second report seeks to identify the economic interests that are enabling the Myanmar military to fund and sustain its oppression. These reports are followed by an analysis revealing the extent of fact-finding efforts undertaken by civil society groups working in and on Myanmar.

DETAILED FINDINGS OF THE UN HUMAN RIGHTS COUNCIL'S INDEPENDENT INTERNATIONAL FACT-FINDING MISSION ON MYANMAR UN DOC. A/HRC/42/CRP.5 (2019)

...

The situation of the Rohingya

2. The situation of the Rohingya continues to be of grave concern to the Mission. The Mission did not document in relation to the last year violations of a similar gravity to the Tatmadaw's "clearance operations" after attacks on police and military posts on 25 August 2017, described in its last report. However, it confirmed that the Rohingya remain the target of a Government attack aimed at erasing the identity and removing them from Myanmar, and that this has caused them great suffering. Additionally, many of the factors that contributed to the killings, rapes and gang rapes, torture, forced displacement and other grave human rights violations by the Tatmadaw and other government authorities that the Mission documented in its 2018 report are still present. This has led to the conclusion that the situation of the Rohingya in Rakhine State has remained largely unchanged since last year. The laws, policies and practices that formed the basis of the Government's persecution against the Rohingya have been maintained. With another year having passed without improvements to their dire living conditions, prospects for accountability or legal recognition as citizens of Myanmar, their plight can only be considered as having deteriorated.

3. The Government of Myanmar has made no progress towards addressing the underlying structural discrimination against the Rohingya by amending the discriminatory laws, including the 1982 Citizenship Law. State policies that impose and force Rohingya to accept national verification cards (NVCs) have intensified. The Rohingya continue to perceive the NVCs with scepticism due to their history as a tool of persecution, having been used to disenfranchise and "other" them from the rest of the population.

---

[392] See, for example, the Global Code of Conduct for Gathering and Using Information about Systematic and Conflict-Related Sexual Violence, named the 'Murad Code', after the Nobel Peace Prize laureate, Nadia Murad, who was sexually enslaved by ISIS in 2014; Witness, *Using Video to Support Justice and Accountability for Sexual and Gender-Based Violence* (2021); and K. Bergtora Sandvik and K. Lohne, 'The Struggle against Sexual Violence in Conflict: Investigating the Digital Turn', 102 (913) *Int'l Rev. Red Cross* (2020) 95.

4. The Mission found that movement restrictions, applied to the Rohingya in a discriminatory and arbitrary manner, touch almost every aspect of the lives of the 600,000 Rohingya remaining in Rakhine State, affecting basic economic, social and cultural rights, including their ability to sustain themselves, obtain an education, seek medical assistance or even pray and congregate.

5. The lack of safe and viable homes and land for Rohingya to return to is further exacerbating their situation. The Mission found that Rohingya villages continue to be bulldozed and razed. An estimated 40,600 structures were destroyed between August 2017 and April 2019, with over 200 settlements almost completely wiped out. Instead, new structures are being built on land that used to be cultivated and lived on by those who fled. Paradoxically, the Mission found that Rohingya have been forced to work in constructing new housing developments, in conditions that amount to forced labour.

6. Against the backdrop of these unbearable conditions, insecurity has been heightened as a result of the conflict between the Arakan Army and the Tatmadaw in northern Rakhine, in areas from which Rohingya were expelled. This has been an additional contributing factor to making a safe, dignified and sustainable return of the Rohingya population impossible at this time.

7. Justice remains elusive for the victims of grave crimes under international law that the Mission documented in its last report, in particular those perpetrated during the 2016 and 2017 "clearance operations". The Government of Myanmar has not taken the necessary measures to effectively investigate or prosecute those responsible.

8. The cumulative effect of these factors has led the Mission to conclude on reasonable grounds that the Government's acts continue to be part of a widespread and systematic attack against the remaining Rohingya in Rakhine State, amounting to the crimes against humanity of inhumane acts and persecution.

9. Furthermore, having considered the Government's hostile policies towards the Rohingya, including its continued denial of their citizenship and ethnic identity, the living conditions to which it subjects them, its failure to reform laws that subjugate the Rohingya people, the continuation of hate speech directed at the Rohingya, its prior commission of genocide and its disregard for accountability in relation to the "clearances operations" of 2016 and 2017, the Mission also has reasonable grounds to conclude that the evidence that infers genocidal intent on the part of the State, identified in its last report, has strengthened, that there is a serious risk that genocidal actions may occur or recur, and that Myanmar is failing in its obligation to prevent genocide, to investigate genocide and to enact effective legislation criminalizing and punishing genocide. Against this background, the Mission deems that the conditions enabling the safe, voluntary, dignified and sustainable return of close to one million Rohingya refugees from Bangladesh do not yet exist. The current conditions makes their return impossible at this time. Because of the absence of positive change over the past two years, the Mission cannot foresee when repatriation will be feasible.

…

THE ECONOMIC INTERESTS OF THE MYANMAR MILITARY, REPORT BY THE INDEPENDENT INTERNATIONAL FACT-FINDING MISSION ON MYANMAR UN DOC. A/HRC/42/CRP.3 (2019)

Executive summary and key recommendations

3. The Mission is issuing this report on the Tatmadaw's economic interests to assist the Government of Myanmar, United Nations Security Council, Member States, relevant regional and international inter-governmental organizations, investors and businesses, international financial institutions, and the United Nations, its funds, programmes and agencies, in implementing [its] recommendations.

4. The outsize power of the Tatmadaw has affected Myanmar's transition from full direct military dictatorship following the November 2010 and subsequent November 2015 elections. The National League for Democracy, led by Aung San Suu Kyi, won the 2015 election and took over the civilian side of the Government in March 2016. However, as prescribed by the 2008 constitution, the Tatmadaw is an autonomous institution free from

any civilian control or oversight. It controls the ministries of defence, home affairs and border affairs, whose ministers are serving military officers selected by the Commander-in-Chief. It retains 25 per cent of the seats in the legislature, giving it the power to veto any constitutional change.

…

6. This report does not provide an exhaustive list of all businesses, individuals and States that provide economic benefit to the Tatmadaw and its senior generals. That was not possible in the time and with the resources available to the Mission. However, it provides an overview and a foundation upon which other investigators and researchers can continue to build. The findings described below are supported with information listed in the annexes to this report. Based on its investigations, the Mission has concluded on reasonable grounds that:

> (a) Two Tatmadaw conglomerates, Myanmar Economic Holdings Limited (MEHL) and Myanmar Economic Corporation (MEC), are owned and influenced by senior Tatmadaw leaders, including the Commander-in-Chief Senior General Min Aung Hlaing and the Deputy Commander-in-Chief Vice Senior General Soe Win, responsible for gross violations of international human rights law and serious violations of international humanitarian law. The Mission identified 106 MEHL and MEC owned businesses across diverse sectors of the economy … . The revenue that these military businesses generate strengthens the Tatmadaw's autonomy … .
>
> There are strong and persistent business and familial links between the Tatmadaw, its conglomerates MEHL and MEC, and a number of private Myanmar companies and conglomerates, colloquially known as "crony companies".
>
> (b) Human rights and international humanitarian law violations, including forced labour and sexual violence, have been perpetrated by the Tatmadaw in mining areas, particularly in Kachin State, in connection with their business activities. …
>
> (c) At least 45 companies and organizations provided the Tatmadaw with USD 6.15 million in financial donations … in support of the "clearance operations" that began in August 2017 against the Rohingya in northern Rakhine. The Mission also found that private companies with enduring links to the Tatmadaw are financing development projects in northern Rakhine in furtherance of the Tatmadaw's objective of re-engineering the region in a way that erases evidence of Rohingya belonging in Myanmar, and preventing their return to access their homeland and communities. … [T]he Mission has identified private companies with officials who may have made a substantial and direct contribution to the commission of crimes under international law, including the crime against humanity of "other inhumane acts" and persecution, warranting their criminal investigation.
>
> (d) 14 foreign companies have joint ventures and at least 44 foreign companies have other forms of commercial ties with Tatmadaw businesses. Through such joint venture and commercial relationships, the Mission finds that any foreign business activity involving the Tatmadaw and its conglomerates MEHL and MEC poses a high risk of contributing to, or being linked to, violations … .
>
> (e) At least 14 foreign companies from seven States have provided arms and related equipment to the Tatmadaw since 2016, after the Tatmadaw's dismal human rights record was widely and publicly known. Moreover, the public record made it clear that the Tatmadaw used many of the types of arms and related equipment that these entities were providing to commit gross violations of human rights and serious violations of international humanitarian law. Many of these companies and States therefore knew, or ought to have known, that their arms transfers could have a direct and reasonably foreseeable impact on the human rights situation in Myanmar. Among the arms suppliers identified by the Mission, 12 companies are State-owned enterprises.

The Mission also received credible information regarding seven foreign private companies from which the Tatmadaw procured or sought to procure dual-use goods and technology since 2016. The technology includes telecommunications services, tracking and precision systems, unmanned aerial vehicles, and internet and data transmission technology.

7. ... [T]he United Nations Security Council, Member States, relevant regional and international inter-governmental organizations should impose targeted financial sanctions against all Tatmadaw-owned companies, especially MEHL, MEC and their subsidiaries, and do so in a manner that respects human rights and gives due consideration to any negative socio-economic impact of such sanctions on the civilian population. This should be accompanied by a comprehensive arms embargo on Myanmar, with a monitoring and enforcement mechanism.

8. The Mission reiterates its recommendation from its 2018 report that "targeted individual sanctions, including travel bans and asset freezes, could support a reduction in violations of international law ... . This report also indicates areas that deserve greater attention, recalling that investigations leading to the tracing, freezing, seizure and recovery of assets linked to persons responsible for crimes under international law is a critical component in the pursuit of accountability. It is also critical for Member States to exercise jurisdiction to investigate and, if appropriate, prosecute officials of companies who allegedly participated in the commission of serious crimes under international law committed in relation to Myanmar's human rights crisis.

...

NOTE

In addition to the UN COI, and an ILO Commission set up in 2022 to investigate violations of freedom of association and the prohibition on forced labour, a wide range of other initiatives have focused on this situation.[393] An illustration of the intermingling of governmental and non-governmental fact-finding is a report funded by the U.S. State Department, which enabled a team of 20 investigators to interview 1,024 Rohingya refugees in camps in Cox's Bazaar, Bangladesh, in a very short space of time in 2018. The report, by the Public International Law and Policy Group, was published as *Documenting Atrocity Crimes Committed Against the Rohingya in Myanmar's Rakhine State*, but it also provided the content for an official State Department report entitled *Documentation of Atrocities in Northern Rakhine State* (August 2018). The former version was subsequently cited some 29 times in the International Criminal Court's Pre-Trial Chamber's decision to authorize an investigation into the Situation in Bangladesh/Myanmar (Doc. ICC-01/19, of 14 November 2019).

According to press reports, the Trump Administration had labeled the situation as 'ethnic cleansing', but was unable to agree on the next steps. But in December 2018, the U.S. House of Representatives voted 394 to 1 to characterize it as 'crimes against humanity and genocide' (Resolution 1091 (116th Congress)). The State Department report, along with reports by 11 different civil society groups, provided the backdrop for this action.[394] The Resolution also called upon the Secretary of State to make a determination along the same lines. But Secretary Pompeo refused, reportedly for fear of driving the Myanmar Government 'into China's orbit' and in order not to distract attention from Pompeo's declaration that China was committing genocide against the Uighurs.[395]

Under the Biden Administration, Secretary Blinken determined, on 21 March 2022, 'following a rigorous factual and legal analysis', that members of the Burmese military committed genocide and crimes against humanity

[393] P. Pillai, 'A "Patchwork Quilt" of Fact-Finding and International Accountability in Myanmar', in M. Hasan et al. (eds.), *The Rohingya Crisis: Humanitarian and Legal Approaches* (2022) 163.
[394] M. Martin, 'Burmese Security Forces and Personnel Implicated in Serious Human Rights Abuses and Accountability Options', Congressional Research Service, Report R45388 (5 March 2019). The groups were: Amnesty International, Fortify Rights, Human Rights Watch, Kachin Women's Association in Thailand, Karen Human Rights Group, Legal Aid Network, Network for Human Rights Documentation—Burma, Physicians for Human Rights, Refugees International, Ta'ang Women's Organization, and the Women's League of Burma.
[395] S. Lewis and H. Pamuk, 'Special Report: Pompeo rejected U.S. effort to declare 'genocide' in Myanmar on eve of coup, officials say', *Reuters* (25 March 2021).

against Rohingya (https://www.state.gov/burma-genocide/). It was only the eighth time since the Holocaust that such a determination had been made by the United States.

Maaike Matelski et al., in 'Multi-Layered Civil Society Documentation of Human Rights Violations in Myanmar: The Potential for Accountability and Truth-Telling', 14 *J. Hum Rts. Practice* (2022) 794, review some of the challenges resulting from the fact that so many different fact-finding initiatives have been launched.

3.1 The risk of over-documentation

The risk of over-documentation may arise, particularly when it comes to the collection of statements. Over-documentation entails situations where victims and victim communities are asked to repeatedly tell and retell their stories to different documenters or audiences, often without fully understanding who is taking down their story or for what purpose it will be used. ...

There are two main concerns associated with over-documentation. First, there are concerns related to safety and wellbeing. If there are multiple actors collecting statements from victims and witnesses, they may not all be adhering to best practice when collecting and storing the information. This can potentially put individuals at risk. Likewise, if multiple actors are collecting statements, a process referred to as 'interview fatigue' may arise. The repetition can have a negative impact on the health and wellbeing of those interviewed. Being asked to recount horrific experiences, often to strangers, can re-traumatize the person. Having to do so multiple times can have serious negative effects on a person's mental condition, especially if they are not also given tools and psycho-social support to process their experiences. ...

The re-traumatization can also lead to another concern, which relates to the accuracy of the information provided. Research has shown that the reliability of witness statements deteriorates when recounted multiple times. ... Unsurprisingly, individuals may start asking for reimbursement for repeatedly telling their stories for use by others. In the long run, this could lead to people becoming what some sociologists have called 'professional victims' whose identity becomes centered around victimhood because it generates attention and sometimes much needed resources. ...

3.2 Hierarchy and contestation between documentation efforts

Another complicating factor concerning human rights documentation efforts by CSOs [civil society organizations] is the issue of hierarchy and contestation of information. Inevitably, the question of which human rights violations get taken up by CSOs and their counterparts is dependent not only on the severity of the violations and the trustworthiness of the source, but also on logistics, finances and political context, a process that has been referred to as 'filtering'. Traditionally marginalized groups, for example those with lower socio-economic status or residing in remote territories, tend to receive less attention than victimized high profile activists. ...

...

As many activists had to flee the country in response to repression, contestation also emerged between local activists and diaspora communities. Transnational activists have combined reporting on human rights violations with advocacy messages that do not always resonate with local needs and priorities in Myanmar, for example by prioritizing political over economic rights, or by calling for punitive measures that may further marginalize local populations. Other hierarchies are also visible with regard to documentation by CSOs in Myanmar. Gender-based violence, for example, is more likely to be viewed as 'collateral damage of warfare' than as a serious violation in itself. Activities such as the training offered to local communities by [Karen Human Rights Group] may help to balance existing inequalities but may also perpetuate divisions. It has been observed, for example, that the preferred local treatment of perpetrators of human rights violations may be less focused on punishment when the person is from the same ethnicity as the victims (that is a Burman soldier accused of rape should be tried in court, but for a soldier of the same ethnicity as the victim, this should be dealt with internally, if at all), which shows that local views on justice may vary. Moreover, CSOs that consult local communities may choose to prioritize violations that do not traditionally appear in international justice initiatives, such as arbitrary taxation.

These examples remind us that shared victimhood does not necessarily result in shared experiences in terms of human rights violations, or a uniform agenda in terms of potential responses. ... .

In *Crimes in Archival Form: Human Rights, Fact Production, and Myanmar* (2022), Ken MacLean examines fact-finding practices used by a variety of actors in Myanmar.[396] After analyzing 'the investigative decisions made, field methods employed, analytical practices utilized, and advocacy strategies mobilized' he concludes that persuasion 'is an inescapable element of human rights documentation from the very start. ... [I]t is not information per se that matters, but rather "what kind of information, produced by whom, and authorized by what symbolic and material powers that make it persuasive"' (at 3).

> Fact-finding ... is fundamentally concerned with documenting "what happened." But "what happened," when expressed in idiomatic form, is not always intelligible to influential actors in a position to take action in response to the stated "facts." The cultural specificity of "what happened" typically needs to be stripped away to recast separate incidents into patterns, such as crimes against humanity, that are then communicated through the frameworks and procedures that international law provides. The process of decontextualization (the removal of idiomatic expression and interpretation) followed by recontextualization (the addition of legalistic expression and interpretation) arguably impoverishes our understanding of how affected populations understand the meaning of what reportedly took place. It does so by making the recontextualized descriptions intellectually inaccessible to the people who experienced and/or witnessed the violations. Conflicts between the resulting "social truth"; "judicial truth," if legal proceedings occur; and "state truth," which may or may not accept a degree of responsibility for the violence, are often the result. Unfortunately, the long history of preemptive violence in Myanmar, which has produced conflicting social, judicial, and state "truth" claims, promises to continue to hamper any efforts to reconcile them in the foreseeable future and, especially, in a manner that promotes transitional justice—which, it should be noted, is far from a universal desire.
>
> ... [T]he praxis of fact-finding, even in its most basic forms, contains embedded within it a range of epistemological, methodological, and ethical quandaries that warrant careful, well-reasoned, and informed decisions and subsequent critical self-reflection. ... [W]hen these decisions are fully taken into account as they shape data collection and processing, publication, and advocacy, an inescapable and unsettling conclusion presents itself. Human rights "facts" – the determination of what occurred, who bears responsibility for it, and what kinds of action are recommended in response—are quite often fashioned rather than found. The implications of this conclusion are profound, particularly given ongoing technological developments in fact-finding ... . The time has come to not only grapple with how these developments are transforming human rights documentation both for better and for worse in the present. ... (at 211-13)

MacLean's conclusion as to the challenges confronting fact-finders in their efforts to communicate and persuade is further complicated by an anthropological perspective provided by Amy Doffegnies and Tamas Wells in 'The Vernacularisation of Human Rights Discourse in Myanmar: Rejection, Hybridisation and Strategic Avoidance', 52 *J. Contemp. Asia* (2022) 247, at 262:

---

[396] See also K. MacLean, 'Digital Human Rights Storytelling and its Palimpsests: (De-)constructed Images of Ethnic Cleansing in Myanmar', 23 *J. Hum. Rts.* (2024) 000

… Many of the participants in this study [including certain Burmese political leaders, activists and Buddhist monks] frequently engaged in discourse about human rights and played a translation role between, for example, international representatives of aid agencies and grassroots members of their parties, organisations or institutions. This intermediary role did not mean that leaders, activists and monks gave meaning to human rights in homogenous ways and nor did sustained relationships with Western human rights actors always lead to a convergence of meaning around the global referent. Rather the study revealed a splintering of the ways that participants engaged with and gave meaning to the language of human rights. Some participants rejected the language of human rights, others drew on various hybridised meanings in ways that often supported, rather than opposed, the exclusion of Muslim minorities. Meanwhile, some activists and networks strategically avoided the language of human rights in order to continue to work for social justice and what they understood to be the universal and underlying emancipatory aims of human rights as a global discourse. Through describing this variety of meanings attached to human rights the article unsettles common portrayals of Myanmar political actors as either rejecting or endorsing human rights discourse.

This splintering of meanings attached to human rights coincided with a major shift in donor agency and diplomatic attention from military authoritarianism to the marginalisation of religious – and most obviously Muslim – minorities. As the transition progressed, "human rights" was no longer a concept that could be mobilised in opposition to a military government. For many activists and Buddhist leaders, "human rights" came to be seen as a political tool that could be wielded by international agencies in support of Muslim communities, which in turn brought Myanmar Buddhism "under threat." At the same time, other activists – who were more sympathetic to Muslim populations – began to avoid the words "human rights" while attempting to promote their universal applicability. For those seeking to use the language of human rights to promote justice in Myanmar, strategic engagement with intermediaries and sensitivity towards divergent meanings of rights, are crucial. More analysis of meanings of human rights could inform local and international considerations on how human rights frameworks can be best approached and deployed to realise their emancipatory intentions.

On 21 December 2022, the UN Security Council adopted its first ever resolution on Myanmar. Previously, many countries had insisted that the matter be left to the regional organization – ASEAN (the Association of Southeast Asian Nations) – which in April 2021 adopted a 'five-point consensus'. But the military junta largely ignored that effort and civil society groups estimated that between the February 2021 military coup and December 2022, 2,600 people had been killed and 16,000 arrested by security forces.

Twelve Security Council members voted for Resolution 2669 (2022), and three abstained (China, India, and Russia):

> The Security Council,
>
> …
>
> Reaffirming its support for the people of Myanmar and its strong commitment to the sovereignty, political independence, territorial integrity and unity of Myanmar,
>
> 1. Demands an immediate end to all forms of violence throughout the country, and urges restraint and de-escalation of tensions;
>
> 2. Urges the Myanmar military to immediately release all arbitrarily detained prisoners, including President Win Myint and State Counsellor Aung San Suu Kyi;
>
> 3. Reiterates its call to uphold democratic institutions and processes …;

4. Urges all parties to respect human rights, fundamental freedoms and the rule of law;

5. Acknowledges ASEAN's central role in helping to find a peaceful solution to the crisis in Myanmar in the interests of the people of Myanmar, and encourages the international community to support the ASEAN-led mechanism and process …;

…

9. Reiterates the necessity for full, safe and unhindered humanitarian access … ;

10. Underscores the need to address the root causes of the crisis in Rakhine State … ;

11. Decides to remain seized of the matter.

After the vote (UN Press Release SC/15159 (2022)), China's representative said it preferred a presidential statement rather than a resolution and stressed 'that there is no quick fix for the Myanmar issue and the solution to the conflict depends on Myanmar itself.' He also 'reiterat[ed] China's policy of friendship towards Myanmar'.[397] The United States representative said that the resolution 'does not go far enough' and should have addressed 'the regime's severe violations of freedom of religion and belief' and should have called 'for the regime to face justice for the crimes it has reportedly committed.' The representative of Russia said 'the situation in Myanmar does not represent a threat to international peace and security', and that only the situation in Rakhine State should be on the Council's agenda. The representative of India noted its long border with Myanmar and said that 'the complex situation … calls for quiet, patient diplomacy' and the avoidance of measures such as resolutions that might 'entrench the parties in inflexible positions'.

QUESTIONS

1. What overall conclusions would you draw from the proliferation of fact-finding initiatives in relation to Myanmar? What are the strengths and weaknesses of the different approaches, and how complementary are they?

2. How do these various initiatives measure up against the critique of 'extractive' approaches to fact-finding in which the flow of information is all one-way (essentially from the South to the North) by Sarah Knuckey et al., in 'Power in Human Rights Advocate and Rightsholder Relationships: Critiques, Reforms, and Challenges', 33 *Harv. Hum. Rts. J.* (2020) 1, at 42, in which they emphasize the importance of consultation and participation:

To overcome top-down, extractive, and objectifying fact-finding, advocates have … [sought to] ensure that rightsholders' expertise about violations, causes of abuse, culture, and context inform investigation processes and outcomes … . [Ideally] … fact-finding would typically follow extensive dialogue between rightsholders and advocates … .

… [W]here advocates themselves undertake [fact-finding, they] … have worked to promote trust and transparency with rightsholders by fully explaining the purposes of the investigation, the advocate's interest in the issue, information about funders, and how any information the rightsholders share will be used. … Consultation and reporting back also provide an opportunity for advocates and rightsholders to together strategize [about next steps].

3. Is it possible for a COI to write a report that will satisfy the expectations of all of the various stakeholders, including victims, domestic civil society groups, the state, and various outside actors?

---

[397] See generally R. Gowan, 'Accommodation Available: China, Western powers and the Operation of Structural Power in the UN Security Council', 15 *Global Policy* (2024) Suppl. 2, 29, at 33.

B. NEW TECHNOLOGIES AND FACT-FINDING

In recent years, human rights fact-finding has been transformed by the application of a range of new technologies such as crisis mapping, crowd sourcing, remote sensing, big data analytics and machine learning, video analysis, open-source data mining, forensic architecture, interactive data visualization, cryptographic hashing, and many others. At the end of a very detailed survey, Catherine Harwood observes that COIs 'are not likely to be rendered obsolete by the emergence of new information technologies or investigative mechanisms. However, their roles and functions may evolve in response to the changing fact-finding landscape. ... [T]he original function of finding facts may be revitalized and complement the narrow focus of criminal mechanisms.'[398]

In the materials that follow we look at a cross section of some of these new technologies and assess their advantages and risks. But first we consider two contrasting case studies, one involving local, low-tech, feminist fact-finding, and the other employing the latest techniques, in response to the killing of a journalist.

Case Study: Feminicide in Mexico

Fact-finding does not always have an international dimension, nor is it confined to the use of highly sophisticated techniques or technology. Consider the example described by Catherine D'Ignazio in *Counting Feminicide: Data Feminism in Action* (3 November 2022 version of a book in progress, at https://mitpressonpubpub.mitpress.mit.edu/counting-feminicide

She defines feminicide (or femicide) as 'the misogynous and gender-related killing of women' and notes that the term 'is used to denote domestic violence or intimate partner violence that is fatal, and also murders perpetrated where a woman's gender, and her gender subordination, are part of the motivation for the crime.' The book starts by recounting the story of María Salguero, a solo activist, who devotes herself to mapping feminicides in Mexico. 'For each feminicide, Salguero plots a point on the map and logs up to 300 fields in her database, everything from name, age, whether the victim was transgender, and relationship with the perpetrator; to mode of death, the case status in the judicial system, and whether organized crime was involved. She also includes the full content of the news report where she sourced the information. ... [O]ne of her many goals is to show that each murdered woman or girl had a name and a life and a place and a community.'

D'Ignazio reflects on why such a project is needed:

> Official government data on gender violence and feminicide are often absent, difficult to access, infrequently updated, contested, and underreported. The reasons for these gaps range from stigma and victim-blaming to matters of legal interpretation and plain old pervasive patriarchy. ... Citizen data monitoring of feminicide has stepped into the data gaps that exist in many countries and regions around the world. Such projects have proliferated particularly since a 2015 report from the UN Special Rapporteur on Violence Against Women called for the creation of femicide observatories in every country ... .
>
> ...
>
> [There are] five major ways that counterdata are used to contest feminicide. Activists that engage in *repair* work use their data to provide direct support and services to relatives and communities who have lost beloved members. ... [C]ounterdata production serves activist efforts to *remember* and memorialize killed people. Often these take creative forms, like videos, music, plays, and art installations that tell stories that seek to bring life and humanity to individuals, and try not to reduce a woman to her death. Many activists are focused on narrative change efforts to *reframe* feminicide. They use data to communicate about lives lost on social media, or through data journalism. These accounts challenge the cultural stereotypes around the killings of women as isolated events perpetrated by

---

[398] C. Harwood, *The Roles and Functions of Atrocity-Related United Nations Commissions of Inquiry in the International Legal Order: Navigating between Principle and Pragmatism* (2019), at 323.

pathological individuals and reframe them as a structural phenomenon and matters of public concern. Counterdata are also used to push to *reform* existing institutional practices around feminicide, and there are examples of collaboration and communication between government and activist groups around the production of feminicide data. In these cases, counterdata and official data begin to mix in fascinating and sometimes uneasy ways. Finally, there are efforts to *revolt* – to use counterdata to support large-scale mobilizations, usually in conjunction with social movements tied to specific political demands.

Case Study: Killing of a Journalist in the West Bank

A well-known Palestinian-American journalist working for Al Jazeera, Shireen Abu Akleh, was shot and killed on 11 May 2022 while covering an Israeli military operation in the West Bank. The following excerpts reflect the evolving understanding of what happened, how key actors responded, and the central role of fact-finding in the ensuing dispute.

13 May 2022: The initial investigation by the Israeli Defense Forces (IDF) 'concluded that it is not possible to unequivocally determine the source of the gunfire' and identified two possible sources. The first was the 'hundreds of bullets … fired by Palestinian gunmen from a number of locations. Dozens of bullets were also fired toward IDF vehicles, which is also the direction where Ms. Abu Akleh was, making this a possible source of the gunfire that hit and killed her.' The second was that 'during the exchange of fire between the Palestinian gunmen and IDF soldiers, a soldier fired a few bullets from a designated firing hole in an IDF vehicle using a telescopic scope at a Palestinian gunman who was shooting at the aforementioned vehicle. The Palestinian gunman fired multiple barrages of gunfire at the IDF soldier, and there is the possibility that Ms. Abu Akleh, who was near the Palestinian gunman from behind, was hit by the soldier's fire toward the Palestinian gunmen.' The IDF expressed its deep condolences over the death and acknowledged the importance of press freedom. It concluded by stating that the 'IDF will continue to thwart terrorism wherever it is required to and uphold its missions, while continuing its efforts to avoid harming non-combatants.'[399]

13 May 2022: Four UN Special Rapporteurs demanded 'a prompt, independent, impartial, effective, thorough and transparent investigation into the killing'.[400]

26 May 2022: Palestinian Attorney-General, Akram al-Khatib, announced that an investigation by the Palestinian Authority found that the journalist had been intentionally shot dead by an Israeli soldier and that 'the only shooting was by the occupation forces, with the aim of killing'. The BBC reported that the 'Israeli defence minister rejected the report, calling it "a blatant lie"'.[401]

22 June 2022: *The New York Times* published an in-depth investigative story entitled 'The Killing of Shireen Abu Akleh: Tracing a Bullet to an Israeli Convoy', with a sub heading: 'A New York Times investigation found that the bullet that killed a Palestinian-American journalist was fired from the approximate position of an Israeli military vehicle.'[402] The Times found no evidence that the person who fired recognized Ms. Abu Akleh and targeted her personally and its inquiry was unable to determine whether the shooter saw that she and her colleagues were wearing protective vests emblazoned with the word 'Press'.

24 June 2022: The OHCHR issued a report. Its staff had 'inspected photo, video and audio material, visited the scene, consulted experts, reviewed official communications and interviewed witnesses.' Its 'findings indicate that no warnings were issued and no shooting was taking place' when the journalists arrived. 'At around 06h30, as four of the journalists turned into the street leading to the camp, wearing bulletproof helmets and flak jackets with "PRESS" markings, several single, seemingly well-aimed bullets were fired towards them from the direction of the Israeli Security Forces. One … bullet hit Abu Akleh in the head and killed her instantly. Several further

---

[399] IDF Editorial Team, 'Findings from the Initial Investigation into the Shooting Incident in which the Journalist Shireen Abu Akleh was Killed', 13 May 2022.

[400] 'UN experts condemn journalist killing amid rising West Bank violence', *UN Press Release*, 13 May 2022.

[401] R. Berg, 'Palestinian report says Israel deliberately killed Al Jazeera's Shireen Abu Aqla', *BBC News*, 27 May 2022.

[402] R. Abdulrahim et. al., 'The Killing of Shireen Abu Akleh: Tracing a Bullet to an Israeli Convoy', *The New York Times*, 20 June 2022.

single bullets were fired as an unarmed man attempted to approach Abu Akleh's body and another uninjured journalist sheltering behind a tree. Shots continued to be fired as this individual eventually managed to carry away Abu Akleh's body.' The Office concluded that that the shots had come from the IDF and not from indiscriminate firing by armed Palestinians, and it 'found no information suggesting that there was activity by armed Palestinians in the immediate vicinity of the journalists.' The report added that '"[m]ore than six weeks after the killing … it is deeply disturbing that Israeli authorities have not conducted a criminal investigation.'[403]

24 June 2022: Israeli Finance Minister Avigdor Liberman tweeted that OHCHR's determination 'that the Al Jazeera journalist was killed by IDF gunfire … is a disgusting allegation that cannot be accepted by us.'[404]

26 June 2022: Israeli Defense Minister Beeny Gantz said that the 'IDF operates day and night to thwart bloodthirsty terrorists who seek to conduct terror attacks and murder Israeli citizens. At the same time, the IDF takes all the possible measures to prevent harm to uninvolved civilians. In addition, the IDF conducts thorough investigations.'[405]

4 July 2022: U.S. State Department spokesperson, Ned Price announced that '[a]fter an extremely detailed forensic analysis, independent, third-party examiners, as part of a process overseen by the U.S. Security Coordinator (USSC), could not reach a definitive conclusion regarding the origin of the bullet'. But he said that after reviewing investigations by the IDF and the Palestinian Authority, the USSC concluded that gunfire from IDF positions was likely responsible for the death of Shireen Abu Akleh. The USSC found no reason to believe that this was intentional but rather the result of tragic circumstances.'

5 September 2022: the same U.S. spokesperson announced that '[t]oday, the IDF reported that it had concluded its investigation … and stated there is a high possibility that Ms. Abu Akleh was accidentally hit by IDF gunfire. We welcome Israel's review of this tragic incident, and again underscore the importance of accountability in this case.' The following day, the State Department announced that it had pressed Israel to 'closely review its policies and practices on rules of engagement and consider additional steps to mitigate the risk of civilian harm'.[406] In response, Israeli Prime Minister Yair Lapid said 'I will not allow an [Israeli military] soldier that was protecting himself from terrorist fire to be prosecuted just to receive applause from abroad'. He added that 'No one will dictate our rules of engagement to us'.[407]

15 September 2022: U. S. Senator Patrick Leahy (D-Vermont) criticized the State Department response, saying that '[w]hether her killing was intentional, reckless, or a tragic mistake, there must be accountability', adding that 'if it was intentional, and if no one is held accountable, then the Leahy Law must be applied.'[408] The 'Leahy law' is legislation that prohibits 'the U.S. Government from using funds for assistance to units of foreign security forces where there is credible information implicating that unit in the commission of gross violations of human rights'.[409]

19 September 2022: After heated debate, a proposed European Union call for an independent inquiry into the killing was amended to omit the word 'independent', despite a report showing that in 2019 and 2020, only 2% of complaints about IDF violence against Palestinians resulted in prosecutions.[410]

20 September 2022: An NGO, Forensic Architecture, released a video reconstructing the killing in minute detail and a report entitled 'Shireen Abu Akleh: The Extrajudicial Killing of a Journalist'.[411] Excerpts follow:

---

[403] OHCHR Press Briefing Notes, 'Killing of journalist in the occupied Palestinian territory', 24 June 2022.

[404] E. Fabian, '"Where's the bullet": Israel rejects UN probe blaming reporter's death on IDF', *The Times of Israel*, 24 June 2022.

[405] A. Savir, '"Unfounded": Israel Rejects Latest UN Inquiry into Death of Al Jazeera Reporter', *Jewish Press*, 26 June 2022.

[406] State Department Press Briefing, 6 September 2022.

[407] 'Israeli PM opposes prosecuting soldier who likely shot Abu Akleh', *Al Jazeera*, 7 September 2022.

[408] 'Israeli Investigation of Shireen Abu Akleh's Death Fails to Convince Key U.S. Lawmakers', *Haaretz*, 18 September 2022.

[409] 'About the Leahy Law: Fact Sheet', Bureau of Democracy, Human Rights and Labor, 20 January 2021.

[410] A. Rettman, 'EU drops call for "independent" probe into Abu Akleh killing', *EUobserver*, 19 September 2022.

[411] Available at https://forensic-architecture.org/investigation/shireen-abu-akleh-the-targeted-killing-of-a-journalist

Timeline

At 6:31:06, a video taken by a witness to the incident shows the journalists, including Shireen, slowly walking down the road towards the IOF's [Israeli occupying forces] position, following standard press protocols for self-identification.

…

At 6:31:07, less than a second after the photograph above was taken, the first round of shooting begins, with six single shots fired at the journalists in rapid succession from the IOF's position.

[At] 06:31:10, the Al Jazeera camera starts rolling. … [T]his footage shows Ali running …, while Shireen hides by the wall.

At 06:31:17 … a second round begins with 7 shots, again fired in rapid succession. We identified the last moment Shireen is seen still alive, crouching near the wall, after the first shot in this second round.

…

A minute after Shireen is shot, a civilian initially tries to provide aid to Shireen, but holds back from crossing the street for fear of being targeted; when he does manage to cross about a minute later, he is shot at within seconds of entering the shooter's field of vision, and forced to retreat. After helping journalist Shatha Hanaysha escape, he returns twenty seconds later to try to administer aid to Shireen and is again shot at twice by the IOF.

…

Our investigation is the first to employ a precise digital reconstruction of the incident. Using advanced spatial and audio analysis, we tracked the location and movements of the various key actors throughout the unfolding incident—journalists, civilians, and military vehicles.

We analysed a previously unseen video recorded by an Al Jazeera cameraperson at the scene, directly obtained other videos taken by witnesses to the incident, and gathered other available open-source videos of the events. Altogether we examined, synchronised and geolocated dozens of videos and photographs.

We were given special access to unpublished autopsy documents and examined images of the bullet extracted from Shireen's head. We identified the bullet, with its distinctive green tip, as an M855 SS109 5.56 x 45mm armour-piercing bullet, the type of munition common to IOF marksmen.

Spatial reconstruction

We commissioned a surveying company to conduct an extensive, professional drone survey of the site and sourced ground photography of the entire length of the road, which allowed us to create a highly accurate 3D photogrammetry model of the scene.

…

By geolocating individual frames from the videos we sourced, we could establish and reconstruct within our digital model the exact positions of Shireen and the other journalists throughout the incident, as well as the position of the military vehicles in relation to them. …

…

The shots were fired from a hole in the side of an MDT David Toyota armoured vehicle.

…

Identifying the distance between the last frame in which Shireen is seen alive and the first frame in which she is seen lying on the ground allowed us to establish her distance from the shooter at the exact moment she was hit. This study reveals that she was facing away from the marksman, with her 'PRESS' vest fully legible at the moment the fatal gunshot was fired.

Trajectory and dispersion

By reconstructing Ali and Shireen's exact positions when each of them was shot and the bullets' precise points of impact, and modelling the location of four other impact points on a tree at the site of the incident, we were able to trace the trajectory of six of the sixteen shots fired during the incident.

…

In studying the position of these six shots, we can also establish that all shots were aimed above the shoulders with the intent to kill their targets.

…

Optics and visibility

We conducted a visual reconstruction of the IOF marksman's view both digitally and optically. Using our digital model, we simulated how Shireen and the other journalists would appear from the marksman's position 190 metres away when the first shots were fired … .

…

According to both the digital and optical reconstructions of the shooter's vision, the journalists' press vests would have been clearly visible throughout the incident.

By marking the impact points of the six spatially located shots from the perspective of the IOF marksman, we can see their close proximity to one another, confirming that they were fired in a targeted effort to hit the journalists.

…

Audio analysis

Audio analysis of the videos capturing the incident allowed us to compare the sound signatures of all shots fired during and preceding the incident and trace them back to the IOF marksman's position. In the two minutes before the shooting begins, no shots are fired at all. No other shots in any of the footage analysed came from the vicinity of the journalists.

…

Testimony

With members of Al-Haq on the ground in Jenin, we conducted a 'situated testimony'—an on-site physical re-enactment and witness account-taking—with journalist Shatha Hanaysha, who was standing near Shireen when she was shot and killed. …

Findings

Shireen and her colleagues were clearly identifiable as journalists when they were shot at. Reconstruction based on digital modelling, physical reconstruction and optical analysis confirms that the journalists followed standard protocols for self-identification and that their large 'PRESS' insignia were clearly visible from the position of the IOF shooter in the moments surrounding the shooting. Furthermore, the autopsy report demonstrated that Shireen was positioned away from the shooter in such a way that her PRESS vest should have been easily legible.

Shireen and her fellow journalists were deliberately and repeatedly targeted, with an aim to kill. We identified the bullet retrieved from Shireen's skull as common to IOF military 'marksmen', whose guns are commonly equipped with an optical scope (Trijicon) that magnifies their vision 4x, and would have made their targets clearly visible. The reconstruction of the timeline of events confirms that the marksman had at least twenty seconds in which to visually assess the journalists before shooting the first round, and eight seconds in which to look at them in between the first and second rounds. Trajectory analysis of shots fired reveals a clear line of fire from the IOF's position toward the group of journalists; close proximity between the gunshots' impact points, suggesting precise aim; and the consistent positioning of those impact points at above-shoulder height, indicating intent to kill.

5 September 2023: The UN Independent Commission of Inquiry called upon Israel to cooperate with the investigation by the U.S. Federal Bureau of Investigation into the killing and with the International Criminal Court's broader investigation (UN Doc. A/78/198).

New Technologies

The following materials look at some of the new technologies being used in human rights fact-finding.

a. Video Evidence

In surveying the role of user-generated content, Jay Aronson, in 'The Utility of User-Generated Content in Human Rights Investigations', in Molly Land and Jay Aronson (eds.), *New Technologies for Human Rights Law and Practice* (2018) 129, begins by quoting a 2011 report by WITNESS, entitled *Cameras Everywhere:*

> Video has a key role to play, not just in exposing and providing evidence of human rights abuses, but across the spectrum of transparency, accountability and good governance. Video and other communication technologies present new opportunities for freedom of expression and information, but also pose significant new vulnerabilities. As more people understand the power of video, including human rights violators, the more the safety and security of those filming and of those being filmed will need to be considered at each stage of video production and distribution.

Aronson elaborates:

> A wide range of people produce video content and share it through social media, the Internet, semiprivate communication channels like Telegram and Snapchat, or privately via e-mail or physical storage. Conflict events, protests, riots, and other similar events are increasingly being live-streamed as they happen. Some of the creators of this content have been trained in human rights documentation, while others have not. In many cases, damning video will come from the perpetrators themselves, who use the content to boast of their power and accomplishments or seek funding from sympathetic outsiders.

> Courts, tribunals, truth commissions, and other fact-finding (or perhaps fact-generating) bodies, as well as journalists and human rights advocates, need to be sensitive to the wide-ranging quality, completeness, and utility of user-generated content. They cannot assume that the content was intentionally created or that the people represented in this material know that their images and activities are being stored, processed, and analyzed for human rights purposes. Extra care must be taken to ensure the privacy, security, and other basic rights of people who produce such content or appear in it. In the case of perpetrator video, they must assume that the content has public relations goals, and they must take care not to spread messages of hate or extremism. Additionally, it is crucial to keep in mind that many war crimes and human rights abuses will continue to leave few electronic traces. Like all other forms of evidence, video is not a magic bullet or panacea that will put an end to atrocities. Nor does it mitigate the need for eyewitnesses and victims to provide testimony and for investigators to visit the scenes of crimes and conduct thorough investigations.

> Nonetheless, video has potential value at every stage of a human rights investigation, whether that investigation is designed to feed into advocacy or legal proceedings. Most commonly, video generates leads that can be used to start an investigation. It can also provide evidence to establish that a crime or violation occurred, or it can be used to support a particular factual finding, such as whether a particular weapon was used in a conflict or whether pollution from a particular mining site is polluting a water source. Sometimes, it can also link a particular person, group, government, or company to the violation in question.

But he also warns of the challenges involved:

> ... Audiences might grow tired of viewing traumatic video and become desensitized to its effects. On the other hand, they might become less likely to believe accounts that are not supported by convincing audiovisual evidence. The persistent creation of falsified media

by states, pranksters, and other nefarious actors could also impugn legitimate content. Further, any good defense attorney, government operative, or rights violator can challenge the authenticity of the video or the interpretation of its content (e.g., that victims were indeed dead but were not killed by the claimed perpetrator, or that the victims did not heed warnings to disperse in the moments before the video was shot). They can also offer alternative explanations for what is seen (e.g., that the munitions in question were stolen from the army by a rebel force, or that anti-government forces were dressed up as army personnel). Video evidence cannot always help dispute claims made by perpetrators that their actions were justified on national or internal security grounds, that the victims posed a threat, or that the action captured on video was wrong but the matter has already been dealt with internally.

b. Digital Authentification

Bailey Ulbricht et al., in 'Digital Eyewitnesses: Using New Technologies to Authenticate Evidence in Human Rights Litigation, 74 *Stan. L. Rev.* (2022) 851, explore the benefits of being able to use digital evidence, but also note that it presents challenges in each phase of the evidentiary life cycle:

> For example, at the storage phase, securely preserving countless hours of film footage or thousands of photos for years is a monumental logistical challenge. Additionally, retaining proof of human rights violations can entail serious risks: Government forces have tortured and killed civilians in Syria over the contents of their phones. Individuals and civil-society organizations have published videos of human rights violations on YouTube to create an internet record, only for thousands of those videos to be taken down by YouTube's content-moderation algorithms, complicating efforts to pin down an original, authentic source. These issues at the storage stage are compounded by struggles to find witnesses who can attest to the authenticity of stored evidence, especially given that proceedings often take place years after events and in far-off jurisdictions. Though it is best to involve witnesses in accountability proceedings whenever possible, the international legal community should explore ways to guarantee safe storage so that digital evidence can be authenticated when live testimony is sparse

They then explain how hashing and distributed-ledger technology (DLT) work:

> Digital records are given a hash after collection, freezing the data and rendering it nearly impossible to alter without detection. Many organizations then store records and their hashes using DLT, a storage mechanism that uses decentralized systems to protect against hackers and others who might tamper with data over long periods of time. When used together, DLT and hashing have far-reaching applications in human rights advocacy and accountability efforts. Perhaps most important is the potential of these technologies to facilitate the authentication of evidence when witnesses are unavailable, allowing cases previously barred from court to proceed.

c. Satellite Imagery

The value of satellite imagery is explored by Micah Farfour, in 'The Role and Use of Satellite Imagery for Human Rights Investigations', in Sam Dubberley, Alexa Koenig and Daragh Murray (eds.), *Digital Witness: Using Open Source Information for Human Rights Investigation, Documentation, and Accountability* (2019) 228:

> Satellite imagery can provide an unbiased, scientific analysis of an area on the planet. And the methodology used to analyse the imagery can also be replicated to verify analytical findings. The actual interpretation of satellite imagery can lead to certain biases, but in the case of human rights research, many other datasets are typically incorporated to triangulate a responsible understanding of the situation.

A satellite is also able to access visually areas of the globe that are often inaccessible to human rights abuse investigators, such as North Korea, Rakhine State, Myanmar, and Jebel Marra, Sudan. In other instances, satellite imagery can provide a very prompt look into a remote region after, for example, a massacre, before a researcher is able to visit the area.

The ability to look back in time, pinpoint activities geospatially, detect changes unobservable by the human eye, and use high-resolution imagery to see specific items provides an incredible advantage to information collected in human rights investigations. When compared with traditional styles of evidence gathering, which relied heavily on witness testimony, satellite imagery offers a check of visual evidence over time that may run counter to the effects of trauma on a person's memory of events or the ulterior motives of a perpetrator to insist upon a different sequence of events on the ground. Satellite imagery, in most situations, cannot independently prove an abuse has been committed, but it can add— sometimes essential—information to what may have transpired. Advancements in spatial, spectral, and temporal resolutions, as mentioned earlier, have led to increased and more accurate documentation of situations involving environmental rights, indiscriminate violence, forced relocation, and violence visited upon civilians, along with other human rights abuses.

3.1 Spatial Resolution

The highest spatial resolution of satellite imagery allowed commercially in the United States is 31cm. Before 2014, laws only allowed the public to view imagery at 50cm resolution. Though the technology is available to capture higher resolutions of satellite imagery, the government restricts the satellite imaging companies.

However, the leap from 50 to 31cm resolution is making satellite imagery into a more robust piece of information difficult to deny. In an increasing number of situations, the higher resolution imagery is making its way into court cases as evidence, such as in the Al- Mahdi case at the International Criminal Court (ICC).
…

3.2 Spectral Resolution

Satellites are measuring the reflectance of light off the surface of the earth in many different wavelengths apart from the visible, red, green, and blue bands. This allows analysts the ability to detect reflectance in other wavelengths invisible to the human eye. Though there are satellite sensors with the ability to measures hundreds of bands, only a few are used regularly in documenting human rights abuses.
…
Places such as the Niger Delta have been horribly polluted by oil spills, which has had a grave impact on the local communities reliant on the land and water. In many spill areas, vegetation has completely died out, and the impact is readily visible in satellite imagery highlighting the NIR [near infrared] band. Information like this is helpful in building cases against the oil companies in the region that allowed oil spills to occur and did not provide sufficient clean-up and the remediation needed to preserve the ecology of the region.

The NIR band is not only helpful in seeing vegetation health, but also highlights areas that have been burned.
…
…
Research has also been conducted to determine areas of potential mass graves using satellite imagery and other remotely sensed data. …

3.3 Temporal Resolution

In many cases of human rights abuse, there is a delay between when the event occurred and when it comes to light. In some instances, the abuses occurred many years earlier and the people affected may not have been aware of their rights or that information was available to protect their rights in retrospect. In other instances, the abuses might span a long time period where looking at a range of historical data is needed to understand events happening now, including the long-term effects of mining on a village.

Today, with so many commercial satellites covering the globe, capturing a weekly image of a location on the planet is feasible. Compared with the original revisit rate of eighteen days, the better temporal resolutions are leading to more accurate documentation of when events happen, potentially aligning with certain actors being present in an area.

With such a growing library of imagery, events and changes detected can be mapped at a larger scale with more frequency. Geospatial patterns over space and time can be used to better understand the situation and the factors that might be involved. If a group has been committing human rights abuses for some time, it is possible to understand the specific types of people that are at risk and predict sensitive areas for future monitoring. For example, the people in Jebel Marra have been subjected to military operations against them year after year. This knowledge, along with frequent revisit rates of satellites, allows researchers to monitor the areas for potential increases in troops and the potential for further human rights abuses to be committed. This documentation could also be used to show the scale of a problem and to create pressure to protect the population against future attacks.

d. Open-Source Investigations

Open-source investigations are increasingly ubiquitous. The following materials begin by illustrating the use of this technique in the Ukraine context, and then look at an important effort to set best practices standards.

HENNING LAHMANN, UKRAINE, OPEN-SOURCE INVESTIGATIONS, AND THE FUTURE OF INTERNATIONAL LEGAL DISCOURSE
116 AM. J. INT'L L. (2022) 810

… [T]he digital transformation and the emergence of social media have vastly expanded the volume and types of data circulated through online platforms and other digital infrastructures. Today, novel tools exist to sift, parse, and analyze the aggregated information for evidentiary clues and patterns to poke holes into states' narratives. Widely available and freely accessible digital means of communication can be used to distribute, amplify, and present the findings and conclusions in ways previously unimaginable.

The practice of open-source counter-narration by civil society actors first came to prominence in the aftermath of the downing of Malaysia Air MH17 over eastern Ukraine on July 17, 2014, when the organization Bellingcat used a vast quantity of digital information to establish the responsibility of Russian separatists in the Donbas as well as Russia's complicity. …

[In 2022, at the beginning of Russia's invasion of Ukraine] after Russia claimed that Ukrainian forces had shelled a kindergarten in the Donbas on February 17, a team of online investigators [including Bellingcat researchers] collaboratively analyzed available photos and video footage to assess the direction of the attack by examining pictures of the crater and spray pattern left by the projectile, demonstrating a separatist-held area as the most likely point of origin. The investigation was subsequently introduced as evidence by the counsel for Ukraine during … ICJ proceedings … . … [By comparison, an OSCE] Special Monitoring Mission to Ukraine from February 18, which had experts on the ground, … could merely state that it "assessed the damage as recent but was unable to determine the weapon used or the direction of fire." A New York Times news article also pointed to separatist fabrications but only cited unnamed sources in the U.S. and Ukrainian governments. At a UN Security Council meeting four days after the shelling, the UN under-secretary-general for political and peacebuilding affairs acknowledged that "the United Nations is not in a position to verify the numerous claims and allegations made by various actors." Further revelations about Russia's factual manipulations ensued. On February 20, for instance, a group of open-source investigators discounted a video ostensibly showing a sabotage operation targeting chlorine tanks in the Donbas using an analysis of its metadata and matching the audio with an older YouTube video of military exercises in Finland. A few days later, Bellingcat published an entire online spreadsheet compiling various "dubious" and "debunked" factual claims made by Russia.

What is genuinely novel about this emerging practice of open-source counter-narration and potentially transformative for international legal discourse is the idea of "open verification," meaning that individual pieces of raw information, to the greatest extent possible, ought to remain in the open and accessible so that any interested person can independently check and verify their accuracy and authenticity. … [C]ounter-narrating a state's justifications thus turns into a social and collective practice of "assembling credibility," ultimately leading to more robust and credible investigatory outcomes.

…

[Conclusion]

…

[W]e should not naïvely take civil society actors engaging in open-source investigations as neutral arbiters of truth by default. The principle of "open verification" seeks to ensure that a narrative's individual evidentiary components can always undergo peer review; yet the narrator's own biases and preconceptions might still be introduced in manifold ways, not least through the investigation's larger framing. Moreover, not all types of evidence are accessible to open-source methods. Finally, any type of publicly available digital information is in principle vulnerable to manipulation and tampering. But if safeguards and best practices can be established, open-source counter-narration has the potential to fundamentally shift the ways we expect international legal discourse to unfold in the future.

BERKELEY PROTOCOL ON DIGITAL OPEN SOURCE INVESTIGATIONS: A PRACTICAL GUIDE ON THE EFFECTIVE USE OF DIGITAL OPEN SOURCE INFORMATION IN INVESTIGATING VIOLATIONS OF INTERNATIONAL CRIMINAL, HUMAN RIGHTS AND HUMANITARIAN LAW (2022)

[Jointly developed by the Human Rights Center, University of California Berkeley School of Law and the UN Office of the High Commissioner for Human Rights.][412]

I. Introduction

1. The Berkeley Protocol on Digital Open Source Investigations describes the professional standards that should be applied in the identification, collection, preservation, analysis and presentation of digital open source information and its use in international criminal and human rights investigations. … [It] comprises both user-generated and machine-generated data, and may include, for example: content posted on social media; documents, images, videos and audio recordings on websites and information-sharing platforms; satellite imagery; and government-published data. …

…

3. While a growing number of international criminal and human rights investigators now use the Internet to facilitate their work, no universal references, guidelines or standards for open source investigations currently exist. …

4. … As open source investigations can contribute to different types of efforts to ensure accountability, the methodology and documentation requirements outlined in the Protocol may be more rigorous than those traditionally employed in other fields, such as journalism and human rights advocacy. …

…

6. Ultimately, the Protocol is designed to assist open source investigators to conduct their work in accordance with a professional methodology that is broadly consistent with legal requirements and ethical norms. …

…

8. Open source information … plays a particularly critical role in international criminal and human rights investigations. This is true for a number of reasons. First, internationally mandated investigations, including those conducted by United Nations commissions of inquiry and fact-finding missions, or those authorized by the International Criminal Court, are dependent on legal and political processes permitting the investigation to take place. Thus, they are often conducted long after the events. Second, often, international investigations may not have access to the physical location at which the incidents under investigation took place, for example, due to a State's refusal to cooperate or grant access. Third, even if granted access to a region or territory, investigators may have limited physical access to the location in question or may be impeded from in situ investigations or in-person interviewing due to concerns about protection. Finally, most investigators will not have full law enforcement powers over the territories in which the alleged crimes or violations occurred, and thus may be

---

[412] For background and analysis, see D. Murray, Y. McDermott, and A. Koenig, 'Mapping the Use of Open Source Research in UN Human Rights Investigations', 14 J. *Hum. Rts. Prac.* (2022) 554.

unable to collect the necessary information. Even in cases in which there is State cooperation, cross-border evidence collection can be an arduous process, slowed down by cumbersome bureaucratic procedures. All of these factors demonstrate why open source investigation techniques, which can be carried out remotely and conducted contemporaneously as events take place, are both powerful and necessary.

...

10. The Protocol is designed to standardize procedures and provide methodological guidance across disparate investigations, institutions and jurisdictions to assist open source investigators in understanding the importance of:

>   (a) Tracing the provenance of online content and attributing it to its original source, where possible;
>
>   (b) Evaluating the credibility and reliability of online sources;
>
>   (c) Verifying online content and assessing its veracity and reliability;
>
>   (d) Complying with legal requirements and ethical norms;
>
>   (e) Minimizing any risk of harm to themselves, their organizations and third parties;
>
>   (f) Enhancing protection of the human rights of sources, including the right to privacy.

...

e. Risks of Digital Fact-Finding

Many challenges lie ahead as human rights actors seek to take advantage of new technologies but also avoid the many pitfalls that await. Mark Latonero, in 'Big Data Analytics and Human Rights: Privacy Considerations in Context', in Molly Land and Jay Aronson (eds.), *New Technologies for Human Rights Law and Practice* (2018) 149 warns of the tensions that need to be resolved when using big data analytics in human rights work. He sees 'a sustained knowledge gap in this area [which] puts vulnerable populations at greater risk.' And he also notes that these problems will be compounded once artificial intelligence (AI) comes to be widely used in this context. Ella McPherson identifies a range of risks in this general area:

ELLA MCPHERSON, RISK AND THE PLURALISM OF DIGITAL HUMAN RIGHTS FACT-FINDING AND ADVOCACY
MOLLY LAND AND JAY ARONSON (EDS.), NEW TECHNOLOGIES FOR HUMAN RIGHTS LAW AND PRACTICE (2018) 188.

I. Introduction

... In theory, now anyone with a cell phone and Internet access can document and disseminate evidence of human rights abuses. But what happens when this theory is put into practice? What happens when ICTs [information and communication technologies] are adopted in empirical realities shaped by unique contexts, distributions of resources, and power relations? ...

...

III. Digital fact-finding and communication risk

Human rights practitioners have adopted ICTs for fact-finding in a variety of ways, including using high-technology information sources like satellite images, drone videos, big data, and statistics as well as open source social media content. ... I focus on practitioners' use of digital information that documents human rights violations and has been produced and transmitted by civilian witnesses – "civilian" in contrast with professional to highlight their inexpert status, and "witness" as someone who is purposively communicating experienced or observed suffering. Civilian witnesses can be spontaneous or solicited. In the digital age, spontaneous witnesses might use their smartphones to document violations that they then share with broader audiences via social media or messaging apps; sometimes this information is gathered, curated, and connected to human rights

NGOs by networks of activists. Solicited witnesses may be answering a human rights NGO's open call for information made via a digital crowdsourcing project or a digital reporting application.

Digital information from civilian witnesses affords human rights practitioners a number of fact-finding advantages. First, the images and video civilian witnesses produce can provide much more detailed evidence than witness interviews that rely on memory. Second, consulting civilian witnesses can tap wells of knowledge, particularly expertise relating to local contexts unfamiliar to foreign practitioners. Third, a wider incorporation of civilians via ICTs can fire up public enthusiasm about human rights and thus receptivity to advocacy. Fourth, and most important for our concern with pluralism, these new sources can support the variety and volume of voices speaking and being heard on human rights. They supplement interviewing's traditional co-production of information between witnesses and practitioners with both the more autonomous production of spontaneous digital witnesses and new forms of co-production via solicited digital witnesses. If these witnesses are situated in closed-country contexts or rapidly unfolding events, they might otherwise be inaccessible to human rights practitioners. ...

...

A. Surveillance and Physical Security

Surveillance, understood broadly as monitoring information about others for purposes including management and control, is a risk that civilian witnesses and human rights practitioners have always faced. Surveillance of their identities, networks, and activities is a key tactic deployed by state adversaries in a "cat-and-mouse" game over truth-claims. Human rights practitioners who pioneered the use of ICTs may have had a momentary advantage in this battle by using these technologies to transmit information quickly and widely. Many state actors, however, have caught up quickly and even surpassed human rights actors in their strategic use of ICTs. The surveillance opportunities ICTs afford center on a metadata paradox. ICTs can both reveal and conceal communication metadata; the first facilitates mass surveillance, while the second facilitates spyware.

ICTs are built to collect metadata on their users, often without users understanding just how significant their data trails are. Many ICT companies routinely collect users' metadata for reasons ranging from marketing to legal compliance. This profit-driven surveillance produces information about communications that also meets the surveillance imperatives of states. ... Even if the content of these communications remains private, metadata can reveal connections between civilian witnesses and human rights practitioners and, through social network analysis, identify individuals as human rights practitioners.

While mass surveillance depends on ICTs' revelation of communication metadata, spyware depends on its obfuscation, afforded by ICTs' complexity. Spyware hides in victims' communications equipment to track and share information about their activities. ...

...

B. Deception and Reputational Integrity

Human rights practitioners' use of digital information from civilian witnesses generates another category of risk: susceptibility to misinterpretation through deception. By dint of their accusations of violations, human rights practitioners often engage in battles over truth-claims with their adversaries. Though the manipulation of truth-claims with an intent to deceive has always been a feature of these battles, human rights practitioners may be more exposed to them in the digital age for several reasons. First, ICTs afford a greater number and variety of sources of information, many of whom are outside of the trusted networks that human rights organizations traditionally consult. Deceptive actors can camouflage themselves among this broader pool of sources. Second, unlike in a traditional face-to-face interview, human rights practitioners using spontaneous or solicited digital information from civilian witnesses are not present at the moment of production. As such, they cannot rely on their direct perceptions of identity clues, communication cues, and contexts to verify civilian witnesses' accounts. Instead, they must use digitally mediated content and metadata as a starting point, which can be distorted and manipulated. Third, this information is often in image or video format that appears to be amateur. This lends it an aura of authenticity – rooted, perhaps, in a "seeing is believing" epistemology – that may belie manipulation.

Deception through truth-claims manipulation can be divided into at least three categories: outright staging of content, doctoring of content, and doctoring of metadata. …

… [T]he doctoring of metadata … involves scraping videos or images from one context and repackaging them as evidence of violations in another context. …

Though some instances of deception may be malevolent, other instances may be backed by the best of intentions. For example, civilian witnesses may use images from one event to illustrate another, similar event that was not recorded. Nevertheless, using any kind of manipulated information as evidence creates a follow-on risk to the reputations of human rights practitioners and their organizations. For these, credibility is a fundamental asset, not only for the persuasiveness of their advocacy, but also for garnering donations and volunteers, influencing policy-making, and motivating mobilization. Credibility is also a human rights organization's Achilles' heel, as it can be damaged in an instant with the publication of truth-claims that others convincingly expose as false. Though the verification of information has always been a cornerstone of human rights work as a truth-claim profession, information mediated by ICTs is challenging established verification practices. This is not only because of the new sources and formats of information ICTs enable, but also because verifying digital information requires expertise that, though increasingly standardized, is still emergent.
…

VII. Conclusion

Techno-optimism has surfaced in the human rights world, as in many others, based in part on the perceived benefits of ICTs for the pluralism of human rights communication. These benefits have been realized in a number of cases, but the application of ICTs has also materialized risk. …

Furthermore, the use of ICTs introduces new intermediary actors to the human rights communication chain, and the technical complexity of ICTs makes these actors and their impact on communication more difficult to identify and assess. Of particular note here are new commercial actors with profit motives. To be sure, human rights reporters have interacted with commercial motives before in their communication practices, such as in considering the marketability of newsworthiness decisions. Never before, however, have commercial actors been so influential over and yet so hidden in mediation. Cases in point are the commercial-political surveillance nexus, the lucrative gray market for spyware, and the proprietary, revenue-maximizing algorithms of social media platforms. Incorporating ICTs into human rights fact-finding and advocacy contributes to new risk assemblages for human rights practitioners.
…

C. UKRAINE AND FUTURE DIRECTIONS FOR FACT-FINDING

The extent to which the scope of the mandates given to international fact-finding bodies has expanded in recent years is illustrated by the response to the Russian invasion of Ukraine. In March 2022, for example, the Human Rights Council (by a vote of 32-2-13) established 'an independent international commission of inquiry, comprising three human rights experts, to be appointed by the President of the Human Rights Council … with the following mandate:

  a) To investigate all alleged violations and abuses of human rights and violations of international humanitarian law, and related crimes in the context of the aggression against Ukraine by the Russian Federation, and to establish the facts, circumstances and root causes of any such violations and abuses;

  b) To collect, consolidate and analyse evidence of such violations and abuses, including their gender dimension, and to systematically record and preserve all information, documentation and evidence, including interviews, witness testimony and forensic material, consistent with international law standards, in view of any future legal proceedings;

c) To document and verify relevant information and evidence, including through field engagement, and to cooperate with judicial and other entities, as appropriate;

d) To identify, where possible, those individuals and entities responsible for violations or abuses of human rights or violations of international humanitarian law, or other related crimes, in Ukraine, with a view to ensuring that those responsible are held accountable;

e) To make recommendations, in particular on accountability measures, all with a view to ending impunity and ensuring accountability, including, as appropriate, individual criminal responsibility, and access to justice for victims;

f) [To report to the Human Rights Council and the General Assembly].

In a blogpost entitled 'Fact-Finding in Ukraine: Can Anything Be Learned from Yemen?', on Articles of War, 14 March 14 2022, Charles Garraway, who was a member of the UN Human Rights Council's Group of Eminent Experts (GEE), which studied the situation in Yemen from 2017 to 2021, compared that fact-finding exercise with the nascent COI in Ukraine. The establishment of the Yemen GEE was strongly resisted by some Arab States, and it was disbanded in a controversial decision by the Council, despite a strong recommendation that much remained to be done (UN Doc. A/HRC/48/20 (2021)):

> [The tension between IHL and IHRL] inevitably affected the methodology of fact-finding. Whereas under "Geneva Law" it is normal to start with the result—for example a torture victim—and work backwards from there, that methodology does not work necessarily for "Hague Law" allegations, particularly the laws on targeting. Most fact-finding has tended to concentrate on the principle of proportionality … best defined in Article 51(5)(b) of Additional Protocol I … .[413] However, the fact that a particular object has been hit by an air strike does not tell you whether it was the intended target, and still less what might have been the anticipated military advantage or the expected civilian loss and damage from that particular strike. That is information that could only be gained from the attacking side. …
>
> …
>
> The Yemen GEE [concentrated] on Article 57 of Additional Protocol I which requires that in the conduct of military operations "constant care shall be taken to spare the civilian population, civilians and civilian objects." In their first Report, although due to the lack of detailed targeting information on individual strikes, it was not possible to reach definite conclusions on any particular incident, it was possible to look at patterns. These revealed, as a result of the number of civilian casualties, the timing of some attacks, and the choice of weapons, that there were "serious concerns" about the targeting process itself. The GEE went on to say "If there are errors in the targeting process that effectively remove the protections provided by international humanitarian law, these would amount to violations". …
>
> [A detailed 2019 legal analysis by the GEE noted] … that the patterns they had observed had continued "casts a serious doubt about whether the targeting process adopted by the coalition complied with these fundamental provisions of international humanitarian law."
>
> … [I]t was possible to use the evidence gained from general patterns to identify possible flaws in the targeting process. … [T]he continuation of the patterns would indicate with increasing clarity that the flaws were continuing, and no remedial steps had been taken …
>
> .
>
> …

---

[413] This article describes as indiscriminate 'an attack which may be expected to cause incidental loss of civilian life, injury to civilians, damage to civilian objects, or a combination thereof, which would be excessive in relation to the concrete and direct military advantage anticipated.'

Towards More Institutionalized Fact-Finding

In 2001, a highly experienced international fact-finder, Cherif Bassiouni, lamented the absence of standard operating procedures for fact-finding missions:

> [N]o manual exists to describe how an investigation should be conducted and there is no standard, though adaptable, computer program to input collected data. Worst of all, there is no continuity. In short, there is nothing to guide, instruct, or assist the heads and appointees to these missions of how to better carry out their mandates. It strains one's belief that in fifty years the most elementary aspects of standardized organization, planning, documentation, and reporting have not been developed. Thus, each mission has to reinvent the wheel … . The results are usually poor or mediocre performance, except where particularly competent persons are appointed to these missions … . [T]here is little consistency and predictability as to the methods and outcomes. …
>
> The lack of standardized methods, particularly as to empirical research and field investigation, means that there is no basis to test the validity of the research in order to assess the plausibility of the conclusions. It is safe to say that no scientific research methodology would consider the above-described approach as anything but selective, insufficient, unreliable, and, at best, anecdotal.[414]

One proposed solution was to adopt regulations outlining 'the structure, powers and functioning of fact-finding commissions, so that, once the need arises to investigate a situation, all the relevant rules are already in place.'[415] One response, by the OHCHR was to produce a book entitled *Commissions of Inquiry and Fact-Finding Missions on International Human Rights Law and Humanitarian Law: Guidance and Practice* (2015).

An earlier attempt to set up a standing body to carry out fact-finding has so far been unsuccessful. Article 90 of the First Additional Protocol to the Geneva Conventions of 1949 provides for the creation of an International Humanitarian Fact-Finding Commission. It was set up in 1991 as a permanent body of 15 experts. Although 76 states have recognized its competence, its services have only been sought once, by the Organization for Security and Co-operation in Europe in relation to a particular incident occurring in Ukraine in 2017. When a major conflict breaks out, the Commission generally proffers its services, but states have been remarkably reticent to make use of them. Robert Heinsch, in 'The Future of the International Humanitarian Fact-Finding Commission: A Possibility to Overcome the Weakness of IHL Compliance Mechanisms?', in Dražan Djukić and Niccolò Pons (eds.), *The Companion to International Humanitarian Law* (2018) 79, has identified four main problems relating to its mandate: (i) an inquiry can only take place with consent from the parties; (2) there was some doubt as to whether its mandate was limited to international armed conflicts, although the Commission has insisted this is not the case; (3) the complexity and perhaps unworkability of the fact that the Commission is authorized to establish facts and make recommendations, but not to conduct a legal evaluation; most commentators consider the two to be inseparably linked; and (4) its findings are confidential unless all parties to the conflict agree otherwise.

In 2022, two major studies called for the creation of some form of 'investigative mechanism' that would be permanent and assuredly independent. One, drafted by a group at Oxford University (Federica D'Alessandra et al., *Anchoring Accountability for Mass Atrocities* (2022)) called for either the establishment of a standing, independent UN investigative support mechanism (ISM) or the establishment of a permanent investigative support division (ISD) within the OHCHR. The second study was prepared by the International Commission of Jurists:

INTERNATIONAL COMMISSION OF JURISTS, OPTIONS FOR THE ESTABLISHMENT OF A STANDING INDEPENDENT INVESTIGATIVE MECHANISM (SIIM)
(2022)

---

[414] M. C. Bassiouni, 'Appraising UN Justice-Related Fact-Finding Missions', 5 *Wash. U. J. L. & Pol'y.* (2001) 35.

[415] A. Cassese, 'How to Ensure Increased Compliance with International Standards: Monitoring and Institutional Fact-Finding', in *ibid.* (ed.), *Realizing Utopia: The Future of International Law* (2012), 303. Cf. a set of guidelines developed for NGO fact-finding: Raoul Wallenberg Institute and the International Bar Association, *Lund-London Guidelines on International Human Rights Fact-Finding Visits and Reports* (2009).

[Note: This report uses the term 'Accountability Mandates' to refer to all UN-mandated investigations with one or more accountability functions.]

UN-mandated investigations have been broadly categorized as being of two types:

> a. UN investigative mechanisms tasked with sophisticated forms of evidence gathering (IIIM[416], UNITAD[417] and the IIMM[418]); and

> b. UN human rights investigations (all other UN mandated investigations).

There has been a misperception that only the former mechanisms carry out criminal investigations into individual criminal responsibility, whereas the latter only monitor, document, report and make recommendations on human rights violations.

However, the ICJ [International Commission of Jurists] considers this categorization of UN-mandated investigations does not reflect reality. Rather, it is more accurate to think of all UN-mandated investigations with at least one accountability function as belonging to the same family and existing on a spectrum, with mandates that weigh more towards traditional human rights investigations and reporting at one end, and UN investigative mechanisms that focus essentially on establishing the evidentiary basis for criminal prosecutions at the other. While in the middle of the spectrum – where most of the Human Rights Council-created Accountability Mandates now operate - there are increasingly sophisticated "*blended*," or "*mixed*" mandates requiring both human rights and criminal investigative capacity. All these Accountability Mandates address, to some extent, aspects of both State responsibility and individual criminal responsibility but use at least some different working methodologies in the gathering of information and evidence.

The ICJ further considers this dual classification scheme has been unhelpful in addressing many of the challenges ..., particularly regarding the resources and staffing that have been allocated to the various Accountability Mandates. Particularly problematic is the belief that those mandates that are perceived to fall into category b. do not need the same resources and specialist staffing that is required by those mandates in category a., notwithstanding the real requirements of their increasingly complex mandates.

The clearest example is the ... Independent International Commission of Inquiry on Ukraine, whose expansive mandate appears to have borrowed from the mandates of Accountability Mandates at both ends of the spectrum.

The blending of functions has been deliberate for a variety of reasons. UN bodies often act with regard to situations where there are strong allegations of human rights or international humanitarian law violations constituting crimes under international law that warrant an investigation into individual criminal responsibility, particularly where ongoing widespread or systematic violations of human rights and/or international humanitarian law are being committed, and States are unable or unwilling to undertake investigations that meet international law and standards.

Other major factors dictating the design of Accountability Mandates - and the emergence of increasingly mixed mandates - are the powers and political dynamics of the various UN bodies establishing them. ...
...

2. Opportunities and challenges faced by Accountability Mandates

In short, Accountability Mandates, whether mixed or essentially focused on individual criminal responsibility, contribute toward accountability by carrying out investigations where an accountability gap exists, by:

---

[416] The IIIM is the International, Impartial and Independent Mechanism to assist in the investigation and prosecution of persons responsible for the most serious crimes under International Law committed in the Syrian Arab Republic since March 2011. It was established in 2016 pursuant to a resolution of the General Assembly (A/71/248).

[417] UNITAD is the UN Investigative Team to Promote Accountability for Crimes Committed by Da'esh/ISIL. It was set up pursuant to Security Council Res. 2379 (2017).

[418] The Independent Investigative Mechanism for Myanmar, discussed above.

a. identifying perpetrators;

b. collecting and preserving evidence for use in national, regional and international legal proceedings, including for use in non-criminal judicial and non-judicial proceedings aimed at providing victims with effective remedies and reparation for violations, before it is lost, destroyed or deteriorates;

c. monitoring and documenting violations and making recommendations to States and other actors on how to protect and remedy human rights, in the case of those Accountability Mandates with mixed mandates; and

d. having a deterrent effect against future violations.

However, the ICJ and Oxford have found that nearly all Accountability Mandates face common challenges each time a new one is established, including:

a. **Political challenges** inside the UN Human Rights Council or other UN bodies to establish or renew a mandate, often against hurdles unrelated to merit;

b. **Financial challenges**, including at the budget allocation stage;

c. **Administrative challenges**, relating to the start-up phase of operations, including the need to secure appropriate staffing with the right substantive expertise and resources to adequately fulfill the mandate; and

d. **System challenges**, to record, store, analyze and preserve massive amounts of digital evidence securely, and the need to develop policies, procedures and protocols to ensure the Accountability Mandates fulfil their functions effectively, efficiently and without doing harm to victims and witnesses.

[The report then proposes two alternative options.]

Option 1: Establish a SIIM

…

A SIIM should be independent of OHCHR and other UN Agencies but linked to them in a consultative and operational capacity - and reliant on them for certain services - in the same way as the IIIM, IIMM and UNITAD. It would have two functions:

- conduct investigations with a view to gathering information and evidence for potential use in criminal and other legal and administrative proceedings; and

- use its capacity to act as a specialist service provider to existing and future UN body-created Accountability Mandates, including relevant fact-finding missions and commissions of inquiry.

Investigation function

The SIIM would conduct its own investigations when its mandate is triggered [by relevant UN bodies or by an independent authority set up for the purpose]

A SIIM would need to put in place the specialized capacity required for when an investigation is warranted into individual criminal responsibility, for example:

a. digital technology infrastructure and expertise;

b. witness and victim protection infrastructure and expertise; and

c. dedicated expertise on international criminal law, forensics and military structures.

This capacity is already in place to varying degrees inside the IIIM, IIMM and UNITAD. A particular area that requires specific resources is "*digitization*", as the capacity to manage digital data and evidence is one of the biggest challenges facing all Accountability Mandates, demanding experience with existing systems as well as capacity to provide customized solutions.

Once collected and preserved, the material could also be appropriate for use in other legal proceedings before human rights courts, truth commissions, and civil and administrative proceedings.

A SIIM should also have a core group of investigators, analysts, and lawyers, including with thematic expertise in areas such as crimes against or involving children and conflict-related sexual violence. This would help in creating consistency and standing expertise and avoiding duplication and double standards. …

…

One of the benefits of a SIIM would be that it would obviate the need for victims to advocate with States for various functions to be included each time a new Accountability Mandate is proposed, some of which may not be feasible in a particular political climate. For instance, it might not always be possible for a mandate to include the *"collection, consolidation and preservation of evidence for use in future legal proceedings."* This would also mitigate against the challenge of *"selectivity"* where some Accountability Mandates get *"stronger"* mandates than others, much to the puzzlement and frustration of victims.

Option 2: Establish an independent, investigation support service provider

This option would entail the establishment a [sic] stand-alone, independent, investigation support service provider, independent of OHCHR and other UN Agencies, but linked to them and reliant on them for certain services.

Unlike a SIIM envisioned by Option 1, such a model would not conduct its own investigations. Rather, it would simply establish a standing specialized capacity that could be drawn upon when an expert, essentially criminal, or other complex investigation is undertaken by existing and future Accountability Mandates such as fact-finding missions and commissions of inquiry, and UN Special Procedure and treaty body support, upon a request for specialist assistance. For example, it could provide support and services such as those listed above (specialized digital storage capacity and expertise, witness and victim protection infrastructure and expertise, expertise on forensics and military matters, and expertise in international criminal law, including on conflict-related sexual violence).

Its independence should allow for greater nimbleness in responding to the needs of those requesting support as it would not be subject to the bureaucratic constraints that all UN agencies face.

…

QUESTIONS

1. What are the arguments for and against the proposal for regulations outlining the powers, structure and functioning of all UN COIs? Is it possible to develop meaningful guidelines to govern such a broad array of circumstances and challenges? Are existing guidelines so general as to provide little real guidance? Or are the interests of human rights better served by avoiding the constraining effects of excessive professionalization and leaving maximum room for creativity and innovation?

2. In 2009, the Guinean army brutally suppressed demonstrations against the ruling junta, leading to over 150 deaths, hundreds of injuries, widespread sexual assault, and cases of enforced disappearances. The UN, Human Rights Watch, and various other groups produced detailed reports. In response, the government commissioned private consultants, CW Group International, who published a report later that year in Washington DC, entitled *Report of Inquiry: Incident at the National Stadium on 9-28-09 in Conakry, Guinea.* This report challenged the findings of the other sources and largely exonerated the government. Are there circumstances under which you see a legitimate role for private, for-profit, groups in human rights fact-finding?

3. Which of the new technologies do you think might bring about the biggest changes in traditional approaches to fact-finding?

Chapter 11. Regional Human Rights Systems[419]

In the realm of human rights, regional intergovernmental systems have played a major role. The Council of Europe moved as early as 1950 to adopt the European Convention on Human Rights (ECHR) and various proposals were made in the early 1950s to include human rights in the frameworks that eventually led to the European Union.[420] It was not until 1969 that the analogous American Convention was adopted, but the Inter-American system began with the adoption of the American Declaration of the Rights and Duties of Man in 1948, and saw steady institutional and normative development thereafter. In 1977, the UN General Assembly (Res. 32/127 (1977)) sought to stimulate the establishment of 'suitable regional machinery' in regions where none then existed. Four years later, in 1981, the African Charter of Human and Peoples' Rights was adopted.

In addition to these three major regional human rights systems, which are the focus of this chapter, various other groups have adopted declarations of human rights and established commissions to promote them.[421] These include the Arab Charter on Human Rights of 2004 overseen by the Arab Human Rights Committee, the Organization of Islamic Cooperation's 1990 Cairo Declaration on Human Rights in Islam, revised by the 2020 OIC Declaration on Human Rights, and the ASEAN Intergovernmental Commission on Human Rights, established in 2009.[422] Sub-regional courts have also been important in some contexts.[423]

The following analysis puts the three major regional systems into broader perspective and emphasises their centrality to the overall international regime.

ALEXANDRA HUNEEUS AND MIKAEL RASK MADSEN, BETWEEN UNIVERSALISM AND REGIONAL LAW AND POLITICS: A COMPARATIVE HISTORY OF THE AMERICAN, EUROPEAN, AND AFRICAN HUMAN RIGHTS SYSTEMS
16 INT'L J. CONSTIT. L. (2018) 136

Our approach … cuts directly against tendencies in recent scholarship to concentrate on the universal system and to emphasize the role of the West in the genesis of human rights institutions. Most scholars who have given a global account of human rights have tended to slight the regional systems and focus instead on the UN-based system, perhaps because it claims the mantle of universality.[424] It is nevertheless in the regional systems where much—if not most—of the human rights action has unfolded, and not only in recent years but from the very beginning. Most decisively, the regional systems have developed judicial institutions that render binding judgments on the member states. Consequently, they have also come to engage in increasingly dense interaction with domestic courts, becoming far more deeply embedded in national systems than the UN system. To slight them is to distort the history of human rights.

Our comparative regional approach moreover allows us to push back on the tendency to view human rights institutions and international courts as creations of the West that are transplanted, copied, or otherwise vernacularized by the South. It is of course possible to describe the Inter-American Court, for example, as a transplant at a formal and purely institutional level. Yet, such a narrow perspective leaves out how this system—like the European and African ones—is embedded in and responsive to a region with distinct cultural, political, and social contexts. This contextual embeddedness in large part explains the trajectory of the system. …

… [N]o single actor, state, or region can claim sole authorship of international or regional human rights. This has historic reasons: at the time of the genesis of all three systems, the repertoire of ideas and concepts from

---

[419] See generally C. Roberts, *Alternative Approaches to Human Rights: The Disparate Historical Paths of the European, Inter-American, and African Regional Human Rights Systems* (2023).

[420] G. de Búrca, 'The Road Not Taken: The European Union as a Global Human Rights Actor', 105 *Am. J. Int'l L.* 649 (2011).

[421] J. Pevehouse, 'Regional Human Rights and Democracy Governance', in T. Börzel and T. Risse (eds.), *The Oxford Handbook of Comparative Regionalism* (2016) 486.

[422] A. Collins and E. Bon Tai Soon, 'The Spiral Model, Scope Conditions, and Contestation in the ASEAN Intergovernmental Commission on Human Rights', 36 *The Pacific Rev.* (2023) 1.

[423] See Jo Un Eom and L. Helfer, 'Human Rights Litigation Before Sub-Regional Courts in East and West Africa', in N. Jain and M. Versteeg (eds.), *Oxford Handbook of Comparative Human Rights Law* (2024) 000; and O. Okafor et al., 'On the Modest Impact of West Africa's International Human Rights Court on the Executive Branch of Government in Nigeria', 35 Harv. *Hum. Rts. J* (2022) 169.

[424] See, e.g., Moyn, who pays very little attention to the early European and American human rights systems; and, when he does, tends to belittle their significance. S. Moyn, *The Last Utopia: Human Rights in History* (2010).

which they drew had already emerged in both legal and political discourse—and this influenced both regional and international developments. Thus, the regional systems are neither the consequence of transplants going from the North to the South nor the result of a larger UN or US-driven master plan of international human rights. Rather, the fact that the systems share relatively similar institutional models is revelatory of how these actors have borrowed from and contributed to a collective bank of ideas about international human rights. Where the regional systems differ the most is therefore not in their institutional designs, which are generally rather similar at a formal legal level, but the temporality of when they have managed to turn ideas into actual institutions. Moreover, as our analysis suggests, even similar institutions, for example, Commissions, have sometimes played out differently on the regional terrains due to specific contextual constraints. We consequently argue that the single most decisive factor explaining differences in regional human rights are contextual differences between the regions. Simultaneously, however, the fact that exchange between the systems and the larger international regime have taken place for decades provides countering processes of unification. This ultimately places the regional systems at the crossroads of a universalizing discourse on human rights and the specific constraints derived from local legal and political contexts. ... [I]nternational human rights have provided a global "script" which has been enacted in radically different settings in Europe, Latin America, and Africa and has resulted in a relative diversity of institutions and practices.

* * *

We turn now to explore the oldest of the regional systems.

A. THE EUROPEAN CONVENTION SYSTEM

1. Introduction and Overview

The European Convention for the Protection of Human Rights and Fundamental Freedoms (ECHR) was signed in 1950 and entered into force in 1953. The ECHR is of particular importance for several reasons: it was the first comprehensive treaty in the world in this field; it established the first international complaints procedure and the first international court for the determination of human rights matters; it remains the most judicially developed of all the human rights systems; it has generated a more extensive jurisprudence than any other part of the international system; and it applies to almost 25 percent of the nations in the world. Our principal concern in this selective examination of the European Convention is with its evolving institutional architecture, particularly with the European Court of Human Rights (ECtHR) and the manner in which it has performed the judicial function.

Elsewhere in this coursebook, we encounter many cases decided by the ECtHR. But a leaflet published by the Court itself provides a reminder of the potential to confuse this court with other key parts of the overall human rights regime. The second page of the four-page *Court in Brief* is headed 'NOT TO BE CONFUSED WITH'. It lists thereunder: the Court of Justice of the European Union (CJEU), the International Court of Justice (ICJ), the Universal Declaration of Human Rights (UDHR), and the European Union's Charter of Fundamental Rights.

The impetus for the adoption of a European Convention came from three factors. It was first a regional response to the atrocities committed in Europe during the Second World War and an affirmation of the belief that governments respecting human rights are less likely to wage war on their neighbours. Second, both the Council of Europe, which was set up in 1949 (and under whose auspices the Convention was adopted), and the European Union (previously the European Community or Communities, the first of which was established in 1952) were partly based on the assumption that the best way to ensure that Germany would be a force for peace, in partnership with France, the United Kingdom, and other West European states, was through regional integration and the institutionalization of common values. This strategy contrasted strongly with the punitive, reparations-based approach embodied in the 1919 Versailles Treaty after the First World War.

The Preamble to the ECHR refers (perhaps somewhat optimistically, especially at the time) to the 'European countries which are likeminded and have a common heritage of political traditions, ideals, freedom and the rule of law ...'. But this statement also points to the third major impetus towards a Convention — the desire to bring the non-Communist countries of Europe together within a common ideological framework and to consolidate their unity in the face of the Communist threat. 'Genuine democracy' (to which the Statute of the Council of Europe commits its members) or the 'effective political democracy' to which the Preamble of the Convention refers, had to be clearly distinguished from the 'people's democracy' which was promoted by the Soviet Union and its allies.

The European Convention's transformation of abstract human rights ideals into a concrete legal framework followed a path which was to become familiar in this field. The initial enthusiasm was soon tempered by concerns over sovereignty and a reluctance to take the concept of a state's accountability too far. Thus, a call by the Congress of Europe in 1948 for the adoption of a Charter of Human Rights to be enforced by a Court of Justice 'with adequate sanctions for the implementation of this Charter' went further than West European governments were prepared to go. Instead, the final version of the Convention acknowledges in the Preamble that it constitutes only 'the first steps for the collective enforcement of certain of the Rights stated in the Universal Declaration'.

Both during the drafting of the Convention and in the years after its adoption there was considerable reluctance on the part of key states to adopt many of its key provisions. In this regard the most detailed historical analyses have been undertaken in relation to the United Kingdom and it is an instructive example. During the Second World War, Prime Minister Churchill often returned to the theme that the war was being fought 'to establish, on impregnable rocks, the rights of the individual', and commentators such as Hersch Lauterpacht insisted that the war was, in large part, about 'the enthronement of the rights of man' and the correlative limitation of state sovereignty.[425] But when victory brought the opportunity to draft a human rights treaty, other considerations would be prominent.

Marco Duranti observes, in *The Conservative Human Rights Revolution: European Identity, Transnational Politics, and the Origins of the European Convention* (2017) at 392, that human rights in Europe 'had widely divergent lineages and have served opposing purposes and taken on conflicting valences.' Contrary to some early accounts, there was no single linear trajectory.

A. W. Brian Simpson, in *Human Rights and the End of Empire: Britain and the Genesis of the European Convention* (2004) at 347, explains that the British, in common with other major powers such as the United States and the then Soviet Union, followed an 'export theory of human rights' according to which 'human rights were for foreigners, who did not enjoy them, not for the British, who enjoyed them anyway. They were for export.' Simpson adds that, on the British side, there were mixed motivations for supporting the Convention:

> simple and honest humanitarianism, the wish of the officials to honour ministerial statements, ... the belief that violations of human rights could threaten peace, a detestation of the Soviet system, and ... the feeling that there needed to be an international response to the horrors of the recent past, though ... [t]he prominence given to the uniqueness of the destruction of European Jewry is a phenomenon of the 1960s and thereafter ... . [The major powers were motivated not by a desire for] self-improvement but self-protection against a return to the oppression ... which might come about through the rise of a new totalitarianism. Those who had not suffered occupation never seemed to have fully grasped the importance of this factor.

Duranti's analysis emphasizes the role of 'conservatives operating through transnational assemblies and nongovernmental organizations' as the ones who 'prompted governments to draft the ECHR and decisively shaped its normative content ... [and its] institutional mechanisms ... .' He notes (at 402) that:

> Conservatives took advantage of the favorable political conditions present in pan-European assemblies to implement a free-market and social Catholic agenda unachievable in national parliaments. ...
>
> ... [T]hey sought to forge a European human rights system that would replace majority rule with the rule of law, the unitary state with a more pluralistic system, the absolute

---

[425] See M. Mazower, *Dark Continent: Europe's Twentieth Century* (1998), 193–4.

sovereignty of nations and parliaments with greater autonomy for individuals, families, localities, minorities, and civil society. ...

... [Conservatives believed] that the legitimacy of supranational institutions would depend on coupling technocratic expertise with an attention to the cultural and ethical bases of European unity. Rejecting liberal cosmopolitanism and technocracy in favor of a nostalgic Christian internationalism, these conservative Europeanists conceived of human rights using conservative moral frameworks that had emerged in reaction to industrialization, Enlightenment rationalism, and the French Revolution. ... [T]he cultural inheritance of Western Christendom could provide a foundation for uniting the manifold communities in which Europeans formed their ethical obligations.

All the same, the good that the conservative human rights revolution did cannot be readily disentangled from the ill. Appeals to the principles of democracy and human rights provided a perch to attack groups who purportedly did not believe in them. Churchill framed human rights as products of Christian civilization so as to extend democratic freedoms to some peoples while excluding others. Though believing in the necessity of preserving the distinctive attributes of different nations, he fixated on a monolithic, static idea of Europe premised on an essentialist conception of European culture and identity. His aim was to fight the fires of hatred in the region, but in so doing he fanned them.

The conservative politicians who championed a European human rights court believed that colonized peoples were not entitled to the same rights protections as Europeans. So, too, did they hold that communist parties were not to enjoy representation in European organizations of states despite enjoying significant electoral support in much of Western Europe, while states with dubious democratic credentials and former Axis powers were welcomed to the "European family." Their views on women's rights were retrograde; extraordinarily, they included no prohibition on discrimination on the basis of gender in their early drafts of a European human rights treaty, even following the inclusion of such a provision in the Universal Declaration.

The conservative human rights revolution was brimming with other contradictions and rank hypocrisies. Churchill lent his support to rightwing authoritarian regimes in the interests of containing communism. Alexandre Marc and Louis Salleron were disturbingly close to the anti- Semitic, authoritarian Far Right in their own country. François de Menthon and Pierre-Henri Teitgen showed a callous disregard toward the plight of Jewish compatriots and refugees. When David Maxwell Fyfe later assumed the position of home secretary, he set out to curtail the rights of British homosexuals with a zeal that was exceptional even in the intolerant climate of that age. The conservative mobilization of the language of human rights in the service of reconciliation meant amnesty for right-wing political prisoners and an end to denazification. As much as this may have assisted in the stabilization of continental democracies, it also strengthened the hand of apologists for collaborationist regimes and those refusing to acknowledge widespread complicity in the Holocaust.

Andrew Moravcsik, in 'The Origins of Human Rights Regimes: Democratic Delegation in Postwar Europe', 54 *Int. Org.* (2000) 217, at 238, explains British concerns:

> As W. E. Beckett, legal advisor to the Foreign Office ... put it, "We ... are dead against anything like an international court to which individuals who think they are aggrieved in this way could go." ...

> ...

> ... British officials and politicians — most notably in Cabinet discussions — dwelled primarily on the fear that the convention would threaten idiosyncratic (but not

unambiguously undemocratic) political practices and institutions in the United Kingdom ... .

The defense of British institutional idiosyncrasy elicited the most violent rhetoric from British politicians and officials. Lord Chancellor Jowitt's official paper criticized the draft convention ... as:

> so vague and woolly that it may mean almost anything. ... It completely passes the wit of man to guess what results would be arrived at by a tribunal composed of elected persons who need not even be lawyers, drawn from various European states possessing completely different systems of law, and whose deliberations take place behind closed doors ... . Any student of our legal institutions must recoil from this document with a feeling of horror.

A common complaint was that judicial review would undermine parliamentary sovereignty. Beckett wrote: "It seems inconceivable that any Government, ... would take the risk of entrusting these unprecedented powers to an international court, legislative powers which Parliament would never agree to entrust to the courts of this country which are known and which command the confidence and admiration of the world." ...

The specific issue cited most often by the government's legal authorities was the British policy toward political extremists. ... Lord Chancellor Jowitt's complaint was that "the Convention would prevent a future British government from detaining people without trial during a period of emergency ... or judges sending litigants to prison for throwing eggs at them; or the Home Secretary from banning Communist or Fascist demonstrations."

...

In the minds of British officials, however, the primacy of domestic sovereignty over collective defense of the democratic peace remained unchallenged. The cabinet mandated efforts to water down the force of any agreement in Britain. British representatives ... [called] for the careful enumeration and definition of human rights ... . Foreign Minister Ernest Bevin himself instructed British negotiators to veto any mandatory right of individual petition "even if it [means] being in a minority of one." ...

Having secured these concessions, which essentially rendered the convention unenforceable in Britain, the cabinet unanimously accepted the desirability of signing it...

.

Christopher Roberts, in *Alternative Approaches to Human Rights: The Disparate Historical Paths of the European, Inter-American, and African Regional Human Rights Systems* (2023) at 27, adds that 'the British demanded that the text be more specific; they called for a strengthened role for the Committee of Ministers; they resisted the idea that the Convention might apply to colonial territories; they opposed the idea of strong domestic legal applicability; and they resisted the ability of individuals to bring petitions, and the existence of a court with mandatory oversight. This resistance was successful on all fronts.'

An Overview

This historical review seems a long way from the world of the twenty-first century in which the rights recognized in the Convention form an integral part of domestic law in most European states. More generally, major institutional reforms have helped to move the system closer to that envisaged by the maximalists of the early 1950s. But, as we shall see below, these successes have brought other forms of governmental resistance to the fore.

The Council of Europe was established in 1949 by a group of ten states, primarily to promote democracy, the rule of law, and greater unity among the nations of Western Europe. It represented both a principled commitment of its members to these values and an ideological stance against Communism. Over the years its activities have included the promotion of cooperation in relation to social, cultural, sporting, and a range of other matters. Until 1990, the Council had 23 members, all from Western Europe. Post-Cold War developments, however, prompted most states of Eastern and Central Europe to join, and today it has 46.[426] Only Belarus, and Russia which was expelled in 2022, are now outside the Council.

The conditions for the admission of a state to the Council of Europe are laid down in Article 3 of its Statute. The state must be a genuine democracy that respects the rule of law and human rights and must 'collaborate sincerely and effectively' with the Council in these domains. In practice, such collaboration involves becoming a party to the European Convention on Human Rights. An applicant state must satisfy the Council's Committee of Ministers that its legal order conforms with the requirements of Article 3. The opinion of the Parliamentary Assembly is sought and the Assembly in turn will appoint an expert group to advise it. A 1994 report concluded that Russia did not meet the requirements,[427] but it was nonetheless admitted in 1996, despite strong criticism of the decision.

The Rights Recognized

Although the initial moves to create a European Convention pre-dated the UN's adoption of the UDHR, the text of the latter was available to those responsible for the final drafting of the Convention. Eventually the drafters defined rights in terms similar to the early version of the draft ICCPR. Since the Covenant went through numerous changes before adoption, the formulations used in the two treaties sometimes differ significantly. Several weighty provisions appear in only one or the other. For example, the European Convention contains no provision relating to self-determination or to the rights of members of minority groups (Arts. 1 and 27 of the ICCPR). Each treaty limits freedoms of expression, association, and religion in similar ways (e.g., criteria of public safety or national security), but the European Convention consistently requires that a limitation be 'necessary in a democratic society' (Arts. 8–11). The derogation clauses (Art. 4 of the ICCPR, Art. 15 of the European Convention) differ with respect to the list of non-derogable provisions.

Article 1 requires the parties to 'secure [these rights] to everyone within their jurisdiction', while Article 13 requires the state to provide 'an effective remedy before a national authority' for everyone whose rights are violated. Compare the more demanding Article 2 of the ICCPR, which refers to states' duty to adopt legislative and other measures to give effect to the recognized rights and to 'develop the possibilities of judicial remedy'.

When the Convention was adopted in 1950, there were several outstanding proposals on which final agreement could not be reached. It was therefore agreed to adopt Protocols containing additional provisions. Since 1952, 16 protocols have been adopted. While the majority are devoted to procedural matters, others have recognized the following additional rights: the right to property ('the peaceful enjoyment of [one's] possessions'), the right to education, and the obligation to hold free elections (Protocol 1 of 1952); freedom from imprisonment for civil debts, freedom of movement and residence, freedom to leave any country, freedom from exile, the right to enter the country of which one is a national, and no collective expulsion of aliens (Protocol 4 of 1963); abolition of the death penalty (Protocol 6 of 1983); the right of an alien not to be expelled without due process, the right to appeal in criminal cases, the right to compensation for a miscarriage of justice, immunity of double prosecution for the same offence, and equality of rights and responsibility of spouses (Protocol 7 of 1984); the general prohibition of discrimination (Protocol 12 of 2000); and abolition of the death penalty, in all circumstances (Protocol 13 of 2002). Acceptance of each of the Protocols is optional.

2. The European Court and its Procedures

The ECHR provides for both individual petitions (Art. 34) and interstate complaints (Art. 33). The latter were once rare, but are now thriving. The former, which may be brought by individuals, legal persons (such as

---

[426] Albania, Andorra, Armenia, Austria, Azerbaijan, Belgium, Bosnia and Herzegovina, Bulgaria, Croatia, Cyprus, Czech Republic, Denmark, Estonia, Finland, France, Georgia, Germany, Greece, Hungary, Iceland, Ireland, Italy, Latvia, Liechtenstein, Lithuania, Luxembourg, Malta, Monaco, Montenegro, Netherlands, North Macedonia, Norway, Poland, Portugal, Republic of Moldova, Romania, San Marino, Serbia, Slovak Republic, Slovenia, Spain, Sweden, Switzerland, Türkiye, Ukraine, and the United Kingdom.

[427] R. Bernhardt et al., 'Report on the Conformity of the Legal Order of the Russian Federation with Council of Europe Standards' (7 October 1994).

corporations), groups of individuals, or nongovernmental organizations, have grown exponentially in numerical terms since the 1990s.

The Convention makes clear that the primary responsibility for implementation rests with the member states themselves. The implementation machinery of the Convention comes into play only after domestic remedies are considered to have been exhausted. A great many complaints are deemed inadmissible, frequently on the ground that domestic law provides an effective remedy for any violation that may have taken place. Contracting States' obligations under Articles 1 and 13 are to 'secure to everyone' the Convention's rights and to provide 'an effective remedy before a national authority' for violations of those rights. This preference for domestic resolution is also reinforced by the requirement to seek a 'friendly settlement' wherever possible and by the procedures for full government consultation in the examination of complaints.

The remedy given by a domestic court may be pursuant to provisions of domestic law that stand relatively independently of the Convention, although perhaps influenced by it, such as a human rights Act, a code of criminal procedure, or a constitutional provision drafted to be consistent with the Convention. Alternatively, a remedy may be given as a result of the incorporation of the Convention into domestic law, which may be achieved as an automatic consequence of ratification or through the adoption of special legislation.

The Evolution of the ECHR System

The system of considering individual complaints is the hallmark of the ECHR regime. Its evolution from a tentative and optional procedure which was used relatively sparingly to one which is now compulsory and extremely widely used has compelled the Contracting States to undertake a series of fundamental reforms. Driven by a flood of applications, concerns that the system will collapse from overload, and complaints by some states that the Court has over-reached, European governments and the Court itself have been in a constant state of reform since the late 1990s.

When originally devised in the 1950s, and for several decades thereafter, the petition procedure was optional. Only three of the original ten members accepted it from the outset, while many of the rest made clear that they wanted no part of it. For example, it was not until 1981 that France accepted the right of individual complaint for its citizens, and during the 1970s the British Government regularly raised the prospect that it might withdraw its acceptance of the procedure. Until the late 1990s the procedures used were much less 'judicial' than they are today, and were surrounded by safeguards aimed at providing reassurances to governments that they need not fear too much encroachment on their national sovereignty.

Initially, all complaints were first considered by the European Commission on Human Rights ('the Commission'). If a complaint was deemed admissible, an effort had to be made to broker a 'friendly settlement'. In the absence of such a settlement, the Commission reported on the facts and expressed its opinion on the merits of the case. That report went to the Committee of Ministers, a political body, which could endorse or reject it. Where the state concerned had opted to accept the compulsory jurisdiction of the Court, either the Commission or that state could refer the case to the Court for a final, binding adjudication.

Over time, more and more states accepted the compulsory jurisdiction of the Court and acceptance of the complaints procedure itself had become unanimous by 1990. A major reform introduced in 1994 (when Protocol No. 9 entered into force) allowed applicants to submit their case to a screening panel composed of three judges, which decided whether the Court should take up the case. There have since been several waves of reform, considered below. The entire system was streamlined by Protocol No. 11 of 1994, by which the right of individual petition became compulsory, the Commission ceased to exist (as of October 1999), the Court became full-time and assumed all the relevant functions of the Commission, individuals gained direct access to the Court, and the political (and too often problematic) role played by the Committee of Ministers was limited to matters of enforcement.

Protocol No. 14 came into force in 2014, enabling lower priority and repeat cases to be dealt with by three-judge panels. Between 2010 and 2019, the so-called Interlaken process (involving high-level meetings in Interlaken in 2010, Izmir in 2011, and Brighton in 2012), yielded further procedural refinements and led to the adoption of Protocol No. 15 which added this paragraph to the Convention's preamble:

> Affirming that the High Contracting Parties, in accordance with the principle of subsidiarity, have the primary responsibility to secure the rights and freedoms defined in this Convention and the Protocols thereto, and that in doing so they enjoy a margin of appreciation, subject to the supervisory jurisdiction of the European Court of Human Rights established by this Convention … .

This was a concession to significantly stronger demands put forward by the United Kingdom and Denmark. In principle it only reiterated existing approaches, but in practice the reiteration carried important political significance, as explained below. The official 'explanatory report' on the protocol states that:

> 7. … [The new text refers] to the principle of subsidiarity and the doctrine of the margin of appreciation. It is intended to enhance the transparency and accessibility of these characteristics of the Convention system and to be consistent with the doctrine of the margin of appreciation as developed by the Court in its case law. …
>
> …
>
> 9. The jurisprudence of the Court makes clear that the States Parties enjoy a margin of appreciation in how they apply and implement the Convention, depending on the circumstances of the case and the rights and freedoms engaged. This reflects that the Convention system is subsidiary to the safeguarding of human rights at national level and that national authorities are in principle better placed than an international court to evaluate local needs and conditions. The margin of appreciation goes hand in hand with supervision under the Convention system. In this respect, the role of the Court is to review whether decisions taken by national authorities are compatible with the Convention, having due regard to the State's margin of appreciation.

Protocol No. 16, which entered into force in 2018, enables the Court to issue Advisory Opinions (see below).

Interpretative Principles

Steven Greer and Lewis Graham, in 'Europe', in Daniel Moeckli, Sangeeta Shah, and Sandesh Sivakumaran (eds.), *International Human Rights Law* (4th ed., 2022) 463, at 477 provide an overview of some of the principles developed by the ECtHR:

> The Court also applies a number of 'principles of interpretation' not found in the text of the Convention … . … The principle of effective protection of individual rights holds that … rights should be interpreted broadly and exceptions narrowly. This is linked to the principle of non-abuse of rights and limitations, which prohibits states and others from undermining rights by abusing either the rights themselves or their limitations. … The principle of positive obligations permits the Court to interpret the ECHR so as to impose obligations upon states actively to protect Convention rights, and not merely the negative obligation to avoid violating them.
>
> Armed with the principle of autonomous interpretation, the Court can define some of the Convention's key terms in order to prevent states conveniently redefining their way around their obligations, for instance, by redesignating crimes as mere 'administrative infractions'. Similarly, the principle of evolutive, or dynamic, interpretation enables outmoded conceptions of how terms in the Convention were originally understood to be abandoned when significant, durable, and … pan-European changes in the climate of European public opinion have occurred … . The twin principles of subsidiarity and supervision … indicate that the role of the Court is subordinate to that of member states … .
>
> The principle of proportionality limits interference with Convention rights to that which is least intrusive in pursuit of a legitimate objective, while the closely related doctrine of the margin of appreciation refers to the room for manoeuvre the Strasbourg institutions

are prepared to accord national authorities in fulfilling their Convention obligations. Pervasive in the ECHR are the closely related principles of legality, the rule of law, and procedural fairness - which seek to subject the exercise of public power to effective, formal legal constraints in order to avoid arbitrariness - and the principle of democracy, which assumes that human rights flourish best in the context of democratic political institutions and a tolerant social climate.

… [B]ecause the Court considers itself less well placed than national authorities to prescribe what should be done, adverse judgments typically declare only that the ECHR has been breached. Where this is the case, an award of compensation, though not automatic, is now the norm. Excluding claims under Article 1 Protocol No 1 (which reflect the value of the property involved) and other outliers, the average compensation per applicant is in the region of €8,300 … .

The Judges

The Court is composed of 46 judges, the same number as there are state parties to the Convention. They are elected in their individual capacity and not as a representative of any state. The position is full-time and salaried and judges cannot engage in any activities that would be incompatible with their independence, impartiality, and demands of their judicial role. They are elected for a non-renewable nine-year term, and must not be over 65 when nominated. The first step in electing a judge is a national selection procedure, in which the State party selects three qualified candidates. Their qualifications, as well as the process followed, are then assessed by the Committee on the Election of Judges to the ECtHR, which interviews the candidates and ranks them. Judges are elected by the 306-member Parliamentary Assembly of the Council of Europe, in a secret ballot.[428]

The plenary Court elects its President and two Vice-Presidents for a three-year period, with the possibility of re-election. Administratively, the Court consists of five geographically and gender-balanced Sections, each with its own President. They work in four formations: (i) a single judge, who may decide only on clearly inadmissible complaints; (ii) a three-judge committee which may rule on admissibility, and on the merits if a case falls clearly within well-established case law; (iii) a Chamber of seven judges may decide cases, by majority vote; and (iv) the Grand Chamber (17 judges, including the Court's President and Vice-President, the Presidents of the five Sections, and a judge with the same nationality as the defendant State. The Grand Chamber hears appeals from a Chamber judgment, and cases relinquished by a Chamber that involves an important or novel question. The Registry, headed by an elected Registrar, provides legal and administrative support to the Court and its 640 staff members play an important role in drafting majority judgments. In 2023, the Court's budget was 77 million euros.

Individual Petitions

Individual petition proceedings under Article 34 begin with a complaint by an individual, group or NGO against a state party. To be declared admissible a petition must not be anonymous, manifestly ill-founded, or constitute an abuse of the right of petition. Domestic remedies must have been exhausted, the petition must be presented within four months of the final decision in the domestic forum, and it must not concern a matter which is substantially the same as one which has already been examined under the ECHR or submitted to another procedure of international investigation or settlement.

The procedure before the Court is adversarial and public and is largely written. Hearings take place only in a very small minority of cases. Individual applicants should be legally represented once the application has been communicated to the respondent state, and legal aid is available. Applications may be submitted in any official state language, but the Court itself operates in English and French.

In 2022, 1,718 cases were the subject of 'friendly settlements.' Although by December 2019, some 10,500 cases had been settled, this procedure is now being pushed much more systematically. Veronika Fikfak, in 'Against

---

[428] 'Procedure for the election of judges to the European Court of Human Rights', Parliamentary Assembly Doc. SG-AS (2023) 01rev06 (26 April 2023).

Settlement before the European Court of Human Rights', 20 *Int'l J. Const. L.* (2022) 942, describes this as being designed 'to nudge individual victims towards settlement, accelerate proceedings in less contentious cases, and free up time for the Court to dedicate to cases raising new issues.' While cases challenging the undue length of domestic judicial proceedings are the most commonly settled, 20 percent of all settled cases involve Article 3 violations (torture etc.). While 202 such cases had been settled by the end of 2009, 1,392 Article 3 cases were settled between 2010 and 2020. Fikfak warns that the trend may be problematic:

> The motives of the Registry and the interests of the state are in synergy—both want cases to go away, and they are willing to work together to make sure this happens. …
> [I]ndividual victims [are affected] in several ways: first, the new default rule that all cases have to go through a settlement phase necessarily acts as a "nudge," encouraging individuals to settle their cases and renounce the examination of their complaints in substance. Second, the close relationship between the state and the Registry acts to reinforce certain biases that favor the state and its position as a repeat player. …
> [S]ettlement provides little or no room for long-term justice. Not only can the settlement remain unenforced, if a unilateral declaration closes a dispute which is part of a general, systemic problem, these infringements will remain hidden and unreported, and they will keep recurring. The settlement has resolved little or nothing.

In seeking to prioritize certain cases, the Court's 'Priority Policy' lists seven categories of applications, in descending order:

I.   Urgent – such as risk to life or health, deprivation of liberty, well-being of a child.
II. Raising questions capable of having an impact on the effectiveness of the Convention system or an important question of general interest.
III. Raising issues affecting 'core rights' (Articles 2, 3, 4 or 5(1) involving direct threats to physical integrity and dignity.
IV. Potentially well-founded applications based on other Articles.
V.   Raising issues already dealt with in well-established case-law.
VI. Problematic admissibility.
VII. Manifestly inadmissible.

Since 2021 the Court has used a targeted strategy aimed for processing 'impact' cases. While these do not concern core Article 2 or 3 rights, they raise issues of considerable relevance for the State concerned and for the Convention system as a whole. Efforts to process them more expeditiously have been successful. Examples cited in the *Court's Annual Report 2022* (2023) include cases on sexual harassment in the workplace; wheelchair access to public buildings; judges' freedom of expression; shortcomings of a national minority voting system; and the failure to implement swift and comprehensive desegregation measures in an elementary school.

In 2022, the Court ruled on 39,570 applications, including handing down judgments on 4,168 cases; although because many applications were joined, there were only 1,163 separate judgments. Of the total, 3,554 were decided by three-judge Committees, and 30,600 applications were dealt with by single-judge formations. In January 2023, 74,650 applications were pending. Of those, 74 percent concerned five countries: Türkiye (20,100 applications); Russia (16,750); Ukraine (10,400); Romania (4,800); and Italy (3,550).[429]

In terms of specific violations, well over half of all those found between 1959 and 2022 (12,520 of a total of 21,784) concerned the right to a fair trial (Article 6). There were 4,495 violations relating to Article 3 (torture/inhuman or degrading treatment), 3,115 relating to the right to an effective remedy (Article 13), and 3,810 relating to the right to property (Protocol No. 1).[430]

---

[429] Council of Europe, *Analysis of statistics* 2022 (2023).
[430] Council of Europe, *Violations by Article and by State* 1959-2022 (2023).

Interim Measures [431]

The Convention contains no provision authorizing the Court to issue interim measures. Rule 39 of the Rules of Court, as revised, provides that the Court may 'indicate to the parties any interim measure which they consider should be adopted in the interests of the parties or of the proper conduct of the proceedings.' It was originally considered non-binding and in 1991, the Court voted 10-9 against finding an implied right to order binding interim measures (*Cruz Varas and Others v. Sweden*). But in 2003, following a precedent set by the International Court of Justice in the *LaGrand (Germany v. United States of America)* case (I.C.J. Reports 2001, para. 109), the ECtHR based itself on general principles of international law and the approach adopted by UN treaty bodies and the ICJ to authorize such measures.[432] In 2005, in *Mamatkulov and Askarov v. Turkey*, the Grand Chamber stated that interim measures could be granted if there is (a) the presence of an imminent risk of (b) irreparable harm to (c) a 'core right'.

This approach has gradually expanded to a range of situations in which applicants would otherwise face a real risk of serious and irreversible harm. The most typical cases are those where, if the expulsion or extradition takes place, the applicants would fear for their lives or would face ill-treatment prohibited by Article 3. Interim measures have also been indicated in relation to the right to a fair trial, the right to respect for private and family life, and freedom of expression. Such measures are not indicated 'to prevent the imminent demolition of property, imminent insolvency, or the enforcement of an obligation to do military service; to obtain the release of an applicant who is in prison pending the Court's decision as to the fairness of the proceedings; to ensure the holding of a referendum; to prevent the dissolution of a political party; or to freeze the adoption of constitutional amendments affecting the term of office of members of the judiciary.'[433]

But in recent years, the Court has issued an increasing number of atypical interim measures. In March 2022, for example, it indicated to the Russian Government in the aftermath of the invasion of Ukraine that they 'should refrain from military attacks against civilians and civilian objects, including residential premises, emergency vehicles and other specially protected civilian objects such as schools and hospitals, and to ensure immediately the safety of the medical establishments, personnel and emergency vehicles within the territory under attack or siege by Russian troops', and should ensure unimpeded access of the civilian population to safe evacuation routes, healthcare, food and other essential supplies, rapid and unconstrained passage of humanitarian aid and movement of humanitarian workers.[434]

In June 2022, interim measures were granted at the request of an asylum-seeker from Iraq who was facing imminent removal from the United Kingdom to Rwanda under an asylum partnership agreement between those two governments. Immediately before the planned departure of a charter flight to Rwanda the Court indicated that the UK Government should not act until three weeks after the delivery of the final domestic decision in ongoing judicial review proceedings. The removal was subsequently halted.[435]

These orders were part of a major increase in decisions on interim measures. In 2022, 3,106 applications were received, of which 1,094 were granted.[436] But compliance with these measures remains a major problem as indicated by Giulia Gentile and Daria Sartori, in 'Interim Measures as "Weapons of Democracy" in the European Legal Space', 1 *Eur. Hum. Rts. L. Rev.* (2023) 18, at 29:

> In the ECHR system, interim measures do not benefit from ad hoc supervision by a separate body acting *proprio motu*. The ECtHR itself carries out control over compliance, but it can do so only if the applicant pursues the case further—which is not always the case … . [T]he only power that the ECtHR has when confronted with non-respect of an interim measure is that of declaring, in the final judgment on the case, that a violation of art. 34 ECHR has occurred and ordering the state to pay an "award of just satisfaction" to the applicant. This will have very limited practical consequences, as the final judgment

---

[431] See generally E. Rieter and K. Zwaan (eds.), *Urgency and Human Rights: The Protective Potential and Legitimacy of Interim Measures* (2021); and F. Palombino, R. Virzo and G. Zarra (eds.), *Provisional Measures Issued by International Courts and Tribunals* (2021).

[432] *Mamatkulov and Abdurasulovic v. Turkey*, Application Nos. 46827/99 and 46951/99, Judgment (6 February 2003), paras. 100-10.

[433] ECHR, *Factsheet – Interim measures*, (February 2023), at 3.

[434] Press Release ECHR 073 (2022) of 4 March 2022.

[435] Press Release ECHR 199 (2022) of 15 June 2022.

[436] ECHR, *Analysis of Statistics 2022* (2023).

will be delivered after quite some years, and the amount of the award is generally so low that states' officials have publicly ridiculed its effectiveness in preventing non-compliance.

...

Pilot Judgments[437]

A major challenge for the ECHR system has been large numbers of 'repetitive cases' which result from a dysfunction in the national legal system. One solution has been the adoption of 'pilot judgments', a procedure that emerged from a cluster of cases involving property rights in Poland (*Broniowski v. Poland* (2004)). After World War II and the redrawing of Poland's eastern border the Government undertook to compensate Polish citizens who had been repatriated and had had to abandon their property. Eventually, there were 78,380 claimants who had not received the compensatory property to which they were entitled. The Court requested the Government to ensure the claimants' property rights, through appropriate legal and administrative measures, or provide them with equivalent redress in lieu. As a result, Poland passed an appropriate new Law in 2005 and the Court found that the law and the compensation scheme were effective and struck out remaining applications.

The procedure was codified in Rule 61 of the Rules of Court. The Court can adopt such a procedure in situations involving 'the existence of a structural or systemic problem or other similar dysfunction' giving rise to multiple similar applications. It first seeks the views of the parties to determine the suitability of this approach in the circumstances, and gives priority attention to all applications included under the umbrella of the pilot judgment. In its judgment the Court identifies the nature of the systemic problems and the type of remedial measures that must be taken. It can prescribe a time limit for this purpose. The Court may adjourn its examination of all similar applications pending the adoption of the prescribed remedial measures, but may resume its examination at any time 'where the interests of the proper administration of justice so require'.

The procedure has been applied successfully in many instances, but it can also fail dismally, as pointed out by Angelika Nussberger in *The European Court of Human Rights* (2020) 172:

> ... [In] *Yuriy Nikolayevich Ivanov v Ukraine* (2009) ... an army veteran had complained of the prolonged non-enforcement of judgments ordering the authorities to pay him retirement payment arrears. This complaint revealed the systemic problem that Ukraine generally failed to honour judgment debts. In the Court's pilot judgment Ukraine was ordered to introduce an effective remedy affording adequate and sufficient redress. It failed to do so, and the number of applications grew exponentially. In the follow-up case *Burmych v Ukraine* the Court was already confronted with 12,143 similar applications ... .
> ... [T]he Court ... decided to strike out all the cases. It held that it had discharged its function [by] identifying the systemic shortcoming, finding a violation ... and giving guidance as to the general measures to be taken. ... [Thus] the Committee of Ministers supervising the execution of the pilot procedure [should] deal with all the remaining cases. ...

> This can be seen as a measure of self-defence or as a declaration of bankruptcy. In any case it shows the limits of the Court's capacity to cure human rights violations where the states concerned refuse to cooperate.

Third Party Interventions

Since 1998, the Convention has given Contracting Parties the right to submit a third party observation if one of its nationals is an applicant in a case, a right invoked only ten times up until 2023, and may request permission to do so in any other case before the Court. Kanstantsin Dzehtsiarou, in 'Conversations with Friends: "Friends of the Court" Interventions of the States Parties to the European Convention on Human Rights', 43 *Legal Studies* (2023) 381 calculates that states have intervened in 11 per cent of cases before the Grand Chamber. Since

---

[437] J. Czepek, 'The Application of the Pilot Judgment Procedure and Other Forms of Handling Large-Scale Dysfunctions in the Case Law of the European Court of Human Rights', 20 *Int'l Community L. Rev.* (2018) 347.

2005 this has states intervening on average in three such cases each year. By comparison, NGOs, academics, and other international actors (such as the OHCHR) have intervened in 124 cases, or 30 per cent of the total.

Supervision of Judgments and the Situation of Russia

Article 46 of the ECHR obliges Contracting States to 'abide by the final judgment of the Court', and the task of ensuring that this happens is entrusted to the Committee of Ministers which meets quarterly to review progress. In principle, it is for the State to decide the means by which it will comply with a judgment, but it must notify the Committee first through a plan and then an 'action report'. Once all necessary measures have been taken, the Committee closes the report. National parliaments, NGOs, national ombudsmen, and other actors can play a role in the process.[438]

In its annual report entitled *Supervision of the Execution of Judgments and Decisions of the European Court of Human Rights 2022* (2023) at 12, the Committee notes that it successfully closed its supervision of 880 cases 'following the adoption by respondent States of individual and/or general measures including, in some cases, constitutional and statutory reforms.' It cited some of the results achieved:

> … in Armenia, constitutional and statutory amendments concerning the Government's competence to declare a state of emergency and judicial review of such decisions (*Dareskizb Ltd);* Croatia amended its legislation to enhance investigations into war crimes and adopted a new law on missing persons (*Skendzic and Krznaric* group); Greece amended its criminal legislation to enhance investigations into racially motivated crime (*Sakir*); Lithuania amended its constitution in order to allow impeached politicians to stand for election to Parliament after a certain period of time (*Paksas*); and Türkiye's prison administration practice has changed in order to enhance protection of LGBTI inmates (*X.*)

Nevertheless, there were still 6,081 cases pending full execution, and the number was rising steadily. If a question of interpretation is thought to be hindering execution, the Committee may seek a clarifying ruling from the Court. Where a State refuses to abide by a final judgment, the Committee can refer the matter to the court. If the latter then finds a violation of Article 46, the case returns to the Committee to consider what might be done. An example of this procedure, only the second time it has been invoked, appears below. If all else fails, the Committee might consider proposing that the State's voting rights in the Council of Europe be suspended or that it be expelled altogether. Neither option is attractive in practice.

The first case in which infringement proceedings have been taken was against Azerbaijan in 2019.[439] The second case, against Türkiye, involved Mehmet Osman Kavala, described by the Court as 'a businessman, [and] human-rights defender in Türkiye [who] has been involved in setting up numerous [NGOs] … active in the areas of human rights, culture, social studies, historical reconciliation and environmental protection.' He was detained on 18 October 2017 on suspicion of attempting to overthrow the government and the constitutional order through force and violence. After convoluted proceedings at the national level, a Chamber of the ECHR in 2019 found a violation of Articles 5 (right to liberty and security) and 18 (limitation on use of restrictions on rights) of the ECHR. It held that 'the authorities had been unable to demonstrate that the applicant's initial and continued pre-trial detention had been justified by reasonable suspicions based on an objective assessment of the acts attributed to him'. Following that judgment, a Turkish court acquitted Mr Kavala on the charge of attempting to overthrow the government and ordered his provisional release. However, he was then rearrested on new charges, including military and political espionage. The ECtHR concluded that the true purpose of his detention was 'reducing him to silence'. The Committee of Ministers raised the case repeatedly with the Government, but to no avail, and in February 2022, it referred the case to the Court. In *Proceedings Under Article 46 § 4, in the Case of Kavala v. Türkiye,* the ECHR Grand Chamber judgment of 11 July 2022 held that Türkiye violated Article 46:

> 173. … [T]he Court considers that the measures indicated by Türkiye do not permit it to conclude that the State Party acted in "good faith", in a manner compatible with the

---

[438] ECHR, 'Guide on Article 46 of the European Convention on Human Rights: Binding force and execution of judgments' (31 August 2022).
[439] *Proceedings Under Article 46 § 4 in the Case of Ilgar Mammadov v. Azerbaijan* (Application no. 15172/13) Grand Chamber, (29 May 2019).

"conclusions and spirit" of the *Kavala* judgment, or in a way that would make practical and effective the protection of the Convention rights which the Court found to have been violated in that judgment.

In response, Türkiye stated that 'the ECtHR has unfortunately failed to meet our expectations by the decision … and once again called into question the credibility of the European human rights system.' It called upon the Committee of Ministers to set 'aside its previous biased and selective approach, [act] in common sense and [avoid] certain circles' efforts to politicize the matter.'[440]

The harshest penalty is expulsion from the Council of Europe, which happened to Russia in 2022. James L. Bischoff, in 'Introductory Note … on Russia's Exclusion …', 62 *Int'l Legal Mat.* (2022) 295 explains the process:

> … Under Article 8 [of the Statute], the Committee of Ministers may, by a two-thirds majority, suspend a member's "rights of representation" if the state "has seriously violated Article 3" [committing it to respect the principles of the rule of law and human rights]. …
>
> Russia launched its full-scale invasion of Ukraine on February 24, 2022. The same day, the Committee of Ministers [condemned] the invasion. On February 25, the Committee voted 42 to 2 … to suspend Russia's rights of representation …, finding a "serious violation" of Article 3. On March 1, the [ECHR] issued interim measures calling on Russia to refrain from military attacks against civilians and civilian objects in Ukraine. On March 3, the Committee … [specified] the bodies in which Russia could no longer participate and [clarified] that suspension did not relieve Russia of its financial obligations, nor did it end the European Court's jurisdiction over Russia.
>
> On March 10, as evidence of atrocities mounted, the Committee of Ministers sought the views of the Parliamentary Assembly on "potential further use of Article 8." … Apparently seeing the writing on the wall, Russia filed a letter [on March 15] with the CoE Secretary-General conveying its decision to withdraw – as Greece's military junta had done in 1969 to successfully avoid expulsion – and to denounce the ECHR. …
>
> … [O]n March 15, the Parliamentary Assembly found by … 216 to 0 … that "the Russian Federation has committed serious violations of the Statute …" and "can therefore no longer be a member … ."
>
> … In a consensus resolution on March 16, the Committee of Ministers noted [Russia's] March 15 letter but proceeded under Article 8 to end Russia's membership immediately, rather than wait for its withdrawal to take effect.
>
> The resolution did not explain how Article 8 could be read to permit immediate expulsion of a member that has already announced its withdrawal. …
>
> … [Under Article 8, the] sanction of expulsion would appear to become available only if the Committee requests withdrawal and the member refuses. … On this reading, assuming Russia's March 15 withdrawal letter was valid, expulsion should have been unavailable and the withdrawal would have taken effect at the end of 2022. …
>
> … [But] the Committee … proceeded directly to expulsion, an interpretation that seems rooted in member states' determination not to allow Russia to exploit the rules to delay the consequences of its actions. … Russia thus became the only state ever expelled from the CoE. On March 23, the Committee … [clarified that Russia] could not remain a party to CoE conventions such as the ECHR that are closed to nonmembers of the CoE.

---

[440] Spokesperson of the Ministry of Foreign Affairs, Ambassador Tanju Bilgiç, 'QA-19: Statement in Response to a Question Regarding the Decision by the ECtHR on the Execution of the Kavala Judgment', (11 July 2022).

The European Court, in turn, declared that Russia would cease to be a party to the ECHR on September 16, interpreting an ambiguous provision of the ECHR as providing a six-month period of continued party status even after a member's expulsion from the CoE. The European Court clarified that it remained competent to "deal with" petitions alleging violations committed before September 16. Numerous petitions have since been filed despite dim prospects for Russia's participation in proceedings or compliance. ...

In its 2022 *Supervision* report (at 15), the Committee of Ministers noted that 'as from 3 March 2022, the Russian authorities ceased all communication with the DEJ [Department for the Execution of Judgments] and did not participate in any Committee of Ministers' Human Rights (DH) meetings in 2022.' The Committee's continuing agenda in relation to Russia included two inter-state cases, *Georgia v. Russia (I)* and *(II)*, and cases relating to: the detention of opposition leader, Alexei Navalny; violations in the Transnistrian region of Moldova; the actions of Russian security forces during anti-terrorist operations in the Northern Caucasus; ill-treatment and excessive use of force by police and other state agents; the absence of adequate safeguards to protect women from domestic violence; and restrictions on freedom of assembly.

QUESTION

1. There is a judge on the Court from every one of the contracting states and if that judge cannot serve on a case involving her home state, an ad hoc judge of that nationality is nominated. Commentators have argued that the nationality link for international judges is 'contrary to standard conceptions of independence and impartiality', as well as 'anachronistic and self-defeating'.441 What are the consequences in terms of professionalism and judicial independence of retaining the nationality link?

2. Do you agree with a former Vice-President of the ECtHR that 'execution is crucial—judgments that are not implemented are not worth the paper they are written on'?442

3. It has been suggested, in the wake of Russia's expulsion/withdrawal that the 'inflexibility of the CoE system of sanctions reflects the - rather old-fashioned - state-centric structure of international law, which traditionally relies on state consent and sovereignty. It is now time to [design] more resilient, effective, and efficient international human rights regimes.'443 What would such a regime look like?

---

3. The Interstate Procedure: Article 33

Article 33 of the revised Convention contains a procedure by which one or more states may allege breaches of the Convention by another state party. Unlike the traditional approach to such cases under the international law of state responsibility for injury to aliens (Ch. 2B, above), it is not necessary for an applicant state to allege that the rights of its own nationals have been violated.

In general, states are reluctant to set in motion a formal condemnation procedure when they do not have a direct stake in the matter or when they perceive a serious risk of antagonizing the target state through what will be seen as a hostile act. One predictable result of such litigation would be the filing of a countersuit. There have so far been some 30 inter-State cases, but the Court's docket has been especially crowded in recent years.

Between 1956 and 1999, the former Commission considered 17 interstate applications, the most significant of which addressed only seven different situations: (1) *Greece v. United Kingdom* (1956, 1957) relating to the declaration of a state of exception in Cyprus (then a British colony); (2) *Austria v. Italy* (1960) concerning the murder trial of six members of the German-speaking minority in the South Tyrol; (3) *Denmark, Netherlands,*

---

441 T. Dannenbaum, 'Nationality and the International Judge: The Nationalist Presumption Governing the International Judiciary and Why It Must Be Reversed', 45 *Cornell Int'l. L. J.* 77 (2012), at 183.

442 Nussberger, at 156.

443 K. Dzehtsiarou and V. Tzevelekos, 'The Aggression Against Ukraine and the Effectiveness of Inter-state Cases in Case of War', 3 *Eur. Conv. Hum. Rts. L. Rev.* (2022) 165.

Norway and Sweden v. Greece (1967, 1970) relating to the coup d'état carried out by the Greek colonels in 1967; (4) *Ireland v. United Kingdom* (1971, 1972) relating to the state of emergency in Northern Ireland; (5) *Cyprus v. Turkey* (1974, 1975, 1977, 1996) cases arising out of the Turkish armed intervention in Cyprus; (6) *Denmark, France, the Netherlands, Norway and Sweden v. Turkey* (1982), alleging violations, including torture, by the military government. A settlement approved by the Commission was widely criticized on the ground that it was not based on respect for human rights; and (7) *Denmark v. Turkey* (1997) alleging torture of a Danish citizen during detention by Turkish authorities, and resulting in a friendly settlement.

Inter-state cases are initially heard by a seven-judge Chamber that includes those judges elected in respect of the applicant and respondent States. Rule 39 interim measures have often been granted. As of April 2023, Chamber and/or Grand Chamber hearings have been held in: (i) *Cyprus v. Turkey*; (ii) *Georgia v. Russia (I) and (II)* (Chamber and GC in each case); and *Slovenia v. Croatia* (GC) involving proceedings brought by a Slovenian bank to collect debts owed by Croatian companies.

In April 2023, there were 14 inter-state cases pending before the Court:

Georgia v. Russia (IV): lodged in 2018, relating to the human rights situation between Georgian-controlled territory and Abkhazia and South Ossetia.

Ukraine v. Russia: Two Grand Chamber cases: (i) *Ukraine v. Russia (re Crimea)*, based on applications lodged in 2014, 2015 and 2018; and (ii) *Ukraine and the Netherlands v. Russia* which joined together four inter-state applications relating to the downing of Flight MH17 and Russia's military operations in Ukraine since 24 February 2022. In addition: (iii) a Chamber case about a 2018 Kerch Strait naval incident involving the capture of Ukrainian sailors; and (iv) a 2021 case about targeted assassinations of perceived opponents of Russia.

Russia v. Ukraine: a 2021 case brought by Russia alleging killings, abductions, forced displacement, and restrictions on the use of the Russian language, as well as interruptions to the water supply in Crimea and Ukraine's alleged responsibility for the deaths of those on MH17 because it failed to close its airspace.

Liechtenstein v. the Czech Republic: a 2020 case concerning the latter's classification of Liechtenstein citizens as having German nationality for the purposes of a decree relating to the confiscation of property after World War II.

Armenia, Azerbaijan, Türkiye: Seven cases related to the 2020 conflict between Armenia and Azerbaijan/Nagorno Karabakh alleging widespread human rights violations of the Convention.

In inter-state cases, the ECtHR can award compensation ('just satisfaction'). In *Georgia v. Russia (I)* – involving Russia's collective expulsion of Georgians in 2006-07 – Russia had to pay Georgia 10,000,000 euros in non-pecuniary damage to be distributed to some 1,500 victims. In *Georgia v. Russia (II)*, the Grand Chamber, recalling its approach in *Varnava and Others v. Turkey*, explained its approach to damages:

> "224. ... [T]here is no express provision for non-pecuniary or moral damage. Evolving case by case, the Court's approach in awarding just satisfaction has distinguished situations where the applicant has suffered evident trauma, whether physical or psychological, pain and suffering, distress, anxiety, frustration, feelings of injustice or humiliation, prolonged uncertainty, disruption to life, or real loss of opportunity ... and those situations where the public vindication of the wrong suffered by the applicant, in a judgment binding on the Contracting State, is a powerful form of redress in itself. In many cases where a law, procedure or practice has been found to fall short of Convention standards this is enough to put matters right. ... In some situations, however, the impact of the violation may be regarded as being of a nature and degree as to have impinged so significantly on the moral well-being of the applicant as to require something further. Such elements do not lend themselves to a process of calculation or precise quantification. Nor is it the Court's role to function akin to a domestic tort mechanism court in apportioning fault and compensatory damages between civil parties. Its guiding principle is equity, which above all involves flexibility and an objective consideration of

what is just, fair and reasonable in all the circumstances of the case, including not only the position of the applicant but the overall context in which the breach occurred. Its non-pecuniary awards serve to give recognition to the fact that moral damage occurred as a result of a breach of a fundamental human right and reflect in the broadest of terms the severity of the damage; they are not, nor should they be, intended to give financial comfort or sympathetic enrichment at the expense of the Contracting Party concerned."

In its judgment of 28 April 2023, the Grand Chamber ruled that Russia had to pay Georgia a total of almost 130 million euros in relation to specified claims on behalf of affected individuals.

Kanstantsin Dzehtsiarou and Vassilis P. Tzevelekos, in 'The Aggression Against Ukraine and the Effectiveness of Inter-state Cases in Case of War', 3 *Eur. Conv. Hum. Rts. L. Rev.* (2022) 165 note some of the challenges that such cases pose for the ECtHR:

> … *Resource Implications*
>
> … inter-state cases, especially in the context of military confrontation, require the Court to examine and assess an enormous amount of evidence, witnesses, and claims concerning a major number of victims. The Court is expected to establish facts that are highly contested and which often require onsite visits. Such visits are difficult and costly … . Each of such cases involves hundreds of volumes of documents and other relevant materials. The ECtHR needs to review these materials, establish their authenticity, and make rulings on their basis. This task is time and resource consuming.
>
> … The Court might not have the capacity to process even a relatively low number of inter-state applications. [Since] a well-resourced special 'court' … to exclusively deal with this type of [case] is unlikely to happen any time soon … the Court has to admit its limited capacity … .
>
> … [In] *Georgia v Russia (II)*, the Court … stated:
>
>> … Having regard in particular to the large number of alleged victims and contested incidents, the magnitude of the evidence produced, the difficulty in establishing the relevant circumstances and the fact that such situations are predominantly regulated by legal norms other than those of the Convention (specifically, international humanitarian law or the law of armed conflict), the Court considers that it is not in a position to develop its case-law beyond the understanding of the notion of "jurisdiction" as established to date.
>
> …
>
> The challenge of inter-state cases is in the fact that they can 'overwhelm' the Court. The ECtHR can easily spend all its resources on a handful of inter-state cases. … [The only available option is for the Court to] choose how to deal with such applications. It has been argued that the Court can be active in suggesting friendly settlements in some cases, allowing counter-claims, and endorsing more adversarial proceedings which would place a higher burden on the parties to the case rather than on the Court itself.
>
> … *Legitimacy and Effectiveness*
>
> Apart from resource implications, inter-state applications are politically sensitive and confrontational … [and] require a lot of dedication and careful decision-making. …
>
> … [First] the Court can be accused of applying varying standards in its decision making depending on the respondent state. …
>
> Second, inter-state cases last for years; often, when the judgment in an inter-state case is delivered, the key effects that it produces are rather 'symbolic', establishing the liability of

a state, and the potential allocation of monetary compensation to the victims. Such delayed judgments can only serve to a limited extent any purposes of conflict resolution or prevent new conflicts in the future. For instance, … *Georgia v Russia (II)* was delivered in 2021 and dealt with the situation that happened in August 2008. …

Third, the implementation of inter-state judgments is problematic, and every unimplemented judgment can undermine the reputation of an international tribunal. Even … establishing the appropriate remedies can prove to be a challenge. … [In inter-state cases which are highly sensitive and compensation amounts are high] it is unlikely that these judgments will easily be executed. …

4. The Court's Jurisdiction

The ECtHR cannot consider an application unless it ascertains that it has jurisdiction over the case. If an event occurred prior to the state becoming a party to the ECHR and has no continuing dimension, if the state whose conduct is complained about is not a party to the Convention, and so on, the Court will have no jurisdiction. One of the most controversial and complex issues currently subject to debate is the extent to which the Court has jurisdiction over events which occur beyond the territory of a Contracting Party. The issue of extraterritorial jurisdiction arises in connection with situations which have become increasingly common. They include, to take the examples dealt with below, situations in which a military strike is launched from within the legal space (*l'éspace juridique*) of the Council of Europe but results in damage outside that area, actions taken by armed forces of one state operating in the territory of another which may or may not be a member of the Council of Europe, and the responsibility of a state contributing troops to a UN or other multilateral peacekeeping force under the auspices of the UN Security Council.

These issues highlight tensions that arise as the Court's approach evolves in response to challenges that were not foreseen at the time of drafting the ECHR. The Court has often affirmed the importance of a dynamic, evolutive or teleological approach to interpretation, but in relation to territorial jurisdiction it seems surprisingly reticent to adopt such an approach. The challenges discussed below also underscore the impact of globalization and the extent to which it remains possible to defend the notion that the Convention is essentially designed to uphold the human rights of those within the *éspace juridique*. As boundaries become ever more porous and European states deepen their involvement in complex ways in neighbouring countries and beyond, such a restrictive notion will be increasingly challenged.

The most contentious of the cases below is *Banković*, decided in 2001, in which forces operating under the control of the North Atlantic Treaty Organization (NATO) fired a missile which killed and injured civilians in the course of an air strike on a television station. The Court rejected jurisdiction in that case but subsequently adjusted its position in the *Issa* case which follows. That case concerns the acts of Turkish Government troops in neighbouring Iraq which resulted in the killing of a number of individuals. Next is *Al-Skeini and Others v. United Kingdom* in which, after extensive litigation in the British courts, the ECtHR was called upon to determine whether six individuals killed by UK forces as the occupying power in an area of Iraq in 2003 could be considered to fall under the UK's ECHR jurisdiction. Finally, the 2021 Grand Chamber case of *Georgia v. Russia (II)* suggests that while *Banković* still reigns, its approach continues to be strongly contested within the Court.

BANKOVIĆ AND OTHERS V. BELGIUM AND OTHERS
EUROPEAN COURT OF HUMAN RIGHTS, GRAND CHAMBER, APPLICATION NO.
52207/99 (12 DECEMBER 2001)

[On 23 April 1999 a missile launched from a NATO forces aircraft hit a building in Belgrade housing the master control room of RTS, which operated three television channels and four radio stations. In total 24 targets were hit in the Former Republic of Yugoslavia (FRY) on the same night, including three in Belgrade. The applicants in the case included one person injured and five relatives of some of the 16 persons killed in the RTS attack. The respondent governments were all NATO members who were party to the ECHR: Belgium, the Czech

Republic, Denmark, France, Germany, Greece, Hungary, Iceland, Italy, Luxembourg, the Netherlands, Norway, Poland, Portugal, Spain, Turkey, and the United Kingdom.

After considering a range of issues the Court concluded that 'the essential question to be examined therefore is whether the applicants and their deceased relatives were, as a result of that extra-territorial act [of firing a missile], capable of falling within the jurisdiction of the respondent States.' Before addressing the jurisdiction issue, the Court noted the applicable rules of interpretation. The framework is that reflected in the rules set out in the Vienna Convention on the Law of Treaties (VCLT). The Court also noted that 'it must remain mindful of the Convention's special character as a human rights treaty', as well as interpreting it 'as far as possible in harmony with other principles of international law of which it forms part'.]

(b) The meaning of the words "within their jurisdiction"

59. As to the "ordinary meaning" of the relevant term in Article 1 of the Convention, the Court is satisfied that, from the standpoint of public international law, the jurisdictional competence of a State is primarily territorial. While international law does not exclude a State's exercise of jurisdiction extra-territorially, the suggested bases of such jurisdiction (including nationality, flag, diplomatic and consular relations, effect, protection, passive personality and universality) are, as a general rule, defined and limited by the sovereign territorial rights of the other relevant States.

…

61. The Court is of the view, therefore, that Article 1 of the Convention must be considered to reflect this ordinary and essentially territorial notion of jurisdiction, other bases of jurisdiction being exceptional and requiring special justification in the particular circumstances of each case.

62. … [In terms of state practice] no State has indicated a belief that its extraterritorial actions involved an exercise of jurisdiction within the meaning of Article 1 of the Convention by making a derogation pursuant to Article 15 of the Convention …

63. Finally, the Court finds clear confirmation of this essentially territorial notion of jurisdiction in the *travaux préparatoires* which demonstrate that the Expert Intergovernmental Committee replaced the words "all persons residing within their territories" with a reference to persons "within their jurisdiction" with a view to expanding the Convention's application to others who may not reside, in a legal sense, but who are, nevertheless, on the territory of the Contracting States.

64. It is true that the notion of the Convention being a living instrument to be interpreted in light of present-day conditions is firmly rooted in the Court's case-law. …

65. However, the scope of Article 1, at issue in the present case, is determinative of the very scope of the Contracting Parties' positive obligations and, as such, of the scope and reach of the entire Convention system of human rights' protection as opposed to the question, under discussion in the *Loizidou* case (*preliminary objections*), of the competence of the Convention organs to examine a case. In any event, the extracts from the *travaux préparatoires* detailed above constitute a clear indication of the intended meaning of Article 1 of the Convention which cannot be ignored. The Court would emphasise that it is not interpreting Article 1 "solely" in accordance with the *travaux préparatoires* or finding those *travaux* "decisive"; rather this preparatory material constitutes clear confirmatory evidence of the ordinary meaning of Article 1 of the Convention as already identified by the Court (Article 32 of the Vienna Convention 1969).

66. Accordingly, and as the Court stated in the *Soering* case:

> "Article 1 sets a limit, notably territorial, on the reach of the Convention. In particular,
> the engagement undertaken by a Contracting State is confined to 'securing' ('*reconnaître*' in
> the French text) the listed rights and freedoms to persons within its own 'jurisdiction'.
> Further, the Convention does not govern the actions of States not Parties to it, nor does
> it purport to be a means of requiring the Contracting States to impose Convention
> standards on other States."

(c) Extra-territorial acts recognised as constituting an exercise of jurisdiction

67. In keeping with the essentially territorial notion of jurisdiction, the Court has accepted only in exceptional cases that acts of the Contracting States performed, or producing effects, outside their territories can constitute an exercise of jurisdiction by them within the meaning of Article 1 of the Convention.

68. Reference has been made in the Court's case-law, as an example of jurisdiction "not restricted to the national territory" of the respondent State (the *Loizidou* judgment *(preliminary objections)*, at § 62), to situations where the extradition or expulsion of a person by a Contracting State may give rise to an issue under Articles 2 and/or 3 (or, exceptionally, under Articles 5 and or 6) and hence engage the responsibility of that State under the Convention.

However, the Court notes that liability is incurred in such cases by an action of the respondent State concerning a person while he or she is on its territory, clearly within its jurisdiction, and that such cases do not concern the actual exercise of a State's competence or jurisdiction abroad.

...

70. Moreover, in that first *Loizidou* judgment *(preliminary objections)*, the Court found that, bearing in mind the object and purpose of the Convention, the responsibility of a Contracting Party was capable of being engaged when as a consequence of military action (lawful or unlawful) it exercised effective control of an area outside its national territory. The obligation to secure, in such an area, the Convention rights and freedoms was found to derive from the fact of such control whether it was exercised directly, through the respondent State's armed forces, or through a subordinate local administration. The Court concluded that the acts of which the applicant complained were capable of falling within Turkish jurisdiction within the meaning of Article 1 of the Convention.

...

In its subsequent *Cyprus v. Turkey* judgment, the Court added that since Turkey had such "effective control", its responsibility could not be confined to the acts of its own agents therein but was engaged by the acts of the local administration which survived by virtue of Turkish support. Turkey's "jurisdiction" under Article 1 was therefore considered to extend to securing the entire range of substantive Convention rights in northern Cyprus.

71. In sum, the case-law of the Court demonstrates that its recognition of the exercise of extra-territorial jurisdiction by a Contracting State is exceptional: it has done so when the respondent State, through the effective control of the relevant territory and its inhabitants abroad as a consequence of military occupation or through the consent, invitation or acquiescence of the Government of that territory, exercises all or some of the public powers normally to be exercised by that Government.

...

73. Additionally, the Court notes that other recognised instances of the extraterritorial exercise of jurisdiction by a State include cases involving the activities of its diplomatic or consular agents abroad and on board craft and vessels registered in, or flying the flag of, that State. In these specific situations, customary international law and treaty provisions have recognised the extra-territorial exercise of jurisdiction by the relevant State.

(d) Were the present applicants therefore capable of coming within the "jurisdiction" of the respondent States?

74. The applicants maintain that the bombing of RTS by the respondent States constitutes yet a further example of an extra-territorial act which can be accommodated by the notion of "jurisdiction" in Article 1 … .

75. In the first place, the applicants suggest a specific application of the "effective control" criteria developed in the northern Cyprus cases... . The Court considers that the applicants' submission is tantamount to arguing that anyone adversely affected by an act imputable to a Contracting State, wherever in the world that act may have been committed or its consequences felt, is thereby brought within the jurisdiction of that State for the purpose of Article 1 of the Convention.

The Court is inclined to agree with the Governments' submission that the text of Article 1 does not accommodate such an approach to "jurisdiction". Admittedly, the applicants accept that jurisdiction, and any consequent State Convention responsibility, would be limited in the circumstances to the commission and consequences of that particular act. However, the Court is of the view that the wording of Article 1 does not provide any support for the applicants' suggestion that the positive obligation in Article 1 to secure "the rights and freedoms defined in Section I of this Convention" can be divided and tailored in accordance with the particular circumstances of the extra-territorial act in question and, it considers its view in this respect supported by the text of Article 19 of the Convention. Indeed the applicants' approach does not explain the application of the words "within their jurisdiction" in Article 1 and it even goes so far as to render those words superfluous and devoid of any purpose. Had the drafters of the Convention wished to ensure jurisdiction as extensive as that advocated by the applicants, they could have adopted a text the same as or similar to the contemporaneous Articles 1 of the four Geneva Conventions of 1949.

Furthermore, the applicants' notion of jurisdiction equates the determination of whether an individual falls within the jurisdiction of a Contracting State with the question of whether that person can be considered to be a victim of a violation of rights guaranteed by the Convention. These are separate and distinct admissibility conditions, each of which has to be satisfied in the afore-mentioned order, before an individual can invoke the Convention provisions against a Contracting State.

76. Secondly, the applicants' alternative suggestion is that the limited scope of the airspace control only circumscribed the scope of the respondent States' positive obligation to protect the applicants and did not exclude it. The Court finds this to be essentially the same argument as their principal proposition and rejects it for the same reasons.

...

79. Fifthly and more generally, the applicants maintain that any failure to accept that they fell within the jurisdiction of the respondent States would defeat the *ordre public* mission of the Convention and leave a regrettable vacuum in the Convention system of human rights' protection.

80. The Court's obligation, in this respect, is to have regard to the special character of the Convention as a constitutional instrument of *European* public order for the protection of individual human beings and its role, as set out in Article 19 of the Convention, is to ensure the observance of *the engagements undertaken* by the Contracting Parties. It is therefore difficult to contend that a failure to accept the extra-territorial jurisdiction of the respondent States would fall foul of the Convention's *ordre public* objective, which itself underlines the essentially regional vocation of the Convention system, or of Article 19 of the Convention which does not shed any particular light on the territorial ambit of that system.

It is true that, in its above-cited *Cyprus v. Turkey* judgment (at § 78), the Court was conscious of the need to avoid "a regrettable vacuum in the system of human-rights protection" in northern Cyprus. However, and as noted by the Governments, that comment related to an entirely different situation to the present: the inhabitants of northern Cyprus would have found themselves excluded from the benefits of the Convention safeguards and system which they had previously enjoyed, by Turkey's "effective control" of the territory and by the accompanying inability of the Cypriot Government, as a Contracting State, to fulfil the obligations it had undertaken under the Convention.

In short, the Convention is a multi-lateral treaty operating, subject to Article 56 of the Convention, in an essentially regional context and notably in the legal space (*espace juridique*) of the Contracting States. The FRY clearly does not fall within this legal space. The Convention was not designed to be applied throughout the world, even in respect of the conduct of Contracting States. Accordingly, the desirability of avoiding a gap or vacuum in human rights' protection has so far been relied on by the Court in favour of establishing jurisdiction only when the territory in question was one that, but for the specific circumstances, would normally be covered by the Convention.

...

4. The Court's conclusion

82. The Court is not therefore persuaded that there was any jurisdictional link between the persons who were victims of the act complained of and the respondent States. Accordingly, it is not satisfied that the applicants

and their deceased relatives were capable of coming within the jurisdiction of the respondent States on account of the extra-territorial act in question.

...

ISSA AND OTHERS V. TURKEY
EUROPEAN COURT OF HUMAN RIGHTS, CHAMBER JUDGMENT, APPLICATION NO. 31821/96 (16 NOVEMBER 2004)

[The case was brought by six Iraqi nationals, who were shepherds and complained of the alleged unlawful arrest, detention, ill-treatment, and subsequent killing of their relatives in the course of a military operation conducted by the Turkish army in northern Iraq in April 1995. The Turkish Government responded that while a military operation had taken place in this region at the relevant time, its forces had not been within ten kilometres of the area where the alleged violations occurred.]

II. Whether the applicants' relatives came within the jurisdiction of Turkey

...

B. The Court's assessment

...

68. ... [T]he concept of "jurisdiction" within the meaning of Article 1 of the Convention is not necessarily restricted to the national territory of the High Contracting Parties. In exceptional circumstances the acts of Contracting States performed outside their territory or which produce effects there ("extra-territorial act") may amount to exercise by them of their jurisdiction within the meaning of Article 1 of the Convention.

69. According to the relevant principles of international law, a State's responsibility may be engaged where, as a consequence of military action — whether lawful or unlawful — that State in practice exercises effective control of an area situated outside its national territory. The obligation to secure, in such an area, the rights and freedoms set out in the Convention derives from the fact of such control, whether it be exercised directly, through its armed forces, or through a subordinate local administration.

70. It is not necessary to determine whether a Contracting Party actually exercises detailed control over the policies and actions of the authorities in the area situated outside its national territory, since even overall control of the area may engage the responsibility of the Contracting Party concerned.

71. Moreover, a State may also be held accountable for violation of the Convention rights and freedoms of persons who are in the territory of another State but who are found to be under the former State's authority and control through its agents operating — whether lawfully or unlawfully — in the latter State ... . Accountability in such situations stems from the fact that Article 1 of the Convention cannot be interpreted so as to allow a State party to perpetrate violations of the Convention on the territory of another State, which it could not perpetrate on its own territory.

2. Application of the above principles

72. In the light of the above principles the Court must ascertain whether the applicants' relatives were under the authority and/or effective control, and therefore within the jurisdiction, of the respondent State as a result of the latter's extraterritorial acts.

73. In this connection, the Court notes that it is undisputed between the parties that the Turkish armed forces carried out military operations in [the relevant area at the time]... .

74. The Court does not exclude the possibility that, as a consequence of this military action, the respondent State could be considered to have exercised, temporarily, effective overall control of a particular portion of the territory of northern Iraq. Accordingly, if there is a sufficient factual basis for holding that, at the relevant time, the victims were within that specific area, it would follow logically that they were within the jurisdiction of

Turkey (and not that of Iraq, which is not a Contracting State and clearly does not fall within the legal space (*espace juridique*) of the Contracting States).

75. However, notwithstanding the large number of troops involved in the aforementioned military operations, it does not appear that Turkey exercised effective overall control of the entire area of northern Iraq... .

76. The essential question to be examined in the instant case is whether at the relevant time Turkish troops conducted operations in the area where the killings took place. The fate of the applicants' complaints in respect of the killing of their relatives depends on the prior establishment of that premise. The Government have vigorously denied that their troops were active in or around Azadi village in the Spna area. The reasonableness of that assertion must be tested in the light of the documentary and other evidence which the parties have submitted to the Court, having regard to the standard of proof which it habitually employs when ascertaining whether there is a basis in fact for an allegation of unlawful killing, namely proof "beyond reasonable doubt", it being understood that such proof may follow from the coexistence of sufficiently strong, clear and concordant inferences or of similar unrebutted presumptions of fact.

...

81. On the basis of all the material in its possession, the Court considers that it has not been established to the required standard of proof that the Turkish armed forces conducted operations in the area in question, and, more precisely, in the hills above the village of Azadi where, according to the applicants' statements, the victims were at that time.

3. The Court's conclusion

82. In the light of the above, the Court is not satisfied that the applicants' relatives were within the "jurisdiction" of the respondent State for the purposes of Article 1 of the Convention... .

AL-SKEINI AND OTHERS V. UNITED KINGDOM
EUROPEAN COURT OF HUMAN RIGHTS, GRAND CHAMBER, APPLICATION NO. 55721/07 (7 JULY 2011)

[Following the invasion of Iraq in March 2003 by the United States, the United Kingdom, and other coalition members, the United States and the United Kingdom, became occupying powers in May 2003. The United Kingdom was put in charge of the South East, including the province of Al-Basrah, with responsibility for maintaining security and supporting the civil administration. This case was brought by the relatives of six persons killed during that period. Three of the victims were shot dead by British soldiers; one was fatally wounded in an exchange of fire between a British patrol and unknown gunmen; one was beaten by British soldiers and forced into a river, where he drowned; and one, Baha Mousa, died of asphyxiation at a British military base, with 93 separate bodily injuries. The two principal issues before the Court were (1) whether it had jurisdiction over events in Iraq, as a non-party to the Convention and (2) whether the UK Government had fulfilled its Article 2 obligation to carry out an effective investigation into the killings. In relation to the latter, it held that there had been a violation, although it tailored the test to the circumstances ('the authorities must take the reasonable steps available to them'). The following excerpt concerns only the jurisdiction issue.

In the United Kingdom, the then House of Lords[444] held that the death of Baha Mousa was within the UK's jurisdiction by analogizing a prison 'with the extra-territorial exception made for embassies'. In relation to the other five victims, killed by UK soldiers on patrol, the House of Lords followed *Banković* in concluding that they were not within the UK's jurisdiction.]

...

1. Jurisdiction

...

(b) The Court's assessment

(i) General principles relevant to jurisdiction under Article 1 of the Convention

---

[444] [2007] UKHL 26.

...

(a) The territorial principle

...

132. To date, the Court in its case-law has recognised a number of exceptional circumstances capable of giving rise to the exercise of jurisdiction by a Contracting State outside its own territorial boundaries. [E]ach case ... must be determined with reference to the particular facts.

(β) State agent authority and control

133. The Court has recognised in its case-law that, as an exception to the principle of territoriality, a Contracting State's jurisdiction under Article 1 may extend to acts of its authorities which produce effects outside its own territory ... .

134. First, it is clear that the acts of diplomatic and consular agents, who are present on foreign territory in accordance with provisions of international law, may amount to an exercise of jurisdiction when these agents exert authority and control over others.

135. Secondly, the Court has recognised the exercise of extra-territorial jurisdiction by a Contracting State when, through the consent, invitation or acquiescence of the Government of that territory, it exercises all or some of the public powers normally to be exercised by that Government... .

136. In addition, the Court's case-law demonstrates that, in certain circumstances, the use of force by a State's agents operating outside its territory may bring the individual thereby brought under the control of the State's authorities into the State's Article 1 jurisdiction. This principle has been applied where an individual is taken into the custody of State agents abroad. For example, in *Öcalan v. Turkey* [GC], no. 46221/99, § 91, ECHR 2005-IV, the Court held that "directly after being handed over to the Turkish officials by the Kenyan officials, the applicant was effectively under Turkish authority and therefore within the 'jurisdiction' of that State for the purposes of Article 1 of the Convention, even though in this instance Turkey exercised its authority outside its territory". In *Issa and Others v. Turkey*, the Court indicated that, had it been established that Turkish soldiers had taken the applicants' relatives into custody in Northern Iraq, taken them to a nearby cave and executed them, the deceased would have been within Turkish jurisdiction by virtue of the soldiers' authority and control over them. In *Al-Saadoon and Mufdhi v. the United Kingdom* (dec.), no. 61498/08, §§ 86–89, 30 June 2009, the Court held that two Iraqi nationals detained in British-controlled military prisons in Iraq fell within the jurisdiction of the United Kingdom, since the United Kingdom exercised total and exclusive control over the prisons and the individuals detained in them. Finally, in *Medvedyev and Others v. France* [GC], no. 3394/03, §67, ECHR 2010-... , the Court held that the applicants were within French jurisdiction by virtue of the exercise by French agents of full and exclusive control over a ship and its crew from the time of its interception in international waters. The Court does not consider that jurisdiction in the above cases arose solely from the control exercised by the Contracting State over the buildings, aircraft or ship in which the individuals were held. What is decisive in such cases is the exercise of physical power and control over the person in question.

137. It is clear that, whenever the State through its agents exercises control and authority over an individual, and thus jurisdiction, the State is under an obligation under Article 1 to secure to that individual the rights and freedoms under Section 1 of the Convention that are relevant to the situation of that individual. In this sense, therefore, the Convention rights can be "divided and tailored".

(γ) Effective control over an area

138. Another exception to the principle that jurisdiction under Article 1 is limited to a State's own territory occurs when, as a consequence of lawful or unlawful military action, a Contracting State exercises effective control of an area outside that national territory. The obligation to secure, in such an area, the rights and freedoms set out in the Convention, derives from the fact of such control, whether it be exercised directly, through the Contracting State's own armed forces, or through a subordinate local administration. Where the fact of such domination over the territory is established, it is not necessary to determine whether the Contracting State exercises detailed control over the policies and actions of the subordinate local administration. The fact

that the local administration survives as a result of the Contracting State's military and other support entails that State's responsibility for its policies and actions. The controlling State has the responsibility under Article 1 to secure, within the area under its control, the entire range of substantive rights set out in the Convention and those additional Protocols which it has ratified. It will be liable for any violations of those rights.

139. It is a question of fact whether a Contracting State exercises effective control over an area outside its own territory. In determining whether effective control exists, the Court will primarily have reference to the strength of the State's military presence in the area. Other indicators may also be relevant, such as the extent to which its military, economic and political support for the local subordinate administration provides it with influence and control over the region.

...

(δ) The Convention legal space ("espace juridique")

141. The Convention … does not … purport to be a means of requiring the Contracting States to impose Convention standards on other States.

142. The Court has emphasised that, where the territory of one Convention State is occupied by the armed forces of another, the occupying State should in principle be held accountable under the Convention for breaches of human rights within the occupied territory, because to hold otherwise would be to deprive the population of that territory of the rights and freedoms hitherto enjoyed and would result in a "vacuum" of protection within the "Convention legal space". However, the importance of establishing the occupying State's jurisdiction in such cases does not imply, *a contrario*, that jurisdiction under Article 1 of the Convention can never exist outside the territory covered by the Council of Europe Member States. The Court has not in its case-law applied any such restriction.

...

(iii) Conclusion as regards jurisdiction

149. [F]ollowing the removal from power of the Ba'ath regime and until the accession of the Interim Government, the United Kingdom (together with the United States) assumed in Iraq the exercise of some of the public powers normally to be exercised by a sovereign government. In particular, the United Kingdom assumed authority and responsibility for the maintenance of security in South East Iraq. In these exceptional circumstances, the Court considers that the United Kingdom, through its soldiers engaged in security operations in Basrah during the period in question, exercised authority and control over individuals killed in the course of such security operations, so as to establish a jurisdictional link between the deceased and the United Kingdom for the purposes of Article 1 of the Convention.

...

CONCURRING OPINION OF JUDGE BONELLO

...

5. Up until now, the Court has, in matters concerning the extra-territorial jurisdiction of Contracting Parties, spawned a number of "leading" judgments based on a need-to-decide basis, patchwork case-law at best. Inevitably, the doctrines established seem to go too far to some, and not far enough to others. As the Court has, in these cases, always tailored its tenets to sets of specific facts, it is hardly surprising that those tenets then seem to limp when applied to sets of different facts... .

...

7. … [T]he judicial decision-making process in Strasbourg has, so far, squandered more energy in attempting to reconcile the barely reconcilable than in trying to erect intellectual constructs of more universal application. A considerable number of different approaches to extra-territorial jurisdiction have so far been experimented with by the Court on a case-by-case basis, some not completely exempt from internal contradiction.

...

16. In my view, the one honest test, in *all* circumstances (including extra-territoriality), is the following: did it depend on the agents of the State whether the alleged violation would be committed or would not be committed? Was it within the power of the State to punish the perpetrators and to compensate the victims? If the answer is yes, self-evidently the facts fall squarely within the jurisdiction of the State. All the rest seems to me clumsy, self-serving alibi hunting, unworthy of any State that has grandiosely undertaken to secure the "universal" observance of human rights whenever and wherever it is within its power to secure them, and, may I add, of courts whose only *raison d'etre* should be to ensure that those obligations are not avoided or evaded.

The Court has, in the present judgment, thankfully placed a sanitary cordon between itself and some of these approaches.

...

* * *

A related issue, addressed by the Court in a judgment issued on the same day as *Al-Skeini*, is whether actions taken by national forces in furtherance of a binding UN Security Council resolution could be evaluated for compliance with the ECHR. In *Al-Jedda v. United Kingdom* (App. No. 27021/08, judgment of 7 July 2011) the Court unanimously rejected the government's claim that the internment action impugned in the application was attributable to the UN and not to the United Kingdom.

> The Court ... noted that, at the time of the invasion in March 2003, there was no UN Security Council (UNSC) resolution providing for the allocation of roles in Iraq if the existing regime was displaced. In May 2003 the US and the UK, having displaced the previous regime, assumed control over the provision of security in Iraq; the UN was allocated a role in providing humanitarian relief, supporting the reconstruction of Iraq and helping in the formation of an Iraqi interim government, but had no role as regards security. The Court did not consider that subsequent UNSC Resolutions altered that position. As the UNSC had neither effective control nor ultimate authority and control over the acts and omissions of troops within the Multi-National Force, Mr Al-Jedda's internment was not attributable to the UN. It took place within a detention facility in Basrah City, controlled exclusively by British forces. He was therefore within the authority and control of the UK throughout ... .[445]

GEORGIA V. RUSSIA (II)
EUROPEAN COURT OF HUMAN RIGHTS, GRAND CHAMBER, APPLICATION NO. 38263/08 (21 JANUARY 2021)

[In August 2008, following a period of tension, provocation and incidents between Georgia and Russia, Russia invaded and occupied the disputed territories of Abkhazia and South Ossetia. During the active phase of the conflict, Russian troops also invaded areas of undisputed Georgian territory (the 'buffer zone'). Georgia alleged that acts committed by Russian armed forces in the course of the invasion violated several articles of the Convention and Protocols. The Court examined the case in terms of two separate time periods: (i) the active phase of hostilities during the five-day war after the intervention by the Russian armed forces (from 8 to 12 August 2008); and (ii) the occupation phase after the cessation of hostilities (ceasefire agreement of 12 August 2008). The key issue concerned the jurisdiction of the Court.]

IV. ACTIVE PHASE OF HOSTILITIES DURING THE FIVE DAY WAR (FROM 8 TO 12 AUGUST 2008)

105. The applicant Government submitted that the military operations (bombing, shelling, artillery fire) by the Russian armed forces and/or South Ossetian forces during the conflict had breached Article 2 of the Convention.

A. Jurisdiction

...

3. The Court's assessment

(a) General principles ...

113. The present case marks the first time since the decision in *Banković and Others* ... that the Court has been required to examine the question of jurisdiction in relation to military operations (armed attacks, bombing, shelling) in the context of an international armed conflict, the existence of which is not disputed by the parties.

---

[445] ECtHR, Factsheet on Extra-territorial Jurisdiction of ECHR States (December 2011). 4.

114. However, the Court's case-law on the concept of extraterritorial jurisdiction has evolved since that decision, in that the Court has indicated, inter alia, that the rights under the Convention could be "divided and tailored" and has introduced a nuance into the concept of the Contracting States' "legal space" ... . In addition, it has established a number of criteria for the exercise of extraterritorial jurisdiction by a State, which must remain exceptional ... .

115. The two main criteria established by the Court in this regard are that of "effective control" by the State over an area (spatial concept of jurisdiction) and that of "State agent authority and control" over individuals (personal concept of jurisdiction) ... .

...

(b) Application of the above principles to the facts of the case

125. In the present case the Court is required to examine whether the conditions applied by the Court in its case-law to determine the exercise of extraterritorial jurisdiction by a State may be regarded as fulfilled in respect of military operations carried out during an international armed conflict.

126. In ... the event of military operations – including, for example, armed attacks, bombing or shelling – carried out during an international armed conflict, one cannot generally speak of "effective control" over an area. ...

...

130. In most of the cases that it has examined since its decision in *Banković and Others*, the Court has found that the decisive factor in establishing "State agent authority and control" over individuals outside the State's borders was the exercise of physical power and control over the persons in question ... .

131. Admittedly, in other cases concerning fire aimed by the armed forces/police of the States concerned, the Court has applied the concept of "State agent authority and control" over individuals to scenarios going beyond physical power and control exercised in the context of arrest or detention ... .

132. However, those cases concerned isolated and specific acts involving an element of proximity.

133. By contrast, the active phase of hostilities which the Court is required to examine in the present case in the context of an international armed conflict is very different, as it concerns bombing and artillery shelling by Russian armed forces seeking to put the Georgian army hors de combat and to establish control over areas forming part of Georgia.

134. [The Court quotes in detail from para. 75 of *Banković and Others*].

...

136. The Court sees no reason to decide otherwise in the present case. The obligation which Article 1 imposes on the Contracting States to secure to everyone within their jurisdiction the rights and freedoms guaranteed by the Convention is, as indicated above, closely linked to the notion of "control", whether it be "State agent authority and control" over individuals or "effective control" by a State over a territory.

137. In this connection, the Court attaches decisive weight to the fact that the very reality of armed confrontation and fighting between enemy military forces seeking to establish control over an area in a context of chaos not only means that there is no "effective control" over an area as indicated above (see paragraph 126), but also excludes any form of "State agent authority and control" over individuals.

138. The Court therefore considers that the conditions it has applied in its case-law to determine whether there was an exercise of extraterritorial jurisdiction by a State have not been met in respect of the military operations that it is required to examine in the instant case during the active phase of hostilities in the context of an international armed conflict.

...

140. That said, the Court is sensitive to the fact that such an interpretation of the notion of "jurisdiction" in Article 1 of the Convention may seem unsatisfactory to the alleged victims of acts and omissions by a

respondent State during the active phase of hostilities in the context of an international armed conflict outside its territory but in the territory of another Contracting State, as well as to the State in whose territory the active hostilities take place.

141. However, having regard in particular to the large number of alleged victims and contested incidents, the magnitude of the evidence produced, the difficulty in establishing the relevant circumstances and the fact that such situations are predominantly regulated by legal norms other than those of the Convention (specifically, international humanitarian law or the law of armed conflict), the Court considers that it is not in a position to develop its case-law beyond the understanding of the notion of "jurisdiction" as established to date.

142. If, as in the present case, the Court is to be entrusted with the task of assessing acts of war and active hostilities in the context of an international armed conflict outside the territory of a respondent State, it must be for the Contracting Parties to provide the necessary legal basis for such a task.

143. The Court reiterates in this connection that this does not mean that States can act outside any legal framework; as indicated above, they are obliged to comply with the very detailed rules of international humanitarian law in such a context.

144. Having regard to all those factors, the Court concludes that the events which occurred during the active phase of the hostilities (8-12 August 2008) did not fall within the jurisdiction of the Russian Federation for the purposes of Article 1 of the Convention. Accordingly, this part of the application must be declared inadmissible, in accordance with Article 35 §§ 3 (a) and 4 of the Convention.

[The Court did, however, find that Russia exercised effective control over South Ossetia, Abkhazia and the buffer zone during its occupation of these areas from 12 August to 10 October 2008, and that events in those areas were therefore within its jurisdiction. After examining considerable evidence regarding the actions of Russian troops in this period, the Court found that Russia had committed violations of the Convention and Protocols in respect of the systematic killing of civilians and torching and looting of houses after the cessation of hostilities; arbitrary detention of Georgian civilians; ill-treatment and torture of prisoners of war; refusal to allow Georgians displaced by the invasion to return; and failure to investigate or provide remedies in respect of these violations.]

JOINT PARTLY DISSENTING OPINION OF JUDGES YUDKIVSKA, WOJTYCZEK AND CHANTURIA

…

II. The question of jurisdiction during armed conflicts

6. … It is obvious that combat is a different army mission from rescue operations or policing. Yet there can be no doubt that the use of the army to combat insurgents in a civil war is a form of exercise of public power and therefore of exercise of jurisdiction (*ultima ratio regum*). From the perspective of State power, the use of the army for fighting against the troops of another State is exactly the same in nature as the use of troops for fighting against insurgents in a civil war. Both situations are forms of exercise of State sovereignty and at the same time of exercise of public power over the persons affected. An order to bomb specific targets in a city is an act of public power, not only in respect of the troops which will execute it but also over the persons who are in the city in question and who will suffer.

…

8. To sum up this part of our opinion: the victims of the alleged human rights violations in the instant case committed during the active phase of the hostilities (8 to 12 August 2008) fell within the jurisdiction of the Russian Federation for the purposes of Article 1 of the Convention.

III. The reasoning adopted by the majority

9. The instant judgment is based upon a series of assumptions and arguments with which we disagree.

…

We disagree with [the statement in para. 125]. In the present case the Court was required to establish whether there was a jurisdictional link between the persons affected by the actions of the respondent State, identified in the application submitted by Georgia, and the respondent State. As rightly stated in paragraph 115 of the judgment, "[t]he two main criteria established by the Court in this regard are that of 'effective control' by the State over an area (spatial concept of jurisdiction) and that of 'State agent authority and control' over individuals (personal concept of jurisdiction) ... . "State agent authority and control" over individuals and "effective control" over an area are the main types of jurisdictional link, yet they are not the only ones.

Secondly, ... [w]e do not see why proximity [para. 132] should be relevant. In any event, we note that the criterion of proximity is fulfilled in the instant case, the military operations having been carried out close to an area under the effective control of the respondent State. More importantly, if jurisdiction has been established in respect of "isolated and specific acts", it is obvious that the respondent State exercises jurisdiction within the meaning of Article 1 when it undertakes a large-scale operation involving innumerable acts with far reaching consequences (*argumentum a fortiori*).

Thirdly, ... [w]e disagree with [the position stated in para. 137]. As shown above, the very conduct of modern military operations presupposes certain forms of "State agent authority and control" over individuals. If the very reality of armed confrontation and fighting between enemy military forces seeking to establish control over an area in a context of chaos makes it necessary to exclude any form of "State agent authority and control" over individuals, then it is not possible to apply international humanitarian law.

Fourthly, ... [w]e are simply astonished by [the arguments in para. 141]. In our view, the role of this Court consists precisely in dealing in priority with difficult cases characterised by "the large number of alleged victims and contested incidents, the magnitude of the evidence produced, the difficulty in establishing the relevant circumstances". Moreover, "the fact that such situations are predominantly regulated by legal norms other than those of the Convention" should not be an obstacle for the application of the Convention. Furthermore, we are not proposing that the Court should "develop its case-law beyond the understanding of the notion of 'jurisdiction' as established to date" but rather that it should confer more consistency on the general principles established in the case-law and apply those principles in a more coherent way.

...

VI. Conclusion

15. ... It is true that the scope of a State's jurisdiction in armed conflict is limited but its legal existence cannot be denied. ...

... [T]o deny the jurisdiction of belligerent States over civilian populations in an area of military combat in an international conflict undermines the very logic of international humanitarian law, which, precisely, shifts civilians to the core of the military decision-making process and places them in complex legal relationships with the belligerent States, even before the first bullets are fired.

...

Partly Dissenting Opinion of Judge Pinto De Albuquerque
...
27. In my view, large-scale military operations outside national territory are no less the expression of State power than targeted policing operations within the State's borders, and the conduct of hostilities abroad is no less a State prerogative than any law-enforcement activity on national territory. In principled terms, engaging in an armed conflict is no less a State function than controlling borders. Hence the Court cannot evade this principle with the argument that "the very reality of armed confrontation and fighting between enemy military forces seeking to establish control over an area in a context of chaos" excludes jurisdiction. If detaining, injuring or killing a person abroad triggers jurisdiction, [as the Court accepted in other cases]... killing many more people cannot exclude jurisdiction, at least personal jurisdiction, regardless of any element of proximity between the State agents and the targeted population. It is not because the State acts far away from its borders that it can do abroad what it cannot do at home. ...

28. The absence of an Article 15 derogation has obviously nothing to do with jurisdiction, as the Court itself has previously admitted. The Court cannot give away its own *Kompetenz-Kompetenz* under Article 1 of the Convention just because the Contracting Parties have simply ignored Article 15. [For relevant state practice

under Article 15, See Banković, para. 62, above.] Confusing the jurisdictional issue and the issue of the law applicable to the facts, as the majority do in the present judgment, only diverts from the fundamental question of the irrationality of the majority's position that the graver the State military conduct, the less intensive the Strasbourg oversight. Nor does it help to argue that the Court's jurisdiction should be determined by the practical difficulties it may face when dealing with a "large number of alleged victims and contested incidents", or with "the magnitude of the evidence produced", in sum, with "the difficulty in establishing the relevant circumstances". It is inconceivable that the Court should delimit its jurisdiction not in accordance with the legal criteria set out in the Convention, but in view of possible future procedural and technical complications in gathering and evaluating evidence. Moreover, the Court itself has long since adopted rather successful techniques of evidence-gathering and evaluation in complicated military situations ... .

29. Equally unconvincing is the argument that the Court should not delve into "such situations [that] are predominantly regulated by legal norms other than those of the Convention" , since it is oblivious to the patent fact that the majority themselves compare and contrast Convention-based substantive obligations and obligations derived from international humanitarian law . ...

...

30. In sum, the Court will face a gargantuan task to restore the damage to its credibility caused by this judgment. The revival of *Banković and Others* ... is indeed deeply regrettable in the eyes of the victims ... .

Partly Dissenting Opinion of Judge Chanturia

A. A closer look at the majority's arguments
...
14. What the majority have done was not merely resuscitate the otherwise lifeless *Banković* precedent (for which the Court was heavily criticised, and probably rightly so, in the past); they took a step backwards by deviating from the spatial concept of extraterritorial jurisdiction introduced by the very same *Banković* case on which the majority themselves relied. In *Banković and Others* the Court at least attempted to justify its position by coming up with the "legal space" argument. By contrast, in the present case the majority failed to give due consideration to the fact that the applicant and respondent States were both High Contracting Parties to the Convention at the material time of the events, and that the shelling and bombing during the active phase of the hostilities had clearly occurred within the legal space (*espace juridique*) of the Convention ... .

B. An issue with the approach to extraterritorial jurisdiction during an international armed conflict

1. Methodology
...
33. In my opinion, the fallacy of the methodology applied by the majority started with the separation of the active phase of the military conflict between Georgia and Russia from the subsequent period of occupation ...
.

34. It would have been more logical and compatible with the scope of the application as lodged by the applicant State to examine, for the purposes of determining the issues of jurisdiction, attributability and imputability, the active phase of the conflict not as a distinct, instantaneous event detached from the historical background but rather as a part of a continuing situation which included both the events that had occurred prior to the outbreak of the military conflict and those which happened afterwards. ...

5. The European Court in Action: Some Illustrative Cases

The role of the European Court is of particular importance for several reasons. First, in quantitative terms, is the fact that it now has the final say in relation to the interpretation of the human rights standards applicable in relation to 46 different nations and covering some 675 million people. Second, its caseload has expanded exponentially over the past two decades and this has important consequences in terms of the quantity and range of case law or jurisprudence being generated. This, in turn, is inevitably an important reference point, acknowledged or not, for the work of the other leading human rights adjudicatory organs such as the African and Inter-American Courts and the ICCPR Committee.

Third, in qualitative terms, the jurisdiction of the Court now spans a diverse array of cultural contexts, political systems, social perspectives, and levels of economic development. As a result, where once it might have been portrayed as a Court whose docket covered only a rather limited range of issues, and often not necessarily those which were seen to be the most pressing, today it is confronted on a daily basis with virtually the full range of human rights challenges of the utmost importance within the societies concerned. A fourth reason for its importance is the crucial role it now plays both as a constitutional court in its own right, and in relation to national constitutional courts, across the whole of Europe. This role has been further enhanced by its capacity to provide Advisory Opinions, when requested, and by the increased emphasis it now places on active engagement with national constitutional courts. While it does not enjoy formal hierarchical superiority vis-à-vis the highest court in the EU, the Court of Justice of the European Union, the latter now gives careful attention to the normative pronouncements of the ECtHR, even though the EU's proposed accession to the Convention has so far failed to eventuate.

The decisions below explore some of the characteristic problems that arise when international tribunals decide human rights issues that may deeply affect the internal order of states. The cases excerpted are, however, limited in scope. They deal with the right to life, democracy, and the independence of the judiciary. The focus here is narrow because there are many ECtHR cases scattered elsewhere throughout this coursebook.

The differences between the handling of complaints within the UN system by a body such as the ICCPR Human Rights Committee and the European Court are striking. Of course, deep and often disputed moral and political premises inform the work of both types of body and sometimes enter into explicit debate. But the Court's opinions take the traditional forms of the law — the facts of the dispute, argument about the interpretation of the text and related argument about the policies or principles involved, reflection on the institutional role of the Court in relation to national political orders, the ultimate decision applying the Convention in a decision binding the states parties, and possible recourse to a political body if a state does not comply with the Court's decision. From this point of view, a study of the European Court's decisions best illustrates the promise of an international (regional) *legal* order brought to bear on national human rights issues.

a. The Right to Life

Article 2 of the Convention states:

> 1. Everyone's right to life shall be protected by law. No one shall be deprived of his life intentionally save in the execution of a sentence of a court following his conviction of a crime for which this penalty is provided by law.

> 2. Deprivation of life shall not be regarded as inflicted in contravention of this Article when it results from the use of force which is no more than absolutely necessary:

> (a) in defence of any person from unlawful violence;

> (b) in order to effect a lawful arrest or to prevent the escape of a person lawfully detained;

> (c) in action lawfully taken for the purpose of quelling a riot or insurrection.

The cases that follow serve to highlight just a few of the very complex issues that have arisen in relation to the right to life. Recall that in Chapter 4 we saw the Indian Supreme Court relying heavily on this right in order to render a range of economic and social rights justiciable, and in Chapter 9 we saw the ICCPR Committee proposing an expansive approach to the right to life in a couple of its General Comments. Although the ECHR recognizes no social rights (other than the right to education in Protocol No. 1), and the ECtHR has been rather conservative in relation to such matters, it has also developed jurisprudence under Article 2 that would support a much more robust notion of positive obligations in certain areas, such as in relation to the environment and climate change. Compare the ways in which it has approached the right to life in four representative cases.

MCCANN AND OTHERS V. UNITED KINGDOM
EUROPEAN COURT OF HUMAN RIGHTS, GRAND CHAMBER, APPLICATION NO. 18984/91 (27 SEPTEMBER 1995)

[Three members of the Provisional IRA [Irish Republican Army] were shot dead on 6 March 1988 in Gibraltar by the British Army's 'special forces', the Special Air Service (SAS). The UK, Spanish, and Gibraltar authorities had been alerted to a planned terrorist attack, and were tracking the members of the group with a view to arresting them at the appropriate time. One of the group was seen parking a car and then joined the other two. It was decided to arrest them and the SAS soldiers on the scene were alerted. Fearing that they would be armed and were trying to detonate remote control devices, the soldiers shot them at close range. No weapons or detonator devices were found on the bodies of the suspects; nor did the car that had been observed contain any explosive device, although another car did. A Gibraltar jury returned verdicts of lawful killing, and judicial review was refused. The applicants claimed a violation of ECHR Article 2. The Court rejected as unsubstantiated the contention that the killings had been premeditated either by the soldiers or their superior officers.]

...

200. The Court accepts that the soldiers honestly believed, in the light of the information that they had been given, ... that it was necessary to shoot the suspects in order to prevent them from detonating a bomb and causing serious loss of life. The actions which they took, in obedience to superior orders, were thus perceived by them as absolutely necessary in order to safeguard innocent lives.

It considers that the use of force by agents of the State in pursuit of one of the aims delineated in [Article 2(2)] of the Convention may be justified under this provision where it is based on an honest belief which is perceived, for good reasons, to be valid at the time but which subsequently turns out to be mistaken. To hold otherwise would be to impose an unrealistic burden on the State and its law-enforcement personnel in the execution of their duty, perhaps to the detriment of their lives and those of others.

It follows that, having regard to the dilemma confronting the authorities in the circumstances of the case, the actions of the soldiers do not, in themselves, give rise to a violation of this provision.

201. The question arises, however, whether the anti-terrorist operation as a whole was controlled and organised in a manner which respected the requirements of Article 2 and whether the information and instructions given to the soldiers which, in effect, rendered inevitable the use of lethal force, took adequately into consideration the right to life of the three suspects.

(3) Control and organisation of the operation

202. ... [I]t had been the intention of the authorities to arrest the suspects at an appropriate stage ... .

203. It may be questioned why the three suspects were not arrested at the border immediately on their arrival in Gibraltar ... if they were believed to be on a bombing mission. Having had advance warning of the terrorists' intentions it would certainly have been possible for the authorities to have mounted an arrest operation ... .

204. [T]he Government submitted that at that moment there might not have been sufficient evidence to warrant the detention and trial of the suspects. Moreover, to release them, having alerted them to the authorities' state of awareness but leaving them or others free to try again, would obviously increase the risks. Nor could the authorities be sure that those three were the only terrorists they had to deal with or of the manner in which it was proposed to carry out the bombing.

205. The Court [observes] that the danger to the population of Gibraltar — which is at the heart of the Government's submissions in this case — in not preventing their entry must be considered to outweigh the possible consequences of having insufficient evidence to warrant their detention and trial. In its view, either the authorities knew that there was no bomb in the car — which the Court has already discounted — or there was a serious miscalculation by those responsible for controlling the operation. As a result, the scene was set in

which the fatal shooting, given the intelligence assessments which had been made, was a foreseeable possibility if not a likelihood ... .

206. The Court notes that at the briefing on 5 March attended by Soldiers A, B, C, and D it was considered likely that the attack would be by way of a large car bomb. A number of key assessments were made. In particular, it was thought that the terrorists would not use a blocking car; that the bomb would be detonated by a radio-control device; that the detonation could be effected by the pressing of a button; that it was likely that the suspects would detonate the bomb if challenged; that they would be armed and would be likely to use their arms if confronted.

207. In the event, all of these crucial assumptions, apart from the terrorists' intentions to carry out an attack, turned out to be erroneous [although] they were all possible hypotheses in a situation where the true facts were unknown and where the authorities operated on the basis of limited intelligence information.

208. In fact, insufficient allowances appear to have been made for other assumptions. For example, since the bombing was not expected until 8 March when the changing of the guard ceremony was to take place, there was equally the possibility that the three terrorists were on a reconnaissance mission. While this was a factor which was briefly considered, it does not appear to have been regarded as a serious possibility.

In addition, at the briefings or after the suspects had been spotted, it might have been thought unlikely that they would have been prepared to explode the bomb, thereby killing many civilians, as Mr McCann and Ms Farrell strolled towards the border area since this would have increased the risk of detection and capture. It might also have been thought improbable that at that point they would have set up the transmitter in anticipation to enable them to detonate the supposed bomb immediately if confronted.

Moreover, even if allowances are made for the technological skills of the IRA, the description of the detonation device as a "button job" without the qualifications subsequently described by the experts at the inquest, of which the competent authorities must have been aware, over-simplifies the true nature of these devices.

209. It is further disquieting in this context that the assessment made by Soldier G, after a cursory external examination of the car, that there was a "suspect car bomb" was conveyed to the soldiers, according to their own testimony, as a definite identification that there was such a bomb. It is recalled that while Soldier G had experience in car bombs, it transpired that he was not an expert in radio communications or explosives ... .

210. In the absence of sufficient allowances being made for alternative possibilities, and the definite reporting of the existence of a car bomb which, according to the assessments that had been made, could be detonated at the press of a button, a series of working hypotheses were conveyed to Soldiers A, B, C and D as certainties, thereby making the use of lethal force almost unavoidable.

211. However, the failure to make provision for a margin of error must also be considered in combination with the training of the soldiers to continue shooting once they opened fire until the suspect was dead. [A]ll four soldiers shot to kill the suspects ... . Against this background, the authorities were bound by their obligation to respect the right to life of the suspects to exercise the greatest of care in evaluating the information at their disposal before transmitting it to soldiers whose use of firearms automatically involved shooting to kill.

212. ... [I]t is not clear whether [the soldiers] had been trained or instructed to assess whether the use of firearms to wound their targets may have been warranted by the specific circumstances that confronted them at the moment of arrest.

Their reflex action in this vital respect lacks the degree of caution in the use of firearms to be expected from law enforcement personnel in a democratic society, even when dealing with dangerous terrorist suspects, and stands in marked contrast to the standard of care reflected in the instructions in the use of firearms by the police which had been drawn to their attention and which emphasised the legal responsibilities of the individual officer in the light of conditions prevailing at the moment of engagement.

This failure by the authorities also suggests a lack of appropriate care in the control and organisation of the arrest operation.

213. In sum, having regard to the decision not to prevent the suspects from travelling into Gibraltar, to the failure of the authorities to make sufficient allowances for the possibility that their intelligence assessments might, in some respects at least, be erroneous and to the automatic recourse to lethal force when the soldiers opened fire, the Court is not persuaded that the killing of the three terrorists constituted the use of force which was no more than absolutely necessary in defence of persons from unlawful violence within the meaning of Article 2[a] ... .

...

FOR THESE REASONS, THE COURT

Holds by *ten votes to nine* that there has been a violation of Article 2 of the Convention;

...

FINOGENOV AND OTHERS V. RUSSIA
EUROPEAN COURT OF HUMAN RIGHTS, CHAMBER JUDGMENT, APPLICATIONS NOS. 18299/03 AND 27311/03 (20 DECEMBER 2011)

[On 23 October 2002, 40 Chechen separatists seized over 900 people in a Moscow theatre and held them hostage for three days. The theatre was also booby-trapped and 18 suicide bombers were positioned among the hostages. The terrorists demanded, *inter alia*, the withdrawal of Russian troops from Chechnya. The Federal Security Service (FSB) set up a 'crisis cell' to negotiate and free the hostages. Although several hostages were released, others were killed. The applicants believed that further negotiations were possible, but the authorities felt that all hostages might be killed. At around 5 a.m. on 26 October security forces pumped an unknown narcotic gas into the building and then stormed it. All the terrorists were killed and the majority of the hostages were freed. But 125 of them died either on the spot or in hospital. The applicants claimed that the rescue operation was chaotic in almost every respect.

Subsequently, the Moscow City Prosecution Office (MPO) opened a criminal investigation. An accomplice to the terrorists was convicted but the MPO repeatedly refused to investigate the actions of the authorities during the crisis. The investigation concluded that the 125 hostages had died from a combination of individual weaknesses and chronic illnesses, exacerbated by the stress of three days of captivity, and that the gas used had at best had an 'indirect effect' on their demise. The death of the hostages was therefore attributed to 'natural' factors and not the use of the gas by the FSB.]

I. ALLEGED VIOLATION OF ARTICLE 2 OF THE CONVENTION

...

C. The Court's assessment

...

1. *Whether the case falls within the ambit of Article 2 of the Convention*

...

201. ... [T]he general conclusion of the expert report ... is difficult to accept. It is unthinkable that 125 people of different ages and physical conditions died almost simultaneously and in the same place because of various pre-existing health problems... .

202. ... [I]t is safe to conclude that the gas remained a primary cause of the death of a large number of the victims.

203. In sum, the present case is about the use of a dangerous substance (no matter how it is described) by the authorities within a rescue operation which resulted in the death of many of those whom the authorities were trying to liberate and in mortal danger for many others. The situation is thus covered by Article 2... . The Court has now to examine whether the use of force was compatible with the requirements of this provision.

...

4. *Standard of scrutiny to be applied*

...

212. The Court is acutely conscious of the difficulties faced by States in protecting their populations from terrorist violence, and recognises the complexity of this problem [as well as the particular problems faced by Russia].

213. ... The hostage-taking came as a surprise for the authorities... . so the military preparations for the storming had to be made very quickly and in full secrecy. It should be noted that the authorities were not in control of the situation inside the building. In such a situation the Court accepts that difficult and agonising decisions had to be made by the domestic authorities. It is prepared to grant them a margin of appreciation, at least in so far as the military and technical aspects of the situation are concerned, even if now, with hindsight, some of the decisions taken by the authorities may appear open to doubt.

214. In contrast, the subsequent phases of the operation may require a closer scrutiny by the Court; this is especially true in respect of such phases where no serious time constraints existed and the authorities were in control of the situation.

...

5. The use of force

(a) Decision to storm

...

219. The question is whether [the Government's] aims could have been attained by other, less drastic, means...

.

220. [G]enerally speaking, there is no necessity to use lethal force "where it is known that the person to be arrested poses no threat to life or limb and is not suspected of having committed a violent offence"... . [T]he situation in the present case was quite different: the threat posed by the terrorists was real and very serious. The authorities knew that many of the terrorists ... were well-trained, well-armed and dedicated to their cause ... ; that the explosion of the devices installed in the main auditorium would probably have killed all of the hostages; and that the terrorists were prepared to detonate those devices if their demands were not met.

...

226. In sum, the situation appeared very alarming. Heavily armed separatists dedicated to their cause had taken hostages and put forward unrealistic demands. The first days of negotiations did not bring any visible success; in addition, the humanitarian situation (the hostages' physical and psychological condition) had been worsening and made the hostages even more vulnerable. The Court concludes that there existed a real, serious and immediate risk of mass human losses and that the authorities had every reason to believe that a forced intervention was the "lesser evil" in the circumstances. Therefore, the authorities' decision to end the negotiations and storm the building in the circumstances did not run counter to Article 2 of the Convention.

(b) Decision to use the gas

...

228. [The Court's case law and relevant UN Principles] indicate that laws and regulations on the use of force should be sufficiently detailed and should prescribe, inter alia, the types of arms and ammunition permitted.

229. The legislative framework for the use of the gas in the present case remains unclear... . The exact formula of the gas was not revealed by the authorities; consequently, it is impossible for the Court to establish whether or not the gas was a "conventional weapon", and to identify the rules for its use. In the circumstances the Court is prepared to admit that the gas was an ad hoc solution, not described in the regulations and manuals for law-enforcement officials.

230. ... [But the] general vagueness of the Russian anti-terrorism law does not necessarily mean that in every particular case the authorities failed to respect the applicants' right to life. Even if necessary regulations did exist, they probably would be of limited use in the situation at hand, which was totally unpredictable, exceptional and required a tailor-made response ...

231. The Court will now move to the applicants' main argument. They claimed that the gas had been a lethal weapon which was used indiscriminately against both terrorists and innocent hostages. That claim deserves the most serious consideration, since "the massive use of indiscriminate weapons ... cannot be considered compatible with the standard of care prerequisite to an operation involving use of lethal force by state agents". The Court observes that the German Constitutional Court in a judgment of 15 February 2006 found incompatible with the right to life, as guaranteed by the German Constitution, a law authorising the use of force to shoot down a hijacked aircraft believed to be intended for a terrorist attack. It found, inter alia, that the use of lethal force against the persons on board who were not participants in the crime would be incompatible with their right to life and human dignity... .

232. In the present case, however, the gas used by the Russian security forces, while dangerous, was not supposed to kill ... . [A]lthough the gas was dangerous and even potentially lethal, it was not used "indiscriminately" as it left the hostages a high chance of survival, which depended on the efficiency of the authorities' rescue effort. The hostages in the present case were not in the same desperate situation as all the passengers of a hijacked airplane.

...

235. Another of the applicants' argument was that the concentration of the gas had been grossly miscalculated, and that the risks to the hostages' life and limb associated with its use outweighed the benefits ... . The Government claimed that the gas dosage had been calculated on the basis of an "average person's reaction". The Court notes that even that dose turned out to be insufficient to send everybody to sleep ... . In any event, the Court is not in a position to evaluate the issue of the dosage of the gas... .

236. In sum, the Court concludes that the use of gas during the storming was not in the circumstances a disproportionate measure, and, as such, did not breach Article 2 of the Convention.

6. Rescue and evacuation operation

237. ... [Was the operation] planned and implemented in compliance with the authorities' positive obligations under Article 2 of the Convention, namely whether the authorities took all necessary precautions to minimise the effects of the gas on the hostages, to evacuate them quickly and to provide them with necessary medical assistance ... .

...

265. In other words, many important factual details in this case are missing. That being said, the Court stresses that its role is not to establish the individual liability of those involved in the planning and coordination of the rescue operation. The Court is called upon to decide whether the State as a whole complied with its international obligations under the Convention, namely its obligation to "take all feasible precautions in the choice of means and methods of a security operation mounted against an opposing group with a view to avoiding and, in any event, minimising, incidental loss of civilian life".

266. The Court acknowledges that in such situations some measure of disorder is unavoidable. It also recognises the need to keep certain aspects of security operations secret. However, in the circumstances the rescue operation of 26 October 2002 was not sufficiently prepared, in particular because of the inadequate information exchange between various services, belated beginning of the evacuation, limited on-the-field coordination of various services, lack of appropriate medical treatment and equipment on the spot, and inadequate logistics. The Court concludes that the State breached its positive obligations under Article 2 of the Convention.

7. Effectiveness of the investigation

...

i. Whether the official investigation was "effective"

273. The present case clearly falls into the category of cases where the authorities must investigate the circumstances of the victims' deaths ... . [T]he events in issue "lay wholly, or in large part, within the exclusive knowledge of the authorities" in the sense that it was virtually impossible for the applicants to obtain any evidence independently from the authorities. In such circumstances the authorities were under an obligation to

carry out an effective official investigation in order to provide a "satisfactory and convincing" explanation of the victims' deaths and the degree of the authorities' responsibility for it.

274. The Court stresses that it is not concerned with the investigation into the terrorist act itself. In this part the investigation appeared to be quite ample and successful ... . The question is whether the investigation was equally successful in examining the authorities' own actions during the hostage crisis.

275. The Court notes that the investigation was opened and continued under Articles 205 ("Terrorist acts") and 206 ("Hostage-taking") of the Criminal Code. Negligence by the authorities cannot be characterised under either of those two provisions ... .

276. Although the investigation is not yet formally completed, the prosecution repeatedly decided that, as regards the authorities' alleged negligence, there was no case to answer. The first decision in that sense was taken ... slightly over one month after the events ... .

277. [While the investigation did address some relevant questions] in some other respects [it] was manifestly incomplete. First and foremost, the formula of the gas has never been revealed by the FSB to the domestic investigative authorities, despite the latter's request to that end, although the investigative team included FSB officers and most of the experts in the case were also from the FSB, and thus, at least in theory, could have been trusted.

...

279. The Court is surprised by the fact that ... all of the crisis cell's working papers were destroyed. In the Court's opinion those papers could have been an essential source of information about the planning and conduct of the rescue operation ... . The Government did not explain when those papers were destroyed, why, on whose authority and on what legal basis ... . Even assuming that some of them might have contained sensitive information, indiscriminate destruction of all documents ... was not justified.

280. Amongst others, the investigators did not try to establish certain facts which, in the Court's opinion, were relevant and even crucial for addressing the question of the authorities' alleged negligence ... .

281. Lastly, the investigative team was not independent ... . [T]he members of the investigative team and the experts whose conclusions were heavily relied on by the lead investigator had conflicts of interests, so manifest that in themselves those conflicts could have undermined the effectiveness of the investigation and the reliability of its conclusions.

282. Other elements of the investigative process are probably also worthy of attention (such as the limited access to the materials of the case by the victims' relatives, and their inability to formulate questions to the officially appointed experts and examine witnesses). However, the Court does not need to examine these aspects of the proceedings separately. It has sufficient evidence to conclude that the investigation into the authorities' alleged negligence in this case was neither thorough nor independent, and, therefore, not "effective". The Court concludes that there was a breach of the State's positive obligation under Article 2 of the Convention on this account.

OSMAN V. UNITED KINGDOM
EUROPEAN COURT OF HUMAN RIGHTS, GRAND CHAMBER, APPLICATION NO. 87/1997/871/1083 (28 OCTOBER 1998)

[A schoolteacher named Paul Paget-Lewis developed an obsession with Ahmet Osman, a teenage schoolboy. After a long series of incidents in which Paget-Lewis was suspected but never charged, he shot and wounded Ahmet and killed his father Ali Osman. Ahmet's mother and the wife of Ali complained that the authorities had failed to appreciate and act on a series of clear warning signs that Paget-Lewis represented a serious threat to the family's physical safety.]

I. ALLEGED VIOLATION OF ARTICLE 2 OF THE CONVENTION

B. The Court's assessment

...

2. As to the alleged failure of the authorities to protect the rights to life of Ali and Ahmet Osman

115. The Court notes that the first sentence of Article 2 § 1 enjoins the State not only to refrain from the intentional and unlawful taking of life, but also to take appropriate steps to safeguard the lives of those within its jurisdiction. It is common ground that the State's obligation in this respect extends beyond its primary duty to secure the right to life by putting in place effective criminal-law provisions to deter the commission of offences against the person backed up by law-enforcement machinery for the prevention, suppression and sanctioning of breaches of such provisions. It is thus accepted by those appearing before the Court that Article 2 of the Convention may also imply in certain well-defined circumstances a positive obligation on the authorities to take preventive operational measures to protect an individual whose life is at risk from the criminal acts of another individual. The scope of this obligation is a matter of dispute between the parties.

116. For the Court, and bearing in mind the difficulties involved in policing modern societies, the unpredictability of human conduct and the operational choices which must be made in terms of priorities and resources, such an obligation must be interpreted in a way which does not impose an impossible or disproportionate burden on the authorities. Accordingly, not every claimed risk to life can entail for the authorities a Convention requirement to take operational measures to prevent that risk from materialising. Another relevant consideration is the need to ensure that the police exercise their powers to control and prevent crime in a manner which fully respects the due process and other guarantees which legitimately place restraints on the scope of their action to investigate crime and bring offenders to justice ... .

[Where the authorities are alleged to have violated their positive obligations] it must be established to [the Court's] satisfaction that the authorities knew or ought to have known at the time of the existence of a real and immediate risk to the life of an identified individual or individuals from the criminal acts of a third party and that they failed to take measures within the scope of their powers which, judged reasonably, might have been expected to avoid that risk. The Court does not accept the Government's view that the failure to perceive the risk to life in the circumstances known at the time or to take preventive measures to avoid that risk must be tantamount to gross negligence or wilful disregard of the duty to protect life. Such a rigid standard must be considered to be incompatible with the requirements of Article 1 of the Convention and the obligations of Contracting States under that Article to secure the practical and effective protection of the rights and freedoms laid down therein, including Article 2 ... . [I]t is sufficient for an applicant to show that the authorities did not do all that could be reasonably expected of them to avoid a real and immediate risk to life of which they have or ought to have knowledge. This is a question which can only be answered in the light of all the circumstances of any particular case.

On the above understanding the Court will examine the particular circumstances of this case.

...

121. In the view of the Court the applicants have failed to point to any decisive stage in the sequence of the events leading up to the tragic shooting when it could be said that the police knew or ought to have known that the lives of the Osman family were at real and immediate risk from Paget-Lewis ... . [The police] cannot be criticised for attaching weight to the presumption of innocence or failing to use powers of arrest, search and seizure having regard to their reasonably held view that they lacked at relevant times the required standard of suspicion to use those powers or that any action taken would in fact have produced concrete results.

122. For the above reasons, the Court concludes that there has been no violation of Article 2 of the Convention in this case.

...

CARTER V. RUSSIA
EUROPEAN COURT OF HUMAN RIGHTS, CHAMBER JUDGMENT, APPLICATION NO.
20914/07 (21 SEPTEMBER 2021)

[On 23 November 2006, Alexander Litvinenko, a Russian political exile and businessman living in the United Kingdom, died of acute radiation syndrome caused by ingesting polonium 210. Litvinenko was a former member of the KGB and FSB (the security agency of the USSR and Russia respectively) who fled to the UK in 2000 after making statements to international media alleging that he had received unlawful orders from his FSB superiors. He became a vocal critic of corruption within Russia's political and intelligence infrastructure.

Litvinenko also undertook private security work, which involved liaising with contacts in Russia. One of these contacts was Andrey Lugovoy, another former FSB officer. After meeting with Lugovoy in the UK a number of times during October and November 2006, Litvinenko became severely ill from radiation poisoning. Radiation contamination was found in hotel rooms in which Lugovoy and his associate, Mr Kovtun, had stayed, as well as in a teapot from which Litvinenko had drunk during a meeting.

The UK police investigated the poisoning and charged Lugovoy and Kovtun with Litvinenko's murder; however, Russia refused to extradite the men on the ground that extradition of nationals is prohibited by its Constitution. In response, Russia's Prosecutor General launched its own criminal investigation, but brought no charges. In 2007, despite having no previous political experience, Lugovoy was made a member of Russia's parliament and acquired parliamentary immunity. Notably, in these proceedings the Russian government failed to produce any documents requested by the Court relating to its own investigation of the affair.

In 2016, the UK published the results of an inquiry into the affair which found, to the criminal standard of proof ('beyond reasonable doubt'), that Litvinenko had been intentionally poisoned by Lugovy and Kovtun by polonium placed in a teapot during their meeting.

The applicant, Litvinenko's widow, claimed before the Court that her husband's murder was carried out under the direction or with the acquiescence or connivance of the Russian state, and that Russia had failed to effectively investigate his murder. She asserted that this amounted to a violation of Articles 2 (the right to life) and 3 (the prohibition on torture) of the Convention.]

III. ALLEGED VIOLATION OF ARTICLE 2 OF THE CONVENTION

111. The applicant complained under Articles 2 and 3 of the Convention that her husband, Mr Litvinenko, had been murdered in a particularly painful manner by Mr Lugovoy (with others) while acting as an agent for, or in connivance with, or with the knowledge and support of, the Russian authorities, and that the Russian authorities had failed to conduct an effective investigation into the murder. The Court will consider this complaint from the standpoint of the right to life ... .

…

B. The Court's assessment

3. Merits

(a) Procedural obligation under Article 2[446]

[The Court found that Russia's investigation was ineffective and inadequate, and that the procedural limb of Article 2 had therefore been violated. Although Russia claimed to have taken some steps to establish the facts of the case, such as conducting interviews and carrying out polonium testing, no documentation to support any investigation was submitted to the Court. Further, the Court noted that the Russian government appeared to have attempted to thwart the UK inquiry by failing to make evidence and witnesses available. The Court dismissed Russia's argument that it had not been able to further investigate the matter because of the UK

---

[446] The Court held that it had jurisdiction over the procedural violation of Article 2 since Russia had instituted an investigation into Litvinenko's death. [ed.]

authorities' failure to comply with requests for legal assistance, noting that Russia had already exonerated Lugovoy and Kovtun of their involvement in Litvinenko's murder at the time it requested assistance and indicated that it was not investigating other suspects.]

...

(b) Substantive obligation under Article 2 of the Convention

149. At the time he was poisoned Mr Litvinenko was in the United Kingdom and therefore not present in an area over which the Russian State exercised "effective control". It remains therefore to be established whether the Russian State can be held accountable for the alleged violation of his right to life under the personal concept of jurisdiction.

150. ... [T]he fate of the applicant's complaint about the assassination of her husband depends on the answers to the following two interrelated questions: (i) whether the assassination of Mr Litvinenko amounted to the exercise of physical power and control over his life in a situation of proximate targeting, and (ii) whether it was carried out by individuals acting as State agents. The Court will establish the facts on the basis of the evidence available in the case-file.

(i) Evaluation of evidence by the Court

151. In assessing evidence in cases concerning an alleged violation of the right to life, the Court has adopted the standard of proof "beyond reasonable doubt". However, it has not borrowed the approach of the national legal systems that use that standard, since its role is not to rule on criminal guilt or civil liability but on Contracting States' responsibility under the Convention. ...

152. In addition, the conduct of the parties in relation to the Court's efforts to obtain evidence may constitute an element to be taken into account ... .

153. The Court has found a violation of Article 2 where a prima facie case had been made that an individual was killed by State agents and the Government failed to provide any other satisfactory and convincing explanation of the events. It also found that it could draw inferences from the Government's conduct in respect of the investigation documents ... . It has not, however, found a violation in cases where the applicant's allegations are tenable but the circumstances of the death nevertheless remain a matter of speculation and assumption ... .

(ii) Establishment of the facts

154. In the present case, the circumstances of Mr Litvinenko's death are no longer a "matter of speculation and assumption". It has been established, beyond reasonable doubt, that he was poisoned with polonium 210, a rare radioactive isotope. It has been further established, also beyond reasonable doubt, that the poison was administered by Mr Lugovoy and Mr Kovtun.

...

(α) Whether Mr Lugovoy and Mr Kovtun exercised physical power and control over the life of Mr Litvinenko in a situation of proximate targeting

158. ... [T]he Court's inquiry will first address the issue whether the assassination of Mr Litvinenko amounted to the exercise of physical power and control over his life in a situation of proximate targeting.

159. The evidence of premeditation strongly indicates that the death of Mr Litvinenko had been the result of a planned and complex operation involving the procurement of a rare deadly poison, the travel arrangements for Mr Lugovoy and Mr Kovtun, and multiple attempts to administer the poison. Mr Litvinenko was not an accidental victim of the operation or merely adversely affected by it; the possibility that he may have ingested polonium 210 by accident is not borne out by the evidence. On the contrary, repeated and sustained attempts to put poison in his drink demonstrate that Mr Litvinenko was the target of the planned operation for his assassination.

160. The Court further notes that the evidence has established, beyond reasonable doubt, that Mr Lugovoy and Mr Kovtun knew that they were using a deadly poison rather than a truth serum or a sleeping pill. When putting the poison in the teapot from which Mr Litvinenko poured a drink, they knew that, once ingested, the poison would kill Mr Litvinenko. The latter was unable to do anything to escape the situation. In that sense, he was under physical control of Mr Lugovoy and Mr Kovtun who wielded power over his life.

161. In the Court's view, the administration of poison to Mr Litvinenko by Mr Lugovoy and Mr Kovtun amounted to the exercise of physical power and control over his life in a situation of proximate targeting. That being so, if this act was imputable to the respondent State, the Court considers that it was capable of falling within the jurisdiction of that State ... .

(β) Whether Mr Lugovoy and Mr Kovtun acted as State agents
...
166. While there existed a theoretical possibility that the assassination of Mr Litvinenko might have been a "rogue operation" not involving State responsibility, the information needed to corroborate this theory lies wholly, or in large part, within the exclusive knowledge of the Russian authorities which moreover asserted exclusive jurisdiction over Mr Lugovoy and Mr Kovtun by invoking the constitutional protection against extradition. In these circumstances, the burden of proof was shifted onto the authorities of the respondent State which were expected to carry out a meticulous investigation into that possibility, identify those involved in the operation and determine whether or not Mr Lugovoy's and Mr Kovtun's conduct was directed or controlled by any State entity or official, which is a factor indicative of State responsibility ... .

167. The Government, however, have not made any serious attempt either to elucidate the facts or to counter the findings arrived at by the United Kingdom authorities. ...

168. Most significantly, ... the Russian authorities failed to carry out an effective investigation themselves. ...

169. ... Noting the Government's failure to displace the prima facie evidence of State involvement, the Court cannot but conclude that Mr Litvinenko was poisoned by Mr Lugovoy and Mr Kovtun acting as agents of the respondent State. The act complained of is attributable to that State.

170. ...[T]he Court has accepted that when they poisoned Mr Litvinenko, Mr Lugovoy and Mr Kovtun were acting as agents of the respondent State and that they exercised physical power and control over his life in a manner sufficient to establish a jurisdictional link with the respondent State for the purposes of Article 1 of the Convention. Accordingly, the Government's objection of inadmissibility ratione loci must be dismissed.

[The Court awarded the applicant EUR100,000 in non-pecuniary damages and EUR 22,500 in legal fees. As the applicant did not specify an amount claimed for pecuniary damages, the Court did not make an award under this head.]
...

QUESTIONS

1. How do you respond to the claim in the dissenting judgment in *Banković* that 'an order to bomb specific targets in a city is an act of public power', and should therefore be treated as an exercise of jurisdiction for the purposes of the ECHR?

2. Should the Court's approach to "proximate targeting" in *Carter* apply to all rights, such as the right to privacy, rather than only to the right to life?

2. Do you agree with Nigel Biggar, who argues in *What's Wrong with Rights?* (2020) at 330 that:

[An] ill-effect of rights-fundamentalism, whether judicial or philosophical, is that, when applied to military affairs, it places unreasonable and demoralizing burdens on troops, and undermines their military effectiveness. And since it is only liberal governments that pay attention to rights-rhetoric, partly because they half-believe it and partly for electoral reasons, it is only their militaries that are weakened. Thus, rights-fundamentalism increases the prospect of the military victory of the enemies of liberal rights. ...

By way of background, the United Kingdom Government announced plans on 4 October 2016 to derogate from the ECHR to ensure that its armed forces would not be constrained by its human rights obligations in future overseas operations. Prime Minister Theresa May said: 'We will repay [our Armed Forces] with gratitude and put an end to the industry of vexatious claims that has pursued those who served in previous conflicts.' On 22 June 2022, the Government introduced 'The Bill of Rights Bill', which provided that there would be no right 'to bring proceedings, or rely on a Convention right, in relation to an act (or proposed act) of a public authority which is done (or is proposed to be done) outside the British Islands in the course of overseas military operations.' Several months later, the Bill was withdrawn.

b. Democracy and Political Participation

The following materials address the links between political participation, elections, and democratic government.[447] They focus on two of a significant number of cases decided by the European Court since 1998 involving the banning or dissolution of political parties in Turkey, and on an Advisory Opinion relating to Lithuania given by the Court in 2022 in relation to bans restricting the right of individuals to run for elected office.

The literature in this area often distinguishes between 'procedural' and 'militant' democracy.[448] Procedural approaches are comparatively permissive and do not seek to limit the political rights even of those seeking to undermine or overthrow the constitutional order. They will, of course, use the criminal law in individual cases of transgression but will not ban political parties. Militant democracy, on the other hand, refers to an approach which seeks to place certain core foundational values beyond the reach of the democratic process. This might involve legislative restrictions on the rights to freedom of expression, participation, and assembly of those who seek to undermine democracy. The classic example of militant democracy is the post-World War II German Basic Law. Article 79(3) prohibits amendments to the basic principles included in Articles 1 (dignity of man) and 20 (democratic, federal, and social state based on the rule of law). In addition, anti-democratic parties may be disbanded (Art. 21(2)); anti-democratic associations dissolved (Art. 9(2)); those seeking to subvert the liberal democratic order may lose their individual freedoms (Art. 18); and citizens have the right to resist attempts, including by the public authorities, to abolish the constitutional order (Art. 20(4)).[449]

The Code of Good Practice in Electoral Matters (Doc. CDL-AD(2002)023rev2-cor-e) adopted in 2002 by the Venice Commission, provides that the withdrawal of political rights 'may only be imposed by express decision of a court of law'. But it adds (para. 6) that '[t]he conditions for depriving individuals of the right to stand for election may be less strict than for disenfranchising them, as the holding of a public office is at stake and it may be legitimate to debar persons whose activities in such an office would violate a greater public interest.'

The dilemma is simple:

> Must a democratic system stand idly by and watch antidemocratic forces gather strength?
> Must liberal constitutions, because they support tolerance and openness, function as
> suicide pacts, preventing effective self-defense? ...

---

[447] There are, of course, many other dimensions. See ECtHR, 'Factsheet – Right to vote' (November 2022); and E. Shattock, 'Free and Informed Elections? Disinformation and Democratic Elections Under Article 3 of Protocol 1 of the ECHR', 22 *Hum. Rts. L. Rev.* (2022) 1.
[448] L. Vinx, 'Democratic Equality and Militant Democracy', 27 *Constellations* (2020) 685.
[449] G. Capoccia, 'Militant Democracy: The Institutional Bases of Democratic Self-Preservation', 9 *Ann. Rev. L. & Soc. Sci.* (2013) 207.

> The correct answer is "no". Constitutional democracies can and do act preemptively; for instance, by banning extremist parties while they are still relatively weak. Endangered democracies can curtail freedom of speech, freedom of association, and associated political rights to vote and compete for office and still remain recognizably liberal and democratic. To be sure, honest debate remains possible about the most effective and least restrictive ways of defending democracy against its most virulent enemies. And there is another important question that remains unanswered: What constitutional obstacles can be put in place to prevent political incumbents from opportunistically invoking the defense of democracy against antidemocratic forces as a justification for cracking down on perfectly legitimate political rivals?[450]

While many of the cases in this area relate to those promulgating forms of fascism or communism that have been seen to be subversive of democracy, the rise of populist authoritarian and other illiberal parties over the past decade have given renewed relevance to many of the debates.

A collection of essays edited by Anthoula Malkopoulou and Alexander S. Kirshner, *Militant Democracy and Its Critics: Populism, Parties, Extremism* (2019) reflects the diverse responses to such 'militancy'. Stefan Rummens, in 'Resolving the Paradox of Tolerance', *ibid.*, at 112, argues in favour of giving more leeway to extremist actors in the informal public sphere, on the "periphery" of the political system, while being increasingly intolerant of such actors at the "core" of decision-making, such as those in parliament or government, to ensure that extremist views "are never translated into actual legislation or polices."

Jan-Werner Müller, in 'Individual Militant Democracy', *ibid.*, at 32, urges caution:

> Something like a permanent banishment of an individual from the polity – literally or figuratively, in the case of a complete forfeiture of political rights – cannot be justified. However, not all participation rights are equally important. There is a space for temporarily restricting some rights as a result of a pattern of action that suggests a particularly resourceful individual is intent on undermining or destroying democracy outright. Some forms of impeachment – when impeachment is also forward-looking, taking into account the damage that might be done in the future by an irresponsible office-holder abusing their powers – can be justified in similar fashion.
>
> … [Such measures should leave open] the possibility of anti-democratic actors changing their minds (or, rather, changing their conduct – the depths of their character are not the issue, and in a sense not our business). … [T]he most plausible approach is to disaggregate the general interest in political participation and restrict rights (or otherwise exclude from the political process) selectively and temporarily only.

Finally, András Sajó, in 'Militant Constitutionalism', *ibid.*, at 203, warns that legal approaches might not hold the key in such contexts:

> The institutions of militant constitutionalism may work against populism in conditions of social inertia but not where populists systematically mobilise hatred and disparagement against the institutions; where democracy is understood simply as regular voting and where constitutional freedoms are not cherished, democracy will fail. A democracy cannot be sustained in the absence of (reasonable) democrats. And it cannot be sustained when people believe that they are still good democrats even as they work to undermine it.

The ECtHR has considered a significant number of relevant cases, involving a diverse range of countries.[451] We turn now to look at two classic cases, along with a more recent example from Lithuania which also illustrates the operation of the Court's relatively new advisory opinion jurisdiction.[452]

---

[450] S. Holmes, 'Book Review', 4 *Int'l. J. Const. L.* (2006) 586.

[451] For a summary see ECtHR, 'Factsheet – Political parties and associations' (May 2022).

[452] See E. Albanesi, 'The European Court of Human Rights' Advisory Opinions Legally Affect Non-ratifying States', 28 *Eur. Pub.* L. (2022) 1; T. Moonen and L. Lavrysen, 'Abstract but Concrete, or Concrete but Abstract? A Guide to the Nature of Advisory Opinions Under Protocol No 16 to the ECHR', 21 *Hum. Rts. L. Rev.* (2021) 752; and K. Lemmens, 'Protocol No 16 to the ECHR: Managing Backlog through Complex Judicial Dialogue?', 15 *Eur. Const. L. Rev.* (2019) 691.

UNITED COMMUNIST PARTY OF TURKEY V. TURKEY
EUROPEAN COURT OF HUMAN RIGHTS, GRAND CHAMBER, APPLICATION NO. 133/1996/752/951 (30 JANUARY 1998)

...

7. The United Communist Party of Turkey ('the TBKP'), the first applicant, was a political party that was dissolved by the Constitutional Court. Mr Nihat Sargin and Mr Nabi Yagci, the second and third applicants, were respectively Chairman and General Secretary of the TBKP. They live in Istanbul.

8. The TBKP was formed on 4 June 1990. On the same day, its constitution and programme were submitted to the office of Principal State Counsel at the Court of Cassation for assessment of their compatibility with the Constitution and Law no. 2820 on the regulation of political parties.

9. On 14 June 1990, when the TBKP was preparing to participate in a general election, Principal State Counsel at the Court of Cassation ('Principal State Counsel') applied to the Constitutional Court for an order dissolving the TBKP. He accused the party of having sought to establish the domination of one social class over the others ... of having incorporated the word 'communist' into its name ... of having carried on activities likely to undermine the territorial integrity of the State and the unity of the nation ... and of having declared itself to be the successor to a previously dissolved political party, the Turkish Workers' Party... .

[The following excerpts from the opinion concern almost exclusively the principal charge of undermining the unity of the nation. In omitted portions, the opinion found the other three grounds inadequate to justify interference with the right of association under Article 11.]

In support of his application Principal State Counsel relied in particular on passages from the TBKP's programme, mainly taken from a chapter entitled 'Towards a peaceful, democratic and fair solution for the Kurdish problem'; that chapter read as follows:

...

The TBKP will strive for a peaceful, democratic and fair solution of the Kurdish problem, so that the Kurdish and Turkish peoples may live together of their free will within the borders of the Turkish Republic, on the basis of equal rights and with a view to democratic restructuring founded on their common interests.

...

10. On 16 July 1991 the Constitutional Court made an order dissolving the TBKP, [resulting in the liquidation of the party, the transfer of its assets to the Treasury, and the banning of its founders and managers from holding similar office in any other political body].

...

As to the allegation that the TBKP's constitution and programme contained statements likely to undermine the territorial integrity of the State and the unity of the nation, the Constitutional Court noted, inter alia, that those documents referred to two nations: the Kurdish nation and the Turkish nation. But it could not be accepted that there were two nations within the Republic of Turkey, whose citizens, whatever their ethnic origin, had Turkish nationality. In reality the proposals in the party constitution covering support for non-Turkish languages and cultures were intended to create minorities, to the detriment of the unity of the Turkish nation.

Reiterating that self-determination and regional autonomy were prohibited by the Constitution, the Constitutional Court said that the State was unitary, the country indivisible and that there was only one nation...

.

...

AS TO THE LAW

I. Alleged Violation of Article 11 of the Convention[453]

...

---

[453] Article 11 provides that:

(1) Everyone has the right to freedom of ... association with others, including the right to form and to join trade unions. ...

2. No restrictions shall be placed on the exercise of these rights other than such as are prescribed by law and are necessary in a democratic society in the interests of national security ... or for the protection of the rights and freedoms of others.

25. ... [P]olitical parties are a form of association essential to the proper functioning of democracy. In view of the importance of democracy in the Convention system, there can be no doubt that political parties come within the scope of Article 11.

...

27. ... [A]n association, including a political party, is not excluded from the protection afforded by the Convention simply because its activities are regarded by the national authorities as undermining the constitutional structures of the State ... .

[W]hile it is in principle open to the national authorities to take such action as they consider necessary to respect the rule of law or to give effect to constitutional rights, they must do so in a manner which is compatible with their obligations under the Convention and subject to review by the Convention institutions.

28. The Preamble to the Convention refers to the 'common heritage of political traditions, ideals, freedom and the rule of law', of which national constitutions are in fact often the first embodiment ... .

...

30. The political and institutional organization of the member States must accordingly respect the rights and principles enshrined in the Convention. It matters little in this context whether the provisions in issue are constitutional or merely legislative ... .

...

32. It does not, however, follow that the authorities of a State in which an association, through its activities, jeopardizes that State's institutions are deprived of the right to protect those institutions. In this connection, the Court points out that it has previously held that some compromise between the requirements of defending democratic society and individual rights is inherent in the system of the Convention. For there to be a compromise of that sort any intervention by the authorities must be in accordance with paragraph 2 of Article 11, which the Court considers below ... .

...

37. Such an interference [by Turkey with Article 11] will constitute a breach of Article 11 unless it was 'prescribed by law', pursued one or more legitimate aims under paragraph 2 and was 'necessary in a democratic society' for the achievement of those aims.

...

(b) Legitimate aim

...

41. [T]he Court considers that the dissolution of the TBKP pursued at least one of the 'legitimate aims' set out in Article 11: the protection of 'national security'.

(c) 'Necessary in a democratic society'

42. The Court reiterates that notwithstanding its autonomous role and particular sphere of application, Article 11 must also be considered in the light of Article 10. The protection of opinions and the freedom to express them is one of the objectives of the freedoms of assembly and association as enshrined in Article 11.

43. That applies all the more in relation to political parties in view of their essential role in ensuring pluralism and the proper functioning of democracy.

As the Court has said many times, there can be no democracy without pluralism... .

...

45. Democracy is without doubt a fundamental feature of the European public order... . The Court has ... pointed out several times that the Convention was designed to maintain and promote the ideals and values of a democratic society.

... The only type of necessity capable of justifying an interference with any of those rights is, therefore, one which may claim to spring from 'democratic society'. Democracy thus appears to be the only political model contemplated by the Convention and, accordingly, the only one compatible with it ... .

46. Consequently, ... only convincing and compelling reasons can justify restrictions on such parties' freedom of association. In determining whether a necessity within the meaning of Article 11(2) exists, the Contracting States have only a limited margin of appreciation, which goes hand in hand with rigorous European supervision embracing both the law and the decisions applying it, including those given by independent courts ... .

47. When the Court carries out its scrutiny, [it does not have] to confine itself to ascertaining whether the respondent State exercised its discretion reasonably, carefully and in good faith; it must look at the interference complained of in the light of the case as a whole and determine whether it was 'proportionate to the legitimate aim pursued' and whether the reasons adduced by the national authorities to justify it are 'relevant and sufficient' ... .

2. Application of the principles to the present case

...

49. The Government pointed out that ... faced with a challenge to the fundamental interests of the national community, such as national security and territorial integrity, the Turkish authorities had not in any way exceeded the margin of appreciation conferred on them by the Convention.

...

51. The Court notes at the outset that the TBKP was dissolved even before it had been able to start its activities and that the dissolution was therefore ordered solely on the basis of the TBKP's constitution and programme, which ... contain nothing to suggest that they did not reflect the party's true objectives and its leaders' true intentions. Like the national authorities, the Court will therefore take those documents as a basis for assessing whether the interference in question was necessary.

...

55. The second submission accepted by the Constitutional Court was that the TBKP sought to promote separatism and the division of the Turkish nation ... .

56. The Court notes that although the TBKP refers in its programme to the Kurdish 'people' and 'nation' and Kurdish 'citizens', it neither describes them as a 'minority' nor makes any claim — other than for recognition of their existence — for them to enjoy special treatment or rights, still less a right to secede from the rest of the Turkish population. On the contrary, the programme states: 'The TBKP will strive for a peaceful, democratic and fair solution of the Kurdish problem, so that the Kurdish and Turkish peoples may live together of their free will within the borders of the Turkish Republic, on the basis of equal rights and with a view to democratic restructuring founded on their common interests'. With regard to the right to self-determination, the TBKP does no more in its programme than deplore the fact that because of the use of violence, it was not 'exercised jointly, but separately and unilaterally', adding that 'the remedy for this problem is political' and that '[i]f the oppression of the Kurdish people and discrimination against them are to end, Turks and Kurds must unite'.

...

57. The Court considers one of the principal characteristics of democracy to be the possibility it offers of resolving a country's problems through dialogue, without recourse to violence, even when they are irksome. Democracy thrives on freedom of expression. From that point of view, there can be no justification for hindering a political group solely because it seeks to debate in public the situation of part of the State's population and to take part in the nation's political life in order to find, according to democratic rules, solutions capable of satisfying everyone concerned ... .

...

59. The Court is also prepared to take into account the background of cases before it, in particular the difficulties associated with the fight against terrorism ... .

...

61. Regard being had to all the above, a measure as drastic as the immediate and permanent dissolution of the TBKP, ordered before its activities had even started and coupled with a ban barring its leaders from discharging any other political responsibility, is disproportionate to the aim pursued and consequently unnecessary in a democratic society. It follows that the measure infringed Article 11 of the Convention.

...

REFAH PARTISI (THE WELFARE PARTY) AND OTHERS V. TURKEY
EUROPEAN COURT OF HUMAN RIGHTS, GRAND CHAMBER, APPLICATION NOS.
41340/98, 41342/98, 41343/98 AND 41344/98 (13 FEBRUARY 2003)

[Four applications were submitted by the Turkish Welfare Party (Refah) and three of its members in May 1998. They alleged that the dissolution of Refah by the Turkish Constitutional Court and the suspension of certain political rights of the party leaders breached Articles 9, 10, 11, 14, 17, and 18 of the ECHR and Articles 1 and 3 of Protocol No. 1. The case was first heard by a Chamber. In July 2001 it held by a vote of four to three that there had been no violation of Article 11 and that it was unnecessary to examine the other alleged breaches. In December 2001, after a request by the applicants, the case was referred to the Grand Chamber.]

THE FACTS

...

11. Refah took part in a number of general and local elections. In the local elections in March 1989 Refah obtained about 10% of the votes ...

Ultimately, Refah obtained approximately 22% of the votes in the general election of 24 December 1995 and about 35% of the votes in the local elections of 3 November 1996.

The results of the 1995 general election made Refah the largest political party in Turkey... . On 28 June 1996 Refah came to power by forming a coalition government with the centre-right... . According to an opinion poll carried out in January 1997, ... Refah might obtain 67% of the votes in the general election to be held roughly four years later.

B. Proceedings in the Constitutional Court

...

12. On 21 May 1997 Principal State Counsel at the Court of Cassation applied to the Turkish Constitutional Court to have Refah dissolved on the grounds that it was a "centre" (*mihrak*) of activities contrary to the principles of secularism. In support of his application, he referred to the following acts and remarks by certain leaders and members of Refah.

– Whenever they spoke in public Refah's chairman and other leaders advocated the wearing of Islamic headscarves in State schools and buildings occupied by public administrative authorities, whereas the Constitutional Court had already ruled that this infringed the principle of secularism enshrined in the Constitution.

– At a meeting on constitutional reform Refah's chairman, Mr Necmettin Erbakan, had made proposals tending towards the abolition of secularism in Turkey. He had suggested that the adherents of each religious movement should obey their own rules rather than the rules of Turkish law.

– On 13 April 1994 Mr Necmettin Erbakan had asked Refah's representatives in the Grand National Assembly to consider whether the change in the social order which the party sought would be "peaceful or violent" and would be achieved "harmoniously or by bloodshed".

– At a seminar held in January 1991 in Sivas, Mr Necmettin Erbakan had called on Muslims to join Refah, saying that only his party could establish the supremacy of the Koran through a holy war (jihad) and that Muslims should therefore make donations to Refah rather than distributing alms to third parties.

...

– Several members of Refah, including some in high office, had made speeches calling for the secular political system to be replaced by a theocratic system. These persons had also advocated the elimination of the opponents of this policy, if necessary by force. Refah, by refusing to open disciplinary proceedings against the members concerned and even, in certain cases, facilitating the dissemination of their speeches, had tacitly approved the views expressed.

– On 8 May 1997 a Refah MP, Mr Ibrahim Halil Çelik, had said in front of journalists in the corridors of the parliament building that blood would flow if an attempt was made to close the "*Imam-Hatip*" theological colleges ... .

...

THE LAW

I. Alleged Violation of Article 11 of the Convention

[The Court considered whether the interference had been 'prescribed by law' and had been in pursuance of a 'legitimate aim'. It responded affirmatively on both issues.]

...

3. "Necessary in a democratic society"

...

98. [T]he Court considers that a political party may promote a change in the law or the legal and constitutional structures of the State on two conditions: firstly, the means used to that end must be legal and democratic; secondly, the change proposed must itself be compatible with fundamental democratic principles. It necessarily follows that a political party whose leaders incite to violence or put forward a policy which fails to respect democracy or which is aimed at the destruction of democracy and the flouting of the rights and freedoms recognised in a democracy cannot lay claim to the Convention's protection against penalties imposed on those grounds ... .

99. The possibility cannot be excluded that a political party, in pleading the rights enshrined in Article 11 and also in Articles 9 and 10 of the Convention, might attempt to derive therefrom the right to conduct what amounts in practice to activities intended to destroy the rights or freedoms set forth in the Convention and thus bring about the destruction of democracy (see *Communist Party (KPD) v. Germany*, no. 250/57, Commission decision of 20 July 1957, Yearbook 1, p. 222). In view of the very clear link between the Convention and democracy, no one must be authorised to rely on the Convention's provisions in order to weaken or destroy the ideals and values of a democratic society. Pluralism and democracy are based on a compromise that requires various concessions by individuals or groups of individuals, who must sometimes agree to limit some of the freedoms they enjoy in order to guarantee greater stability of the country as a whole.

In that context, the Court considers that it is not at all improbable that totalitarian movements, organised in the form of political parties, might do away with democracy, after prospering under the democratic regime, there being examples of this in modern European history.

100. The Court reiterates, however, that the exceptions set out in Article 11 are, where political parties are concerned, to be construed strictly; only convincing and compelling reasons can justify restrictions on such parties' freedom of association. In determining whether a necessity within the meaning of Article 11 § 2 exists, the Contracting States have only a limited margin of appreciation. Although it is not for the Court to take the place of the national authorities, which are better placed than an international court to decide, for example, the appropriate timing for interference, it must exercise rigorous supervision embracing both the law and the decisions applying it, including those given by independent courts. Drastic measures, such as the dissolution of an entire political party and a disability barring its leaders from carrying on any similar activity for a specified period, may be taken only in the most serious cases ... . Provided that it satisfies the conditions set out in paragraph 98 above, a political party animated by the moral values imposed by a religion cannot be regarded as intrinsically inimical to the fundamental principles of democracy, as set forth in the Convention.

...

(ε) The appropriate timing for dissolution

102. In addition, the Court considers that a State cannot be required to wait, before intervening, until a political party has seized power and begun to take concrete steps to implement a policy incompatible with the standards of the Convention and democracy, even though the danger of that policy for democracy is sufficiently established and imminent. The Court accepts that where the presence of such a danger has been established by the national courts, after detailed scrutiny subjected to rigorous European supervision, a State may "reasonably forestall the execution of such a policy, which is incompatible with the Convention's provisions, before an

attempt is made to implement it through concrete steps that might prejudice civil peace and the country's democratic regime" (see the Chamber's judgment, § 81).

103. ... A Contracting State may be justified under its positive obligations in imposing on political parties, which are bodies whose *raison d'être* is to accede to power and direct the work of a considerable portion of the State apparatus, the duty to respect and safeguard the rights and freedoms guaranteed by the Convention and the obligation not to put forward a political programme in contradiction with the fundamental principles of democracy.

(ζ) Overall examination

104. In the light of the above considerations, the Court's overall examination ... must concentrate on the following points: (i) whether there was plausible evidence that the risk to democracy, supposing it had been proved to exist, was sufficiently imminent; (ii) whether the acts and speeches of the leaders and members of the political party concerned were imputable to the party as a whole; and (iii) whether the acts and speeches imputable to the political party formed a whole which gave a clear picture of a model of society conceived and advocated by the party which was incompatible with the concept of a "democratic society".

105. ... [T]he Court must [also] take account of the historical context in which the dissolution of the party concerned took place and the general interest in preserving the principle of secularism in that context in the country concerned to ensure the proper functioning of "democratic society".

(ii) Application of the above principles to the present case
...
(a) Pressing social need

The appropriate timing for dissolution
...
108. The Court ... considers that at the time of its dissolution Refah had the real potential to seize political power without being restricted by the compromises inherent in a coalition. If Refah had proposed a programme contrary to democratic principles, its monopoly of political power would have enabled it to establish the model of society envisaged in that programme.
...
110. While it can be considered, in the present case, that Refah's policies were dangerous for the rights and freedoms guaranteed by the Convention, the real chances that Refah would implement its programme after gaining power made that danger more tangible and more immediate... .

In short, the Court considers that in electing to intervene at the time when they did in the present case the national authorities did not go beyond the margin of appreciation left to them under the Convention.
...
The main grounds for dissolution cited by the Constitutional Court

116. The Court considers on this point that among the arguments for dissolution pleaded by Principal State Counsel at the Court of Cassation those cited by the Constitutional Court as grounds for its finding that Refah had become a centre of anti-constitutional activities can be classified into three main groups: (i) the arguments that Refah intended to set up a plurality of legal systems, leading to discrimination based on religious beliefs; (ii) the arguments that Refah intended to apply sharia to the internal or external relations of the Muslim community within the context of this plurality of legal systems; and (iii) the arguments based on the references made by Refah members to the possibility of recourse to force as a political method. The Court must therefore limit its examination to those three groups of arguments cited by the Constitutional Court.

(a) The plan to set up a plurality of legal systems
...
119. The Court sees no reason to depart from the Chamber's conclusion that a plurality of legal systems, as proposed by Refah, cannot be considered to be compatible with the Convention system. In its judgment, the Chamber gave the following reasoning:

"70 ... . the Court considers that Refah's proposal that there should be a plurality of legal systems would introduce into all legal relationships a distinction between individuals grounded on religion, would categorise everyone according to his religious beliefs and would allow him rights and freedoms not as an individual but according to his allegiance to a religious movement.

The Court takes the view that such a societal model cannot be considered compatible with the Convention system, for two reasons.

Firstly, it would do away with the State's role as the guarantor of individual rights and freedoms... .

Secondly, such a system would undeniably infringe the principle of non discrimination between individuals as regards their enjoyment of public freedoms... . "

(b) Sharia

122. ... [After examining the various comments attributed to Refah leaders the Court accepted] the Constitutional Court's conclusion that these remarks and stances of Refah's leaders formed a whole and gave a clear picture of a model conceived and proposed by the party of a State and society organised according to religious rules.

123. The Court concurs in the Chamber's view that sharia is incompatible with the fundamental principles of democracy, as set forth in the Convention:

> "72. Like the Constitutional Court, the Court considers that sharia, which faithfully reflects the dogmas and divine rules laid down by religion, is stable and invariable. Principles such as pluralism in the political sphere or the constant evolution of public freedoms have no place in it. ... It is difficult to declare one's respect for democracy and human rights while at the same time supporting a regime based on sharia, which clearly diverges from Convention values, particularly with regard to its criminal law and criminal procedure, its rules on the legal status of women and the way it intervenes in all spheres of private and public life in accordance with religious precepts... . In the Court's view, a political party whose actions seem to be aimed at introducing sharia in a State party to the Convention can hardly be regarded as an association complying with the democratic ideal that underlies the whole of the Convention."

124. The Court must not lose sight of the fact that in the past political movements based on religious fundamentalism have been able to seize political power in certain States and have had the opportunity to set up the model of society which they had in mind. It considers that, in accordance with the Convention's provisions, each Contracting State may oppose such political movements in the light of its historical experience.

125. The Court further observes that there was already an Islamic theocratic regime under Ottoman law. When the former theocratic regime was dismantled and the republican regime was being set up, Turkey opted for a form of secularism which confined Islam and other religions to the sphere of private religious practice. Mindful of the importance for survival of the democratic regime of ensuring respect for the principle of secularism in Turkey, the Court considers that the Constitutional Court was justified in holding that Refah's policy of establishing sharia was incompatible with democracy.

...

(d) The possibility of recourse to force

...

130. The Court considers that, whatever meaning is ascribed to the term "jihad" used in most of the speeches mentioned above (whose primary meaning is holy war and the struggle to be waged until the total domination of Islam in society is achieved), there was ambiguity in the terminology used to refer to the method to be employed to gain political power. In all of these speeches the possibility was mentioned of resorting "legitimately" to force in order to overcome various obstacles Refah expected to meet in the political route by which it intended to gain and retain power.

131. Furthermore, the Court endorses the following finding of the Chamber:

> "74 ... . While it is true that [Refah's] leaders did not, in government documents, call for the use of force and violence as a political weapon, they did not take prompt practical steps to distance themselves from those members of [Refah] who had publicly referred with approval to the possibility of using force against politicians who opposed them. Consequently, Refah's leaders did not dispel the ambiguity of these statements about the possibility of having recourse to violent methods in order to gain power and retain it."

Overall examination of "pressing social need"

132. ... [Taking account of the factors above the Court concluded that the dissolution order] may reasonably be considered to have met a "pressing social need".

Proportionality of the measure complained of

133. After considering the parties' arguments, the Court sees no good reason to depart from the following considerations in the Chamber's judgment:

> "82. ... [A]fter [Refah's] dissolution only five of its MPs (including the applicants) temporarily forfeited their parliamentary office and their role as leaders of a political party. The 152 remaining MPs continued to sit in Parliament and pursued their political careers normally ... . The Court considers in that connection that the nature and severity of the interference are also factors to be taken into account when assessing its proportionality ... ."

4. The Court's conclusion regarding Article 11 of the Convention

135. Consequently, following a rigorous review to verify that there were convincing and compelling reasons justifying Refah's dissolution and the temporary forfeiture of certain political rights imposed on the other applicants, the Court considers that those interferences met a "pressing social need" and were "proportionate to the aims pursued". It follows that Refah's dissolution may be regarded as "necessary in a democratic society" within the meaning of Article 11 § 2.

136. Accordingly, there has been no violation of Article 11 of the Convention. [The Court therefore concluded that there was no need to examine the same issues in relation to the other provisions of the Convention cited by the applicants.]

...

CONCURRING OPINION OF JUDGE KOVLER

...

[The judge agrees that there is no violation of Article 11.] What bothers me about some of the Court's findings is that in places they are unmodulated, especially as regards the extremely sensitive issues raised by religion and its values. I would prefer an international court to avoid terms borrowed from politico-ideological discourse, such as "Islamic fundamentalism" ... , "totalitarian movements" ... , "threat to the democratic regime" ... , etc., whose connotations, in the context of the present case, might be too forceful.

I also regret that the Court, in reproducing the Chamber's conclusions (paragraph 119 of the judgment), missed the opportunity to analyse in more detail the concept of a plurality of legal systems, which is linked to that of legal pluralism and is well-established in ancient and modern legal theory and practice ... . Not only legal anthropology but also modern constitutional law accepts that under certain conditions members of minorities of all kinds may have more than one type of personal status ... . Admittedly, this pluralism, which impinges mainly on an individual's private and family life, is limited by the requirements of the general interest. But it is of course more difficult in practice to find a compromise between the interests of the communities concerned and civil society as a whole than to reject the very idea of such a compromise from the outset.

This general remark also applies to the assessment to be made of sharia, the legal expression of a religion whose traditions go back more than a thousand years, and which has its fixed points of reference and its excesses, like any other complex system ... .

ADVISORY OPINION REQUESTED BY THE LITHUANIAN SUPREME ADMINISTRATIVE COURT
EUROPEAN COURT OF HUMAN RIGHTS, GRAND CHAMBER, REQUEST NO. P16-2020-002 (8 APRIL 2022)

[From 2009-2012, both Ms N.V. (at that time sitting as a regional court judge) and her brother were central figures in a high-profile child custody case that received extensive media coverage and online attention in Lithuania. This case involved claims by Ms N.V's brother, Drąsius Kedys, that his child had been trafficked by her mother to a paedophile ring which, he alleged, included a prominent Lithuanian politician and a judge. [454] While none of these allegations were ever accepted by Lithuanian courts, Kedys' claims of corruption and paedophilia generated substantial popular outrage against a political system perceived as corrupt, as well as support for Kedys himself. Attention on the case and the conspiracy theories surrounding it heightened over the next three years as each of the two individuals Kedys identified, as well as Kedys himself, were killed in mysterious circumstances.

Ms N.V., a vocal supporter of her brother's claims, was given temporary guardianship of his daughter following his death in 2010. After a court dismissed the allegations of abuse, however, Ms N.V. was later ordered to return her niece to the girl's mother. She refused to do so. In May 2012, police attended Ms. N.V.'s house in Garliava to carry out the court's order, but were obstructed by Ms. N.V. and crowds of supporters outside her house who attempted to prevent the removal of the child. [455]

The *Drąsos kelias* (Way of Courage) party grew out of this movement of popular support for Kedys, after whom it is named, and Ms N.V. The latter was elected to the Seimas in October 2012, thus acquiring immunity. In early 2013, the Seimas agreed to lift that immunity so that she could be prosecuted for criminal acts stemming from the Garliava protest. She immediately fled to the United States.

In June 2014, Ms N.V. was impeached in absentia for failing to perform her duties as a member of the Seimas and her mandate as a member of parliament revoked. She was arrested in the United States in February 2018 and extradited to Lithuania in November 2019 to face criminal prosecution.

In 2020, Ms N.V. asked to be registered as a candidate for the October 2020 Seimas elections, but was refused by the Electoral Commission (CEC) on the basis that her impeachment made her permanently ineligible for a parliamentary mandate under Article 2 § 5 of the Law on Elections to the Seimas. Ms. N.V. challenged this decision before Lithuania's Supreme Administrative Court. The Lithuanian court in turn requested an advisory opinion from the Court on the operation of Article 3 of Protocol No. 1 to the Convention, which relates to the right to free elections. This decision also had implications for Constitutional revisions proposed in order to execute an earlier judgment of the Grand Chamber of the Court in *Paksas v. Lithuania*. That case involved a former President of Lithuania, removed from office on 6 April 2004 following impeachment for gross violations of the Constitution. On 15 July 2004 the Seimas amended the Law on Elections to the effect that any official who had been removed from office in impeachment proceedings was permanently disqualified from being a member of parliament.

In a judgment of 6 January 2011 ..., the Court held that the permanent and irreversible nature of Mr Paksas' disqualification from holding parliamentary office was a disproportionate restriction and that therefore there had been a violation of Article 3 of Protocol No. 1.]

I. PRELIMINARY CONSIDERATIONS

---

[454] See 'Moral panic of the decade: former judge's extradition rekindles 10-year-old story', *Lithuanian National Radio and Television* (8 November 2019); S. Daniunaite, 'Extradition of judge Neringa Venckienė who alleges a paedophile ring in Lithuania', *Lithuania Tribune* (14 August 2019).
[455] *ibid.*

60. Under Article 1 § 1 of Protocol No. 16, designated highest courts or tribunals may request the Court to give advisory opinions on "questions of principle relating to the interpretation and application of the rights and freedoms defined in the Convention and the Protocol's thereto". ... [Such bodies] may do so "only in the context of a case pending before it".

61. ...[T]he aim of the advisory opinion procedure is to further enhance the interaction between the Court and national authorities and thereby reinforce the implementation of the Convention, in accordance with the principle of subsidiarity. The aim of the procedure is not to transfer the dispute to the Court, but rather to give the requesting court guidance on Convention issues when determining the case before it. The Court has no jurisdiction either to assess the facts of a case or to evaluate the merits of the parties' views on the interpretation of domestic law in the light of Convention law, or to rule on the outcome of the proceedings. Its role is limited to furnishing an opinion in relation to the questions submitted to it. It is for the requesting court or tribunal to resolve the issues raised by the case and to draw, as appropriate, the conclusions which flow from the opinion delivered by the Court for the provisions of national law invoked in the case and for the outcome of the case ... .

62. ...[Advisory opinions] must be confined to points that are directly connected to the proceedings pending at domestic level. Their value also lies in providing the national courts with guidance on questions of principle relating to the Convention that are applicable in similar cases ... .
...

II. THE QUESTIONS ASKED BY THE SUPREME ADMINISTRATIVE COURT
...
A. The second question asked by the Supreme Administrative Court

68. The Court considers that the Supreme Administrative Court is asking, in substance, which criteria are to be applied by a competent Lithuanian court in the assessment of whether, in the concrete circumstances of a given case, the ban preventing a former member of the Seimas who has been removed in impeachment proceedings from standing for election to the Seimas has become disproportionate with the consequence that it breaches Article 3 of Protocol No. 1.
...

2. Relevance of these principles to the facts relating to the present advisory opinion

90. The Court refers to its finding in *Paksas* according to which in assessing the proportionality of a general measure restricting the exercise of the rights guaranteed by Article 3 of Protocol No. 1, decisive weight should be attached to the existence of a time-limit and the possibility of reviewing the measure in question. The need for such a possibility is linked to the fact that the assessment of this issue must have regard to the historical and political context in the State concerned; since this context is capable of evolving, not least in terms of the perceptions which voters may have of the circumstances that led to the introduction of such a general restriction, the initial justification for the restriction may subside with the passing of time... .

91. The Court also observes that under Article 3 of Protocol No. 1 to the Convention, States have a wide margin of appreciation in regulating the right to stand for election. In particular, they enjoy considerable latitude to establish in their constitutional order rules governing the status of parliamentarians, and the criteria may vary according to the historical and political factors peculiar to each State ... . However, these rules should not be such as to exclude some persons or groups of persons from participating in the political life of a country and in the choice of the legislature ... . Moreover, even if legitimate considerations may provide justification for restrictions on the right to stand for election, such restrictions may become incompatible with Article 3 of Protocol No. 1 when applied long after the threat to democracy which had justified their earlier application has ceased to be relevant in light of the greater stability enjoyed by the country concerned, for example by reason of its full European integration ... . The Court has also recognised that, with the passage of time, general restrictions on electoral rights become more difficult to justify, thus requiring restrictive measures to be individualised ... . Thus, the margin of appreciation enjoyed by the States in this field is not unlimited, and it

remains for the Court to determine in the last resort whether the requirements of Article 3 of Protocol No. 1 have been met … .

92. It follows from this that the reference in *Paksas* … to the weight to be attached to the existence of a time-limit and the possibility of reviewing the ban in question is not necessarily to be understood as requiring these two elements to be combined. Nor does it specify whether the time-limit applicable in a given case should be set in the abstract or on a case-by-case basis. What matters in the end is for the ban in question to remain proportionate within the meaning of the *Paksas* judgment. This can be achieved by way of an appropriate legislative framework or judicial review of the duration, nature and extent of such a ban as applicable to the person concerned, performed on the basis of objective criteria and having regard to the particular circumstances of that person as they present themselves at the time of the review. The Court notes in this context that the findings in *Paksas* that a lifelong disqualification, on account of its permanent and irreversible nature, was a disproportionate restriction does not in itself imply that a decision to refuse to allow a person to stand for election, at the time of such a refusal, will necessarily amount to a disproportionate restriction. Whether that is the case will depend on an individual assessment of the refusal and the specific circumstances of the case based on objective criteria, including the individual's past and current behaviour.

…

94. …[T]urning to the criteria which are relevant in deciding [whether impeachment should justify a ban on running for office], in the Court's opinion they should be objective in nature and allow relevant circumstances connected not only with the events which led to the impeachment of the person concerned, but also – and primarily – with the functions sought to be exercised in the future by that person to be taken into account in a transparent way. This is because the purpose of the impeachment and the subsequent ban is not primarily to impose another sanction on the person concerned in addition to a criminal sanction which may already have been imposed, but to protect parliamentary institutions. The relevant criteria should therefore be identified mainly from the perspective of the requirements of the proper functioning of the institution of which that person seeks to become a member, and indeed of the constitutional system and democracy as a whole in the State concerned … .

95. This comes down to evaluating the objective impact which that person's potential membership of the institution concerned would have on the latter's functioning, having regard to such considerations as the past and current behaviour of the person who has been removed from office in impeachment proceedings and the nature of the wrongdoing which led to his or her impeachment, but also – and more importantly – the institutional and democratic stability of the institution concerned, the nature of the latter's duties and responsibilities, and the likelihood of the person in question having the potential to significantly disrupt the functioning of that institution, or indeed of democracy as a whole in the State concerned. Aspects such as that person's loyalty to the State, encompassing his or her respect for the country's Constitution, laws, institutions and independence, may also be relevant in this respect … . It is in the light of all those aspects that a determination should be made as to the appropriate and proportionate length of a ban precluding persons who have been removed from office in impeachment proceedings from being eligible for any function to which the ban applies.

96. Lastly, the procedure leading to such a determination in an individual case should be surrounded by sufficient safeguards designed to ensure respect for the rule of law and protection against arbitrariness. This will include the need for the procedure to be held before an independent body and for the person concerned to be heard by the latter and be provided with a reasoned decision … .

…

QUESTION

How does the jurisprudence of the ECtHR measure up against the view that Europe needs to be militant in defending its democracy? Consider the view of Gerald Neuman, in 'Impeachment, Disqualification, and Human Rights', 54 *Colum. Hum. Rts. L. Rev.* (2023) 627, at 671, that the ECtHR's approach 'seems to rest on excessive confidence in the ability of a threatened democracy to maintain the independence of a politically salient court or other adjudicatory body.'

c. Judicial Independence and the Rule of Law

A key battlefront in the fight against authoritarian, illiberal and populist governments is the independence of the judiciary. The range of such measures was outlined by Margaret Satterthwaite, UN Special Rapporteur on the independence of judges and lawyers (UN Doc. A/HRC/53/31 (2023)), at para. 19:

> [Concerns include] … new limits on courts' jurisdiction to review the legality of executive or parliamentary action or reforms to the nature or composition of courts – particularly high courts – that effectively diminish their independence and ability to remedy human rights violations. These may include politically strategic reductions in the size of the highest court, arbitrary removal of judges or reductions in their terms, or the subjection of judges to early retirement in a manner that politicizes their role. Alternatively, such situations may include the appointment or retention of judges seen as favourable to those in other branches of government through a politicized expansion of the size of the highest court, the arbitrary abolishment of a retirement age or extension of terms, or the irregular creation of extraordinary chambers. [Other problems arise when] the process or rules around selection and appointment are altered in a way that reduces the focus on potential judges' capability and integrity and increases the role of candidates' presumed or stated political affiliations. … Even seemingly neutral rules of judicial administration may be politicized and used as tools to discipline or reward judges for their decisions. …

The cases below examine responses by the ECtHR to situations in Turkey and Poland.

TURAN V. TURKEY
EUROPEAN COURT OF HUMAN RIGHTS, CHAMBER JUDGMENT, APPLICATION NO. 75805/16 AND 426 OTHERS (4 APRIL 2022)

[On 15-16 July 2016, members of the Turkish armed forces attempted to carry out a coup against the National Assembly, government and President of Turkey. In the aftermath, the Turkish government commenced criminal investigations into persons suspected of being members of or linked to the organization allegedly responsible for the coup (referred to as FETÖ/PDY). Many of these were members of the judiciary, thousands of whom were charged as members of an armed terrorist organisation in the weeks following the coup attempt.

The applicants were a group of 427 judges and prosecutors who had been arrested and detained on suspicion of associations with FETÖ/PDY. The government justified their arrest and detention in accordance with provisions of the ordinary law applicable to cases of discovery *in flagrante delicto*, and on the basis that the crime with which they were charged was a 'continuing offence'. The applicants countered that their detention breached special rules of procedure under domestic law which imposed specific requirements in relation to the arrest and pre-trial detention of members of the judiciary. On this basis, they asserted that their detention was in violation of Article 5 § 1 of the Convention, which requires that any deprivation of liberty be in accordance with a procedure prescribed by law.]

80. [The Court] reiterates …that where the "lawfulness" of detention is at issue, including the question whether "a procedure prescribed by law" has been followed, the Convention refers essentially to national law and lays down the obligation to conform to the substantive and procedural rules thereof. This primarily requires any arrest or detention to have a legal basis in domestic law. Compliance with national law is not, however, sufficient: Article 5 § 1 requires in addition that any deprivation of liberty should be in keeping with the purpose of protecting the individual from arbitrariness. The Court must further ascertain in this connection whether domestic law itself is in conformity with the Convention, including the general principles expressed or implied therein, notably the principle of legal certainty… .

…

82. The Court notes, moreover, that it has on many occasions emphasised the special role in society of the judiciary, which, as the guarantor of justice, a fundamental value in a State governed by the rule of law, must enjoy public confidence if it is to be successful in carrying out its duties … . … In particular, where domestic

law has granted judicial protection to members of the judiciary in order to safeguard the independent exercise of their functions, it is essential that such arrangements should be properly complied with. Given the prominent place that the judiciary occupies among State organs in a democratic society and the growing importance attached to the separation of powers and to the necessity of safeguarding the independence of the judiciary ... , the Court must be particularly attentive to the protection of members of the judiciary when reviewing the manner in which a detention order was implemented from the standpoint of the provisions of the Convention ... .

...

[The Court held that the pre-trial detention of the applicants was unlawful and constituted a violation of Article 5 § 1. However, it held by six votes to one that there was 'no need to examine the admissibility and merits of the applicants' remaining complaints under Article 5 of the Convention'. These included individual applicants' claims that they had been detained absent reasonable suspicion that they had committed an offence, that courts had not provided relevant and sufficient reasons for decisions, that their pre-trial detention had been excessively long, that reviews of their detention did not comply with procedural safeguards, and that they lacked effective domestic remedies to obtain compensation.]

...

98. ... Having regard to the significance and implications of [the Court's finding that the applicants' detention was not prescribed by law], which goes to the heart of the protection afforded under Article 5 and entails a violation of one of the core rights guaranteed by the Convention, and to the accumulation of thousands of similar applications on its docket concerning detentions in the aftermath of the attempted coup d'état in Turkey, which puts a considerable strain on its limited resources, the Court considers – as a matter of judicial policy – that it is justified in these compelling circumstances to dispense with the separate examination of the admissibility and merits of each remaining complaint raised by each individual applicant under Article 5. The Court also points out in this connection that an individualised examination of the remaining complaints brought by each applicant would significantly delay the processing of these cases, without a commensurate benefit to the applicants or contribution to the development of the case-law. It notes furthermore that it has already addressed the legal issues raised by these complaints for the most part ... . It is precisely within this exceptional context that the Court, guided by the overriding interest to ensure the long-term effectiveness of the Convention system, which is under threat by the constantly growing inflow of applications ..., decides not to examine the applicants' remaining complaints under Article 5.

CONCURRING OPINION OF JUDGE KOSKELO, JOINED BY JUDGE RANZONI

108. The present judgment is remarkable in an unusual and highly problematic sense. The Court concludes, in effect, that it is faced with a situation that renders it unable to fulfil its function, and this conclusion is reached, moreover, in the context of core aspects of core rights enshrined in Article 5 of the Convention. ...

109. I have voted in favour of this extraordinary outcome, reluctantly and with great misgivings. Why so?

110. It is well established that there are situations where complaints raised under different provisions of the Convention rely on a factual basis and on legal arguments which present similarities, to the extent that the Court may be justified in considering that, once a violation is found under one provision, it is not necessary to separately examine the issue from the standpoint of another provision also invoked by the applicant. The present joined cases, however, do not fall into that category of situations because, in this instance, the Court refrains from examining all other complaints raised under Article 5 apart from the issue of lawfulness. ...The issues raised under those complaints and the complaints based on the lack of lawfulness are not "overlapping". In fact they concern Convention safeguards which are distinct and fundamentally important.

...

116. The decision not to examine the applicants' other complaints raised under Article 5 of the Convention thus has a critically novel quality. I have nonetheless arrived at the conclusion that the time has come to acknowledge the reality as it presents itself: if alleged violations occur on a large scale and the rights concerned are no longer protected through domestic remedies, even the international supervision entrusted to the Court reaches its practical limits. ... In circumstances where it has become clear that the complaints cannot, and therefore will not, be processed within a reasonable time-frame, or without paralysing the Court's activity more generally, it is better to make this impasse transparent rather than maintain illusions about the situation. Any further conclusions remain for other bodies to consider.

PARTLY DISSENTING OPINION OF JUDGE KŪRIS

1. I voted against point 5 of the operative part of the judgment. At the same time, I agree with the outcome, because, hard as I try, I am unable to propose any pragmatic alternative to the majority's audacious decision to terminate the examination of the numerous applicants' complaints … . My disagreement thus concerns not the very outcome but the wording of operative point 5: had it been worded without using the formula "no need to examine", which it now contains, and had it thus corresponded to the reasoning intended to substantiate it (paragraph 98 of the judgment), I would have voted for it … . Regrettably, the formula "no need to examine" is certainly not adequate for the extraordinary situation in which the Court has found itself in the present case. That formula had to be avoided – and it could have been avoided at no cost. It is most unfortunate. It is faulty. It is misleading, because its employment in the operative part suggests that the respective complaints are not meritorious.

But they certainly are.

…

38. There is a risk that some may read this judgment … as a signal that a member State can escape responsibility for violating the Convention *en masse*, since the Court may be flooded with complaints against that State to such an extent that it becomes unable to cope with them and decides not to examine them.

To be frank: if a regime decides to go rogue, it should *do it in a big way*. And if responsibility can be escaped by "doing it big", why not give it a try?

GRZĘDA V. POLAND
EUROPEAN COURT OF HUMAN RIGHTS, GRAND CHAMBER, APPLICATION NO. 43572/18 (15 MARCH 2022)

[In 2017, Poland's government announced reforms that would in effect increase the power of the Minister for Justice to change the internal organization of the courts and to appoint and dismiss court presidents and vice-presidents.

The same year, the lower house of Parliament (Sejm) approved another amendment (the 2017 Amending Act) transferring the power to elect the National Council of the Judiciary (NCJ), the body tasked by the Constitution with safeguarding the independence of courts and judges as well as evaluating and nominating judges, to the lower house of Parliament controlled by the governing party. Following the passage of this law, Parliament terminated the appointment of all NCJ members appointed under earlier regulations.

While this case concerns the application of the 2017 Amending Act, it is also relevant to understand the broader context of legislative reforms introduced by the government which increased the executive's power over the courts. These included measures creating two new disciplinary and review chambers within the Supreme Court and enhancing the power of the Minister of Justice over judicial discipline, including the power to sanction judges who questioned the lawfulness of judicial appointments made by the new NCJ. Several disciplinary investigations were opened into judges who opposed the government's reforms.]

…

I. ALLEGED VIOLATION OF ARTICLE 6 § 1 OF THE CONVENTION

172. The applicant complained that he had been denied access to a court in order to contest the premature and allegedly arbitrary termination of his term of office as a judicial member of the NCJ. He had been elected as a member of this body for a four-year term… and had the right to remain in office for the duration of that term … . The applicant claimed that the premature termination of his term of office had violated the Constitution and breached the rule of law. He relied on Article 6 § 1 of the Convention, of which, the relevant part, reads as follows:

"In the determination of his civil rights and obligations … everyone is entitled to a fair … hearing … by an independent and impartial tribunal established by law."

…

A. Admissibility

…

[The Court considered the submissions of several third-party interveners in relation to questions of the rule of law and judicial independence, including Amnesty International and the International Commission of Jurists, the Polish Judges' Association Iustitia, the Commissioner for Human Rights of the Republic of Poland, and the UN Special Rapporteur on the Independence of Judges and Lawyers.]

…

(d) The Court's assessment

(i) General principles

…

261. As regards public servants employed in the civil service, according to the criteria established in *Vilho Eskelinen and Others* … the respondent State cannot rely before the Court on an applicant's status as a civil servant to exclude the protection embodied in Article 6 unless two conditions are fulfilled. First, the State in its national law must have expressly excluded access to a court for the post or category of staff in question. Secondly, the exclusion must be justified on objective grounds in the State's interest. In order for the exclusion to be justified, it is not enough for the State to establish that the civil servant in question participates in the exercise of public power or that there exists a special bond of trust and loyalty between the civil servant and the State, as employer. It is also for the respondent State to show that the subject matter of the dispute in issue is related to the exercise of State power or that it has called into question the special bond. Thus, there can in principle be no justification for the exclusion from the Article 6 guarantees of ordinary labour disputes, such as those relating to salaries, allowances or similar entitlements, on the basis of the special nature of the relationship between the particular civil servant and the State in question. There will, in effect, be a presumption that Article 6 applies. It will be for the respondent State to demonstrate, first, that a civil servant applicant does not have a right of access to a court under national law and, secondly, that the exclusion of the rights under Article 6 for the civil servant is justified … .

…

The second condition of the Eskelinen *test*

[The Court considered whether the exclusion of the applicant's access to a court was justified on objective grounds in the State's interest.]

…

298. … [T]he Preamble to the Convention … declares the rule of law to be part of the common heritage of the Contracting Parties … . The Committee of Ministers has also taken the view that judicial independence constitutes a fundamental aspect of the rule of law … .

299. The Court reiterates that, in order for national legislation excluding access to a court to have any effect under Article 6 § 1 in a particular case, it should be compatible with the rule of law. This concept, which is not only expressly mentioned in the Preamble but is also inherent in all the Articles of the Convention, requires, *inter alia*, that any interference must in principle be based on an instrument of general application … . Section 6 of the 2017 Amending Act cannot be regarded as such an instrument since it was directed at a specific group of fifteen clearly identifiable persons – judicial members of the NCJ elected under the previous regulation, including the applicant – and its primary purpose was to remove them from their seats on that body. It was a one-off statutory amendment that terminated *ex lege* the constitutionally prescribed tenure of the NCJ's judicial members. The Court has already held that laws which are directed against specific persons are contrary to the rule of law … .

300. … [T]he present case is closely related to judicial independence, since the dispute at issue concerns a judicial member of the NCJ … … …[I]ts very *raison d'être* and its task of safeguarding judicial independence require that the NCJ enjoy autonomy *vis-à-vis* the political branches of State power. The Court accepts the view of the third-party interveners that the removal, or threat of removal, of a judicial member of the Council during his or her term of office has the potential to affect the personal independence of that member in the exercise of his or her

NCJ duties ... . By extension, the Council's mission to safeguard judicial independence may also be adversely affected, and this would raise a number of rule-of-law issues, including those pertaining to the safeguarding of rights enshrined in and protected by the Convention.

301. ... First, all Contracting Parties to the Convention have explicit, formal guarantees of judicial independence in their laws, whether of constitutional or of statutory rank. Second, judicial independence is a *sine qua non* for the right to a fair hearing under Article 6 of the Convention. Third, judicial independence is operationalised in the persons who are vested with judicial power.

302. ... [T]he Court has ... emphasised the special role in society of the judiciary which, as the guarantor of justice, a fundamental value in a State governed by the rule of law, must enjoy public confidence if judges are to be successful in carrying out their duties ... . Given the prominent place that the judiciary occupies among State organs in a democratic society and the importance attached to the separation of powers and to the necessity of safeguarding the independence of the judiciary ..., the Court must be particularly attentive to the protection of members of the judiciary against measures that can threaten their judicial independence and autonomy ... .

303. Given the role played by judicial councils, the same considerations should apply as regards the tenure of judges, such as the applicant in the present case, who are elected to serve on them because of their status and in view of the need to safeguard judicial independence, which is a prerequisite to the rule of law. ...

304. As regards the regulation of the NCJ under domestic law, the Court notes that this body is constitutionally mandated to safeguard the independence of the courts and judges (Article 186 § 1 of the Constitution). In the Court's view, the effective exercise of this essential role is only possible when the council in question is sufficiently independent from the executive and legislative powers.
...
306. One of the key manifestations of the NCJ's role of safeguarding judicial independence is its exclusive competence to propose candidates for appointment at every level of the judiciary and to every type of court. To make it perfectly clear, this covers both initial appointments to judicial office, and every promotion to a higher level of the judiciary. Formally, the President of the Republic appoints judges, but he may only do so on the basis of proposals submitted by the NCJ ... .

307. While there exists a widespread practice, endorsed by the Council of Europe, to put in place a judicial council as a body responsible for the selection of judges, the Convention does not contain any explicit requirement to this effect. In the Court's view, whatever system is chosen by member States, they must abide by their obligation to secure judicial independence. Consequently, where a judicial council is established, the Court considers that the State's authorities should be under an obligation to ensure its independence from the executive and legislative powers in order to, inter alia, safeguard the integrity of the judicial appointment process.
...

308. The Court has held that "independence" refers to the necessary personal and institutional independence that is required for impartial decision-making, and it is thus a prerequisite for impartiality. It characterises both (i) a state of mind, which denotes a judge's imperviousness to external pressure as a matter of moral integrity and (ii) a set of institutional and operational arrangements – involving both a procedure by which judges can be appointed in a manner that ensures their independence and selection criteria based on merit – which must provide safeguards against undue influence and/or unfettered discretion of the other State powers, both at the initial stage of the appointment of a judge and during the exercise of his or her duties ... . The Court has also discerned a common thread running through the institutional requirements of Article 6 § 1, in that they are guided by the aim of upholding the fundamental principles of the rule of law and the separation of powers ...
.

309. ... [T]here exists a clear link between the integrity of the judicial appointment process and the requirement of judicial independence in Article 6 § 1 ... .
...
322. ... [T]he Court finds that the fundamental change in the manner of electing the NCJ's judicial members, considered jointly with the early termination of the terms of office of the previous judicial members ..., means

that its independence is no longer guaranteed ... . [T]he NCJ's independence was determined precisely by the rule that its judicial members were elected by judges for a constitutionally prescribed term of office.

323. ... [T]he Convention does not prevent States from taking legitimate and necessary decisions to reform the judiciary .... However, any reform of the judicial system should not result in undermining the independence of the judiciary and its governing bodies. ...

...

325. ... [T]he Court concludes that the second condition of the Eskelinen test, namely that the applicant's exclusion from access to a court be justified on objective grounds in the State's interest, has not been met.

...

327. Members of the judiciary should enjoy – as do other citizens – protection from arbitrariness on the part of the legislative and executive powers, and only oversight by an independent judicial body of the legality of a measure such as removal from office is able to render such protection effective ... .

...

B. Merits

...

4. The Court's assessment

...

(c.) Application of the general principles to the present case

...

348. The Court notes that the whole sequence of events in Poland ... vividly demonstrates that successive judicial reforms were aimed at weakening judicial independence, starting with the grave irregularities in the election of judges of the Constitutional Court in December 2015, then, in particular, remodelling the NCJ and setting up new chambers in the Supreme Court, while extending the Minister of Justice's control over the courts and increasing his role in matters of judicial discipline. ... . As a result of the successive reforms, the judiciary – an autonomous branch of State power – has been exposed to interference by the executive and legislative powers and thus substantially weakened. The applicant's case is one exemplification of this general trend.

349. Having regard to the foregoing, the Court finds that on account of the lack of judicial review in this case the respondent State impaired the very essence of the applicant's right of access to a court ... .

...

* * *

The program of judicial reforms introduced by Poland's governing Law and Justice Party between 2015 and 2022 was the subject of public protests, as well as a number of challenges in the Polish and European courts. In 2021, the European Commission found that the new disciplinary regime imposed on judges undermined the independence of the judiciary and 'was incompatible with the primacy of EU law'.[456] The Court of Justice of the European Union granted interim measures, requiring Poland to suspend the new disciplinary regime or pay penalties of 1,000,000 euros per day.

The Polish government, however, resisted pressure from Europe to reverse course. Following the interim measures decision, the Minister of Justice applied to Poland's reconstituted Constitutional Court (an institution whose independence from the ruling party was questionable) for holdings that Article 6 § 1 of the Convention was unconstitutional under Polish law. In February 2023, the government informed the European Court of Human Rights that it would not comply with the orders to reinstate judges who opposed its reforms.[457] But in December 2023, following elections, the new Polish Government began the process of dismantling the measures previously adopted and seeking to restore the independence of the judiciary.

For details about the European Union's response to the situation in Poland before the change of government, see Ch. 11A 7, below.

---

[456] *Grzęda v. Poland* (App. No. 43572/18), Judgment (15 March 2022), para. 25.
[457] A. Ptak, 'Poland informs European court it will not comply with order to reinstate judges', *Notes from Poland*, (17 February 2023).

6. Evaluating the System

Despite the effectiveness of the various waves of reform, the Court inevitably faces considerable pressure to change its approach in a variety of ways. Many observers see the problems as flowing primarily from the great success of the system and see the solutions consisting largely of administrative reforms and enhanced political will. Others identify deeper political problems because various states feel that the system has become too intrusive and that it is starting to 'bite' in ways that they are not willing to accept. In some states, there has been a populist dimension to this resentment at being 'dictated to by Strasbourg'; in others the problem may lie with the self-proclaimed illiberal character of some of the governments.

The following excerpts reflect on the ways in which the Court has responded to these various pressures. Laurence Helfer and Erik Voeten, in 'Walking Back Human Rights in Europe?', 31 *Eur. J. Int'l L.* (2020) 797 discern caution and even regression in some of the Court's pronouncements. They analyse all separate opinions attached to Grand Chamber judgments between 1999 and 2018 and identify the 'walking back dissents', or those that assert that the Grand Chamber has overturned prior rulings or settled doctrine in a way that favours the respondent government.

> … Beginning in the mid-2000s … the member states, especially the established democracies that have long been the ECtHR's staunch supporters, began to impose new restrictions on disfavoured groups, especially immigrants, criminal defendants and suspected terrorists. They also publicly criticized the Court for expanding rights and freedoms too far and for giving insufficient deference to governments. First hesitantly and then more frequently after 2012, the Grand Chamber started to narrow its interpretation of the Convention, especially in cases against consolidated democracies.

> What the ECtHR has not done – at least not explicitly – is overturn its prior case law in a rights-restrictive direction. … Instead, the Grand Chamber may be achieving the same result indirectly by purporting to reconcile earlier rights-protective rulings with later decisions that are more favourable to respondent states. …

> The rise of what we label as 'walking back dissents' reveals that some members of the ECtHR themselves believe that the Grand Chamber is overturning prior judgments in a regressive direction. It also suggests that the Court is, in fact, constricting human rights in Europe. We show that walking back dissents have increased in both absolute and percentage terms over the last two decades, with the sharpest uptick following the 2012 Brighton Declaration. We also find that such dissents are especially common in cases

against established democracies, and in cases – often brought by prisoners, immigrants and suspected terrorists – whose Convention protections have provoked significant backlash against the Court.

... [T]wo plausible explanations ... [are, first], the Grand Chamber may be responding to political signals from the member states ... . Second, the ECtHR may be tacitly taking account of the growing number of member states that have restricted the rights of certain disfavoured individuals and minority groups, in effect applying the living instrument and European consensus doctrines in reverse. ... [Another possible factor might be] the appointment of judges who favour more restrained interpretations of human rights. ...

...

... Grand Chamber judgments that walk back human rights, even tacitly, are normatively and jurisprudentially fraught. Most obviously, such rulings have immediate adverse effects for the thousands of vulnerable individuals who seek legal redress from the Court. But the rulings also have consequences beyond the litigants. When the ECtHR expounds the meaning of a particular right or freedom, its interpretation has ripple effects across the [then] 47 member states, all of which have incorporated the Convention into domestic law, and across national judiciaries, many of whose members give significant weight to ECtHR rulings when interpreting rights or freedoms in their respective constitutions. Pro-government rulings that disappoint these actors risk undermining the Court's influence and its legitimacy.

At the same time, the ECtHR depends upon the political, institutional and financial backing of the member states, especially established democracies. When that support wanes, it is ... perilous for the ECtHR to 'double down' on a strategy of expanding rights and freedoms. ... [It is] not unreasonable for Strasbourg judges to consider the criticisms expressed by governments and to take account of regressive trends in national laws and policies.

...

On the one hand, tacit overturning has real costs. It undermines the consistency and predictability of ECtHR case law and risks inconsistent treatment of similarly situated litigants. It also generates separate opinions that expose normative fractures among the judges over foundational principles. ...

Yet tacit overturning may also have advantages. Studies of national and international courts have found that judges issue vague or ambiguous rulings when faced with political uncertainty. Vagueness can 'provide state officials with a measure of discretion ...'. ...

In the ECtHR context, ambiguity may reduce compliance pressures on all member states.
...

Alec Stone Sweet, Wayne Sandholtz, and Mads Andenas, in 'The Failure to Destroy the Authority of the European Court of Human Rights: 2010–2018', 21 *L. & Prac. Int'l Cts. & Trib.* (2022) 244, push back against the thesis of Helfer and Voeten:[458]

The [ECtHR] is the most active and influential human rights court in the world. Since the 1990s, it has received, annually, more individual applications, produced more rulings on the merits, and is cited more often than any other court in the world. High courts as diverse as the Canadian Supreme Court, the Hong Kong Court of Final Appeal, and the Colombian and South African Constitutional Courts routinely consider the jurisprudence of the ECtHR, when they adjudicate domestic charters of rights. The Inter-American

---

[458] The debate, which largely concerns competing methodological approaches, is developed in A. Stone Sweet, W. Sandholtz and M. Andenas, 'Dissenting Opinions and Rights Protection in the European Court: A Reply to Laurence Helfer and Erik Voeten', 32 *Eur. J. Int'l L.* (2021) 897; followed by a rejoinder by Helfer and Voeten, at 32 *Eur. J. Int'l L.* (2021) 907.

Court of Human Rights and the various African regional courts virtually never issue an important judgment without consulting the relevant rulings of the European Court. Indeed, the case law of the ECtHR is today a focal point for inter-judicial coordination within a rights-based commons of global scope and significance.

The prominence of the Strasbourg Court rests on its jurisprudence, which features a steadfast commitment to maximizing the effectiveness of the European Convention on Human Rights (ECHR) within national legal orders. Its success ultimately depends on the willingness of national judges to enforce the Convention which is, in turn, contingent upon the tolerance of legislative and executive officials of highly intrusive modes of judicial scrutiny. ...

...

Between 2010 and 2018, the Member States of the Council of Europe staged a series of extraordinary "High Level Conferences", the purpose of which was to evaluate the Court's performance and potential reforms. The agenda was dominated by two issues: (i) how to deal with a chronically overloaded docket ...; and (ii) whether to dismantle the components of judicial supremacy that had been established though the ECtHR's precedents. The latter question had been placed on the agenda by those seeking to force or persuade the Court to soften review and to grant more deference to the policy preferences of governments. ...

... Helfer and Voeten concede that the High Level Conferences did not induce the ECtHR to roll back protections explicitly; they nonetheless accuse the Court of having done so surreptitiously, betraying its own doctrinal commitments while lying about it. We reject these claims. ...

...

7 Conclusion.

There are several clear reasons for the failure of States and reformers to curb the powers of the Court. First, the decision-rules governing treaty revision (consensus-based unanimity) are protective of the Court and its authority. Second, only a small minority of States were committed to rolling back the ECtHR's progressive jurisprudence. A majority of States recognized and supported the Court's achievements, which include helping to maintain peace in Europe, bolstering transitions to rights-based democracy, operating a system of monitoring and enforcement of human rights, and raising standards of protection. Third, States proved willing to pay the tax for these collective goods, which entails tolerating enhanced supervision of their own rights-regarding activities. Of course, they may well protest judgments finding violations in sensitive policy areas, and high court judges will be unhappy with rulings they would not have produced on their own. For its part, the ECtHR has noted and responded to these reactions, while maintaining its core commitments.

...

Although the Court has been beset by regular political "crises" well before the High Level Conferences, the latter provided fora in which some Member States could express their dissatisfactions with the regime. British governments at times even threatened to abolish the 1999 Human Rights Act and to withdraw from the Court. Still, the efforts of the United Kingdom at Brighton, and of Denmark at Copenhagen, failed. In the end, the interpretation and application of subsidiarity and margin of appreciation remain in the hands of the Court.

A former Judge on the Court, Paul Lemmens, in 'The European Court of Human Rights—Can There Be Too Much Success?', 14 *J. Hum. Rts. Prac.* (2022) 169, explains the judicial techniques the Court has used in response to the various criticisms:

> ... Faced with accusations of activism and challenges to its legitimacy, the Court has opted for a course of action in line with its subsidiary role within the Convention system. ... [T]he Court has entered a new phase, which can be defined as the 'age of subsidiarity'. It is not a completely new age, but to some extent a return to the roots of the Convention system. What is new ... is the emphasis on what is called a 'process-based' review. This starts with a review of the procedural guarantees offered to the parties in administrative and judicial proceedings. ... The Court holds that the decision-making process leading to measures of interference with the rights of a given individual must be fair and such as to afford due respect to the interests safeguarded to the individual by the Convention. ...

> However, the process-based review, as it operates nowadays ... [is] related to the substance of the decision taken at the domestic level. ... [T]he domestic authorities must strike a fair balance between the rights of the individual and the general interests pursued by the public authorities. Such balancing is a matter for which the authorities enjoy a 'margin of appreciation' ... . It is not for the Court to decide what is the best policy in a given field. What counts is that, whatever policy choice is made, a 'fair' balance is struck.

> ...

> ...[A]n unsatisfactory balancing exercise will lead to the conclusion that the end result is disproportionate and constitutes a (substantive) violation of the applicant's rights.

> [Where there has been] a satisfactory balancing exercise ... the Court regularly states that it would require 'strong reasons' to substitute its own view for that of the national authorities. ...

> ... [T]he process-based review, characterized by the fact that the Court respects to a considerable degree the balancing exercise appropriately undertaken by the national authorities, is an answer to the criticism that it received from a number of governments and that culminated in the Brighton Declaration. Does this answer mean that the level of human rights protection is lowered? ...

> Looking only at what the Court does in the cases brought before it, is missing the complete picture. The general idea behind the Court's approach is to strengthen the 'shared responsibility' between national authorities and itself. ... The more the national authorities display 'due diligence' in the application of the Convention principles, the more deference the Court will show to them; conversely, the more defective the national process is, the more interventionist the Court will be. ...

> *4. Outlook and prospects*

> ...

> In order to remain relevant, [the Court] will have to enjoy the confidence not only of a large majority of the States parties to the Convention, but also of the citizens of Europe. This means that it must drive and not look back, allow for a margin of appreciation but at the same time insist on respect for the principles of the Convention, act vigorously (and in a timely manner) where governments ignore the Convention and go against its basic principles, and pay special attention to the rights of the most vulnerable and powerless persons.

Responding to Lemmens, Stefanie Schmahl, in 'The European Court of Human Rights—Can There Be Too Much Success? A Comment', 14 *J. Hum. Rts. Prac.* (2022) 191 emphasizes the importance of judicial self-restraint, the subsidiarity principle and the margin of appreciation, all of which have important implications for the Court's role:

> By transferring the interpretation of the [ECHR] to an independent international authority, States relinquish part of their power. They will only accept this transfer of power permanently if the judicial interpretation by the Strasbourg Court remains consistent, comprehensible and plausible. The Court should therefore not act as a human rights' 'trendsetter' or a 'judicial activist'. In the vast majority of cases, the Court has respected this barrier. ... The common ground has to be legally based on the overwhelming agreement of the Contracting States and not on international or European soft law instruments, as convincing in substance as they might be. Human rights are not an 'optimization programme' for which there are no limits, since this would transgress the regulatory function of the law and the limit of law-making, which is first and foremost entrusted to the democratically legitimized legislator.

> *4. Conclusion*

> Overall, three principles are decisive[:]the judicial self-restraint of the Court, the subsidiarity principle and a margin of appreciation ... If the Court ventures too far beyond the wording of the treaty, it risks that its judgments will not be implemented in the national legal orders ... .

7. The Broader European Institutional Context

a. The European Union

The origins of the European Union lie in the Treaty of Paris of 1952 establishing the European Coal and Steel Community (ECSC) and subsequently in the two Treaties of Rome of 1957 creating the European Economic Community (EEC) and the European Atomic Energy Community. Upon the entry into force in 1993 of the Treaty on Economic Union these communities became the European Union, and the Treaty of Paris expired in 2002. From six founding members in 1957 the EU had 27 in 2023, following the exit of the United Kingdom in 2020.

The impetus for the first step of creating the ECSC came essentially from a desire to ensure that the heavy industries of the Ruhr, which had underpinned Germany's military might in two World Wars, would be 'contained' within an intergovernmental structure bringing together West Germany and its former antagonists. The expansion into an EEC in 1957 was an attempt to promote closer economic integration within Europe for both federalist and economic reasons. While the adoption of a bill of rights based on the ECHR had been proposed in the early 1950s, none of the subsequent treaties contained such a bill or a list of enumerated rights. The 1957 treaties were more concerned with the freedom of the marketplace than the rights of individuals. The latter were seen to be appropriately protected at the national level.

The Court of Justice of the European Union (CJEU), which is the judicial organ of the EU, was known as the European Court of Justice (ECJ) until 2009. In the absence of a bill of rights, the Court began in 1969 to evolve a specific doctrine of human rights, the original motivation for which probably owed more to a desire to protect the primacy of EC law over national law than to any concern to provide extended protection to individuals. Over the years during which the human rights doctrine has evolved, the Court has identified several different normative underpinnings for 'the general principles of EC law' of which human rights (referred to by the European Court of Justice as 'fundamental rights') were one category. These normative underpinnings include certain provisions of the Treaty of Rome, the constitutional traditions of the member states, and international treaties accepted by member states. The European Court of Justice has applied this concept of human rights to the actions of the Community itself, and, with certain qualifications, to the actions of the member states.[459] The

---

[459] See P. Alston, M. Bustelo, & J. Heenan (eds.), *The EU and Human Rights* (1999).

Court's jurisprudence was subsequently reflected in the Treaty on European Union (TEU or 'Lisbon Treaty'), which entered into force in 2009. Relevant provisions include:

Article 2

The Union is founded on the values of respect for human dignity, freedom, democracy, equality, the rule of law and respect for human rights, including the rights of persons belonging to minorities. These values are common to the Member States in a society in which pluralism, non-discrimination, tolerance, justice, solidarity and equality between women and men prevail.

Article 3

...

5. In its relations with the wider world, the Union shall uphold and promote its values and interests and contribute to the protection of its citizens. It shall contribute to ... the protection of human rights, in particular the rights of the child, as well as to the strict observance and the development of international law, including respect for the principles of the United Nations Charter.

Article 6

...

2. The Union shall accede to the [ECHR]. Such accession shall not affect the Union's competences as defined in the Treaties.

3. Fundamental rights, as guaranteed by the [ECHR] and as they result from the constitutional traditions common to the Member States, shall constitute general principles of the Union's law.

The resulting state of the law has been summarized thus:

ii. There are three formal sources for EU human rights law listed in Article 6 TEU. [They are: the EU Charter of Fundamental Rights; the ECHR; and 'general principles of EU law'.] ... These three sources overlap, creating some legal confusion, and other sources of international human rights law have occasionally been invoked by the ECJ.

iii. The CJEU has made it clear in recent years that the Charter is now the principal basis on which the EU Courts will ensure that human rights are observed, and the proportion of cases in which the CJEU has drawn on ECHR case law has declined since the coming into force of the Charter.

iv. Article 6(2) TEU declares that the EU shall accede to the ECHR. ... However, the CJEU dealt a surprising blow to the prospects for EU accession when it ruled in 2014 that the long-negotiated draft Agreement on Accession of the EU to the ECHR was incompatible with the EU Treaties and with the autonomy of the EU legal order in several fundamental ways.

v. EU human rights standards ... are binding on the EU and its institutions and bodies in all of their activities, and on the Member States when they act within the scope of EU law ... .[460]

The TEU also provides (Art. 7) for the suspension of certain EU membership rights if 'a serious and persistent breach' of human rights is deemed to exist within a member state. But the EU has been reluctant even to take

---

[460] P. Craig and G. de Búrca, *EU Law: Text, Cases, and Materials* (7th ed., 2020), 430.

such measures, as demonstrated in the cases of Poland and Hungary. Gráinne de Búrca, in 'Poland and Hungary's EU Membership: On Not Confronting Authoritarian Governments', 20 *Int'l J. Con. L.* (2022) 13, notes that reports by the Venice Commission, the EU Commission, and judgments of the Court of Justice of the EU, *inter alia*, confirm that Poland and Hungary have undermined the EU's basic values by:

(i) Poland and Hungary subjecting the courts to political control …;

(ii) establishing government-approved disciplinary procedures … and using these to discipline or terminate the appointment of judges who question aspects of the government's agenda …;

(iii) repressing and de-funding civil society groups who challenge or question aspects of governmental policy …;

(iv) exercising increasing control over media freedom and dismantling media pluralism …;

(v) smearing and harassing critics, including through civil and criminal defamation actions, and repressing freedom of expression …;

(vi) repression of particular disfavored groups and minorities, including LGBTQ+ communities …, targeting asylum seekers …;

(vii) using the apparatus of law and order, and in particular the public prosecution offices, in a highly selective way to protect ruling elites; refusing to investigate prominent cases of corruption and illegality, and using the police and powers of prosecution to discipline and harass political opponents …;

…

Nevertheless, Craig and de Búrca note that both states retain full EU membership, with all their rights and privileges intact. Because of a 'notable *political* unwillingness to confront Poland or Hungary in a robust way', there has been 'little by way of response from the Council of Ministers, the European Union's main intergovernmental institution.' In response to the question of why there has been such reticence, she suggests: (i) the typical reluctance of states within international organizations to sanction one another; (ii) institutions of democracy or the rule of law have been weakened or undermined in other member states in recent times; (iii) a belief that 'tough confrontation … will not help to resolve the problem of growing authoritarianism'; (iv) the shadow of Brexit; and (v) a 'fear of driving states like Hungary closer towards actors like Russia, creating further geopolitical instability'.

> The gamble that EU member states are taking in failing to confront Hungary and Poland is that the nature of the European Union itself will gradually change, both with the breakdown of mutual trust and mutual recognition on which the internal market and the area of judicial cooperation depends, and with the spread of authoritarianism both within the EU institutions and in other member states. Even the values themselves—the meanings given to democracy, the rule of law, and human rights within EU law and policy—are constantly weakened and eroded by the toleration of and the failure to challenge authoritarian practices. The temptation to stand back and let things unfold.

b. The Venice Commission

The European Commission for Democracy through Law, known as the 'Venice Commission' was established in 1990 under an agreement among 18 Council of Europe member states. It has since become a major player in offering analysis and advice on a wide range of issues. Its 2002 Statute provides that it is 'an independent consultative body', designed to promote the rule of law and democracy. Its prime function, described in its *Annual Report of Activities 2022* (2023) 7, is to provide constitutional assistance to member states, mainly in the form of Opinions. At the request of a constitutional court or the ECtHR, it may also provide amicus curiae briefs on comparative constitutional and international law issues.

c. The Organization for Security and Co-operation in Europe (OSCE)

The Conference on Security and Co-operation in Europe (CSCE) opened in 1973 and concluded in August 1975 with the signing of the Final Act of Helsinki (known as the Helsinki Accord) by the 35 participating states (including all European states except Albania, plus Canada and the United States). The Soviet Union sought formal recognition of its European frontiers, while the West sought concessions primarily in relation to security matters. Human rights were of only secondary concern. In 1995 the CSCE became the OSCE, and by 2023 it had 57 member states.

In 2011, the OSCE had over 2,800 staff and an annual budget of 151 million euros. In 2022, the staff was down to 152 and the budget was 23 million euros.[461] Its principal institutions are its Secretariat in Vienna, the Office for Democratic Institutions and Human Rights (ODIHR) based in Warsaw, a Representative on Freedom of the Media based in Vienna, and a High Commissioner on National Minorities based in The Hague. The OSCE has been especially active in electoral observation.[462]

8. Other Human Rights Conventions Adopted by the Council of Europe

a. The European Social Charter[463]

Although economic and social rights were reflected in the post-Second World War constitutions of France, Germany, and Italy, they were not included in the European Convention. One of the key drafters, Pierre-Henri Teitgen, explained this decision in 1949 on the grounds that it was first necessary 'to guarantee political democracy in the European Union and then to co-ordinate our economies, before undertaking the generalisation of social democracy.' These rights were subsequently recognized in the European Social Charter of 1961.

The core ESC system consists of the original Charter of 1961 and a revised Charter of 1996. As of 2023, 42 of the 46 Council of Europe member states have ratified one or the other treaty (the exceptions are Liechtenstein, Monaco, San Marino and Switzerland). Only 16 states have accepted the collective complaints procedure.

The Charter and its Additional Protocol of 1988 guarantee a series of 'rights and principles' with respect to employment conditions and 'social cohesion'. The former relate to non-discrimination, prohibition of forced labour, trade union rights, decent working conditions, equal pay for equal work, prohibition of child labour, and maternity protection. Among the latter are: health protection; social security; and certain rights for children, families, migrant workers, and the elderly. These rights are not legally binding *per se*. The legal obligations designed to ensure their effective exercise are contained in Part II, which details the specific measures to be taken in relation to each of the rights. Part III reflects the principle of progressive implementation tailored to suit the circumstances of individual states. Each contracting party must agree to be bound by at least five of seven rights which are considered to be of central importance. It must also accept at least five of the other rights as listed in Part II.

Part IV provides for a monitoring system based on the submission of regular reports by contracting parties. The reports are examined by the European Committee of Social Rights, whose 15 independent expert members hold seven sessions per year of one week each. Its assessments of compliance and non-compliance are then considered by the Parliamentary Assembly and a Governmental Committee. Finally, on the basis of all these views, the Committee of Ministers may make specific recommendations to the state concerned. The Additional Protocol providing for collective complaints entered into force in July 1998. By December 2022, a total of 223

---

[461] OSCE, *Democracy and Human Rights in the OSCE: Office for Democratic Institutions and Human Rights, Annual Report* (2023) 7.

[462] OSCE, *Handbook on Observing the Work of Election Management Bodies* (2023).

[463] See S. Angeleri and C. Nivard, *The European Social Charter: A Commentary* (2022); and K. Lukas, *The Revised European Social Charter: An Article by Article Commentary* (2021). The European Union also plays an important role in relation to social rights: S. Garben, 'The European Pillar of Social Rights: An Assessment of its Meaning and Significance', 21 *Camb. Y.B. Eur. Leg. Stud.* (2019) 101.

complaints against 16 different countries had been registered (57 concerned France, 39 Italy, and 23 Greece). 17 complaints were registered in 2022. A comprehensive overview is provided in the Council of Europe's *Digest of the Case Law of the European Committee of Social Rights* (2022).[464]

b. The European Convention for the Prevention of Torture

In 1987, the Council of Europe adopted the European Convention for the Prevention of Torture and Inhuman or Degrading Treatment or Punishment (ECPT) which emphasizes prevention. It has been ratified by all 46 states. The ECPT can include states that are non-members of the Council of Europe: following Russia's departure from the Council, notably, it continued to be a party to the Convention.

The Convention establishes a Committee for the Prevention of Torture (CPT) which is composed of 46 independent experts. Its function is 'to examine the treatment of persons deprived of their liberty with a view to strengthening, if necessary, the protection of such persons' from torture, inhuman or degrading treatment (Art. 1). The Convention is not concerned solely with prisoners but with any 'persons deprived of their liberty by a public authority'. Each state party is required to permit the Committee to visit any such place within the state's jurisdiction (Art. 2), unless there are exceptional circumstances (which will rarely be the case). Most visits are routine and scheduled well in advance, but there is also provision for ad hoc visits with little advance notice (Art. 7).

The Committee undertakes some 15-18 visits per year, ranging in length from a few days to two weeks.[465] In 2022 there were seven periodic and nine ad hoc visits, totalling 140 days. It meets *in camera* and its visits and discussions are confidential; as, in principle, are its reports. The latter, however, may be released, either at the request of the state concerned or if a state refuses to cooperate and the Committee decides by a two-thirds majority to make a public statement. Most reports are released. An indication of the scope of its mandate is provided by this description of issues to which particular attention was paid in 2022 *(32nd General Report of the CPT* (2023) 7):

> … persons detained by the police, to patients and residents held in psychiatric establishments and social care homes (Croatia), patients in psychiatric wards of civil hospitals and non-autonomous elderly persons accommodated in nursing homes (Italy), life-sentenced prisoners (Latvia), persons detained over terrorist offences and those deprived of their liberty under immigration legislation (Netherlands), foreign nationals detained in Border Guard establishments, remand prisoners, and forensic psychiatric patients (Poland), women held in prisons, persons held on remand and patients held in psychiatric or forensic establishments (Portugal), persons undergoing "compulsory health treatment" (involuntary psychiatric hospitalisation) and residents in a home for the elderly (San Marino).

c. Framework Convention for the Protection of National Minorities

Despite the importance of national minorities within Europe and discussions about appropriate measures since 1949, the issue proved too controversial and complex for the Council of Europe to adopt specific standards until 1994, when the Framework Convention was adopted. In part, the impetus was the adoption of the 1992 UN Declaration on Rights of Persons Belonging to Minorities, and the development of non-binding standards and promotional activities in this field by the CSCE. The Council sought to avoid longstanding controversies by, among other things, confining the Convention to programmatic obligations that are not directly applicable and that leave considerable discretion about implementation to the state concerned. International supervision is undertaken by the Committee of Ministers of the Council based upon periodic reports to be submitted by states parties. The Convention entered into force in February 1998 and as of 2024 had been ratified by 39 states.

---

[464] C. O'Cinneide, 'The European System(s) of Social Rights Protection', in J. Dugard et al. (eds.), *Research Handbook on Economic, Social and Cultural Rights as Human Rights* (2020) 48; and K. Lukas and C. O'Cinnéide, 'Gender Equality within the Framework of the European Social Charter' in R. Cook (ed.), *Frontiers of Gender Equality: Transnational Legal Perspectives* (2023) 219.

[465] See generally: C. Bicknell, M. Evans and R. Morgan, *Preventing Torture in Europe* (2018).

The Convention does not define a 'national minority', leaving each state to define which groups are covered. But the state's definition is required to be non-discriminatory, made in good faith, and consistent with general principles of international law. It applies the principle of 'free self-identification', according to which individuals have the right to decide for themselves whether they wish to be treated as belonging to a national minority, as long as that decision is based on objective criteria connected with their identity, such as their religion, language, traditions and cultural heritage.[466]

B. THE INTER-AMERICAN SYSTEM

The Inter-American human rights system consists of the Inter-American Commission on Human Rights (IACHR) and the Inter-American Court of Human Rights (IACtHR). They apply the standards contained in the originally non-binding American Declaration on the Rights and Duties of Man (1948) and the American Convention on Human Rights (1969). The relationship between the Declaration and the Convention is broadly comparable to that between the UDHR and the two International Covenants. Similarly, many of the techniques that are used by the Commission and Court will be familiar from our study of the UN and ECHR systems. By the same token, the Inter-American system is distinctive in many ways.

1. Background and Institutions

During the first half of the twentieth century, Latin American states took important initiatives designed to protect the rights of women, workers, and indigenous peoples. These initiatives were developed in parallel with an emphasis on the principles of non-intervention and the equality of states. The latter preoccupations came in response to persistent interventions over the years by the United States, often under the pretext of providing diplomatic protection for its nationals. In 1944 the Inter-American Juridical Committee prepared a draft declaration of rights, an initiative that was viewed both as a means to promote international protection and to eliminate the pretexts for U.S. intervention.

a. History of the Organization of American States

In May 1948 the ninth Inter-American Conference, held in Bogotá, established the Organization of American States (OAS). Its predecessor organizations date back to the International Union of American Republics of 1890. The 1948 Charter entered into force in 1951 and has been amended several times since. The United States saw the organization as a bulwark against communism, while Latin American states had more complex reasons for supporting it.

Article 2 of the Charter declares the purposes of the Organization to be:

> to strengthen the peace and security of the continent; to promote and consolidate representative democracy, with due respect for the principle of nonintervention; to prevent possible causes of difficulties and to ensure the pacific settlement of disputes that may arise among the member states; to provide for common action on the part of those States in the event of aggression; to seek the solution of political, juridical and economic problems that may arise among them; to promote by cooperative action, their economic, social and cultural development, and to achieve an effective limitation of conventional weapons that will make it possible to devote the largest amount of resources to the economic and social development of the member states.

Its principal organs are the General Assembly that meets annually as well as in additional special sessions if required, the Meeting of Consultation of Ministers of Foreign Affairs that considers urgent matters, the Permanent Council, and the General Secretariat. The latter two organs are based in Washington DC.

At the 1948 Bogotá Conference, Uruguay pressed for the inclusion of human rights in the OAS Charter and the creation of an Inter-American court, while others insisted on nothing more than a non-binding declaration.

---

[466] See *Framework Convention for the Protection of National Minorities, Collected Texts* (10th ed., 2023); and *Compilation of Thematic Commentaries of the Advisory Committee* (2nd ed., 2018).

Mexico and the United States took the lead in opposing the creation of institutional arrangements. The result was the American Declaration of the Rights and Duties of Man, adopted seven months before the UN's UDHR and two-and-a-half years before the European Convention. But it was to take much longer before there was a regional treaty monitored by an effective supervisory machinery. The Inter-American Commission on Human Rights was created in 1959 and the American Convention on Human Rights was adopted in 1969. It entered into force in 1978.

In 2001, the Inter-American Democratic Charter was adopted. It recognized that '[t]he peoples of the Americas have a right to democracy and their governments have an obligation to promote and defend it' (Art. 1), declared the 'effective exercise of representative democracy [to be] the basis for the rule of law' (Art. 2) and defined representative democracy to include essential elements such as 'respect for human rights and fundamental freedoms, access to and the exercise of power in accordance with the rule of law, the holding of periodic, free, and fair elections ..., the pluralistic system of political parties and organizations, and the separation of powers and independence of the branches of government' (Art. 3). The Charter also lays down various procedures to be followed when democracy is threatened. Thus, for example, '[i]n the event of an unconstitutional alteration of the constitutional regime that seriously impairs the democratic order in a member state' the OAS Permanent Council may be convoked and may initiate diplomatic initiatives. If necessary, the General Assembly can also act and can suspend the membership rights of the state concerned, although this does not affect that state's human rights obligations (Arts. 20–1).

Stefano Palestini, in 'Why is the Collective Protection of Democracy in the Americas Doomed to Fail?', *Rev. Democ.* (4 October 2021) is critical of the IADC in practice:

> Since its adoption in 2001, 38 political crises have been brought to the attention of the OAS. ... In 42 percent of the cases, the OAS member states arrived at the conclusion that the crisis at stake did not amount either to an "interruption of the democratic order" or an "alteration of the constitutional regime" and hence there was no enforcement. ... In a series of crises, the IADC was not enforced because the most powerful member states simply decided against it.

> ...

> A relationship of tutelage emerges in which big states are perceived as the enforcers and small states the targets. In fact, with the partial exception of Venezuela a medium state in which the IADC has been enforced four times, the more frequent targets of the IADC have all been relatively small states like Bolivia (4), Nicaragua (3), and Ecuador (2). ...

As of 2024 there were 35 member states of the OAS, of which 24 were parties to the American Convention on Human Rights[467] (Trinidad and Tobago withdrew in 1998 in disagreement over the death penalty, and Venezuela in 2013, alleging that the Court admitted politicized cases, failed to respect the exhaustion of domestic remedies rule, and overreached vis-à-vis the domestic constitutional order.) Twenty states have recognized the jurisdiction of the Court to consider contentious cases against them.[468] Although the United States signed the Convention in 1978, it has yet to ratify, and neither has Canada. Cuba remains, technically, a member of the OAS, but its Communist government has been excluded from participation in the Organization's work since 1962. As we shall see below, these facts have not prevented the Inter-American Commission from scrutinizing the human rights records of the relevant states. The two major human rights bodies within the OAS are the Commission and the Court.

b. The Commission

The Commission's principal roles are to consider individual petitions, monitor country situations, and develop thematic analyses of key issues. The Court's primary function is to consider contentious cases brought to it by

---

[467] Argentina, Barbados, Bolivia, Brazil, Chile, Colombia, Costa Rica, Dominica, Ecuador, El Salvador, Grenada, Guatemala, Haiti, Honduras, Jamaica, Mexico, Nicaragua, Panama, Paraguay, Peru, Dominican Republic, Suriname, Uruguay, and Venezuela.

[468] Argentina, Barbados, Bolivia, Brazil, Chile, Colombia, Costa Rica, Dominican Republic, Ecuador, El Salvador, Guatemala, Haiti, Honduras, Mexico, Nicaragua, Panama, Paraguay, Peru, Suriname and Uruguay.

States or referred by the Commission. But it also plays an important role in providing 'advisory opinions,' prescribing 'provisional measures' in urgent cases where people are at risk of irreparable damage, and promoting and monitoring compliance with its judgments and other orders.

Petitions may be filed by individuals alleging that any OAS Member State has violated the human rights guaranteed in applicable instruments. If the Commission finds the state responsible, it may make detailed recommendations to the state, and will monitor compliance. In the case of States that have accepted the contentious jurisdiction of the Court, either generally or for a particular case, non-compliance may lead the Commission to refer the case to the Court, which in turn can adopt a judgment that is legally binding for the state concerned.

The Commission was created in 1959 in the shadow of the Cuban revolution. It first met in 1960, began onsite visits in 1961, and was authorized to hear complaints in 1965. It consists of seven independent expert members, each from a different state, elected for a four-year term, renewable once. Its main function is to promote respect for and defence of human rights. States Parties to the Convention undertake in Article 43 to provide it with information it requests 'as to the manner in which their domestic law ensures the effective application' of the treaty. Commissioners are part-time and unpaid, but each takes responsibility as a 'thematic rapporteur' for an issue such as human rights defenders, persons of African descent and indigenous peoples, or the rights of the child. Each Commissioner also acts as a 'country rapporteur,' with lead responsibility for 3-6 countries. In addition, there are two separate independent special rapporteurs dealing with (i) Freedom of Expression and (ii) Economic, Social, Cultural, and Environmental Rights. The mandates of these rapporteurs are reviewed every three years, and may be terminated or renewed.

The Commission usually meets for four sessions of one to two weeks each year, with occasional additional 'extraordinary' sessions. In 2022, sessions were hybrid, thus enabling virtual as well as in-person participation. In that year, 56 public hearings were held, the great majority of which were focused on a specific country situation. When public hearings are held on the admissibility or merits of individual cases, which is entirely discretionary, one commentary notes that:

> they ordinarily last one hour and are not dedicated primarily to taking live evidence from witnesses. When witnesses do appear, they ordinarily give a brief statement and are not subject to examination or cross-examination. Thus, as currently structured, the Commission's fact-finding process in individual cases cannot be termed judicial. While one might imagine enhancing the procedures of the Commission to enable it to become the authoritative judicial fact-finder of the system, doing so would require significant changes that we do not foresee in the near future.[469]

The *Strategic Plan 2023-2027* identifies nine strategic objectives: 1) to increase access to inter-American justice, particularly for persons in historical situations of exclusion; 2) to strengthen the protection of persons by States when faced with the risk of serious, imminent and irreparable harm to human rights; 3) to promote compliance with the recommendations and standards of the inter-American human rights system; 4) to increase the capacity of the IACHR to have an impact on the prevention of human rights violations and on the timely response to human rights crises ...; 5) to deepen the awareness of human rights defenders of their rights ...; 5) deepen the awareness of state agents of the structural problems that give rise to human rights violations in the hemisphere; 6) strengthen the capacity of state agents and civil society organizations ...; 7) increase access to IACHR mechanisms by historically excluded persons, civil society organizations, and States; 8) improve IACHR mechanisms with a focus on gender, intersectionality, and results-based management; and 9) improve the management of human talent, as well as financial, administrative, and technological resources, with a human rights approach.

c. The Court

The Court's principal functions are to decide contentious cases, issue advisory opinions which may be requested by the Commission, OAS organs, and OAS Member States, and prescribe provisional measures. It has seven

---

[469] J. Cavallaro and S. Brewer, 'Reevaluating Regional Human Rights Litigation in the Twenty-First Century: The Case of the Inter-American Court,' 102 *Am. J. Int'l. L.* 678 (2008), at 778.

judges, elected by the States Parties, for a six-year term, renewable once. They must be qualified to exercise 'the highest judicial functions.' In 2015, none were female; in 2024, three were. In 2023, the Court met for nine regular sessions over a period of 22 weeks. It also met in one special sessions, and held two sessions away from San José (in Chile and Colombia).

During 2023, the Court delivered 33 judgments, including 26 on preliminary objections, merits, reparations, and costs, and seven interpretation judgments, this being the year in which the largest number of judgments on merits was issued. It also issued 28 resolutions on provisional measures and 68 resolutions on monitoring compliance with judgments. It retains jurisdiction over a case until full compliance is achieved. As of 31 December 2023, the Court had 69 cases pending resolution. It also had a staff of 73 permanent officials,[470] and a budget of US$7.05 million, of which 71 percent came from the regular budget of the OAS.

The IACtHR has been at the forefront of a movement to develop more detailed, structural, and tailored remedial measures. Many of its judgments finish with a long list of orders directed primarily to the state concerned. This gives rise to concern that such onerous requirements will discourage compliance and be ignored by some states. Precisely to counteract such problems, the Court has developed an intensive and original system for monitoring compliance, something which was not envisaged in the Convention, but which the Court has argued to be 'inherent in the exercise of its jurisdictional powers'.

The Court's judgments generally call for the state to report on measures taken within one year. The Court then follows up by issuing orders, holding hearings, and sometimes undertaking visits to the state. Separate judgments against the same state might be joined for monitoring purposes. According to the Court's *Annual Report 2023* (2024) at 81, this allows common issues to be discussed, facilitates discussions among the representatives of victims, encourages more 'dynamic participation' by state officials, and brings disputed issues to the fore. In its Decision 1/19 (2019) the Court has also sought to broaden the discussions further by providing that other entities such as domestic courts and domestic human rights groups can play a role in encouraging the adoption of appropriate measures. Any such engagements are then noted on the relevant webpage of the Court. At the end of 2023, 295 cases were subject to monitoring compliance, entailing the monitoring 1577 measures of reparation.

Advisory opinions are designed 'to clarify the meaning, purpose and rationale' of the provisions in question to enable Member States and OAS organs to meet their 'international obligations fully and effectively, and to define and implement public policies in the area of human rights ….' (Advisory Opinion No. OC-21/14, Series A, No. 21 (19 August 2014), para. 29).[471] As of June 2023, the Court had issued 30 advisory opinions, and two important references are pending. The first was submitted by Mexico on 1 November 2022 concerning 'the activities of private arms companies and their impact on human rights'. The second, submitted by Chile and Colombia on 9 January 2023 concerns 'the scope of state obligations for responding to the climate emergency under the frame of international human rights law and, specifically, under the American Convention on Human Rights' (see Ch 11B, below).

Recent Advisory Opinions have dealt with:

- Differentiated approaches with respect to certain groups of persons in detention (Advisory Opinion OC-29/22, Series A, No. 29 (30 May 2022));
- Indefinite Presidential Re-election in Presidential Systems in the context of the Inter-American System of Human Rights (OC-28/21);
- Rights to freedom to organize, collective bargaining, and strike, and their relation to other rights, with a gender perspective (OC-27/21);
- Denunciation of the American Convention on Human Rights and the Charter of the Organization of American States and the consequences for State human rights obligations (OC-26/20);

---

[470] Pablo González Domínguez, 'The Role of the Secretariat in the Inter-American Court of Human Rights: A Comparative Analysis', 116 *Am. J. Int'l L. Unbound* (2022) 390.

[471] See generally W. Arévalo Ramirez and A. Rousset Siri, Compliance with Advisory Opinions in the Inter-American Human Rights System,' 117 *AJIL Unbound* (2023) 298.

- The institution of asylum, and its recognition as a human right under the Inter-American System of Protection (OC-25/18);
- Gender identity, and equality and non-discrimination with regard to same-sex couples. State obligations in relation to change of name, gender identity, and rights deriving from a relationship between same-sex couples (OC-24/17);
- The Environment and Human Rights (State obligations in relation to the environment in the context of the protection and guarantee of the rights to life and to personal integrity (OC-23/17); and
- Entitlement of legal entities to hold rights under the Inter-American Human Rights System (OC-22/16).

The Court has so far rejected five requests for Advisory Opinions. The most recent was in 2017, when it rejected one submitted by the Commission for an opinion relating to due process rights in the context of impeachment proceedings. This was triggered by the process against President Rousseff of Brazil. The Court pointed out that advisory opinions should not address an actual or potential contentious case, be used to obtain an indirect ruling on a domestic dispute, be used as an instrument of internal political debates, relate exclusively to a matter already disposed of in the Court's jurisprudence, or seek to resolve factual issues.

The type of issue brought to the Court in contentious cases has evolved significantly over the years. Initially the decision to submit cases to the Court was entirely at the discretion of a reluctant Commission, and between 1979 and 1986 it transmitted no contentious cases. But in 2001, the Commission's new Rules of Procedure put in place a presumption that cases would be submitted to the Court where a State had failed to implement the Commission's recommendations. This virtually tripled the Court's workload, forcing it to significantly adapt its procedures.

The history of military dictatorships in Latin America during the 1970s and 1980s ensured that all but two of the cases decided by the court dealt with state-sanctioned acts of violence such as torture and disappearances. The Court was thus able to generate an important and innovative body of jurisprudence on these issues, as illustrated by its first and arguably most important judgment in the *Velásquez Rodríguez* case. The Court's role began to change significantly not just because the end of the dictatorship era brought new types of challenges, but also because of the changing landscape of constitutionalism in Latin America. The result was the emergence of 'a transnational network of lawyers who advance a liberal vision of constitutional law that emphasizes judicial power, rights-based review, and Dworkinian-style interpretive practices, and who embrace the view that constitutional rights are grounded not only in positive domestic law but also in international human rights instruments.'[472] This in turn has enhanced the power of the Court and its jurisprudence at the national level. Before examining this evolution more fully, we consider the basic elements of the regime, including the rights recognized and the different regimes that apply according to the ratification record of the state concerned, as well as exploring some examples of the role played by the Commission.

d. Rights Recognized in the American Declaration and Convention

In terms of rights, the American Declaration on the Rights and Duties of Man (adopted on 2 May 1948) is similar in content to the Universal Declaration (adopted on 10 December 1948), although the approach to economic and social rights differed importantly. But what especially distinguishes the America Declaration are ten articles setting out the duties of the citizen: the duty 'so to conduct himself in relation to others that each and every one may fully form and develop his personality'; to 'aid support, educate and protect his minor children'; to 'acquire at least an elementary education'; to vote in popular elections; to 'obey the law and other legitimate commands of the authorities'; to 'render whatever civil and military service his country may require for its defence and preservation'; to cooperate with the state with respect to social security and welfare; to pay taxes; and to work. By comparison, the UDHR says only that 'Everyone has duties to the community in which alone the free and full development of his personality is possible' (Art 29(1)).[473]

---

[472] A. Huneeus, 'Constitutional Lawyers and the Inter-American Court's Varied Authority,' 79 *L. & Contemp. Probs.* 179 (2016), at 181.

[473] On duties in human rights instruments generally, see Chapter 6, above.

The process of drafting an inter-American treaty began in 1959. The result was the American Convention on Human Rights of 1969 (also known as the Pact of San José, Costa Rica) which contains 26 rights and freedoms, 21 of which are formulated in similar terms to the provisions of the ICCPR. Consider some comparisons:

(1) Article 27 of the ICCPR, which recognizes the rights of members of minority groups, has no counterpart in the American Convention.

(2) The five provisions which are in that Convention but not in the ICCPR are the right of reply (Art. 14), the right to property (Art. 21), freedom from exile (Art. 22(5)), the right to asylum (Art. 22(7)), and prohibition of 'the collective expulsion of aliens' (Art. 21(9)).

(3) Some provisions in the American Convention express the same general idea as in other human rights treaties but do so in a distinctive manner — for example, Article 4 (1) on the right to life provides that the right 'shall be protected by law and, in general, from the moment of conception'.

(4) Article 23 on participation in government contains the same rights and requirements as the analogous Article 21 of the UDHR and Article 25 of the ICCPR.

When the Convention was adopted in 1969 it was decided not to have a separate treaty relating to economic, social, and cultural rights but rather to include a general provision (Art. 26) in the following terms:

> The States Parties undertake to adopt measures, both internally and through international cooperation, especially those of an economic and technical nature, with a view to achieving progressively by legislation or other means, the full realization of the rights implicit in the economic, social, educational, scientific and cultural standards set forth in the Charter of the Organization of American States as amended by the Protocol of Buenos Aires.

The OAS Charter, as amended, sets up an Inter-American Council for Education, Science and Culture, as well as an Economic and Social Council, both of which are supposed to set standards, consider reports made by states, and make recommendations. In response to the ineffectiveness of that machinery, the OAS adopted, in 1988, an Additional Protocol to the American Convention on Human Rights in the Area of Economic, Social and Cultural Rights (known as the Protocol of San Salvador). It obliges parties to adopt measures, 'to the extent allowed by their available resources, and taking into account their degree of development', for the progressive achievement of the rights listed. The Protocol became effective in 1999 and had, as of June 2023, 18 states parties.

The rights recognized in the Protocol are similar to those in the International Covenant on Economic, Social and Cultural Rights, although the formulations differ significantly. The Protocol does not recognize the rights to adequate clothing and housing or to an adequate standard of living (Art. 11 of the ICESCR), but it does include the right to a healthy environment, the right to special protection in old age, and the rights of persons with disabilities, none of which are explicitly recognized in the ICESCR.[474]

2. The Standards to be Applied to Different States

In recent years the Commission has sought to transcend the problem that different standards apply to different states by promoting 'universal ratification' within the Americas of the Convention and other relevant human rights treaties.[475] But the pattern of ratifications is very uneven and results in a somewhat complex architecture for the inter-American system. A key question concerns the implications of a state's non-ratification of the Convention. For the Commission:

> First, it may represent a significant constraint on the full exercise of citizenship and the development of standards, public policies, and measures intended to protect and ensure

---

[474] For a comprehensive analysis, see *Compendium on Economic, Social, Cultural and Environmental Rights: Inter-American Standards*, OEA/Ser.L/V/II., Doc. 465, 31 December 2021).

[475] These include: the Convention to Prevent and Punish Torture (1985), the Protocol to Abolish the Death Penalty (1990), the Convention on Forced Disappearance of Persons (1994), the Convention on the Prevention, Punishment and Eradication of Violence against Women (1994), the Convention on the Elimination of All Forms of Discrimination against Persons with Disability (1999), the Convention against All Forms of Discrimination and Intolerance (2013), the Convention against Racism, Racial Discrimination and Related Forms of Intolerance (2013), and the Convention on Protecting the Human Rights of Older Persons (2015).

everyone's enjoyment of rights, essential elements for an inclusive democracy. It maintains the door shut to a protection system of a complementary nature which may be vital for persons in a specific situation of vulnerability and thus subject to violations of their human rights, such as those affected by poverty and historical situations of discrimination. Second, it limits the effectiveness of discourse on human rights as expressed by those States that have not ratified, as well as their regional and international leadership on these subjects. Third, it constitutes an obstacle to OAS regional integration goals and to sustainable opportunities for multilateral cooperation in the Americas and at the international level.[476]

The Commission has also noted that fewer petitions are submitted, fewer hearings requested, and fewer invitations for on-site visits are received in the case of states that have not ratified the Convention. The Commission and the Court have, however, acted to ensure that minimum standards will still apply, as illustrated by the especially significant examples of Cuba and the United States, neither of which has ratified the Convention.

Cuba

The coming to power of the Communist government in 1959 provided a major impetus to develop the OAS's human rights activities. The challenge was to reconcile Cuba's suspension from the Organization with a desire to monitor and report on the human rights situation. This excerpt explains the legal analysis by which this was achieved:

> Cuba is a member state of the Organization of American States since July 16, 1952... . The Commission has maintained that the Cuban State "is juridically answerable to the Inter-American Commission in matters that concern human rights" inasmuch as it "is party to the first international instruments established in the American hemisphere to protect human rights" and because "Resolution VI of [January 31, 1962] excluded the Government of Cuba, not the State, from participating in the inter-American system." In this connection the IACHR stated: ... it was not the intention of the Organization of American States to leave the Cuban people without protection. That Government's exclusion from the regional system in no way means that it is no longer bound by its international human rights obligations.[477]

After the resumption of diplomatic ties between the USA and Cuba, President Raúl Castro Ruz participated in the OAS General Assembly in April 2015, thus marking the first occasion in history when all 35 OAS heads of state and government had come together. The Commission continues to issue regular reports on Cuba, including one in 2020, supplemented by a 50-page analysis in its *Annual Report 2022* (Chapter IV.B). The latter observed 'the failure to uphold the essential elements of representative democracy and its institutions, as well as the lack of provisions to ensure the separation of powers and the absence of guarantees of judicial independence, are persistent structural factors that profoundly affect the exercise of human rights and fundamental freedoms in Cuba.' But the Commission's report also notes (paras. 220-21) that while it has often called for 'the lifting of the U.S. economic blockade on account of its impact on the Cuban people and their rights', 'the blockade "does not release the State of Cuba from its ... international obligations"'. It also noted UN General Assembly resolution 77/7 (2022) which called for the end of the economic embargo and was adopted by 185 votes in favour to 2 against (Israel, United States), with 2 abstentions (Brazil, Ukraine).

USA

The United States has signed, but not ratified, the American Convention. Its official position is that the American Declaration is clearly non-binding. It is a 'noble statement of human rights aspirations' which 'lacks the precision necessary to resolve complex legal questions'. 'It would seriously undermine the process of

---

[476] *Considerations Related to the Universal Ratification of the American Convention and other Inter-American Human Rights Treaties*, OAS/Ser.L/V/II.152, Doc. 21 (14 August 2014), para. 13.
[477] IACHR Annual Report 2006, para. 54.

international lawmaking ... to impose legal obligations on states through a process of "reinterpretation" or "inference" from a non-binding statement of principles.' It is hardly surprising then, given (1) the willingness of the United States to apply to other nations the Universal Declaration of Human Rights, the status of which is very similar, and (2) the enthusiasm of the United States for holding its Latin American neighbours to their human rights obligations, that other states within the inter-American system were keen to clarify the status of the American Declaration. The Advisory Opinion below does not focus specifically on the United States, but its target is fairly clear.

ADVISORY OPINION OC-10/89
INTER-AMERICAN COURT OF HUMAN RIGHTS, INTERPRETATION OF THE AMERICAN DECLARATION OF THE RIGHTS AND DUTIES OF MAN WITHIN THE FRAMEWORK OF ARTICLE 64 OF THE AMERICAN CONVENTION ON HUMAN RIGHTS, REQUESTED BY THE GOVERNMENT OF THE REPUBLIC OF COLOMBIA (14 JULY 1989)

...

2. [In February 1988, the Government of Colombia sought an advisory opinion on] the following question:

> Does Article 64 authorize the Inter-American Court of Human Rights to render advisory opinions at the request of a member state or one of the organs of the OAS, regarding the interpretation of the American Declaration of the Rights and Duties of Man, adopted by the Ninth International Conference of American States in Bogotá in 1948?

...

30. Article 64(1) of the Convention authorizes the Court to render advisory opinions "regarding the interpretation of this Convention or of other treaties concerning the protection of human rights in the American states." ...

...

33. [It is clear] that the Declaration is not a treaty as defined by the Vienna Conventions [on the law of treaties].because it was not approved as such ... .

34. Here it must be recalled that the American Declaration was adopted by the Ninth International Conference of American States (Bogotá, 1948) through a resolution adopted by the Conference itself. It was neither conceived nor drafted as a treaty ... .

...

[As noted] on September 26, 1949, by the Inter-American Committee of Jurisconsults ...:

> It is evident that the Declaration of Bogotá does not create a contractual juridical obligation, but it is also clear that it demonstrates a well-defined orientation toward the international protection of the fundamental rights of the human person ... .

35. The mere fact that the Declaration is not a treaty does not necessarily compel the conclusion that the Court lacks the power to render an advisory opinion containing an interpretation of the American Declaration.

36. In fact, the American Convention refers to the Declaration in paragraph three of its Preamble which reads as follows:

> *Considering* that these principles have been set forth in the Charter of the Organization of the American States, in the American Declaration of the Rights and Duties of Man, and in the Universal Declaration of Human Rights, and that they have been reaffirmed and refined in other international instruments, worldwide as well as regional in scope.

And in Article 29(d) which indicates:

> ... No provision of this convention shall be interpreted as:

> ...

> d. excluding or limiting the effect that the American Declaration of the Rights and
> Duties of Man and other international acts of the same nature may have.

From the foregoing, it follows that, in interpreting the Convention in the exercise of its advisory jurisdiction, the Court may have to interpret the Declaration.

37. ... [T]o determine the legal status of the American Declaration it is appropriate to look to the inter-American system of today in the light of the evolution it has undergone since the adoption of the Declaration, rather than to examine the normative value and significance which that instrument was believed to have had in 1948.

38. The evolution of the here relevant "inter-American law" mirrors on the regional level the developments in contemporary international law and specially in human rights law, which distinguished that law from classical international law to a significant extent. That is the case, for example, with the duty to respect certain essential human rights, which is today considered to be an *erga omnes* obligation ... .

39. The Charter of the Organization refers to the fundamental rights of man in [various provisions] ... but it does not list or define them. The member states of the Organization have, through its diverse organs, given specificity to the human rights mentioned in the Charter and to which the Declaration refers.

40. This is the case of Article 112 of the Charter ...:

> There shall be an Inter-American Commission on Human Rights, whose principal
> function shall be to promote the observance and protection of human rights and to serve
> as a consultative organ of the Organization in these matters.

> An inter-American convention on human rights shall determine the structure,
> competence, and procedure of this Commission, as well as those of other organs
> responsible for these matters.

Article 150 of the Charter provides as follows:

> Until the inter-American convention on human rights, referred to in Chapter XVIII
> (Chapter XVI of the Charter as amended by the Protocol of Cartagena de Indias), enters
> into force, the present Inter-American Commission on Human Rights shall keep vigilance
> over the observance of human rights.

41. These norms authorize the Inter-American Commission to protect human rights. These rights are none other than those enunciated and defined in the American Declaration. That conclusion results from Article 1 of the Commission's Statute ... [adopted in 1979]:

> 1. The Inter-American Commission on Human Rights is an organ of the Organization of
> the American States, created to promote the observance and defense of human rights and
> to serve as consultative organ of the Organization in this matter.

> 2. For the purposes of the present Statute, human rights are understood to be:

> > a. The rights set forth in the American Convention on Human Rights, in relation
> > to the States Parties thereto;

> > b. The rights set forth in the American Declaration of the Rights and Duties of
> > Man, in relation to the other member states.

Articles 18, 19 and 20 of the Statute enumerate these functions.

42. The General Assembly of the Organization has also repeatedly recognized that the American Declaration is a source of international obligations for the member states of the OAS... .

43. Hence it may be said that by means of an authoritative interpretation, the member states of the Organization have signalled their agreement that the Declaration contains and defines the fundamental human rights referred to in the Charter. Thus the Charter of the Organization cannot be interpreted and applied as far as human rights are concerned without relating its norms, consistent with the practice of the organs of the OAS, to the corresponding provisions of the Declaration.

44. In view of the fact that the Charter of the Organization and the American Convention are treaties with respect to which the Court has advisory jurisdiction by virtue of Article 64(1), it follows that the Court is authorized, within the framework and limits of its competence, to interpret the American Declaration and to render an advisory opinion relating to it whenever it is necessary to do so in interpreting those instruments.

QUESTIONS

1. Is the Commission's rationale for continuing to examine the human rights situation in Cuba convincing?

2. On the basis of the Court's Advisory Opinion, what is the legal status of the American Declaration, and how would you compare it in that respect with the Universal Declaration?

---

3. The Commission at Work

Over the years, the Inter-American Commission has evolved significantly in terms of its techniques. Its early emphasis was on country reports. A 1980 report on Argentina at the height of the problem of disappearances remains a classic in terms of effective fact-finding and follow-up. As recounted by Tom Farer, one of its members, the Commission, '[w]ith the grudging consent of the military government, ... roamed the country, recording thousands of denunciations of the regime's exterminatory assault on left-wing insurgents and anyone suspected of assisting them, whether materially or intellectually.' It 'privately interviewed hundreds of political prisoners and secured testimony from the fortunate few who ... had been released.' In Farer's assessment, the resulting report 'began the process of regime de-legitimation which culminated in the restoration of democracy four years later.'[478]

The continuing evolution of the approach adopted by the Commission and the Court from that early phase until 2020 is traced by Christopher Roberts, in *Alternative Approaches to Human Rights: The Disparate Historical Paths of the European, Inter-American and African Regional Human Rights Systems* (2022) 147:

> [F]our sets of cases – concerning the reform of repressive public order systems,
> indigenous peoples' rights, violence against women, and the rights of marginalized groups
> – were at the forefront of the system's ongoing development of a progressive and
> assertive approach to its work in the new millennium. That approach had multiple,
> interrelated characteristics, including the tendency on the part of both the Commission
> and the Court to adopt a wide-angled perspective, taking in broader structural issues; the
> assertion of the strength and hierarchical supremacy of human rights law, understood as
> having a degree of force on the national as well as on the international legal level; a
> willingness to prescribe sweeping, multifaceted, and forceful remedial measures; and a
> recognition of the interrelationship between rights and democracy, and of the need for
> rights work to be focused on rewriting the fundamental rules of society, with the aim
> both of addressing past wrongs, and of achieving more inclusive political cultures going
> forwards. In sum, the period saw the system continuing to evolve from its past focus on

---

[478] T. Farer, 'I Cried for you, Argentina', 38 *Hum. Rts Q.* (2016) 851.

calling out widespread and serious violations, to a new emphasis on combatting structural forms of violence and inequality within societies.

We now consider briefly each of the main functions the Commission currently performs, within the constraints of its budget of US$18,000,000 (for 2023), of which $10 million comes from the OAS regular budget.

a. Individual Complaints

The number of complaints received annually by the Commission has grown steadily. In 1997 there were 435, in 2001 there were 885, and by 2022 there were 2,440. Of those, 631 were from Colombia, 625 from Mexico, 282 from Peru, 182 from Brazil, 150 from Argentina, and 68 from the United States. One of the major developments in recent years has been the rapid diminution in the Commission's backlog in dealing with complaints. In 2015, for example, 9,673 complaints were pending evaluation. At that time, the Commission was rejecting around 75 percent as not having met the procedural requirements. Following Resolution 1/16 (2016), designed to reduce the backlog, it was systematically reduced. In part this also reflected a higher rejection rate, which reached 86 percent in 2022. In its *Annual Report 2022*, the Commission noted that:

> This rigorous analysis process enables the Commission, through its initial evaluation decisions, to protect the subsidiary and complementary nature of the inter-American system, both from a procedural standpoint (when domestic remedies have not been exhausted or an exception does not apply) as well as a substantive one (when the acts in question do not constitute a violation of rights recognized in the instruments under its jurisdiction).

b. Precautionary Measures

One of the most significant but also controversial activities of the Commission is the issuance of precautionary measures. These are the inter-American system's equivalent of the interim measures adopted by the ICCPR Committee (Ch. 9, above). Just as with the Covenant, the Inter-American Convention makes no provision for such measures, but the Commission argued that they are inherent in its other powers. Article 25 of the Commission's Rules of Procedure provides that:

> … in serious and urgent situations, the Commission may, on its own initiative or at the request of a party, request that a State adopt precautionary measures to prevent irreparable harm to persons or to the subject matter of the proceedings in connection with a pending petition or case. The measures may be of a collective nature to prevent irreparable harm to persons or groups of persons. In this regard, the number of precautionary measures granted does not reflect the number of persons protected by their adoption. Moreover, … the granting of such measures and their adoption by the State shall not constitute a prejudgment on the violation of the rights protected … .

The Commission's *Annual Report 2022* notes that 1,033 requests for precautionary measures were received. 'The Commission granted and/or expanded 50 precautionary measures, thus protecting more than 1648 people … . In total, 80 resolutions on precautionary measures were issued in 2022.'

Perhaps the most controversial example of such measures was an order made in 2011 in relation to the building of a dam in Brazil:

> On April 1, 2011, the IACHR granted precautionary measures for the members of [11 specified] indigenous communities … . The request for precautionary measure alleges that the life and physical integrity of the beneficiaries is at risk due to the impact of the construction of the Belo Monte hydroelectric power plant. The [Commission requested that Brazil] immediately suspend the licensing process for the [plant] and stop any construction work from moving forward until certain minimum conditions are met. The State must (1) conduct consultation processes, in fulfillment of its international obligations — meaning prior consultations that are free, informed, of good faith, culturally appropriate, and with the aim of reaching an agreement — in relation to each of

the affected indigenous communities that are beneficiaries of these precautionary measures; (2) guarantee that, in order for this to be an informed consultation process, the indigenous communities have access beforehand to the project's Social and Environmental Impact Study, in an accessible format, including translation into the respective indigenous languages; (3) adopt measures to protect the life and physical integrity of the members of the indigenous peoples in voluntary isolation of the Xingu Basin, and to prevent the spread of diseases and epidemics... .[479]

Brazil deemed the proposed measures 'precipitous and unwarranted', severed formal relations with the Commission, recalled its OAS ambassador, and froze its annual US$800,000 contribution to the IACHR. A key Senator stated that the request 'threatens Brazilian sovereignty'. Critics of the project noted that it had been controversial since 1975, would flood nearly 200 square miles in the Amazon and displace 50,000 people, and lead to the disappearance of 1,000 species of plants and animals. Protests had been led by FUNAI (the National Indian Foundation of Brazil), Amazon Watch, the vocalist Sting and movie director James Cameron. For its part, the Brazilian Government claimed that it would be the world's third largest dam, provide thousands of construction jobs, supply electricity to 23 million homes, and be a source of clean and renewable energy. It was said to be the first of as many as 70 dams scheduled for construction in the region.[480]

Another example is Precautionary Measure No. 731–18 (16 August 2018) concerning Migrant Children affected by the 'Zero Tolerance' Policy regarding the United States of America:

> 1. On June 18, 2018, [the Commission] received a request for precautionary measures presented by the National Commission of Human Rights of Mexico, the Ombudsman's Office of Colombia, the Ombudsman's Office of Ecuador, the Attorney General's Office of Guatemala, the National Commissioner of Human Rights of El Salvador, the National Commissioner of Human Rights of Honduras, … in favor of migrant children that had been detained and separated from their families in the United States as a result of the implementation of the "Zero Tolerance" policy [pursued by the Trump Administration]. Among other conditions, the applicants allege that the separation of parents from their children could cause irreparable harm to their rights, particularly in the context of the children's best interest.
>
> …
>
> 3. After analyzing the factual and legal allegations submitted by the parties, the Commission concludes that the rights to family life and personal integrity, as well as the right to identity of the children … are prima facie in a situation of risk. …
>
> …
>
> VI. DECISION
>
> 39. The Commission considers that this matter meets *prima facie* the requirements of seriousness, urgency and risk of irreparable harm set forth in Article 25 of its Rules of Procedure. Consequently, the Commission requests that the United States:
>
>> a) Adopt the necessary measures to protect the rights to a family life, personal integrity, and identity of the proposed beneficiaries. Particularly, assuring that these rights are protected through the reunification of the children with their biological families and in support of the children's best interests;
>>
>> b) Adopt the necessary measures, while the reunification is carried out, to immediately guarantee an appropriate, free, and regular communication between

---

[479] PM 382/10 — Indigenous Communities of the Xingu River Basin, Pará, Brazil, in *Annual Report of the* IACHR (2012), Chap. III.
[480] See generally L. Birns and K. Soltis, 'Controversy in the Amazon: Brazil Disregards the Inter-American Commission on Human Rights at Potentially Great Cost', *Council on Hemispheric Affairs* (9 June 2011), at www.coha.org/controversy-in-the-amazon/.

the beneficiaries and their families[;] … provide medical and psychological assistance … [and] provide interpreting services when necessary … .

c) In case any of the proposed beneficiaries was deported separately from their children, adopt immediately the necessary measures in the framework of international cooperation to guarantee their reunification, taking into account the child's best interest and the necessary support and care;

d) Suspend any migration procedure that may result in the separation of the children from their parents; … .

In a commentary on this measure, and by way of contrast to Brazil's response, Berta Esperanza Hernández-Truyol, in 58 *Int'l Leg. Mat.* (2019) 371, noted that the Commission's intervention had, in practice, complemented the resistance shown by U.S. domestic courts in relation to these particular policies.

c. Interstate Complaints

The American Convention establishes an optional interstate complaints procedure (Arts. 45–51), but to date it has only been used twice. Assuming the states in question have recognized the Commission's competence for this purpose, and if the complaint is deemed admissible, the Commission will seek to reach a friendly settlement (Art. 48). If a settlement is not reached, the Commission shall report and may 'make such proposals and recommendations as it sees fit' (Art. 50). In March 2007 the Commission presented its first report on such a complaint.[481] It concerned allegations of systematic discrimination against Nicaraguan citizens resident in Costa Rica. The complaint was deemed inadmissible by virtue of the complainant's failure to submit the complaint within six months of its having been notified of a final decision being handed down in Costa Rica. Nonetheless, the Commission took the opportunity, in a 69-page judgment, to explore the applicable procedures, develop its jurisprudence on admissibility in such cases, exculpate Costa Rica in relation to some of the most serious charges, acknowledge Costa Rica's admission of the existence of discrimination and xenophobia in its territory, and to conclude by condemning 'all acts of discrimination or xenophobia against migrant persons of any origin' and recalling the 'obligation of states to protect individuals against discrimination, whether this occurs within the public sphere or among private parties'.

In October 2010, the Commission declared an application by Ecuador against Colombia to be admissible. It resulted from the killing of an Ecuadorian national during a military operation by Colombian forces on Ecuadorian territory to fight guerrilla fighters. Ecuador alleged violations of the rights to life, humane treatment, judicial guarantees, and judicial protection. The Commission rejected Colombia's claims that international humanitarian law should apply and that domestic remedies had not been exhausted.[482] The case was resolved through a friendly settlement.

One explanation, offered by Jorge Contesse, in 'Inter-States Disputes under the Inter-American Human Rights System', 13 *Int'l Hum. Rts. L. Rev.* (2024) 74, for the paucity of interstate complaints is that Latin American states resort to advisory opinions as a 'covert' interstate dispute mechanism.

d. Country Reports

In many cases, country visits by the Commission are undertaken by a single Commissioner in the framework of a 'working visit'. The outcome is a detailed press release outlining any major problems identified. But such visits do not count as an 'in loco' visit by the Commission, which requires the participation of at least two commissioners. Between October 1961 and 2021, the Commission undertook 102 such country visits.

A January 2020 visit to Chile is an example of a visit involving all seven Commissioners, as well as the Special Rapporteurs on Freedom of Expression and on Economic, Social, Cultural and Environmental Rights. It was scheduled in the aftermath of the 2019 social unrest involving mass demonstrations and what the Commission

---

[481] Report No. 11/07, Interstate Case 01/06, *Nicaragua v. Costa Rica* (8 March 2007).
[482] Report No. 112/10, Inter-State Petition IP-02, Admissibility, *Franklin Guillermo Aisalla Molina (Ecuador – Colombia)* OEA/Ser.L/V/II.140, Doc. 10 (21 October 2010).

found to be a disproportionate response by the security forces to the 'democratic and legitimate expressions of its population'. The visit resulted in a 125-page report appended to the Commission's 2022 Annual Report. In addition, the latter report provides details of the measures taken by the Government in response to the Commission's extensive recommendations (Chapter IV.A, paras. 209-37).

The Commission has adopted a detailed set of 'General Guidelines' on the follow-up of its recommendations and decisions (OEA/Ser.L/V/II.173, Doc. 177 (30 September 2019)).

Chapter IV of the Annual Report is entitled 'Human Rights Developments in the Region'. Part A provides an overview of the human rights situation in each country. For example, the entry on the United States provides this introductory overview to a nine-page analysis:

> 400. Regarding challenges, the IACHR reiterates its concern over the persistence of patterns of racism and institutional and structural inequalities, the application of the death penalty, and the increase in mass shootings. Also, of particular concern continues to be the prolongation of migration policies that restrict the rights of persons in a situation of human mobility. The Commission is also concerned about the barriers implemented during 2022 to the exercise of sexual and reproductive rights.

Chapter IV.B contains 'special reports' which, in 2022, were directed at Cuba, Nicaragua, Venezuela, and Guatemala. Inclusion in Part B is considered an unwelcome 'honour' for any state. Traditionally, the Commission has sought to apply five criteria in selecting countries for this purpose: (1) states ruled by governments that have not come to power through secret, genuine, periodic, and free elections; (2) states in which human rights 'have been, in effect, suspended totally or in part, by virtue of the imposition of exceptional measures'; (3) states which commit 'massive and grave violations'; (4) 'states that are in a process of transition from any of the above three situations'; and (5) where 'temporary or structural situations', such as major institutional crises, 'seriously affect the enjoyment of fundamental rights'.

e. Friendly Settlements[483]

The Commission's first approved friendly settlement was not until 1985, but by 1994 it had become a well-established part of proceedings. When it revised its Rules of Procedure in 2001, governments were strongly incentivized to consider such a settlement in order to avoid a virtually automatic referral of the case to the Court. As a result, friendly settlements were achieved in response to 27 percent of admissible petitions between 2001 and 2018 (compared to 15 percent in 1992-2000).[484]

Since 2003, the Commission has also innovated by introducing 'compliance agreements'. Unlike friendly settlements, these are negotiated only after the Commission has issued its 'merits report' and its recommendations, but before that report is acted upon by the Court. This technique is reported to have significantly increased compliance rates.[485]

In 2022, 29 new friendly settlement agreements were signed, and 23 reports approving friendly settlements were published. Under the *Strategic Plan 2023-2027* (at 60) the Commission has undertaken to strongly promote friendly settlements, to promote negotiation processes, to encourage compliance agreements, and to reduce the existing backlog of settlement processes.

An example of a potentially far-reaching settlement is the following (*Annual Report 2022*, at 126):

> **Report No. 305/22, Petition 1256 05, Ivana Emilce Rosales, Argentina:** the case relates to the international responsibility of the Argentine State due to the alleged violation of [a range of human rights] ... to the detriment of Ivana Emilce Rosales and her daughters Mayka and Abril, by virtue of an arbitrary, discriminatory judicial decision

---

[483] IACHR, *Impact of the Friendly Settlement Procedure* (2nd ed, 2018) OEA/Ser.L/V/II.167, Doc. 31 (1 March 2018).
[484] F. Parente, 'Settle or Litigate? Consequences of Institutional Design in the Inter-American System of Human Rights Protection', 17 *Rev. of Int'l Org.* (2022) 39.
[485] A. Pérez-Liñán et al., 'Compliance Agreements in the Inter-American Human Rights System', *Max Planck Institute*, MPIL Research Paper, Series No. 2021-26 (2021).

during the criminal investigation for attempted homicide in a context of gender violence of which Ivana and her daughters, Mayka and Abril, were victims. … The friendly settlement agreement [was] signed on September 23, 2021 … .

[It] contains several measures, including (a) holding an official public ceremony to acknowledge international responsibility; (b) the publication of the friendly settlement agreement; … (e) the provision of legal assistance to enable Abril to change her paternal surname; (f) the granting of a house; (g) economic compensation; (h) the creation of the Ivana and Mayka Rosales Comprehensive Protection Center for victims of gender violence; (i) measures to provide free, comprehensive, expert legal representation to victims of gender violence; … and (l) the implementation of a National Registry of Gender Violence. …

As is also the case in relation to the ECHR system, friendly settlements in the Inter-American system have been relatively neglected by scholars. One recent analysis, by Jorge Contesse, in 'Settling Human Rights Violations', 60 *Harv. Int'l L. J.* (2019) 317, identifies advantages including enabling governments to avoid 'naming and shaming' associated with litigation, obtaining reparations more quickly for victims, and alleviating the backlog of cases. But he also identifies four key problems:

(1) the misperception that settling human rights violations is normatively inferior than obtaining judicial decisions;

(2) the unnecessary exclusion of third parties from the settlement process;

(3) the inconsistent function of individual commissioners and underutilization of their institutional participation in settlements; and

(4) the difficulty of adequately enforcing settlement terms post-resolution.

Contesse concludes that disputes concerning individual violations should be treated differently to those seeking structural remedies. In particular, the Commission could 'explore ways to give voice to all interested and potentially affected parties', such as enabling the submission of *amicus curiae* briefs, or involving them in thematic hearings (at 365).

f. Backlash

The rapid evolution of the system and the key role played by the Commission has given rise to instances of backlash. Most notably, after Brazil's rejection of the Belo Monte Dam precautionary measures, the OAS established a 'Special Working Group to Reflect on the Workings of the IACHR with a View to Strengthening the [Inter-American system]'. One month later, on 29 July 2011, the Commission modified its Belo Monte order. And following recommendations by the Working Group, the Commission amended 13 of its Rules of Procedure. On precautionary measures, the resolution defined the terms 'serious,' 'urgent,' and 'irreparable harm,' spelled out information required from applicants, specified the procedures to be followed and the elements to be taken into account in evaluating the situation, specified the form that orders should take, and provided that they could be reconsidered at any time.

Soon after, Venezuela, Ecuador, and Bolivia launched a concerted attack on the Commission in June 2012, alleging persistent bias against left-leaning governments. Another attack came in a 23 April 2019 Declaration in Asunción by the governments of Argentina, Brazil, Chile, Colombia and Paraguay. Again, the stated goal was constructive: to improve 'the operability, functionality and effectiveness of the Inter-American Human Rights System', but the approach adopted was very similar to that taken by the United Kingdom and Denmark in their pushback against the European system:

1. They emphasize that the principle of subsidiarity, which underlies the legal requirements for admissibility of a petition, has a twofold dimension. … [I]t assumes that the State concerned has the obligation to investigate any violation of the Convention that occurs in its territory, and … that the State concerned has the right to have its own

jurisdictional system resolve the situation before being submitted to an international instance.

2. They consider that the legitimate space of autonomy available to States to ensure all persons subject to their jurisdiction, through their own democratic processes, the rights and guarantees enshrined in the Convention in accordance with their constitutional systems must be respected.

3. They also consider that, in the context of the measures taken to reduce the procedural backlog at the Commission, the rights of the defence, legal certainty and procedural equality must be guaranteed.

4. They stress the importance of a strict application of the sources of international human rights law and the recognition of the margin of appreciation of the States in the fulfillment of the obligations established in the Convention. They also recall that the resolutions and judgments of the organs of the inter-American system have effect only for the parties to the litigation.

5. They emphasize the importance of due knowledge and consideration of the political, economic, and social realities of the States by the organs of the inter-American human rights system. In this context, they underscore the need for the forms of reparation to be duly proportionate and to respect both the constitutional and legal systems of the States, as well as the requirements of the rule of law.

In response, Amnesty International accused the group of 'seeking to impose constraints on the actions of the regional Inter-American mechanism in their own interests and so put the rights of victims at risk' (AMR 01/0294/2019 (6 May 2019)). While the relevant claims made little overt headway, it is clear that a significant message was sent to the Commission and that it was heard. The *Strategic Plan 2023-2027* envisages: i) streamlining processes and progressive reduction of the procedural backlog; ii) strengthening and expansion of friendly settlements; iii) prioritization of petitions and cases to ensure more timely justice and the development of standards with a structural impact; and iv) expansion of management capacity.

QUESTIONS

1. What factors should the Commission take into account in considering precautionary measures such as those issued in relation to Brazil in 2011 and the United States in 2019?

2. How would the overall inter-American system change if the Commission were to implement the approach proposed by the five governments in the Asunción Declaration?

---

4. The Inter-American Court in Action[486]

Although its functions are comparable, the Inter-American Court plays a more restricted role than its European counterpart. In particular, acceptance of its contentious jurisdiction is not compulsory for States parties to the Convention and it can only hear cases referred to it by States parties or the Commission. Initially the Court and the Commission saw each other as rivals. The Commission, established over two decades earlier, was very reluctant to refer contentious cases to the Court. The situation changed only in the late 1980s, beginning with the referral of three cases involving enforced disappearances in Honduras. The principal case, *Velásquez Rodríguez*, appears below. It was the first contentious case initiated by an individual that involved systemic state violence. Outside as well as inside the inter-American system, it has proved to be one of the most influential and cited decisions of an international human rights tribunal.

---

[486] For a thorough analysis of the jurisprudence of the IACtHR, see L. Hennebel and H. Tigroudja, *The American Convention on Human Rights: A Commentary* (2022). More generally, see N. Zúñiga, *The Inter American Court of Human Rights: The Legitimacy of International Courts and Tribunals* (2023).

VELÁSQUEZ RODRÍGUEZ CASE
INTER-AMERICAN COURT OF HUMAN RIGHTS, SER. C, NO. 4 (29 JULY 1988)

[This case arose out of a period of political turbulence, violence, and repression in Honduras. A petition to the Commission in 1981 alleged that Angel Manfredo Velásquez Rodríguez was arrested without warrant in 1981 by members of the National Office of Investigations (DNI) and the G-2 of the Armed Forces. The 'arrest' involved his seizure by seven armed men dressed in civilian clothes and driving an unlicensed car. Eyewitnesses reported his later detention, 'harsh interrogation and cruel torture'. Police and security forces continued to deny the arrest and detention. Velásquez had disappeared. The petition alleged that this conduct, attributable to Honduras, violated several articles of the American Convention on Human Rights.

In 1986, Velásquez was still missing, and the Commission concluded that the Government of Honduras 'had not offered convincing proof that would allow [it] to determine that the allegations are not true'. The Commission referred the matter to the Court since Honduras had recognized its contentious jurisdiction. The Court held closed and open hearings, called witnesses, and requested the production of evidence and documents. The statement of facts below is taken from the Court's opinion and consists both of its independent findings and its affirmation of some findings of the Commission.

The Commission presented witnesses to testify that there were numerous cases of disappearances between 1981 and 1984, that these were 'imputable to the Armed Forces of Honduras and enjoying the acquiescence of the Government of Honduras', and that there were at the time no effective domestic remedies to protect such kidnapped persons. Several witnesses testified that they were kidnapped, imprisoned in clandestine jails, and tortured by members of the Armed Forces. Explicit testimony described the severity of the torture — including beatings, electric shocks, hanging, burning, drugs, and sexual abuse — to which witnesses had been subjected. Several witnesses indicated how they knew that their captors and torturers were connected with the military. Testimony indicated that 'somewhere between 112 and 130 individuals were disappeared from 1981 to 1984'.

The President of the Committee for the Defense of Human Rights in Honduras testified about the existence of a unit in the Armed Forces that carried out the disappearance, giving details about its organization and commanders. A former member of the Armed Forces testified that he had belonged to the battalion carrying out the kidnapping, and claimed that he had been told of the kidnapping and later torture and killing of Velásquez. All such testimony was denied by military officers and the Director of Honduran Intelligence.

The Commission also presented evidence that domestic judicial remedies were inadequate. Courts were slow and judges were often ignored by police. Authorities denied detentions. Judges charged with executing the writs of *habeas corpus* were threatened and on several occasions imprisoned. Law professors and lawyers defending political prisoners were pressured not to act; one of the two lawyers to bring a writ of *habeas corpus* was arrested. In no case was the writ effective in relation to a disappeared person.

In view of threats against witnesses it had called, the Commission asked the Court to take provisional measures contemplated by the Convention. Soon thereafter, the Commission reported the death of a Honduran summoned by the Court to appear as a witness, killed 'on a public thoroughfare [in the capital city] by a group of armed men who ... fled in a vehicle'. Four days later the Court was informed of two more assassinations, one victim being a man who had testified before the Court as a witness hostile to the government. After a public hearing, the Court decided on 'additional provisional measures' requiring Honduras to report within two weeks: (1) on measures that it adopted to protect persons connected with the case; (2) on its judicial investigations of threats against such persons; and (3) on its investigations of the assassinations.]

...

[VII]

...

123. Because the Commission is accusing the Government of the disappearance of Manfredo Velásquez, it, in principle, should bear the burden of proving the facts underlying its petition.

124. The Commission's argument relies upon the proposition that the policy of disappearances, supported or tolerated by the Government, is designed to conceal and destroy evidence of disappearances. When the

existence of such a policy or practice has been shown, the disappearance of a particular individual may be proved through circumstantial or indirect evidence or by logical inference. Otherwise, it would be impossible to prove that an individual has been disappeared... .

126. ... If it can be shown that there was an official practice of disappearances in Honduras, carried out by the Government or at least tolerated by it, and if the disappearance of Manfredo Velásquez can be linked to that practice, the Commission's allegations will have been proven to the Court's satisfaction, so long as the evidence presented on both points meets the standard of proof required in cases such as this.

127. The Court must determine what the standards of proof should be in the instant case. Neither the Convention, the Statute of the Court, nor its Rules of Procedure speak to this matter. Nevertheless, international jurisprudence has recognized the power of the courts to weigh the evidence freely, although it has always avoided a rigid rule regarding the amount of proof necessary to support the judgment.

...

130. The practice of international and domestic courts shows that direct evidence, whether testimonial or documentary, is not the only type of evidence that may be legitimately considered in reaching a decision. ...

131. Circumstantial or presumptive evidence is especially important in allegations of disappearances, because this type of repression is characterized by an attempt to suppress any information about the kidnapping or the whereabouts and fate of the victim.

...

134. The international protection of human rights should not be confused with criminal justice. States do not appear before the Court as defendants in a criminal action. The objective of international human rights law is not to punish those individuals who are guilty of violations, but rather to protect the victims and to provide for the reparation of damages resulting from the acts of the States responsible.

135. In contrast to domestic criminal law, in proceedings to determine human rights violations the State cannot rely on the defense that the complainant has failed to present evidence when it cannot be obtained without the State's cooperation.

136. The State controls the means to verify acts occurring within its territory. Although the Commission has investigatory powers, it cannot exercise them within a State's jurisdiction unless it has the cooperation of that State.

...

138. The manner in which the Government conducted its defense would have sufficed to prove many of the Commission's allegations by virtue of the principle that the silence of the accused or elusive or ambiguous answers on its part may be interpreted as an acknowledgment of the truth of the allegations, so long as the contrary is not indicated by the record or is not compelled as a matter of law. This result would not hold under criminal law, which does not apply in the instant case ...

...

[IX]

147. The Court now turns to the relevant facts that it finds to have been proven. They are as follows:

> a. During the period 1981 to 1984, 100 to 150 persons disappeared in the Republic of Honduras, and many were never heard from again... .

> b. Those disappearances followed a similar pattern... .

> c. It was public and notorious knowledge in Honduras that the kidnappings were carried out by military personnel, police or persons acting under their orders... .

> d. The disappearances were carried out in a systematic manner, regarding which the Court considers the following circumstances particularly relevant:

i. The victims were usually persons whom Honduran officials considered dangerous to State security... . [Omitted paragraphs deal with arms used, details of the kidnappings and interrogations, denials by officials of any knowledge about the disappeared person, and the failure of any investigative committees to produce results.]

e. On September 12, 1981, between 4:30 and 5:00 p. m., several heavily armed men in civilian clothes driving a white Ford without license plates kidnapped Manfredo Velásquez from a parking lot in downtown Tegucigalpa. Today, nearly seven years later, he remains disappeared, which creates a reasonable presumption that he is dead... .

f. Persons connected with the Armed Forces or under its direction carried out that kidnapping... .

g. The kidnapping and disappearance of Manfredo Velásquez falls within the systematic practice of disappearances referred to by the facts deemed proved in paragraphs a–d.

...

[X]

149. Disappearances are not new in the history of human rights violations. However, their systematic and repeated nature and their use, not only for causing certain individuals to disappear, either briefly or permanently, but also as a means of creating a general state of anguish, insecurity and fear, is a recent phenomenon. Although this practice exists virtually worldwide, it has occurred with exceptional intensity in Latin America in the last few years.

150. The phenomenon of disappearances is a complex form of human rights violation that must be understood and confronted in an integral fashion.

151. The establishment of [the UN Working Group on Disappearances in 1980] is a clear demonstration of general censure and repudiation of the practice of disappearances ... .

152. Within the inter-American system, the [OAS] General Assembly ... and the Commission have repeatedly referred to the practice of disappearances and have urged that disappearances be investigated and that the practice be stopped ... .

153. International practice and doctrine have often categorized disappearances as a crime against humanity, although there is no treaty in force which is applicable to the States Parties to the Convention and which uses this terminology ... .

...

155. The forced disappearance of human beings is a multiple and continuous violation of many rights under the Convention that the States Parties are obligated to respect and guarantee. The kidnapping of a person is an arbitrary deprivation of liberty, an infringement of a detainee's right to be taken without delay before a judge and to invoke the appropriate procedures to review the legality of the arrest, all in violation of Article 7 of the Convention. [Every person has 'the right to personal liberty and security', 'arbitrary arrest or imprisonment' are prohibited, and procedural rights must be respected.] ...

156. Moreover, prolonged isolation and deprivation of communication are in themselves cruel and inhuman treatment, harmful to the psychological and moral integrity of the person and a violation of the right of any detainee to respect for his inherent dignity as a human being. Such treatment, therefore, violates Article 5 of the Convention. [No one 'shall be subjected to torture or to cruel, inhuman, or degrading punishment or treatment'.] ...

157. The practice of disappearances often involves secret execution without trial, followed by concealment of the body to eliminate any material evidence of the crime and to ensure the impunity of those responsible. This

is a flagrant violation of the right to life, recognized in Article 4 of the Convention. [Every person has 'the right to have his life respected... . No one shall be arbitrarily deprived of his life.'] ...

158. The practice of disappearances, in addition to directly violating many provisions of the Convention, such as those noted above, constitutes a radical breach of that treaty in that it implies a crass abandonment of the values which emanate from the concept of human dignity and of the most basic principles of the inter-American system and the Convention ... .

...

[The part of the Court's opinion examining the obligation of a state not only to respect individual rights (such as by not 'disappearing' the government's opponents), but also to ensure free exercise of rights (such as by protecting those expressing political opinions against violence by private, nongovernmental actors), appears above.]

[XII]

...

190. During this proceeding, the Commission requested the payment of compensation, but did not offer evidence regarding the amount of damages or the manner of payment. Nor did the parties discuss these matters.

191. The Court believes that the parties can agree on the damages. If an agreement cannot be reached, the Court shall award an amount. The case shall, therefore, remain open for that purpose. The Court reserves the right to approve the agreement and, in the event no agreement is reached, to set the amount and order the manner of payment.

[In the concluding paragraphs, the Court unanimously declared that Honduras violated Articles 4, 5, and 7 of the Convention, all three read in conjunction with Article 1(1); and unanimously decided that Honduras was required to pay fair compensation to the victim's next of kin.]

* * *

Various judgments of the Inter-American Court are reproduced in chapters throughout this casebook. For that reason, the following materials do not seek to provide a comprehensive overview of its jurisprudence or evolution. Instead, the focus is on three issues: the development of the 'conventionality control doctrine (analysed by Jorge Contesse); the significance of the Court's approach to monitoring compliance and the structural orientation of its analyses (Rene Urueña); and its approach to the rights of indigenous peoples.

JORGE CONTESSE, HUMAN RIGHTS AS TRANSNATIONAL LAW
116 AJIL UNBOUND (2022) 313

...

International Law as Constitutional Law

At the end of the 1980s, many Latin American countries began the transition to become constitutional democracies. Many adopted new constitutions, while some reformed existing constitutions. States that experienced a sort of "new constitutional beginning," and which did so through new legal regulations, made an explicit commitment to international human rights law. If one reviews the new constitutions adopted at that time—Brazil in 1988, Colombia in 1991, and Peru in 1993—or the important constitutional reforms that other countries carried out, such as Chile in 1989 or Argentina in 1994, all of them provided that international human rights law would now form an integral part of constitutional law.

This step was key to what would become the use of international law by domestic courts, especially constitutional courts. With varying intensity, national courts started incorporating in their reasoning international human rights norms that subsequently gave rise to a common law in Latin America, the so-called *ius constitutionale commune*. This phenomenon would crystallize, as I show in the following section, with the Inter-American Court's adoption of the doctrine of conventionality control, thus cementing Latin America international human rights law as constitutional law.

In the mid-1990s, a Peruvian district court declared the country's amnesty law unconstitutional for violating due process and affecting the rights of the victims of a massacre that occurred in November 1991 under Alberto Fujimori's regime—"the Barrios Altos massacre." Interestingly, in its ruling, the court determined that the unconstitutionality of the amnesty law stemmed not only from its incompatibility with the Peruvian Constitution, but also with the Universal Declaration of Human Rights and the American Convention on Human Rights. International law was unequivocally now part of Peru's domestic law.

At the same time, the Constitutional Court of Colombia, established by the 1991 Constitution, created one of its most important doctrines: the "block of constitutionality." Under this doctrine, the Colombian Court found that it should not only take into account the norms of the national Constitution, but also the norms and principles of international human rights law. According to the court, international human rights norms, "without appearing formally in the articles of the constitutional text, are used as parameters for the control of the constitutionality of laws," thus generating a single normative "block" to be used by the Constitutional Court.

A few years later, the Chilean courts—known for their reticence toward the use of international law and especially their acquiescence to the military dictatorship of Augusto Pinochet—did the same with the self-amnesty laws passed by the Pinochet regime. Resorting to the Geneva Conventions, the Chilean Supreme Court modified its prior interpretation of self-amnesty laws which had rejected all efforts to hold accountable those responsible for serious human rights violations. With the new interpretation, the Chilean Court determined that international law (in this case, international humanitarian law) took precedence over domestic law.
....

Constitutional Law as International Law

... [T]he Inter-American Court of Human Rights ... progressively took on the role of a type of regional constitutional court. ...

... [In] *Barrios Altos v. Peru* ... the Inter-American Court determined that Peru was responsible for the lack of proper investigation and punishment of those responsible for the Barrios Altos massacre. [The Court declared] that self-amnesty laws "lack legal effect," pursuant to which [it] ordered the reopening of the investigations by the national courts.

... [T]he claim that such incompatibility [with the Convention] renders these laws "devoid of legal effect" is what ... turned the Inter-American Court into a sort of regional constitutional court. Declaring a national law inapplicable—or null and void—is typically a decision that a *domestic* (that is, "constitutional") court may take, not one that is left to the decision of an *international* tribunal.

... [I]n 2006 [it] issued another landmark judgment: *Almonacid-Arellano v. Chile*, in which [it] created its doctrine of "conventionality control." According to this doctrine, all national judges are directly bound to follow the norms of the Convention and the interpretations of the Inter-American Court. ... Thus, the separation between international law and constitutional law progressively unravels, as the Court seems to understand national judges as genuine "inter-American judges."

RENE URUEÑA, COMPLIANCE AS TRANSFORMATION: THE INTER-AMERICAN SYSTEM OF HUMAN RIGHTS AND ITS IMPACT(S) RAINER GROTE ET AL. (EDS.), RESEARCH HANDBOOK ON COMPLIANCE IN INTERNATIONAL HUMAN RIGHTS LAW (2021) 225

3.2 A New Approach: Compliance as Transformation

... [F]our things are noteworthy in [the compliance] initiatives. First, their sheer volume. The organs of the IASHR clearly think that they themselves are primarily responsible for supervising compliance with their remedial orders and have developed a wide range of tools to do so. The IASHR represents, in this sense, a clear choice for a legalized system of compliance – in sharp contrast with more political systems of compliance review, such as the European system of human rights. ...

The second ... is the wide variety of orders. ... Many of the tools created to supervise orders from the system are different in the Commission and the Court, and the standards applied by each institution (and by the same institution in different moments) often vary. This may be a consequence of the piecemeal fashion in which most of these mechanisms have emerged. ...

Third, ... the System conceives of compliance monitoring as part of a wider process of transformation. ... Most of the supervising mechanisms ... seem to be less concerned with enforcing certain orders, but rather with creating cognitive frameworks and domestic political dynamics that will, eventually, lead to the wider compliance with its orders. ... [Through] informational requirements ... on-site visits and decentralized compliance hearings ... the System is striving to create the cognitive and political frameworks that will facilitate local pressure towards compliance, usually by domestic civil society groups. ... [T]he organs in the system use compliance monitoring mechanisms as a tool to open spaces of dialogue with local stakeholders, in order to work in tandem with civil society, and change, through the process of compliance monitoring, the very conditions that prevent compliance.

... In most traditional readings of compliance with international judicial decisions, both the judicial decision and the context of implementation are read as static, and compliance is read as a mechanical process in which the political 'leverages' in the context of implementation are activated, in order to achieve behavioural changes in the addressees of the decision. ...

The Inter-American approach ... rejects the idea that the judicial decision is already crystallized, or carved in stone. ... An order by the IASHR is ... the first (and fundamental) statement in a conversation, defining the scope and limits of the possibilities of implementation, but lacking the details of concrete policy, whose definition fall within the scope of competence of the state. Moreover, the IASHR questions the idea that the context of implementation is static. ... [Instead, the regime] creates a continuum between the decision (or order) and the shaping of the conditions for its implementation, reading the latter as essentially malleable. ... [T]he question of compliance is not only whether there are tools to 'force' the state to comply (what kind of leverage is there to induce, for example, domestic prosecution of perpetrators? Is there an active domestic judiciary? Is there a powerful civil society?) but also how can this very decision be used to mobilize such tools and change the equation towards compliance (how can the local judiciary use this decision to bring about compliance with it? How can civil society mobilize around this decision?). This essentially dynamic process of compliance monitoring draws its inspiration from domestic models of transformative constitutionalism in Latin America. In particular, the Colombian Constitutional Court has adopted a nuanced strategy of compliance supervision ... .

... Compliance review [is thus] part of a dialectic process of interaction with domestic civil society, in which compliance is not an end in itself, but a process of transformation in which domestic pro-rights constituencies, including civil society organizations, national human rights institutions, and domestic tribunals, use the process of compliance to push for social transformation.

QUESTION

The facts of a case before the IACtHR are contested. What method does the Court employ to resolve them? Does it employ such traditional notions of the law of evidence in systems of national law as burdens of proof (burdens of persuasion) or presumptions? For example:

(a)   What is the relevance to the Court's finding of Honduran responsibility of the Court's use of terms like (the Honduran) 'practice' or 'policy', or the characterization of disappearances as 'systemic'?

(b)   What is the significance of the Court's observation that the state 'controls the means to verify acts occurring within its territory'? Is the Court threatening the state with an adverse finding if it fails to make that effort?

THE RIGHTS OF INDIGENOUS PEOPLES

The Inter-American Court has played an especially important role in relation to the rights of indigenous peoples. It is estimated that some 50 million indigenous people in Latin America belong to 500 different ethnic groups, with the largest populations living in Mexico, Guatemala, Peru and Bolivia. They make up 8 percent of the region's total population, but 17 percent of the population living in extreme poverty.

In 2016, the Court reviewed its own jurisprudence in the context of Advisory Opinion OC-22/16 (26 February 2016): 'Entitlement of Legal Entities to Hold Rights under the Inter-American Human Rights System …'. The Court affirmed that 'legal entities', such as corporations, are not entitled to claim the rights recognized in the American Convention, regardless of whether domestic State law defines them as cooperatives, companies or firms. It then continued to examine the situation in relation to indigenous peoples. Based on a review of its own case law, as well as various domestic and international legal sources, the Court held that "indigenous and tribal communities are entitled to some of the rights protected under the Convention and, therefore, can access the inter-American system."

SAWHOYAMAXA INDIGENOUS COMMUNITY V. PARAGUAY
INTER-AMERICAN COURT OF HUMAN RIGHTS, SER. C, NO. 146 (29 MARCH 2006)

…

73. Having assessed [all the evidence] … . the Court finds the following facts to be proven:

…

73(1) Towards the end of the 19th century vast stretches of land in the Paraguayan Chaco were acquired by British businessmen through the London Stock Exchange as a consequence of the debt owed by Paraguay after the so-called War of the Triple Alliance. The division and sale of such territories were made while their inhabitants, who, at the time, were exclusively Indians, were kept in full ignorance of the facts.

…

73(2) The economy of the indigenous peoples in the Chaco was mainly based on hunting, fishing, and gathering, and therefore, they had to roam their lands to make use of nature … .

73(3) Over the years, and particularly after the Chaco War between Bolivia and Paraguay (1933–1936), the non-indigenous occupation of the Northern Chaco which had started by the end of the 19th century was extended. The estates that started settling in the area used the Indians who had traditionally lived there as workers, who thus became farmhands and employees of new owners. Although the indigenous peoples continued occupying their traditional lands, the effect of the market economy activities into which they were incorporated turned out to be the restriction of their mobility, whereby they ended by becoming sedentary.

73(4) Since then, the lands of the Paraguayan Chaco have been transferred to private owners and gradually divided. …

73(5) The Sawhoyamaxa ("from the place where coconuts have run out") Community is an indigenous community, typical of those traditionally living in the Paraguayan Chaco that has become sedentary … .

…

73(8) [In 2006], the Community has 407 members, grouped in approximately eighty-three dwelling places.

73(9) The lands claimed … are within the lands which they have traditionally occupied and which are part of their traditional habitat.

73(10) The lands claimed are suitable for the Indigenous Community members to continue with their current subsistence activities and to ensure their short and mid-term survival, as well as the beginning of a long-term process of development of alternative activities which will allow their subsistence to become sustainable.

[The Court considered several issues including whether the plea of non-exhaustion of domestic remedies could be invoked at this late stage, whether the existing indigenous land-claim administrative procedure was effective, and whether the time taken to consider claims had been reasonable. It reached negative conclusions on each issue.]

[Right to property — Article 21]

...

116. Article 21 of the American Convention declares that:

> 1.   Everyone has the right to the use and enjoyment of his property. The law may subordinate such use and enjoyment to the interest of society.
>
> 2.   No one shall be deprived of his property except upon payment of just compensation, for reasons of public utility or social interest, and in the cases and according to the forms established by law. ...

117. In analyzing [Article 21] in relation to the communal property of the members of indigenous communities, the Court has taken into account Convention No. 169 of the ILO in the light of the general interpretation rules established under Article 29 of the Convention, in order to construe ... Article 21 in accordance with the evolution of the Inter-American system ... . The State ratified Convention No. 169 and incorporated its provisions to domestic legislation by Law No. 234/93.

118. ... [T]he close ties the members of indigenous communities have with their traditional lands and the natural resources associated with their culture ..., must be secured under Article 21 of the American Convention. The culture of the members of indigenous communities reflects a particular way of life, of being, seeing and acting in the world, the starting point of which is their close relation with their traditional lands and natural resources, not only because they are their main means of survival, but also because they form part of their worldview, of their religiousness, and consequently, of their cultural identity.

119. [Article 13 of Convention No. 169 requires states to] respect "the special importance for the cultures and spiritual values of the peoples concerned of their relationship with the lands or territories, or both as applicable, which they occupy or otherwise use, and in particular the collective aspects of this relationship."

120. Likewise, this Court considers that indigenous communities might have a collective understanding of the concepts of property and possession, in the sense that ownership of the land "is not centered on an individual but rather on the group and its community." This notion of ownership and possession of land does not necessarily conform to the classic concept of property, but deserves equal protection under Article 21. ... . Disregard for specific versions of use and enjoyment of property, springing from the culture, uses, customs, and beliefs of each people, would be tantamount to holding that there is only one way of using and disposing of property, which, in turn, would render protection under Article 21 ... illusory for millions of persons.

121. Consequently, the close ties of indigenous peoples with their traditional lands and the native natural resources thereof, associated with their culture, as well as any incorporeal element deriving therefrom, must be secured under Article 21 ... . [In the Court's jurisprudence] "property" as used in Article 21, includes "material things which can be possessed, as well as any right which may be part of a person's patrimony; that concept includes all movable and immovable, corporeal and incorporeal elements and any other intangible object capable of having value".

122. The Paraguayan Constitution recognizes the existence of indigenous peoples as groups which have preceded the formation of the State, as well as their cultural identity, the relation with their respective habitat and their communal characteristics of their land-tenure system, and further grants them a series of specific rights which serve as basis for the Court to define the scope of Article 21 of the Convention.

123. On the other hand, Article 3 of Law No. 43/89 points out that settlements of indigenous communities are "constituted by a physical area made up of a core of houses, natural resources, crops, plantations, and their environs, linked insofar as possible to their cultural tradition ...]"

...

125. The State has pointed out that it "does not deny its obligation to restore rights to these peoples," but the members of the Sawhoyamaxa Community "claim title to a piece of real estate based exclusively on an anthropologic report that, worthy as it is, collides with a property title which has been registered and has been conveyed from one owner to another for a long time." Likewise, the State fears that, would [the] claim by the Community be granted, "it would be convicted for the 'sins' committed during the [C]onquest" (inner quotation marks as used in the original text), and that this could lead to the "absurd situation in which the whole country could be claimed by indigenous peoples, for they are the primitive inhabitants of the stretch of territory that is nowadays called Paraguay."

126. [T]he Court will proceed to examine, in the first place, whether possession of the lands by the indigenous people is a requisite for official recognition of property title thereto. In the event that possession not be a requisite for restitution rights, the Court will analyze, in the second place, whether enforcement of said rights is time-restricted. Finally, the Court will address the actions that the State must take to enforce indigenous communal property rights.

i) The possession of the lands

127. Acting within the scope of its adjudicatory jurisdiction, the Court has had the opportunity to decide on indigenous land possession in three different situations. On the one hand, in the *Case of the Mayagna (Sumo) Awas Tingni Community*, the Court pointed out [in 2001] that possession of the land should suffice for indigenous communities lacking real title to property of the land to obtain official recognition of that property, and for consequent registration. On the other hand, in the *Case of the Moiwana Community*, the Court considered [in 2005] that the members of the N'djuka people were the "legitimate owners of their traditional lands" although they did not have possession thereof, because they left them as a result of the acts of violence perpetrated against them. In this case, the traditional lands have not been occupied by third parties. Finally, in the *Case of the Indigenous Community Yakye Axa*, the court [in 2005] considered that the members of the Community were empowered, even under domestic law, to file claims for traditional lands and ordered the State, as measure of reparation, to individualize those lands and transfer them on a for no consideration basis.

128. The following conclusions are drawn from the foregoing: 1) traditional possession of their lands by indigenous people has equivalent effects to those of a state-granted full property title; 2) traditional possession entitles indigenous people to demand official recognition and registration of property title; 3) the members of indigenous peoples who have unwillingly left their traditional lands, or lost possession therof, maintain property rights thereto, even though they lack legal title, unless the lands have been lawfully transferred to third parties in good faith; and 4) the members of indigenous peoples who have unwillingly lost possession of their lands, when those lands have been lawfully transferred to innocent third parties, are entitled to restitution thereof or to obtain other lands of equal extension and quality. Consequently, possession is not a requisite conditioning the existence of indigenous land restitution rights. The instant case is categorized under this last conclusion.

129. Paraguay acknowledges the right of indigenous peoples to claim restitution of their lost traditional lands
. . . .
...

iii) Actions to enforce the rights of the community members over their traditional lands

135. [W]hen a State is unable, on objective and reasoned grounds, to adopt measures aimed at returning traditional lands and communal resources to indigenous populations, it must surrender alternative lands of equal extension and quality, which will be chosen by agreement with the members of the indigenous peoples, according to their own consultation and decision procedures.

136. Nevertheless, the Court can not ... decide that Sawhoyamaxa Community's property rights to traditional lands prevail over the right to property of private owners or *vice versa*, since the Court is not a domestic judicial authority with jurisdiction to decide disputes among private parties. This power is vested exclusively in the Paraguayan State. Nevertheless, the Court has competence to analyze whether the State ensured the human rights of the members of the Sawhoyamaxa Community.

137. ... [T]he [three] arguments put forth by the State to justify non-enforcement of the indigenous people's property rights have not sufficed to release it from international responsibility. ...

138. [First] ... the fact that the claimed lands are privately held by third parties is not in itself an "objective and reasoned" ground for dismissing *prima facie* the claims by the indigenous people. Otherwise, restitution rights become meaningless and would not entail an actual possibility of recovering traditional lands, as it would be exclusively limited to an expectation on the will of the current holders, forcing indigenous communities to accept alternative lands or economic compensations. In this respect, the Court has pointed out that, when there be conflicting interests in indigenous claims, it must assess in each case the legality, necessity, proportionality and fulfillment of a lawful purpose in a democratic society ... to impose restrictions on the right to property, on the one hand, or the right to traditional lands, on the other ... .

139. [The same rationale applies to the second argument which suggests] that indigenous communities are not entitled, under any circumstances, to claim traditional lands when they are exploited and fully productive, viewing the indigenous issue exclusively from the standpoint of land productivity and agrarian law, something which is insufficient for it fails to address the distinctive characteristics of such peoples.

140. [The third argument is that the owner's right is protected under a bilateral agreement between Paraguay and Germany which, because of its treaty status, has become part of the law of the land.] ... [T]he Court has not been furnished with the aforementioned treaty [but it is said to allow] ... for capital investments made by a contracting party to be condemned or nationalized for a "public purpose or interest", which could justify land restitution to indigenous people ... . [The] enforcement [of such bilateral treaties] should always be compatible with the American Convention, which is a multilateral treaty on human rights that stands in a class of its own and that generates rights for individual human beings and does not depend entirely on reciprocity among States.
...

142. Finally, it is worth recalling that, under Article 1(1) of the Convention, the State is under the obligation to respect the rights recognized therein and to organize public authority in such a way as to ensure to all persons under its jurisdiction the free and full exercise of human rights.

143. Even though the right to communal property of the lands and of the natural resources of indigenous people is recognized in Paraguayan laws, such merely abstract or legal recognition becomes meaningless in practice if the lands have not been physically delimited and surrendered because the adequate domestic measures necessary to secure effective use and enjoyment of said right by the members of the Sawhoyamaxa Community are lacking. The free development and transmission of their culture and traditional rites have thus been threatened.

144. For the aforementioned reasons, the Court concludes that the State violated Article 21 of the American Convention, to the detriment of the members of the Sawhoyamaxa Community, in relation to Articles 1(1) and 2 therein.

[Right to juridical personality — Article 3]
...

187. In the instant case, neither the Commission nor the representatives have alleged the violation of Article 3 of the American Convention. However, from the facts of the case, it ... appears that there has been no registration or official documentation of the existence of several members of the indigenous Sawhoyamaxa Community. The Court considers that the parties have had the opportunity of addressing such situation [sic], thus, it is pertinent to examine the obligations stemming from Article 3 of the American Convention which provides as follows:

> "Every person has the right to recognition as a person before the law."

...

192. The above mentioned members of the Community have remained in a legal limbo in which, though they have been born and have died in Paraguay, their existence and identity were never legally recognized, that is to say, they did not have personality before the law. Indeed, the State, in the instant proceeding before the Court,

has intended to use this situation for its own benefit. In fact, at the time of referring to the right to life, the State alleged:

> If neither the existence of these persons nor even their death has even been proved, it is not possible to claim liability from anyone, lest [sic] the State, where are their birth and death certificates?

...

194. On the basis of the above considerations, and notwithstanding the fact that other members of the Community may be in the same situation, the Court finds that the State violated the right to personality before the law enshrined in Article 3 ... .

[Reparations]

[Based on Article 63(1), the Court ordered 'the State [to] adopt all legislative, administrative or other type of measures necessary to guarantee the members of the Community ownership rights over their traditional lands' and required it to consider the possibility of purchasing or acquiring those lands, or to make available alternative lands, selected with the Community's agreement. This was to be completed within three years.]

219. Non-pecuniary damage may include distress and suffering caused directly to the victims or their relatives [which] may only be compensated [either] by paying an amount of money or delivering property or services [or] through public actions or works .. .

235. ... [T]he State shall, within a reasonable time, enact into its domestic legislation ... the legislative, administrative and other measures necessary to provide an efficient mechanism to claim the ancestral lands of indigenous peoples enforcing their property rights and taking into consideration their customary law, values, practices and customs.

...

236. [The State shall publish parts of the judgment in the media and on radio in appropriate languages and on a regular basis.]

...

248 The Court shall monitor full compliance with this Judgment and shall consider the instant case closed upon full compliance by the State with the provisions therein. Within a year ... the State shall submit to the Court a report on the measures adopted to comply herewith ... .

* * *

The Sawhoyamaxa case also illustrates the fact that litigation in a regional human rights court is very often only one part of a much more complex ongoing process. Joel E. Correia, in 'Adjudication and Its After Effects in Three Inter-American Court Cases Brought against Paraguay: Indigenous Land Rights', 111 *Erasmus L. Rev.* (2018) 43, traced the aftermath of the IACtHR ruling:

> ... [The] Sawhoyamaxa decided to reoccupy their communal territory because the Paraguayan state systemically delayed implementing the IACtHR judgment and its recommendations for land restitution. In 2013, 7 years following the IACtHR judgment, community members from Sawhoyamaxa reoccupied their communal territory and embarked on an intensive advocacy campaign with the assistance of Tierraviva and Amnesty International. To the surprise of the community and Tierraviva, the Paraguayan Senate approved a Law 5124 in 2014 to expropriate 14,404 hectares of land to the community.
>
> The law of expropriation, like the IACtHR judgment, was a remarkable legal victory that bolstered the community's claim to its communal territory. Despite the momentous victory, state officials refused to force the landowners to accept payment for the 14,404 hectares, surrender the title to the property, or vacate ranch buildings contained therein. Moreover, the Paraguayan Supreme Court entertained two challenges made by the

landowner to question the constitutionality of Law 5124 because he argued the land was 'rationally exploited' and therefore ineligible for expropriation. ... [The result is that the] Sawhoyamaxa enjoys de facto usage of their land but limited de jure protection because the property technically remains under the legal control of the ranching company that refuses to cede the title.

QUESTION

What could be done, at the institutional level, to improve the prospects that IACtHR judgments in cases relating to indigenous peoples are implemented in practice? In a chapter devoted to 'remedies for violations of indigenous rights', Kent Roach in *Remedies for Human Rights Violations: A Two-Track Approach to Supra-national and National Law* (2021) 454-515, calls on the Court itself and national courts to pay more heed to the communities themselves in devising remedies. How might that help?

C. THE AFRICAN SYSTEM

The youngest of the regional systems, but the one covering the largest number of states, is the African one. The African Charter on Human and Peoples' Rights was adopted in 1981, entered into force in 1986, and as of 2024, had 54 states parties (all of the members of the African Union, except for Morocco).[487]

In discussing rights and duties (Ch. 6B, above), the African Charter served to illustrate a human rights regime that was more duty-oriented than the universal human rights system or the two other regional systems. These materials do not repeat that discussion, but instead focus on the work of the two principal institutions, the African Commission on Human and Peoples' Rights and the African Court of Human and Peoples' Rights. Nor do they address the broader issue of Africa's influence in shaping the overall international regime.[488]

1. The African Union

In 1963 the Organization of African Unity was established as the official regional body of African states. It was inspired by the anti-colonial struggles of the late 1950s, and was primarily dedicated to the eradication of colonialism. The emergent African states created through it a political bloc to facilitate intra-African relations and to forge a regional approach to Africa's relationships with external powers. In 2001 the OAU was replaced by the African Union (AU). Today, all 55 African states are members of the AU, with Morocco which withdrew in 1984 after the organization recognized Western Sahara, having re-joined in 2017.

For a variety of reasons, especially its experience of colonialism, the OAU Charter attached major importance to 'unity and solidarity' among African states, and defence of 'their sovereignty, their territorial integrity and independence'. Thus, the inviolability of territorial borders, expressed through the principle of non-interference in the internal affairs of member states, was one of the OAU's central creeds. But concern at its failure to react to various gross violations of human rights committed by dictators like Idi Amin in Uganda, Jean-Bédel Bokassa in the then Central African Empire, and Francisco Macias Nguema in Equatorial Guinea, combined with a growing recognition of the importance of human rights, led the OAU to adopt, in 1981, the African Charter on Human and Peoples' Rights.[489]

This development, in addition to the steady accumulation of national constitutions within Africa which contained detailed human rights provisions, facilitated the inclusion of a wide range of human rights objectives and principles in the AU Charter, unlike the OAU Charter which had said very little. Thus, among the AU's objectives, listed in Article 3, are to '(e) encourage international cooperation, taking due account of' the UN Charter and the UDHR and to '(h) promote and protect human and peoples' rights'. Similarly, Article 4 lists

---

[487] See R. Murray, *The African Charter on Human and Peoples' Rights: A Commentary* (2019).
[488] See D. Nault, *Africa and the Shaping of International Human Rights* (2020); M. Izarali, O. Masakure and B. Ibhawoh (eds.), *Expanding Perspectives on Human Rights in Africa* (2019).
[489] For a compilation of all key AU human rights documents, see *Compendium of African Human and Peoples' Rights Law* (2022).

key AU principles, including: non-interference in internal affairs; the AU Assembly's 'right ... to intervene in a Member State ... in respect of grave circumstances, namely: war crimes, genocide and crimes against humanity; promotion of gender equality; 'respect for democratic principles, human rights, the rule of law and good governance'; promotion of social justice; respect for the sanctity of human life; and 'condemnation and rejection of unconstitutional changes of governments'.

While the AU Charter does not contain any human rights requirements relating to admission to the Union, it does provide for the possible suspension of certain institutional rights or the imposition of sanctions upon states that fail to comply with AU decisions and policies (Art. 23(2)). In addition, governments that 'come to power through unconstitutional means shall not be allowed to participate' in AU activities (Art. 30).

The OAU also adopted several other important human rights instruments. The best known is the Protocol to the Charter on the Rights of Women in Africa (2003) (the 'Maputo Protocol').[490] As of 2024 it had 42 ratifications. The Protocol defines 'discrimination against women' to include 'any distinction, exclusion or restriction or any differential treatment based on sex and whose objectives or effects compromise or destroy the recognition, enjoyment or the exercise by women, regardless of their marital status, of human rights and fundamental freedoms in all spheres of life.' It has detailed provisions dealing, *inter alia*, with 'harmful practices' ('all behaviour, attitudes and/or practices which negatively affect the fundamental rights of women and girls, such as their right to life, health, dignity, education and physical integrity' (Art. 5)), violence against women (Art. 4), equality in and after marriage (Arts. 6 and 7), the right to political participation (Art. 9), protection of women in armed conflicts (Art. 11), health and reproductive rights (Art. 14), and widow's rights (Art. 20). Its implementation is to be overseen in the same way as the African Charter.

Other instruments include the African Charter on the Rights and Welfare of the Child (1990), with 50 ratifications as of 2024; the Protocol on the Rights of Older Persons (2016), with 11 ratifications; and the Protocol on the Rights of Persons with Disabilities (2018) with 8 ratifications. The African Committee of Experts on the Rights and Welfare of the Child has been very active, although its activities are not covered below.[491]

2. The African Commission

The 11 members of the Commission are elected by secret ballot by the Assembly of Heads of State and Government from a list of persons nominated by parties to the Charter. They serve (Art. 31) 'in their personal capacity'. Article 45 defines the mandate or functions of the Commission to be: (1) to 'promote Human and Peoples' Rights'; (2) to 'ensure the protection' of those rights; (3) to 'interpret all the provisions of the Charter' when so requested by states or AU institutions; and (4) to perform other tasks that may be committed to it by the Assembly. Thus, its three main functions are promotion, protection, and interpretation.

Promotion includes (Art. 45) undertaking 'studies and researches on African problems in the field of human and peoples' rights', as well as organizing seminars and conferences, disseminating information, encouraging 'local institutions concerned with human and peoples' rights', giving its views or making recommendations to governments, and formulating principles and rules 'aimed at solving legal problems related to human and peoples' rights ... upon which African Governments may base their legislation.' Under Article 46 the Commission 'may resort to any appropriate method of investigation'.

Before surveying the Commission's various activities, it is helpful to get a sense of what it sees as the main challenges. In reviewing the 'state of human rights in Africa' in its *Strategic Framework 2021-2025* (2020) at 7, the Commission began by recalling that 'Africa has developed an impressive array of normative and institutional frameworks on human rights ... .' It added:

> Over the past few decades, Africa has built an extensive body of instruments and policies
> to push forward the women's rights agenda ... [although] women's rights continue to be

---

[490] L. Chenwi, 'Protocol to the African Charter on Human and Peoples' Rights on the Rights of Women in Africa (Maputo Protocol)', in C. Binder et al. (eds.), *Elgar Encyclopedia of Human Rights* (2022) 104.

[491] For more information, see the website of the ACERWC at www.acerwc.africa/en.

undermined by inadequate implementation, institutional barriers, discriminatory and patriarchal social norms and practices, as well as by violence and intimidation. …

The continent has recorded significant gains over the years … [yet] challenges related to slow compliance, implementation of and reporting on continental and regional commitments by Member States persist. … Human rights defenders … continue to face widespread harassment, intimidation, abuse and death threats. …

… Extra-judicial killings are prevalent in countries where freedom of expression is unjustly restricted by the State – where there is little room for dissent. … [Political] rights have often been restricted under the guise of security concerns, attempts to curb defamation as well as fake news. This has led to, in some cases, complete internet and telecommunication shutdowns and in others, partial blockades of online spaces and platforms, taxes on social media, shutdowns of media houses and/or restrictions on their operation, surveillance and censorship. This is particularly the case during elections. Electoral related violence and unrest has often exacerbated and/or triggered human rights violations.

…

While armed groups and violent extremist elements wreak havoc …, counter-terrorism laws and practices that entail extra-judicial killings, arbitrary arrest and detention, disappearances and torture, can be equally counter-productive. …

Similarly, in its 2022 annual report to the AU's Heads of State and Government, the Commission identifies many 'areas of concern',[492] including: the largest number of military coups in Africa in over a decade in less than a year between April 2021 and February 2022; the low level of women's representation in parliaments and decision-making bodies in most African countries; persistence of the death penalty in some countries; the fact that only 16 African countries have ratified the Second Optional Protocol to the ICCPR aimed at the abolition of the death penalty; non-ratification of numerous international and regional treaty instruments; lack of legislation to regulate online violence against women in many African countries; persistence of police brutality, excessive use of force and the resulting culture of impunity within the police force in many countries, particularly in Kenya; illegal practices by law enforcement and security officials, including arbitrary arrests, excessive use of force, torture, cruel and inhumane treatment, and the state of detention facilities in Nigeria; the challenge of prison overcrowding, the lack of disaggregated data on prison overcrowding in most states and the dilapidated state of prisons, most of which are over half a century old; restriction of civic space, criminalization of bloggers, and restrictions on Internet access in some countries, which continue to impede the independence and freedom of journalists and interest groups.

Amnesty International highlights another major challenge which it describes as a 'chronic lack of cooperation by African states with the three regional human rights bodies, a pattern of lack of political will that is reflected in their indifference and open hostility.' The same report is also critical of the calibre of some of the Commissioners. This is reflected in 'the lack of enough candidates to allow for meaningful, genuine, competitive and merit based election. … [Elections] have almost always attracted unacceptably low numbers of nominations. Importantly, national nomination processes have often lacked transparency and openness. They have been historically shrouded in secrecy and rarely based on merit.' Rachel Murray also notes that 'more needs to be done to ensure those appointed to this important and influential position are individuals with the necessary experience, commitment and credibility.'[493]

The Commission engages in many activities that are comparable to those used by other inter-governmental human rights bodies. The following list provides an overview of its work, drawing mainly on its 2022 annual report.

1.   State reporting

---

[492] ACHPR, *52nd and 53rd Combined Activity Reports* (2023), para. 54.
[493] R. Murray, *The African Charter on Human and Peoples' Rights: A Commentary* (2019) 609.

States are required by the Charter (Article 62) to report to the Commission every two years. In 2022, only 12 of 54 states were up to date with their reports. 24 had three or more reports outstanding, meaning that they had not reported for at least six years. Six states have never reported, and five of those have been a party to the Charter since at least 1986.

2. **Individual complaints**

In 2022 there were 220 communications pending. During that year, 18 were admitted, nine were declared admissible and seven inadmissible, 13 were struck-off, and two removed from its roll. There were 12 decisions on merits.

3. **Interstate complaints**

The interstate complaints procedure contained in the Charter (Articles 47-52) has been used 'only three (or maybe four)' times by States. The only complaint to reach the merits phase was Communication 227/99 (2003), Democratic Republic of Congo v Burundi, Rwanda and Uganda.[494]

4. **Provisional measures**

Only one is reported upon for 2022 and that was objected to on various grounds by the target state, Ethiopia.

5. **Urgent appeals**

In 2022 the Commission sent 23 'letters of concern and urgent appeal'. Only Algeria, the addressee of two of the letters, responded.

6. **Fact-finding missions**

In 2022, the Commission sent no fact-finding missions. In 2021 it decided to establish a Commission of Inquiry into the human rights situation in Tigray, Ethiopia (Res. 482 (EXT.OS/XXXII) 2021), but efforts to reach agreement with the government were unsuccessful.

7. **Statements**

The Commission's 2021 report (para. 61) provides an example of a thematic statement which addressed the 'Human Rights Situation in the context of the COVID-19 pandemic'. Attention was drawn to issues such as: 'i. Limited access of vaccines to low-income countries and communities …; and the refusal to temporarily waive the COVID-19 patents …'; 'ii. Human rights abuses reported in the context of continuing states of emergency, disaster and calamity declared in many State Parties in relation to the COVID-19 pandemic …'; 'iii. The excessive use of force by law enforcement officers in the implementation of COVID-19 response measures …;" iv. The continued restrictions on freedom of expression and of the press, and the often-lengthy detention of civil society activists, as well as the unjustified prosecution of journalists under the guise of enforcing COVID-19 regulations;' … 'viii. The increased rate of girls being raped in many African countries due to the imposition of lockdown measures' … .

8. **Publication of guidelines**

Recent examples include: Guidelines on adhering to human and peoples' rights under the African Charter in the context of states of emergency or disaster (2023); Guidelines on Shadow Reports of the African Commission on Human and Peoples' Rights (2022); Guidelines on the protection of all persons against enforced disappearances in Africa (2022); Declaration of Principles on Freedom of Expression and Access to Information in Africa (2019); Guidelines on the Right to Water in Africa (2019); State Reporting Guidelines and Principles on Articles 21 And 24 of the African Charter relating to Extractive Industries, Human Rights and the Environment (2018); Principles on the Decriminalisation of Petty Offences in Africa (2018); Guidelines on Access to Information and Elections in Africa (2017); and Guidelines on Combating Sexual Violence and its Consequences in Africa (2017).

9. **Special Rapporteurs and Working Groups**

Special mechanisms include:

---

[494] *ibid.*, 656.

- Special Rapporteurs on: Freedom of Expression and Access to Information; Prisons, Conditions of Detention and Policing in Africa; Human Rights Defenders and Focal Point on Reprisals in Africa; Refugees, Asylum Seekers, Internally Displaced Persons and Migrant in Africa; and Rights of Women in Africa.

- Committees for: Prevention of Torture in Africa (and its 2022 Alert and Reporting Mechanism on Situations of Torture and Other Cruel, Inhuman or Degrading Treatment or Punishment); and Protection of the Rights of People Living with HIV

- Working Groups on: Economic, Social and Cultural Rights; Death Penalty, Extra-Judicial, Summary or Arbitrary Killings and Enforced Disappearances in Africa; Indigenous Populations/Communities and Minorities in Africa; Rights of Older Persons and People with Disabilities; and Extractive Industries, Environment and Human Rights Violations in Africa; and Fair Trial.

Assessing Compliance

Commentators on the African system have long pointed out that a focus on formal compliance fails to capture the full impact of the processes that take place around regional human rights institutions.[495] Nevertheless, a 2007 study by Frans Viljoen and Lirrette Louw[496] found that:

> [T]he attempt to chart compliance empirically and analytically is fraught with methodological difficulties. The most important of these is the Commission's failure to enunciate clear and specific remedies, leaving an unreliable yardstick for measuring compliance. Even when the yardstick is clearer, linking the steps toward compliance to the required remedial action often remains a matter of causal conjecture.
>
> Our analysis of cases of full and clear noncompliance suggests that the most important factors predictive of compliance are political, rather than legal. The only factor relating to the treaty body itself that shows a significant link to improved compliance is its follow-up activities. This finding lends support to arguments for a fully developed and effectively functional follow-up mechanism in the secretariat of the Commission, the consistent integration of follow-up activities into the Commission's mandate, and the appointment of a Special Rapporteur on follow-up ... .

The authors conclude that while the AU Charter has brought significant improvements in institutional arrangements, it still remains to be seen whether the AU will take effective action based on the opportunities available to it. In a 2022 update, one of the authors notes that little has changed since the 2007 study was published.[497]

The Commission, in its *Strategic Framework 2021-2025* (2020) at 7, observed that:

> ... [C]hallenges to implementation ... [include] weak, ineffective institutions, limited political will and action to enforce human rights and freedoms as well as to technical blockades. It is also important to note that financial resources remain [inadequate]. ... Africans are not sufficiently aware of key AU instruments such as the Charter. This is exacerbated by limited translation of these texts into local languages, which undermines

[495] O. Okafor, *The African Human Rights System: Activist Forces and International Institutions* (2007) 285.
[496] F. Viljoen Y L. Louw, 'State Compliance with the Recommendations of the African Commission on Human and Peoples' Rights, 1994–2004', 101 *Am. J. Int'l. L.* (2007) 1, at 32.
[497] L. Louw, 'Member States' Compliance with the Recommendations of the African Commission on Human and Peoples' Rights', in A. Adeola (ed.), *Compliance with International Human Rights Law in Africa: Essays in Honour of Frans Viljoen* (2022) 165.

local ownership. The conflation of these factors leads to poor human rights education and subsequently low legal literacy and citizen demand for rights.

It is widely accepted that one of the most important factors in predicting the impact of judgments is social mobilization.[498] But this starting point raises the issue of the effectiveness of the African regional institutions in building constituencies, educating the populace, and facilitating the involvement of civil society actors within the system.

Relations with NGOs and NHRIs

According to Rachel Murray, 'NGOs and CSOs have been crucial to the successes of the African human rights system. They have helped develop the standards …; they have worked closely with the [Commission and Court] to enhance their working procedures and practices'.[499] She adds (at 13) that if 'the credibility and legitimacy of a human rights system at the regional or international levels is measured in terms of its openness and level of engagement with civil society and non-governmental organisations, then the African Commission would score very well.'

By 2023, under its Resolution 361 on the Criteria for Granting and Maintaining Observer Status to Human Rights NGOs in Africa, the Commission had granted Observer Status to 544 NGOs. But this impressive figure masks tensions that first arose after its 2014 Resolution 275, on Protection against Violence and other Human Rights Violations against Persons on the basis of their real or imputed Sexual Orientation or Gender Identity. The AU and many states reacted negatively and in 2015 the AU called on the Commission to withdraw the observer status that it had granted to the Coalition of African Lesbians (CAL). Eventually the Commission complied.[500] In 2023, it rejected applications from three NGOs on the grounds that 'sexual orientation is not an expressly recognised right or freedom under the African Charter, and [is] contrary to the virtues of African values, as envisaged by the African Charter'. In reporting the decision, the International Service for Human Rights warned that it 'could seriously undermine and question the integrity and impartiality of the protection mechanism' and 'could potentially constrain NGOs wishing to collaborate with the Commission'.[501]

In 2022, the Commission adopted Guidelines on Shadow Reports. In principle, such an initiative would seem to be designed to encourage the submission of civil society reports that provide information that will add to and often contradict claims made by governments. These reports have played an especially important role in the context of the UN treaty bodies, where their content and orientation is not specifically regulated. The African Commission's guidelines provide that (para. 3):

> a. The Shadow Report should be concise, specific, and clearly structured. It should use simple and free flowing language.
>
> b. The Shadow Report must contain reliable, and objective information that is supported by a body of evidence including court cases, official reports, NHRIs annual reports, academic research, surveys, NGO reports, news articles. Sources used in the Report must be clearly cited, where at all possible, and up-to-date statistical information should be provided.
>
> c. The Shadow Report should be accompanied by copies of the relevant provisions of the principal legislative, judicial, administrative, and other texts referred to in the report, where applicable.
>
> …

[498] V. Ayeni, 'Beyond Compliance: Do Decisions of Regional Human Rights Tribunals in Africa Make a Difference?', in A. Adeola (ed.), *Compliance with International Human Rights Law in Africa: Essays in Honour of Frans Viljoen* (2022) 71.

[499] R. Murray, *The African Charter on Human and Peoples' Rights: A Commentary* (2019) 643.

[500] See S. Ayele Dersso, 'The Future of Human Rights and the African Human Rights System', 40 *Nordic J. Hum. Rts.* (2022) 28.

[501] International Service for Human Rights, *Outcomes of the 73rd session of the African Commission* (13 December 2022), at https://ishr.ch/latest-updates/outcome-of-the-73rd-session-of-the-african-commission/.

e. The Shadow Report should be submitted at least 30 days prior to the examination of the State Report.

f. The report should not include abusive, insulting, or defamatory language against individuals, institutions, or other entities.

...

The Commission has recognized the importance of the 47 national Human Rights Institutions (NHRIs) that exist in Africa. But it also notes that 'although they have increased the profile of human rights on the continent, they face challenges such as duplication of mandates with other State institutions, inadequate resources and lack autonomy considering that most are dependent on the executive branch for their financing.'[502] At the same time, civil society actors have suggested that the Commission needs the targeted support of NHRIs in order to protect its autonomy.[503]

3. The African Court on Human and Peoples' Rights

When the African Charter was adopted in 1981, a clear decision was taken to opt for a Commission rather than a Court as the principal institutional arrangement. Negotiations to establish a Court continued, however, and in 1998 the OAU Assembly adopted a Protocol to the African Charter on Human and Peoples' Rights to establish an African Court on Human and Peoples' Rights. The Protocol entered into force in 2004, after 15 states parties to the Charter had ratified it.

As of 2024, the Protocol had been ratified by 34 Member States of the African Union, namely: Algeria, Benin, Burkina Faso, Burundi, Cameroon, Chad, Côte d'Ivoire, Comoros, Congo, Democratic Republic of Congo, Gabon, The Gambia, Ghana, Guinea-Bissau, Kenya, Libya, Lesotho, Madagascar, Mali, Malawi, Mozambique, Mauritania, Mauritius, Nigeria, Niger, Rwanda, Sahrawi Arab Democratic Republic, South Africa, Senegal, Tanzania, Togo, Tunisia, Uganda and Zambia.

But, of those, only eight currently accept the Court's jurisdiction to receive cases directly from individuals and NGOs: Burkina Faso, Gambia, Ghana, Guinea-Bissau, Malawi, Mali, Niger and Tunisia.

As of January 2024, the Court's website reported a total of 338 cases received. Although it finalized 205 cases, almost half of those were dismissed as being inadmissible. The most cases came from Tanzania (156), Benin (43), Cote d'Ivoire (40), Mali (31), Tunisia (20), Rwanda (17), and Burkina Faso (10). Those figures perhaps help to explain why, between 2016 and 2020, four States withdrew their Declaration to allow individuals and NGOs to file cases before the Court: Rwanda (2016), Tanzania (2019), Benin (2020) and Côte d'Ivoire (2020). These withdrawals represented a considerable setback for the Court. In total, 46 percent of the Court's cases have come from Tanzania, the country that hosts the Court. At the time of its withdrawal, 28 of the Court's 70 judgments related to Tanzania. We consider below some of the explanations for the withdrawal.

On 27 June 2014, the African Union adopted the 'Malabo Protocol' to the Protocol on the Statute of the Court. If it enters into force, it would transform the Court into the African Court of Justice and Human Rights and would grant it a wide-ranging criminal jurisdiction, in addition to that prescribed by the Charter. As of 2024, 15 states have signed the Malabo Protocol, but none has ratified. The background to this initiative is described in Chapter 16B 4, below. A 2017 report by Amnesty International suggests why there has been no movement:

> With a jurisdiction covering three areas of international law, it is questionable whether the new court ... will have the capacity to effectively and efficiently deliver on its mandate. The proposed Court will have jurisdiction over 14 crimes ... [including] unconstitutional changes of government and illicit exploitation of natural resources. ... Yet, the proposed ACJHR will have only 6 judges dedicated to the International Crimes Section ... .[504]

---

[502] ACHPR, *Strategic Framework, 2021-2025* (2020) 9.
[503] L. Murugu Mute, *Protecting the mandate and autonomy of the African Commission on Human and Peoples' Rights: Leveraging the Roles of National Human Rights Institutions* (2021).
[504] *Malabo Protocol: Legal and Institutional Implications of the Merged and Expanded African Court: Snapshots,* Index No. AFR 01/6137/2017 (2017).

The African Court on Human and Peoples' Rights is based in Arusha, Tanzania, and consists of 11 judges 'elected in an individual capacity'. No two judges may be nationals of the same state (Art. 11). Its membership is to include 'representation of the main regions of Africa and of their principal legal traditions', and in the election of judges the Assembly 'shall ensure that there is adequate gender representation' (Art. 14). Judicial independence is to be fully ensured (Art. 17). All judges must be from Africa and a judge must not sit in a case concerning his or her own state of nationality. The President of the Court works full time, while the other ten judges work on a part-time basis. In 2024, five were women, including the President.

The Court's jurisdiction extends to cases and disputes 'concerning the interpretation and application' of the Charter, Protocol, 'and any other relevant human rights instrument ratified by the States concerned' (Art. 3). Although the Court's Rules of Procedure provide for third party interventions, they have only occurred in the context of advisory opinions. At the request of a member state of the OAU or the AU, the Court may give its advisory opinion 'on any legal matter related to the Charter or any other relevant human rights instruments', provided that the matter is not then being examined by the Commission (Art. 4). Of 15 requests, the Court has only accepted (and finalized) four, with the rest being 'struck out'.[505] They are:

- No 001/2021, On the application of the principle of regional rotation in the election of the bureau of the Pan African Parliament (PAP);
- No 001/2020, On the right to participate in the government of one's country in the context of an election held during a public health emergency or a pandemic, such as the Covid-19 crisis;
- No 001/2018, On the compatibility of Vagrancy Laws with the African Charter; and
- No.002/2013, On the Standing of the African Committee of Experts on the Rights and Welfare of the Child before the ACtHPR.

If the Court finds a violation, 'it shall make appropriate orders to remedy the violation' (Art. 27). States parties to the Protocol 'undertake to comply with the judgment in any case to which they are parties ... and to guarantee its execution' (Art. 30). The OAU Council of Ministers is to 'monitor' a judgment's execution (Art. 29). In 2022, the Court's annual budget was US$12,000,000, of which 89 percent came from Members States and 11 percent from 'international partners' (Doc. EX.CL/1409(XLII) (2023)).

The Case Law of the Court

One author has argued that the African Court can be seen as a 'continental (super) constitutional court'.[506] In support of this thesis he notes several relevant judgments:

ADEM K ABEBE, 'HORIZONTAL' COMPLIANCE WITH DECISIONS OF THE AFRICAN COURT ON HUMAN AND PEOPLES' RIGHTS
ADEROMOLA ADEOLA (ED.), COMPLIANCE WITH INTERNATIONAL HUMAN RIGHTS LAW IN AFRICA: ESSAYS IN HONOUR OF FRANS VILJOEN (2022) 169

...

In its first judgment on merits,[507] the African Court found unconstitutional the provision banning independent candidates from local, parliamentary and presidential elections in Tanzania. ... [T]he Supreme Court of Appeal ... ruled that all provisions of the Tanzanian Constitution could be amended as long as the prescribed procedure was followed [thereby rejecting] any implied limits on the power of amendment ... .

... The [African] Court ruled that the ban on independent candidacy violated the individual right to equal protection of the law and the prohibition against discrimination, the right to association, which specifically includes the right not to associate, and the right to political participation guaranteed in the African Charter. The Court also held that Tanzania did not satisfactorily argue that the ban on independent candidacy served a

---

[505] See generally, C. A. Odinkalu, 'Advice without Consent?: Assessing the Advisory Jurisdiction of the African Court on Human and Peoples' Rights', 45 *Hum. Rts. Q.* (2023) 365.

[506] A. Abebe, 'Taming Regressive Constitutional Amendments: The African Court as a Continental (super) Constitutional Court', 17 *Int. J. Const L.* (2019) 89.

[507] *Mtikila and Others v Republic of Tanzania,* Application Nos. 009/2011 and 011/2011 (14 June 2013).

legitimate interest. In any case, the Court found that the absolute ban on independent candidacy was disproportional to any stated aim of fostering national unity and solidarity. ...

In a case against Cote d'Ivoire,[508] the Court was confronted with the question of the compatibility of the Composition of the Independent Electoral Commission with continental standards, notably guarantees of independence and impartiality of election management bodies in the African Charter on Democracy, Elections and Governance and the ECOWAS Protocol on Good Governance and Democracy. The Court ruled that the composition of the Commission with representatives of political parties and office- holders violated the principle of impartiality. It also ruled that the disproportionate representation of the ruling party and the head of executive in the Commission, compared to representatives of opposition groups, violated not only the independence and impartiality of the Commission but also the principle of equality before the law. ...

In another case involving Burkina Faso,[509] the African Court found that legal provisions providing for sentences of imprisonment for the crime of defamation were incompatible with the African Charter, therefore necessitating non- custodial sentences. Four of the Court's judges added dissenting opinions finding the crime of defamation incompatible with the freedom of expression, thus suggesting that civil suits should replace criminal defamation laws. ... In addition, the Court ruled that the requirements to hold a press-card, which can be equated to licensing requirements, to practise journalism were incompatible with the freedom of expression. This was in addition to finding violations of the rights of the specific journalist imprisoned for defamation and granting of an order for compensation.

In 2019, the African Court found that the inclusion of mandatory death penalty sentences in Tanzania in relation to certain crimes, which requires judges to impose death sentences if the material facts of murder have been proven, was found to be 'automatic and mechanical' and, therefore, incompatible with the right to life, and also principles of fairness, due process and judicial impendence.[510] ... A few days before the official delivery of the judgment, the Tanzanian government submitted a letter to the AU withdrawing the [Article 34(6)] declaration allowing individuals and NGOs to submit cases before the Court. ...

* * *

The death penalty case was, however, only one of a number of reasons why Tanzania might have opted to withdraw its Article 34(6) declaration. A 28 October 2019 press release by Amnesty International, 'Tanzania: Climate of fear, censorship as repression mounts', provides a broader explanation:

> [A new] report by Amnesty International, "The price we pay: Targeted for dissent by the Tanzanian State" and [another] by Human Rights Watch, "As long as I am quiet, I am safe: Threats to Independent Media and Civil Society in Tanzania" were researched and documented separately but their findings were similar.
>
> ...
>
> They found that the president and senior government officials frequently made anti- human rights statements, at times followed by cracking down on individuals and organizations. The remarks, coupled with arbitrary arrests and threats to deregister non- governmental groups, has stifled independent reporting by journalists and public discussions on human rights violations ahead of the upcoming elections.
>
> Both organizations found that Tanzanian authorities undermined the rights to freedom of expression and association by enforcing new and existing repressive laws and regulations governing media, non-governmental organizations, and political parties.

Another perspective is provided by Nicole De Silva and Misha Plagis, in 'NGOs, International Courts, and State Backlash against Human Rights Accountability: Evidence from NGO Mobilization against Tanzania at the

---

[508] *Actions Pour la Protection des Droits de L'Homme (APDH) v. The Republic of Cote d'Ivoire*, Application No. 001/2014, Judgment (18 November 2016).
[509] *Konaté v. Burkina Faso*, Application No 004/2013, Judgment (5 December 2014).
[510] *Ally Rajabu and Others v. United Republic of Tanzania*, Application No. 007/2015, Judgment (28 November 2019).

African Court on Human and Peoples' Rights', 57 *L. & Soc. Rev.* (2023) 36. They analyze the role of NGOs in promoting strategic litigation against the Tanzanian Government:

> How does state backlash against human rights accountability, which may occur at the domestic and/or international levels, influence whether and how NGOs use international courts for their human rights advocacy? We develop a new two-level framework for explaining how specific forms of state backlash against human rights accountability can influence whether and how NGOs strategically litigate at IHRCs. ... Our framework focuses on the potential for backlash at two levels (domestic and international) and its consequences for NGOs, as key human rights defenders and IHRC constituencies.
>
> ... [W]e empirically analyze the impact of Tanzania's two-level backlash tactics on NGOs' mobilization at the African Court ... . [W]e provide an overview of cases of NGO participation in litigation against Tanzania at the African Court. From this, we select three cases of NGO-led litigation ... .
>
> ...

Abolishing the death penalty

[This analysis focuses on the case noted in the article above by Abebe.]

Rights of persons with albinism

PWA face a range of human rights issues including discrimination, special health and educational needs, harmful traditional practices, violence (e.g., killings, ritual attacks), witchcraft-related trade and trafficking of body parts, infanticide, and child abandonment. In recent decades, given a surge in violence against them, PWA in Tanzania received significant attention and advocacy from media, local and international NGOs, and international organizations. Under tremendous pressure to protect PWA and their human rights, the Tanzanian government introduced some protective measures ... .

...

[A complaint was filed with the African Court in 2020, shortly before the expiry of the one-year grace period after which Tanzania's withdrawal became fully effective.]

Rights of pregnant schoolgirls and mothers

In 2017, the Tanzanian government announced that it would enforce a law, which had existed since 2002, allowing pregnant schoolgirls to be expelled or excluded from school and denying them the right to study in public schools. By one estimate, over 8000 girls are expelled from school in Tanzania each year, while other pregnant girls stop attending school because they fear expulsion or stigma. ... NGOs have advocated for the inclusion of pregnant schoolgirls and young mothers in regular education at public schools, but they had limited domestic political opportunities for this advocacy and were subject to targeted domestic-level state backlash. In 2017, President Magufuli accused these NGOs of being used by foreign agents, and Tanzania's Home Affairs Minister threatened to rescind the registration of organizations advocating on this issue.

...

[A complaint was also filed with the African Court in this case in 2020.]

...

Conclusion

...

... NGOs' persistent human rights advocacy in the face of state backlash is a double-edged sword. On the one hand, it counters the state backlash objective of regressing to a previous condition, and it continues to support the development of international human rights law and the pursuit of human rights accountability. On the other hand, NGOs' continued mobilization amid state backlash may also risk further, more extreme state backlash, potentially drawing in a wider set of states and having deleterious systemic effects—internationally on the relatively nascent international judiciary, and domestically on already vulnerable human rights defenders. ...

Rwanda has also been much criticized for its human rights record, but when it withdrew its declaration in 2016 it focused solely on one case. Its official letter to the Court (24 February 2016) stated:

> CONSIDERING that a Genocide convict who is a fugitive from justice has ... secured a right to be heard by the Honourable Court, ultimately gaining a platform for re-invention and sanitization, in the guise of defending the human rights of the Rwandan citizens;
>
> CONSIDERING that the Republic of Rwanda, in making [its] Declaration never envisaged that the kind of person described above would ever seek and be granted a platform on the basis of the said Declaration;
>
> CONSIDERING that Rwanda has set up strong legal and judicial institutions entrusted with and capable of resolving any injustice and human rights issues;
>
> NOW THEREFORE, ... withdraws the Declaration ... and shall make it afresh after a comprehensive review.

4. The African Court in Action

The materials that follow provide examples of the Court's case law. The first case was brought by the Commission against Kenya and involves indigenous peoples' rights. The second concerns the functioning of the courts and the democratic system in Tunisia. And the third is an example of an Advisory Opinion which addresses the problem of vagrancy laws, or what is sometimes called the criminalization of poverty.

Kenya has not made the declaration under Article 34(6) of the Charter permitting individuals and accredited NGOs to bring cases before the Court. The following case against Kenya was brought instead by the African Commission. To date, only three such cases have been brought. Under its 2010 Rules of Procedure, the African Commission could refer communications to the African Court: (a) when a respondent state has manifestly refused to comply with a decision of the African Commission; (b) when a respondent state has not complied with provisional measures issued by the African Commission; (c) when a communication reveals a situation of serious or massive violations of human rights; and (d) at any stage of the examination of a communication if the African Commission deems necessary. This rule was amended in 2020 and the relevant Rule 130 says only that the Commission may refer cases when it has not yet decided on admissibility. In the view of Amnesty International it is now 'unclear under what specific circumstances would the Commission make a referral'. The rule also introduces 'additional hurdles in the referral process' which 'potentially [foreclose] any real prospects of more cases ever [being] referred to the African Court by the African Commission.'[511]

AFRICAN COMMISSION ON HUMAN AND PEOPLES' RIGHTS V. REPUBLIC OF KENYA AFRICAN COURT OF HUMAN RIGHTS, APPLICATION NO. 006/2012, JUDGMENT (26 MAY 2017)

[The Applicant is the African Commission and the Respondent is the Republic of Kenya. The case was brought to the Commission on 14 November 2009 through a Communication from the Centre for Minority Rights Development (CEMIRIDE) and Minority Rights Group International (MRGI), both acting on behalf of the

---

[511] Amnesty International, *The State of African Regional Human Rights Bodies and Mechanisms*, 2019-2020, Index No. AFR 01/3089/2020 (2020), 20.

Ogiek Community of the Mau Forest. On 23 November 2009, the Commission issued an Order for Provisional Measures requesting Kenya to suspend implementation of an eviction notice issued in October 2009.]

On 12 July 2012, following the lack of response from the Respondent, the Commission seised this Court with the present Application … .

A) Facts of the Matter

… The Applicant alleges that the Ogieks are an indigenous minority ethnic group in Kenya comprising about 20,000 members, about 15,000 of whom inhabit the greater Mau Forest Complex, a land mass of about 400,000 hectares … .

…

The Applicant states that the eviction notice was issued on the grounds that the forest constitutes a reserved water catchment zone, and was in any event part of government land … .. The Applicant states further that the Forestry Service's action failed to take into account the importance of the Mau Forest for the survival of the Ogieks, and that the latter were not involved in the decision leading to their eviction. The Applicant contends that the Ogieks have been subjected to several eviction measures since the colonial period, which continued after [Kenya's] independence … . According to the Applicant, the October 2009 eviction notice is a perpetuation of the historical injustices suffered by the Ogieks.

The Applicant further avers that the Ogieks have consistently raised objections to these evictions with local and national administrations, task forces and commissions and have instituted judicial proceedings, to no avail.

[On 15 March 2013, the Court issued an Order for Provisional Measures, and on 24 September 2014 granted leave to MRGI to intervene. On 27-28 November 2014 the Court held a public hearing, at which all parties were represented. The Court dismissed several jurisdictional challenges and found that domestic remedies had been exhausted.]

…

V. ON THE MERITS

… [T]he Applicant alleges violation of Articles 1, 2, 4, 8, 14, 17(2) and (3), 21 and 22 of the Charter. … [T]he Court will commence with the alleged violation of Article 14 ['[t]he right to property shall be guaranteed'.]

…

[But the central issue, on which all others hinge, is] whether or not the Ogieks constitute an indigenous population. …

A. The Ogieks as an Indigenous Population

…

The Applicant argues that the Ogiek are an "indigenous people" … .

…

The Respondent's position is that the Ogieks are not a distinct ethnic group but rather a mixture of various ethnic communities. During the Public Hearing however, the Respondent admitted that the Ogieks constitute an indigenous population in Kenya but that the Ogieks of today are different from those of the 1930s and 1990s having transformed their way of life through time and adapted themselves to modern life and are currently like all other Kenyans.

The Court's Assessment

The Court notes that the concept of indigenous population is not defined in the Charter. For that matter, there is no universally accepted definition of "indigenous population" in other international human rights instruments. [It notes, however, the work of the African Commission's Working Group on Indigenous Populations/Communities and of the UN Sub-Commission's Rapporteur on Minorities.]

…

From the foregoing, the Court deduces that for the identification and understanding of the concept of indigenous populations, the relevant factors to consider are the presence of priority in time with respect to the occupation and use of a specific territory; a voluntary perpetuation of cultural distinctiveness, which may include aspects of language, social organisation, religion and spiritual values, modes of production, laws and institutions; self-identification as well as recognition by other groups, or by State authorities that they are a distinct collectivity; and an experience of subjugation, marginalisation, dispossession, exclusion or discrimination, whether or not these conditions persist.

These criteria generally reflect the current normative standards to identify indigenous populations in international law. The Court deems it appropriate, by virtue of Article 60 and 61 of the Charter, which allows it to draw inspiration from other human rights instruments to apply these criteria to this Application.

... [Reports before the Court] affirm the Applicant's assertion that the Mau Forest is the Ogieks' ancestral home. The most salient feature of most indigenous populations is their strong attachment with nature, particularly, land and the natural environment. Their survival in a particular way depends on unhindered access to and use of their traditional land and the natural resources thereon. In this regard, the Ogieks, as a hunter-gatherer community, have for centuries depended on the Mau Forest for their residence and as a source of their livelihood.

The Ogieks also exhibit a voluntary perpetuation of cultural distinctiveness, which includes aspects of language, social organisation, religious, cultural and spiritual values, modes of production, laws and institutions through self-identification and recognition by other groups and by State authorities, as a distinct group. Despite the fact that the Ogieks are divided into clans made up of patrilineal lineages each with its own name and area of habitation, they have their own language, albeit currently spoken by very few and more importantly, social norms and forms of subsistence, which make them distinct from other neighbouring tribes. They are also identified by these neighbouring tribes, such as the Maasai, Kipsigis and Nandi, with whom they have had regular interaction, as distinct 'neighbours' and as a distinct group.

The records before this Court show that the Ogieks have suffered from continued subjugation, and marginalisation. Their suffering as a result of evictions from their ancestral lands and forced assimilation and the very lack of recognition of their status as a tribe or indigenous population attest to the persistent marginalisation that the Ogieks have experienced for decades.

In view of the above, the Court recognises the Ogieks as an indigenous population that is part of the Kenyan people having a particular status and deserving special protection deriving from their vulnerability.
...

Alleged violation of Article 14 of the Charter

Applicant's Submission

The Applicant contends that the failure of the Respondent to recognise the Ogieks as an indigenous community denies them the right to communal ownership of land as provided in Article 14 of the Charter. ...
...

The Court's Assessment

Article 14 of the Charter provides as follows:

> "The right to property shall be guaranteed. It may only be encroached upon in the
> interest of public need or in the general interest of the community and in accordance with
> the provisions of appropriate laws."

The Court observes that, although addressed in the part of the Charter which enshrines the rights recognised for individuals, the right to property as guaranteed by Article 14 may also apply to groups or communities; in effect, the right can be individual or collective.

The Court is also of the view that, in its classical conception, the right to property usually refers to three elements namely: the right to use the thing that is the subject of the right (*usus*), the right to enjoy the fruit thereof (*fructus*) and the right to dispose of the thing, that is, the right to transfer it (*abusus*).

However, to determine the extent of the rights recognised for indigenous communities in their ancestral lands as in the instant case, the Court holds that Article 14 of the Charter must be interpreted in light of the applicable principles especially by the United Nations.

In this regard, Article 26 of the [UN Declaration on the Rights of Indigenous Peoples of 2007], provides as follows:

> "1. Indigenous peoples have the right to the lands, territories and resources which they have traditionally owned, occupied or otherwise used or acquired.
>
> 2. Indigenous peoples have the right to own, use, develop and control the lands, territories and resources that they possess by reason of traditional ownership or other traditional occupation or use, as well as those which they have otherwise acquired.
>
> 3. States shall give legal recognition and protection to these lands, territories and resources. Such recognition shall be conducted with due respect to the customs, traditions and land tenure systems of the indigenous peoples concerned."

It follows in particular from Article 26 (2) of the Declaration that the rights that can be recognised for indigenous peoples/communities on their ancestral lands are variable and do not necessarily entail the right of ownership in its classical meaning, including the right to dispose thereof (*abusus*). Without excluding the right to property in the traditional sense, this provision places greater emphasis on the rights of possession, occupation, use/utilization of land.

… [S]ince the Court has already held that the Ogieks constitute an indigenous community, it holds, on the basis of Article 14 of the Charter read in light of the above-mentioned [UN] Declaration, that they have the right to occupy their ancestral lands, as well as use and enjoy the said lands.

However, Article 14 envisages [restrictions] provided that such restriction is in the public interest and is also necessary and proportional.

… [T]he Respondent's public interest justification for evicting the Ogieks from the Mau Forest has been the preservation of the natural ecosystem. Nevertheless, it has not provided any evidence to the effect that the Ogieks' continued presence in the area is the main cause for the depletion of natural environment in the area. … [T]he Court is of the view that the continued denial of access to and eviction from the Mau Forest of the Ogiek population cannot be necessary or proportionate to achieve the purported justification of preserving the natural ecosystem of the Mau Forest.

… [T]he Court holds that by expelling the Ogieks from their ancestral lands against their will, without prior consultation and without respecting the conditions of expulsion in the interest of public need, the Respondent violated their rights to land as defined above and as guaranteed by Article 14 of the Charter read in light of the [UN Declaration].

Alleged violation of Article 2 of the Charter

Applicant's Submission

The Applicant submits that Article 2 of the Charter provides a non-exhaustive list of prohibited grounds of discrimination and that the expression "or other status", widens the list to include statuses not expressly noted. The Applicant notes that any discrimination against the Ogiek Community would fall within the definition of "race", "ethnic group", "religion" and "social origin" referred to in Article 2. …

... The Applicant stresses that the Respondent has, since independence, been pursuing a policy of assimilation and marginalisation, presumably in an attempt to ensure national unity and, in the case of land and natural resource rights, in the name of conservation of the Mau Forest. According to the Applicant, while such aims of national unity or conservation may be legitimate and serve the common interest, the means employed, including the non-recognition of the tribal and ethnic identity of the Ogieks and their corresponding rights is entirely disproportionate to such an aim and, is ultimately counterproductive to its achievement. ...

...

The Court's Assessment

Article 2 of the Charter provides that:

> "Every individual shall be entitled to the enjoyment of the rights and freedoms
> recognised and guaranteed in the present Charter without distinction of any kind such as
> race, ethnic group, colour, sex, language, religion, political or any other opinion, birth or
> any status."

...

In terms of Article 2 of the Charter, while distinctions or differential treatment on grounds specified therein are generally proscribed, ... not all forms of distinction can be considered as discrimination. A distinction or differential treatment becomes discrimination, and hence, contrary to Article 2, when it does not have objective and reasonable justification and, in the circumstances where it is not necessary and proportional.

...

In so far as the Ogieks are concerned, the Court notes from the records available before it that their request for recognition as a tribe goes back to the colonial period, where their request was rejected by the then Kenya Land Commission in 1933, asserting that "they [the Ogieks] were a savage and barbaric people who deserved no tribal status" and consequently, the Commission proposed that "they should become members of and be absorbed into the tribe in which they have the most affinity". The denial of their request for recognition as a tribe also denied them access to their own land as, at the time, only those who had tribal status were given land as "special reserves" or "communal reserves". This has been the case since independence and is still continuing. In contrast, other ethnic groups such as the Maasai, have been recognised as tribes and consequently, been able to enjoy all related rights derived from such recognition, thus proving differential treatment.

The Court accordingly finds that, if other groups which are in the same category of communities, which lead a traditional way of life and with cultural distinctiveness highly dependent on the natural environment as the Ogieks, were granted recognition of their status and the resultant rights, the refusal of the Respondent to recognise and grant the same rights to the Ogieks, due to their way of life as a hunter-gatherer community amounts to 'distinction·based on ethnicity and/or 'other status' in terms of Article 2 of the Charter.

...

[T]he Court finds that the Respondent, by failing to recognise the Ogieks' status as a distinct tribe like other similar groups and thereby denying them the rights available to other tribes, violated Article 2 of the Charter.

Alleged violation of Article 4 of the Charter

Applicant's Submission

... The Applicant contends that forced evictions may violate the right to life when they generate conditions that impede or obstruct access to a decent existence.

The Court's Assessment

Article 4 of the Charter stipulates that:

> "Human beings are inviolable. Every human being shall be entitled to respect for his life
> and the integrity of his person. No one may be arbitrarily deprived of this right"

... Contrary to other human rights instruments, the Charter establishes the link between the right to life and the inviolable nature and integrity of the human being. The Court finds that this formulation reflects the indispensable correlation between these two rights.

The Court notes that the right to life under Article 4 of the Charter is a right to be enjoyed by an individual irrespective of the group to which he or she belongs. The Court also understands that the violation of economic, social and cultural rights (including through forced evictions) may generally engender conditions unfavourable to a decent life.[39] However, the Court is of the view that the sole fact of eviction and deprivation of economic, social and cultural rights may not necessarily result in the violation of the right to life under Article 4 of the Charter.

The Court considers that it is necessary to make a distinction between the classical meaning of the right to life and the right to decent existence of a group. Article 4 of the Charter relates to the physical rather than the existential understanding of the right to life.

In the instant case, it is not in dispute between the Parties that that the Mau Forest has, for generations, been the environment in which the Ogiek population has always lived and that their livelihood depends on it. As a hunter-gatherer population, the Ogieks have established their homes, collected and produced food, medicine and ensured other means of survival in the Mau Forest. There is no doubt that their eviction has adversely affected their decent existence in the forest. According to the Applicant, some members of the Ogiek population died at different times, due to lack of basic necessities such as food, water, shelter, medicine, exposure to the elements, and diseases, subsequent to their forced evictions. The Court notes however that the Applicant has not established the causal connection between the evictions of the Ogieks by the Respondent and the deaths alleged to have occurred as a result. The Applicant has not adduced evidence to this effect.

In view of the above, the Court finds that there is no violation of Article 4 of the Charter.

Alleged violation of Article 8 of the Charter

Applicant's Submission

The Applicant contends that the Ogieks practise a monotheistic religion closely tied to their environment and that their beliefs and spiritual practices are protected by Article 8 of the Charter and constitute a religion under international law. ...

...

Respondent's Submission

The Respondent contends that the Applicant has failed to adduce evidence to show the exact places where the alleged ceremonies for the religious sites of the Ogieks are located. They argue that the Ogieks have abandoned their religion as they have converted to Christianity and that the religious practices of the Ogieks are a threat to law and order, thereby necessitating the Respondent's interference, to protect and preserve law and order. The Respondent contends that the Ogieks are free to access the Mau Forest, except between 6 p.m. and 9 a.m. and that they are prohibited from carrying out certain activities, unless they have a licence permitting them to do so.

The Court's Assessment

Article 8 of the Charter ... requires State Parties to fully guarantee freedom of conscience, the profession and free practice of religion. The right to freedom of worship offers protection to all forms of beliefs regardless of denominations: theistic, non-theistic and atheistic beliefs, as well as the right not to profess any religion or belief. ...

The Court notes that, in the context of traditional societies, where formal religious institutions often do not exist, the practice and profession of religion are usually inextricably linked with land and the environment. ...

... The Mau Forest constitutes [the Ogiek's] spiritual home and is central to the practice of their religion. It is where they bury the dead according to their traditional rituals[45], where certain types of trees are found for use to worship and it is where they have kept their sacred sites for generations.

...

Article 8 of the Charter however allows restrictions on the exercise of freedom of religion in the interest of maintaining law and order. Though the Respondent can interfere with the religious practices of the Ogieks to protect public health and maintain law and order, these restrictions must be examined with regard to their necessity and reasonableness. The Court is of the view that, rather than evicting the Ogieks ..., there were other less onerous measures that the Respondent could have put in place ... [including] sensitisation campaigns to the Ogieks on the requirement to bury their dead in accordance with the requirements of the Public Health Act ... .

... [T]he Respondent has not submitted any evidence to support its position that the adoption of Christianity means a total abandonment of the Ogiek traditional religious practices. Even though some members of the Ogieks might have been converted to Christianity, the evidence before this Court show that they still practice their traditional religious rites. Accordingly, the alleged transformation in the way of life of the Ogieks and their manner of worship cannot be said to have entirely eliminated their traditional spiritual values and rituals.

... The Court therefore finds that the Respondent is in violation of Article 8 of the Charter.

Alleged violation of Articles 17(2) and (3) of the Charter

Applicant's Submission

The Applicant, citing [the Commission's] own jurisprudence in the Endorois Case avers that "Culture could be taken to mean that complex whole which includes a spiritual and physical association with one's ancestral land, knowledge, belief, art, law, morals, customs and any other capabilities and habits acquired by humankind as a member of society - the sum total of the material and spiritual activities and products of a given social group that distinguish it from other similar groups and in that it encompasses a group's religion, language, and other defining characteristics". On the basis of this, the Applicant submits that the cultural rights of the Ogieks have been violated ...

The Applicant maintains that the Ogieks should be allowed to determine what culture is good for them rather than the Respondent doing so. ...

...

Respondent's Submission

... The Respondent urges the Court to bear in mind the intricate balance between the right to culture and environmental conservation for future generations.

Furthermore, the ... Ogieks ... life style has metamorphosed and the cultural and traditional practices which made them distinct no longer exist, thus, the group itself no longer exists and it cannot therefore claim any cultural rights. [They] no longer live as hunters and gatherers, thus, they cannot be said to conserve the environment. They have adopted new and modern ways of living, including building permanent structures, livestock keeping and farming which would have a serious negative impact on the forest if they are allowed to reside there.

The Court's Assessment

Article 17 of the Charter provides:

> "1. Every individual shall have the right to education.

> 2. Every individual may freely, take part in the cultural life of his community.

3. The promotion and protection of morals and traditional values Recognised by the community shall be the duty of the State".

The right to culture ... is to be considered in ... both its individual and collective nature. It ensures protection, on the one hand, of individuals' participation in the cultural life of their community and, on the other, obliges the State to promote and protect traditional values of the community.

Article 17 of the Charter protects all forms of culture and places strict obligations on State Parties to protect and promote traditional values. In a similar fashion, the Cultural Charter for Africa obliges States to adopt a national policy which creates conditions conducive for the promotion and development of culture. ...

The protection of the right to culture goes beyond the duty, not to destroy or deliberately weaken minority groups, but requires respect for, and protection of, their cultural heritage essential to the group's identity. In this respect, culture should be construed in its widest sense encompassing the total way of life of a particular group, including the group's languages, symbols such as dressing codes and the manner the group constructs shelters; engages in certain economic activities, produces items for survival; rituals such as the group's particular way of dealing with problems and practicing spiritual ceremonies; identification and veneration of its own heroes or models and shared values of its members which reflect its distinctive character and personality.

The Court notes that in the context of indigenous populations, the preservation of their culture is of particular importance. ...

The UN Declaration on Indigenous Peoples, states that "indigenous peoples and individuals have the right not to be subjected to forced assimilation or destruction of their culture" and States shall provide effective mechanisms to prevent any action that deprives them of "their integrity as distinct peoples, or of their cultural values or ethnic identities". ...

... [T]he Court notes ... that the Ogiek population has a distinct way of life centred and dependent on the Mau Forest Complex. As a hunter-gatherer community, they get their means of survival through hunting animals and gathering honey and fruits, they have their own traditional clothes, their own language, distinct way of entombing the dead, practicing rituals and traditional medicine, and their own spiritual and traditional values ...
.

... [Evidence shows] that the Ogieks have been peacefully carrying out their cultural practices until their territory was encroached upon by outsiders and they were evicted from the Mau Forest. Even in the face of this, the Ogieks still undertake their traditional activities: traditional wedding ceremonies, oral traditions, folklores, and songs. They still maintain their clan boundaries in the Mau Forest and each clan ensures the maintenance of the environment within the boundary it is allocated. ...
...
The Court therefore finds that the Respondent has violated the right to culture of the Ogiek population ... .
...
[The Court's analysis of alleged violation of Article 21 (the right to freely dispose of their wealth) and Article 22 (the right to development) is excerpted above, in Chapter 4.]

Alleged violation of Article 1 of the Charter
...

The Court's Assessment

Article 1 of the Charter declares that

> "The Member States of the Organization of African Unity parties to the present Charter
> shall recognise the rights, duties and freedoms enshrined in this Charter and shall
> undertake to adopt legislative or other measures to give effect to them".

...

… [T]he Respondent has violated article 1 of the Charter by not taking adequate legislative and other measures to give effect to the rights enshrined under article 2, 8, 14, 17 (2) and (3), 21 and 22 of the Charter. …

AFRICAN COMMISSION ON HUMAN AND PEOPLES' RIGHTS V. REPUBLIC OF KENYA AFRICAN COURT OF HUMAN RIGHTS, APPLICATION NO. 006/2012, JUDGMENT (REPARATIONS) (23 JUNE 2022)

…

VIII. OPERATIVE PART

160. … The Court unanimously …

i. Dismisses all the Respondent State's objections;

On pecuniary reparations

> ii. *Orders* the Respondent State to pay the sum of KES 57 850 000 [just under US$500,000], free from any government tax, as compensation for the material prejudice suffered by the Ogiek;

> iii. *Orders* the Respondent State to pay the sum of KES 100 000 000 [US$835,000] … as compensation for the moral prejudice suffered by the Ogiek;

On non-pecuniary reparations

> iv. *Orders* the Respondent State to take all necessary measures, legislative, administrative or otherwise to identify, in consultation with the Ogiek and/or their representatives, and delimit, demarcate and title Ogiek ancestral land and to grant collective title to such land in order to ensure, with legal certainty, the Ogiek's use and enjoyment of the same.;

> v. *Orders* the Respondent State, where concessions and/or leases have been granted over Ogiek ancestral land, to commence dialogue and consultations between the Ogiek and their representatives and the other concerned parties for purposes of reaching an agreement on whether or not they can be allowed to continue their operations by way of lease and/or royalty and benefit sharing with the Ogiek in line with all applicable laws. Where it proves impossible to reach a compromise, the Respondent State is ordered to compensate the concerned third parties and return such land to the Ogiek;

> vi. *Orders* that the Respondent State must take all appropriate measures, within one (1) year, to guarantee full recognition of the Ogiek as an indigenous people of Kenya in an effective manner, including but not limited to according full recognition to the Ogiek language and Ogiek cultural and religious practices;

> vii. *Dismisses* the Applicant's prayer for a public apology;

> viii. *Dismisses* the Applicant's prayer for the erection of a monument to commemorate the human rights violations suffered by the Ogiek;

> ix. *Orders* the Respondent State to take all necessary legislative, administrative or other measures to recognise, respect and protect the right of the Ogiek to be effectively consulted, in accordance with their tradition/customs in respect of all development, conservation or investment projects on Ogiek ancestral land;

> x. *Orders* the Respondent State to ensure the full consultation and participation of the Ogiek, in accordance with their traditions/customs, in the reparation process as ordered in this judgment;

xi. *Orders* the Respondent State to adopt legislative, administrative and/or any other measures to give full effect to the terms of this judgment as a means of guaranteeing the non-repetition of the violations identified;

xii. *Orders* the Respondent State to take the necessary administrative, legislative and any other measures within twelve (12) months of the notification of this judgment to establish a community development fund for the Ogiek which should be a repository of all the funds ordered as compensation in this case;

xiii. *Orders* the Respondent State, within twelve (12) months of notification of this judgment, to take legislative, administrative or any other measures to establish and operationalise the Committee for the management of the development fund ordered in this Judgment;

On implementation and reporting

xiv. *Orders* that the Respondent State must, within six (6) months [publish both reports in the Government Gazette and on a government website];

xv. *Orders* the Respondent State to submit, within twelve (12) months from the date of notification of this Judgment, a report on the status of implementation of all the Orders herein;

xvi. *Holds*, that it shall conduct a hearing on the status of implementation of the orders made in this judgment on a date to be appointed by the Court twelve (12) months from the date of this judgment.

IBRAHIM BEN MOHAMED BEN IBRAHIM BELGUITH V. REPUBLIC OF TUNISIA AFRICAN COURT OF HUMAN RIGHTS, APPLICATION NO. 017/2021, JUDGMENT (22 SEPTEMBER 2022)

[By way of background to this case, Human Rights Watch notes that President Kais Saied, who was elected in 2019, 'granted himself extraordinary powers in July 2021, claiming they were needed to deal with a crisis of governance. He suspended much of the post-revolutionary Constitution of 2014 and dissolved the Parliament … . [The authorities subsequently took] a range of repressive measures against opponents, critics, and political figures'. In July 2022, before the Court judgment below, a new Constitution was approved by 94.6 percent of voters in a referendum. The *New York Times* observed that 'the referendum … was undercut by mass boycotts, voter apathy and a setup heavily tilted toward Mr. Saied.' It reported that the result cemented one-man rule and dealt a 'body blow to a democracy built with immense effort and high hopes after the overthrow of the country's dictator' at the start of the Arab Spring in 2011.[512]

The broader significance of the case is illustrated by developments in various other African states in the months before and after the judgment. Between 2020 and September 2023, nine successful coups occurred in Africa.]

…

II. SUBJECT OF THE APPLICATION

A. Facts of the matter

3. The Applicant alleges in his Application that the President of the Respondent State, abrogated the Constitution, halted the democratic process and arrogated to himself more powers by promulgating the following presidential decrees:

---

[512] Vivian Yee, 'Tunisians Approve New Constitution That Undercuts Democracy', *New York Times*, July 26, 2022.

[No. 69, No. 80, No. 109, No. 117, No. 137 and No. 138.]

4. The Applicant asserts that the above decrees unlawfully terminated the functions and appointment of the Head and members of Government, and suspended the powers of Parliament and the provisions of the Constitution, except the preamble and Chapters I and II.

...

VII. MERITS

...

A. Alleged violation of the right to have one's cause heard

...

92. The Applicant further avers that the Presidential Decree No. 2021-117 violates the right to be heard before the courts by stipulating in its Article 7 that decrees issued by the President of the Republic are not subject to appeal.

...

94. The Respondent State did not respond on the alleged violation of this right.

95. The Court notes that, Article 7(1)(a) of the Charter provides that:

> Every individual shall have the right to have his cause heard. This comprises:
>
> > (a) the right to an appeal to competent national organs against acts of violating his fundamental rights as recognized and guaranteed by conventions, laws, regulations and customs in force.

...

97. The Court emphasises that Article 7(1)(a) of the Charter makes it clear that the existence of a competent tribunal is a *sine qua non* to the enjoyment of the right to be heard, including the right to appeal. This must be read together with Article 26 of the Charter which imposes on State Parties the obligation to establish and improve appropriate national institutions for the promotion and protection of human rights and freedoms and to guarantee the independence of the courts.

...

100. [A]t the time the Application was filed before this Court, the Constitutional Court [authorized by Law No. 50 of 2015] had not been operationalised. The Court notes that there was also no other Court or authority in the Respondent State that could consider constitutional disputes relating to the powers of the President. ...

101. As a result, it is evident that the Applicant was not able to challenge the constitutionality of the Presidential decrees. This in effect left him with no legal avenue to seek a remedy for his grievances and deprived him of his right to be heard.

102. In view of the foregoing, the Court holds that the Respondent State violated the Applicant's right to be heard contrary to Article 7(1)(a) of the Charter as read together with Article 26 of the Charter.

B. Alleged violation of the people's right to self-determination and the right to political participation

...

106. [T]he Applicant submits that the Respondent State has violated his and Tunisian peoples' right to political participation and right to self-determination contrary to its obligations under Articles 13 and 20 of the Charter.

107. The Respondent State did not respond to both alleged violations.

108. The Court notes that the Applicant alleges violations of both the right to self- determination and the right to political participation, which are guaranteed in Articles 13 and 20 of the Charter. The Court acknowledges in this regard the fundamental importance of the individual's right to political participation under Article 13 and to the peoples' free determination of their political status within the terms of Article 20 (1) of the Charter.

109. However, the Court finds that in the instant Application, the main issues raised by the Applicant relate to the right to political participation, and thus, the Court limits its determination to this aspect of the Applicant's allegation. In the circumstances of this case and considering the nature the Applicant's submissions, the Court does not find it necessary to consider the allegation relating to the violation of the right to self-determination.

…

113. … [T]he exceptional measures taken by the Respondent State were implemented within the framework of Presidential decrees issued by a democratically elected President owing to certain situations. The decrees were passed in accordance with Article 80 of the Respondent State's Constitution (2014), which provided that:

> In the event of imminent danger threatening the nation's institutions or the security or independence of the country, and hampering the normal functioning of the state, the President of the Republic may take any measures necessitated by the exceptional circumstances, after consultation with the Head of Government and the Speaker of the Assembly of the Representatives of the People and informing the President of the Constitutional Court. The President shall announce the measures in a statement to the people.

…

116. The Court notes that there is nothing on record showing that the substantive conditions of an imminent danger to the nation's institutions or the security and independence of the country or the abovementioned procedural requirements were met before the President issued the decrees in question. …

117. Furthermore, the Court finds that the decrees in question disproportionately disrupted the work of the government including that of elected institutions such as the House of People's Representatives. …

118. In this vein, the Court notes that the Respondent State was under an obligation to consider other least restrictive measures to deal with the said dispute prior to taking such drastic measures as the suspension of the powers of Parliament, and limiting the immunity of its members … . The Respondent State's failure to do so made the adopted measures not only disproportionate in relation to the stated goals but also with the Respondent State's own Constitutional dispensation.

119. Accordingly, the Court finds that the Respondent State's restrictive measures were neither adopted in accordance with the law nor were they proportionate for the purpose for which they were adopted.

120. Consequently, the Court holds that the Respondent State has violated the right of the people to participate in the conduct of public affairs contrary to Article 13 (1) of the Charter.

…

VIII. REPARATIONS

129. The Court notes that in the present case, the Applicant does not seek pecuniary reparations because, according to him, even if it is present, real and continuous, the material harm caused by the violations, is not personal or direct, and that he has no standing to seek compensation on behalf of the Tunisian people.

130. However, the Applicant requests the Court to order the Respondent State to repeal all the decrees mentioned in paragraph 3 of this judgment in order to guarantee the human rights set out, by taking the following measures:

> i. Adopt the necessary legislative and regulatory instruments to ensure the supremacy of the Constitution, including the speedy establishment of the Constitutional Court and the removal of all legislative, regulatory, political and realistic impediments hindering it;
>
> ii. Pass laws that criminalize participation in, and support of, unconstitutional change of power;
>
> iii. Adopt laws that guarantee the inculcation of democratic culture among the people, especially young people;

iv. Provide procedural avenues and effective solutions to remedy violations of the Constitution, pending the establishment of the Constitutional Court, such as obliging it to submit to the Court a report on judgment enforcement procedures and guarantees of non-repetition.

131. The Respondent State does not address the issue of reparations and only requests that the case be declared inadmissible and be dismissed on the merits.

…

XI. OPERATIVE PART

For these reasons, THE COURT *Unanimously,*

…

On Merits

i. *Finds* that the Respondent State violated the Applicant's [rights under Article 7(1)(a), Article 13(1), and Article 1, of the Charter]

…

On Reparations

iv. *Orders* the Respondent State to repeal [each of the challenged] Presidential Decrees … and to return to constitutional democracy within two (2) years from the date of notification of this judgment.

v. *Orders* the Respondent State to take all measures necessary for the operationalisation of an independent Constitutional Court and remove all legal impediments thereto within two (2) years from the date of notification of this judgment.

On implementation and reporting

vi. *Orders* the Respondent State to report to the Court, within six (6) months …

ADVISORY OPINION NO. 001/2018
AFRICAN COURT OF HUMAN RIGHTS, ON THE COMPATIBILITY OF VAGRANCY LAWS WITH THE AFRICAN CHARTER ON HUMAN AND PEOPLES' RIGHTS AND OTHER HUMAN RIGHTS INSTRUMENTS APPLICABLE IN AFRICA, REQUESTED BY THE PAN AFRICAN LAWYERS UNION (PALU) (4 DECEMBER 2020)

I. THE AUTHOR

1. This Request for Advisory Opinion … was filed by the Pan African Lawyers Union [PALU].

…

4. According to PALU "[m]any countries abuse [vagrancy laws] to arrest and detain persons where there has been no proof of a criminal act." PALU submits, therefore, that these laws are overly broad and confer too wide a discretion on law enforcement agencies to decide who to arrest which impacts disproportionately on vulnerable individuals in society. PALU also submits that arrests for violation of vagrancy laws contribute to congestion in police cells and prison overcrowding. It is PALU's further submission that the manner in which vagrancy offences are enforced is contrary to the basic principles of criminal law i.e. it undermines the presumption of innocence and thereby threatens the rule of law.

5. PALU, therefore, requests for an opinion from the Court on [four] questions … .

…

A. Compatibility of vagrancy laws and the Charter

38. ... PALU has requested the Court to provide an opinion on:

> Whether vagrancy laws and by-laws, including but not limited to, those that contain offences which criminalise the status of a person as being without a fixed home, employment or means of subsistence; as having no fixed abode nor means of subsistence, and trade or profession; as being a suspected person or reputed thief who has no visible means of subsistence and cannot give a good account of him or herself; and as being idle and who does not have visible means of subsistence and cannot give good account of him or herself violate [Articles 2, 3, 5, 6, 7, 12 and 18 of the Charter].

39. ...

> Whether vagrancy laws and by-laws, including but not limited to, those containing offences which, once a person has been declared a vagrant or rogue and vagabond, summarily orders such person's deportation to another area, violate Articles 5, 12, 18 of the Charter.

40. ...

> Whether vagrancy laws and by-laws, including but not limited to, those that allow for the arrest of someone without a warrant simply because the person has no "means of subsistence and cannot give a satisfactory account" of him or herself, violate Articles 2, 3, 5, 6 and 7 of the Charter.

iii. The Court's position

...

58. Although many countries have had vagrancy laws on their statute books, there have always been nuances across legal systems in terms of the formulation of the offences and the manner of enforcement. In this Advisory Opinion, therefore, the Court remains alive to the fact that the term "vagrancy" is often used in a generic sense to allude to various offences commonly grouped under this umbrella including but not limited to: being idle and disorderly, begging, being without a fixed abode, being a rogue and vagabond, being a reputed thief and being homeless or a wanderer.

59. From a sociological perspective, it has been suggested that there were three main reasons that motivated the adoption of vagrancy laws. First, to curtail the mobility of persons and criminalise begging, thereby ensuring the availability of cheap labour to land owners and industrialists whilst limiting the presence of undesirable persons in the cities; second, to reduce the costs incurred by local municipalities and parishes to look after the poor; lastly, and to prevent property crimes by creating broad crimes providing wide discretion to law enforcement officials. ...

60. ... [I]n the Penal Codes of at least eighteen (18) African countries, a vagrant is defined as any person who does not have a fixed abode nor means of subsistence, and who does not practice a trade or profession. In at least eight (8) African countries; a "suspected person or reputed thief who has no visible means of subsistence and cannot give a good account" of him or herself commits an offence of being a "rogue" or a "vagabond". The Court also notes that in South Africa, for instance, by-laws prohibit a person without a fixed abode from loitering or sleeping in a public amenity, public space or in the beach. The Court further notes that in at least three (3) African countries, the offence of being an idle and disorderly person is defined to include someone who loiters or is idle and who does not have a visible means of subsistence and cannot give a good account of him or herself.

61. ... [T]he Court observes that other African countries ... have repealed some of their vagrancy laws [and that] courts, in some African countries, have also nullified some vagrancy laws for being unconstitutional. ...

...

a. Vagrancy laws and the right to non-discrimination and equality

...

66. [T]he right to non-discrimination under Article 2 of the Charter, is related to the right to equality before the law and equal protection of the law as guaranteed under Article 3. ...

...

70. [T]he Court notes that vagrancy laws, effectively, punish the poor and underprivileged, including but not limited to the homeless, the disabled, the gender-nonconforming, sex workers, hawkers, street vendors, and individuals who otherwise use public spaces to earn a living. Notably, however, individuals under such difficult circumstances are already challenged in enjoying their other rights including more specifically their socio-economic rights. Vagrancy laws, therefore, serve to exacerbate their situation by further depriving them of their right to be treated equally before the law.

71. The Court also notes that while an eternal attribute of all good laws is that they must always be clear and precise, vagrancy laws often employ vague, unclear and imprecise language. Common terminology used in framing vagrancy offences include expressions such as "loitering", "having no visible means of support" and "failing to give a good account of oneself". Such language does not provide sufficient indication to the citizens on what the law prohibits while at the same time conferring broad discretion on law enforcement agencies in terms of how to enforce vagrancy laws. This, automatically, makes vagrancy laws prone to abuse, often to the detriment of the marginalized sections of society.

72. The Court recalls that the status of an individual is one of the prohibited grounds for discrimination under Article 2 of the Charter. In relation to the application of vagrancy laws, no reasonable justification exists for the distinction that the law imposes between those classified as vagrants and the rest of the population except their economic status. The individual classified as a vagrant will, often times, have no connection to the commission of any criminal offence hence making any consequential arrest and detention unnecessary. The arrest of persons classified as vagrants, clearly, is largely unnecessary in achieving the purpose of preventing crimes or keeping people off the streets.

73. The Court further recalls that the right to equality before the law requires that "all persons shall be equal before the courts and tribunals". ... [L]aws with discriminatory effects towards the marginalized sections of society are not compatible with both Articles 2 and 3 of the Charter.

74. The Court also recalls that any arrest without a warrant requires reasonable suspicion or grounds that an offence has been committed or is about to be committed. Notably, where vagrancy-related offences are concerned, most arrests are made on the basis of an individual's underprivileged status and the inability to give an account of oneself. In this context, therefore, arrests are substantially connected to the status of the individual ... . Arrests without a warrant for vagrancy offences, therefore, are also incompatible with Articles 2 and 3 of the Charter.

75. In light of the above, the Court holds that vagrancy laws, both in their formulation as well as in their application, by, among other things, criminalizing the status of an individual, enabling the discriminatory treatment of the underprivileged and marginalized, and also by depriving individuals of their equality before the law are not compatible with Articles 2 and 3 of the Charter. The Court also finds that arrests for vagrancy-related offences, where they occur without a warrant, are not only a disproportionate response to socio-economic challenges but also discriminatory since they target individuals because of their economic status.

b. Vagrancy laws and the right to dignity

76. Under Article 5, the Charter provides as follows:

> Every individual shall have the right to the respect of the dignity inherent in a human being ... .

...

79. The Court also recalls that the Commission in *Purohit and Moore v. The Gambia* concluded that the use of the words "lunatics" and "idiots" to refer to persons with mental disabilities dehumanizes and denies them their dignity. In the same vein, the Court notes that vagrancy laws commonly use the terms "rogue", "vagabond", "idle" and "disorderly" to label persons deemed to be vagrants. These terms, the Court holds, are a reflection

of an outdated and largely colonial perception of individuals without any rights and their use dehumanizes and degrades individuals with a perceived lower status.

80. The Court also holds that the application of vagrancy laws often deprives the underprivileged and marginalized of their dignity by unlawfully interfering with their efforts to maintain or build a decent life or to enjoy a lifestyle they pursue. ... Consequently, the Court finds that vagrancy laws are incompatible with the notion of human dignity as protected under Article 5 of the Charter.

81. The Court also holds that labelling an individual as a "vagrant", "vagabond", "rogue" or in any other derogatory manner and summarily ordering them to be forcefully relocated to another area denigrates the dignity of a human being. If the implementation of such order is accompanied by the use of force, it may also amount to physical abuse. The Court thus finds that the forcible removal of persons deemed to be vagrants is not compatible with Article 5 of the Charter.

...

c. Vagrancy laws and the right to liberty

83. The Court notes that Article 6 of the Charter provides that:

> Every individual shall have the right to liberty and the security of his person. No one may be deprived of his freedom except for reasons and conditions previously laid down by law. In particular, no one may be arbitrary arrested or detained.

...

85. ... [I]n practice, the enforcement of these laws often results in pretextual arrests, arrests without warrants and illegal pre-trial detention. This exposes vagrancy laws to constant potential abuse.

86. The Court concedes that arrests under vagrancy laws may, ostensibly, satisfy the requirement that the deprivation of freedom must be based on reasons and conditions prescribed by law. Nevertheless, the manner in which vagrancy offences are framed, in most African countries, presents a danger due to their overly broad and ambiguous nature. One of the major challenges is that vagrancy laws do not, ex ante, sufficiently and clearly lay down the reasons and conditions on which one can be arrested and detained to enable the public to know what is within the scope of prohibition. In practice, therefore, many arrests for vagrancy offences are arbitrary.

...

d. Vagrancy laws and the right to fair trial

88. Article 7 of the Charter provides ...:

> b) the right to be presumed innocent until proved guilty by a competent court or tribunal
> .... .

...

92. The Court observes that because vagrancy laws often punish an individual's perceived status, such as being "idle", "disorderly" or "a reputed thief", which status does not have an objective definition, law enforcement officers can arbitrarily arrest individuals without the sufficient level of prima facie proof that they committed a crime. Once they are taken into custody, such arrested persons would have to explain themselves to the law enforcement officer(s) to demonstrate that, for example, they were not idle or disorderly, are not a reputed thief or that they practice a trade or profession. ...

93. ... [F]orcing a suspect to explain himself/herself may be tantamount to coercing a suspect to make self-incriminating statements. Law enforcement officers may exert undue pressure on suspected criminals by pretextually arresting them under vagrancy laws and then soliciting incriminatory evidence even in relation to crimes not connected to vagrancy.

...

e. Vagrancy laws and the right to freedom of movement

95. The Court recalls that Article 12 of the Charter provides, so far as is material, that:

> 1. Every individual shall have the right to freedom of movement and residence within the borders of a State provided he abides by the law.

...

99. ... [A]ny limitation of the freedom of movement must ... be provided by law, ... be necessary to protect national security, public order, public health or morals or the rights and freedom of others [and] be consistent with the other rights recognized in the Charter. ...

100. ... [While vagrancy law limitations are prescribed by law, they fail] to satisfy the second and third conditions. This is because vagrancy laws are not necessary for any of the purposes for which they are often cited. ...

101. The Court is also mindful that even if vagrancy laws contribute to the prevention of crimes in some cases, other less-restrictive measures such as offering vocational training for the unemployed and providing shelter for the homeless adults and children are readily available for dealing with the situation of persons caught by vagrancy laws. ...

102. [T]he enforcement of vagrancy laws, generally, is incompatible with the right to freedom of movement as guaranteed under Article 12 [as is] forced relocation ... .

f. Vagrancy laws and the right to the protection of the family
...
104. The Court notes that underlying Article 18 of the Charter is the responsibility of Member States to take care of the physical and moral health of the family. ...

105. The Court observes that arrests and detentions under vagrancy laws may result in the forcible removal of the suspected "vagrants" from their families. Due to this, other family members that rely on those arrested under vagrancy laws, most notably children, the elderly and the disabled may suffer from the deprivation of financial and emotional support. ...

[The following two sections of the Opinion are omitted:
B. *Vagrancy laws and the Children's Rights Charter*
C. *Vagrancy laws and the Women's Rights Protocol*]

D. *The obligations of State Parties to the Charter in respect of vagrancy laws*
...
ii. *The Court's position*
...
152. The Court observes that there are two dimensions to PALU's final question and these are, first, whether an obligation to amend vagrancy laws exist and, second, the precise nature of this obligation.

153. ... [T]he Court holds that Article 1 of the Charter, Article 1 of the Children's Rights Charter and Article 1 of the Women's Rights Protocol obligates all State Parties to, inter alia, either amend or repeal their vagrancy-laws and by-laws to bring them in conformity with these instruments. This would be in line with the obligation to take all necessary measures including the adoption of legislative or other measures in order to give full effect to the Charter, the Children's Rights Charter and the Women's Rights Protocol.

154. ... [T]his obligation requires all State Parties to amend or repeal all their vagrancy laws, related by-laws and other laws and regulations so as to bring them in conformity with the provisions of the Charter, the Children's Rights Charter and the Women's Rights Protocol.

...

* * *

In a Case Note in 117 *Am. J. Int'l L.* (2023) 121, Jacquelene W. Mwangi puts the Advisory Opinion into context:

> In sociopolitical contexts where colonial legacies pervade law and institutions despite constitutional transitions, courts and social movements can co-create legal openings. The combination of PALU's advocacy and the Court's expansive approach in handling this Request is instrumental toward building an accessible forum for legal reform through advisory opinions. ... A big part of this success seems to be a fortunate but contingent institutional alignment within the African Human Rights System, between PALU, the Commission, and the Court. First, PALU's wide experience in strategic litigation ...[and a Memorandum of Understanding (MOU)] with the AU provided it with legal standing. Second, ... the AU Commission's "Principles on the Decriminalisation of Petty Offences in Africa" provided an authoritative text for reference by PALU and the Court ... . Most significantly, the Court took the opportunity to expand its own powers by stating in obiter that its Advisory Opinions provide guidance to all member states of the AU regardless of whether they have ratified various human rights instruments. ...

> But, on the other hand, the Court did not here explicitly turn away from its past restrictive interpretation [of the entities entitled to request an advisory opinion]. ... The Court has repeatedly held that ... NGOs have no standing to bring requests for advisory opinions because they are not recognized by the AU. This position has been heavily criticized and is a highly restrictive reading of the Court's jurisdiction ... . [I]t is not clear whether there are other African civil society organizations besides PALU that have an MOU with the AU. ...

> Lastly, while the Opinion may provide leverage to individuals and local/regional organizations that litigate rights nationally, the highlighting of intersections between vagrancy laws, poverty, underdevelopment, and degradation of human rights calls for more institutional linkages between AU organs and national institutions. ...

An optimistic response to developments such as this Advisory Opinion is provided by Marius Pieterse, in 'The Relevance of the African Regional Human Rights System in the Urban Age', 36 *Leiden J. Int'l L.* (2023) 1:

> [The Commission and the Court] have read the ACHPR as operating in harmony with other international human rights treaties, have embraced the interdependence and indivisibility of civil and political and social, economic and cultural rights, have frequently vindicated different groupings and intersections of individual and collective rights in particular factual contexts, have acknowledged the rights-related obligations of local government and have displayed a willingness to extend both the reach and content of the rights to contemporary urban contexts. ...

The Record of the Court

The Court itself is concerned about the current situation. In *the Annual Report of the Court 2021*, it observes:

72. One of the major challenges facing the Court at the moment is the perceived lack of cooperation from Member States of the African Union, in particular, in relation to the low level of compliance with the decisions of the Court. Of the over 200 decisions rendered by the Court, as at the time of writing this Report, only one State Party, that is, Burkina Faso, had fully complied with the judgments of the Court. As at July 2021, only 7% of judgments of the Court had been fully complied with, 18% partially complied and 75% non-compliance. Some States have stated clearly before the Executive Council that they will not comply with the Court's decisions.

73. The African Court would like to underscore that its success as a human rights court, and indeed, that of the African human rights or justice system as a whole, is a collective responsibility, and requires the active and constructive participation of all stakeholders.

Compliance with the Court's judgment is one way for States to manifest their commitment to not only the protection of human rights but also a commitment to the ideals of the African Union.

74. A worrying trend which seems to be emerging is for States against which the Court has rendered a judgment to withdraw or threaten to withdraw their Article 34(6) Declaration, which allows individuals and NGOs to seize the Court directly. Within a period of four years, four State Parties to the Protocol have withdrawn their Declarations.

75. The Court views these withdrawals as a decline in the efforts already made in building democracy, defense of human rights and the promotion of the rule of law, and these withdrawals may undermine the human rights protection mechanisms on the continent.

The important role of civil society and the need for better official follow-up mechanisms are emphasized by Victor Ayeni and Andreas von Staden, in 'Monitoring Second-order Compliance in the African Human Rights System', 6 *Afr. Hum. Rts. Y.B.* (2022) 3:

> [T]he driving force for most implementation monitoring activities of AHRBs [African Human Rights Bodies] have been CSOs, yet little attention has been given to them so far in regard to implementation monitoring. … Since there are limited prospects for political monitoring due to a lack of political will by members of the AU Executive Council, implementation monitoring at least in the immediate future will depend on civil society actors and the AHRBs themselves. We remain skeptical as to the prospects of effective political monitoring in Africa and are concerned about the capacity of the African Court, a judicial institution that is constrained by institutional design, to monitor the implementation of its decisions to the same extent and using a comparable range of monitoring tools as the African Commission and the African Children's Committee. Post-judgment, the African Court may need to focus primarily on developing dialogical processes with critical compliance constituencies in respondent states rather than hoping that AU political organs will enforce its decisions through sanctions and other measures.
>
> … [A]mong the biggest impediments to implementation monitoring in Africa is a lack of consistency and clarity in the procedures and practices of the AHRBs. Each of the three AHRBs should establish a unit within its respective secretariat dedicated exclusively to the supervision of the execution of its judgments and decisions …, appoint a special rapporteur for follow-up, … [and] adopt guidelines for the conduct of implementation hearings, including for joint hearings and hearings in situ. …

Many commentators have drawn attention to the reluctance of the various bodies of the African Union to follow up on the findings of the Commission and the Court and to raise the political stakes of non-compliance. Adem Abebe, at p. 179, focuses on the concept of 'horizontal compliance' to argue that judgments invalidating legal provisions in one country should also have implications for other countries in which comparable laws exist. In order to foster broader reflection across borders, he suggests that the organ in charge of monitoring states' compliance, the AU Executive Council, should be prompted by a report from the Court to alert all states to the potential domestic implications of judgments directed against other states. The Court could also seek to engage the Assembly of Heads of States and Governments in this process.

QUESTIONS

1. 'The constraints specified in the Commission's Guidelines on shadow reports would seem likely to make it rather difficult for under-resourced NGOs to be able to submit shadow reports that comply with the guidelines, and to provide ample justifications for states and other actors to object to reports they do not appreciate.' Discuss.

2. Why might the judgment relating to Kenya's Ogiek Community be considered path-breaking?

3. If military coups are again becoming commonplace in Africa, should the Commission and/or the Court be at the forefront of efforts to deter such events?

4. The problems addressed by the Court in its Advisory Opinion on vagrancy laws exist in many countries. Why would the African Court be at the forefront of identifying the many human rights violations often associated with such laws?

PART E: STATES AND OTHER ACTORS IN THE REGIME

Chapter 12. States

Ultimately, effective protection of human rights must come from within the state. The international system has, as we have seen, a range of means that it uses to encourage states to fulfil their obligations, but ultimately it is domestic actors who will determine the extent of compliance. This chapter looks first (Section A) at the ways in which states interact with international norms, and specifically how they 'internalize' treaties and customary international law — that is, how states absorb international human rights norms within their domestic legal and political systems so that international human rights obligations can be implemented and enforced by state authorities. It also considers some of the principal institutional mechanisms used at the national level to promote and uphold international human rights standards.

The next four sections (B-E) of the chapter focus on what can be thought of as horizontal modes of implementing and enforcing human rights. This is in contrast to vertical modes of enforcement through the efforts explored in the preceding chapters, where intergovernmental institutions and their organs sought to secure compliance by non-compliant (violator) states. Pressures are exerted and perhaps sanctions applied by international organs 'above' the state. Such organs apply international law.

Section B looks at sanctions imposed in response to human rights violations. This is a practice long adopted by the United States, with increasing participation by the European Union and other Western states. Such sanctions have had an especially high profile in the wake of Russia's invasion of Ukraine in 2022. Section C examines jurisdictional principles, with particular emphasis on the exercise of universal jurisdiction which involves enforcement by national bodies in cases where there is no direct nexus to the forum state. Section D turns to the role of national courts in providing remedies to victims of human rights violations that occurred in other countries. The principal historical example was the Alien Tort Statute in the United States, but in recent years it has declined dramatically in importance. Finally, Section E considers sovereign and official immunity. It discusses the prospect of achieving justice in light of the ability of states and some officials to invoke such defences to shield themselves from prosecution.

As a matter of international law, a threshold question is whether a national body has legal authority to exercise jurisdiction. Should courts, for example, be presumed to have such power unless international law expressly prohibits it? Or should courts be presumed not to have such power unless international law affirmatively authorizes it? Also consider different classes of defendants. That is, in addition to those thorny jurisdictional issues, should high state officials be immune from criminal and civil proceedings in foreign courts? In particular, should standard forms of diplomatic and sovereign immunity protect individuals who have allegedly engaged in crimes against humanity and other gross human rights violations? What is the proper balance between the need to protect sovereign prerogatives and the need to redress human rights abuses in these contexts? What principles should be developed to strike the correct balance and who should decide? These are some of the issues we explore in the sections that follow.

These issues variously concern the lawful authority and desirability of different forms of influence over foreign human rights practices. They demand answers to questions about the proper allocation of power between private individuals and public authorities. They also invite an exploration of the vices and virtues of criminal prosecution and civil litigation, as well as the impact on foreign policy relationships in taking such cases to court.

A. DOMESTIC INTERNALIZATION OF INTERNATIONAL LAW

Part A begins with a reflection by Ryan Goodman and Derek Jinks on how international human rights law might be able to change state behaviour. It then moves to focus on the incorporation of human rights treaties in domestic legal and political systems. It examines the interpenetration of the international and national systems, and the significance of treaties within states. Our discussion then expands to include relationships between customary international law and national systems. The broad questions explored are: how do these international norms influence the national legal and political systems of states? Are they automatically absorbed into a state legal system, or reproduced in state legislation, and with what effects on the different branches of government such as the executive and judiciary? Or do they remain distinct from the state system, 'above' it as part of international law? While the readings by David Sloss relate primarily to United States law,[513] the broader principles hold true elsewhere.[514]

RYAN GOODMAN AND DEREK JINKS, SOCIALIZING STATES: PROMOTING HUMAN RIGHTS THROUGH INTERNATIONAL LAW
(2013) 21

...

Chapter 2: Three Mechanisms of Social Influence

...

A. Material inducement

The first and most obvious social mechanism is material inducement — whereby states and institutions influence the behavior of other states by increasing the benefits of conformity or the costs of nonconformity through material rewards and punishments. ...

B. Persuasion

... Persuasion theory suggests that the practices of actors are influenced through processes of social "learning" and other forms of information conveyance that occur in exchanges within international organizations and transnational networks. Persuasion "requires argument and deliberation in an effort to change the minds of others." Persuaded actors "internalize" new norms and rules of appropriate behavior and redefine their interests and identities accordingly. ... The touchstone of the overall process is that actors are consciously convinced of the truth, validity, or appropriateness of a norm, belief, or practice. ... [They] change their minds on the basis of the norm's congruence with their existing beliefs and values.

C. Acculturation

... Whereas persuasion emphasizes the content of a norm, acculturation emphasizes the relationship of the actor to a reference group or wider cultural environment. ... [It] encompasses processes such as mimicry and status maximization. The general mechanism induces behavioral changes through pressures to conform. Individual behavior (and community-level behavioral regularity) is in part a function of social structure — the relations between individual actors and some reference group. Actors are impelled to adopt the behavioral practices and attitudes of similar actors in their surrounding social environment.

The touchstone of acculturation is that varying degrees of identification with a reference group generate varying degrees of cognitive and social pressures to conform. ... Social influence is a rich process — one that also includes "normative social influence" whereby actors are impelled to adopt appropriate attitudes and behaviors. An actor need not be unaware of these influences — these processes can be subconscious or fully apparent. ...

...

Despite the obvious similarities, acculturation differs from persuasion in important respects. First, persuasion requires acceptance of the validity or legitimacy of a belief, practice, or norm — acculturation requires only that an actor perceive that an important reference group harbors the belief, engages in the practice, or subscribes to the norm. Accordingly, persuasion involves complete internalization. Acculturation can involve complete or incomplete internalization. Second, persuasion requires active assessment of the merits of a belief. Acculturation processes, in contrast, frequently (though not invariably) operate tacitly; it is often the very act of conforming that garners social approval and alleviates cognitive discomfort. Persuasion involves assessment of the content of the message (even if only indirectly); acculturation involves assessment of the social relation (the degree of identification) between the target audience and some group (and of the importance of the issue to the group).

---

[513] See C. *Bradley, International Law in the US Legal System* (3rd edn., 2020).

[514] See A. Byrnes and C. Renshaw, 'Within the State', in D. Moeckli, S. Shah and S. Sivakumaran (eds.), *International Human Rights Law* (4th edn., 2022) 505; A. Edgar and R. Thwaites, 'Implementing Treaties in Domestic Law: Translation, Enforcement and Administrative Law', 19 *Melb. J. Int'l L.* (2018) 1; and European Commission for Democracy Through Law (Venice Commission), 'Report on the Implementation of International Human Rights Treaties in Domestic Law and the Role of Courts' (2014).

Acculturation occurs not as a result of the content of the relevant rule or norm but rather as a function of social structure. Acculturation depends less on the properties of the rule than on the properties of the relationship of the actor to the community. Because the acculturation process does not involve actually agreeing with the merits of a group's position, it may (but does not necessarily) result in outward conformity with a social convention without private acceptance or corresponding changes in private practices.

…

DAVID SLOSS, DOMESTIC APPLICATION OF TREATIES
DUNCAN HOLLIS (ED.), THE OXFORD GUIDE TO TREATIES (2ND ED., 2020) 355

I. Monism and Dualism

…

Dualist States are States in which no treaties have the status of law in the domestic legal system; all treaties require implementing legislation to have domestic legal force. Monist States are States in which some treaties have the status of law in the domestic legal system, even in the absence of implementing legislation. In most monist States, there are some treaties that require implementing legislation and others that do not. There is substantial variation among monist States as to which treaties require implementing legislation. Moreover, monist States differ considerably in terms of the hierarchical rank of treaties within the domestic legal order. Despite these variations, all monist States have one common feature: at least some treaties have the status of law within the domestic legal order.

…

II. Horizontal, Transnational, and Vertical Treaty Provisions

… States conclude treaties to regulate three different types of relationships: horizontal relations between and among States, vertical relations between States and private actors (including natural persons and corporations), and transnational relations between private actors who interact across national boundaries. The role of domestic courts in applying treaties varies greatly depending on whether the treaty provision at issue is horizontal, vertical, or transnational.

Domestic courts rarely apply treaties that regulate horizontal relationships among States. …

In contrast …, domestic courts routinely apply transnational treaty provisions that regulate cross-border relationships between private actors [such as the 1980 Convention on the International Sale of Goods and the 1980 Hague Convention on Child Abduction]. Although States negotiated and ratified these treaties, they are designed primarily to regulate cross-border relationships among private actors, not horizontal relationships among States. … [S]uch transnational treaties 'have generated thousands of reported opinions' from domestic courts, including more than 10,000 domestic judicial opinions applying the CISG, at least 1,750 applying the New York Convention, and almost 1,000 applying the Hague Convention. …

…

The most significant differences among States relate to the judicial application of vertical treaty provisions— provisions that regulate relations between States and private parties [such as the ICCPR or the Refugee Protocol]. …

Whereas both vertical and transnational treaty provisions implicate the rights of private parties … vertical treaty provisions implicate the public functions of government in a way that is not true for transnational treaty provisions. …

This distinction between vertical and transnational treaty provisions helps explain the distinction between nationalist and transnationalist approaches to the judicial application of treaties. 'Transnationalist' decisions manifest a belief that the judiciary has an independent responsibility to ensure that domestic government officials act in accordance with international treaty obligations. 'Nationalist' decisions manifest a belief that courts should not scrutinize too closely government conduct that is arguably inconsistent with international treaty obligations. In countries where courts adopt a more 'transnationalist' approach—such as Albania, Argentina, the Netherlands, and South Africa—domestic courts apply both vertical and transnational treaty provisions with equal vigour. However, in States where courts adopt a more 'nationalist' approach—such as the United States and Israel—domestic courts are hesitant to apply vertical treaty provisions, even though they routinely apply transnational provisions.

The contrast between nationalist and transnationalist approaches manifests different judicial attitudes about the relative weight assigned to two competing factors: the judicial responsibility to protect the rights of private parties and the judicial responsibility to refrain from interfering with public governmental functions. …

…

A. Statutory interpretation

Courts in both monist and dualist States frequently apply an interpretive presumption that statutes should be construed in conformity with the nation's international legal obligations, including obligations derived from both treaties and customary international law. This interpretive presumption is sometimes called a 'presumption of conformity' or a 'presumption of compatibility'. In the United States, the presumption is referred to as the '*Charming Betsy* canon'. Labels aside, the presumption of conformity is probably the most widely used transnationalist tool. …

…

B. Treaty interpretation

Domestic courts in both monist and dualist States are frequently asked to interpret treaties. In dualist States, this situation commonly arises when the legislature enacts a statute that is expressly intended to implement a treaty. In monist States, courts sometimes interpret treaties when a litigant asks the court to apply a treaty directly, and sometimes when the treaty is applied indirectly. …

Courts applying a transnationalist approach interpret treaties in accordance with the shared understanding of the parties. In accordance with this approach, transnationalist judges cite the Vienna Convention on the Law of Treaties, decisions of foreign courts and international tribunals, as well as views adopted by non-judicial international bodies to support their interpretations of particular treaty provisions. …

In contrast, courts applying a nationalist approach emphasize that treaty interpretation is primarily an executive function, not a judicial function. …

…

C. Constitutional interpretation

Courts in both monist and dualist States apply treaties to help elucidate the meaning of constitutional provisions. Argentina, South Africa, and India are leading examples of States where courts routinely invoke treaties and other provisions of international law in the context of constitutional interpretation. …

DAVID SLOSS, THE DEATH OF TREATY SUPREMACY: AN INVISIBLE CONSTITUTIONAL CHANGE
(2016) 1515

When the Framers of the U.S. Constitution met in Philadelphia in 1787, they drafted a Constitution designed to ensure that states would not violate the nation's treaty commitments. …

On August 5, 2008, the State of Texas executed José Ernesto Medellín. His execution violated the nation's legal obligations under the U.N. Charter … . President George W. Bush … tried to block Medellín's execution, precisely because it violated U.S. treaty obligations. However, the Supreme Court ruled in … *Medellín v. Texas* [552 U.S. 491] that President Bush could not prevent Texas from putting Medellín to death, even though the execution violated international law. The Supreme Court based its decision on an understanding of the Constitution that differed sharply from the Framers' understanding. …

---

[515] For a review of the book by a long-time State Department lawyer, see D. Stewart, 112 *Am. J. Int'l* L. (2018) 779.

...The "treaty supremacy rule" is codified in Article VI of the Constitution, known as the Supremacy Clause. The rule, as traditionally understood, provided that treaties automatically supersede conflicting state laws. ... [This rule] helped ensure that state governments would not violate U.S. treaty obligations unless the federal political branches authorized them to do so. ... Articles 55 and 56 of the Charter obligate the United States to promote "human rights ... for all without distinction as to race." In the late 1940s and early 1950s, human rights activists in the United States invoked the Charter's human rights provisions, together with the Constitution's treaty supremacy rule, to challenge the validity of state laws that discriminated on the basis of race or nationality. In 1950, in *Fujii v. California* [242 P. 2d 617] a California court ruled in favor of human rights claimants, striking down a California law that discriminated against Japanese nationals because it conflicted with the Charter's human rights provisions. The potential implications of that decision were shocking. If the court was right, the United States had effectively abrogated Jim Crow laws throughout the South by ratifying the U.N. Charter. That result was unacceptable to many Americans at the time. Responding to *Fujii*, conservatives mobilized support for a constitutional amendment, known as the Bricker Amendment, whose aim was to abolish the treaty supremacy rule. ... [P]roponents of the Bricker Amendment realized some of their goals without a formal constitutional amendment. I refer to that constitutional transformation as the "de facto Bricker Amendment."

... [This] is not a story about the triumph of democracy and popular sovereignty [but] about invisible constitutional transformation. ... [M]ost lawyers in the United States today are unaware that the Constitution's treaty supremacy rule was dramatically transformed in the 1950s. The substance of that transformation was initially expressed in American Bar Association (ABA) reports and Senate testimony by Eisenhower administration officials in the early 1950s. Later, the de facto Bricker Amendment was "codified" in the Restatement (Second) of Foreign Relations Law [1965]. None of those sources were readily accessible to the American public. Moreover, neither the ABA nor the ALI exercises formal governmental authority.

The de facto Bricker Amendment remained largely invisible because the results were expressed in technical legal jargon that obscured the magnitude of the constitutional change. Before 1950, the treaty supremacy rule was simple: all treaties prevail over conflicting state laws because the Supremacy Clause says so. By 1965, though, a new constitutional understanding had emerged - "self-executing" treaties prevail over conflicting state laws, but states are free to violate "non-self-executing" treaties. ... The de facto Bricker Amendment expanded the scope of self-execution doctrine to encompass the relationship between treaties and state law. In the process, lawyers created the "NSE exception to the treaty supremacy rule." The NSE exception allows state government officers to violate U.S. treaty obligations without authorization from the federal political branches.

...
... In *Medellín v. Texas*, the Supreme Court held that Article 94 of the U.N. Charter is not self-executing. The Court's decision was based on the NSE exception to the treaty supremacy rule that arose from the de facto Bricker Amendment (although the Court claimed, incorrectly, that it was applying nineteenth-century self-execution doctrine). As a practical matter, the Court's decision meant that Texas was allowed to violate U.S. treaty obligations. Moreover, Texas's actions meant that the federal political branches were forced to deal with the foreign policy consequences of a treaty violation that they did not authorize and that the president tried to prevent. This was precisely the type of situation that the Framers sought to avoid by codifying the treaty supremacy rule in Article VI of the Constitution.

The de facto Bricker Amendment gained acceptance because the NSE exception to the treaty supremacy rule was responsive to widely shared sentiments about American constitutional identity. ...

... [T]he Bricker debate generated an atmosphere in which human rights treaties are seen as political poison. Consequently, the United States refuses to ratify most human rights treaties, and the treaties we do ratify include unilateral reservations and declarations designed to ensure that ratification does not affect human rights protection in the United States. The net result is that we cling to our faith in the superiority of the U.S. constitutional system, but domestic protection for human rights falls short of international standards. ...

COMMITTEE ON ECONOMIC, SOCIAL AND CULTURAL RIGHTS, GENERAL COMMENT NO. 9: DOMESTIC APPLICATION OF THE COVENANT UN DOC. E/C.12/1998/24 (1998)

…

A. *The duty to give effect to the Covenant in the domestic legal order*

…

2. [The Covenant requires] each State Party to use all the means at its disposal to give effect to the rights recognized in the Covenant … . Thus the norms themselves must be recognised in appropriate ways within the domestic legal order, appropriate means of redress, or remedies, must be available to any aggrieved individual or group, and appropriate means of ensuring governmental accountability must be put in place.

…

B. *The status of the Covenant in the domestic legal order*

4. In general, legally binding international human rights standards should operate directly and immediately within the domestic legal system of each State party, thereby enabling individuals concerned to seek enforcement of their rights before national courts and tribunals. The rule requiring the exhaustion of domestic remedies reinforces the primacy of national remedies in this respect. …

5. The Covenant itself does not stipulate the specific means by which its terms are to be implemented in the national legal order. And there is no provision obligating its comprehensive incorporation or requiring it to be accorded any specific type of status in national law. Although the precise method by which Covenant rights are given effect in national law is a matter for each State Party to decide, the means used should be appropriate in the sense of producing results which are consistent with the full discharge of its obligations by the State Party. The means chosen are also subject to review as part of the Committee's examination of the State Party's compliance with its Covenant obligations.

…

C. *The role of legal remedies*

…

11. The Covenant itself does not negate the possibility that the rights may be considered self-executing in systems where that option is provided for. Indeed, when it was being drafted, attempts to include a specific provision in the Covenant providing that it be considered 'non-self-executing' were strongly rejected. In most States the determination of whether or not a treaty provision is self-executing will be a matter for the courts, not the executive or the legislature. In order to perform that function effectively the relevant courts and tribunals must be made aware of the nature and implications of the Covenant and of the important role of judicial remedies in its implementation … . [W]hen Governments are involved in court proceedings, they should promote interpretations of domestic laws which give effect to their Covenant obligations … .

…

D. *The treatment of the Covenant in domestic courts*

…

13. … [S]ome courts have applied the provisions of the Covenant either directly or as interpretive standards. Other courts are willing to acknowledge, in principle, the relevance of the Covenant for interpreting domestic law, but in practice, the impact of the Covenant on the reasoning or outcome of cases is very limited. Still other courts have refused to give any degree of legal effect to the Covenant in cases in which individuals have sought to rely on it. …

14. Within the limits of the appropriate exercise of their functions of judicial review, courts should take account of Covenant rights where this is necessary to ensure that the State's conduct is consistent with its obligations under the Covenant. Neglect by the courts of this responsibility is incompatible with the principle of the Rule of Law which must always be taken to include respect for international human rights obligations.

…

HUMAN RIGHTS COMMITTEE, GENERAL COMMENT NO. 31: THE NATURE OF THE GENERAL LEGAL OBLIGATION IMPOSED ON STATES PARTIES TO THE COVENANT (2004)

...

13. Article 2, paragraph 2, requires that States Parties take the necessary steps to give effect to the Covenant rights in the domestic order. It follows that, unless Covenant rights are already protected by their domestic laws or practices, States Parties are required on ratification to make such changes to domestic laws and practices as are necessary to ensure their conformity with the Covenant. Where there are inconsistencies between domestic law and the Covenant, article 2 requires that the domestic law or practice be changed to meet the standards imposed by the Covenant's substantive guarantees. Article 2 allows a State Party to pursue this in accordance with its own domestic constitutional structure and accordingly does not require that the Covenant be directly applicable in the courts, by incorporation of the Covenant into national law. The Committee takes the view, however, that Covenant guarantees may receive enhanced protection in those States where the Covenant is automatically or through specific incorporation part of the domestic legal order. The Committee invites those States Parties in which the Covenant does not form part of the domestic legal order to consider incorporation of the Covenant to render it part of domestic law to facilitate full realization of Covenant rights as required by article 2.

14. The requirement under article 2, paragraph 2, to take steps to give effect to the Covenant rights is unqualified and of immediate effect. A failure to comply with this obligation cannot be justified by reference to political, social, cultural or economic considerations within the State.

15. Article 2, paragraph 3, requires that in addition to effective protection of Covenant rights States Parties must ensure that individuals also have accessible and effective remedies to vindicate those rights. Such remedies should be appropriately adapted so as to take account of the special vulnerability of certain categories of person, including in particular children. The Committee attaches importance to States Parties' establishing appropriate judicial and administrative mechanisms for addressing claims of rights violations under domestic law. The Committee notes that the enjoyment of the rights recognized under the Covenant can be effectively assured by the judiciary in many different ways, including direct applicability of the Covenant, application of comparable constitutional or other provisions of law, or the interpretive effect of the Covenant in the application of national law. Administrative mechanisms are particularly required to give effect to the general obligation to investigate allegations of violations promptly, thoroughly and effectively through independent and impartial bodies. National human rights institutions, endowed with appropriate powers, can contribute to this end. A failure by a State Party to investigate allegations of violations could in and of itself give rise to a separate breach of the Covenant. Cessation of an ongoing violation is an essential element of the right to an effective remedy.

...

* * *

Traditionally, the main focus of national level human rights efforts has been on domestic constitutional and legislative provisions, and especially Bills of Rights.[516] Examples of this phenomenon appear throughout the casebook. Suffice it for present purposes to note that, while the experience of states differs greatly from one to another, constitutional rights are clearly not sufficient on their own to ensure compliance by states with their international human rights obligations. Consider, for example, the following assessment by Adam Chilton and Mila Versteeg, 'The Politics of Constitutional Rights', in Mark Tishnet and Dimitry Kochenov (eds.), *Research Handbook on the Politics of Constitutional Law* (2023) 432:

> Some rights may be adopted by some countries as a genuine attempt to prevent repression, while others are adopted to advance strategic goals, such as entrenching economic interests, attracting investors, appeasing the international community, and even paving the way for greater authoritarianism. Once adopted, some rights, like the right to form political parties, may be associated with improved rights practices; but other rights, like the right to education, might not be associated with any changes in school funding or educational attainment. And even if some rights may individually be associated with

---

[516] See S. Fredman, *Comparative Human Rights Law* (2018).

better rights practices, it is still possible that the inclusion of more rights in constitutions still may weaken respect for rights overall.[517]

One of the most important exercises in domestic internalization of international norms was the adoption in the United Kingdom of the Human Rights Act in 1998. The Act 'gives further effect' to the rights guaranteed under the European Convention. Public bodies are generally required to act in ways compatible with the Convention, and the courts must take account of the jurisprudence of the European Court of Human Rights, including interpreting legislation, as far as possible, in a way compatible with Convention rights. If a court finds a statute to be incompatible it must issue a ruling to that effect. Such a ruling does not set aside the offending provisions but calls their attention to the Parliament, which must indicate what remedial legislation, if any, will be proposed. The Act has brought major changes to domestic law, but has also been the subject of political controversy and a series of inquiries into its impact and legislative proposals to substitute it by a British Bill of Rights.

Roger Masterman, in 'The United Kingdom's Human Rights Act as a Catalyst of Constitutional Migration: Patterns and Limitations of Rights Importation by Design', 19 *Eur. Const. L. Rev.* (2023) 88, at 109, assesses its impact:

> … the Act has also provoked opposition to the extent to which it permits 'foreign' authorities to influence domestic judicial decision-making. The consequence of the international heritage of the Convention rights and the courts' internationalist approach to their application has been a significant convergence between the substance of Convention norms and protections at the UK national level. This is, first, attributable to the design of the Human Right Act which … leaves 'little scope' for divergence between the Strasbourg Court and UK apex court in relation to the definition and meaning of the Convention rights. It is, secondly, a product of the cumulative judicial approach to 'taking into account' the Convention case law … which has generated a perception of domestic courts abdicating decision-making responsibility as regards the substance of the domestically applicable rights and remedial extent of the Act. A narrative of legal subjection to the European Court of Human Rights – of transplantation and overweening influence – is firmly embedded in UK human rights discourse. This is even though the Human Rights Act facilitates a fluid and multi-directional migration of authorities; it has not operated to the exclusion of the common law (or other foreign) authorities in rights adjudication and has empowered domestic courts to interact with Strasbourg jurisprudence in ways which allow it to be integrated with – rather than supplant – domestic laws. … While the Human Rights Act scheme holds the potential to allow for the critical assimilation of domestic and international norms – to facilitate a context-sensitive rather than overriding migration of constitutional standards – the tenor of recent reform proposals points towards a future parochialisation (and significant dilution) of the UK's legal rights regime and a further post-Brexit step towards insulating the domestic legal order from external influences.

Institutional Dimensions of Internalization

Many scholars have criticised the extent to which the international human rights regime has focused on the issues discussed in the preceding readings, and failed to address adequately the essential role of a more diverse and pluralistic approach that goes well beyond both legal incorporation and a preoccupation with the role of the state as legislator and enforcer of rights. Julie Fraser, in *Social Institutions and International Human Rights Law Implementation: Every Organ of Society* (2020) at 9, argues that treating state law 'as *the* law' leads to an approach that 'recognises only the modern state model and marginalises other plural legal systems beneath and beyond the state that exist in virtually all countries in the world.' In terms of alternative approaches, she suggests (at 287) that domestic implementation measures should involve 'broad consultation and seek to identify culturally sensitive approaches'. This includes engagement with non-state actors, 'including representatives or members of social institutions', and the development of National Human Rights Institutions. 'States should identify

---

[517] See also A. Chilton and M. Versteeg, 'Do Constitutional Rights Make a Difference?', 60 *Am. J. Pol. Sci.* (2016) 575.

domestic constituents from within local communities and support them to develop a culture of rights from the bottom up.' States, in turn, when reporting to UN treaty bodies, should provide an account of how such processes have worked, and treaty bodies should tailor their recommendations to take full account of the role played by social institutions, broadly defined.

National systems for implementing, monitoring and enforcing international human rights norms have proliferated greatly in recent years.[518]

a. National Human Rights Institutions (NHRIs)

In the early 1990s, the UN General Assembly encouraged Member States to establish or strengthen national human rights institutions (NHRIs), a term that has been interpreted to include human rights commissions, human rights ombuds institutions, consultative and advisory bodies, institutes and centres, and hybrid institutions. The General Assembly adopted the 'Paris Principles' in Resolution 48/134 (1993):

UN GENERAL ASSEMBLY, PRINCIPLES RELATING TO THE STATUS OF NATIONAL INSTITUTIONS (THE PARIS PRINCIPLES) RESOLUTION 48/134 (1993)

Competence and responsibilities

1. A national institution shall be vested with competence to promote and protect human rights.

2. A national institution shall be given as broad a mandate as possible, which shall be clearly set forth in a constitutional or legislative text, specifying its composition and its sphere of competence.

3. A national institution shall, inter alia, have the following responsibilities:

(a) To submit to the Government, Parliament and any other competent Body ... opinions, recommendations, proposals and reports on any matters concerning ... human rights; [such actions] shall relate to the following areas:

(i) Any legislative or administrative provisions ... intended to [protect] human rights ...;

(ii) Any situation of violation of human rights which it decides to take up;

(iii) The preparation of reports on the national [human rights] situation ...;

(iv) Drawing the attention of the Government to [domestic] situations ... where human rights are violated and making proposals to ... end to such situations ...;

(b) To promote and ensure the harmonization of national legislation regulations and practices with the [State's human rights obligations], and their effective implementation;

(c) To encourage ratification ...;

(d) To contribute to ... reports [submitted] to United Nations bodies and ... regional institutions ... , with due respect for their independence;

(e) To cooperate with [international and other national human rights institutions];

...

Composition and guarantees of independence and pluralism

---

[518] S. Jensen, S. Lagoutte and S. Lorion, 'The Domestic Institutionalisation of Human Rights: An Introduction', 37 *Nordic J. Hum. Rts.* (2019) 165.

1. The composition of the … [NHRI shall] ensure the pluralist representation of the social forces (of civilian society) …
2. The national institution shall have [a suitable] infrastructure …, in particular adequate funding … to enable it to have its own staff and premises, in order to be independent of the Government … .

Methods of operation
Within the framework of its operation, the national institution shall:
(a) Freely consider any questions falling within its competence …;
(b) Hear any person and obtain any information and any documents necessary for assessing situations falling within its competence;
(c) Address public opinion directly …;
(d) Meet on a regular basis …;
…

Additional principles …
A national institution may be authorized to hear and consider complaints and petitions concerning individual situations. Cases may be brought before it by individuals, their representatives, third parties, non-governmental organizations, associations of trade unions or any other representative organizations. …

* * *

An important innovation, building on the NHRI concept, is reflected in Article 33 of the Convention on the Rights of Persons with Disabilities (CRPD):[519]

1. States Parties … shall designate one or more focal points within government for matters relating to the implementation of the [CRPD] … .

2. States Parties shall … maintain, strengthen, designate or establish … a framework, including one or more independent mechanisms, as appropriate, to promote, protect and monitor implementation of the [CPRD]. When designating or establishing such a mechanism, States Parties shall take into account the [Paris Principles].

3. Civil society, in particular persons with disabilities and their representative organizations, shall be involved and participate fully in the monitoring process.

Similarly, Article 3 of the 2002 Optional Protocol to the Convention against Torture requires each State Party to 'set up, designate or maintain at the domestic level one or several visiting bodies for the prevention of torture and other cruel, inhuman or degrading treatment or punishment'. The Protocol also addresses questions of the independence, mandate and budgetary resources of these 'national preventive mechanisms', or NPMs. In addition to visiting places of detention, they complement the work of international bodies.[520]

In 1993, NHRIs set up an International Coordinating Committee which, in 2016, became the Global Alliance of National Human Rights Institutions (GANHRI). One of its most important functions is accreditation. NHRIs accorded 'A status' comply fully with the Paris Principles, and those with 'B status' have achieved only partial compliance. In 2023, there were 88 with A status and 32 with B status. Accreditation involves a peer-based review undertaken by a Sub-Committee on Accreditation (SCA) at the outset, every five years thereafter, or when a significant change of circumstances occurs.[521]

---

[519] C. Lichuma and D. Tatic, 'Human Rights Experimentalism in Action: The Potential of National Human Rights Institutions in Enhancing the Implementation and Monitoring of the Convention on the Rights of Persons with Disabilities', 14 J. *Hum. Rts. Prac.* (2022) 108.

[520] See OHCHR, *The Role of National Preventive Mechanisms: A Practical Guide* (2018).

[521] D. Langtry and K. Roberts Lyer, *National Human Rights Institutions: Rules, Requirements, and Practice* (2021); and H. Takata, 'How Are the Paris Principles on NHRIs Interpreted? Towards a Clear, Transparent, and Consistent Interpretative Framework', 40 *Nordic J. Hum. Rts.* (2022) 285.

In 2023, for example, the SCA again deferred re-accrediting the National Human Rights Commission of India (NHRC) for a range of reasons, including that: it involved police officers in its investigations, thus compromising its impartiality; three of six commissioner positions were vacant, and no women were members; the appointments process lacked transparency and participation by civil society and was not conducive to a merit-based selection that ensures pluralism; the Commission's executive head, the Secretary-General, is seconded by the government from the public service, thus affecting the Commission's actual and perceived independence; and its relationships with civil society were neither effective nor constructive. The SCA also gave credence to a third-party submission alleging: that the Commission had failed to review important legislation, such as the Foreign Contribution (Regulation) Act 2010, Citizenship (Amendment) Act 2019, and Unlawful Activities (Prevention) Act 1967, each of which seriously restricted human rights; that it had not been active in protecting religious minorities; and that it dismissed a high number of complaints at the first stage of the process.[522]

There is now an extensive literature on NHRIs and their effectiveness or otherwise.[523] Despite the binary A or B status adopted by the GANHRI, there is huge variation in: the design of such institutions, the scope of their activities, their actual as opposed to formal relationship with the government, and their preparedness to stand up for human rights in difficult situations. Specific institutions also fluctuate over time between strong and weak, influential and powerless, well-resourced and starved for funding, and respected and dismissed. An illustration of the challenges is provided by Tomer Broude and Natan Milikowsky, in 'Establishing an NHRI in a Contested Political Space: A Deliberative Process in Israel', 37 *Nordic J. Hum. Rts.* (2019) 281. They ask, in the context of a heavily contested space for human rights in Israel, how a NHRI can be meaningfully established and whether, in reality, the effectiveness of domestic human rights actors might be enhanced without a formal NHRI. They describe the results of a deliberative process that considered key questions such as:

> ... (1) should the goal be a 'first-best' NHRI or second-best alternatives ('ideal' vs 'realist' scenarios)? (2) what would be the role of an NHRI given reduced chances of addressing the most politically contested human rights concerns, such as the situation of Palestinians in East Jerusalem and the West Bank, and unequal family status in Israeli society; (3) might NHRI establishment in the current political climate in Israel result in adverse effects for human rights through co-optation and political capture? And (4) how best to design an NHRI that satisfies not only formal requirements but also localised effectiveness?

Their conclusion is that the Paris Principle model might be too demanding politically in a contested space such as that in Israel today. This pragmatic conclusion inevitably also raises questions as to the effectiveness of the 88 NHRIs around the world that are considered to comply with the demands of the Principles, even though many of them operate in countries with terrible human rights records.

Another assessment of the institutional arrangements that have evolved in relation to NHRIs places particular emphasis on the role played by the SCA through its accreditation process.

KATERINA LINOS AND TOM PEGRAM, WHAT WORKS IN HUMAN RIGHTS INSTITUTIONS?
111 AM. J. INT'L L. (2017) 628

...

An important prior quantitative study ... concludes that countries that set up NHRIs perform better on critical physical integrity measures, such as freedom from torture, extrajudicial killing, political imprisonment, and disappearance, than countries that lack NHRIs. However, qualitative case studies reveal surprising variation among NHRIs, praising some for robust, even heroic, protection efforts, while condemning other bodies as sham institutions.

---

[522] https://ganhri.org/accreditation/sca-reports/.
[523] For a literature review, see R. Welch, J. DeMeritt and C. Conrad, 'Conceptualizing and Measuring Institutional Variation in National Human Rights Institutions (NHRIs)', 65 *J. Conflict Resol.* (2021) 1010.

... We collected fine-grained quantitative data on twenty-two formal institutional design features of all NHRIs around the world, focusing on four critical dimensions: independence safeguards, investigatory powers, promotion functions, and inclusiveness. ...

Broadly, our study demonstrates that formal institutional safeguards influence human rights outcomes, in part because formal institutional design remains relatively stable over time. Whereas governments can often resist NHRI advocacy by pulling on other levers—notably by manipulating personnel appointments and cutting budgets—they find it harder to change formal safeguards. In turn, formal safeguards structure the initial hiring and priorities of NHRIs, shape modes of resistance, and contribute to the development of positive or negative feedback loops over time.

Our study suggests that one institutional safeguard above all, the power to initiate, execute, and complete investigations on receipt of complaints, stands out as particularly important in enabling NHRI effectiveness, including in developing country settings displaying weak rule of law. Other design features strongly promoted by international NHRI templates, such as independence safeguards and broad promotional powers, may not correlate generally with more effective organizational outcomes across countries, but emerge as important under certain conditions ... .

... [T]he diffusion of NHRIs around the world marks a big success for the United Nations. Almost 120 countries now have NHRIs, and the vast majority of these closely follow the UN-sponsored Paris Principles. Moreover, the United Nations has begun building on the success of NHRIs by giving NHRIs formal speaking rights and incorporating them into treaty structures—notably as national preventive mechanisms under the OPCAT. The establishment of ex novo structures has also set in motion important design feedback effects, serving as a focal point for mobilizing compliance levels above an expected baseline ... .

... [T]he ultimate test of the United Nations' influence does not concern the diffusion of NHRIs, but the diffusion of effective NHRIs. ... By showing that formal design features are in fact connected to greater effectiveness, this study documents a particularly strong influence of the United Nations. Formal rules have provided NHRI practitioners and their supporters with a rare lever of influence over instituting structures at the national level, but ... adopting states retain significant prerogatives over the resulting NHRI form, as well as the individuals who populate the organization.

The United Nations has few levers other than formal design recommendations to influence NHRI behavior—for instance, it cannot directly appoint NHRI staff members, or contribute significantly to NHRI financing. This greatly increases the importance of issuing the correct formal design recommendations. ...

Our study highlights one particular limitation of the UN-promoted Paris Principles—the de-prioritization of protective functions, and especially complaint-handling powers. How can one best ensure that the UN template is updated in light of current knowledge? Amending the Paris Principles seems unlikely ... . However, another avenue for reform seems promising: the SCA, the peer review monitoring mechanism that grades NHRIs. Lacking a direct means to implement policy, the UN system has strongly promoted the role of the SCA as a third-party monitor of NHRI design integrity and performance. Delegation of monitoring duties to a third party can enhance compliance, especially where—as is the case of the SCA—a central body collects information from diverse sources and issues highly specific assessments in the form of letter grades to individual NHRIs. In recent years, the SCA has sought to ratchet up the specificity of the Paris Principles still further through authoritative interpretations.

...

b. Parliaments

Two other initiatives warrant a mention in terms of efforts to encourage internalization of international norms. The first is the role played by national parliaments.[524] The Inter-Parliamentary Union (IPU) encourages its member institutions to establish human rights committees and lists well over 100 states in which such bodies have been created. A well-known example, which at one stage was especially active and effective, is the United

---

[524] Council of Europe, *National Parliaments as Guarantors of Human Rights in Europe: Handbook for Parliamentarians* (2018).

Kingdom Parliamentary Joint Committee on Human Rights. It scrutinizes government Bills for compatibility with human rights, monitors the government's response to relevant court judgments, scrutinizes the UK's compliance with international human rights treaty obligations, and conducts thematic inquiries. In Australia, the Human Rights (Parliamentary Scrutiny) Act 2011 established a similar Joint Committee.[525] Some parliaments, as with the United States Congress, have standing and other committees that regularly consider human rights performance in other countries, but rarely do so domestically.

A 2018 Policy Brief prepared by the Commonwealth and the Universal Rights Group on *The Role of National Parliaments* underlined the importance of 'leveraging parliaments' legislative, oversight and budgetary roles to support the effective domestic implementation of the recommendations of the UN's human rights mechanisms, the transparent monitoring of progress, and objective and balanced international reporting.' In practice, the human rights record of parliaments, even in democratic countries, is often rather poor. They may well be on the frontlines of adopting legislation that deprives certain groups of their rights and of taking measures to resist accountability.[526] In addition, parliamentarians themselves are not infrequently the victims of human rights violations, as indicated by the hundreds of cases documented by the IPU.

In 2018, the UN Office of the High Commissioner for Human Rights proposed a set of Draft Principles on Parliaments and human rights, prompted by the role of parliaments in relation to the Universal Periodic Review process (Ch. 8B, above).[527] The Draft Principles call on all parliaments to set up a human rights committee and to give it the following responsibilities:

> (a) To encourage the ratification of … human rights instruments;

> (b) To introduce and review bills and existing legislation to ensure [human rights] compatibility …;

> (c) To lead the parliamentary oversight of the [human rights-related] work of the Government …;

> …

> (e) To review draft national budgets from the perspective of … human rights;

> (f) To ensure that development assistance and cooperation funds support the implementation of recommendations from international and regional human rights mechanisms in countries recipient of such funds;

> (g) To call for the elaboration of national human rights action plan and oversee its implementation;

> (h) To engage and consult with the national human rights institution and civil society representatives …;

> (i) To lead parliamentary action in response to national human rights developments and issues, including through legislative initiatives, parliamentary inquiries, public hearings, public debates, and the issuing of reports …;

> (j) To hold public hearings …;

> …

The Principles spell out the roles that such a committee should have as well as its ideal composition and working methods. Although this approach draws its inspiration from the Paris Principles for NHRIs, commentators have been critical of the 'one size fits all' approach, the assumption that parliamentary committees can act

---

[525] L. Grenfell and J. Debeljak (eds.), *Law Making and Human Rights* (2020).
[526] See generally, M. Hunt, H. Hooper and P. Yowell (eds.), *Parliaments and Human Rights* (2015); and M. Saul, A. Follesdal and G. Ulfstein (eds.), *The International Human Rights Judiciary and National Parliaments: Europe and Beyond* (2017).
[527] 'Contribution of parliaments to the work of the Human Rights Council and its universal periodic review', UN Doc. A/HRC/38/25 (2018), Annex.

independently of governments in many contexts, and have drawn attention to the risk that such committees might 'open rights up to negative politicization'. Kirsten Roberts Lyer, in 'Parliaments as Human Rights Actors: The Potential for International Principles on Parliamentary Human Rights Committees', 37 *Nordic J. Hum. Rts.* (2019) 195 suggests that one response to such concerns is for the OHCHR and perhaps the IPU to set up a body comparable to the SCA under the Paris Principles, so that parliamentary committees are peer-reviewed and compliance ranked.

c. Local authorities

In 'Transnational Human Rights and Local Activism: Mapping the Middle', 108 *American Anthropologist* (2006) 38, Sally Engle Merry asked how transnational ideas such as human rights are 'adopted in local social settings'. 'How do they move across the gap between a cosmopolitan awareness of human rights and local sociocultural understandings …'. While her focus was on the concepts of vernacularization and translation discussed in Ch. 7 above, the potentially important role of local authorities such as cities and municipalities in localizing human rights norms has gained increased attention in recent years.[528] Their importance has been enhanced by steadily increasing urbanization around the world, and growing decentralization all too often accompanied by de facto budget cuts that place the burden of making the hard decisions on local governments. Barbara Oomen and Moritz Baumgärtel, in 'Frontier Cities: The Rise of Local Authorities as an Opportunity for International Human Rights Law, 29 *Eur. J. Int'l L.* (2018) 607 also link this phenomenon to the 'right to the city' that was spelled out by Henri Lefebvre, in *Le Droit à la ville* (1968), and emphasized the importance of all residents being able to shape the city in which they live. The concept is now reflected in the Brazilian Constitution and in local ordinances in Mexico City and elsewhere.

In Canada cities and municipalities have launched various initiatives, including 'local recognition of human rights through an ordinance, declaration, or charter …; … rights-based audits of policies, plans and budgets, setting aside adequate staff and financial resources to embed a culture of rights, and providing relevant training to municipal staff; participatory governance and inclusion …; and [adopting] accountability mechanisms, such as human rights ombudspersons, local human rights commissions, and citizen juries … .[529]

In the United States, since 2013, a Cities for CEDAW has encouraged US municipalities to become CEDAW Cities by adopting some sort of municipal code requiring them to '(1) conduct a gender analysis of city operations and laws; (2) establish a convention oversight body; and (3) financially underwrite any convention initiatives.' By 2021, 41 US cities had adopted such initiatives.[530]

QUESTIONS

1. Compare Sloss's analysis with the comment quoted above by Jack Goldsmith, arguing that U.S. '[d]omestic incorporation of the ICCPR … would constitute a massive, largely standardless delegation of power to federal courts to rethink the content and scope of nearly every aspect of domestic human rights law.' Is the U.S. alone in this dilemma, and what solutions might be available?

2. Welch et al., above, describe NHRIs as 'domestic institutions that increase the (perceived) costs of repression for government leaders and their agents' and as 'abuse-limiting … institutions'. What does this say about the role envisaged for such institutions? Should NHRIs play a significant role in relation to ESCR norms?

3. The Universal Periodic Review process, described in Chapter 8, is a relatively successful peer review process. So is GANHRI's Sub-Committee on Accreditation. Would such a process also work in relation to parliamentary human rights committees?

---

[528] See J. Miaz et al. (eds.), *Engaging with Human Rights: How Subnational Actors use Human Rights Treaties in Policy Processes* (2024); and M. Saul, Local Authorities at the European Court of Human Rights', *Int'l J. Hum. Rts.* (2024) 000.

[529] N. Dragicevic and B. Porter, *Human Rights Cities: The Power and Potential of Local Government to Advance Economic and Social Rights* (2020).

[530] See M. Och, 'More Than Just Moral Urbanism? The Incorporation of CEDAW Principles into Local Governance Structures in the United States', 14 *J. Hum. Rts. Prac.* (2022) 1060; and A. Sisson Runyan and R. Sanders, 'Prospects for Realizing International Women's Rights Law Through Local Governance: The Case of Cities for CEDAW,' 22 *Hum. Rts. Rev.* (2021) 303.

B. SANCTIONS

Economic and other forms of sanctions became commonplace in international relations after World War II. They were enshrined in the UN Charter as one of the most powerful tools available to the UN if the Security Council agreed to their imposition. In the 1970s and 1980s, states from the Global South were strong advocates of their use against South Africa and other racist regimes. Following Iraq's invasion of Kuwait in 1991, the Security Council imposed very harsh sanctions against the government of Saddam Hussein which, according to Nicholas Mulder, in *The Economic Weapon: The Rise of Sanctions as a Tool of Modern War* (2022) 'cost hundreds of thousands of lives and permanently damaged the country's economic and social fabric.'

The United States has long used economic, trade and financial sanctions to promote foreign policy goals,[531] as illustrated problematically by the case of Cuba. In 2023, the U.S. Treasury's Office of Foreign Assets Control (OFAC) listed 25 countries sanctioned by the United States.[532] This reflects the military dominance of the U.S., its longstanding record of intervening in other countries to promote its foreign policy goals, and the powerful role of U.S. financial markets. But other countries have now followed this lead,[533] as we will see below. While a range of stated objectives have been used to justify such sanctions, human rights and countering terrorism are now the most commonly invoked.

A key question is whether such sanctions work. This is Mulder's assessment:

> While the success rate differs depending on the objective, the historical record is relatively clear: most economic sanctions have not worked. In the twentieth century, only one in three uses of sanctions was "at least partially successful." More modest goals have better chances of success. But from the available data it is clear that the history of sanctions is largely a history of disappointment.

> What is striking is that this limited utility has not affected frequency of use. To the contrary: sanctions use doubled in the 1990s and 2000s com- pared to the period from 1950 to 1985; by the 2010s it had doubled again. Yet while in the 1985–1995 period, at a moment of great relative Western power, the chances of sanctions success were still around 35–40 percent, by 2016 this had fallen below 20 percent. In other words, while the use of sanctions has surged, their odds of success have plummeted.

> …

> Perhaps the most confounding aspect of sanctions is that regardless of their technical sophistication, their outcome is never a matter of economic factors alone. … Given the power of [nationalism and other related] ideas to move entire societies, how would economic pressure alone dissuade them from repeating such collective struggle? While history shows the power of material calculations, it illustrates equally important countervailing motives. …

> The same aspect of economic sanctions that makes them philosophically appealing to liberal internationalism—their reliance on a *homo economicus* rationale—also limits their salience. Economic sanctions do not project only material force; they also project political, social, and cultural values. Sanctions would no doubt work better in a world of perfectly rational, consistently self-interested subjects, but this is not the world that we actually inhabit. Most people in most places at most times make collective choices on the basis of a wider set of considerations. The economic weapon may be a form of politics by

---

[531] See generally A. Hofer, 'The Efficacy of Targeted Sanctions in Enforcing Compliance with International Law', 113 AJIL *Unbound* (2019) 163.

[532] Afghanistan, The Balkans, Belarus, Burma, Central African Republic, China, Cuba, Democratic Republic of Congo, Ethiopia, Hong Kong, Iran, Iraq, Lebanon, Libya, Mali, Nicaragua, North Korea, Russia, Somalia, Sudan, South Sudan, Syria, Ukraine, Venezuela, Yemen, and Zimbabwe. For a critique of OFAC's approach, see D. Leclercq, 'Rights-Based Sanctions Procedures', 75 *Admin. L. Rev.* (2023) 105.

[533] See T. Ruys, C. Ryngaert, and F. Rodríguez Silvestre (eds.), *The Cambridge Handbook of Secondary Sanctions and International Law* (2024).

other means. But ultimately, stitching animosity into the fabric of international affairs and human exchange is of limited use in changing the world.[534]

Given reasonably broad acceptance of the view that sanctions generally don't achieve their stated goal,[535] the question then becomes: why the United States continues to use economic sanctions so often? Richard Hanania, in 'Ineffective, Immoral, Politically Convenient: America's Overreliance on Economic Sanctions and What to Do About It' (Cato Institute, Policy Analysis No. 884 (2020)), offers this answer:

> The popularity of sanctions owes more to the domestic interests of politicians than their ability to achieve geopolitical goals. American policymakers show little interest in the empirical research on sanctions and they often do not supplement trade restrictions with diplomatic efforts that can help achieve a bargain. In contrast, sanctions make sense from the perspective of domestic politics and political psychology. They provide a middle ground between military force and doing nothing and are unlikely to cause a domestic backlash because the damage they inflict is indirect and largely unobserved.

But the sanctions weapon of choice has changed significantly over the past two decades, as noted by Gary Clyde Hufbauer and Euijin Jung, in 'Economic sanctions in the twenty-first century', in Peter A.G. van Bergeijk (ed.), *Research Handbook on Economic Sanctions* (2021) 26:

> In earlier decades, the United States enacted statutes (e.g., the Helms–Burton Law in 1996) and issued regulations designed to force foreign subsidiaries of US firms, and even foreign firms, not to do business with targets such as Cuba and China. These laws and regulations sparked nationalist backlashes in Canada, France, and other US allies because US measures were perceived to intrude on sovereign powers abroad.

> In recent decades, the United States has devised a more direct technique—offer banks and industrial firms in Europe, Japan, Korea, and elsewhere a choice: Do business in the target country, or do business in the United States, but not both. ... Moreover, the surveillance techniques of the National Security Agency (NSA) and the Central Intelligence Agency (CIA) provide powerful deterrence against 'cheating.' ...

> ...

> Seldom acknowledged but hard to deny, broad economic sanctions are akin to area bombing, also known as carpet bombing ... [which] inevitably kills innocent children and other civilians; broad sanctions inevitably inflict privation, disease, and hunger on the poorer strata of society, often the young and old.

> ...

> ... [T]he overwhelming trend in the past two decades is away from comprehensive sanctions to 'smart' or 'targeted' sanctions. In the scores of cases unknown to the public, limited sanctions are the preferred tool – sanctions aimed at specific individuals, companies, or transactions, without inflicting humanitarian harm on the broader population. However, in high-profile cases – ... such as Iran, Cuba, North Korea, and Venezuela – the flavor is comprehensive sanctions. Humanitarian exceptions thus remain a key component of sanctions policy.

> ...

Human rights groups have played a central role in many of these developments, but generally in demanding new and stronger sanctions rather than questioning their use. Following the push for sanctions against apartheid South Africa in the 1980s, various other campaigns were launched including those against the trade in 'conflict diamonds' and against countries engaged in 'modern slavery'. More recently, civil society groups have campaigned strongly for sanctions against military leaders in Myanmar and those responsible for China's

---

[534] N. Mulder, *The Economic Weapon: The Rise of Sanctions as a Tool of Modern War* (2022), at 295.
[535] A. Demarais, *Backfire: How Sanctions Reshape the World Against U.S. Interests* (2022).

repression of the Uighur population and the crackdown against democracy protesters in Hong Kong. But one of the most effective lobbying efforts related to sanctions against Russia for the death in detention of a whistle-blowing tax lawyer:

CONGRESSIONAL RESEARCH SERVICE, THE GLOBAL MAGNITSKY HUMAN RIGHTS ACCOUNTABILITY ACT: SCOPE, IMPLEMENTATION, AND CONSIDERATIONS FOR CONGRESS DOC. NO. R46981 (3 DECEMBER 2021)

...

Origins

The Global Magnitsky Act is based, in part, on a 2012 law that focuses on Russia, the Sergei Magnitsky Rule of Law Accountability Act (hereafter, the Sergei Magnitsky Act). Sergei Magnitsky, a tax lawyer and auditor in Russia, documented the expropriation of the assets of Hermitage Capital—once the largest foreign investment brokerage in Russia—through rampant Russian government corruption. Russian authorities arrested Magnitsky in November 2008, reportedly for tax evasion, and denied him medical care, family visits, and legal due process. Magnitsky was reportedly beaten while in detention, and ultimately died in prison in November 2009. [In August 2019, the European Court of Human Rights concluded that the case had involved multiple violations of human rights.] ...

In 2012, Congress passed the Sergei Magnitsky Act to require the President to identify and impose sanctions on any person determined to have been involved in the detention, abuse, or death of Magnitsky; the ensuing cover-up; or the alleged criminal conspiracy that Magnitsky had uncovered. ... [In 2016, the Global Magnitsky Human Rights Accountability Act was enacted.]

Numerous Members [of Congress described these Acts] as providing the United States with tools to impose some measure of accountability against foreign perpetrators, particularly when relevant foreign governments are unable or unwilling to do so. ... [Some see them] as providing the executive branch with a tool to impose sanctions against specific persons in countries with which the United States shares important bilateral relations without necessarily provoking a broader rupture to these relations.

The Global Magnitsky Act contrasts with some other provisions in law that contemplate broader restrictions on relations with foreign governments on the basis of human rights violations. It also differs from country-specific targeted sanctions regimes, the creation of which can be time consuming and diplomatically challenging or disadvantageous ... .

Overview of the Law and Executive Order

The Global Magnitsky Act was enacted on December 23, 2016. The executive branch has used Executive Order 13818, issued on December 20, 2017, to implement and build on the act's provisions. When issuing E.O. 13818, the President additionally invoked emergency authorities set out in the National Emergencies Act (NEA) and International Emergency Economic Powers Act (IEEPA), as well as authority under the Immigration and Nationality Act (INA). The President determined that serious human rights abuse and corruption "constitute an unusual and extraordinary threat to the national security, foreign policy, and economy of the United States," declaring that they "undermine the values that form an essential foundation of stable, secure, and functioning societies; have devastating impacts on individuals; weaken democratic institutions; degrade the rule of law; perpetuate violent conflicts; facilitate the activities of dangerous persons; and undermine economic markets." ...

Type of Sanctions

... The law authorizes two types of restrictions:

- Economic sanctions (asset blocking and prohibitions on transactions): Freezing any property held within U.S. jurisdiction and prohibiting U.S. individuals or entities from entering into transactions with the designated person.

- Visa restrictions: Denying entry into the United States and revoking any already-issued visas.

...

Scope of Sanctionable Behavior and Targets

...

With regard to human rights, the Global Magnitsky Act authorizes the President to impose sanctions on any foreign person that the President identifies as "responsible for extrajudicial killings, torture, or other gross violations of internationally recognized human rights" against an individual in any foreign country who seeks to

- "expose illegal activity carried out by government officials," or

- "obtain, exercise, defend, or promote internationally recognized human rights and freedoms, such as the freedoms of religion, expression, association, and assembly, and the rights to fair trial and democratic elections."

...

* * *

As of 10 December 2022, 450 foreign individuals and entities had been made subject to Global Magnitsky sanctions. Those sanctioned are included in the OFAC 'Specially Designated Nationals and Blocked Persons List', which as of 28 July 2023 ran to 2,206 pages of small print in three columns.

Other states with Magnitsky laws include Australia (Autonomous Sanctions Amendment (Magnitsky-style and Other Thematic Sanctions) Act 2021), the United Kingdom, Canada, and quite a few others.

In the United Kingdom, the Sanctions and Anti-Money Laundering Act 2018 is supplemented by the Global Human Rights Sanctions Regulations 2020 to create a Magnitsky-style law. By November 2022, 'designations' had been made in relation to the following countries: Belarus, Bosnia and Herzegovina, Central African Republic, Democratic People's Republic of Korea, Democratic Republic of the Congo, Guinea-Bissau, Iran, Iraq, Libya, Mali, Myanmar, Nicaragua, Pakistan, Russia, Somalia, South Sudan, Sudan, Syria, The Gambia, Venezuela, Yemen, and Zimbabwe.[536]

Canada adopted the Justice for Victims of Corrupt Foreign Officials Act in 2017. Meredith Lilly, in 'Symbolic Act, Real Consequences: Passing Canada's Magnitsky Law to Combat Human Rights Violations and Corruption', 75 *Int'l J.* (2020) 163, notes that all of the sanctions imposed in the first three years could have been adopted under the pre-existing legislative framework and concluded that the law had been adopted for largely symbolic reasons. But she also cautions that the Act's existence will generate more pressure to act, and thereby 'politicize those actions for domestic political purposes, and to pursue uneven policy decisions that could result in dramatic policy swings over time.'

COUNCIL OF THE EUROPEAN UNION, REGULATION 2020/1998 CONCERNING RESTRICTIVE MEASURES AGAINST SERIOUS HUMAN RIGHTS VIOLATIONS AND ABUSES (7 DECEMBER 2020)

...

<u>Article 2</u>

1. This Regulation applies to:

---

[536] https://www.gov.uk/government/publications/the-uk-sanctions-list#full-publication-update-history.

(a) genocide;

(b) crimes against humanity;

(c) the following serious human rights violations or abuses:

　　(i) torture and other cruel, inhuman or degrading treatment or punishment;

　　(ii) slavery;

　　(iii) extrajudicial, summary or arbitrary executions and killings;

　　(iv) enforced disappearance of persons;

　　(v) arbitrary arrests or detentions;

(d) other human rights violations or abuses, including but not limited to the following, in so far as those violations or abuses are widespread, systematic or are otherwise of serious concern as regards the objectives of the common foreign and security policy set out in Article 21 TEU:

　　(i) (trafficking in human beings, as well as abuses of human rights by migrant smugglers as referred to

　　in this Article;

　　(ii) sexual and gender-based violence;

　　(iii) violations or abuses of freedom of peaceful assembly and of association;

　　(iv) violations or abuses of freedom of opinion and expression;

　　(v) violations or abuses of freedom of religion or belief.

2. For the purpose of applying paragraph 1, regard should be had to customary international law and widely accepted instruments of international law, such as: [the ICCPR, the ICESCR, Genocide Convention, CAT, CERD, CEDAW, CRC, Convention on Disappearances, CRPD, the Trafficking Protocol, the ICC Statute; and the ECHR.]

3. For the purposes of applying this Regulation, natural or legal persons, entities or bodies may include:

(a) State actors;

(b) other actors exercising effective control or authority over a territory;

(c) other non-State actors … .

<u>Article 3</u>

1. All funds and economic resources belonging to, owned, held or controlled by any natural or legal person, entity or body as listed in Annex I shall be frozen.

2. No funds or economic resources shall be made available, directly or indirectly, to or for the benefit of natural or legal persons, entities or bodies listed in Annex I.
…

* * *

The EU sanctions regime reflects a Magnitsky-style approach, but it carefully avoids that name in order not to antagonize Russia. And unlike the U.S. approach, it does not cover acts of corruption. The listing of individuals pursuant to the EU Regulation requires a unanimous decision by all EU member states, thus leaving open the question of whether individual states might seek to supplement the system with their own national initiatives. The jurisdictional basis of the EU regime has been clarified by Tom Ruys, in 'Introductory Note to The European Union Global Human Rights Sanctions Regime (EUGHRSR)', 60 *Int'l Legal Mat.* (2021) 298, who notes that:

> The Commission Guidance Note stresses, somewhat confusingly, that the financial sanctions "do not apply extra-territorially." The more accurate formulation would be that the scope of application of Regulation 2020/1998 … remains within the bounds of permissive principles of jurisdiction by refraining from creating obligations for non-EU operators unless the business is conducted at least partly within the EU.
>
> …
>
> On a more general level, debate remains regarding whether sanctions against human rights offenders have (only) a signaling and deterring objective, or are also punitive in nature. Related to this is the question of exit strategy—under what conditions will sanctions be lifted? The unilateral (non-UN) character also raises the question of legitimacy and may fuel accusations of double standards, as certain individuals are listed and other obvious candidates left out. Most in the Western world will regard the EUGHRSR and consorts as an important tool in the fight against impunity and for the promotion of human rights. Yet dissenting voices may criticize the proliferation of unilateral Magnitsky-style sanctions—with the lists of designated persons differing from one jurisdiction to another—as a *lex horrenda* and a recipe for international tension. Against this background, one question that remains largely unanswered concerns the effectiveness of sanctions (sectoral and targeted) in changing behavior. Either way, the introduction of a "Magnitsky-style" sanctions regime by a bloc of 27 EU Member States is bound to give further impetus to the spread of such regimes to other countries. Already in December 2020, nine other European countries "aligned" themselves with Council Decision (CFSP) 2020/1999. Several other countries are reportedly preparing or considering similar legislation.

CHRISTINA ECKES, EU HUMAN RIGHTS SANCTIONS REGIME: STRIVING FOR UTOPIA BACKED BY SOVEREIGN POWER? 26 EUR. FOR. AFF. REV. (2021) 219

…

The EU HRSR may be inspired by the US regime but the US model of *Global Magnitsky* cannot and should not be followed too closely as it does not offer judicial protection to those sanctioned in a way that would meet due process guarantees under the Charter of Fundamental Rights. For the EU HRSR, it will be a challenge to ensure compliance with the human rights guaranteed under EU and national law, including the rights to the defence of those sanctioned. The high numbers of annulments in the past, both of counterterrorist and country sanctions, have seriously damaged the legitimacy of these sanction regimes. The EU HRSR has to make a credible claim of contributing to the protection of human rights without itself infringing them.

…

The very objective of protecting human rights requires that such a regime must be endowed with particularly robust legal safeguards to ensure that those committed to fighting human rights violations do not become perpetrators themselves. The EU HRSR would have done well in stipulating the need for a clear and distinct link based on personal conduct between the targeted person and a grave rights violation; an express and sufficient evidentiary threshold; and the commitment to meet this threshold on the basis of publicly available and reliable information. It did not do so. These stipulations could have contributed to ensuring a practice of self-restraint needed in view to the broad scope of a sanction regime addressing grave human rights violations across the globe. They could have ensured that all designations rest on a robust factual basis that can be made available to those sanctioned and, in the event of a legal challenge, to the CJEU. The EU HRSR leaves these points open and it is now for the Council to develop a credible practice that respects the rights of those sanctioned.

Rules on the burden of proof, the commitment to formality by establishing clear and precise listing criteria, as well as the use of presumptions are in their core about accepting that inevitably mistakes will be made. All three mechanisms could have been used to ensure strategically and in the long-term that when mistakes are made they are made because the EU is not able to list someone who committed a serious human rights violation rather than that it targets an innocent person. Only time and potentially a series of legal challenges might tell us more about the EU's use of the EU HRSR in practice.

The EU HRSR may become a successful attempt to reach beyond the existing means of holding perpetrators of serious human rights violations responsible. Yet, we cannot expect it to be applied neutrally and impartially, exclusively focused on the gravity of the violation. As [with] all sanction instruments, the EU HRSR cannot but conform to the foreign policy objectives and interests of those applying it. It is best to acknowledge the link between human rights sanctions and sovereign power than to pretend neutrality.

The Lawfulness of Sanctions: Venezuela and Russia/Ukraine

Venezuela ratified the ICC Statute in June 2000. On 26 September 2018, Argentina, Colombia, Chile, Paraguay, and Peru referred the situation in Venezuela to the Prosecutor of the court, alleging that the Maduro government had committed crimes against humanity. Invoking various reports prepared within the Inter-American system, they cited '(i) murder; (ii) imprisonment or other severe deprivation of physical liberty; (iii) torture; (iv) rape; (v) the persecution of an identifiable group or collectivity on political grounds; and (vi) the enforced disappearance of persons'. On 3 November 2021, the Prosecutor announced both a decision to proceed with investigations and an agreement with Venezuela to foster mechanisms to support genuine proceedings at the national level.

On 13 February 2020, Venezuela submitted its own referral to the court (Referral II) in relation to U.S. sanctions. In 2017 the U.S. had imposed sanctions under EI 13808 prohibiting U.S. individuals and entities from dealing with the Venezuelan government and the state-owned oil company (PDVSA). Additional targeted sanctions were imposed in 2018 against senior Venezuelan officials, and in 2019, oil shipments and Central Bank transactions were targeted.

In its claim, Venezuela cited an analysis by Mark Weisbrot and Jeffrey Sachs, entitled *Economic Sanctions as Collective Punishment: The Case of Venezuela* (2019) which found that 'most of the impact of [U.S.] sanctions [had] not been on the government but on the civilian population':

> The sanctions reduced the public's caloric intake, increased disease and mortality (for both adults and infants), and displaced millions of Venezuelans … . They exacerbated Venezuela's economic crisis and made it nearly impossible to stabilize the economy, contributing further to excess deaths. …
>
> …
>
> We find that the sanctions have inflicted, and increasingly inflict, very serious harm to human life and health, including an estimated more than 40,000 deaths from 2017 to 2018; and that these sanctions would fit the definition of collective punishment of the civilian population … .

In 2021, the UN Special Rapporteur on the negative impact of unilateral coercive measures on the enjoyment of human rights, Alena Douhan, visited Venezuela and noted sanctions imposed not just by the United States but also the European Union, the United Kingdom, Canada, Switzerland, Mexico and other countries in Latin America. She reported (UN Doc. A/HRC/48/59/Add.2) that:

> … [S]ectoral sanctions on the oil, gold and mining industries, the economic blockade, the freezing of Central Bank assets, the targeted sanctions imposed on Venezuelans and third-country nationals and companies and the overcompliance by banks and third-country companies have exacerbated the pre-existing economic and social crisis and had a devastating effect on the entire population, especially those living in poverty, women, children, older persons, persons with disabilities or life-threatening or chronic diseases,

and the indigenous population. No strata of society has been untouched. She recommends that these sanctions, which were imposed mostly in the name of human rights, democracy and the rule of law, be lifted, as they undermine those very principles, values and norms.

Venezuela's referral made similar claims:

> … Such measures contravene international law …, have caused enormous hardship for the people of Venezuela, … have contributed to very significant increases in mortality of children and adults, and negatively affected a range of other human rights … . Such unilateral coercive measures of unprecedented scale constitute a widespread or systematic attack upon a civilian population [thus amounting to crimes against humanity under Article 7(1) of the Rome Statute].

By way of background, the UN Committee on Economic, Social and Cultural Rights adopted General Comment No. 8 in 1997, focused on 'the relationship between economic sanctions and respect for economic, social and cultural rights'. It was adopted at a time when there was a strong backlash against very severe sanctions against Iraq in response to its invasion of Kuwait in 1990 and the subsequent military intervention by an UN-authorized coalition, led by the United States.

...

3. [Sanctions] often cause significant disruption in the distribution of food, pharmaceuticals and sanitation supplies, jeopardise the quality of food and the availability of clean drinking water, severely interfere with the functioning of basic health and education systems, and undermine the right to work. In addition, their unintended consequences can include reinforcement of the power of oppressive elites, the emergence, almost invariably, of a black market and the generation of huge windfall profits for the privileged elites which manage it, enhancement of the control of the governing elites over the population at large, and restriction of opportunities to seek asylum or to manifest political opposition. ...

4. In considering sanctions, it is essential to distinguish between the basic objective of applying political and economic pressure upon the governing elite of the country to persuade them to conform to international law, and the collateral infliction of suffering upon the most vulnerable groups within the targeted country. ...

5. However, a number of recent United Nations and other studies which have analysed the impact of sanctions, have concluded that [humanitarian exemptions do not protect ESCR].

...

7. The Committee considers that the provisions of the Covenant, virtually all of which are also reflected in a range of other human rights treaties as well as the Universal Declaration of Human Rights, cannot be considered to be inoperative, or in any way inapplicable, solely because a decision has been taken that considerations of international peace and security warrant the imposition of sanctions. Just as the international community insists that any targeted State must respect the civil and political rights of its citizens, so too must that State and the international community itself do everything possible to protect at least the core content of the economic, social and cultural rights of the affected peoples of that State.

...

10. ... The imposition of sanctions does not in any way nullify or diminish the relevant obligations of [the target state]. As in other comparable situations, those obligations assume greater practical importance in times of particular hardship. ...

11. The second set of obligations relates to the party or parties responsible for the imposition, maintenance or implementation of the sanctions, whether it be the international community, an international or regional organization, or a State or group of States. In this respect, the Committee considers that there are three conclusions which follow logically from the recognition of economic, social and cultural human rights.

12. First, these rights must be taken fully into account when designing an appropriate sanctions regime. ...

13. Second, effective monitoring, which is always required under the terms of the Covenant, should be undertaken throughout the period that sanctions are in force. When an external party takes upon itself even partial responsibility for the situation within a country (whether under Chapter VII of the Charter or otherwise), it also unavoidably assumes a responsibility to do all within its power to protect the [ESCR] of the affected population.

14. Third, the external entity has an obligation "to take steps, individually and through international assistance and co-operation, especially economic and technical" in order to respond to any disproportionate suffering experienced by vulnerable groups within the targeted country.

15. In anticipating the objection that sanctions must, almost by definition, result in the grave violations of [ESCR] if they are to achieve their objectives, the Committee notes the conclusion of a major United Nations study to the effect that "decisions to reduce the suffering of children or minimize other adverse consequences can be taken without jeopardizing the policy aim of sanctions". This applies equally to the situation of all vulnerable groups.

...

DEVIKA HOVELL, UNFINISHED BUSINESS OF INTERNATIONAL LAW: THE QUESTIONABLE LEGALITY OF AUTONOMOUS SANCTIONS
113 AJIL UNBOUND (2019) 140

...

... U.S. domestic law [on sanctions] appears to leave the President with impressive latitude. The most common domestic legal basis for U.S. sanctions programs is the International Emergency Economic Powers Act (IEEPA), which grants the President power that has been described by the U.S. Supreme Court as "sweeping and unqualified." Sanctions are commonly implemented by executive orders under which the President declares a national emergency justifying the imposition of sanctions measures. ...

...

[The Trump] White House not only uses sanctions more widely, but also shows a greater tendency to deploy them unilaterally. ... [T]here is a legally relevant difference between UN-authorized sanctions and "autonomous" sanctions, with the latter term denoting sanctions either lacking or exceeding authorization by the UN Security Council. The distinction between UN-authorized and autonomous sanctions is not one the United States clearly draws. While the EU website clearly sets out the source of sanctions in either UN, EU, or combined acts, the Office of Foreign Assets Control (OFAC) declines to provide information explaining the degree of convergence between U.S. sanctions programs and those authorized by the United Nations. ...

Opposition to U.S. autonomous sanctions is not new. Since 1992, the General Assembly has annually passed a resolution urging all states to "refrain from promulgating laws and measures" such as the U.S. Helms-Burton Act imposing autonomous sanctions against Cuba and those trading with Cuba, "the extraterritorial effects of which affect the sovereignty of other states, the legitimate interests of entities or persons under their jurisdiction and the freedom of trade and navigation." The latest resolution passed by 189 votes to 2 (the United States and Israel voting against). ...

... The European Union is a key player in the autonomous sanctions game, with twenty-five of its forty-three sanctions regimes imposed on non-EU member states without UN authorization. ...

...

Unilateral Corrective Sanctions: The Maverick Enforcer

The main basis for the legality of autonomous sanctions derives from the law relating to countermeasures. The ILC's Articles on State Responsibility clarify and refine the scope of a state's right to deploy countermeasures, setting out a number of conditions. These include:

> (1) The targeted state must have committed an internationally wrongful act.
>
> (2) The sanctioning state must establish it is an "injured state."
>
> (3) The measures must aim to induce the targeted state to comply with its obligations.
>
> (4) The measures must be proportionate to the injury suffered.
>
> (5) The measures may not affect fundamental human rights norms or jus cogens norms. These include the due process rights of individuals or entities targeted by sanctions measures.
>
> (6) The measures must be terminated when the wrongful act has ceased.

Uncertainty remains as to the definition of "injured state." This is relevant as many of the violations that U.S. sanctions, and indeed EU sanctions, seek to redress could be said not to affect U.S. or EU citizens directly, although they would fall within the category of violations of an obligation that protects the collective interest of the group (e.g., a multilateral disarmament regime, as in the case of Iran) or of an erga omnes obligation owed to the international community as a whole (e.g., grave human rights violations, as in the case of Syria or Myanmar). The ILC expressly reserved its position on this question, leaving "resolution of the matter to the further development of international law."

Unilateral Coercive Sanctions: The Rogue Enforcer

At the end of the day, the key difference between lawful and unlawful autonomous sanctions is that the former serve the corrective purpose of bringing wrongdoing states back into line with their treaty or customary international law obligations. The idea is that sanctions should not cross the line from inducing a state to comply with legal obligations it has accepted to coercing a state to do something it is not bound to do under international law. Unilateral acts "become especially contentious where they are associated with one community imposing its values on another, where that other community has not consented to the imposition of such values." Sanctions should not be a wager on a state's weakness, but on its wisdom to conform with agreed principles of international law.

There is a growing movement of states arguing for the illegality of unilateral coercive measures. ... [H]owever, until states declare themselves willing to agree on defined legal parameters, the precise line between lawful and unlawful autonomous measures remains a matter of debate rather than law.

...

DAPO AKANDE, PAYAM AKHAVAN, AND EIRIK BJORGE, ECONOMIC SANCTIONS, INTERNATIONAL LAW, AND CRIMES AGAINST HUMANITY: VENEZUELA'S ICC REFERRAL
115 AM. J. INT'L L. (2021) 493

...

There is no doubt that the ... Trump administration['s] ... policy has had a devastating impact. The question [is] whether it constitutes crimes against humanity.

...

G. The UN Human Rights Covenants

The [ICCPR and the ICESCR] both provide, in common Article 1(2), that: "In no case may a people be deprived of its own means of subsistence." ... Thus, "measures taken in the framework of inter-state relations should not be such as to threaten starvation of the people of a State." To the extent that economic sanctions breach that rule—and have the effect of threatening the starvation of a whole people—they are illegal under international law. ...

...

I. ICESCR

The provisions of the ICESCR are more directly relevant to economic sanctions and frequently invoked by Venezuela in Referral II. Article 2(1) obliges states parties "to take steps, individually and through international assistance and co-operation, especially economic and technical, to the maximum of its available resources, with a view to achieving progressively the full realization of the rights recognized in the present Covenant by all appropriate means, including particularly the adoption of legislative measures." This obligation of conduct is "programmatic and promotional," and requires good faith efforts to realize progressively the relevant rights, rather than achieving a particular result. The ICJ has clarified that the ICESCR guarantees rights that are "essentially territorial," though "it is not be excluded that it applies both to territories over which a State party has sovereignty and to those over which that State exercises territorial jurisdiction." ...

[The authors quote briefly from General Comment No. 8, above.]

It is thus very difficult to conclude as a general principle that sanctions would necessarily violate obligations under the ICESCR. Customary international law does not bar the use of economic coercion. In the absence of specific legal obligations to engage in trade with another state, an embargo will in principle be a lawful measure. Where general international law does impose a limit is in the extreme circumstance where unilateral sanctions rise to the level of depriving a people of its own means of subsistence or threatens the starvation of the people of a state. There is in general international law a "duty not to use economic coercion for the purpose of destroying or dismembering a State." This would seem to be some way removed from the U.S. sanctions against Venezuela, whether their ostensible objective is merely to confront human rights violations or to achieve "regime change." ...

ELENA CHACHKO AND J. BENTON HEATH, A WATERSHED MOMENT FOR SANCTIONS? RUSSIA, UKRAINE, AND THE ECONOMIC BATTLEFIELD
116 AJIL UNBOUND (2022) 135

...

The Russian invasion of Ukraine has opened the sanctions floodgates. A trickle of preexisting sanctions that the United States, the European Union, and others had imposed against Russia over its annexation of Crimea, malicious cyber activity, and human rights violations has turned into a tsunami of increasingly severe economic measures. The Russia sanctions regime continues to evolve daily, but the sanctions imposed to date can be divided into roughly six categories. [(i) full asset freezes against the Russian leadership and elites; (ii) blocking sanctions against major Russian banks and financial institutions, limitations on transactions with others, and the removal of certain financial institutions from the Swift financial messaging system; (iii) bans on the import of Russian oil, liquefied natural gas, and coal, as well as any new U.S. investment in Russia's energy sector; (iv) export controls designed to curtail Russian access to necessary commodities and technologies and to hinder Russia's military buildup; (v) bans on Russian airlines and the repossession of planes leased to Russian airlines; and (vi) an exodus of private actors which have suspended operations in Russia.]

...

The overwhelming response, in the short term, reaffirms the central role of sanctions as a tool of the post-1945 legal order, and reaffirms a "laissez faire" approach to their application. Today, sanctions are a widely recognized pressure valve in international relations—an ostensibly non-violent measure that can be applied to influence state and increasingly individual behavior and punish violations of the law. This is a break with the older law of neutrality, in which the decision to restrain trade with only one party to a conflict could be considered a hostile act. The legal distinction between economic force and war is widely accepted today, and it is reaffirmed in contemporary commentary that treats the allies' sanctions as wisely avoiding, rather than contributing to, military escalation.

The "pressure valve" view has become coupled with a relative absence of strong legal constraints on a state's decision on whether to deploy sanctions. The International Court of Justice's finding that even a comprehensive embargo does not breach customary international law, though it may violate an applicable commercial treaty, remains the point of departure. In practice, rules of general international law that might have constrained a state's decision to use sanctions—such as non-intervention or limits on national jurisdiction—often seem to be at best a minimal constraint. If sanctions do not violate a primary norm, then rules governing countermeasures, such as notice and proportionality, do not apply.

Domestic legal institutions in key sanction-imposing jurisdictions have also acquiesced in the practice and the fundamental legitimacy of sanctions as a tool of statecraft. In the United States in particular, a series of Supreme Court decisions in the 1980s "freed the president . . . to conduct widespread economic warfare merely by declaring a national emergency with respect to a particular country," while sidelining congressional oversight.

...

Conclusion

Going forward, the question is whether this high-profile economic war heralds any significant legal change. We are skeptical that the international legal order stands at the precipice of any kind of grand regulatory moment for economic sanctions, though legal reform is a worthy long-term goal. The present moment, instead, offers a set of overlapping and competing narratives, which are likely to be refracted through the overlapping and competing institutions that purport to govern economic warfare. If there is any call for optimism today, it is the hope that the renewed public focus on economic conflict will generate an ethic of responsibility around sanctions, along with a toolbox of ideas that might be combined and experimented with as international politics lurches from crisis to crisis.

QUESTIONS

1. Some of the governments that have been most active in imposing Magnitsky sanctions have significantly downgraded human rights in terms of their other foreign policy priorities. Is this a reasonable trade-off to be making?

2. Sanctions regimes have often made the provision of humanitarian assistance virtually impossible. In December 2022, the Security Council (Res. 2664) decided that 'the provision, processing or payment of funds, other financial assets, or economic resources, or the provision of goods and services necessary to ensure the timely delivery of humanitarian assistance or to support other activities that support basic human needs ... are permitted and are not a violation of the asset freezes imposed [by the Council].' India abstained from voting on the grounds (UN Doc. SC/15134) that 'terrorist groups [take] full advantage of humanitarian carve-outs and [make] a mockery of sanctions regimes'. They 'use the umbrella of the humanitarian assistance space to raise funds and recruit fighters'. Should and could sanctions regimes be made humanitarian-friendly?

3. In rejecting part of the claims made by Venezuela, Akande et al. conclude that ESCR are merely 'programmatic and promotional' and that the Covenant only 'requires good faith efforts to realize progressively the relevant rights'. Is this an appropriate understanding, based on the materials considered in Chapter 4, above, and if you agree with it, does it mean that there is no role for the analysis in General Comment No. 8 of the ESCR Committee?

C. UNIVERSAL JURISDICTION

The principle of universal jurisdiction emerged primarily in the context of criminal prosecutions and subsequently extended to areas of civil litigation. It is accordingly helpful to review basic jurisdictional principles on which states prescribe (make law), particularly laws imposing individual criminal responsibility, and the basic jurisdictional principles on which a state's courts hear civil and criminal cases.

Criminal litigation, unlike civil litigation, ordinarily requires that the state whose courts are trying a case have custody of the defendant. Holding criminal trials *in absentia* is rare. Choice of law, so vital an element of many civil cases, generally does not figure in criminal litigation; the court applies only the law of the state from which it derives its authority, almost always the one in which it sits, even if the conduct occurred or the effects were felt in other states. The principle of universal jurisdiction examined below, constitutes a major exception to this generalization.

The bases on which states enact the criminal laws to which their courts look therefore becomes a critical issue. There are certain conventional categories, some of which are more broadly accepted internationally than others. This is reflected in the list included in the American Law Institute, Restatement (Fourth), Foreign Relations Law of the United States (2019), section 402:

> (1) … [T]he United States exercises jurisdiction to prescribe law with respect to:
>
> > (a) persons, property, and conduct within its territory;
> >
> > (b) conduct that has a substantial effect within its territory;
> >
> > (c) the conduct, interests, status, and relations of its nationals and residents outside its territory;
> >
> > (d) certain conduct outside its territory that harms its nationals;
> >
> > (e) certain conduct outside its territory by persons not its nationals or residents that is directed against the security of the United States or against a limited class of other fundamental U.S. interests; and
> >
> > (f) certain offenses of universal concern …
>
> (2) In exercising jurisdiction to prescribe, the United States takes account of the legitimate interests of other nations as a matter of prescriptive comity.

The *Restatement* elaborates on the offenses in 1(b) above in section 413:

> International law recognizes a state's jurisdiction to prescribe law with respect to certain offenses of universal concern, such as genocide, crimes against humanity, war crimes, certain acts of terrorism, piracy, the slave trade, and torture, even if no specific connection exists between the state and the persons or conduct being regulated.

A 'comment' attached to that section notes that:

> *e. Common limits.* Some states impose additional limits on exercises of universal jurisdiction, such as: (1) the territorial presence of the suspect before initiation of a

criminal investigation or commencement of trial proceedings; (2) commission of the crime during a specified conflict or time period; (3) authorization or approval of the prosecution by an executive or judicial body; and (4) deference to the territorial state or the suspect's state of nationality if either state is willing and able to prosecute (i.e., complementarity). Considerations of international comity, rather than the obligations of international law, appear to motivate these limitations.

1. THE EICHMANN TRIAL

The *Eichmann* trial and conviction in 1961 illustrate issues concerning the application of universal jurisdiction at an early stage of the post-Nuremberg evolution of human rights law.

Adolf Eichmann, operationally in charge of the mass murder of Jews in Germany and German-occupied countries, fled Germany after the war. He was abducted from Argentina by Israelis, and brought to trial in Israel under the Nazi and Nazi Collaborators (Punishment) Law, enacted after Israel became a state. Section 1(a) of the Law provided:

> A person who has committed one of the following offences — (1) did, during the period of the Nazi regime, in a hostile country, an act constituting a crime against the Jewish people; (2) did, during the period of the Nazi regime, in a hostile country, an act constituting a crime against humanity; (3) did, during the period of the Second World War, in a hostile country, an act constituting a war crime; is liable to the death penalty.

The Law defined 'crimes against the Jewish people' to consist principally of acts intended to bring about physical destruction. The other two crimes were defined similarly to the like charges at Nuremberg. The 15 counts against Eichmann involved all three crimes. The charges stressed Eichmann's active and significant participation in the 'final solution to the Jewish problem' developed and administered by Nazi officials. Eichmann was convicted in 1961 and later executed. There appear below summaries of portions of the opinions of the trial and appellate courts.

THE ATTORNEY-GENERAL OF THE GOVERNMENT OF ISRAEL V. EICHMANN[537]

Eichmann argued that the prosecution violated international law by inflicting punishment (1) upon persons who were not Israeli citizens (2) for acts done by them outside Israel and before its establishment, (3) in the course of duty and (4) on behalf of a foreign country. In reply, the Court noted that, in the event of a conflict between an Israeli statute and principles of international law, it would be bound to apply the statute. However, it then concluded that 'the law in question conforms to the best traditions of the law of nations. The power of the State of Israel to enact the law in question or Israel's "right to punish" is based … from the point of view of international law, on a dual foundation: The universal character of the crimes in question and their specific character as being designed to exterminate the Jewish people.'

Thus the Court relied primarily on the universality and protective principles to justify its assertion of jurisdiction to try the crimes defined in the Law. It held such crimes to be offences against the law of nations, much as was the traditional crime of piracy. It compared the conduct made criminal under the Israeli statute (particularly the 'crime against the Jewish people') and the crime of genocide, as defined in Article 1 of the Convention for the Prevention and Punishment of Genocide.

> The Contracting Parties confirm that genocide, whether committed in time of peace or in time of war, is a crime under international law which they undertake to prevent and to punish.[538]

---

[537] District Court of Jerusalem, Judgment of 11 December 1961. This summary and the selective quotations are drawn from 56 *Am. J. Int'l. L.* (1962) 805 (unofficial translation).

[538] Article 6 of the Convention, the meaning and implications of which were viewed differently by the parties, states: 'Persons charged with genocide or any of the other acts enumerated in Article III shall be tried by a competent tribunal of the State in the territory of which the act was committed, or by such international penal tribunal as may have jurisdiction with respect to those Contracting Parties which shall have accepted its jurisdiction.'

The Court also stressed the relationship between the Law's definition of 'war crime' and the pattern of crimes defined in the Nuremberg Charter. It rejected arguments of Eichmann based upon the retroactive application of the legislation, and stated that 'all the reasons justifying the Nuremberg judgments justify *eo ipse* the retroactive legislation of the Israeli legislator'.

The Court then discussed another 'foundation' for the prosecution — the offence specifically aimed at the Jewish people.

> [This foundation] of penal jurisdiction conforms, according to [the] acknowledged terminology, to the protective principle. ... The 'crime against the Jewish people,' as defined in the Law, constitutes in effect an attempt to exterminate the Jewish people. ... If there is an effective link (and not necessarily an identity) between the State of Israel and the Jewish people, then a crime intended to exterminate the Jewish people has a very striking connection with the State of Israel. ... The connection between the State of Israel and the Jewish people needs no explanation.

EICHMANN V. THE ATTORNEY-GENERAL OF THE GOVERNMENT OF ISRAEL[539]

After stating that it fully concurred in the holding and reasoning of the district court, the Supreme Court proceeded to develop arguments in different directions. It stressed that Eichmann could not claim to have been unaware at the time of his conduct that he was violating deeply rooted and universal moral principles. Particularly in its relatively underdeveloped criminal side, international law could be analogized to the early common law, which would be similarly open to charges of retroactive law-making. Because the international legal system lacked adjudicatory or executive institutions, it authorized, for the time being, national officials to punish individuals for violations of its principles, either directly under international law or by virtue of municipal legislation adopting those principles.

Moreover, in this case Israel was the most appropriate jurisdiction for trial, a *forum conveniens* where witnesses were readily available. It was relevant that there had been no requests for extradition of Eichmann to other states for trial, or indeed protests by other states against a trial in Israel.

The Court affirmed the holding of the district court that each charge could be sustained. It noted, however, much overlap among the charges, and that all could be grouped within the inclusive category of 'crimes against humanity'.

PNINA LAHAV, JUDGMENT IN JERUSALEM
(1997) 150

[In this portion of her biography of Simon Agranat, Justice and later Chief Justice of the Israeli Supreme Court, Lahav analyses his role in the Supreme Court's affirmance of Eichmann's conviction and death sentence. The Court delivered its judgment in a *per curiam* opinion. Justice Agranat had prepared the section of that opinion dealing with jurisdictional challenges to the trial.]

Agranat also understood that more than appearance was at stake: the soul of the Zionist project was reshaped by the brutal confrontation with the Holocaust. The old tension within Zionism between universalism and particularism now tilted in favor of particularism. Israelis were perceiving themselves as special: a special target for genocide and special in their right to ignore international norms in pursuit of justice. Popular hubris was growing, nurturing a victim mentality, a sense of self-righteousness and excessive nationalism, threatening to weaken the already shaky foundations of universalism in Israeli political culture.

...

Agranat understood that the legal reasoning he chose would affect the resolution of the tension between particularism and universalism. The Supreme Court could either let the conviction stand on the basis of crimes against the Jewish people, thereby lending force to the contention that Israel operated by its own rules,

---

[539] Supreme Court sitting as Court of Criminal Appeals, 29 May 1962. See 36 *Int'l. L.* Rep. (1968) 277.

impervious to the laws developed by the community of nations, or it could try to show that Eichmann's trial was compatible with international norms of justice and fairness.

Most of the legal arguments advanced by Eichmann were designed to prove that Israel lacked jurisdiction to try him. Two of these arguments received extensive attention from the international community. The first was that the 1950 Israeli Law against the Nazis and Nazi Collaborators, which vested jurisdiction in the Israeli courts, was an ex post facto criminal law and as such could not apply to foreign nationals; the second was that, because the crimes were 'extra-territorial offenses' committed by a foreign national, Israel could not prosecute Eichmann according to the territoriality principle of international law.

In rejecting these arguments, the district court stressed the superiority of Israeli law in the sovereign state of Israel. The Law against the Nazis and Nazi Collaborators, the district court held, was a part of Israeli positive law and, as such, was binding on the courts of the land. It did hold that the law agreed with international norms, but emphasized the impact of the Holocaust on the evolution of the law of nations. This holding contained a symbolic message: Jewish national pride and self-assertion ruled the day. There was poetic justice in this interpretation. If the Final Solution was about the lawless murder of Jews, the *Eichmann* case was about the subjection of the perpetrators to Jewish justice, conceived and applied by the very heirs of those murdered.

There was ambivalence in Agranat's handling of this theme. On one hand, he endorsed the district court's analysis; on the other, his own reasoning went in a different direction. He sought to prove that the validity of the Law against the Nazis and Nazi Collaborators stemmed not from its superiority to the law of nations but from its compatibility with international law. Jewish justice was thereby not different from or superior to the law of nations; rather, it was a part of it.
...
... Citing scholarly works and judicial opinions, he asserted that international law did not prohibit ex post facto laws and was not dogmatic about the territoriality principle. Thus Israel's decision to prosecute, far from being a violation of international law, was simply a perfectly legitimate reluctance to recognize principles not fully endorsed by the community of nations. ... He wanted to show that Israel's law was not an aberration but an affirmation of the law of nations.

The Law against the Nazis and Nazi Collaborators created a new category of crimes: crimes against the Jewish people. As such, it was a unique ex post facto law. The crime was specific to Jews and created a category hitherto unknown in any legal system. It was precisely for this reason that the crime formed a coherent part of Zionism. ... Zionism portrayed the Holocaust less as the vile fruit of totalitarianism and more as the culmination of two millennia of anti-Semitism. The Jews had been defenseless because they did not possess political power. Even in Nuremberg the Allies refused to recognize that the Jews as a nation were especially targeted by the Nazis. The offense, 'crimes against the Jewish people', was designed to correct that myopia and to assert, ex post facto and forever, the Jewish point of view. ...

Speaking for the Supreme Court, Agranat raised a different voice. He reviewed the four categories of the indictment, and he concluded that they had a common denominator, a 'special universal characteristic'. About 'crimes against the Jewish people' he had this to say: 'Thus, the category of "crimes against the Jewish people" is nothing but ... "the gravest crime against humanity". It is true that there are certain differences between them ... but these are not differences material to our case'. Therefore, he concluded, in order to determine whether international law recognized Israeli jurisdiction stemming from this ex post facto statute, the Court could simply collapse the entire indictment into 'the inclusive category of "crimes against humanity"'. This 'simple' technique enabled Agranat to devote the bulk of his opinion to the universal aspects of the *Eichmann* case.

QUESTIONS

1. Consider the alternatives to trial of Eichmann by the Israeli court. Would any international tribunal have been competent? What would have been involved in an effort to establish another ad hoc international criminal tribunal like Nuremberg, and would that effort have been likely to succeed? Would trial before the courts of another state have been preferable? Which state?

2. What problems, if any, do you see in reliance on 'crimes against the Jewish people'? How would you distinguish it from, for example, legislation by an African state defining 'crimes against the black people' that could reach persons in Western or other states who are accused of violence against black people? Are both types of statutes good ideas?

2. Ex Parte Pinochet and Universal Jurisdiction

General Augusto Pinochet resigned as head of state of Chile in 1990 and became a 'Senator for life'. In 1998, he travelled to the United Kingdom for medical treatment. Judicial authorities in Spain sought to extradite him to stand criminal trial in Spain on several charges, including torture, related to the right-wing military overthrow of President Allende on 11 September 1973 and the subsequent political repression during Pinochet's term as head of state. An international warrant for his arrest was issued in Spain, and a British magistrate issued a provisional warrant under the UK Extradition Act 1989. None of the conduct alleged by the Spanish authorities was committed against UK citizens or in the United Kingdom. Seeking to return to Chile, Pinochet initiated proceedings for habeas corpus and for judicial review of the warrant.

On appeal, the House of Lords decided the case, but this judgment was set aside due to a conflict of interest involving one of the Law Lords. A differently constituted seven-member panel reheard the appeal in 1999. Six of the seven Law Lords upheld the extradition process, but (in the majority of their opinions) only with respect to a small number of the charges. Extradition was appropriate only for charges satisfying the 'double criminality' principle, which requires the conduct in question to have been criminal in both Spain and the United Kingdom at the time it was committed. A majority of the Law Lords concluded that because a section of the Criminal Justice Act 1988, incorporating the United Kingdom's obligations under the Convention Against Torture, had created a new domestic crime for torture committed outside the country, only the charges of torture committed after the Act's entry into force could proceed.

Lord Browne-Wilkinson discussed the foundation for universal jurisdiction over torture:

> I have no doubt that long before the Torture Convention of 1984 state torture was an international crime in the highest sense.

> But there was no tribunal or court to punish international crimes of torture. Local courts could take jurisdiction: see … *Attorney-General of Israel v. Eichmann*. But the objective was to ensure a general jurisdiction so that the torturer was not safe wherever he went. … The Torture Convention was agreed not in order to create an international crime which had not previously existed but to provide an international system under which the international criminal — the torturer — could find no safe haven. …

> …

> Under Article 5(2) a state party has to take jurisdiction over any alleged offender who is found within its territory.

> …

> [I]n my judgment the Torture Convention did provide what was missing: a worldwide universal jurisdiction.

Other Law Lords expressed a range of opinions concerning universal jurisdiction. Consider, for example, Lord Millett's opinion:

> … [C]rimes prohibited by international law attract universal jurisdiction under customary international law if two criteria are satisfied. First, they must be contrary to a peremptory norm of international law so as to infringe a jus cogens. Secondly, they must be so serious and on such a scale that they can justly be regarded as an attack on the international legal

order. Isolated offences, even if committed by public officials, would not satisfy these criteria. …

…

… Customary international law is part of the common law, and accordingly I consider that the English courts have and always have had extra-territorial criminal jurisdiction in respect of crimes of universal jurisdiction under customary international law.

In my opinion, the systematic use of torture on a large scale and as an instrument of state policy had joined piracy, war crimes and crimes against peace as an international crime of universal jurisdiction well before 1984. I consider that it had done so by 1973. For my own part, therefore, I would hold that the courts of this country already possessed extra-territorial jurisdiction in respect of torture and conspiracy to torture on the scale of the charges in the present case and did not require the authority of statute to exercise it. …

…

Whereas the international community had condemned the widespread and systematic use of torture as an instrument of state policy, the Convention extended the offence to cover isolated and individual instances of torture provided that they were committed by a public official. I do not consider that offences of this kind were previously regarded as international crimes attracting universal jurisdiction. … Whereas previously states were entitled to take jurisdiction in respect of the offence wherever it was committed, they were now placed under an obligation to do so.

In contrast, Lord Phillips remarked:

I believe that it is still an open question whether international law recognises universal jurisdiction in respect of international crimes — that is the right, under international law, of the courts of any state to prosecute for such crimes wherever they occur. In relation to war crimes, such a jurisdiction has been asserted by the State of Israel, notably in the prosecution of Adolf Eichmann, but this assertion of jurisdiction does not reflect any general state practice in relation to international crimes. Rather, states have tended to agree, or to attempt to agree, on the creation of international tribunals to try international crimes. They have however, on occasion, agreed by conventions, that their national courts should enjoy jurisdiction to prosecute for a particular category of international crime wherever occurring.

After the decision, the extradition case continued while Pinochet remained under house arrest. France, Belgium and Switzerland also made extradition requests. In 2000, the British Home Secretary stated that medical examinations of Pinochet led him to conclude that the 84-year-old general was incapable of standing trial and should be released to return to Chile. Later that year, Pinochet was permitted to fly home, to a radically different political context in which he was an isolated, far less influential and potent figure. Judicial steps were underway towards intense investigation into Pinochet's connection with the killings and torture. The Chilean Supreme Court stripped Pinochet of immunity, and several charges were brought against him. However, on 10 December 2006, Pinochet died before any prosecution was brought.

3. The Belgian Arrest Warrant Case

A leading treatment of the scope and viability of universal jurisdiction arose in proceedings before the International Court of Justice (ICJ). The case involved Belgium's 'universal jurisdiction' law, which has since been modified. At the time, the law permitted Belgian judicial authorities to prosecute violations of international humanitarian law regardless of where the acts were committed and regardless of the nationality of the perpetrators and victims. In late 1998, 12 individuals lodged a complaint with a Belgian investigating judge at the Brussels Court of First Instance. Of the 12 complainants, five were of Belgian nationality, seven were of

Congolese nationality and all were resident in Belgium. The complaint concerned events that had taken place in the Democratic Republic of the Congo (DRC).

In mid-2000, the Belgian judge issued an arrest warrant *in absentia* against Mr Abdulaye Yerodia Ndombasi, who was the DRC's Minister for Foreign Affairs at the time. The warrant accused Mr Yerodia of committing war crimes and crimes against humanity before serving in his ministerial post. The complaint alleged that he made public speeches that incited the massacre of several hundred people, mainly of Tutsi origin, in the DRC. The Government of the DRC initiated proceedings against the Government of Belgium before the ICJ claiming that the issuance and international distribution of the arrest warrant unlawfully infringed the foreign minister's immunity and violated international rules on jurisdiction. A majority of the ICJ did not reach the issue of universal jurisdiction, holding instead that the promulgation and circulation of the arrest warrant violated Mr Yerodia's official immunity as Foreign Minister. A separate opinion joined by Judges Rosalyn Higgins, Peter Kooijmans and Thomas Buergenthal squarely addressed the issue of universal jurisdiction in one of the most extensive treatments of the subject to date. We return to the majority's assessment of the official immunity claim later in this chapter. Excerpts of the joint separate opinion follow.

CASE CONCERNING THE ARREST WARRANT OF 11 APRIL 2000 (DEMOCRATIC REPUBLIC OF THE CONGO V. BELGIUM) INTERNATIONAL COURT OF JUSTICE, GENERAL LIST NO. 121 (14 FEBRUARY 2002)

JOINT SEPARATE OPINION OF JUDGES HIGGINS, KOOIJMANS AND BUERGENTHAL:

19. We ... turn to the question whether States are entitled to exercise jurisdiction over persons having no connection with the forum State when the accused is not present in the State's territory. ...

20. Our analysis may begin with national legislation, to see if it evidences a State practice. ... [N]ational legislation, whether in fulfilment of international treaty obligations to make certain international crimes offences also in national law, or otherwise, does not suggest a universal jurisdiction over these offences. Various examples typify the more qualified practice. [The Opinion then reviews the Australian War Crimes Act of 1945, the United Kingdom War Crimes Act of 1991 and the Criminal Code of Canada 1985.]

21. All of these illustrate the trend to provide for the trial and punishment under international law of certain crimes that have been committed extraterritorially. But none of them, nor the many others that have been studied by the Court, represent a classical assertion of a universal jurisdiction over particular offences committed elsewhere by persons having no relationship or connection with the forum State.

22. The case law under these provisions has largely been cautious so far as reliance on universal jurisdiction is concerned. In the Pinochet case in the English courts, the jurisdictional basis was clearly treaty based, with the double criminality rule required for extradition being met by English legislation in September 1988, after which date torture committed abroad was a crime in the United Kingdom as it already was in Spain. ...

...

26. In some of the literature on the subject it is asserted that the great international treaties on crimes and offences evidence universality as a ground for the exercise of jurisdiction recognized in international law. This is doubtful.

27. Article VI of the Convention on the Prevention and Punishment of the Crime of Genocide, 9 December 1948, provides:

> "Persons charged with genocide or any of the other acts enumerated in Article III shall be
> tried by a competent tribunal of the State in the territory of which the act was committed,
> or by such international penal tribunal as may have jurisdiction with respect to those
> Contracting Parties which shall have accepted its jurisdiction."

This is an obligation to assert territorial jurisdiction, though the *travaux préparatoires* do reveal an understanding that this obligation was not intended to affect the right of a State to exercise criminal jurisdiction on its own nationals for acts committed outside the State (A/C 6/SR, 134; p. 5). Article VI also provides a potential grant of non-territorial competence to a possible future international tribunal — even this not being automatic under the Genocide Convention but being restricted to those Contracting Parties which would accept its jurisdiction. In recent years it has been suggested in the literature that Article VI does not prevent a State from exercising universal jurisdiction in a genocide case.

28. Article 49 of the First Geneva Convention, Article 50 of the Second Geneva Convention, Article 129 of the Third Geneva Convention and Article 146 of the Fourth Geneva Convention, all of 12 August 1949, provide:

> "Each High Contracting Party shall be under the obligation to search for persons alleged to have committed, or to have ordered to be committed, … grave breaches, and shall bring such persons, regardless of their nationality, before its own courts. It may also, if it prefers, and in accordance with the provisions of its own legislation, hand such persons over for trial to another High Contracting Party concerned, provided such High Contracting Party has made out a prima facie case."

29. Article 85, paragraph 1, of the First Additional Protocol to the 1949 Geneva Convention incorporates this provision by reference.

30. The stated purpose of the provision was that the offences would not be left unpunished (the extradition provisions playing their role in this objective). It may immediately be noted that this is an early form of the *aut dedere aut prosequi* to be seen in later conventions. But the obligation to prosecute is primary, making it even stronger.

31. No territorial or nationality linkage is envisaged, suggesting a true universality principle. But a different interpretation is given in the authoritative Pictet *Commentary: Geneva Convention for the Amelioration of the Condition of the Wounded and Sick in Armed Forces in the Field* (1952), which contends that this obligation was understood as being an obligation upon States parties to search for offenders who may be on their territory. Is it a true example of universality, if the obligation to search is restricted to the own territory? Does the obligation to search imply a permission to prosecute in absentia, if the search had no result?

…

38. The Convention against Torture, of 10 December 1984, establishes in Article 5 an obligation to establish jurisdiction

> "(a) When the offences are committed in any territory under its jurisdiction or on board a ship or aircraft registered in that State;
>
> (b) When the alleged offender is a national of that State;
>
> (c) When the victim is a national of that State if that State considers it appropriate."

If the person alleged to have committed the offence is found in the territory of a State party and is not extradited, submission of the case to the prosecuting authorities shall follow (Art. 7). Other grounds of criminal jurisdiction exercised in accordance with the relevant national law are not excluded (Art. 5, para. 3), making clear that Article 5, paragraphs 1 and 2, must not be interpreted *a contrario*.

39. The passage of time changes perceptions. The jurisdictional ground that in 1961 had been referred to as the principle of "primary universal repression" came now to be widely referred to by delegates as "universal jurisdiction" — moreover, a universal jurisdiction thought appropriate, since torture, like piracy, could be considered an "offence against the law of nations." (United States: E/CN.4/1367, 1980). Australia, France, the Netherlands and the United Kingdom eventually dropped their objection that "universal jurisdiction" over torture would create problems under their domestic legal systems. (See E/CN. 4/1984/72.)

40. This short historical survey may be summarized as follows.

41. The parties to these treaties agreed both to grounds of jurisdiction and as to the obligation to take the measures necessary to establish such jurisdiction. The specified grounds relied on links of nationality of the

offender, or the ship or aircraft concerned, or of the victim. ... These may properly be described as treaty-based broad extraterritorial jurisdiction. But in addition to these were the parallel provisions whereby a State party in whose jurisdiction the alleged perpetrator of such offences is found, shall prosecute him or extradite him. By the loose use of language the latter has come to be referred to as "universal jurisdiction," though this is really an obligatory territorial jurisdiction over persons, albeit in relation to acts committed elsewhere.

42. Whether this obligation (whether described as the duty to establish universal jurisdiction, or, more accurately, the jurisdiction to establish a territorial jurisdiction over persons for extraterritorial events) is an obligation only of treaty law, *inter partes* or, whether it is now, at least as regards the offences articulated in the treaties, an obligation of customary international law was pleaded by the Parties in this case but not addressed in any great detail.

...

44. However, we note that the inaccurately termed "universal jurisdiction principle" in these treaties is a principle of obligation, while the question in this case is whether Belgium had the right to issue and circulate the arrest warrant if it so chose. ...

45. That there is no established practice in which States exercise universal jurisdiction, properly so called, is undeniable. As we have seen, virtually all national legislation envisages links of some sort to the forum State; and no case law exists in which pure universal jurisdiction has formed the basis of jurisdiction. This does not necessarily indicate, however, that such an exercise would be unlawful. In the first place, national legislation reflects the circumstances in which a State provides in its own law the ability to exercise jurisdiction. But a State is not required to legislate up to the full scope of the jurisdiction allowed by international law. The war crimes legislation of Australia and the United Kingdom afford examples of countries making more confined choices for the exercise of jurisdiction. ... Moreover, while none of the national case law to which we have referred happens to be based on the exercise of a universal jurisdiction properly so called, there is equally nothing in this case law which evidences an *opinio juris* on the illegality of such a jurisdiction. In short, national legislation and case law, — that is, State practice — is neutral as to exercise of universal jurisdiction.

46. There are, moreover, certain indications that a universal criminal jurisdiction for certain international crimes is clearly not regarded as unlawful. The duty to prosecute under those treaties which contain the *aut dedere aut prosequi* provisions opens the door to a jurisdiction based on the heinous nature of the crime rather than on links of territoriality or nationality (whether as perpetrator or victim). The 1949 Geneva Conventions lend support to this possibility, and are widely regarded as today reflecting customary international law.

47. The contemporary trends, reflecting international relations as they stand at the beginning of the new century, are striking. The movement is towards bases of jurisdiction other than territoriality. "Effects" or "impact" jurisdiction is embraced both by the United States and, with certain qualifications, by the European Union. Passive personality jurisdiction, for so long regarded as controversial, is now reflected not only in the legislation of various countries, and today meets with relatively little opposition, at least so far as a particular category of offences is concerned.

...

53. This brings us once more to the particular point that divides the Parties in this case: is it a precondition of the assertion of universal jurisdiction that the accused be within the territory?

54. Considerable confusion surrounds this topic, not helped by the fact that legislators, courts and writers alike frequently fail to specify the precise temporal moment at which any such requirement is said to be in play. Is the presence of the accused within the jurisdiction said to be required at the time the offence was committed? At the time the arrest warrant is issued? Or at the time of the trial itself? ... The only prohibitive rule ... is that criminal jurisdiction should not be exercised, without permission, within the territory of another State. The Belgian arrest warrant envisaged the arrest of Mr. Yerodia in Belgium, or the possibility of his arrest in third States at the discretion of the States concerned. This would in principle seem to violate no existing prohibiting rule of international law.

...

58. If the underlying purpose of designating certain acts as international crimes is to authorize a wide jurisdiction to be asserted over persons committing them, there is no rule of international law (and certainly not the *aut*

dedere principle) which makes illegal co-operative overt acts designed to secure their presence within a State wishing to exercise jurisdiction.

59. If, as we believe to be the case, a State may choose to exercise a universal criminal jurisdiction in absentia, it must also ensure that certain safeguards are in place. They are absolutely essential to prevent abuse and to ensure that the rejection of impunity does not jeopardize stable relations between States.

No exercise of criminal jurisdiction may occur which fails to respect the inviolability or infringes the immunities of the person concerned. ... [C]ommencing an investigation on the basis of which an arrest warrant may later be issued does not of itself violate those principles. The function served by the international law of immunities does not require that States fail to keep themselves informed.

A State contemplating bringing criminal charges based on universal jurisdiction must first offer to the national State of the prospective accused person the opportunity itself to act upon the charges concerned. The Court makes reference to these elements in the context of this case at paragraph 16 of its Judgment.

Further, such charges may only be laid by a prosecutor or *juge d'instruction* who acts in full independence, without links to or control by the government of that State. Moreover, the desired equilibrium between the battle against impunity and the promotion of good inter-State relations will only be maintained if there are some special circumstances that do require the exercise of an international criminal jurisdiction and if this has been brought to the attention of the prosecutor or *juge d'instruction*. For example, persons related to the victims of the case will have requested the commencement of legal proceedings.

60. It is equally necessary that universal criminal jurisdiction be exercised only over those crimes regarded as the most heinous by the international community.
...
64. The arrest warrant issued against Mr. Yerodia accuses him both of war crimes and of crimes against humanity. As regards the latter, charges of incitement to racial hatred, which are said to have led to murders and lynchings, were specified. Fitting of this charge within the generally understood substantive context of crimes against humanity is not without its problems. "Racial hatred" would need to be assimilated to "persecution on racial grounds," or, on the particular facts, to mass murder and extermination. [The opinion analyses whether incitement is an acceptable form of liability under international criminal law, and concludes that it is.]

65. It would seem (without in any way pronouncing upon whether Mr. Yerodia did or did not perform the acts with which he is charged in the warrant) that the acts alleged do fall within the concept of "crimes against humanity" and would be within that small category in respect of which an exercise of universal jurisdiction is not precluded under international law.

4. The Fall and Rise of Universal Jurisdiction

The 1993 Belgian law on universal jurisdiction led to a handful of cases being brought against prominent international leaders, including Fidel Castro and Saddam Hussein. Following charges brought in June 2001 against Israeli Prime Minister Ariel Sharon, which led to strong protests by Israel, and the ICJ judgment upholding Yerodia's immunity as Foreign Minister, Belgium decided to amend its law. Before it could do so, in 2003, seven Iraqi families living in Belgium requested an investigation of former U.S. President George H. W. Bush, Vice-President Dick Cheney, Secretary of State Colin Powell, and General Norman Schwarzkopf for war crimes during the first Gulf War in 1991. Then U.S. Secretary of Defense, Donald Rumsfeld, called the charges 'absurd', denied the authority of Belgian courts to try American officials, and threatened to withhold funding for the new NATO headquarters in Brussels. Belgium repealed the 1993 law and introduced a much more restrictive law.

A similar dynamic played out in Spain. After the Pinochet case, as well as charges brought against officials from the United States and Israel, the Spanish court in June 2014 issued warrants for China's former President Jiang

Zemin and former Prime Minister Li Peng in relation to human rights abuses in Tibet. In the face of a powerful diplomatic backlash, the Spanish law was amended to greatly reduce its scope.

On 30 November 2018, and again on 12 April 2023, Israel drew lessons from its experience. It told the UN Sixth Committee, during a debate on the ILC Draft Articles on Crimes against Humanity, that the following safeguards should apply to the exercise of universal jurisdiction:

> … a requirement that any initiation of legal proceedings would be conducted only with the prior approval of high-level legal officials in the executive branch at the earliest stage; assertion of universal jurisdiction should be regarded as a measure of last resort in appropriate circumstances only; adherence to the principle of subsidiarity; and a requirement that prior to issuing requests for mutual legal assistance, provisional arrest, or extradition, States take appropriate measures to determine whether the party that filed the complaint has filed complaints about the alleged incident or suspect in other fora, and if so, whether an investigation has taken place or is ongoing there.

But in the past few years, universal jurisdiction has made a comeback. In November 2023, French investigative judges issued an arrest warrant for Syrian President Bashar al-Assad relating to the use of chemical weapons. The following materials explore the impact of the situation in Syria, especially in Europe.

BETH VAN SCHAACK, IMAGINING JUSTICE FOR SYRIA
(2020) 447

… [T]he failures of the Security Council when it comes to Syria have eroded our faith in the U.N. system of collective security. With Russia readily wielding its veto in defense of Assad, the Council has been unable to invoke Chapter VII and deploy its strongest accountability tools: the creation of an ad hoc tribunal or even an investigative mechanism with teeth, the referral of the situation to the International Criminal Court, or the imposition of targeted sanctions on responsible individuals. … [S]tates have turned to other multilateral fora, such as the Organisation for the Prohibition of Chemical Weapons, and [the General Assembly created] the International, Impartial and Independent Mechanism for Syria—which is collecting, collating, and analyzing evidence of international crimes for any national, regional, or international proceedings that materialize. …

… [I]t is not clear … that the ICC offers the best solution to the imperative of justice in Syria given the sheer magnitude of the criminality on display and limitations in the Court's subject matter jurisdiction over war crimes committed in non-international armed conflicts. In addition, the shortcomings of prior Security Council referrals are legion. Besides the obvious problems associated with the Council exercising political control over the Court in violation of the trias politica, detractors point to controversial textual elements in the resolutions that were deemed essential to achieve consensus (such as the provision effectively granting immunity to personnel from non-member states); the failure of the Council to provide any meaningful follow-up to effectuate its referrals (particularly when it comes to the arrest of suspects); and the fact that such referrals amount to an unfunded mandate. Indeed, Security Council referrals have been described by Court insiders as a "poisoned chalice." Furthermore, the limitations of the ICC are becoming increasingly apparent as cases fail and resources become even more thinly spread.

…

… [T]he war in Syria has re-enlivened the principle of universal jurisdiction alongside other extraterritorial jurisdictional principles, rendering domestic courts the situs of the most aggressive and creative accountability exercises. … A number of juridical innovations have facilitated this trend toward the empowerment of domestic courts, including the incorporation of international criminal law and expansive jurisdictional principles into national penal codes, the establishment of specialized—and globally networked—war crimes units, and the creation of increasingly frictionless systems of mutual legal assistance. On the ground, the fact that a fourth of the Syrian prewar population has fled the country means that perpetrators, victims, and witnesses are on the move and often find themselves in close proximity to each other in their states of refuge. With no international forum capable of exercising plenary jurisdiction, domestic courts have stepped up to fill the jurisdictional void. The enforcement of international criminal law is now more decentralized, but also more coordinated, than ever. And so, like flowing water, justice finds its outlets wherever it can.

EYAD A. CASE
KOBLENZ HIGHER REGIONAL COURT, CASE NO. 1 STE 3/21 (24 FEBRUARY 2021)
[MACHINE TRANSLATION FROM THE ORIGINAL GERMAN CASE REPORT.]

...

As part of this widespread and systematic attack on the civilian population, the accused Eyad A., as an employee of the Syrian General Intelligence Service, helped to seriously deprive a total of 30 people of their physical liberty in branch 251 prison and to torture them while they were held there as a member of Branch 40 of the Syrian General Intelligence Service in September/October 2011, after the violent breakup of a demonstration in Douma, he and colleagues searched the streets for fleeing demonstrators and finally arrested 30 people and took them to Branch 251 prison. The accused accompanied the transport of the demonstrators in one of the buses and saw that they were being beaten on the way to the prison as well as on arrival at the prison. In prison, the detainees were then brutally mistreated and systematically tortured. The accused, Eyad A., was already aware of the regular and systematic torture in Ward 251 prison when the demonstrators were arrested and accepted the torture of those arrested with approval. He also expected the torture to be part of a planned, organized government crackdown on opposition forces.

These findings of the Senate are based on the statements of the numerous witnesses questioned, on the information provided by the experts, the documentary and visual evidence collected and, to a large extent, on the information provided by the accused Eyad A. himself. He did not comment on the allegation throughout the criminal proceedings. In May 2018, however, he revealed his work for the secret service in a hearing in the asylum procedure, but initially only revealed himself as an " eyewitness" to violent attacks. Finally, during a police interrogation in August 2018, he disclosed his involvement in the persecution ... .

...

ROGER LU PHILLIPS, A DROP IN THE OCEAN: A PRELIMINARY ASSESSMENT OF THE KOBLENZ TRIAL ON SYRIAN TORTURE
JUST SECURITY, (22 APRIL 2021)[540]

...

... The case had special resonance because some of the victims from Branch 251 were depicted in the Caesar Files which show the bodies of several thousand victims of torture in photographs smuggled out of Syria by a military photographer. ...

...

So far, universal jurisdiction has proven to be the most viable option for Syrians to obtain a measure of justice in the near term, particularly in Germany, Sweden, the Netherlands, and France where there are sizeable populations of Syrians and special war crimes units mandated to conduct such investigations. ...

Limits of Universal Jurisdiction

...

Hundreds of thousands of Syrians have sought refuge in Germany, yet very few have attended the proceedings in Koblenz or even know what is happening there. The German Federal Prosecutor chose to file charges in the provincial court likely to avoid a backlog of cases in other locales such as Berlin, where there is a large Syrian population. But the result was to deprive many Syrians of an opportunity to see justice at work. When they did attend, they were not permitted access to the Arabic language interpretation, which is produced for the benefit of the defendants and plaintiffs. ...

The court's approach to witness protection could also be described as clumsy. On several occasions, witnesses were hesitant to speak and expressed concerns for the safety of family members living in Syria, Turkey, and even Europe. It was not apparent that the court had advance notice of these concerns and the issues were addressed as they arose in court. ...

Syrian audiences were likewise perplexed by the decision to charge Eyad Al-Gharib despite his low rank and the fact that he defected from the regime, not to mention his apparent cooperation with authorities in the investigation of [another accused] Anwar Raslan. Other witnesses with the same or more significant

---

[540] Analysis based on The Syria Justice and Accountability Centre, *Between Hope and Despair: A Way Forward after the Koblenz Trial* (2022)

responsibility testified in the trial and were not charged by the prosecutor. This created confusion as to the German Federal Prosecutor's policy, leading Al-Gharib's counsel to question what criteria were used to open criminal proceedings in Germany. It also contributed to the reticence of insider witnesses to cooperate with investigators and prosecutors. This will likely create obstacles to building cases against senior leaders and begs the question as to who of the millions of Syrians with some connection to the Syrian government should be prosecuted. This will be a significant challenge as Syrians grapple with the conflict of the last 10 years and chart a path forward that includes comprehensive justice and the possibility of reconciliation.

Sweden[541]

Sweden ratified the Rome Statute of the International Criminal Court in 2002. The Swedish Criminal Code (SCC) and the Swedish Act on Criminal Responsibility for Genocide already covered some of the relevant crimes, but in 2014 a new law codifying the Rome Statute was incorporated into Swedish law through the Swedish Act on Criminal Responsibility for Genocide, Crimes Against Humanity and War Crimes incorporated the Rome Statute into Swedish law. Its coverage includes genocide, crimes against humanity, and war crimes, and a range of other crimes provided for in the Statute. It also allows for universal jurisdiction for those crimes as well as any other crime which carries a minimum sentence of four years under Swedish law.

LENA BJURSTRÖM, SWEDEN ON THE FRONTLINE WITH SYRIA CASES
JUSTICEINFO.NET (11 FEBRUARY 2021)

…

On 10 February 2015, Syrian rebel Mouhannad Droubi appeared before the District Court of Södertörn, south of Stockholm. Droubi, a veteran of the Free Syrian Army (ASL) and refugee in Sweden since September 2013, was charged with particularly aggravated assault and accused of war crimes. In a video broadcast on Facebook in the summer of 2012, he is seen beating up a supposed soldier of the Syrian loyalist army and threatening to cut out his tongue. The video, which he himself posted online, got lost in the limbo of social networks before being anonymously transmitted to the Swedish police in July 2014, leading to an investigation and his arrest three months later.

… After several twists and turns in the trial and appeal, Droubi was finally sentenced to eight years in prison for this crime in August 2016.

…

This created controversy in the Syrian community in exile [because it] concerned a member of the opposition. At a time when evidence of the multiple crimes committed by the regime were accumulating, the conviction of the former ASL soldier rubbed some people up the wrong way, especially when this case was followed a few months later in Sweden by a life sentence on another rebel fighter, Haisam Omar Sakhanh, for the execution of seven regular army soldiers.

… [In order to educate the public, the] Swedish police then developed brochures in several languages, including Arabic, explaining the work carried out and calling on Syrians to testify.

Founded in 2008, the International Crimes Unit of the Swedish Public Prosecutor's Office now has 16 prosecutors, assisted by 15 officers from the war crimes unit of the national police. …

In September 2017, … a former soldier in Bashar Al-Assad's army [was convicted]. Mohammed Abdullah had been spotted on his arrival in Sweden in 2015 by the Syrian human rights organization Al Kawakibi and reported to the asylum office and then the police. First arrested in 2016, the former soldier was first released for lack of evidence, despite strong suspicions. It was a photo in which he posed smiling, with his foot on a pile of corpses, that allowed him to be charged the following year and sentenced to eight months in prison for "outrages upon human dignity" as a war crime. [The murder charge had to be dropped, for lack of sufficient evidence.]

At the same time, the Swedish Public Prosecutor's Office opened a wide-ranging investigation as early as 2015. …[According to Hanna Lemoine, a prosecutor:] "We learned lessons from investigations in Rwanda, where we

---

[541] See Open Society Justice Initiative and Trial International, *Universal Jurisdiction Law and Practice in Sweden*, (April 2020).

heard victims and witnesses of events that happened more than 20 years ago. We understood that if we could have catalogued evidence and documented these events earlier, it would have been better. ... Since we have an important Syrian community in Sweden, we understood there was potentially a lot of evidence in our country regarding the crimes committed in Syria" ... .

[A]bout 50 individual investigations are now underway in Sweden ... . While the majority concern former members of Daesh, particularly foreign fighters, a few cases concern individuals affiliated with other rebel groups, and about ten concern individuals linked to the Syrian regime. ...

[But the future of such prosecutions in Sweden remains uncertain. In] any case involving universal jurisdiction, Swedish prosecutors must seek express authorization from the government before any indictment. "No criteria [for justification] are mentioned in the law, which gives the government wide discretionary power," notes a report by the NGOs Trial International and Open Society Justice Initiative on Swedish universal jurisdiction. "This could potentially be a major obstacle to prosecution of foreigners, especially high ranking ones, and there is no recourse available to challenge the government's exercise of decision." To date, this authorization has never been refused. But the Syrian suspects pursued in Sweden were only subordinates, present on the territory. And so far, Sweden has never issued international arrest warrants in such cases.

...

WOLFGANG KALECK AND PATRICK KROKER, SYRIAN TORTURE INVESTIGATIONS IN GERMANY AND BEYOND: BREATHING NEW LIFE INTO UNIVERSAL JURISDICTION IN EUROPE? 16 J. INT'L CRIM. JUST. (2018) 165

The structural investigations regarding Syria ... demonstrate that a more nuanced approach to UJ offers an avenue to fill the gaps in (the incomplete and imperfect) system of international criminal law. Additionally, they allow for strategic investigations into atrocity crimes for which there are no other judicial forum. This prosecutorial technique further enables the authorities to investigate powerful actors at least in the beginning, without directly being exposed to political pressure since they are not focused on specific incidents or suspects, thus avoiding strong political reactions and interference by states whose elite might be under investigation. Yet, structural investigations can ultimately yield tangible results in the form of arrest warrants issued against persons most responsible for heinous crimes if individual investigations against them are opened. They thus allow the German Federal Prosecutor to balance the rationale of 'no-safe haven' approach and to avoid what Langer calls the 'high political cost', namely an approach that takes into consideration the important role of national jurisdictions in the patchwork of international justice.

The combination of trials against suspects arrested on European territory and the initiation of broader investigations against those who bear the most responsibility... show that the 'no-safe haven' and the 'global-enforcer approach' can complement each other and that this combination can serve as an interesting model for a modern and pragmatic approach to revitalizing UJ in Europe.

MÁXIMO LANGER AND MACKENZIE EASON, THE QUIET EXPANSION OF UNIVERSAL JURISDICTION 30 EUR. J. INT'L L. (2019) 779

...

2 The Numerical Expansion of Universal Jurisdiction

...

A. Complaints and Cases Considered by Authorities by Their Own Motion (Propio Motu Investigations)

...Before 1988, there were 286 universal jurisdiction cases initiated. In the decade between 1988 and 1997, 342 universal jurisdiction cases were initiated. In the following decade – 1998–2007 – there were 503 such cases.

And, [between 2008 and 2017] there were 815 new universal jurisdiction cases, which represents a total nearly as high as the two previous decades combined.

...

B. Completed Trials

[T]here were 32 universal jurisdiction cases that resulted in a completed trial between 1961 and June 2010. In our 2016–2018 updating of the Langer-Eason Database, we found 29 universal jurisdiction trials that were completed between July 2010 and 2017. ...

...

C. Explanatory Factors

...

1 ICC Implementing Legislation

One such factor could be the adoption of new universal jurisdiction provisions, generally as part of the domestic implementation of the Rome Statute. Such statutory changes set the stage for the expansion in both universal jurisdiction complaints and trials by increasing the range of venues in which it is possible for universal jurisdiction claims to be heard.

2 Creation of Specialized Investigative Units

In addition to these statutory changes leading to a greater number of venues in which universal jurisdiction litigation is permitted, the increasing frequency and regularity of universal jurisdiction cases and trials is also likely due in part to a series of institutional changes and processes that have increased the number of venues in which universal jurisdiction is logistically possible. One of these institutional changes has been the creation of special international crimes units in the police and/or in the office of the prosecutor or among investigating judges. ...

3 Institutional Learning

... The term 'institutional learning' refers to the 'capability' of complex institutions to 'learn about, adapt and change' both their institutional frameworks and operational strategies over time. ...
We can see evidence of ... state officials involved with universal jurisdiction investigations and trials ... 'learning by doing' and 'learning by using', becoming more effective/efficient the more cases they conduct. ...
[E]xperience conducting universal jurisdiction cases generates institutional knowledge that facilitates holding more universal jurisdiction trials in the future.

...

4 Technological Change

... [T]echnological shifts ... have reduced the logistical difficulty and economic cost of universal jurisdiction investigations and litigation. The first of these is the increase in the availability of Internet-connected devices capable of audio/video/photo recording and the use of this technology to document the kinds of abuses criminalized under international law. As smartphones are becoming ubiquitous even in the poorest and most conflict prone areas of the world, more and more individuals have the means to reliably and clearly 'record and document acts of atrocity'. As these devices are also connected to the Internet, this same technological shift has made it easier for victims to send this documentary evidence directly to advocates or to share it with others via social media.

...

1 The Trial of Hissène Habré in Senegal

... Hissène Habré was the president of Chad from 1982 to 1990. During his rule, arbitrary arrests, torture, enforced disappearances, extrajudicial executions and other abuses were committed against political opponents and members of different ethnic groups. When Habré was deposed in 1990, he fled to Senegal. … On 25 January 2000, seven Chadian nationals, together with an association of victims, filed a complaint before an investigating judge in Senegal, with a civil party application. On 4 July 2000, the Appeals Chamber in Senegal held that Senegalese courts did not have jurisdiction over the case given that the Senegalese Criminal Procedure Code did not provide for universal jurisdiction. In 30 November 2000, a group of victims filed another complaint against Habré in Belgium based on the principle of universal jurisdiction. In 2001, victims filed a case against Senegal with the United Nations Committee against Torture that called Senegal to keep Habré there.

On 19 September 2005, the Belgian investigating judge issued an arrest warrant against Habré for torture, genocide, crimes against humanity and war crimes and requested his extradition from Senegal. On 25 November 2005, the Appeals Chamber of Senegal held that it could not extend its jurisdiction to matters relating to the investigation or prosecution of a former head of state for acts allegedly committed during the exercise of his functions. The day after the delivery of this judgment, Senegal referred to the African Union the issue of the institution of proceedings against this former head of state. In early 2006, the United Nations Committee against Torture ruled that Senegal had violated the Convention against Torture by failing to extradite or prosecute Habré. In July 2006, the African Union's Assembly of Heads of State and Government 'decid[ed] to consider the Hissène Habré case as falling within the competence of the African Union, … mandate[d] the Republic of Senegal to prosecute and ensure that Hissène Habré is tried, on behalf of Africa, by a competent Senegalese court with guarantees of a fair trial' and 'mandate[d] the Chairperson of the [African] Union … to provide Senegal with the necessary assistance for the effective conduct of the trial'.

In 2007, Senegal amended its laws to give universal jurisdiction to its courts over core international crimes and to establish the rest of the legal framework to be able to try Habré in Senegal. In 2010, Senegal negotiated with donors to pay a budget of €8.6 million for the costs of the trial. In the meantime, Belgium instituted proceedings against Senegal in 2009 before the International Court of Justice (ICJ), and, on 20 July 2012, the ICJ ruled that Senegal had the duty to prosecute or extradite the case under the Convention against Torture. Only four days later, Senegal and the African Union agreed to establish the 'Extraordinary African Chambers in the Senegalese Courts'. The Statute of the Extraordinary African Chambers, annexed to the agreement, established that the official capacity of the accused did not relieve him of criminal responsibility. On 30 May 2016, the Trial Chamber composed by two Senegalese judges and a judge from Burkina Faso convicted Habré for [crimes against humanity, torture, and war crimes]. It sentenced him to life imprisonment. On 27 April 2017, the Appeals Chamber – a body composed of three judges, one from the Republic of Mali and two from Senegal – confirmed most of the convictions against Habré issued by the Trial Chamber and further ordered Habré to pay 82.290 million West African francs (€123 million) in compensation to victims.

…

B Quiet Expansion

The quiet character of this expansion of universal jurisdiction can also be considered a positive development. First, against predictions that universal jurisdiction would deeply disrupt international relations among states or interfere with transitions to democracy or to peace, the quiet expansion of it suggests that it has not. Similarly, against concerns that universal jurisdiction trials would engage in global vigilante justice that would infringe on the sovereignty of other states, the quiet expansion of universal jurisdiction also suggests that this has not happened either. …

…

* * *

Trial International's *Universal Jurisdiction Annual Review 2023*, at 10, notes that 'countries, with little or no experience with the specificities of investigating international crimes, also took legal action to respond to the atrocities committed in Ukraine,' partly in response to an influx of Ukrainian asylum-seekers. The review noted the resulting 'real risk of duplication, overdocumentation and re-traumatization of victims, in particular taking into account [the] varying levels of expertise [of the investigators.' This is consistent with the cases in Germany and Sweden in which migrants from countries in which they were persecuted act as a stimulus to universal jurisdiction cases. Leslie Johns, Máximo Langer, and Margaret E. Peters, in 'Migration and the Demand for Transnational Justice', 116 *Am. Pol. Sci. Rev.* (2022) 1184 reflect on the dynamics involved:

… [W]hen individuals migrate from repressive societies, they often have grievances that were not adequately remedied in their sending state. These grievances can motivate migrants to seek transnational justice when they arrive in a receiving state.1 Migrants have numerous tactics for achieving transnational justice including reporting crimes to authorities, providing evidence and witness testimony, increasing public awareness of atrocities, and lobbying government elites to take action. In some states, they can even launch private prosecutions. However, these demands will only yield transnational justice if enough migrants demand that the receiving state take action. Our main theoretical claim is that higher migrant stocks from a sending state increase the likelihood of criminal cases by the receiving state for acts that occurred in the sending state. We additionally argue that universal jurisdiction cases are more likely when there are more severe atrocities in the sending state; the government of the receiving state is more responsive to political demands; and the economic, legal, and political costs of prosecutions are lower. In sum, transnational justice is a justice remittance, in which migrants provide accountability and remedies for crimes in their sending states. …

…

… [O]ur evidence counters the claim that universal jurisdiction is a form of "judicial tyranny" by domestic courts seeking to intervene in foreign states. [D]omestic courts … usually have links to the alleged crimes because victims are living in the prosecuting state. Additionally, most states do not allow actual trials to occur unless the defendant is physically present, meaning that prosecuting states often deny "safe harbor" to an international criminal within their borders, rather than to merely project neo-imperial power abroad. Indeed, the UK's refusal to extradite Pinochet ultimately stymied the Spanish prosecution. Extradition proceedings therefore serve as a check on overzealous domestic prosecutions.

While most of the commentaries above reflect an assumption that the growth in universal jurisdiction cases is clearly a positive development, Brianne McGonigle Leyh, in 'Using Strategic Litigation and Universal Jurisdiction to Advance Accountability for Serious International Crimes', 16 *Int'l J. Transitional Just.* (2022) 363, draws attention to three risks involved:

Over-Documentation and Contestation Amongst Civil Society Actors

… [O]ver-documentation … is a risk both for the safety and well-being of the victims as well as for the reliability and usability of the information gathered. The risk of over-documentation involves situations where victims are repeatedly asked, by numerous and varied actors, to retell their stories again and again. In many of these situations, victims are unaware of who is recording their story or what it will be used for.

Having to recount traumatic experiences multiple times to multiple actors, who are often strangers, can lead to what experts call 'interview fatigue,' and re-traumatization. …

Concerns around the well-being and re-traumatization of victims are also connected to questions about the quality and accuracy of the information collected. Research indicates that when victims or witnesses recount something multiple times, the reliability of their statement declines. Inaccurate and unreliable statements harm justice processes, and present obstacles to building successful cases. …

Poor Conduct and Lack of Oversight

Another risk has to do with limited codes of conduct and a lack of oversight. The same ethical and professional standards that apply to domestic investigators and prosecutors do not apply to private investigators. … Furthermore, the lack of democratic legitimacy, oversight and accountability (coupled in some cases with geographic distance between the victim communities and the international NGOs) is problematic in relation to the rights of others as well as the reliability of the process as a whole.

...

Dominance of the Domestic Criminal Law of European States

With a few exceptions, such as the Hissène Habré case in Senegal and recent developments in Argentina, European states are dominating the accountability landscape when it comes to universal jurisdiction cases for serious international crimes. Since 2009, there has been a 'significant' shift in terms of which European states are pursuing investigations and prosecutions. ... [W]hat does this dominance mean for the international criminal law landscape and how does it pose a risk?

... A shift to European domestic systems, away from global institutions, carries three risks: (i) a reproduction of colonial dynamics whereby actors in the Global North exercise jurisdiction over 'others' in the South, marginalizing local groups and contributing to a two-tiered system of justice; (ii) substantive fragmentation whereby domestic crime interpretation may prevail over that of global institutions; and (iii) procedural obstacles for participating and non-participating victims and affected communities in the foreign domestic jurisdiction.

... European interest will in all likelihood prevail when it comes to case selection or any other politically sensitive topic. If cases become too sensitive (for instance they begin to target Western allies) ... there will likely be a curtailing of universal jurisdiction. There is an obvious hypocrisy here. This is also the case when funding comes directly from Western states known to oppose foreign accountability processes directed at their own citizens or allies. Additionally, there is a 'danger of a colonial power dynamic (white saviour complex)' between the Western-based NGOs and the grassroot organizations and populations they are working with and 'assisting.' Care must be taken not to marginalize the voices and interests of affected groups. ...

QUESTION

Do you see any downsides, from a human rights perspective, in the rapid increase in cases invoking universal jurisdiction? Is the North-South dynamic problematic? What might the alternative be?

D. CIVIL LITIGATION IN THE UNITED STATES AND GLOBAL COMPARISONS

As with universal jurisdiction, which has waxed, waned and now appears to be on the rise once more, efforts by victims of human rights violations by governments or corporations to obtain redress through civil action in domestic courts have seen mixed results over the last two decades. From the 1980s to the early 2000s, an important line of cases in the United States successfully utilized the 1789 Alien Tort Statute (ATS) (28 U.S.C. 1350) to secure accountability for perpetrators of human rights abuses located in the U.S. It provides that: 'The district courts shall have original jurisdiction of any civil action by an alien for a tort only, committed in violation of the law of nations or a treaty of the United States.'

Largely overlooked for almost two centuries, it was given new life by in *Filártiga v. Peña-Irala* (630 F.2d 876 (2d Cir. 1980)) in which the court permitted two Paraguayan citizens, Dr Joel Filártiga and his daughter, to file an ATS suit against a Paraguayan official for allegedly torturing to death Dr Filártiga's teenage son. That decision has since been cited, for various propositions, in well over two hundred U.S. federal court cases. Other federal courts subsequently permitted suits to be brought under the ATS for international law violations including genocide, slavery, disappearances and war crimes. Congressional passage of the U.S. Torture Victim Protection Act of 1991 added another dimension to the opportunities afforded by the ATS for human rights litigation in U.S. courts.

However, in 2004 the Supreme Court significantly limited the causes of action under the ATS (*Sosa v. Alvarez Machain* (542 U.S. 692). Since then, the Court has continued to narrow the scope of the ATS further in a series of cases, to the point where it has now effectively eliminated its utility as a route to compensation for victims of human rights violations. In contrast, other Global North jurisdictions are becoming more hospitable to such litigation. Thus, the European Union has mandated human rights due diligence for larger companies, while courts in Canada, the United Kingdom and the Netherlands have recently ruled in favour of victims of human rights abuses.

1. The Alien Tort Statute

The early successes of the ATS had political as well as legal consequences. As noted by Oona A. Hathaway et al. in 'Has the Alien Tort Statute Made a Difference?: A Historical, Empirical, and Normative Assessment', 107 *Cornell L. Rev.* (2022) 1205, at 1207:

> Even as it was celebrated by human rights advocates, the ATS became the bane of some scholars, lawyers, judges, and U.S. administrations who came to regard its use by human rights advocates as an inappropriate effort to challenge U.S. foreign policy through the courts. When advocates began using the ATS against U.S. and foreign officials, the U.S. government treated the ATS as a growing threat. In the 2000s, the Bush Administration regularly weighed into ATS suits in favor of defendants. Around the same period, ATS lawyers trained their sites on corporations they alleged were complicit in human rights abuses. These corporations had deep pockets that offered the potential of meaningful compensation for plaintiff victims.

Further, while earlier cases like *Filártiga* had targeted foreign government officials, litigants also began to bring ATS claims against the U.S. government in relation to the interventions in Afghanistan and Iraq in the early 2000s. It was against the background of these broader political considerations that the Supreme Court was called upon to decide the future of the ATS in *Sosa v Alvarez-Machain*.

a. *Sosa v. Alvarez-Machain*, 542 U.S. 692 (2004)

The Court summarised the background to this case as follows:

> In 1985, an agent of the Drug Enforcement Administration (DEA), Enrique Camarena-Salazar, was captured on assignment in Mexico and taken to a house in Guadalajara, where he was tortured over the course of a 2-day interrogation, then murdered. Based in part on eyewitness testimony, DEA officials in the United States came to believe that respondent Humberto Alvarez-Machain (Alvarez), a Mexican physician, was present at the house and acted to prolong the agent's life in order to extend the interrogation and torture.

> In 1990, a federal grand jury indicted Alvarez for the torture and murder of Camarena-Salazar, and the United States District Court for the Central District of California issued a warrant for his arrest. The DEA asked the Mexican Government for help in getting Alvarez into the United States, but when the requests and negotiations proved fruitless, the DEA approved a plan to hire Mexican nationals to seize Alvarez and bring him to the United States for trial. As so planned, a group of Mexicans, including petitioner Jose Francisco Sosa, abducted Alvarez from his house, held him overnight in a motel, and brought him by private plane to El Paso, Texas, where he was arrested by federal officers.

Alvarez was acquitted of the charges brought against him in 1992 and subsequently sought damages from Sosa under the ATS. He was successful before the Ninth Circuit, and certiorari was granted to the Supreme Court to clarify the scope of the ATS. That is, in the absence of statutory clarification of what constituted 'a tort ... committed in violation of the law of nations or a treaty of the United States', what kinds of claims could be brought under the statute? Did the ATS create a substantive right to bring claims for violation of customary international law, or was it merely 'a jurisdictional statute creating no new causes of action'?

The majority leaned toward the latter conclusion. It held that the scope of the international norms and violations thereof covered by the ATS was restricted to those which had been in the conception of the drafters at the time of its passage in 1789:

> ... There is no record of congressional discussion about private actions that might be subject to the jurisdictional provision, or about any need for further legislation to create private remedies; there is no record even of debate on the section... . Still, the history does tend to support ... [the proposition] that Congress intended the ATS to furnish jurisdiction for a relatively modest set of actions alleging violations of the law of nations. Uppermost in the legislative mind appears to have been offenses against ambassadors; violations of safe conduct were probably understood to be actionable, and individual actions arising out of prize captures and piracy may well have also been contemplated. But the common law appears to have understood only those three of the hybrid variety as definite and actionable, or at any rate, to have assumed only a very limited set of claims.

However, the majority did not entirely foreclose the possibility that the ATS could be extended by analogy to *some* causes of action under modern customary international law:

> We assume, too, that no development in the two centuries from the enactment of [the ATS] to the birth of the modern line of cases beginning with *Filartiga v. Pena-Irala,* has categorically precluded federal courts from recognizing a claim under the law of nations as an element of common law... . ...Accordingly, we think courts should require any claim based on the present-day law of nations to rest on a norm of international character accepted by the civilized world and defined with a specificity comparable to the features of the 18th-century paradigms we have recognized. ...

The majority warned that significant judicial caution should be exercised in expanding the scope of the ATS beyond 'offenses against ambassadors; violations of safe conduct ... and individual actions arising out of prize captures and piracy'. Reasons for this caution included the 1938 decision of *Erie R. Co. v. Tompkins*, 304 U.S. 64, which 'denied the existence of any federal "general" common law'; the Court's preference for leaving to Congress any decision to create a private right of action; concerns about the foreign policy implications of ATS claims; and a wariness towards 'judicial creativity' in seeking out violations of the law of nations.

In contrast, Justice Scalia's concurring judgment (Chief Justice Rehnquist and Justice Thomas joining) powerfully disagreed that any new causes of action could be created under the ATS:

> We Americans have a method for making the laws that are over us. We elect representatives to two Houses of Congress, each of which must enact the new law and present it for the approval of a President, whom we also elect. For over two decades now, unelected federal judges have been usurping this lawmaking power by converting what they regard as norms of international law into American law. Today's opinion approves that process in principle, though urging the lower courts to be more restrained.

> This Court seems incapable of admitting that some matters — any matters — are none of its business. ...In today's latest victory for its Never Say Never Jurisprudence, the Court ignores its own conclusion that the ATS provides only jurisdiction, wags a finger at the lower courts for going too far, and then — repeating the same formula the ambitious lower courts themselves have used — invites them to try again.

b. The ATS after *Sosa*

The lower courts did, as Scalia warned, try again. In *Kiobel v. Royal Dutch Petroleum Co.* 569 U.S. 108 (2013), applicants argued that oil companies headquartered in the Netherlands, Britain and Nigeria had aided and abetted violations of the law of nations committed by the Nigerian government against the Ogoni people in the Niger Delta. In the 1990s, Ogoni communities had protested the environmental damage caused by oil drilling in the region, and – per the complaint – oil companies had 'enlisted the Nigerian Government to violently suppress the burgeoning demonstrations.' The claimants alleged that the respondents had assisted in the commission of the atrocities by 'providing the Nigerian forces with food, transportation, and compensation, as well as by allowing the Nigerian military to use respondents' property as a staging ground for attacks.'

The lack of a clear nexus with the United States, however, proved fatal to the claim. As Oona A. Hathaway et al. (above) describe, at 1237:

> In its decision in 2013, the Supreme Court held that the ATS cause of action did not apply to wholly extraterritorial conduct. Only claims that "touch and concern the territory of the United States . . . with sufficient force" will "displace the presumption against extraterritoriality," and that "mere corporate presence" in the United States is insufficient. In the end, the Court did not rule on the question of corporate liability, though each side found language in the opinion to favor their view.

The Supreme Court went further in *Jesner v. Arab Bank, PLC*, 138 S. Ct. 1386 (2018). In this case, the petitioners were victims of terror attacks in Israel and Palestine to which, they alleged, the Jordanian bank had made financial contributions. The Court held that foreign corporations could not be subject to ATS liability under any circumstances, on the basis that (a) it was not clear that a universal norm of corporate responsibility for human rights violations had coalesced as a 'violation of the law of nations'; and (b) the foreign policy implications of imposing liability on foreign corporations make it appropriate for the Court to defer to Congress to determine whether it is 'prudent and necessary' to do so. But if *Jesner* established that foreign companies were immune from ATS prosecution, what of domestic corporations?

In 2021, the Supreme Court handed down its decision in *Nestlé USA, Inc. v. Doe et al.*, 141 S. Ct. 1931, concerning allegations that U.S.-based chocolate companies Nestlé and Cargill had aided and abetted the use of child labour and forced labour on cacao plantations in West Africa. Oona A. Hathaway, in '*Nestlé USA, Inc. v. Doe and Cargill, Inc. v. Doe*: The Twists and Turns of the Alien Tort Statute', 5 *Am. Const. Soc. Sup. Ct. Rev.* (2021) 163, summarizes the majority's reasoning at 173:

> Justice Thomas, writing for eight justices (only Justice Alito declined to join), did not apply the "touch and concern" test from *Kiobel*, but instead relied on an intervening decision, *RJR Nabisco, Inc. v. European Community*, in which the Court articulated a two-step framework. First, "we presume that a statute only applies domestically" and ask "'whether the statute gives a clear, affirmative indication' that rebuts this presumption." Second, where the statute does not overcome the presumption against extraterritorially, "plaintiffs must establish that 'the conduct relevant to the statute's focus occurred in the United States.'" Here, Justice Thomas writes, the statute does not apply extraterritorially, so the question is whether the conduct meets the second step of RJR. Justice Thomas, joined by seven other justices, says no: "Nearly all the conduct that they say aided and abetted forced labor—providing training, fertilizer, tools, and cash to overseas farms—occurred in Ivory Coast." The Ninth Circuit had allowed the case to proceed because plaintiffs— respondents here—pleaded that "every major operational decision by both companies is made in or approved in the U.S." But "general corporate activity— like decisionmaking— cannot alone establish domestic application of the ATS." In *Kiobel*, the Court had held that it was not enough to simply allege "mere corporate presence." Here, Justice Thomas writes, "Pleading general corporate activity is no better." He elaborates, "generic allegations of this sort do not draw a sufficient connection between the cause of actions respondents seek—aiding and abetting forced labor overseas—and domestic conduct." He concludes, "To plead facts sufficient to support a domestic application of the ATS, plaintiffs must allege more domestic conduct than general corporate activity."

For many commentators, the Court's reasoning on jurisdiction effectively foreclosed the ATS as a route to corporate accountability for human rights abuses. If 'general corporate activity' – such as operational decision-making, payments and other assistance to alleged violators, and lobbying against transparency regulations – was insufficiently connected with the statute's focus to rebut the presumption against extraterritoriality, it is unclear which, if any, activities would suffice to establish jurisdiction.

In some respects, however, the Court's decision did not neuter the ATS to the extent some had feared. The majority did not favour an interpretation of the ATS which would involve total immunity for corporate defendants: five judges made it clear in their opinions that they would reject such an interpretation, while the remainder were silent on the issue. Further, only Justices Thomas, Gorsuch and Kavanaugh would have followed Justice Scalia in limiting causes of action under the ATS to the three historical offences identified in *Sosa*. Oona A. Hathaway (above, 5 *Am. Const. Soc. Sup. Ct. Rev.* (2021) at 174 provides a tentatively optimistic interpretation of the Court's reasoning:

> But what about corporate cases? It's possible that the Court means exactly what it says— it's not enough to assert "general corporate activity." Instead, the pleadings should have done more to connect the dots between the human rights violations that took place in Ivory Coast and the corporate decisions made in the United States. …
>
> …
>
> Some or all of the justices (though, interestingly, not Justice Alito himself) may have come away from [the plaintiffs' oral argument] convinced that the pleadings were not sufficiently specific to establish that corporate conduct that supported aiding and abetting liability took place in the United States. If that is correct, then the impact of *Nestlé* might be less significant, at least for corporate cases. It would simply mean that plaintiffs must more specifically allege that the corporate conduct in the United States specifically aided and abetted the human rights violations abroad.

c. The future of the ATS

Many commentators do not, however, share Hathaway's optimism for the future of corporate accountability claims under the ATS. The post-*Nestlé* ATS has been described as 'functionally … dead letter as a tool to address transnational human-rights violations by companies'.[542] Clara Petch, in 'What Remains of the Alien Tort Statute after *Nestlé USA, Inc. v. Doe?*', 42 *Nw. J. Int'l L. & Bus.* (2022) 397 at 420 is circumspect in her analysis:

> …despite the Supreme Court's continual chipping away of the ATS's jurisdictional reach, the ATS still formally provides avenues for bringing suit. As far as named defendants are concerned, ATS precedent permits suit against domestic parties. While there is debate over whether the ATS authorizes liability for any foreign party, the Supreme Court has not yet foreclosed the option to sue a foreign individual. With respect to causes of action, plaintiffs can bring suit for specifically defined and universally accepted international offenses under *Sosa*, including genocide, war crimes, crimes against humanity, slavery, and terrorism.
>
> However, neither an egregious violation of international law nor a domestic defendant engaging in activities within the United States alone will establish grounds for jurisdiction. The pattern of litigation over the past decade indicates that the presumption against extraterritoriality and foreign policy concerns enshrined in the modern ATS framework present significant obstacles. As a practical matter, it is striking that the Supreme Court has never permitted jurisdiction for an ATS suit and has progressively carved away at the scope of the statute. While, from a doctrinal standpoint, there may still be available avenues for bringing ATS claims, the current trend suggests that the Supreme Court would foreclose them when given the opportunity. Therefore, it would be inadvisable for potential litigants to deplete their resources in the pursuit of ATS litigation at this time.

---

[542] C. Ryerson, D. Pinkert, and A. Kelly, 'Seeking Justice: The State of Transnational Corporate Accountability', *The Yale* L. J. F. (22 December 2022), 806.

Legislative reform of the ATS has been proposed as one solution. The Alien Tort Statute Clarification Act (ATSCA) was introduced in 2022 by Senators Dick Durbin (D-IL) and Sherrod Brown (D-OH). It aims to clarify that the statute's extraterritorial application extends to 'any tort…if … an alleged defendant is a national of the United States or an alien lawfully admitted for permanent residence … or an alleged defendant is present in the United States, irrespective of the nationality of the alleged defendant'. This language mirrors the 2008 amendment to the Trafficking Victims Protection Reauthorization Act (TVPRA), which has been accepted by U.S. courts as extending the statute's extraterritorial application to corporations as well as natural persons, as well as European Union regulations limiting *forum non conveniens* and extraterritoriality doctrines. However, Hassan M. Ahmad, in 'Judicial Activism in Transnational Business and Human Rights Litigation', 42 *Berkeley J. Int'l L.* (2024) cautions that:

> … the ATSCA is unlikely to pass into law. Distinct from the Torture Victim Protection Act (TVPA) and the Trafficking Victims Protections Reauthorization Act that cannot compel corporations to compensate foreign plaintiffs, the ATSCA … would allow for foreign plaintiffs to access corporate revenues. Given that some of the largest U.S-headquartered MNCs that undertake extractive and manufacturing operations in the Global South have considerable lobbying power over Congress and have previously avowed to oppose attempts at finding them liable for human rights violations abroad "until hell freezes over", it is improbable they will likely let up now. …

Unless a reformed ATS becomes a reality, or the Supreme Court signals a change of course, it is likely that suits under the statute will continue to decline. In their retrospective on the ATS, Oona A. Hathaway et al. (above) suggest (at 1299) that this may be a helpful juncture to critically evaluate both the statute's impact and the role of strategic litigation generally:

> Has the ATS made a difference? Yes, but not necessarily in the ways one might expect. ATS suits have not been very successful in bringing about monetary awards that are actually paid. Nonetheless, the process of litigation has led to a number of significant monetary settlements, including for the plaintiffs in Nestle. … Moreover, the incidence of private settlement of ATS complaints has brought to the fore the tension between the material and normative aims of human rights cases, because private dispute resolution generally precludes public scrutiny of the human rights violations, and it often represents a missed opportunity to affirm and develop legal norms and standards of accountability.

> ATS litigation has also brought normative benefits not always reflected in financial payments: Through the process of litigation, survivors of human rights abuse have been able to exercise their voices and reclaim a measure of dignity by defending their rights. ATS suits have also exposed inadequacies in the current legal regime, providing ammunition to human rights organizations that advocate for legal and policy reform. Perhaps the greatest contribution of ATS suits to the collective interest in greater accountability for human rights abuse has been the exposure of the mismatch between social expectations about the protection of human rights and the actual legal protection of these rights. …

> The story of the ATS offers [broader] lessons … . By design, litigation alone cannot bring about broad social change. Instead, litigation is most effective when used in tandem with other strategies—including activism, harnessing media attention, and highlighting the individual stories of those who have long been ignored to bring about legislative reform and change in practice on the ground. … It may be that the ATS will make its greatest difference by exposing the limits of litigation alone to secure even the most basic human rights.

QUESTIONS

1. Other than the three historical paradigms identified in Sosa and subsequent cases, which violations of the law of nations might plausibly constitute causes of action under the ATS? Do you agree with the Supreme Court's decision to restrict possible causes of action in this manner?

2. What challenges might a claimant face in pleading specific corporate activity tying a company's actions in the United States to human rights abuses in other countries?

3. How do you explain the evolution of the Court's approach to jurisdiction, from the 'touch and concern' test in *Kiobel* to its application of the *Nabisco* test in *Nestlé*?

2. Other Avenues for Civil Litigation in the United States

Some alternative statutory avenues exist through which victims of foreign human rights abuses may seek compensation.[543] However, the extent to which these can provide broad-based relief, particularly in cases against corporations, remains unclear.

a. The Torture Victim Protection Act (TVPA)[544]

The TVPA, passed in 1991, was intended to complement the ATS and carry out the intent of the Convention Against Torture, which the United States had ratified the year prior. It provides rights for both citizens and non-citizens to bring civil suits against natural persons for acts of torture and extrajudicial killing committed outside the United States. The TVPA is in some respects more favourable to claimants than the ATS: extraterritorial jurisdiction under the TVPA is explicitly authorized and unambiguous, and plaintiffs may be either aliens or U.S. nationals. While the statute commenced in 1992, plaintiffs have in some circumstances been able to recover for conduct well before that date, provided that the conduct complained of constituted a violation of relevant customary international law at the time. In *Cabello v. Fernández-Larios,* 402 F.3d 1148, (11th Circuit 2005), for example, the court granted compensation to the estate of a Chilean economist executed by officials of the Pinochet regime during the 1973 'Caravan of Death'.

However, the TVPA has important limitations as a route to civil compensation for victims of overseas human rights abuses. Victims can only recover against natural persons – that is, there is no right of action, including for aiding and abetting, against states, organizations or corporate defendants[545] – and must have exhausted domestic remedies in the jurisdiction where the torture occurred. Further, a defendant must have acted 'under actual or apparent authority, or color of law, of any foreign nation'.[546] It is therefore only available where a victim has been subjected to torture by agents of a foreign power, and only against those agents – not, for example, a corporation which aided and abetted the torture.

b. The Trafficking Victims Protection Reauthorization Act (TVPRA)[547]

The TVPRA has been proposed as a promising alternative route to corporate liability. In addition to providing extraterritorial jurisdiction over crimes associated with forced labour and human trafficking, the TVPRA allows trafficking victims to file civil suits against any defendant who 'knowingly benefits, or attempts or conspires to benefit, financially or by receiving anything of value from participation in a venture which that person knew or should have known has engaged in [human trafficking or forced labour]'.

TVPRA lawsuits against corporations using forced labour have seen some success. In 2021, the United States District Court for the Northern Mariana Islands awarded almost $6,000,000 to Chinese construction workers who had been lured to the island with promises of good wages and U.S. green cards.[548] The defendant corporations (based in mainland China and Hong Kong) charged the plaintiffs large recruitment fees, smuggled

---

[543] See generally E. Aristova and U. Grusic (eds.), *Civil Remedies and Human Rights in Flux: Key Legal Developments in Selected Jurisdictions* (2023).
[544] Pub. L. No. 102–256, 106 Stat.73 (1992).
[545] See, e.g., *Mohamad v. Palestinian Authority*, 566 U.S. 449 (2012).
[546] TVPA, section 2(a).
[547] 18 U.S.C. § 1589, 18 U.S.C. § 1590, 18 U.S.C. § 1595 and 18 U.S.C. § 1596.
[548] *Wang et al. v. Gold Mantis Construction Decoration* LLC., United States District Court for the Northern Mariana Islands, Civil Action No. 1:18-cv-00030 (24 May 2021).

them into the island on tourist visas and confiscated their passports, subjected them to up to 24-hour workdays, provided cramped and unsanitary quarters, denied them medical treatment for workplace injuries, and threatened harm or deportation if they reported these conditions.

Attempts to use the TVPRA against corporations for violations that occur further down their supply chains, however, have so far been unsuccessful. In 2021 decision, the District Court of Columbia dismissed a petition brought against a number of large electronic companies by a group of Congolese children forced to work in cobalt mines which supplied the raw materials for the companies' products.[549] Notably, the court held that the global supply chains of Apple, Microsoft and others did not constitute a 'venture' within the meaning of the TVPRA.

c. Consumer Protection Litigation

As environmental and social governance (ESG) becomes a branding strategy for corporations, State laws governing misleading or deceptive advertising are emerging as a route through which consumers can make companies accountable for these claims. Two cases before State courts as of 2023 illustrate this trend:

- In *Walker v. Nestlé USA*, the plaintiff consumer sued under California consumer and competition statutes in respect of statements displayed on Nestlé products, including that the cocoa was 'sustainably sourced', certified by a social auditing agency, and that the company is '[s]upporting farmers for better chocolate'. The plaintiff argues that she relied on these claims in purchasing the products, and that these statements are deceptive because the company 'sources its cocoa from West African plantations which rely on child labor and child slave labor, …[and that] the child labor conditions have worsened rather than improved since the inception of the "NESTLÉ® Cocoa Plan"'.[550] In March 2022, a judge of the California District Court denied Nestlé's motion to dismiss the case.

- In October 2021, NGO Corporate Accountability Lab commenced proceedings against Hershey and social auditing scheme Rainforest Alliance for false and deceptive marketing representations under Washington, D.C. consumer laws. Its complaint notes that the worst forms of child labour are endemic and well-known in farms in West Africa, from which Hershey sources most of its cocoa.[551]

If these cases are successful, strategic consumer protection litigation may be the next frontier for corporate accountability in the United States. These types of cases can incentivize meaningful transparency and better supply chain practices by multinational corporations. However, they offer limited scope for remediating third-party victims of corporate human rights abuses.

d. International Arbitration

Some scholars have proposed that international investment arbitration may be the next frontier for human rights claims against corporations. In 2016, in *Urbaser v. Argentina*, an arbitral tribunal accepted that 'the human right for everyone's dignity and its right for adequate housing and living conditions are complemented by an obligation on all parts, public and private parties, not to engage in activity aimed at destroying such rights'.[552] However, it did not find that this founded an obligation on the part of an investor to provide water and sanitation services in a manner consistent with the local community's right to water.[553]

The treatment of corporate human rights obligations in *Urbaser* remained somewhat ambivalent. More ambitious proposals exist for incorporating human rights into the investment treaty system: for example, some treaties drafted recently make express reference to human rights. A group of international lawyers published

---

[549] *John Doe v. Apple Inc., et al.*, United States District Court, District of Columbia, Civil Action No. 1:19-cv-03737 (2 November 2021).

[550] *Walker v. Nestlé USA, Inc.*, United States District Court, S.D. California, Case No.: 3:19-cv-723-L-DEB (28 March 2022).

[551] https://corpaccountabilitylab.org/calblog/2021/11/2/cal-files-suit-against-hershey-and-rainforest-alliancenbsp.

[552] *Urbaser S.A. et al. v. The Argentine Republic* (Award of 8 December 2016), ICSID Case No. ARB/07/26, at 1199.

[553] *ibid.*, 1207.

model Rules on Business and Human Rights Arbitration in 2019,[554] and others have even proposed an international tribunal to resolve human rights complaints related to corporate activity.[555] However, whether investment arbitration can serve as a suitable vehicle for human rights claims will also depend on whether it can overcome the structural hurdles of confidential proceedings, limited opportunities for third-party intervention, and narrow grounds for appeal.

QUESTIONS

1. Which, if any, of the paradigms above do you think are a convincing alternative to the ATS for victims of overseas human rights violations seeking a civil remedy?

2. How far should a corporation's liability for human rights abuses in its supply chain extend?

---

3. Civil Litigation of Human Rights Claims in Other Jurisdictions

As ATS suits recede, plaintiffs are increasingly seeing success in other jurisdictions. Recent decisions in Canada and the United Kingdom, as well as the introduction of mandatory due diligence laws in the European Union, signal a more progressive approach to corporate accountability.

a. Canada

In 2020, the British Columbia Supreme Court handed down a decision in *Nevsun Resources Ltd. v. Araya*.[556] The defendant, a Vancouver-based mining company, had developed and held a majority stake in an Eritrean mine, pursuant to an agreement with the government. The case was brought by a group of Eritrean refugees living in Canada, who had been indefinitely conscripted to work at the mine pursuant to a national service program. They claimed that their treatment violated prohibitions against slavery, forced labour, cruel, inhuman and degrading treatment and crimes against humanity under customary international law. Nevsun sought to strike out the claim on the basis that (a) the Canadian courts could not assess the sovereign acts of Eritrea's government (the 'act of state' doctrine); and (b) that claims based on customary international law were bound to fail.

The Court dismissed Nevsun's motion. It held by a 7:2 majority that the 'act of state' doctrine did not apply in Canada, and by a 5:4 majority, that customary international law formed part of Canadian common law. It could thus to some degree bind corporations, and be considered by a trial court. The case would not, however, go to trial: the parties reached a confidential settlement later that year.

Although the question whether Nevsun was bound by the customary human rights norms was never judicially resolved, *Nevsun v. Araya* is a landmark case. Beatrice A. Walton, in a case note on the decision, suggests that:

> … *Nevsun* may well prove a watershed moment for human rights plaintiffs in Canada seeking to invoke customary international law. The opinion also provides a model for other national courts looking to make use of customary international law more generally. *Nevsun* is equally important as a case about corporate social responsibility, particularly in finding that it is possible for a court to apply customary international law to corporations in a suit at common law. After the U.S. Supreme Court's decision in *Arab Bank v. Jesner* that foreign corporations cannot be held liable under the ATS, *Nevsun* provides a

---

[554] B. Simma et al., *The Hague Rules on Business and Human Rights Arbitration* (June 2019), https://www.cilc.nl/cms/wp-content/uploads/2019/06/Draft-BHR-Rules-Final-version-for-Public-consultation.pdf.
[555] C. Cronstedt and R. C. Thompson, 'A Proposal for an International Arbitration Tribunal on Business and Human Rights', 57 *Harvard Int'l L. J.* (2016) 66.
[556] [2020] S.C.C. 5 (Can.).

resounding reply in substance and in form to the U.S. Supreme Court's increasing hostility to transnational human rights litigation. …

…

At the most basic level, the fact that customary international law is "part of" the common law means that Canadian courts can fashion new torts inspired by custom, as common law courts do in other areas of law. But the fact that custom is "part of" Canadian law also has significant ramifications for the claims said to be brought under international law "directly." Even with respect to these claims, the majority's approach acknowledges, even embraces, a reasonable degree of discretion in translating international law into the common law. An important example of this comes in relation to the debate over which body of law supplies the various aspects of these claims. …

…

… The *Nevsun* majority suggests that even if a norm has a strictly interstate character, it may be possible for the common law to "evolve so as to extend the scope of th[e] norm to bind corporations" to corporations (para. 113). Whether these more flexible approaches to custom take hold, and the ultimate success of customary international law claims in Canada, remains to be seen in further appeals.[557]

b. The United Kingdom

In two recent cases, the Supreme Court of the United Kingdom has held that a parent company based in the Global North can in some circumstances owe a duty of care to people affected by the impact of its subsidiaries' activities in other countries.

Vedanta Resources PLC & Anor v Lungowe & Ors [2019] 1 CLC 619 involved negligence and breach of statutory duty claims brought by a group of Zambian citizens against Vedanta and its subsidiary, KCM, claiming that a copper mine run by KCM had polluted local watercourses. In support of their claim against the parent company, the plaintiffs argued that Vedanta had '…exercised a sufficiently high level of supervision and control of the activities at the mine, with sufficient knowledge of the propensity of those activities to cause toxic escapes into surrounding watercourses, as to incur a duty of care to the claimants.'[558] This supervision, they alleged, was supported by 'material published by Vedanta in which it asserted its responsibility for the establishment of appropriate group-wide environmental control and sustainability standards, for their implementation throughout the group by training, and for their monitoring and enforcement.'[559]

The Supreme Court, considering Vedanta's jurisdictional challenge, found that the claimants' case was arguable and not an abuse of EU law. In relation to the question whether a parent company could have a duty of care to third parties in respect of its subsidiary's actions, the court stated:

> Even where group-wide policies do not of themselves give rise to such a duty of care to third parties, they may do so if the parent does not merely proclaim them, but takes active steps, by training, supervision and enforcement, to see that they are implemented by relevant subsidiaries. Similarly, … the parent may incur the relevant responsibility to third parties if, in published materials, it holds itself out as exercising that degree of supervision and control of its subsidiaries, even if it does not in fact do so. In such circumstances its very omission may constitute the abdication of a responsibility which it has publicly undertaken.[560]

---

557 Beatrice A. Walton, 'Case Note: *Nevsun Resources Ltd. v. Araya*, Case No. 37919' 115 *Am. J. Int'l L.* (2021) 107.
558 *Vedanta Resources* PLC & *Anor v. Lungowe & Ors* [2019] 1 CLC 619, para. 55.
559 *Ibid.*
560 *Ibid.*, para 53.

The court found the question of whether England (and not Zambia) was the proper forum for the litigation a more difficult question, stating:

> This case seeks compensation for a large number of extremely poor Zambian residents for negligence or breach of Zambian statutory duty in connection with the escape within Zambia of noxious substances arising in connection with the operation of a Zambian mine. If substantial justice was available to the parties in Zambia as it is in England, it would offend the common sense of all reasonable observers to think that the proper place for this litigation to be conducted was England, if the risk of irreconcilable judgments arose purely from the claimants' choice to proceed against one of the defendants in England rather than, as is available to them, against both of them in Zambia. …[561]

However, after carefully considering the poverty of the applicants and the lack of funding available to class action participants in Zambia (including the failure of similar cases where claimants had been unable to afford to obtain expert evidence), the court found that it would be unjust to remove the case to Zambian courts.

The reasoning in *Vedanta* was subsequently applied in *Okpabi & Ors v. Royal Dutch Shell Plc & Anor* [2021] WLR 1294, a jurisdictional appeal involving claims by Nigerian plaintiffs that Royal Dutch Shell (RDS) had failed to fulfil its duty of care to properly clean and remediate oil spills from its subsidiary's infrastructure. As in *Vedanta*, the claimants adduced evidence that RDS 'exercised significant control over material aspects of SPDC's operations and/or assumed responsibility for SPDC's operations, including by the promulgation and imposition of mandatory health, safety and environmental policies, standards and manuals which allegedly failed to protect the appellants against the risk of foreseeable harm arising from SPDC's operations.'[562] Applying *Vedanta*, the Court held that the plaintiffs had an arguable case.

c. The European Union

Commentators have noted that a 'growth of legal activism among campaigning NGOs in Europe' in recent years has strengthened the culture of public interest and impact litigation in the EU.[563] In the Netherlands, for example, Friends of the Earth supported a group of Nigerian farmers to file claims against Royal Dutch Shell concerning – as in the UK case of *Okpabi* – oil pipeline leaks. This litigation, commenced in 2008, eventually produced a settlement of 15 million euros for the plaintiffs in December 2022.[564]

Another important development in this context is the 2024 European Commission due diligence directive, considered in Ch. 13A, below.

* * *

The developments above indicate that some parts of the Global North are broadening the scope for civil claims against multinational corporations for overseas human rights violations. On one view, this indicates that wealthy countries are increasingly prepared to accept responsibility for damage caused by businesses headquartered in their jurisdictions and from whose profits their economies benefit. On another, confining this kind of litigation to courts outside the countries in which the relevant harms occurred reflects legal imperialism and stunts the development of the law in Global South countries.[565]

E. SOVEREIGN AND OFFICIAL IMMUNITY

Civil suits, especially those pursued under the ATS and TVPA, often end in default judgments and generally do not result in actual payment of damages. Several obstacles thwart the attainment of financial compensation.

---

[561] *Ibid.*, para 87.
[562] *Okpabi & Ors v. Royal Dutch Shell Plc & Anor* [2021] WLR 1294, para 7.
[563] See, e.g., R. Chambers and G. Berger Walliser, 'The Future of International Corporate Human Rights Litigation: A Transatlantic Comparison', 58 *Am. Bus. L. J.* (2021) 579, 634.
[564] Reuters, 'Shell to pay 15 mln euros in settlement over Nigerian oil spills' (23 December 2022).
[565] D. Palombo, 'Rejecting Jurisdiction to Avoid Imperialism – That Simple?', *Opinio Juris* (25 June 2021).

Individual defendants often do not have deep pockets. In contrast with criminal cases, defendants may also freely leave the country. Also, foreign enforcement of judgments is usually difficult if not practically impossible. Suits against two types of defendants — corporations and governments — do not pose such obstacles. This part considers obstacles that uniquely affect suits against states and state officials, the type of cases in which plaintiffs might have a real prospect of achieving compensation but where principles of immunity can close off such avenues. Indeed, questions of immunity have frequently arisen in cases under the ATS. The first group of cases set out below concerns the ability of plaintiffs to sue a foreign state directly. The second involves attempts to sue particular individuals in their official or personal capacity when those individuals claim to be protected by immunity.

1. Foreign State Immunity from Human Rights Prosecutions

Depending on the jurisdiction in which a claim is brought, foreign state immunity will be governed by complementary and often overlapping regimes derived from customary international law, treaties, and domestic legislation. The principle that a foreign state is (subject to certain enumerated exceptions) immune from the jurisdiction of the courts of another state is well-established in customary international law.[566] It is also set out the 1972 European Convention on State Immunity (Basle Convention) and the 2004 United Nations Convention on Jurisdictional Immunities of State and Their Property. In the United States, the Foreign Sovereign Immunities Act of 1976 (FSIA), codified principally at 22 U.S.C.A. 1602–11, provides a comprehensive legislative framework for claims of immunity by foreign states, including 'an agency or instrumentality' thereof.

Both international and domestic law provide for limited exceptions to the principle of foreign state immunity. The customary law distinction between a state's *acta jure gestionis* (act of management) and *acta jure imperii* (act of government) is reflected in the exclusion of immunity where a state is engaged in a commercial transaction. Other generally accepted exceptions include circumstances where a state has waived its immunity or submitted itself to the jurisdiction; for employment contracts performed in the territory of a foreign state; in proceedings for pecuniary compensation for death, injury or property damage occurring in a foreign state; and in relation to intellectual and industrial property.

The following cases illustrate how domestic, regional and international courts have examined and applied the law of state immunity.

Argentine Republic v. Amerada Hess Shipping Corp., 488 U.S. 428 (1989), involved an ATS action with origins in the Falklands (Malvinas) war between the United Kingdom and Argentina. It was based on damage to the plaintiff's ship by an attack of Argentinian aircraft. The Supreme Court refused to find an exception to the rule of immunity for suits under the ATS because of Argentina's alleged violation of international law. The Court held that the FSIA is 'the sole basis for obtaining jurisdiction over a foreign state in our courts'. It drew from the FSIA 'the plain implication that immunity is granted in those cases involving alleged violations of international law that do not come within one of the FSIA's exceptions.' Plaintiffs were accordingly required as a threshold matter to satisfy one of the conditions under the FSIA for suspending sovereign immunity. In *Siderman de Blake v. Republic of Argentina*, 965 F.2d 699 (9th Cir. 1992), the Court of Appeals agreed with the plaintiff's argument that official acts of torture attributed to Argentina constituted a violation of a *jus cogens* norm of the 'highest status within international law'. Nonetheless, taking its lesson from the *Amareda Hess* decision in which the Supreme Court was so specific, the court concluded that it was Congress that would have to make any further exceptions to sovereign immunity. 'The fact that there has been a violation of *jus cogens* does not confer jurisdiction under the FSIA.'

In *Al-Adsani v. United Kingdom*, European Court of Human Rights (Grand Chamber), Application No. 35763/97, (21 November 2001), a dual British-Kuwaiti national initiated civil proceedings in the United Kingdom against the Government of Kuwait and individual Kuwaitis for his alleged torture in Kuwait. The UK appellate court permitted Mr Al-Adsani to proceed against the individual Kuwaitis but held that the State Immunity Act 1978

---

[566] See, e.g. International Law Commission, 'Jurisdictional Immunities of States and their Property', 2 Y.B. *Int'l L. Comm'n* (1980) 137 (A/CN.4/SER.A/1980/Add.1 (Part 2)); *Jurisdictional Immunities of the State (Germany v. Italy: Greece Intervening)*, Judgment of 3 February 2012, I.C.J. Rep. 99, paras. 55-57.

barred suit against the Government of Kuwait. Mr Al-Adsani appealed to the European Court of Human Rights, claiming in significant part that the application of state immunity denied him access to a court in violation of Article 6 of the European Convention. The Grand Chamber, by a slim majority (9 votes to 8), rejected his claim, holding that:

> 66. The Court, while noting the growing recognition of the overriding importance of the prohibition of torture, does not accordingly find it established that there is yet acceptance in international law of the proposition that States are not entitled to immunity in respect of civil claims for damages for alleged torture committed outside the forum State. The 1978 Act, which grants immunity to States in respect of personal injury claims unless the damage was caused within the United Kingdom, is not inconsistent with those limitations generally accepted by the community of nations as part of the doctrine of State immunity.

In 2014, the ECtHR affirmed this position in *Jones v. United Kingdom*. This case involved a similar claim by British citizens subjected to torture in Saudi Arabian prisons. Before the European Court, they argued that that the approach in *Al-Adsani* should be reconsidered. The Court declined to do so, holding that it 'was acting in accordance with its obligation to take account of the relevant rules and principles of international law and to interpret the Convention so far as possible in harmony with other rules of international law of which it forms part'.[567]

Jurisdictional Immunities of the State (Germany v. Italy: Greece Intervening), Judgment of 3 February 2012, *I.C.J. Rep.* 99 was a case brought by Germany in response to a series of decisions by Italian courts holding that sovereign immunity did not apply in respect of compensation claims filed by victims of crimes committed by Nazi Germany. The ICJ held that Germany was entitled to immunity, even if the actions of its armed forces and other organs of the state during World War II amounted to violations of *jus cogens* norms:

> 91. The Court concludes that, under customary international law as it presently stands, a State is not deprived of immunity by reason of the fact that it is accused of serious violations of international human rights law or the international law of armed conflict. In reaching that conclusion, the Court must emphasize that it is addressing only the immunity of the State itself from the jurisdiction of the courts of other States; the question of whether, and if so to what extent, immunity might apply in criminal proceedings against an official of the State is not in issue in the present case.

The Court also rejected Italy's argument that sovereign immunity created an inconsistency with states' obligations to have regard to *jus cogens* violations of international law, holding that, 'the two sets of rules address different matters. The rules of State immunity are procedural in character ... . They do not bear upon the question whether or not the conduct in respect of which the proceedings are brought was lawful or unlawful'.

In *Kazemi Estate v. Islamic Republic of Iran* (2014) S.C.C. 62, Canada's Supreme Court came to a similar conclusion. The applicant brought a civil case against Iran for the wrongful detention and torture of himself and his mother, who died as a result of her treatment by the Iranian authorities. The Supreme Court took note of the recent decisions in *Jones* and *Germany v. Italy*. It concluded that the applicant could not take advantage of the 'personal or physical injury' exception to state immunity, as this does not apply if the act causing the injury did not occur in Canada. Further, it held that:

> [104] ... The fact of the matter is that Canada has expressly created an exception to immunity for criminal proceedings, and has stopped short of doing so for civil suits involving *jus cogens* violations ... . Much like the I.C.J., I am convinced that the fact that universal criminal jurisdiction exists has no bearing in the present case (*Germany v. Italy*, at para. 87). The two types of proceeding are seen as fundamentally different by a majority of actors in the international community.

In coming to this decision, the court noted the potential impact on Canada's foreign relations of recognizing universal civil jurisdictions for violations of customary human rights law.

---

[567] *Jones and Others v. The United Kingdom*, European Court of Human Rights, Applications Nos. 34356/06 and 40528/06 (2 June 2014), para. 195.

The cases of *Germany v. Philipp*, 592 U.S. __ (2021) and *Republic of Hungary v. Simon*, 592 U.S. __ (2021) involved attempts by Holocaust survivors to obtain compensation for property expropriated by state authorities during World War II. The plaintiffs claimed that this taking was an act of genocide and thus fell within the FSIA's expropriation exception, which excluded sovereign immunity in respect of 'rights in property taken in violation of international law'. In *Philipp*, the Supreme Court of the United States held unanimously that international law at the time of the FSIA's enactment only prohibited expropriating the property of aliens: expropriation of a state's own citizens' property ('domestic takings') was a matter for domestic law. The expropriation exception in the FSIA was therefore only applicable where a government confiscated the property of foreigners.

The Court in *Philipp* chose not to address the second argument raised by Germany: that it was obligated to abstain from deciding the case on international comity grounds. In *Hungary v. Simon*, which raised only the comity question, the Court vacated the judgment of the D.C. Circuit and remanded it for reconsideration in light of *Philipp*.

2. Immunity of State Officials from Human Rights Prosecutions

Domestic and international courts have also considered whether the acts of state officials can be made the subject of civil claims. State officials may be immune from prosecution on one of two bases: (1) immunity *ratione materiae*, which is applicable to any state official to the extent that they are performing acts of an official nature; and (2) immunity *ratione personae*, which is applicable only to incumbent holders of high office (i.e. heads of state, heads of government, foreign affairs ministers, and diplomatic agents) but covers both official and private acts committed prior to or during their term of office. The cases below involve judicial consideration of the circumstances where immunity *ratione materiae* and *ratione personae* exist in the context of human rights claims.

As discussed above in the context of universal jurisdiction, the case of *Rex v. Bow Street Magistrate, ex parte Pinochet*[568] stems from the 1998 arrest of the former dictator of Chile in London at the request of Spain. The Spanish prosecutor charged Pinochet with authorizing the torture, disappearances and murder of citizens of Chile, as well as Spanish nationals. The question before the House of Lords was whether Pinochet should be extradited to Spain. In order to determine this, they needed to determine whether Pinochet was immune from the jurisdiction of UK courts in respect of his violations of international law. Six of the seven Law Lords concluded that Pinochet did not enjoy immunity from prosecution for these acts and should therefore be extradited. However, their reasoning for so doing varied, with some indicating that they would not have decided in this manner if the case concerned a violation of a *jus cogens* norm, rather than a violation of the Torture Convention.

Lord Saville reasoned that the Torture Convention necessarily eliminated Pinochet's official immunity for the crime of torture. Lord Browne-Wilkinson agreed, indicating his view that there was a 'strong ground for saying that the implementation of torture as defined by the Torture Convention cannot be a state function.' However, he expressed doubt that a crime against customary international law or *jus cogens* would be sufficient to overcome an immunity:

> I have doubts whether, before the coming into force of the Torture Convention, the existence of the international crime of torture as *jus cogens* was enough to justify the conclusion that the organisation of state torture could not rank for immunity purposes as performance of an official function. At that stage there was no international tribunal to punish torture and no general jurisdiction to permit or require its punishment in domestic courts. Not until there was some form of universal jurisdiction for the punishment of the crime of torture could it really be talked about as a fully constituted international crime.

Lord Hope of Craighead added:

> … [T]here remains the question whether the immunity can survive Chile's agreement to the Torture Convention if the torture which is alleged was of such a kind or on such a scale as to amount to an international crime. …

---

[568] *R v. Bow Street Metropolitan Stipendiary Magistrate, ex parte Pinochet Ugarte* (No. 3), 2 WLR 827 (1999).

...

> Despite the difficulties which I have mentioned, I think that there are sufficient signs that
> the necessary developments in international law were in place by [29 September 1998, the
> date of entry into force of the Criminal Justice Act].

...

> I would not regard this as a case of waiver. Nor would I accept that it was an implied
> term of the Torture Convention that former heads of state were to be deprived of their
> immunity *ratione materiae* with respect to all acts of official torture as defined in article 1. It
> is just that the obligations which were recognised by customary international law in the
> case of such serious international crimes by the date when Chile ratified the Convention
> are so strong as to override any objection by it on the ground of immunity *ratione materiae*
> to the exercise of the jurisdiction over crimes committed after that date which the United
> Kingdom had made available.

Three years later, in *Arrest Warrant Of 11 April 2000 (Democratic Republic of The Congo v. Belgium)*,[569] the International Court of Justice was called upon to determine the validity of Belgium's issue and circulation of an arrest warrant against the incumbent foreign minister of the DRC. The ICJ held by 13 votes to three that no exception to the principle of immunity *ratione personae* exists in customary international law, even where an incumbent holder of high office is suspected of having committed war crimes or crimes against humanity. However, it emphasized '...that the immunity from jurisdiction enjoyed by incumbent Ministers for Foreign Affairs does not mean that they enjoy impunity in respect of any crimes they might have committed, irrespective of their gravity.'[570] It set out four circumstances in which immunity would not bar the prosecution of a high-ranking state official: (1) in cases brought against them by their courts of their own countries; (2) if the state they represent waives their immunity; (3) when they cease to hold office, in which case they may be tried in respect of 'acts committed prior or subsequent to his or her period of office, as well as in respect of acts committed during that period of office in a private capacity'; and (4) where they are subject to proceedings before specific international criminal courts with jurisdiction, such as the ICTY, ICTR or ICC.[571] In particular, the court noted that the ICC Statute expressly states that immunities do not bar the Court from exercising its jurisdiction over defendants.

In *Samantar v. Yousuf* 560 U.S. 305 (2010), the Supreme Court of the U.S. was called upon to decide a case brought against a former member of the Somali government. The plaintiffs had sued under the ATS and TVPA, alleging that they had suffered torture and other human rights violations at his hands. The defendant claimed that he was entitled to immunity under the FSIA; as, he argued, this statute immunized a foreign official for acts taken on behalf of the foreign state. The Supreme Court disagreed, holding that Congress did not intend the FSIA to codify the immunity of officials – only of states – and remanded the matter to the District Court to determine whether he was entitled to immunity under the common law. However, the Court observed that sovereign immunity might still preclude the exercise of jurisdiction in some circumstances:

> [N]ot every suit can successfully be pleaded against an individual official alone. Even
> when a plaintiff names only a foreign official, it may be the case that the foreign state
> itself, its political subdivision, or an agency or instrumentality is a required party, because
> that party has "an interest relating to the subject of the action" and "disposing of the
> action in the person's absence may ... as a practical matter impair or impede the person's
> ability to protect the interest." Fed. Rule Civ. Proc. 19(a)(1)(B). If this is the case, and the
> entity is immune from suit under the FSIA, the district court may have to dismiss the suit,
> regardless of whether the official is immune or not under the common law. ... Or it may
> be the case that some actions against an official in his official capacity should be treated
> as actions against the foreign state itself, as the state is the real party in interest. ...

[569] Judgment of 14 February 2002, I.C.J. *Rep.* 3.
[570] Para. 60.
[571] Para. 61.

In January 2021, the German Federal Court of Justice (BGH), delivered a landmark judgment concerning the immunity of foreign state officials who committed grave violations of international law.[572] The case concerned an officer in the Afghan army who had mistreated captured Taliban officers and desecrated the body of a deceased Taliban member; there was some debate as to whether these actions amounted to torture or a war crime. Ultimately, the BGH held that war crimes prosecutions would not be precluded on the basis of immunity where the acts were 'committed by a foreign, lower-ranking defendant in the exercise of foreign sovereign activity against non-domestic persons.'[573] It therefore abstained from referring this question to the German Federal Constitutional Court.[574]

Tom Syring, in 'Judgment on Foreign Soldiers' Immunity for War Crimes Committed Abroad (BGH)' 61 *Int'l Legal Materials* (2022) 483, at 485, notes that:

> While the Court's reasoning and concomitant decision not to refer the question of functional immunity to the Federal Constitutional Court may be contestable from the vantage point of legal theory, it is all the more understandable from a practical perspective: a referral would likely have taken several years and put on hold—if not jeopardized altogether—several current and future cases. ... [F]rom a legal policy perspective, this is an important judgment ... .

QUESTIONS

1. Is there a consistent thread that runs between the treatment of immunity in the Pinochet case and the 2021 BGH decision? Should other courts follow the BGH decision?

2. What role should international comity play in relation to claims of immunity?

---

[572] Bundesgerichtshof [BHG], 3 StR 654/19, Case No. ECLI:DE:BGH:2021:280121U3STR564.19.0 (28 January 2021).

[573] Translation provided in T. Syring, 'Judgment on Foreign Soldiers' Immunity for War Crimes Committed Abroad (BGH)' 61 *Int'l Legal Materials* (2022) 483, 487.

[574] For more detail, see L. Sadat, 'New Developments in State Practice on Immunity of State Officials for International Crimes' 25 ASIL *Insights* (23 September 2021).

Chapter 13. Non-State Actors: Businesses and Others

One of the most dramatic developments within international human rights law over the past three decades has been the growing importance of a range of non-state actors. The centrality of the state is one of the defining features of international law and the human rights system builds upon this by seeking to bind states through a network of treaty obligations to which, in the vast majority of cases, only states can become parties. Non-state actors are thus, by definition, placed at the margins of the resulting legal regime. The problem is that actors such as corporations and other businesses, civil society groups, international organizations and armed opposition groups, to name just the most prominent among a wide range of potentially important non-state actors, have all assumed major roles in relation to the enjoyment of human rights, especially in recent years.

Various factors have contributed to this development. They include: (1) the privatization of functions previously performed by governments, including in relation to social welfare services, prisons, asylum processing, schools, adoptions, health-care provision for the poor, and the supply of water, gas and electricity; (2) the ever-increasing mobility of capital and the increased importance of foreign investment flows, facilitated by market deregulation and trade liberalization; (3) the expanding responsibilities of multilateral organizations, some of which have been called upon to exercise a wide range of governmental functions in areas ranging from Kosovo and East Timor to Afghanistan and Iraq; (4) the enormous growth in the role played by transnational civil society organizations, many of which now have multimillion dollar budgets, employ very large staffs, and perform public-type functions in many countries; (5) the changing nature of conflicts, which has seen a growth in the number and proportion of internal conflicts and a subsequent rise in the importance of organized armed groups controlling territory and population and aspiring to gain international legitimacy; and (6) the growth of international terrorist and criminal networks, which are not confined to any one state and some of whose activities have become global in scope.

These developments have increased the risk that a human rights regime that addresses itself effectively only to states will become increasingly marginalized in the years ahead. The phenomenon of privatizing security through the 'outsourcing' of military and military-support functions, even in wartime, provides a good illustration. As recently as the 1980s, there was widespread opposition to the role played by such 'mercenaries'. But the twenty-first century has witnessed a broad and potentially almost unlimited role being accorded to private contractors in conflict situations, from Afghanistan to Ukraine. A similar phenomenon is also occurring in many other sectors of society, including prisons, policing, healthcare, education, and public transport.

This chapter looks at the role of non-state actors in three specific situations. The first concerns the endeavours, primarily within the UN setting, to articulate and implement human rights obligations for corporations. The second examines the extent to which the existing framework of human rights law is capable of addressing the role of armed opposition groups. And the third looks at the human rights obligations of international organizations, including the UN itself, the World Bank and other major institutional actors.

Before engaging with these specific contexts, note should be taken of the approach to non-state actors adopted by human rights bodies, such as the UN Human Rights Committee and the Committee on Economic and Social Rights.

The Human Right Committee stated in its General Comment No. 31 (2004) on 'the nature of the general legal obligation imposed on States Parties to the Covenant' that:

> The article 2, paragraph 1, obligations ['to respect and to ensure to all individuals within its territory and subject to its jurisdiction the rights recognized …'] are binding on States Parties and do not, as such, have direct horizontal effect as a matter of international law. The Covenant cannot be viewed as a substitute for domestic criminal or civil law. However, the positive obligations on States Parties to ensure Covenant rights will only be fully discharged if individuals are protected by the State, not just against violations of Covenant rights by its agents, but also against acts committed by private persons or entities that would impair the enjoyment of Covenant rights in so far as they are amenable to application between private persons or entities. There may be circumstances in which a failure to ensure Covenant rights as required by article 2 would give rise to

violations by States Parties of those rights, as a result of States Parties' permitting or failing to take appropriate measures or to exercise due diligence to prevent, punish, investigate or redress the harm caused by such acts by private persons or entities. ...

In General Comment No. 36, on the right to life, the same Committee said in 2018:

> 22. States parties must take appropriate measures to protect individuals against deprivation of life by other States, international organizations and foreign corporations operating within their territory or in other areas subject to their jurisdiction. They must also take appropriate legislative and other measures to ensure that all activities taking place in whole or in part within their territory and in other places subject to their jurisdiction, but having a direct and reasonably foreseeable impact on the right to life of individuals outside their territory, including activities taken by corporate entities based in their territory or subject to their jurisdiction, are consistent with article 6, taking due account of related international standards of corporate responsibility, and of the right of victims to obtain an effective remedy.

In 2011, a group of international experts, convened by Maastricht University and the International Commission of Jurists, adopted the Maastricht Principles on Extraterritorial Obligations of States in the Area of Economic, Social and Cultural Rights, which provide, inter alia:[575]

> ...

> *8. Definition of extraterritorial obligations*

> For the purposes of these Principles, extraterritorial obligations encompass:

> a) obligations relating to the acts and omissions of a State, within or beyond its territory, that have effects on the enjoyment of human rights outside of that State's territory; ...

> ...

> *24. Obligation to regulate*

> All States must take necessary measures to ensure that non-State actors which they are in a position to regulate, as set out in Principle 25, such as private individuals and organisations, and transnational corporations and other business enterprises, do not nullify or impair the enjoyment of economic, social and cultural rights. ...

> *25. Bases for protection*

> States must adopt and enforce measures to protect economic, social and cultural rights through legal and other means, including diplomatic means, in each of the following circumstances:

> a) the harm or threat of harm originates or occurs on its territory;

> b) where the non-State actor has the nationality of the State concerned;

> c) as regards business enterprises, where the corporation, or its parent or controlling company, has its centre of activity, is registered or domiciled, or has its main place of business or substantial business activities, in the State concerned;

---

[575] See O. De Schutter et al., 'Commentary to the Maastricht Principles on Extraterritorial Obligations of States in the Area of Economic, Social and Cultural Rights', 34 *Hum. Rts.* Q. (2012) 1084; but cf. R. Wilde, 'Socioeconomic Rights, Extraterritorially', in E. Benvenisti and G. Nolte (eds.), *Community Interests Across International Law* (2018) 381.

d) where there is a reasonable link between the State concerned and the conduct it seeks to regulate, including where relevant aspects of a non-State actor's activities are carried out in that State's territory; …

Apparently drawing inspiration from the Maastricht Principles, the UN Committee on Economic, Social and Cultural Rights adopted General Comment No. 24 (2017) on State obligations under the [ICESCR] in the context of business activities:[576]

11. The present general comment addresses the States parties to the Covenant, and in that context it only deals with the conduct of private actors — including business entities — indirectly. In accordance with international law, however, States parties may be held directly responsible for the action or inaction of business entities: (a) if the entity concerned is in fact acting on that State party's instructions or is under its control or direction in carrying out the particular conduct at issue, as may be the case in the context of public contracts; (b) when a business entity is empowered under the State party's legislation to exercise elements of governmental authority or if the circumstances call for such exercise of governmental functions in the absence or default of the official authorities; or (c) if and to the extent that the State party acknowledges and adopts the conduct as its own.

…

28. Extraterritorial obligations arise when a State party may influence situations located outside its territory, consistent with the limits imposed by international law, by controlling the activities of corporations domiciled in its territory and/or under its jurisdiction, and thus may contribute to the effective enjoyment of economic, social and cultural rights outside its national territory

2. Extraterritorial obligation to protect

30. The extraterritorial obligation to protect requires States parties to take steps to prevent and redress infringements of Covenant rights that occur outside their territories due to the activities of business entities over which they can exercise control, … .

…

33. In discharging their duty to protect, States parties should also require corporations to deploy their best efforts to ensure that entities whose conduct those corporations may influence, such as subsidiaries (including all business entities in which they have invested, whether registered under the State party's laws or under the laws of another State) or business partners (including suppliers, franchisees and subcontractors), respect Covenant rights. Corporations domiciled in the territory and/or jurisdiction of States parties should be required to act with due diligence to identify, prevent and address abuses to Covenant rights by such subsidiaries and business partners, wherever they may be located. The Committee underlines that, although the imposition of such due diligence obligations does have impacts on situations located outside these States' national territories since potential violations of Covenant rights in global supply chains or in multinational groups of companies should be prevented or addressed, this does not imply the exercise of extraterritorial jurisdiction by the States concerned. …

---

[576] For a critique, see D. Birchall, 'Reconstructing State Obligations to Protect and Fulfil Socio-Economic Rights in an Era of Marketisation', 71 *I.C.L.Q.* (2022) 227.

A. BUSINESS AND HUMAN RIGHTS (BHR)

The relationships between states and corporations, especially regarding issues of human rights, must be considered in their historical context. This involves recognizing elements of continuity running from colonial times through to today. The excerpt below from Doreen Lustig provides both a historical overview and an outline of the formal framework of international law that applies. It is also important to understand that, notwithstanding efforts to develop forms of accountability as described later in this chapter, international law and multilateral institutions have played a central role in shaping and facilitating the continuities between colonialism and the current legal regime. This is described by Karen Alter, whose approach also highlights the fact that the North-South logic that has dominated much of the BHR discourse is increasingly inadequate to capture the dynamics at play in the debates over human rights-based accountability.

DOREEN LUSTIG, THE ENDURING CHARTER: CORPORATIONS, STATES, AND INTERNATIONAL LAW
M. J. DURKEE (ED.), STATES, FIRMS, AND THEIR LEGAL FICTIONS: ATTRIBUTING IDENTITY AND RESPONSIBILITY TO ARTIFICIAL ENTITIES (2024) 87

(1) Introduction

The corporation as a legal entity and a form of governance has no innate conceptual identity; rather, its legal identity is the product of historical developments. During the nineteenth century, a corporation came to be considered a private entity formed for the purpose of pursuing commercial ends. Prior to that time, the identity of corporations was less clearly defined, and they owed their existence to the governments that chartered them. They were frequently granted monopolistic privileges and tasked with building infrastructure projects, such as roads and canals. As noted by Philip Stern, during the early modern period "[i]ncorporation … had nothing to do with the nature of the business at hand. It was a legal and political institution that allowed groups of students, merchants, townsmen, or monarchical subjects to make claims on property, rights, and privileges, and to pass these on to later generations in perpetuity." Over the course of the nineteenth century, the corporation gradually came to be governed by private and contract law principles.

In the context of international law, this transition would gain prominence in the latter part of nineteenth century in debates among scholars in the field about the involvement of chartered companies in the scramble for Africa. During this period, scholars of international law scrutinized the involvement of business corporations in Africa and ultimately criticized the use of the chartered company for colonial purposes. As the nineteenth century drew to an end, most chartered companies were dissolved. …

Yet, the formal dissolution of the charter hardly put an end to the close relationship between governments and corporations. …

(2) The Separate Spheres Presumption in the Articles on Responsibility of States for Internationally Wrongful Acts

The Articles on Responsibility of States for Internationally Wrongful Acts (ARSIWA) are the primary source for defining the doctrine of attribution in international law. Of particular interest here is their definition of the circumstances under which "conduct consisting of an act or omission or a series of acts or omissions is to be considered as the conduct of the State."

As noted in the ILC commentaries, "the conduct of private persons or entities is not attributable to the State under international law." While the ILC has presented rules for entities, or organizations, and international criminal law has developed rules for holding natural personals responsible, the responsibility of non-state actors in international law remains underdeveloped.

In the context of state responsibility, the circumstances for imputing the acts of corporate actors to a state are limited to situations in which the private corporation is operating *as a state organ* (Article 4), *like a state organ* (Article 5), or in cases when it is *directed or controlled by the state* (Article 8). This approach to attribution presumes a clear distinction between the private sphere of the corporation and the public sphere of the state as the underlying logic for defining the extent of state responsibility. As the ILC commentary explains:

> In theory, the conduct of all human beings, corporations or collectivities linked to the State by nationality, habitual residence or incorporation might be attributed to the State, whether or not they have any connection to the Government. In international law, such an approach is avoided, both with a view to *limiting responsibility to conduct which engages the State as an organization, and also so as to recognize the autonomy of persons acting on their own account* and not at the instigation of a public authority.

...

V. The Positivist Turn in Corporate Responsibility and the Separate Spheres Presumption

The international law of the post-charter era not only leveraged the commercial interests of business corporations; it also further contributed to the insulation of corporations from legal scrutiny when they operated in colonial settings. Once the charters of these companies were revoked, they were legally considered as private corporations. As the last vestiges of the chartered corporation disappeared, corporations, as such, would no longer be subjects of international legal scrutiny. The classic public–private distinction situated corporations on the private side of that divide. The fact that at this point (the 1880s onward), corporations could be freely incorporated made this transition from chartered to private companies relatively easy, with little or no negative impact on the businesses or the businessmen involved.

In an interstate legal order, concerns over corporate involvement in dubious practices translated to positivist concerns over the obligation of the state to regulate such practices. But the demand that powerful imperial governments assume control over their territories did not result in an attempt to regulate the conduct of corporations. Almost to the contrary, historical accounts of this period in the African context document how the close collaboration between colonial officials and African authorities "formed a patriarchal alliance to bolster their respective power and control over younger men, women and children." Amid the end of imperial governments' control over foreign territories, the involvement of corporations in the exploitation of labor and resources, as well as their destabilizing effect on political communities in postcolonial settings remained invisible to international legal scrutiny for decades to come. Until recently, even though the home state of transnational corporations usually had the regulatory capacity to hold such corporate actors accountable, it could only be held internationally responsible in the exceptional circumstances of effective control over the territory in which the corporation operates. States had no international responsibility to regulate corporate actors operating outside their national territory, even in situations where the corporate actor had the nationality of the state concerned. As noted by Cristina Lafont:

> [T]he "veil of sovereignty" gives rise to the "veil of ignorance" that allows other states to single-mindedly protect and promote the interests and rights of those under their jurisdiction while disclaiming that they have any obligation to be aware of, let alone to take into account, the impact that their actions might have upon the human rights of those outside their jurisdiction. Such impacts are simply conceptualized as someone else's responsibility.[577]

While home states were conceived as having limited to no responsibility to regulate the conduct of corporations beyond their borders, governments of host states are often unwilling or unable to provide their citizens with access to remedies for international legal violations caused by corporations (either as direct perpetrators or as possible accomplices to such violations). The regulatory weakness of host states and limited to no regulatory responsibility of home states is often viewed as a governance gap. Indeed, applying the nineteenth-century shift to territoriality as a defining feature of sovereignty in a world of uneven regulatory capacities proved particularly consequential in the context of private corporations. Global value chains (GVCs) enable the coordination of production across national borders while maintaining their high-value activities in affluent countries. ...

---

[577] C. Lafont, *Sovereignty and the International Protection of Human Rights* (2015) 427.

While international lawyers' opposition to the legitimacy of corporate actors exercising sovereign authority continued to shape the law on state responsibility in the post-charter era, freely incorporated corporations were conceived as nationals and could use the doctrine of diplomatic protection to call upon their incorporating (powerful) governments to protect their interests if such were undermined by, frequently, less powerful governments. Yet, as noted in the landmark 1970 *Barcelona Traction* decision, "the process of "lifting the corporate veil" or "disregarding the legal entity" has been found justified and equitable in certain circumstances or for certain purposes. The wealth of practice already accumulated on the subject in municipal law indicates that the veil is lifted, for instance, to prevent the misuse of the privileges of legal personality, as in certain cases of fraud or malfeasance." The incorporation of the corporate actor by the same (powerful) government" was not sufficient as a basis for the attribution to the state of the subsequent conduct of that entity." Thus, while a corporation could be protected as a national of a particular state under the doctrine of diplomatic protection, and later, under the regulatory umbrella of bilateral investment treaties and international human rights, that nexus of nationality was not a sufficient basis for state responsibility.

While corporations are conceived by international law as "nationals" in the context of diplomatic protection or "investors" and "individuals" in international investment law and international human rights, the practice of corporations in the post-charter era often blurs the distinction between the corporation as a private (individual) and the state as the architype for public governance authority. The influence of corporations on governmental lawmaking and their prominent role as regulators and lawmakers in global governance are prominent challenges to such public/private distinctions. As noted earlier, international lawyers of the late nineteenth century ignored Adam Smith's critique of the influence of chartered companies as interest groups who shaped governmental positions to advance their limited interests. Even in later periods, long after the revocation of the charter, scholars continue to criticize the failure to regulate the significant role of corporations as inhibitors or influential interest groups in international lawmaking processes. Corporations not only exercise their influence on global regulation as lobbyists and interest groups. They also exercise regulatory functions themselves. The literature on global private authority, transnational private regulation, voluntary sustainability standards, and corporate social responsibility offers different conceptual framings for their regulatory influence. Beyond the new governance context, corporations could be conceived as lawmakers in the context of concessionary agreements and international investment law. Such non-statist regulatory perspective on the role and influence of corporations undermines the presumption of separateness between the public and the private and marks a transition to a theory of international legal ordering in which the state is but one regulator among others.

…

KAREN J. ALTER, FROM COLONIAL TO MULTILATERAL INTERNATIONAL LAW: A GLOBAL CAPITALISM AND LAW INVESTIGATION
19 INT'L J. CONSTIT. L. (2021) 798

The shift from a colonial to multilateral international order was full of great promise. Colonialism was built on coercive domination. European colonial systems were famous for locating the most profitable economic elements in the metropole, while treating peripheral countries as producers of raw materials, as sites of grueling cheap and slave labor, and as captive markets for European finished products. The 1941 Atlantic Charter signaled the hopes of multilateralism, promising an end to territorial domination, a recognition of the right to self-determination, an effort to work collectively towards lowering trade barriers, improved labor standards and economic advancement, promoting freedom of the seas, and creating a world free of want and fear. The United Nations (UN) enshrined these goals, recognizing that nations would interact as sovereign equals drafting international law through multilateral processes. Multilateral institutions created new international legal rules to promote free trade, to keep oceans open for all, to create a stable currency exchange system, and to help secure peace and security. Colonial prerogatives including the right to use force to open markets or to compel the repayment of debts were eliminated.

The shift to multilateralism created profound changes in international law, usually in the direction of creating international agreements and institutions that could garner greater international political support from states. Yet global capitalism operated alongside this international legal and institutional transformation. The forces of global capitalism served as a break on what was politically possible. Newly independent states hoped that their growing numbers would translate into a multilateral power to renegotiate the set of global economic rules that had been created by and for colonial powers. Their hopeful ideals—for permanent sovereignty over their own natural resources, for a New International Economic Order (NIEO), and for a set of more equal and fair international economic agreements—failed in large part because of the refusal of wealthy states to accede to developing country demands. Multilateralism therefore also served as a break on what was possible.

[The author defines global economic law as encompassing 'international law, transnational law and transnational legal orderings, and binding private contracts between firms, banks, and states that are then upheld by domestic courts.' This enlarged categorization reflects the options that state and economic actors have in being able to rely upon 'multilateral international law' or on 'transnational law, private contracts, bilateral agreements', which might better reflect the goals of powerful economic actors.]

… [A] lack of an agreed-upon legal hierarchy across the elemental institutions and agreements allows actors within to play the different layers of authority against each other. For example, by moving from one institutional venue to another, actors can either escape or draw on legal obligations that are present in one system but lacking in another. …

[W]hile both the laws and lacunae of the colonial and multilateral global economic systems reflect state decisions, economic actors can act independently in ways that constrain state action. In both the colonial and multilateral eras, global firms asked for and Sovereigns provided domestic and international law and international relations support to secure these firms' global operations. Yet it is also true that firms have used jurisdiction jumping to escape state efforts to curb business excesses. The Marxist notion that states are mere handmaidens of capitalist interests misses how firms also work through and across the international regime complex to escape individual and collective efforts by states to regulate the global market.

… [Looking ahead] we should not expect these trends to change even if Western power declines and Asian power ascends. The nature of global capitalism is that it is adaptive and driven by an extractive and profit-seeking logic. Global capitalism can shed entire regimes—like slavery and colonialism—and then reform and reproduce inequality and exploitative relationships in new forms. Meanwhile global economic law, in its multilateral, bilateral, coalition of the willing and private law forms, remains the legal infrastructure that facilitates and structures global capitalism, enabling firms to jump jurisdictions to escape state regulation and to exploit gaps in the international regime complex of global economic law. … [N]ew emerging powers … are likely to replicate or reproduce pieces of the American-led multilateral order, even as they aspire to get beyond it. And these powers are likely to do so using the existing tools of global economic law.

1. Types of Challenge

The range of human rights abuses of which corporations have been accused is vast. The online Business and Human Rights Resource Centre collects detailed information about situations globally, and the following excerpts provide a flavour of the challenges.

A report on Africa (*Africa Quarterly*, May 2022), which focuses on litigation brought by local communities in foreign and domestic courts, illustrates some of the key issues:

> In Zambia, local communities have sued Anglo-American for alleged lead poisoning caused by one of its mines, while in Liberia, Salala Rubber Corporation is in court facing allegations of land grabbing, water pollution, and desecration of cemeteries and sacred sites. In South Africa, Indigenous peoples won a court ruling which halted the construction of an Amazon headquarters on their ancestral lands subject to free and inclusive consultation. Poor working conditions and lack of respect for workers' rights have also led to legal proceedings against British American Tobacco in Malawi, Panda International in the Democratic Republic of Congo and Sama, Meta's (formerly Facebook) content moderation subsidiary in Kenya. Even MTN [Africa's largest mobile network operator] has been sued over internet blackouts in eSwatini, while other companies have been accused of complicity in war crimes and crimes against humanity in connection with their activities in Sudan.

Another report, Business and Human Rights Defenders in Southeast Asia (November 2022), focuses on Asia:

Between 2015 and 2021, we recorded more than 4,200 attacks on human rights defenders (HRDs) raising concerns about business-related human rights abuses. During this seven-year period, Asia-Pacific and Latin America have consistently been the two most dangerous regions for HRDs focused on business and nearly a quarter of all attacks globally (22% or 916 attacks) have occurred in Southeast Asia. In 2021, three out of the four most dangerous countries for HRDs in Asia-Pacific were … the Philippines, Cambodia and Indonesia.

The report notes that the most dangerous sectors for HRDs in Asia were mining (230 cases), agribusiness (207), and logging and lumber (89). Seventy percent of attacks in Southeast Asia in 2021 were against climate, land and environmental rights defenders, while 27 percent were against labour rights activists and trade unionists. A very prominent feature is the extent of 'judicial harassment', defined as including arbitrary detention, criminalisation of protests and other activities, and strategic lawsuits against public participation (SLAPPs).

Mining activities, especially on the lands of indigenous peoples, also give rise to many disputes. This story illustrates one such case:[578]

> … [L]ocals from Asunción Mita, Guatemala, voiced their opposition in a referendum on the mining projects that have affected their community for decades. Eighty nine per cent of them voted "no" … in a municipal consultation held last month … .

> … Bluestone Resources [a Canadian company], Guatemala's Ministry of Energy and Mines and a local pro-mining group tried to contest the legality of the voting process … .

> … [T]he Guatemalan Constitutional Court nullified the consultation results after an injunction filed by a Bluestone Resources subsidary, Elevar Resources. The community, along with social and environmental organizations in the neighbouring countries of El Salvador and Honduras, plan to take the consultation case to the Inter-American Court of Human Rights. …

> The ministry approved an Environmental Impact Assesment that overlooked the concerns, such as the pollution of the Lempa river, presented by the Guatemalan Madre Selva environmental collective and locals from Asunción Mita … . Until now, the Guatemalan government has never conducted a consultation before awarding an extraction license. …

> … The Cerro Blanco mining activity in Guatemala poses a great threat to El Salvador and Honduras as well because they rely on the Lempa river to meet the water requirements of their 3.8 million residents.

> Bluestone Resources said an independent international consulting firm collected data from locals and found "a positive attitude toward the project." The company obtained the support of some locals by investing in infrastructure, education and promises of employment, creating divisions within the community as those who oppose the mine are stigmatized and further marginalized...

2. Towards Regulation

For human rights proponents, the growth of corporate power raises the question of how to ensure that the activities of corporations in general, and transnational corporations (TNCs) in particular, are consistent with human rights standards, and of how to promote accountability when violations of those standards occur. In principle, the answer is straightforward. The human rights obligations assumed by each government require it to use all appropriate means to ensure that actors operating within its territory or otherwise subject to its jurisdiction comply with national legislation designed to give effect to human rights.

---

[578] G. Ferrucci, 'Canadian mining project in Guatemala opposed in local vote over environmental concerns', *The Conversation* (27 October 2022).

In practice, however, various problems arise: (1) governments are often loathe to take the measures necessary to ensure compliance by TNCs, especially, but not only, in relation to labour matters; (2) such measures are costly and perceived to be beyond the resource capabilities of governments in developing countries; (3) in the context of increasing global mobility of capital, competition among potential host countries discourages initiatives that may push up labour costs and make one country less attractive than others with lower regulatory standards (the so-called 'race to the bottom'); (4) the transnational complexity of manufacturing and related arrangements in an era of globalization makes it increasingly difficult to identify who is responsible for what activities and where; and (5) especially in the labour area, difficult issues arise about the different levels of minimum acceptable standards from one country to another.

In the 1970s, in the context of demands by developing countries for the establishment of a New International Economic Order, efforts began to draft a Code of Conduct for Transnational Corporations. Although a draft was completed in 1983, developed countries sought to circumvent the process by pursuing a separate initiative through the rich countries' club — the Organisation for Economic Co-operation and Development (OECD). The OECD adopted its Guidelines for Multinational Enterprises in 1976, and they continue to be regularly updated. In the meantime, the Code, which reflected a much more stringent approach to regulating the conduct of TNCs, was finally abandoned in 1992. The end of the Cold War brought much greater competition to attract foreign direct investment to developing countries, and with it came increased pressure to accept the terms on offer from the TNCs rather than making human rights or related demands. Gradually, however, the pendulum has swung back again over the past decade or more.

Codes of conduct have been adopted by thousands of TNCs and they vary hugely in their content, participation, arrangements for monitoring, follow-up, etc. In 1999, then-UN Secretary-General Kofi Annan launched the Ten Principles of the UN Global Compact, designed to encourage corporations to commit to following a list of principles in their activities. In addition to principles governing the environment and anti-corruption efforts, the Compact includes the following:

Human Rights

> Principle 1: support and respect the protection of international human rights within their sphere of influence;

> Principle 2: make sure their own corporations are not complicit in human rights abuses.

Labour Standards

> Principle 3: freedom of association and the effective recognition of the right to collective bargaining;

> Principle 4: the elimination of all forms of forced and compulsory labour;

> Principle 5: the effective abolition of child labour;

> Principle 6: the elimination of discrimination in respect of employment and occupation.

The Global Compact (www.unglobalcompact.org) has attracted significant corporate support but has generally elicited scepticism from human rights proponents because of the vagueness of the Ten Principles, and their apparent failure to generate significant pressure upon corporations to improve their performance. As of 2020, the Compact listed over 10,000 participating companies in 160 countries, representing more than 70 million employees.

According to the *Annual Report for 2020*, prepared for the Global Compact by DNV, A Norway-based consultancy firm working in the area of renewable energy and the oil and gas industry:

> More than 90 per cent of survey respondents have corporate policies in place that reflect the four issue areas of the Ten Principles: human rights (90%), labour (94%), environment (94%) and anti-corruption (90%). ...
>
> ...
>
> ... [W]hile 62 per cent of companies conduct an environmental impact assessment, impact assessments are only conducted by 18 per cent for human rights, 25 per cent for anti-corruption and 29 per cent for labour.
>
> ...
>
> ...[O]nly 17 per cent of respondents require supply chain partners to adhere to the Ten Principles of the UN Global Compact.[579]

Some commentators have described the Compact as little more than a platform for sharing best practices, while others have criticized it on the grounds that there are few incentives to keep subscribers in line and that its governance structure 'inhibits both accountability for actions and transparency in external communications, further highlighting the absence of meaningful programme evaluation and credible reporting.'[580]

In essence, the strategy reflected in the Global Compact is gradually to ratchet up the levels of commitment and accountability. Many in the human rights field, however, have expressed frustration with such incrementalism, and have pressed instead for progress towards binding legal rules. A first step in this direction was thought to have been the adoption of a set of Norms on the Responsibilities of Transnational Corporations and Other Business Enterprises with Regard to Human Rights (the so-called 'UN Norms'). The Norms were drafted in 2003 by a working group of the UN Sub-Commission on the Promotion and Protection of Human Rights, chaired by David Weissbrodt.[581] The Sub-Commission was abolished in 2006 and effectively replaced by the Human Rights Council Advisory Committee.

Responses to the UN Norms varied dramatically. The NGOs who were most engaged — notably Amnesty International, Human Rights Watch and the International Commission of Jurists — all endorsed them as an appropriate starting point from which to develop corporate accountability. While the views of scholars were deeply divided, governmental reaction was largely negative. Most developing countries were not keen on intrusive regulation, and most developed countries felt that the Norms were either unnecessary or overreaching. The United States, for example, spoke of an 'anti-business agenda'. The response of industry representatives was mixed, but most were hostile. In 2004, the UN Commission on Human Rights (the predecessor to the Human Rights Council) noted that the Norms contained 'useful elements and ideas', but stated that the draft had no legal standing. The following year, it opted (CHR Res. 2005/69) instead to appoint an independent expert as Special Representative of the Secretary-General (SRSG) with a mandate:

> (a) To identify and clarify standards of corporate responsibility and accountability ...; (b) To elaborate on the role of States in effectively regulating [corporations] ..., including through international cooperation; (c) To research and clarify the implications ... of concepts such as 'complicity' and 'sphere of influence'; (d) To develop materials and methodologies for undertaking human rights impact assessments of [corporate activities]; and (e) To compile a compendium of best practices of States and [corporations].

John Ruggie was appointed as SRSG on the issue of human rights and transnational corporations and other business enterprises. Ruggie assembled a staff of ten researchers/advisors, obtained free legal assistance from over 24 law firms worldwide, mobilized academic institutions and other researchers, engaged in 47 consultations with stakeholders around the world, conducted 20 site visits, drafted detailed studies and analyses of key issues, and placed his mandate at the centre of most discussions about corporate human rights responsibilities. He raised millions of dollars from governments and corporations to facilitate his work, and he avoided explicit

---

[579] Uniting Business in the Decade of Action (Global Compact & DNV GL, 2020), at 16.

[580] N. Andrews, 'Normative Spaces and the UN Global Compact for Transnational Corporations: The Norm Diffusion Paradox,' 47 *J. Int. Relat. Dev.* (2017) 1.

[581] D. Weissbrodt and M. Kruger, 'Norms on the Responsibilities of Transnational Corporations and Other Business Enterprises with Regard to Human Rights', 97 *Am.J. Int'l L.* (2003) 901.

criticism of particular corporations.[582] The intellectual framework that he developed was organized around the three principles of 'protect, respect and remedy' and he submitted his final report in 2011. It consisted almost entirely of a set of Guiding Principles (the UNGPs), on which comments from governments and other stakeholders had been solicited and reflected in advance.

GUIDING PRINCIPLES ON BUSINESS AND HUMAN RIGHTS: IMPLEMENTING THE UNITED NATIONS 'PROTECT, RESPECT AND REMEDY' FRAMEWORK
UN DOC. A/HRC/17/31, ANNEX (21 MARCH 2011)

General principles

These Guiding Principles are grounded in recognition of:

> (a) States' existing obligations to respect, protect and fulfil human rights and fundamental freedoms;

> (b) The role of business enterprises as specialized organs of society performing specialized functions, required to comply with all applicable laws and to respect human rights;

> (c) The need for rights and obligations to be matched to appropriate and effective remedies when breached.

These Guiding Principles apply to all States and to all business enterprises, both transnational and others, regardless of their size, sector, location, ownership and structure.
…
Nothing in these Guiding Principles should be read as creating new international law obligations. . . .
…

I. The State duty to protect human rights

A. Foundational principles

1. States must protect against human rights abuse within their territory and/or jurisdiction by third parties, including business enterprises. This requires taking appropriate steps to prevent, investigate, punish and redress such abuse through effective policies, legislation, regulations and adjudication.
…
2. States should set out clearly the expectation that all business enterprises domiciled in their territory and/or jurisdiction respect human rights throughout their operations.
…

B. Operational principles

General State regulatory and policy functions

3. In meeting their duty to protect, States should:

> (a) Enforce laws that are aimed at, or have the effect of, requiring business enterprises to respect human rights, and periodically to assess the adequacy of such laws and address any gaps;

---

[582] See generally, J. Ruggie, *Just Business: Multinational Corporations and Human Rights* (2013).

(b) Ensure that other laws and policies governing the creation and ongoing operation of business enterprises, such as corporate law, do not constrain but enable business respect for human rights;

(c) Provide effective guidance to business enterprises on how to respect human rights throughout their operations;

(d) Encourage, and where appropriate require, business enterprises to communicate how they address their human rights impacts.

The State-business nexus

4. States should take additional steps to protect against human rights abuses by business enterprises that are owned or controlled by the State, or that receive substantial support and services from State agencies such as export credit agencies and official investment insurance or guarantee agencies, including, where appropriate, by requiring human rights due diligence.
...
5. States should exercise adequate oversight in order to meet their international human rights obligations when they contract with, or legislate for, business enterprises to provide services that may impact upon the enjoyment of human rights.
...
6. States should promote respect for human rights by business enterprises with which they conduct commercial transactions.
...

Supporting business respect for human rights in conflict-affected areas

7. Because the risk of gross human rights abuses is heightened in conflict-affected areas, States should help ensure that business enterprises operating in those contexts are not involved with such abuses, including by:

> (a) Engaging at the earliest stage possible with business enterprises to help them identify, prevent and mitigate the human rights-related risks of their activities and business relationships;

> ...

Ensuring policy coherence

8. States should ensure that governmental departments, agencies and other State-based institutions that shape business practices are aware of and observe the State's human rights obligations when fulfilling their respective mandates, including by providing them with relevant information, training and support.
...
9. States should maintain adequate domestic policy space to meet their human rights obligations when pursuing business-related policy objectives with other States or business enterprises, for instance through investment treaties or contracts.

10. States, when acting as members of multilateral institutions that deal with business-related issues, should:

> (a) Seek to ensure that those institutions neither restrain the ability of their member States to meet their duty to protect nor hinder business enterprises from respecting human rights;

> (b) Encourage those institutions, within their respective mandates and capacities, to promote business respect for human rights and, where requested, to help States meet their duty to protect against human rights abuse by business enterprises, including through technical assistance, capacity-building and awareness-raising;

(c) Draw on these Guiding Principles to promote shared understanding and advance international cooperation in the management of business and human rights challenges.

II. The corporate responsibility to respect human rights

A. Foundational principles

11. Business enterprises should respect human rights. This means that they should avoid infringing on the human rights of others and should address adverse human rights impacts with which they are involved.

12. The responsibility of business enterprises to respect human rights refers to internationally recognized human rights — understood, at a minimum, as those expressed in the International Bill of Human Rights and the principles concerning fundamental rights set out in the International Labour Organization's Declaration on Fundamental Principles and Rights at Work.

...

13. The responsibility to respect human rights requires that business enterprises:

> (a) Avoid causing or contributing to adverse human rights impacts through their own activities, and address such impacts when they occur;

> (b) Seek to prevent or mitigate adverse human rights impacts that are directly linked to their operations, products or services by their business relationships, even if they have not contributed to those impacts.

14. The responsibility of business enterprises to respect human rights applies to all enterprises regardless of their size, sector, operational context, ownership and structure. Nevertheless, the scale and complexity of the means through which enterprises meet that responsibility may vary according to these factors and with the severity of the enterprise's adverse human rights impacts.

...

15. In order to meet their responsibility to respect human rights, business enterprises should have in place policies and processes appropriate to their size and circumstances, including:

> (a) A policy commitment to meet their responsibility to respect human rights;

> (b) A human rights due-diligence process to identify, prevent, mitigate and account for how they address their impacts on human rights;

> (c)   Processes to enable the remediation of any adverse human rights impacts they cause or to which they contribute.

...

B. Operational principles

Policy commitment

16. As the basis for embedding their responsibility to respect human rights, business enterprises should express their commitment to meet this responsibility through a statement of policy that:

> (a) Is approved at the most senior level of the business enterprise;

> (b) Is informed by relevant internal and/or external expertise;

> (c) Stipulates the enterprise's human rights expectations of personnel, business partners and other parties directly linked to its operations, products or services;

(d) Is publicly available and communicated internally and externally to all personnel, business partners and other relevant parties;

(e) Is reflected in operational policies and procedures necessary to embed it throughout the business enterprise.

...

Human rights due diligence

17. In order to identify, prevent, mitigate and account for how they address their adverse human rights impacts, business enterprises should carry out human rights due diligence. The process should include assessing actual and potential human rights impacts, integrating and acting upon the findings, tracking responses, and communicating how impacts are addressed. Human rights due diligence:

> (a) Should cover adverse human rights impacts that the business enterprise may cause or contribute to through its own activities, or which may be directly linked to its operations, products or services by its business relationships;

> (b) Will vary in complexity with the size of the business enterprise, the risk of severe human rights impacts, and the nature and context of its operations;

> (c) Should be ongoing, recognizing that the human rights risks may change over time as the business enterprise's operations and operating context evolve.

18. In order to gauge human rights risks, business enterprises should identify and assess any actual or potential adverse human rights impacts with which they may be involved either through their own activities or as a result of their business relationships. This process should:

> (a) Draw on internal and/or independent external human rights expertise;

> (b) Involve meaningful consultation with potentially affected groups and other relevant stakeholders, as appropriate to the size of the business enterprise and the nature and context of the operation.

...

19. In order to prevent and mitigate adverse human rights impacts, business enterprises should integrate the findings from their impact assessments across relevant internal functions and processes, and take appropriate action.

> (a) Effective integration requires that:

> > (i) Responsibility for addressing such impacts is assigned to the appropriate level and function within the business enterprise;

> > (ii) Internal decision-making, budget allocations and oversight processes enable effective responses to such impacts.

> (b) Appropriate action will vary according to:

> > (i) Whether the business enterprise causes or contributes to an adverse impact, or whether it is involved solely because the impact is directly linked to its operations, products or services by a business relationship;

> > (ii) The extent of its leverage in addressing the adverse impact.

...

20. In order to verify whether adverse human rights impacts are being addressed, business enterprises should track the effectiveness of their response. Tracking should:

> (a) Be based on appropriate qualitative and quantitative indicators;

(b) Draw on feedback from both internal and external sources, including affected stakeholders.

...

21. In order to account for how they address their human rights impacts, business enterprises should be prepared to communicate this externally, particularly when concerns are raised by or on behalf of affected stakeholders. Business enterprises whose operations or operating contexts pose risks of severe human rights impacts should report formally on how they address them. In all instances, communications should:

> (a) Be of a form and frequency that reflect an enterprise's human rights impacts and that are accessible to its intended audiences;

> (b) Provide information that is sufficient to evaluate the adequacy of an enterprise's response to the particular human rights impact involved;

> (c) In turn not pose risks to affected stakeholders, personnel or to legitimate requirements of commercial confidentiality.

...

Remediation

22. Where business enterprises identify that they have caused or contributed to adverse impacts, they should provide for or cooperate in their remediation through legitimate processes.
...

Issues of context

23. In all contexts, business enterprises should:

> (a) Comply with all applicable laws and respect internationally recognized human rights, wherever they operate;

> (b) Seek ways to honour the principles of internationally recognized human rights when faced with conflicting requirements;

> (c) Treat the risk of causing or contributing to gross human rights abuses as a legal compliance issue wherever they operate.

24. Where it is necessary to prioritize actions to address actual and potential adverse human rights impacts, business enterprises should first seek to prevent and mitigate those that are most severe or where delayed response would make them irremediable.
...

III. Access to remedy

A. Foundational principle

25. As part of their duty to protect against business-related human rights abuse, States must take appropriate steps to ensure, through judicial, administrative, legislative or other appropriate means, that when such abuses occur within their territory and/or jurisdiction those affected have access to effective remedy.
...

B. Operational principles

State-based judicial mechanisms

26. States should take appropriate steps to ensure the effectiveness of domestic judicial mechanisms when addressing business-related human rights abuses, including considering ways to reduce legal, practical and other relevant barriers that could lead to a denial of access to remedy. ...

State-based non-judicial grievance mechanisms

27. States should provide effective and appropriate non-judicial grievance mechanisms, alongside judicial mechanisms, as part of a comprehensive State-based system for the remedy of business-related human rights abuse.
...
Non-State-based grievance mechanisms

28. States should consider ways to facilitate access to effective non-State-based grievance mechanisms dealing with business-related human rights harms. ...

29. To make it possible for grievances to be addressed early and remediated directly, business enterprises should establish or participate in effective operational-level grievance mechanisms for individuals and communities who may be adversely impacted. ...

30. Industry, multi-stakeholder and other collaborative initiatives that are based on respect for human rights-related standards should ensure that effective grievance mechanisms are available. ...

Effectiveness criteria for non-judicial grievance mechanisms

31. In order to ensure their effectiveness, non-judicial grievance mechanisms, both State-based and non-State-based, should be:

> (a) Legitimate: enabling trust from the stakeholder groups for whose use they are intended, and being accountable for the fair conduct of grievance processes;

> (b) Accessible: being known to all stakeholder groups for whose use they are intended, and providing adequate assistance for those who may face particular barriers to access;

> (c) Predictable: providing a clear and known procedure with an indicative timeframe for each stage, and clarity on the types of process and outcome available and means of monitoring implementation;

> (d) Equitable: seeking to ensure that aggrieved parties have reasonable access to sources of information, advice and expertise necessary to engage in a grievance process on fair, informed and respectful terms;

> (e) Transparent: keeping parties to a grievance informed about its progress, and providing sufficient information about the mechanism's performance to build confidence in its effectiveness and meet any public interest at stake;

> (f) Rights-compatible: ensuring that outcomes and remedies accord with internationally recognized human rights;

> (g) A source of continuous learning: drawing on relevant measures to identify lessons for improving the mechanism and preventing future grievances and harms;

Operational-level mechanisms should also be:
...

> (h) Based on engagement and dialogue: consulting the stakeholder groups for whose use they are intended on their design and performance, and focusing on dialogue as the means to address and resolve grievances.

NOTE

In response to the SRSG's final report, the Human Rights Council 'endorsed' the Guiding Principles and noted that Ruggie's work did not foreclose 'any other long-term development, including further enhancement of standards'. But rather than appointing a new SRSG, it appointed a five-member Working Group to promote the Guiding Principles, to gather good practices and lessons learned, to support capacity-building and, potentially most significantly, to 'explore options and make recommendations for enhancing access to effective remedies available to those whose human rights are affected by corporate activities, including those in conflict areas' (HRC Res. 17/4 (2011)). While Ruggie explicitly disparaged suggestions that the next phase should include the drafting of a binding international legal instrument, he diplomatically suggested that 'a multilateral approach to providing greater legal clarification may be warranted in response to the diverging national interpretations of the applicability to business enterprises of international standards prohibiting 'gross' human rights abuses, possibly amounting to the level of international crimes.'[583] The Council chose to ignore this proposal.

The Working Group decided to undertake two country missions per year focused on good practices, to receive information from all sources, and to adopt a thematic focus for the annual Forum on Business and Human Rights authorized by the Council. It also stated that, '[g]iven the broad scope of its mandate, the vast scale and complexity of the issue at hand, and resource constraints, the Working Group is not in a position to investigate individual cases of alleged business-related human rights abuse.'[584]

TAKING STOCK

Although most international institutional actors and many states have warmly embraced the UNGPs,[585] Tara Melish, in 'Putting "Human Rights" Back into the UN Guiding Principles on Business and Human Rights: Shifting Frames and Embedding Participation Rights', in César Rodriguez-Garavito (ed.), *Business and Human Rights: Beyond the End of the Beginning* (2017) 62, notes that some human rights NGOs have seen them 'as "regressive," a "step backward" in the protection of human rights, one based on a corporate good will model that not only has proven itself ineffective over decades of trial and creative experimentation, but that … ignores the critical elements of a human rights approach to social change.' In her view, the price for high-level corporate and state buy-in was the systematic removal from the UNGPs framework and regulatory logic of 'the very essence of a "human rights approach" to community problem-solving' revolving around empowerment, participation, and accountability.

In 2021, the Working Group issued a major report entitled *UNGPs 10+: A Roadmap for the Next Decade of Business and Human Rights*. In its annual report that year it acknowledged that '[t]he persistence of business-related abuses is a major concern and a source of deep frustration, and should be a matter of urgent priority attention by States and business. … [V]oluntary approaches alone are not enough. The rise of mandatory measures will undoubtedly accelerate both uptake and progress. At the same time, the experience of many decades has demonstrated that legal measures are essential but not sufficient … . (UN Doc. A/HRC/47/39 (2021), para. 114).

Steven R. Ratner, in his 'Introduction to the Symposium on Soft and Hard Law on Business and Human Rights', 114 *AJIL Unbound* (2020) 163, identified three main criticisms of the UNGPs: (i) 'as a nonbinding instrument, they place no new obligations on states or corporations under international law or domestic law'; (ii) Pillar I 'does not resolve the precise duties of the home state of a company to regulate its activities beyond the state's borders' and nor does it 'create or propose any institutional mechanism to evaluate states' performance'; and (iii) Pillar II deliberately leaves companies with 'flexibility on how to carry out due diligence as well as on how to mitigate violations by suppliers, distributors, and others with whom they have business relationships.' He concluded that the strong multi-stakeholder support for the UNGPs was a consequence of 'their lack of legal bindingness, their imprecise provisions on key issues, and their absence of any true control mechanism.'

---

[583] www.business-humanrights.org/media/documents/ruggie-statement-to-un-human-rights-council-30-may-2011.pdf.
[584] UN Doc. A/HRC/20/29 (10 April 2012), para. 89.
[585] See generally B. Choudhury (ed.), *The UN Guiding Principles on Business and Human Rights* (2023).

Nicola Jägers, in 'UN Guiding Principles at 10: Permeating Narratives or Yet Another Silo?', 6 *Bus. & Hum. Rts. J.* (2021) 198, argues that:

> The success of the UNGPs lies in a process of 'norm-cascading', influencing other powerful narratives that ultimately help shape policy responses. Arguably, the design and language of the UNGPs hold promise to penetrate the notoriously fragmented regulatory and policy responses to global problems and the incoherence that arises from such a siloed approach. Corporate (ir)responsible behaviour plays a significant role in many of the challenges faced today. In the critical area of climate change, this is certainly the case. Yet, … the Paris Climate Agreement and the SDGs, two global instruments central to the narrative on (environmental) sustainability, reflect remarkably little uptake of the BHR narrative by states. …

> … [T]he lack of reference to corporate responsibility and accountability in competing narratives indicates that BHR to date does not seem to function as the guidepost for states on how to involve the private sector in reaching (environmental) sustainability goals in a manner that recognizes their human rights responsibilities. In fact, [we see] the prevalence of perpetuating the [corporate social responsibility] narrative of linking responsible business conduct to philanthropy. As Deva has pointed out, … most businesses are continuing with their leisurely 'human rights journey' and states often remain mute on the responsibilities of corporations. Moreover, 'states continue to pursue a "development first, human rights later" strategy and "cashstrapped UN Agencies increasingly flirt with business to forge unprincipled partnerships"'. In light of the immense challenges and the need to mobilize vast resources, seeking the partnership of the private sector is a necessity, but this should not come at the expense of the vulnerable whose human rights are negatively affected by corporate activity.

The role of codes of conduct and related initiatives continues to be robustly contested. One strong proponent is Erika George, in *Incorporating Rights: Strategies to Advance Corporate Accountability* (2021), at 325:

> In the ecology of global governance, new business and human rights indicators, rankings, and benchmarks now provide rights advocates with greater power and the ability to inform and influence investors. Taken together, this mix of strategies has the potential to play an important role in solidifying emerging soft law standards and strengthening future regulation. The commitments contained in voluntary codes of conduct to respect human rights are becoming obligatory through being incorporated into supplier contracts that link global supply chains. …

> … [O]ver time the extent to which codes incorporate reference to human rights standards has increased. Similarly, the rhetorical framing used in corporate sustainability reporting is incorporating rights and increasingly treats voluntary standards as de facto obligatory for maintaining a "social license" to operate.

> …

> … Responsible business practices and corporate codes of conduct consistent with the responsibility to respect international human rights will serve to create a body of soft law to supplement the human rights regime and strengthen protections. Domestic laws in some countries are incorporating the concepts contained in international standards. …

> This mix of standards and strategies to actually operationalize respect for human rights in business enterprises is likely to be a more promising avenue for progress than promulgating still more international human rights treaties. This is not to say that there is no place for law. Rather, I argue that more than law will be required to bridge the human rights regulatory gap.

> …

… [A] new approach to corporate social responsibility in the international arena may be the best option for improving standards and practices … . Indeed, a broader business ethic, one that embraces human rights, is imperative. Significantly, corporate culture and committed leadership are important in driving change.

A more skeptical assessment of codes of conduct is presented by Cristina Aibar-Guzmán, Isabel-María García-Sánchez and Celia Salvador-González, in 'Do Codes of Conduct Really Mean a Change in Corporate Practices with Regard to Human Rights? Evidence from the Largest Garment Companies Worldwide', 26 *Int'l J. Hum. Rts.* (2022) 282:

> One of the consequences of globalisation is the rise of outsourcing and the relocation of certain links of companies' value chains to developing countries, characterised by low wages, weak enforcement of labour law, and precarious working conditions. This has resulted in abuse and human rights violations, such as forced and child labour, physical and sexual abuse, exploitation, and discrimination as well as health problems, injuries, and workers' death caused by poor working conditions.

> As a result, global corporations have been subjected to significant pressure from stakeholders (e.g. international NGOs, customers, the media, creditors, shareholders, and investors) concerned about working conditions at their supply factories in other countries and the status of their workers' human rights, which has led global corporations to assume their responsibility in this regard and insert the human rights agenda into their social responsibility policies.

> An instrument for integrating human rights obligations into corporate social responsibility is the development of voluntary codes of conduct. They define the 'baseline expectations or responsibilities to which companies are expected to adhere by a wide range of stakeholders'. Corporate codes of conduct state the management's formal commitment to behave ethically and set the actions to be adopted in this regard. In this sense, the reasons why global corporations adopt a voluntary code of conduct are varied, including enhanced reputation, a response to stakeholder pressures, and the actual desire of modifying procedures and preventing misconduct. Given their voluntary nature, codes of conduct lack any 'legally binding effect'; instead, they are 'self-regulatory governance systems' which define the firm's social aspirations and moral obligations.

> …

> Our analysis shows that the adoption of a code of conduct by the analysed companies expressing their formal commitment to respect labour and human rights can be considered a legitimation strategy with no reflection in the actual corporate behaviour.

QUESTIONS

1. What do you see as the principal strengths and weaknesses of the UNGPs?

2. What significance, if any, do you attach to the Working Group's decision not to 'investigate' any alleged corporate violations?

3. A press release dated 19 August 2019, announced 'Business Roundtable Redefines the Purpose of a Corporation to Promote "An Economy That Serves All Americans"'. The group brought together the CEOs of America's leading companies. In what was lauded as a breakthrough statement, they committed to: delivering value to our customers; investing in our employees; dealing fairly and ethically with our suppliers; supporting the communities in which we work; and generating long-term value for shareholders. No mention was made of rights. In light of the analyses by Lustig and Alter, how might deep change be brought about in this area?

4. Thousands of participants now attend the annual UN Annual Forum on BHR. Michael Hobbes, in 'Saving the World, One Meaningless Buzzword at a Time', Foreign Policy (21 February 2017), argued that it involved 'corporations, activists, and politicians [turning] the language of human rights into meaningless babble'. He also suggested that the businesses participating in BHR discussions are an unrepresentative sample:

Most of the world, after all, is not companies you've heard of. There are no state-owned enterprises here, no business-to-business firms, no steel smelters or brandless megasuppliers. The companies here, the ones that are scared of you, are just a tiny sliver of the global economy, a few billion in revenue, a few hundred thousand workers. The rest of it is firms no one knows, that no one is watching, that do not produce marketing messages that can be turned against them.

How would a BHR proponent respond to such a challenge?

BEYOND THE UNGPS

In September 2013, Ecuador led a group of 84 governments in the Human Rights Council calling for a legally binding 'instrument' to regulate business and human rights. The group welcomed the UNGPs and the creation of the Working Group, but called this only 'a first step'. The Council responded in Res 26/9 (2014) by establishing 'an open-ended intergovernmental working group [OEIGWG] on a legally binding instrument on transnational corporations and other business enterprises with respect to human rights…'. Between 2015 and 2022, the OEIGWG held eight sessions. The original resolution envisaged a central role for the Chair-Rapporteur of the group, who has so far always been an Ecuadorian. A succinct overview of the process is provided by Claire O'Brien, and Daniel Schönfelder, in 'A Defining Moment for the UN Business and Human Rights Treaty Process', *Verfassungsblog* (26 October 2022):

> … [The] … process has seen geographically uneven participation, with many globally and regionally significant economies notably absent. Earlier texts, moreover, adopted a prescriptive approach, seeking to legislate in close detail over matters such as civil and criminal procedure in cross-border cases. They would also have pre-committed states parties to a raft of premature design choices around due diligence laws. At the same time, they regressed from the ambition of the UNGPs to address all business activity by dropping state-businesses and small and medium-sized enterprises from their focus.

> Out of kilter with the form of most human rights treaties, this approach, perhaps unsurprisingly, drew many detractors. Participating states, often with good reason, raised incompatibilities with national constitutional commitments and court procedure, particularly in the domain of civil litigation. Many (including initially the United States) stayed away, while registering discontent or, like the European Union, either reserved positions on the whole text and remained largely silent, while nevertheless embarking on unilateral national regulatory initiatives.

> Until now, it was often attempted to solve such problems by simply adding more text, in an attempt to cover all national eventualities. Yet this resulted in long and complex clauses that still failed to reflect the subsidiarity or discretion commonly afforded states in other areas.

At its October 2023 session, the OEIGWG focused on the following text, along with amendments submitted by States in advance of the session.

DRAFT LEGALLY BINDING INSTRUMENT [LBI] TO REGULATE, IN INTERNATIONAL HUMAN RIGHTS LAW, THE ACTIVITIES OF TRANSNATIONAL CORPORATIONS AND OTHER BUSINESS ENTERPRISES
JULY 2023

[Preamble omitted]

Article 1. Definitions

1.1. "**Victim**" shall mean any person or group of persons who suffered a human rights abuse in the context of business activities, irrespective of the nationality or domicile of the victim. ...

1.2. "**Adverse human rights impact**" shall mean a harm which corresponds to a reduction in or removal of a person's ability to enjoy an internationally recognized human right.

1.3. "**Human rights abuse**" shall mean any acts or omissions that take place in connection with business activities and results in an adverse human rights impact.

1.4. "**Business activities**" means any economic or other activity, including but not limited to the manufacturing, production, transportation, distribution, commercialization, marketing and retailing of goods and services, undertaken by a natural or legal person, including State-owned enterprises, financial institutions and investment funds, transnational corporations, other business enterprises, joint ventures, and any other business relationship undertaken by a natural or legal person. This includes activities undertaken by electronic means.

1.5. "**Business activities of a transnational character**" means any business activity described in Article 1.4. above, when:

> a. It is undertaken in more than one jurisdiction or State; or
>
> b. It is undertaken in one State but a significant part ... takes place through any business relationship in another State or jurisdiction; or
>
> c. It is undertaken in one State but has significant effect in another State or jurisdiction.

1.6. "**Business relationship**" refers to any relationship between natural or legal persons, including State and non-State entities, to conduct business activities, including those activities conducted through affiliates, subsidiaries, agents, suppliers, partnerships, joint venture, beneficial proprietorship, or any other structure or relationship, including throughout their value chains, as provided under the domestic law of the State, including activities undertaken by electronic means.
...
1.8. "**Human rights due diligence**" shall mean the processes by which business enterprises identify, prevent, mitigate and account for how they address their adverse human rights impacts. While these processes will vary in complexity with the size of a business enterprise, the risk of severe adverse human rights impacts, and the nature and context of the operations of that business enterprise, these processes will in every case comprise the following elements:

> (a) identifying and assessing any adverse human rights impacts with which the business enterprise may be involved through its own activities or as a result of its business relationships;
>
> (b) taking appropriate measures to prevent and mitigate such adverse human rights impacts;
>
> (c) monitoring the effectiveness of its measures to address such adverse human rights impacts; and

(d) communicating how the relevant business enterprise addresses such adverse human rights impacts regularly and in an accessible manner to stakeholders, particularly to affected and potentially affected persons.

1.9. "**Remedy**" shall mean the restoration of a victim of a human rights abuse to the position they would have been had the abuse not occurred, or as nearly as is possible in the circumstances. An "effective remedy" involves reparations that are adequate, effective, and prompt; are gender and age responsive; and may draw from a range of forms of remedy such as restitution, compensation, rehabilitation, satisfaction, such as cessation of abuse, apologies, and sanctions, as well as and guarantees of non-repetition.

Article 2. Statement of Purpose

2.1. The purpose of this [LBI] is:
   a) To clarify and facilitate effective implementation of the obligation of States to respect, protect, fulfill and promote human rights in the context of business activities, particularly those of transnational character;

   b) To clarify and ensure respect and fulfillment of the human rights obligations of business enterprises;

   c) To prevent and mitigate the occurrence of human rights abuses in the context of business activities by effective mechanisms of monitoring and enforceability;

   d) To ensure access to gender responsive, child sensitive and victim centred justice and effective, adequate and timely remedy for victims of human rights abuses in the context of business activities;

   e) To facilitate and strengthen mutual legal assistance and international cooperation ... .

Article 3. Scope

3.1. This [LBI] shall apply to all business activities, including business activities of a transnational character.

3.2. ... States Parties may establish in their law, a non-discriminatory basis to differentiate how business enterprises discharge these obligations commensurate with their size, sector, operational context or the severity of impacts on human rights.

3.3. This [LBI] shall cover all internationally recognized human rights and fundamental freedoms binding on the State Parties of this [LBI].

Article 4. Rights of Victims

4.1. Victims of human rights abuses in the context of business activities shall enjoy all internationally recognized human rights and fundamental freedoms.
...

Article 5. Protection of Victims

...
5.3 States Parties shall investigate all human rights abuses covered under this [LBI], effectively, promptly, thoroughly and impartially, and where appropriate, take action against those natural and/or legal persons found responsible, in accordance with domestic and international law.
...

Article 6. Prevention

6.1. States Parties shall regulate effectively the activities of all business enterprises within their territory, jurisdiction, or otherwise under their control, including transnational corporations and other business enterprises that undertake activities of a transnational character.

6.2. State Parties shall adopt appropriate legislative, regulatory, and other measures to:

a) prevent the involvement of business enterprises in human rights abuse;

b) ensure respect by business enterprises for internationally recognized human rights and fundamental freedoms;

c) ensure the practice of human rights due diligence by business enterprises; and,

d) promote the active and meaningful participation of individuals and groups, ... in the development and implementation of laws, policies and other measures to prevent the involvement of business enterprises in human rights abuse.

...

6.4. Measures to achieve the ends referred to in Article 6.2 shall include legally enforceable requirements for business enterprises to undertake human rights due diligence as well as such supporting or ancillary measures as may be needed to ensure that business enterprises while carrying out human rights due diligence:

a) undertake and publish on a regular basis human rights impact assessments prior and throughout their operations;

b) integrate a gender and age perspective, and takes full and proper account of the differentiated human rights-related risks and adverse human rights impacts experienced by women and girls;

c) take particular account of the needs of those who may be at heightened risks of vulnerability or marginalization;

d) meaningful consult with potentially affected groups and other relevant stakeholders;

e) protect the safety of human rights defenders, journalists, workers, members of indigenous peoples, among others, as well as those who may be subject to retaliation; and

f) insofar as engagement with indigenous peoples takes place, undertake such process in accordance with the internationally recognized standards of free, prior, and informed consent.

6.5. Each Party shall take necessary measures to ensure that business enterprises take appropriate steps to prevent human rights abuse by third parties where the enterprise controls, manages or supervises the third party, including through the imposition of a legal duty to prevent such abuse in appropriate cases.
...

Article 7. Access to Remedy

7.1. States Parties shall provide their relevant State agencies, with the necessary competence in accordance with this [LBI] to enable victims' access to adequate, timely and effective remedy and access to justice, and to overcome the specific obstacles which women and groups in vulnerable or marginalized situations face in accessing such mechanisms and remedies.
...

Article 8. Legal Liability

8.1. Each State Party shall adopt such measures as may be necessary to establish a comprehensive and adequate system of legal liability of legal and natural persons conducting business activities, within their territory, jurisdiction, or otherwise under their control, for human rights abuses that may arise from their business activities or relationships, including those of transnational character.
...

Article 9. Jurisdiction

9.1. State Parties shall take such measures as may be necessary to establish its jurisdiction in respect of human rights abuse in cases where:

a) the human rights abuse took place, in whole or inpart, within the territory or jurisdiction of that State Party;

b) the relevant harm was sustained, in whole or in part, within the territory or jurisdiction of that State Party;

c) the human rights abuse was carried out by either:

    i. a legal person domiciled in the territory or jurisdiction of that State Party; or
    j. a natural person who is a national of, or who has his or her habitual residence in the territory or jurisdiction of, that State Party; and

d) a victim seeking remedy through civil law proceedings is a national of, or has his or her habitual residence in the territory or jurisdiction of, that State Party.

...

A strong critique of the process is provided by Dena Freeman, in 'Sovereignty, Human Rights and the Regulation of Transnational Corporations: A Critical Spatial Analysis of Civil Society Proposals for a Binding Treaty', 21 *Globalizations* (2024) 000

> My argument in brief is as follows. Starting from critical spatial histories of international law that argue that Northern states use international law to facilitate global capital accumulation by diminishing sovereignty beyond their borders and intentionally *not* extending their sovereignty over capital operating in these non- or low-sovereign spaces, I argue that considering ways to reconfigure spatial patterns of sovereignty is fundamental to devising ways to regulate contemporary TNCs. I show that the two main civil society groupings active in the current UN negotiations make proposals that elaborate spatial orderings of sovereignty in significantly different ways and that would lead to vastly different global spatial orders if implemented. The Human Rights NGOs [a loose network of many, largely Northern-based, human rights and social justice NGOs, including FIDH, ESCR-Net, the ICJ, CIDSE and others] would elaborate what I call 'imperial sovereignty', in which Northern states would extend their sovereignty into the spaces where they had previously sought to keep sovereignty diminished. This imperial sovereignty might limit capital accumulation and enable TNC regulation but it would also further an imperial spatial order. The Global Campaign, [made up predominantly of Southern-based NGOs and grassroots social movements] in contrast, seek to elaborate what I call 'global sovereignty', in which sovereignty is vertically dispersed upwards to a global level and downwards to the people. This formulation, I argue, would both enable TNC regulation and also promote an emancipatory global spatial order. ...

QUESTION

Why would it be in the interests of various key countries to consider agreeing to the approach reflected in the draft? How compelling is the case put by Olivier De Schutter, in 'Reclaiming states' economic sovereignty: the crux of the new treaty on business and human rights', Business and Human Rights Resource Center, 24 Oct 2023:

Rich countries have an interest in seeking to counter the blackmailing of corporations which routinely threaten to outsource production to locations where human rights are regularly flouted with impunity. Developing nations have an interest in ensuring transnational corporations will not coerce them into granting investors exorbitant privileges, which largely annul any benefit host countries might have expected from the arrival of investors.

All governments, in fact, have a common interest in reclaiming control of globalisation: the urgency is to tame the new leviathans, the corporate groups integrated at transnational level, that 40 years of globalisation have allowed to emerge – undermining the sovereignty of all states.

3. Facebook Case Study

A decade or so ago, the sectors that preoccupied BHR debates and initiatives were the extractive industries, footwear and garment manufacturers, electronics producers, private security companies, and discount retailers. In today's world, Big Tech is in the spotlight,[586] and for good reason:

> Information technology is embedded in global society and used daily by billions of people. The internet, personal electronic devices and social media are intrinsic to our economic and social future and offer important opportunities to tackle social and sustainability challenges. Yet concern at tech giants' negative human rights impacts is growing and society's trust in them is being corroded. ...

> Tech giants' human rights impacts range widely. Besides workforce and other supply chain issues, they include impacts linked to the gathering, use and commercialisation of personal data; facilitating the spread of hate speech, misinformation, political extremism, terrorism, electoral manipulation and the suppression of democratic dissent; the impacts of content moderation and encryption; discrimination and other human rights abuses resulting from algorithmic bias; and impacts on at-risk groups including children and human rights defenders. At system level, further impacts relate to concentration of wealth and reinforcement of inequalities, large-scale tax avoidance and its consequences for public revenues, economic instability and criminality linked to cryptocurrencies, for example. Many such issues have assumed new dimensions in the context of the COVID-19 pandemic.

> Regulators face difficulties in addressing such risks and securing compliance by powerful tech giants whose activities are dynamic, diversified, transnational and technically complex. In many cases, root causes of risks to human rights go beyond individual products or services to implicate tech giants' business models, corporate governance and incentives structures, as well as the effects of dominant market positions that assume, but also transcend, the decisions and conduct of individual corporations.[587]

In addition to all of these factors, the major tech companies are leviathans in terms of their revenues, profits and stock market valuations. In the United States, for example, in 2021 the stock market value of the five largest American firms (Apple, Microsoft, Google, Amazon and Facebook) was $9.3 trillion, which was 'more than the value of the next 27 most valuable U.S. companies put together, including corporate giants like Tesla, Walmart and JPMorgan Chase'. Apple's profits in a three-month period in 2021 reached $21.7 billion, which 'was nearly double the combined annual profits of the five largest U.S. airlines in pre-pandemic 2019'. And, in the same time period, Google earned $50 billion in advertising revenue.[588]

Facebook was founded in 2004 and, by 2023, had 3.03 billion monthly active users, with 2.064 billion users visiting at least one of Facebook's core products (Facebook, WhatsApp, Instagram, and Messenger) every day. It is available in 112 languages worldwide. In the United States, 70 percent of the total population use Facebook,

---

[586] See OHCHR, 'The practical application of the Guiding Principles on Business and Human Rights to the activities of technology companies', UN Doc. A/HRC/50/56 (2022).

[587] C. O'Brien, R. Jørgensen and B. Hogan, *Tech Giants and Human Rights: Investor Expectations* (2021). This is a report prepared for the Council on Ethics of the Swedish National Pension Funds by the Danish Institute for Human Rights.

[588] S. Ovide, 'Big Tech Has Outgrown This Planet', *The New York Times* (29 July 2021).

and in the United Kingdom it is used by 66 percent of the population. It is the leading social platform, used by 61.8 percent of social media users.[589] On 30 September 2023, Meta (Facebook's parent) had 66,185 full-time employees, down from 86,482 nine months earlier. In 2006, it had 150 employees. On 1 October 2021 the *Wall Street Journal* published 'The Facebook Files', aimed at showing that Facebook 'knows, in acute detail, that its platforms are riddled with flaws that cause harm, often in ways only the company fully understands.'

For all of these reasons, the following case study focuses on Facebook (and its parent company, Meta).[590] We look first at its official human rights policy and its policy guidance on 'dangerous organizations'.[591] Then we consider the work of its Oversight Board, set up in 2020, and originally described by Mark Zuckerberg as a kind of 'Facebook Supreme Court'.

META/FACEBOOK, CORPORATE HUMAN RIGHTS POLICY
(2021)

Meta's mission is to give people the power to build community and bring the world closer together. We build social technologies to enable the best of what people can do together. Our principles are: give people a voice; serve everyone; promote economic opportunity; build connection and community; keep people safe and protect privacy. We recognize all people are equal in dignity and rights. We are all equally entitled to our human rights, without discrimination. Human rights are interrelated, interdependent and indivisible.

OUR COMMITMENTS

We are committed to respecting human rights as set out in the [UNGPs]. This commitment encompasses internationally recognized human rights as defined by the International Bill of Human Rights [the UDHR and the two Covenants], as well as the [ILO] Declaration on Fundamental Principles and Rights at Work.

Depending on circumstances, we also utilize other widely accepted international human rights instruments, including [CERD, CEDAW, CRC, CRPD, the EU Charter of Fundamental Rights, and the American Convention].

We specifically recognize that the universal obligation of non-discrimination is a necessary — but not sufficient — condition for real, lived, equality.

We are committed to implementing the Global Network Initiative (GNI) Principles on Freedom of Expression and Privacy, and their associated Implementation Guidelines. Human rights also guide our work developing responsible innovation practices, including when building, testing, and deploying products and services enabled by Artificial Intelligence (AI).

We recognize the importance of the OECD Principles on Artificial Intelligence, which are widely adopted and endorsed by the G20. In particular, we note the framework's recommendation that:

> "AI actors should respect the rule of law, human rights and democratic values,
> throughout the AI system lifecycle. These include freedom, dignity and autonomy,
> privacy and data protection, non-discrimination and equality, diversity, fairness, social
> justice, and internationally recognised labour rights."

We recognize the diversity of laws in the locations where we operate, and where people use our products. We strive to respect domestic laws. When faced with conflicts between such laws and our human rights commitments, we seek to honor the principles of internationally recognized human rights to the greatest extent possible. In these circumstances we seek to promote international human rights standards by engaging with governments, and by collaborating with other stakeholders and companies.

---

[589] www.demandsage/facebook-statistics/
[590] See Meta, Human Rights Report: Insights and Actions 2022 (2023).
[591] For a description of the evolution of these policies, see K. Stylianou, N. Zingales and S. Di Stefano, *Is Facebook Keeping Up with International Standards on Freedom of Expression? A Time-Series Analysis, 2005-2020* (2022).

HOW WE IMPLEMENT

We implement our commitment to human rights using approaches set out in the [UNGPs]. …

…

02 Conducting Human Rights Due Diligence and Disclosure

The potential human rights impacts of Meta's products and operations varies significantly across time, location, content, and affected communities. We thus identify and prioritize the most salient human rights issues in each context using the UNGP framework of likelihood and severity (the latter defined by scope, scale, and remediability).

We conduct human rights due diligence to identify such risks, and to help us create strategies to avoid, prevent and mitigate them. We also seek to identify and support opportunities for our products, policies, and operations to promote human rights.

We use a variety of due diligence methodologies, including, but not limited to, human rights impact assessments.

We pay particular attention to the rights and needs of users from groups or populations that may be at heightened risk of becoming vulnerable or marginalized. We are committed to identifying relevant such groups for each context, undertaking meaningful engagement to hear their hopes and concerns, and to protecting and promoting their rights when using our products.

…

FACEBOOK COMMUNITY STANDARDS: DANGEROUS INDIVIDUALS AND ORGANIZATIONS POLICY (ACCESSED 9 NOVEMBER 2022)

Policy Rationale

In an effort to prevent and disrupt real-world harm, we do not allow organizations or individuals that proclaim a violent mission or are engaged in violence to have a presence on Facebook. We assess these entities based on their behavior both online and offline, most significantly, their ties to violence. Under this policy, we designate individuals, organizations, and networks of people. These designations are divided into three tiers that indicate the level of content enforcement, with Tier 1 resulting in the most extensive enforcement because we believe these entities have the most direct ties to offline harm.

Tier 1 focuses on entities that engage in serious offline harms - including organizing or advocating for violence against civilians, repeatedly dehumanizing or advocating for harm against people based on protected characteristics, or engaging in systematic criminal operations. Tier 1 entities include terrorist, hate, and criminal organizations. We remove praise, substantive support, and representation of Tier 1 entities as well as their leaders, founders, or prominent members. Tier 1 includes hate organizations; criminal organizations, including those designated by the United States government as Specially Designated Narcotics Trafficking Kingpins (SDNTKs); and terrorist organizations, including entities and individuals designated by the United States government as Foreign Terrorist Organizations (FTOs) or Specially Designated Global Terrorists (SDGTs).
….

In addition, we do not allow content that praises, substantively supports, or represents events that Facebook designates as violating violent events - including terrorist attacks, hate events, multiple-victim violence or attempted multiple-victim violence, multiple murders, or hate crimes. Nor do we allow praise, substantive support, or representation of the perpetrator(s) of such attacks. We also remove content that praises, substantively supports or represents ideologies that promote hate, such as nazism and white supremacy.

Tier 2 focuses on entities that engage in violence against state or military actors but do not generally target civilians -- what we call "Violent Non-State Actors." We remove all substantive support and representation of these entities, their leaders, and their prominent members. We remove any praise of these groups' violent activities.

Tier 3 focuses on entities that may repeatedly engage in violations of our Hate Speech or Dangerous Organizations policies on-or-off the platform or demonstrate strong intent to engage in offline violence in the near future, but have not necessarily engaged in violence to date or advocated for violence against others based on their protected characteristics. This includes Militarized Social Movements, Violence-Inducing Conspiracy Networks, and individuals and groups banned for promoting hatred. Tier 3 entities may not have a presence or coordinate on our platforms.

We recognize that users may share content that includes references to designated dangerous organizations and individuals to report on, condemn, or neutrally discuss them or their activities. Our policies are designed to allow room for these types of discussions while simultaneously limiting risks of potential offline harm. We thus require people to clearly indicate their intent when creating or sharing such content. If a user's intention is ambiguous or unclear, we default to removing content.

In line with international human rights law, our policies allow discussions about the human rights of designated individuals or members of designated dangerous entities, unless the content includes other praise, substantive support, or representation of designated entities or other policy violations, such as incitement to violence.
…

OVERSIGHT BOARD CHARTER
(SEPTEMBER 2019)

Introduction

Freedom of expression is a fundamental human right. Facebook seeks to give people a voice so we can connect, share ideas and experiences, and understand each other.
…
… The purpose of the [Oversight Board] is to protect free expression by making principled, independent decisions about important pieces of content and by issuing policy advisory opinions on Facebook's content policies.

The board will operate transparently and its reasoning will be explained clearly to the public, while respecting the privacy and confidentiality of the people who use Facebook, Inc.'s services, including Instagram (collectively referred to as "Facebook"). It will provide an accessible opportunity for people to request its review and be heard.
…

Article 1. Members
The board will be composed of a diverse set of members whose names will be public. They will exercise neutral, independent judgment and render decisions impartially.

SECTION 1. SIZE
The board will consist of [between 11 and 40 members. As of January 2023, there were 23].

SECTION 2. BOARD COMPOSITION AND MEMBER QUALIFICATIONS
… [M]embers must possess and exhibit a broad range of knowledge, competencies, diversity, and expertise.

Members must not have actual or perceived conflicts of interest that could compromise their independent judgment and decision-making. Members must have demonstrated experience at deliberating thoughtfully and as an open-minded contributor on a team; be skilled at making and explaining decisions based on a set of policies or standards; and have familiarity with matters relating to digital content and governance, including free expression, civic discourse, safety, privacy and technology.

SECTION 3. TERM

Each member will serve for a three-year term, for a maximum of three terms. Trustees will oversee the approval of term renewals.

...

SECTION 4. COLLECTIVE POWERS

The board will have the following expressly defined authorities for content properly brought to the board for review:

> 1. Request that Facebook provide information reasonably required for board deliberations in a timely and transparent manner;
>
> 2. Interpret Facebook's Community Standards and other relevant policies (collectively referred to as "content policies") in light of Facebook's articulated values;
>
> 3. Instruct Facebook to allow or remove content;
>
> 4. Instruct Facebook to uphold or reverse a designation that led to an enforcement outcome;
>
> 5. Issue prompt, written explanations of the board's decisions.

In addition, the board can provide policy guidance, specific to a case decision or upon Facebook's request, on Facebook's content policies. The board will have no authority or powers beyond those expressly defined by this charter.

...

Article 2. Authority to Review

People using Facebook's services and Facebook itself may bring forward content for board review. The board will review and decide on content in accordance with Facebook's content policies and values.

SECTION 1. SCOPE

In instances where people disagree with the outcome of Facebook's decision and have exhausted appeals, a request for review can be submitted to the board by either the original poster of the content or a person who previously submitted the content to Facebook for review. Separately, Facebook can submit requests for review, including additional questions related to the treatment of content beyond whether the content should be allowed or removed completely. Detailed procedures on submission and requirements for review by the board will be publicly available.

The board has the discretion to choose which requests it will review and decide upon. In its selection, the board will seek to consider cases that have the greatest potential to guide future decisions and policies. In limited circumstances where the board's decision on a case could result in criminal liability or regulatory sanctions, the board will not take the case for review.

The board will establish its own set of procedures that its staff will use to select a pool of cases from which the board can choose. Once a case is selected, the board will notify the submitting person, the person who originally posted the content, and Facebook.

SECTION 2. BASIS OF DECISION- MAKING

Facebook has a set of values that guide its content policies and decisions. The board will review content enforcement decisions and determine whether they were consistent with Facebook's content policies and values.

For each decision, any prior board decisions will have precedential value and should be viewed as highly persuasive when the facts, applicable policies, or other factors are substantially similar.

...

* * *

The Oversight Board has used the following formulation to summarize its own status and role:

> The Oversight Board is a separate entity from Meta and will provide its independent judgment on both individual cases and questions of policy.[592] Both the Board and its administration are funded by an independent trust. The Board has the authority to decide whether Facebook and Instagram should allow or remove content. These decisions are binding, unless implementing them could violate the law. The Board can also choose to issue recommendations on the company's content policies.

The Board's 'decisions' are prepared by five-member panels, and approved by a majority of the Board. Membership of the panels is not public, and majority and minority views are not attributed to named individuals.

OVERSIGHT BOARD, THE TRUMP CASE
CASE DECISION 2021-001-FB-FBR (2021)

Full case decision

In this case, Facebook asked the Board to answer two questions:

> Considering Facebook's values, specifically its commitment to voice and safety, did it correctly decide on January 7, 2021, to prohibit Donald J. Trump's access to posting content on Facebook and Instagram for an indefinite amount of time?

> In addition to the board's determination on whether to uphold or overturn the indefinite suspension, Facebook welcomes observations or recommendations from the board about suspensions when the user is a political leader.

…

2. Case description

Elections are a crucial part of democracy. They allow people throughout the world to govern and to resolve social conflicts peacefully. In the United States of America, the Constitution says the president is selected by counting electoral college votes. On January 6, 2021, during the counting of the 2020 electoral votes, a mob forcibly entered the Capitol where the electoral votes were being counted and threatened the constitutional process. Five people died and many more were injured during the violence.

Prior to January 6, then-President Donald Trump had asserted without evidence that the November 2020 presidential election had been stolen. Legal claims brought by Mr. Trump and others of election fraud were rejected in over 70 cases, and the then-Attorney General, after investigation, stated that there had been no fraud "on a scale that could have effected a different outcome in the election." Nevertheless, Mr. Trump continued to make these unfounded claims, including through using Facebook, and referred to a rally planned for January 6:

> a. On December 19, 2020, the Trump Facebook page posted: "Peter Navarro releases 36-page report alleging election fraud 'more than sufficient' to swing victory to Trump - A great report by Peter. Statistically impossible to have lost the 2020 Election. Big protest in D.C. on January 6th. Be there, will be wild!"

> b. On January 1, 2021, the Trump Facebook page posted: "The BIG Protest Rally in Washington, D.C., will take place at 11.00 A.M. on January 6th. Locational details to follow. StopTheSteal!"

…

---

[592] https://www.oversightboard.com/.

During [the mob attack on the Capitol], Mr. Trump posted a video and a statement to his Facebook page (which had at least 35 million followers), and the video was also shared to his Instagram account (which had at least 24 million followers). The posts stated the 2020 election was "stolen" and "stripped away." The posts also praised and supported those who were at the time rioting inside the Capitol, while also calling on them to remain peaceful. ...

...

Mr. Trump posted the following written statement at 6:07 pm EST, as police were securing the Capitol:

> These are the things and events that happen when a sacred landslide election victory is so unceremoniously & viciously stripped away from great patriots who have been badly & unfairly treated for so long. Go home with love & in peace. Remember this day forever!

At 6:15 pm EST, Facebook removed this post for violating its Community Standard on Dangerous Individuals and Organizations and imposed a 24-hour block on Mr. Trump's ability to post on Facebook or Instagram.

On January 7, 2021, after further reviewing Mr. Trump's posts, his recent communications off Facebook, and additional information about the severity of the violence at the Capitol, Facebook extended the block "indefinitely and for at least the next two weeks until the peaceful transition of power is complete." Facebook cited Mr. Trump's "use of our platform to incite violent insurrection against a democratically elected government."

...

4. Relevant standards

Under the Oversight Board's Charter, it must consider all cases in light of the following standards:

I. Facebook's content policies:

...

Facebook's Community Standard on Dangerous Individuals and Organizations prohibits [certain content.]

...

II. Facebook's values:

Facebook has five values outlined in the introduction to the Community Standards which it claims guide what is allowed on its platforms. Three of these values are "Voice," "Safety," and "Dignity."

...

III. Human rights standards:

...

The Board analyzed Facebook's human rights responsibilities in this case by considering human rights standards including:

- The right to freedom of expression: ... (ICCPR), Articles 19 and 20; as interpreted in General Comment No. 34, Human Rights Committee (2011); the Rabat Plan of Action [on the prohibition of advocacy of national, racial or religious hatred that constitutes incitement to discrimination, hostility or violence, published by OHCHR], (2012); UN Special Rapporteur on freedom of opinion and expression report A/HRC/38/35 (2018); Joint Statement of international freedom of expression monitors on COVID-19 (March, 2020).
- The right to life: ICCPR Article 6.
- The right to security of person: ICCPR Article 9, para. 1.
- The right to non-discrimination: ICCPR Articles 2 and 26; [ICERD], Articles 1 and 4.
- Participation in public affairs and the right to vote: ICCPR Article 25.
- The right to remedy: ICCPR Article 2; General Comment No. 31, Human Rights Committee (2004); UNGPs, Principle 22.

5. Content creator's statement

When Facebook refers a case to the Board, the Board gives the person responsible for the content the opportunity to submit a statement. In this case, a statement to the Board was submitted on Mr. Trump's behalf … .

…

6. Facebook's explanation of its decision

…

Facebook states that its decision was "informed by Article 19 of the ICCPR, and U.N. General Comment No. 34 on freedom of expression, which permits necessary and proportionate restrictions of freedom of expression in situations of public emergency that threatens the life of the nation. In this case, the District of Columbia was operating under a state of emergency that had been declared to protect the U.S. Capitol complex." Facebook notes that it also took into account the six contextual factors from the Rabat Plan of Action on the prohibition of advocacy of national, racial or religious hatred. The Rabat Plan of Action was developed by experts with the support of the United Nations to guide states in addressing when advocacy of racial, religious or national hatred that incites discrimination, hostility or violence is so serious that resort to state-imposed criminal sanctions is appropriate, while protecting freedom of expression, in line with states' obligations under Article 19 and Article 20, para. 2 of the ICCPR.

Facebook argues that the events of January 6 represented an unprecedented threat to the democratic processes and constitutional system of the United States. While Facebook asserts that it strives to act proportionately and accountably in curtailing public speech, given the unprecedented and volatile circumstances, Facebook believes it should retain operational flexibility to take further action including a permanent ban.

In this case, the Board asked Facebook 46 questions, and Facebook declined to answer seven entirely, and two partially. The questions that Facebook did not answer included questions about how Facebook's news feed and other features impacted the visibility of Mr. Trump's content; whether Facebook has researched, or plans to research, those design decisions in relation to the events of January 6, 2021; and information about violating content from followers of Mr. Trump's accounts. The Board also asked questions related to the suspension of other political figures and removal of other content; whether Facebook had been contacted by political officeholders or their staff about the suspension of Mr. Trump's accounts; and whether account suspension or deletion impacts the ability of advertisers to target the accounts of followers. Facebook stated that this information was not reasonably required for decision-making in accordance with the intent of the Charter; was not technically feasible to provide; was covered by attorney/client privilege; and/or could not or should not be provided because of legal, privacy, safety, or data protection concerns.

7. Third-party submissions

The Oversight Board received 9,666 public comments related to this case. …

…

8. Oversight Board analysis

8.1 Compliance with content policies

The Board agrees with Facebook's decision that the two posts by Mr. Trump on January 6 violated Facebook's Community Standards and Instagram's Community Guidelines. Facebook's Community Standard on Dangerous Individuals and Organizations says that users should not post content "expressing support or praise for groups, leaders, or individuals involved in" violating events. …

…

The Board notes that other Community Standards may have been violated in this case, including the Standard on Violence and Incitement. Because Facebook's decision was not based on this Standard and an additional finding of violation would not affect the outcome of this proceeding, a majority of the Board refrains from reaching any judgment on this alternative ground. …

A minority of the Board would consider the additional ground and find that the Violence and Incitement Standard was violated. The minority would hold that, read in context, the posts stating the election was being "stolen from us" and "so unceremoniously & viciously stripped," coupled with praise of the rioters, qualifies as "calls for actions," "advocating for violence" and "misinformation and unverifiable rumors that contribute[d] to the risk of imminent violence or physical harm" prohibited by the Violence and Incitement Community Standard.

The Board finds that the two posts severely violated Facebook policies and concludes that Facebook was justified in restricting the account and page on January 6 and 7.

...

8.2 Compliance with Facebook's values

The analysis above is consistent with Facebook's stated values of "Voice" and "Safety." For the reasons stated in this opinion, in this case the protection of public order justified limiting freedom of expression.

A minority believes it is particularly important to emphasize that "Dignity" was also relevant. Facebook relates "Dignity" to equality and that people should not "harass or degrade" others. The minority considers below that previous posts on the platform by Mr. Trump contributed to racial tension and exclusion and that this context was key to understanding the impact of Mr. Trump's content. Having dealt with this case on other grounds, the majority does not comment on these posts.

8.3 Compliance with Facebook's human rights responsibilities

... [The UNGPs] which Facebook has endorsed, establish what businesses should do on a voluntary basis to meet these responsibilities. ...

Facebook has become a virtually indispensable medium for political discourse, and especially so in election periods. It has a responsibility both to allow political expression and to avoid serious risks to other human rights. Facebook, like other digital platforms and media companies, has been heavily criticized for distributing misinformation and amplifying controversial and inflammatory material. Facebook's human rights responsibilities must be understood in the light of those sometimes competing considerations.

The Board analyzes Facebook's human rights responsibilities through international standards on freedom of expression and the rights to life, security, and political participation. Article 19 of the ICCPR sets out the right to freedom of expression.

... The Board does not apply the First Amendment of the U.S. Constitution, which does not govern the conduct of private companies. However, the Board notes that in many relevant respects the principles of freedom of expression reflected in the First Amendment are similar or analogous to the principles of freedom of expression in ICCPR Article 19.

Political speech receives high protection under human rights law because of its importance to democratic debate. The UN Human Rights Committee provided authoritative guidance on Article 19 ICCPR in General Comment No. 34 ... .

...

International law allows for expression to be limited when certain conditions are met. Any restrictions must meet three requirements – rules must be clear and accessible, they must be designed for a legitimate aim, and they must be necessary and proportionate to the risk of harm. The Board uses this three-part test to analyze Facebook's actions when it restricts content or accounts. First Amendment principles under U.S. law also insist that restrictions on freedom of speech imposed through state action may not be vague, must be for important governmental reasons and must be narrowly tailored to the risk of harm.

I. Legality (clarity and accessibility of the rules)

...

The clarity of the Standard against praise and support of Dangerous Individuals and Organizations leaves much to be desired ... . The UN Special Rapporteur on Freedom of Expression has also raised concerns about the vagueness of the [Standard]. ... Any vagueness under the terms of the Standard does not render its application to the circumstances of this case doubtful. The January 6 riot at the Capitol fell squarely within the types of harmful events set out in Facebook's policy, and Mr. Trump's posts praised and supported those involved at the very time the violence was going on, and while Members of Congress were calling on him for help. In relation to these facts, Facebook's policies gave adequate notice to the user and guidance to those enforcing the rule.

With regard to penalties for violations, ... the Board reiterates that the patchwork of applicable rules makes it difficult for users to understand why and when Facebook restricts accounts, and raises legality concerns.

... Facebook's imposition of an "indefinite" restriction is vague and uncertain. "Indefinite" restrictions are not described in the Community Standards and it is unclear what standards would trigger this penalty or what standards will be employed to maintain or remove it. Facebook provided no information of any prior imposition of indefinite suspensions in any other cases. The Board recognizes the necessity of some discretion on Facebook's part to suspend accounts in urgent situations like that of January, but users cannot be left in a state of uncertainty for an indefinite time.

The Board rejects Facebook's request for it to endorse indefinite restrictions, imposed and lifted without clear criteria. Appropriate limits on discretionary powers are crucial to distinguish the legitimate use of discretion from possible scenarios around the world in which Facebook may unduly silence speech not linked to harm or delay action critical to protecting people.

II. Legitimate aim
...

III. Necessity and proportionality
The requirement of necessity and proportionality means that any restriction on expression must, among other things, be the least intrusive way to achieve a legitimate aim (General Comment No. 34, para. 34).
...
The crucial question is whether Facebook's decision to restrict access to Mr. Trump's accounts on January 6 and 7 was necessary and proportionate to protect the rights of others. ...

As part of its analysis, the Board drew upon the six factors from the Rabat Plan of Action to assess the capacity of speech to create a serious risk of inciting discrimination, violence, or other lawless action: [Context; status of the speaker; intent; content and form; extent and reach; and imminence of harm.]
...

Analyzing these factors, the Board concludes that the violation in this case was severe in terms of its human rights harms. Facebook's imposition of account-level restrictions on January 6 and the extension of those restrictions on January 7 was necessary and proportionate.
...

9. Oversight Board decision
On January 6, Facebook's decision to impose restrictions on Mr. Trump's accounts was justified. ...

However, it was not appropriate for Facebook to impose an indefinite suspension.

Facebook did not follow a clear published procedure in this case. Facebook's normal account-level penalties for violations of its rules are to impose either a time-limited suspension or to permanently disable the user's account. The Board finds that it is not permissible for Facebook to keep a user off the platform for an undefined period, with no criteria for when or whether the account will be restored.
...
Facebook must, within six months of this decision, reexamine the arbitrary penalty it imposed on January 7 and decide the appropriate penalty. This penalty must be based on the gravity of the violation and the prospect of future harm. It must also be consistent with Facebook's rules for severe violations which must in turn be clear, necessary, and proportionate.
...

… A minority of the Board emphasizes that Facebook's rules should ensure that users who seek reinstatement after suspension recognize their wrongdoing and commit to observing the rules in the future. In this case, the minority suggests that, before Mr. Trump's account can be restored, Facebook must also aim to ensure the withdrawal of praise or support for those involved in the riots.

10. Policy advisory statement

…

Finally, the Board urges Facebook to develop and publish a policy that governs its response to crises or novel situations where its regular processes would not prevent or avoid imminent harm. While these situations cannot always be anticipated, Facebook's guidance should set appropriate parameters for such actions, including a requirement to review its decision within a fixed time.

OVERSIGHT BOARD, THE 'BLACK PETE' CASE
CASE 2021-002-FB-UA (2021)

On December 5, 2020, a Facebook user in the Netherlands shared a post including text in Dutch and a 17-second-long video on their timeline. The video showed a young child meeting three adults, one dressed to portray "Sinterklaas" and two portraying "Zwarte Piet," also referred to as "Black Pete."

The two adults portraying Zwarte Piets had their faces painted black and wore Afro wigs under hats and colorful renaissance-style clothes. All the people in the video appear to be white, including those with their faces painted black. In the video, festive music plays and one Zwarte Piet says to the child, "[l]ook here, and I found your hat. Do you want to put it on? You'll be looking like an actual Pete!"

Facebook removed the post for violating its Hate Speech Community Standard.

Key findings

While Zwarte Piet represents a cultural tradition shared by many Dutch people without apparent racist intent, it includes the use of blackface which is widely recognized as a harmful racial stereotype.

Since August 2020, Facebook has explicitly prohibited caricatures of Black people in the form of blackface as part of its Hate Speech Community Standard. As such, the Board found that Facebook made it sufficiently clear to users that content featuring blackface would be removed unless shared to condemn the practice or raise awareness.

A majority of the Board saw sufficient evidence of harm to justify removing the content. They argued the content included caricatures that are inextricably linked to negative and racist stereotypes, and are considered by parts of Dutch society to sustain systemic racism in the Netherlands. They took note of documented cases of Black people experiencing racial discrimination and violence in the Netherlands linked to Zwarte Piet. These included reports that during the Sinterklaas festival Black children felt scared and unsafe in their homes and were afraid to go to school.

A majority found that allowing such posts to accumulate on Facebook would help create a discriminatory environment for Black people that would be degrading and harassing. They believed that the impacts of blackface justified Facebook's policy and that removing the content was consistent with the company's human rights responsibilities.

A minority of the Board, however, saw insufficient evidence to directly link this piece of content to the harm supposedly being reduced by removing it. They noted that Facebook's value of "Voice" specifically protects disagreeable content and that, while blackface is offensive, depictions on Facebook will not always cause harm to others. They also argued that restricting expression based on cumulative harm can be hard to distinguish from attempts to protect people from subjective feelings of offense.

…

The Oversight Board's decision
The Oversight Board upholds Facebook's decision to remove the content.
...

OVERSIGHT BOARD, TIGRAY COMMUNICATION AFFAIRS BUREAU
CASE 2022-006-FB-MR (2022)593

Case Summary and Outcome

On October 4, 2022, the Oversight Board upheld Meta's decision to remove a Facebook post that threatened violence during the conflict in Ethiopia. The content was posted on the official page of the Tigray Regional State's Communication Affairs Bureau and was viewed more than 300,000 times. The post discussed the losses suffered by federal forces, encouraged the national army to "turn its gun" toward Prime Minister Abiy Ahmed's group, and warned government forces that they would die if they refused to surrender. ...

[T]he Board held that by removing this post, Meta complied with Facebook's Violence and Incitement Community Standard, Meta's values, and the company's human rights responsibilities. Moreover, the Board considered that the "context in Ethiopia, the status and intent of the speaker; the content of the speech as well as its reach; and the likelihood of offline harm all contributed to a heightened risk of offline violence".

While the Board recognized Meta had taken positive steps to improve content moderation in some conflict zones, it highlighted that Meta should do more to meet its human rights responsibility to establish a principled, transparent system for moderating content in such contexts to reduce the risk of its platforms being used to incite violence or violations of international law. ...

OVERSIGHT BOARD, CALL FOR WOMEN'S PROTEST IN CUBA
CASE 2023-014-IG-UA (2023)

...

2. Case description and background

In July 2022, a news platform's verified Instagram account, describing itself as critical of the government in Cuba, posted a video in which a woman calls on other women to join her in the streets to protest. A caption in Spanish includes quotes from the video, hashtags that refer to the "dictatorship" and "regime" in Cuba, and calls for international attention to the humanitarian situation in the country, including by using #SOSCuba. At one point in the video, the woman says that Cuban men are "rats" because they cannot be counted on to defend those who are being repressed by the government. At another point, she says that Cuban men are "mares" who carry urinal pots. The text overlaying the video connects political change to women's protests. The video was played more than 90,000 times and shared fewer than 1,000 times.
...
The post was shared around the first anniversary of the historic nationwide protests that occurred in July 2021 when Cubans took to the streets in what the Inter-American Commission on Human Rights (IACHR) described as "a peaceful protest to claim their civil liberties and demand changes to the country's political structure." ...
...
The [government's] legislative response to the July 2021 protests also included further criminalization of online speech, including new penal code regulation establishing heightened penalties for alleged offenses such as spreading "fake information" or offending someone's "honor" on social media, or in online or offline media. This is supplementary to existing provisions of the penal code, which cover "public disorder," "resistance," and "contempt," and have historically been used to stifle dissent and criminalize protests. ...

Near-complete government control of the internet's technical infrastructure in Cuba, in addition to censorship, obstruction of communications, and the very high cost of accessing the internet, "prevents all but a small fraction of Cubans from reading independent news website and blogs" (IACHR, 2022 Annual Report, para.

---

593 For a critique, see D. Wong, and L. Floridi, 'Meta's Oversight Board: A Review and Critical Assessment', 33 *Minds & Machines* (2023) 261.

69). The Board also makes note of the attempts by government-linked networks described by Meta in its February 2023 report on Adversarial Threat to "create the perception of widespread support for the Cuban government across many internet platforms, including Facebook, Instagram, Telegram, Twitter, YouTube and Picta, a Cuban social network." … [Meta's] investigation found links between the Cuban government and the people behind a network of 363 Facebook accounts, 270 pages, 229 groups and 72 accounts on Instagram, which violated Meta's policy against coordinated inauthentic behavior.

…

6. Meta's submissions

…

The Board asked 17 questions in writing. The questions addressed issues relating to Meta's content-moderation approach in Cuba; the bearing that asymmetrical power dynamics have on the Hate Speech Community Standard, as well as its enforcement following automated and human review; and opportunities for context assessment, specifically within the part of Meta's cross-check system called Early Response Secondary Review (ERSR). ERSR is a type of cross-check that provides additional levels of human review for certain posts initially identified as violating Meta's policies while keeping the content online. All 17 questions were answered by Meta.

…

8. Oversight Board analysis

…

8.1 Compliance with Meta's content policies

I. Content rules

The Board finds that the content in this case is not hate speech as per Meta's Community Standards, but a *qualified behavioral statement* and, as such, is allowed under the Hate Speech policy. Consequently, the removal of the content is inconsistent with this policy. …

According to public comments and experts consulted by the Board, epithets such as "rats" or "mares" are used in the vernacular Spanish spoken in Cuba in heated discussions to imply cowardice. As such, the terms should not be read literally and do not indicate that men have inherently negative characteristics by virtue of being men. Rather, they mean that Cuban men have not acted with the necessary forcefulness to defend those who are being repressed by the government in the context of the protests.

…

In conclusion, the Board finds that, when read as a whole, the post does not intend to dehumanize men, generate violence against them or exclude them from conversations about the Cuban protests. On the contrary, the woman in the video is questioning what, in her opinion, the behavior of Cuban men has been in the precise context of the protests, and she aims to galvanize them to participate in such historic events. The content in this case is, therefore, a statement of qualified behavior on an issue of significant public interest related to the historic protests and the wave of repression that followed.

…

Finally, the Board agrees that the post falls directly within Meta's paramount value of "Voice." Therefore, its removal was not consistent with Meta's values. …

…

NOTE

Following the Board's decision in the Trump case, Meta's Vice-President of Global Affairs issued a statement on 4 June 2021. Trump's accounts were suspended for two years, a term that could be extended if Facebook determines that there remains a serious risk to public safety.

> When the suspension is eventually lifted, there will be a strict set of rapidly escalating
> sanctions that will be triggered if Mr. Trump commits further violations in future, up to
> and including permanent removal of his pages and accounts.

> …

… [Now that we have enforcement protocols] … we hope and expect they will only be applicable in the rarest circumstances.

We know that any penalty we apply — or choose not to apply — will be controversial. There are many people who believe it was not appropriate for a private company like Facebook to suspend an outgoing President from its platform, and many others who believe Mr. Trump should have immediately been banned for life. …

Of course, this penalty only applies to our services — Mr. Trump is and will remain free to express himself publicly via other means….

…

The Oversight Board's decision is accountability in action. It is a significant check on Facebook's power, and an authoritative way of publicly holding the company to account for its decisions. …

… Facebook shouldn't be making so many decisions about content by ourselves. In the absence of frameworks agreed upon by democratically accountable lawmakers, the board's model of independent and thoughtful deliberation is a strong one that ensures important decisions are made in as transparent and judicious a manner as possible. The Oversight Board is not a replacement for regulation, and we continue to call for thoughtful regulation in this space.

We are also committing to being more transparent about the decisions we make and how they impact our users. … [594]

The transparency commitment was challenged several months later by Faiza Patel and Mary Pat Dwyer, in 'So, What Does Facebook Take Down? The Secret List of 'Dangerous' Individuals and Organizations', *Just Security* (1 November 2021):

… [N]ew information has emerged about the content that the company routinely removes from the platform on the theory that it is legally required to do so. Because Facebook maintains that these takedowns are legally mandated, it has erected a wall around debates about those decisions. Its own Oversight Board is barred from hearing cases where a decision to reinstate a post "could" lead to "criminal liability" or "adverse governmental action." This rule insulates from review decisions about how Facebook interprets its legal obligations and how it evaluates the risks of a country's reaction.

Recently, the Intercept published the lists of people and groups that Facebook deems "dangerous," a jumble of well-known terrorist groups, street gangs, drug cartels, media organizations, and far-right militias that are covered under the company's Dangerous Individuals and Organizations (DIO) Community Standard. Facebook itself had only disclosed the existence of these lists and their overall policy rationale, but not the specific content of the lists. Upon publication of the lists, Facebook defended them with a familiar refrain; its departing Director of Counterterrorism and Dangerous Organizations stated that the company "has a legal obligation to follow U.S. law related to entities designated as foreign terrorist organizations, global terrorists and other sanctioned parties."

In fact, Facebook's lists include hundreds of groups and individuals that have not been designated or sanctioned by the U.S. government. Many of them are unsavory and under U.S. law Facebook is legally permitted to keep them off its platform, but no U.S. law requires it to do so.

---

[594] N. Clegg, 'In Response to Oversight Board, Trump Suspended for Two Years; Will Only Be Reinstated if Conditions Permit', *Meta Newsroom*, 4 June 2021.

Even for those groups that are drawn from U.S. government designations, the question remains: does U.S. law require social media platforms to take down praise and positive comments about groups and individuals if the government designates them as terrorists? Despite the repeated assertions of Facebook and Instagram, the answer is no.

The issue has significance far beyond the United States too. Does Facebook, for example, consider itself bound by Israel's recent, controversial designation of six human rights groups as terrorist organizations? Only when Facebook acknowledges that its decisions on who to include on its banned lists are its own can the company (and its peers, many of which also rely on similar lists) address the harms from this approach – a form of content moderation that is designed to capture a swath of speech that has little relationship to real world harms.

American commentators have also pushed back against Facebook's call for more effective government regulation of the Internet. Will Duffield, in 'About Those Facebook Ads Calling for More Internet Regulation', *National Review* (Online, 7 February 2022) argues that:

A "standardized approach" would eliminate competition among platforms to provide the best content moderation. At present, if Facebook users deem the platform's rules too restrictive, they can use more liberally governed services such as Reddit or Gab. Switching between rules is as easy as switching tabs. But standardizing the speech rules "all across the board" would erase many of these platforms' distinguishing features. Because of Facebook's size and ubiquity, any standardized rules would probably look more like Facebook's than those of other platforms.

…

Facebook seems to forget that America already provides a set of standardized speech rules. First Amendment jurisprudence allows the prohibition of obscenity, imminent threats, copyright violations, and other longstanding categories of unprotected speech. …

…

Standardizing the moderation practices of platforms would require government either to promulgate rules for the removal of protected speech or to prohibit platforms from removing protected speech entirely. In the former case, government would violate constitutional prohibitions on government censorship; in the latter, it would usurp the editorial rights of private platforms. Without the ability to moderate, platforms would struggle to attract the advertisers that fund their free publishing tools.

Although Facebook might wish to give its editorial rights to the government, our Constitution prevents the government from accepting them. If Facebook's power over speech is concerning, it would be more concerning in the hands of the state. One size of speech rules cannot possibly fit all. Facebook's desired homogenization of content policies would harm its competitors and leave Internet users worse off.

ANDREAS KULICK, META'S OVERSIGHT BOARD AND BEYOND– CORPORATIONS AS INTERPRETERS AND ADJUDICATORS OF INTERNATIONAL HUMAN RIGHTS NORMS 22 L. & PRAC. INT'L CTS. & TRIBUNALS (2023) 167

2.2. Flawed, But Without Alternative

Global Tech companies interpret human rights. …

… But they are flawed interpreters. Decision-making based on such interpretation lacks legitimacy in at least three respects. First of all, corporations in general lack democratic legitimacy to decide matters of individuals' human rights protection. …

Second, corporations … lack judicial legitimacy, i.e. the ability to settle a dispute authoritatively between two sides as an independent, neutral and impartial third party. [Tech companies are none of these.] … [S]ignificant differences exist between state courts as opposed to (quasi-) adjudicatory bodies set up by corporations. … First, corporations' internal structure may provide for some power-sharing and checks and balances and thus some 'corporate governance', but still is not tailored towards a separation of power into three branches of government that include a judiciary. Second, corporations are accountable only to their shareholders and not to an entire polis. Above all, corporations are not obliged to serve the public interest but instead have a duty to serve the shareholders' interests, which primarily means profit-making.

Third, there is the danger of what may be called corporate human rights imperialism: Global Tech companies usually lack socio-cultural legitimacy to interpret international human rights norms and to issue binding decisions based on such interpretations. … [T]here is the palpable possibility that companies hailing from the Western hemisphere apply predominantly Western views on how certain human rights standards should be interpreted. …

… [I]n the foreseeable future there seems to be hardly an alternative to corporations as flawed interpreters in the area of online speech regulation. … Furthermore, public regulation of online discourse does not seem an attractive alternative, considering the vast opportunities this would open for authoritarian governmental control. Also, the sheer number of instances in which decisions between two or several human rights issues on a platform with hundreds of millions or even several billion users need to be taken means that only a very small fraction of them will ever come before a domestic or international court. This is why domestic or regional regulation of online speech usually defers to corporations to realize and enforce human rights matters in the first – and often in the last – instance. It therefore seems that we are … stuck with corporations as flawed interpreters of human rights. Therefore, we need to think how to improve on such flaws. …

3. Case Study: The Jurisprudence of the OB [Oversight Board]

…

… [T]he OB's 'independence' as enshrined in its Charter and Bylaws should not distract from the fact that the OB remains very much Meta's creature: set up, (initially) selected and financed by the corporation. Meta has created an entity that it has bestowed with the competence to make, in a few select 'hard cases', individual content decisions in its stead. The OB's interpretations of human rights norms thereby remain attributable to Meta, Inc. and thus remain very much corporate interpretation – even more so given that the OB's 'independence' has limits … .

3.2. Analysis of the Case Law Thus Far

Turning to the analysis of its case law, as of mid-August 2022, the OB had deliberated on 26 disputes and had issued 25 decisions. …

…

… [A]ll 25 decisions are unanimous in concentrating on the interpretation of international human rights norms. In all decisions thus far, the OB starts with the Facebook Community Standards and Values but then dedicates usually about two thirds of the analysis to international human rights law.

…

… [E]stablished customary rules on treaty interpretation, as arguably enshrined in Articles 31-33 of the Vienna Convention on the Law of Treaties (VCLT), find neither mention nor recognizable application in the OB's decisions thus far. In fact, the board does not seem to burden itself with any form of textual interpretation of the human right norms it refers to. … [T]he OB relies for the most part on interpreting interpretations of human rights norms. What instructs its analysis are mostly secondary documents by U.N. and treaty bodies … . … Most frequently referred to are the [Human Rights Committee's General Comment No. 34], which is mentioned in each of the 25 decisions and 90 times overall, and various reports of the U.N. Special Rapporteur on Freedom of Expression, which all decisions but four refer to and which are cited 64 times in total. Other general comments or observations of the [Committee] or other treaty bodies as well as a few documents of U.N. (sub)bodies, such as the Rabat Plan of Action, feature regularly, but less frequently.

… The lack of consideration of [Human Rights Committee] case law on Article 19 ICCPR and similar jurisprudence on other provisions and by other treaty bodies is particularly striking. …

…

3.3. Conclusions on the OB 'Case Law'

… [T]he board's rather idiosyncratic method of interpretation, disguised as a mere application of authoritative interpretations of international human rights treaty provisions, bears the high potential of changing the content of these norms in the interest and image of the social media corporation … .

…

* * *

Some observers are more optimistic about the OB's role. Laurence Helfer and Molly Land, in 'The Meta Oversight Board's Human Rights Future', 44 *Cardozo L. Rev.* (2023) 2233, at 2299, conclude that:

> the Board is already making noteworthy contributions to advancing human rights. As it
> continues to provide Meta with interpretive guidance and recommendations, the OB will
> gradually shape the company's content moderation decisions and policies as well as
> international human rights law writ large. The Board may also assist national and regional
> lawmakers and courts in regulating social media companies and particularizing their due
> diligence obligations. And Meta's engagement with the OB may affect the company's
> culture, helping to inculcate the values of transparency, information sharing, and fair
> process.

> …

But a key question is whether the OB is achieving legitimacy by ticking the relevant procedural boxes – accessibility, selection criteria, legal reasoning, and the invocation of IHRL standards – while failing to explore the tailored substantive norms that are required in the context of content moderation by a private actor. Evelyn Douek, in 'The Meta Oversight Board and the Empty Promise of Legitimacy', 37 *Harv. J. L & Tech.* (2024) 000, notes that:

> The Board has barely discussed the differences between state and private speech
> regulators—it has not even discussed the ways in which the UNGPs explicitly distinguish
> a State's and a company's obligations under IHRL. Indeed, it more often emphasizes the
> way companies and states might face similar questions, rather than their differences. In
> no case has the use of IHRL meaningfully constrained the Board, nor could it. This is not
> a weakness of IHRL alone—because there is so little precedent about how to think about
> free speech interests in the context of private platforms, *no* body of pre-existing norms
> answers the difficult questions for making rights-respecting content moderation
> decisions. …

> …

> The Board instead regularly cites rules that apply to states and then proceeds to apply
> them to Meta, without comment, often using general and passive language like
> "restrictions on freedom of expression must [meet IHRL criteria]," eliding that the
> authorities they cite to are exclusively state-based jurisprudence. …[595]

---

[595] See also E. Douek, 'The Limits of International Law in Content Moderation', 6 *UC Irvine J. Int'l, Trans International, Transnational, and Comp. L.* (2021) 37.

She argues that this failure is even more important since other key actors moving to regulate platform operators, from the European Union to national efforts in India and Germany, are increasingly adopting an OB-style approach.

QUESTIONS

1. In assessing the potential of self-regulatory schemes such as that put in place by Facebook, consider the implications of this analysis by Ronald J. Deibert, in 'The Road to Digital Unfreedom: Three Painful Truths About Social Media', 30 *J. of Democracy* (2019) 25:

The first painful truth is that the social-media business is built around personal-data surveillance, with products ultimately designed to spy on us in order to push advertising in our direction. The second painful truth is that we have consented to this, but not entirely wittingly: social media are designed as addiction machines, expressly programmed to draw upon our emotions. The third painful truth is that the attention-grabbing algorithms underlying social media also propel authoritarian practices that aim to sow confusion, ignorance, prejudice, and chaos, thereby facilitating manipulation and undermining accountability. Moreover, the fine-grained surveillance that companies perform for economic reasons is a valuable proxy for authoritarian control.

2. Richard Wilson, in 'Digital Authoritarianism and The Global Assault on Human Rights', 44 *Hum. Rts. Q* (2022) 704, at 738 argues that '[p]latforms must move away from a one-size-fits-all content moderation policy towards a context-specific approach that is informed by, and responsive to, the circumstances on the ground. Content moderation policies must facilitate a pluralization of speech norms and a decentralization of their operations while conforming to international human rights principles …'. Is this what the Board did in the Cuban case?

3. In thinking about the desirability of internal or external 'oversight', consider the example of Twitter. One week after Elon Musk became owner and CEO of Twitter in October 2022, the company's Human Rights Counsel tweeted that 'the entire Human Rights team has been cut from the company', adding that he was proud of the work the team had done to implement the UNGPs 'to protect those at-risk in global conflicts & crises'.

---

4. Other Approaches to Regulation

Codes of conduct, various forms of Corporate Social Responsibility, voluntary self-regulation, and other techniques have often been found wanting in this context. In the materials that follow, we consider the approaches adopted by different judicial actors, note emerging regulatory approaches around human rights due diligence and, finally, consider some alternative ways forward, as suggested by Katarina Pistor and Surya Deva.

Judicial Remedies

Courts are increasingly involved in different aspects of the BHR debate, at both the national and international levels.

Historically, there are many examples of corporations being involved in crimes against humanity and war crimes, including unlawful killings, torture, and deprivation of liberty. Such crimes are committed in 'host states suffering from armed conflict and/or authoritarian regimes, in which the corporations operate or have business interests.'[596] During the drafting of the Rome Statute, France proposed the inclusion of an article stating that '[w]ithout prejudice to any individual criminal responsibility of natural persons under this Statute, the Court may also have jurisdiction over a juridical person under this Statute.' This amendment was not adopted and the

---

[596] W. Huisman, S. Karstedt and A. van Baar, 'The Involvement of Corporations in Atrocity Crimes', in B. Holá et al. (eds.), *The Oxford Handbook of Atrocity Crimes* (2022) 393, at 417.

Statute applies only to natural persons.[597] Nevertheless, efforts continue in this direction. Article 46C of the Statute of the African Court of Justice and Human Rights,[598] as amended by the Malabo Protocol of 2014, which has not yet entered into force, provides for corporate criminal liability:

1. … [T]he Court shall have jurisdiction over legal persons, with the exception of States.

2. Corporate intention to commit an offence may be established by proof that it was the policy of the corporation to do the act which constituted the offence.

3. A policy may be attributed to a corporation where it provides the most reasonable explanation of the conduct of that corporation.

4. Corporate knowledge of the commission of an offence may be established by proof that the actual or constructive knowledge of the relevant information was possessed within the corporation. …

And the Draft Articles on Crimes Against Humanity adopted by the International Law Commission in 2019 also address legal persons:

> Subject to the provisions of its national law, each State shall take measures, where appropriate, to establish the liability of legal persons for the offences referred to in this draft article. Subject to the legal principles of the State, such liability of legal persons may be criminal, civil or administrative (UN Doc. A/74/10 (2019), 14).

In terms of judicial remedies in domestic courts, Gwynne Skinner, in *Transnational Corporations and Human Rights: Overcoming Barriers to Judicial Remedy* (2020) 158 sees them as a crucial element in attaining a just outcome:

> … [V]ictims of business-related human rights abuses face numerous obstacles when they attempt to seek judicial remedy from a TNC from within the host state. TNCs often operate in high-risk countries whose legal systems lack causes of action, encompass an ineffective and non-independent judiciary, and fail to properly induce lawyers to take on cases about human rights violations. Additionally, these countries often fail to physically protect advocates and victims from retaliation or other forms of intimidation. Their legal codes often impose burdensome rules on victims (such as loser pays rules) that mean the case is both physically and logistically difficult to sustain. Such hurdles at the outset of a case mean that the legal system is already stacked against the victim, who usually lacks the financial resources of a TNC.

> When faced with such hurdles within the host country, victims should be able to turn to another jurisdiction for remedy. But in home states, too, … victims usually face similar hurdles: they lack a cause of action, such that the foreign court cannot establish subject matter jurisdiction (in the US, this is framed as a restriction on the extraterritorial jurisdiction of American courts). Moreover, rules limiting shareholder liability have pushed parent companies to the fringes of responsibility. Legal doctrines such as *forum non conveniens*, and restrictive rules for example on choice of law and limitation periods, are additional hurdles that victims encounter. …

> Non-judicial types of remedy, while theoretically an alternate source of redress, are often not as successful. Schemes at the company- or project-level, or initiatives such as the OECD's [National Contact Points], rarely achieve success for individual victims. Moreover, because their scope is so limited, their wider impact on human rights issues is too narrow to be effective.

---

[597] A. Clapham, 'The Question of Jurisdiction under International Criminal Law over Legal Persons: Lessons from the Rome Conference on an International Criminal Court', in M. Kamminga and S. Zia-Zarifi (eds.), *Liability of Multinational Corporations Under International Law* (2000) 139.
[598] T. Michalakea, 'Article 46C of the Malabo Protocol: A Contextually Tailored Approach to Corporate Criminal Liability and Its Contours', 7 *Int'l Hum. Rts L. Rev.* (2018) 225.

Together, these obstacles prevent victims from obtaining a remedy for their harm in two ways. First, they make the legal system financially and practically inaccessible to victims of business-related human rights violations. Second, for those victims who decide to pursue judicial remedy, it raises the emotional, financial, and physical costs to an overwhelming height.

…

… [H]ome states [should] legislate that parent corporations are strictly liable for any harm resulting from the extraterritorial acts of majority-owned subsidiaries and other affiliates they control which breach international human rights law, at least in those instances where the plaintiffs cannot realistically obtain a remedy from the subsidiary or affiliate in the host country. …

In *Vedanta Resources PLC v Lungowe*, [2019] UKSC 20, 1,800 Zambian citizens claimed that their health and livelihoods had been damaged by toxic discharges from the Nchanga Copper Mine, operated by Konkola Copper Mines (KCM), a Zambian company. The latter's parent company was the UK-domiciled Vedanta Resources. The suit alleged common law negligence and breach of statutory duty by both KCM as the operator of the Mine, and Vedanta on the basis that exercised control and direction at all material times over the mining operations.

The UK Supreme Court concluded that the public claims Vedanta had made about its responsibility for maintaining environmental control over its subsidiaries and its ongoing monitoring, training, and enforcement role gave rise to a possible duty of care. The Court explained that its main rationale for providing the claimants access to justice in the UK by asserting its jurisdiction was that the claimants had insufficient resources to fund litigation, had no access to legal aid, and could not rely on conditional fee agreements, which were illegal in Zambia. The Court also questioned the capacity of Zambian legal professionals 'in terms of numbers in the legal team, or experience' in order to conduct such complex litigation. The case has been widely welcomed as opening a potential door for litigants against parent companies for the operations of their subsidiaries. But critics have argued that the 'company's duty of care is construed as a product of its will (as conveyed in its "published materials") rather than on its potential impact and influence on the conduct of its subsidiaries. Such reasoning reifies the power relations between the British (Court) and the Zambian (victims and legal system). The voice, presence, and agency of the litigants are all missing from the decision.'[599]

The regional human rights courts have also addressed many issues of corporate responsibility. The European Court of Human Rights, for example, has an extensive body of case law dealing with state-owned corporate entities.[600] It also has a complex jurisprudence dealing with the *human* rights of corporations.[601] We turn now to an important case from the Inter-American system which relies heavily on the UNGPs in its reasoning.

INTER-AMERICAN COURT OF HUMAN RIGHTS, MISKITO DIVERS (LEMOTH MORRIS ET AL.) V. HONDURAS
JUDGMENT OF 31 AUGUST 2021
[UNOFFICIAL TRANSLATION FROM SPANISH]

[The case began with a 2004 petition to the Inter-American Commission on Human Rights alleging that Honduras had violated the human rights of a group of 42 lobster and shrimp divers from the indigenous Miskito community in the east of the country by failing to regulate safe working conditions, prevent labour exploitation, and provide effective administrative and judicial mechanisms for redress. In 2018, the Commission and the government reached a Friendly Settlement Agreement and the Court was called upon to approve the settlement.]

---

[599] D. Lustig, 'The Vedanta Challenge to Multilateralism: Piercing the Boundaries of the Global Legal Order', 20 *Int'l J. Const L.* (2022) 35, at 44.

[600] M. Barnes, 'The European Court of Human Rights and State-Owned Entities: Engagement and Development of a *Jurisprudence Constante*', 21 *The Law & Practice of International Courts and Tribunals* (2022) 369.

[601] A. Kulick, 'Corporate Human Rights?', 32 *Eur. J. Int'l L* (2021) 537.

31. According to PAHO [the Pan American Health Organization, male members of the Miskito community traditionally] practiced 'free diving' (without equipment) to obtain lobster for family consumption, not going deeper than 40 to 60 feet in their dives. However, due to their greater commercialization, which represents an important source of income for the Honduran economy, they began to fish on the Atlantic Coast of Honduras and Nicaragua, by diving, and not by artisanal fishing. PAHO noted that the Miskitos begin this activity at the age of 14, and that it ... causes occupational accidents, intoxications and disabilities for people of productive age. ... [O]f the 9,000 lobster divers, 98% of whom are Miskitos, 97% have suffered some type of syndrome and 4,200 have some type of disability.

32. [The Court noted the grave dangers of such deep-sea fishing and PAHO's evidence that most diving accidents are preventable if a range of precautionary measures are taken.]

33. [T]he Inter-American Development Bank [IDB] reported that ... the fishing companies do not have the minimum standards necessary ..., there are no contracts to support the labor relationship, the appropriate equipment for this activity is not provided, so divers lack adequate safety conditions. In addition, the IDB noted that some divers have been offered drugs to be able to resist as long as possible underwater fishing for lobster, even in some cases receiving part of their salary in cash and part with drugs.

34. ... [T]he National Commissioner for Human Rights ... indicated that, since 2001, Miskitos who are recruited to be divers do not receive training on diving techniques or on the safety measures that should be adopted. They also reported that the people affected by accidents have not received compensation for the damages suffered or the illnesses or disabilities resulting from such accidents. For this reason, due to injuries and lack of treatment and compensation, most Miskito divers with disabilities engage in begging.
...
38. ... According to the information received, there are no mechanisms to supervise the working conditions of Miskito divers. On the other hand, there is little State presence to offer protection and judicial guarantees to the divers in the area. The State stated that it would look further into the issue to find a solution.
...

Considerations of the court with respect to human rights violations to the detriment of the victims

41. ... [T]his Court deems it appropriate to analyze the content of the rights that were affected ... with special emphasis on the rights to life, personal integrity, health and social security, work and fair and satisfactory conditions that guarantee the health and safety of the worker ... .

A. Preliminary consideration: the responsibility of business with respect to human rights

42. ... [T]he first obligation assumed by the States Parties [to] the Convention, is to "respect the rights and freedoms" recognized ... . [T]he protection of human rights necessarily includes the notion of restricting the exercise of state power.

43. The second obligation of States is to "guarantee" the free and full exercise of the rights ... . This obligation implies the duty of the States Parties to organize the entire governmental apparatus and, in general, all structures through which the exercise of public power is manifested, in such a way that they are capable of legally ensuring the free and full exercise of human rights. As a consequence of this obligation, States must prevent, investigate and punish any violation of the rights recognized ... .

44. ... [T]he obligation to guarantee extends beyond the relationship between State agents and persons subject to their jurisdiction, and encompasses the duty to prevent, in the private sphere, third parties from violating protected legal rights. [But any liability on the part of the State for private acts will depend on the particular circumstances and the concreteness of the relevant obligations.]

45. ... Article 2 of the Convention contemplates the general duty of the States Parties to adapt their domestic law to ... to guarantee [Convention rights]. This duty implies the adoption of measures in two areas. On the one hand, the elimination of norms and practices of any nature that violate the guarantees set forth in the Convention. On the other hand, the issuance of norms and the development of practices conducive to the

effective observance of these guarantees. Precisely with respect to the adoption of such measures, this Court has recognized that all the authorities of a State Party to the Convention have the obligation to exercise a control of conventionality, so that the interpretation and application of the Convention may be based on the principle of the right to a fair trial.

46. [The Court's responsibility is not] to determine the individual responsibility of private parties, but to establish whether States are responsible for the violation of the human rights recognized in the Convention. [The Court recalls General Comment No. 24 of the ESCR Committee].

47. [The Court then 'highlights', and quotes at length from, the three pillars of the UNGPs,] as well as the foundational principles derived from these pillars, which are fundamental in determining the scope of the human rights obligations of States and companies … .

48. Therefore, and in the framework of the obligations to guarantee and the duty to adopt domestic law provisions derived from Articles 1(1) and 2 of the American Convention, this Court emphasizes that the States have the duty to prevent violations of the Convention. The States must adopt legislative and other measures to prevent such violations and to investigate, punish and redress such violations when they occur. States are thus obliged to regulate that companies adopt actions aimed at respecting the human rights recognized in the various [Inter-American human rights instruments] … especially in relation to risky activities. By virtue of this regulation, companies must prevent their activities from causing or contributing to human rights violations, and adopt measures aimed at remedying such violations. The Court considers that the responsibility of companies is applicable regardless of size or sector; however, their responsibilities may be differentiated in the legislation by virtue of the activity and the risk they pose to human rights.

49. In addition, this Court considers that, in order to achieve the aforementioned goals, States should adopt measures to ensure that companies have: a) appropriate policies for the protection of human rights; b) due diligence processes for the identification, prevention and correction of human rights violations, as well as to guarantee decent and dignified work; and c) processes that allow the company to repair human rights violations that occur as a result of its activities, especially when these affect people living in poverty or belonging to groups in vulnerable situations. The Court considers that, within this framework of action, States should encourage companies to incorporate good corporate governance practices with a stakeholder approach, which entail actions aimed at orienting business activity towards human rights violations. …

50. … States must guarantee the existence of judicial or extrajudicial mechanisms that are effective in remedying human rights violations. …

51. … [I]t is the companies that are primarily responsible for behaving responsibly in the activities they carry out, since their active participation is fundamental for the respect and enforcement of human rights. Companies must adopt, on their own, preventive measures for the protection of the human rights of their workers, as well as those aimed at preventing their activities from having a negative impact on the communities in which they operate or on the environment. In this sense, the Court considers that the regulation of business activity does not require companies to guarantee results, but should be aimed at ensuring that they carry out continuous assessments of the risks to human rights, and respond through effective and proportional measures to mitigate the risks caused by their activities, in consideration of their resources and possibilities, as well as with accountability mechanisms for the damages that have been produced. This is an obligation that must be adopted by companies and regulated by the State.

52. … States must adopt measures aimed at ensuring that transnational corporations are held accountable for human rights violations committed in their territory, or when they benefit from the activity of national companies that participate in their chain of productivity.
…

[In a unanimous Judgment, the Court endorsed the Friendly Settlement Agreement, accepted the State's acknowledgement of international responsibility, found violations of the rights to life, to life with dignity, to personal integrity, to judicial guarantees, to the rights of the child, to equal protection of the law, to judicial protection, to health, to work in just, equitable and satisfactory conditions, to social security, and to equality and non-discrimination, and it ordered a wide range of specific actions to be undertaken by the State (para. 162).]

Due Diligence-Based Regulatory Options

The UNGPs have succeeded in turning much of the regulatory focus on to the principle of due diligence. But it has done so in a way that poses risks to the original meaning(s) of the term. The emphasis of international regulatory efforts is now on the notion of 'human rights due diligence' or HRDD, which is assuming an increasingly narrow and specialized meaning. When the concept first entered the mainstream of human rights jurisprudence through the *Velásquez Rodríguez* case (see Ch. 3, above) it had a broad and open-ended connotation, which was then transposed into issue areas such as violence against women. Recall the Human Rights Committee's use of the concept in 2004 (Ch 9, above) as an obligation on states 'to prevent, punish, investigate or redress the harm caused' by private actors. In 2018, it expanded upon this approach in General Comment No. 36, observing that States parties have 'a due diligence obligation to undertake reasonable positive measures, which do not impose on them disproportionate burdens, in response to reasonably foreseeable threats to life originating from private persons and entities, whose conduct is not attributable to the State. … States parties must further take adequate measures of protection, including continuous supervision, in order to prevent, investigate, punish and remedy arbitrary deprivation of life by private entities, such as private transportation companies, private hospitals and private security firms (para. 21).

John Ruggie defined HRDD as 'a comprehensive, proactive attempt to uncover human rights risks, actual and potential, over the entire life cycle of a project or business activity, with the aim of avoiding and mitigating those risks' (UN Doc. A/HRC/11/13 (2009), para. 71). The emphasis was thus on risk and the notion that was imported owed much more to the field of corporate law and risk management than to human rights.[602]

European Due Diligence Laws

In 2017, France adopted a law mandating large companies to adopt due diligence policies. The Law Relating to the Duty of Vigilance of Parent and Contracting Companies requires companies to identify and prevent adverse human rights and environmental impacts. The results have been mixed.[603] Germany, the Netherlands, Norway, and Switzerland also adopted such laws, but with widely varying coverage and standards. Partly in order to avoid such fragmentation, the European Union (EU) adopted, on 15 March 2024, a Directive on Corporate Sustainability Due Diligence (the CSDDD). It was the outcome of over two years of heavily contested negotiations and extensive last minute attempts to scuttle it or at least water it down. Some of the latter succeeded. EU member states must incorporate the Directive into national legislation within two years.

It applies to very large EU companies employing over 1,000 employees and generating a net worldwide annual turnover of €450 million, and to non-EU companies generating €450 million turnover in the EU. In total, some 5,300 companies in the EU are affected. The Directive's due diligence obligations draw on the UNGPs, the OECD Guidelines for Multinational Enterprises and the OECD Due Diligence Guidance for Responsible Business Conduct.

Companies are required to companies to conduct risk-based HRDD to prevent, mitigate and bring to an end adverse environmental and human rights impacts. These are defined as impacts on persons arising from human rights abuses, including, rights of liberty, freedom of thought and religion; interference with privacy; just working conditions; adequate workforce housing; the rights of children and prohibition of child labour; the prohibition of forced labour; and unequal treatment in employment.

---

[602] J. Bonnitcha and R. McCorquodale, 'The Concept of "Due Diligence" in the UN Guiding Principles on Business and Human Rights', 28 *Eur. J. Int'l L.* (2017) 899.

[603] See E. Savourey and S. Brabant, 'The French Law on the Duty of Vigilance: Theoretical and Practical Challenges Since its Adoption', 6 *J. Bus & Hum. Rts.* (2021) 141; and A. Schilling-Vacaflor and M.-T. Gustafsson, 'Towards More Sustainable Global Supply Chains? Company Compliance with New Human Rights and Environmental Due Diligence Laws', 32 *Environmental Politics* (2023) 000.

Companies are also required to pay special attention to individuals in marginalised or vulnerable groups, such as indigenous peoples, and use their influence to contribute to an adequate standard of living (particularly, a living wage) in supply chains, as well as to take into account corruption and bribery factors.

Stakeholder engagement is a feature of the Directive. Affected parties who must be consulted include employees, communities, and civil society organizations. Companies must regularly monitor the effectiveness of their due diligence processes and provide annual public reports detailing their findings and actions taken.

In addition, companies must establish or participate in effective remediation processes to address adverse impacts. This may require setting up grievance mechanisms to provide affected individuals and communities with access to remedies.

Enforcement and Sanctions

Each EU member state will appoint authorities responsible for overseeing compliance with the directive. Fines for non-compliance are potentially as high as five percent of a company's global turnover, and there is civil liability for damages caused by failure to meet due diligence obligations.

An early assessment is provided by Nicolas Bueno, Nadia Bernaz, Gabrielle Holly, and Olga Martin-Ortega, in 'The EU Directive on Corporate Sustainability Due Diligence (CSDDD): The Final Political Compromise', 9 *Bus. & Hum. Rts. J.* (2024) 000:

> [The Directive's conditions for fault-based civil liability] … are quite restrictive: damage arising from an adverse impact 'to a person'…, a negligent or intentional failure to comply with the obligation to prevent or end an adverse impact, and causation between this specific failure and the damage. Causation is further excluded if the damage is caused 'only' by the business partners. All these elements must be proven by the claimant.

> To attenuate the onerous burden of proof for claimants, domestic courts must be able to order the disclosure of evidence that lies in the control of the company 'in accordance with national procedural law'. This should be read as requiring the member states to introduce or adapt a mechanism of disclosure in accordance with their existing laws, otherwise, it would be meaningless. …

> ### III. Implications of the Directive Beyond Europe

> *A. Impact on Companies along the Value Chain*

> The CSDDD will have extraterritorial implications, including prompting changes in the policies and practises of companies along value chains. …

> *B. New Legislation in Third Countries*

> [Anu] Bradford has … theorised and documented the 'de jure Brussels effect', whereby third countries adopt their legislation in response to EU laws with extraterritorial implications. Third countries do so to level the playing field in their jurisdiction between companies who have to follow EU law, and companies who only operate domestically. The adoption of the CSDDD may lead third countries to pass their own sustainability due diligence laws … . …

> *C. Implications for the Business and Human Rights Treaty Negotiation*

… [T]he adoption of the CSDDD shows that it is possible to turn aspects of existing soft law instruments into actual binding legislation, albeit with important compromises in terms of scope and content. …

IV. The Way Forward

…

… [T]he Directive is, at its core, a 'do no harm' instrument inspired by the UNGPs. Its impact on human rights, the environment and climate will greatly depend on how member states implement it, how the Commission reviews it, how civil society engages with it, and whether there are sufficient drivers for companies to engage meaningfully with the process, rather than adopting a compliance-driven approach. The UNGPs will continue to be a reference point to ensure that the CSDDD is adhered to not just in accordance with the letter of the law, but also in the spirit of the UNGPs.

Alternative Approaches

If a binding treaty is far from finished, and HRDD approaches are only just beginning to be implemented in binding legislative form, the question arises as to what other approaches might be pursued. Mark Goodale, in *Reinventing Human Rights* (2022) 153 calls for a deeply transformative approach:

> Perhaps nothing quite captures the unique combination of self-interestedness and folly in the international human rights system as the idea that multinational corporations should be trusted to restructure their operations so as to protect human rights around the world, all because of an earnest commitment to the value of corporate social responsibility (CSR) and a willingness to perform human rights 'due diligence.'

Arguing that 'it would be the height of naivety to imagine that corporations could be reliable allies in the struggle against the economic, environmental, and social problems that are an inevitable consequence of capitalism as a mode of production', he calls for the 'reinvention' of human rights in order to 'break the shackles of inevitability … and to ground a vision of the future in which profit maximization is relegated as the dominant value so that a more radically 'ambitious and successful moral program' can be given shape and form.

Views on HRDD differ greatly. Daniel Litwin, in 'Business Impacts on Economic Inequality: An Agenda for Defining Related Human Rights Impacts and Economic Inequality Due Diligence', 8 *Bus. & Hum. Rts J.* (2023) 90, argues that if HRDD is seen 'as a management process rather than a source of tortuous liability', businesses could be required 'to identify, assess and address their actual and potential economic inequality-related adverse human rights impacts' as part of their HRDD responsibilities. But a major study by Ingrid Landau, *Human Rights Due Diligence and Labour Governance* (2024) concludes that by deferring to managerial understandings of the concept, decision-makers have 'shorn HRDD of much of its transformative potential'. She adds that (p. 184):

> … HRDD so far appears to be lending a technical and apolitical veneer to questions around the corporate management of labour rights in supply chains and thus potentially impeding, rather than facilitating, the capacity of workers and their organisations to challenge corporate practices. …

…

> … [There is] a real possibility that HRDD's legalisation will ultimately reinforce existing private governance approaches and further entrench those very business models and power dynamics that lead to labour exploitation in the first place. There is also a risk that ongoing momentum surrounding HRDD in transnational governance may overshadow, or detract from, efforts to expand other more promising approaches and mechanisms in transnational labour governance.

Taking the example of Big Tech, Katarina Pistor calls for more imaginative forms of accountability to be explored. Finally, Surya Deva, a former member of the UN Working Group, surveys a broad range of 'alternative approaches' to the BHR puzzle.

KATARINA PISTOR, STATEHOOD IN THE DIGITAL AGE
27 CONSTELLATIONS (2020) 3

…

7 Accountability of Digital Power Wielders

[Grant and Keohane][604] discuss the landscape of power wielders in an increasingly globalized world and the various means by which they can be held accountable. They surveyed the bewildering number and range of power wielders in global relations that included states and multinational corporations, along with non-governmental and multilateral organizations. The authors argue that while many of these power wielders are not subject to the classic accountability mechanisms associated with democratic forms of governance, such as elections and the division of powers, neither do they operate beyond anyone's control. Rather, they respond to different accountability mechanisms and different constituencies or "accountability holders." Some are part of a hierarchical organization or are fiscally constrained, others can be held liable in a court of law or have to endure regular supervision, and yet others are subject to a competitive market or peer pressure, or risk their reputation if they misbehave. As long as some effective accountability mechanisms exist, power wielders can be kept in check. Grant and Keohane offer a minimalist vision of accountability, but this makes their framework especially useful for inquiring into the accountability of the digital power wielders. If they are not even subject to the mechanisms Grant and Keohane identify, they may in fact be largely unconstrained.

When applied to the new digital power wielders, foremost the Big Tech companies among them, one is indeed struck by the absence of truly effective accountability mechanisms that might keep these companies in check. As corporations with shareholders, one might assume that Big Tech companies should be subject to capital market pressure. Yet … many Big Tech companies have chosen capital structures that mute the shareholder voice. A single or just a handful of founding shareholders exerts full control over the company. Neither are these companies likely to have to return to capital markets to raise additional funds, because they can more easily monetize their control over consumer data and use these earnings for future investments or their own shares for acquiring other companies.

There are two other "market" forces to consider: the market for the users or consumers of digital platforms on one hand, and the market for the clients that buy access to the user data the digital platforms harvest, organize, and analyze. …

…

The relation between Big Tech and their clients also is a far cry from the ideal of a market transaction. The clients are buying access to the predictive power of the data the Big Tech companies have amassed in order to place targeted ads or select information that is meant to influence the behavior of the platform customers. Importantly, each client's needs and interests in the data differ so that there cannot be a truly competitive auction for data, but only tailored access to them. And just as consumers do, the clients of Big Tech companies suffer from information asymmetry because they do not have sufficient information about the data or the algorithms that are used to organize and analyze them.

If digital power wielders are not subject to market forces, what other accountability mechanisms might keep them in check? As it turns out, none of the mechanisms that Grant and Keohane identified work for Big Tech companies. First, Big Tech companies do not face a binding budget constraint. The data they constantly harvest from billions of users is their revenue stream—a resource that is potentially infinite. As consumers grow increasingly dependent on the services of platform providers and clients on the insights the data these customers generate, Big Tech's future revenue streams are all but assured. They hardly fear peer pressure, because the handful of Big Tech companies have carved out spheres of interests for themselves that free them both from competition and from peer pressure. Neither do they have to fear reputational harm, as they can control the

---

[604] R. Grant and R. Keohane, 'Accountability and Abuses of Power in World Politics', 99 *Am. Pol. Sci. Rev.* (2005) 29.

dissemination of information about themselves, both negative and positive. They can create their own image and ensure that deviations from it will be suppressed.

This leaves supervisory and regulatory control by state institutions. Such control has not been absent entirely. Regulators in the USA and the EU have launched investigations into anti-competitive conduct, tax evasion, and illegal state aid schemes. As discussed, on occasion they have imposed fines of these companies. However, these sanctions have not had any lasting effects, in part because they were too small to ensure compliance in the future. In response, some US politicians (including Senator Warren) have called for the break-up of Big Tech companies. This is perhaps the greatest threat these companies face, but one should not be too optimistic about the lasting effects of such measures. Digital platforms exhibit powerful network effects, making true competition all but elusive. Moreover, unless these companies are restrained from future acquisition sprees that would allow them to rebuild their empires and thwart competition yet again, not much will be gained.

Where accountability mechanisms do not exist yet, they could nonetheless be created. One mechanism that has been widely discussed in the literature is to give consumers full property rights over their data. Another would be to give human data the status of *ius communis* of things that may not be appropriated by anyone. The first solution is unlikely to have much effect on Big Tech's business model. Consumers already contract away most uses of their data; it is difficult to see why allocating property rights to them would make them more cautious in trading them away. Holding property rights to their data will also not give them much in terms of monetary gain, as the raw information an individual produces is not worth much. Only the aggregation of similar information from millions, if not billions, of users produces the kind of predictive power that can be monetized.

This leaves the idea of data as a common good, for the management of which a public trust might be created. Ideally, such a measure should have been implemented long ago. Turning back the clock on the vast amounts of data that have already been collected and stored and the extensive surveillance apparatus private companies and state agencies have established over the last two decades seems almost an impossible task. Still, this is worth trying as it would diminish access to data in the future and thus cut the income stream of Big Tech companies. For this to work, the state with its power of coercion would have to act and restrain Big Tech. This, unfortunately, is the Achilles heel of this scheme. States are among the greatest harvesters and aggregators of data, and not only in China. They too have benefited from the legal grey zone that has surrounded data, arguing that collecting vast amounts of data, even from their own citizens, is not subject to legal or even constitutional constraints that protect individuals against them, including the need for court warrants for wire or phone tapping, because they allegedly do not target specific individuals (although they can be attributed to them with ease). Moreover, states have on occasion taken advantage of the data that Big Tech companies have amassed; they collaborate with these companies in creating new surveilling techniques, separate platforms for state agencies (such as the Central Intelligence Agency), and storage facilities for their data. In short, the only force that might establish accountability over Big Tech is not only conflicted, if not complicit in the very practices it should regulate. States may be competing with Big Tech over monetary sovereignty; but when it comes to the unconstrained access to the data of their citizens, their interests are aligned.

SURYA DEVA, BUSINESS AND HUMAN RIGHTS: ALTERNATIVE APPROACHES TO TRANSNATIONAL REGULATION
17 ANNU. REV. LAW SOC. SCI. (2021) 139, 151

...

7. Conclusion

From a critical review of selected alternative approaches to transnational regulation of business, several conclusions and insights for the future can be drawn. First, the influence of the UNGPs, embodying polycentric governance, on diverse regulatory pathways is clear. What is less clear is whether UNGP-induced approaches will bring systemic changes needed to humanize business. For example, mandatory HRDD laws might end up becoming a tick-box compliance exercise with no effective remedy for victims of corporate human rights abuses. ...

...

Third, it seems that states remain a critical, if not central, player in guiding business behavior, even in polycentric governance or non-state-centric regulatory approaches. For example, transparency and disclosure rules by state agencies enable market actors like consumers, investors, and CSOs to assume a regulatory role. At the same time, states continue to show lack of political will, at both individual and collective levels, in regulating business behavior effectively. They often act incohesively and put profit (i.e., creating a business- and investment-friendly environment) over people and the planet (i.e., building an inclusive and sustainable society). ...

Fourth, ... rights in BHR do not really mean legally enforceable rights on paper or in practice. Going forward, regulatory approaches should respond to the needs of rightsholders rather than deliver what is acceptable to businesses. ...

Fifth, assuming that most businesses are rational actors, different regulatory approaches should be employed in tandem to make corporate human rights abuses a costly business. A range of incentives and disincentives should also be employed to change the corporate culture that gives priority to profit over people and the planet. Corporate laws will be vital in internalizing human rights in all business decision-making processes.

Sixth, greater attention should be paid to the role of businesses to protect and fulfil human rights, rather than merely respect human rights. Equally critical will be to focus on corporate responsibility for abuses of socioeconomic rights, contributing to poverty or tax evasion. The COVID-19 pandemic has exposed many inequalities and vulnerabilities that would not be overcome by merely adopting a do-no-harm approach.

Seventh, developing an effective transnational framework combining various regulatory strands in the BHR field requires more clarity on several issues. How will soft social expectations under Pillar II of the UNGPs interact with hard HRDD regulations and legalization of business responsibility to respect human rights on the regional or international level? Should businesses have an obligation of result in certain situations, and should conducting HRDD operate as a defense to legal liability? In what circumstances, and how, could states be held accountable for breach of their duty to protect against human rights abuses by businesses? How to deal with hard cases of corporate impunity in the BHR field, situations in which there is no obvious business case to respect human rights and the concerned states are unable or unwilling to hold the relevant business actors accountable?

QUESTION

The prospects for the successful negotiation of a binding treaty, followed by its ratification by the key states, do not seem especially bright. Meanwhile, most of the governmental momentum seems to be focused on HRDD laws. How do you evaluate this trend in light of this comment by Claire O'Brien, and Daniel Schönfelder:

... [Such] responses are still a patchwork, full of loopholes and discrepancies, that remains wide open to gaming by corporate malefactors. Such initiatives are also, so far, largely restricted to jurisdictions of the Global North, while their impacts redound 'elsewhere', on the rights and livelihoods of people who have had almost no part in their design. Yet both inclusion and coordination are as imperative in devising human rights rules for the global economy, as they will be in their future oversight, evaluation and review: principles of universality and democracy demand no less, making it hard to see how legitimacy or effectiveness can be achieved without them. The science of due diligence regulation is, further, in its infancy, with little evidence to hand regarding the merits or challenges associated with models espoused by different national jurisdictions. Without an international binding instrument, then, a global level playing field remains out of sight. The interests of responsible businesses, therefore, are equally served by a widely-endorsed global business and human rights framework.

B. NON-STATE ARMED GROUPS

At one level, non-state armed groups (NSAGs), opposed to the relevant government, are simply outlaws. They have rejected or resisted the authority of the state and opted to act outside the applicable legal framework. But at another level, such groups are often involved in a quest for legitimacy, designed to convince the relevant population and the world at large of the illegitimacy of the existing form of state power, and perhaps invoking by way of justification the state's violations of the rights of the group concerned. Two questions arise. First, should we seek to encourage such groups to accept human rights commitments? Second, what would the legal basis for any such obligations be?[605]

International humanitarian law (IHL) has long accepted that armed opposition groups engaged in an internal armed conflict are bound by IHL, even though they are not parties to the relevant treaties. Even though the structure and assumptions of human rights law are different, there have been examples of governments and opposition groups consenting to abide by both human rights and IHL commitments in a single agreement. In 2021, the International Committee of the Red Cross estimated that there are over 100 armed conflicts around the world and that, worldwide, 'around 600 armed groups have the capacity to cause violence of humanitarian concern'. In IHL terms, more than 100 of those qualify as parties to a non-international armed conflict (NIAC), and are thus bound by IHL. Some of these groups perform functions typically reserved for states, administering territory, providing a wide range of services to populations that number in the millions, and demanding tax contributions from those within their area of control.

In the readings that follow, Sivakumaran outlines the theoretical bases upon which the application of IHL to armed opposition groups might be grounded,[606] and Clapham considers how the UN has dealt with such groups. The section concludes with some reflections on the current state of the law.

SANDESH SIVAKUMARAN, BINDING ARMED OPPOSITION GROUPS
55 INT'L. & COMP. L. Q. (2006) 369

The vast majority of conflicts being fought today are internal in character. Internal armed conflicts are fought between a state and an armed opposition group, or between two armed opposition groups, within the boundaries of a single state. Armed opposition groups are becoming increasingly sophisticated and are responsible for some of the most egregious atrocities committed in conflicts. Given the proliferation of internal armed conflicts, the number of armed opposition groups that take part in them, and the atrocities that are committed by such groups, it is essential that international humanitarian law regulates such conflicts and governs the behaviour of such groups.

There exist, however, only a minimum of international humanitarian law rules that pertain to armed conflict of an internal character. [They include, in particular, Common Article 3 of the four Geneva Conventions, and Additional Protocol II.] …

A treaty binds parties to it, thus these instruments bind states parties fighting in an internal armed conflict. The language of these instruments also purports to bind armed opposition groups fighting in such a conflict. This raises the question of how armed opposition groups are bound by the law governing internal armed conflict when they are not party to the relevant treaties. …
…
Four reasons that are commonly put forward to explain the binding nature of the rules governing internal armed conflict on armed opposition groups — customary international law; general principles; the rules governing the effect of treaties on third parties; and the principle of succession — are not in fact capable of binding all types of armed opposition groups by all the rules of internal armed conflict. This is so even when all four reasons are used in conjunction with one another. The legislative jurisdiction explanation — the principle whereby the state binds all individuals within its territory upon ratification of a treaty — is the only one that is capable of binding all types of armed opposition groups by all the rules that govern internal armed conflict.

There is a more fundamental theoretical difference between the four limited explanations on the one hand and the legislative jurisdiction explanation on the other hand. The four limited explanations apply the rules that are applied to states to armed opposition groups. In this way, they are treated like states. The legislative jurisdiction

---

[605] See generally, Special Issue on Non-state armed groups, 915 *Int'l Rev. Red Cross* (2022); E. Heffes, 'International Human Rights Law and Non-State Armed Groups: The (De)construction of an International Legal Discourse', in R. Kolb et al. (eds.), *Research Handbook on Human Rights and Humanitarian Law* (2022) 265; and A. Callamard, 'Towards International Human Rights Law Applied to Armed Groups', 37 *Neth. Q. Hum. Rts.* (2019) 85.
[606] See also S. Sivakumaran, *The Law of Non-International Armed Conflict* (2012).

approach treats armed opposition groups as entities subordinate to states. The default positions of the two also differ. The four limited explanations start off from the position that armed opposition groups are not bound by the rules governing internal armed conflict while the legislative jurisdiction explanation begins from the view that armed opposition groups are so bound. Consequently, the four limited explanations are more attractive to armed opposition groups while the legislative jurisdiction approach is more appealing to states. As a result, a question that has to be asked is whether using the legislative jurisdiction approach will lead to a decrease in compliance with the rules on the part of the armed opposition group.

Compliance in this regard is likely affected more by the degree of legitimacy the armed opposition group sees in the rules than the precise manner in which they are bound. One of the threads underlying this article has been the degree of legitimacy of the rules from the perspective of the armed opposition group. In order to increase the degree of legitimacy of and foster a sense of respect for the laws governing internal armed conflict, participation of armed opposition groups in the formation of the rules is vital. Participation may range from the formal — for example involvement of armed opposition groups in the conclusion of new international humanitarian law treaties using their practice for the purposes of customary international law, concluding Common Article 3 agreements and encouraging unilateral declarations of acceptance — to the less formal — such as creating linkages with armed opposition groups that do respect international humanitarian law and pointing to the positive practice of other armed opposition groups.

That armed opposition groups are bound by the rules governing internal armed conflict is beyond doubt; quite how to increase their compliance with these rules is the next big question.

ANDREW CLAPHAM, DILEMMAS FACING COMMISSIONS OF INQUIRY NEHAL BHUTA ET AL. (EDS.), THE STRUGGLE FOR HUMAN RIGHTS (2021) 251

… [I]nternational bodies such as the Security Council, the General Assembly, and the HRC use the expressions 'human rights violations' and 'human rights abuses' rather arbitrarily even if COIs generally favour the word violations, although some human rights lawyers still prefer to draw a strict distinction, reserving the word abuses to describe the transgressive acts of non-state actors. …

In the practice of special rapporteurs, the Security Council, and COIs, any dichotomy between legal obligations and non-legal moral responsibility is dissolved when reporting on armed groups that are considered to be carrying out governmental type functions and controlling territory. … The Security Council monitors six 'grave violations' of children's rights in armed conflict, listing governments and armed groups without distinction. COIs often report on the acts of non- state actors as violating human rights obligations under international law and determine responsibility for both governmental and opposition forces without nuance.
…
… [A 2006 report on Sri Lanka, by the UN Special Rapporteur on extrajudicial, summary or arbitrary executions (UN Doc. E/CN.4/2006/53/Add.5)] grappled with the dilemma of how to report on and engage non- state actors, without seemingly lending them legitimacy by treating them 'like a state'. …:

> As a non- State actor, the LTTE [the Liberation Tigers of Tamil Eelam] does not have legal obligations under ICCPR, but it remains subject to the demand of the international community, first expressed in the [UDHR], that every organ of society respect and promote human rights.

> I have previously noted that it is especially appropriate and feasible to call for an armed group to respect human rights norms when it 'exercises significant control over territory and population and has an identifiable political structure. This visit clarified both the complexity and the necessity of applying human rights norms to armed groups. The LTTE plays a dual role. On the one hand, it is an organization with effective control over a significant stretch of territory, engaged in civil planning and administration, maintaining its own form of police force and judiciary. On the other hand, it is an armed group that has been subject to proscription, travel bans, and financial sanctions in various Member States. The tension between these two roles is at the root of the international

community's hesitation to address the LTTE and other armed groups in the terms of human rights law. The international community does have human rights expectations to which it will hold the LTTE, but it has long been reluctant to press these demands directly if doing so would be to 'treat it like a State.

It is increasingly understood, however, that the human rights expectations of the international community operate to protect people, while not thereby affecting the legitimacy of the actors to whom they are addressed. The Security Council has long called upon various groups that Member States do not recognize as having the capacity to formally assume international obligations to respect human rights. The LTTE and other armed groups must accept that insofar as they aspire to represent a people before the world, the international community will evaluate their conduct according to the Universal Declaration's 'common standard of achievement.

… [One] complexity of the current situation … is that some of the armed groups are more like criminal enterprises than governments-in-waiting. Some may have minimal control over territory, and yet move around with their child abductees and targeting those they come across. Some victims may find that control over their town changes from week-to-week or even day-to-day. … [T]hese days many of the groups may be oscillating between opposition and government. … [T]he idea that there is at all times a clear distinction between state and non-state groups is fallacious. In some contexts armed groups can be better described as 'spin offs' from the state rather than non- state actors, and those same groups may at various stages take on functions that the state chooses not to entrust to its own forces. Add to this the ambiguity over whether some groups have joined or left the government, along with the factor that we may often have different governments within the same state recognized as *de lege* authorities by different parts of the international community, and one can see the impossibility of … drawing watertight distinctions when labelling specific incidents as violations or abuses. …

Looking Ahead

Cordula Droege and Eirini Giorgou, in 'How International Humanitarian Law Develops', 920-921 *Int'l Rev. Red Cross* (2022) 1, note that while it is widely accepted that NSAGs are bound by the IHL rules applicable to NIACs, they:

> are not involved in the development of IHL by means of treaty or custom: they do not participate in treaty negotiations or become party to such instruments, and their practice does not constitute "State practice" constituent of customary law.

> Nevertheless, some submit that, with their activities, such actors "have consistently and conspicuously affected the evolution of IHL for a long time", in particular through the conclusion of special agreements among parties to the conflict on the application of IHL or through the adoption of action plans with the UN. Similarly, there are signs that the practice of NSAGs is, if not accepted on a formal normative level by States, at least accepted for practical reasons in many respects. In that way, the contribution of NSAGs to the interpretation of the rules through practice might be more substantial than meets the eye.

Katharine Fortin, in *The Accountability of Armed Groups under Human Rights Law* (2017) 391, notes the value of parallel accountability processes, including those of Geneva Call, an independent humanitarian NGO, and the UN's Monitoring and Reporting Mechanism on Children and Armed Conflict. The rationale is that NSAGs 'are more likely to adhere to norms which they have signed themselves, than to norms which have been imposed upon them by the State against whom they are fighting.' Under these mechanisms, 'the voices of the armed groups are valid and can be heard', and their declaration can be monitored on the ground.

Marco Sassòli, in 'How Will International Humanitarian Law Develop in the Future?', 920-921 *Int'l Rev. Red Cross* (2022) 2052, calls for the involvement of NSAGs in developing IHL, although he acknowledges that 'States are nearly unanimously opposed' for fear of conferring legitimacy on 'terrorist' groups. There are, however, other ways of ensuring their input, such as through Geneva Call. In relation to the relevance of NSAG practice in determining custom, he argues that 'it is useless to consider a rule to be "customary" law if half of the addressees … do not respect it out of a sense of conviction.' But he notes that conceptual difficulties arise in considering NSAG practice in determining custom applicable in NIACs: (i) such groups are not meant to be permanent which makes the notion of assessing their practice more complicated; (ii) their practice generally relates only to one state or one other armed group; (iii) the problem of whether the diversity of NSAGs should be reflected in the relevant rules; and (iv) the problem of whether the rules resulting from the practice of NSAGs should bind only them or states as well. But, whatever the difficulties, he concludes that NSAGs 'must gain more voice in the development of IHL of NIACs.'

But despite the strong trend reflected above, the resistance of states remains a major obstacle. The extent of legitimacy and legal standing granted to NSAGs has varied enormously with the winds of international politics. National Liberation Movements in the twentieth century achieved considerable rights of participation and substantial legitimation of their armed struggle as a result of the geopolitical climate in which they emerged: the rise of the Third World majority in the General Assembly, and a Cold War dynamic in which each superpower sought to court, or avoid alienating, the newly emerging states, and so cooperated in different degrees with their normative agenda at the United Nations. In the contemporary world, the pendulum appears to have swung far in the other direction. The utility of declaring armed groups as 'terrorist' — and thus confining them categorically to the status of criminals — appears widely understood among states facing internal armed conflicts, with few states willing to contest such labels even if the facts are more complex. Thus, while there is no doubt that the Islamic Resistance Movement in Palestine (Hamas) engages in terrorist tactics, it is equally beyond doubt that they now effectively control the Gaza Strip and its population and conduct a full range of governance functions. Continuing to label the group terrorist as a means of inducing compliance with humanitarian and human rights law has had limited success, and greatly limits the avenues through which 'carrots' can be used to induce moderation, compromise, and conflict resolution. [607]

Laws prohibiting the provision of 'material support' to terrorist groups can come into conflict with the humanitarian goal of engaging with NSAGs in order to protect civilian populations and seek an end to conflict. In *Holder v. Humanitarian Law Project*,[608] the HLP sought to train members of the Kurdistan Worker's Party (PKK) in international law for dispute resolution and for bringing petitions to UN bodies and to engage in political advocacy. The U.S. Supreme Court held that while some U.S. government-designated Foreign Terrorist Organizations engage in political and humanitarian activities, they are nonetheless 'so tainted by their criminal conduct that any contribution to such an organization facilitates that conduct'. Three dissenting justices argued that the government should have to show that the 'defendants provided support that they knew was significantly likely to help the organization pursue its unlawful terrorist aims'. The contradictions between such criminal law approaches to counter-terrorism and initiatives to bring armed groups within the humanitarian umbrella have created serious unresolved dilemmas on the ground.[609]

QUESTION

'Arguments based upon the approach of IHL to armed opposition groups have no relevance to human rights law. The latter's assumptions are fundamentally different and the label of human rights respecter is one that, by definition, can and should only be conferred on a legitimate state actor.' Discuss.

C. INTERNATIONAL ORGANIZATIONS

Like other non-state actors, international organizations (IOs) are not states, and in most cases they are not able to become parties to human rights treaties. But the conclusion that they are not therefore bound to respect

---

[607] N. Bhuta, 'The Role International Actors Other Than States Can Play in the New World Order', in A. Cassese (ed.), *Realizing Utopia: The Future of International Law* (2012) 61, at 70.
[608] 130 S. Ct 2705 (2010).
[609] See N. K. Modirzadeh et al., 'Humanitarian Engagement Under Counter-Terrorism: A Conflict of Norms and the Emerging Policy Landscape', 883 *Int'l. Rev. Red Cross* (2011) 1.

human rights is generally considered to be untenable. The challenge, however, is to identify legal grounds for asserting that relevant obligations apply. Three main routes have been identified.

Derivation from Member States' Obligations

In principle, it can be argued that IOs are agents of the States that are their members and that they are therefore bound to act in accordance with their principals' treaty obligations. But this does not take adequate account of the fact that most IOs have independent legal personalities, and thus must consent to be bound by treaties. In addition, as argued by Gerald Neuman, in 'International Organizations and Human Rights – the Need for Substance', Human Rights Program at Harvard Law School (HRP 19-001 (2019)) the states will have overlapping and inconsistent treaty obligations, making it difficult to determine which ones apply.

It has also been suggested, especially by the UN Committee on ESCR, that IOs must take the human rights obligations of the relevant states into account when interacting with them, so that they do not become complicit in some way in relation to violations. See, for example, General comment No. 12: The right to adequate food (1999), para. 19). An extension of this argument is that IOs derive from the obligations of Member States an obligation to interpret their statutes consistently with human rights law.[610]

The International Law Commission's 2011 Draft articles on the responsibility of international organizations (DARIO) suggest four routes through which an IO may be responsible for violations of human rights law: aid or assistance in the commission of an internationally wrongful act; direction and control exercised over the commission of an internationally wrongful act; coercion of a state or another international organization; or circumvention of its own international obligations through directing or authorising a member state to commit an act that would be wrongful if committed by the IO.[611] However each of these options – with the exception of coercion – requires that the act must have been wrongful for the IO, and thus that the IO must have had human rights obligations independent of the state through which it acted.

Separate Legal Capacity

It has been long accepted that IOs have a separate legal personality provided they meet certain requirements: that is, they are a permanent association of states with a decision-making structure and the capacity to enter into relations and conclude agreements with other IOs and nations.[612] This definition would include the UN specialized agencies listed in the 1947 Immunities Convention (the ILO, WHO, IMF, World Bank, etc.) as well as organizations with similar functions like the WTO. IOs may therefore be subject to human rights obligations in the same manner as states: consent, customary international law, or general principles of law.[613] These obligations also extend to the employees or agents of IOs, as well as organs of states placed at their disposal (for example, in joint peacekeeping operations).[614] But IOs' powers and obligations are generally limited to what is necessary for, or related to, the exercise of their functions in the fulfilment of their purposes.

a. Explicit Consent or Internal Requirements

An IO is subject to human rights obligations where its governing documents specify that it must act in accordance with human rights (or a specific Convention), or where it is a party to a treaty. The latter is extremely rare: the only example to date is the European Union's (EU) accession to the Convention on the Rights of Persons with Disabilities in 2009. And few IOs have explicit human rights requirements in their constitutive documents. Again, the exception is the EU (see Chapter 11, above).

The UN Charter makes various references to human rights and requires the organization's purposes to be carried out 'in conformity with the principles of justice and international law'. But it does not, *per se*, require UN

---

[610] G. M. Zagel, 'International Organisations and Human Rights: The Role of the UN Covenants in Overcoming the Accountability Gap', 36 *Nordic J. Hum. Rts.* (2018) 74, 80.

[611] ILC, Draft articles on the responsibility of international organizations [DARIO], UN Doc. A/66/10 (2011), para. 87, Arts. 14-17.

[612] See, e.g., *Reparation for Injuries Suffered in the Service of the United Nations (Advisory Opinion)* [1949] ICJ Rep 174.

[613] See C. Ferstman, *International Organizations and the Fight for Accountability: The Remedies and Reparations Gap* (2017), 16.

[614] DARIO, Arts. 6-9.

bodies to respect human rights. An increasingly common approach is for IOs to require compliance with or consideration of human rights and/or international humanitarian law through internal resolutions, policies and mandates.[615] Examples include: (1) the 1999 UN Secretary-General's Bulletin on 'Observance by United Nations forces of international humanitarian law' (UN Doc. ST/SGB/1999/13); (2) the 2013 'due diligence' Policy and Guidance Note (UN Doc. A/67/775), which applies to peacekeeping and police missions as well as collaboration with migration and border security authorities (the UN has 'obligations under international law to respect, promote and encourage respect for international humanitarian, human rights and refugee law'); and (3) Security Council acknowledgements that human rights and humanitarian considerations are relevant to counter-terrorism and sanctions decisions (see, e.g., S/RES/2615 (2021)). By contrast, the World Bank and IMF have insisted that human rights are not part of their mandate.[616]

b. Custom and General Principles of Law

There is general agreement that IOs are obligated to respect *jus cogens* norms, such as prohibitions on the crime of aggression, genocide, discrimination, crimes against humanity, and torture.[617] The extent to which a particular IO is required to protect or advance a wider range of rights, including social and economic rights, remains a matter of debate. Scholars have contended that human rights are binding on IOs if (a) the right has attained the status of customary international law or is a general principle of law; and (b) if the exercise of the right is relevant to or impacted by the IO's purposes and functions.

Most rights in the UDHR are arguably part of customary international law. In addition, IOs' internal measures requiring human rights compliance also strengthen claims relating to practice and *opinio juris*. Stian Øby Johansen argues in *The Human Rights Accountability Mechanisms of International Organizations* (2020), at 54, that a rule-by-rule approach is required: 'Only those rules that concern the sphere of competences of a specific organization may be applied to that organization.' In his view, positive obligations require more careful suitability assessments than negative rights, and will bind an IO only to the extent that it has the power to act.

The bottom line is that, despite gradual concessions by different IOs in the direction of accepting some human rights obligations, a significant accountability gap continues to exist.

---

[615] See further M. Heupel and M. Zürn (eds.) *Protecting the Individual from International Authority: Human Rights in International Organizations* (2017).
[616] See UN Doc. A/70/274 (2015); cf. D. van den Meerssche, *The World Bank's Lawyers* (2023).
[617] Ferstman, above, 19.

Chapter 14. Social Movements and Civil Society

This book is replete with illustrations of the many ways in which social movements, civil society, non-governmental organizations and an array of activists and advocates have helped shape the international human rights regime. They have invariably been the prime movers in pushing governments, corporations, international organizations and others to take greater account of human rights, and they have succeeded in imposing forms of accountability that go well beyond the formal institutional arrangements that have been the focus of several of the preceding chapters.

But perceptions differ as to the contributions made by different parts of the overall movement. Writing in 2003, Balakrishnan Rajagopal, in *International Law from Below: Development, Social Movements and Third World Resistance* (2003), at 174, criticized human rights historiographies 'in which the agency of rights-transformation is the state or statist forms such as international organizations and the direction of rights transformation is ineluctably from the "traditional" to a (Eurocentric) "modern". Excluded from this historiography is the role that ordinary individuals and social movements may have played.'[618] He added that this 'discourse retains many elements which are directly descended from colonial ideology and practices.' In his view, recent accounts had acknowledged 'the contributions made by NGOs but these are usually restricted to 'Third World watchers' located in the First World such as Human Rights Watch [HRW] or Amnesty International.'

Almost a decade later, Aryeh Neier, one of HRW's founders, wrote *The International Human Rights Movement: A History*. He argued that that 'the driving force behind the protection of human rights worldwide, today and for roughly the past thirty-five years, has been the nongovernmental human rights movement' (at 7). This chronology reflects the emergence of HRW and Amnesty, and much of his book is devoted to their roles. In a chapter on 'the worldwide movement' (at 233), he acknowledges that 'literally thousands of other organizations are also active in the field', but the pages that follow recount the work of a host of groups based in the United States or western Europe. They include the Lawyers Committee for Human Rights (now Human Rights First), Physicians for Human Rights, the Committee to Protect Journalists, the International Human Rights Law Group (now Global Rights), the Washington Office on Latin America, Freedom House, the International Center for Transitional Justice, and the Center for Justice and International Law (CEJIL). The account then refers to a handful of groups not based or originating in the United States, including some in the United Kingdom and eastern Europe.

In mainstream histories focusing on the United Nations human rights system, it is not difficult to trace the decisive influence of civil society actors, working individually or in coalitions, on the great majority of progressive steps taken towards recognizing the human rights of particular groups or the rights most in need of protection in particular contexts. Examples include the indispensable role of Amnesty International and, subsequently, the International Commission of Jurists in pushing for the Convention against Torture; the role played by indigenous groups in propelling efforts that led to the adoption, in 2007, of the UN Declaration on the Rights of Indigenous Peoples; and the role of diverse coalitions from both North and South in driving the processes that culminated in the adoption of the Convention on the Rights of the Child in 1989 and the Convention on the Rights of Persons with Disabilities in 2007, and in putting LGBTQI+ rights definitively on the international community's agenda in subsequent years.

Whatever the history books tell us, it is clear that the role played by what we might generically term 'social movements' in relation to the evolution of the human rights regime in all parts of the world has changed immensely in recent decades. In 2004, Charles Tilly defined social movements as consisting of sustained, organized public efforts making collective claims on target authorities and employing certain forms of political action, including associations and coalitions, public meetings, processions, vigils, rallies, demonstrations, petition drives, statements to and in public media and pamphleteering, and concerted public representations regarding the strength of the movement.[619]

---

[618] For a powerful critique of the relationship between scholarship and social movements, see Aziz Choudry, 'Reflections on Academia, Activism, and the Politics of Knowledge and Learning', 24 *Int'l J. Hum. Rts.* (2020) 28.
[619] C. Tilly, E. Castañeda and L. Wood, *Social Movements*, 1768 – 2018 (4th ed., 2020).

Building on this definition, a 2022 report by the UN Special Rapporteur on the rights to freedom of peaceful assembly and of association, Clément Nyaletsossi Voule (UN Doc. A/77/171), added that social movements 'are predominantly informal in nature, … often emerge from the grassroots, and many are leaderless and horizontal in nature.' They provide sites of agency and solidarity, thus 'fostering social engagement, democratic participation and responsive governance.' He described their effective presence as 'a key indicator of a healthy society', enabling 'particular communities, including those marginalized, … to raise their voices and make their concerns visible.'

In recent years, there has been a steady rise in protests around the world, which has led governments of all persuasions to impose limitations on the right to protest.[620] A study by Isabel Ortiz et al. in *World Protests: A Study of Key Protest Issues in the 21st Century* (2022) tracks 2,809 protests between 2006 and 2020 in 101 countries that together account for 93 percent of the world population. Although protests have increased everywhere, they found more in middle- and high-income countries, and an increasing number of global protests (239 events) organized across regions.

Their study notes that the 'protests were not random, unorganized riots; the majority of world protests were planned, and their demands were articulated. The main grievances and causes of outrage were:' failure of political representation and political systems; economic justice and anti-austerity; civil rights; and global justice. The participants were 'not only traditional protesters (e.g. activists, NGOs/CSOs, trade unions); [but also the] middle classes, women, students and youth, pensioners, indigenous, ethnic and racial groups, as well as other grassroot citizens'. They record 52 events with one million or more protesters: 'the largest recorded was the 2020 strike in India against the government's plan to liberalize farming and labor, estimated to have involved 250 million protestors.' The most common methods of protest were marches and rallies, blockades, strikes, and occupations. They also describe 'the advent of a new era of civil disobedience/direct action carried out by computer hackers and whistleblowers'. 'Riots and protests involving violence and vandalism/looting represent only 20% of the total. Though only used by a few, 5% of protests record desperate methods such as hunger strikes and self-inflicted violence (e.g. self-immolation, protesters sewing their own lips).'

But another important part of the picture is the claim that these mass movements are becoming less successful in the third decade of the 21st century. Erica Chenoweth, in 'Can Nonviolent Resistance Survive COVID-19?', 21 *J. Hum. Rts.* (2022) 304, suggests that there has been a steady decline in the success rates of people-power campaigns over the preceding twenty years, and that 2020 and 2021 were the worst years on record for people power since the 1930s:

> For the first time since the 1940s—a decade dominated by state-backed partisan rebellions against Nazi occupations—nonviolent resistance does not have a statistically significant advantage over armed insurrection in terms of discrete success rates.
>
> …
>
> … [O]ne of the most important factors relates to the adaptive measures states have taken to prevent, deter, and suppress mass movements. These "smart repression" techniques involve a combination of divide and rule strategies, digital repression, propaganda and misinformation, and the declaration of emergency powers in the context of crises. …

Chenoweth draws attention to the proliferation of rights restrictions that accompanied governmental responses to COVID-19, citing statistics from the International Center for Not-for-Profit Law showing that 153 countries restricted assembly rights, 59 restricted rights to expression, and 110 made emergency declarations. Governments also cracked down against human rights defenders, activists, organizers, and dissidents by relying on expanded 'surveillance, adept use of social media to spread disinformation and mobilize their own supporters, jailing or terrorizing dissidents or their families, and purging or shoring up their inner entourage and security forces to ensure their loyalty in crucial moments.' She also notes the frequency with which authoritarians denounce protesters and dissidents as terrorists, criminals, and traitors, and incite attacks upon them.

---

[620] E. Page and N. Robinson, 'Legal Threats to the Right to Protest', in *Oxford Handbook of Peaceful Assembly* (2024) 000.

Another question raised in this context is whether groups promoting anti-human rights goals should be considered 'social movements'. Ortiz et al. note that, although 'the overwhelming majority of large protests were related to progressive issues', some were also 'led by radical right groups such as the QAnon protests in 2020 in the United States and globally; opposition to Muslims, migrants, and refugees in Germany; or the protests against the Workers Party in Brazil in 2013 and 2015.' Chenoweth also observes that 'the techniques of people power—long associated with progressive aims and causes—have been cynically appropriated by those who would use these techniques to dispossess, disenfranchise, or subjugate others.' But the report by the UN Special Rapporteur specifically includes only social movements that 'act in conformity with the aims and principles' of the UN Charter and the UDHR. One question to consider is, what criteria would best serve to differentiate the various groups in this regard?

For all of their contributions, most human rights INGOs based in the West have traditionally pursued relatively narrow agendas, marginalized issues of economic and social rights, focused primarily on advocacy and trying to influence government policies, and generally operated at a considerable distance from the grassroots, or the 'field' as they would have called it.

Today, the landscape is changing. The human rights regime and the 'movement' supporting it are under pressure to expand their focus to respond to a global pandemic, with the likelihood of more to come, to dramatic global warming, rapidly growing inequality, upheavals caused by technologies, and the consequences of the near global embrace of neoliberal policies involving austerity, privatization, deregulation, shrinking government budgets and capacities, and the outsourcing to the private sector of a great many functions that were formerly performed by governments. With this expansion of the overall agenda has come the growing realization that the old-style human rights movement will need to engage much more systematically with a wider array of partners and issues, and to adopt new strategies and tactics. While path dependence makes it difficult for the largest groups to respond, adapt, and adjust, other social movements are already very active.

A. CRITIQUES OF MAINSTREAM GROUPS

Despite the importance of viewing human rights social movements in their global context, many of the harshest recent critiques of the human rights regime, some of which are reflected in Chapter 17 below, are largely based, either implicitly or explicitly, on the work of HRW and Amnesty. While these groups clearly should not be seen as proxies for the much broader and more diverse movement, their role has nonetheless been very important.

In terms of magnitude, Amnesty and HRW are still the behemoths in the field. In 2021, HRW's budget was $97 million, and it had 510 staff based in 105 cities, researched 100 countries, and generated 6,000 publications. In the same year, Amnesty raised €357 million and called itself 'the largest human rights movement globally, with a global presence including offices in more than 70 countries, 2,600 staff and seven million members, volunteers and supporters worldwide.' Although Amnesty's budget was over three times larger than HRW's, 30 percent was devoted to building the 'supporter base' (membership), and 2 percent to maintaining democratic internal governance. While 74 percent of Amnesty's budget came from donations from over 2 million individuals, HRW does not disclose how many individual members it has, and wealthy donors play a key role in its governance structures.[621]

In terms of impact, the two organizations have played an outsized role in shaping certain parts of the international regime, and they continue to be among the most prolific and oft-cited sources of information about many of the most pressing human rights situations around the world. But there is also no shortage of criticism directed at them. A prominent critic is Stephen Hopgood whose book, *The Endtimes of Human Rights* (2013), focuses heavily on what he terms an elite concept of Human Rights (written in upper case) which is 'a New York-Geneva-London-centered ideology' based on 'top-down authoritative rules' and focused on international law, criminal justice, and global governance institutions. The relevant organizations 'raise money, write reports, run international campaigns, open local offices, lobby governments, and claim to speak with singular authority in the name of humanity as a whole.' This is said to be the very opposite of the 'bottom-up democratic norms' that make up the lower-case notion of human rights, favored by the other 99 percent of the

---

[621] See generally, P. Alston, *Human Rights Watch Inc.* (forthcoming, 2025).

world, and which are 'malleable, adaptable, pragmatic and diverse'. As a result, 'we are on the verge of the imminent decay of the Global Human Rights Regime.' And 'when international NGOs speak, their narrow funding base makes them little more than the private foreign policies of middle-class professionals' (at 172). In describing global/local dynamics, he says (at x-xi) that:

> … the global inevitably structures, disciplines, channels, institutionalizes, and eventually colonizes the local reproducing hierarchies of power and influence …'. This is partly because the transnational space is structured by a political economy that is almost wholly controlled by global Human Rights centers (in western Europe and the United States). But it is also because the singularity of the Human Rights message resists local adaptation on any basis other than a transient and tactical one. What is at issue is who gets to decide global rules and to define legitimate exceptions to them. This is the essence of sovereign power— setting, and breaking, the rules. To become the supreme authority—a court of law above all politics, national and international—is the inner logic of Human Rights.

> …

> What changed, what turned human rights into Human Rights, was American power. From the 1970s onward, a new kind of advocacy emerged that sought to pressure the American state into using its vast resources to coerce, cajole, and induce improved human rights abroad. New organizations, of which by far the most successful has been Human Rights Watch, were the product not of a popular movement but of elite mobilization. The language of human rights soon took root, creating a large constituency of supporters, but these new activists were only in some cases like the solidarity-inspired members of the postwar years. Seismic shifts had taken place in transforming the narrow middle class of old Europe into a wide, transnational class of consumers. The majority adopted human rights as a kind of lifestyle choice, joining and campaigning for human rights as a global language of freedom and justice rather than for any specific cause with which they were personally linked. They were a paying audience as much as an activist base. The global membership model Amnesty International had pioneered proved a singular one, and while it persisted it was not replicated.

In Hopgood's view, 'it is only as a by-product of American power and money that human rights have been globalized'. As for Amnesty, it sought to rely on a model of 'secular religiosity' which 'anchored moral authority on detachment from power politics'. But this approach 'had very limited capacity to affect world politics in any deep way. Its achievement was to keep open the idea of impartial, neutral space over and above politics and conflict. Yet this virtue was also its weakness in terms of impact' because it was 'a symbolically powerful but politically ineffectual form of activism against determined opposition.'

More recently, Makau Mutua, in 'Human Rights: A TWAILBlazer Critique', 52 *Denv. J. Int'l L. & Pol'y* (2024) 185, 205 has reprised his earlier critiques of the same groups:

> … [T]he human rights movement has a grand narrative on race in which the peoples of the Global South—who are Black and Brown—are subordinate and inferior to the white, European races of the Global North. The movement hews closely to global hierarchies of power. It is part of the geopolitical hegemonic calculus that drives the international legal order. It promises too much and delivers too little to societies in the Global South. This relationship of the inferior to the superior in racial terms has been cultivated by dominant human rights NGOs and INGOs in the Global North and powerful states in North America, especially the United States, and in the European Union. Powerful NGOs such as the London-based Amnesty International and the New York-based Human Rights Watch have styled themselves the guardians of human rights. These organizations focus mostly on human worked closely with Western governments, prominent funders, and large media houses in the West to marshal influence and power over states in the Global South. These asymmetries of power have correspondingly diminished the voices of human rights NGOs in the Global South in favor of their counterparts in the West. Further, this is why the Western-dominated human rights movement have done little to

document and expose violations of economic and social rights, especially by multinational corporations.

Hopgood's provocations predictably drew many critical responses from scholars such as Kathryn Sikkink and Gráinne de Búrca (see Chapter 17, below), as well as from Kenneth Roth ('The End of Human Rights?', *New York Review of Books* (23 October 2014)), then head of HRW. He conceded that while there was 'an element of truth in Hopgood's critique', it also involves 'much caricature':

> ... [T]he movement is powerful because of its ability, often at great risk, to conduct detailed, on-the-ground investigations of human rights abuses and then to use the information gathered to shame and pressure governments that fall short of public expectations for their conduct. One of the most important assets of the human rights movement is its ability to focus public attention on the abuses that it investigates and documents. The work of [HRW] is cited in the global media dozens of times a day.
>
> ...
>
> ... Hopgood decries the human rights movement for not doing more to solicit direct action by members of the public, but the movement's primary methods of investigation and exposure are intimately linked to public opinion. If publicizing a rights violation does not lead to condemnation in the media and by concerned members of the public, the written law will make little difference.
>
> The same dynamic lies behind the human rights movement's enlisting of powerful governments. Appeals to the dictates of international law are far less important in moving such governments to use their influence to defend rights than are reports in the media informing people of serious abuses. The public, in turn, often demands that its government avoid complicity in abuses by repressive regimes and use its clout to curb them. The US and other governments, for their part, can make abusive leaders pay a price for that abuse, whether in lost military aid, targeted sanctions, or diplomatic snubbing. That price can make a leader decide to stop committing human rights violations.
>
> ...
>
> These are powerful tools. Yet Hopgood belittles them as "elite mobilization," in contrast with the popular mobilization that he prefers. But behind the verbiage seems to be a dislike for the means used to influence public opinion. It is true that groups like [HRW] tend to focus on better-informed media, because they are more likely to have the sophistication needed to address these often complex issues. To dismiss this use of media as "elite" is to neglect its enormous impact in shaping public opinion throughout society.
>
> ...

Even scholars who emphasize the achievements of groups like HRW and Amnesty frequently concede the need for change, especially in terms of relationships between human rights groups and the broader array of social movements.[622] Antoine Buyse and Verónica Gómez, 'Human Rights Organizations and Civil Society', in Kees Biekart and Alan Fowler (eds.), *A Research Agenda for Civil Society* (2022) 99, point to more recent initiatives ranging from:

> [S]ocial justice movements in Latin America, to the #MilkTea Alliance of democracy movements in South East Asia, the #BlackLivesMatter protests against racial discrimination and the #FridaysforFuture protests of children and teenagers against climate change in many places. ... [T]hese forms of activism have been much more vocal, often more radical and certainly much more visible and locally rooted than the work of human rights NGOs. At the same time, their success has varied greatly, often because street tactics do not always easily translate into policy or legal changes and may be

---

[622] For a different perspective, see R. O'Dell and L. Veazey, 'Is Amnesty International Still a Grassroots, Member-Led Organization? An Assessment of Its Democratic Viability', 15 *J. Hum. Rts. Prac.* (2023) 186.

difficult to sustain. On the other hand, the traditional advocacy, lobbying and research work of human rights NGOs has been perceived by such movements as too slow, too moderate and too much intertwined with existing power structures. The professionalization of human rights organizations in the last few decades, including the preferred methods of action and a partial shift to paid staff as opposed to volunteers, may have increased their effectiveness within international institutions, but at the same time have widened the gap with grassroots movements. The need for rootedness for human rights NGOs and the need for long-term effect for social movements makes for a plausible argument for more cooperation, also because many of the demands of social movements could be translated into and framed as human rights issues. However, the very different ways of organizing, the specific goals and the tactics used make for two uneasy bedfellows. …

Other critiques have addressed the field as a whole. César Rodríguez-Garavito, in 'Human Rights 2030: Existential Challenges and A New Paradigm for the Field', in Nehal Bhuta et al. (eds.), *The Struggle for Human Rights: Law, Politics, Practice* (2021) 328, has identified five field-wide challenges that the movement must address. They are (i) fragmentation and a lack of collaboration and learning across the field; (ii) strategic stagnation and limited innovation; (iii) slowness and a tendency to focus on the short term; (iv) a relatively narrow membership and audience; and (v) shortcomings in managing the complexity of new challenges such as inequality or climate change. Similarly, Martín Abregú, a senior Ford Foundation official and former NGO leader has criticized the movement both for its failure to address the structural causes underlying human rights violations, and for not '[m]aking human rights real for the vast majority of the world's people' by engaging 'in more comprehensive and collaborative work with non-human rights sectors.'[623]

A collaborative venture calling itself Reimagining International NGOs (RINGO) argues that the 'current model of the INGO seems no longer fit for purpose.'[624] Participants in one of its one of its workshops identified barriers to change, including concerns that: the large groups are not engaging in the internal reflections that are needed to bring change; these groups are unprepared to relinquish their power; they are reluctant to take a systems perspective; they do not encourage risk-taking or work on transformative change; and they are overly bureaucratized. And global North-based funders were criticized for perpetuating existing asymmetries. The group concluded by identifying eight 'areas in which the INGO system needs to be reimagined: structural racism; patriarchy and feminist leadership; resource flows; incentives; solidarity and collaboration; governance and accountability; INGO impact; [and] government role.'[625]

Another detailed study focused on the negative consequences that may be generated at the local level by outside advocacy groups.[626] The authors generally refrain from criticizing specific INGOs, but it seems that HRW and Amnesty are clearly among their target group:

> … [T]op-down advocacy models risk increasing rightsholders' experience of marginalization, and lead to interventions that are unresponsive to rightsholders' needs and priorities. They can risk adopting strategies that produce backlash and negative consequences for rightsholders, including serious security risks, and reinforce structural barriers to the exercise of rightsholder power. Such practices may also have the effect of undermining rightsholder or grassroots-led efforts to achieve social justice. For example, an advocate's intervention may provide a temporary, palliative reprieve from a violation at the expense of the broader structural change around which rightsholders had been mobilizing, or, funders may direct their limited resources to interventions designed and implemented by outside advocates rather than the rightsholders themselves. The critique of top-down advocacy is of critical importance because of its focus on power. Much human rights work is fundamentally about challenging the structural power imbalances— whether rooted in economic, political, social, or cultural systems or relationships—that operate to deprive rightsholders of the agency to affect change in their own lives. The

---

[623] M. Abregú, 'What strengthening human rights has to do with challenging inequality', Ford Foundation (22 May 2017).
[624] The RINGO Project: Re-Imagining the INGO and the Role of Global Civil Society, at https://rightscolab.org/ringo/.
[625] Rights CoLAB and Reos Partners, 'Inception Workshop: A Discovery Journey of the Ringo system' (May 2021).
[626] S. Knuckey et al., 'Power in Human Rights Advocate and Rightsholder Relationships: Critiques, Reforms, and Challenges', 33 *Harv. Hum. Rts J.* (2020) 1.

critique calls into question to what extent outside advocates' own actions vis-à-vis rightsholders might undermine that very goal by recreating and reinforcing the imbalances of power that the advocates seek to disrupt. Advocacy practices may stunt the exercise of rightsholders' agency in decision-making processes that affect them, processes that are fundamentally important to their being able to counter a sense of invisibility and reclaim their dignity, and also to building local capacity and self-reliance to sustainably address future issues or abuses. Human rights practice that fails to empower rightsholders may therefore unwittingly further entrench human rights abuses.

B. ALTERNATIVE APPROACHES

The most powerful response to the criticisms of Hopgood, Posner, Moyn and others writing in a similar vein is that their focus is both too narrow and somewhat dated. The materials that follow aim to give a sense of the greater variety of perspectives, approaches, tactics, and techniques used by other social movement actors within the human rights community. The first reading, by Mette Eilstrup-Sangiovanni and J. C. Sharman, raises the question of whether human rights groups tend to rely on an unduly limited range of tactics. The example of 'peoples' tribunals' suggests that acting completely outside official structures might be rewarding. Then, Jochen von Bernstorff suggests that a significantly new approach that gives the 'most affected' centre stage is increasingly dominant. And several readings provide a case study of the approaches used by 'disability activists'.

1. 'Vigilante Enforcement'

METTE EILSTRUP-SANGIOVANNI AND J. C. SHARMAN, VIGILANTES BEYOND BORDERS:
NGOS AS ENFORCERS OF INTERNATIONAL LAW
(2022) 159

Nonstate actors increasingly play the role of vigilante enforcers of international law. ... [We need] to shift our view to a more pluralistic understanding which recognizes the multiple enforcement roles of other actors in world politics, especially NGOs. So far we have illustrated the rise of autonomous NGO enforcement in three broad domains of international law: human rights, the environment, and anti-corruption. We have explained this trend by several facilitating factors: a growing mismatch between increasing legalization and limited state enforcement; legal and technological innovations empowering nonstate enforcers; and the changing ecologies of NGO populations. In some cases, states have deliberately or inadvertently created conditions for NGOs to step into an autonomous enforcement role, particularly when governments have committed to wide-ranging legal obligations and then failed to supply adequate enforcement, or when unintended consequences of law have opened new doors to nonstate enforcement. In other cases, NGOs have wrested power from states by turning domestic or international enforcement mechanisms against governments in response to sins of omission or commission.

...

... Although there are ... plenty of exceptions, human rights and anti-corruption NGOs have so far been primarily concerned with holding individuals accountable for breaches of international law. In contrast, environmental groups are more likely to target companies and governments. ...

...

The Legitimacy of Vigilante Enforcement

...

... Given that vigilante justice is sometimes seen as a contradiction in terms, what defence can be offered in terms of legitimacy for transnational enforcement by NGOs?

Scholars often distinguish between procedural and substantive legitimacy. Procedural legitimacy is taken to flow from proper procedure. Thus, if a treaty prescribes that only governments have authority to enforce, then only state-sanctioned enforcement shall be deemed legitimate. Substantive legitimacy is more concerned with the contents of rules and institutions. Hence, insofar as NGOs duly enforce laws which are passed and ratified by states in cases where states lack the means or will to do so, this may be deemed legitimate. It is a commonplace that contracts are enforced by private parties via the courts. Why not accept that legitimacy in regard to international enforcement arises from the legitimacy of international laws— not from who enforces them? This is especially so when ... the international laws in question enjoy near-universal acceptance. On these grounds transnational enforcement could be interpreted and welcomed as a trend towards greater inclusiveness and empowerment of a wider range of global actors.

In terms of the rule of law and due process, it is important to emphasize that NGOs are not above the law. Ultimately, like companies, NGOs are creatures of law and are only distinguished from collections of individuals by formal registration and recognition that ultimately comes from the state. Whether or not they are engaged in enforcement, NGOs enjoy none of the immunities granted to the police. NGOs can be and are occasionally prosecuted and sued for their transgressions. The shortcomings of NGO enforcement, which are real, need to be compared not against some ideal standard but against the practical alternative of state enforcement, warts and all. 'NGO brutality' is not a common problem, whereas police brutality is. The same goes for corruption. ...

... NGOs have often become more rather than less legalistic as they have taken on an enforcement role. Strategic litigation and the 'Pinochet effect' have meant that NGOs are increasingly operating through courts, using the laws as they exist to promote their objectives. Even when NGOs are not in court themselves, the more indirect side of enforcement commonly centres on prompting and supporting police action via preliminary investigations and evidence gathering. Vigilante NGOs are more likely to be in tacit alliance with law enforcement agencies than protest and advocacy groups are. ...
...
... World politics in the twenty-first century is increasingly a hybrid system in which the enforcement of international rules is both delegated but also independently practiced by nonstate actors. From the perspective of states, inter-governmental organizations, and NGOs alike, this hybrid approach raises the possibility of achieving more effective and efficient enforcement of international laws. In the absence of a unitary world state with a police force to match, a combination of public and private enforcement may be the only way to maintain the operability of an ever more ambitious body of international law. In supplying law enforcement, NGOs make a plausible claim to be supplying a public good, since a lack of enforcement ultimately risks making international law irrelevant.

2. People's Tribunals

International peoples' tribunals have been a prominent feature of the civil society landscape since the initiative led by Bertrand Russell and Jean-Paul Sartre to hold the United States and its allies to account for their violations, during the Vietnam War, of human rights and humanitarian law and the law on the use of force. The 25 panel members, acting in their personal capacities, consisted of writers, philosophers, activists, Nobel laureates and others, including James Baldwin, Stokely Carmichael, Simone de Beauvoir, and Alice Walker. The United States, and various allies, were found guilty in 1967 of 'the deliberate, systematic and large-scale bombardment of civilian targets ... [and] repeated violations of the sovereignty, neutrality and territorial integrity of Cambodia ...'. In the mid-1970s, another tribunal deliberated on the crimes committed by Latin American dictatorships.

The same technique of detailed hearings and collection of evidence, followed by a reasoned verdict, was subsequently adopted by the Permanent Peoples' Tribunals led by Italian leftist politician, Lelio Basso. By 2023, the Tribunal had held 49 Sessions on a wide range of issues, including COVID-19 related crimes by President Bolsonaro in Brazil, the murders of journalists worldwide, and crimes committed in Sri Lanka, Syria, Turkey, Myanmar and elsewhere (see https://permanentpeoplestribunal.org/).

Consider the following assessment by Andrew Byrnes and Gabrielle Simm (eds.), in *Peoples' Tribunals and International Law* (2017), at 273:

> [Such tribunals generally share certain features.] The first is that they all represent a 'formal' response to the (perceived) failures or inability of state-sponsored national and international institutions to prevent or redress systematic violations of human rights.

Secondly, they manifest a belief in the emancipatory and protective power of international law, and those involved claim the right as the beneficiaries of that law to own it, interpret it and call states to account for violating it. Thirdly, they challenge the state monopoly on the creation of law, maintaining that it is for peoples and people to formulate a law that promotes the realisation of their rights. … [Many of the tribunals also] critique those international legal concepts and structures that bolster and are invoked in support of injustice and seek to challenge the oppressive dimensions of international law. As a result, they regularly seek to push existing international law to develop in a direction that will provide enhanced protection to oppressed peoples and marginalised groups. The criticisms levelled at peoples' tribunals and the practice of individual tribunals frequently reflect states' desires to reassert their monopoly on authoritative lawmaking and the interpretation and application of international law. Critics also castigate peoples' tribunals for their failure to comply with a formalist and limited model of adversarial litigation and fail to understand the nature of the social activity in which peoples' tribunals are engaged. Peoples' tribunals perform multiple roles that official institutions and procedures still fail to adequately perform. This is why peoples' tribunals have been growing in popularity and have become a common form of resistance for social movements.

3. Involving the 'Most Affected'

**JOCHEN VON BERNSTORFF, NEW RESPONSES TO THE LEGITIMACY CRISIS OF INTERNATIONAL INSTITUTIONS:
THE ROLE OF 'CIVIL SOCIETY' AND THE RISE OF THE PRINCIPLE OF PARTICIPATION OF 'THE MOST AFFECTED' IN INTERNATIONAL INSTITUTIONAL LAW
32 EUR. J. INT'L L. (2021) 125**

1 Introduction

… Classic NGOs in various fields of law and policy-making are increasingly being replaced by local and transnational social movements, so-called 'affected persons' organizations' (APOs), in reaction to a perceived crisis of legitimacy and a backlash against both international institutions and international NGOs. This trend has, over the last 10 years, already transformed rules of civil-society participation in at least 20 prominent international organizations.

For example, members of indigenous groups and peasant organizations have successfully lobbied for new rights instruments and institutional reform to ensure protection, participation and influence. Persons affected by HIV/AIDS, tuberculosis and malaria have been accorded designated seats on decision-making bodies in the Global Fund, UNITAID and other institutions of global health governance. Organizations that represent disabled people took on a strong role in the negotiations of the UN's Convention on the Rights of Persons with Disabilities. Working children movements from the Global South challenged the Western understandings of child labour at various intergovernmental organizations (IOs). Among the first institutions which modified their rules of procedure accordingly were the Committee on World Food Security (CFS) in Rome, the Monitoring Mechanism of the Convention on the Rights of Persons with Disabilities (CRPD) and the World Health Organization (WHO). …

Activists involved in these movements do not want to exercise formalized decision-making powers. Rather, the general idea is to participate in institutionalized deliberation in order to influence the content of adopted decisions. For social movements, participation in international institutions is one strategy among others aimed at fostering the transnational mobilization of social resistance against perceived hegemonic networks of powerful national administrations, scientific expertise and influential corporate actors. The status of speaking, if credible and well-coordinated, for those who are being negatively affected on the ground by certain norms and policies can give these voices a high moral and empirical persuasiveness in these institutional settings. Usually, however, positions taken by APOs are more radical and uncompromising than those of classic NGO representatives. Even without formal voting rights, APOs can have a considerable impact on the content of new international norms, standards and decisions; one striking example being the negotiations on the UN

Convention on the Rights of Persons with Disabilities, during which many persons with disabilities representing disability APOs participated under the motto 'nothing about us without us!' and exerted considerable influence on the content of the new document.

The general concept of affectedness is … a basic and longstanding democratic ideal that those affected should have a say on issues that concern them. In traditional Western democratic theory, from Kant to Rawls, being affected by rules enforced in a certain delimited territory has been conceptualized as requiring elections of representative bodies on a 'one citizen, one vote' basis … . … Nancy Fraser proposed to replace the 'all-affected principle' with a more specific principle of involving all those groups 'subjected' to a given transnational governance structure ('all-subjected principle'). Legal scholars in this context have framed new forms of participatory and multi-level policy-making as 'global experimentalist governance', or … [developed] a global administrative law (GAL) perspective … .

…

5 Conclusion

…

The quest for involving affected persons' organizations can be understood as an attempt to redraw the constructed boundaries between private and public spheres, aiming at expanding the public sphere at the cost of 'market solutions' and expert and elite-driven regulation. … [W]e are thus witnessing a struggle for the extension of global, national and local publics, a struggle for attention and visibility in public institutions so-far dominated by hegemonic expert networks. The move to participation of the most affected does not really aim to democratize international institutions in the sense of equal representation; the aim is, instead, to give a voice to those groups that are existentially affected by policy and rule-making of a particular institution.

In international legal debates, two options for the future of international institutions have been put forward in this context. GAL scholars propose to reform international institutions through greater civil-society participation and various other measures enhancing 'accountability' taken from the toolbox of national administrative law. The second option is to dismantle international institutions and to redirect energy and mobilization of affected groups to the domestic level as suggested by Chimni. Both positions on civil-society participation and the legitimacy problem of international institutions have their inherent limitations and drawbacks. For one, the reformist agenda comes with the structural limitations posed by one of root causes of prior exclusions and blind spots of expert-driven global governance: fragmentation. It is no coincidence that the involvement of APOs, including marginalized and impoverished segments of the global society, is already well underway in all those international institutions that deal with the so-called 'negative externalities' of globalized markets and property protection regimes, such as the human rights and the environmental law field. But to assume that institutions like the WTO, the World Bank, the IMF or the UN Security Council would give affected persons' organizations an influential voice regarding their global policies and rule-making seems unrealistic. … [A] regime that has been erected to promote free trade will refrain from integrating movements which campaign for reintroducing highly protected and subsidized national and local markets guaranteeing the survival of smallholders and non-industrial forms of traditional agriculture. … [T]he public law framework of economic globalization, protecting the operations of powerful private economic actors and a status-quo-oriented distribution of wealth, poverty and adverse environmental effects, will not be fundamentally changed by such measures. Even if these regimes should introduce the whole GAL accountability agenda, including effective judicial review, their foundational actor and value-configuration would not allow for major concessions vis-à-vis the global poor and the climate. More accountability in the form of judicial review could eventually even destroy political concessions vis-à-vis these 'external' or second-order values (exceptions) because of the internal regime biases that have usually been internalized by specialized judges and arbitrators.

At the same time, relegating mobilization of the most affected to the national level, as proposed by Chimni, is by no means a panacea, either. Many of the problems faced by the most affected require global solutions to be developed and enforced by global institutions. The main reason is that without significant redistribution of wealth and resources from the Global North to the Global South, and without restructuring the global economy, climate change-induced catastrophes and deprivations will, in the near future, fundamentally challenge existing living conditions in all parts of the globe. The world is in need of a profound economic and social transformation … . Some international legal and institutional structures will certainly have to be dismantled during this phase. States will remain crucial actors, but … global political and economic transformations require a new value configuration promoted by a hegemonic discourse including private actors. This time, however, it needs to be in the form of a solid transnational solidarity movement, involving governments, cross-sectorial international institutions, NGOs and – hopefully setting the tone – the most affected.

4. Disability Activism

Gerard Quinn, as UN Special Rapporteur on the rights of persons with disabilities, noted (UN Doc. A/HRC/46/27 (2021) para. 25) the extent to which the Convention on the Rights of Persons with Disabilities (CRPD) provided an impetus to what some have called 'disability activism':

> Article 4 (3) of the Convention famously requires that the voices of persons with disabilities and their representative organizations be heard, that persons with disabilities should be closely consulted and actively involved in the development and implementation of legislation and policies to implement the Convention and in other decision-making processes concerning issues that affect them. Furthermore, article 33 (3) requires that civil society, in particular persons with disabilities and their representative organizations, be actively engaged in the process of monitoring the implementation of the Convention at the domestic level. Clearly, the Convention envisages a domestic institutional architecture of change involving power (Government), voice (civil society) and ideas (the checking value of national human rights institutions and the value added of innovative blueprints for change generated by dedicated research bodies working with civil society). At the heart of this new architecture for change is the voice of persons with disabilities.

The background to this disability activism is described by Maria Berghs, Tsitsi Chataika, Kudakwashe Dube, and Yahya El-Lahib, 'Introducing Disability Activism', in *ibid.* (eds.), *The Routledge Handbook of Disability Activism* (2020) 3:

> We are living through 'activist' times with differing formal and informal expressions of what activism looks like from individual actions, artistic movements, mass protest marches, hashtag activism (e.g. #ArabSpring, #BlackLivesMatter, #JeSuisCharlie, #MeToo movement, #ThisFlag), consumer activism, climate activism, peace activism; to ensure collective institutional, legislative or political change. These campaigns are viewed as more inclusive, democratic, 'liquid' and horizontal in nature, in that anyone can join. With the impact of social media, boundaries between public and private life collapse. The personal now can become political and part of public discourses, as well as imagery, and experienced as individually empowering. Public spaces become 'occupied' and appropriated for direct action, political slogans of resistance and mass protests. Most activists now use technology, such as mobile phones and the Internet, as well as email, photographs, videos, podcasts, crowdfunding and blogs, making it accessible to a wider global audience.
>
> Much of the physical and emotional labour of activism and advocacy, in terms of writing letters or calling, recruiting new members, ensuring funding, thinking of campaign slogans and planning innovative actions and tactics for attention, has thus profoundly altered with this new media landscape. At the same time, there have been criticisms of this 'new activism', with some despairingly calling it mainly 'online', 'cyber' or 'digital' activism, 'clicktivism', or 'slacktivism'.
>
> …
>
> What is missing from many of the above criticisms and analysis of new forms and impetus of activism is 'disability'. … While everyone is involved in new forms of activism – from local to global (this is inclusive of age, ethnicity, gender, socio-economic class and so on), disability theory, people with impairments, illness and chronic conditions, as well as different forms of new activisms, have been neglected. …

Disability activism is also incorrectly viewed as only about disability 'rights' or with inadequate cross-cultural or interdisciplinary reach. It is often erroneously seen as something 'special' or 'different', with limited political or human rights impact that only those with a 'disability' identity can do. However, there is often no nuanced understanding of what 'disability issues' involve. We have nonetheless seen a surge of disability advocacy, activism, campaigning and research on activism, from confrontational protests and symbolic direct action … , to the start of a disability movement and advocacy on disability issues in China and its intersectionality to other movements like #MeToo. …

But despite the neglect of disability issues in mainstream analyses of human rights activism, there is actually a rich history behind the evolution of radically different approaches to activism in this field, culminating in the emergence of a human rights model of disability.

One of the most elaborate descriptions of the evolution of the various models and approaches to disability is provided by Hisayo Katsui and Lieketseng Ned, 'Discussing Models of Disability of Health in a Global Context', in Lieketseng Ned et al. (eds.), *The Routledge International Handbook of Disability and Global Health* (2024) 19, at 21-22. They suggest the possible negative and positive impacts of various approaches including a: traditional model, charity-based approach, medical model, religious model, social model, political model, human rights-based approach, 'crip theory', decolonial approach, and a neoliberalism-based approach.

Gerard Quinn (UN Doc. A/HRC/52/32 (2023)) has described the difference between the medical and human rights models and their impact in terms of transforming services for persons with disabilities:

19. Our inherited disability service system owes much to the medical model of disability. It is commonly said to focus on deviations from a norm (how "normal" humans function) and then on the design of interventions to "fix" the deviation in the person. This contributed to a narrow social support philosophy mainly seeking to "compensate" the person with a disability for their "loss". The focus was on the impairment, not the person. Moral agency, and legal capacity – the control of persons over their own lives – was not the goal. Still less was the goal to forge inclusive pathways into communal life. Left out altogether was the connection between the advancement of disability rights and community development.

20. … The Convention departs radically from the medical model of disability. The various social models that helped pave the way for a human rights-based approach to disability challenged the underlying basis and effects of the medical model. Rejected was the fixation on impairment that devalued people. Instead, the starting point is the humanity and the just claims of persons with disabilities as human beings with equal rights, hopes and dreams.

21. Taking common humanity rather than impairment as the core departure point means taking the person seriously as an end in themselves and as a free moral agent. Thus, the objective of services must no longer be about maintenance, care or protection. … It should be about autonomy – voice, choice and control – and social inclusion. Services of the future should primarily be about enabling one to self-actualize in the world.

22. Second, in addition to the general rejection of the medical model, a web of core rights in the Convention points strongly to the need for the reconceptualization of services. Personhood and moral agency form the bedrock of the Convention. Article 12, on equal recognition before the law, seeks to give persons with disabilities the ability to shape their own lives and thus change the way in which the world interacts with them. The provision is an antidote to the tendency of traditional service systems to bypass the wishes of the person and to entrap them

in a world not of their own making. It points strongly towards the personalization of services. This does not mean fixating on the myth of the completely atomistic individual, but taking human interdependence seriously, especially in support models for decision-making.

23. Article 19, on living independently and being included in the community, is intimately connected with this mission. It is directed at enabling the free development of one's personality, in a home of one's own, and with free interaction in the community: a mix of moral agency with social inclusion. Home is an intensely private place for repose and the evolution of identity, and it is spatially connected with the community, allowing one to engage on one's own terms.

24. The implications for the future of services are clear. For persons with disabilities to lead in all matters concerning their own lives, a reorientation will be required away from fixation on impairments and towards consciousness of the importance of the life choices of the person. Since social inclusion is vital to the evolution of our sense of self, it follows that services should stitch together social capital to ensure an equal right to belong, to grow and to be connected with others. Article 19 (b) speaks more directly to the need for personalized services and support.

...

The CRPD illustrates well the role played by civil society mobilization around the Convention, which can take many different forms. The examples of Argentina and Nigeria are instructive. Gráinne de Búrca, in *Reframing Human Rights in a Turbulent Era* (2021) describes the process followed in Argentina:

> ... [In Argentina] the paradigm introduced by the CRPD has been particularly successful in galvanizing and strengthening the role of relevant civil society organizations and has had a notable impact on mobilization, advocacy, and policy reform in the disability field.
> ...
>
> While a variety of organizations of persons with disabilities and their advocates was already active in relation to disability issues well before the adoption of the CRPD in Argentina, the state's ratification and constitutional incorporation of that treaty galvanized many of these groups around an explicit disability rights agenda. Activists worked to build a more collective and coordinated movement, to highlight and publicize issues ..., to identify and advance particular cases, and to use legal and other strategies to challenge a range of injustices both in domestic and international fora. At the national level they sought and generated information from the state as well as from affected individuals and families, and attempted to educate the public and state officials on the issues facing people with disabilities, as well as mobilizing affected constituencies and their supporters. At the international level they used the treaty-body reporting process to organize collaboration amongst themselves, draft shadow reports, highlight particular issues, and generate international attention. They worked to inform and influence the jurisprudence and output of the treaty body and other human rights actors ... . These normative sources—General Comments, Reports, and Concluding Observations—were then later invoked and relied on in domestic litigation to advance disability rights and to influence prosecutors, judges, and advocates general, ... leading ultimately to reforms aimed at advancing the rights of persons with disabilities ... . [R]eform is rarely achieved through a single or discrete event, but is usually the product of an ongoing struggle and an often slow process that includes setbacks and losses rather than only successes.
>
> ...
>
> ... [I]nternational human rights institutions and actors ... [provided] a focal point for information-generation and normative elaboration as well as a forum for accountability enhancement, rather than one of conventionally understood 'enforcement'. Similarly,

while local and national actors within Argentina undoubtedly drew upon and mobilized international resources and networks just as the 'boomerang' model originally described,[627] bringing issues to the attention of international monitoring bodies and preparing petitions and shadow reports to highlight problems and abuses, they have also had an important ongoing domestic role in following up on the interventions of international actors, using the outputs of international bodies at the national and local level to challenge, contest, advocate, explain, and promote change. …

Nigeria also provides an instructive case study in relation to the CRPD and social mobilization. The Government signed the treaty in 2007 and ratified it in 2010. But after the National Assembly adopted a Bill to implement its provisions, successive Presidents refused to sign. The Bill finally gained Presidential assent in January 2019, after what HRW described as '9 years of relentless advocacy by disability rights groups and activists.'[628]

Audrey Comstock, in *Committed to Rights: UN Human Rights Treaties and Legal Paths for Commitment and Compliance* (2021) 88, describes the positive impact of this process:

> Signing the CRPD brought the treaty and Nigerian disability rights issues to the forefront of domestic and international recognition. With signature, the Nigerian government opened itself to support from the United Nations and other programs promoting disability rights. The president could not contest the programs as imposing outside or Western rights on Nigeria because he had already committed through signing the treaty. [S]igning … allowed for international development measures to send aid and programs into Nigeria and enact parts of the treaty. Signing the CRPD also legitimated the disability rights movement in Nigeria, fueling further domestic support and mobilization. [The federal government funded small-scale programs, and at the state] and community level, leaders were able to … proceed with their own implementation independent of national-level implementation.

The need for such an entry point for advocacy was highlighted by HRW in a report, *Nigeria: People with Mental Health Conditions Chained, Abused* (2019), which claimed that '[t]housands of people with mental health conditions across Nigeria are chained and locked up in various facilities where they face terrible abuse':

> Deep-rooted problems in Nigeria's healthcare and welfare systems leave most Nigerians unable to get adequate mental health care or support in their communities. Stigma and misunderstanding about mental health conditions, including the misperception that they are caused by evil spirits or supernatural forces, often prompt relatives to take their loved ones to religious or traditional healing places.

> Human Rights Watch found that people with actual or perceived mental health conditions, including children, are placed in facilities without their consent, usually by relatives. In some cases, police arrest people with actual or perceived mental health conditions and send them to government-run rehabilitation centers. Once there, many are shackled with iron chains, around one or both ankles, to heavy objects or to other detainees, in some cases for months or years. They cannot leave, are often confined in overcrowded, unhygienic conditions, and are sometimes forced to sleep, eat, and defecate within the same confined place. Many are physically and emotionally abused as well as forced to take treatments.

---

[627] The 'boomerang model' is a term coined by M. Keck and K. *Sikkink, in Activists beyond Borders: Advocacy Networks in International* Politics (1998). It describes how, especially in a repressive state, international and transnational networks provide alternative sources of human rights information, which they draw to the attention of states, international organizations, and others to pressure the government into honouring its international commitments. For an 'updated' version, see C. Pallas and E. Bloodgood (eds.), *Beyond the Boomerang: From Transnational Advocacy Networks to Transcalar Advocacy in International Politics* (2022).

[628] A. Ewang, 'Nigeria Passes Disability Rights Law', Human Rights Watch (25 January 2019).

5. Other Perspectives

ANN MARIE CLARK, DEMANDS OF JUSTICE: THE CREATION OF A GLOBAL HUMAN RIGHTS PRACTICE
(2022)

Conclusion

…

As leading human rights NGOs have become more authoritative, their positioning in the human rights universe may constrain their modes of action, making them less willing to be bold, and more comfortable with status quo politics. Their established reputations, their power as gatekeepers, and their capacity in comparison to smaller NGOs bolster their authority. In addition, critical scholars point out that a human rights frame privileges classical liberal, individualist views originating in the wealthy Global North while expressing wariness of the potential to reproduce social relations that contributed to the structural injustices of colonialism, racism, and gender bias. …

… The human rights framework as a path to justice may at some point reach its limits, but human rights possess two unique features that, to some extent, keep human rights practices from losing their edge as tools of justice. The first feature is that the users of human rights tools become subject to critique from the very standpoint of human rights that they propound, and their legitimacy depends on how well they respond to those critiques. …

The second feature is the malleability of human rights practice, despite the level of institutionalization in law and international organization. Even where tailored protections in international human rights law are incomplete, local, regional, and global activists use human rights in new and uncharted ways. …

Many expressions of justice concerns draw on the language of human rights: environmental justice, racial justice, indigenous rights, LGBTQI rights, gender equity, and economic and social justice concerns. The variation illustrates the broad applicability of human rights as tools of justice. …

…

To paraphrase Beitz, human rights may be the closest thing we have to a common language of justice in global politics. Human rights practice has changed the terms of engagement in global politics by providing a common standard for the normative evaluation of political realities. The human rights culture of argument now operates against a background of institutionalized monitoring procedures in intergovernmental organizations. In addition, human rights language has become a medium for justice-related claims people make of their governments. Even with these developments, however, it is a mistake to see human rights as a finished project. Economic, social, and cultural rights have yet to be fully supplied with dedicated human rights tools at the global level. …

…

MOHAMED EL HACHIMI AND RACHID TOUHTOU, CIVIL SOCIETY, NGOS, AND HUMAN RIGHTS IN AFRICA
R. SOORYAMOORTHY AND NENE ERNEST KHALEMA (EDS.), THE OXFORD HANDBOOK OF SOCIOLOGY OF AFRICA (2022) C27.S1

…

Conceptualizing Civil Society and Human Rights in Africa

…

The concept of civil society that originated with the writings of Friedrich Hegel, Karl Marx, and, later, Antonio Gramsci is endemic in Western political thought. To the extent that this concept grew out of the evolution of state-society interactions in Western societies, it can travel outside the West only with some methodological precautions. This is not to say that civil society cannot appear in other sociocultural contexts or that it is the only valid form that can emerge out of state-society interaction and perform the functions of Western civil society. It only means that, as with any other concept, the use of civil society as an analytical tool requires considering how well it is adapted to the reality of the state-society relations it seeks to grasp.

The liberal concept of civil society comprises a least three essential elements: civility, a public sphere, and a relationship with democracy. ...

...

In Africa, however, a large majority of civil society organizations operate in sociopolitical contexts that lack one or more of the aforementioned three essentials. Civil society organizations in most African societies share three peculiarities that make it difficult to assert that they meet the core criteria. First, they mainly operate in authoritarian or semi-authoritarian political systems, where even when a political reform is introduced, it rarely meets the requirements of a liberal democracy. Second, under these authoritarian political systems, the public sphere is yet to emerge, and in many African countries there is no social arena where citizens can exchange views and opinions free from state control. Last, because the existing civil society organizations take either the form of service providers or are self-organized based on ethnic origin, they do not embody the civic spirit that is so important to the concept of civil society.

Is There an African Indigenous Concept of Civil Society?

Given these missing elements, is it possible to talk about an indigenous conception of civil society in Africa? ...

Unlike the NGOs, considered to have been imposed by colonial powers, local forms of African societal self-organization are thought to be anchored in history. These local forms cover a broad spectrum and range from local political organizations and institutions, such as chiefdoms, councils of elders, and local defense communities, to vigilante or militia groups, militant social movements, youth organizations, and violence entrepreneurs. Regardless of whether they meet the requirements for a Western civil society, the functions these groups perform are similar to those a civil society organization today is supposed to play, especially that of mediating between the society and the state, and some have filled the vacuum created by a typically weak central power.

Some scholars in fact argue that "elements of civil society may be found among political systems in Africa". This attempt to forge an alternative concept of civil society takes the traditional Akan political environment and philosophy as an illustrative example. ...

This understanding of the notion of civil society has two serious limitations. First, restructuring the concept of civil society along the lines of the traditional African political systems is likely to be perceived as legitimizing the enduring authoritarian systems prevailing in most African countries. Second, rejecting the universal understanding of human rights because it is based on Western liberal ideology has proven to be merely a subtle maneuver instrumentalized by authoritarian regimes to justify human rights violations in the name of cultural specificities.

... We recognize the validity of some of the arguments in favor of an alternative African concept of civil society; however, these efforts are yet to come up with an operational concept able to serve as an adequate analytical tool to shed light on the peculiarities of state-society interactions in the African context. The only way we can enrich the debate on the indigenous African civil society is to analyze the dynamism of organizations that defend their civil society identities. Instead of dwelling on the theoretical, liberal, and normative discussion, we should observe how these organizations operate in their various contexts and how they define their work. ... [T]he functions performed by organizations claiming a civil society identity are shaped, inter alia, by a twofold constraint: on the one hand, by their struggle against various forms of repressive power, as shown by their roles in transitional justice and peacebuilding processes, and on the other hand, by coping with the traditions and cultural specificities of local societies, as reflected in their involvement in women's rights and minority rights issues.

Conclusion

... The African civil sphere, mainly as it relates to the discourses and practices of human rights, does not follow the Western, liberal perspective of states and societies that influence the civil sphere. The colonial and postcolonial trajectories of African societies have ruptures from the old, traditional lost systems of social capital and solidarity safety nets. The postcolonial trajectories of these societies when they try to imitate Western development models seem to have failed in major African societies, giving rise to forms of civic engagement from the perspective of the people trying to help themselves. ...

Associations and NGOs in Africa thrive in traditional societies where notions of tribe, family relations, and primordial forms of solidarity appear to be obstacles to the emergence of modern civil society. Although modern NGOs bloomed in Africa from the 1990s because of international aid, pressures from global civil society, and transnational corporations, the hybrid civil society specific to Africa could not break from the chains of traditionalism flourishing in African societies. Even this hybrid modern civil society could not craft the democratic civic space, the condition *sine qua non* for the emergence of a civil society in the Western model. Transitional justice mechanisms and women's rights are proof that the boundaries between traditionalism and modern civil society are not easily crossed. Indeed, it seems that cultural specificities still have a strong weight when dealing with these two issues in this hybrid civil society that tends to mobilize identity, cultural specificity, and anti-modernity arguments when dealing with transitional justice mechanism and women's rights. To large segments of African societies, civil society was not a natural evolving process but one which was created with the availability of aid and donor organizations.

Civil society in Africa ... is increasingly challenged by the emergence of new forms of activism, mainly mobilizing in the arts, the street, and online. These new forms of activism have become widespread in Africa. The future of human rights and democracy in Africa is likely to depend more on these new forms of activism rather than on traditional civil society. ... [Although] many forms of societal organizations in Africa do not meet the universal requirements of the conception of civil society ... this did not prevent them from struggling against authoritarian regimes. ...

C. THE ACCOUNTABILITY OF HUMAN RIGHTS NGOS

Since human rights NGOs systematically demand accountability from states, international organizations, businesses, and other actors, it is unsurprising that they themselves are subject to such demands. Two decades ago there was a vibrant debate around the question of 'who elected the NGOs?'. Today, however, states that seek to repress NGOs have, for the most part moved from debating accountability to suppressing civil society space. The materials below consider both of these responses.

'Who elected the NGOs?' has been a rallying cry for those who felt that NGOs wielded too much power. At the same time, human rights proponents have agreed that greater accountability and transparency should ideally make NGOs more effective and more strongly supported. Attacks on human rights NGOs are often led by officials and supporters of particular states whose policies have been criticized. Such attacks are, of course, evidence of the impact of the reports themselves, and the contested facts and interpretations can be fought out in the public domain in light of constantly emerging new evidence. More problematic, from the perspective of NGOs in general, have been the generic critiques of the very legitimacy of such organizations. After the Seattle riots against the WTO in 1999, *The Economist* asked whether NGOs were 'the first steps towards an "international civil society" (whatever that might be)', or whether they instead represented 'a dangerous shift of power to unelected and unaccountable special-interest groups'.[629] A year later, the same magazine asked:

> ... who elected Oxfam ... ? Bodies such as these are, to varying degrees, extorting admissions of fault from law-abiding companies and changes in policy from democratically elected governments. They may claim to be acting in the interests of the people — but then so do the objects of their criticism, governments and the despised international institutions. In the West, governments and their agencies are, in the end, accountable to voters. Who holds the activists accountable?[630]

Kenneth Anderson, in 'The Ottawa Convention Banning Landmines, The Role of International Non-Governmental Organizations and the Idea of International Civil Society', 11 *Eur. J. Int'l. L.* (2000) 92 applies this critique to international NGOs as well as the international organizations that provide them with a forum:

---

[629] 'The Non-Governmental Order', *The Economist* (18 December 1999).
[630] 'Angry and Effective', *The Economist* (23 September 2000).

... [I]nternational lawyers ... fundamentally believe that international organizations, and their underlying concept of 'world government' — what is today taken as the vision of Grotius — are legitimate, and deserve to be understood as the world's constitutionally supreme sources of authority and the exercise of power. ...

... [They] tend to form a church of those converted to belief in supranationalism. ...

...

... [But] the brutal fact remains that international organizations as they exist today do not have the perception of legitimacy to carry out the functions that international elites would assign to them. ...

...

... Yet now it is urgently needed, and where to get it?

... International organizations claim to have overcome the democratic deficit as an impediment to their legitimacy by having as their partners, and having the moral and political approval of, international NGOs, the voice of 'world opinion', and the loud and incessant invocation of 'international civil society'. ...

...

... International NGOs, for their part, are happy to accept the accolade of 'international civil society', the voice of the people, and so on, for the obvious reason that it increases their power and authority within international organizations, international elites, and beyond. ...

...

[The author suggests that some legitimacy might inhere in INGOs if they could claim to be] authentic intermediaries of the 'people'. ... But this is implausible, for at least two reasons.

First, [INGOs] are not very often connected, in any direct way, to masses of 'people'. International NGOs, in virtue of their role to operate globally rather than locally, are fundamentally elite organizations. There are exceptions, to be sure, but they are prototypically large religious affiliations. ... There are certain large secular exceptions, as well; Amnesty International is perhaps one, in that at least it has a large base membership. But that membership comes mostly from wealthy countries, and its membership even in those countries tends to be educated and at least middle class ... [T]he far more typical 'international' NGO of the kind whose approval and favour international organizations seek is much closer to the model of Human Rights Watch — a relatively small, highly professional, entirely elite organization funded by foundations and wealthy individuals in the Western democracies, and having no discernible base outside international elites. This is not to denigrate Human Rights Watch or the vital work it does, but it would be the first to declare that its legitimacy is not based on democratic roots among the masses but on its fidelity to its own conception of the meaning of international human rights. ...

The dilemma is straightforward. On the one hand, as Benedict Kingsbury has observed, '[i]nternational civil society in its widest sense is bound to be a largely unregulated free-for-all, with markets in prestige, influence, membership, fundraising capability, and other markers of organizational success.'[631] Efforts to regulate or control NGOs are, in some respects, contrary to their nature and ethos. They are inevitably suspect when coming from those who have been obliged to change their policies and practices as a result of NGO campaigning. On the other hand, the NGOs' unyielding demands for accountability on the part of others

---

[631] B. Kingsbury, 'First Amendment Liberalism as Global Legal Architecture: Ascriptive Groups and the Problems of the Liberal NGO Model of International Civil Society', 3 *Chicago J. Int'l. L.* (2002) 183, at 193.

necessarily serve to focus attention on shortcomings in terms of their own accountability. Some have argued that they could not be held to the same standards of accountability as those who hold 'real' power. As one study put it,'[i]n the grand scheme of societal relations, NGOs ultimately have very little power. They do not have coercive power, financial power, or even the authority and power that derives from representation.'[632] Others note that they are in any event answerable to their supporters and funders, and that their impact and effectiveness is largely dependent upon their perceived legitimacy and credibility.

One starting point is to ask what 'accountability' might actually mean in this context. Ruth Grant and Robert Keohane, in 'Accountability and Abuses of Power in World Politics', 99 *Am. Pol. Sci. Rev.* (2005) 29, identify seven accountability mechanisms of relevance in this regard:

> **Hierarchical accountability** is a characteristic of bureaucracies and of virtually any large organization. Superiors can remove subordinates from office, constrain their tasks and room for discretion, and adjust their financial compensation. ...

> **Supervisory accountability** refers to relations between organizations where one organization acts as principal with respect to specified agents. For instance, the World Bank and IMF are subject to supervision by states and by institutions within states, such as courts. ...

> **Fiscal accountability** describes mechanisms through which funding agencies can demand reports from, and ultimately sanction, agencies that are recipients of funding. ...

> **Legal accountability** refers to the requirement that agents abide by formal rules and be prepared to justify their actions in those terms, in courts or quasi-judicial arenas. ... Courts do not have the broad general authority of governments or of electorates in democracies. Instead, the courts apply a narrow version of the trusteeship model, asking whether the power-wielders performed the duties of their offices faithfully in a limited sense: whether they obeyed the law. ...

> **Market accountability** is [important. It] is not to an abstract force called "the market," but to investors and consumers, whose influence is exercised in whole or in part through markets. ...

> **Peer accountability** arises as the result of mutual evaluation of organizations by their counterparts. NGOs, for example, evaluate the quality of information they receive from other NGOs and the ease of cooperating with them. Organizations that are poorly rated by their peers are likely to have difficulty in persuading them to cooperate and, therefore, to have trouble achieving their own purposes.

> **Public reputational accountability** is pervasive because reputation is involved in all the other forms of accountability. Superiors, supervisory boards, courts, fiscal watchdogs, markets, and peers all take the reputations of agents into account. Indeed, reputation is a form of "soft power," defined as "the ability to shape the preferences of others". The category of public reputational accountability is meant to apply to situations in which reputation, widely and publicly known, provides a mechanism for accountability even in the absence of other mechanisms as well as in conjunction with them.

Isobelle Jaques, in 'Strengthening Democratic Governance: The Role of Civil Society', Report on Wilton Park Conference S06/10 (2006), suggests what the goals of legitimacy, openness and transparency might mean for NGOs:

> Legitimacy stems from several sources: firstly, from a strong moral conviction, through acting on the basis of universally-recognised rights and freedoms of speech, assembly and association to articulate public concerns inadequately addressed by government; secondly, a political legitimacy or credibility, through approval of the community or constituency

[632] L. Jordan, 'Mechanisms for NGO Accountability', Global Public Policy Institute, Research Paper Series No. 3 (2005) 13.

represented by the voluntary association, asserting people's sovereignty and community control; thirdly, competence or performance legitimacy, by delivering results through being closer to local reality than governmental institutions, helping to bridge a government-community gap and promote social cohesion; fourthly, legal recognition …; and, most importantly, legitimacy comes from accountability and transparency.

NGOs should be accountable to a wide range of stakeholders: peoples whose rights they seek to protect and advance; their own members, supporters and staff; to those who contribute finance, goods or services; to partner institutions, both governmental and non-governmental; to regulatory bodies; to those whose policies, programmes or behaviour they wish to influence; and, more broadly, to the media and general public. They should be able to demonstrate a democratic structure, participative decision-making and non-partisan approach if they claim legitimacy on political grounds. They should focus on whatever is their primary agenda and not be diverted from this by demands of donors or obstacles in their operational environment. Some express concern that … some civil society organisations … have veered away from contentious issues like political reform and redistributive justice … . …

Fiscal accountability is … vital, with effective reporting and monitoring systems, and sources of funding fully divulged. Some argue against accepting government support and foreign funding if civil society organisations are involved in promoting political and democratic reform; others, acknowledging the potential sensitivity of this, believe assuring a diversity of funding from public and private sources will overcome accusations of undue influence of donors.

The evolution towards national and international codes of conduct for voluntary self-regulation is regarded as a healthy development, although given the tremendous difference in size and scope of civil society organisations all cannot be brought under one approach. It will, however, introduce common principles which all can use in their work. …

In practice, while some groups such as Amnesty International and Transparency International have signed on to codes of conduct such as that overseen by Accountable Now (which is now also responsible for the International Non-Governmental Organizations' Accountability Charter of 2005), they generally rely on internal mechanisms should major challenges arise. One notable exception occurred following the tragic suicide of two Amnesty staff members in 2018. This raised broader questions of staff well-being and led Amnesty to commission independent legal reviews of the two cases. It also asked KonTerra, a group specializing in 'staff care and organizational resilience' to undertake a thorough review. This resulted in far-reaching recommendations that Amnesty promised to review and implement. Five senior staff members subsequently resigned.[633]

In another situation, in 2022, Amnesty accused Ukrainian forces of putting 'civilians in harm's way by establishing bases and operating weapons systems in populated residential areas, including in schools and hospitals'.[634] The organization found that '[s]uch tactics violate international humanitarian law and endanger civilians, as they turn civilian objects into military targets.' The same day, the Russian Ministry of Foreign Affairs retweeted the report and noted that this was 'exactly what #Russia has been saying all along.' Several senior Amnesty officials resigned, arguing that the organization should not be focusing on a country defending itself from brutal attacks.

Responding to the ensuing controversy, Amnesty appointed an external review panel of five IHL experts. They concluded that the evidence supported the reporting but that the legal assessment 'was made in overly emphatic and categorical terms'. More generally they found that the 'legal and factual analysis' was insufficiently 'detailed and reasoned', and that '[p]arts of the overarching narrative … were written in language that was ambiguous,

---

[633] The KonTerra Group, *Amnesty International, Staff Wellbeing Review* (January 2019).
[634] Amnesty International, 'Ukrainian fighting tactics endanger civilians' (4 August 2022).

imprecise, and in some respects legally questionable.' Amnesty did not release the review publicly, but in April 2023 it was leaked to, and published by, the *New York Times*.[635]

In 2020, a reporter revealed that HRW had accepted a donation in 2012, reported to be $470,000, for its work in the Middle East and North Africa but allegedly on condition that it would not support work on LGBT rights.[636] The Saudi donor was also the owner of a company that HRW had previously criticized for being complicit in labour rights abuses. Both the conditionality and the donation itself raised questions under HRW's internal guidelines. HRW's Board subsequently issued a press release describing the acceptance of the donation as 'a serious error' and 'a deeply regrettable decision', and announcing the return of the money.[637]

The broader area of humanitarian and development NGO scandals, especially involving alleged sexual exploitation and abuse (SEA) by aid workers, have led to calls for more institutionalized external forms of accountability.[638] One resulting report (Dorothea Hilhorst, Asmita Naik and Andrew Cunningham, *International Ombuds for Humanitarian and Development Aid: Scoping Study* (2018)) proposed the creation of a 'Joint Sectoral Aid Ombuds' which would be 'nested in an international body and governed by different parts of the sector, with the work carried out by a small secretariat supported by a flexible roster of technical experts and on-the-ground specialists.' If existing mechanisms had not resolved an issue, an appeal could be made to the Ombuds, which would accept complaints from 'all affected populations', would make recommendations, possibly publicly, but would have 'no direct authority to sanction'. The proposal garnered little support from key stakeholders and has been criticized by scholars.[639]

Consider the following very different approach proposed by Domenico Carolei and Nadia Bernaz, in 'Accountability for Human Rights: Applying Business and Human Rights Instruments to Non-Governmental Organizations', 14 *J. Hum. Rts. Prac.* (2022) 507, at 523, which relies upon the UN Guiding Principles on Business and Human Rights (see Ch. 13, above):

> … [A]lthough not primarily designed for them, business and human rights instruments may be applicable to NGOs. At a minimum business and human rights instruments are relevant to NGOs when they undertake business-like activities, but arguably other activities as well. Second, … business and human rights instruments [are suitable] for the NGO sector, [but] they should go hand in hand with self-regulation and other accountability mechanisms. … Applying existing instruments, which requires no further drafting, … provides an attractive, moderate avenue for NGO accountability. … The due diligence process described in the UNGPs mandates organizations to identify, prevent, mitigate and remedy their human rights impact in order to meet the (corporate) responsibility to respect human rights. Undertaking this process is challenging for all organizations, whether non-profit or for-profit. If NGOs, like corporations, undertook a transparent human rights due diligence process, communicated about it, and shared best practices, they would make a concrete contribution to the diffusion of the business and human rights standards, particularly the UNGPs. …

'Foreign Agent' Designations

In Chapter 8, we read a report by the UN Special Rapporteur on the situation of human rights defenders which described the extent to which these groups have come under sustained assault in many countries around the world. In *People Power Under Attack 2022* (2023), Civicus reported that 'the number of countries where harassment against activists was documented increased from 65 in 2018 to 106 in 2022.' It added that '[a]lthough harassment is perceived as a relatively subtle form of repression and, in some instances, is used intentionally to

---

[635] C. Savage, 'Unreleased Report Finds Faults in Amnesty International's Criticism of Ukraine', *New York Times* (27 April 2023).

[636] A. Emmons, 'Human Rights Watch Took Money from Saudi Businessman after Documenting His Coercive Labor Practices', *The Intercept* (2 March 2020).

[637] Human Rights Watch, 'Statement on Return of Donation' (27 February 2020).

[638] See M. Polizzi and A. Murdie, 'NGOs and human rights', and A. Crack, 'NGO accountability', in T. Davies (ed.), *Routledge Handbook of NGOs and International Relations* (2019).

[639] D. Carolei, 'An International Ombudsman to Make Non-Governmental Organizations More Accountable? Too Good to be True …', 35 *Leiden J. Int'l L.* (2022) 867.

leave little trace and ensure impunity, it is highly effective in deterring HRDs from their work and can strategically restrict the space for CSOs.

One particular form of harassment that has grown in popularity is to declare persons or groups who advocate for human rights to be 'foreign agents' if they meet certain conditions. Russia provides a prominent example in this regard.[640]

ECODEFENCE AND OTHERS V. RUSSIA
EUROPEAN COURT OF HUMAN RIGHTS, THIRD SECTION, APPLICATION NOS. 9988/13 AND 60 OTHERS (14 JUNE 2022)

[The case was brought by 73 Russian NGOs, active in civil society issues, human rights, environmental protection, cultural heritage, education, social security and migration.]

5. [The] 2012 ... Foreign Agents Act ... required Russian NGOs which were deemed to engage in "political activity" and to have been in receipt of "foreign funding" to seek registration as "foreign agents", under the threat of administrative and criminal sanctions. They were also required to label their publications as originating from a "foreign-agent" organisation, post information on their activities on the Internet and submit to more extensive accounting and reporting requirements.

...

RELEVANT LEGAL FRAMEWORK AND MATERIAL

1. THE FOREIGN AGENTS ACT

A. Enactment of the Foreign Agents Act
1. Definitions

15. ... [The] Foreign Agents Act ... defin[ed] such an agent as:

> "... a Russian non-commercial organisation receiving funds and other property from foreign States, their governmental bodies, international and foreign organisations, foreign nationals, stateless persons or persons authorised by [any of the above], or Russian legal entities receiving funds and other property from the above-mentioned sources ... ('foreign sources') and which engages in political activity, including political activity carried out in the interests of foreign providers of funds, in the territory of the Russian Federation."

...

E. Updated definition of "political activity"

28. On 2 June 2016 the definition of political activity was updated to read:

> "A non-commercial organisation, except for a political party, is considered to carry out a political activity in Russian territory if, regardless of its statutory goals and purposes, it engages in activities in the fields of statehood, the protection of the Russian constitutional system, federalism, the protection of the Russian Federation's sovereignty and territorial integrity, the rule of law, public security, national security and defence, external policy, the Russian Federation's social, economic and national development, the development of the political system, the structure of State and local authorities, [or] human rights, for the purpose of influencing State policy, the structure of State and local authorities, or their decisions and actions.

---

[640] G. Goncharenko and I. Khadaroo, 'Disciplining Human Rights Organisations Through an Accounting Regulation: A Case of the "Foreign Agents" Law in Russia', 72 *Critical Perspectives on Accounting* (2020) 102129.

[The legislation defined political activities as including, inter alia, 'organising and holding public events', 'attempting to obtain specific outcomes in elections or referenda', 'engaging in the activities of political parties', 'submitting public petitions to State and local authorities and officials', 'disseminating … views on State authorities' decisions and policy', 'shaping opinion on social and political issues', involving citizens in any of those activities, and financing such activities.]

LEGAL MATERIAL REFERRED TO BY THE PARTIES

A. Fundamental Principles on the Status of Non-governmental Organisations in Europe …, 13 November 2002, and Recommendation CM/Rec(2007)14 of the Council of Europe Committee of Ministers to member states on the legal status of non-governmental organisations in Europe (10 October 2007)

42. NGOs may solicit and receive funding – cash or donations in kind – from another country, multilateral agencies or an institutional or individual donor, subject to generally applicable foreign exchange and customs laws … . … [This] is a fundamental principle, a natural consequence of their non-profit-making nature. Such contributions, along with the proceeds of any economic activity, are an NGO's vital means of financing the pursuit of its objectives. However, this possibility for NGOs to collect funding is not absolute and may be subject to regulation, with a view to protecting the target audience … .
…

B. The United States Foreign Agents Registration Act

44. The Foreign Agents Registration Act … of 1938 … as amended in 1942 and 1966 (22 U.S.C. §§ 611-621), was originally adopted to require that agents representing the interests of foreign powers in a "political or quasi-political capacity" disclose their relationship with the foreign government, so that "the government and the American people" could evaluate "the statements and activities of such persons". In 1966 the Act was amended to target agents actually working with foreign powers who sought economic or political advantage by influencing governmental decision-making. The amendments shifted the focus of the law from propaganda to political lobbying and narrowed the meaning of "foreign agent". …
…
[Under the current text:]

> (o) The term 'political activities' means any activity that the person engaging in believes will, or that the person intends to, in any way influence any agency or official of the Government of the United States or any section of the public within the United States with reference to formulating, adopting, or changing the domestic or foreign policies of the United States or with reference to the political or public interests, policies, or relations of a government of a foreign country or a foreign political party ..."

C. Hungary's Transparency Act

45. Hungary's Act no. LXXVI of 2017 on the Transparency of Organisations Financed from Abroad ("the Transparency Act") required associations and foundations (except for sport and religious associations), political parties and ethnic minority associations to apply to be on a special register if the foreign funding part of their budget exceeded … (approximately EUR 22,100) annually, under the threat of fines or dissolution. Organisations financed from abroad were subject to additional labelling and reporting requirements.

46. The Act was repealed in April 2021 following a finding by the Court of Justice of the European Union (Grand Chamber) that it was contrary to EU law (see judgment of 18 June 2020, *Commission v Hungary (Transparency of associations)*, C-78/18, EU:C:2020:476). The Court held in particular that the objective of increasing the transparency of the financing of associations, although legitimate, cannot justify the introduction of legislation based on a presumption – made on principle and applied indiscriminately – that any financial support paid by a non-national natural or legal person, and any civil society organisation receiving such financial support, were intrinsically liable to jeopardise the State's political and economic interests and the ability of its

institutions to operate free from interference (§ 86). As concerns the grounds of public policy or public security, the Court found that the financial thresholds triggering the application of the obligations put in place by the Transparency Act were fixed at amounts which clearly did not appear to correspond with the scenario of a sufficiently serious threat to a fundamental interest of society which those obligations are supposed to prevent (§ 94).

47. The Court further considered that the obligations put in place by Transparency Act constituted limitations on the right to freedom of association ... . Those obligations ... create a generalised climate of mistrust vis-à-vis the associations ... [so as] to stigmatise them. ...

...

RELEVANT LEGAL MATERIAL

...

A. Intergovernmental organisations and advisory bodies

1. The Venice Commission

50. On 27 June 2014 the ... Venice Commission reached the following conclusions ... (CDL-AD(2014)025).

> "132. ... The use of the term 'foreign agent' is highly controversial. By bringing back the rhetoric used during the communist period, this term stigmatises the NCOs to which it is applied, tarnishing their reputation and seriously hampering their activities. The Venice Commission therefore recommends that the term be abandoned.
>
> 133. The Venice Commission further considers that the legitimate aim of ensuring transparency of NCOs receiving funding from abroad cannot justify measures which hamper the activities of NCOs operating in the field of human rights, democracy and the rule of law. It therefore recommends reconsidering the creation of a special regime with autonomous registration, special register and a host of additional legal obligations.

...

THE LAW

...

ALLEGED VIOLATION OF ARTICLES 10 AND 11 OF THE CONVENTION

[The applicants claimed violations of Article 10, on freedom of expression, and Article 11, on freedom of association. The Court, having found that these rights had been interfered with, then considered whether the interference could be justified under the terms of the Convention. It found (para. 104) that the authorities had 'applied an extensive and unforeseeable interpretation to the term "political activities"' and did not distinguish actions taken in a personal capacity from those of the organizations. In the Court's view, the 'authorities extended the concept of "political activity" to any form of public advocacy on an extremely wide set of issues' and the overall policy 'produced incoherent results and engendered uncertainty among NGOs'. As to whether the impact of the requirements was sufficiently foreseeable, it found (para. 112) that the legislation was interpreted in practice in an 'overbroad and unpredictable' way that did 'not meet the "quality of law" requirement and deprive[d] the applicants of the possibility to regulate their financial situation.' As to the legitimacy of the aim of the legislation, the Court devoted particular attention to the question of whether it was 'necessary in a democratic society' to restrict the relevant sources of funding.]

165. ... While States may have legitimate reasons to monitor financial operations in accordance with international law, with a view to preventing money laundering and terrorism and extremism financing, the ability of an association to solicit, receive and use funding in order to be able to promote and defend its cause constitutes an integral part of the right to freedom of association. The limits placed on a generalised restriction on the right to freedom of association and the availability of alternatives are also important factors in the assessment of its proportionality.

166. The Court concurs with the CJEU in that the objective of increasing the transparency of the financing of associations, although legitimate, cannot justify legislation which is based on a presumption, made on principle and applied indiscriminately, that any financial support by a non-national entity and any civil society organisation receiving such financial support are intrinsically liable to jeopardise the State's political and economic interests and the ability of its institutions to operate free from interference. A regulatory framework needs to correspond with the scenario of a sufficiently serious threat to a fundamental interest of society, which those obligations are supposed to prevent.

167. The Foreign Agents Act does not contain provisions prohibiting foreign funding altogether. However, it also does not establish a minimum amount or share of "foreign funding" in an organisation's budget, with the result that an organisation regularly funded from abroad, an organisation which has been awarded an international prize for its work, and an organisation receiving a computer or software licence from an international company would all indiscriminately be considered to be funded by "foreign sources". If an organisation receiving such funding is also deemed to have engaged in "political activities", it is liable to be registered as a "foreign agent". The Court has established above that in practice the domestic authorities gave an extremely wide and unforeseeable interpretation of the concepts of "foreign sources" and "political activities". Even the usual activities of civil society organisations which were explicitly excluded from the scope of "political activity" were construed in such a way that almost any actions were taken to constitute "political activity". This situation rendered it difficult for the applicants to foresee which specific actions on their part could lead to their registration as "foreign agents" … .

…

169. The Court considers that an enforced choice between accepting foreign funding and soliciting domestic State funding represents a false alternative. In order to ensure that NGOs are able to perform their role as the "watchdogs of society", they should be free to solicit and receive funding from a variety of sources. The diversity of these sources may enhance the independence of the recipients of such funding in a democratic society.

…

(v) Nature and severity of the penalties

…

185. Taking into account the essentially regulatory nature of the offences, the substantial amounts of the administrative fines imposed and their frequent accumulation, and the fact that the applicants were not-for-profit civil society organisations which suffered a reduction in their budgets due to restrictions on foreign funding, the Court holds that the fines provided for by the Foreign Agents Act cannot be regarded as being proportionate to the legitimate aim pursued. This finding would be applicable a fortiori to criminal sanctions … .

(vi) Conclusion on the necessity requirement

186. The Court has found above that the Government have not shown relevant and sufficient reasons for creating a special status of "foreign agents", imposing additional reporting and accounting requirements on organisations registered as "foreign agents", restricting their access to funding options, and punishing any breaches of the Foreign Agents Act in an unforeseeable and disproportionately severe manner. The cumulative effect of these restrictions – whether by design or effect – is a legal regime that places a significant "chilling effect" on the choice to seek or accept any amount of foreign funding, however insignificant, in a context where opportunities for domestic funding are rather limited, especially in respect of politically or socially sensitive topics or domestically unpopular causes. The measures accordingly cannot be considered "necessary in a democratic society".

(e) Overall conclusion

187. … [T]here has been a violation of Article 11 of the Convention interpreted in the light of Article 10.

…

* * *

Within weeks of the Court's judgment, Russia adopted a new law, in force from December 2022. According to Human Rights Watch, 'Russia: New Restrictions for "Foreign Agents"' (1 December 2022), the new law replaces the previous definitions:

> … with a consolidated, simplified, but endlessly broad definition to cover any person – Russian, foreign or stateless; any legal entity, domestic or international; or any group without official registration, if they are considered to have received foreign support and/or are considered to be "under foreign influence" and engaged in activities that Russian authorities would deem to be "political." …

> The law defines "foreign influence" as "support" from foreign sources that includes funding, technical assistance, or other undefined kinds of assistance and/or open-ended "impact" that constitutes coercion, persuasion, and/or "other means."

> …

> [It] also excludes "foreign agents" from key aspects of public life. These include bans on joining the civil service, participating in electoral commissions, acting in an advisory or expert capacity in official or public environmental impact assessments, in independent anti-corruption expertise of draft laws and by-laws, or electoral campaigns or even donating to such campaigns or to political parties.

> Foreign agents are also banned from teaching or engaging in other education activities for minors or producing informational materials for them. They cannot participate in organizing public assemblies or support them through donations and are barred from a number of other activities.

> …

As already noted, various other countries have followed a comparable approach. In June 2024 the Law on Transparency of Foreign Influence was adopted in Georgia despite massive demonstrations and a presidential veto. It requires organizations receiving more than 20% of their funding from overseas to register as 'agents of foreign influence', and imposes onerous disclosure requirements and fines for violations. India has also continued to ratchet up restrictions on civil society, as explained by Amnesty International and nine other groups in 'India Should Stop Using Abusive Foreign Funding Law' (19 January 2022):

> The Centre for Promotion of Social Concerns, a prominent human rights organisation better known by its program unit People's Watch, monitors human rights abuses, works with socially and economically marginalized victims of abuses, including by police, and conducts human rights education and training. In 2016, the Ministry of Home Affairs rejected the group's application for renewal under the Foreign Contribution Regulation Act. They said it was "on the basis of a field agency report," which civil society leaders widely believe refer to reports of intelligence agencies or law enforcement personnel.

> When the Centre for Promotion of Social Concerns challenged the government's decision in the Delhi High Court, the Home Affairs Ministry told the court that the group used foreign funding to share information with United Nations special rapporteurs and foreign embassies, "portraying India's human rights record in negative light…to the detriment of India's image." The government characterized this as "undesirable activities detrimental to national interest."

> …

> This crackdown is part of a wider repression of civil society in India, including through the use of draconian laws such as sedition and terrorism. Since 2016, the authorities have revoked, suspended, refused to renew the FCRA license of hundreds of civil society groups, or accused them of evading the law and frozen their bank accounts. …

...

> [Despite criticism from the UN High Commissioner for Human Rights, and UN experts],
> in 2020, the Indian parliament [added] intrusive governmental oversight, additional
> regulations and certification processes, and operational requirements, which have further
> adversely affected civil society groups' access to foreign funding and their ability to carry
> out human rights work. ...

The UN's NGO Committee

The only UN mechanism for promoting NGO accountability has long been deeply politicized, with Russia playing a leading role. Article 71 of the UN Charter provides that:

> The Economic and Social Council [ECOSOC] may make suitable arrangements for
> consultation with non-governmental organizations which are concerned with matters
> within its competence. Such arrangements may be made with international organizations
> and, where appropriate, with national organizations after consultation with the Member
> of the United Nations concerned.

The consultative status envisaged enables organizations to access UN premises, and to attend and often participate in the work of many UN bodies, including making written or oral statements, organizing 'side events', and meeting with government and other representatives. A UN website (www.csonet.org) states that '[t]o be eligible for consultative status, an NGO must have been in existence (officially recognized by a government) for at least two years, must have an established headquarters, a democratically-adopted constitution, authority to speak for its members, a representative structure, appropriate mechanisms of accountability and democratic and transparent decision-making processes. The basic resources of the organization must be derived mainly from contributions of the national affiliates or other components or from individual members.' To make an application, an organization must submit copies of its constitution, statutes etc.; its official registration; financial statements; and representative publications and statements. Over 6,000 organizations have consultative status.[641]

ECOSOC's Committee on Non-Governmental Organizations (NGO Committee) is made up of 19 UN member States and makes recommendations on NGO applications for ECOSOC accreditation – also called consultative status. It plays the key role in recommending, or withholding, the grant of status. Rana Siu Inboden, in 'China at the UN: Choking Civil Society', 32 *J. of Democ.* (2021) 124 explains why its approach has been problematic:

> The NGO Committee, which effectively acts as a gatekeeper to the UN for civil society
> organizations, comprises nineteen UN member states ... , ... [They] serve four-year
> terms with no term limits ... . The workload of the Committee ... makes it hard for
> smaller delegations with fewer resources to devote the time and energy to participate.
> Thus, the Committee is heavily dominated by large countries with resources, such as
> China and Russia, and strongly motivated ones, including Cuba and Pakistan, with
> repressive agendas. This has allowed authoritarian countries ... to dominate the
> Committee.
>
> ... States sitting on the Committee are allowed to raise questions, even mundane,
> arbitrary, or seemingly innocuous ones about income or activities, that automatically delay
> the application, usually until the next session six months later. ...

Inboden reports that, between 2016 and 2019, additional information was sought primarily by China (340 times), South Africa (337), India (283), Cuba (220), and Russia (172). Applications by 964 NGOs were deferred at least once as a result of questions.

---

[641] See generally B. Ramcharan et al. (eds.), *The Protection Roles of Human Rights NGOs: Essays in Honour of Adrien-Claude Zoller* (2023).

International Service for Human Rights, an organization devoted to facilitating the participation of civil society in UN activities, confirms that '[t]he Committee's membership overwhelmingly comprises States that do not support a vibrant civil society at the UN, … and the body itself is known for excessive politicisation, even gaining the notorious reference of the 'Anti-NGO Committee'. At one typical session, in September 2022, 319 applications were deferred and nine NGOs were rejected, including groups working on 'human rights, genocide prevention, caste-based discrimination and religious freedom.' All of those nine had been blocked for some years, but the International Dalit Solidarity Network 'has now been deferred for fifteen years and has received 105 written questions from the Committee, including several repeat questions to which it has provided full and timely responses.'[642]

QUESTIONS

1. What considerations might inhibit greater partnership and cooperation among human rights NGOs?

2. How can social movements, including 'affected persons' organizations', contribute to bringing about the profound transformations that von Bernstorff suggests are needed? Are human rights groups likely to be major players in such endeavours? Should they be?

3. Does the closing of civil society space worldwide mean that the role of the large INGOs based mainly in the North is even more important, or does it instead mean that new models are needed?

4. What lessons might human rights groups learn from disability activists?

5. How would you analyze the accountability of human rights INGOs on the basis of the mechanisms described by Grant and Keohane? Should Amnesty's practice of commissioning external reviews in controversial cases be more widely followed?

6. How would you distinguish Russia's approach from that in the U.S. Foreign Agents Registration Act? Consider also this analysis from Canada's Public Safety Department:[643]

The global threat landscape Canada faces has significantly evolved, with threats from a variety of both state and non-state actors becoming sophisticated and pervasive. Today, Canada's security and intelligence community is focused, among other threats, on foreign interference. Foreign interference is activity undertaken by foreign states, or those individuals and entities acting on behalf of a foreign state, to advance their own strategic objectives to the detriment of Canada's national interests. Such activity is deceptive, coercive, threatening and/or illegal. Foreign interference is distinct from normal activities undertaken by foreign states to exert influence, such as legitimate lobbying, advocacy efforts, and regular diplomatic activity.

[The Consultation Paper provides a scenario to illustrate the notion of 'malign foreign influence'.]

Scenario #2: An individual, employed by a foreign government, asks a prominent Canadian academic to write an op-ed opposing the Government of Canada's approach to a particular international issue, and urging Canadians to likewise disagree. The academic writes the op-ed and it is published in a widely circulated national newspaper. The academic is also asked to engage with student groups on campus to advocate a viewpoint that is favorable to the foreign government. The academic does not disclose their relationship with the individual employed by the foreign government. This is an example of malign foreign influence because the influence activities are undertaken covertly. The foreign interests being represented in the article, and in the engagement with student groups, is not transparent.

---

[642] International Service for Human Rights, 'ECOSOC: States must end unjustified barriers to 9 civil society groups in upcoming vote' (5 December 2022).
[643] Public Safety Canada, 'Enhancing Foreign Influence Transparency: Exploring Measures to Strengthen Canada's Approach, Public and Stakeholder Consultation Paper' (10 March 2023).

PART F: CURRENT TOPICS

Chapter 15. Climate Change, the Environment and the Right to Development

In 1972, the UN Conference on the Human Environment, in Stockholm, proclaimed that the environment is essential to human 'well-being and to the enjoyment of basic human rights – even the right to life itself' (UN Doc. A/CONF.48/14/Rev.1 (1973), 3). This realization prompted many states to accord constitutional recognition to the right to live in a healthy environment, starting with Portugal (1976) and Spain (1978). In 1994 a UN Sub-Commission Special Rapporteur, Fatma Zohra Ksentini, proposed 27 'draft principles on human rights and the environment', the second of which was that 'all persons have the right to a secure, healthy and ecologically sound environment.' (UN Doc. E/CN.4/Sub.2/1994/9). Governments took no action on her report.

But by 2022, the UN Special Rapporteur on human rights and the environment, David Boyd, reported that the right was recognized in the constitutions of 110 States and incorporated in national legislation in over 100 states (see UN Docs. A/77/284 (2022) and A/HRC/43/53 (2019)). It is also reflected in regional treaties ratified by 133 States, including the African Charter on Human and Peoples' Rights, the Aarhus Convention on Access to Information, Public Participation in Decision-making and Access to Justice in Environmental Matters (1998) and its Inter-American counterpart, the Escazú Agreement (2018), the San Salvador Protocol to the American Convention, and the Arab Charter on Human Rights.

The culmination of these efforts was the recognition of a 'human right to a clean, healthy and sustainable environment' by the UN Human Rights Council in 2021 (Res. 48/13) and the General Assembly in 2022 (Res. 76/300).

Parallel to these developments, the existential threat to the planet and humankind posed by climate change has been on the international agenda since the 1992 UN Framework Convention on Climate Change (FCCC), supplemented first by the Kyoto Protocol of 1997, and then by the Paris Agreement of 2015. By 2024, there were 198 parties to the UNFCCC. A vital component in promoting informed awareness has been the work of the Intergovernmental Panel on Climate Change (IPCC), set up by the UN Environment Program and the World Meteorological Organization in 1988 to provide the best available scientific evidence to governments. In 2024, it consisted of 195 experts.

The IPCC's 2023 Sixth Assessment Report confirmed that:

> A.1 Human activities, principally through emissions of greenhouse gases, have unequivocally caused global warming ... . [42 percent of cumulative net CO2 emissions between 1850 and 2019 occurred after 1990.]
>
> ...
>
> A.2.1 It is unequivocal that human influence has warmed the atmosphere, ocean and land. ... Evidence of observed changes in extremes such as heatwaves, heavy precipitation, droughts, and tropical cyclones, and, in particular, their attribution to human influence, has further strengthened since [the previous assessment in 2014]. Human influence has likely increased the chance of compound extreme events since the 1950s, including increases in the frequency of concurrent heatwaves and droughts ... .
>
> A.2.2 Approximately 3.3–3.6 billion people live in contexts that are highly vulnerable to climate change. Human and ecosystem vulnerability are interdependent. Regions and people with considerable development constraints have high vulnerability to climatic hazards. ... Between 2010 and 2020, human mortality from floods, droughts and storms was 15 times higher in highly vulnerable regions, compared to regions with very low vulnerability. ...
>
> A.2.3 Climate change has caused substantial damages, and increasingly irreversible losses, in terrestrial, freshwater, cryospheric, and coastal and open ocean ecosystems (high confidence). Hundreds of local losses of species have been driven by increases in the magnitude of heat extremes (high confidence) with mass mortality events recorded on

land and in the ocean (very high confidence). Impacts on some ecosystems are approaching irreversibility such as the impacts of hydrological changes resulting from the retreat of glaciers, or the changes in some mountain (medium confidence) and Arctic ecosystems driven by permafrost thaw (high confidence).

Jeff Goodell, in *The Heat Will Kill You First: Life and Death on a Scorched Planet* (2023), at 18, puts the case in less technical terms:

> The harshest truth about life on a superheated planet is this: as temperatures rise, a lot of living things will die, and that may include people you know and love. A study in *The Lancet* … estimated that 489,000 people worldwide died from extreme heat in 2019. That's far more than all other natural disasters combined, including hurricanes and wildfires. It is also more than the number of deaths from guns or illegal drugs. And those are only the deaths that are directly attributable to heat. There are also deaths caused by the heat-related amplification of ground-level ozone pollution (aka smog), or the smoke from wildfires in desiccated forests. The smoke can drift thousands of miles, lofting tiny particulates into the atmosphere. When you inhale them, they can trigger a variety of health problems, from asthma to heart attacks. The toll is enormous: globally, between 260,000 and 600,000 people die each year inhaling smoke from wildfires. …

Despite the overwhelming strength of the scientific evidence, over the past three decades, climate denialism, often funded and promoted by fossil fuel companies like ExxonMobil and other corporate interests, has flourished (see UN Doc. A/HRC/41/39, paras. 32-35). Misinformation campaigns, large-scale advertising efforts, political campaign contributions, intensive lobbying, and reinforcement from major media actors such as News Corporation and its Fox News outlet, have provided the material on the basis of which conservative politicians in many countries have opposed efforts to mitigate global warming. U.S. President Donald Trump called climate change a 'hoax'.

Each year there is a Conference of the Parties (COP) to the FCCC to negotiate specific targets and commitments. In opening COP27 on 7 November 2022, UN Secretary-General, António Guterres, sought to ring the alarm bells:

> We are in the fight of our lives. And we are losing. Greenhouse gas emissions keep growing. Global temperatures keep rising. And our planet is fast approaching tipping points that will make climate chaos irreversible. We are on a highway to climate hell with our foot still on the accelerator. … It is unacceptable, outrageous and self-defeating to put it on the back burner.

Except for an 'in principle' agreement to establish a 'loss and damage' fund to compensate poorer nations, the conference achieved little in concrete terms. At COP28 in 2023, the major achievement was acknowledging for the first time the need for 'transitioning away from fossil fuels', but governments stopped short of calling for a 'phaseout' of reliance on oil, coal and gas.

In retrospect, the human rights community has been slow to react to the threat posed by climate change, although the former UN High Commissioner for Human Rights, Mary Robinson, has long called for a human rights approach to climate change, and climate justice. In 2005 she argued that:

> [W]e can no longer think about climate change as an issue where the rich give charity to the poor to help them to cope with its adverse impacts. Rather, this has now become an issue of global injustice that will need a radically different framing to bring about global justice.[644]

The OHCHR began issuing regular climate change reports in 2009 (UN Doc. A/HRC/10/61; and for 2023, see A/HRC/53/45). The major international NGOs showed little interest until recently. In 2015, Amnesty's senior leadership team decided that 'climate change was not … a priority in Amnesty's strategic goals for 2016–

---

[644] M. Robinson, 'Climate Change and Justice', Barbara Ward Lecture, London (11 December 2006).

2019'.[645] And the Executive Director of Human Rights Watch from 1993 to 2022, Kenneth Roth, often suggested that human rights were of marginal relevance and added little to environmental and climate change concerns.[646] Some scholars also questioned the value of the linkage. Kathryn Sikkink noted that 'climate change is one of the most pressing issues of our age, but it is not an issue where the framing in terms of human rights is particularly helpful.'[647] Instead, in her view, the emphasis should be on the responsibilities of governments, corporations, and other actors.

The following report provides a snapshot of some of the human rights-related challenges:

PHILIP ALSTON, CLIMATE CHANGE AND POVERTY: REPORT OF THE SPECIAL RAPPORTEUR ON EXTREME POVERTY AND HUMAN RIGHTS
UN DOC. A/HRC/41/39 (2019)

…

II. The scale of the challenge

3. David Wallace-Wells began *The Uninhabitable Earth* by observing that global warming "is worse, much worse, than you think". Carbon is being added to the atmosphere 100 times faster than at any point in pre-industrial human history and more damage has been done in the three decades since the [IPCC was established] in 1988 than in the whole of human history up to that time.

4. The last five years have been the hottest in the modern record and global carbon dioxide emissions began rising again in 2017 after three years of levelling off. World energy consumption is projected to grow 28 per cent between 2015 and 2040. The consequences today are attested to by record temperatures, rapidly melting icecaps, unprecedented wildfires, frequent so-called "thousand year" floods and devastating, more frequent hurricanes. Millions face malnutrition due to devastating drought and many more will have to choose between starvation and migration. Rising ocean temperatures are killing marine ecosystems that support food systems for hundreds of millions of people and climate change is threatening food production and posing dire economic and social threats.

5. The most widespread scientific benchmark for measuring global warming is the rise in temperature relative to pre-industrial levels, already 1°C. The 2015 Paris Agreement aims to ensure no higher than a 2°C rise by 2100 and endeavours to limit it to 1.5°C, but even those increases would be catastrophic for many people.

6. A rise of only 1.5°C rather than 2°C could mean reducing the number of people vulnerable to climate-related risks by up to 457 million; 10 million fewer people exposed to the risk of sea level rise; reducing exposure to floods, droughts, and forest fires; limiting damage to ecosystems and reductions in food and livestock; cutting the number of people exposed to water scarcity by half; and up to 190 million fewer premature deaths over the century.

7. However, the scale of change required to limit warming to 1.5°C is historically unprecedented and could only be achieved through "societal transformation" and ambitious emissions reduction measures. Even 1.5°C of warming – an unrealistic, best-case scenario – will lead to extreme temperatures in many regions and leave disadvantaged populations with food insecurity, lost incomes and livelihoods, and worse health. As many as 500 million people will be exposed and vulnerable to water stress, 36 million people could see lower crop yields and up to 4.5 billion people could be exposed to heat waves. In all of these scenarios, the worst affected are the least well-off members of society.

III. The impact on human rights, poverty and inequality

A. Human rights

---

[645] Amnesty International 33rd International Council meeting, 'Circular 10: human rights aspects of climate change'.

[646] See, for example, K. Roth, 'Discussion: Accountability Beyond States', in C. Booth Walling and S. Waltz (eds.), *Human Rights: From Practice to Policy* (2010) 68; and, at http://bigthink.com/ideas/4064 (2007), he noted that 'rhetorical rights language doesn't add appreciable weight to the arguments against global warming'.

[647] K. Sikkink, 'Human Rights, Responsibilities, and Democracy', 52 *Vand J. Transnat'l L.* (2019) 1315.

8. Climate change threatens the full enjoyment of a wide range of rights (A/HRC/31/52, paras. 23–32). Rapid action and adaptation can mitigate much of this, but only if done in a way that protects people in poverty from the worst effects.

9. According to the World Bank, at 2°C of warming, 100–400 million more people could be at risk of hunger and 1–2 billion more people may no longer have adequate water. Climate change could result in global crop yield losses of 30 per cent by 2080, even with adaptation measures. Between 2030 and 2050, it is expected to cause approximately 250,000 additional deaths per year from malnutrition, malaria, diarrhoea and heat stress....

10. People in poverty face a very real threat of losing their homes [on displacement, see A/HRC/56/47 (2024)]. By 2050, climate change could displace 140 million people in sub-Saharan Africa, South Asia and Latin America alone. Flooding and landslides can weaken already degraded infrastructure and housing, especially for people living in unplanned or unserviced settlements. Since 2000, people in poor countries have died from disasters at rates seven times higher than in wealthy countries. In addition, the authorities have a history of prioritizing wealthier areas for protection, further endangering people in poverty.

B. Poverty

11. Climate change will ... have the most severe impact in poor countries and regions, and the places where poor people live and work. Developing countries will bear an estimated 75–80 per cent of the cost of climate change.

12. People in poverty tend to live in areas more susceptible to climate change and in housing that is less resistant; lose relatively more when affected; have fewer resources to mitigate the effects; and get less support from social safety nets or the financial system to prevent or recover from the impact. Their livelihoods and assets are more exposed and they are more vulnerable to natural disasters that bring disease, crop failure, spikes in food prices and death or disability.
...

C. Inequality

14. Perversely, the richest people, who have the greatest capacity to adapt and are responsible for and have benefited from the vast majority of greenhouse gas emissions, will be the best placed to cope with climate change, while the poorest, who have contributed the least to emissions and have the least capacity to react, will be the most harmed. The poorest half of the world's population – 3.5 billion people – is responsible for just 10 per cent of carbon emissions, while the richest 10 per cent are responsible for a full half. A person in the wealthiest 1 per cent uses 175 times more carbon than one in the bottom 10 per cent.

15. In addition to the economic benefits rich countries have already reaped from fossil fuels, one recent study found that climate change itself has already worsened global inequality and that the gap in per capita income between the richest and poorest countries is 25 percentage points larger than it would be without climate change.
...
50. Rather than helping the world adapt to climate change, privatizing basic services and social protection may be a form of maladaptation. When hurricane Sandy wreaked havoc in New York in 2012, stranding low-income and vulnerable New Yorkers without access to power and healthcare, the Goldman Sachs headquarters was protected by tens of thousands of its own sandbags and power from its generator. Private white-glove firefighters have been dispatched to save the mansions of high-end insurance customers from wildfires. An over-reliance on the private sector could lead to a climate apartheid scenario in which the wealthy pay to escape overheating, hunger, and conflict, while the rest of the world is left to suffer.

A. RECOGNIZING A RIGHT TO A CLEAN, HEALTHY AND SUSTAINABLE ENVIRONMENT

1. The United Nations

Between 2012 and 2021, the UN Human Rights Council adopted seven resolutions on human rights and the environment. In 2012, John Knox was appointed an independent expert on the issue, and became Special Rapporteur in 2015. He and his successor, David Boyd, played an important role in cajoling and facilitating more significant engagement on the part of the Council, which finally paid off with its 2021 resolution, followed by General Assembly Res. 76/300 (28 July 2022) entitled 'The human right to a clean, healthy and sustainable environment':[648]

> The General Assembly,
>
> …
>
> *Reaffirming* the [UDHR, the outcomes of the Vienna, Stockholm and Rio conferences, and the Declaration on the right to development] and relevant international human rights treaties, and noting other relevant regional human rights instruments,
>
> *Reaffirming also* that all human rights are universal, indivisible, interdependent and interrelated,
>
> …
>
> *Recalling* States' obligations and commitments under multilateral environmental instruments and agreements, including on climate change …,
>
> *Recalling also* Human Rights Council resolution 48/13 of 8 October 2021, entitled "The human right to a clean, healthy and sustainable environment",
>
> …
>
> *Recalling* the Guiding Principles on Business and Human Rights …,
>
> …
>
> *Noting also* that a vast majority of States have recognized some form of the right to a clean, healthy and sustainable environment through international agreements, their national constitutions, legislation, laws or policies,
>
> 1. *Recognizes* the right to a clean, healthy and sustainable environment as a human right;
>
> 2. *Notes* that the right to a clean, healthy and sustainable environment is related to other rights and existing international law;
>
> 3. *Affirms* that the promotion of the human right to a clean, healthy and sustainable environment requires the full implementation of the multilateral environmental agreements under the principles of international environmental law;
>
> 4. *Calls upon* States, international organizations, business enterprises and other relevant stakeholders to adopt policies, to enhance international cooperation, strengthen capacity-building and continue to share good practices in order to scale up efforts to ensure a clean, healthy and sustainable environment for all.

---

[648] See Symposium on UN Recognition of the Human Right to a Healthy Environment, 117 *Am. J. Int'l L. Unbound* (2023) 162.

The resolution, initially co-sponsored by Costa Rica, Maldives, Morocco, Slovenia and Switzerland, was adopted by a vote of 161-0-8 (States abstaining were: Belarus, Cambodia, China, Ethiopia, Iran, Kyrgyzstan, Russia, Syria). China explained its position by noting that there is no agreement as 'to the definition and scope of the right to the environment and its relationship with other human rights.' It also regretted that 'the principle of common but differentiated responsibilities is … not included in the text'. India noted that because the terms clean, healthy and sustainable were not defined, they 'remain open to subjective interpretation, thereby diluting the very objective of the recognition' of the right (UN Doc. A/76/PV.97).

In an 'Explanation of Position' (28 July 2022), the United States indicated its acceptance of the importance of such a right, but added:

> We note that [the resolution] is not legally binding or a statement of current international law. International law has yet to establish [such] a right … as a matter of customary international law, nor does treaty law provide for such a right. … [I]n voting "YES" on this resolution the United States does not recognize any change in the current state of conventional or customary international law. There is not yet a shared understanding of what the basis for the right would be and/or what its scope would entail. …

> [In relation to paragraph 3, we] do not agree with any suggestion that multilateral environmental agreements are implemented "under the principles of international environmental law" or have any bearing on any State's international legal obligations. There is no single set of principles under which multilateral environmental agreements operate, and such agreements are each implemented in accordance with their own provisions and are applicable only to those States that have joined them. We emphasize that development and enforcement of strong domestic environmental laws and policies is what leads to a healthy environment.

> U.S. support for the resolution … does not establish or support legally binding requirements on the United States or a private right of action under U.S. law. …

The United Kingdom took a more nuanced position. It stated that: '[t]here is no international consensus on the legal basis' of this right: '[r]ecognizing rights without due consideration and a common understanding at an international level of what those rights comprise creates ambiguity'; General Assembly resolutions are not legally binding; and this right 'derives from existing international economic and social rights law as a component of the right to an adequate standard of living or the right to the enjoyment of the highest attainable standard of physical and mental health' (UN Doc. A/76/PV.97, 11-12).

2. The Council of Europe

In 2021, the Parliamentary Assembly of the Council of Europe (Recommendation 2211) called upon the Member States to adopt an additional protocol to the European Convention on Human Rights (ECHR) concerning the right to a safe, clean, healthy and sustainable environment.[649] The recommendation proposed the following text:

Section I – Definition

Article 1

> For the purposes of this Additional Protocol, "the right to a safe, clean, healthy and sustainable environment" means the right of present and future generations to live in a non-degraded, viable and decent environment that is conducive to their health, development and well-being.

---

[649] See also Council of Europe Parliamentary Assembly, Doc. 15955 of 28 March 2024.

Section 2 – General principles

[Article 2]

Every generation has a duty to protect the environment and biodiversity and to prevent any irreparable and irreversible damage to life on Earth, so as to ensure the right of subsequent generations to live in a safe, clean, healthy and sustainable environment.

Every generation shall ensure that natural resources are used and managed in an environmentally sustainable manner, and that scientific and technological progress in all areas does not harm life on Earth.

Every generation is responsible for protection of the environment and has a duty to:

a. prevent environmental damage;

b. remedy environmental damage.

[Article 3]

a. No one can be discriminated against on account of his/her belonging to a particular generation.

b. Each High Contracting Party shall see to it that discrimination is prohibited and shall ensure equal and effective protection against discrimination to enable all individuals, groups and peoples to enjoy a safe, clean, healthy and sustainable environment.

c. Each High Contracting Party shall ensure that additional measures are taken to protect the rights of persons who are more vulnerable to or particularly threatened by environmental harm.

[Article 4]

Where a risk of harm to the environment and biodiversity has been established, measures for preventive action and rectification, as a priority at source, shall be put in to avoid the occurrence of environmental damage.

Where there are threats of severe damage to the environment or to human, animal or plant health, lack of scientific certainty shall not be used as a reason for postponing cost-effective measures to prevent the degradation of the environmental and biodiversity.

a. Any rolling back of legal protection of the environment or of access to environmental justice shall be prohibited.

b. National and international provisions on the environment may be subject only to continuous improvement, having regard to the current state of scientific and technological knowledge.

In case of doubt, all matters before courts, administrative agencies and other decision-makers must be resolved in a way most likely to favour the protection and conservation of nature, with preference to be given to alternatives that are least harmful to the environment.

Section 3 – Substantive right

[Article 5]

Everyone has the right to a safe, clean, healthy and sustainable environment.

[Article 6]

Everyone is entitled to access information relating to the environment held by public authorities, without having to prove an interest.

If a project, programme or policy has an impact on the environment and biodiversity, everyone shall be entitled to be consulted in advance in order to be heard by the decision-making bodies regarding the authorization and development of that project.

Everyone has the right of access to justice in matters relating to the environment.

Everyone whose rights set forth in this Protocol are violated shall have an effective remedy.

A 2022 Briefing Paper by the UK-based Environmental Rights Recognition Project suggested the following benefits of such a protocol: (1) symbolism; (2) putting environmental considerations at the heart of policy making; (3) requiring legislators to factor environmental impact into their work; (4) increasing civic participation; (5) filling the gap that results from only 13 of the 46 Member States having no existing constitutional or legislative right to a healthy environment; (6) creating a level playing field by setting a 'pan-European baseline'; (7) clarifying obligations and promoting legal certainty; and (8) improving overall environmental performance.

But rather than deciding to draft a new protocol, the Committee of Ministers of the Council of Europe recommended to its 46 member governments that they 'reflect on the nature, content and implications of the right to a clean, healthy and sustainable environment and, on that basis, actively consider recognising [it] at the national level' (Recommendation CM/Rec(2022)20 (27 September 2022)). It added that in implementing the recommendation, they should 'ensure the respect of general principles of international environmental law, such as the no harm principle, the principle of prevention, the principle of precaution and the polluter pays principle, and take into account the need for intergenerational equity.' In relation to the role of corporations, they recommended that:

> Member States should encourage or, where appropriate, require business enterprises to act in compliance with their human rights responsibilities related to the environment, including by applying a smart mix of measures– national and international, mandatory and voluntary.

3. The Regional Systems

As early as 2001, the African Commission on Human and Peoples' Rights decided that the right to a healthy environment imposed on States the obligation to take reasonable measures to prevent pollution and ecological degradation, to promote conservation, and to secure ecologically sustainable development and use of natural resources.[650]

Until 2024, the European Court of Human Rights had interpreted the 'right to respect for private and family life' in Article 8 of the ECHR cautiously in relation to environmental harm. But several major cases that had been referred to the Grand Chamber were decided on 9 April 2024. In the lead-up to these cases, commentators questioned whether the 'Court's often deferential, inconsistent and unreasoned remedial practice' was likely to provide an adequate basis for remedies in relation to climate change.[651] But while two of the cases were declared inadmissible, the third proved to be a major turning point in climate litigation.

In the first of the cases, *Carême v. France* (Grand Chamber, Application No. 7189/21 (9 April 2024) the Court held inadmissible a complaint by the former mayor of the municipality of Grande-Synthe that France had failed to take sufficient steps to prevent climate change thereby violating his right to life and the right to respect for

---

[650] African Commission on Human and Peoples' Rights, Social and Economic Rights Center (SERAC) and Center for Economic and Social Rights (CESR) v. Nigeria, Communication 155/96 (Decision of 27 October 2001) paras. 52 and 53.
[651] H. Keller, C. Heri, and R. Piskóty, 'Something Ventured, Nothing Gained?: Remedies Before the ECtHR and Their Potential for Climate Change Cases', 22 *Hum. Rts L. Rev.* (2022) 000; N. Kobylarz and E. Grant (eds.), *Human Rights and the Planet: The Future of Environmental Human Rights in the European Court of Human Rights* (2022).

his private and family life and home. The complaint emphasized the risk of climate-change-induced flooding in the period 2030-40. But after submitting the complaint, the applicant had ceased to be mayor and had moved to another country, and retained no significant links to Grande-Synthe. Accordingly, the court found that he could not claim to have victim status under the approach spelled out in the *KlimaSeniorinnen* case below.

In the second case, *Duarte Agostinho and Others v. Portugal and 32 Others* (application No. 39371/20) of 9 April 2024, six young Portuguese nationals complained of the present and future impacts of climate change. They cited increased temperatures and extreme heat and resulting wildfires and claimed that Portugal and 32 other respondent states bore responsibility. They relied on provisions of the ECHR, the 2015 Paris Agreement, the UN Convention on the Rights of the Child, and various reports and expert findings. Most notably, they argued that their generation was particularly affected by climate change and that, given their ages, the interference with their rights was more marked than in the case of previous generations. The court held that territorial jurisdiction was established in respect of Portugal, but not in relation to the other states.

> 208. In sum, extending the Contracting Parties' extraterritorial jurisdiction on the basis of the proposed criterion of "control over the applicants' Convention interests" in the field of climate change – be it within or outside the Convention's legal space – would lead to an untenable level of uncertainty for the States. Action taken in relation to some of the basic human activities … or any omission in managing the activity's potential harmful effects on climate change, could lead to the establishment of a State's extraterritorial jurisdiction over the interests of persons outside its territory and without any particular link with the State concerned. More importantly, accepting the applicants' arguments would entail an unlimited expansion of States' extraterritorial jurisdiction under the Convention and responsibilities under the Convention towards people practically anywhere in the world. …

And since the applicants had not pursued any legal avenue in Portugal that complaint was also inadmissible for non-exhaustion of domestic remedies. But, it was the 260-page judgment in the third case that proved to be path-breaking in many respects:

VEREIN KLIMASENIORINNEN SCHWEIZ AND OTHERS V. SWITZERLAND
EUROPEAN COURT OF HUMAN RIGHTS, GRAND CHAMBER, APPLICATION NO.
53600/20 (9 APRIL 2024)

[The first applicant is Verein KlimaSeniorinnen Schweiz, a non-profit association established under Swiss law to promote and implement effective climate protection on behalf of its members. The latter are women living in Switzerland, and the average age of the more than 2,000 members is 73. The second to fifth applicants are individual members of the same association.]
…

C. The Court's assessment
1. Preliminary points

410. At the outset, the Court notes that climate change is one of the most pressing issues of our times. …
…
412. Judicial intervention, including by this Court, cannot replace or provide any substitute for the action which must be taken by the legislative and executive branches of government. However, democracy cannot be reduced to the will of the majority of the electorate and elected representatives, in disregard of the requirements of the rule of law. The remit of domestic courts and the Court is therefore complementary to those democratic processes. The task of the judiciary is to ensure the necessary oversight of compliance with legal requirements. The legal basis for the Court's intervention is always limited to the Convention … . …
…
414. … The particular nature of the problems arising from climate change in terms of the Convention issues raised has not so far been addressed in the Court's case law. …

415. The Court's existing case law in environmental matters concerns situations involving specific sources from which environmental harm emanates. …

416. In the context of climate change, the key characteristics and circumstances are significantly different. First, there is no single or specific source of harm. GHG emissions arise from a multitude of sources. The harm derives from aggregate levels of such emissions. Secondly, CO_2 – the primary GHG – is not toxic per se at ordinary concentrations. The emissions produce harmful consequences as a result of a complex chain of effects. These emissions have no regard for national borders.

417. Thirdly, that chain of effects is both complex and more unpredictable in terms of time and place than in the case of other emissions of specific toxic pollutants. … In the longer term, some of the consequences risk destroying the basis for human livelihoods and survival in the worst affected areas. …

418. Fourthly, the sources of GHG emissions are not limited to specific activities that could be labelled as dangerous. …

419. Fifthly, combating climate change, and halting it, does not depend on the adoption of specific localised or single sector measures. Climate change is a polycentric issue. Decarbonisation of the economies and ways of life can only be achieved through a comprehensive and profound transformation in various sectors. …

420. … [I]ntergenerational burden sharing assumes particular importance … … … [F]uture generations are likely to bear an increasingly severe burden of the consequences of present failures and omissions to combat climate change … . By their commitment to the UNFCCC, the States Parties have undertaken the obligation to protect the climate system for the benefit of present and future generations of humankind … . …

421. Lastly, while the challenges of combating climate change are global, both the relative importance of various sources of emissions and the necessary policies and measures required for achieving adequate mitigation and adaptation may vary to some extent from one State to another depending on several factors such as the structure of the economy, geographical and demographic conditions and other societal circumstances. …

422. Because of these fundamental differences, it would be neither adequate nor appropriate to follow an approach consisting in directly transposing the existing environmental case law to the context of climate change. …
…

(b) Issues of proof

427. One of the key features of climate change cases is the necessity for the relevant court to engage with a body of complex scientific evidence. …

428. A mere allegation that the State failed to comply with certain domestic rules and environmental or technical standards is not in itself sufficient … … … [I]n some cases, the Court may need to have regard to the relevant international standards … .

429. The Court also relies on studies and reports by relevant international bodies … . As regards climate change, the Court points to the particular importance of the reports prepared by the IPCC … … … These reports provide scientific guidance on climate change regionally and globally, its impact and future risks, and options for adaptation and mitigation .
…

(c) Effects of climate change on the enjoyment of Convention rights
…
432. The findings of the IPCC … have not been challenged or called into doubt by the respondent or intervening States. …

433. Moreover, the IPCC findings correspond to the position taken, in principle, by the States in the context of their international commitments to tackle climate change. … Moreover, the respondent Government in the

present case, as well as the many third-party intervener Governments, have not contested that there is a climate emergency.

...

436. In sum, on the basis of the above findings, the Court will proceed with its assessment of the issues arising in the present case by taking it as a matter of fact that there are sufficiently reliable indications that anthropogenic climate change exists, that it poses a serious current and future threat to the enjoyment of human rights guaranteed under the Convention, that States are aware of it and capable of taking measures to effectively address it, that the relevant risks are projected to be lower if the rise in temperature is limited to 1.5oC above pre-industrial levels and if action is taken urgently, and that current global mitigation efforts are not sufficient to meet the latter target.

...

(e) The issue of the proportion of State responsibility

...

442. ... [T]he global climate regime established under the UNFCCC rests on the principle of common but differentiated responsibilities and respective capabilities of States. ... [A] respondent State should not evade its responsibility by pointing to the responsibility of other States, whether Contracting Parties to the Convention or not.

...

444. Lastly, as regards the "drop in the ocean" argument implicit in the Government's submissions – namely, the capacity of individual States to affect global climate change – it should be noted that in the context of a State's positive obligations under the Convention, the Court has consistently held that it need not be determined with certainty that matters would have turned out differently if the authorities had acted otherwise. The relevant test does not require it to be shown that "but for" the failing or omission of the authorities the harm would not have occurred. Rather, what is important, and sufficient to engage the responsibility of the State, is that reasonable measures which the domestic authorities failed to take could have had a real prospect of altering the outcome or mitigating the harm. ...

(f) Scope of the Court's assessment

...

451. ... [T]here is force in the argument put forward by the UN Special Rapporteurs that the question is no longer whether, but how, human rights courts should address the impacts of environmental harms on the enjoyment of human rights.

...

3. Admissibility

(a) Victim status/locus standi (representation)

...

464. The Court reiterates that the issue of victim status should be distinguished from the issue of locus standi. The latter relates to the questions of representation of the (direct) victims' complaints before the Court. ...

<u>(α) Victim status of individuals</u>

465. In order to fall into the category of direct victims, the applicant must be able to show that he or she was "directly affected" by the measure complained of. ...

466. However, this does not necessarily mean that the applicant needed to be personally targeted by the act or omission complained of. What is important is that the impugned conduct personally and directly affected him or her.

...

<u>(β) Locus standi (representation) by associations</u>

...

475. ... [A]lthough in the absence of a measure directly affecting them the Court does not normally grant victim status to associations, even if the interests of their members could be at stake, there may be "special

considerations" where an association represents individuals, even in the absence of a measure directly affecting the association in question.

...

487. In sum, the Court finds that in order to claim victim status [in the climate change context] ... an applicant needs to show that he or she was personally and directly affected by the impugned failures. This would require the Court to establish ... the following ...:

(a) the applicant must be subject to a high intensity of exposure to the adverse effects of climate change, that is, the level and severity of (the risk of) adverse consequences of governmental action or inaction affecting the applicant must be significant; and

(b) there must be a pressing need to ensure the applicant's individual protection, owing to the absence or inadequacy of any reasonable measures to reduce harm.

488. The threshold for fulfilling these criteria is especially high. ... [T]he Court will have due regard to circumstances such as the prevailing local conditions and individual specificities and vulnerabilities. The Court's assessment will also include, but will not necessarily be limited to, considerations relating to: the nature and scope of the applicant's Convention complaint, the actuality/remoteness and/or probability of the adverse effects of climate change in time, the specific impact on the applicant's life, health or well-being, the magnitude and duration of the harmful effects, the scope of the risk (localised or general), and the nature of the applicant's vulnerability.

(β) Standing of associations
...

502. ... In order to be recognised as having locus standi to lodge an application [in a climate change case] ... the association in question must be: (a) lawfully established in the jurisdiction concerned or have standing to act there; (b) able to demonstrate that it pursues a dedicated purpose in accordance with its statutory objectives in the defence of the human rights of its members or other affected individuals within the jurisdiction concerned, whether limited to or including collective action for the protection of those rights against the threats arising from climate change; and (c) able to demonstrate that it can be regarded as genuinely qualified and representative to act on behalf of members or other affected individuals within the jurisdiction who are subject to specific threats or adverse effects of climate change on their lives, health or well-being as protected under the Convention.

In this connection, the Court will have regard to such factors as the purpose for which the association was established, that it is of non-profit character, the nature and extent of its activities within the relevant jurisdiction, its membership and representativeness, its principles and transparency of governance and whether on the whole, in the particular circumstances of a case, the grant of such standing is in the interests of the proper administration of justice. ...

...

(iii) Application of these principles to the present case
...

(b) Applicability of the relevant Convention provisions
...

(α) Article 2
...

513. In sum, in order for Article 2 to apply to complaints of State action and/or inaction in the context of climate change, it needs to be determined that there is a "real and imminent" risk to life. However, such risk to life in the climate-change context must be understood in the light of the fact that there is a grave risk of inevitability and irreversibility of the adverse effects of climate change, the occurrences of which are most likely to increase in frequency and gravity. Thus, the "real and imminent" test may be understood as referring to a serious, genuine and sufficiently ascertainable threat to life, containing an element of material and temporal proximity of the threat to the harm complained of by the applicant. This would also imply that where the victim status of an individual applicant has been established ..., it would be possible to assume that a serious risk of a

significant decline in a person's life expectancy owing to climate change ought also to trigger the applicability of Article 2.

(β) Article 8

…

519. … Article 8 must be seen as encompassing a right for individuals to effective protection by the State authorities from serious adverse effects of climate change on their life, health, well-being and quality of life.

520. However, in this context, the question of "actual interference" or the existence of a relevant and sufficiently serious risk entailing the applicability of Article 8 essentially depends on the assessment of similar criteria to those set out in paragraphs 487 to 488 above concerning the victim status of individuals, or in paragraph 502 above concerning the standing of associations. These criteria are therefore determinative for establishing whether Article 8 rights are at stake and whether this provision applies. …

(ii) Application of these principles to the present case

(α) Article 8 of the Convention

[The court found, on the basis of the criteria it had established, that the applicant association had the necessary locus standi in this case.]

…

533. However, while it may be accepted that heatwaves affected the [quality of life of applicants 2-5], it is not apparent from the available materials that they were exposed to the adverse effects of climate change, or were at risk of being exposed at any relevant point in the future, with a degree of intensity giving rise to a pressing need to ensure their individual protection … . It cannot be said that the applicants suffered from any critical medical condition whose possible aggravation linked to heatwaves could not be alleviated by the adaptation measures available in Switzerland or by means of reasonable measures of personal adaptation given the extent of heatwaves affecting that country. It should also be reiterated that victim status in relation to future risk is only exceptionally admitted by the Court and the individual applicants have failed to demonstrate that such exceptional circumstances exist in their regard.

…

535. … [A]pplicants nos. 2 5 do not fulfil the victim-status criteria … [and so] their complaints should be declared inadmissible … .

…

[The Court decided to examine the association's complaint solely in terms of Article 8, but noted that the same principles were largely applicable to an Article 2 analysis relating to environmental issues.]

…

(ii) Content of the States' positive obligations

544. … [T]he Court already held long ago that the scope of protection under Article 8 of the Convention extends to adverse effects on human health, well-being and quality of life arising from various sources of environmental harm and risk of harm. Similarly, the Court derives from Article 8 a right for individuals to enjoy effective protection by the State authorities from serious adverse effects on their life, health, well-being and quality of life arising from the harmful effects and risks caused by climate change.

545. … In this context, the State's primary duty is to adopt, and to effectively apply in practice, regulations and measures capable of mitigating the existing and potentially irreversible, future effects of climate change. This obligation flows from the causal relationship between climate change and the enjoyment of Convention rights … and the fact that the object and purpose of the Convention, as an instrument for the protection of human rights, requires that its provisions must be interpreted and applied such as to guarantee rights that are practical and effective, not theoretical and illusory

…

548. … [E]ffective respect for the rights protected by Article 8 of the Convention requires that each Contracting State undertake measures for the substantial and progressive reduction of their respective GHG emission levels,

with a view to reaching net neutrality within, in principle, the next three decades. ... [F]or the measures to be effective, it is incumbent on the public authorities to act in good time, in an appropriate and consistent manner.

549. Moreover, in order for this to be genuinely feasible, and to avoid a disproportionate burden on future generations, immediate action needs to be taken and adequate intermediate reduction goals must be set for the period leading to net neutrality. Such measures should, in the first place, be incorporated into a binding regulatory framework at the national level, followed by adequate implementation. The relevant targets and timelines must form an integral part of the domestic regulatory framework, as a basis for general and sectoral mitigation measures. ...

550. When assessing whether a State has remained within its margin of appreciation, the Court will examine whether the competent domestic authorities, be it at the legislative, executive or judicial level, have had due regard to the need to:

> (a) adopt general measures specifying a target timeline for achieving carbon neutrality and the overall remaining carbon budget for the same time frame, or another equivalent method of quantification of future GHG emissions, in line with the overarching goal for national and/or global climate-change mitigation commitments;

> (b) set out intermediate GHG emissions reduction targets and pathways (by sector or other relevant methodologies) that are deemed capable, in principle, of meeting the overall national GHG reduction goals within the relevant time frames undertaken in national policies;

> (c) provide evidence showing whether they have duly complied, or are in the process of complying, with the relevant GHG reduction targets (see sub-paragraphs (a) (b) above);

> (d) keep the relevant GHG reduction targets updated with due diligence, and based on the best available evidence; and

> (e) act in good time and in an appropriate and consistent manner when devising and implementing the relevant legislation and measures.

...

(c) Application of the above principles to the present case
...
567. In these circumstances, given the pressing urgency of climate change and the current absence of a satisfactory regulatory framework, the Court has difficulty accepting that the mere legislative commitment to adopt the concrete measures "in good time", as envisaged in the Climate Act, satisfies the State's duty to provide, and effectively apply in practice, effective protection of individuals within its jurisdiction from the adverse effects of climate change on their life and health.
...
573. In conclusion, there were some critical lacunae in the Swiss authorities' process of putting in place the relevant domestic regulatory framework, including a failure by them to quantify, through a carbon budget or otherwise, national GHG emissions limitations. Furthermore, ... the State had previously failed to meet its past GHG emission reduction targets. By failing to act in good time and in an appropriate and consistent manner regarding the devising, development and implementation of the relevant legislative and administrative framework, the respondent State exceeded its margin of appreciation and failed to comply with its positive obligations in the present context.

574. The above findings suffice for the Court to find that there has been a violation of Article 8 of the Convention.
...

657. In the present case, having regard to the complexity and the nature of the issues involved, the Court is unable to be detailed or prescriptive as regards any measures to be implemented in order to effectively comply

with the present judgment. Given the differentiated margin of appreciation accorded to the State in this area (see paragraph 543 above), the Court considers that the respondent State, with the assistance of the Committee of Ministers, is better placed than the Court to assess the specific measures to be taken. It should thus be left to the Committee of Ministers to supervise, on the basis of the information provided by the respondent State, the adoption of measures aimed at ensuring that the domestic authorities comply with Convention requirements, as clarified in the present judgment.

…

PARTLY CONCURRING PARTLY DISSENTING OPINION OF JUDGE EICKE

INTRODUCTION

1. To my regret, I am unable to agree with the majority either in relation to the methodology they have adopted or on the conclusions which they have come to both in relation to the admissibility (and, in particular, the question of "victim" status) as well as on the merits. …

2. … The disagreement is of a more fundamental nature and, at least in part, goes to the very heart of the role of the Court within the Convention system and, more generally, the role of a court in the context of the unique and unprecedented challenges posed to humanity (including in but also across our societies) by anthropogenic climate change.

3. … [T]he majority in this case has gone well beyond what I consider to be, as a matter of international law, the permissible limits of evolutive interpretation.

4. In doing so, it has, in particular, unnecessarily expanded the concept of "victim" status/standing … and has created a new right (under Article 8 and, possibly, Article 2) [see paras. 519 and 544 above] … and/or imposed a new "primary duty" on Contracting Parties [see para. 545 above] … .

BACKGROUND

5. … [M]y disagreement with the majority does not relate in any way to the nature or magnitude of the risks and the challenges posed by anthropogenic climate change. I completely share their understanding of the urgent need to address this issue … .

…

CONCLUSION

68. … [T]he Court would already have achieved much if it had focussed on a violation of Article 6 of the Convention and, at a push, a procedural violation of Article 8 relating in particular to (again) the right of access to court and of access to information necessary to enable effective public participation in the process of devising the necessary policies and regulations and to ensure proper compliance with and enforcement of those policies and regulations as well as those already undertaken under domestic law. However, in my view, the majority clearly "tried to run before it could walk" and, thereby, went beyond what was legitimate for this Court … by means of "interpretation and application of the Convention", to do.

69. I also do worry that, in having taken the approach and come to the conclusion they have, the majority are, in effect, giving (false) hope that litigation and the courts can provide "the answer" without there being, in effect, any prospect of litigation (especially before this Court) accelerating the taking of the necessary measures towards the fight against anthropogenic climate change. In fact, there is a significant risk that the new right/obligation created by the majority (alone or in combination with the much enlarged standing rules for associations) will prove an unwelcome and unnecessary distraction for the national and international authorities, both executive and legislative, in that it detracts attention from the on-going legislative and negotiating efforts being undertaken as we speak to address the – generally accepted – need for urgent action. Not only will those authorities now have to assess and, if considered necessary, design and adopt (or have adopted) new "regulations and measures capable of mitigating the existing and potentially irreversible, future effects of climate change" but there is also a significant risk that they will now be tied up in litigation about whatever regulations and measures they have adopted (whether as a result or independently) or how those regulations and measures have

been applied in practice and, where an applicant was successful, lengthy and uncertain execution processes in relation to any judgments. ...

...

QUESTION

Did the Court succeed in striking a balance among the many competing considerations in the *Verein KlimaSeniorinnen Schweiz* case, or did it overstep as argued by the sole dissenting member of the 17-judge Grand Chamber?

The Inter-American system has gone furthest in recognizing environmental rights.[652] The foundation was laid in an Advisory Opinion (OC-23/17, of 15 November 2017) by the Court on 'The Environment and Human Rights'. Colombia had sought clarification of states' environment-related obligations under the Convention by reference to the right to life (Art. 4) and the right to humane treatment (Art. 5) in light of the Convention's general Article 1 obligation to respect rights. The context involved largescale infrastructure projects that threatened transboundary harm to the Caribbean marine environment, thereby jeopardizing the human rights of coastal and island residents. Colombia's dispute with Nicaragua before the International Court of Justice lay behind the request, but Nicaragua was not actually mentioned in the application.

The Court noted that Article 11 of the Protocol of San Salvador expressly recognizes 'the right to live in a healthy environment'. But since only 16 states have ratified that treaty, it was highly significant that the Court also determined that the right is covered by the American Convention by virtue of the general provision in Article 26 relating to economic, social and cultural rights. It then addressed the nature of the right and its broader application to nature:

59. The human right to a healthy environment has been understood as a right that has both individual and also collective connotations. In its collective dimension, the right to a healthy environment constitutes a universal value that is owed to both present and future generations. That said, the right to a healthy environment also has an individual dimension insofar as its violation may have a direct and an indirect impact on the individual owing to its connectivity to other rights, such as the rights to health, personal integrity, and life. Environmental degradation may cause irreparable harm to human beings; thus, a healthy environment is a fundamental right for the existence of humankind.

...

62. The Court considers it important to stress that, as an autonomous right, the right to a healthy environment, unlike other rights, protects the components of the environment, such as forests, rivers and seas, as legal interests in themselves, even in the absence of the certainty or evidence of a risk to individuals. This means that it protects nature and the environment ... because of their importance to the other living organisms with which we share the planet that also merit protection in their own right. In this regard, the Court notes a tendency, not only in court judgments, but also in Constitutions, to recognize legal personality and, consequently, rights to nature.

The Court also had to determine that it had jurisdiction in these matters, and held unanimously (para. 244) that:

...

2. The concept of jurisdiction under Article 1(1) ... encompasses any situation in which a State exercises authority or effective control over an individual, either within or outside its territory ... .

...

4. ... [I]ndividuals whose rights under the Convention have been violated owing to transboundary harm are subject to the jurisdiction of the State of origin of the harm, because that State exercises effective control over the activities carried out in its territory or under its jurisdiction ... .

---

[652] See D. Mejía-Lemos, 'The Protection of the Environment through International Human Rights Litigation: Taking Stock of Challenges and Opportunities in the Inter-American System', 22 *Hum. Rts L. Rev.* (2022) 000.

5. … States have the obligation to prevent significant environmental damage within or outside their territory and, to this end, must regulate, supervise and monitor activities within their jurisdiction that could produce significant environmental damage … .

6. States must act in accordance with the precautionary principle … .

7. … States have the obligation to cooperate, in good faith, to ensure protection against significant transboundary harm to the environment. …

8. … States have the obligation to ensure the right of access to information concerning potential environmental damage, the right to public participation of persons subject to their jurisdiction in policies and decision-making that could affect the environment, and also the right of access to justice in relation to the State environmental obligations … .

The Inter-American Court subsequently applied this reasoning in relation to the right to a healthy environment in the *Case of Indigenous Communities of the Lhaka Honhat Association (Our Land) v. Argentina*, IACtHR Series C400 (6 February 2020), although there was also a strong dissent.[653] On 9 January 2023, Chile and Colombia requested an Advisory Opinion from the Court on states' climate change-related obligations. An indication of the wide-ranging nature of the request is provided by the first of six sets of questions put to the Court:[654]

2. … [W]hat measures should States take to minimize the impact of the damages …? … [W]hat differentiated measures should be taken with respect to populations in situations of vulnerability or intersectional considerations?

2.A. What considerations should a State take to implement its obligation to (i) regulate; (ii) monitor and oversee; (iii) require and approve social and environmental impact studies; (iv) establish a contingency plan; and (v) mitigate activities within its jurisdiction that aggravate or may aggravate the climate emergency?

2.B. What principles should inspire mitigation, adaptation and response actions to the losses and damages generated by the climate emergency in the affected communities?

For its part, the Inter-American Commission, in Res. 3/2021 entitled 'Climate Emergency: Scope of Inter-American Human Rights Obligations' called on states to 'adopt and implement policies aimed at reducing greenhouse gas emissions that reflect the greatest possible ambition, foster resilience to climate change and ensure that public and private investments are consistent with low-carbon and climate-resilient development' (paragraph 1); to ensure 'that climate norms, policies and actions are constructed, updated and/or reexamined in a transparent and participatory manner with all social actors ensuring that climate actions do not adversely affect people's rights' (paragraph 3); and 'to move towards a gradual but determined decarbonization of the economies of the region' (paragraph 4).

B. LITIGATION

Although litigation is only one of the many measures that can be taken to stem global warming and compel key actors to change their policies, there has been a surge of litigation in this area in recent years. The first major international case was lodged in 2005, when Sheila Watt-Cloutier, an Inuk woman and Chair of the Inuit Circumpolar Conference, petitioned the Inter-American Commission on Human Rights 'seeking relief from violations resulting from global warming caused by acts and omissions of the United States'. She submitted it 'on behalf of herself, 62 other named individuals, and all Inuit of the arctic regions of the United States of America and Canada who have been affected by the impacts of climate change described in [the 175-page] petition.' Almost one year later, the Commission's Assistant Executive Secretary, Ariel Dulitzky, indicated that it would not be taken up because 'the information provided does not enable us to determine whether the alleged

---

[653] For a critique of the judgment, see L. Mardikian, 'The Right to a Healthy Environment Before the Inter-American Court of Human Rights', 72 *ICLQ* (2023) 945.
[654] Electronic translation from Spanish.

facts would tend to characterize a violation of rights protected by the American Declaration.' Despite its rejection, the petition gave an important impetus to advocacy in international organizations and litigation in national and international courts invoking human rights-based claims to challenge governments, corporations, and other actors for fueling global warming. Since that time, litigation has expanded rapidly, as explained below.

CÉSAR RODRÍGUEZ-GARAVITO, LITIGATING THE CLIMATE EMERGENCY IBID. (ED.), LITIGATING THE CLIMATE EMERGENCY: HOW HUMAN RIGHTS, COURTS, AND LEGAL MOBILIZATION CAN BOLSTER CLIMATE ACTION (2022) 9.

… [L]itigants have predominantly followed a two-pronged strategy. They have (1) asked courts to take the goals of the climate regime (as set out in the Paris Agreement, IPCC reports, and other authoritative sources) as benchmarks to assess governments' climate action and (2) invoked the norms, frames, and enforcement mechanisms of human rights to hold governments legally accountable for such goals. In the face of governments' reluctance or hostility toward taking the urgent measures that are needed to address the climate emergency, HRCC [Human Rights and Climate Change] litigation can be fruitfully viewed as a bottom-up mechanism … .

…

1.1 The Post-Paris Regime and Climate Rights Litigation

… [I]nternational climate governance went from an unsuccessful effort to establish an integrated, top-down regime (the 1997 Kyoto Protocol to the UN Framework Convention on Climate Change) to an ongoing attempt to consolidate a bottom-up, experimental regime (the Paris Agreement) that creates incentives for states to act on climate change through an iterative process of international negotiations, domestic civil society pressure, emissions reporting based on IPCC methodologies, and periodic stocktaking and peer review of progress on climate mitigation and adaptation.

The Paris Agreement does not establish a binding obligation for states to implement their nationally determined contributions (NDCs) to emission cuts, nor does it specify any procedure to ensure that states are transparent in their accounting of those contributions. Since the success of the Paris system hinges on transparency, the model will only work if states have material and reputational incentives … .

The large majority of HRCC suits and complaints (which focus on emissions cuts) can be understood as strategies to provide the post-Paris climate regime with procedural and substantive mechanisms for translating the aforementioned targets into legally binding commitments at the domestic level. … [S]tates are the target of all but 22 of the 148 cases filed between 2015 and 2021. …

…

1.2 Key Questions and Emerging Norms in Climate Rights Litigation

Despite the diversity of jurisdictions, litigants, and adjudicators involved in them, HRCC lawsuits tend to revolve around a common set of questions and norms. …

…

The ideal-typical HRCC case proceeds in three steps …:

…

1.2.1 The Baseline Norms: An International "Common Ground" on Climate Rights

… In determining the relevant legal standards … litigants and courts have often used the European Court of Human Rights' (ECtHR) doctrine of the legal "common ground" applicable to domestic human rights cases [which] includes other "elements of international law," states' interpretations of such elements, and state practice reflecting common values. As the ECtHR put it in *Demir and Baykara v. Turkey*, a judgment widely used by litigants and courts in European climate rights cases: "It is not necessary for the respondent State to have ratified the entire collection of instruments that are applicable in respect of the precise subject matter of the

case concerned. It will be sufficient for the Court that the relevant international instruments denote a continuous evolution in the norms and principles applied in international law or in the majority of member States of the Council of Europe and show, in a precise area, that there is common ground in modern society."
…
Importantly, the common ground [includes] the Paris Agreement and the IPCC's reports. …
…
If confirmed by future litigation, the emerging recognition of an international normative common ground would consolidate the convergence of human rights, environmental protection, and climate governance. …

1.2.2 A Justiciable Right to Climate Action

… The key question here is: Do governments have justiciable legal obligations, as a matter of international human rights and climate change law, to reduce GHG emissions?

… [In] almost invariably answer[ing] this question in the affirmative … two emerging norms have been upheld … .. First, a justiciable right to a climate system capable of sustaining human life … . [S]ome rulings have homed in on the rights of young people and future generations to a livable planet. …

The second norm relates to the legal competence of courts to enforce governments' duties regarding climate action in general and emissions reduction in particular. The question of justiciability raises issues concerning the harmonization of (1) the protection of rights with deference for governmental policy discretion and (2) the duty of courts to provide remedies for rights violations with the principle of the separation of powers. Although common in human rights and public interest litigation writ large, those issues are compounded by the scale, temporality, and uncertainty that characterize the problem of global warming.

Unsurprisingly, judges have given a range of different answers to this question, in line with contrasting jurisprudential traditions on the redressability of rights violations by courts in different jurisdictions. … Although granting governments latitude in setting climate goals and choosing policies to attain them, most courts have held that such decisions are not exempt from judicial review and that governmental discretion is not absolute. …

… While adjudicators have recognized that governments have a wide margin of appreciation in dealing with the complexities of climate policy, they have tended to conclude that climate change is a regulatory and scientific issue that is amenable to judicial scrutiny based on national and international standards on climate change and human rights, as opposed to a political issue in which governments have full policy discretion. …

1.2.3 The Legally Enforceable "Fair Share" of Climate Mitigation

The final step [is to inquire]: What levels of ambition and urgency with regard to national emission reductions are compatible with such rights and duties? This is the question, for instance, at the core of the average European lawsuit … . … In other suits, rather than the level of ambition itself, plaintiffs challenge the consistency of government-authorized projects or policies with the mitigation target that the government has formally adopted through national or international law. …

Both modalities of litigation raise complex questions about how to set and enforce a country's level of mitigation ambition. The controversy over different criteria of equity for determining countries' appropriate share of GHG emission cuts involves core issues of climate ethics and politics … . … [L]itigants and courts … have tended to take a cautious approach by closely tying their claims and remedies to the ambition levels prescribed by the Paris Agreement and the IPCC.

This approach has been translated into two embryonic norms. First, with regard to a country's share of emission reductions, HRCC cases have articulated a view that stresses individual states' duties. States' line of defense in mitigation lawsuits has hinged on the nature of the climate system as a public good. From this perspective, since emission reductions by one country will not make a dent in preventing global warming without other countries contributing their share, citizens have no justiciable rights-based claim to state climate action.

In contrast, litigants and courts have relied on a responsibility-based interpretation of the Paris Agreement. In this view, states have a duty to contribute their "minimum fair share" to emissions reduction, regardless of other countries' actions. As noted, the determination of a country's fair share has been guided by estimates stemming from the IPCC's recommendations and reports.

The most explicit articulation of the "minimum fair share" norm can be found in the Dutch Supreme Court's decision in [*State of the Netherlands v. Stichting Urgenda* (2019)]. According to the court, under the European Convention on Human Rights and the global climate regime, "the Netherlands is obliged to do 'its part' in order to prevent dangerous climate change, even if it is a global problem." The court bases its legal opinion on an interpretation of the UNFCCC whereby "all countries will have to do the necessary" to attain global emission targets, as well as on the generally accepted principle of international law according to which countries must avoid causing harm to others. "This approach justifies partial responsibility: each country is responsible for its part and can therefore be called to account in that respect" in judicial forums. Using the heuristics of a "carbon budget" – the amount of GHG that is left for humanity to burn before surpassing the 1.5 degrees Celsius to 2 degrees Celsius threshold of global warming – the court concludes that "no reduction is negligible," as all emissions contribute to using up the global budget, regardless of the size of the country or its emissions.
…
… [T]his norm remains underspecified. Given that the meaning of "minimum fair share" varies according to the criterion of fairness used, this remains an open question in HRCC litigation. …
…

1. National Courts

Litigation in national courts faces many obstacles. In *Friends of the Irish Environment v. Ireland*, (Appeal No: 205/19 (judgment of 31 July 2020)) a domestic advocacy group challenged the 2017 National Mitigation Plan, claiming that it violated the relevant legislation as well as the Irish Constitution and the government's European Convention on Human Rights obligations relating to the right to life and the right to private and family life. On appeal, the Supreme Court ultimately ruled that the Plan was insufficient to meet the legislative obligation and ordered that a new plan be drawn up. But the court also held that FIE lacked standing to bring its rights-based claims under the Constitution or the ECHR, and Chief Justice Clarke, writing for the court, was deeply skeptical of the claim that there was or should be a derived constitutional right to a healthy environment:

> 8.10 … What exactly does it mean? How does it fit into the constitutional order? Does it really advance rights beyond the right to life and the right to bodily integrity? If not, then what is the point of recognising such a right? If so, then in what way and within what parameters?

> 8.11 … [The right] either does not bring matters beyond the right to life or the right to bodily integrity, in which case there is no need for it. If it does go beyond those rights, then there is not a sufficient general definition (even one which might, in principle, be filled in by later cases) about the sort of parameters within which it is to operate.

In *Juliana v. United States*, 947 F.3d 1159 (9th Cir. 2020), 'twenty-one young citizens, an environmental organization, and a "representative of future generations"' sought 'an order requiring the government to develop a plan to "phase out fossil fuel emissions and draw down excess atmospheric CO2."' The court noted that '[s]ome plaintiffs claim psychological harm, others impairment to recreational interests, others exacerbated medical conditions, and others damage to property' and that the causes of action were based on due process, equal protection, and the public trust doctrine. Writing for the panel, Judge Hurwitz began by noting that 'the federal government has long promoted fossil fuel use despite knowing that it can cause catastrophic climate change, and that failure to change existing policy may hasten an environmental apocalypse.'

To establish redressability, the court held that the plaintiffs needed to identify relief that was both "(1) substantially likely to redress [its] injuries" and "(2) within the district court's power to award." In terms of the latter, the court said:

There is much to recommend the adoption of a comprehensive scheme to decrease fossil fuel emissions and combat climate change, both as a policy matter in general and a matter of national survival in particular. But it is beyond the power of an Article III court to order, design, supervise, or implement the plaintiffs' requested remedial plan. As the opinions of their experts make plain, any effective plan would necessarily require a host of complex policy decisions entrusted, for better or worse, to the wisdom and discretion of the executive and legislative branches. … These decisions range, for example, from determining how much to invest in public transit to how quickly to transition to renewable energy, and plainly require consideration of "competing social, political, and economic forces," which must be made by the People's "elected representatives, rather than by federal judges interpreting the basic charter of Government for the entire country."

In dissent, Judge Staton replied:

My colleagues throw up their hands, concluding that this case presents nothing fit for the Judiciary. … But a federal court need not manage all of the delicate foreign relations and regulatory minutiae implicated by climate change to offer real relief, and the mere fact that this suit cannot alone halt climate change does not mean that it presents no claim suitable for judicial resolution.

Plaintiffs bring suit to enforce the most basic structural principle embedded in our system of ordered liberty: that the Constitution does not condone the Nation's willful destruction. So viewed, plaintiffs' claims adhere to a judicially administrable standard. … [E]ven a partial and temporary reprieve would constitute meaningful redress [and would be] much like the desegregation orders and statewide prison injunctions the Supreme Court has sanctioned … ., …

Compare the *Juliana* case with this case from the Supreme Court of the State of Hawai'i:

HAWAI'I ELECTRIC LIGHT COMPANY, INC., APPEAL FROM THE PUBLIC UTILITIES COMMISSION
DOCKET NO. 2017-0122 (13 MARCH 2023)

OPINION OF THE COURT BY EDDINS, J.

Over ten years ago, energy company Hu Honua … sought regulatory approval to supply energy to Hawai'i Island using a biomass power plant. Last summer, approval for that energy deal was denied. Hu Honua appeals the denial, arguing that the Public Utilities Commission (PUC) misunderstood its mandate and held Hu Honua to an unfair standard.

We disagree. The PUC understood its public interest-minded mission. It faithfully followed our remand instructions to consider the reasonableness of the proposed project's costs in light of its greenhouse gas emissions and the project's impact on intervenor Life of the Land's members' right to a clean and healthful environment. …

…

II. … B.

Hu Honua's interpretation of HRS § 269-6(b) is equally strained. "HRS Chapter 269 is a law relating to environmental quality that defines the right to a clean and healthful environment under article XI, section 9 by providing that express consideration be given to reduction of greenhouse gas emissions in the decision-making of the Commission." …

HRS § 269-6(b) sets out specific factors the PUC must consider to determine whether the costs of a proposed energy project are reasonable. These include (1) price volatility; (2) export of funds for fuel imports; (3) fuel supply reliability risk; and (4) greenhouse gas emissions. The PUC then subjects these factors to "public interest-minded balancing."…

Hu Honua maintains that when applying these factors to a renewable energy project, the "only permissible" comparison for the PUC to draw is with fossil-fuel plants. … If Hu Honua is right, the only relevant question before the PUC was: is burning trees better than burning coal?

Neither the language of HRS § 269-6(b) nor the legislative intent behind it supports this blinkered approach. …

But the legislature intended the PUC to consider "potentially harmful climate change due to the release of harmful greenhouse gases." … We do not lightly assume that the legislature would sabotage its climate goals by limiting the PUC to artificial and unhelpful analyses.

…

C.

…

The people of Hawai'i have declared "a climate emergency." Hawai'i faces immediate threats to our cultural and economic survival: sea level rise, eroding the coast and flooding the land; ocean warming and acidification, bleaching coral reefs and devastating marine life; more frequent and more extreme droughts and storms. For the human race as a whole, the threat is no less existential.

…

The reality is that yesterday's good enough has become today's unacceptable. The PUC was under no obligation to evaluate an energy project conceived of in 2012 the same way in 2022. Indeed, doing so would have betrayed its constitutional duty.

Because the PUC's actions aligned with its statutory and constitutional obligations, we affirm PUC Order Nos. 38395 and 38443.

CONCURRING OPINION BY WILSON, J.

I. Introduction

… In its emergency declaration, the Hawai'i legislature called for "an immense increase of scale in endeavors to conserve our biosphere[.]" …

The [PUC] … has the daunting task of saving Hawai'i from the existential threat of climate change by reducing carbon emissions from Hawai'i's energy system. In so doing, the PUC protects the constitutional right of Hawai'i's people to a life-sustaining climate system. …

IV. Urgent State Action is Necessary

Although climate change is an international issue, the United States is responsible for approximately 20% of the world's historic and cumulative greenhouse gas emissions. … Unlike [some other] jurisdictions … the federal courts of the United States have thus far abdicated responsibility to apply the rule of law to claims that allege knowing contamination of the atmosphere with deleterious levels of greenhouse gas emissions.

One of the most prominent examples of a federal court abdicating its responsibility to leave future generations a habitable planet is the Ninth Circuit's [decision] … in Juliana v. United States. …

…

The conclusion that the due process right to "life, liberty [and] property" under Article I, section 5 subsumes the right to a life-sustaining climate is supported by the fact that a life-sustaining climate system underlies all other constitutional guarantees. Juliana, 217 F. Supp. 3d at 1248-49 (D. Or. 2016) ("Often, an unenumerated fundamental right draws on more than one [c]onstitutional source. The idea is that certain rights may be necessary to enable the exercise of other rights, whether enumerated or unenumerated") … . In other words, the right to a life-sustaining climate system is deserving of fundamental status as essential to our scheme of ordered liberty because it is "preservative of all rights." …

...

... A stable climate system is fundamental to Hawai'i's constitutional guarantees, including "the right to personal security[,]"and the right to bodily integrity.If the PUC continues to permit energy projects which emit high levels of greenhouse gases, it will be contributing to the destruction of resources essential to public health and Hawaiian culture, which in turn undermines all fundamental rights guaranteed by the Hawai'i Constitution.

...

The climate system is a "natural resource" held in trust by the State for the benefit of present and future generations. ...

...

... The public trust "does not remain fixed for all time, but must conform to changing needs and circumstances." ...

...

In applying the PUC's public trust duty to its decision whether to approve or deny the amended PPA, Article XI, section 1 of the Hawai'i Constitution requires the PUC to consider the Project's contribution to, or mitigation of, the climate emergency. An agency's constitutional public trust obligations are independent of its statutory mandates, but they operate in tandem. ...

...

VII. Conclusion

We are facing a sui generis climate emergency. The lives of our children and future generations are at stake. With the destruction of our life-sustaining biosphere underway, the State of Hawai'i is constitutionally mandated to urgently reduce its greenhouse gas emissions ... .

***

In addition to the *Urgenda* case, described by Rodriguez-Garavito, two other cases are especially important in illustrating different issues and approaches in this area, the first from Germany and the second from the Netherlands.

NEUBAUER ET AL. V. GERMANY
FEDERAL CONSTITUTIONAL COURT OF GERMANY (ORDER OF 24 MARCH 2021)

Facts of the case:

[Four different groups filed complaints. Two were groups of young people, one was an environmental NGO, and another was a group of individuals from Bangladesh and Nepal. The complaints were considered jointly by the court.]

...[T]he complainants primarily claim that the state, in enacting § 3(1) and § 4(1) third sentence [of the Federal Climate Change Act of 12 December 2019 (the KSG)] in conjunction with Annex 2, has failed to introduce a legal framework sufficient for swiftly reducing greenhouse gases, ... to limit the increase in the Earth's temperature to 1.5°C, or at least to well below 2°C. ... [T]he complainants − some of whom live in Bangladesh and Nepal − rely primarily on constitutional duties of protection arising from Art. 2(2) first sentence GG and Art. 14(1) GG, as well as on a fundamental right to a future in accordance with human dignity and a fundamental right to an ecological minimum standard of living, which they derive from Art. 2(1) GG in conjunction with Art. 20a GG and from Art. 2(1) GG in conjunction with Art. 1(1) first sentence GG. With regard to future burdens arising from the obligations to reduce emissions for periods after 2030 – which they describe as an "emergency stop" – the complainants rely on fundamental freedoms more generally.

[*Note* the following provisions of the Basic Law (the GG):

> Art. 1(1): Human dignity shall be inviolable. To respect and protect it shall be the duty of all state authority.

Art. 2(1) Every person shall have the right to free development of his personality insofar as he does not violate the rights of others or offend against the constitutional order or the moral law.

Art. 2(2): Every person shall have the right to life and physical integrity. Freedom of the person shall be inviolable. These rights may be interfered with only pursuant to a law.

Art. 20a: Mindful also of its responsibility towards future generations, the state shall protect the natural foundations of life and animals by legislation and, in accordance with law and justice, by executive and judicial action, all within the framework of the constitutional order.]

Key considerations of the Senate:

..

I. Where the complainants are natural persons, their constitutional complaints are admissible. The two environmental associations, however, have no standing to lodge a constitutional complaint. ...

II. It cannot be ascertained that duties of protection arising from Art. 2(2) first sentence GG and Art. 14(1) GG are violated due to the risks posed by climate change.

The protection of life and physical integrity under Art. 2(2) first sentence GG encompasses protection against impairments caused by environmental pollution, regardless of who or what circumstances are the source of the impairment. The state's duty of protection arising from Art. 2(2) first sentence GG also encompasses the duty to protect life and health against the risks posed by climate change, including climate-related extreme weather events such as heat waves, forest fires, hurricanes, heavy rainfall, floods, avalanches and landslides. It can furthermore give rise to an objective duty to protect future generations. Since climate change can moreover result in damage being caused to property such as agricultural land or real estate (e.g. due to rising sea levels or droughts), the fundamental right to property under Art. 14(1) GG also imposes a duty of protection on the state with regard to the property risks caused by climate change.

Given the leeway afforded to the legislator in fulfilling these duties of protection, no violation of these duties can be ascertained. ...

There is no need to decide at this point whether duties of protection arising from fundamental rights also place Germany under an obligation vis-à-vis the complainants living in Bangladesh and Nepal to take action against impairments – both potential and actual – caused by global climate change. Ultimately, no violation of a duty of protection arising from fundamental rights could be ascertained here either.

III. However, fundamental rights are violated by the fact that the emission amounts allowed until 2030 ... substantially narrow the remaining options for reducing emissions after 2030, thereby jeopardising practically every type of freedom protected by fundamental rights. As intertemporal guarantees of freedom, fundamental rights afford the complainants protection against comprehensive threats to freedom caused by the greenhouse gas reduction burdens that are mandatory under Art. 20a GG being unilaterally offloaded onto the future. The legislator should have taken precautionary steps to ensure a transition to climate neutrality that respects freedom – steps that have so far been lacking.

1. The challenged provisions have an advance interference-like effect on the freedom comprehensively protected by the Basic Law. ...

...

2. It cannot presently be ascertained that § 3(1) second sentence and § 4(1) third sentence KSG in conjunction with Annex 2 violate Art. 20a GG.

a) Art. 20a GG places the state under an obligation to take climate action and is aimed at achieving climate neutrality. Climate action does not take absolute precedence over other interests. In cases of conflict, it must be balanced with other constitutional interests and principles. However, given that climate change is currently deemed to be almost entirely irreversible, any behaviour that leads to an exceeding of the critical temperature threshold for achieving the constitutional climate goal would only be justifiable under strict conditions – such as for the purpose of protecting fundamental rights. Within the balancing process, the obligation to take climate action is accorded increasing weight as climate change intensifies.

The obligation to take climate action arising from Art. 20a GG is not invalidated by the fact that the climate and global warming are worldwide phenomena and that the problems of climate change cannot therefore be resolved by the mitigation efforts of any one state on its own. The climate action mandate enshrined in Art. 20a GG possesses a special international dimension. Art. 20a GG obliges the state to involve the supranational level in seeking to resolve the climate problem. The state cannot evade its responsibility by pointing to greenhouse gas emissions in other states. On the contrary, the particular reliance on the international community here gives rise to the constitutional necessity to actually implement one's own climate action measures at the national level and not to create incentives for other states to undermine the required cooperation.

The open normative content of Art. 20a GG and its explicitly formulated reference to legislation do not preclude constitutional review of compliance with the obligation to take climate action; Art. 20a GG is a justiciable legal provision designed to commit the political process to a favouring of ecological interests, partly with a view to future generations who will be particularly affected.

In declaring under § 1 third sentence KSG that the Act is based on the Paris target, the legislator is exercising its mandate and prerogative to specify the constitution by formulating the climate goal of Art. 20a GG in a permissible manner, setting out that the increase in the global average temperature should be limited to well below 2°C and preferably 1.5°C above pre-industrial levels. This must also form part of the basis for constitutional review.

b) ...
... [Based on IPCC figures], the German Advisory Council on the Environment has calculated a specific remaining national budget for Germany from 2020 onwards that would be compatible with the Paris target. Due to the uncertainties and assumptions involved in the approach, the calculated size of the budget cannot, at this point, serve as an exact numerical benchmark for constitutional review. Some decision-making leeway is retained by the legislator. However, the legislator is not entirely free when it comes to using this leeway. If there is scientific uncertainty regarding causal relationships of environmental relevance, Art. 20a GG imposes a special duty of care on the legislator. This entails an obligation to even take account of mere indications pointing to the possibility of serious or irreversible impairments, as long as these indications are sufficiently reliable.

At this point, no violation of the aforementioned duty of care can be ascertained. ...

3. § 3(1) second sentence and § 4(1) third sentence KSG in conjunction with Annex 2 do not, however, satisfy the requirement arising from the principle of proportionality that the reduction in CO_2 emissions to the point of climate neutrality that is constitutionally necessary under Art. 20a GG be distributed over time in a forward-looking manner that respects fundamental rights.

a) According to this requirement, one generation must not be allowed to consume large portions of the CO_2 budget while bearing a relatively minor share of the reduction effort if this would involve leaving subsequent generations with a drastic reduction burden and expose their lives to comprehensive losses of freedom. At some point in the future, even serious losses of freedom may be deemed proportionate and justified under constitutional law in order to prevent climate change. This is precisely what gives rise to the risk of having to accept considerable losses of freedom. However, since the current provisions on allowable emission amounts have now already established a path to future burdens on freedom, the impacts on future freedom must be proportionate from today's perspective. Furthermore, the objective duty of protection arising from Art. 20a GG encompasses the necessity to treat the natural foundations of life with such care and to leave them in such condition that future generations who wish to continue preserving these foundations are not forced to engage in radical abstinence.

The efforts required under constitutional law to reduce greenhouse gas emissions after 2030 will be considerable. Whether they will be so drastic as to entail unacceptable impairments of fundamental rights from today's perspective is impossible to determine. However, the risk of serious burdens is significant and can only be reconciled with the potentially affected fundamental rights if precautionary steps are taken to manage the reduction efforts anticipated after 2030 in ways that respect fundamental rights. This also requires initiating the transition to climate neutrality in good time. In specific terms, this means that transparent guidelines for the further structuring of greenhouse gas reduction must be formulated at an early stage, providing orientation for the required development and implementation processes and conveying a sufficient degree of developmental urgency and planning certainty. Here, it is imperative under constitutional law that further reduction measures are defined in good time for the post-2030 period, extending sufficiently far into the future. Moreover, further annual emission amounts and reduction measures must be defined in such detail that sufficiently specific orientation is provided.

...

c) ... The legislator must at the very least determine the size of the annual emission amounts to be set for periods after 2030 itself or impose more detailed requirements for their definition by the executive authority responsible for issuing the ordinance.

[*Note*: In response, the legislature adopted new reduction targets, effective from 31 August 2021, to achieve a 65 percent reduction in GHGs from 1990 levels by 2030.]

MILIEUDEFENSIE ET AL. V. ROYAL DUTCH SHELL PLC
THE HAGUE DISTRICT COURT (JUDGMENT OF 26 MAY 2021)

[The co-plaintiffs were Milieudefensie, Greenpeace Nederland, Fossielvrij NL, Waddenvereniging, Both Ends, Jongeren Milieu Actief, ActionAid, and 17,379 individual claimants. Royal Dutch Shell (RDS) is a public limited company, established under the laws of England and Wales, and with its head office in The Hague. It is the top holding company of the Shell group, which also includes 'intermediate parents, Operating Companies and Service Companies'. RDS is the direct or indirect shareholder of over 1,100 separate companies worldwide. It was claimed that Shell's contributions to global warming violated its duty of care under Dutch law and human rights.]

...

4.2. Admissibility

1. Admissibility of class actions

...

4.2.2.   The class actions of Milieudefensie et al. are public interest actions. Such actions seek to protect public interests, which cannot be individualized because they accrue to a much larger group of persons, which is undefined and unspecified. The common interest of preventing dangerous climate change by reducing CO_2 emissions can be protected in a class action. ... [The issue is whether] the interests in question [are] suitable for bundling so as to safeguard an efficient and effective legal protection of the stakeholders.

4.2.3.   The court is of the opinion that the interests of current and future generations of the world's population ... is not suitable for bundling. Although the entire world population is served by curbing dangerous climate change, there are huge differences in the time and manner in which the global population at various locations will be affected by global warming ... .

4.2.4.   However, the interests of current and future generations of Dutch residents and ... of the inhabitants of the Wadden Sea area, a part of which is located in the Netherlands ... are suitable for bundling, even though in the Netherlands and in the Wadden region there are differences in time, extent and intensity [of future climate change] caused by CO_2 emissions. ...

4.2.5.   The interest served with the class action must align with the objects stated in the articles of association and must also actually be promoted. Milieudefensie, Greenpeace Nederland, Fossielvrij NL, Waddenvereniging, Both Ends and Jongeren Milieu Actief meet this requirement. ActionAid does not meet this requirement, as it does not promote the interests of Dutch residents sufficiently for its collective claim to be allowable. ActionAid's object ... pertains to the world with a special focus on Africa. ...

...

2. *Locus standi of individual claimants*

4.2.7. … [B]esides a class action there is only room for the claims of individual claimants if they have a sufficiently concrete individual interest. That is not the case here … .

…

4.4. RDS' reduction obligation

4.4.1. RDS' reduction obligation ensues from the unwritten standard of care laid down in Book 6 Section 162 Dutch Civil Code, which means that acting in conflict with what is generally accepted according to unwritten law is unlawful. From this standard of care ensues that when determining the Shell group's corporate policy, RDS must observe the due care exercised in society. The interpretation of the unwritten standard of care calls for an assessment of all circumstances of the case in question.

4.4.2. In its interpretation of the unwritten standard of care, the court has included: (1.) the policy- setting position of RDS in the Shell group, (2.) the Shell group's CO_2 emissions, (3.) the consequences of the CO_2 emissions for the Netherlands and the Wadden region, (4.) the right to life and the right to respect for private and family life of Dutch residents and the inhabitants of the Wadden region, (5.) the UN Guiding Principles, (6.) RDS' check and influence of the CO_2 emissions of the Shell group and its business relations, (7.) what is needed to prevent dangerous climate change, (8.) possible reduction pathways, (9.) the twin challenge of curbing dangerous climate change and meeting the growing global population energy demand, (10.) the ETS system and other 'cap and trade' emission systems that apply elsewhere in the world, permits and current obligations of the Shell group, (11.) the effectiveness of the reduction obligation, (12.) the responsibility of states and society, (13.) the onerousness for RDS and the Shell group to meet the reduction obligation, and (14.) the proportionality of RDS' reduction obligation. …

…

(1.) the policy-setting position of RDS in the Shell group

4.4.4. From the facts as presented … it follows that RDS determines the general policy of the Shell group. The companies in the Shell group are responsible for the implementation and execution of the policy, and must comply with applicable legislation and their contractual obligations. The implementation responsibility of the Shell companies does not alter the fact that RDS determines the general policy of the Shell group.

(2.) the Shell group's CO2 emissions

4.4.5. … [T]he Shell group is a major player on the worldwide market of fossil fuels [and] … is responsible for significant CO_2 emissions all over the world. …

(3.) the consequences of CO2 emissions for the Netherlands and the Wadden region

4.4.6. The temperature rise in the Netherlands (approximately 1.7 degrees above the pre- industrial temperature) has so far developed about twice as fast as the global average … … …

…

(4.) the right to life and the right to respect for private and family life of Dutch residents and the inhabitants of the Wadden region

4.4.9. Milieudefensie et al invoke the right to life and the right to respect for private and family life [in the ECHR and the ICCPR]. … [They] cannot directly invoke these human rights with respect to RDS. Due to the fundamental interest of human rights and the value for society as a whole they embody, the human rights may play a role in the relationship between Milieudefensie et al. and RDS. Therefore, the court will factor in the human rights and the values they embody in its interpretation of the unwritten standard of care.

4.4.10. From the Urgenda ruling it can be deduced that Articles 2 and 8 ECHR offer protection against the consequences of dangerous climate change due to CO_2 emissions induced global warming. [The court then refers to the Human Rights Committee's General Comment No. 36 and the 2019 report of the Special Rapporteur on environment.] ...

RDS' argument that the human rights invoked by Milieudefensie et al. offer no protection against dangerous climate change therefore does not hold. The serious and irreversible consequences of dangerous climate change ... pose a threat to the human rights of Dutch residents and the inhabitants of the Wadden region.

(5.) the UN Guiding Principles (UNGP)

4.4.11. In its interpretation of the unwritten standard of care, the court follows the UN Guiding Principles (UNGP). The UNGP constitute an authoritative and internationally endorsed 'soft law' instrument ... . Due to the universally endorsed content of the UNGP, it is irrelevant whether or not RDS has committed itself to the UNGP, although RDS states on its website to support the UNGP.
[The court then undertakes a lengthy analysis of the UNGP.]
...

4.4.37. In answering the question what can be expected of RDS, the court considers that an important characteristic of the imminent environmental damage in the Netherlands and the Wadden region at issue here is that every emission of CO_2 and other greenhouse gases, anywhere in the world and caused in whatever manner, contributes to this damage and its increase. ... [The fact] that RDS is not the only party responsible for tackling dangerous climate change in the Netherlands and the Wadden region does not absolve RDS of its individual partial responsibility to contribute to the fight against dangerous climate change according to its ability. ... [M]uch may be expected of RDS in this regard, considering it is the policy- setting head of the Shell group, a major player on the fossil fuel market and responsible for significant CO_2 emissions, which incidentally exceed the emissions of many states ... ...
...

(11.) the effectiveness of the reduction obligation

4.4.49. RDS argues that the reduction obligation will have no effect, or even be counterproductive, because the place of the Shell group will be taken by competitors. Even if this were true, it will not benefit RDS. Due to the compelling interests which are served with the reduction obligation, this argument cannot justify assuming beforehand there is no need for RDS to not meet this obligation. ...

4.4.50. The question also is whether this argument of RDS is actually valid. What this argument assumes is perfect substitution, whereby the place of the Shell group will be taken over one-on-one by other parties. However, it remains to be seen whether this circumstance will transpire. ...

(12.) the responsibility of states and society

4.4.51. ... According to RDS, private parties cannot take any steps until states determine the frameworks. RDS also argues that government policy is needed to bring about the required change of the energy market. RDS also claims that the energy transition must be achieved by society as a whole, not by just one private party. ...

4.4.52. ... [The undisputed] responsibility of other parties and the uncertainty whether states and society as a whole will manage to achieve the goals of the Paris Agreement, do not absolve RDS of its individual responsibility ... . Due to the compelling interests which are served with the reduction obligation, RDS must do its part with respect to the emissions over it has control and influence. It is an individual responsibility that falls on RDS, of which much may be expected. ...

(13.) the onerousness of the reduction obligation on RDS

4.4.53. RDS argues that imposing a reduction obligation on it will lead to unfair competition and a disruption of the 'level playing field' on the oil and gas market. RDS has failed to specify this argument. ... The court assumes that the reduction obligation will have far-reaching consequences for RDS and the Shell group. ... However, the interest served with the reduction obligation outweighs the Shell group's commercial interests ...

. Due to the serious threats and risks to the human rights of Dutch residents and the inhabitants of the Wadden region, private companies such as RDS may also be required to take drastic measures and make financial sacrifices to limit CO2 emissions to prevent dangerous climate change. For these reasons, RDS' argument, namely that accepting the reduction obligation, as advocated by Milieudefensie et al., is highly unusual and has no precedent, does not benefit RDS.

…

Conclusion on RDS' reduction obligation

4.4.55. The court concludes that RDS is obliged to reduce the CO2 emissions of the Shell group's activities by net 45% at end 2030, relative to 2019, through the Shell group's corporate policy. This reduction obligation relates to the Shell group's entire energy portfolio and to the aggregate volume of all emissions … . It is up to RDS to design the reduction obligation, taking account of its current obligations. The reduction obligation is an obligation of result for the activities of the Shell group. …

4.5. Policy …
…
4.5.3. … There is no room for weighing interests. Therefore, the court disregards RDS' argument about the desirability/undesirability of claims such as this one, and whether or not this invites everyone in global society to lodge claims against each other. RDS' argument that it is not appropriate to impose a court order on one private party fails on the basis of the considerations on RDS' legal obligation … .

…
[*Note*: On 20 July 2022, Shell appealed the decision.]

M K RANJITSINH & ORS. V. UNION OF INDIA & ORS.
SUPREME COURT OF INDIA ORIGINAL CIVIL JURISDICTION, WRIT PETITION (CIVIL) NO. 838 OF 2019
JUDGMENT OF MARCH 21, 2024

DR DHANANJAYA Y, CHANDRACHUD, CJI

[The case involved an application for measures to protect the Great Indian Bustard and the Lesser Florican, both of which are threatened with extinction. The Indian Government and others objected to the sweeping nature of the orders given by the Court on 19 April 2021, and appealed for modifications.]

…
C. The mission to combat climate change

I. India's commitment under international conventions

[The Court reviewed India's engagement in the Kyoto Protocol, the UNFCC, and the Paris Agreement.]

II. The right to a healthy environment and the right to be free from the adverse effects of climate change

19. … [T]here is no single or umbrella legislation in India which relates to climate change and the attendant concerns. However, this does not mean that the people of India do not have a right against the adverse effects of climate change.

20. Article 48A of the Constitution provides that the State shall endeavour to protect and improve the environment and to safeguard the forests and wild life of the country. Clause (g) of Article 51A stipulates that it shall be the duty of every citizen of India to protect and improve the natural environment … . Although these are not justiciable provisions of the Constitution, they are indications that the Constitution recognises the importance of the natural world. The importance of the environment … becomes a right in other parts of the Constitution. Article 21 recognises the right to life and personal liberty while Article 14 indicates that all persons

shall have equality before law and the equal protection of laws. These articles are important sources of the right to a clean environment and the right against the adverse effects of climate change.

21.   In *M.C. Mehta v. Kamal Nath*, this Court held that Articles 48A and 51A(g) must be interpreted in light of Article 21 ... .

22.   In *Virender Gaur v. State of Haryana*, this Court recognised the right to a clean environment in the following terms:

> "7. ... The State, in particular has duty in that behalf and to shed its extravagant
> unbridled sovereign power and to forge in its policy to maintain ecological balance and
> hygienic environment. ... [T]here is a constitutional imperative on the State Government
> and the municipalities, not only to ensure and safeguard proper environment but also an
> imperative duty to take adequate measures to promote, protect and improve both the
> man-made and the natural environment."

23.   In *Karnataka Industrial Areas Development Board v. C. Kenchappa,* this Court took note of the adverse effects of rising sea levels and rising global temperatures. In *Bombay Dyeing & Mfg. Co. Ltd. (3) v. Bombay Environmental Action Group*, this Court recognised that climate change posed a "major threat" to the environment.

24.   Despite a plethora of decisions on the right to a clean environment ..., it is yet to be articulated that the people have a right against the adverse effects of climate change. ... As the havoc caused by climate change increases year by year, it becomes necessary to articulate this as a distinct right. It is recognised by Articles 14 and 21.

25.   Without a clean environment which is stable and unimpacted by the vagaries of climate change, the right to life is not fully realised. The right to health (which is a part of the right to life under Article 21) is impacted due to ... [many factors]. The inability of underserved communities to adapt to climate change or cope with its effects violates the right to life as well as the right to equality. ...

...

27.   The right to equality under Article 14 and the right to life under Article 21 must be appreciated in the context of the decisions of this Court, the actions and commitments of the state on the national and international level, and scientific consensus on climate change and its adverse effects. ...

28.   [The Court quoted extensively from a 2019 joint statement by five UN treaty bodies noting that] "...State parties have obligations, including extra-territorial obligations, to respect, protect and fulfil all human rights of all peoples. Failure to take measures to prevent foreseeable human rights harm caused by climate change, or to regulate activities contributing to such harm, could constitute a violation of States' human rights obligations."

[The Court invoked the preamble of the Paris Agreement linking climate change and human rights, referred to analyses by the UN Special Rapporteur on Human Rights and the Environment, and noted the Inter-American Court's 2017 advisory opinion in 2017 on the right to a healthy environment.]

35.   ... [T]he right to a healthy environment encapsulates the principle that every individual has the entitlement to live in an environment that is clean, safe, and conducive to their well-being. By recognizing the right to a healthy environment and the right to be free from the adverse effects of climate change, states are compelled to prioritize environmental protection and sustainable development, thereby addressing the root causes of climate change and safeguarding the well- being of present and future generations. It is imperative for states like India, to uphold their obligations under international law, including their responsibilities to mitigate greenhouse gas emissions, adapt to climate impacts, and protect the fundamental rights of all individuals to live in a healthy and sustainable environment.

...

IV. Climate change litigation in other jurisdictions

44.   Climate change litigation serves as a pivotal tool in advancing rights-based energy transitions and promoting energy justice, intertwined with human rights principles. ...

45.   Internationally, courts have been confronted with the challenging task of adjudicating cases where significant issues related to climate change are at stake....

[The Court then recounts the details of several cases, including *State of the Netherlands v. Urgenda Foundation, Sacchi, et al. v. Argentina* (UN Committee on the Rights of the Child), *Ioane Teitiota v. New Zealand* (UN Human Rights Committee).]

50.   These cases, all instituted and decided in the past decade, indicate the type of concerns which will travel to the courts in the next few years.

...

58.   India's international obligations and commitments in the present case (detailed in the preceding segments of this judgment) have not been enacted in domestic law. Regardless, the Court must be alive to these obligations while adjudicating writ petitions which seek reliefs that may hinder these obligations from being fulfilled or otherwise interfere with India's international commitments as well as the right to be free from the adverse effects of climate change.

...

61.   Moreover, the decision on whether to convert the overhead power transmission lines into underground lines is a matter of environmental policy. While adjudicating writ petitions which seek reliefs which are of the nature sought in the present case, this Court must conduct judicial review while relying on domain experts. Those who are equipped and trained to assess the various facets of a problem which is litigated before the Court must be consulted before a decision is taken. If this is not done, the Court may be in danger of passing directions without a full understanding of the issue in question. Consequently, in the absence of evidence which forms a certain basis for the directions sought, this Court must be circumspect in issuing sweeping directions. ... [I]t will be appropriate if an expert committee is appointed. The committee may balance the need for the preservation of the GIB which is non-negotiable, on one hand, with the need for sustainable development, especially in the context of meeting the international commitments of the country towards promoting renewable sources of energy, on the other hand. By leveraging scientific expertise and engaging stakeholders in meaningful consultations, this approach ensures that conservation efforts are grounded in evidence and inclusive of diverse perspectives.

...

70.   We request the Committee to complete its task and submit a report to this Court through the Union Government on or before 31 July 2024.

...

2. International and Regional human Rights Bodies

The Human Rights Committee, the Committee on the Rights of the Child, and the Inter-American Commission and Court have all made important contributions to the climate change debate. Before reading those, consider the caution urged by Benoit Mayer, in 'Climate Change Mitigation as an Obligation Under Human Rights Treaties?', 115 *Am. J. Int'l L.* (2021) 409:

> [H]ow far a human rights treaty requires a state to comply with its general mitigation obligations ... depends on the personal scope of the treaty and the importance of the right at issue, as well as the potential benefits of climate change mitigation for the enjoyment of the right, and its unintended consequences for the enjoyment of rights, within the state's territory or under its jurisdiction.
>
> ... [H]uman rights treaties may have a rather limited role to play with regard to climate change mitigation. In fact, the interpretation of human rights treaties as the source of mitigation obligations faces some of the major hurdles that have hindered international cooperation on climate change mitigation in the last three decades. For one thing, human rights treaties view nature mostly in instrumental terms, and largely ignore the interests of future generations. Overall, international human rights law encourages each state to

protect the rights of individuals within its territory rather than to cooperate on the global common good. This inherent tension between national interests and international cooperation will not be solved through an incremental extension of international human rights law, be it through the recognition of new rights (e.g., to a healthy environment or a sustainable climate), the identification of fictitious rights-holders (e.g., "future generations" or "Mother Earth"), or the extension of the extraterritorial application of human rights treaties—not, that is, without betraying the text, and the object and purpose, of human rights treaties, and using them as a Trojan horse at the service of extraneous objectives.

IOANE TEITIOTA V. NEW ZEALAND
U.N. HUMAN RIGHTS COMMITTEE, FINAL VIEWS, UN DOC. CCPR/C/127/D/2728/2016 (24 OCTOBER 2019)

…

1.1 The author of the communication is Ioane Teitiota, a national of Kiribati born in the 1970s. His application for refugee status in New Zealand was rejected. He claims that the State party violated his right to life under the Covenant by removing him to Kiribati in September 2015. …

…

Factual background

2.1 The author claims that the effects of climate change and sea level rise forced him to migrate from the island of Tarawa in Kiribati to New Zealand. The situation in Tarawa has become increasingly unstable and precarious due to sea level rise caused by global warming. Fresh water has become scarce because of saltwater contamination and overcrowding on Tarawa. Attempts to combat sea level rise have largely been ineffective. Inhabitable land on Tarawa has eroded, resulting in a housing crisis and land disputes that have caused numerous fatalities. Kiribati has thus become an untenable and violent environment for the author and his family.

2.2 The author has sought asylum in New Zealand, but the Immigration and Protection Tribunal issued a negative decision concerning his claim for asylum. … The Court of Appeal and the Supreme Court each denied the author's subsequent appeals concerning the same matter.

…

Issues and proceedings before the Committee …
Consideration of the merits

…

9.2 The Committee notes the author's claim that by removing him to Kiribati, the State party subjected him to a risk to his life in violation of article 6 of the Covenant, and that the State party's authorities did not properly assess the risk inherent in his removal.

[The Committee recalls relevant provisions of its General Comment No. 31 (2004) and No. 36 (2018).]

9.5 … [E]nvironmental degradation can compromise effective enjoyment of the right to life, and … severe environmental degradation can adversely affect an individual's well-being and lead to a violation of the right to life.

9.6 In the present case, … the Immigration and Protection Tribunal found … that there was no evidence that: (a) the author had been in any land disputes in the past, or faced a real chance of being physically harmed in such a dispute in the future; (b) the author would be unable to find land to provide accommodation for himself and his family; (c) the author would be unable to grow food or access potable water; (d) the author would face life-threatening environmental conditions; (e) the author's situation was materially different from that of every other resident of Kiribati; or (f) the Government of Kiribati had failed to take programmatic steps to provide for the basic necessities of life, in order to meet its positive obligation to fulfil the author's right to life. …

9.7 In assessing whether the State party's authorities provided the author with an adequate and individualized assessment of the risk of a threat to his right to life, the Committee first notes the author's claim that the increasing scarcity of habitable land on Tarawa has led to violent land disputes that have resulted in fatalities. In that connection, the Committee considers that a general situation of violence is only of sufficient intensity to create a real risk of irreparable harm under articles 6 or 7 of the Covenant in the most extreme cases, where there is a real risk of harm simply by virtue of an individual being exposed to such violence on return, or where the individual in question is in a particularly vulnerable situation. In assessing the author's circumstances, the Committee notes the absence of a situation of general conflict in Kiribati. … While the Committee does not dispute the evidence proffered by the author, it considers that the author has not demonstrated clear arbitrariness or error in the domestic authorities' assessment as to whether he faced a real, personal and reasonably foreseeable risk of a threat to his right to life as a result of violent acts resulting from overcrowding or private land disputes in Kiribati.

9.8 The Committee also notes the author's claims before the domestic authorities that he would be seriously harmed by the lack of access to potable water on Tarawa … [but concludes] that the author has not provided sufficient information indicating that the supply of fresh water is inaccessible, insufficient or unsafe so as to produce a reasonably foreseeable threat of a health risk that would impair his right to enjoy a life with dignity or cause his unnatural or premature death.

9.9 The Committee further notes the author's claim before the domestic authorities that his right to life had been violated because he had been deprived of his means of subsistence, as his crops had been destroyed due to salt deposits on the ground. … The information made available to the Committee does not indicate that when the author's removal occurred, there was a real and reasonably foreseeable risk that he would be exposed to a situation of indigence, deprivation of food and extreme precarity that could threaten his right to life, including his right to a life with dignity. …

…

9.12 In the present case, the Committee accepts the author's claim that sea level rise is likely to render Kiribati uninhabitable. However, it notes that the time frame of 10 to 15 years, as suggested by the author, could allow for intervening acts by Kiribati, with the assistance of the international community, to take affirmative measures to protect and, where necessary, relocate its population. …

…

9.14 Without prejudice to the continuing responsibility of the State party to take into account in future deportation cases the situation at the time in Kiribati and new and updated data on the effects of climate change and rising sea levels thereupon, the Committee is not in a position to hold that the author's rights under article 6 of the Covenant were violated upon his deportation to Kiribati in 2015.

…

CHIARA SACCHI ET AL. V. TURKEY
COMMITTEE ON THE RIGHTS OF THE CHILD, DECISION UNDER THE OPTIONAL PROTOCOL TO THE CONVENTION ON THE RIGHTS OF THE CHILD ON COMMUNICATION NO. 108/2019, UN DOC. CRC/C/88/D/108/2019 (22 SEPTEMBER 2021)

[Complaints were also brought by the same authors against Argentina, Brazil, France, and Germany, resulting in separate but virtually identical analyses by the Committee.][655]

1.1 The authors of the communication are Chiara Sacchi, a national of Argentina [and nationals from Brazil, France, Germany, India, the Marshall Islands, Nigeria, Palau, South Africa, Sweden, Tunisia, and the USA. All were then under the age of 18.] They claim that, by failing to prevent and mitigate the consequences of climate change, the State party has violated their rights under articles 6, 24 and 30, read in conjunction with article 3, of the Convention. The Optional Protocol entered into force for [Turkey] on 26 March 2018.

…

---

[655] See also Committee on the Rights of the Child, General Comment No. 26 (2023) on children's rights and the environment, with a special focus on climate change.

Facts as submitted by the authors

2. The authors claim that, by causing and perpetuating climate change, the State party has failed to take the necessary preventive and precautionary measures to respect, protect and fulfil the authors' rights to life, health and culture. They claim that the climate crisis is not an abstract future threat. The 1.1°C rise in global average temperature is currently causing devastating heat waves, forest fires, extreme weather patterns, floods and sea level rise, and fostering the spread of infectious diseases, infringing on the human rights of millions of people globally. Given that children are among the most vulnerable, physiologically and mentally, to these life-threatening impacts, they will bear a far heavier burden and for far longer than adults.

Complaint

...

3.7 The authors request that the Committee find: (a) that climate change is a children's rights crisis; (b) that the State party, along with other States, has caused and is perpetuating the climate crisis by knowingly acting in disregard of the available scientific evidence regarding the measures needed to prevent and mitigate climate change; and (c) that, by perpetuating life-threatening climate change, the State party is violating the authors' rights to life, health and the prioritization of the best interests of the child, as well as the cultural rights of the authors from indigenous communities.

3.8 The authors further request that the Committee recommend: (a) that the State party review and, where necessary, amend its laws and policies to ensure that mitigation and adaptation efforts are accelerated to the maximum extent of available resources and on the basis of the best available scientific evidence to protect the authors' rights and make the best interests of the child a primary consideration, particularly in allocating the costs and burdens of climate change mitigation and adaption; (b) that the State party initiate cooperative international action – and increase its efforts with respect to existing cooperative initiatives – to establish binding and enforceable measures to mitigate the climate crisis, prevent further harm to the authors and other children, and secure their inalienable rights; and (c) that, pursuant to article 12 of the Convention, the State party ensure the child's right to be heard and to express his or her views freely, in all international, national and subnational efforts to mitigate or adapt to the climate crisis and in all efforts taken in response to the authors' communication.

...

Issues and proceedings before the Committee
Consideration of admissibility

...

Jurisdiction

9.2 The Committee notes the State party's submission that the complaint is inadmissible for lack of jurisdiction as none of the authors reside in the State party and as they have no legal or factual relationship with it. The Committee also notes that authors' argument that they are within the State party's jurisdiction as victims of the foreseeable consequences of the State party's domestic and cross-border contributions to climate change and the carbon pollution knowingly emitted, permitted or promoted by the State party from within its territory. The Committee further notes the authors' claims that the State party's acts and omissions perpetuating the climate crisis have already exposed them throughout their childhood to the foreseeable, life-threatening risks of climate change caused by humans.

9.3 Under article 2 (1) of the Convention, States parties have the obligation to respect and ensure the rights of "each child within their jurisdiction". Under article 5 (1) of the Optional Protocol, the Committee may receive and consider communications submitted by or on behalf of an individual or group of individuals, within the jurisdiction of a State party, claiming to be victims of a violation by that State party of any of the rights set forth in the Convention. The Committee observes that, while neither the Convention nor the Optional Protocol make any reference to the term "territory" in its application of jurisdiction, extraterritorial jurisdiction should be interpreted restrictively.

9.4 The Committee notes the relevant jurisprudence of the Human Rights Committee and the European Court of Human Rights referring to extraterritorial jurisdiction. Nevertheless, that jurisprudence was developed and

applied to factual situations that are very different to the facts and circumstance of this case. The authors' communication raises novel jurisdictional issues of transboundary harm related to climate change.
…

9.7 [T]he Committee finds that the appropriate test for jurisdiction in the present case is that adopted by the Inter-American Court of Human Rights in its Advisory Opinion on the environment and human rights. This implies that, when transboundary harm occurs, children are under the jurisdiction of the State on whose territory the emissions originated for the purposes of article 5 (1) of the Optional Protocol if there is a causal link between the acts or omissions of the State in question and the negative impact on the rights of children located outside its territory, when the State of origin exercises effective control over the sources of the emissions in question. The Committee considers that, while the required elements to establish the responsibility of the State are a matter of merits, the alleged harm suffered by the victims needs to have been reasonably foreseeable to the State party at the time of its acts or omissions even for the purpose of establishing jurisdiction.

9.8 The Committee notes the authors' claims that, while climate change and the subsequent environmental damage and impact on human rights it causes are global collective issues that require a global response, States parties still carry individual responsibility for their own acts or omissions in relation to climate change and their contribution to it. The Committee also notes the authors' argument that the State party has effective control over the source of carbon emissions within its territory, which have a transboundary effect.

9.9 The Committee considers that it is generally accepted and corroborated by scientific evidence that the carbon emissions originating in the State party contribute to the worsening of climate change, and that climate change has an adverse effect on the enjoyment of rights by individuals both within and beyond the territory of the State party. The Committee considers that, through its ability to regulate activities that are the source of these emissions and to enforce such regulations, the State party has effective control over the emissions.

9.10 In accordance with the principle of common but differentiated responsibilities, as reflected in the Paris Agreement, the Committee finds that the collective nature of the causation of climate change does not absolve the State party of its individual responsibility that may derive from the harm that the emissions originating within its territory may cause to children, whatever their location.

9.11 Regarding the issue of foreseeability, the Committee notes the authors' uncontested argument that the State party has known about the harmful effects of its contributions to climate change for decades … . [Thus] the potential harm of the State party's acts or omissions regarding the carbon emissions originating in its territory was reasonably foreseeable to the State party.

9.12 … [T]he Committee must now determine whether there is a sufficient causal link between the harm alleged by the authors and the State party's actions or omissions for the purposes of establishing jurisdiction. …

Victim status

9.13 … The Committee considers that, as children, the authors are particularly affected by the effects of climate change, both in terms of the manner in which they experience its effects and the potential of climate change to have an impact on them throughout their lifetimes, particularly if immediate action is not taken. Due to the particular impact on children, and the recognition by States parties to the Convention that children are entitled to special safeguards, including appropriate legal protection, States have heightened obligations to protect children from foreseeable harm.

9.14   Taking the above-mentioned factors into account, the Committee concludes that the authors have sufficiently justified, for the purposes of establishing jurisdiction, that the impairment of their Convention rights as a result of the State party's acts or omissions regarding the carbon emissions originating within its territory was reasonably foreseeable. It also concludes that the authors have established prima facie that they have personally experienced real and significant harm in order to justify their victim status. …

Exhaustion of domestic remedies

9.15 ... [T]he Committee notes the State party's argument that domestic remedies are available to the authors ... [and] that non-nationals, including children, have standing in said procedures and that legal aid is available. The Committee further notes the authors' argument that it is most likely that the domestic courts would dismiss their claims for lack of standing.

...

9.17 In the present case, the Committee notes that the authors have not attempted to initiate any domestic proceedings in the State party ... ... In the absence of further reasoning from the authors as to why they did not attempt to pursue these remedies, other than generally expressing doubts about the prospects of success of any remedy, the Committee considers that the authors have failed to exhaust all domestic remedies that were reasonably effective and available to them to challenge the alleged violation of their rights under the Convention.

...

9.19 The Committee notes the authors' argument that pursuing remedies in the State party would be unreasonably prolonged and notes that the authors refer to one case in the State party which took 14 years to decide. Nevertheless, the Committee considers that the authors have failed to establish the connection of that case with the remedies that would be available within the State party to address their specific claims or to otherwise indicate how the deciding periods would be unreasonably prolonged or unlikely to bring relief ... . The Committee concludes that ... the authors have failed to exhaust domestic remedies.

9.20 Consequently, the Committee finds the communication inadmissible for failure to exhaust domestic remedies under article 7 (e) of the Optional Protocol.

...

DANIEL BILLY ET AL. V. AUSTRALIA
HUMAN RIGHTS COMMITTEE, VIEWS UNDER THE OPTIONAL PROTOCOL, COMMUNICATION NO. 3624/2019 (21 JULY 2022)

1.1   The eight authors of the communication are Daniel Billy, Ted Billy, Nazareth Fauid, Stanley Marama, Yessie Mosby, Keith Pabai, Kabay Tamu and Nazareth Warria, born in 1983, 1957, 1965, 1967, 1982, 1964, 1991 and 1973, respectively. They are nationals of Australia and residents of the Torres Strait region. They act in their own names and on behalf of five children ... .

...

The facts as submitted by the authors

2.1 The authors belong to the indigenous minority group of the Torres Strait Islands and live on ... four islands ... . The indigenous people of the Torres Strait Islands, especially the authors who reside in low-lying islands, are among the most vulnerable populations to the impact of climate change.

...

2.3 Sea level rise already caused flooding and erosion on the authors' islands, and higher temperature and ocean acidification produced coral bleaching, reef death, and the decline of seagrass beds and other nutritionally and culturally important marine species. ...

2.4 With respect to the impact of climate change on the islands, the village on Boigu ... is flooded each year. Erosion has caused the shoreline to advance and has detached a small area from the island. On Masig, a cyclone in March 2019 caused severe flooding and erosion and destroyed buildings. The cyclone resulted in the loss of three metres of shoreline. Approximately one metre of land is lost every year. In addition, a tidal surge in recent years has destroyed family graves, scattering human remains. On Warraber, high tides and strong winds cause seawater to flood the village centre every two to three years. On Poruma, erosion has washed away much of the island's sand over the past few decades.

2.5 Sea level rise has caused saltwater to intrude into soil of the islands, such that areas previously used for traditional gardening can no longer be cultivated. ... Patterns of seasons and winds play a key role in ensuring the authors' livelihoods and subsistence but are no longer predictable. Precipitation, temperature and monsoon seasons have changed, making it harder for the authors to pass on their traditional ecological knowledge. Seagrass beds and dependent species have disappeared. While crayfish is a fundamental source of food and income for the authors, they no longer find crayfish in areas where coral bleaching has occurred.

...

2.7 The State party has failed to implement an adaptation programme ... [d]espite numerous requests for assistance and funding made to the state and federal authorities ... .

2.8 The State party has also failed to mitigate the impact of climate change. ... The State party ranked 43rd out of 45 developed countries in reducing its greenhouse gas emissions [between 1990 and 2016 and] has actively pursued policies that have increased emissions by promoting the extraction and use of fossil fuels, in particular thermal coal for electricity generation.

2.9 There are no available or effective domestic remedies to enforce their rights under articles 2, 6, 17, 24 and 27 of the Covenant. The authors' rights under the Covenant are not protected in the Constitution or any other legislation applicable to the federal Government. ...

...

Observations of the State party on admissibility and the merits

4.1 ... [T]he State party maintains that the communication is inadmissible. The alleged violations of international climate change treaties [and the ICESCR], are inadmissible ratione materiae because they are outside the scope of the present Covenant. ... [T]here are stark and significant differences between the Paris Agreement and the Covenant. The two instruments have different aims and scopes. ... [I]nterpreting the Covenant through the Paris Agreement would be contrary to the fundamental principles of international law. The ordinary meaning of one treaty cannot be used to supplant the clear language of the Covenant.

4.2 ... [As for the authors claim to be victims, there] is no evidence that [they] face any current or imminent threat of a violation of any of the rights they invoked. Moreover, the authors have not shown any meaningful causation or connection between the alleged violations of their rights and the State party's measures or alleged failure to take measures. ... It is not possible, under the rules of State responsibility under international law, to attribute climate change to Australia. ... [T]he authors invoke a risk that has not yet materialized.

4.3 ... None of the alleged failures to take mitigation measures fall within the scope of the Covenant. It is not possible under international human rights law to attribute climate change to the State party. As a legal matter, it is not possible to trace causal links between the State party's contribution to climate change, its efforts to address climate change, and the alleged effects of climate change on the enjoyment of the authors' rights. ...

4.4 The authors' claims with respect to adaptation measures are also without merit, as the alleged adverse effects of climate change have yet to be suffered, if at all, by the authors. Nor are such alleged violations imminent.

4.5 The State party describes in detail the adaptation and mitigation measures it is taking with respect to climate change. ...

...

Issues and proceedings before the Committee
Consideration of admissibility

...

7.5 ... The Committee observes that it is not competent to determine compliance with other international treaties or agreements. However, to the extent that the authors are not seeking relief for violations of the other treaties before the Committee but rather refer to them in interpreting the State party's obligations under the Covenant, the Committee considers that the appropriateness of such interpretations relates to the merits of the authors' claims under the Covenant. ...

7.6 [Australia's claim that it] ... cannot be held responsible – as a legal or practical matter – for the [relevant] climate change impacts ... require[s] the Committee to contemplate whether ... a State party may be considered to have committed a violation of the Covenant rights of an individual, where the harm to the individual allegedly resulted from the failure of the State party to implement adaptation and/or mitigation measures ... .

7.7 With respect to adaptation measures, the [authors] have invoked articles 6, 17, 24 (1) and 27, each of which entails positive obligations of States parties to ensure the protection of individuals under their jurisdiction against violations of those provisions.

7.8 With respect to mitigation ... information provided by both parties indicates that the State party is and has been in recent decades among the countries in which large amounts of greenhouse gas emissions have been produced. The Committee also notes that the State party ranks high on world economic and human development indicators. In view of the above, the Committee considers that the alleged actions and omissions fall under the State party's jurisdiction ... .

7.9 ... [A] person can only claim to be a victim in the sense of article 1 of the Optional Protocol if he or she is actually affected. It is a matter of degree how concretely that requirement should be taken. However, individuals claiming to be a victim of a violation of a right protected under the Covenant must demonstrate either that a State party has, by act or omission, already impaired the exercise of their right or that such impairment is imminent ... . If the law or practice has not already been concretely applied to the detriment of such an individual, it must in any event be applicable in such a way that the individual's risk of being affected is more than a theoretical possibility.

7.10 ... [T]he authors – as members of peoples who are the longstanding inhabitants of traditional lands consisting of small, low-lying islands that presumably offer scant opportunities for safe internal relocation – are highly exposed to adverse climate change impacts. It is uncontested that the authors' lives and cultures are highly dependent on the availability of the limited natural resources to which they have access, and on the predictability of the natural phenomena that surround them. ... [They] would likely be unable to finance adequate adaptation measures themselves, on an individual or community level, to adjust to actual or expected climate and its effects in order to moderate harm. The Committee therefore considers that the authors are among those who are extremely vulnerable to intensely experiencing severely disruptive climate change impacts.
...
...

Consideration of the merits
...
Article 6

8.3 The Committee notes the authors' claim that the events in this case constitute a violation by act and omission of their right to a life with dignity under article 6 of the Covenant, owing to the State party's failure to perform its duty to provide adaptation and mitigation measures to address climate change impacts that adversely affect their lives, including their way of life. With respect to the State party's position that article 6 (1) of the Covenant does not obligate it to prevent foreseeable loss of life from climate change, the Committee recalls that the right to life cannot be properly understood if it is interpreted in a restrictive manner, and that the protection of that right requires States parties to adopt positive measures to protect the right to life. The Committee also recalls its general comment No. 36 (2018) on the right to life, in which it established that the right to life also includes the right of individuals to enjoy a life with dignity and to be free from acts or omissions that would cause their unnatural or premature death (para. 3). The Committee further recalls that the obligation of States parties to respect and ensure the right to life extends to reasonably foreseeable threats and life-threatening situations that can result in loss of life. States parties may be in violation of article 6 of the Covenant even if such threats and situations do not result in the loss of life. The Committee considers that such threats may include adverse climate change impacts, and recalls that environmental degradation, climate change and unsustainable development constitute some of the most pressing and serious threats to the ability of present and future generations to enjoy the right to life. The Committee recalls that States parties should take all appropriate measures to address the general conditions in society that may give rise to direct threats to the right to life or prevent individuals from enjoying their right to life with dignity.

8.4 ... While the State party notes that socioeconomic entitlements are protected under a separate Covenant, the Committee observes that the preamble of the present Covenant recognizes that the ideal of free human beings enjoying freedom from fear and want can only be achieved if conditions are created whereby everyone may enjoy their civil and political rights, as well as their economic, social and cultural rights.

8.5 The Committee observes that both it and regional human rights tribunals have established that environmental degradation can compromise effective enjoyment of the right to life ... the Committee notes that the TSRA, a government agency, recognised in its report entitled "Torres Strait Climate Change Strategy 2014-18" the vulnerability of the Torres Strait Islands to significant and adverse climate change impacts that affect ecosystems and livelihoods of the Islands' inhabitants. ...

8.6 The Committee ... notes that while the authors evoke feelings of insecurity engendered by a loss of predictability of seasonal weather patterns, seasonal timing, tides and availability of traditional and culturally important food sources, they have not indicated that they have faced or presently face adverse impacts to their own health or a real and reasonably foreseeable risk of being exposed to a situation of physical endangerment or extreme precarity that could threaten their right to life, including their right to a life with dignity. [Their claims] mainly relate to their ability to maintain their culture, which falls under the scope of article 27 of the Covenant.

8.7 Regarding the authors' assertion that their islands will become uninhabitable in 10 years (Boigu and Masig) or 10 to 15 years (Poruma and Warraber) in the absence of urgent action, the Committee recalls that without robust national and international efforts, the effects of climate change may expose individuals to a violation of their rights under article 6 of the Covenant. Furthermore, given that the risk of an entire country becoming submerged under water is such an extreme risk, the conditions of life in such a country may become incompatible with the right to life with dignity before the risk is realized. ... The Committee considers that the time frame of 10 to 15 years, as suggested by the authors, could allow for intervening acts by the State party to take affirmative measures to protect and, where necessary, relocate the alleged victims. The Committee considers that the information provided by the State party indicates that it is taking adaptive measures to reduce existing vulnerabilities and build resilience to climate change-related harms in the Islands. Based on the information made available to it, the Committee is not in a position to conclude that the adaptation measures taken by the State party would be insufficient so as to represent a direct threat to the authors' right to life with dignity.

8.8 In view of the foregoing, the Committee considers that the information before it does not disclose a violation by the State party of the authors' rights under article 6 of the Covenant.

Article 17

8.9 ... The Committee recalls that States parties must prevent interference with a person's privacy, family or home that arises from conduct not attributable to the State, at least where such interference is foreseeable and serious. Thus, when environmental damage threatens disruption to privacy, family and the home, States parties must prevent serious interference with the privacy, family and home of individuals under their jurisdiction.

8.10 The Committee recalls that the authors depend on fish, other marine resources, land crops, and trees for their subsistence and livelihoods, and depend on the health of their surrounding ecosystems for their own wellbeing. The State party has not contested the authors' assertions in that regard. The Committee considers that the aforementioned elements constitute components of the traditional indigenous way of life of the authors, who enjoy a special relationship with their territory, and that these elements can be considered to fall under the scope of protection of article 17 of the Covenant. ... [It] obligates States parties to adopt positive measures ...

8.11 The Committee takes note of the State party's extensive and detailed information that it has taken numerous actions to address adverse impacts caused by climate change and carbon emissions generated within its territory. ...

8.12 ... [The State party] has not contested the factual allegations set forth by the authors concerning the concrete climate change impacts on their home, private life and family. ... The Committee considers that when climate change impacts – including environmental degradation on traditional [indigenous] lands in communities where subsistence is highly dependent on available natural resources and where alternative means of subsistence and humanitarian aid are unavailable – have direct repercussions on the right to one's home, and the adverse consequences of those impacts are serious because of their intensity or duration and the physical or mental harm that they cause, then the degradation of the environment may adversely affect the well-being of individuals and constitute foreseeable and serious violations of private and family life and the home. ... [B]y failing to discharge its positive obligation to implement adequate adaptation measures to protect the authors' home, private life and family, the State party violated the authors' rights under article 17 of the Covenant.

Article 27

8.13 The Committee recalls that article 27 establishes and recognizes a right which is conferred on individuals belonging to minority indigenous groups and which is distinct from, and additional to, the other rights which all persons are entitled to enjoy under the Covenant. The Committee recalls that, in the case of indigenous peoples, the enjoyment of culture may relate to a way of life which is closely associated with territory and the use of its resources, including such traditional activities as fishing or hunting. Thus, the protection of this right is directed towards ensuring the survival and continued development of the cultural identity. The Committee further recalls that article 27 of the Covenant, interpreted in the light of the United Nations Declaration on the Rights of Indigenous Peoples, enshrines the inalienable right of indigenous peoples to enjoy the territories and natural resources that they have traditionally used for their subsistence and cultural identity. Although the rights protected under article 27 are individual rights, they depend in turn on the ability of the minority group to maintain its culture, language or religion.

8.14 The Committee notes the authors' assertion that their ability to maintain their culture has already been impaired ... . [T]he State party has not refuted the authors' arguments that they could not practice their culture on mainland Australia, where they would not have land that would allow them to maintain their traditional way of life. The Committee considers that the climate impacts mentioned by the authors represent a threat that could have reasonably been foreseen by the State party, as the authors' community members began raising the issue in the 1990s. While noting the completed and ongoing seawall construction on the islands where the authors live, the Committee considers that the delay in initiating these projects indicates an inadequate response by the State party to the threat faced by the authors. ... [T]he Committee considers that the information made available to it indicates that the State party's failure to adopt timely adequate adaptation measures to protect the authors' collective ability to maintain their traditional way of life, to transmit to their children and future generations their culture and traditions and use of land and sea resources discloses a violation of the State party's positive obligation to protect the authors' right to enjoy their minority culture. Accordingly, the Committee considers that the facts before it amount to a violation of the authors' rights under article 27 of the Covenant.
...

* * *

The adoption of these different sets of views by the Human Rights Committee and the Committee on the Rights of the Child has, as was to be expected, significantly increased the relevant committee's level of awareness and concern in these areas. In August 2023, for example, the latter committee adopted General Comment No. 26 (2023) on 'children's rights and the environment, with a special focus on climate change'.

C. CIVIL AND POLITICAL RIGHTS

An important but neglected dimension of the relationship between climate change and human rights is the threat posed to democracy and civil and political rights. These threats come from various directions. Eve Darian-Smith, in *Global Burning: Rising Antidemocracy and the Climate Crisis* (2022) 136, draws attention to the relevance of growing authoritarianism:

> As far-right leaders roll back environmental protections and promote extractive industries
> such as logging, mining, and industrial-scale agriculture, they are also rolling back
> elements of democracy such as a free press, nonpartisan judges, public health programs,
> public education, and the right to vote and protest injustice and suppression. The call for
> law and order and the mobilization of militarized police are common among authoritarian

leaders anxious to prevent public demonstrations against them. Violently suppressing citizens opposing the government is deeply entangled with leaders defending extractive industries through state-backed military and police force. Anti-environmentalism has become a marker of extreme-right parties and political agendas as well as a common theme among the radical media and movements that support them.

Declarations of emergency are increasingly common in the context of severe weather upheavals and these often involve significant restrictions on the exercise of rights. As popular protests grow in response to the widespread reluctance of governments to take the measures needed to meet the Paris goals, many governments have sought to restrict protests. In October 2022, the Home Secretary of the United Kingdom successfully amended a bill to restrict protests to allow her to apply for injunctions against anyone she deems 'likely' to carry out protests that could cause 'serious disruption' to 'key national infrastructure', prevent access to 'essential' goods or services, or have a 'serious adverse effect on public safety'. The police could arrest anyone suspected of breaching such an injunction.[656]

In the United States, many comparable measures are already in place, according to the International Center for Not-for-profit Law, 'Analysis of US Anti-Protest Bills', updated 12 January 2022:

> Many anti-protest bills restrict the freedom of assembly by creating extreme penalties for common infractions connected to protests. A 2020 law enacted in Tennessee makes obstructing a sidewalk or street an offense punishable by a year in jail, even though most protests occur on sidewalks and streets. … In Louisiana, a law enacted in 2018 makes it a felony, punishable by five years in jail, to trespass near a pipeline … .

> …

> Many anti-protest bills use sweeping definitions of "rioting" and other offenses that can penalize nonviolent protest activity. In Florida, a law enacted in 2021 makes it a felony to "riot." However, "rioting" is defined in a manner that can capture peaceful protesters who are simply part of a larger crowd where a few individuals engage in property destruction—even something as minor as kicking over a trash can. In fact, under the law, no actual property destruction needs to occur for those in a crowd to be guilty of "rioting"—just the "imminent danger" of damage is sufficient. …

> …

> A number of anti-protest bills create chilling new risks for organizations and individuals who are not directly involved in protests. Under a 2017 law enacted in Oklahoma, organizations that "conspire" with protesters who trespass near an oil or gas pipeline are liable for up to $1 million … .

> …

> Many anti-protest bills create new protections for individuals who harm protesters. An Iowa law enacted in 2021 … shields drivers from civil liability if they injure or kill someone who is unlawfully blocking a road during a "protest, demonstration, riot, or unlawful assembly," as long as the driver was exercising "due care." In 2020 alone, there were over one hundred instances of protesters being hit by vehicles. … [A] Florida law enacted in 2021, protect someone who injures or even kills a protester from being sued, as long as the victim was most likely participating in a "riot." …

Another dimension is that the uncertainty and insecurity generated by global warming, combined with large-scale movements of people both internally and across borders, will pose immense and unprecedented challenges to governance. Migration flows through Mexico to the United States and from Syria and other countries into Europe have already caused upheavals. Mass migration is likely to stimulate nationalist, xenophobic, racist and

---

[656] https://bills.parliament.uk/bills/3153/stages/16631/amendments/10001084.

other responses. Maintaining a balanced approach to civil and political rights, whether in a society that is determinedly seeking to mitigate climate change or one that is in denial, will be extremely challenging.

Finally, there is the attraction of authoritarian responses to intractable problems. Ross Mittiga, in 'Political Legitimacy, Authoritarianism, and Climate Change', 116 *Am. Pol. Sci. Rev.* (2022) 998, discerns a 'growing chorus of praise for "authoritarian environmentalism." … [W]hile authoritarianism is in general lamentable, having a government unencumbered by democratic procedures or constitutional limits on power could be advantageous when it comes to implementing urgently needed climate action.' He concludes that:

> [L]egitimacy requires that governments ensure the safety and security of their citizens, now and into the future; governments that cannot or will not perform this function, are, for that reason, illegitimate. … Legitimacy also requires that governments exercise their power in broadly acceptable ways. What counts as acceptable, however, varies considerably across generational and cultural lines and in light of different circumstances. For this reason, even the most widely celebrated standards—including the protection of basic rights and adherence to democratic processes—remain open to contestation and reconfiguration and, in this sense, are contingent.

D. FUTURE DIRECTIONS

There is no shortage of proposed measures to combat global warming while using the framework of human rights and seeking to ensure that any measures taken are compatible with human rights standards. Consider three such options. At the international level, states have endorsed several requests for advisory opinions from international courts. Strategic litigation, often funded by private investors, is also playing an increasingly important role. We then consider the role that might be played by a national human rights institution, and the options outlined by a UN Special Rapporteur.

In addition to the advisory opinion sought from the Inter-American Court of Human Rights in January 2023, the UN General Assembly, on a proposal initially coming from Vanuatu, requested an advisory opinion from the International Court of Justice on the following question (Res. 77/276 of 29 March 2023, adopted unanimously):

> Having particular regard to the Charter of the United Nations, the International Covenant on Civil and Political Rights, the International Covenant on Economic, Social and Cultural Rights, the United Nations Framework Convention on Climate Change, the Paris Agreement, the United Nations Convention on the Law of the Sea, the duty of due diligence, the rights recognized in the Universal Declaration of Human Rights, the principle of prevention of significant harm to the environment and the duty to protect and preserve the marine environment,
>
> (a) What are the obligations of States under international law to ensure the protection of the climate system and other parts of the environment from anthropogenic emissions of greenhouse gases for States and for present and future generations;
>
> (b) What are the legal consequences under these obligations for States where they, by their acts and omissions, have caused significant harm to the climate system and other parts of the environment, with respect to:
>
>> (i) States, including, in particular, small island developing States, which due to their geographical circumstances and level of development, are injured or specially affected by or are particularly vulnerable to the adverse effects of climate change?
>>
>> (ii) Peoples and individuals of the present and future generations affected by the adverse effects of climate change?

While an advisory opinion from the Court could give strong impetus to the development of international obligations to combat global warming, it could also amount to a significant setback if the Court does not move beyond its existing jurisprudence.[657]

In 2021 Antigua and Barbuda and Tuvalu set up the Commission of Small Island States on Climate Change and International Law (COSIS). By 2024, it had nine member states. As an international organization, it was able to request an advisory opinion from the International Tribunal on the Law of the Sea (ITLOS). On 12 December 2022 it requested one on the scope of state obligations under the UN Convention on the Law of the Sea (UNCLOS) in relation to greenhouse gas emissions. Thirty-four states, nine international organizations, and a number of other groups subsequently made submissions to the Tribunal and participated in the proceedings.

The Tribunal's unanimous Advisory Opinion, delivered on 21 May 2024, based itself on international environmental law, broadly defined, but made only one single fleeting reference to human rights and none to the implications of international human rights obligations. The Opinion found that greenhouse gas emissions (GHG) constitute pollution of the marine environment under the Convention and that States have an obligation to take all necessary measures to control such pollution. The Tribunal also found that States have special obligations to protect and preserve the marine environment in relation to climate change impacts. It characterized the findings of the IPCC as reflecting the scientific consensus (para. 208) but added that in the absence of scientific certainty, States must apply the precautionary approach (para. 213).

The Tribunal recognized that the 'principle of common but differentiated responsibilities', acknowledged in the UNFCCC and the Paris Agreement, applies in relation to the law of the sea (para. 229). This meant that States parties 'with greater means and capabilities must do more to reduce such emissions than States with less means and capabilities' (para. 227), and that developed States have a specific duty to assist developing States, and especially those vulnerable to climate change, in their efforts to address GHG-related marine pollution (paras. 338-339).

Obligation to exercise 'stringent' due diligence

The Tribunal held that the Convention's Art. 194 due diligence-type obligation in relation to marine pollution requires each state to put in place a national system, including legislation, administrative procedures, and an enforcement mechanism to regulate GHG emitting activities (para. 235), but no mention was made of human rights due diligence obligations.

Strategic Litigation

Amnesty International (https://www.amnesty.org/en/strategic-litigation/) defines 'strategic human rights litigation' as litigation that is 'consciously designed to advance the clarification, respect, protection and fulfilment of rights. The idea is to change laws, policies and practice, and to secure remedies or relief following violations. [It] is also often about raising public awareness of an injustice.' While this technique has long been used in a wide range of cases, as illustrated by *Brown v. Board of Education of Topeka* (347 U.S. 483, 1954) which found school racial segregation in the United States to be unconstitutional, it is assuming particular prominence today in the areas of environmental protection and climate change.[658]

Prominent public interest actors working in the human rights field include the Open Society Justice Initiative[659] and the European Center for Constitutional and Human Rights.[660] But private investors and commercial law firms are also increasingly involved. Suneal Bedia and William C. Marra, in 'The Shadows of Litigation Finance', 74 *Vand. L. Rev.* (2021) 563, define litigation finance as 'the practice where a third party provides capital to a litigant or law firm in connection with a legal claim. [It] is usually provided to plaintiffs seeking money damages … [and] provided by a funder with a profit motive.' They note that the starting premise for those in this business is 'that a legal claim is an asset, the same way a person's home or a company's inventory is an asset. Litigation

---

[657] See D. Bodansky, *An ICJ Advisory Opinion on Climate Change: Ten Questions and Answers*, Center for Climate and Energy Solutions, (October 2022).
[658] See generally S. Baer, 'Democracy in Peril: A Call for Amici and Amicae Curiae and Critical Lawyering', 10 *Transnat'l Legal Theory* (2019) 140; J. Goldston, 'Human Rights in the Crosshairs', *Just Security* 23 August 2022.
[659] OSJI, *Strategic Litigation Impacts: Insights from Global Experience* (2018).
[660] W. Kaleck, *Law versus Power: Our Global Fight for Human Rights* (2019).

finance allows claimholders, or law firms with contingent fee interests in claims, to secure financing against those assets ... .'

One of the principal benefits, according to the authors, is that such litigation promotes the goals of the legal system 'by ensuring legal outcomes track the strength of a party's claim, not the size of its bank account.' But they also note concerns that 'litigation finance will spur frivolous litigation and allow profit-seeking investors to take over our civil justice system [and questions about] whether litigation finance threatens the legal profession, interferes with counsel's professional independence, and impairs the principle of party control.' In their view, litigation financiers: (i) introduce greater competition into the market for legal services; (ii) provide capital that allows law firms to litigate plaintiff-side cases that they otherwise would be reluctant to pursue; and (iii) provide a broader suite of options to liquidity- and risk-constrained clients.

One of the largest groups working on environmental and climate litigation is ClientEarth (https://www.clientearth.org/). In the Netherlands, the non-profit Planet Prosperity Foundation enabled Roger Cox to litigate both the *Urgenda and Milieudefensie* cases, excerpted above. But a recent example of for-profit litigation financing is provided by Camilla Hodgson, in 'The Money Behind the Coming Wave of Climate Litigation', *The Financial Times* (5 June 2023). After a 2009 oil spill in the Timor Sea, a petroleum exploration company, PTTEP Australasia, without admitting liability, paid compensation of US$127 million to settle the claims of some 15,000 Indonesian farmers. A British firm, Harbour Litigation Funding, spent over $21 million on the case, and received $53 million in return, or just over 40 percent of the award.

A report by the European Parliamentary Research Service, *Responsible Private Funding of Litigation* (2021) acknowledged that third-party litigation funding (TPLF) 'may represent a tool to support private citizens and businesses in accessing justice and constitute a mechanism for transferring the risk of the uncertain outcome of the dispute to the litigation funder.' But it also cautioned that 'it may pose risks and entail conflicts of interests. If not properly regulated, it could lead to excessive economic costs and to the multiplication of opportunity claims, problematic claims and so called "frivolous claims".' For victims of human rights violations and groups advising or representing them, the question is whether, or under what circumstances, such approaches are an ideal, or perhaps just adequate, way to proceed. What are the advantages and disadvantages, and the potential pitfalls of strategic litigation, both in general and when privately funded?

COMMISSION ON HUMAN RIGHTS OF THE PHILIPPINES, NATIONAL INQUIRY ON CLIMATE CHANGE REPORT
(DECEMBER 2022)

On 22 September 2015, Greenpeace Southeast Asia, Philippine Rural Reconstruction Movement, Philippine Alliance of Human Rights Advocates, Philippine Human Rights Information Center, and other groups and individuals petitioned the Commission on Human Rights of The Philippines (CHRP) to investigate the role of the 'Carbon Majors' in relation to climate change-caused human rights violations. They named the world's largest 47 fossil fuel producers, including Chevron, ExxonMobil, British Petroleum, and Royal Dutch Shell. The Philippines is hit by some twenty typhoons each year and Typhoon Haiyan in 2013 killed over 6,000 people.

The CHRP is an independent office created by the Constitution and is the official National Human Rights Institution (NHRI). The Commission reported in May 2022, having held eight public hearings in Manila, two in New York, and two in London, hearing 65 witnesses and receiving 239 submissions. It had neither subpoena power nor the capacity to issue penalties, and proceeded on the basis of persuasion and cooperation. It summed up the spirit in which it proceeded by observing that:

> The challenge to NHRIs is to test boundaries and create new paths; to be bold and creative, instead of timid and docile; to be more idealistic or less pragmatic; to promote soft laws into becoming hard laws; to see beyond technicalities and establish guiding principles that can later become binding treaties; in sum, to set the bar of human rights protection to higher standards.

> ...

It took administrative notice of IPCC reports. It found that the Carbon Majors had 'engaged in willful obfuscation of climate science, which has prejudiced the right of the public to make informed decisions about their products, concealing that their products posed significant harms to the environment and the climate system [and delaying] meaningful environmental and climate action (at 108). It concluded that carbon majors within Philippine jurisdiction 'may be compelled to undertake human rights due diligence and to provide remediation.' It noted that the 'non-binding nature' of the UNGPs did not prevent their incorporation into domestic law. It also found that, on the basis of the 'enterprise theory of corporate personhood', the responsibility to refrain from contributing to climate change impacts extends to all business enterprises within each Carbon Major's respective value chains (at 112-13).

In its extensive recommendations, the Commission called upon states to, inter alia: discourage dependence on fossil fuels, including by terminating tax breaks and subsidies, offering tax credits and other incentives for renewable or clean energy technologies; require private actors and businesses receiving any form of assistance to have decarbonization and net-zero plans; collaborate on innovative climate action and guarantee that the benefits of science and technology are enjoyed by all, including ensuring that global intellectual property regimes do not obstruct climate change efforts; cooperate in creating a legally binding instrument to strengthen the implementation of the UNGPs, and provide redress mechanisms for victims of human rights harms caused by businesses; concretize the responsibility of businesses in the context of climate change; ensure that all persons have the necessary capacity to adapt to climate change, and guarantee equality and non-discrimination in climate adaptation and mitigation measures; ensure a just transition towards an environmentally sustainable economy; fulfill climate finance commitments and devise new mechanisms for loss and damage; support and provide adequate legal protection to environmental defenders and climate activists; promote climate change awareness and education; include the military in carbon accounting; and strengthen shared efforts to conserve and accelerate the restoration of forests and other terrestrial ecosystems.

For their part, the Carbon Majors (and other carbon-intensive industries) should: publicly disclose due diligence and climate and human rights impact assessment results; desist from all activities that undermine the findings of climate science; cease further exploration of new oil fields, keep fossil fuel reserves in the ground, and lead the transition to clean energy; contribute to a green climate fund for the implementation of mitigation and adaptation measures; and continually engage with experts, CSOs and other stakeholder for the assessment and improvement of corporate climate response.

Other recommendations were also addressed to financial institutions and investors, the UN and other international bodies, NHRIs, courts, NGOs, CSOs and the legal profession, and global citizens.

* * *

In October 2021, the UN Human Rights Council appointed a Special Rapporteur to address climate change. Resolution 48/14 received 42 votes in favor, one against (Russia), and four abstentions (China, Eritrea, India and Japan). In his first report to the General Assembly (UN Doc. A/77/226 (2022)), the 'Special Rapporteur on the promotion and protection of human rights in the context of climate change' laid out an ambitious and wide-ranging agenda:

> 90. [With respect to mitigation, the General Assembly should]
>
> (a) Request the Secretary-General to host a high-level mitigation commitment forum …
> to reduce global emissions by at least 55 per cent by 2030;
>
> (b) Recommend the repeal of the Energy Charter Treaty;
>
> I Agree to establish an internationally legally binding fossil fuel financial disclosure
> mechanism, to require Governments, businesses and financial institutions to disclose
> their investments in the fossil fuel and carbon intensive industries;
>
> (d) Establish an international human rights tribunal to hold accountable Governments,
> business and financial institutions for their ongoing investments in fossil fuels and carbon
> intensive industries and the related human rights effects that such investments invokI(e)

Pass a resolution to ban any further development of fossil fuel mining and other harmful mitigation actions;

(f) Recommend that the International Criminal Court include an indictable offense of ecocide.

91. Also with respect to mitigation, [COP27 should]:

> (a) Include human rights considerations in their nationally determined contributions and other planning processes and ensure that market-based mechanisms have effective means for protecting human rights and effective compliance and redress mechanisms to this effect;

> (b) Ensure that food security and the protection of the rights of indigenous peoples take precedent over land-based mitigation actions.

92. [With respect to loss and damage, a fund should be created and the General Assembly should, inter alia]:

> …

> (h) Create a redress and grievance mechanism to allow vulnerable communities to seek recourse for damages incurred, including legal measures to determine criminal, civil or administrative liability, and providing comprehensive restitution and guarantee of non-repetition;

> (i) Establish international legal protections to persons internally displaced and displaced across international borders as a consequence of climate change;

> (j) Explore legal options to close down tax havens as a means of freeing up taxation revenue for loss and damage.

> …

94. The Special Rapporteur recommends that the International Law Commission be mandated to develop, within a two-year time frame, an international legal procedure to give full and effective protection to environmental and indigenous human rights defenders, including by establishing an international tribunal for the prosecution of perpetrators of violence against and the killing of environmental and indigenous human rights defenders.

95. The Special Rapporteur recommends that the International Law Commission be mandated to include in the definition of ecocide those actions against environmental and indigenous human rights defenders.

> …

98. The Special Rapporteur further recommends that the General Assembly encourage all States to give standing to children and young people, including indigenous children and young people international, national and subnational court systems.

…

QUESTIONS

1. In an ideal scenario, what would be the impact of the UN's recognition of the human right to a clean, healthy and sustainable environment in General Assembly Resolution 76/300 (28 July 2022)?

2. In its 'Explanation of Position' on the resolution, the United States objected that there is still no 'shared understanding' of what such a right entails. Is that a fatal flaw, or can a right be recognized before all of its implications have been identified? How helpful is the Council of Europe's Parliamentary Assembly's resolution in this regard?

3. Researchers have claimed that global warming projections documented by—and in many cases modeled by—Exxon and ExxonMobil Corp scientists between 1977 and 2003 accurately forecast much of what has happened in terms of climate change, while at the same time the company's public statements denying the reality of global warming contradicted the relevant data.[661] Under the UN Guiding Principles on Business and Human Rights, would the company have any obligations to publicly acknowledge such findings, or to take any action as a result?

4. What are the main threats that climate change might pose to the enjoyment of civil and political rights, today, in ten years, and in fifty years?

5. What are the strengths and weaknesses of strategic litigation in this area? Use examples from the cases studied above.

6. Consider the following criticisms[662] of the approach adopted in *Billy v. Australia*: (i) 'the majority did not rigorously apply General Comment 36 on the right to life', see Ch. 9, above; (ii) the 'real and foreseeable risk' standard applied is appropriate in a refugee case such as *Teitiota v. New Zealand*, but sets the bar too high in this situation;[663] and (iii) the Committee overlooked Article 6 violations that have already occurred, while accepting assurances about projects yet to be completed.

7. A common approach in both litigation and broader advocacy is to rely in part on the interests of future generations.[664] In 2023, a group of experts adopted the Maastricht Principles on the Human Rights of Future Generations.[665] Principle 13 provides that:

a) States have obligations to respect, protect, and fulfil the human rights of future generations.
b) These obligations extend to all conduct of States, whether through actions and omissions, and whether undertaken individually or collectively, including decisions made in their capacity as members of international or regional organizations. Such conduct includes, but is not limited to, the adoption or implementation of policies, practices, programs and legislation.
c) Failure to comply with these obligations constitutes a violation of the rights of future generations.
d) States must ensure an effective remedy for failure to respect, protect and fulfil these rights as set out in section.

Compare that approach with the following analysis:

An appeal to the responsibility towards future generations is attractively simple: an exhortation to act, drawing on a powerful imagery of obligation, an altruistic duty towards our children and grandchildren, an invitation to global solidarity. [But, in fact, such an appeal] instead stands to elide numerous existing loci of responsibility in climate matters that are more concrete, more coherent, more demanding, more easily understood and more effectively articulated in law. It tends to fold those to whom responsibility is owed in the present into those owing responsibility and so annihilates the former's claim to a present and a future alike. Responsibilities towards those alive today surround us; they swell, if we choose to see them. And, if acted upon, the consequences will flow into the future … .[666]

---

[661] G. Supran et al., 'Assessing ExxonMobil's Global Warming Projections', 379 *Science* (2023).

[662] N. Barrett and A. Gupta, 'Why Did the UN Human Rights Committee Refuse Broader Protections for Climate Change Victims?', *Opinio Juris* (10 May 2022).

[663] Cf. M. Foster and J. McAdam, 'Analysis of "Imminence" in International Protection Claims: *Teitiota v New Zealand* and Beyond', 71 *Int'l & Comp. L. Q.* (2022) 975.

[664] B. Lewis, 'Protecting Environmental Human Rights for Future Generations', in W. Baber and J. May (eds.), *Environmental Human Rights in the Anthropocene: Concepts, Contexts, and Challenges* (2023) 31.

[665] A. M. Suárez Franco and S. Liebenberg, 'The Maastricht Principles on the Human Rights of Future Generations', *Spotlight on Global Multilateralism* (2023) 58.

[666] S. Humphreys, 'Against Future Generations', 33 *Eur. J. Int'l L.* (2022) 1061, at 1091.

E. THE RIGHT TO DEVELOPMENT

Claims for a right to development emerged at around the same time as the environmental rights considered above. Some commentators have pointed to the links between the two, but much depends on the way in which the right to development is defined.

Article 56 of the UN Charter commits all member states to take 'joint and separate action in co-operation' with the UN for the achievement of the purposes identified in Article 55, which includes human rights, 'higher standards of living … and conditions of economic and social progress and development' and 'solutions of international economic, social, health and related problems'. Similarly, Article 28 of the UDHR provides that '[e]very one is entitled to a social and international order in which the rights and freedoms set forth in this Declaration can be fully realized'. These provisions, although expressed at a level of great generality, have often been invoked by those who posit the existence of a broad international 'duty to cooperate' or a 'right to solidarity'. In a world of deep-rooted and growing inequalities among nations, the question inevitably arises whether the international community bears some responsibility for assisting states whose resources are inadequate to ensure the human rights of their own citizens, or for providing direct assistance to those individuals in dire need.

Since 1977 much of this debate has been pursued within the field of human rights under the rubric of the 'right to development'. The debate touches upon a number of themes raised in earlier chapters: the basis for recognition of new rights, the priority to be accorded to the different sets of rights, the links between human rights and democratic governance and the relationship between individual and collective rights (including peoples' rights).

The list of internationally recognized human rights is by no means immutable. Just as the British sociologist T. H. Marshall characterized the eighteenth century as the century of civil rights, the nineteenth as that of political rights and the twentieth as that of social rights so, too, have some commentators over the past three decades put forward claims for the recognition of the new rights, in particular a category known as the 'third generation of solidarity rights'. By analogy with the slogan of the French Revolution these rights have been said to correspond to the theme of *fraternité*, while first-generation civil and political rights correspond with *liberté* and second-generation economic and social rights with *egalité*. Karel Vasak's list of solidarity rights included 'the right to development, the right to peace, the right to environment, the right to the ownership of the common heritage of mankind, and the right to communication'.[667]

Of these, the most debated and contentious at the international level has been the right to development. First recognized by the UN Commission on Human Rights in 1977 (CHR Res. 4 (XXXIII)), it was enshrined in the Declaration on the Right to Development (General Assembly Res. 41/28 (1986)). The 1993 Vienna World Conference on Human Rights declared it to be 'a universal and inalienable right and an integral part of fundamental human rights'. Subsequently, a Working Group was established in 1998, a Special Rapporteur was appointed in 2016,[668] and an Expert Mechanism created in 2019. In October 2023, The Human Rights Council (Res. 54/18 adopted by a vote of 29-13-5) submitted this draft 'covenant' to the General Assembly 'for its consideration, negotiation and subsequent adoption'.

DRAFT INTERNATIONAL COVENANT ON THE RIGHT TO DEVELOPMENT
UN DOC A/HRC/54/50 (2023)

Preamble

…

Part I

Article 1 Object and purpose

---

[667] K. Vasak, 'A 30-Year Struggle', UNESCO Courier, November 1977, 29; for a critique, see S. Jensen and C. Walton, 'Not "Second-Generation Rights": Rethinking the History of Social Rights', in ibid., *Social Rights and the Politics of Obligation in History* (2022) 1.

[668] Special Rapporteur Surya Deva has spelled out a new vision for the right to development in UN Docs. A/HRC/54/27 (2023) and A/78/160 (2023.

The object and purpose of the present Covenant is to promote and ensure the full, equal and meaningful enjoyment of the right to development by every individual and all peoples everywhere, and to guarantee its effective operationalization and full implementation at the national and international levels.

…

Article 3 General principles

To achieve the object and purpose of the present Covenant and to implement its provisions, the States Parties shall be guided by, inter alia, the principles set out below:

(a) Development centred on the individual and peoples: the individual and peoples are the central subjects of development and must be the active participants and beneficiaries of the right to development;

(b) Principles common to all human rights: the right to development should be realized in a manner that reflects the universality, inalienability, indivisibility, interdependence and interrelatedness of all human rights and integrates the principles of equality, non-discrimination, intersectionality, empowerment, participation, transparency, accountability, equity, inclusion, accessibility and subsidiarity;

(c) Human rights-based development: as development is a human right that is indivisible from and interrelated and interdependent with all other human rights, the laws, policies and practices of development, including development cooperation, must be normatively anchored in a system of rights and corresponding obligations established by international law. Accordingly, the promotion of, respect for and enjoyment of certain human rights and fundamental freedoms cannot justify the denial of other human rights and fundamental freedoms;

…

Part II
Article 4 Right to development

1. Every individual and all peoples have the inalienable right to development, by virtue of which they are entitled to participate in, contribute to and enjoy civil, cultural, economic, environmental, political and social development that is indivisible from and interdependent and interrelated with all other human rights and fundamental freedoms.

2. Every individual and all peoples have the right to active, free and meaningful participation in development and in the fair distribution of benefits resulting therefrom.

Article 5 Relationship with the right of peoples to self-determination

1. The right to development implies the full realization of the right of all peoples to self- determination.

…

Article 6 Relationship with other human rights

States Parties reaffirm that all human rights, including the right to development, are universal, inalienable, interrelated, interdependent, indivisible and equally important.

States Parties agree that the right to development is an integral part of human rights and must be realized in conformity with the full range of civil, cultural, economic, environmental, political and social rights.

Article 7
Relationship with the responsibility of everyone to respect human rights under international law

… [A]ll natural and legal persons, peoples, groups and States have the general duty under international law to refrain from participating in the violation of the right to development.

Part III

Article 8 General obligations of States Parties

States Parties shall respect, protect and fulfil the right to development for all, without discrimination of any kind
... .

Article 9 General obligations of international organizations

... [I]nternational organizations also have the obligation to refrain from conduct that aids, assists, directs, controls or coerces, with knowledge of the circumstances of the act, a State or another international organization to breach any obligation that the State or the latter organization may have with regard to the right to development.

Article 10 Obligation to respect

States Parties shall refrain from conduct, whether expressed through law, policy or practice, that:

(a) Nullifies or impairs the enjoyment and exercise of the right to development;

(b) Impairs the ability of another State or an international organization to comply with that State's or that international organization's obligations with regard to the right to development;

(c) Aids, assists, directs, controls or coerces, with knowledge of the circumstances of the act, another State or an international organization to breach that State's or that international organization's obligations with regard to the right to development;
...

Article 11 Obligation to protect

States Parties shall adopt and enforce all necessary, appropriate and reasonable measures, including administrative, legislative, investigative, judicial, diplomatic and others, to ensure that natural or legal persons, peoples, groups or any other State or agents that the State is in a position to regulate do not nullify or impair the enjoyment and exercise of the right to development within or outside their territories when:

(a) Such conduct occurs, partially or fully, on the territory of the State Party;

(b) The natural or legal person has the nationality of the State Party;

(c) The State Party has the requisite legal duty under either domestic or international law to supervise, regulate or otherwise exercise oversight, through, *inter alia*, requiring human rights due diligence, of the conduct of the legal person engaging in business activities, including those of a transnational character.

Article 12 Obligation to fulfil

1. Each State Party shall take measures, individually and through international assistance and cooperation, with a view to progressively enhancing the right to development ... .

2. To this end, each State Party shall take all necessary measures at the national level, and shall ensure, inter alia, non-discrimination and equality of opportunity, including through digital inclusion where applicable, for all individuals and peoples in their access to basic resources, education, health services, food, housing, water and sanitation, employment, and social security and protection, and in the fair distribution of income, and shall carry out appropriate economic and social reforms with a view to eradicating all social injustices.

Article 13 Duty to cooperate

States Parties reaffirm and shall implement their duty to cooperate with each other, through joint and separate action, in order to:

(a) Solve international problems of an economic, social, cultural, political, environmental, health-related, educational, technological or humanitarian character;

(b) End poverty in all its forms and dimensions, including by eradicating extreme poverty;
...

2. To this end, States Parties have primary responsibility, in accordance with the general principle of international solidarity described in the present Covenant, for the creation of international conditions favourable for the realization of the right to development for all, and shall take deliberate, concrete and targeted steps, individually and jointly, including through cooperation within international organizations and engagement with civil society:

(a) To ensure that natural and legal persons, groups and States do not impair the enjoyment of the right to development;
...

3. States Parties shall ensure that financing for development and all other forms of aid and assistance given or received by them, whether bilateral or under any institutional or other international framework, adhere to internationally recognized development cooperation effectiveness principles and are consistent with the provisions of the present Covenant.

4. States Parties recognize their duty to cooperate to create a social and international order conducive to the realization of the right to development by, inter alia:

(a) Promoting a universal, rules-based, open, non-discriminatory, equitable, transparent and inclusive multilateral trading system;

(b) Implementing the principle of special and differential treatment for developing countries, in particular least developed countries, as defined in applicable trade and investment agreements;

(c) Improving the regulation and monitoring of global financial markets and institutions, and strengthening the implementation of such regulations;

(d) Ensuring enhanced representation and voice for developing countries, including least developed countries, in decision-making in all international economic and financial institutions, in order to deliver more effective, credible, accountable and legitimate institutions;
...

Part IV
[In terms of implementation, the draft envisages the establishment of a Conference of States Parties which would 'periodically examine voluntary reports by States Parties' and an 'implementation mechanism' of independent experts 'to facilitate, coordinate and assist, in a non-adversarial and non-punitive manner, the implementation and promotion of compliance' with the Covenant. This treaty body would 'make suggestions and general recommendations' based on states' reports, and 'review requests by rights holders to comment on situations in which their right to development has been adversely affected'.]

* * *

The right to development has never ceased to be controversial among governments as well as among scholars and commentators, although it has achieved constitutional recognition in 31 countries.[669] In international debates, the right is generally grounded in claims relating to the material conditions required to ensure realization of the full range of existing human rights, but it is also sometimes grounded in claims of appropriate reparations for colonialism and other forms of exploitation of the South by the North, or on arguments that the existing

---

[669] R. Hirschl, 'Economic and Social Rights in National Constitutions', 62 *Am. J. Comp. L.* (2015) 1043, n. 35.

international economic order is loaded against developing countries and that compensation should follow.[670] China has been an enthusiastic promoter and an official 2016 government White Paper (The Right to Development: China's Philosophy, Practice and Contribution) states that:

> Development is a universal human theme, providing for people's basic needs and giving them hope of better life. The right to development is an inalienable human right, symbolizing dignity and honor. Only through development can we address global challenges; only through development can we protect basic civil rights of the people; only through development can we promote the progress of human society.

In 2023, the United States explained its opposition to the proposed covenant:

> ... [T]he Right to Development resolution creates a detrimental narrative which would elevate the process of development above human rights, undermine the human rights system, and harm development rather than promote it. ... [T]he text appears to protect states instead of individuals. States do not have human rights; they guarantee them to individual human beings.

> [The right] is not recognized in any of the core UN human rights conventions, does not have an agreed international meaning, and is not recognized as a universal right held and enjoyed by individuals. We are also concerned about ... the lack of meaningful negotiations' on the draft covenant.[671]

The contrast between the 2023 formulation of the right to development and the historical vision of some of its early Global South proponents is dramatic. The 'genealogical starting point' for the right is the set of demands for economic and political justice contained in the NIEO.[672]

James Thuo Gathii, in 'Africa and the Radical Origins of the Right to Development', 1 *TWAIL Review* (2020) 28, notes that in 1967 Senegal's Foreign Minister, Doudou Thiam, argued that 'the right to development belonged to the third world ...'. He conceptualized it as a collective right to correct the wrongs wrought by colonial rule. The revolutionary agenda that he envisaged would require developing countries to:

> tear down all the practices, institutions and rules on which international economic relations are based, in so far as these practices, institutions and rules sanction injustice and exploitation and maintain the unjustified domination of a minority over the majority of men ... . The right of peoples to self-determination, the sovereign equality of peoples, international solidarity - all these will remain empty words ... until relations between nations are viewed in the light of economic and social facts. ...

In 1979, a former Algerian Foreign Minister, later to become a judge on the International Court of Justice (from 1982 to 2001), Mohamed Bedjaoui, published a manifesto entitled *Towards a New International Economic Order* underscoring the extent to which international law had facilitated colonial subjugation and insisting that the new order must provide 'for the development of all nations in the world'.[673] He further developed the role of the right to development in that context in 'The Right to Development', in M. Bedjaoui (ed.), *International Law: Achievements and Prospects* (1991) 1182. He characterized it as 'the *core right* from which all the others stem', and described its international dimension as being 'nothing other than *the right to an equitable share in the economic and social well-being of the world.*' He understood its basis in the following terms:

> 22. The 'right to development' flows from this right to self-determination and has the *same nature*. There is little sense in recognizing self-determination as a superior and inviolable principle if one does not recognize *at the same time* a 'right to development' for the peoples that have achieved self-determination. This right to development can only be

---

[670] These arguments were examined in detail in the first major UN report on the right to development. See UN Doc. E/CN.4/1334 (1978).

[671] Eric Merron (USA), Explanation of Vote, Third Committee of the UN General Assembly, November 7, 2023.

[672] N. Gilman, 'The New International Economic Order: A Reintroduction', 6 *Humanity* (2015) 1 at 7.

[673] See generally, U. Özsu, '"In the Interests of Mankind as a Whole": Mohammed Bedjaoui's New International Economic Order', 6 *Humanity* (2015) 129.

an 'inherent' and 'built-in' right forming an inseparable part of the right to self-determination.

> 23. ... [This makes the right to development] much more a right of the State or of the people, than a right of the individual, and it seems to me that it is better that way.

In terms of the content of the right, he identified several aspects including that the state must be able to 'claim a *'fair price'* for its raw materials and for whatever it offers in its trade with the more developed countries', and that 'the State is *entitled if not to the satisfaction of its needs at least to receive a fair share of what belongs to all, and therefore to that State also.*' He elaborated that this 'should be perceived as a right and not as an act of charity' and that it 'should be made effective by *norms and institutions.*' In stark contrast to other jurists who argued about the degree of normativity of the right, Bedjaoui insisted that 'the right to development is, by its nature, so incontrovertible that it *should* be regarded as belonging to *jus cogens.*'

A more nuanced perspective is provided below by another iconic Global South scholar, Georges Abi-Saab (Egypt). That excerpt is followed by another from the same era, by Jack Donnelly who calls the right unfounded and dangerous.

GEORGES ABI-SAAB, THE LEGAL FORMULATION OF A RIGHT TO DEVELOPMENT HAGUE ACADEMY OF INTERNATIONAL LAW, THE RIGHT TO DEVELOPMENT AT THE INTERNATIONAL LEVEL (1980) 163

[Abi-Saab begins by noting that, for the right to development to be considered a legal right, it must be possible to identify the active and passive subjects of the right and its content. But those elements depend on the legal basis of the right, which in turn depends on whether the right is an individual or collective one.]

It is possible to think of different legal bases of the right to development as a collective right. The first possibility ... is to consider the right to development as the aggregate of the social, economic and cultural rights not of each individual, but of all the individuals constituting a collectivity. In other words, it is the sum total of a double aggregation of the rights and of the individuals. This version ... has the merit of shedding light on the link between the rights of the individual and the right of the collectivity; a link which is crucial. ...

Another way ... is to approach it directly from a collective perspective ... by considering it either as the economic dimension of the right of self-determination, or alternatively as a parallel right to self-determination, partaking of the same nature and belonging to the same category of collective rights.
...
As far as the beneficiaries or active subjects are concerned, the first answer that comes to mind is that they are those societies possessing certain characteristics which lead the international community to consider them wanting in terms of development and to classify them as 'developing' or 'less developed' countries (LDC). ...
...
... Up to now, we have used societies, communities, countries and States as interchangeable, which they are not. In fact, here as with self-determination, the common denominator of these different ways of describing the beneficiary collectivity is the 'people' they designate, which constitutes the socially relevant entity or group in this context. ... Suffice it to say here that the distinction between 'people' and 'State', though in theory it is as important in relation to the right to development as to the right of self-determination, in practice it is not. ...
...
... [T]he passive subject of the right to development can only be the international community as such. But as the international community does not have at its disposal the means (organs, resources) of directly fulfilling its obligations under the right to development, it can only discharge them through a category of its members, that of the 'developed' States. ...
...
... [S]atisfaction of the collective right is a necessary condition, a condition-precedent or a prerequisite for the materialization of the individual rights. Thus without self-determination it is impossible to imagine a total realization of the civil and political rights of the individuals constituting the collectivity in question. Such rights

can be granted and exercised at lower levels, such as villages and municipalities, but they cannot reach their full scope and logical conclusion if the community is subject to colonial or alien rule.

...

The same with the right to development, which is a necessary precondition for the satisfaction of the social and economic rights of the individuals. And here, even more than in the case of self-determination, the causal link between the two levels is particularly strong; for without a tolerable degree of development, the society will not be materially in a position to grant and guarantee these rights to its members, i.e., of providing the positive services and securing the minimum economic standards which are required by these rights.

...

JACK DONNELLY, IN SEARCH OF THE UNICORN: THE JURISPRUDENCE AND POLITICS OF THE RIGHT TO DEVELOPMENT
15 CALIF. WESTERN INT'L. L. J. (1985) 473, 482

III. Legal Sources of the Right to Development

...

... If the right to development means the right of peoples freely to pursue their development, then it can be plausibly argued to be implied by the Covenants' right to self-determination. However, such a right to development is without interest; it is already firmly established as the right to self-determination.

A substantially broader right to development, however, cannot be extracted from this right to self-determination. The right to self-determination recognized in the Covenants does not imply a right to live in a developing society; it is explicitly only a right to *pursue* development. Neither does it imply an *individual* right to development; self-determination, again explicitly, is a right of peoples only. In no sense does it imply a right to be developed. Thus the claim that the right to development is simply the realization of the right to self-determination is not based on the Covenants' understanding of self-determination.

It might also be argued that because development is necessary for self-determination, development is itself a human right. Such an argument, however, is fallacious. ... Even assuming that development is necessary for, rather than a consequence of, full enjoyment of the right to self-determination, it simply does not follow that peoples have a right to development.

Allowing such an argument to prevail would result in a proliferation of bizarre or misguided rights. ...

...

[Second, one] might question whether 'development' falls under the notion of a social and international order referred to in Article 28 [of the UDHR]. 'Development' suggests a process or result; the process of development or the condition of being developed. 'Order', by contrast, implies a set of principles, rules, practices or institutions; neither a process nor a result but a structure. Article 28, therefore, is most plausibly interpreted as prohibiting *structures* that deny opportunities or resources for the realization of civil, political, economic, social or cultural human rights. ...

...

Suppose, though, that Article 28 *were* to be taken to imply a human right to development. What would that right look like? It would be an *individual* right, and only an individual right; a right of persons, not peoples, and certainly not States. It would be a right to the enjoyment of traditional human rights, not a substantively new right. It would be as much a civil and political as an economic and social right – Article 28 refers to *all* human rights – and would be held equally against one's national government and the international community. ...

...

[V. Subjects of the Right to Development]

...

If human rights derive from the inherent dignity of the human person, collective human rights are logically possible only if we see social membership as an inherent part of human personality, and if we argue that as part of a nation or people, persons hold human rights substantively different from, and in no way reducible to, individual human rights. This last proposition is extremely controversial. ...

The very concept of human rights, as it has heretofore been understood, rests on a view of the individual person as separate from, and endowed with inalienable rights held primarily in relation to, society, and especially the state. Furthermore, within the area defined by these rights, the individual is superior to society in the sense that ordinarily, in cases of conflict between individual human rights and social goals or interests, individual rights must prevail. The idea of collective *human* rights represents a major, and at best confusing, conceptual deviation.

I do not want to challenge the idea of collective rights *per se* or even the notion of peoples' rights; groups, including nations, can and do hold a variety of rights. But these are not *human* rights as that term is ordinarily understood. …

…

A further problem with collective human rights is determining who is to exercise the right; the right-holder is not a physical person, and thus an institutional 'person' must exercise it. In the case of a right held by a people, or by society as a whole, the most plausible 'person' to exercise the right is, unfortunately, the state. Again this represents a radical reconceptualization of human rights – and an especially dangerous one.

…

* * *

Nico Schrijver has argued, in 'A New Convention on the Human Right to Development: Putting the Cart before the Horse?', 38 *Neth. Q. Hum. Rts* (2020) 84, that the right should be taken more seriously than it has been for three reasons: (i) it is a 'cluster right' that brings together the rights to a decent standard of living, food, water, clothing, housing, work, education, life, and freedom of expression and association; (ii) it is an 'integrative right' that brings together CPR, ESCR, and peoples' rights; and (iii) it is a 'bridging right' connecting the 'rights of individuals (citizens) with those of groups and peoples'.

James Thuo Gathii, in 'Africa and the Radical Origins of the Right to Development', 1 *TWAIL Rev.* (2020) 28 emphasizes a radical approach to the right to development which:

> examines the international order through a lens of marginalization and domination of the third world and its peoples by international law. … Critical scholars in the TWAIL movement reveal how … liberatory goals [such as sovereign equality, self-determination, human rights, development and equality] coexist alongside economic hierarchy and subordination between nations and carry forward within them the legacy of colonial conquest and European imperialism.

He contrasts this with '[t]he reconceptualizing of development as a right … by donor agencies in cooperation with formerly colonial countries, abandoning the more radical vision … in at least three ways': (i) shifting the 'focus away from external and north-south issues and the constitutive role of colonial rule and its legacies [to] domestic and internal development issues'; (ii) presenting North-South development relationships 'as cooperative instead of confrontational'; and (iii) enabling 'international financial institutions, western donors and investors to identify non-western peoples and states as development failures in need of assistance, which lays the basis for their intervention as experts with specialized knowledge and resources.'

Elsabé Boshoff, in 'Rethinking the Premises Underlying the Right to Development in African Human Rights Jurisprudence', 31 *Rev. Eur. Comp and Int'l Env. L.* (2022) 27, argues that the African Charter, as interpreted by the African Commission and Court, opens up possibilities for 'a revised understanding of development, not as wealth-based, but rather as centred on human well-being situated within a healthy and satisfactory environment.' She calls for 'elements of African environmental ethics' to be recognized in interpreting the right to development'. An important case in this regard is one already encountered in Chapter 11:

AFRICAN COMMISSION ON HUMAN AND PEOPLES' RIGHTS V. REPUBLIC OF KENYA APPLICATION NO. 006/2012, JUDGMENT (26 MAY 2017)

Alleged violation of Article 21 of the Charter

…

The Applicant [the African Commission] contends that the Respondent [Kenya] has violated the rights of the Ogieks to freely dispose of their wealth and natural resources in two ways. Firstly, by evicting them from the Mau Forest and denying them access to the vital resources therein, and secondly, by granting logging concessions on Ogiek ancestral land without their prior consent and without giving them a share of the benefits in those resources.

...

The Court's Assessment

Article 21 of the Charter states that:

"1. All peoples shall freely dispose of their wealth and natural resources. This right shall be exercised in the exclusive interest of the people. In no case shall a people be deprived of it.

...

... [T]he Charter does not define the notion of "peoples". ... [Its drafters] deliberately omitted to define the notion in order to "permit a certain flexibility in the application and subsequent interpretation by future users of the legal instrument, the task of fleshing out the Charter being left to the human rights protection bodies."

It is generally accepted that, in the context of the struggle against foreign domination in all its forms, the Charter primarily targets the peoples comprising the populations of the countries struggling to attain independence and national sovereignty.

In the circumstances, the question is whether the notion "people" used by the Charter covers not only the population as the constituent elements of the State, but also the ethnic groups or communities identified as forming part of the said population within a constituted State. ...

In the view of the Court, the answer to this question is in the affirmative, provided such groups or communities do not call into question the sovereignty and territorial integrity of the State without the latter's consent. ... [N]othing prevents other peoples' rights, such as the right to development (Article 22), the right to peace and security (Article 23) or the right to a healthy environment (Article. 24) from being recognised, where necessary, specifically for the ethnic groups and communities that constitute the population of a State.

...

The Court ... has already recognised for the Ogieks a number of rights to their ancestral land ... . In so far as those rights have been violated by the Respondent, the Court holds that the latter has also violated Article 21 of the Charter since the Ogieks have been deprived of the right to enjoy and freely dispose of the abundance of food produced by their ancestral lands.

Alleged violation of Article 22 of the Charter

Applicant's Submission

The Applicant contends that the Respondent has violated the Ogieks' right to development by evicting them from their ancestral land in the Mau Forest and by failing to consult with and/or seek the consent of the Ogiek Community in relation to the development of their shared cultural, economic and social life within the Mau Forest. ...

...

Respondent's Submission

The Respondent argues that it has not violated the right to development of the Ogieks ... [and] that the Applicant has not demonstrated how it has failed in undertaking development initiatives for the benefit of the Ogieks or how they have been discriminated against and excluded in the process of conducting development initiatives.

...

The Court's Assessment

Article 22 of the Charter provides that:

> "1. All peoples shall have the right to their economic, social and cultural development with due regard to their freedom and identity and in the equal enjoyment of the common heritage of mankind.
>
> 2. States shall have the duty, individually or collectively, to ensure the exercise of the right to development."

The Court reiterates its view above with respect to Article 21 of the Charter that the term "peoples" in the Charter comprises all populations as a constitutive element of a State. These populations are entitled to social, economic and cultural development being part of the peoples of a State. Accordingly, the Ogiek population, has the right under Article 22 of the Charter to enjoy their right to development.

...

...[T]he Ogieks have been continuously evicted from the Mau Forest by the Respondent, without being effectively consulted. The evictions have adversely impacted on their economic, social and cultural development. They have also not been actively involved in developing and determining health, housing and other economic and social programmes affecting them.

146. The Court therefore holds that the Respondent violated Article 22 of the Charter.

QUESTIONS

1. Compare the different conceptions of the right to development put forward by Abi-Saab, Bedjaoui and Donnelly with the text of the 1986 General Assembly Declaration. Key concerns voiced by some of the governmental and other opponents of the right to development include objections to collective human rights and especially to any idea that a human right can be vested in a state, resistance to the idea that resource transfers from the North to the South are obligatory and fears that a right to development gives priority to development over human rights. To what extent does the Declaration provide a foundation for each of these concerns?

2. Does the African Commission's approach in the Ogiek case suggest a way forward for making the right to development operational beyond the realm of indigenous peoples' rights?

Chapter 16. Responding to Mass Violations: Prosecutions and Transitional Justice

This chapter looks at the responses of international law in general, and of the international human rights regime in particular, to mass violations of *human* rights and humanitarian law. The primary focus is on the evolution of the field of international criminal law (ICL) since the Nuremberg judgment, with emphasis on the role of the International Criminal Court (ICC). The ICC was created by the Rome Statute of 1998, and brought into existence when the Statute entered into force on 1 July 2002, after sixty states had ratified the treaty. The ad hoc tribunals set up by the Security Council in relation to the former Yugoslavia in 1993 and Rwanda in 1994 played a crucial role in developing both the legal and procedural foundations of this body of law.[674]

THE EVOLUTION OF INTERNATIONAL CRIMINAL LAW

The creation of an international criminal tribunal was agreed upon in the Treaty of Versailles after World War I. Although German Kaiser Wilhelm II was the principal target, the Netherlands refused to extradite him, and a few desultory trials were held in Leipzig in 1921 before German courts. The Nuremberg and Tokyo war crimes trials of the late 1940s set important precedents but the Cold War quickly dimmed enthusiasm for institutionalizing such a system on a continuing global basis. While scholars such as Georg Schwarzenberger and Cherif Bassiouni sought to rekindle the debates,[675] it was not until after the fall of the Berlin Wall in 1989, combined with the outrage generated by well-documented atrocities in the former Yugoslavia and Rwanda in the early 1990s, that sufficient political will could be mustered. The first step was the creation of the two ad hoc tribunals, followed by agreement on the ICC Statute in 1998. The record of the ICC over the past two decades has been somewhat chequered, with various missteps along the way. By 2019, the barrage of criticism of the Court's record was so great that the Assembly of States Parties appointed a group of independent experts to provide 'concrete, achievable and actionable recommendations aimed at enhancing the performance, efficiency and effectiveness of the Court and the Rome Statute system as a whole'. The review, chaired by Richard Goldstone, made 384 recommendations in a 348-page report.[676] Nevertheless, most observers acknowledge that the court's very existence is an immense achievement, that the standards enshrined in the Statute have definitively changed the legal landscape, and that much potential remains to be realized. The flurry of activity around the situations in Ukraine and Gaza since 2022 has also breathed new life into the overall ICL system.

When the ad hoc tribunals were established, they were given primacy over national court systems, which had to yield to the relevant international tribunal. Over time, both began to develop a more nuanced division of responsibility with the national legal systems. In contrast, Articles 17 and 19 of the Rome Statute embody the crucial principle of complementarity which ensures that primacy is given to national-level jurisdictions, as long as the relevant case is being 'genuinely' investigated or prosecuted by a state that has jurisdiction.[677]

Despite the many overlaps between ICL on the one hand, and human rights and humanitarian law on the other, they are by no means synonymous, as noted by Darryl Robinson, in 'The Identity Crisis of International Criminal Law', 21 *Leiden J. Int'l L.* (2008) 925, at 946:

> … ICL practitioners often assume that the ICL norms are coextensive with their human rights or humanitarian law counterparts, and uncritically transplant concepts and jurisprudence from other domains to flesh out their content. Such assumptions overlook the fact that these bodies of law have different purposes and consequences and thus entail different philosophical commitments.
>
> Human rights law and humanitarian law apply to collective entities – states or parties to conflict. They focus on systems, seeking to improve the practices of states (or parties to

---

[674] See generally R. Cryer, D. Robinson and S. Vasiliev, *An Introduction to International Criminal Law and Procedure* (4th edn., 2019).

[675] See G. Schwarzenberger, 'The Problem of an International Criminal Law', 3 *Current Legal Problems* (1950) 263; and M. C. Bassiouni, *International Criminal Law* (3 vols., 3rd edn., 2008).

[676] *Independent Expert Review of the International Criminal Court and the Rome Statute System: Final Report* (30 September 2020).

[677] P. Seils, *Handbook on Complementarity* (International Center for Transitional Justice, 2016).

conflict) in order to advance protection of and respect for identified beneficiaries. The remedies in each area of law are roughly comparable to civil remedies, such as a cessation of the conduct, an apology, an undertaking of non-repetition, and possibly compensation or other efforts to restore the status quo ante.

The primary focus of ICL, on the other hand, is on the culpability of individuals. ... [T]he scope of ICL is much narrower: it addresses only the most serious crimes of concern to the international community as a whole. Moreover, ICL is enforced through a particularly robust method – the arrest, stigmatization, punishment, and imprisonment of individual human beings found responsible for crimes. ...

...

[Two kinds of] substantive and structural conflation [are common]. The crude form is the assumption that, because a prohibition is recognized in human rights or humanitarian law, it therefore must be (or ought to be) criminalized in ICL as well. Such arguments tend to overlook questions of legality and personal culpability and whether criminal law is the appropriate tool to deal with the problem.

The more subtle, and more interesting, variation occurs with respect to those norms that are indisputably recognized as criminalized in ICL, and which are drawn from human rights law or humanitarian law. Where an ICL prohibition is drawn from another area of law, it is understandable to assume that the norms have the same scope as they have in their original domain. Through the resulting unreflective transplantation or mimicry of human rights or humanitarian law norms, norms are absorbed into criminal law without awareness that they may be novel to criminal law and hence without scrutiny as to whether they comply with the fundamental principles peculiar to criminal law.

The existing regime of ICL accords priority to four 'core' crimes: genocide, crimes against humanity, war crimes, and the crime of aggression. These are increasingly referred to as 'atrocity crimes', a label that, as we shall see below, is not without its critics. International law recognizes various other crimes, including piracy, slavery, torture, terrorism and drug trafficking, and new crimes have also been proposed such as 'ecocide'[678] and 'domicide' (the systematic and deliberate mass destruction of homes during violent conflict (UN Doc. A/77/190 (2022)).

In the materials that follow, we first take note of the legacy of the ICTY and ICTR, the work of which significantly influenced today's ICC. We then introduce the ICC and the scope of its jurisdiction, before considering definitions of the core crimes and examining a major recent case.

A. INTERNATIONAL CRIMINAL TRIBUNALS FOR THE FORMER YUGOSLAVIA AND RWANDA

The two ad hoc tribunals were the result of very specific historical circumstances, as Milena Sterio and Michael Scharf explain in their introduction to *The Legacy of Ad Hoc Tribunals in International Criminal Law: Assessing the ICTY's and the ICTR's Most Significant Legal Accomplishments* (2019) 1:

> Prior to its dissolution in 1991–92, Yugoslavia was not so much an ethnic melting pot as a boiling cauldron of ethnic tension with deep historic roots. The ascent of a hardline Serbian nationalist government in Serbia headed by Slobodan Milosevic prompted Croatia and Slovenia to declare their independence on June 25, 1991, with Bosnia following suit on March 1, 1992. The Bosnian Serbs, under the leadership of their self-styled president, Radovan Karadzic, and military leader, Ratko Mladic, immediately

---

[678] Provisionally defined as 'unlawful or wanton acts committed with knowledge that there is a substantial likelihood of severe and either widespread or long-term damage to the environment being caused by those acts': Stop Ecocide Foundation, Independent Expert Panel for the Legal Definition of Ecocide (June 2021), Art. 8 *ter* (1); see also R. Mwanza, 'The Right to a Healthy Environment as a Catalyst for the Codification of the Crime of Ecocide', 117 AJIL *Unbound* (2023) 189; and C. G. Gonzalez, 'Racial Capitalism, Climate Change, and Ecocide', 41 *Wisconsin Int'l L. J.* (2024) 479 ('the move to codify ecocide does not challenge the laws, institutions, or ideologies that reproduce racial capitalism').

launched attacks against the Croatian and Muslim populations in northeast and southern Bosnia, with the goal of connecting Serb-populated regions in north and west Bosnia to Serbia in the east. Within a few months, the Serbs had expelled, killed, or imprisoned 90 percent of the 1.7 million non-Serbs who once lived in Serbian-held areas of Bosnia.

With Russia's assumption of the permanent seat and veto of the Soviet Union in the Security Council in December 1991, the Security Council emerged from the Cold War paralysis of the previous forty years and was experiencing a rare (though short-lived) era of cooperation. The first test for the reinvigorated Council was the deepening crisis in the Balkans. The Security Council adopted a series of measures aimed at restoring peace and halting the bloodshed, including imposing economic sanctions on Serbia, establishing a no-fly zone, creating safe areas, authorizing force to ensure the delivery of humanitarian aid, and excluding Serbia from participating in the General Assembly. Finally, on May 25, 1993, the Security Council adopted Resolution 827, establishing "an international tribunal for the sole purpose of prosecuting persons responsible for serious violations of international humanitarian law committed in the territory of the former Yugoslavia since January 1, 1991." Within two years, the Tribunal had been set up at The Hague, its eleven judges had been elected by the General Assembly, its Chief Prosecutor had been selected by the Security Council, and its first trial was ready to begin.

While the ICTY was preparing its first case, a genocidal conflagration was ignited in the small African nation of Rwanda by the death of its Hutu president when his plane was shot down by a surface-to-air missile on April 6, 1994. Nearly 800,000 people (mostly of the minority Tutsi tribe) were slaughtered during the next hundred days at a rate nearly three times greater than the rate of the loss of Jewish lives during the Holocaust. When the massacres began in Rwanda, the Security Council's first reaction was to withdraw nearly all the United Nations peacekeeping troops from the country for their safety. In July 1994, the Security Council established a Commission of Experts, which issued a report on October 2, 1994, confirming that genocide had been committed by the Hutus against the Tutsis and recommending the establishment of an International Criminal Tribunal to prosecute the perpetrators. A month later, on November 8, 1994, the Security Council adopted Resolution 955, providing for the establishment of a second ad hoc tribunal for Rwanda, which would have its own trial chambers to be headquartered in Arusha, Tanzania, but share the Prosecutor and the Appeals Chamber of the ICTY.

In 2010, the Security Council established the International Residual Mechanism for Criminal Tribunals (IRMCT) to carry out the remaining essential functions of the two ad hoc tribunals. Among its tasks are to locate and arrest the four remaining persons indicted by the ICTR, and assist national jurisdictions in handling requests related to prosecuting international crimes committed in the former Yugoslavia and Rwanda. The Council's resolution (Res. 1966 of 2010) directed that the IRMCT 'should be a small, temporary and efficient structure, whose functions and size will diminish over time, but it is currently scheduled to operate until the end of 2024.

Legacies of the Ad Hoc Tribunals

By the time the ICTY closed in December 2017, it had indicted 161 individuals, resulting in 91 convictions, 18 acquittals, and 13 cases being referred to national courts. Thirty-seven of those indicted either died (including, most notably, Slobodan Milošević, the former Serbian President) or had their indictments withdrawn. Other prominent defendants included Ratko Mladic, head of the Bosnian Serb army which carried out the Srebrenica massacre, sentenced to life imprisonment, and Radovan Karadžić, president of the Republika Srpska (a Serbian enclave in Bosnia) who evaded capture until 2008 and in 2016 was sentenced to 40 years in prison.

On its own legacy website, the ICTY claims to have 'irreversibly changed the landscape of international humanitarian law, provided victims an opportunity to voice the horrors they witnessed and experienced, and proved that those suspected of bearing the greatest responsibility for atrocities committed during armed conflicts can be called to account' (https://www.icty.org/).

The ICTR closed down in December 2015, having indicted 93 individuals, of whom 62 were convicted, 14 were acquitted or released, and two died before judgment. Those convicted included a former Rwandan Prime Minister, former army chief of staff, the former Defence Ministry chief of staff, as well as corporate and media figures.

On its legacy website, the ICTR notes that it was 'at the forefront of the global fight against impunity, prosecuting those considered most responsible for the gravest crimes committed in 1994. ... [I]ts legacy lays the foundation for a new era in international criminal justice'(https://unictr.irmct.org/). Sara Kendall and Sarah Nouwen, in 'Speaking of Legacy: Toward an Ethos of Modesty at the International Criminal Tribunal for Rwanda', 110 *Am. J. Int'l L.* (2016) 212 note, however, that the website 'foregrounds ICTR trials without noting the thousands of domestic criminal trials that took place under Rwanda's 1996 law governing the prosecution of genocide-related crimes or the prosecution of around 400,000 individuals through community-based *gacaca* courts.' It 'also claims that the ICTR has also led to "healing" without mentioning the work of other actors, such as civil society organizations and the Rwandan state. Meanwhile, accounts of decreasing political freedom in Rwanda are conspicuously absent.'

The following readings provide insights into different aspects of the legacy of the two tribunals.

CARSTEN STAHN, THE ICTY IS DEAD! LONG LIVE THE ICTY! STAHN ET AL. (EDS.), LEGACIES OF THE INTERNATIONAL CRIMINAL TRIBUNAL FOR THE FORMER YUGOSLAVIA (2020) 71

Historically, the Tribunal went through different phases. ... [It] was created in what we now view as the 'heroic' age of international justice. Like other criminal institutions, the ICTY had teething problems. Initially, there was a feeling that the Tribunal would not get off the ground. Some feared that a failure of the ICTY 'would also mark the end of any international criminal justice'. Relatively small cases broke the ice. The ICTY used a 'pyramid strategy', through which it sought to gradually build cases against senior leaders through investigation and prosecution of mid- or low-level perpetrators. The Tadić case[679] became the signature case ... although Duško Tadić was overall a relatively minor figure in the Yugoslav conflict. ...

... Tadić's story formed the backbone of some of the most important legal moments in the development of international criminal justice: the famous 1995 Interlocutory Appeal on Jurisdiction, which articulated the modern law on non-international armed conflict, or the legendary 1999 Appeals Judgment which reframed the test for the qualification of international armed conflicts ('overall control') and (re-) invented Joint Criminal Enterprise (JCE) beyond its post-Second World War context. Most importantly, Tadić illustrated like hardly any other case the emancipation of international criminal justice in the United Nations system after 1945. Both ad hoc tribunals asserted their independence from their creator. Criminal adjudication was formally separated from the executive authority.

Then, the Tribunal faced the 'big fish versus small fish' dilemma. It was questionable whether the ICTY had enough power to go after the most responsible leaders. With growing arrests through international forces and political pressure, the tribunal was expected to try high-level defendants. It ran mega trials, like the Slobodan Milošević trial. This practice showed the complexity of cases, but also the risks of extensive charging and the limits of self-representation. The ICTY became a laboratory for procedural adjustment and innovation. It sought to devise a system that is best suited to atrocity crimes. Initially, rules were largely drafted in analogy to domestic systems. But they had to adjust to the context of international criminal proceedings. One of the biggest successes of the procedural law is that it managed to identify certain weaknesses of a purely adversarial culture and to develop certain special rules for effective adjudication of international crimes. In some areas, such as sexual and gender-based violence, they are ahead of domestic systems.

Over time, the tribunal almost became a victim of its success. Its caseload grew. This led to heightened expectations by affected communities, including victim groups. But it also posed capacity constraints. States soon became interested in downsizing. The tribunal solved this partly through the Completion Strategy. It had

---

[679] *Prosecutor v Dusko Tadić* (Appeals Chamber Decision) IT- 94- 1- AR72 (2 October 1995).

some positive spin-offs. It led to a 'rediscovery of complementarity', which has become crucial for other international criminal courts and tribunals as well. ...

...

A ... major innovation of the ICTY is that it adjusted the law to changing patterns of violence, including the role of non- State actors in the commission of crimes. This is reflected, inter alia, in the wide definition of armed conflict, which includes conflicts between armed groups, the reading of the policy element of crimes against humanity, or the extension of torture or command responsibility to civilian structures. The ICTY also adapted to changing means of warfare. It established, *inter alia*, that rape was used as a weapon of war in the municipality of Foča, and that the shelling and sniping of Sarajevo constituted an act of terror against the civilian population.

Through its jurisprudence, the ICTY tried not only to establish individual criminal responsibility but to contribute to the coherence of the international legal order. The Tribunal partly constituted the law that it enacted. In particular, it has taken an active stance on the development of international customary law. It found that *opinio juris* may be more important than practice for the establishment of customary law in the humanitarian field and grounded crimes in custom. The reliance on customary law as a source was also a means to preserve its own legacy, namely to ensure that other courts follow its interpretations.

* * *

The ICTY also had a significant impact *within* Serbia, as documented by Diane Orentlicher in *Some Kind of Justice: The ICTY's Impact in Bosnia and Serbia* (2018) 424:

> The ICTY helped catalyze a serious, if plainly incomplete, process of judicial reckoning in Serbia ... . [T]he [Office of the Prosecutor] bolstered the professionalism and independence of its Serbian partner ... [and] Serbian lawyers' participation in the ICTY's Visiting Young Professionals and Liaison Prosecutors programs ... helped seed a new generation of professionals committed to principles of impartial justice. ...

> The domestic institutions have always operated in a constrained environment, and have come under heightened pressure during the era of "reformed" nationalist leadership. Serbia's government has ... "actively engaged in creating a social environment where the prosecution of those responsible for war crimes, especially those who held medium or high ranks, has become virtually impossible.' To be sure, recent reversals are not unusual. Looking to experience in other post-conflict settings, transitional justice processes are anything but "neat and straightforward" but instead are "complex and messy." Progress is often followed by setbacks, which, in turn, might be followed by further advances.

> ... In time, what began as a modest enterprise can take root, deepen into a habit of accountability, mold public expectations and deepen a society's moral commitments.

An overview of the legacy of the ad hoc tribunals is provided by Michael Scharf and Milena Sterio, in 'Conclusion' in Sterio and Scharf, p. 000 above, at 357:

> ... The tribunals have successfully prosecuted several defendants of genocide and other genocidal offenses; they have prosecuted defendants and developed important case law regarding crimes of sexual violence; they have fine-tuned various modes of liability useful toward the prosecution of various defendants, such as superior responsibility and joint criminal enterprise liability; they have established a legacy of cooperation with national prosecutorial authorities and an operational legacy regarding complex case management; they have developed a procedural legacy regarding international criminal proceedings, through the elaboration of sophisticated rules of procedure and evidence; and they have established a legacy of defense rights, applicable to all defendants, including those accused of the most heinous violations of international criminal law. On the other hand, the ICTY and the ICTR have been far less successful in achieving national reconciliation and goals of societal transformation. This may be an important lesson for future tribunals: while it may be appropriate to ask such future international criminal courts to render justice and

develop international criminal law, it may be futile to demand that such courts accomplish extrajudicial goals of societal change and reconciliation. ...

Second, ... the ICTY and the ICTR have contributed significantly to the development of international criminal law in both the normative as well as the operational sense. ... [They] have established that the same principles of individual liability apply to international as well as to internal armed conflict; in addition, they have successfully convicted defendants of genocidal offenses, and thereby confirmed the importance of imposing genocide liability on particular defendants within particular conflicts. Moreover, the ICTY and the ICTR have developed case law on the prosecution of speech crimes, by imposing additional liability on defendants for inciting the commission of serious crimes within international criminal law. The tribunals have elaborated on various modes of liability, including superior responsibility and advanced modes of joint criminal enterprise, which have enabled the prosecution of nondirect perpetrators of international crimes. The ICTY and the ICTR have also focused on defense rights, by establishing that duress can be a mitigating factor in the imposition of a criminal sentence, and both tribunals have contributed to a sentencing legacy, by establishing a uniform and coherent sentencing approach in the field of international criminal law. In addition, the tribunals have created an operational legacy, by creating specific case management procedures and courtroom management techniques which ensure that international criminal trials proceed in a fair and just manner. ...

While less has been written about the ICTR's legacy, it too is both impressive and less comprehensive than once hoped, as noted by Sara Kendall and Sarah Nouwen, at p. 000 above, 218:

Perhaps the least contested element of the ICTR's legacy is the fact that its case law has made significant contributions to doctrinal international criminal law and has demonstrated that individuals in certain positions can be held to account for grave crimes. The ICTR legacy website claims that the Tribunal is responsible for many inaugural moments in the field: it was "the first" international tribunal to enter a judgment for genocide; to interpret the definition of genocide set out in the 1948 Genocide Convention; to define rape in international criminal law and to recognize it as a means of perpetrating genocide; and, since Nuremberg, to issue a judgment against a former head of state, among other things. ...

The Tribunal has also promoted international criminal law as a professional field. As anthropologist Nigel Eltringham has argued, "there can be no doubt that a significant legacy of the ICTR is . . . the creation of a cadre of lawyers and judges who are equipped to populate international courtrooms in the future." ...

Finally, the ICTR, like the ICTY, has helped make individual criminal accountability a response to mass atrocity. ... The institutionalization of international criminal law has resulted in this particular conception of justice becoming more preeminent than alternative conceptions, such as restorative and distributive justice. The ICTR has thus contributed to the idea of international criminal law being the path towards "justice to all people, everywhere." According to some commentators, the development and preservation of that legacy requires that the application of international criminal law becomes a standard and universal response to mass atrocity.

...

By rendering judgment against seventy defendants, the ICTR has "done" a considerable amount of retributive justice. The Tribunal promoted individual criminal responsibility for genocide, crimes against humanity, and war crimes in Rwanda and beyond, by holding people to account who might have otherwise escaped accountability. From the perspective of promoting the rule of law, the fact that it has prosecuted senior members of the former government, including a prime minister, is particularly significant, as it demonstrates that even those once in the highest positions of power can be held legally accountable for their actions.

Nonetheless, the pro-accountability and anti-impunity message has been weakened by the fact that the ICTR has opened no cases against people with ties to the incumbent government for crimes allegedly committed by the RPF/Army during the 1994 conflict. According to ... Alison Des Forges, at least 25,000 to 30,000 people, including civilians, may have been killed by the RPF. Des Forges argued that these killings were widespread and systematic rather than "unconnected crimes" carried out by individual soldiers, and that RPF commanders must have known about and at least tolerated these abuses. ...

... Key among [the reasons why the ICTR did not move against the RPF] is the Tribunal's extensive dependence upon the Rwandan government for cooperation, ranging from granting permission for its investigators to enter Rwanda to not blocking Rwandans from testifying before the ICTR. Rather than fearing international condemnation or even sanctions for noncooperation, the Rwandan government has managed to maintain financial and political support by leveraging the West's guilt for its failures during the genocide.

While the achievements of the ad hoc tribunals are important, along with their jurisprudential legacy, their perceived excesses and shortcomings also shaped the debates around a future ICC, as traced by Stuart Ford, in 'The Impact of the Ad Hoc Tribunals on the International Criminal Court', in Sterio and Scharf, p. 000 above, at 307:

> While states had expressed a belief at their creation that the ad hoc tribunals would not have the ability to create new international law, the reality was slightly different. The text of the ICTY Statute was, for political reasons, quite vague about the details of the crimes within the jurisdiction of the court. This gave the judges considerable latitude to interpret the text. And interpret it they did. For example, in one of its earliest decisions, the ICTY Appeals Chamber held that the court had jurisdiction over crimes committed in noninternational conflicts, and that there was individual criminal responsibility for violations committed during noninternational conflicts. This was arguably inconsistent with the most straightforward reading of the Statute and contrary to the position taken by many states when these issues were debated during the negotiation of Additional Protocol II to the Geneva Conventions. Moreover, the ICTY Appeals Chamber justified this decision, in part, on the grounds that international law had moved away from a "State-sovereignty-oriented approach," and had moved toward a "human-being-oriented approach." In the same decision, the court went on to adopt a definition of "armed conflict" that was broader than that which states had accepted in the Additional Protocols. The decision "stunned" international lawyers with its breadth. And states were probably not happy to hear judges at the ICTY declare that state sovereignty was no longer at the center of international law.

> While the Rome Statute ended up incorporating most of the changes to the laws of war that were pioneered by the judges at the ICTR and ICTY, states were concerned that the judges had gone too far in expanding the scope of international law. This made states nervous, particularly as many of the accused at international criminal tribunals are agents of a state. Thus, the drafters of the Rome Statute did several things designed to limit the ability of the judges at the ICC to create new international law.

> One thing the drafters did was to define the crimes within the jurisdiction of the ICC in great detail. While the crime of genocide is laid out quite briefly in the Rome Statute, the definition of crimes against humanity has more than twenty sub-parts, and that of war crimes has more than fifty sub-parts. These crimes are then further expanded upon in the Elements of Crimes. Contrast this with the Statute of the ICTY, which is far less detailed. For example, the ICTY Statute simply lists "persecutions on political, racial and religious grounds" as a crime against humanity. The Rome Statute has a much longer and more

detailed definition of persecution. It is then further defined in a separate definitions section. The components of the crime are then also explained in the Elements of Crimes. The difference is even more striking for war crimes. The Statute of the ICTY granted the court jurisdiction over violations of "the laws and customs of war." It then provided a nonexhaustive list of such violations. The Rome Statute takes a completely different approach. It grants the court jurisdiction over war crimes, but it provides the judges with an extremely detailed definition of war crimes. There is no provision in Article 8 of the Rome Statute like the open-ended "including but not limited to" language in Article 3 of the ICTY Statute. The effect is to constrain the ability of judges to expand the scope of international criminal law through their decisions.

Hybrid Courts

Before turning to the ICC, it should be noted that a range of hybrid or partly internationalized criminal courts have been set up. Laura Dickinson, in 'The Promise of Hybrid Courts', 97 *Am. J. Int'l L.* (2003) 295, at 310, argues that such bodies 'may be more likely to be perceived as legitimate by local and international populations because both have representation on the court'. In addition, they increase the capacity of domestic legal institutions, and might facilitate broader adaptation and dissemination of the relevant norms and processes.

The most prominent examples include:

> (i) the Special Court for Sierra Leone,[680] set up following a civil war between 1991 and 2002. Sierra Leone appointed a minority of the judges, with the UN Secretary-General appointing the rest. Between 2002 and 2013, it convicted eight of thirteen persons indicted, including former President Charles Taylor, who was sentenced to 50 years' imprisonment for war crimes and crimes against humanity.

> (ii) the Extraordinary Chambers in the Courts of Cambodia,[681] which conducted investigations and trials between 2006 and 2022. It will continue its operations until 2025, with a promotional mandate, and to consider reparations. The tribunal's purpose was to try leaders of the Khmer Rouge regime, which governed from 1975 to 1979, during which 1.7 million people are estimated to have died by execution, forced labour, or starvation. It was a national court involving local and foreign judges. The former Head of State, Khieu Samphan, was convicted of genocide, crimes against humanity and war crimes,[682] and he and two others ('Duch', the former head of a notorious interrogation centre, and Nuon Chea, former Deputy Secretary of the Communist Party) were sentenced to life imprisonment. The court had originally been expected to try as many as 30 defendants. One achievement was that 165,000 Cambodians attended the first two trials between 2009 and 2015.

> A media report marking the closing of the tribunal summed up its challenges:

>> The tribunal's awkward pairing of two judicial systems, and two often-conflicting views of its purpose, led to delays and sometimes-acrimonious disputes. Besides coming under criticism for its high cost and slow pace, the tribunal was marred by corruption and succumbed to pressure from Prime Minister Hun Sen, himself a former Khmer Rouge cadre, to limit the scope of the prosecutions.[683]

> (iii) the Special Tribunal for Lebanon,[684] which was set up in 2009 to prosecute those responsible for the 2005 killing of Lebanese Prime Minister Rafik Hariri and 21 others. All the judges were appointed by the UN Secretary-General, but the Tribunal applied

---

[680] C. Jalloh, *The Legal Legacy of the Special Court for Sierra Leone* (2020).
[681] J. Bernath, *The Khmer Rouge Tribunal: Power, Politics, and Resistance in Transitional Justice* (2023); and S. Meisenberg and I. Stegmiller (eds.), *The Extraordinary Chambers in the Courts of Cambodia: Assessing their Contribution to International Criminal Law* (2016).
[682] J. Ciorciari, 'Case 002/02 Against Khieu Samphan', 62 *Int'l Leg. Mat.* (2023) 937.
[683] S. Mydans, '6 Years, 3 Convictions: The Khmer Rouge Trials Come to an End', *The New York Times* (22 September 2022).
[684] O. Kavran, 'The Special Tribunal for Lebanon and its Outreach Programme', 20 *J. Int'l Crim. Just.* (2022) 81.

Lebanese law and criminal procedures. Three individuals were tried in absentia and ultimately convicted, after the Appeals Chamber reversed two earlier acquittals. The court held 499 hearings and gathered 174,000 pages of evidence before its mandate ended in December 2023. This assessment of the most significant conviction is instructive:

> … [The Trial] Chamber must settle with a story and a finding that is incomplete and at least a little unconvincing. … At best, the decision might serve as a resource to inform dialogue and discussion within Lebanon about how to apportion responsibility within its fragile political system. At worst, it will further destabilize the Lebanese polity and render any positive reading of [international criminal justice] suspect and unconvincing. …[685]

(iv) the Extraordinary African Chambers of the Courts of Senegal. For details see Ch. 12, above.[686]

(v) the Kosovo Specialist Chambers[687] were set up in 2015 with jurisdiction over crimes against humanity, war crimes and other crimes under Kosovo law, committed in Kosovo between 1998 and 2000 by or against citizens of Kosovo or the Federal Republic of Yugoslavia. This followed a report by the Parliamentary Assembly of the Council of Europe (Doc. 12462 of 7 January 2011) alleging that Serbians and Albanian Kosovars had been imprisoned 'in secret places of detention under [Kosovo Liberation Army] control in northern Albania and were subjected to inhuman and degrading treatment, before ultimately disappearing.' Trafficking in human organs was also alleged. The Chambers were set up under an international agreement with the European Union, ratified by the Kosovo Assembly. They are based in The Hague, composed of international judges and other personnel, and funded by the EU, Canada, Norway, Switzerland, Turkey, and the United States. In April 2023, an especially important case began against the former KLA leader and President of Kosovo, Hashim Thaçi, and three other former senior officials for war crimes and crimes against humanity.

The tribunals in Sierra Leone, Cambodia, and Lebanon were all set up following negotiated agreements with the UN. In the latter case, the Security Council had to pass a resolution to bring the provisions of the agreement into force. The Kosovo tribunal resulted from negotiations with the European Union.

B. THE INTERNATIONAL CRIMINAL COURT[688]

The General Assembly first instructed the International Law Commission to study the possibility of establishing a permanent criminal court in 1948. While extensive work was undertaken, it was not until 1992 that the Assembly requested the Commission to draft a statute, which then became the basis for intensive negotiations at the Rome Conference in 1998. The ICC treaty came into force in 2002 and, as of 2024, 123 countries are states parties to it (33 from Africa, 19 from Asia-Pacific, 18 from Eastern Europe, 28 from Latin America and the Caribbean, and 25 from the group of 'Western European and other' States). Burundi withdrew from the Statute in 2017 and the Philippines in 2019, each after preliminary investigations had been opened in relation to situations in those countries. Non-parties include China, Egypt, India, Indonesia, Iran, Israel, Libya, Pakistan, Russia, Rwanda, Sudan, Syria, the United States and Zimbabwe.

In addition to the Court, the Rome Statute established the Assembly of States Parties, which oversees the management of the Court, elects the judges and the Prosecutor, and approves the budget. There is also a Trust Fund for Victims, which implements reparations ordered by the court and provides physical, psychological, and material support to victims and their families. The court itself consists of four principal organs: the Presidency;

---

[685] M. Burgis-Kasthala, 'Time for Justice? Reflections on Narrative Absences and Presences in the Special Tribunal for Lebanon's *Ayyash* Decision', 33 *Eur. J. Int'l. L.* (2022) 1213, at 1241.

[686] J. P. Perez-Leon-Acevedo, 'The Extraordinary African Chambers in the Senegalese Courts and the Development of International Criminal Law in Africa', in J. Sarkin and E. Siang'andu (eds.), *Africa's Role and Contribution to International Criminal Justice* (2021) 53.

[687] https://www.scp-ks.org/en.

[688] See C. Stahn (ed.), *The International Criminal Court in Its Third Decade: Reflecting on Law and Practices* (2024).

the Judicial Divisions (18 judges are allocated among the Pre-Trial, Trial and Appeals divisions); the Office of the Prosecutor (OTP), which investigates crimes and initiates criminal proceedings; and the Registry, which manages the court's administration, including its headquarters, detention unit, and public defense office. For 2024, the ICC had a budget of €197 million, and employed over 900 personnel from some 100 countries.

By 2024, 31 cases had been brought before the court and 17 investigations were ongoing by the OTP into the following situations: Uganda, the DRC, Darfur (Sudan), Kenya, Libya, Côte d'Ivoire, Central African Republic (I and II), Mali, Georgia, Burundi, Bangladesh/Myanmar, Afghanistan, Palestine, the Philippines, Venezuela I and Ukraine. The situations in Nigeria and Venezuela (II) were being monitored as part of preliminary examinations. Seven persons were in custody and 14 suspects remained at large.

The ICC held its first hearing in 2006, concerning war crimes charges against Thomas Lubanga Dyilo, a Congolese warlord accused of recruiting child soldiers; his subsequent conviction in 2012 was the first in the court's history. The OTP has opened twelve official investigations and is conducting an additional nine preliminary examinations. A total of 46 individuals have been indicted. High-ranking individuals have included Ugandan rebel leader Joseph Kony, former President Omar al-Bashir of Sudan, President Uhuru Kenyatta of Kenya, Libyan head of state Muammar Gaddafi, President Laurent Gbagbo of Ivory Coast and former Vice President Jean-Pierre Bemba of the Democratic Republic of the Congo, although of these only the last was so far convicted.

1. The ICC Statute: Jurisdiction

The extent of the court's jurisdiction was at the core of debates at the Rome Conference. Issues included the respective roles to be played by the Prosecutor, states parties and the Security Council in relation to investigations and prosecutions, the circumstances under which non-parties could consent to jurisdiction, the powers of the Security Council to make referrals and to pause cases, and the limits to be placed upon the independence of the Prosecutor.

The agreed starting points were that the court's jurisdiction was 'limited to the most serious crimes of concern to the international community as a whole' (Article 5), namely the four core crimes, and that the complementarity principle would prioritize effective action at the national level over international involvement.[689] In temporal terms, the ICC has jurisdiction only over crimes committed after 1 July 2002 and, in relation to a given state, only after the Statute enters into force for it.

The jurisdictional arrangements are of critical importance because of the legal and political compromises struck, and of how carefully they were negotiated. There is no substitute for studying the key provisions, and they are reproduced below. As reflected in Articles 12-14, the court has jurisdiction in situations where the accused is the national of a state party, or of a state that consents to the court's jurisdiction, or where the conduct occurred on a state party's territory, or that of a consenting state. In situations in which neither the state where the crime occurred nor the accused's state of nationality is a party to the Statute, the only option is for the Security Council to refer the case under Chapter VII of the UN Charter.

Among the most contentious issues at the Rome Conference were those relating to the jurisdiction of the court:

<u>Article 12</u>
<u>Preconditions to the exercise of jurisdiction</u>

1. A State which becomes a Party to this Statute thereby accepts the jurisdiction of the Court with respect to [genocide, crimes against humanity, and war crimes].

2. In the case of article 13, paragraph (a) or (c), the Court may exercise its jurisdiction if one or more of the following States are Parties to this Statute or have accepted the jurisdiction of the Court in accordance with paragraph 3:

---

[689] P. Labuda, *International Criminal Tribunals and Domestic Accountability* (2023).

(a) The State on the territory of which the conduct in question occurred or, if the crime was committed on board a vessel or aircraft, the State of registration of that vessel or aircraft;

(b) The State of which the person accused of the crime is a national.

3. If the acceptance of a State which is not a Party to this Statute is required under paragraph 2, that State may, by declaration lodged with the Registrar, accept the exercise of jurisdiction by the Court with respect to the crime in question. ...

Article 13
Exercise of jurisdiction

The Court may exercise its jurisdiction with respect to a crime referred to in article 5 in accordance with the provisions of this Statute if:

(a) A situation in which one or more of such crimes appears to have been committed is referred to the Prosecutor by a State Party in accordance with article 14;

(b) A situation in which one or more of such crimes appears to have been committed is referred to the Prosecutor by the Security Council acting under Chapter VII of the Charter of the United Nations; or

(c) The Prosecutor has initiated an investigation in respect of such a crime in accordance with article 15.

Article 14
Referral of a situation by a State Party

1. A State Party may refer to the Prosecutor a situation in which one or more crimes within the jurisdiction of the Court appear to have been committed requesting the Prosecutor to investigate the situation for the purpose of determining whether one or more specific persons should be charged with the commission of such crimes. ...

Article 15
Prosecutor

1. The Prosecutor may initiate investigations proprio motu on the basis of information on crimes within the jurisdiction of the Court.
...
3. If the Prosecutor concludes that there is a reasonable basis to proceed with an investigation, he or she shall submit to the Pre-Trial Chamber a request for authorization of an investigation, together with any supporting material collected. Victims may make representations to the Pre-Trial Chamber ... .

4. If the Pre-Trial Chamber ... considers that there is a reasonable basis to proceed with an investigation, and that the case appears to fall within the jurisdiction of the Court, it shall authorize the commencement of the investigation ... .
...

Article 16
Deferral of investigation or prosecution

No investigation or prosecution may be commenced or proceeded with under this Statute for a period of 12 months after the Security Council, in a resolution adopted under Chapter VII of the Charter of the United Nations, has requested the Court to that effect; that request may be renewed by the Council under the same conditions.
...

Article 17
Issues of admissibility

1. … [T]he Court shall determine that a case is inadmissible where:

(a) The case is being investigated or prosecuted by a State which has jurisdiction over it, unless the State is unwilling or unable genuinely to carry out the investigation or prosecution;

(b) The case has been investigated by a State which has jurisdiction over it and the State has decided not to prosecute the person concerned, unless the decision resulted from the unwillingness or inability of the State genuinely to prosecute;

(c) The person concerned has already been tried for conduct which is the subject of the complaint, …;

(d) The case is not of sufficient gravity to justify further action by the Court.
…

Article 53
Initiation of an investigation

1. The Prosecutor shall, having evaluated the information made available to him or her, initiate an investigation unless he or she determines that there is no reasonable basis to proceed under this Statute. In deciding whether to initiate an investigation, the Prosecutor shall consider whether:

> (a) The information available to the Prosecutor provides a reasonable basis to believe that a crime within the jurisdiction of the Court has been or is being committed;

> (b) The case is or would be admissible under article 17; and

> (c) Taking into account the gravity of the crime and the interests of victims, there are nonetheless substantial reasons to believe that an investigation would not serve the interests of justice.

Security Council Referral

Until 2024, the Security Council had used its authority under Article 13(b) to refer a situation to the ICC only in relation to Sudan in 2005 and Libya in 2011. But various other such cases have been mooted and the role of the Council has generated considerable controversy. Three of the Council's permanent five members are not parties to the Rome Statute (China, Russia and the United States), and both referrals have related to African states, while atrocity situations elsewhere have not obtained the necessary consensus. The referrals have also been problematic because they impose an additional financial burden on the Court which must be borne only by states parties, and because nationals of Security Council members who are not state parties have been exempted from the ICC's jurisdiction.

In the view of Tom Dannenbaum, in 'Legitimacy in War and Punishment: The Security Council and the ICC', in Kevin Heller et al. (eds.), *The Oxford Handbook of International Criminal Law* (2020) 129, at 151, such referrals present a major legitimacy challenge to the Court:

> … Unless permanent members discard the veto altogether in this context, an uptick in Security Council referrals to the ICC would likely exacerbate, rather than remedy the divide between legality and legitimacy. Short of Rome Statute ratification by the current non-party permanent members, two options for strengthening the Court's legitimacy in this respect stand out. First, the Court could move to a universal jurisdiction model, as proposed during Rome Statute drafting. …Realistically, however, such a reform is unlikely to gain political traction. …

The alternative route to a more legitimate ICC would be for the Court to revert to a nationality and territorial jurisdiction model. Short of an unlikely statutory amendment eliminating the Security Council referral trigger, this could be achieved in two ways. First, in direct contrast to the path to legitimacy in responding to atrocity with appropriate force, the Council could step back from referring atrocity situations to the Court. Second, and more radically, the prosecutor could use her discretion to refrain from opening investigations or pursuing charges in Council-referred situations on the grounds that pursuing those avenues would not be in the 'interests of justice'. …

2. The Definition of Crimes

While the definition of genocide is taken directly from the 1948 Convention on the Prevention and Punishment of the Crime of Genocide, the definitions of crimes against humanity and war crimes were, as Stuart Ford noted at p. 000 above, intensively debated at the Rome Conference. One proposal pushed from the outset by the United States was for the Conference to adopt a statement of the 'elements of the crime', which would clarify and elaborate upon the elements that would need to be proven in relation to each of the offences specified in Articles 6-8. Most delegations were reluctant to impose a checklist on the court but, in order to obtain a consensus, agreed that such a document could be adopted if it were non-binding. The elements were developed after the conference by the Preparatory Commission and adopted by the Assembly of States Parties by a two-thirds majority. Article 9 indicates that their role is to 'assist' the court in interpreting the relevant crimes. They are thus a primary source of law for the Court, but subject to its interpretation of the specific provisions of the Statute itself.[690]

The ICTY had a major impact on the understanding of the term genocide. Carsten Stahn, 'ICTY and the New Law on Genocide', in Steven van Hoogstraten (ed.) *New Challenges to International Law: A View from The Hague* (2018) 126, at 130, notes that:

> … [Its] main innovation lies in the fact that it adjusted the interpretation of genocide to different contexts, in particular killings and destruction carried out against parts of groups in limited geographic areas, such as enclaves and towns. It accepted that genocide is not a game of numbers. It ruled that destruction of a part of a group is sufficient if that part is 'emblematic' of the overall group. …

> In its first genocide conviction in relating to events in Srebrenica, namely the Krstić case, the ICTY accepted the argument that genocide may occur even when the exterminatory intent extends only to a limited geographic zone— something that has been called 'localized genocide'. The ICJ has shown a rather wide degree of deference to ICTY case law in its genocide cases. …

> The message in relation to genocidal intent in relation to attacks in other municipalities has remained more ambiguous. The Prosecution sought to establish that genocide took place in all of Bosnia and Herzegovina. However, Karadžić and Mladić were acquitted for counts of genocide relating to other Bosnian municipalities, based on different reasons, such as the failure to establish specific genocidal intent or to destroy a substantial part of the group. This may fuel a perception that genocide only occurred in Srebrenica. The overall record contains certain gaps and loopholes. …

While treaties exist defining genocide and war crimes, there is no equivalent for crimes against humanity. In 2019, after five years of work by Sean Murphy, its Rapporteur on the subject, the International Law Commission sent a set of draft articles on prevention and punishment of crimes against humanity to the UN General Assembly for its consideration (UN Doc. A/74/10 (2019), 11). Russia's invasion of Ukraine in 2022 led to the breaking of a deadlock in the Assembly's Sixth Committee, and a resolution seeking to consider a final draft in

---

[690] See W. Schabas, *The International Criminal Court: A Commentary on the Rome Statute* (2nd ed., 2016) 322; and K. Dörmann, *Elements of War Crimes under the Rome Statute of the International Criminal Court: Sources and Commentary* (2003).

2024 (Res. 77/249 (2022)). Successful adoption of a treaty would provide greater clarity on the relevant crimes, oblige states parties to incorporate the definition and prohibition of the relevant offences into their national law, and provide additional protections for civilian populations.

Articles 6-8 of the Rome Statute, spelling out the definitions of genocide, crimes against humanity, and war crimes, follow.

<u>Article 6</u>
<u>Genocide</u>

For the purpose of this Statute, "genocide" means any of the following acts committed with intent to destroy, in whole or in part, a national, ethnical, racial or religious group, as such:

(a) Killing members of the group;

(b) Causing serious bodily or mental harm to members of the group;

(c) Deliberately inflicting on the group conditions of life calculated to bring about its physical destruction in whole or in part;

(d) Imposing measures intended to prevent births within the group;

(e) Forcibly transferring children of the group to another group.

<u>Article 7</u>
<u>Crimes against humanity</u>

1. For the purpose of this Statute, "crime against humanity" means any of the following acts when committed as part of a widespread or systematic attack directed against any civilian population, with knowledge of the attack:

(a) Murder;

(b) Extermination;

(c) Enslavement;

(d) Deportation or forcible transfer of population;

(e) Imprisonment or other severe deprivation of physical liberty in violation of fundamental rules of international law;

(f) Torture;

(g) Rape, sexual slavery, enforced prostitution, forced pregnancy, enforced sterilization, or any other form of sexual violence of comparable gravity;

(h) Persecution against any identifiable group or collectivity on political, racial, national, ethnic, cultural, religious, gender as defined in paragraph 3, or other grounds that are universally recognized as impermissible under international law, in connection with any act referred to in this paragraph or any crime within the jurisdiction of the Court;

(i) Enforced disappearance of persons;

(j) The crime of apartheid;

(k) Other inhumane acts of a similar character intentionally causing great suffering, or serious injury to body or to mental or physical health.

. . .

Article 8
War crimes

1. The Court shall have jurisdiction in respect of war crimes in particular when committed as part of a plan or policy or as part of a large-scale commission of such crimes.

2. For the purpose of this Statute, "war crimes" means:

(a) Grave breaches of the Geneva Conventions of 12 August 1949, namely, any of the following acts against persons or property protected under the provisions of the relevant Geneva Convention:

(i) Wilful killing;

(ii) Torture or inhuman treatment, including biological experiments;

(iii) Wilfully causing great suffering, or serious injury to body or health;

(iv) Extensive destruction and appropriation of property, not justified by military necessity and carried out unlawfully and wantonly;

(v) Compelling a prisoner of war or other protected person to serve in the forces of a hostile Power;

(vi) Wilfully depriving a prisoner of war or other protected person of the rights of fair and regular trial;

(vii) Unlawful deportation or transfer or unlawful confinement;

(viii) Taking of hostages.

(b) Other serious violations of the laws and customs applicable in international armed conflict, within the established framework of international law, namely, any of the following acts:

(i) Intentionally directing attacks against the civilian population as such or against individual civilians not taking direct part in hostilities;

(ii) Intentionally directing attacks against civilian objects, that is, objects which are not military objectives;

(iii) Intentionally directing attacks against personnel, installations, material, units or vehicles involved in a humanitarian assistance or peacekeeping mission in accordance with the Charter of the United Nations, as long as they are entitled to the protection given to civilians or civilian objects under the international law of armed conflict;

(iv) Intentionally launching an attack in the knowledge that such attack will cause incidental loss of life or injury to civilians or damage to civilian objects or widespread, long-term and severe damage to the natural environment which would be clearly excessive in relation to the concrete and direct overall military advantage anticipated;

(v) Attacking or bombarding, by whatever means, towns, villages, dwellings or buildings which are undefended and which are not military objectives;

(vi) Killing or wounding a combatant who, having laid down his arms or having no longer means of defence, has surrendered at discretion;

...

(c) In the case of an armed conflict not of an international character, serious violations of article 3 common to the four Geneva Conventions of 12 August 1949, namely, any of the following acts committed against persons taking no active part in the hostilities, including members of armed forces who have laid down their arms and those placed <u>hors de combat</u> by sickness, wounds, detention or any other cause:

> (i) Violence to life and person, in particular murder of all kinds, mutilation, cruel treatment and torture;

> (ii) Committing outrages upon personal dignity, in particular humiliating and degrading treatment;

> (iii) Taking of hostages;

> (iv) The passing of sentences and the carrying out of executions without previous judgement pronounced by a regularly constituted court, affording all judicial guarantees which are generally recognized as indispensable.

(d) Paragraph 2 (c) applies to armed conflicts not of an international character and thus does not apply to situations of internal disturbances and tensions, such as riots, isolated and sporadic acts of violence or other acts of a similar nature.

(e) Other serious violations of the laws and customs applicable in armed conflicts not of an international character, within the established framework of international law, namely, any of the following acts:

> (i) Intentionally directing attacks against the civilian population as such or against individual civilians not taking direct part in hostilities;

> (ii) Intentionally directing attacks against buildings, material, medical units and transport, and personnel using the distinctive emblems of the Geneva Conventions in conformity with international law;

...

3. The *Ongwen* Case

In order to bring these provisions alive, the following materials focus on the ICC case of Dominic Ongwen, which began with a warrant issued in 2005 and ended with the completion of the appeals phase in December 2022. The case is significant for many reasons. It was the first case to be self-referred to the court by a state party, it involved the largest number of charges brought and the most modes of liability invoked against a single defendant, it was the first time a defendant pleaded defenses such as mental disease and duress, and it led to convictions for previously untried crimes.

Ongwen was a high-level member of the Lord's Resistance Army (LRA), established by Joseph Kony in the 1980s to further an armed rebellion against the Ugandan government. The LRA also targeted civilians in Northern Uganda whom they considered to be pro-government, especially those living in government-established camps for Internally Displaced Persons (IDP camps). The camps were part of an anti-insurgency strategy to remove people from rural areas where they might assist the rebels. Ongwen himself was abducted by the LRA in 1987 at around nine years of age and experienced brutality and suffering. He eventually rose to become a battalion commander of the LRA's Sinia Brigade.

Uganda became a party to the Rome Statute on 14 June 2002, and referred the situation in northern Uganda to the Court on 16 December 2003. On 29 July 2004, the Prosecutor launched an investigation and, on 8 July 2005, the Trial Chamber issued sealed warrants for five LRA leaders, including Joseph Kony and Dominic Ongwen. Starting in 2010, United States Special Forces and others made extensive but unsuccessful efforts to capture them. Ongwen voluntarily surrendered to forces in the Central African Republic, and was transferred to ICC custody on 20 January 2015. His case was separated from that of the other leaders, and the trial ran from December 2016 to November 2019. A total of 116 witnesses testified for the prosecution and 63 for the defence. Over 4,000 victims were represented by two separate legal teams, which made submissions, presented evidence, and called seven witnesses.[691]

Ongwen was charged with 70 counts of war crimes and crimes against humanity that took place between 1 July 2002 and 31 December 2005. On 4 February 2021, the Trial Chamber convicted him of 61 crimes. He was found responsible as: (i) an indirect perpetrator of crimes including attacks against the civilian population, murder, torture, enslavement, pillaging, destruction of property and persecution, committed in the context of attacks against two IDP camps (in Lukodi and Abok) in May-June 2004; (ii) an indirect co-perpetrator of similar crimes committed in attacks on two other IDP camps (Pajule and Odek) in 2003-2004; (iii) an indirect co-perpetrator of sexual and gender-based crimes (SGBC), including forced marriage as a form of other inhumane acts, torture, rape, sexual slavery, and enslavement, and the crime of conscription of children under the age of 15 years and their use in armed hostilities; and (iv) as a direct perpetrator of a number of other SGBC, including forced marriage as a form of other inhumane acts, torture, rape, sexual slavery, enslavement, forced pregnancy, and outrages upon personal dignity.

In appealing the convictions, the defence raised 90 separate grounds, alleging legal, factual and procedural errors. In particular, the defence alleged that Ongwen's fair trial rights had been violated, including in relation to the notice and scope of the charges brought against him. It challenged the modes of liability and criminal responsibility under which he was convicted as an indirect perpetrator and co-perpetrator, the Trial Chamber's failure to have adequate regard to his defences of mental disease and duress, the Chamber's interpretation and factual findings concerning SGBC, and the appropriateness of imposing cumulative convictions. All the convictions were upheld in the judgment of the Appeals Chamber on 15 December 2022. The sentence of 25 years' imprisonment was also upheld. The Trial Chamber's judgment was 1,077 pages long, and the judgment of the Appeals Chamber totalled 811 pages, giving some sense of the magnitude and complexity of the case.

The following materials explore selected aspects of the case, starting with the Court's overview of the charges relating to crimes against humanity, and in particular SGBC. These materials should be read against the background of significant criticism of the ways in which the ad hoc tribunals had dealt with such issues. This includes, in particular, their approach to gender-related crimes. Indira Rosenthal, Valerie Oosterveld, and Susana SáCouto, in 'Introduction', in *ibid. (eds.), Gender and International Criminal Law* (2022) 1, note that:

> Despite nearly thirty years of unprecedented attention on the commission of sexual violence and other gender-based crimes under international law, these crimes, their causes, and their consequences remain poorly understood. The result has been a series of investigative, prosecutorial, and judicial decisions in international criminal courts and tribunals that reveal deeply held misconceptions about the role of gender in the commission, experience, investigation, prosecution, and punishment of crimes under international law. … [T]hese mistaken beliefs … remain pervasive among ICL practitioners— investigators, prosecutors, defence counsel, and judges— as well as in the media.

In a subsequent chapter in the same book, Kirsten Campbell and Gorana Mlinarević, in 'A Feminist Critique of Approaches to International Criminal Justice in the Age of Identity Politics', at 75, observe that the ICTY charged 78 persons with sexual violence, of whom 32 were convicted. They acknowledge that the ICTY and the ICTR 'shifted conflict-related sexual violence from being an "invisible crime" to being seen as prosecutable as an international crime as such.' However, they also criticize its approach:

> The ICTY Statute only provided for individual criminal responsibility … in contrast to the approach taken at … Nuremberg … which treated the SS, Gestapo, and other groups as criminal organizations, as well as providing for individual criminal responsibility. …

---

[691] See generally: Special issue on the *Ongwen* Case, 23 *Int'l Crim. L. Rev.* 667 (2023).

Because of this ... the ICTY confronted a crucial problem concerning its prosecutions of mass atrocities. On the one hand, it focused on the individual, to the exclusion of the systems, structures, and collectivities that enabled mass atrocities to occur. On the other hand, it needed to account for the collective nature of these crimes.

... [T]he ICTY addressed what it called 'collective criminality' through the doctrine of joint criminal enterprise (JCE) ... [requiring]: (1) a plurality of persons; (2) the existence of common plan, design, or purpose; and (3) participation of the accused in the common design of the crimes under the Statute. ... JCE is conceptualized as a form of individual liability for participation in group criminality.

...

Without addressing system criminality, it was neither possible to adequately address the patriarchal nature of the conflict, criminality, and victimization, nor to properly prosecute gender-based crimes. ... [T]he individualized conceptualization of criminal responsibility hides the gender 'dimension' of crimes by obscuring (1) the gendered patterns and effects of CRSV [conflict-related sexual violence] and (2) the gendered structures that create these crimes. ...

...

Taking a broader perspective ... shows how gender shapes patterns of victimization and perpetration, both in terms of who become victims and perpetrators and what crimes are committed. It also shows that these patterns of victimization and perpetration are connected to the wider gendered power relations of war, in that it reveals that the majority of perpetrators of CRSV were men participating in patriarchal masculinized (valued) military, police, and political groups, and the majority of the victims were women who were unarmed, feminized (devalued) civilians. Understood as such, patterns of sexual violence are an important aspect of understanding how CRSV is a gender-based crime, and how those crimes are connected to gender power relations.

THE PROSECUTOR V. DOMINIC ONGWEN
TRIAL JUDGMENT, NO. ICC-02/04-01/15 (4 FEBRUARY 2021)

...

IV. ASSESSMENT OF EVIDENCE
...
D. Grounds excluding criminal responsibility
...
2. Duress
i. Introduction

2581. Duress in Article 31(1)(d) of the Statute has three elements. The first element is that the conduct alleged to constitute the crime has been caused by duress resulting from a threat of imminent death or of continuing or imminent serious bodily harm against that person or another person. The threat in question may either be: (i) made by other persons or (ii) constituted by other circumstances beyond that person's control. The threat is to be assessed at the time of that person's conduct.

2582. From the plain language of the provision, the words 'imminent' and 'continuing' refer to the nature of the threatened harm, and not the threat itself. It is not an 'imminent threat' of death or a 'continuing or imminent threat' of serious bodily harm – the Statute does not contain such terms. Rather, the threatened harm in question must be either to be killed immediately ('imminent death'), or to suffer serious bodily harm immediately or in an ongoing manner ('continuing or imminent serious bodily harm'). On this understanding, duress is unavailable if the accused is threatened with serious bodily harm that is not going to materialise sufficiently soon. A merely abstract danger or simply an elevated probability that a dangerous situation might occur – even if continuously present – does not suffice.

2583. The second element … is that the person acts necessarily and reasonably to avoid the threat. The person is not required to take all conceivable action to avoid the threat, irrespective of considerations of proportionality or feasibility. The Chamber must specifically consider what, if any, acts could 'necessarily and reasonably' avoid the threat, and what the person should have done must be assessed under the totality of the circumstances in which the person found themselves. Whether others in comparable circumstances were able to necessarily and reasonably avoid the same threat is relevant in assessing what acts were necessarily and reasonably available.

2584. Finally, the third element … is that the person does not intend to cause a greater harm than the one sought to be avoided. This is a subjective element – it is not required that the person actually avoided the greater harm, only that he/she intended to do so. The Chamber considers that assessment of whether one intended harm is 'greater' than another depends on the character of the harms under comparison.
…

viii. Conclusion

2668. … [T]here is no basis in the evidence to hold that Dominic Ongwen was subjected to a threat of imminent death or imminent or continuing serious bodily harm to himself or another person at the time of his conduct underlying the charged crimes. … [He] was not in a situation of complete subordination vis-à-vis Joseph Kony, but frequently acted independently and even contested orders received from Joseph Kony. … [I]n the period of the charges [he] did not face any prospective punishment by death or serious bodily harm when he disobeyed Joseph Kony. Dominic Ongwen also had a realistic possibility of leaving the LRA, which he did not pursue. Rather, he rose in rank and position, including during the period of the charges. Finally, he committed some of the charged crimes in private, in circumstances where any threats otherwise made to him could have no effect.
…

2672. … [T]he Defence also made some legally unspecified submissions emphasising that Dominic Ongwen was himself a victim of crimes, on account of his abduction at a young age by the LRA. The Chamber … notes that [he] committed the relevant crimes when he was an adult and, importantly, that, in any case, the fact of having been (or being) a victim of a crime does not constitute, in and of itself, a justification of any sort for the commission of similar or other crimes – beyond the potential relevance of the underlying facts to the grounds excluding criminal responsibility expressly regulated under the Statute. The separate and more specific Defence assertion that 'Article 21(3)[692] prohibits charging a victim of a crime with the same crime' is equally without merit: a rule that would immunize persons who suffer human rights violations from responsibility for all similar human rights violations that they may themselves commit thereafter manifestly does not exist in international human rights law.
…

V. LEGAL FINDINGS
A. Applicable law
…
i. Contextual elements
a. Crimes against humanity

[The Chamber recalls the provisions of Article 7(1) of the Statute.]

i Attack against any civilian population

2674. An 'attack' in this context means a 'course of conduct involving the multiple commission of acts referred to in [Article 7(1)]'. The requirement that the acts form part of a 'course of conduct' indicates that Article 7 is meant to cover a series or overall flow of events, as opposed to a mere aggregate of random or isolated acts.

---

[692] Article 21(3): 'The application and interpretation of law pursuant to this article must be consistent with internationally recognized human rights, and be without any adverse distinction founded on grounds such as gender … age, race, colour, language, religion or belief, political or other opinion, national, ethnic or social origin, wealth, birth or other status.'

The 'multiple commission of acts' sets a quantitative threshold involving a certain number of acts falling within the course of conduct.

2675. The course of conduct must be 'directed against any civilian population', namely a collective, as opposed to individual civilians. The civilian population must be the primary target of the attack and not an incidental victim of it. The presence within a civilian population of individuals who do not fall under the definition of 'civilians' does not deprive the population of its civilian character. ...

ii Organisational policy

2676. The 'course of conduct involving the multiple commission of acts' must take place 'pursuant to or in furtherance of a State or organizational policy to commit such attack' ... . The Elements of Crimes specify that the '"policy to commit such attack" requires that the [...] organization actively promote[s] or encourage[s] such an attack against a civilian population'. For the purposes of this judgment, only the 'organisational policy' prong is relevant.

2677. As regards the 'organisation' pursuing the policy, the Chamber adheres to the definition established by Trial Chamber II:

> In the Chamber's view, the connection of the term "organisation" to the very existence of the attack and not to its systematic or widespread nature presupposes that the organisation has sufficient resources, means and capacity to bring about the course of conduct or the operation involving the multiple commission of acts referred to in article 7(2)(a) of the Statute. It therefore suffices that the organisation [has] a set of structures or mechanisms, whatever those may be, that are sufficiently efficient to ensure the coordination necessary to carry out an attack directed against a civilian population.

2678. As the terms 'pursuant to or in furtherance of' imply, the policy requirement ensures that the multiple acts forming the course of conduct are linked. It ensures that acts which are unrelated or perpetrated by individuals acting randomly on their own are excluded.

2679. A policy may consist of a pre-established design or plan, but it may also crystallise and develop only as actions are undertaken by the perpetrators. The 'policy' may be inferred from a variety of factors, such as: (i) a recurrent pattern of violence; (ii) the existence of preparations or collective mobilisation orchestrated and coordinated by the organisation; (iii) the use of public or private resources to further the policy; (iv) the involvement of organisational forces in the commission of crimes; (v) statements, instructions or documentation attributable to the organisation condoning or encouraging the commission of crimes; and (vi) an underlying motivation. In principle, a state or organisation committing a systematic attack against a civilian population will satisfy the policy requirement.

iii Widespread or systematic attack

2680. The alternative qualifiers of 'widespread' or 'systematic' serve to characterise the 'attack' itself.

2681. The term 'widespread' connotes the large-scale nature of the attack and the number of targeted persons. The assessment of whether the attack is widespread is neither exclusively quantitative nor geographical, but must be carried out on the basis of all the relevant facts of the case.

2682. The term 'systematic' reflects the organised nature of the violent acts, referring often to the existence of 'patterns of crimes' and the improbability of their random or accidental occurrence.

b. War crimes – armed conflict not of an international character

2683. The war crimes charged in this case exclusively concern a non-international armed conflict. An armed conflict not of an international character exists when there is protracted armed violence between governmental authorities and organised armed groups or between such groups within a State. Such a conflict exceeds situations of internal disturbances and tensions, such as riots, isolated and sporadic acts of violence or other acts of similar nature.

2684. When evaluating the intensity of the conflict to determine its 'protracted' character, chambers consider factors such as: (i) the seriousness and frequency of attacks and armed clashes; (ii) the spread of clashes over territory and the group's ability to control territory over a period of time; (iii) whether any ceasefire orders had been issued or agreed to; (iv) the type and number of armed forces deployed, including any involvement of the government; (v) the type of weapons used; (vi) whether the situation had attracted the attention of the UN Security Council, or involvement of other international organisations; (vii) whether those fighting considered themselves bound by international humanitarian law and (viii) the effects of the violence on the civilian population, including the extent to which civilians left the relevant area, the extent of destruction, and the number of persons killed. Exercise of control over a part of the territory is not required, though the importance of this factor increases in the absence of active hostilities. It is also not required that the violence be continuous and uninterrupted – the Chamber need only find that the violence goes beyond isolated or sporadic acts.

2685. When evaluating whether an entity qualifies as an 'organised armed group', chambers consider factors such as: (i) the existence of a command structure, the existence of headquarters, the issuing of political statements, and the use of official spokespersons; (ii) the military (operational) capacity of the armed group, which may be shown by, for example, the ability to define a unified military strategy, the use of military tactics, the ability to carry out (large scale or coordinated) operations, the control of territory, and having a territorial division into zones of responsibility; (iii) the logistical capacity of the armed group, indicated, among others, by the existence of a supply chain for military equipment, as well as by the group's ability to move troops around and to recruit and train personnel; (iv) the existence of an internal disciplinary system and the ability to implement international humanitarian law; and (v) the group's ability to speak with one voice, indicated, for example, by the capacity of the leadership to act on behalf of its members in political negotiations and to conclude agreements, such as cease-fire or peace agreements.

2686. A situation that starts out as a non-international armed conflict may become international, if another State intervenes in the conflict directly (through its troops) or indirectly (when some of the groups involved act on behalf of that other State). ...

2687. To assess whether an international armed conflict exists as a result of such indirect participation of a State, the Chamber must appraise the degree of control exerted by that State over the armed group in question. In doing so, the Chamber will rely on the 'overall control' test, whereby it must be established that the State had 'a role in organising, coordinating or planning the military actions of the military group, in addition to financing, training and equipping or providing operational support to that group'. An international armed conflict therefore exists if a degree of control is exercised by the intervening third State over a non-State actor fighting in opposition to, or without the consent of, the government, that goes beyond the mere financing and equipping of the armed group. It does not require, however, that such control extends to the issuance of specific orders or instructions relating to single military actions.

c. Nexus requirement and perpetrators' awareness
...
2689. The war crimes charged in the present case require, as their contextual elements, that the relevant took [sic] place in the context of and was associated with an armed conflict not of an international character. The perpetrator's conduct need not take place as part of hostilities, meaning that the nexus requirement could still be satisfied for crimes temporally or geographically remote from the actual fighting. ...
...

ii. The crimes

2694. In the following, the Chamber will set forth the relevant applicable law of the individual crimes with which Dominic Ongwen is charged. The crimes are embedded in the context that gives them their international character and differentiates them from ordinary crimes.

2695. Unless otherwise provided in the Statute, the material elements of the crimes must have been committed with 'intent' and 'knowledge' within the meaning of Article 30 of the Statute. ...

a. Murder and attempted murder (Article 7(1)(a) and Article 8(2)(c)(i))

2696. The crime of murder is committed in case a person is killed as a result of the perpetrator's act or omission. In the case of attempted murder, substantial steps have been taken to execute the crime but it does not occur because of circumstances independent of the perpetrator's intentions.

2697. For the purpose of murder as a war crime, Article 8(2)(c) of the Statute prescribes that the crime must be committed 'against persons taking no active part in the hostilities, including members of armed forces who have laid down their arms and those placed hors de combat by sickness, wounds, detention or any other cause'. Taking an active part in the hostilities is understood as acts of war that by their nature or purpose strike at the personnel and matériel of enemy armed forces. It is not considered taking an active part in the hostilities when persons otherwise protected under international humanitarian law exercise their right to individual self-defence.

2698. Lastly, while the Prosecutor must demonstrate, to the extent possible, the location, date and means of killing, she is not required to demonstrate for each killing the identity of the victim or that the corpse of the deceased has been found.
...

b. Torture (Article 7(1)(f) and Article 8(2)(c)(i))

2700. The crime of torture, whether as a crime against humanity or war crime, is committed either by act or omission and has a common material element that '[t]he perpetrator inflicted severe physical or mental pain or suffering upon one or more persons'.

2701. The severity implies an important degree of pain and suffering and may be met by a single act or by a combination of acts when viewed as a whole. This can be assessed only on a case-by-case basis in the light of all the circumstances of the case. It is not necessary to prove that the pain or suffering involved specific physical injury (such as organ failure), impairment of a bodily function or death. The pain and suffering may be either physical or mental. The consequences of torture do not have to be visible, nor must the injury be permanent.

2702. There are some notable differences between the elements of torture as a crime against humanity versus a war crime.

2703. For torture as a crime against humanity, Article 7(2)(e) of the Statute further requires that '[s]uch person or persons were in the custody or under the control of the perpetrator'. Torture as a crime against humanity also requires that the pain or suffering did not arise only from, and was not inherent or incidental to, lawful sanctions.

2704. In contrast, for torture as a war crime, the custody/control element is not required. Instead, for the war crime of torture there is an additional mental element specified below. The war crime must also be committed against persons taking no active part in the hostilities, including members of armed forces who have laid down their arms and those placed *hors de combat*.

2705. In addition to the mental elements specified in Article 30, the war crime of torture further requires that:

> The perpetrator inflicted the pain or suffering for such purposes as: obtaining information or a confession, punishment, intimidation or coercion or for any reason based on discrimination of any kind.

...

c. Rape (Article 7(1)(g) and Article 8(2)(e)(vi))

2708. The crime of rape, whether as a crime against humanity or war crime, is committed when the following two material elements are fulfilled:

> 1. The perpetrator invaded the body of a person by conduct resulting in penetration, however slight, of any part of the body of the victim or of the perpetrator with a sexual organ, or of the anal or genital opening of the victim with any object or any other part of the body.

> 2. The invasion was committed by force, or by threat of force or coercion, such as that caused by fear of violence, duress, detention, psychological oppression or abuse of power, against such person or another person, or by taking advantage of a coercive environment, or the invasion was committed against a person incapable of giving genuine consent.

2709. The establishment of one of the coercive circumstances or conditions set out in the second element is sufficient for penetration to amount to rape. It is not necessary to prove the victim's lack of consent and there is no requirement of resistance on the part of the victim.

2710. Coercive circumstances need not be evidenced by a show of physical force – threats, intimidation, extortion, and other forms of duress which prey on fear or desperation may constitute coercion. Coercion may be inherent in certain circumstances, such as armed conflict or the military presence of hostile forces amongst the civilian population. Several factors may contribute to creating a coercive environment, such as the number of people involved in the commission of the crime, or whether the rape is committed during or immediately following a combat situation, or is committed together with other crimes.

d. Enslavement (Article 7(1)(c))

2711. Article 7(2)(c) of the Statute defines 'enslavement' as the exercise of any or all of the powers attaching to the right of ownership over a person and includes the exercise of such power in the course of trafficking in persons, in particular women and children. The Elements of Crimes include a non-exhaustive list of the various forms in which ownership over a person may be exercised, namely 'by purchasing, selling, lending or bartering such a person or persons, or by imposing on them a similar deprivation of liberty'.

2712. Indicia for the exercise of the powers attaching to the right of ownership include: (i) control or restrictions of someone's movement and, more generally, measures taken to prevent or deter escape; (ii) control of physical environment; (iii) psychological control or pressure; (iv) force, threat of force or coercion; (v) duration of the exercise of powers attaching to the right of ownership; (vi) assertion of exclusivity; (vii) subjection to cruel treatment and abuse; (viii) control of sexuality; (ix) forced labour or subjecting the person to servile status; and (x) the person's vulnerability and the socio-economic conditions in which the power is exerted.
…

e. Sexual Slavery (Article 7(1)(g) and Article 8(2)(e)(vi))

2715. The crime of sexual slavery is a specific form of the crime of 'enslavement', penalising the perpetrator's restriction or control of the victim's sexual autonomy while held in the state of enslavement. The crime of sexual slavery, whether as a crime against humanity or war crime, is committed when the material element of enslavement is fulfilled and the perpetrator also caused such person or persons to engage in one or more acts of a sexual nature.
…

f. Forced pregnancy (Article 7(1)(g) and Article 8(2)(e)(vi))

2717. This is the first time forced pregnancy is to be considered by a trial chamber of this Court. The crime of forced pregnancy is grounded in the woman's right to personal and reproductive autonomy and the right to family.

2718. The Statute adopted a 'narrow' definition of forced pregnancy, largely because the provision was 'one of the most difficult and controversial to draft'. Negotiations for the crime of forced pregnancy were largely driven with atrocities of the Bosnian conflict in mind, where Bosnian women were raped and then unlawfully detained with the intent to change the ethnic composition of their group by giving birth to half-Serb children.

...

2721. The resulting definition of forced pregnancy in the Statute is a delicate compromise that specified the *mens rea* requirement as 'affecting the ethnic composition of any population or carrying out other grave violations of international law'. A final sentence was added, saying that this crime 'shall not in any way be interpreted as affecting national laws related to pregnancy'. This final sentence does not add a new element to the offence – and is thus not reproduced in the Elements of Crimes – but allays the concern that criminalising forced pregnancy may be seen as legalising abortion.

2722. As with any crime, forced pregnancy must be interpreted in a manner which gives this crime independent meaning from the other sexual and gender based violence crimes in the Statute. This is demanded by the rule against surplusage, a basic principle of statutory interpretation that presumes that the legislator does nothing in vain and that the court must endeavour to give significance to every word of a statutory instrument. This also implicates the principle of fair labelling, and how the proper characterisation of the evil committed, that is to say, calling the crime by its true name, is part of the justice sought by the victims. It is not enough to punish it merely as a combination of other crimes (e.g., rape and unlawful detention), or subsumed under the generic "any other form of sexual violence'. The crime of forced pregnancy depends on the unlawful confinement of a (forcibly made) pregnant woman, with the effect that the woman is deprived of reproductive autonomy.

i Material elements (actus reus)

2723. The crime of forced pregnancy, whether as a crime against humanity or a war crime, is committed when the perpetrator 'confined one or more women forcibly made pregnant'. The forcible conception of the woman could occur prior to or during the unlawful confinement. The perpetrator need not have personally made the victim forcibly pregnant – confining a woman made forcibly pregnant by another is necessary and sufficient for the crime of forced pregnancy.

2724. The material element of this crime can be split into two components. The first of these is 'unlawful confinement', which means that the woman must have been restricted in her physical movement contrary to standards of international law. ...

2725. The second component of the material element is that the woman has been 'forcibly made pregnant'. This is understood as encompassing the same coercive circumstances described for other sexual violence crimes in the Statute. This means that the woman need not have been made pregnant through physical violence alone. 'Forcibly' in this context means force, or threat of force or coercion, such as that caused by fear of violence, duress, detention, psychological oppression or abuse of power, against her or another person, or by taking advantage of a coercive environment, or that the woman made pregnant was a person incapable of giving genuine consent. The existence of such coercive circumstances undermines the woman's ability to give voluntary and genuine consent.

ii Mental elements (mens rea)

2726. Not every confinement of a forcibly impregnated woman constitutes the crime of forced pregnancy. In addition to the mental elements specified in Article 30, the perpetrator must act with the specific intent of 'affecting the ethnic composition of any population or carrying out other grave violations of international law'.

2727. This requirement of special intent is phrased alternatively, meaning that the crime of forced pregnancy under the Statute is committed with the intent either to affect the ethnic composition of the population or to carry out other grave violations of international law, e.g., confining a woman with the intent to rape, sexually enslave, enslave and/or torture her.

...

2729. On this understanding, the crime of forced pregnancy consists in the confinement of a forcibly pregnant woman in order to carry out other grave violations of international law, regardless of whether the accused specifically intended to keep the woman pregnant.

...

h. Other inhumane acts, including forced marriage (Article 7(1)(k))

2741. Dominic Ongwen is charged with the crime of other inhumane acts, including forced marriage, within the meaning of Article 7(1)(k) of the Statute. In conformity with the principle of legality, this category of crimes against humanity must be interpreted conservatively and – with due regard to Article 22(2) of the Statute – must not be used to expand uncritically the scope of crimes against humanity. Judicial interpretation within Article 7(1)(k) of the Statute must be consistent with the essence of the offence and in a manner which could have been reasonably foreseen.

...

2743. The crime of other inhumane acts is committed, either by act or omission, when the following two material elements are fulfilled:

> 1. The perpetrator inflicted great suffering, or serious injury to body or to mental or physical health, by means of an inhumane act.

> 2. Such act was of a character similar to any other act referred to in article 7, paragraph 1, of the Statute.

2744. International case-law suggests that serious beatings, subjection to deplorable conditions of detention and requiring persons to witness the beatings or killings of others can constitute other inhumane acts. Other international jurisdictions have also recognised forced marriage as an 'other inhumane act' falling under crimes against humanity.

...

2747. ... The Chamber can enter a conviction under Article 7(1)(k) if the perpetrator inflicts great suffering, or serious injury to body or to mental or physical health, by means of a course of conduct which, despite comprising also acts falling under one or more of the enumerated crimes, is, in its entirety, not identical, but is nonetheless 'similar' in character in terms of nature and gravity, to those enumerated crimes.

2748. The Chamber considers forced marriage – and the enumerated acts charged out of the same overall course of conduct in this case – to be just such an example. Every person enjoys the fundamental right to enter a marriage with the free and full consent of another person. Marriage creates a status based on a consensual and contractual relationship – it is an institution and also an act or rite. The central element, and underlying act of forced marriage is the imposition of this status on the victim, i.e. the imposition, regardless of the will of the victim, of duties that are associated with marriage – including in terms of exclusivity of the (forced) conjugal union imposed on the victim – as well as the consequent social stigma. Such a state, beyond its illegality, has also social, ethical and even religious effects which have a serious impact on the victim's physical and psychological well-being. The victim may see themselves as being bonded or united to another person despite the lack of consent. Additionally, a given social group may see the victim as being a 'legitimate' spouse. To the extent forced marriage results in the birth of children, this creates even more complex emotional and psychological effects on the victim and their children beyond the obvious physical effects of pregnancy and child- bearing.

2749. Accordingly, the harm suffered from forced marriage can consist of being ostracised from the community, mental trauma, the serious attack on the victim's dignity, and the deprivation of the victim's fundamental rights to choose his or her spouse.

...

B. Legal characterisation of the facts

...

7. Sexual and gender-based crimes perpetrated directly by Dominic Ongwen (Counts 50 to 60)

i. Forced marriage (Count 50)

...

3023. [The numbers used by the court, such as P-0099, enable witnesses to be identified but to remain anonymous.] P-0099, P-0101, P-0214, P-0226 and P-0227, who were 'distributed' to Dominic Ongwen, were not allowed to leave. Dominic Ongwen placed them under heavy guard. They were told or came to understand that if they tried to escape they would be killed. These women were ultimately considered Dominic Ongwen's so-called 'wives' and had to maintain an exclusive conjugal relationship with him. Being Dominic Ongwen's so-called 'wife' did not cease until P-0099, P-0101, P-0214, P-0226 and P-0227 escaped or were released from the LRA.

3024. ... [T]he Chamber finds that Dominic Ongwen executed the specific legal elements of forced marriage as an other inhumane act, pursuant to Article 7(1)(k) of the Statute.

3025. As concerns the mental elements, due to the nature of the acts performed by Dominic Ongwen and due to the sustained character of the acts over a long period of time, the Chamber considers that Dominic Ongwen meant both to engage in his relevant conduct and to cause the consequence.
...

ii. Torture (Counts 51-52)
...
3028. The Chamber found that P-0101, P-0214, P-0226 and P-0227 were subjected to beating at Dominic Ongwen's command at any time. They were hit with canes and sticks. Some beatings knocked them unconscious, left them unable to walk and left permanent scars. On this basis, the Chamber finds that the first element of torture as a crime against humanity, ... and torture as a war crime ..., i.e. that the perpetrator inflicted on the victim severe physical or mental pain or suffering, is met.

3029. At the relevant times P-0101, P-0214, P-0226 and P-0227 were abducted and as so-called 'wives' they were in custody and under control of Dominic Ongwen. The second element of torture as a crime against humanity, pursuant to Article 7(1)(f) of the Statute is also met.
...
3031. Considering in particular the circumstances of their abduction, as well as of their stay within the LRA, and more specifically in Dominic Ongwen's household, the Chamber is also satisfied that P-0101, P-0214, P-0226 and P-0227 were civilians at the relevant time. ...

3032. As concerns the mental elements, due to the nature of the acts performed by Dominic Ongwen and due to the sustained character of the acts over a long period of time, the Chamber considers that Dominic Ongwen meant to engage in his relevant conduct and to cause the consequence. Considering that Dominic Ongwen knew the victims personally, he also knew of their civilian status.

3033. Finally, and recalling again that failure on the part of P-0101, P-0214, P-0226 and P-0227 to perform the domestic duties assigned to them led to punishment by beating, the Chamber is also satisfied that Dominic Ongwen acted with the purpose of coercing, intimidating or punishing, and that the special intent requirement applicable to torture as a war crime, pursuant to Article 8(2)(c)(i) of the Statute, is therefore met.
...

iii. Rape (Counts 53-54)
...
3040. ... [D]uring the period relevant to the charges, Dominic Ongwen had sex by force with P-0101, P-0214, P-0226 and P-0227. This happened on a repeated basis whenever Dominic Ongwen wanted. On this basis, the Chamber finds that the first legal element of rape as a crime against humanity, ... and rape as a war crime, ... is met.

3041. Likewise, considering that P-0101, P-0214, P-0226 and P-0227 were abductees, detained and beaten on Dominic Ongwen's command, and thus living under threat of force in a coercive environment, the Chamber finds that the second legal element of rape as a crime against humanity, pursuant to Article 7(1)(g) of the Statute, and rape as a war crime, pursuant to Article 8(2)(e)(vi) of the Statute is met.

3042. As concerns the mental elements, due to the nature of the acts performed by Dominic Ongwen and due to the sustained character of the acts over a long period of time, the Chamber considers that Dominic Ongwen meant to engage in the relevant conduct.

...

iv. Sexual slavery (Counts 55-56)

...

3045. The Chamber found that the seven women 'distributed' to Dominic Ongwen were not allowed to leave. Dominic Ongwen placed them under heavy guard. They were told or came to understand that if they tried to escape they would be killed. They were also subjected to beating at Dominic Ongwen's command at any time. They were hit with canes and sticks. Some beatings knocked them unconscious, left them unable to walk and left permanent scars. The seven women had to perform different domestic duties ... . Failing to perform these tasks led to punishment by beating.

3046. ... Considering that Dominic Ongwen, as described, deprived them of their personal liberty, restricted and dictated their movement, including by threats and subjecting them to armed guard, subjected them to forced labour, and physically and psychologically abused them, the Chamber finds that Dominic Ongwen exercised powers attaching to the right of ownership over these women by imposing on them a deprivation of liberty ... . The first element of sexual slavery as a crime against humanity, ... and sexual slavery as a war crime, ... is therefore met.

3047. The Chamber further found that Dominic Ongwen had sex by force with P-0101, P-0214, P-0226 and P-0227. This happened on a repeated basis whenever Dominic Ongwen wanted during the time in which these women were deprived of their personal freedom. Accordingly, the Chamber finds that the second element of sexual slavery as a crime against humanity, ... and sexual slavery as a war crime, ... – i.e. that the victims were caused to engage in one or more acts of sexual nature, which, in the present case took the form of repeated rapes – is also met.

3048. As concerns the mental elements, due to the nature of the acts performed by Dominic Ongwen and due to the sustained character of the acts over a long period of time, the Chamber considers that Dominic Ongwen meant to engage in the relevant conduct.

...

vi. Forced pregnancy (Counts 58-59)

...

3057. The Chamber found that Dominic Ongwen had sex by force with his so-called 'wives', including with P-0101 and P-0214 [each of whom gave birth to children]. ...

3058. ... [D]uring their pregnancies [they] were not allowed to leave. Dominic Ongwen placed them under heavy guard. They were told or came to understand that if they tried to escape they would be killed.

3059. On this basis, the Chamber finds that Dominic Ongwen confined P-0101 and P-0214, who had been forcibly made pregnant. The objective element of forced pregnancy as a crime against humanity, ... and forced pregnancy as a war crime, ... is met.

3060. As concerns the mental elements, due to the nature of the acts performed by Dominic Ongwen and due to the sustained character of the acts over a long period of time, the Chamber considers that Dominic Ongwen meant to engage in the relevant conduct.

3061. Moreover, the Chamber finds that Dominic Ongwen confined P-0101 and P-0214, who had been forcibly made pregnant, with the intent of sustaining the continued commission of other crimes found, in particular of forced marriage, torture, rape and sexual slavery. The special intent requirement of the crime of forced pregnancy is therefore equally met.

...

vii. Outrages upon personal dignity (Count 60)

...

3064. The Chamber found that on 1 July 2002, Dominic Ongwen forced P-0226 to beat to death a captured UPDF soldier near Patongo, Northern Uganda. P-0226 hit him once, as did other girls. She had blood splattered on her clothes. P-0226 had never killed anyone before, and this was part of the reason Dominic Ongwen gave as to why he selected her to do this. This experience caused her severe anguish. ...

3065. The Chamber finds that by forcing P-0226 to beat a person to death, in the circumstances as described, constituted a violation of her dignity, and that this violation of the dignity was so severe as to be generally recognised as an outrage upon personal dignity. ... The first and second elements of outrages upon personal dignity as a war crime, pursuant to Article 8(2)(c)(ii) of the Statute are met.
...

THE PROSECUTOR V. DOMINIC ONGWEN SENTENCE, TRIAL CHAMBER IX (6 MAY 2021)

...

386. ... [F]rom the perspective of the extreme gravity of the crimes committed by Dominic Ongwen, including the degree of his culpable conduct, a joint sentence of life imprisonment would surely be in order ... ... [T]he Chamber has, however, decided not to sentence Dominic Ongwen to life imprisonment ... .

...

388. The Chamber is confronted in the present case with a unique situation of a perpetrator who willfully and lucidly brought tremendous suffering upon his victims, but who himself had previously endured grave suffering at the hands of the group of which he later became a prominent member and leader. ... The fact [of Ongwen's abduction and brutal socialization] ... in no way justifies or rationalises the heinous crimes he willfully chose to commit as a fully responsible adult; however, these circumstances ... make the prospective of committing him to spend the rest of his life in prison ... excessive.

389. ... By no means does Dominic Ongwen's personal background overshadow his culpable conduct and the suffering of the victims ... . Nevertheless, the specificity of his situation cannot be put aside in deciding whether he must be sentenced to life imprisonment for his crimes. ...

390. Envisaging a concrete prospect for Dominic Ongwen to eventually re-build his life – while adequately punished for the crimes committed – in a new, more healthy environment ... is one of the conflicting driving forces for the Chamber's ultimate consideration ... ...

391. It is with these considerations in mind that the Chamber has decided not to sentence Dominic Ongwen to the – exceptional – penalty of life imprisonment.
...

393. ... [N]o imprisonment for a period shorter than 25 years could constitute an adequate, proportionate and just joint sentence in light of all relevant circumstances of the present case. ...

394. In addition, while not an aggravating factor in and of itself or an element otherwise impinging as such on the length of the prison sentence to be imposed in the present case, the Chamber cannot overlook the absence, in Dominic Ongwen's submissions during the hearing on sentence, of any expression of empathy for the numerous victims of his crimes – and even less of any genuine remorse – supplanted by a lucid, constant focus on himself and his own suffering eclipsing that of anyone else.
...

PARTLY DISSENTING OPINION OF JUDGE RAUL C. PANGALANGAN

...

11. Indeed we must take into account Dominic Ongwen's circumstance as former child soldier whose life might have taken a different turn altogether had it not been for that fateful morning of his abduction. ...

12. However, the Court must weigh those individual circumstances against the 'gravity of the crime' under Article 78 and other factors, among them, "the extent of the damage caused, in particular the harm caused to the victims and their families" (Rule 145(1)(c).

13. It is exactly because of the extreme gravity of the crimes, including the degree of Dominic Ongwen's culpable conduct and, in particular, the deep and permanent physical and psychological harm caused to the victims and their families, that I find that the 'adequate, proportionate and just joint sentence in light of all relevant circumstances of the present case' is a sentence of imprisonment for 30 years.

…

THE PROSECUTOR V. DOMINIC ONGWEN
THE APPEALS CHAMBER (15 DECEMBER 2022)

[The Appeals Chamber unanimously rejected the 90 grounds of appeal against conviction put forward by Ongwen's defence team. It also unanimously rejected ten out of the 11 grounds of appeal raised in the sentencing appeal. The principal area of contention was whether the approach used by the Trial Chamber had inappropriately double-counted certain offences. The other contested issue concerned the significance that should be attached to Ongwen's abduction and brutalization as a child soldier himself. Four of the five judges in the Appeals Chamber agreed with the Trial Chamber that it was appropriate to address the issue only in the context of sentencing. The President of the Appeals Chamber dissented. Her Opinion follows.]

PARTLY DISSENTING OPINION OF JUDGE LUZ DEL CARMEN IBÁÑEZ CARRANZA

…

XI. CONCLUSION

…

196. The dissenting judge considers it appropriate at this concluding stage to recapitulate all the points made in this opinion.

a. There has been a clear legal error in the reasoning of the Trial Chamber. It attached weight twice to the number of victims, as part of the gravity assessment and as an aggravating factor in relation to 20 out of the 61 individual sentences imposed on Mr Ongwen. This resulted in unfairness in the sentencing proceedings … .

b. The most appropriate relief in this case is to reverse the joint sentence impose and to remand the matter for the Trial Chamber to impose a new sentence;

c. Mr Ongwen's abduction, conscription, violent indoctrination, being forced to carry out and participate in criminal acts, when he was still a defenceless child of about nine years of age and his upbringing in the coercive environment of the LRA had a long-lasting impact on his personality, the development of his brain and moral values, and future opportunities. These circumstances merit significant weight in mitigation when imposing a new sentence on Mr Ongwen;

d. In addition, Judge Ibáñez Carranza wishes to use this opportunity to acknowledge the violation of Mr Ongwen's basic human rights that affected his dignity as a human being. Given the expressive nature of judicial decisions, and specifically of international criminal judgments, recognising in this case the crimes of which Mr Ongwen was a victim provides the means to acknowledge his victim status and re-instate the dignity that was taken away from him when he was a defenceless child;

…

Issues Raised by the *Ongwen* Case

The excerpts above from the 2021 Trial Chamber judgments and the 2022 Appeals Chamber illustrate many aspects of the way in which the ICC functions. They also illustrate the Statute's narrow definition of duress which would exclude criminal responsibility, the elements of specific crimes, definitional approaches, how different crimes relate to one another, and the type of evidence considered by the court. In the materials that follow, we focus on several of the more contentious issues raised.

A. GENDER

The *Ongwen* case was path-breaking in relation to the emphasis placed upon sexual and gender-based crimes and in charging certain crimes for the first time. Nonetheless, critics have suggested that it did not go far enough. It has been argued, for example, that the crime of forced pregnancy could have been treated in greater depth, thereby better situating 'this crime and its impact as well as plac[ing] the victims at the forefront of consideration.'[693] Others have argued that the separate crime of gender persecution should have been investigated and prosecuted in order to increase the visibility of this issue, to recognize the direct harms suffered by victims, and to lay the groundwork to address the situation of people of different sexual orientations and gender identities in future prosecutions.[694]

Following the *Ongwen* case, and in response to a range of suggestions that a more systematic approach be adopted in future, the Office of the Prosecutor, announced a new Policy on the Crime of Gender Persecution in December 2022. The policy specified (para. 4) that '[g]ender persecution is committed against persons because of sex characteristics and/or because of the social constructs and criteria used to define gender', and noted that (para. 5) LGBTQI+ persons were included in this regard. The Policy states (para. 10) that the 'perpetrators' discriminatory intent may intersect with other grounds for persecution prohibited under the Statute, and also reflect existing social constructs or criteria used to define targeted groups based on, for example, race, ethnicity or culture, or impose new ones.' In December 2023, the OTP announced a 'Policy on Gender-based Crimes' covering crimes involving sexual, reproductive and other gender-based crimes.

B. SENTENCING

Article 77 of the Rome Statute authorizes the Court to impose: '(a) Imprisonment for a specified number of years, which may not exceed a maximum of 30 years; or (b) A term of life imprisonment when justified by the extreme gravity of the crime and the individual circumstances of the convicted person.' While the *Ongwen* case illustrates different perspectives on the appropriate sentence, the ICC has been very significantly influenced by the practice of the ICTY in this area, as described by Margaret M. deGuzman, in 'Punishing for Humanity', in Carsten Stahn et al. (eds.), *Legacies of the International Criminal Tribunal for the Former Yugoslavia* (2020) 391:

> The ICTY's judges chose to forge new global norms rather than adhere to, or even be strongly guided by, the sentencing norms of the former Yugoslavia. The ICTY Statute itself diverged from national norms in some respects, in particular by rejecting the death penalty, but also required the judges to consult national practices in determining sentences. The judges interpreted this requirement loosely, reserving to themselves a wide discretion that enabled them to identify a range of global sentencing objectives and factors to apply in pursuit of those objectives.
>
> … [T]the Rome Statute and the ICC Rules of Procedure draw significantly on the norms developed at the ICTY. The ICC's judges have followed ICTY jurisprudence, for instance, in holding that the gravity of the offense 'is a principal consideration in imposing a sentence'[, and in emphasizing] their discretion to determine relevant factors in the gravity analysis as well as aggravating circumstances. ICC judges have cited ICTY judgments liberally in support of their gravity analyses, … for their holding that gravity factors cannot be double counted as aggravating factors … that admission of guilt can be a mitigating circumstance, that efforts to promote peace and reconciliation can be counted in mitigation, and that statements of remorse can affect sentencing.

C. THE VICTIM-PERPETRATOR DILEMMA

The Trial Chamber gave greater consideration to this issue in the sentencing phase than in its original judgment. Consider the following comments:

Ayodele Akenroye and Kamari Clarke, 'Deconstructing the Complexities of Violence: Uganda and the Case against Dominic Ongwen', in Sarah Federman and Ronald Niezen (eds.), *Narratives of Mass Atrocity: Victims and Perpetrators in the Aftermath* (2022) 78, at 101:

---

[693] T. Kirabira, A. Ringin and R. Grey, 'Feminist Judgments at the International Criminal Court: The Case of Dominic Ongwen', iCourts Working Paper Series, no. 294, (2022).

[694] M. Kumskova, 'Invisible Crimes against Humanity of Gender Persecution: Taking a Feminist Lens to the ICC's *Ntaganda* and *Ongwen* Cases', 57 *Tex. Int'l L. J.* (2022) 239.

… During the sentencing hearing, Dominic Ongwen spoke extensively for more than one hour where he gave chilling accounts of how he was made to kill people, drank human blood, was forced to commit inhumane acts while a minor, and the life changing consequence on him. Yet, the ICC judgment failed to deal with the impact of trauma and Dominic's "loss of humanity," and instead found him not to be damaged and that immediately he turned eighteen he had the agency to decide what is morally right from what is morally wrong, including choosing not to escape like other abductees.

Mark Drumbl, '"Getting" an Unforgettable Gettable: The Trial of Dominic Ongwen', *Justice in Conflict* blog (5 February 2021):

… Now we have a former child soldier convicted in the solemnity and seriousness of a vaunted and vaulted one-of-a-kind court designed to prosecute those most responsible world-wide for atrocity. Yes, this man hurt many others. No one denies it. Had the ICC wished to convict, however, a more honest track would have been to explicitly say: this man is broken, he was kidnapped at the age of ten, brutalized and beaten so he brutalized and beat others, he raped and killed so many and so cruelly, but we just don't care about his childhood, we just don't care about his victimization, we don't care about his neurological development – all we care about is what he did, regardless of why, and *tout comprendre c'est tout pardonner* [to understand all is to forgive all], and we refuse that for reasons that have nothing to do with him, as perpetrator, but instead with us, as judges, hungry for a role, and for the victims, achingly deserving of redress.

Instead, the judgment leaves us with an artifice of sorts. We have a man who had no childhood, shoehorned into one box, a reductionism of sorts.

…

… [I]n pursuing this case the ICC continues its trajectory of specializing its judicial efforts on rebels who lost their rebellions, mostly in Africa, and its path of successfully prosecuting implicated mid-level characters. This, too, is fine; these characters have committed terrible crimes. But is it not fair to wonder whether this is what was intended on that euphoric day, July 17, 1998, when all this formally began?

In convicting and spectacularizing Ongwen, while pursuing its goals of convicting who it can, the ICC also indirectly buoys those it cannot, will not, or lacks the spine to try to convict. While Ongwen faces his reckoning for violence between 2002 and 2005, President Museveni benefits from impunity for his conduct … . But without President Museveni's nod, the ICC would not have delivered judgment against Ongwen. …

…

[M]uch of life 'just happens', perhaps, and so too with much of atrocity, which tragically is part of human condition. Yet this is not how international criminal law constructs its accused. International criminal law constructs them as plotters and planners, as intentional movers and shakers, as willful and wanton. It needs to construct them this way. After all, courts punish to deter others. Courts punish to ensure that others not make the same patterned choices. The immediate lesson from Ongwen, then, is that little children and adolescents kidnapped into invidious armed groups should try not to become socialized into hurtful adults. They should try to 'grow up right', on their own. They should resist. They should act far more respectfully than the adults and authority figures around them. They should be disobedient. This is the conduct immediately encouraged by the Ongwen verdict.

…

To 'us', to the judges, to the legal industry of international criminal law, Ongwen is truly the 'other'. Hence, his trial becomes a bit of a spectacle. Perhaps a jury of actual peers tasked with processing all of this and authenticating it in some sort of judgment would have proceeded differently, and spoken and written in an alternate cadence, even if arriving at a similar outcome.

QUESTIONS

How do you react to the suggestion that international criminal justice is still very much a concept in the making and that the ICC is learning from past mistakes and changing its approach as new cases arise? Consider the following comment, comparing the approach adopted in the Ongwen case with that reflected in three earlier cases, all of which involved suspects from the DRC. Those cases were contentious and led to two acquittals as well as two convictions:

The mixed record of the Congo trials prompted widespread reflection among Court stakeholders – but any lessons learned seemed to widen the gaps. Both Prosecution and Defense repositioned themselves in tactical ways, seeking to avoid prior hazards. Judges in all phases were unable to hide the rifts that surfaced in the *Bemba* appeals process, while remaining as decorous as possible in their disagreements.

1. *The Prosecution multiplied charges and modes of liability.* In contrast to the simple charges and single events tested out in the Ituri trials, the Prosecution now asserted all of its charging options at the pre-trial confirmation stage. The next trials would encompass multiple criminal charges, all modes of liability, and a proliferation of criminal events or attacks, swelling the "facts and circumstances" controlling the scope of proceedings. …

2. *The Prosecution submitted mountains of evidence,* confident of avoiding early filters of admissibility, and hopeful that the mantra of holism would leverage the weaker parts – including quantities of anonymous hearsay and circumstantial evidence. …

3. *The Defense spread itself thin to meet these shape-changing master narratives,* while searching for some overarching doctrinal backstop. For Ntaganda, that line of defense was standard military necessity; for Ongwen, it was the embattled doctrine of psychological duress. Both were unable to block the evidentiary flood. …695

---

4. Backlash Against African Prosecution

By 2017, the ICC had been in existence for 15 years, but all of the situations it had under review were in Africa. The situations in Uganda, the Central African Republic, the Democratic Republic of the Congo and Mali were all referred by the respective governments, and all involved rebel leaders. Two other situations, Darfur (Sudan) and Libya were referred by the Security Council and led to indictments against the respective heads of state, Omar al-Bashir, and Muammar Gaddafi. Two other situations, involving Kenya and Côte d'Ivoire, were initiated by the Prosecutor using his *proprio motu* powers.

This stark imbalance led to backlash from different quarters. Various African governments accused the Court of racial bias. Several African states—led by Kenya, whose prominent political figures, including two future presidents, were under indictment—mounted a powerful counter-attack. Non-African governments were aware of the unsustainability of the situation and the OTP began to engage in more determined inquiries and investigations elsewhere. Scholars also weighed in to this battle.696 Christopher Gevers, in 'Africa and International Criminal Law', in Kevin Heller et al. (eds.), *The Oxford Handbook of International Criminal Law* (2020) 154 argues that the relationship between Africa and international criminal law needs to be seen in light of a much longer history than just that of the ICC. '[T]he question [then] becomes not whether ICL (or the ICC)

---

695 R. Gaskins, *The Congo Trials in the International Criminal Court* (2020) 457.
696 A. B. Rukooko and J. Silverman II, 'The International Criminal Court and Africa: A Fractious Relationship Assessed', 19 *Afr. Hum. Rts. L. J.* (2019) 85.

might be a field that operates on neo-colonial and racist lines, but whether it might have been anything else (or might yet be).' Consider the following critique of the Court for 'criminalizing Blackness'.

RACHEL LÓPEZ, BLACK GUILT, WHITE GUILT AT THE INTERNATIONAL CRIMINAL COURT
MATIANGAI SIRLEAF (ED.), RACE AND NATIONAL SECURITY (2023) 211

Introduction

All but one defendant convicted at the International Criminal Court (ICC) has been a Black man. This is not a coincidence. ... [T]he jurisdictional and substantive law that governs the ICC systematically results in Black guilt being heightened while White guilt is minimized. With these convictions, the ICC builds on a long history of criminalizing Blackness .... Since the ICC supposedly prosecutes only "the most serious crimes of international concern," these convictions express the not-so-subtle suggestion that the "worst of the worst" criminals on the planet are Black men. More troubling still, given the longstanding characterization of international crimes as evil, it perpetuates well-documented stereotypes of darker skin being associated with wickedness, thereby building on a pernicious narrative of the "evil Black body."
...

I. Institutionalizing Black Guilt
...
... [T]he outsized role of the U.N. Security Council in the matters handled by the court is partly to blame. ...

... The Security Council has only asked the ICC to investigate crimes in two African nations, Sudan and Libya, but issued no referrals for documented torture and war crimes by the United States and United Kingdom in Iraq and Afghanistan. While Article 16 of the Rome Statute was meant to allow the Security Council to step in and delay prosecutions if doing so is in the interest of maintaining peace and security, so far, it has only been used to immunize White guilt, shielding the citizens of majority White nations from the court's reach. In fact, the first evocation of the Security Council's deferral power was only made after the United States threatened to veto a resolution renewing the U.N. peacekeeping mission in Bosnia (as well as all other future peacekeeping operations) unless a provision immunizing its troops from criminal liability was included. Since then, the Security Council has invoked Article 16 two additional times, each time at the United States' behest to immunize soldiers from any criminal liability resulting from military operations authorized by the Security Council.

While the Security Council has used Article 16 to minimize the guilt of White majority nations, it refused to use this power to defer investigations in two African nations, Sudan and Kenya, despite repeated requests from the African Union to do so. Functionally, this has meant that White leaders who authorized torture like George W. Bush and Donald Rumsfeld have evaded criminal liability before the ICC, while Black and Arab-African heads of state like Uhuru Muigai Kenyatta and Omar al-Bashir faced charges.

... [T]he temporal and definitional limitations on what counts as a prosecutable crime before the ICC renders White violence less visible and consequential. ... [T]he crimes committed before the Rome Statute entered into force on July 1, 2002 are off the table. ... [T]his narrow temporal gaze often obfuscates the role of colonial powers in the violence under investigation by the ICC and shields them from prosecution for their past empire-building crimes, most notably slavery and genocide. In a broader sense, these rules have criminalized the processes by which Global North became wealthy, at the same time as effectively granting them de facto amnesty for those same acts.

The impunity for colonial era crimes of the Global North is compounded by the fact that the type of violence currently perpetrated by these majority White nations also tends to be untouched by international criminal law, while those crimes which typify Western stereotypes of Black men have been vigorously pursued. First, as Kamari Clarke illuminated in her groundbreaking book, *Fictions of Justice*, the choice of acts considered to be the "most serious crimes of international concern" under the Rome Statute and therefore prosecutable by the ICC exacerbates Black guilt, while mitigating White guilt. Omitted from actionable crimes are those most likely to be committed by majority White nations, such as colonial domination, economic aggression, the use of nuclear weapons, the recruitment, use, financing, and training of mercenaries, and environmental atrocities. These crimes were all dropped during the negotiation of the Rome Statute because they were considered to "devalu[e] the concept of crimes against the peace and security of mankind." …

…

II. Prosecuting Evil

In response to allegations of anti-African bias, supporters of the ICC have claimed that the focus on Africa is not racially motivated, but rather is just the unfortunate result of following the rules. For example, former ICC prosecutor, Luis Moreno Ocampo … characterized allegations of African bias as "hypocrisy," saying "we are in Africa for two reasons: the most serious crimes under ICC jurisdiction are in Africa…and African leaders requested the court's intervention." In essence, his argument, much like those of other proponents of the ICC, is that we should not be concerned with racism at the court, because the exclusive prosecution of African defendants resulted from a race-neutral application of the law.

…

Conclusion

… The broader effect of such systemic bias at the ICC is particularly invidious because it reinforces well-documented racialized associations of dark skin with evil. A deeper reckoning with the rules that yield such consistently racially discriminatory results is imperative especially given the increased prominence of expressive theories of punishment in international criminal law, which justify criminal prosecutions for their role in communicating the international community's sense of right and wrong. …

Kenya and the ICC

In seeking to understand how the Court got into this situation, it is helpful to explore two of the situations – those relating to Uganda and to Kenya – in more detail.

The ICC's attempted engagement with the situation in Kenya stands in marked contrast to the Ongwen case. The latter involved a single individual who had eventually surrendered and who had no political support. He was charged with specific crimes, and the ICC was able to obtain access to and detailed evidence from many key witnesses. In Kenya, the principal defendants were very high-level politicians, with continuing links to the government in power, access to a well-funded and high-powered defence team, and in a position to obstruct investigations within Kenya.

By way of background, post-election violence in six of Kenya's eight provinces, in 2007-2008 led to the killing of over 1,000 people, 900 documented acts of rape and sexual violence, 350,000 people displaced, and over 3,500 seriously injured. On 31 March 2010, Pre-Trial Chamber II granted the Prosecutor's request to open an investigation *proprio motu* (on their own initiative). It did so after noting the Prosecutor's submission alleging '…elements of brutality, for example burning victims alive, attacking places sheltering IDPs, beheadings, and using pangas and machetes to hack people to death', and that perpetrators, among other acts, allegedly 'terrorized communities by installing checkpoints where they would select their victims based on ethnicity, and hack them to death, commonly committed gang rape, genital mutilation and forced circumcision, and often forced family members to watch.'

The ICC's website (https://www.icc-cpi.int/kenya) notes dryly that:

> The investigation has produced two main cases, originally with six suspects, involving charges which include the following crimes: crimes against humanity: murder, deportation or forcible transfer of population, persecution, rape, and other inhumane acts. However, charges were not confirmed or were withdrawn concerning these six suspects.

The suspects included two senior politicians: Uhuru Kenyatta, a member of the Kikuyu ethnic group, and William Ruto, a Kalenjin, who were accused of masterminding the ethnic violence against one another's communities in the 2007 election. As the threat of international prosecution before the ICC grew, the two formed a successful alliance in the 2013 election. Kenyatta was elected President, and Ruto Vice-President. What happened thereafter is recounted by Susanne D. Mueller, in 'Kenya and the International Criminal Court (ICC): Politics, the Election and the Law', 8 *J. East. Afr. Stud.* (2014) 25:

> Winning the election was part of a key defense strategy to undercut the ICC by seizing political power, flexing it to deflect the ICC, and opening up the possibility of not showing up for trial if all else failed. The strategy entailed using a series of delaying tactics to ensure that the ICC trials would not start until after the defendants had won the election and gained power at the highest level. The tactics ranged from mobilizing international organizations against the ICC, making numerous, legal challenges designed to delay the court, and the intimidation of potential witnesses, allegedly by defense sympathizers and go betweens, to keep them from assisting the ICC. The tactics were part of a larger design to undercut the ICC. Demonizing opponents, politicizing ethnicity, and attacking the ICC as a tool of the West both before and during the presidential campaign served this end and victory in the election. …

> …

> Indicative of attempts to undermine the ICC process were the plethora of attacks against witnesses. This included intimidating, bribing, and killing them. The message being sent both by the state, which did nothing to protect witnesses and victims as required by the Rome Statute, and allegedly by the defendants and their supporters, was that if individuals cooperated with the ICC's investigations, they would pay heavy costs. Many did. As each trial date neared, more witnesses dropped out, thereby forcing the ICC to find others. This compelled the defense to ask for more time to review the new evidence, precipitating a vicious circle of delays and the need for more witnesses and more time. Politics began to trump the law as the defendants' political risk increased. Early on it appears there was a plan to eliminate, intimidate, and bribe people who knew too much about the [post-election violence], key individuals who were part of it, and civil society activists who were assisting and sheltering potential witnesses. Leaving none to tell the story was an apparent tactic to get rid of key witnesses while simultaneously attacking the credibility of others. The aim was to get the cases dropped for lack of evidence even before the ICC's investigation began and charges were confirmed. Later, it was to destroy the credibility of other witnesses who remained and to delay or halt the onset of trials both before and after the 2013 presidential election.

Eventually, all six cases collapsed and the ICC was left to try two defendants for 'offences against the administration of justice consisting in corruptly influencing witnesses regarding cases from the situation in Kenya'. Only one defendant came into the Court's custody, and he died in October 2022 before his trial could be completed.

Mark Kersten, in 'Will Justice catch up with those responsible for Post-Election Violence in Kenya?', *Justice in Conflict* blog (1 September 2022), focuses on another dimension of the situation:

> Over this period, Kenya's government and its allies focused on two claims. The first was that the ICC was an illegitimate court and 'plaything' of colonial powers. To this end, Kenyatta's government hired British public relations experts to spread its word and undermine the standing of the Court.

> Kenyatta and Ruto's second claim was that Kenya was able and willing to investigate any alleged wrongdoing itself. Senior officials, including the Attorney General Githu Muigai, repeatedly stated that Nairobi would set up an International and Organized Crimes Division as part of its judiciary capable of investigating and prosecuting any perpetrators of atrocities. It never happened. What did transpire, however, was that Kenyatta and Ruto stayed in and consolidated their power, as much of the world slowly forgot about the 2007/08 atrocities.

Kenyatta and Ruto remained in office until August 2022, but by then had fallen out over various issues. Ruto won the election in that year and became President. Kersten draws an important lesson from this series of events:

> ...[T]his means that the country's last two heads of state will have been implicated in atrocities and tried, unsuccessfully, at the ICC.

> Where does that leave justice and accountability efforts in Kenya?

> Exactly as they were. There is no reason to believe that a Ruto government will show any interest in revisiting, let alone doing something, about the rights violations committed in 2007/08.

> ...

> One of the most important yet neglected lessons of the world's experiment with international criminal law is that it is not the ICC, the United Nations or any international body which is most responsible for those rare moments when justice and accountability is delivered; it is changes in the domestic political arena. When investigating and prosecuting atrocities becomes important to the national leaders in charge, it becomes possible.

> The context in Kenya has never been ripe for justice and accountability. Not once since 2007/08 has there been a serious attempt to address the widespread and systematic crimes that were committed following the presidential election. There has been a lot of talk and a many empty promises.

> If ever accountability is to be pursued, it won't be because of the ICC or any international institution, but because the Kenyan people want it and because leaders not implicated in violence, atrocity, and corruption can successfully run for office.

Uganda and the ICC

It is also helpful to see the Ugandan case in its broader political and legal context. Compare the next two readings. The first, by a leading Ugandan scholar, explains how the referral of the situation involving the Lord's Resistance Army to the ICC fitted in with the interests of the Ugandan Government. The second, by a German scholar who observed the trial of Dominic Ongwen, raises the question of whether the trial was little more than the continuation of colonialism by different means.

JOE OLOKA-ONYANGO, UNPACKING THE AFRICAN BACKLASH TO THE INTERNATIONAL CRIMINAL COURT (ICC): THE CASE OF UGANDA AND KENYA
4 STRATHMORE L. J. (2020) 41

...The initial reference of the Northern Uganda situation by President Museveni to the ICC in December 2003 was done over strenuous objections from domestic civil society and the local human rights community ...

... President Museveni's actions were not simply to internationalise the conflict in northern Uganda. They were also designed to buttress his credentials as the regional power broker, and to divert attention from a costly misadventure in the DRC. It is not by coincidence that the overtures to the ICC were taken in parallel to the judicial claim filed by the DRC at the International Court of Justice (ICJ) with the proceedings against Uganda being commenced in mid-2003 while a judgment was eventually returned against the country at the end of 2005. Meanwhile, arrest warrants were issued on 8 July 2005 and 27 September 2005 for Joseph Kony and four members of the LRA high command on 33 separate counts of war crimes and crimes against humanity, including murder, rape, enlisting of children, and sexual enslavement.

When peace talks were initiated between the Government and the LRA in mid-2006, the ICC insisted on pursuing the referrals irrespective of the Juba peace negotiations taking place between the two sides. This angered the Ugandan President and led to the first souring in the relationship. Although the ICC made a pretense of supporting the measures taken by Uganda with regard to the traditional justice rites of *Mato Oput* and its ilk, it was a lukewarm embrace. In a way however, the ICC process did undermine efforts at a victim-oriented resolution of the conflict by focusing attention on capture, prosecution and conviction of only the LRA. At an international conference in Nuremburg, the ICC Prosecutor was quoted as saying, 'calling for amnesties, the granting of immunities and other ways to avoid prosecutions.... are not consistent with the Rome Statute.... there can be no political compromise on legality and accountability'. Regardless of local developments, these remarks demonstrated that the ICC wanted to see the LRA prosecution through to its logical conclusion. Additionally, international organisations had a role to play in influencing the Prosecutor not to back down.

Matters were also not helped by the fact that the ICC approach was opposed by the local political leadership in Acholi land, Ugandan civil society at large, as well as by several academics and media pundits. Given the prominent manner in which the traditional justice elements featured in the peace settlement alongside the question of amnesty, the ICC felt that it was being blind-sided by the Ugandan Government. The referrals of the LRA obviously raised many questions about the role of the other party to the conflict, the Uganda Peoples' Defence Forces (UPDF).

... [After] the Kenyan referrals were announced. Museveni must have felt they were too close to home for comfort. Hence, at the inauguration of President Kenyatta in early 2013, Museveni saluted the Kenyan voters for rejecting what he described as ICC 'blackmail', even claiming that 'the usual opinionated and arrogant actors' wanted to install leaders of their choice in Africa and '... eliminate the ones they do not like'.
...
An element of duplicity on the part of the Ugandan Government with regard to the ICC becomes even more apparent [with] its reaction to Sudanese President Bashir's referral to the Court in 2009 ... . [In] 2014, Uganda had accused Sudan of resuming its support for the LRA rebels to the extent that Uganda filed a complaint with the Organisation of Islamic Cooperation (OIC). One would imagine that Uganda would not be quick in leaping to the defence of Bashir as against the ICC when in the past, it accused him of supporting/funding rebels in a case it 'voluntarily' referred to the same Court. That it would do so can only, *ipso facto*, point to double standards. It is plausible to thus assume that although Uganda joined the cacophony of African states expressing concern about the Sudan referrals, Kampala was not overly distressed about the lodestone placed on Bashir's neck.

... [T]he referral of Libya to the ICC was another matter because it involved President Gaddafi, a long-time ally of the regime in Uganda. Museveni then declared that he was 'totally allergic to foreign, political, and military involvement in sovereign countries, especially the African countries'. True to his (new) word, Museveni became one of the most vociferous opponents of the ICC within the African Union (AU) and instigated some of the discussions around not simply non-cooperation with the office of the Prosecutor, but complete withdrawal from the Rome Statute.

However, duplicity was not just confined to Kampala or The Hague. Behind the scenes, the United States saw an opportunity in the Kony referrals to pursue its global anti-terrorism agenda, and hence supported the actions of the Ugandan Government against the LRA up to its elusive search for Kony and his lieutenants in the jungles of the DRC and the CAR.

The Government's mixed signals over its 'Kony problem'-to wit seeking the prosecution of the LRA rebels internationally (before the ICC) on the one hand, while also advocating for domestic prosecution (and traditional forms of justice or 'peaceful reconciliation') ... [did not lead it to object] to the Hague trial of Dominic Ongwen ... . The inconsistency in the Government's position was thus stark and logically suggestive of duplicity.

At the end of the day, in his relations with the ICC, Museveni was both able to have his cake and to eat it, deftly selecting when, where, how and on what terms and issues he chose to cooperate with the institution and on those over which he did not. He was also adept at jumping on the victimisation band-wagon when circumstances suited him, pushing the AU to adopt increasingly more hostile positions towards the institution. Ultimately, the Ugandan victims of both the LRA and the UPDF were short-changed in the process as efforts directed towards truth and reconciliation were given short shrift and wider questions of accountability thus ignored. In contradistinction to the noble 'justice-oriented' aims for which the Rome Statute and the Court under it were envisioned, Uganda and the ICC had resorted to an alliance without 'righteous foundation'. Little good could therefore come out of it.

JONAS BENS, THE SENTIMENTAL COURT: THE AFFECTIVE LIFE OF INTERNATIONAL CRIMINAL JUSTICE (2022) 171

Epilogue: Affect and Colonialism

On February 4, 2021, … the judges of the ICC found Dominic Ongwen guilty of war crimes and crimes against humanity. Two weeks earlier, Yoweri Kaguta Museveni had won the general election and, despite allegations of election fraud and violent suppression of the political opposition, entered his sixth term as president of Uganda. Ongwen's conviction, which carries a prison sentence of twenty-five years, most likely marks the end of the ICC's criminal prosecution in northern Uganda. …

The judgment was presented by the presiding judge, Bertram Schmitt, from Germany. He made his remarks slowly and carefully, his face showing a solemn expression. … [He stated:]

> Let me emphasise that it was difficult for the Chamber to ascertain the names of every victim of the several crimes. Yet, in many cases the Chamber was able to do so. These victims have a right not to be forgotten. They have the right to be mentioned explicitly today, as they are in the judgment as well. Please bear with me if I pronounce names incorrectly.

This brief scene profoundly affected me, but in several quite ambivalent ways. It triggered an intense awareness of the colonial structure of our contemporary world. What struck me immediately, and maybe this was just on the surface of the arrangement, was the constellation of bodies: a white European man sitting in judgment over a black African, deciding his fate. This encapsulates the colonial constellation in a nutshell. Second, Schmitt evokes the African victims of violence to legitimize this constellation of bodies in which he speaks. He presents himself and his colleagues at the bench as people who take the side of the victims and do not want them to be forgotten. The "specter of the victim" as a prevalent trope of colonialism at the center of international criminal justice has been formidably and critically analyzed by Kamari Clarke in *Fictions of Justice* (2009). Colonialism can mean many different things, but at its core, it means intervening in the sphere of others and deriving the legitimation for this intervention from one's own system of rules. Schmitt is aware that he is meddling in the affairs of others whose names he has difficulty pronouncing. He is doomed to let this awareness show in his awkward apology to the audience. This small scene brings the colonial constellation to life in an uncanny way – it is a colonial awkwardness that feels all too familiar.

…

[The author then refers to the critique by Mahmood Mamdani, in Ch. 2, above, of the Nuremberg model as the wrong template for bringing justice in the aftermath of violence.] … In Mamdani's analysis, the Nuremberg tribunals did not even work in Germany in the late 1940s. In his book, Mamdani proposes something else: instead of constructing victims and perpetrators after violent conflict, a society should come together as survivors of violence … .

I agree with Mamdani's analysis, which is shared by most of the anthropologists who write about transitional justice, that the system of international criminal justice cannot be separated from the colonial structures governing the global capitalist order in which it was conceived and in which it operates. But … I find Mamdani's suggestion that "Nuremberg" was a mistake, that it was the wrong thing to do, thoroughly repellent. It feels inconceivable to me that Jewish Germans who survived the death camps and former Nazi officials could ever somehow come together as "survivors of the Third Reich." … The proposition that it would have been better to avoid a criminal justice approach to Nazi perpetrators would probably only find support on the very extreme right in Germany.

…

... Colonialism is such an omnipresent structure that shapes the sentiments of people. One cannot but navigate and partly reproduce these sentiments. When people are in a position to reproduce colonial sentiment, when they feel compelled by forces larger than themselves and try to do the right thing nevertheless, then the kind of colonial awkwardness emerges that one can feel in Judge Schmitt's apology. Even those who see themselves as fighters against colonial injustice will not be able to avoid feeling such colonial awkwardness. The question is: Do we perceive these affective dynamics of colonialism merely as a mechanism of subjugation, or as an unavoidable starting point for resistance against a world that produces and reproduces enormous inequality every day? ...

THE BROADER RACE ISSUE

Moving beyond the specifics of the Ongwen and other Ugandan cases, it has been argued that the ICC needs to move beyond a posture of race-neutrality and confront the deeper structures involved.[697] Although the following critiques preceded the warrants sought in relation to the situations in Ukraine and Palestine (Gaza), they have not lost their relevance.

RANDLE C. DEFALCO AND FRÉDÉRIC MÉGRET, THE INVISIBILITY OF RACE AT THE ICC: LESSONS FROM THE U.S. CRIMINAL JUSTICE SYSTEM 7 LONDON REV. INT'L. L. (2019) 55

...

Conclusion: The Unbearable 'Whiteness' of the ICC?

Accusations that the ICC is racist have created a degree of panic among certain international criminal justice advocates. The threatened and actual withdrawal of African states from the Court has been widely perceived as a catastrophe. We are concerned, by contrast, that the blanket dismissal of race-based critiques of the ICC may inhibit critical assessments of how the ICC and other international criminal justice institutions are actually operating, and what their effects are, including in terms of their roles in the global production of race and racism. ...

Much like the U.S. Supreme Court in its selective blindness to certain manifestations of racism, especially structural racism, international criminal justice actors at times behave as if any acknowledgement of the multi-dimensional complexities of race and racism will necessarily open a Pandora's box of insurmountable racial justice challenges that the law is ill-equipped to address. The perceived safer avenue selected by the ICC, at least thus far, has been selectively to see race in much the same way as US courts do—that is, to acknowledge the role of race/racism as a cause or consequence of crime and atrocity, but not to see race when it comes to questions of structural or distributive justice that the Court itself is implicated in.

The most evident danger is that the ICC will become a forum exclusively for prosecuting atrocity crimes committed by or within predominantly Black, Arab or other racialised communities, whilst exempting itself from the need to ever see itself as part of the ongoing perpetuation of a racially fragmented and polarised world. ...

... [W]hat is at stake in these and other cases concerning intersections between race and criminal justice are questions of distributive justice. How are the burdens inherent in employing the technique of criminal law—investigatory actions, surveillance and intrusions of privacy, arrest, detention, prosecution, social stigma, and the like, and, in the international arena, the possibility of sanctions or even foreign intervention—distributed amongst the populations subject to a given criminal justice system? Who benefits from the law most in terms of being made safer (or at least being made to feel subjectively safer) and less at risk of being victimised, be it by criminals or criminal justice actors (such as police officers or prosecutors) themselves? Under the cover of working to prevent atrocities in Africa, the international community may appear to be engaged in systemic global policing of racialised Africans.

---

[697] See also S. Manley, P. Tehrani and R. Rasiah, 'The (Non-) Use of African Law by the International Criminal Court', 34 *Eur. J. Int'l L.* (2023) 555.

… International criminal justice does not proceed from a safe place of racial innocence. It exists in a world that is structured by racial constructions, and it ignores those constructions and their relevance at its peril. … [H]ow might one go about decolonising or improving the racial politics of international criminal justice?

In recent years, the ICC has inched towards a more nuanced approach to grappling with the racialised dimensions of international criminal justice. During the mandate of former ICC Prosecutor Moreno-Ocampo, the rhetoric emanating from the OTP was especially tone deaf, characterised by bombastic all-or-nothing claims about the Court's unimpeachable virtue. Under the guidance of Fatou Bensouda, the OTP has at least made efforts to address crimes beyond those committed by Black and/or Arab-African men, by investigating potential international crimes occurring in Afghanistan, Georgia, the Ukraine, Israel/Palestine, and Iraq, including those allegedly committed by (mostly White) US and British nationals. Such initiatives may have the potential to begin to subvert dominant racialising narratives, but, if anything, the rebalancing of prosecutorial focus beyond Africa is framed more in geographic and national terms than explicitly racial ones, once again avoiding the discomfort of acknowledging the significance race continues to exhibit globally.

The ICC's anti-racist credentials have been challenged for a while by those who are on the receiving end of international criminal justice's racial politics. To discuss race and to challenge its construction, is to discuss power and to challenge its production. Doing so requires that individuals and institutions acknowledge their own roles in perpetuating—as enablers, bystanders, and/or uncritical conduits—such power structures, along with the privileges they enjoy because of their racial associations (or various other identity categories) that others do not. It also requires an urgent emphasis on transparency and accountability in prosecutorial decisions, given the importance of discretion in allowing racial prejudice to seep into the substance of criminal justice, be it domestically or internationally. And it requires doing so in ways that do not unwittingly end up reinforcing and reifying racial categorisations in the name of anti-racism, but that constantly locate the problem of racism in the very construction of such categories.

One need look no further than the US for a cautionary example of how the dogged refusal to see certain forms of racism, especially structural ones, can deeply undermine the credibility of a criminal justice system, to the point that it becomes a source of—rather than a bulwark against—pervasive human rights violations and the perpetuation of racialised oppression. Dogmatic adherence to race-neutrality, in this context, risks blinding international criminal justice to its own role in historical and structural patterns of racial production and thereby further eroding its already precarious credibility.

QUESTIONS

1. What lessons might be drawn from the successful undermining of the Kenyan cases?

2. Given Joe Oloka-Onyango's description of the politics surrounding the LRA referral, under what circumstances do you think the OTP should accept self-referrals of rebels by the governments that they are fighting?

3. What conclusions do you draw from Jonas Bens' description of what he sees as the colonialist overtones reflected in the *Ongwen* case?

---

5. The United States and the ICC

The U.S. participated actively in drafting and shaping the Rome Statute. But it was one of seven countries that voted against its adoption in 1998. The others were China, Iraq, Israel, Libya, Qatar, and Yemen. On 31 December 2000, the last day on which it was possible to do so, President Clinton signed the treaty. But he also recommended that the Senate should not be asked for its advice and consent to ratification until fundamental concerns were satisfied. In particular, these related to the 'unchecked' power of the Prosecutor and the risk that U.S. soldiers and officials could be subjected to politicized prosecutions. Under Article 18 of the Vienna

Convention on the Law of Treaties, a signatory State is obliged not to 'defeat the object and purpose of a treaty prior to its entry into force'. On 6 May 2002, some eight months after the attacks of 9/11, and as the U.S. invasion of Afghanistan was in full force, President Bush 'unsigned' the Rome Statute (which is not in fact possible) by informing the UN Secretary-General that 'the United States does not intend to become a party to the treaty [as a result of which it] has no legal obligations arising from its signature ...'. Israel used the same formula to 'unsign' three months later.

In 2002, the American Service-Members' Protection Act prohibited certain forms of U.S. cooperation with the ICC, required military and other aid to states parties to the Rome Statute to be cut unless those states signed an agreement not to surrender U.S. personnel to the Court, and authorized 'all means necessary, including military force' to be used to release U.S. persons arrested by the ICC. It was informally called 'The Hague Invasion Act'.

The Bush administration also negotiated bilateral agreements with some 100 states, not all of which were states parties. The agreements provided that no nationals, current or former officials, or military personnel of either party may be surrendered or transferred by the other state to the ICC for any purpose. These were said to be based on Article 98(2) of the Statute,[698] but this claim was widely contested. In 2002, the administration threatened not to support a peace-keeping operation unless the Security Council used its power under Article 16 to defer any investigation or prosecution for a period of 12 months in cases 'involving current or former officials or personnel from a contributing State not a party to the Rome Statute over acts or omissions relating to a United Nations established or authorised operation' (Res. 1422 (2002)). The suspension was renewed again in 2003, but rejected by Council members the following year.

During this period, the U.S. made exceptions when it suited it. In 2005, it permitted the Security Council to refer the Darfur case to the Court and, in 2011, the Obama administration voted to refer Libya for investigation. The U.S. also played a key role in delivering Bosco Ntaganda, of the DRC, and Dominic Ongwen, of Uganda, to the custody of the ICC.

In September 2018, President Trump told the UN General Assembly that the U.S. would 'provide no support or recognition to the ... Court. As far as America is concerned the ICC has no jurisdiction, no legitimacy, and no authority.' In March 2019, Secretary of State Mike Pompeo announced that the U.S. would impose visa bans on ICC officials involved in a potential investigation of U.S. citizens alleged to have committed crimes in Afghanistan. The threat was subsequently extended to cover investigations affecting nationals of allied countries, including Israelis. In 2019, it was confirmed that the U.S. visa of Prosecutor Fatou Bensouda had been revoked. In May 2020, Pompeo threatened 'consequences' if the court pursued its inquiries in relation to Palestine.

On 11 June 2020, President Trump issued Executive Order 13928, entitled 'Blocking Property of Certain Persons Associated with the [ICC]':

...

> I therefore determine that any attempt by the ICC to investigate, arrest, detain, or
> prosecute any United States personnel without the consent of the United States, or of
> personnel of countries that are United States allies and who are not parties to the Rome
> Statute or have not otherwise consented to ICC jurisdiction, constitutes an unusual and
> extraordinary threat to the national security and foreign policy of the United States, and I
> hereby declare a national emergency to deal with that threat. ...

Relevant sanctions included asset freezes and family entry bans against some ICC officials and those who assist certain court investigations, thus deterring other nations from cooperating with the Court. President Biden revoked that Executive Order on 1 April 2021 and sanctions on ICC personnel were lifted. The following day, Secretary of State Blinken emphasized that the U.S. 'disagree[s] strongly with the ICC's actions relating to the Afghanistan and Palestinian situations' and maintained its 'longstanding objection to the Court's efforts to assert jurisdiction over personnel of non-States Parties such as the United States and Israel.'

---

[698] Article 98(2): 'The Court may not proceed with a request for surrender which would require the requested State to act inconsistently with its obligations under international agreements pursuant to which the consent of a sending State is required to surrender a person of that State to the Court ...'.

The U.S. could always avoid a situation in which the Court seeks to exercise jurisdiction over an American by satisfying the complementarity principle and investigating and prosecuting in its domestic courts. But:

> To do so is to concede the authority of the ICC to subject US actions to its scrutiny. This the United States steadfastly refuses to do. In turning the argument into one about jurisdiction, the United States seeks to challenge not the merits of the probe but the Court's very authority to hold non-signatories responsible … . [As a result, we] … hold ourselves out as champions of international law — provided we are not subject to its norms and processes.[699]

Following the invasion of Ukraine, Congress approved a 'War Crimes Accountability' provision, which authorized the U.S. government to render assistance to the ICC 'to assist with investigations and prosecutions of foreign nationals related to the Situation in Ukraine, including to support victims and witnesses.'[700] The U.S. has subsequently provided extensive funding to a wide range of civil society and other groups, as well as to prosecutors in Ukraine, and to the ICC, to support such efforts. In contrast, the U.S. rejected the actions of the ICC in relation to Israel's Prime Minister and Defence Minister in May 2024 as 'outrageous'.

6. Russia and Ukraine: The ICC and the Crime of Aggression

Ukraine is not a state party to the Rome Statute but, in 2013, shortly before Russia's invasion and annexation of Crimea, it accepted the Court's jurisdiction over alleged crimes committed on its territory (Article 12(3) of the Statute). Immediately after Russia's 2022 invasion, the Prosecutor indicated he would seek authorization to open an investigation, but this became unnecessary when 43 states parties formally referred the situation to the Court. Four other states subsequently joined, and an investigation was opened on 2 March 2022, less than one week after the invasion.

After the Prosecutor appealed for assistance, Western States committed unprecedented levels of funding to support the OTP's Trust Fund for Advanced Technology and Specialized Capacity and committed national personnel to assist the Office. The European Union, the United States and the United Kingdom established the Atrocity Crimes Advisory Group to assist the Office of the Prosecutor-General of Ukraine, which has opened thousands of war crimes investigations. And within a year, the ICC Prosecutor had made four visits to Ukraine.

One investigative effort funded by the U.S. led to a report by the Humanitarian Research Lab at Yale School of Public Health, entitled 'Russia's Systematic Program for the Re-education & Adoption of Ukraine's Children' (14 February 2023).

Following an application by the OTP on 22 February 2023, Pre-Trial Chamber II issued arrest warrants on 17 March 2023 for Russian President Vladimir Putin and Maria Lvova-Belova, Russia's Commissioner for Children's Rights. On 24 June 2024, warrants were also issued for the arrest of Sergei Shoigu and Valery Gerasimov, former Minister and First Deputy Minister of Defence of the Russian Federation. The charges relate to a large number of strikes against numerous electric power plants and sub-stations in 2022-23.[701]

Putin and Lvova-Belova were indicted for the war crime of unlawful deportation of population (children) and that of unlawful transfer of population (children) from occupied areas of Ukraine to the Russian Federation (under articles 8(2)(a)(vii) and 8(2)(b)(viii) of the Rome Statute). The Chamber held that '[t]here are reasonable grounds to believe that Mr Putin bears individual criminal responsibility for the aforementioned crimes, (i) for having committed the acts directly, jointly with others and/or through others (article 25(3)(a) of the Rome Statute), and (ii) for his failure to exercise control properly over civilian and military subordinates who

---

[699] L. Douglas, 'The United States and the ICC: The Court that Cannot Operate Against Us', 19 *J. Int'l. Crim. Just.* (2021) 477, at 484.
[700] Consolidate Appropriations Act (2023). See P. Williams et al., 'Introducing the Symposium on U.S. Support for the ICC's Trust Fund for Victims', *Just Security* (13 February 2023).
[701] Each person is charged with the war crime of directing attacks at civilian objects (article 8(2)(b)(ii) of the Rome Statute) and the war crime of causing excessive incidental harm to civilians or damage to civilian objects (article 8(2)(b)(iv) of the Rome Statute), and the crime against humanity of inhumane acts under article 7(1)(k) of the Rome Statute.

committed the acts, or allowed for their commission, and who were under his effective authority and control, pursuant to superior responsibility (article 28(b) of the Rome Statute).'

The warrants remained sealed in order to protect victims and witnesses, and to safeguard continuing investigations. But in a statement on the day the warrants were announced, the Prosecutor, Karim Khan, said:

> Incidents identified by my Office include the deportation of at least hundreds of children taken from orphanages and children's care homes. Many of these children, we allege, have since been given for adoption in the Russian Federation. The law was changed in the Russian Federation, through Presidential decrees issued by President Putin, to expedite the conferral of Russian citizenship, making it easier for them to be adopted by Russian families.
>
> My Office alleges that these acts, amongst others, demonstrate an intention to permanently remove these children from their own country. At the time of these deportations, the Ukrainian children were protected persons under the Fourth Geneva Convention.
>
> We also underlined in our application that most acts in this pattern of deportations were carried out in the context of the acts of aggression committed by Russian military forces against the sovereignty and territorial integrity of Ukraine which began in 2014.[702]

The allusion to acts of aggression was most likely intended to signal that, although the ICC lacks jurisdiction to prosecute Russian officials for the crime of aggression, relevant actions would be addressed indirectly in the war crimes prosecutions.[703] President Putin's spokesperson announced that Russia did not recognize the Court or its jurisdiction and former President, Dmitry Medvedev, called the Court a 'legal non-entity' and warned that any attempt to arrest Putin 'would be a declaration of war on the Russian Federation'. The prosecution of President Putin raises many issues, but two of the most important concern the immunity enjoyed by heads of state, and the possibility of a prosecution for aggression.

Head of State Immunity

Two provisions of the Rome Statute are of particular relevance to the question of whether President Putin could be argued to enjoy immunity from either arrest or prosecution:

Article 27
Irrelevance of official capacity

1. This Statute shall apply equally to all persons without any distinction based on official capacity. In particular, official capacity as a Head of State or Government, ... shall in no case exempt a person from criminal responsibility under this Statute ... .

2. Immunities or special procedural rules which may attach to the official capacity of a person, whether under national or international law, shall not bar the Court from exercising its jurisdiction over such a person.

Article 98
Cooperation with respect to waiver of immunity and consent to surrender

1. The Court may not proceed with a request for surrender or assistance which would require the requested State to act inconsistently with its obligations under international law with respect to the State or diplomatic immunity of a person or property of a third State, unless the Court can first obtain the cooperation of that third State for the waiver of the immunity.

* * *

---

[702] K. A. A. Khan, Statement on the issuance of arrest warrants against President Vladimir Putin and Ms. Maria Lvova-Belova (17 March 2023).

[703] F. Mégret, 'Why Prosecuting Aggression in Ukraine as a Crime Against Humanity Might Make Sense', 28 *J. Conflict and Security L.* (2023) 467.

In the *Case of the Arrest Warrant of 11 April 2000 (Democratic Republic of the Congo v. Belgium)* [2002] ICJ 1, the International Court of Justice confirmed the absolute and functional immunity of current and former heads of state and foreign ministers, based on customary international law. The assumption is that any such arrest is incompatible with the principles of sovereign equality and non-interference. The Court also found that customary international law did not support the existence of any form of exception to the rule in relation to war crimes or crimes against humanity.

Nevertheless, this issue has been extensively litigated in relation to the outstanding arrest warrants issued by the ICC for then President Omar Al-Bashir, of Sudan, on 4 March 2009 and 12 July 2010, for war crimes, crimes against humanity and genocide. Because Sudan was not a party to the Rome Statute, the situation in Darfur had been referred to the Court by the Security Council in Resolution 1593 (2005), which was adopted under Chapter VII of the UN Charter and was thus binding on states. President Al-Bashir subsequently travelled to several states, including Jordan, Malawi, and South Africa, none of which took steps to arrest him and render him to The Hague.

On the application of the Prosecutor, the Pre-Trial Chamber held that the relevant states were required to arrest Al-Bashir. In response, Jordan appealed. The Appeals Chamber agreed with the Pre-Trial Chamber that Article 27(2) meant that states parties to the Rome Statute could not invoke the principle of immunity to justify a failure to arrest and surrender an accused to the Court. It added that Article 27(2) also reflected customary international law, and that the order of the Security Council effectively brought Sudan, a non-state party, into the overall regime requiring cooperation with the Court as if it were a state party. Thus, Al-Bashir would have no immunity, in accordance with Article 27(2). A brief excerpt follows from the Appeals *Chamber's Judgment in the Jordan Referral re Al-Bashir Appeal* (ICC-02/05-01/09-397) (6 May 2019):

> 113. … [T]here is neither State practice nor *opinio juris* that would support the existence of Head of State immunity under customary international law vis-à-vis an international court. To the contrary, … such immunity has never been recognised in international law as a bar to the jurisdiction of an international court. …
>
> 114. The absence of a rule of customary international law recognising Head of State immunity vis-à-vis international courts is relevant not only to the question of whether an international court may issue a warrant for the arrest of a Head of State and conduct proceedings against him or her, but also for the horizontal relationship between States when a State is requested by an international court to arrest and surrender the Head of State of another State. … [N]o immunities under customary international law operate in such a situation to bar an international court in its exercise of its own jurisdiction.

The judgment proved to be very controversial. Consider the following responses:

Leila Nadya Sadat, 'Why the ICC's Judgment in the al-Bashir Case Wasn't So Surprising', *Just Security* (12 July 2019):

> … [T]he decision was (1) unsurprising, (2) correctly decided, and (3) consistent with the Court's judicial mandate. …
>
> …
>
> … [T]he *travaux préparatoires* … indicate that Article 27(1) … codifies the customary international law rule that whatever immunities an official might have before national courts cannot be pled as a bar or a defense to criminal responsibility, *ratione materiae*, before the ICC regarding the *jus cogens* crimes in the Rome Statute. Article 27(2) complements this provision by ensuring that no procedural immunities bar the ICC from exercising this jurisdiction. …
>
> …

... [I]n taking up the question of head of State immunity under customary international law, rather than relying upon the effect of U.N. Security Council Resolution 1593 to answer the question (as it could have done), the Appeals Chamber acted consistent with its judicial mandate and properly reaffirmed the autonomous nature of international criminal law before the ICC.

...

... [T]he political objective of immunizing heads of state (and presumably other high government officials) cannot properly be achieved through judicial reinterpretation of the Rome Statute, but can only be undertaken by the States Parties themselves, as the African Union has attempted in the Malabo Protocol.

... The Appeals Chamber has rendered a very significant decision regarding the scope and nature of the ICC's jurisdiction over core crimes.

Yet questions remain. First, the decision will not stop either the political or the scholarly debate over head of state immunity. Second, it does not answer the "vexing" question of when efforts to change customary international law ... could reach the tipping point necessary for such a change to come into effect. ... Moreover, if the core crimes and the provision of non-immunity for core crimes before international courts are *jus cogens* (peremptory norms), query whether [they can] be changed by contrary state practice at all? ...

Dov Jacobs, 'You have just entered Narnia: ICC Appeals Chamber adopts the worst possible solution on immunities in the *Bashir* case', *Spreading the Jam* (6 May 2019):

... [T]his Judgment means that immunities cannot be claimed by nationals of non-State parties, even when the situation is not referred to the Court by the UNSC. ...

... This is probably one of the weirdest consequences of the Judgment: because the Appeals Chamber claims the existence of a rule not just in the Rome Statute, but in customary international law, that there are no immunities before "international tribunals", one could arguably claim that the obligation to arrest and surrender a person would rest not only on State parties but also on non-State parties, because customary law is binding on all States... this is of course a ridiculous proposition, but it shows the absurdity of the Judgment.

... [T]he AC makes no mention of the Malabo Protocol, which explicitly provides for Head of State immunity. ...

Dapo Akande, 'ICC Appeals Chamber Holds that Heads of State Have No Immunity Under Customary International Law Before International Tribunals', *EJIL:Talk!* (6 May 2019):

This is stunning and appears to be deeply misguided. It is also, in my opinion, a very dangerous and unwise move for the Court to make. This reasoning appears to assert that parties to the Rome Statute, have, by creating the Court, taken away the rights of non-party states under international law. Dangerous because this reasoning is likely to stiffen opposition to the Court by non-parties. The John Bolton's [sic] of this world and many people far more reasonable will point to this ruling to set out precisely why it is important to oppose this court and other international criminal courts. ... [T]he issue of the immunity of heads of state before international criminal courts is not what is at issue ... . What [is] at issue is the immunity of heads of states from arrest by other states acting at the request of an international criminal court. That the head of state may not have immunity before the international criminal court does not, without more, say anything about whether he or she may have immunity before a foreign state.

ICC, Q&A Regarding Appeals Chamber's 6 May 2019 Judgment in The Jordan Referral Re *Al-Bashir* Appeal (ICC-PIOS-Q&A-SUD-02-01/19), May 2019:

...

The judgment has generated animated discussion in blogosphere. what is the court's view on that?

> There is nothing new, extra-ordinary [sic] or wrong about judgments of courts of law generating discussion among those who have a view. ...

> In the era of social media, it is hoped that observers would properly study the Court's judgments and decisions before rushing to comment on them. ...

> Lawyers engaging in public commentary should exercise particular caution and remain mindful of the cardinal principles that guide the conduct of lawyers, including that of honesty, integrity and fairness. This principle adequately covers the need to be fair when criticising courts and judges. ...

The Crime of Aggression

At the Rome Conference in 1998, states were unable to agree on proposals to criminalize aggression. Definitional questions and the possible role of the Security Council were the principal stumbling blocks, in addition to fears on the part of powerful states of the ramifications of such a move.[704] After extensive negotiations, a 2010 Review Conference of the ICC Statute, held in Kampala,[705] agreed by consensus to several amendments, including the following:

Article 8 bis

Crime of aggression

1. For the purpose of this Statute, "crime of aggression" means the planning, preparation, initiation or execution, by a person in a position effectively to exercise control over or to direct the political or military action of a State, of an act of aggression which, by its character, gravity and scale, constitutes a manifest violation of the Charter of the United Nations.

2. For the purpose of paragraph 1, "act of aggression" means the use of armed force by a State against the sovereignty, territorial integrity or political independence of another State, or in any other manner inconsistent with the Charter of the United Nations. Any of the following acts, regardless of a declaration of war, shall, in accordance with United Nations General Assembly resolution 3314 (XXIX) of 14 December 1974, qualify as an act of aggression:

> (a) The invasion or attack by the armed forces of a State of the territory of another State, or any military occupation, however temporary, resulting from such invasion or attack, or any annexation by the use of force of the territory of another State or part thereof;

> (b) Bombardment ...;

> (c) The blockade of the ports or coasts ...;

> ...

> (g)   The sending by or on behalf of a State of armed bands, groups, irregulars or mercenaries, which carry out acts of armed force against another State of such gravity as to amount to the acts listed above, or its substantial involvement therein.

---

[704] '... [T]he United States delegation expressed trepidation that the Kampala amendments might stimulate states to enact implementing statutes giving their domestic courts universal jurisdiction over the crime of aggression.' M. Scharf, 'Universal Jurisdiction and the Crime of Aggression', 53 *Harv. Int'l L. J.* (2012) 357, at 359.

[705] All relevant documents are available at https://asp.icc-cpi.int/reviewconference/crime-of-aggression.

Article 15 bis
Exercise of jurisdiction over the crime of aggression (State referral, *proprio motu*)

...

... 4. The Court may ... exercise jurisdiction over a crime of aggression, arising from an act of aggression committed by a State Party, unless that State Party has previously declared that it does not accept such jurisdiction by lodging a declaration with the Registrar. ...

5. In respect of a State that is not a party to this Statute, the Court shall not exercise its jurisdiction over the crime of aggression when committed by that State's nationals or on its territory.

6. Where the Prosecutor concludes that there is a reasonable basis to proceed with an investigation in respect of a crime of aggression, he or she shall first ascertain whether the Security Council has made a determination of an act of aggression committed by the State concerned. ...

7. Where the Security Council has made such a determination, the Prosecutor may proceed with the investigation in respect of a crime of aggression.

8. Where no such determination is made within six months ..., the Prosecutor may proceed with the investigation ... provided that the Pre-Trial Division has authorized the commencement of the investigation ..., and the Security Council has not decided otherwise ... .

* * *

As of January 2024, 45 states have ratified the amendments relating to the crime of aggression. Sixteen of those states have implemented the relevant provisions into domestic law, and nine have expanded the scope of their universal jurisdiction laws to include aggression.[706]

Agreement on the definition of the crime of aggression represents major progress, but the many limits on the Court's jurisdiction for this crime reflect the determination of major powers to greatly reduce the possibility that they might be subject to such prosecutions. As a result, the most likely scenario for activation of the provisions would involve an outlier state committing an act of aggression which the Permanent Five members of the UN Security Council agree violates Article 8 *bis* and leads them to make a referral to the Court. This would exacerbate the criticism that the Court is only likely to constrain the least powerful, rather than the most powerful and aggressive.

Russia, like the United States, is not a State Party and, because both states wield a veto in the Security Council, neither is ever likely to be the subject of a referral. To make up for this gap, the European Commission opened the International Centre for the Prosecution of the Crime of Aggression against Ukraine (ICPA) in July 2023 as a hub to support national investigations. Including an initial US contribution of US$1 million, the centre has a budget of over US$10 million in its first year.

In response to these developments, various commentators have raised the issue of double standards, with some pointing to the U.S. invasion of Iraq in 2003 which did not lead to any investigations or prosecutions. Others observe that the United States, which has strongly supported initiatives against Russia, is not a party to the ICC, sought to ensure that it would never be the subject of a prosecution for the crime of aggression, and has resisted providing information to the ICC in the Russia case, reportedly because 'American military leaders ... fear setting a precedent that might help pave the way for it to prosecute Americans.'[707] Following the outbreak of the Gaza war in October 2023, many commentators warned of the risk of double standards if the ICC Prosecutor did not pursue both sides in that conflict for alleged crimes.

---

[706] A. Hartig, *Making Aggression a Crime Under Domestic Law: On the Legislative Implementation of Article 8bis of the ICC Statute* (2023) 7-8.

[707] C. Savage, 'Pentagon Blocks Giving Hague Court Evidence of Possible Russian War Crimes', *The New York Times* (8 March 2023).

Double standards have long been a seemingly unavoidable feature in the evolution of international human rights law.[708] Are they any more problematic when the issue is international criminal justice? Consider the following divergent perspectives.

Beth Van Schaack, Ambassador-at-Large for Global Criminal Justice, U.S. State Department, Remarks at Nuremburg Principles Meeting, Catholic University of America (27 March 2023):

> [At Nuremberg and in response to the atrocities committed in the former Yugoslavia and in Rwanda] the world came together to deliver a measure of justice in the face of atrocities. I am proud that at each of these moments, the United States supported the advancement of international criminal law and accountability. ...
>
> Again now, at this critical moment in history, I am pleased to announce that the United States supports the development of an internationalized tribunal dedicated to prosecuting the crime of aggression against Ukraine. Although a number of models have been under consideration, ... we believe an internationalized court that is rooted in Ukraine's judicial system, but that also includes international elements, will provide the clearest path to establishing a new Tribunal and maximizing our chances of achieving meaningful accountability. We envision such a court having significant international elements—in the form of substantive law, personnel, information sources, and structure. It might also be located elsewhere in Europe, at least at first, to reinforce Ukraine's desired European orientation, lend gravitas to the initiative, and enable international involvement, including through Eurojust.
>
> ...
>
> We are committed to working with Ukraine, and peace-loving countries around the world, to stand up, staff, and resource such a tribunal in a way that will achieve comprehensive accountability for the international crimes being committed in Ukraine.
>
> ...
>
> A tribunal of this type will complement the work that will be undertaken by the new International Centre for the Prosecution of the Crime of Aggression (ICPA) ... [which] will coordinate the investigation of acts of aggression committed against Ukraine and build criminal dossiers against those leaders responsible for planning, preparing, initiating, or waging this war of aggression for future trials. ...
>
> ...
>
> The United States remains unwavering in its support of the government and people of Ukraine as they defend their country and their freedom. ...

Alice Speri, 'Momentum Grows on Special Tribunal to Prosecute Putin's Aggression in Ukraine', *The Intercept* (13 February 2023):

> Reed Brody, a human rights attorney specialized in mass atrocities and author of "To Catch a Dictator," stressed that the only reason a special tribunal might be necessary for Ukraine is that countries now calling for it restricted the ICC's jurisdiction over this crime. "People talk about a gap and a loophole. Well, how did that gap get created? It was purposeful," he told The Intercept. "You have to balance, is it better to have some justice at the cost of consecrating double standards? I'm not sure that everyone understands how toxic this justified perception is that international justice only kicks in against, you know, enemies or outcasts or low-value countries."

---

[708] For a strong defence of the proposed special tribunal, see P. Labuda, 'Countering Imperialism in International Law', 49 *Yale J. Int'l L.* (2023) 000.

Asked about the extent to which concerns over double standards have hindered discussions over a special tribunal for Ukraine, Van Schaack told The Intercept "very little." She added, "The reality is that Russian aggression is so egregious, it's such a clear and manifest violation of the U.N. charter. …

[Andriy] Kostin, the Ukrainian [Prosecutor-General], also dismissed those concerns.

"I don't want to spend time discussing the past. We can talk about the double, triple standards in the history of many countries, many organizations, but we have no time for this," he told reporters during his U.S. visit. "After the war, when we win, we will have time to analyze, to discuss and to find out what has happened before."

"We can't leave the situation as it is," he added. "If an aggressor starts an aggression and there is no valid, effective instrument to punish them, we need to invent this instrument together and punish the aggressor. Not only for this aggression, but to deter any other aggressor in any other place or time in the future." …

Kai Ambos, 'Ukraine and the Double Standards of the West', 20 *J. Int'l Crim. Just.* (2022) 875, at 891:

Western claims to be defending a rules-based international order, in the context of the Ukraine situation or beyond, can only legitimately be made if the West itself complies with international law. While one may, arguably, see a difference between the Russian war of aggression and the US-led invasion of Iraq or between the Russian *ius in bello* violations in Ukraine and the Western ones in Iraq and Afghanistan, these differences, if accepted at all, are at best ones of degree but not of principle. The same applies to drone killings by the US outside armed conflict and extra-legal executions by the Russians in the UK or elsewhere. In all these situations international law is violated, and the one violator cannot, legitimately and credibly, lecture the other one about compliance … .

QUESTION

The Parliamentary Assembly of the Council of Europe unanimously adopted Resolution 2482 (26 January 2023) calling upon the 46 member states of the Council (Russia was expelled in 2022) to establish a special tribunal. It proposed that:

7.1 its jurisdiction would be limited to the crime of aggression committed against Ukraine and would extend *ratione temporis* to the aggression started by the Russian Federation in February 2014. Its jurisdiction would include the role and complicity of the leaders of Belarus in the war of aggression against Ukraine … .

What are the arguments for and against extending the jurisdiction of this special tribunal to cover all member states of the Council of Europe?

---

7. Israel and Palestine: The Gaza Crisis

The killings and kidnappings carried out in Israel by Hamas on 7 October 2023, followed by the prolonged invasion of Gaza by Israeli forces and the massive loss of life that ensued, generated renewed pressure on the Prosecutor to act. On 5 February 2021, the ICC's Pre-Trial Chamber I had determined that the Court could, on an ongoing basis, exercise its criminal jurisdiction in the Situation in the State of Palestine, including Gaza and the West Bank. As a result, the Court has jurisdiction over crimes committed by both nationals of States Parties and by the nationals of non-States Parties on the territory of a State Party.[709]

STATEMENT OF ICC PROSECUTOR KARIM A.A. KHAN KC: APPLICATIONS FOR ARREST WARRANTS IN THE SITUATION IN THE STATE OF PALESTINE, 20 MAY 2024

Yahya Sinwar, Mohammed Diab Ibrahim Al-Masri (Deif), Ismail Haniyeh

On the basis of evidence collected and examined by my Office, I have reasonable grounds to believe that **Yahya SINWAR** (Head of the Islamic Resistance Movement ("Hamas") in the Gaza Strip), **Mohammed Diab Ibrahim AL-MASRI**, more commonly known as DEIF (Commander-in-Chief of the military wing of Hamas, known as the *Al-Qassam Brigades*), and **Ismail HANIYEH** (Head of Hamas Political Bureau) bear criminal responsibility for the following war crimes and crimes against humanity committed on the territory of Israel and the State of Palestine (in the Gaza strip) from at least 7 October 2023:

- Extermination as a crime against humanity, contrary to article 7(1)(b) of the Rome Statute;
- Murder as a crime against humanity, contrary to article 7(1)(a), and as a war crime, contrary to article 8(2)(c)(i);
- Taking hostages as a war crime, contrary to article 8(2)(c)(iii);
- Rape and other acts of sexual violence as crimes against humanity, contrary to article 7(1)(g), and also as war crimes pursuant to article 8(2)(e)(vi) in the context of captivity;
- Torture as a crime against humanity, contrary to article 7(1)(f), and also as a war crime, contrary to article 8(2)(c)(i), in the context of captivity;
- Other inhumane acts as a crime against humanity, contrary to article 7(l)(k), in the context of captivity;
- Cruel treatment as a war crime contrary to article 8(2)(c)(i), in the context of captivity; and
- Outrages upon personal dignity as a war crime, contrary to article 8(2)(c)(ii), in the context of captivity.

My Office submits that the war crimes alleged in these applications were committed in the context of an international armed conflict between Israel and Palestine, and a non-international armed conflict between Israel and Hamas running in parallel. We submit that the crimes against humanity charged were part of a widespread and systematic attack against the civilian population of Israel by Hamas and other armed groups pursuant to organisational policies. Some of these crimes, in our assessment, continue to this day.

My Office submits there are reasonable grounds to believe that SINWAR, DEIF and HANIYEH are criminally responsible for the killing of hundreds of Israeli civilians in attacks perpetrated by Hamas (in particular its military wing, the al-Qassam Brigades) and other armed groups on 7 October 2023 and the taking of at least 245 hostages. …

It is the view of my Office that these individuals planned and instigated the commission of crimes on 7 October 2023, and have through their own actions, including personal visits to hostages shortly after their kidnapping, acknowledged their responsibility for those crimes. We submit that these crimes could not have been committed without their actions. They are charged both as co-perpetrators and as superiors pursuant to Articles 25 and 28 of the Rome Statute.

…

My Office also submits there are reasonable grounds to believe that hostages taken from Israel have been kept in inhumane conditions, and that some have been subject to sexual violence, including rape, while being held in captivity. We have reached that conclusion based on medical records, contemporaneous video and documentary evidence, and interviews with victims and survivors. My Office also continues to investigate reports of sexual violence committed on 7 October.

---

[709] For analyses of the jurisdictional and head of state/government immunity issues in this case, see K. Ambos et al, 'Without Fear or Favour: For an Effective International Criminal Court', *VerfBlog*, 14 June 2024, at https://verfassungsblog.de/without-fear-or-favour/; and T. Obel Hansen, 'State Objections to the ICC Prosecutor's Request for Arrest Warrants in the Palestine Investigation', *EJIL: Talk!*, 27 May 2024.

… I again reiterate my call for the immediate release of all hostages taken from Israel and for their safe return to their families. This is a fundamental requirement of international humanitarian law.

Benjamin Netanyahu, Yoav Gallant

On the basis of evidence collected and examined by my Office, I have reasonable grounds to believe that **Benjamin NETANYAHU**, the Prime Minister of Israel, and **Yoav GALLANT**, the Minister of Defence of Israel, bear criminal responsibility for the following war crimes and crimes against humanity committed on the territory of the State of Palestine (in the Gaza strip) from at least 8 October 2023:

- Starvation of civilians as a method of warfare as a war crime contrary to article 8(2)(b)(xxv) of the Statute;
- Wilfully causing great suffering, or serious injury to body or health contrary to article 8(2)(a)(iii), or cruel treatment as a war crime contrary to article 8(2)(c)(i);
- Wilful killing contrary to article 8(2)(a)(i), or Murder as a war crime contrary to article 8(2)(c)(i);
- Intentionally directing attacks against a civilian population as a war crime contrary to articles 8(2)(b)(i), or 8(2)(e)(i);
- Extermination and/or murder contrary to articles 7(1)(b) and 7(1)(a), including in the context of deaths caused by starvation, as a crime against humanity;
- Persecution as a crime against humanity contrary to article 7(1)(h);
- Other inhumane acts as crimes against humanity contrary to article 7(1)(k).

… We submit that the crimes against humanity charged were committed as part of a widespread and systematic attack against the Palestinian civilian population pursuant to State policy. These crimes, in our assessment, continue to this day.

My Office submits that the evidence we have collected … shows that Israel has intentionally and systematically deprived the civilian population in all parts of Gaza of objects indispensable to human survival.

This occurred through the imposition of a total siege over Gaza that involved completely closing the three border crossing points, Rafah, Kerem Shalom and Erez, from 8 October 2023 for extended periods and then by arbitrarily restricting the transfer of essential supplies – including food and medicine – through the border crossings after they were reopened. The siege also included cutting off cross-border water pipelines from Israel to Gaza – Gazans' principal source of clean water – for a prolonged period beginning 9 October 2023, and cutting off and hindering electricity supplies from at least 8 October 2023 until today. This took place alongside other attacks on civilians, including those queuing for food; obstruction of aid delivery by humanitarian agencies; and attacks on and killing of aid workers, which forced many agencies to cease or limit their operations in Gaza.

My Office submits that these acts were committed as part of a common plan to use starvation as a method of war and other acts of violence against the Gazan civilian population as a means to (i) eliminate Hamas; (ii) secure the return of the hostages which Hamas has abducted, and (iii) collectively punish the civilian population of Gaza, whom they perceived as a threat to Israel.

The effects of the use of starvation as a method of warfare, together with other attacks and collective punishment against the civilian population of Gaza are acute, visible and widely known, and have been confirmed by multiple witnesses interviewed by my Office, including local and international medical doctors. They include malnutrition, dehydration, profound suffering and an increasing number of deaths among the Palestinian population, including babies, other children, and women.

Famine is present in some areas of Gaza and is imminent in other areas. As UN Secretary-General António Guterres warned more than two months ago, "1.1 million people in Gaza are facing catastrophic hunger – the highest number of people ever recorded – anywhere, anytime" as a result of an "entirely manmade disaster". Today, my Office seeks to charge two of those most responsible, NETANYAHU and GALLANT, both as co-perpetrators and as superiors pursuant to Articles 25 and 28 of the Rome Statute.

Israel, like all States, has a right to take action to defend its population. That right, however, does not absolve Israel or any State of its obligation to comply with international humanitarian law. Notwithstanding any military goals they may have, the means Israel chose to achieve them in Gaza – namely, intentionally causing death, starvation, great suffering, and serious injury to body or health of the civilian population – are criminal.

…

Today we once again underline that international law and the laws of armed conflict apply to all. No foot soldier, no commander, no civilian leader – no one – can act with impunity. Nothing can justify wilfully depriving human beings, including so many women and children, the basic necessities required for life. Nothing can justify the taking of hostages or the targeting of civilians.

…

It is critical in this moment that my Office and all parts of the Court, including its independent judges, are permitted to conduct their work with full independence and impartiality. I insist that all attempts to impede, intimidate or improperly influence the officials of this Court must cease immediately. My Office will not hesitate to act pursuant to article 70 of the Rome Statute if such conduct continues.

…

Let us today be clear on one core issue: if we do not demonstrate our willingness to apply the law equally, if it is seen as being applied selectively, we will be creating the conditions for its collapse. In doing so, we will be loosening the remaining bonds that hold us together, the stabilising connections between all communities and individuals, the safety net to which all victims look in times of suffering. This is the true risk we face in this moment.

…

Responses to the Prosecutor's statement

Immediately after this statement, it was claimed by *The Guardian* and two Israeli-based magazines *+972* and *Local Call* that, for almost a decade, Israel ran a 'secret "war" against the court. The country deployed its intelligence agencies to surveil, hack, pressure, smear and allegedly threaten senior ICC staff in an effort to derail the court's inquiries.' This allegedly included intercepting phone calls, messages, emails and documents involving the Prosecutor and his predecessor.[710]

Even before the Prosecutor made his announcement, he received a letter dated 24 April 2024 and signed by 12 US Senators warning that any warrants against Israeli officials would amount to actions that are 'illegitimate and lack legal basis, and if carried out will result in severe sanctions against you and your institution.' It characterized any such action as an attempt 'to punish Israel for taking legitimate actions of self-defense against their Iranian-backed aggressors' and argued that the issuance of warrants would call 'into question the legitimacy of Israel's laws, legal system, and democratic form of government.' They also noted that it would expose the ICC's 'hypocrisy and double standards' since it has never issued warrants against the leaders of Iran, Syria, or China.

> Finally, neither Israel nor the United States are members of the ICC and are therefore outside of your organization's supposed jurisdiction. If you issue a warrant for the arrest of the Israeli leadership, we will interpret this not only as a threat to Israel's sovereignty but to the sovereignty of the United States. …

> The United States will not tolerate politicized attacks by the ICC on our allies. Target Israel and we will target you. If you move forward with the measures indicated in the report, we will move to end all American support for the ICC, sanction your employees and associates, and bar you and your families from the United States. You have been warned.

On 4 June 2024, the House of Representatives by a vote of 247-155, adopted 'H.R.8282 - Illegitimate Court Counteraction Act' which essentially proposed the re-enactment of the Trump-era sanctions against the Court.[711] The entirety of President Biden's official response on 20 May 2024 was:

---

[710] 'Spying, hacking and intimidation: Israel's nine-year "war" on the ICC exposed', *The Guardian*, 28 May 2024
[711] https://www.congress.gov/bill/118th-congress/house-bill/8282/text

> The ICC prosecutor's application for arrest warrants against Israeli leaders is outrageous. And let me be clear: whatever this prosecutor might imply, there is no equivalence — none — between Israel and Hamas. We will always stand with Israel against threats to its security.

Prime Minister Netanyahu called the announcement 'a moral outrage of historic proportions', given that Israel was 'waging a just war against Hamas, a genocidal terrorist organisation that perpetrated the worst attack on the Jewish people since the Holocaust.' He also called the Prosecutor one of the 'great antisemites in modern times,' whose warrants against Israeli officials amounted to 'callously pouring gasoline on the fires of antisemitism that are raging around the world.'[712]

QUESTIONS

1. What are the principal legal challenges that the Prosecutor is likely to face?

2. How compelling, legally and politically, are the responses from the United States?

---

8. Evaluating International Criminal Justice and the ICC

Both international criminal law as a field, and the work of the ICC as an institution, have been the subject of sustained criticism from scholars and practitioners.[713] Gerry Simpson suggests, in 'International Criminal Law: The Next Hundred Years', in Kevin Jon Heller et al. (eds.), *The Oxford Handbook of International Criminal Law* (2020) 841, at 849-50, that international criminal law 'may now be the most critiqued field in human history.' He then adds his own critique which is that what the field does 'is to bring into being a narrow and compromised image and practice of justice, enact and reproduce a particular victim and perpetrator subjectivity, and encourage a sometimes distracting form of anti-politics.' In the same volume, at 1, the editors identify three enduring controversies that have marred the discipline's self-understanding:

> … ICL has increasingly raised issues of hierarchy. The very nature of ICL is to create a hierarchy between the norms it backs and all other norms, the latter of which are presumed not to have an (internationally) penal character. But do norms of ICL always trump 'ordinary' norms of international law, as in the case of immunities? Issues of hierarchy can be found within ICL itself between its 'core' crimes and those presumed to lie at its periphery; in the relationship between international criminal tribunals themselves (is the ICC a primus inter pares or merely one among many international criminal jurisdictions?); and between international criminal tribunals and domestic courts (issues of complementarity and primacy). Questions of hierarchy also emerge in the practice of international criminal justice, such as in the tension between the rights of the defence and the rights of victims, or between the pursuit of justice and the pursuit of peace.
>
> ICL also increasingly raises questions of equality that are at least partly in tension with the vertical thrust of hierarchy. How should ICL treat like cases alike? To what extent is international criminal justice the repository of ideological presuppositions that lead it to emphasize the importance of some harm or some evil at the expense of others? Certain hierarchical criteria (e.g., the relative gravity of crimes) inevitably provide the basis for claims that less grave instances of crime are being treated with too much severity—and vice versa. Negotiating this distributive dimension has become the stock and trade of international criminal tribunals, which constantly have to deal with allegations that their choices reflect some a priori bias.

---

[712] 'What the ICC arrest warrants mean for Israel and Hamas', BBC News, 21 May 2024.
[713] See, for example, M. Bergsmo et al. (eds.), *Power in International Criminal Justice* (2020).

Finally, ICL raises intractable questions of authority in a context where its impact on certain constituencies is real and dramatic. Although ICL seems to presuppose consensus in its very definition, that consensus is prone to crumble as soon as one seeks to implement it. What seems agreeable from a distance often looks uglier when the hard political costs for various actors are computed from up close. Who, in such conditions, gets to establish international criminal tribunals? How are international criminal cases constructed—and by whom? Who exercises prosecutorial discretion? Who speaks for international criminal justice? For victims? And why would states, victims, or even defendants decide to defer to certain institutional actors and not others?

SERGEY VASILIEV, THE CRISES AND CRITIQUES OF INTERNATIONAL CRIMINAL JUSTICE
KEVIN JON HELLER ET AL. (EDS.), THE OXFORD HANDBOOK OF INTERNATIONAL CRIMINAL LAW (2020) 626

… Every international criminal tribunal, past or present, has had to face charges of legality and fairness deficits, victor's justice, selectivity, neo-colonialism, or other criticisms … . Such critiques … aim at exposing the project's intimacy with hegemonic power: its provenance, embedding, and complicity in the structures of geopolitical (economic, cultural, gender-based) domination. …

… Instituted by states directly or via international organizations, [the tribunals'] authority comes with strings attached. It can only be enforced on the strength of donors' continued operational, political, and financial support. At the same time, courts pretend that authority to be transcendent, decoupled from any one stakeholder, and universal in addressees. They purport to do justice *pro omnibus*, in the name of the 'international community', 'humanity', 'civilization' or 'us'—the subjects they themselves constitute. Their brand of justice is *erga omnes* and dispensed, among others, vis-à-vis the powers-that-be on which they depend for functioning and survival.

… [The tribunals] seek to transcend politics by proffering justice as a superior alternative. But the rhetoric of legalism holds little sway. Although power camouflages itself artfully in technical juridical enterprises hinging upon expertise and rule-following, the courts are inevitably political actors that pool, process, and deploy power. … Rather than 'speaking truth to power', the tribunals have mostly piggybacked on the latter, with their pursuit of justice only extending as far as political expedience permits.

Selectivity and unequal enforcement—regular features of the international criminal justice landscape—cannot be entirely explained by mere jurisdictional and admissibility constraints, despite *bona fide* attempts. Those features may flow from the anticipation of backlash and internalization of outside pressures … .
…
Mainstream accounts paint international criminal law's history as indivertible and irreversible progress from the heroic primitivism of Nuremberg (and the less presentable Tokyo) to the conveyor belt and technocratic *punctilio* of modern judicial bureaucracies to the glorious culmination in eternity, the permanent [ICC]. Such linear master-narratives, which are also eagerly sustained by the institutions and their insiders themselves, cast the journey 'from Nuremberg to The Hague through Rome and beyond' as an aspect and the premise of the humanity's progress. However, the credibility of sanitized and self-serving histories has increasingly been questioned.

The turn to the critical history of the discipline brings to light blind spots, untested assumptions, and epistemological twists of the mainstream takes. …
…

B. Critical Turn

Increasingly, international criminal law scholarship has opened itself up to critical voices and become more introspective. Accounts highlighting aspects of courts' underperformance have multiplied and criticisms grown ever more strident, which also had an influence on how practitioners and insiders positioned themselves in the debate. The internal (efficacy) critiques belonging to the liberal type and its derivative a-liberal genre have focused respectively on the instances when the law or practice fell short of liberal justice principles or was constrained by their domestic articulations too unreflectively. The liberal ('pre-fab') critiques are essentially benevolent and often practised by the actors of the 'mainstream', i.e. those situated professionally and ideologically within the project.

Even more consequential has been the coming to the fore of the so-called 'radical critiques': a mixed bag of approaches interrogating international criminal law from the Third World Approaches to International Law (TWAIL), postcolonial, Marxist, feminist, and other angles. This genre of critiques fundamentally questions the project's moral and epistemic credentials, its rationality, and virtuousness. Such structural critiques upset the field's certainties, lay bare its contradictions, and arouse its anxieties. By unpacking its contentious origins, workings, and effects, those accounts expose the extent to which international criminal justice may be a part of the problem rather than solution.
…
… It is yet to be seen whether the rise of critique will bring about an epistemological renewal of the discipline.
…

As for the practice, the effects of the 'critical turn' have not been immediately felt or, at least, been very visible. As the proverbial dogs bark, the caravan of international justice goes on. The professionals in The Hague and elsewhere have been carrying on with their chores. …
…

III. Legitimacy Skirmishes and Mediatory Spaces
…
A. What Critics Want
…
… [R]adical critiques seek to expose [ICL's] linkages to the dominant global (or localized) geopolitical, economic, and socio-cultural power structures, and its role in perpetuating rather than remedying injustices and inequalities of the existing order. Insofar as these accounts bring into sharper relief its perceived irrelevance (moral bankruptcy, vacuity, hypocrisy, and irrationality), they are potentially far deadlier to the legitimacy of the international criminal justice enterprise than the critiques performed within a liberal frame of reference, which presume that any defect can be repaired through a stricter adherence to law and/or expansion of its reach. …
…
Other than the motive of unsettling the orthodoxies of the field that animates all radical critiques, there exists no unity regarding the ultimate goals of the critical project, the admissible extent of participation and engagement, or the question of whether critics should invest in improving and reforming the enterprise that is being critiqued. For some, the goal is epistemic: production of transformative knowledge needed to rebuild ICL on new, fairer foundations. Getting closer creates a risk of losing critical detachment and compromising critical identity: a critic 'selling out' for relevance and becoming complicit with the object of critique. Others will pursue engagement beyond critical knowledge production and invest in a 'constructive' agenda to spawn reform and 'fix' the system. Those who still harbour faith in the emancipation and empowerment through international (criminal) law take its transformative promise seriously and are determined to hold it to its professed ideals. They are not prepared to withdraw just yet.
…
The political power of critiques is amplified when they resonate with an 'anti-mainstream' and 'counter-hegemonic' pushback by individual states, intergovernmental organizations, and other actors defying international criminal justice in its current form. Whenever it converges with the politics of structural resistance to the project, the critique itself becomes deeply political and starts being seen as a threat, and not just rhetorically. The critics' situational alignment with those wishing the project's demise may be in discord with their prior involvement with the project and engender mistrust about their loyalties, agendas, and motivations. Some defenders might also still expect the critics to be less vocal in their critiques so as not to further exacerbate the position of the institutions as the real underdogs in their clashes with recalcitrant sovereign powers. The critical agenda of challenging the hegemony incarnated in international criminal justice, they will reason, should logically extend to all hegemons, including those who attack the project. The Al-Bashirs, Dutertes, Boltons, and Putins of this world, who oppress subjects on whose behalf the critics engage (developing peoples, poor classes,

people of colour, women, victims of state-sponsored violence), are now trying to beat the ICC into submission. It is those hegemons, and not the ICC, that ought to become primary targets of critique.

There is an expectation that critics would form a tactical alliance with the defence camp particularly when the project is threatened; this is not unreasonable, unless one embraces the dubious wisdom that 'an enemy of an enemy is a friend'. Directing the sword of critique to the project's 'foes' does not render the critic complicit, because a critique of those who attack it is not the same as defending it; it simply means being true to one's own method. This is why the defenders may consider it inconsistent if the critics do not turn against the powerful detractors of the institutions, and if they do not use their celebrated critical sensibility as readily in order to expose and condemn those attackers' self-interest, hypocrisy, and track record of oppression, exclusion, and atrocity.

While the most radical of the critical projects would be to demand the dismantling of the system of international criminal justice, few critics, if any, would contemplate this outcome or be prepared to push for it to the end. As critique is ontologically dependent—some would say parasitic—on its object, many 'crits' are in fact quite invested in the project that they need as an indispensable target, or a 'convenient punch-bag'. ... Yet, a significant number of critics stop short of rejecting the foundational ideas and rationales underlying international criminal justice. Rather, they endorse it insofar as it carries, if theoretically, a promise for at least starting to address the systemic causes for exclusion and oppression. International criminal justice continues to be seen as a potentially transformative and critical project in itself; a tool that can be wielded by the weak in order to constrain power, not only by the powerful in order to oppress the weak. ...
...

IV. Legitimacy as Crisis Management

Is there a solution to the never-ending legitimacy crises of international criminal justice? ...

[D]iscarding the project's emancipatory promise would mean throwing the baby out with the bathwater. It is the reason why the project continues to arouse strong emotions and interest in those who want to see its promise fulfilled. Some of the 'radical critics' challenge it precisely because they believe it could be reinvented or refashioned as an instrument of justice and equality to the benefit of the invisible, voiceless, and downtrodden. The courts can do little to fix the global power structures of which they are a progeny. But critical sensibility could infiltrate the mainstream and permeate the intimate sphere of decision-making. If and when the project's insiders come to be sensitized to the critical concerns to the point of making them their own, this could become the tipping point for the genuine transformation of institutional politics of international criminal law. ...

To most of the radical critiques, there are no persuasive and ready-made answers (yet). The legitimacy curse of international criminal justice can hardly be undone and most of the available solutions will be partial and attitudinal. That said, the legitimacy 'crises' can be managed more expertly than has been the case so far. Legitimacy is a plant that needs to be watered regularly. ...

PHILIP ALSTON, 'CRIMINALIZING HUMAN RIGHTS'
15 *J. HUM. RTS. PRAC.* (2023) 660

[Note that this analysis is not directed specifically at the work of the ICC, but at the evolution of the broader system.]

The priorities reflected in the overarching system that includes the [IHRL, IHL and ICL regimes] are currently undergoing a gradual but highly significant transformation. The cause is a growing preoccupation with 'atrocity crimes' including their documentation, investigation, and prosecution, the imposition of criminal sanctions in response to an ever-increasing range of violations, and the recasting of other violations as crimes. ...

The pre-occupation with atrocity crimes, and other endeavours to expand the list of such crimes, such as those around ecocide, domicide, and omnicide, and the urge to apply the label of genocide wherever possible, diminishes the attention given to significant violations that do not reach the threshold of an atrocity. It makes it less likely that the most high-profile and well-resourced activities in the field, which are increasingly concerned with atrocity crimes, will seriously engage with the full range of violations and will make use of the spectrum of available responses. It also facilitates the neglect of structural issues such as extreme inequality, entrenched racism and sexism, and extreme poverty. And it leaves even less space for tackling the non-criminal dimensions of newer but equally pressing challenges such as climate change, and human rights threats posed by digital technologies and artificial intelligence. A closely related phenomenon is the trend towards responding to serious violations through the imposition of criminal sanctions, rather than through more nuanced and tailored measures. Criminal law, at both the international and domestic levels, is increasingly becoming the principal fulcrum around which many enforcement responses now revolve.

In the IHRL and ICL fields, some of these issues have been canvassed in instructive debates focused on the preoccupation with combating impunity.[714] But in much of the literature the focus on the opposite of impunity—punishment—leads to an unduly narrow understanding of the consequences of what is happening. For example, some critics focus primarily on how the definition of atrocity crimes might be expanded, while others explore techniques that might be used to broaden the prosecutorial focus.[715] But the spotlight remains on prosecution rather than on the wider spectrum of available tools.[716] 'Criminalization', rather than anti-impunity, is a more encompassing and evocative way of describing a process that has been gathering speed over the past two decades. It is a term … used here in a more encompassing sense than comparable approaches such as 'anti-impunity',[717] the proliferation and legitimation of punitive responses in human rights law,[718] judicialization or juridification,[719] or 'human rights penalty'.[720] The present usage draws upon those insights but seeks to emphasize the combined impact of what are often examined as distinct phenomena.

In broad terms, criminalization reflects a mentality—a way of understanding and implementing the goals of a complex set of regimes. It reflects a particular philosophy of how societies can best be regulated, and it assumes that law enforcement officers, prosecutors and judges should be at the core of the overall system. It thus adopts a very narrow and specific approach to the much broader challenge of how to promote and uphold respect for human rights within societies.

More specifically, examples of the criminalization process can be found in: the preoccupation with 'atrocity crimes' in the work of the International Criminal Court and other tribunals, thus greatly narrowing the effective scope of ICL; the parallel narrowing of principal concerns in the IHL field away from the full range of issues and towards violations that might be prosecuted under ICL; the growing emphasis within UN commissions of inquiry (COIs) on 'atrocity crimes' and on gathering evidence that would satisfy the standards of criminal tribunals in order to establish individual criminal responsibility; and the high levels of funding being invested into international investigative mechanisms and atrocity crime COIs, in contrast to the patently inadequate funding of core activities such as treaty body monitoring and the accountability roles of Special Procedures mandate-holders. An important recent civil society initiative proposing the creation of a Standing Independent Investigative Mechanism, which would have a very broad mandate and a large staff, epitomizes some of these trends. While accountability is a leitmotif for the entire IHRL/IHL/ICL system, this initiative defines it very narrowly so that in order to qualify as an 'accountability mechanism' the relevant body must engage in evidence collection, the identification of perpetrators, or the preparation of casefiles. Another example is the overwhelming emphasis on a plethora of comparatively lavishly funded criminal investigations in Ukraine.

A similar dynamic is occurring within more specific sectors of human rights. Being seen to 'crack down' by prosecuting and punishing individual wrongdoers has become the preferred response in some key areas. In the field of women's rights, for example, governments and international institutions and courts are increasingly focused on those violations that involve criminal conduct, such as rape and violence against women. And as we shall see below, in areas such as counter-terrorism and transitional justice there is a premium on criminalizing certain forms of behaviour and prosecuting violators, rather than on trying to grapple with the broader context in which solutions need to be sought. Other areas, beyond the scope of this article, that warrant future analysis

---

[714] K. Engle,' Anti-Impunity and the Turn to Criminal Law in Human Rights', 100 *Cornell L. Rev.* (2015) 1069.

[715] R. DeFalco, *Invisible Atrocities: The Aesthetic Biases of International Criminal Justice* (2022)

[716] B. Sander, 'The Anti-Impunity Mindset', in M. Bergsmo et al. (eds.), *Power in International Criminal Justice* (2020) 325.

[717] K. Engle, n. 41 above.

[718] M. Pinto, 'Historical Trends of Human Rights Gone Criminal', 42 *Hum. Rts. Q.* (2020) 729.

[719] C. Harwood, *The Roles and Functions of Atrocity-Related United Nations Commissions of Inquiry in the International Legal Order* (2019)

[720] S. Tapia Tapia, *Feminism, Violence Against Women, and Law Reform: Decolonial Lessons from Ecuador* (2022).

in this regard are labour rights and modern slavery laws, and refugee and migration law. States are rapidly expanding their criminal codes, turning to the police and security forces to uphold human rights, and concentrating their efforts on a limited number of wrongdoers.

A similar trend is discernible in terms of the human rights foreign policies of many Western governments that now engage less substantively with a broader range of issues and have instead prioritized the imposition of sanctions against individuals accused of corruption or human rights abuses. These targeted sanctions have become a favoured technique of Western governments, and have been mimicked by China and Russia. Such sanctions are, arguably, a form of criminal punishment, in which named individuals are publicly accused of crimes, and a punishment or sanction is prescribed and implemented. Similarly, very considerable resources are now being invested at the national level, especially in western Europe, in order to prosecute individuals for crimes committed in foreign jurisdictions on the basis of assertions of universal jurisdiction.

In some ways, the most paradoxical aspect of these trends is that few human rights proponents would be likely to oppose any of the developments when looked at individually on their own merits. Who would contest the propositions that accountability is crucial, impunity must be countered, and the guilty must be prosecuted and punished? In addition, the voluminous literature around international criminal justice argues that many other benefits potentially flow from processes of criminalization, such as deterrence, historical record-building, victim-participation, reparations and so on. And, from the perspective of those working in these areas, there is cause for satisfaction: considerable additional resources are being mobilized, new civil society and professional initiatives are flourishing at both the international and national levels by way of adaptation to the new environment, important new skills are being developed, a professional core of investigators, prosecutors, defence counsel, and judges has emerged, some accountability mechanisms are being better-resourced, and entirely new international mechanisms are being created.

But these advantages come at a considerable price … . …

* * *

But many other assessments have been less critical. Nancy Amoury Combs, in 'International Criminal Justice', in Barbora Holá et al. (eds.), *The Oxford Handbook of Atrocity Crimes* (2022) 617, at 626, focuses on the system's more practical achievement in relation to impunity:

> Before the 1990s, no one expected perpetrators of mass atrocities to be held criminally accountable. Today, as a statistical matter, no one should expect perpetrators of mass atrocities to be held criminally accountable, because most still are not. But the advent of the international criminal justice project transformed the world from one in which impunity following international crimes is expected to one in which impunity following international crimes is decried.

And Carsten Stahn, in 'The ICC in Its Third Decade: Setting the Scene', in Carsten Stahn and Rafael Braga da Silva (eds.), *The International Criminal Court in Its Third Decade: Reflecting on Law and Practices* (2024) 3, 10, notes the Court's important jurisprudential contributions:

> to the reading and clarification of substantive criminal law, including the understanding of the policy requirement of crimes against humanity, sexual and gender crimes against women and men, intra- party offences against children, destruction of cultural property, reproductive rights, and the re- conceptionalization of modes of liability beyond the jurisprudence of the *ad hoc* tribunals.

…

> … In some areas, such as sexual and gender- based violence, victim participation60 or reparative practices for victims and survivors, emerging ICC practices are often at the forefront or ahead of developments domestically, despite their imperfections.

Evaluating the ICC

There have been many efforts to evaluate the effectiveness of the ICC.[721] Some of these have focused on the more institutional and procedural dimensions, while others have adopted a broader empirical approach. The former is illustrated by Douglas Guilfoyle, in 'Lacking Conviction: Is the International Criminal Court Broken? An Organisational Failure Analysis', 16 *Melb. J. Int'l. L.* (2019) 401, at 449:

> It is hard to escape the conclusion that the Court has not been well served to date by either its Prosecutors or, collectively, its judiciary. What is required is a new motivating ethic of modesty throughout the entire institution: modesty as to how much it can achieve; modesty among the senior office-holders as to the scope of their roles and the divisions of responsibility among the Court's arms; modesty in terms of strict application of the Rome Statute and avoidance of judicial overreach. In particular, the Court must retire some of its more grandiose universalist rhetoric and set more realistic expectations in its communications with victims and other stakeholders. Universalism may have fostered its legitimacy among some audiences, but it has led to missteps, and risked alienating major constituencies, including among the ASP.

> As regards the OTP, 'it is hard to see how the Court can succeed if the Office of the Prosecutor is failing to present convincing cases'. Numerous factors appear to have led to this result: poor resource allocation (opening too many preliminary investigations or investigations in too many situations); poor strategy (turning quite late to the idea of prosecuting mid-level leaders first); poor case preparation (a lack of 'linking' evidence connecting high leaders with the crimes actually committed); a certain ignorance or naivete about local political conditions; as well as actual obstruction by states and a degree of judicial uncertainty as to applicable standards of evidence.

Many of these concerns were addressed by the 2020 Independent Expert Review of the ICC (p. 000 above) which confined its 348 recommendations to concrete reforms. For example, it observed (at 332) that:

> The Court, and senior management specifically, need to make efforts to rebuild and strengthen internal trust and re-shape the working culture at the Court. The leadership of the Court should adopt and demonstrate a clear commitment to a multi-pronged strategy to deal with predatory behaviour in the workplace, namely bullying, harassment and especially sexual harassment.

But the Review, perhaps wisely, effectively sidestepped the question of the Court's effectiveness:

> 368. Assessing the Court's effectiveness means evaluating the impact of the Court on affected local communities and victims, as well as the Court's deterrent effect. Different indicators and methodology are required, including qualitative indicators assessed through – for example – polls and questionnaires among local communities. For an objective assessment of the Court's impact, such analysis would best be carried out by entities external to the Court. Civil society organisations and academics can play an essential role in this regard … .

Consider, in contrast, the following attempt to arrive at an empirically-grounded assessment.

GEOFFREY DANCY, THE HIDDEN IMPACTS OF THE ICC: AN INNOVATIVE ASSESSMENT USING GOOGLE DATA
34 LEIDEN J. INT'L L. (2021) 729

---

[721] See S. Ford, 'Can the International Criminal Court Succeed? An Analysis of the Empirical Evidence of Violence Prevention', 43 *Loy. L.A. Int'l & Comp. L. Rev.* (2020) 101; H. Jo and B. Simmons, 'Can the International Criminal Court Deter Atrocity?,' 70 *Int'l Org.* (2016) 443; C. Hillebrecht, 'The Deterrent Effects of the International Criminal Court: Evidence from Libya', 42 *Int'l Interactions* (2016) 616; and J. Meernik, 'The International Criminal Court and the Deterrence of Human Rights Atrocities,' 17 *Civil Wars* (2015) 318.

... In evaluation science, assessing the performance of an organization requires a systematic consideration of how efficiently or effectively it operates to produce outputs that translate into intended outcomes. ... Some have wondered whether it is even possible to reliably assess the ICC's accomplishments: the Rome Statute does not clearly outline the Court's aims or objectives; and its extrapolated goals are multi-faceted and possibly contradictory. ...

... [T]his article argues that ... the ICC has diffuse yet measurable impacts on social discourse, and these impacts are overlooked in most assessments. The data presented demonstrate that ICC interventions – including preliminary examinations and investigations – are associated with a significant and sustained increase in Google searches for 'human rights' in situation countries. ... [T]here is a no more significant predictor of sudden spikes in a country's Google searches for human rights than the onset of an OTP investigation. This mostly likely indicates that ICC involvement leads to information-seeking among the public, hinting that the Court may indeed have 'socio-pedagogical' effects that often remain hidden.
...

2. Two perspectives on ICC performance

2.1 The rationalist approach

The most common approach to evaluating the ICC's performance is rationalism. ... This ontology ... assumes social, legal, and political behaviour can be perfected through good insight and design. Journalists informally adopt rationalism when they point to the OTP's low conviction rate, or when they call into question the ICC's sluggish process, great expense, or lack of 'bang for the buck' as evidence of inefficiency. Some ask outright whether the ICC has 'failed', citing the fact that atrocities still take place in states like Syria, Yemen, or Myanmar. The implication is that, if only it followed better procedures or its personnel were more competent, the Court would achieve greater success in deterring violence in the world.

Rationalism also undergirds more formal 'effectiveness criticism' directed at the ICC. This involves identifying the Court's mandated aims – like providing victim satisfaction or deterring future atrocities – and positing that certain operational shortcomings prevent those aims from being reached. One common underlying assumption is that the ICC has carefully calculating audiences that are keeping a close watch. When those audiences observe missteps, they receive signals to update their attitudes and behaviour in relation to the Court. For instance, consider the often disparaged slow pace of investigations and proceedings, which results not only from the institutional structure of the Court but also prosecutorial strategy. Concern over the ICC's expeditiousness, carried over from criticism of the ad hoc tribunals of the 1990s, is rooted in the presumption that slow justice leads to waning hopes among victims. If victims are not satisfied, the thinking goes, the Court will lose legitimacy. Similarly, drawing on criminology, scholars argue that selective prosecutions and infrequent convictions will do little to change the cost–benefit analysis of would-be atrocity criminals. In other words, insufficient trial outputs will fail to achieve deterrence. Why? Because atrocity criminals are plodding, careful actors who follow the Court's record, and update their prior beliefs with new information. But each of these effectiveness critiques is theoretical: we possess very little hard evidence that victims are disappointed with the ICC, or that violent state leaders discount the Court for being toothless.

Rationalist performance evaluations are not just employed for criticism. The ICC itself has adopted a highly rationalist, some say technocratic, approach to monitoring its own operations. The Second Court's Report on Development of Performance Indicators outlines a set of four goals – fair and expeditious trials, effective leadership and management, adequate security, and victim access – and presents a bevy of indicators for auditing the Court's pursuit of those goals. ...

2.2 The constructivist approach

An alternative approach to assessing ICC performance is available. Drawing on international relations theory ... [c]onstructivism is concerned with the ways that ideas and norms permeate interactions, thus conditioning 'the nature of agents and subjects'. Philosophically, this diverges from rationalism in many ways, most notably by assuming that humans are social beings whose preferences are shaped by a dense network of rules that constitute society. In short, people are not individual cost-benefit calculators; they are complex rule navigators.

Constructivist performance evaluation has been proposed by a handful of management scholars, but not widely adopted in the study of law and society. This alternative essentially involves considering how an organization may itself alter social relations. There are two main reasons that reviewers might consider this departure from a rational systems approach. First, the ICC is not easily reduced to a corporate forum for creating predictable legal 'outputs' that produce desired 'outcomes'. The trajectory of Court practice does not follow a clearly designed logic model because some of the Court's outputs and outcomes are unpredictable. For example, the purpose of the OTP's preliminary examinations was given relatively scant attention in the Rome Statute, but over time these examinations have evolved, playing an increasingly important role in monitoring states' compliance with international criminal law. Furthermore, research demonstrates that advancing to the investigation stage has unintended positive impacts on situation countries, encouraging legal mobilization and increasing low-level prosecutions of state agents. ...

A second reason to consider a constructivist approach is that an overly instrumentalized view of the Court's work ignores that international legal institutions and global society are co-constitutive. ... The need to merely belong, or be recognized as belonging, to that community, might alter behaviour. Understanding this means moving beyond a narrow, managerial understanding of organizational outputs and outcomes. ... For example, empirical research demonstrates that Rome Statute ratifications alone are associated with declines in indiscriminate violence committed by government and rebel forces, even while civil war is ongoing. States party to the Rome Statute are home to almost no massacres, and very few new civil wars. That political violence in increasingly concentrated in non-party states suggests the Rome regime is influential, though it is hard to attribute this pattern to individual choices made by rational leaders in direct response to Court actions. It could be that the role of the ICC regime is not just causal, but constitutive.48 It not only produces independent outputs that translate into outcomes; it embodies and defines rules of global society. ...
...

7. Conclusion

... [First, in] countries where the ICC has intervened, interest in human rights spiked, and sustained. The new and higher level of Google searches for human rights is quite enduring, lasting for years. ... It would be a mistake to write off Google search trends as meaningless. The data suggest that the ICC drives sustained curiosity about human rights, which may signal a broader ability to contribute to long- term social and ideational change. ...

Second, an excessively rationalist account [of] ICC outputs and outcomes will probably miss some broader constitutive social effects attributable to the Court. Evaluating performance solely based on its use of resources, the perceived fairness and expeditiousness of trial proceedings, or the extent to which victims participate is too managerial an exercise. ... It is quite possible that most of the ICC's impacts are subtle and indirect. Uncovering these impacts means being open to a holistic understanding of international criminal law and engaging in the persistent and creative search for evidence of law's social effects among audiences in various contexts.

Third ..., evaluators need not choose between ... [r]ationalism and constructivism ... . [Both] can complement one another. ... [C]onsidering the multi-dimensional nature of ICC performance would at the very least push us beyond either blind apology or obsession with crisis, toward a pragmatic grounding in the real opportunities the ICC offers.

Regional Approaches

In looking to the future evolution of this field Leila N. Sadat, in 'The International Criminal Law of the Future', in David L. Sloss (ed.), *Is the International Legal Order Unraveling?* (2022) 397, at 423, draws attention to two important elements. The first is the need for a system of global criminal justice that focuses on the broad range of crimes beyond those dealt with in the Rome Statute. To the extent that such prosecutions are currently pursued unilaterally, she cautions that:

> Efforts by the United States and other countries to extend their national jurisdictions
> extraterritorially to serve as the investigators and police of the world are likely to succeed

only sporadically and are likely to increase interstate tensions. ... For that reason, it may be useful to create mechanisms enabling some transnational crimes to become the subject of international adjudication so that their enforcement becomes more effective and multilateral. Indeed, an effort is now ongoing to establish a new global corruption court.

She also draws attention to the important potential role that might be played by regional criminal courts:

> ... [A]t its best, a global system of criminal justice would have the ICC as its centerpiece, with many satellite courts at the international level and national jurisdictions filling in where regional and international courts are not engaged, are overwhelmed, or cannot exercise jurisdiction. Although the ICC will not directly exercise its jurisdiction in many cases, given its status as a court of last resort, its activities will be central to the system as a whole. Ideally, such a system will be human rights friendly, incorporating protections for the accused found in international human rights law, and state actors engaging in national prosecutions will be encouraged to use best practices in their national systems. It will also respond to modern calls for a more restorative approach to criminal justice. The real danger is not that ICL will disappear. Rather, the risk is that attacks on its international and multilateral manifestations, such as the ICC, will cause it to become increasingly illiberal and unilateral, increasing friction between states and endangering international peace and security.

On 27 June 2014, the African Union adopted a treaty designed to set up such a regional system. But, as of 2024, the Protocol on Amendments to the Protocol on the Statute of the African Court of Justice and Human Rights, known as the Malabo Protocol, has been signed by 15 of the 55 African Union member states and ratified by none of them. Eki Yemisi Omorogbe, in 'The Crisis of International Criminal Law in Africa: A Regional Regime in Response?', 66 *Neth. Int'l L. Rev.* (2019) 287 describes the background to this initiative:

> Between 2009 and 2011 African states reacted negatively to a German court's warrant for the arrest of a Rwandan who at the time had become an aide to Rwandan President Paul Kagame, to the ICC's arrest warrant for Libyan President Gaddafi, and the Kenyan prosecutions in the ICC.

> The AU's response to the ICC proceedings [involving Kenya] was swift. In October 2013, the AU Assembly in extraordinary session expressed its reservation about the effect of these ICC proceedings on the sovereignty, stability, peace and security of that state and the wider region.33 It called for the suspension of ICC proceedings against Ruto and Kenyatta until they leave office.34 It also widened its policy of non-cooperation ... .

> ...

> Significantly, the AU Assembly also requested the speeding up of the process of including international crimes within the mandate of the African Court on Human and Peoples' Rights [leading to the adoption of the Malabo Protocol.] ...

> Certain provisions of the Protocol reflect the AU-ICC conflict. The key provision is Article 46A *bis* of the Protocol which provides:

> No charges shall be commenced or continued before the Court against any serving Head of State or government, or anybody acting or entitled to act in such capacity, or other senior state officials based on their functions, during their tenure of office.

> In parallel, the obligation of states to cooperate with the ICL is limited in Article 46L(g) to 'Any other assistance not prohibited by the law of the requested State' in respect of the arrest, surrender and transfer of accused persons to the Court.39 These provisions when read alongside the AU's policy of non-cooperation with the ICC in the arrest of any African Head of State shows that the objective is to remove incumbent leaders from the overview of all international courts and tribunals.

Finally, no reference is made [to] the Rome Statute or the ICC in the Protocol. That silence is intentional. … [M]aking reference to the ICC would have required engagement with it.

Omorogbe notes that Article 28B of the Protocol incorporates the important jurisprudence of the ICTR in *Prosecutor v. Akayesu*, by including within the definition of genocide: '(f) Acts of rape or any other form of sexual violence when these are committed with the intent to destroy a national, ethnic or religious group.' He also notes that, unlike the Rome Statute, the Protocol (Article 46C) provides jurisdiction over legal persons, thus making it possible to prosecute multinational corporations for crimes against humanity.

But Amnesty International, in *Malabo Protocol: Legal and Institutional Implications of the Merged and Expanded African Court - Snapshots* (2 May 2017) has expressed:

> … concerns about the implications of vague/broadly defined crimes in the ACJHR Statute, and in particular, with respect to the crimes of terrorism and unconstitutional change of government, which may therefore be used to clamp down on the legitimate exercise of freedom of expression, association, assembly and human rights. The broad formulation of the crimes as currently drafted, raise serious concerns as to compliance with the principle of legality established under international law.

Consider the following provisions:

Article 28G
Terrorism

For the purposes of this Statute, 'terrorism' means any of the following acts:

> A. Any act which is a violation of the criminal laws of a State Party, the laws of the African Union or a regional economic community recognized by the African Union, or by international law, and which may endanger the life, physical integrity or freedom of, or cause serious injury or death to, any person, any number or group of persons or causes or may cause damage to public or private property, natural resources, environmental or cultural heritage and is calculated or intended to:

>> 1. intimidate, put in fear, force, coerce or induce any government, body, institution, the general public or any segment thereof, to do or abstain from doing any act, or to adopt or abandon a particular standpoint, or to act according to certain principles; or

>> 2. disrupt any public service, the delivery of any essential service to the public or to create a public emergency; or

>> 3. create general insurrection in a State.

…

Article 28E
The Crime of Unconstitutional Change of Government

1. For the purposes of this Statute, 'unconstitutional change of government' means committing or ordering to be committed the following acts, with the aim of illegally accessing or maintaining power:
   a) A putsch or coup d'état against a democratically elected government;
   b) An intervention by mercenaries to replace a democratically elected government;
   c) Any replacement of a democratically elected government by the use of armed dissidents or rebels or through political assassination;
   d) Any refusal by an incumbent government to relinquish power to the winning party or candidate after free, fair and regular elections;

e) Any amendment or revision of the Constitution or legal instruments, which is an infringement on the principles of democratic change of government or is inconsistent with the Constitution;

f) Any substantial modification to the electoral laws in the last six (6) months before the elections without the consent of the majority of the political actors.

Funding

One element in evaluating the effectiveness of the various criminal courts and tribunals is their cost. By way of comparison, in 2022, the UN regular budget appropriated $134 million for all of the activities undertaken by the Office of the High Commissioner for Human Rights (UN Doc. A/77/6 (Sect. 24) (2022) 60). That amount was supplemented by $227.7 million in extra-budgetary contributions, mostly from states.

For 2024, the ICC's budget was €197 million or around US$217 million. This was a 16 percent increase from 2023. The increase reflected inflation as well as the Court's expanding workload.[722] By comparison the total cost of the two ad hoc tribunals (the ICTY and the ICTR) was $3.8 billion. Unlike the ICC, which is paid for only by States Parties, that budget was covered by regular UN budget assessments applicable to all member states. That meant that the United States paid 22 percent of the total. In Cambodia, the ECCC cost $337 million over 16 years. Of the total, $45 million was from Cambodia with the rest paid for by 39 foreign countries.

Consider the following justification of such expenses by Milena Sterio and Michael Scharf, p. 000 above, at 357:

> … [W]hile international justice has not come cheaply, these costs are a fraction of the costs of a peacekeeping mission or military operation. At the Pentagon, the cost for one B-2 stealth bomber is $3 billion, the cost for a Virginia-class attack submarine is $2.7 billion, and one Arleigh Burke-class guided missile destroyer costs American taxpayers $1.7 billion. In 2017, the United States was spending $3.1 billion per month to wage war in Afghanistan. It is noteworthy that in the two and a half decades since the creation of the ad hoc tribunals, neither war nor genocide has returned to the former Yugoslavia or Rwanda.

QUESTIONS

1. Are many of the critiques of ICL also applicable to some domestic legal systems or do international criminal tribunals have some unique characteristics?

2. Which critiques of ICL seem most compelling and what alternative approaches would you consider in response? Do adjustments need to be made, or is a wholesale reconceptualization necessary to satisfy the strongest critiques?

3. Should radical critics of ICL pay any heed to the possible (probable?) misuse of their work by those opposing the ICL agenda in order to protect the impunity of perpetrators?

4. Randle C. DeFalco, in '(Re)Conceptualizing Atrocity Crimes as Public Health Catastrophes', in Jocelyn Getgen Kestenbaum et al. (eds.), *Public Health, Mental Health, and Mass Atrocity Prevention* (2021) 17, calls for 'a conceptual shift away from a myopic focus on spectacular acts of violence within international criminal justice and toward the recognition of a broader array of manifestations of power over the health and lives of human populations.' In what ways do you think the growing emphasis on 'atrocity crimes', promoted by the limited scope of international criminal law, might have influenced the evolution of the overall human rights regime?

---

[722] S. Ford, 'Funding the ICC for Its Third Decade', in C. Stahn (ed.), *The International Criminal Court in Its Third Decade* (2024) 368.

5. What role does, and should, politics play in international criminal justice. Consider the following observation by Nancy Amoury Combs, in 'International Criminal Justice', in Barbora Holá et al. (eds.), *The Oxford Handbook of Atrocity Crimes* (2022) 617, at 638:

What is innovative—and inspiring—about the modern-day international criminal justice project is not its imposition of accountability per se, but its effort to impose that accountability universally and pursuant to neutral principles. ... [But this rhetoric] obscures the reality that its ideals are unachievable at present. Prosecutors pretend that political considerations play no role in atrocity selection, for instance, when we all know that the practical ability to carry out a prosecution must be an important factor in the decision to initiate the prosecution to begin with. International criminal law must pretend to be apolitical, yet its ultimate success is largely predicated on its ability to navigate around the numerous land mines that politics places in its path.

Chapter 17. Transitional Justice and Reparations

The preceding chapter explored criminal accountability as an essential response to massive violations of human rights, starting with the Nuremberg and Tokyo trials. But for all the benefits of criminal prosecutions, they can only address a small part of the overall set of challenges that arise for the survivors and victims, for the communities, for the affected state(s), and for the international community in the aftermath of such events.

The focus of the materials that follow is on what has come to be called 'transitional justice', and on the rapid expansion of the 'right to an effective remedy' (Article 8 of the UDHR), which is an integral part of international human rights law. International law has long recognized the importance of reparations, especially in the context of a state's obligation to repair the consequences of a breach of international law for which it is responsible. In human rights law, the more common generic term is 'remedies' which is used to encompass reparations, as well as restitution, compensation, satisfaction, and guarantees of non-repetition. These different elements have all become crucial components of the approach to transitional justice, which was originally developed as an approach to facilitate the transition from authoritarianism to democracy, but is now also used to encompass post-conflict transitions. In addition, the relevant principles are increasingly being invoked in situations in which demands are made for comprehensive measures to redress historic and ongoing injustices, including slavery, colonialism, and the ravaging of indigenous societies.

A. TRANSITIONAL JUSTICE

Despite its prominence in the field and a burgeoning literature, transitional justice remains an ill-defined concept that is constantly evolving. The best-known definition was put forward in a 2004 report by the UN Secretary-General on the rule of law and transitional justice in conflict and post-conflict societies (UN Doc. S/2004/616, para. 8):

> The notion of "transitional justice" … comprises the full range of processes and mechanisms associated with a society's attempts to come to terms with a legacy of large-scale past abuses, in order to ensure accountability, serve justice and achieve reconciliation. These may include both judicial and non-judicial mechanisms, with differing levels of international involvement (or none at all) and individual prosecutions, reparations, truth-seeking, institutional reform, vetting and dismissals, or a combination thereof.

In practice, transitional justice generally seeks to bring a flexible and tailored approach and also provides a framework within which complex and controversial trade-offs can be shaped and negotiated, often in ways that might not fit easily into formal human rights frameworks.[723]

A more elaborate definition, offered by Pablo de Greiff, the first UN Special Rapporteur on truth, justice and reparation, who did much to develop the concept in practice, views it:

> … as a comprehensive policy implemented to cope with the legacies of massive and systematic human rights violations and abuses, and to restore or establish anew the currency of human rights. Such a policy has as its core elements truth, justice, reparations, and guarantees of non-recurrence. In addition to the immediate function each element of a comprehensive transitional justice policy is supposed to serve, namely, to impart (criminal) justice, disclose truth, redress violations, and prevent their recurrence, a comprehensive transitional justice also pursues two 'mediate' ends, to provide recognition to victims, not only as victims but as rights-holders, and to promote civic trust. Such a policy also pursues two 'final' goals, to strengthen the rule of law, and to promote social integration or reconciliation.[724]

---

[723] See *Transitional Justice: A Strategic Tool for People, Prevention and Peace,* Guidance Note of the UN Secretary-General (2023).
[724] P. de Greiff, 'The Vernacularization of Transitional Justice: Is Transitional Justice Useful in Pre-conflict Settings?', in P. Alston (ed.), *Capturing the Complexity of Human Rights* (2024) 117.

The implications of the 'right to an effective remedy' in terms of the phenomenon of impunity and the granting of amnesties long remained unclear. Emblematic cases emerged in Chile and Argentina in the aftermath of the military dictatorships of the 1970s. In Chile, the regime of General Augusto Pinochet issued Amnesty Decree Law No. 2191 on 10 March 1978, which provided a wide-ranging amnesty for crimes committed in the years following the 1973 coup d'état.

In Argentina, prosecutions of military personnel that took place after the return to democracy in late 1983 generated a strong military backlash. To avoid chaos, the government of President Raúl Alfonsín invoked a 'compelling need for national reconciliation and consolidation of the democratic system' and passed the 'full stop law' of 24 December 1986 to limit new prosecutions. But continued judicial activity led to the 'due obedience law' of 5 June 1987, which granted automatic immunity from prosecution to all members of the military except top commanders. Within days, the Supreme Court upheld its constitutionality.

Setting Relevant Human Rights Standards

It was against this background that two separate, but ultimately closely related, standard-setting initiatives emerged within the United Nations. In the mid-1980s, Louis Joinet undertook a study of amnesty laws (UN Doc E/CN.4/Sub.2/1985/16/Rev.1 (1987)) which laid the foundations for a 'Set of Principles for the protection and promotion of human rights through action to combat impunity' (UN Doc E/CN.4/Sub.2/1997/20/Rev.1 (1997)). Joinet also introduced transitional justice as a so-called fourth pillar of anti-impunity measures focused on the non-recurrence of violations.

The Joinet principles on impunity were subsequently updated by Diane Orentlicher and presented to the UN Commission on Human Rights in 2004 (UN Doc E/CN.4/2004/88 (2004)). Although the Commission 'noted' them as 'a guideline to assist States', it never formally endorsed them. They have, nevertheless, become an 'authoritative reference point' in discussions about impunity,[725] which they define broadly as arising whenever a state fails: (i) to investigate serious human rights violations; (ii) to prosecute, try, and duly punish perpetrators of such violations; (iii) to provide victims with effective remedies and reparation for the harm suffered; and (iv) to take the appropriate steps to prevent a repetition of violations.

A separate UN process, begun in 1989 and led by Theo van Boven, focused on the 'right to restitution, compensation and rehabilitation for victims of gross violations of human rights'. His study led to the adoption of an important set of guidelines on reparations in 2005. Before examining those, it is important to note that the Joinet study had originally focused also on economic, social and cultural rights, but in 1994 the Commission split the study into two separate tracks. Although a final report by El Hadji Guissé was presented in relation to these rights (UN Doc. E/CN.4/Sub.2/1997/8 (1997)), no tangible outcome emerged as a result. Similarly, because the van Boven study was undertaken against the background of the crimes listed in the Rome Statute, it too failed to explore where these rights fit into the broader picture of reparations. Instead, principle 26 noted that they are relevant to all violations.

BASIC PRINCIPLES AND GUIDELINES ON THE RIGHT TO A REMEDY AND REPARATION FOR VICTIMS OF GROSS VIOLATIONS OF INTERNATIONAL HUMAN RIGHTS LAW AND SERIOUS VIOLATIONS OF INTERNATIONAL HUMANITARIAN LAW GENERAL ASSEMBLY RES. 60/147 (2005)

...

IV. *Statutes of limitations*

6. Where so provided for in an applicable treaty or contained in other international legal obligations, statutes of limitations shall not apply to gross violations of international human rights law and serious violations of international humanitarian law [Note: this phrase is abbreviated below to 'gross/serious violations'] which constitute crimes under international law.

---

[725] F. Haldemann and T. Unger (eds.), *The United Nations Principles to Combat Impunity: A Commentary* (2018) 4.

7. Domestic statutes of limitations for other types of violations ... should not be unduly restrictive.
...

VII.   *Victims' right to remedies*

11.   Remedies for [gross/serious violations] include the victim's right to the following as provided for under international law:
(a) Equal and effective access to justice;
(b) Adequate, effective and prompt reparation for harm suffered;
(c) Access to relevant information concerning violations and reparation mechanisms.
...

IX.   *Reparation for harm suffered*

15.   Adequate, effective and prompt reparation is intended to promote justice by redressing [gross/serious violations]. ... In cases where a person, a legal person, or other entity is found liable for reparation to a victim, such party should provide reparation to the victim or compensate the State if the State has already provided reparation to the victim.
...

18.   In accordance with domestic law and international law, and taking account of individual circumstances, victims of [gross/serious violations] should, as appropriate and proportional to the gravity of the violation and the circumstances of each case, be provided with full and effective reparation, as laid out in principles 19 to 23
... ..

19.   *Restitution* should, whenever possible, restore the victim to the original situation before the [gross/serious violations] occurred. Restitution includes, as appropriate: restoration of liberty, enjoyment of human rights, identity, family life and citizenship, return to one's place of residence, restoration of employment and return of property.

20.   *Compensation* should be provided for any economically assessable damage, as appropriate and proportional to the gravity of the violation and the circumstances of each case, resulting from [gross/serious violations], such as:

(a)   Physical or mental harm;
(b)   Lost opportunities ...;
(c)   Material damages ...;
(d)   Moral damage;
(e)   Costs ... .

21.   *Rehabilitation* should include medical and psychological care as well as legal and social services.

22.   *Satisfaction* should include, where applicable, any or all of the following:

(a)   Effective measures aimed at the cessation of continuing violations;
(b)   Verification of the facts and full and public disclosure of the truth to the extent that such disclosure does not cause further harm or threaten the safety and interests of the victim ... [and others];
(c)   The search for the whereabouts of the disappeared, for the identities of the children abducted, and for the bodies of those killed ...;
(d)   An official declaration or a judicial decision restoring the dignity, the reputation and the rights of the victim and of persons closely connected with the victim;
(e)   Public apology, including acknowledgement of the facts and acceptance of responsibility;
(f)   Judicial and administrative sanctions against persons liable for the violations;
(g)   Commemorations and tributes to the victims;
...

23.   *Guarantees of non-repetition* should include, where applicable, any or all of the following measures, which will also contribute to prevention:

(a)   Ensuring effective civilian control of military and security forces;
(b)   Ensuring that all civilian and military proceedings abide by international standards of due process, fairness and impartiality;
(c)   Strengthening the independence of the judiciary;
(d)   Protecting persons in the legal, medical and health-care professions, the media and other related professions, and human rights defenders;
…
(g)   Promoting mechanisms for preventing and monitoring social conflicts and their resolution;
(h)   Reviewing and reforming laws … .

X.   *Access to relevant information concerning violations and reparation mechanisms*

24.   … [V]ictims and their representatives should be entitled to seek and obtain information on the causes leading to their victimization and on the causes and conditions pertaining to the [gross or serious violations] and to learn the truth in regard to these violations.
…

* * *

Note that the Reparations Guidelines combine a focus on human rights law and international humanitarian law, thus overcoming proposals for the adoption of two separate instruments. The situation of non-state actors, such as corporations, is dealt with obliquely in principle 15.

Both the Reparations Guidelines and the Principles on Impunity reflect the principles contained in the International Law Commission's draft Articles on Responsibility of States for Internationally Wrongful Acts (see Ch. 2, above), which were also adopted in 2001. These two 'soft law' instruments have heavily influenced the approach adopted within the field of transitional justice in the twenty-first century. It has been suggested that transitional justice developed as a response to twentieth century 'atrocity crimes' (defined by reference to the Rome Statute), but this is a retrospective application of a term that was not in use at the time and is much too narrow to describe the broad range of circumstances in which efforts were made to seek remedies that went well beyond condemnations and prosecutions in response to major violations.

Before examining the application of these various principles to historical and current situations involving claims for reparations, we consider three important sets of issues: the 'peace versus justice' debate, the granting of amnesty to offenders, and the role of truth commissions. Then follows a brief review of the current state of the art in transitional justice.[726]

One important set of questions involve how institutional efforts to remedy mass human rights violations should address concerns that such interventions will promote war or social conflict. Efforts to address past wrongdoing, for example, may threaten to unravel a fragile peace agreement or the transition from an authoritarian past. Concerns about such consequences often relate to the prospect of criminal trials. These concerns, however, can also apply to a range of other measures. For instance, a truth commission, under certain circumstances, could be more likely to rupture social relations and foster notions of collective guilt rather than encourage reconciliation. Lustration policies – precluding former perpetrators and their supporters from participating in a successor government – might obstruct social integration and political stability. Civil suits against particular individuals or organizations, such as companies formerly involved in apartheid South Africa, might undermine government efforts to encourage those and other actors to rebuild the country.

The important question may not be whether to adopt particular institutional devices, but that of timing. When is it appropriate, or most feasible, to deal with the past through these justice and accountability mechanisms? A central question may also be about who decides. That is, what institution or set of actors should have the

---

[726] See generally: Security Council Report, *Research Report: Transitional Justice: What Role for the UN Security Council* (2022).

authority to decide whether to pursue various strategies? Are local actors best situated to make those decisions, international actors, judicial or political bodies? Does it matter if local actors generally prefer amnesties? What if local actors prefer prosecution, especially for retributive or symbolic reasons, despite a more pragmatic judgement of international exports and institutions? Should the structure of international and domestic legal institutions include a presumption favouring (or disfavouring) certain justice and accountability mechanisms? What factors should overcome that presumption?

Finally, how should decision-makers weigh justice and peace in the instant case versus the precedent set and consequences for dealing with situations of mass violations in the future? For example, trials in the instant case may be important to promoting norms and expectations of punishment in other countries or in the same country's political future. Alternatively, trials might encourage repressive leaders or combatants in the future to conclude that amnesties are not reliable and that conceding political power is not in their best interest.

1. The 'Peace Versus Justice' Debate

At the international level, this debate has manifested itself most prominently in arguments about whether prosecuting the leader of one of the parties to an ongoing conflict will incentivize that person to prolong the hostilities and thus delay peace. At the national level, as we shall see below, the debate has focused on whether such individuals should be granted an amnesty either before or after prosecution in the name of healing societal wounds more quickly.[727]

The experience of the ICTY and the ICC provide some insights from experience. Analysis by Jacqueline McAllister, in 'The Peace versus Justice Debate Revisited', in Carsten Stahn et al. (eds.) *Legacies of the International Criminal Tribunal for the Former Yugoslavia* (2020) 523, at 537, reached the following conclusions about the impact of ICTY prosecutions on peace efforts:

> First, the ICTY did in fact facilitate peace efforts. Second, [it] did so by providing US mediators with leverage for ensuring that only key leaders participated in talks … … . Third, … [it] also facilitated US mediation efforts by agreeing to monitor and vet entity-level indictments …. [This] helped to deescalate a major post- Dayton crisis by effectively reassuring former belligerents that they would not be subject to victor's justice.
>
> …
>
> … [Why might the ICTY] have facilitated, versus undermined, peace efforts. In order for ICTs to increase the costs of noncompliance with ICL, and thereby generate leverage for mediators, they need to be able to conduct legal proceedings. … ICT officials must negotiate with a range of parties to effectively conduct investigations, secure apprehensions, and hold trials. … Prosecutorial support for ICTs has steadily increased ever since the ICTY's establishment. Indeed, the Tribunal's own successes in eventually apprehending an array of high- level suspects— including Slobodan Milošević— are indicative of this trend … . Kathyrn Sikkink points to such developments as evidence of a 'justice cascade', or 'a fundamental shift [in] legitimacy of the norm of individual criminal accountability for human rights violations and an increase in criminal prosecutions on behalf of that norm'. Thus, it is now harder— especially for the top combatant leaders who are at the centre of the ICC's efforts— to dodge criminal prosecution.
>
> However, recent research suggests that greater prosecutorial support, combined with the ICC's focus on high- level suspects, can actually make the process of negotiating peace far more difficult. For instance, Alyssa Prorok finds that both factors have made it more difficult for top leaders facing possible prosecution to attend talks for fear they might be arrested and transferred to The Hague. In addition, because amnesty is off the table, it is

---

[727] In general, *amnesties* foreclose prosecutions for stated crimes (often by reference to crimes or conduct that took place before a stated date), whereas *pardons* release convicted human rights offenders from serving their sentences (or the remainders thereof if they are prisoners at the time of pardon). Nonetheless, usage often views these terms as interchangeable, so that persons not yet tried are 'pardoned' and prisoners serving sentences are granted an 'amnesty'.

more challenging to negotiate a settlement. The situation was quite different for the ICTY during the Yugoslav wars. The Tribunal had an immensely challenging time securing prosecutorial support, especially early on. ... [T]he OTP did not end up targeting many top leaders until after peace negotiations had concluded. This suggests that regional leaders potentially had much less to fear than their contemporary counterparts in other civil conflicts, assuming they did not run afoul of the ICTY's then-main enforcement partner: the US. Thus, the ICTY perhaps facilitated, versus undermined, peace efforts both because it was cautious in indicting top leaders and because lead mediators effectively exercised discretion over suspect arrests and transfers. ...

The impact of ICC involvement can also cut both ways, according to Alyssa Prorok, 'The (In)compatibility of Peace and Justice? The International Criminal Court and Civil Conflict Termination', 71 *Int'l Org.* (2017) 213, at 239:

> Empirical tests ... support [the] argument [that] ICC involvement significantly reduces the likelihood of conflict termination when the risk of domestic punishment is low. Its impact diminishes, becoming insignificant, as the domestic punishment risk increases. ...
>
> ... [T]he court's broader influence is complex and multifaceted: ICC ratification improves prospects for peace in warring states, while active involvement by the court has the opposite impact. The ICC, therefore, is not universally benign or entirely harmful ... ...
>
> ... [W]hile the ICC's primary mandate is the pursuit of justice, the results indicate that its broader effects on the process of conflict termination must be taken into account by policy-makers and the court itself. In particular, the fact that ICC involvement can prolong conflict has important implications for how the court pursues investigations in ongoing conflict situations in the future. It may be in the best interest of peace, for example, for the ICC to investigate and pursue arrests and trials only after a settlement has been reached. This is particularly true because the court's most detrimental impact comes when conditions for successful settlement improve domestically (that is, as the domestic punishment risk diminishes), suggesting that the court is doing harm in the very settings where successful settlement may otherwise have been possible. ...

An issue that is related to the peace versus justice debate is whether impunity should be considered the greatest threat to respect for human rights, and should thus be the pre-eminent concern of the international community. For some commentators, criminal prosecution might not be the sole path to eliminate impunity, but it is the most important. Thus, Kate Cronin-Furman, in *Hypocrisy and Human Rights: Resisting Accountability for Mass Atrocities* (2022) 117, argues 'that the repeated failures to protect or avenge the victims of mass atrocities' are a deplorable feature of the international system and one that must be countered by determined efforts to gather and process evidence of mass atrocities so that accountability can eventually be exacted from perpetrators. Her view is that victim communities seek, 'more than anything else ... the designation of their persecutors as human rights abusers'.

Oher researchers have reached different conclusions. Payam Akhavan et al., in 'What Justice for the Yazidi Genocide?: Voices from Below', 42 *Hum. Rts. Q.* (2020) 1, describe the results of a survey of the preferences expressed by survivors of the sustained assaults by the Islamic State of Iraq and the Levant (ISIL) on Iraq's Yazidi minority, characterized by many sources as a genocide. The interviewers sought to elicit an understanding of what 'justice' might mean for the survivors. One question concerned the interviewees' preference for retributive justice, such as prosecutions before the ICC or another such tribunal, or restorative justice involving a more wide-ranging set of measures:

> What emerged is an understanding of justice principally focused on local issues, immediate concerns, agency, and prospects of a better future—features more readily achievable through local restorative justice rather than global punitive justice. This included a predilection for financial assistance, truth-telling and public recognition, and a need for healing and reconciliation among local communities and, more intimately, neighbors.

The authors concluded that scholars and advocates need to do more to listen to the voices from below and not assume that they define 'justice' as the pursuit of prosecutions: 'The early and continuing prioritization of the ICC, and the near-singular focus of energy and resources on this objective, has undermined the pursuit of more restorative forms of justice.' The initiatives by the Prosecutor in relation to both Ukraine and Palestine, considered in the preceding chapter, have potentially put the peace versus justice debate in a whole new light. Consider the observations in relation to Ukraine by Carsten Stahn, in 'The ICC in Its Third Decade: Setting the Scene', in Carsten Stahn and Rafael Braga da Silva (eds.), *The International Criminal Court in Its Third Decade: Reflecting on Law and Practices* (2024) 3, 19-20:

> The warrants create a certain point of no return. They signal that there can be no sustainable peace without leadership responsibility. Politically, they may be interpreted as an effort to promote regime change in Russia. This … may create a 'lock in' and prolong hostilities or intensify conflict. It communicates to the Russian government 'that its options are to win or to lose power and face prosecution'. Under such circumstance, the continuation of the war may become 'existential'.

> Russian officials may be reluctant to engage in peace negotiations, while facing the threat of prosecution in their aftermath. Once issued by a Chamber, warrants cannot simply be withdrawn by Prosecution. The power of the Security Council to defer investigations and prosecutions under Art. 16 of the ICC Statute is only temporary. The OTP has adopted a narrow reading of the interests of justice clause, which implies that considerations of peace and security do not *per se* bar accountability. Dealing with the ICC warrants may thus require creative strategies, or even a re-calibration of existing 'no peace without justice' formulas. …

> The Ukraine warrants … [have] contributed to the stigmatization of crimes, restricted potential travel options, and highlighted the global relevance of the Court in the ongoing conflict. They have prompted new discussions on cooperation between the ICC and the US. However, they also carry risks. They reveal political divisions among states parties. They make the ICC vulnerable to lawfare. In case of lack of compliance, the Court will be perceived as a toothless tiger. Those who are critical of the Court's strong focus in Ukraine, and risks of double standards, will likely use the Ukraine as a precedent to assess the decisiveness and effectiveness of response in other ongoing or future ICC situations.

2. Amnesties

A 2009 study by Diane Orentlicher for the UN Office of the High Commissioner for Human Rights entitled *Rule-of-law tools for post-conflict States: Amnesties* (UN Doc. HR/PUB/09/1 (2009)) defines amnesties as legal measures that have the effect of:

> (a) Prospectively barring criminal prosecution and, in some cases, civil actions against certain individuals or categories of individuals in respect of specified criminal conduct committed before the amnesty's adoption; or

> (b) Retroactively nullifying legal liability previously established.

The debate over the acceptability of amnesties in situations involving serious human rights violations involves balancing various elements. These include legal obligations to prosecute, the central importance of ensuring accountability, and an assessment of the impact of an amnesty on other legitimate goals. In 2013, a group of experts adopted the Belfast Guidelines on Amnesty and Accountability, designed to guide decisions made 'in the midst or in the wake of conflict or repression.' The Guidelines acknowledged that amnesties might, at different stages, be used for:

(viii)   encouraging combatants to surrender and disarm

(ix)   persuading authoritarian rulers to hand over power

(x)   building trust between warring factions

(xi)   facilitating peace agreements

(xii)   releasing political prisoners

(xiii) encouraging exiles to return

(xiv)   providing an incentive to offenders to participate in truth recovery or reconciliation
        programmes.

The Guidelines distinguish 'illegitimate amnesties' which 'are generally unconditional and have the effect of preventing investigations and ensuring impunity for persons responsible for serious crimes', from 'legitimate amnesties', which are 'primarily designed to create institutional and security conditions for the sustainable protection of human rights, and require individual offenders to engage with measures to ensure truth, accountability and reparations.'

In seeking to link the concepts of amnesty and accountability, the Guidelines suggest that 'amnesties can be designed to complement or operate sequentially with judicial and non-judicial accountability processes' to:

> a) deliver some form of truth and accountability for cases which are not selected for prosecution
>
> b) focus limited prosecutorial resources on those cases which are deemed to be of a higher priority or where the perpetrator has failed to fulfil the conditions of the amnesty
>
> c) contribute to a broader range of conflict transformation goals than an exclusive focus on prosecutions
>
> d) deliver greater consistency with a state's international obligations than broad amnesties that prevent all prosecutions.

Monika Nalepa, in *After Authoritarianism: Transitional Justice and Democratic Stability* (2022) 1 draws attention to the precedent set by Spain, and suggests that a utilitarian calculus might play some role in framing policy responses:

> After [Generalissimo] Francisco Franco died, the elites who succeeded him resolved on behalf of the Spanish people to let bygones be bygones. Formally, in 1977, they passed an Amnesty Law; informally, they agreed to a "Pact of Forgetting." The rationale offered for this deliberate decision was to [choose] democracy over justice. Although the Francoist regime had committed numerous atrocities during the civil war of 1936–1939 as well as after the Nationalists' victory, Spanish elites decided to "seal the archives" of the Guardia Civil and the Policia Armada (Franco's secret police) and not attempt any reckoning with the past. Even private conversation concerning the civil war and the authoritarian regime that succeeded it was rendered taboo. This "Pact of Forgetting" was shared widely by all sides of the political spectrum, including the communists against whom Franco's Nationalists had fought in the civil war. …
>
> The informal pact became so entrenched that when, in 2007, a socialist government tried to revisit the past by proposing the mildest of transparency measures, victim rehabilitation, it was met with staunch criticism. The Spanish example stood in contrast with its geographic and temporal neighbors, Greece and Portugal, both of which thoroughly purged their former authoritarian leadership and its agencies. …
>
> Incidentally, neither Greece nor Portugal fared as well recovering from their authoritarian pasts as Spain. … Scholars of comparative democratization … overwhelmingly agreed that Spain consolidated because of letting bygones be bygones rather than despite it. …
>
> It is then hardly surprising that when twenty years later, a wave of democratization spread across Eastern Europe, Spain's approach to reckoning with the authoritarian past was

used as a model for (not) dealing with the legacies of communism. In Poland, this approach was summarized with the term "gruba kreska" ("thick line"). Although originally intended to represent the idea of a clean slate for the new noncommunist cabinet, which would only be held accountable for policies implemented after assuming office, it quickly came to represent the idea of forgiving the communists for all human rights violations committed during their 45-year-long tenure in Poland.

…

Conclusion: Beyond Ritual Sacrifices

… In democracies recovering from authoritarian rule or civil war, politicians trying at all costs to prevent their skeletons from coming out of the closet fail at being effective representatives and betray the interests of their voters. In an effort to bury the truth about skeletons in the closet they succumb to blackmail. The advice to "let bygones be bygones," "forgive and forget," or "let sleeping dogs lie" especially when applied to crimes committed secretly under the authoritarian regime may be deadly for a new polity. At the same time, new democracies' temptation to punish known members and collaborators of the former regime is a form of "ritual sacrifice." Although it signals to some voters a clean break with the former regime, it has little beyond symbolic significance and may be equally crippling as the decisions to let sleeping dogs lie. There is a caveat, however, to the advice of forgoing purges of known collaborators of the authoritarian regime. When the interests of those working for the *ancien régime* depart so much from those of the new democratic politicians that their expertise is worth surrendering, purges should be used. The bottom line is then, that purges should be applied sparingly, while transparency should be used widely.

* * *

In relation to Spain, some changes were introduced in the 2007 Historic Memory Law, but these were limited in scope and a range of UN mechanisms called for a very different approach. In 2009, the UN Human Rights Committee (UN Doc. CCPR/C/ESP/CO/5, para. 9) recommended that Spain should:

> (a) consider repealing the 1977 amnesty law; (b) take the necessary legislative measures to guarantee recognition by the domestic courts of the non-applicability of a statute of limitations to crimes against humanity; (c) consider setting up a commission of independent experts to establish the historical truth about human rights violations committed during the civil war and dictatorship; and (d) allow families to exhume and identify victims' bodies, and provide them with compensation where appropriate.

In 2014, the Special Rapporteur on the promotion of truth, justice, reparation and guarantees of non-repetition (UN Doc. A/HRC/27/56/Add.1) refuted many of the government's arguments against such measures. The 2022 Democratic Memory Law represented a considerable but far from comprehensive change of heart:

> The new law creates the public prosecutor's office for human rights and democratic memory, to investigate past violations and to promote the search for the whereabouts of the disappeared. In addition, it broadens the definition of 'victim' and gives due recognition to children, who were abducted and adopted without parental consent, to their parents and siblings. It also stipulates that it is the responsibility of the state to carry out exhumations and the search for persons who disappeared during the Civil War and the Franco dictatorship.[728]

The law also: makes the state responsible for recovering the remains of victims buried in unmarked graves; establishes a national DNA database; requires schools to teach about the civil war and the dictatorship; and pardons people convicted of political crimes during the Franco era. It does not lift the amnesty that prevents prosecutions of state officials who committed crimes during the relevant period, and does not provide financial compensation for victims.

---

[728] C. Fernandez-Torne and P. Ouziel, 'Democratising and decolonising Spain: the limits of the new law on memory', *Justice Info* (5 December 2022).

In September 2023, the United Kingdom Parliament adopted the *Northern Ireland Troubles (Legacy and Reconciliation) Act 2023*. In December 2023, the Government of Ireland announced that it would bring an inter-state case under the ECHR challenging the Act's immunity provisions 'which shut down existing avenues to truth and justice for historic cases, including inquests, police investigations, Police Ombudsman investigations, and civil actions.' It added that reviews by the proposed Independent Commission for Reconciliation and Information Recovery 'are not an adequate substitute for police investigations, carried out independently, adequately, and with sufficient participation of next of kin.'

The examples mentioned above are mostly concerned with historical situations, but the granting of amnesties is also often raised in the context of negotiating peace deals. In 1999, in the context of negotiating the Lomé Accords to end the Sierra Leone civil war, the UN announced a policy of not agreeing to amnesty for war crimes, crimes against humanity, or genocide. Geoff Dancy surveyed all amnesties enacted in civil war contexts since 1946. In 'Deals with the Devil? Conflict Amnesties, Civil War, and Sustainable Peace', *72 Int'l. Org.* (2018) 387, at 416, he concludes that:

> … [O]ffers of legal amnesty can be used to halt intrastate conflicts, … subject to three ancillary rules. The first rule is that amnesties work better if they are enacted in the negotiation phase. … If and when armed combatants get to the negotiation phase, amnesties may serve as a more useful tool. They are still a signal but of costly commitments to peace. The trick is designing them in a way that is balanced, granting some concessions without making the deal too costly for the government in the future.

> … The second finding is that amnesties with explicit immunities for serious violations are not associated with a lower risk of conflict recurrence. This challenges the conventional wisdom among peacemakers that forgiving human rights abuses may be a necessary element of war-ending bargains. In the last sixty years, that is simply not the case. [Immunities for serious violations] are a roll of the dice. On one hand, they may encourage peace discussions with recalcitrant groups but, on the other hand, they weaken the government's position. Immunities for terrible acts create a negative reputation for the governments that offer them. Governments will be punished, by civilian audiences and by rebels, for making deals that are too accommodating. Rebels will see no reason not to fight against such conciliatory leaders in the future. Civilians will pressure those leaders to renege on the deal and go back to war. Negotiators need to be clear with rebel and state leaders that human rights violations—especially if they are extreme—will have to be investigated. That is now part of the political landscape following conflicts. Ignoring the problem of human rights atrocities is no longer realistic and it was never very effective anyway.

> The third finding is that amnesties are also more effective when they are embedded within larger processes of peace. … [W]hen they are passed following lengthy and iterated processes of negotiation—often as part of larger postconflict deals to release political prisoners, forgive former soldiers of crimes against the state, or to help demobilize the opposition— they are sometimes successful.

> … [A]mnesties that bring together various veto players, spoilers, and combatant groups, while being careful not to provide impunity for atrocity, help countries stay at peace following civil war.

Amnesty Laws in the Regional Courts

Both the Inter-American and the European regional courts have ruled on amnesty laws, but a uniform approach is yet to emerge. Jorge Contesse, in 'Resisting the Inter-American Human Rights System', 44 *Yale J. Int'l L.* (2019) 179, at 188, describes the approach of that court:

In … *Barrios Altos v. Peru*, [2011 Inter-Am. Ct. H.R. (ser. C) No. 75, P 39] the Inter-American Court found that Peru had international responsibility for the violation of the right to life, the right to humane treatment, the right to a fair trial, and judicial protection of fifteen individuals killed by a death squad that operated under the autocratic regime of former Peruvian president Alberto Fujimori. The Court declared that amnesty laws "violate non-derogable rights recognized by international human rights law," [and] that such laws "lack legal effect."

Barrios Altos had a major impact on domestic judges. District courts issued rulings ordering the reopening of criminal investigations in cases where courts had applied the amnesty laws. And the Peruvian Constitutional Court embraced the Inter-American Court's jurisprudence in its entirety ... .

...

In 2005, the Argentinean Supreme Court overruled a 1987 decision and declared unconstitutional several of the country's amnesty laws. ... [The Court found that] the *Barrios Altos* case addressed all questions about State obligations under international anti-impunity doctrines ... [and rendered] Argentina's amnesty laws null and void. ...

In Europe, a Grand Chamber of the European Court of Human Rights (ECtHR), in *Marguš v. Croatia* (App. No. 4455/10, judgment of 27 May 2014) considered the case of a Croatian Army commander who was convicted of war crimes in 2007, following an earlier decision in 1997 to grant him amnesty pursuant to the 1996 General Amnesty Act covering all criminal offenses committed in connection with the war in Croatia in the preceding six years:

137. The Court notes the interveners' argument that ... the granting of amnesties as a tool in ending prolonged conflicts may lead to positive outcomes.

138. The Court also notes the jurisprudence of the Inter-American Court of Human Rights, notably the ... cases of *Barrios Altos, Gomes Lund et al., Gelman and The Massacres of El Mozote and Nearby Places*, where that court ... found that no amnesties were acceptable in connection with grave breaches of fundamental human rights since any such amnesty would seriously undermine the States' duty to investigate and punish the perpetrators of such acts. It emphasised that such amnesties contravene irrevocable rights recognised by international human rights law.

(γ) *The Court's conclusion*

139. In the present case the applicant was granted amnesty for acts which amounted to grave breaches of fundamental human rights such as the intentional killing of civilians and inflicting grave bodily injury on a child, and the [Croatian] County Court's reasoning referred to the applicant's merits as a military officer. A growing tendency in international law is to see such amnesties as unacceptable because they are incompatible with the unanimously recognised obligation of States to prosecute and punish grave breaches of fundamental human rights. Even if it were to be accepted that amnesties are possible where there are some particular circumstances, such as a reconciliation process and/or a form of compensation to the victims, the amnesty granted to the applicant in the instant case would still not be acceptable since there is nothing to indicate that there were any such circumstances.

Having reviewed subsequent ECtHR case law, Juan-Pablo Pérez-León-Acevedo, in 'The European Court of Human Rights *vis-à-vis* amnesties and pardons', 26 *Int'l J. Hum. Rts.* (2022) 1107, notes that the Court has still not provided a comprehensive statement of its response to amnesties. Nevertheless, he suggests four factors are central to its approach. The first is:

> [t]he national process through which amnesties/pardons have been adopted, applied, and/or validated ... . This ... includes which organ granted these measures and through which normative instrument, whether these measures apply to serious abuses in national proceedings, and whether subsequent actions adopted ... negatively affected or changed originally admissible amnesties/pardons.
>
> ... [The second is the] margin of ... appreciation has generally been the factor that has most expanded the degree of ECtHR's deference ... .

... [Third], poor levels of state compliance with international obligations on human rights ... require the ECtHR to constrain its deference to states. This occurs particularly (but not exclusively) when state officers committed atrocities ... .

[Fourth], the impact [on] legitimate goals of peace, reconciliation, or democratic transition ... may increase the degree of ECtHR's deference ... . to states as opposed to exemption measures seeking impunity, which constrain such deference ... provided that: the state demonstrates that these measures are genuinely adopted to achieve the said legitimate aim(s) rather than impunity; and/or when these measures are accompanied with other transitional justice mechanisms such as reparations.

In other words, the Court has neither adopted an absolute prohibition on amnesties for certain serious crimes, nor closed the door on doing so. Miles Jackson, in 'Amnesties in Strasbourg', 38 *Oxf. J. Leg. Stud.* (2018) 451, argues that if, when the time comes, it opts for the first approach, it will problematically discount 'the difficult and complex choices facing political decision makers in peace negotiations, and ... the value of amnesties in securing other legitimate ends':

First, ... to treat the duty to prosecute as absolute excludes from consideration other relevant interests. This exclusion prioritises the ends served by criminal trials in the face of genuinely conflicting moral and political demands. Secondly, [it would] inhibit the way that the margin of appreciation ought to operate in amnesty cases. ... Thirdly, [it would inhibit] the scope of deference that courts ought to provide to political decision makers on a question such as this. ... Fourthly, to treat the duty to prosecute as absolute renders it non-derogable under article 15(2) ECHR. This ... [upsets] the delicate structure of article 15(2) ... and closes a valuable means of political flexibility built into the Convention.

QUESTION

What are the most compelling arguments in favour of an absolute prohibition on amnesties for individuals accused of crimes such as murder, torture, or crimes against humanity?

---

3. Truth Commissions

Truth commissions are perhaps the best-known component of transitional justice. They have been defined as:

... temporary, officially sanctioned bodies with mandates to investigate specific periods of past state abuses. They signal an official determination, genuine or not, to establish the truth about past abuses and to avoid their recurrence. Subject to the creativity of their designers, TCs are able to: provide official acknowledgment of abuses and rewrite history; focus on institutional and structural factors that permitted such abuses; make recommendations for legal and institutional reforms; provide information that is useful for subsequent prosecutions and vetting of abusive public officials; and create a basis for victim reparations and memorialization.[729]

The groundwork for the creation of well over fifty such commissions between 1984 and today was laid by the gradual recognition of a 'right to the truth' in international law. General Assembly Resolution 3220 (XXIX) (1974) recognized that 'the desire to know the fate of loved ones in armed conflicts is a basic human need'. Building on this recognition, Article 32 of the 1977 First Additional Protocol to the Geneva Conventions provided for 'the right of families to know the fate of their relatives'. The reference to a 'right' was a subject of considerable debate in the drafting process.

---

[729] G. Dancy and O. T. Thoms, 'Do Truth Commissions Really Improve Democracy?', 55 *Comp. Pol. Studs.* (2022) 555. See also the pioneering text by R. Teitel entitled *Transitional Justice* (2000).

Within institutions dedicated to human rights law, the right to the truth first found expression in the context of missing and disappeared persons. The Inter-American Commission on Human Rights and Court of Human Rights, the UN Working Group on Enforced or Involuntary Disappearances (in its first report: UN Doc. E/CN.4/1435 (1981)) and the Human Rights Committee developed a doctrine recognizing the right of families to know the fate of their close relatives. The right was codified in Article 24 of the 2006 International Convention for the Protection of All Persons from Enforced Disappearance. And, in 2010, the Working Group adopted a General Comment on the Right to the Truth, characterizing it as 'both a collective and an individual right' (UN Doc. A/HRC/16/48 (2011), 14).

Recognition of the right to the truth has expanded well beyond disappearances,[730] as reflected in the Principles on impunity and the Guidelines on reparations. In 2009, the Human Rights Council adopted Resolution 9/11 affirming the right to the truth:

> Stressing the importance for the international community to endeavour to recognize the right of victims of gross violations of human rights and serious violations of international humanitarian law, and their families and society as a whole, to know the truth regarding such violations, to the fullest extent practicable, in particular the identity of the perpetrators, the causes and facts of such violations, and the circumstances under which they occurred.

The organs of the Inter-American system also played a central role in developing the concept, which has also been taken up by the other regional system, as noted in the Report of the Special Rapporteur on the promotion of truth, justice, reparation and guarantees of non-recurrence, Pablo de Greiff (UN Doc. A/HRC/24/42 (2013)):

> 19. At the regional level, the Inter-American Commission … [and Court] were at the forefront of developing jurisprudence on the right to truth of the victim, his or her next of kin, and the whole of society. Regarding the collective nature of this right, the Commission observed [in 1986] that "every society has the inalienable right to know the truth about past events, as well as the motives and circumstances in which aberrant crimes came to be committed, in order to prevent repetition of such acts in the future". In [2013], the Court framed the right to truth in the form of a positive State obligation, stressing that "the next of kin of the victims and society as a whole must be informed of everything that has happened in connection with the said violations". The African Commission on Human and Peoples' Rights has recognized the right to truth as an aspect of the right to an effective remedy for a violation of the African Charter on Human and Peoples' Rights. In connection with gross human rights violations committed in the context of countering terrorism, the European Court of Human Rights acknowledged the right to truth not only for victims and their families but for the general public as well.

> 20. The right to truth entitles the victim, his or her relatives and the public at large to seek and obtain all relevant information concerning the commission of the alleged violation, the fate and whereabouts of the victim and, where appropriate, the process by which the alleged violation was officially authorized. With this legal framework in mind, in the aftermath of repression or conflict, the right to truth should be understood to require States to establish institutions, mechanisms and procedures that are enabled to lead to the revelation of the truth, which is seen as a process to seek information and facts about what has actually taken place, to contribute to the fight against impunity, to the reinstatement of the rule of law, and ultimately to reconciliation.

Over the past two decades, truth-telling has also come to play an important role in a diverse array of contexts. For example, Beth Sundstrom and Cara Delay, in *Catching Fire: Women's Health Activism in Ireland and the Global Movement for Reproductive Justice* (2023) at 14, cite the case of truth-telling among the victims of enforced sterilizations in Peru which served as 'a nonviolent method of historical justice that protected victims' right to

---

[730] L. Bilsky, 'The Right to Truth in International Criminal Law', in K. J. Heller et al. (eds.), *The Oxford Handbook of International Criminal Law* (2020) 473.

the truth as a form of resistance and created the possibility of reparation.' They argue that gender-sensitive truth-telling goes hand-in-hand with reproductive justice, and give an example of civil society-led truth-telling 'which emphasized accountability by listening to women's voices, avoiding reifying or essentializing women's experiences, and affirming local women's meaning making.'

a. Argentina

Most accounts of the emergence of truth commissions begin with post-World War II Germany and efforts to supplement denazification with institutional reforms designed to prevent the recurrence of Nazism, to pay reparations to victims, and to recognize and memorialize what happened. Similar efforts were pursued after the fall of the Berlin Wall and the reunification of Germany. But in more recent history, two commissions have assumed iconic status: those in Argentina and South Africa. In Argentina, a major economic crisis and a crushing military defeat in the Falklands/Malvinas war, led to the election of a democratic government headed by President Raúl Alfonsín. He established the National Commission on the Disappearance of Persons (CONADEP), presided over by the famous writer, Ernesto Sabato.[731] Its report, *Nunca Más* (Never Again) was published in 1984:

ERNESTO SABATO, PROLOGUE TO NUNCA MÁS
(1984)

... [In Argentina] the armed forces responded to the terrorists' crimes with a terrorism far worse than the one they were combating, and after 24 March 1976 they could count on the power and impunity of an absolute state, which they misused to abduct, torture and kill thousands of human beings.

Our Commission was set up not to sit in judgment, because that is the task of the constitutionally appointed judges, but to investigate the fate of the people who disappeared during those ill-omened years of our nation's life. However, after collecting several thousand statements and testimonies, verifying or establishing the existence of hundreds of secret detention centres, and compiling over 50,000 pages of documentation, we are convinced that the recent military dictatorship brought about the greatest and most savage tragedy in the history of Argentina. ... Through the technique of disappearance and its consequences, all the ethical principles which the great religions and the noblest philosophies have evolved through centuries of suffering and calamity have been trampled underfoot, barbarously ignored.

...

... [Human rights were not] violated in a haphazard fashion, but systematically ... with identical kidnappings and tortures taking place throughout the country. How can this be viewed as anything but a planned campaign of terror conceived by the military high command? How could all this have been committed by a few depraved individuals acting on their own initiative, when there was an authoritarian military regime, with all the powers and control of information that this implies? How can one speak of individual excesses? The information we collected confirms that this diabolical technology was employed by people who may well have been sadists, but who were carrying out orders. ...

The abductions were precisely organized operations, sometimes occurring at the victim's place of work, sometimes in the street in broad daylight. They involved the open deployment of military personnel, who were given a free hand by the local police stations. When a victim was sought out in his or her home at night, armed units would surround the block and force their way in, terrorizing parents and children, who were often gagged and forced to watch. They would seize the persons they had come for, beat them mercilessly, hood them, then drag them off to their cars or trucks, while the rest of the unit almost invariably ransacked the house or looted everything that could be carried. The victims were then taken to a chamber over whose doorway might well have been inscribed the words Dante read on the gates of Hell: 'Abandon hope, all ye who enter here',

Thus, in the name of national security, thousands upon thousands of human beings, usually young adults or even adolescents, fell into the sinister, ghostly category of the *desaparecidos* ... .

---

[731] See generally, V. Vegh Weis, 'Exploring the World's First Successful Truth Commission: Argentina's CONADEP and the Role of Victims in Truth-Seeking', 15 *J. Hum. Rts. Prac.* (2023) 100.

Seized by force against their will, the victims no longer existed as citizens. Who exactly was responsible for their abduction? Why had they been abducted? Where were they? There were no precise answers to these questions: the authorities had no record of them; they were not being held in jail; justice was unaware of their existence. Silence was the only reply to all the habeas corpus writs, an ominous silence that engulfed them. No kidnapper was ever arrested, not a single detention centre was ever located, there was never news of those responsible being punished for any of the crimes. ...

A feeling of complete vulnerability spread throughout Argentine society, coupled with the fear that anyone, however innocent, might become a victim of the never-ending witch-hunt. Some people reacted with alarm. Others tended, consciously or unconsciously, to justify the horror. 'There must be some reason for it,' they would whisper ... .

All sectors fell into the net: trade union leaders fighting for better wages; youngsters in student unions, journalists who did not support the regime; psychologists and sociologists simply for belonging to suspicious professions; young pacifists, nuns and priests who had taken the teachings of Christ to shanty areas; the friends of these people, too, and the friends of friends, plus others whose names were given out of motives of personal vengeance, or by the kidnapped under torture. The vast majority of them were innocent not only of any acts of terrorism, but even of belonging to the fighting units of the guerrilla organizations: these latter chose to fight it out, and either died in shootouts or committed suicide before they could be captured. Few of them were alive by the time they were in the hands of the repressive forces.

From the moment of their abduction, the victims lost all rights. Deprived of all communication with the outside world, held in unknown places, subjected to barbaric tortures, kept ignorant of their immediate or ultimate fate, they risked being either thrown into a river or the sea; weighed down with blocks of cement, or burned to ashes.
...
...
In the course of our investigations we have been insulted and threatened by the very people who committed these crimes. Far from expressing any repentance, they continue to repeat the old excuses that they were engaged in a dirty war, or that they were saving the country and its Western, Christian values, when in reality they were responsible for dragging these values inside the bloody walls of the dungeons of repression. They accuse us of hindering national reconciliation, of stirring up hatred and resentment, of not allowing the past to be forgotten. This is not the case. We have not acted out of any feeling of vindictiveness or vengeance. All we are asking for is truth and justice ... . If this does not happen, then the transcendent mission which the judicial power fulfills in all civilized communities will prove completely valueless. Truth and justice, it should be remembered, will allow the innocent members of the armed forces to live with honour; otherwise they risk being besmirched by an unjust, all embracing condemnation. Truth and justice will permit the armed forces as a whole to see themselves once more as the true descendants of those armies which fought so heroically despite their lack of means to bring freedom to half a continent.

We have been accused, finally, of partiality in denouncing only one side of the bloody events which have shaken our nation in recent years, and of remaining silent about the terrorism which occurred prior to March 1976, or even, in a tortuous way, of presenting an apology for it. On the contrary, our Commission has always repudiated that terror ... . Also, Argentinians have had the opportunity of seeing an abundance of television programmes, of reading countless newspaper and magazine articles, as well as a full-length book published by the military government, in which those acts of terrorism were listed, described, and condemned, in minute detail.

Great catastrophes are always instructive. The tragedy which began with the military dictatorship in March 1976, the most terrible our nation has ever suffered, will undoubtedly serve to help us understand that it is only democracy which can save a people from horror on this scale, only democracy which can keep and safeguard the sacred, essential rights of man. Only with democracy will we be certain that NEVER AGAIN will events such as these, which have made Argentina so sadly infamous throughout the world, be repeated in our nation.

RONALD DWORKIN, REPORT FROM HELL
NEW YORK REVIEW OF BOOKS (17 JULY 1986)

...

Two further crucial decisions were necessary ... . First, who should be prosecuted? Alfonsín, ... [had] ordered the arrest and trial of the military men at the top: the nine commanders who formed the three ruling juntas from 1976 to 1982. But should the government also prosecute the staff and junior officers who supervised the abductions and detention centers and the torture, or the thousands of ordinary soldiers who participated in these crimes? Argentine law provided a defense for military subordinates who were merely following orders. But how should this defense be interpreted? Should it protect soldiers who followed orders that were, in fact, illegitimate? Should it protect those who, following orders, committed obvious atrocities?

Second, in which courts should those who were prosecuted be tried? It was at least arguable that ... the law required that military men be tried only in military courts ... . It would violate the spirit of due process the government was anxious to reinforce to change that jurisdictional rule retrospectively and try military men in civilian courts. But the military court—the Supreme Council of the Armed Forces—was unlikely to condemn the military structure as a whole, as it would have to do if it accepted the claims of Nunca Mas.

The government was subject to intense political pressures on both sides of these two issues. The human rights community, and particularly the Mothers of the Plaza, were outraged at the possibility that the army could be left to judge itself, or that those who had actually butchered and tortured their fellow citizens might escape condemnation altogether. But Argentina needed to bury its past as well as to condemn it, and many citizens felt that years of trials would undermine the fresh sense of community Alfonsín's victory had produced. And any general program of prosecution, reaching far down the command structure, might anger the military and make it regard the new government as its enemy, which would be unwise in a nation where military coups had become almost a ritual.

The new government formally declared its intentions in a comprehensive statute, Law 23.049 of February 14, 1984 ...: all prosecutions of the military ... were to be tried in the first instance by the Supreme Council of the Armed Forces ... . But [its decisions] were subject to automatic review by the civilian Federal Chamber of Appeal, which could consider new evidence if it thought this necessary. ...

The law also resolved the issue of criminal responsibility. It provided, in Article 11, that in the absence of any evidence to the contrary, any member of the military who acted "without decision-making capacity" would be presumed justifiably to have regarded all the orders he received as legitimate orders, except that this presumption would not hold if the acts he committed were "atrocious" or "aberrant." ... It was widely understood that abduction, for example, was not atrocious, so that the junior officers who formed the abduction squads would not be guilty under these standards, but that torture, rape, murder, and robbery were atrocities ... .

Law 23.049 was attacked by the human rights groups as much too lenient; they saw it as a capitulation to the military for political reasons.

[In the end, the Supreme Council] refused to participate in the trial of the nine commanders, which was transferred to the civilian court ... .]

* * *

Nunca Más became a bestseller in Argentina and was translated into five other languages, selling over half a million copies. It was also used as a model for other Latin American truth commissions between 1985 and 2003. Emilio Crenzel, in 'Genesis, Uses, and Significations of the Nunca Más Report in Argentina, 42 *Lat. Am. Persp.* (2015) 20 notes that Nunca Más:

> recognized the disappeared as subjects of law without revealing their political activism,
> posited the exclusive responsibility of the dictatorship in the disappearances, and upheld
> democracy as the guarantee for preventing the horror from ever happening again, thus
> obscuring the responsibility of political and civil society before and after the coup. ... [It

thus] publicly challenged with unprecedented strength the dictatorship's denial of the crime. … [It secured] a massive readership.

… Nunca Más became the template for constructing a new memory of [the] past. It became the dominant way of thinking about, remembering, and representing the past. [But, over time, the human rights community challenged the Alfonsín government] … over who was the rightful interpreter of its contents … . … [A]fter the impunity laws were passed and the pardons were granted … the human rights organizations regarded the Nunca Más report as a means for denouncing the crime of forced disappearance and as a sign of the waning willingness of the state and political leaders to seek justice.

From 1995 on, Nunca Más entered a new cycle of mass dissemination as multiple actors sought ways of conveying the past to younger generations. … [I]t was no longer seen as a means for attaining punitive goals and became a vehicle of memory, opening the way for a debate over possible political and historical interpretations. … These accounts introduced new meanings, some even openly challenging the original report's view, by presenting state violence as existing prior to the coup, explaining the disappearances as a result of material goals or of political and religious values that the report posited as being violated by this crime, and abandoning the view of democracy as the political regime that guaranteed the "never again" imperative.

Nonetheless, these interventions reproduced some of the interpretative approaches of the report, eluded the historical examination of the past, overlooked any possible connections between political and civil society and the horrors perpetrated, and ignored the political activism of the disappeared. … [Argentine society has had difficulty] in incorporating this past into a historical account that includes politics as a feature of its protagonists and a cause for ruptures. The uses of Nunca Más illustrate the public's acceptance of the report as a canonical text, while its resignifications evidence that it too was shaped by the political times of collective memory. …

b. South Africa

The establishment of the South African Truth and Reconciliation Commission was part of the negotiated settlement in 1994 to bring an end to apartheid. For various reasons, it captured the public imagination and has been highly influential, although assessments of its contributions vary, as noted by the UN Special Rapporteur in 2017:

> … It is the only truth commission to include an amnesty-for-truth model (a highly conditioned amnesty by design). It integrated a promise of reparations (alas, not completely satisfied), and, importantly, provided a public platform for victims, not the least through highly successful public hearings. Ultimately, the expectation that the amnesty process would generate significant information was not met. Similarly, the idea that those whose amnesty applications had been denied would be liable for prosecution (7,112 applications filed but only 849 amnesties granted) has been emptied of force because of the reluctance to initiate prosecutions. Nonetheless, the model has been extraordinarily influential. Kenya, Liberia and Sierra Leone have adopted elements of this approach.[732]

Other commentators have been even more critical:

> … [The TRC] was widely applauded by international scholars and human rights non-governmental organizations, and it did perform a number of functions admirably. The Commission's public and televised hearings brought the voices of ordinary Africans into the mainstream public space in a way that was unprecedented in South Africa's history. After the TRC hearings, it was apparent to all that apartheid was a vicious system of

---

[732] P. de Greiff, Report of the Special Rapporteur on the promotion of truth, justice, reparation and guarantees of non-recurrence on his global study on transitional justice, UN Doc. A/HRC/36/50/Add.1 (7 August 2017), para. 14.

institutionalized racism that destroyed millions of human lives, through violence and through structural neglect.

... [But] the final TRC Report released in 1998 was a shambolic document comprised of 3,500 jumbled, barely edited pages with no coherent chronology and no index. It contained basic and embarrassing mistakes of fact ... .

Perhaps more significant was the TRC's evasion of the larger historical questions about the nature of the apartheid system and its relationship to violence. The TRC report need not have settled these complex issues, but it ought to have broached them, since a central stated rationale for truth commissions is that they can address the historical questions that criminal courts must eschew in their focus on individual criminal responsibility. In the end, the South African TRC did not leave behind a well-constructed report that offered new insights into apartheid-era violence. In fact, the criminal prosecution of apartheid security policemen such as [Colonel] Eugene De Kock arguably produced more new and substantial information on the day-to day functioning, if not the entire chain of command of the apartheid state security apparatus. In this respect, there is a very wide disjuncture between how international scholars and practitioners and South Africans of various political dispositions perceive the Commission's legacy.

The South African case casts doubt upon the often-stated view that truth commissions inevitably represent a marked improvement upon domestic criminal trials with respect to the histories they write. Instead, some commissions and courts produce meager and impoverished accounts, whereas others write complex and detailed histories of the origins of conflict. ...[733]

c. East Timor and Indonesia

Two very different experiences in this region are recounted by different scholars. The first relates to East Timor:

... After 1999, when the United Nations assumed administration of East Timor following massive violence around the referendum on self-determination, a Serious Crimes Process and a Commission for Reception, Truth and Reconciliation were established. The former was comprised of two hybrid criminal justice mechanisms that focused on perpetrators of the most serious abuses. The Commission complemented this approach by dealing with the aftermath of violence in communities, focusing on mid- or lower-level perpetrators of crimes, through a programme to encourage the "reception" of former militias back home. Another novelty was the joint truth-seeking effort with Indonesia, the Commission on Truth and Friendship. Initially criticized by observers who expected nothing short of a whitewash, that Commission's final report supported many of the politically sensitive findings of the Commission for Reception, Truth and Reconciliation in East Timor regarding crimes against humanity committed by Indonesian forces.[734]

The second relates to events in Indonesia:

In October 1965, ... [the] Indonesian military, with the assistance of co-opted religious and nationalist youth militias, rounded up members and affiliates of the mass-supported Indonesian Communist Party (PKI). Between October 1965 and March 1966, up to 1 million unarmed civilians were murdered due to their alleged political beliefs, with a further estimated 1.5 million held in political detention camps for years afterward.

...

---

[733] R. Ashby Wilson and V. Petrović, 'Transitional Justice Histories: Narrating Mass Atrocities', in J. Meierhenrich, A. Hinton and L. Douglas (eds.), *The Oxford Handbook on Transitional Justice* (2023).
[734] P. de Greiff, above, para. 21.

[Between 2008 and 2012, Indonesia's National Human Rights Commission (Komnas HAM) launched an official inquiry into these events. If the Commission was able to provide 'sufficient preliminary evidence' that gross violations could reasonably be expected to have occurred, a full investigation and possible prosecutions should then be undertaken by the Attorney-General.]

… [The Commission] report, which provided substantial evidence of numerous crimes against humanity perpetrated by state agents and their proxies in 1965–1966, was a landmark achievement in many ways. It refuted the military's own version of events, and instead laid the blame squarely on the Indonesian Army leadership for its role in coordinating and carrying out the murders, exterminations, torture, sexual violence, and the many other forms of widespread violence perpetrated systematically against Communists in the aftermath of the October 1, 1965 coup. Nothing has come of the [report] … .[735]

d. Colombia

Colombia was in a state of civil war between 1958 (or 1964, according to some accounts) and 2016. After a 'final peace agreement' in 2016, a Truth Commission began work in 2018. In July 2022 it published an 896-page summary of findings and recommendations, along with the first two chapters of what will eventually be a ten-chapter report. It estimated that some 450,000 people were killed, nearly twice the number previously believed. Millions of people were displaced. The report drew on more than 14,000 individual and collective interviews, as well as a cache of previously classified Central Intelligence Agency and other U.S. Government reports which disclosed many forms of involvement by U.S. officials and corporate actors.

On 24 November 2016, the Colombian Government and FARC-EP (Revolutionary Armed Forces of Colombia – Army of the People) signed the 'Final Agreement to End the Armed Conflict and Build a Stable and Lasting Peace'. Among other things, the agreement created the 'Holistic System for Truth, Justice, Reparation and Non-Recurrence (SIVJR). Juana Acosta-López and Cindy Espitia-Murcia, in 'The Transitional Justice Model in Colombia *vis-à-vis* the Inter- American Human Rights System', in Alejandro Linares-Cantillo et al. (eds.), *Constitutionalism: Old Dilemmas, New Insights* (2021) 331, explain the role of the three principal organs established by the agreement:

1. *The Truth, Coexistence and Non- Recurrence Commission.* This is a temporary extra- judicial organ tasked with four main functions, namely: (i) to clarify the human rights and international humanitarian law ('IHL') violations and breaches committed in the course of the NIAC [non-international armed conflict]; (ii) to provide the society with ample explanation on the complexity of the Colombian conflict; (iii) to promote the recognition of the victims and the acknowledgement of the individual and collective responsibilities of those who participated in the conflict; (iv) to promote reconciliation and coexistence in the territories as a guarantee of non- recurrence. …

2. *Special Unit for the Search of Persons deemed as Missing in the Context and due to the Conflict.* This is a high- level special unit of a humanitarian and extra- judicial nature, whose goal is to direct, coordinate, and contribute to the implementation of humanitarian actions for the searching and identification of all the people deemed as missing due to the NIAC who are still alive. In the cases of those deceased, whenever possible, the Special Unit should work for the location and dignified delivery of their remains.

3. *Special Jurisdiction for Peace.* This organ is composed of a number of judicial panels for justice. In its twenty-year term it is tasked with judging those who bear most responsibility for crimes that constitute serious violations of international human rights law and grave breaches of IHL that were committed during the sixty-year NIAC. … [Its main function] is to secure, by reasonable means within its reach, truth, justice, reparation, and guarantees of non- recurrence for the victims. …

---

[735] J. Melvin and A. Pohlman, 'Crimes against Humanity in Indonesia (1965–1966)', in B. Holá et al. (eds.), *The Oxford Handbook of Atrocity Crimes* (2022) 829.

An excerpt from the recommendations in the Truth Commission's 2022 report follows. Note that this is an unofficial electronically-generated translation.

COMMISSION FOR THE CLARIFICATION OF TRUTH, COEXISTENCE AND NON-REPETITION, THERE IS A FUTURE IF THERE IS TRUTH: FINAL REPORT, FINDINGS AND RECOMMENDATIONS
(2022) 624

Introduction

… The signing of the Peace Agreement … opened a new opportunity to undertake as a society the transformations that are necessary … . However, [today] … we are facing a scenario of increased violence in some areas of the country. …

The … violence and armed confrontation in some territories has resulted in an increase in displacements, confinements, recruitments, landmine incidents and assassinations of social leaders, human rights defenders and people in the process of reincorporation. Added to this is the blockage of dialogues with the ELN and the absence of a security strategy appropriate to the context and focused on the protection of people. Taken together, all of the above implies a risk of reliving a cycle of violence that was thought to have been overcome … .
…
… [E]ight themes were prioritized … in the recommendations:
1) peace building as a national project, 2) victims, 3) political regime and participation, 4) drug trafficking, 5) impunity, 6) security, 7) territorial peace, 8) culture for peace and education. …
…

Summary of recommendations
…

- … [P]eace as a long-term priority must become a national project that places respect for life and dignity at the center, that guarantees rights to all equally, that recognizes and respects diversity, a peace that is built from the territory and with the communities, and in which dialogue is the main tool for dealing with differences and resolving conflicts. A peace that allows for reconciliation and the reconstruction of citizens' trust in institutions and among themselves … .

- Recognize the victims of the armed conflict in their pain, dignity and resistance; recognize the injustice of what they have experienced and the collective trauma that we share as a society. This should lead us to commit ourselves to comprehensive and transformative reparations for the more than nine million victims of the internal armed conflict … .

…

- To advance in a critical examination of our past in order to build on it a future in peace. For this reason, we need a policy of memory and truth for the construction of peace and non-repetition that commits the State and society as a whole and contributes to the strengthening of democratic values. Furthermore, it must recognize, support and promote the memory initiatives of civil society and its organizations as essential for the construction of a plural and democratic memory; and ensure that the responsible institutions have the necessary independence and autonomy to carry out a policy and decisive action for a living and plural memory that implies a break with the past of stigmatization, justification or denial.

- Rethink the problem of drug trafficking and find the political, economic, ethical and legal ways out of it in in-depth debates, both at the national and international levels, that will allow progress in the regulation of the drug market and overcome prohibitionism. This is based on the recognition of the penetration of drug trafficking at all levels of culture, politics and economy, and that the war against drugs and for illegalized drugs is one of the main and most relevant factors that have facilitated the persistence of conflict and violence … . In the immediate term, it is urgent to adopt a human rights and public health approach in the policy against cultivation and consumption and to rationalize the use of criminal action against the weakest links in the chain, which will allow, among other things, overcoming structural problems of poverty, exclusion and stigmatization. And to implement a proposal for the rigorous regulation of the market and consumption under state and international control in a process in which Colombia can and should play an inspirational and leading role.

- Strengthen and develop investigative mechanisms that allow the State and society to know in depth the system of relationships, alliances and interests involved in drug trafficking and networks of violence. …

- Recover the value of justice to vindicate legality, promote peaceful coexistence, contribute to the satisfaction of victims' rights and rebuild trust in the State. In this sense, given the persistence of violence caused by armed groups and the impact of impunity, it is necessary to improve the State's capacity to guarantee the impartiality and independence of the investigative and judicial entities, as well as the control bodies that must be a guarantee and commitment to the necessary strengthening of democracy … .

…

- Establish a new vision of security for peace building, as a public good centered on people, that allows us to overcome the logics of the armed conflict in which we have lived, change the way the State understands and is present in the territories and rebuild trust based on dialogues between citizens and institutions, particularly the public force, as a fundamental element for territorial peace and institutional strengthening. In this context, the transformation of the security sector, and in particular the role of the security forces in ensuring the prevention of crime and the requirements of the law in the protection of the lives and tranquility of people, starting with those who are most exposed due to poverty and exclusion, becomes relevant … . Finally, the recovery of trust also implies that the sector's institutions face the legacy of human rights violations and breaches of IHL in which their members have been responsible, and guarantee the non-repetition of these events.

- To deepen democracy for peace through the definitive exclusion of weapons from politics … .

- Building peace requires new tools and a break with the past, a positive shock, and not a fragmented vision of the way forward. … A ministry or an entity that promotes State policies for reconciliation and peace-building is one of the tools that the Commission proposes. …

- To guarantee conditions of well-being and dignified life for the communities in the territories … requires a comprehensive, long-term effort that commits not only the State, but society as a whole, based on a participatory, equitable, sustainable and multicultural land-use planning process. To this end, land redistribution, prevention and reversal of dispossession, access to public goods and services, including security and justice, and productive opportunities (financial capital, tertiary roads, access to markets) must be guaranteed for rural inhabitants, which means food security and sovereignty for the country, care for ecosystems, water and land as fundamental elements for the common good and good national living from the local communities.

- … There cannot be full peace without differential treatment of historically excluded groups - ethnic peoples, peasant population, women, children, adolescents and youth, LGBTIQ+ persons, persons with disabilities or functional diversity, and the elderly- and if specific efforts are not made to transform the factors that caused the armed conflict to have a particularly aggravated impact on them. …

* * *

To the extent that generalizations can be valid across a wide range of truth commissions over many decades, Adam Kochanski, in 'Mandating Truth: Patterns and Trends in Truth Commission Design', 21 *Hum. Rts. Rev.*

(2020) 113, identified three emerging trends based on a review of 44 truth commissions, that operated between 1974 and 2015. The first was a move towards more complex mandates. He notes that while the 1990 Chad TC had the singular goal of documenting the abuses committed under Hissène Habré, the 2008 Kenyan Truth, Justice, and Reconciliation Commission had 18 different goals. He notes, however, that the broader focus 'has coincided with a turn away from the early expectation that truth commissions will support human rights prosecutions', but adds that there has been no accompanying 'move toward robust procedural powers for investigation and reporting'. The second trend is a diminished emphasis on seeking prosecutions, for which he offers two possible explanations. The first is that 'a functional division of labour has emerged' between the work of TCs and trials conducted by the courts. The second, and more problematic, explanation 'is that a logic of reduced costs is motivating TC establishment. In other words, TCs are being selected because they offer a substitute for trials – abusive regimes view them as a less harmful policy option that can deflect calls for accountability.' He cites bodies set up in Sri Lanka and Côte d'Ivoire as illustrations of initiatives largely designed to defuse or even silence accountability demands.

The third trend identified by Kochanski is a failure to give TCs strong investigative and reporting powers. He suggests that this might be taken as 'an early indicator of instrumental use given some of the most questionable TCs fall into the range of limited powers (e.g. Algeria, Lebanon, Serbia and Montenegro, Sri Lanka, and so forth).'

4. The Future of Transitional Justice

While the materials above have focused primarily on issues such as amnesties and truth commissions, there are a great many other dimensions to transitional justice, including reparations which are dealt with below (p. 000). In addition, mention should be made of the increasing use of techniques associated with transitional justice to address the violations of rights to which indigenous peoples in many countries have been subjected (see UN Docs. A/76/180 (2021) and A/HRC/51/50 (2022)). Sámi reconciliation commissions have been set up in Norway (2018), Finland (2019) and Sweden (2020), and in 2021, Victoria, the second most populous state in Australia, established the Yoorrook Justice Commission to 'develop a shared understanding among all Victorians of the impact of colonisation, as well as the diversity, strength and resilience of First Peoples' cultures; and to make recommendations for healing, system reform and practical changes to laws, policy and education, as well as to matters to be included in future treaties.'[736] In a different context, transitional justice approaches have also been used to address sexual and other abuses in religious settings.[737]

Looking at the field as a whole, David Tolbert and Marcela Prieto Rudolphy, 'Transitional Justice in the 21st Century: History, Effectiveness, and Challenges', in Barbora Holá et al. (eds.), *The Oxford Handbook of Atrocity Crimes* (2022) 581, note the extent to which deep disagreements remain as to its nature and future directions:

> There is an air of paradox in the goals associated with transitional justice. There are conflicts between substantive and procedural justice, and between reconciliation and nation-building. There is the challenge of achieving criminal accountability when violations have been committed by thousands of perpetrators and achieving reconciliation while simultaneously "opening up old wounds;" and promoting a transformative agenda that at the same time is meant not to imperil the transition. Although tensions may arise in practice, there is nothing in the goals that makes them incompatible … .
>
> … [T]here is no consensus on any conception of transitional justice. Some think transitional justice is just a form of ordinary justice, while others emphasize the particularities of pre-transitional states. Teitel has focused on the particularities of transitional justice and its relation between law and political transformation, while De Greiff has argued that transitional justice is a "principled application of justice in distinct circumstances." More recently, Colleen Murphy has provided a theoretical account of transitional justice and its demands, which contests the idea of transitional justice as a mere compromise between different familiar kinds of justice and underlines transitional

---

[736] https://yoorrookjusticecommission.org.au/overview/.
[737] J. Gallen, *Transitional Justice and the Historical Abuses of Church and State* (2023).

justice's special nature. Others emphasize restorative justice, which aims for reconciliation by seeking to re-establish the relationships between victims and perpetrators and involving the wider community. Initially thought of as applicable only to lesser violations, some now argue it should extend to the most serious crimes. Finally, there is the most recent transitional justice canon, which has been called the "fourth generation of transitional justice scholarship": transitional justice as transformative justice. ...

Thus, there is no consensus on any conception of transitional justice nor on the relationships among transitional justice's goals. This makes the second question—on which there is not much consensus either —even more challenging: Does transitional justice deliver on what its advocates promise? ...

In the following readings, Dustin Sharp and Frank Haldemann offer important reflections on the ways in which the field should evolve in the years ahead.

DUSTIN SHARP, RETHINKING TRANSITIONAL JUSTICE FOR THE TWENTY-FIRST CENTURY:
BEYOND THE END OF HISTORY
(2018) 155

[In concluding his book, Sharp argues that transitional justice policy in the twenty-first century should be (re)oriented around the following five broad themes:]

Transitional justice should embrace more extended concepts of peace, justice, and violence

"Peace" tends to be conceived of as a narrow (neo)liberal peace. "Justice" is typically understood in terms of legal and atrocity justice for a narrow if not egregious band of civil and political rights violations. And the "violence" that is to be condemned (and, hopefully, prevented) is understood as comprising physical violence, for the most part excluding violence of the economic, cultural, and structural kind. These are all, of course, social and political constructions, and there is a sense in which they are mutually reinforcing. That is, narrow constructions of justice and violence lead to a comparatively thin idea of peace, and vice versa.

... Without doubt, justice in its fullest and most expansive sense must necessarily remain a broader concept than transitional justice. However, to the extent that questions of economic violence and distributive justice help to drive conflict, instability, and human rights abuses, their positioning at the periphery of transitional justice concern may ultimately be self-defeating. Thus, whatever the dividing line between abuses that will be addressed or go unaddressed by transitional justice mechanisms, it makes little sense as a matter of policy to draw a simplistic one that reifies historic dichotomies of civil and political versus economic and social rights.
...
Much will depend on context, but whether issues of economic violence are addressed is a question largely bound up with practical and methodological challenges, not fundamental or structural impossibilities. More cautious approaches might, for example, focus on those patterns of economic violence with the greatest negative impact on economic and social rights, or perhaps focus on a small group of those "bearing the greatest responsibility" for economic crimes. Another filtering device to render the inquiry more manageable might be temporal – limiting the investigation to a period of the last ten years, for example. In this, the embrace of economic violence would be little different than historical approaches to violations of civil and political rights, which have tended to be relatively limited and selective.

The question is therefore increasingly less whether facets of economic violence should be addressed than how they should be addressed in view of available resources and the roots and drivers of the conflict. ...

Transitional justice should embrace the idea of "liberal localism"

... Transitional justice has tended to privilege largely Western approaches to and understandings of what it means to "do justice." This has at frequent intervals sparked resistance and backlash, and diminished a sense of badly needed legitimacy and local support for many transitional justice initiatives. The sense that transitional justice is in essence a "Western" enterprise pushed, funded, and supported by the Global North is not entirely accurate, but contains an uncomfortable degree of truth that is ultimately corrosive to the very local ownership and support essential to long-term success. Yet the choice going forward is not a simple one between dogmatic localism and strongly assertive if not imperious global justice. Rather, the dilemmas of "the local" reveal competing liberal principles and commitments that need to be balanced. In and of itself, there is nothing particularly illiberal, for example, in giving greater weight to local autonomy, participation, and decision making when it comes to deciding what justice is supposed to mean and what the appropriate mechanisms for delivering that justice should be. If taken seriously, principles of pluralism and concepts like the "margin of appreciation" worked out in historically liberal societies would also go a long way toward generating locally driven transitional justice practice reflective of greater contextual openness and adaptability. …

…

Transitional justice should strike a better balance between retributive, restorative, and distributive justice

…

Considered most expansively, "justice" could be understood as a broad social project and a condition in society. To "do justice" with such a conception in mind would likely involve a wide spectrum of efforts involving components of retributive, restorative, and distributive justice. Yet this holistic view of justice stands in contrast to a narrower human rights legalism often associated with transitional justice that has tended to see justice as a relationship to the state, has tended to see "accountability" for mass atrocities as synonymous with individual criminal accountability rather that a broader collective or institutional model, and which has imagined justice to be something that can, to some extent, be engineered and delivered through legal mechanisms and reforms. If this is the conception of justice animating the field, we can then ask whether "transitional justice" is not just a simple byword for "law," "legal justice," or "retributive justice." Thus, a necessary step in achieving a more holistic view of justice would be to question the bias of many in the field toward topdown retributivism as the "gold standard" response to mass atrocity. This assumption is particularly hardwired into lawyers for whom courtroom justice is often seen as the only form of "hard" or "real" justice that one should accept, with anything else being a second-best or compromise solution. …

Transitional justice should embrace peacebuilding, the emancipatory kind, supported by a broader range of liberalisms

Transitional justice has in several short decades become the "globally dominant lens" through which we now grapple with legacies of violence and mass atrocity. That lens has not been an apolitical, acultural, or nonideological one, being most accurately viewed as a fairly narrow, mostly Western, (neo)liberal prism with all the reductive concepts of peace, justice, and violence that go with it. Seen through these optics, transitional justice is the harbinger and handmaiden of atrocity justice and liberal democracy. … [T]hese liberal optics … have contributed, at least in part, to some of the blind spots and frictions associated with transitional justice initiatives today, helping to push certain questions and modalities of justice into the foreground, while relegating others to the background of transitional justice concern:

Set in the Foreground	Set in the Background
the global, the Western	the local, the non-Western "other"
the modern, the secular	the traditional, the religious
the legal	the political
civil and political rights	economic and social rights
physical violence	economic and structural violence
the state, the individual	the community, the group
formal, institutional, "top-down" change	informal, cultural, social, "bottom-up" change

A key question is what happens to the chart above if we come to conceptualize transitional justice not simply as a vector for the promotion of atrocity justice and liberal democracy, but as a broader component of peacebuilding. …

…

... [E]mbracing a paradigm of emancipatory peacebuilding, buttressed by constructs from critical peacebuilding theory, would serve to support a number of the policy changes advocated above. For example, an embrace of positive peace would help to generate a default policy assumption that one should evaluate the need [to address] both physical and economic violence, and consider the cocktail of retributive, restorative, and distributive most suited to the context. As another example, embracing a vision of peacebuilding informed by concepts of popular peace, the everyday and hybridity would help to generate a default policy assumption that justice initiatives should in most instances begin from the "bottom up," being planned and driven by local constituencies and cosmovision. ...

...

Transitional justice should embrace a sense of radical humility

...

... Historically, dominant transitional justice practice has been characterized by a sort of overconfidence in its abilities, predicated on the assumption that we know what concepts like "doing justice" and "accountability" actually mean, both in and beyond the West; and that mainstream understandings of such concepts are an unmitigated good for transitional societies and beyond. Dominant practice has also often reflected a lack of humility about the extent to which these concepts can be actualized by outsiders without robust local support.

... And if after deep inquiry more flexible and extended concepts of justice, violence, and peace are indeed to be embraced as a policy matter, they must be accompanied by a sense of "radical humility" that accepts the need for their continued interrogation and contestation. ...

FRANK HALDEMANN, TRANSITIONAL JUSTICE FOR FOXES: CONFLICT, PLURALISM AND THE POLITICS OF COMPROMISE (2023) 201

Nine Theses on Transitional Justice ...

Isaiah Berlin [made famous the] distinction between the hedgehog and the fox – a metaphor for two radically distinct ways of thinking ... . His heart was with foxes, with those eclectic, pluralist thinkers who, unlike hedgehogs, see 'many things' rather than 'one big thing', and who are sceptical about reducing everything to one single framework or system in terms of which all questions can be solved. [The author seeks to think 'like a fox' about transitional justice, and summarizes the findings of his book in nine theses]:

1. *It's time to learn to unlearn the normal model.* Our way of thinking about and doing transitional justice has been for too long straitjacketed by ... 'the normal model' [which] reduces transitional justice to an anti-impunity framework, structured around neatly defined and supposedly complementary legal obligations and rights. It is time to relearn the language of dilemmas, uncertainties, conflicts and failure that the normal model suppresses. ... [This requires posing questions such as:] How do transitions come about? What conflicts arise? Which values, and which interests collide? How can conflicts be accommodated, and how can enduring change occur? Which compromises are acceptable, and which are not? What is a credible alternative to the present state of affairs? What new social contract is needed to build a better future? ...

2. *Rather than wishing value conflict away, the question is how to constructively live with it.* The normal model problematically assumes that transitional justice forms a harmonious whole. The reality of transitional justice is far messier, however. The goods usually associated with transitional justice (truth, justice, peace, the rule of law, democracy, etc.) tend to conflict, and often irreconcilably, and when they do, there is no single correct formula for resolving the conflict. Value conflict, then, is structural rather than incidental to the project of transitional justice. ...

3. *There are no neat solutions, only hard choices.* ... There is no overarching standard, no neat formula, by which such conflicts can be wholly dissolved or resolved. Nothing can make the tensions entirely disappear. Every choice, however well considered, entails regrettable loss. ...

4. *We can be realistic without being hopeless.* ... [We] must engage head-on with the issue of how real change is possible here and now. This ... means being wary of both bright-eyed optimism and simplistic moralising. ...

5. *Context is almost everything.* The practice of transitional justice is inescapably context dependent. ... [I]t is quintessentially a matter of making delicate judgements about what can be done, or even be tried, in some particular circumstances by concrete agents with limited resources and powers. ... Principles and values ... do have a central role to play ... [but] normative generalising is a rather poor guide to practice. It is no substitute for the work of situated judgement.

6. *It's a winding route along an ever-evolving itinerary.* ... [T]ransitional justice ... involves ... hard choices about how to allocate scarce resources and settle deep conflicts among competing values and interests. These choices are inherently political. ...

7. *Compromise always leaves a sour aftertaste, but we can hardly do without it.* ... [Often] compromise is the only viable alternative to continuing war and oppression, and hence a precondition of the very possibility of transitional justice. Compromise in itself is neither 'bad' nor 'good', however. It must be asked in each case whether a particular compromise can stand up to critical scrutiny at a particular point in time. ...

8. *We need to remove our Western blinders.* Even as it pays lip service to 'the local', the normal model leaves virtually no room for practices and approaches other than those from the West. Decolonising transitional justice would mean engaging with 'other' standpoints ... . It would call ... for a critical dialogue between different practices and forms of knowledge, premised on the belief that no framework can be seen as *the* answer to transitional justice's problems. ...

9. *The task is both impossible and necessary.* Any response to radical evil is inescapably incomplete and inadequate. Nothing can ever undo what was done, recover what was lost. The slate cannot be wiped clean. ... If 'something is to be done', we cannot do without ideals of what a better society should look like. Envisioning a credible alternative to the status quo is the very precondition for doing something. Transitional justice can be hopeful without being shallowly optimistic. It is bound up with the hope that social conditions are improvable through genuine human struggle. ...

QUESTIONS

1. What is the significance of the position, expressed by various international human rights bodies, that the right to the truth is: (i) separate from the right to information; and (ii) an individual as well as a collective right?

2. It has been suggested that we are now seeing the fourth generation of approaches to transitional justice, which focuses on bringing transformative justice. Compare the principal characteristics of the approach reflected in *Nunca Más* in 1984 with that in the Colombian Truth Commission report almost forty years later. Is the latter too wide-ranging? If so, what issues would you have left out?

B. REPARATIONS

Reparations are an integral part of the right to an effective remedy, and of transitional justice. But they are also assuming a broader role in terms of redress for historical injustices, such as slavery and colonialism,[738] which are the main focus of the following materials. Before examining those issues, however, it is useful to consider some of the philosophical dimensions of reparations claims. Consider first the analysis of different ethical

---

[738] On 'the duty to provide reparations to peoples, deprived of their means of subsistence, self-determination and development', see Separate Opinion of Judge Cançado Trindade in *Legal Consequences of the Separation of the Chagos Archipelago from Mauritius in 1965*, Advisory Opinion, *I.C.J. Reports 2019*, 156, at 232.

theories of reparations by Eric Posner and Adrian Vermeule, in 'Reparations for Slavery and Other Historical Injustices', 103 *Colum. L. Rev.* (2003) 689:

> ... A theory of reparations explains why the government should require one group of people to pay another group of people even though the latter group, the victims or their descendants or relations, do not have a prior legal right against the first group. Reparations claims thus involve three relationships: (1) the relationship between the original wrongdoer and the original victim; (2) the relationship between the original wrongdoer and the possible payer of reparations; and (3) the relationship between the original victim and the possible claimant or beneficiary of reparations. The claimant must show that each relationship is of the proper type.
>
> The nature of the relationship depends on two separate moral questions. The first concerns the grounds of the moral obligation that gives rise to the reparations claim. Many reparations schemes are based on a claim that one group of people wrongfully harmed another group of people and therefore owe compensation to the extent of the harm. Others are based on a claim that one group of people was unjustly enriched by another group of people and therefore must make restitution of the benefit obtained. The harm and restitution theories have distinctive implications for the generosity and form of reparations and for the validity of the claims of nonwrongdoers and nonvictims.
>
> The second question concerns the nature of the entity that can bear moral obligations. We consider three positions. Under ethical individualism, only individuals can have moral obligations and rights. Under "soft" ethical individualism, a corporate body can also have moral obligations and rights even arising out of circumstances where the individuals who compose the corporation do not. Thus, an individual who belongs to the corporation could be made to pay on account of a wrongful act committed by the corporation even though the individual was not to blame for the act. Under ethical collectivism, a more loosely defined group such as a nation can have moral obligations and rights. Here, even individuals who, though members of the group, did not voluntarily enter the group or accept the benefits of membership (as in the case of soft ethical individualism) can be made to pay for the wrongful acts of the group. As we will discuss, reparations claims become easier to make as individualistic premises are relaxed, but they also become vaguer and less compelling.

Jeremy Waldron, in 'Redressing Historic Injustice', 52 *U. Toronto L. J.* (2002) 135 addresses issues relating to reparations, especially for indigenous peoples. His thesis has been summarized in the following terms:

> [Waldron's] 'thesis of the supersession of historic injustice' or the 'supersession thesis' ... is as follows: If a historical injustice occurs leading to an unjust situation S1 at time T1, morally relevant changes in circumstances can occur between T1 and T2, such that at T2, justice does not require – and may prohibit – returning to the prior situation. So, suppose settlers unjustly seized Indigenous lands in 1840. Just after this, the dispossession remains an ongoing injustice and should be reversed. However, changes in circumstances like population increases and environmental conditions may mean that historical entitlements (judged from a moral perspective) can no longer be justified relative to contemporary needs for lands and resources. The distribution of resources that was unjustly established through the seizure in 1840 may become a just (or not unjust) distribution of resources in 2022. Waldron says that if it is no longer a continuing injustice that Indigenous peoples are deprived of those resources, then the injustice has been 'superseded'. ...[739]

Now, consider Waldron's own analysis:

> It does not follow from what has been said we should attach no importance to historic injustice of the sort that disfigured the colonial history of countries like New Zealand. The arguments made in Parts IV-VIII are directed at a particular way of thinking about

---

[739] L. Meyer and T. Waligore, 'Superseding historical injustice? New critical assessments', 25 *Crit. Rev. Int'l. Soc. & Pol. Phil.* (2022) 319.

that injustice and a particular way of approaching its remediation. I have criticized the approach that aims, as it were, to wind the tape back to the injustice and try to make the world as though the injustice had never happened: I have argued that the counterfactuals that that involves are impossible to figure out (if not incoherent), and I have argued, too, that such an approach tries to do justice to the wrong entities (viz. modern-day successors to the groups that were important at the time the injustice took place) and to vindicate the wrong rights (rights that obtained by virtue of circumstances quite different from those of the modern world). The reparationist enterprise fails to take proper account of the fact that the people, entities, and circumstances in relation to which justice must now be done have changed radically from the peoples, entities, and circumstances in relation to which violations were historically committed. Some of those changes are a result of the historic injustice. But, as I argued in the early sections of the article, that does not mean they can be ignored or reversed. We must come to terms with each other here and now, irrespective of how were [sic] all got here.

Behind the thesis of supersession lies a determination to focus upon present and prospective costs - the suffering and the deprivation over which we still have some control. The idea is that any conception of justice that is to be made practically relevant for the way we act now must be a scheme that takes into account modern circumstances and their impact on the conditions under which people presently live their lives. Arguments for reparation take as conclusive claims of entitlement oriented towards circumstances that are radically different from those we actually face: claims of entitlement based on the habitation of a territory by a small fraction of its present population, and claims of entitlement based on a determination to ignore the present dispersal of persons and peoples on the face of the earth, simply because the historic mechanisms of such dispersal were savagely implicated in injustice. And yet, here we all are. The present circumstances are the ones that are real: it is in the real world that people starve or are hurt or degraded if the demands of justice in relation to their circumstances are not met. Justice, we say, is a matter of the greatest importance. But the importance to be accorded to it is relative to what may actually happen if justice is not done, not to what might have happened if injustice in the past had been avoided.

I want to end by emphasizing two other points that qualify or clarify my thesis of the supersession of historic injustice. First, what I have said applies only if an honest attempt is being made to arrange things justly for the future. If no such attempt is being made, there is nothing to overwhelm or supersede the enterprise of reparation. My thesis is not intended as a defence of complacency or inactivity, and to the extent that opponents of reparation are complacent about the injustice of the status quo, their resistance is rightly condemned. Repairing historic injustice is, as we have seen, a difficult business, and, as a matter of fact, it is almost always undertaken by people of good will. The only thing that can trump that enterprise is an honest and committed resolve to do justice for the future, a resolve to address present circumstances in a way that respects the claims and needs of everyone.

Second, my thesis is not that such resolve has priority over all rectificatory actions. I claim only that it has priority over reparation that might carry us in a direction contrary to that indicated by a prospective theory of justice. Often, and understandably, claims based on reparation and claims based on forward-looking principles will coincide, for, as we saw in Part III, past injustice is not without its present effects. It is a fact that many of the descendants of those who were defrauded and expropriated live demoralized lives of relative poverty - relative, that is, to the descendants of those who defrauded them. If the relief of poverty and the more equal distribution of resources is the aim of a prospective theory of justice, it is likely that the effect of rectifying past wrongs will carry us some distance in this direction. All the same, it is worth stressing that it is the impulse to justice now that should lead the way in this process, not the reparation of something whose wrongness is understood primarily in relation to conditions that no longer obtain.[740]

THOMAS PIKETTY, A BRIEF HISTORY OF EQUALITY
(2022) 68

…

The Question of Reparations

… The case of Haiti was particularly extreme in that the slave population grew very rapidly … . Around 1700, the total population of the island was about 30,000 inhabitants, of which barely half were slaves. … At the end of the 1780s, the colony had more than 470,000 slaves (90 percent of the population), 28,000 Whites (5 percent), and 25,000 métis and free Blacks (5 percent).

… The system was in a phase of accelerated expansion when the French Revolution broke out. In 1789-1790, free Blacks claimed the right to vote and to participate in assemblies. This seemed to them logical, given the resounding proclamations regarding equal rights that were being made in Paris, but they were refused that right. The slave uprising began in August 1791 … . Despite military reinforcements sent from France, the insurgents rapidly gained ground and took control of the plantations, whereupon the planters fled the country. The new commissioners sent from Paris decreed the emancipation of slaves in August 1793, a decision that was extended to all the colonies by the Convention of February 1794 … . There was hardly any time to implement this decision. In 1802, the property owners persuaded Napoleon to reestablish slavery in all the slaveholding islands except Haiti, which declared its independence in 1804, after having once again driven out the French troops sent to take back their property. …

Should the French State Reimburse the Debt Paid by Haiti?

The case of Haiti is emblematic, not only because it was the first abolition of slavery in the modern age after a victorious slave revolt, and the first independence from a European power won by a Black population, but also because this episode ended with a gigantic public debt that undermined Haiti's development over the following two centuries. Although in 1825 France finally agreed to accept the country's independence and to put an end to its threats to send troops to invade the island, that was only because Charles X had obtained from the Haitian government a commitment to repay to France a debt of 150 million gold francs to indemnify the slaveholders for the loss of their property. The Port-au-Prince government did not really have a choice, given France's clear military superiority, the embargo imposed by the French fleet, and the genuine risk that the island would be occupied. This veritable tribute represented more than 300 percent of Haiti's national income in 1825 – more than three years of production – a huge sum that it was materially impossible to repay in a short time. In this case, the treaty stipulated a rapid payment of the whole amount to [a bank], with the Haitian government being responsible for refinancing itself and paying interest to French private banks in order to spread out the repayment. The Haitian debt was the object of multiple, chaotic negotiations, but it was largely repaid (capital and interest), with an average payment of about 5 percent of the Haitian national income per annum between 1840 and 1915 … . With the support of the French government, the banks finally decided to cede the rest of their receivables to the United States, which occupied Haiti from 1915 to 1934 to reestablish order and safeguard its own financial interests.

The 1825 debt, transferred from one creditor to another, was officially extinguished and definitively repaid by the beginning of the 1950s. For more than a century, from 1825 to 1950, the price that France tried to make Haiti pay for its freedom had one main consequence: the island's development was overdetermined by the question of the indemnity, which was sometimes violently denounced and sometimes accepted with resignation, according to the ebb and flow of endless political cycles.

Suppose the French state finally decides to reimburse the debt paid by Haiti, as the Haitian state has been asking it to do for decades. What should the amount of this reparation be? There is no single answer to this question, and it deserves to be the subject of a democratic debate. But it cannot be evaded. A simple, transparent solution

---

[740] An entire symposium on this thesis was published in 2022. See J. Waldron, 'Supersession: A reply', 25 *Crit. Rev. Int'l. Soc. & Pol. Phil.* (2022) 443.

might consist in setting the amount at 300 percent of the Haitian national income in 2020, or about 30 billion euros [which would represent the equivalent of a little more than 1 percent of France's current public debt].
…

[The British approach]
…

… [T]he law of abolition passed by the British Parliament in 1833 put in place full compensation for property owners. Relatively sophisticated scales were drawn up on the basis of the slaves' age, gender, and productivity, so that the compensation might be as fair and as exact as possible. In this way, some 20 million pounds sterling, or about 5 percent of the United Kingdom's national income at the time, was paid to 4,000 slaveholders. Today, if a government decided to devote to such a policy the same proportion of the British national income, it would have to pay approximately 120 billion euros, or about 39 million euros, on average, for each of the 4,000 property owners. … All this was financed by a corresponding increase in the public debt, which was itself repaid by all British taxpayers … .

* * *

The history recounted by Piketty was subsequently supplemented by a remarkable in-depth, long-term, archival study undertaken by the New York Times: Catherine Porter et al., 'The Ransom: The Root of Haiti's Misery: Reparations to Enslavers', *The New York Times* (20 May 2022).[741] Some excerpts follow:

> Though Haiti's government made the last payments connected to its former slaveholders in 1888, the debt was far from settled: To finish paying it off, Haiti borrowed from other foreign lenders who, in league with a few self-serving Haitian officials indifferent to their people's suffering, laid claim to a significant share of the nation's income for decades to come.
>
> Depleted after decades of paying France, Haiti took out even more loans after that. By 1911, $2.53 out of every $3 Haiti took in from coffee taxes, its most important source of revenue, went to paying debts held by French investors … . That left precious little to run a country, much less build one.
>
> In some years of the United States occupation, which began in 1915, more of Haiti's budget went to paying the salaries and expenses of the American officials who controlled its finances than to providing health care to the entire nation of around two million people.
>
> Even after the Americans relinquished fiscal control in the late 1940s, Haitian farmers were living on a diet that was "often close to the starvation level" … . As few as one in six children went to school.
>
> During slavery, Haiti brimmed with such wealth that its largest and most important city, Cap-Français, was known as the "Paris of the Antilles," bursting with bookstores, cafes, gardens, elegant public squares and bubbling fountains. … The harbor, choked with garbage today, was perennially full of ocean-worthy sailing ships.

In 1991, Jean-Bertrand Aristide, a former priest, became Haiti's first democratically elected President. He was ousted in a military coup seven months later, but was re-elected in 2001. In 2003 he launched a campaign to secure reparations from France and calculated that Haiti was owed $21,685,135,571.48. *The New York Times* commented that although French diplomats mocked the figure for its size and precision, 'estimates vetted by economists and historians … [show] his calculations may have been close to the mark – and possibly even modest.' Bertrand was subsequently compelled to leave the country before the end of his term in office, on the grounds that there was otherwise a risk of civil war. But the French Ambassador to Haiti at that time 'told *The Times* … that France and the United States had effectively orchestrated "a coup" against Mr. Aristide by forcing him into exile.' The newspaper added that:

---

[741] See also L. Obregón, 'Empire, Racial Capitalism and International Law', 31 *Leiden J. Int'l L.* (2018) 597.

Since his departure, none of his successors have pressed the issue. In 2003, the French government dismissed his claim of restitution. Twelve years later, [French President François] Hollande acknowledged that France did indeed owe Haiti a debt – before his staff quickly said it was not a monetary one.

Litigation

Litigation has been important in upholding reparations in some contexts but not others. Antony Anghie, in 'Rethinking International Law: A TWAIL Retrospective', 34 *Eur. J. Int'l L.* (2023) 7, at 87, draws a sharp contrast between the rejection of Global South reparations demands and the enthusiastic enforcement of the 'Western law of reparations' (based on notions of state responsibility, p. 000 above), which has required formerly colonized countries to pay vast amounts of compensation for wrongs suffered at their hands by corporate investors. International law has premised both approaches on property rights. In the colonialism context, rights to the property of colonized peoples were quickly transferred to the colonizers. But a very different approach has prevailed in response to the expropriation of investors' property:

> … A law of reparations shaped to compensate corporations is now accepted as logical, coherent, inevitable and, indeed, indispensable to furthering growth and development. This body of law both embodies and extends the neo-liberal vision of the world that is now so dominant. By contrast, efforts to provide reparations for slavery or colonial exploitation are criticized as aberrant and destructive, threatening entire social and economic structures with endless claims and no end in sight. …

The contrast is reflected in a Separate Opinion by Judge Abdulqawi Yusuf, in the International Court of Justice case of *Armed Activities on the Territory of the Congo (Democratic Republic of the Congo v. Uganda): Reparations* (9 February 2022), para. 37:

> 37. In its 2005 Judgment,[742] the Court … [recognized] injuries caused not only to the DRC but also to "persons on its territory"[. This] should have found application in the reparations phase through the award of different types of reparations depending on the nature and scope of the injury and on the addressees of the reparation. This is not unfortunately the case. The Judgment seems to be stuck in a time warp as it reflects the State-centred approach to reparation reminiscent of the law of diplomatic protection, while acknowledging gross violations of human rights and humanitarian law the victims of which should be entitled to compensation or other forms of reparation independently of their State. Recent developments in human rights and international humanitarian law have led to a widespread recognition that, with regard to claims arising from an injury suffered by an individual or a community, reparation should accrue to the injured individual or community.

At the national level, very few court cases claiming reparations have so far succeeded. The following British case, based on a tort claim, and benefiting from unusually abundant documentary proof, illustrates both the challenges and the limited opportunities.

NDIKU MUTUA, PAULO NZILI, WAMBUGU NYINGI, JANE MUTHONI MARA & SUSAN NGONDI V. THE FOREIGN AND COMMONWEALTH OFFICE
HIGH COURT OF JUSTICE, QUEEN'S BENCH DIVISION, [2011] EWHC 1913 (QB) (21 JULY 2011)
[INITIAL HEARING TO DETERMINE THE VIABILITY OF THE CLAIMANTS' CASE]

MR. JUSTICE MCCOMBE

(A) Introduction

---

[742] *Armed Activities on the Territory of the Congo (Democratic Republic of the Congo v. Uganda), Judgment, I.C.J. Reports 2005*, 257, para. 259

1. This is an action for damages for personal injuries brought by five claimants in respect of alleged torts of assault and battery and negligence, for which it is said the defendant is liable as representing Her Majesty's government in the United Kingdom. The injuries in respect of which the claims are made are said to have been deliberately inflicted on the claimants while they were in detention in Kenya, in varying periods between 1954 and 1959, by officers and soldiers of the Kenya police force, the Home Guard and/or the Kenya Regiment. The particulars of the injuries alleged to have been inflicted speak of physical mistreatment of the most serious kind, including torture, rape, castration and severe beatings. ... [I]f the allegations are true ... the treatment of these claimants was utterly appalling.

...

13. The claim is presented under five heads. ... (1) ... the former liability of the Colonial Administration in Kenya simply devolved or was transferred, by operation of the common law, upon the UK Government at the time of independence in 1963. ... (2) ... the UK Government is directly liable to the claimants, as a joint tortfeasor, with the Colonial Administration and the individual perpetrators of the tortious assaults, for having encouraged, procured, acquiesced in, or otherwise having been complicit in, the creation and maintenance of the "system" under which the claimants were mistreated. Such liability is said to arise out of the role of the military/security forces under the command of the British Commander-in- Chief. ... (3) ... the UK Government is similarly jointly liable, through the former Colonial Office, for the acts complained of, because of its role in the creation of the same system under which detainees were knowingly exposed to ill-treatment. ... (4) ... the UK Government is liable to the claimants ... as the result of an instruction, approval or authorisation of particular treatment of claimants given on 16 July 1957. ... (5) ... the UK Government is liable in negligence for breach of a common law duty of care in failing to put a stop to what it knew was the systemic use of torture and other violence upon detainees in the camps when it had a clear ability to do so.

...

148. At this stage of the proceedings it seems to me that there is a substantial body of evidence suggesting that both governments well knew that those in charge of the camps and/or those under their command were "not fit and proper persons" to be given custody of prisoners. ... At trial the evidence may point the other way, but such a conclusion cannot be ruled out at present.

...

[The court considered the government's claim that a duty of care should not be imposed 'in areas where public policy issues, in the sense of political judgments, arise' (para. 151), but concluded that this was an exceptional case and 'of such a nature that judicial policy might positively demand the existence of a duty of care' (para. 153).

154. In my judgment, it may well be thought strange, or perhaps even "dishonourable", that a legal system which will not in any circumstances admit into its proceedings evidence obtained by torture should yet refuse to entertain a claim against the Government in its own jurisdiction for that government's allegedly negligent failure to prevent torture which it had the means to prevent, on the basis of a supposed absence of a duty of care. ...

[The court concluded that the claims, as amended, could go forward.]

HIGH COURT OF JUSTICE, QUEEN'S BENCH DIVISION, [2012] EWHC 2678 (QB) (5 OCTOBER 2012)
[HEARING ON WHETHER THE CASE WAS BARRED BY THE LIMITATION ACT]

Mr. Justice McCombe

1. [In the preceding judgment] I directed that the case be set down "for hearing of limitation as a preliminary issue". The pleaded issues on limitation are as follows.

2. ... [T]he defendant pleads that each claim by the claimants is barred by virtue of the expiry of the three year time limit provided for under section 11(4) of the Limitation Act 1980 ... . [In response] the claimants state ...:

"(i) … [I]t is admitted that the action is outwith the time limit provided by s.11 of [the 1980 Act];

(ii) Notwithstanding the passage of time a fair trial remains possible and there are compelling reasons why the Court should exercise its discretion under s.33 and permit the claims to proceed".

6. [Section 33(1) of the Act provides that 'If it appears to the court that it would be equitable to allow an action to proceed', it may exercise its discretion to do so, having regard to:]

(a) the length of, and the reasons for, the delay on the part of the plaintiff;

…

(c) the conduct of the defendant after the cause of action arose, …;

…

(e) the extent to which the plaintiff acted promptly and reasonably once he knew whether or not the act or omission of the defendant, to which the injury was attributable, might be capable at that time of giving rise to an action for damages;

(f) the steps, if any taken by the plaintiff to obtain medical, legal or other expert advice and the nature of any such advice he may have received."

…

(D) The factual issues arising
…
28. … [I]t seems to me that the following factual issues would arise at trial …:

i) When were the injuries inflicted on each claimant and where did the relevant ill-treatment occur? What was the official status of the perpetrators? Were they soldiers, African home guards, prison officers or other officials? What was the legal status of those individual perpetrators, vis-a-vis the Colonial Government, the British Army (and its Commanders-in-Chief) and the Colonial Office in London respectively and does that status matter?
…
iii) Did General Erskine [Commander in Chief, East Africa Command] (and each of his successors) have full command and the means of control over the entire "security forces" in Kenya? …

iv) Did the British Army commanders have either de jure or de facto control of officials and others serving in the detention facilities and villages …;

v) What role did the War Council in Kenya/the British Army play in the "screening", interrogation and detention system?

vi) Was there a system of torture and/or other ill-treatment of detainees …;

vii) … what was the true nature of the relationship between the Colonial Office in London and the Colonial Administration in Nairobi? …
…
ix) What (if anything) did the Colonial Office know about abuses to detainees occurring in detention facilities and elsewhere and when did it have such knowledge?

x) Was there any cover up of any such abuses and, if so, by whom? …
…
xii) Causation and Quantum of damages

29. In respect of all these matters, the claimants contend that a fair trial is possible on the basis of the substantial documentary base that survives and the oral evidence of surviving witnesses in Kenya and the UK. The defendant says, "No, a fair trial is not possible" ... .

(E) Background facts relating to the Section 33 factors
...
31. Each of the surviving claimants is now elderly. Mr Nyingi is aged 84, Mr Nzili is 85 and Mrs Mara is about 73. Mrs Ngondi was 71 when she died. They each come from remote rural areas of Kenya and have worked in elementary farming communities. They have little education, even in their own languages; none has any significant knowledge or understanding of English. They have no experience, prior to this matter, of legal or other professional advice. They have minimal financial means. The possibility of any legal claim arising out of their now admitted ill-treatment was only brought to their attention by the Kenya Human Rights Commission ("KHRC") in [2006 and 2008]. ...

32. As a matter of historical scholarship, two new works about the Kenya Emergency were published in 2005. Those works were *Imperial Reckoning: the Untold Story of Britain's Gulag in Kenya* by Professor Caroline Elkins of Harvard University and *Histories of the Hanged: Britain's Dirty War in Kenya and the End of Empire* by Professor David Anderson of Oxford University. Both these works, based on extensive research both in Kenya and the UK, reached the conclusion that there was regular and systematic abuse of detainees in screening centres and detention camps. ... Published historical work on these subjects prior to 2005 had been much more limited and the documentary basis of the present claims had not been unearthed. ...
...

(F) The two main rival contentions: Documents and Witnesses
...
[In the earlier phase of the case, it was recounted that the UK Government had been unable to locate 300 boxes of documents relating to the Emergency, that had been removed from Kenya before independence in 1963. But as the trial was underway, those in charge of government records at a facility called Hanslope Park announced that the boxes had been found.]

48. ... In the intervening 12 months a great deal of further work has been conducted on that collection by both sides. The historians robustly maintain ... that the new disclosure has only served to confirm the impressions and conclusions that they had expressed ... .
...
51. At a trial the court would have to conduct its own analysis of the documents ... . However, on the present evidence, ... [I conclude] that the available documentary base is very substantial indeed and capable of giving a very full picture ... .
...

109. Looking at those claimants' evidence, I think that it will be quite possible to determine sufficiently clearly where and when they suffered their injuries and the official status of those responsible for inflicting them. It will also be possible, on the documents arranged and collated chronologically, together with the other evidence, to determine whether or not the injuries occurred because of a breach of duty on the part of the United Kingdom government.
...

[The court noted that although not necessary to the conclusion of the case, it would consider the argument that in cases involving torture and statute of limitations issues, 'the Court may be assisted by considering the approach of international tribunals when adjudicating on claims arising out of torture' (para. 155). The claim was that 'By logical extension [from criminal cases,] the disapproval of time bars for torture cases extends to civil actions'. The Court found, however, that customary international law did not support the existence of such a rule in relation to civil, as opposed to criminal, cases (para. 157). In concluding the judgment, the Court upheld the request that it should exercise its discretion under the Act to allow the case to proceed.]

WILLIAM HAGUE (SECRETARY OF STATE FOR FOREIGN AND COMMONWEALTH AFFAIRS), MAU MAU CLAIMS (SETTLEMENT)
UNITED KINGDOM PARLIAMENTARY DEBATES, HOUSE OF COMMONS (6 JUNE 2013)
COL. 1692

[An emergency was declared between 1952 and 1963 as a result of the armed struggle between the Kenya Land and Freedom Army (known as the Mau Mau), and the British authorities. Widespread violence was committed by both sides, and most of the victims were Kenyan. Many thousands of Mau Mau members were killed, while the Mau Mau themselves were responsible for the deaths of over 2,000 people, including 200 casualties among the British regiments and police. [British statistics estimated that 11,000 Mau Mau were killed, Anderson's estimate is 25,000 and Elkins' estimate has been many times that number.]

Emergency regulations were introduced; political organisations were banned; prohibited areas were created; and provisions for detention without trial were enacted. The colonial authorities made unprecedented use of capital punishment and sanctioned harsh prison, so-called "rehabilitation", regimes. Many of those detained were never tried, and the links of many with the Mau Mau were never proven. …

We recognise that British personnel were called upon to serve in difficult and dangerous circumstances. Many members of the colonial service contributed to establishing the institutions that underpin Kenya today, and we acknowledge their contribution. However, I would like to make it clear now and for the first time on behalf of Her Majesty's Government that we understand the pain and grievance felt by those who were involved in the events of the emergency in Kenya. The British Government recognise that Kenyans were subject to torture and other forms of ill treatment at the hands of the colonial administration. The British Government sincerely regret that these abuses took place and that they marred Kenya's progress towards independence. Torture and ill treatment are abhorrent violations of human dignity, which we unreservedly condemn.
…
In 2012 [the High Court ruled that the cases excerpted above could proceed.] The Court of Appeal was due to hear our appeal against that decision last month. However, I can announce today that the Government have now reached an agreement with Leigh Day, the solicitors acting on behalf of the claimants, in full and final settlement of their clients' claims.

The agreement includes payment of a settlement sum in respect of 5,228 claimants, as well as [costs] of £19.9 million. The Government will also support the construction of a memorial in Nairobi to the victims of torture and ill-treatment during the colonial era. …

This settlement provides recognition of the suffering and injustice that took place in Kenya. …

We continue to deny liability on behalf of the Government and British taxpayers today for the actions of the colonial administration in respect of the claims, and indeed the courts have made no finding of liability against the Government in this case. We do not believe that claims relating to events that occurred overseas outside direct British jurisdiction more than 50 years ago can be resolved satisfactorily through the courts without the testimony of key witnesses, which is no longer available. …

… [W]e do not believe that this settlement establishes a precedent in relation to any other former British colonial administration.

… We do not want our current and future relations with Kenya to be overshadowed by the past. Today, we are bound together by commercial, security and personal links … . Bilateral trade between the UK and Kenya amounts to £1 billion each year, and around 200,000 Britons visit Kenya annually.
…

* * *

Much has been written about this case.[743] But the key question is why other cases have not followed on the same path. Caroline Elkins, in 'History on Trial: Mau Mau Reparations and the High Court of Justice', in *Time for Reparations*, above, at 117, suggests three reasons: (i) cases cannot be filed in British courts for abuses that occurred before 1948; (ii) claimants in such cases must be alive and able to appear in court; and (iii) equally damning historical records have not yet become available in relation to other situations.

On 31 May 2021, six UN Special Procedures mandate-holders (those dealing with transitional justice, right to housing, rights of indigenous peoples, rights of internally displaced persons, racism, and torture) sent a 'communication' to the UK Government (UN Doc. AL GBR 5/2021) alleging that:

> During the pre-colonial and colonial period in Kenya, the Kipsigis and Talai indigenous
> peoples of Kericho County, as was the case with other communities and indigenous
> peoples in Kenya, were subjected to gross violations of human rights, such as unlawful
> killing, sexual violence, torture, inhuman and degrading treatment, arbitrary detention,
> arbitrary displacement and violations of the rights to privacy, family life and property.
> The violations also included the expropriation of extensive land belonging to the Kipsigis
> and Talai peoples of Kericho County, which was considered to be particularly fertile and
> suited to agriculture. Over 500.000 persons belonging to the Kipsigis and Talai peoples
> are estimated to have been affected by these events.

The letter notes however that the Government has already indicated that it had 'no intention to enter any process' to resolve these claims. Unfortunately, the communication contains no legal analysis engaging with the facts or with precedents, but simply an annex entitled 'Reference to international human rights law' which lists a large array of standards and reports of general relevance.

International Initiatives

From time to time, various groups have sought to underscore the importance of the reparations issue. The 'Abuja Proclamation', adopted by the First Pan-African Conference on Reparations held in Abuja, Nigeria, on 27-29 April 1993:

> Calls upon the international community to recognize that there is a unique and
> unprecedented moral debt owed to the African peoples which has yet to be paid - the
> debt of compensation to the Africans as the most humiliated and exploited people of the
> last four centuries of modern history.
>
> …
>
> Further u₁   the OAU [the Organization of African Unity] to call for full monetary
> payment of repayments through capital transfer and debt cancellation.
>
> Convinced that the claim for reparations is well grounded in International Law.
>
> Urges on the OAU to establish a legal Committee on the issue of Reparations. …

In Resolution 543 (LXXIII) of 12 December 2022, the African Commission on Human and People's Rights called upon African Union states to 'establish a committee to consult, seek the truth, and conceptualise reparations from Africa's perspective, describe the harm occasioned by the tragedies of the past, establish a case for reparations (or Africa's claim), and pursue justice for the trade and trafficking in enslaved Africans, colonialism and colonial crimes, and racial segregation and contribute to non-recurrence and reconciliation of the past'.

In the UN context, the 2001 Durban Conference was an important watershed:

---

[743] M. Parry, 'Uncovering the brutal truth about the British empire', *The Guardian*, 18 August 2016; and J. Balint, 'The "Mau Mau" Legal Hearings and Recognizing the Crimes of the British Colonial State: A Limited Constitutive Moment', 3 *Crit. Analysis of L.* (2016) 261.

... [T]he slave-trading nations ... have expressed their abject regret for historical wrongs committed, [but] they have insisted on separating issues of responsibility from reparations and rejected the imposition of ex post facto liability. Although [pre-conference] expert reports endorsed reparations, the 2001 World Conference Against Racism only "acknowledge[d] that slavery and the slave trade are a crime against humanity and should always have been so, especially the transatlantic slave trade" [UN Doc. A/CONF.189/12 (2001), para. 13]. This formulation has consistently been interpreted to mean that slavery was not in fact such a crime at the time it happened. Instead, the Conference recognized a "moral obligation . . . to halt and reverse the lasting consequences of those practices" and invited governments "to honour the memory of the victims of these tragedies."[744]

In 2021, the UN High Commissioner for Human Rights (UN Doc. A/HRC/47/53 (2021)) reported that:

62. Existing initiatives indicate that there is an increasing willingness and emerging practice to acknowledge the need to repair the continuing impacts of enslavement, the transatlantic trade in enslaved Africans and colonialism. Building on these initiatives, States should initiate comprehensive processes to halt, reverse and repair the lasting consequences and ongoing manifestations of these legacies in their specific national context. These processes should be designed to seek the truth, define the harm, pursue justice and reparations and contribute to non-recurrence and reconciliation.

...

64. Measures taken to address the past should seek to transform the future. Structures and systems that were designed and shaped by enslavement, colonialism and successive racially discriminatory policies and systems must be transformed. Reparations should not only be equated with financial compensation.[745]

The most elaborated international proposal to date is from Caribbean Commission:[746]

CARICOM, TEN POINT PLAN FOR REPARATORY JUSTICE
(2014)

In 2013 Caribbean Heads of Governments established the Caricom Reparations Commission (CRC) with a mandate to prepare the case for reparatory justice for the region's indigenous and African descendant communities who are the victims of Crimes against Humanity (CAH) in the forms of genocide, slavery, slave trading, and racial apartheid. ....

THE CRC ASSERTS THAT EUROPEAN GOVERNMENTS:

Were owners and traders of enslaved Africans instructed genocidal actions upon indigenous communities

Created the legal, financial and fiscal policies necessary for the enslavement of Africans

Defined and enforced African enslavement and native genocide as in their 'national interests'

Refused compensation to the enslaved with the ending of their enslavement

Compensated slave owners at emancipation for the loss of legal property rights in enslaved Africans

---

[744] P. Alston, 'Does the Past Matter? On the Origins of Human Rights", 126 *Harv. L. Rev.* (2013) 2043, at 2050. For a refutation of the argument that slavery 'was legal at the time', see E. T. Achiume, below; and K. Schwarz, *Reparations for Slavery in International Law* (2022).

[745] See also, Report of the Secretary-General on reparatory justice for people of African descent, UN Doc. A/78/317 (2023))

[746] See R. Biholar, 'Reparations for Chattel Slavery: A Call from the "Periphery" to Decolonise International (Human Rights) Law', 40 *Nordic J. Hum. Rts.* (2022) 64.

Imposed a further one hundred years of racial apartheid upon the emancipated

Imposed for another one hundred years policies designed to perpetuate suffering upon the emancipated and survivors of genocide

And have refused to acknowledge such crimes or to compensate victims and their descendants

Caricom Ten Point Action Plan

1. Full Formal Apology

The descendants of the indigenous peoples subjected to genocide, the loss of several cultures, and the erasure of numerous languages require a full and formal apology. ...

A full apology accepts responsibility, commits to non-repetition, and pledges to repair the harm caused. Governments from countries responsible for the destruction have refused to offer apologies and have instead issued Statements of Regret. These statements do not acknowledge that crimes have been committed and continue to represent a refusal to take responsibility.

2. Indigenous Peoples Development Programmes

As a result of European conquest and colonisation, the indigenous peoples within the Member States of CARICOM have been subjected to forced migration within countries and across the region; to brutal work conditions, and genocide. Indigenous peoples were brutalized and killed as a result of official instructions to the European military commanders who came to the region. Those who were not immediately killed had their ancestral lands seized and a community of 3 million people in 1700 was decimated to less than 30 thousand in 2000. This also led to the destruction of their languages and unique cultural heritage. Their descendants remain traumatized, landless, and are one of the most marginalized groups in the region as a result of the deliberate and racist discrimination on the part of the European colonizers.

Despite the efforts of the newly developing CARICOM Member States which have inherited the situation, the rebuilding of these communities cannot be done without responsible European States taking on the responsibility of correcting the damage and where possible, restoring the communities that still exist.

3. Funding for Repatriation to Africa

The descendants of African peoples stolen from their homes, lands, people, and cultures have a legal right of return; ... . It is the responsibility of those States that are responsible for the forced movement and enslavement of their ancestors to establish a resettlement programme for those who wish to return. ...

4. The Establishment of Cultural Institutions and the Return of Cultural Heritage
...
The restoration of historical memory through community institutions such as museums and research centres will allow citizens to understand these crimes against humanity as well as other colonial harm and to memorialize their ancestors' contributions ... .
...

5. Assistance in Remedying the Public Health Crisis
...
6. Education Programmes
...
7. The Enhancement of Historical and Cultural Knowledge Exchanges
...
8. Psychological Rehabilitation as a Result of the Transmission of Trauma

9. The Right to Development through the Use of Technology

For 400 years the trade and production policies of Europe could be summed up in the British slogan: "not a nail is to be made in the colonies". This was a deliberate decision to retard the technology available for development within CARICOM Member States.

...

10. Debt Cancellation and Monetary Compensation

CARICOM governments that emerged from slavery and colonialism have inherited the massive crisis of community poverty and an inability to deal with the development of their countries because of the burdens of the legacy of colonialism.

...

... Since correcting the burden of colonialism has fallen on these new States, they are unable to deal with the challenges of development without taking on onerous levels of debt. This debt cycle properly belongs to the governments from the responsible European countries who have made no sustained attempt to deal with debilitating colonial legacies.

Support for the payment of domestic debt, the cancellation of international debt, and direct monetary payments where appropriate, are necessary reparatory actions to correct the harm caused by colonialism.

* * *

In contrast, consider the following perspectives on proposals for international reparations:

Niall Ferguson, *Empire: The Rise and Demise of the British World Order and the Lessons for Global Power* (2004), xx:

[In responding to the question '[w]as the British Empire a good or bad thing', Ferguson acknowledges that its 'involvement in the Atlantic slave trade and slavery itself ... is no longer a question for historical judgement alone; it has become a political, and potentially a legal, issue.']

> ... [F]or much ... of its history, the British Empire acted as an agency for imposing free markets, the rule of law, investor protection and relatively incorrupt government on roughly a quarter of the world. [It encouraged the] 'imperialism of free trade'. Prima facie, therefore, there seems a plausible case that the Empire enhanced global welfare – in other words, was a Good Thing.
>
> Many charges can of course be levelled against the British Empire ... . I do not claim, as John Stuart Mill did, that British rule in India was 'not only the purest in intention but one of the most beneficent in act ever known to mankind'; nor, as Lord Curzon did, that 'the British Empire is under Providence the greatest instrument for good that the world has seen' ... . The Empire was never so altruistic. In the eighteenth century the British were indeed as zealous in the acquisition and exploitation of slaves as they were subsequently zealous in trying to stamp slavery out ... .
>
> Yet the fact remains that no organization in history has done more to promote the free movement of goods, capital and labour than the British Empire ... . And no organization has done more to impose Western norms of law, order and governance around the world.
> ...

Nigel Biggar, *Between Kin and Cosmopolis: An Ethic of the Nation* (2014), 90:

> One obvious apparent problem with empire is that it comprises the imposition of rule by one people upon another, and so involves oppression and exploitation. The imposition of rule, however, is not inherently unjust: all government involves the threat and exercise of coercion against the unwilling ... . Nor is the oppression and exploitation of one group by another peculiar to empires: it happens within nation-states, too ... . Sometimes the imposition of imperial rule can have the salutary effect of imposing a unifying, pacific, and law-abiding order on peoples otherwise inclined to war among themselves. The order

that an empire brings should not be instantly dismissed as intolerably unjust. It might be. On the other hand, sometimes a measure of injustice should be tolerated for the sake of a decent measure of peace, without which nothing at all can flourish. …

Albie Sachs, 'Foreword', in Jacqueline Bhabha, Margareta Matache and Caroline Elkins (eds.), *Time for Reparations: A Global Perspective* (2021) xi:

…

In the course of this process of humanizing international law, it would, in my view, be important not to limit the theme of reparations to seeking monetary compensation. …

…[I]n a libel case in which I sat as a justice of the Constitutional Court in South Africa, a colleague and I strongly criticized the use of money awards as the main mechanism for salvaging the dignity and honor of the traduced person. Our contention, later adopted by the court as a whole, was that apology and suitable restorative justice amends would be far more meaningful than payment of a lump sum that would still leave the parties as enemies.

Money can often be quite the wrong moral currency, the wrong register. It abstracts pain from the human heart and puts it in the marketplace. … [R]estorative justice can be far more enduring, far more meaningful than punitive or compensatory justice, though it can contain elements both of punishment and material recompense. …

E. Tendayi Achiume, 'The Postcolonial Case for Rethinking Borders', in *Dissent,* Summer 2019:

… [I]nternational legal scholars such as Antony Anghie have unpacked the complex ways in which international legal doctrine, and international financial and economic institutions, advance First World nations' interests at the expense of those of the Third World, while stymieing equality-enhancing or reparatory reform. The structural subordination of the Third World as a whole to the First World as a whole should negate the right of any First World country to exclude any Third World person [seeking to enter the First World country], whether or not that specific country colonized the country of nationality of that specific person. The benefits to the First World of neocolonial subordination—and its ethical implications—go far beyond discrete bilateral relations between former colonial powers and the nations they colonized.

Olúfẹmi O. Táíwò, *Reconsidering Reparations* (2022):

[This statement of the author's analysis is taken from his post on the LPE Project blog (21 February 2023), at https://lpeproject.org/blog/reconsidering-reparations/].

… [M]y recent book *Reconsidering Reparations* argues for two things. First, reparations for trans-Atlantic slavery and colonialism should be seen as a future-oriented project engaged in building a just social order. Second, if we accept that view, then reparations and the struggle for racial justice should be directly linked to the struggle for climate justice.

…

[The author advocates a] "constructive view" [that] aims to rebuild our social environment itself in the direction of justice: redistributing resources and social advantages to create a just world. …

Other ways of thinking about reparations focus on retributive or reconciliatory justice. …

Both of these approaches get much right about the moral dimensions of reparations and the history of injustice that makes reparations relevant and important. But focusing repairs on the wealth of particular marginalized groups or the moral relationships between particular groups of marginalized people risks overlooking the rigid aspects of our political and economic systems that impoverished and alienated the groups in the first place. Moreover, these approaches are often used to defend one-off, reversible policy actions: the cash transfer, scholarship program, apology, or memorial. The constructive view accepts the importance of redistributing wealth and resources, as well as rebuilding cultural and interpersonal esteem, and supports many of these policies. But it comes with a further requirement: to root these interventions in a political context that will safeguard rather than erode the gains they make towards justice.

Climate crisis arises out of the same history as the global racial empire. … Given this, we can expect climate change to redistribute social advantages in a way that compounds and locks in the distributional injustices that we have inherited. Left unchecked, the climate crisis threatens to destabilize and overwhelm the past victories won for the cause of racial justice and whatever additional ones we are able to eke out in the near future.

In the face of these links, what should be done? … Bread-and-butter reparations demands, like direct transfers of money to individuals and families or reconciliation processes, must retain their central importance. But we can link the important need for cash and memorials to other important structural concerns, from addressing the destructive role of prisons and pollutants to building food, water, housing, and energy systems that are managed for and by people rather than for profit. Like the fight against the climate crisis itself, these needed interventions will be won or lost on a planetary scale.

Reparations in the United States[747]

While reparations for slavery in the United States are currently the focus of a great many initiatives, including commissions established by the states of California, Illinois and New York, and the city of San Francisco, they are also deeply rooted in the history of struggles against slavery, as illustrated by an example from the late eighteenth century. In 1775, after the defeat of the British in Lexington and Concord, the largest slave owner in Massachusetts fled to England. His property was confiscated by the state in 1778 and his remaining slaves freed. One of them, Belinda Sutton (aka Royall), petitioned the General Court (the state legislature) on 14 February 1783:[748]

The Petition of Belinda an Affrican, humbly shews:

… [B]efore she had Twelve years … when she, in a sacred grove, with each hand in that of a tender Parent, was paying her devotions to the great Orisa who made all things – an armed band of white men, driving many of her Countrymen in Chains, ran into the hallowed shade! … She was ravished from the bosom of her Country, from the arms of her friends – while the advanced age of her Parents, rendering them unfit for servitude, cruelly separated her from them forever!

Scenes which her imagination had never conceived of – a floating World … three hundred Affricans in chains, suffering the most excruciating torments; and some of them rejoicing, that the pangs of death came like a balm to their wounds.

…

Fifty years her faithful hands have been compelled to ignoble servitude for the benefit of an Isaac Royall, until … the present war was Commenced – The terror of men armed in the Cause of freedom, compelled her master to fly … .

---

[747] See generally: V. Ladisch and A. M. Roccatello, 'The Color of Justice: Transitional Justice and the Legacy of Slavery and Racism in the United States (ICTJ Briefing)', International Center for Transitional Justice (26 April 2021); A. Nurse, *Reparations and Anti-Black Racism: A Criminological Exploration of the Harms of Slavery and Racialized Injustice* (2022); and W. Darity and A. Mullen, *From Here to Equality: Reparations for Black Americans in the Twenty-first Century* (2020).
[748] Transcription published by Royall House and Slave Quarters, at https://royallhouse.org/belinda-suttons-1783-petition-full-text/.

The face of your Petitioner, is now marked with the furrows of time, and her frame feebly bending under the oppression of years, while she, by the Laws of the Land, is denied the enjoyment of one morsel of that immense wealth, apart whereof hath been accumilated by her own industry, and the whole augmented by her servitude.

WHEREFORE, casting herself at the feet of your honours, as to a body of men, formed for the extirpation of vassalage, for the reward of Virtue, and the just return of honest industry – she prays, that such allowance may be made her out of the estate of Colonel Royall, as will prevent her and her more infirm daughter from misery in the greatest extreme, and scatter comfort over the short and downward path of their Lives – and she will ever Pray.

Belinda Royall was granted a pension of 15 pounds and 12 shillings, to be paid out of the estate of Isaac Royall. But no precedent was set and the debate continues to unfold in the third decade of the twenty-first century. An important impetus was given to the debate by Ta-Nehisi Coates, in 'The Case for Reparations', *The Atlantic* (15 June 2014). He argued that even after the Civil War, Black people:

> … were terrorized. In the Deep South, a second slavery ruled. In the North, legislatures, mayors, civic associations, banks, and citizens all colluded to pin black people into ghettos, where they were overcrowded, overcharged, and undereducated. Businesses discriminated against them, awarding them the worst jobs and the worst wages. Police brutalized them in the streets. And the notion that black lives, black bodies, and black wealth were rightful targets remained deeply rooted in the broader society. …
>
> …
>
> … [W]hite supremacy is not merely the work of hotheaded demagogues, or a matter of false consciousness, but a force so fundamental to America that it is difficult to imagine the country without it.

In Coates's view, the resulting wealth gap provided the strongest illustration of the fact that Black people had been treated 'as sub-citizens, sub-Americans, and sub-humans' and it led him to advocate reparations as a way of closing the resulting 'chasm', as 'the price we must pay to see ourselves squarely.'

Coates' article drew many critical responses. Consider the following examples. Kevin D. Williamson, wrote in 'The Case against Reparations: A reply to Ta-Nehisi Coates', *National Review* (24 May 2014):

> … Even if we accept the facts of aggregate advantage and disadvantage with their roots in historical injustice, the aggregate cannot be converted into the collective inasmuch as neither advantage nor disadvantage is universal on either side nor linked to a straightforward chain of causality. Some blacks are born into college-educated, well-off households, and some whites are born to heroin-addicted single mothers, and even the totality of racial crimes throughout American history does not mean that one of these things matters and one does not.
>
> Once that fact is acknowledged, then the case for reparations is only moral primitivism: My interests are inextricably linked to my own kin group and directly rivalrous with yours, i.e., the very racism that this program is in theory intended to redress. Mr. Coates also, I think, miscalculates what the real-world effects of converting our liberal conception of justice into a system of racial appropriation might mean. There are still, after all, an awful lot of white people, and though many of them might be inclined to make amends under some sort of racial truce following the process Mr. Coates imagines, many of them might simply be inclined to prevail. … [A] system of exclusive interests in which black and white operate effectively in opposition … is not only morally repugnant, but likely to undermine the genuine political and economic interests of African Americans. …

David Frum, 'The Impossibility of Reparations', *The Atlantic* (3 June 2014):

The United States government launched its reparations program to African Americans in autumn of 1969. Originally known as "the Philadelphia plan," the program set quotas for black employment in construction trades. Over the next decades, such quotas would spread from industry to industry, and would expand into higher education and public contracting.

…

The affirmative action experience since 1969 offers some insights into what is likely to happen next: (1) The program will expand to additional groups. (2) The question of who qualifies will become ever more contested and embittered. (3) Side effects will be large and unexpected. (4) The program will work severe inequities. (5) The legitimacy of the project will rapidly fade.

Affirmative action ranks among the least popular things that U.S. governments do. When surveyed, white Americans crushingly reject race preferences, Hispanic Americans object by a margin of 2 to 1, and black Americans are almost evenly divided, with only the slightest plurality in favor.

Now imagine how Americans will feel when what is redistributed by racial calculus is not university admissions or workplace promotions but actual, foldable cash. …

The most directly relevant litigation on these issues declined to consider claims lodged against leading countries that were alleged to have unjustly profited from slavery:

IN RE AFRICAN-AMERICAN SLAVE DESCENDANTS LITIGATION
307 F. SUPP. 2D 977 (N.D. ILL. 2004)

CHARLES NORGLE, DISTRICT JUDGE

…

Beginning in 2002, a number of lawsuits were filed by descendants of slaves seeking reparations from private corporations, which were alleged to have unjustly profited from the institution of slavery. … This litigation presently consists of nine individual lawsuits, and these individual Plaintiff's [sic] have filed a consolidated complaint.

The Plaintiffs …, on behalf of themselves and the classes they seek to represent, seek reparations on behalf of all "descendants of formerly enslaved Africans" and all living "formerly enslaved African-Americans." Specifically, Plaintiff's seek an accounting, constructive trust, restitution, disgorgement, compensatory and punitive damages arising out of the named defendants' alleged past and continued wrongful conduct relating to the institution of slavery.

…

The named defendants … are eighteen present-day companies whose predecessors are alleged to have been unjustly enriched through profits earned either directly or indirectly from the Trans-Atlantic Slave Trade and slavery between 1619 and 1865, as well as post-Emancipation slavery through the 1960s.

…

V. Conclusion

It is beyond debate that slavery has caused tremendous suffering and ineliminable scars throughout our Nation's history. However, Plaintiffs' claims … fail based on numerous well-settled legal principles. First, Plaintiffs' claims are beyond the constitutional authority of this court. Without alleging any specific connection between themselves and the named Defendants, Plaintiffs lack essential constitutional standing requirements to bring their claims. Second, prudential limitations prohibit the court from deciding such broad questions of social importance when such claims are brought on behalf of absent third parties, as Plaintiffs attempt here. Third, the long-standing and well-reasoned political question doctrine bars the court from deciding the issue of slavery reparations, an issue that has been historically and constitutionally committed to the Legislative and Executive branches of our government. Fourth, Plaintiffs' claims are untimely. Conceding that many of the torts alleged in the Complaint occurred prior to the formal end of slavery, Plaintiffs fail to show how any of these claims fall within the applicable statutes of limitation. Finally, under the rules of procedure which guide the federal judicial system, Plaintiffs' Complaint fails to state a claim upon which relief can be granted, a serious defect the court cannot overlook regardless how egregious the circumstances giving rise to the claims.

In summary, Plaintiffs' attempt to bring these claims more than a century after the end of the Civil War and the formal abolition of slavery fails; this determination is consistent with the position taken by numerous courts which have considered the issue over the last century. Ultimately, the legal obstacles prohibiting judicial resolution of such claims cannot be circumvented by the courts. ... Some may view this ruling as a condonation of ancient wrongs. That view is wrong. To suggest that the lions have won again and that the court is impervious to the human suffering at the core of this case would be absurd. The reasonable prudent person will read this opinion with care. We strive, case by case, within an imperfect system of law, through human endeavors, towards the unattainable perfect justice we seek.

* * *

In conclusion, we note some local initiatives within the United States and then an analysis by the UN Special Rapporteur on racism that rebuts some of the principal objections often made to reparations. The local initiatives are recounted in a report by the UN High Commissioner for Human Rights (UN Doc. A/HRC/47/53 (2021) para. 57):

> In the United States, for example, litigation was instigated against the city of Tulsa, Oklahoma, regarding the 1921 massacre; the Maryland Lynching Truth and Reconciliation Commission has been established; memorialization initiatives have been undertaken in Montgomery, Alabama; reparations will seek to "address the historical wealth and opportunity gaps that African American/Black residents of Evanston experienced"; and, at the federal level, a bill (HR40) has been introduced to establish a commission to study and develop reparation proposals for African-Americans. Mappings, apologies and reparations initiatives have been launched at the state and local levels by universities and religious groups, among others, regarding their historical relationship to enslavement. The private sector has also begun issuing formal apologies and undertaking certain commitments towards reparations.

E. TENDAYI ACHIUME, REPORT OF THE SPECIAL RAPPORTEUR ON CONTEMPORARY FORMS OF RACISM, RACIAL DISCRIMINATION, XENOPHOBIA AND RACIAL INTOLERANCE
UN DOC. A/74/321 (2019)

...

Political and legal resistance to reparations
45. Serious political opposition to reparations for colonialism and slavery remains among the countries that benefited the most from both. ... [I]n Durban in 2001, certain former colonial powers remained staunchly resistant to formal apologies for slavery and colonialism, and to any acknowledgment of the pressing need for reparations. [T]he Regional [preparatory] Conference of the Americas ... adopted the following strong statement acknowledging that:

> the enslavement and other forms of servitude of Africans and their descendants and of the indigenous peoples of the Americas, as well as the slave trade, were morally reprehensible, in some cases constituted crimes under domestic law and, if they occurred today, would constitute crimes under international law. [And that] these practices have resulted in substantial and lasting economic, political and cultural damage to these peoples and that justice now requires that substantial national and international efforts be made to repair such damage. ...

46. Canada and the United States opposed the inclusion of this important paragraph in the report of the Regional Conference. ... The report of the European Conference did not even mention peoples of African or Asian descent.

47. Political opposition to the subject of reparations in some countries is so deep that even attempts to study the issue have been consistently blocked at the legislative level. For example, between 1989 and 2023, Congress has failed to act on a draft bill, H.R. 40, entitled "Commission to Study and Develop Reparation Proposals for African-Americans Act".

48. Conventional analysis of international law, including by former colonial nations, identifies a number of legal hurdles to the pursuit of claims for reparations for slavery and colonialism. Among the most salient legal hurdles identified is the intertemporal principle in international law, codified in article 13 of the articles on responsibility of States for internationally wrongful acts. The intertemporal principle stresses that a State is responsible for violations of international law only if, at the time of the violation or its continuing effects, the State was bound by the legal provisions it transgressed. Numerous States have appealed to the non-retroactive application of international law to deny that they have a legal obligation to provide reparations. For example, ... Germany has argued that its obligations [to the Ovaherero and Nama peoples of Namibia] are "historical" and "moral".

49. First, the intertemporal principle is subject to exception, including when (a) an act is ongoing ... or (b) the wrongful act's direct ongoing consequences extend into a time when the act and its consequences are considered internationally wrongful. That means that racial discrimination rooted in or caused by colonialism and slavery that occurred after each had been outlawed cannot be subject to the intertemporal bar. Second, the intertemporal principle does not apply to present-day racially discriminatory effects of slavery and colonialism, which States are obligated to remediate, including through reparations. The intertemporal principle cannot be said, per se, to bar all claims for reparations for racial discrimination rooted in the events and structures of slavery and colonialism. ...

50. ... [T]he intertemporal principle has a long history of service to both slavery and colonialism. ... [I]nternational law itself played an important role in consolidating the structures of racial discrimination and subordination throughout the colonial period, including through customary international law, which was co-constitutive with colonialism. Part of the problem, then, is that international law has not fully been "decolonized" and remains replete with doctrines that prevent the reparation and remediation of the inequality and injustice entrenched in the colonial era. When Member States and even international lawyers insist on the application of the intertemporal principle as a bar to pursuing reparation and remediation of racial injustice and inequality, they are, in effect, insisting on the application of neocolonial law. Legal efforts are more appropriately directed at developing international doctrine that can ensure the equal treatment and recognition of all human beings irrespective of race, and that is, in part, what is at stake in debates on reparations for slavery and colonialism.

51. Other legal concerns involve the difficulties in potential matters of responsibility and causality, especially with regard to the time that has passed since the transatlantic slave trade and colonialism. The concern is that determining the individuals responsible for horrific acts, the identities of the victims, the descendants of the victims and how much is owed poses insurmountable legal difficulties. The legal complexity that would be and is involved in pursuit of individually and even class-based legal claims for reparations are genuine. However, such difficulties cannot be the basis for nullifying the existence of underlying legal obligations. ...

...

53. Several States have refused to issue a formal apology for their roles in slavery and colonialism, instead issuing expressions of remorse or regret. States appear to be driven by concern that formal apologies could be construed as an admission of legal responsibility, generating lengthy legal claims and financial compensation. Such concerns not only put the [UN Guidelines on reparations] on hold, but also drove the dilution of the strong calls for apologies and reparations articulated ... during the lead-up to [Durban]. ...

54. Development aid and national reform can certainly form part of the suite of reparatory measures for slavery and colonialism. However, if pursued in a manner that completely denies the connection between contemporary problems and their historical origins, such initiatives cannot do the necessary work of repairing structures of racial inequality and discrimination rooted in historic injustice. Such ahistorical and uncontextualized

development aid similarly fails to fulfil specific international human rights obligations relating to the contemporary manifestations of historic racial discrimination and injustice. ...

QUESTIONS

1. Does Waldron's 'supersession thesis' suggest any conclusions that might be relevant in the debate over reparations for slavery or colonialism? Compare Cuneen's approach focusing on the need to assert indigenous sovereignty which 'demands a reimagining of how we conceptualize sovereignty and a rethinking of the institutional and governance arrangements required to give it effect'.[749]

2. Are the causal links suggested in the analyses of the 'reverse reparations' paid by Haiti to France sufficiently clear as to make it a relatively straightforward case in favour of an obligation to pay reparations?

3. At its peak, the British Empire governed a quarter of the world's population and between one-quarter and one-fifth of its land surface.[750] Does this suggest that the United Kingdom bears a special responsibility in terms of the payment of reparations, or that the magnitude of the issues raised is simply too great to warrant consideration?

4. In assessing the case for reparations for slavery and its aftermath in the United States, what weight should be given to predictions of a massive backlash from the white population?

---

[749] C. Cuneen, 'Settler Colonial States and Transitional Justice', in J. Meierhenrich et al (eds.), *The Oxford Handbook of Transitional Justice* (2023) 000.
[750] D. Judd, *Empire: The British Imperial Experience, 1756 to the Present* (1996) 2.

Chapter 18. Critical Perspectives

The preceding chapters of this book have underscored many of the major challenges faced by the international human rights regime (IHRR). Before surveying responses to those challenges, it is helpful to acknowledge that, when we talk about 'human rights' or even about the 'regime' or the 'movement', we are generally not focusing on the totality of the multi-faceted system, but we do not then specify exactly what it is we are talking about. We might be referring to conceptions based on broad philosophical or religious ideas, to local culturally-derived values, to a system that falls under the rubric of human rights in national law, to the specific normative framework embodied in something we call international human rights law, to the interpretations of rights adopted by leading courts and other bodies, or to the institutional framework that has been established at the international or regional levels. This lack of specificity has been a major problem when it comes to some of the sweeping overall assessments published over the past couple of decades, which have too often focused on human rights *tout court* and found 'them' inadequate, ineffectual, problematic, counter-productive, or even destructive.

At the international level, refuge is frequently taken in the term 'implementation', in the sense of giving effect to the agreed norms, but this term is often invoked at such a level of determined generality as to tell us rather little about what is actually happening. For scholars, it might be more productive to consider whether the focus should be on: *vernacularization in* the sense of translating norms at one level into a language in which they can be understood at another; 'awareness-raising and *sensitization*' to use the term adopted by the Inter-American Court of Human Rights; *mobilization* by social movements; *legalization*, juridification, norm domestication, or constitutionalization as the lawyers get their hands on the concept; or *institutionalization*, as governments or inter-governmental actors seek to establish arrangements by which to give effect to the obligations and responsibilities of different actors. Of course, these processes, far from being independent of one another, are often very closely linked. But for analytical purposes, it is helpful to keep such distinctions in mind.

Almost a decade ago, César Rodríguez-Garavito, in 'The Future of Human Rights', 20 *Sur* (2014) 499, noted the extent of the uncertainty facing the IHRR as a result of: '(i) the rise of a multipolar world with new emerging powers, (ii) the emergence of new actors and legal and political strategies, (iii) the challenges and opportunities presented by information and communication technologies, as well as (iv) the threat posed by extreme environmental degradation. He highlighted some specific problems, in particular 'the hierarchical nature of traditional human rights discourse and movement, asymmetry between North and South organisations, over-legalisation of human rights language, and the lack of concrete assessments of human rights outcomes.' He argued that human rights practitioners could either respond in a defensive manner by acting as gatekeepers, or could engage in 'reflexive reconstruction that reimagines practices and boundaries to generate productive symbiosis among diverse human rights actors… .'[751]

Today, the challenges and the questions to which they give rise are even more urgent. Consider the following overview:

NEHAL BHUTA ET AL., INTRODUCTION
IBID. (EDS.), THE STRUGGLE FOR HUMAN RIGHTS (2021) 1

[We live] in an era of faltering democratic institutions and practices, dramatically destructive climate events, collapsing economic growth, renewed attention to systemic racism and police brutality, global pandemics, and some of the most unequal distribution of income and wealth recorded in over a hundred years. These profound crises occur against the background of the collapse of long-standing assumptions that had structured politics and international relations. Even as the previous epoch-making political-economic settlement (whether we call it Keynesianism, Embedded Liberalism, Welfarism, or something else) comes dangerously unwound, it has come under renewed criticism for reproducing the legacies of colonialism, imperialism, and slavery, and for embedding the normative status of a concrete type of social persona: white, male, able-bodied, heterosexual. Can contemporary human rights laws and practices meet these and the many other challenges we face? Should the seventy-year project of legalizing human rights internationally be pushed further, paused, or rethought? …

---

[751] See also L. Fletcher, 'Power and the International Human Rights Imaginary: A Critique of Practice', 14 J. *Hum. Rts. Prac.* (2022) 749.

One productive starting point is that, even as the relationship of human rights to social and political change is everywhere shifting and contested, human rights remain the closest thing to a global lingua franca for representing, framing, labelling, and demanding redress for injustice and social suffering. … [O]rganizations and groups—non-profits, social movements, and loose collectives—embrace the language of human rights in all regions of the globe, and have successfully used human rights to advance justice and accountability. The shared language of rights can be used to express and legitimate values, concerns, and needs, and can be an important organizing tool. Global movements—such as those led by indigenous peoples, peasants, workers, women, and people with disabilities—have organized to claim human rights and demand that their rights be recognized in law. The attention that can be garnered by claims of human rights violations can and has been used to label economic, political, and institutional structures as fundamentally unjust and inadequate. Formal human rights institutions can be used to spotlight abuse, focus attention on issues, serve as platforms for advocacy, and pressure governments to reform. They provide space for advocates to unite across borders, raise the profile of national struggles, and articulate their demands in new ways.

…

* * *

A course book such as this is designed to stimulate the reader's thoughts and reflections rather than to provide answers to the most challenging questions that arise. Accordingly, it cannot pretend to provide an overall evaluation of the regime as a whole. But it would be remiss not to provide some sampling of the flood of assessments or critiques that have emerged over the past two decades.

Probably the most compelling analyses of the effectiveness of human rights have been written in the context of detailed studies focused on particular rights, groups, institutions, or countries. Conversely, the harshest critiques have often been of a general and all-embracing nature, such as Stephen Hopgood's, *The Endtimes of Human Rights* (2013), or Eric Posner's *The Twilight of Human Rights Law* (2014). We have considered above various claims that human rights are irredeemably Western in origin, content and implementation, and will not revisit those arguments here. But other commentators portray the almost complete failure of the IHRR, and sometimes point to unintended consequences that have left the victims of injustice even worse off. This is sometimes attributed to misplaced strategies, unduly narrow interpretations, or unacceptable omissions. However, other critiques suggest that the regime has either knowingly or inadvertently displaced, discouraged, or suppressed alternative approaches that might have been more effective.

One of the most detailed empirical studies, focused on the domestic impact of human rights treaties, is Beth Simmons, *Mobilizing for Human Rights: International Law in Domestic Politics* (2009):

> … [F]ormal commitments to treaties can have noticeably positive consequences. Depending on the domestic context into which they are inserted, treaties can affect domestic politics in ways that tend to exert important influences over how governments behave toward their own citizens. Treaties are the clearest statements available about the content of globally sanctioned decent rights practices. Certainly, it is possible for governments to differ over what a particular treaty requires – this is so with domestic laws as well – but it is less plausible to argue that the right to be free from torture, for example, is not something people have a right to demand and into which the international community has no right to inquire; less plausible to contend that children should be drafted to carry AK-47s; and less plausible to justify educating boys over girls on the basis of limited resources when governments have explicitly and voluntarily agreed to the contrary. Treaties serve notice that governments are accountable – domestically and externally – for refraining from the abuses proscribed by their own mutual agreements. Treaties signal a seriousness of intent that is difficult to replicate in other ways. They reflect politics but they also shape political behavior, setting the stage for new political alliances, empowering new political actors, and heightening public scrutiny. When treaties alter politics in these ways, they have the potential to change government behaviors and public policies. It is precisely because of their potential power to constrain that treaty commitments are contentious in domestic and international politics (at 4).

...

International law is not a panacea for all ills. It will not eliminate ruthless dictators, end racial or gender discrimination for all time, or raise all humans to an acceptable standard of living. These international legal commitments are not magic bullets. They have helped but not cured the rights deficit ... . The principles espoused in [human rights treaties] have garnered broad official acceptance worldwide. There are disagreements among states over the exact meaning of some of their provisions but also widespread acknowledgment of their authoritative character. These treaties have inspired some of the most significant constitutional changes within countries in the past three decades. They have touched off domestic debates, provoked demands, and raised the expectations of ordinary citizens. They have been used at crucial moments and critical junctures by litigants and judges to shape domestic law, institutions, and practices for the future. In many cases, people are much better off because of international human rights law than they would have been in its absence (at 350).

SETTING THE SCENE

Before considering a range of critical snapshots, it is helpful to supplement earlier materials in this book by providing some relevant context in terms of the legal, historical and sociological debates in this area. Robert Howse and Ruti Teitel provide an insightful reminder that a narrow or legalistic understanding of compliance cannot capture the reality of the situation. Ryan Goodman and Derek Jinks examine some of the socialization techniques present in the IHRR, and Philip Alston warns of the pitfalls of selective historical accounts.

ROBERT HOWSE AND RUTI TEITEL, BEYOND COMPLIANCE: RETHINKING WHY INTERNATIONAL LAW REALLY MATTERS 1 GLOBAL POLICY (2010) 127

...

... [T]he conceptual, and more recently empirical, study of compliance has become a central preoccupation, and perhaps the fastest growing subfield, in international legal scholarship ... .

... Looking at the aspirations of international law through the lens of rule compliance leads to inadequate scrutiny and understanding of the diverse complex purposes and projects that multiple actors impose and transpose on international legality, and especially a tendency to oversimplify if not distort the relation of international law to politics.

...

One reason that compliance is often seen as a central problem for international legal scholarship is the challenge (by realists and some but not all positivists) that law is only really law when accompanied by authoritative interpretation and enforcement (see Morgenthau, 1948). A focus on compliance, or more adequately perhaps obedience (see Henkin, 1968), aims to deflect such a claim by asserting that there is a range of considerations including reputational effects/long-term self-interest that lead to compliance with international law, regardless of the absence of authoritative interpretation and enforcement in most instances.

Such a response at once proves too much and too little. ...

... It is worth noting however that one of the most sophisticated positivist accounts of law, that of H. L. A. Hart, rejects the notion that legal obligation implies effective coercive sanctions, specifically informed by a consideration of international law. According to Hart:

> To argue that international law is not binding because of its lack of organized sanctions is tacitly to accept the analysis of obligation contained in the theory that law is essentially a matter of orders backed by threats. This theory, as we have seen, identifies 'having an obligation' or 'being bound' with 'likely to suffer the sanction or punishment threatened for disobedience'. Yet, as we have argued, this identification distorts the role played in all legal thought and discourse of the ideas of obligation and duty (Hart, 1961, pp. 217–218).

...

The following are some of the possible effects of international law that are not captured by the notion of behavioral 'compliance' with a 'rule' of law... .

International law (norms and/or institutions such as courts and tribunals) may shift in whole or in part decision-making, interpretative and/or legitimating power from one set of elite actors to another (for example from diplomats, foreign policy analysts and military planners to legal professionals such as judges, lawyers and law professors). This effect is autonomous from that of compliance: in some cases, legal professionalization may lead to more compliance, and in some cases less. In others, it could even lead to 'ultracompliance': effects which go beyond what is desired from the perspective of the objectives of the legal regime, and which may even be perverse.

...

International law can affect the way that policy makers view international problems and conflicts (for example in terms of clashes of rights as opposed to balancing of political or economic interests) and their perception of the constituencies to whom they are accountable in addressing such problems and conflicts. ...

...

... [There is] an internal difficulty within the 'compliance' perspective. Goldsmith and Posner, for example, maintain that unlike ratification of human rights treaties, 'democracy, peace and economic development' have been shown to enhance human rights protection; however, this contrast assumes that democracy, peace and economic development occur entirely exogenously of the effects of international human rights law. If ... international human rights law helps to lock in transitions to peaceful democratic conditions, then it may ultimately lead to what is usually conceived of as compliance, but only through a normative effect that is caught in the first instances by focusing on something other than rule compliance.

...

While Eric Posner ... tends to dismiss the influence of the International Court of Justice (ICJ), based on the number of judgments it has emitted and their purportedly distant effects on the controversies decided (Posner, 2004), the jurisprudential acquis of the ICJ on such essential questions as state responsibility, countermeasures and treaty interpretation has been repeatedly invoked, in for example, investor–state arbitrations ... .

...

Rather obviously legal agents bargain in the shadow of the law. ... States, instead of simply 'complying' with international legal rules may bargain in light of them, and around them. ...

[In the context of] the international legal duty to punish crimes against humanity, ... the increasing likelihood of such prosecutions given the creation of an international criminal court may well affect peace or regime transition bargains between parties to a conflict, for instance making it more difficult or less plausible to use amnesties as a bargaining chip for acceptance of a peaceful, negotiated transition. On the other hand, with the ICC in the background now, and its ability to enforce international criminal law during an ongoing conflict, more cautious or restrained behavior by some of the participants in the conflict may result, and this could actually make a transitional bargain easier. ... [T]hese effects do not even come into focus if one centers the analysis on effects on 'compliance' with the duty to prosecute and/or the duty to cooperate with the ICC for instance.

RYAN GOODMAN AND DEREK JINKS, SOCIALIZING STATES: PROMOTING HUMAN RIGHTS THROUGH INTERNATIONAL LAW
(2013)

Chapter 1: Introduction

...

First-generation scholarship in international human rights law, in our view, provides an indispensable but plainly incomplete framework. Prevailing approaches suggest that law changes human rights practices either by materially inducing states (and individuals) or by persuading states (and individuals) of the validity and legitimacy of human rights law. In our view, the former approach fails to grasp the complexity of the social environment within which states act, and the latter fails to account for many ways in which the diffusion of social and legal norms occurs. Indeed, a rich cluster of empirical studies in interdisciplinary scholarship documents particular processes that socialize states in the absence of material inducement or persuasion. These studies conclude that the power of social influence can be harnessed even if: (1) collective action problems and political constraints that inhibit effective material inducements are not overcome and (2) the complete internalization sought through persuasion is not achieved. ...

Our aim is to provide a more complete conceptual framework by identifying a third mechanism by which international law might change state behavior — what we call acculturation. ... We do not suggest that international legal scholarship has completely failed to identify aspects of this process. Rather, we maintain that the mechanism is underemphasized, insufficiently specified, and poorly understood, and that it is often conflated or confused with other constructivist mechanisms such as persuasion. ...

Chapter 2: Three Mechanisms of Social Influence

...

A. Material inducement

The first and most obvious social mechanism is material inducement — whereby states and institutions influence the behavior of other states by increasing the benefits of conformity or the costs of nonconformity through material rewards and punishments.

B. Persuasion

Persuasion is a mechanism of social influence documented principally by psychologists and sociologists — and applied by others to the spread of norms across states. Persuasion theory suggests that the practices of actors are influenced through processes of social "learning" and other forms of information conveyance that occur in exchanges within international organizations and transnational networks. Persuasion "requires argument and deliberation in an effort to change the minds of others." Persuaded actors "internalize" new norms and rules of appropriate behavior and redefine their interests and identities accordingly. ... The touchstone of the overall process is that actors are consciously convinced of the truth, validity, or appropriateness of a norm, belief, or practice. ...

...

C. Acculturation

Another important mechanism of social influence, in our view, is acculturation. ... Whereas persuasion emphasizes the content of a norm, acculturation emphasizes the relationship of the actor to a reference group or wider cultural environment. ... Accordingly, acculturation encompasses processes such as mimicry and status maximization. The general mechanism induces behavioral changes through pressures to conform. Individual behavior (and community-level behavioral regularity) is in part a function of social structure — the relations between individual actors and some reference group. Actors are impelled to adopt the behavioral practices and attitudes of similar actors in their surrounding social environment.

... Actors, in an important sense, are influenced by their environment; indeed, this generalized influence is one important way that "culture" is transmitted and reproduced. Although culture is typically understood as "learned behavior," much of what actors absorb from their social environment is not simply "informational social influence." Social influence is a rich process — one that also includes "normative social influence" whereby actors are impelled to adopt appropriate attitudes and behaviors. An actor need not be unaware of these influences — these processes can be subconscious or fully apparent. ...

...

Despite the obvious similarities, acculturation differs from persuasion in important respects. First, persuasion requires acceptance of the validity or legitimacy of a belief, practice, or norm — acculturation requires only that an actor perceive that an important reference group harbors the belief, engages in the practice, or subscribes to the norm. Accordingly, persuasion involves complete internalization. Acculturation can involve complete or incomplete internalization. Second, persuasion requires active assessment of the merits of a belief. Acculturation processes, in contrast, frequently (though not invariably) operate tacitly; it is often the very act of conforming that garners social approval and alleviates cognitive discomfort. Persuasion involves assessment of the content of the message (even if only indirectly); acculturation involves assessment of the social relation (the degree of identification) between the target audience and some group (and of the importance of the issue to the group). Acculturation occurs not as a result of the content of the relevant rule or norm but rather as a function of social structure. Acculturation depends less on the properties of the rule than on the properties of the relationship of the actor to the community. Because the acculturation process does not involve actually agreeing with the merits of a group's position, it may (but does not necessarily) result in outward conformity with a social convention without private acceptance or corresponding changes in private practices.

PHILIP ALSTON, DOES THE PAST MATTER? ON THE ORIGINS OF HUMAN RIGHTS
126 HARV. L. REV. (2013) 2043, 2076

[In *The Last Utopia: Human Rights in History* (2010), at 8-9, Samuel Moyn famously claimed that 'it was … only in the 1970s that a genuine social movement around human rights made its appearance'. He adds that '[f]ew things that are powerful today turn out on inspection to be longstanding and inevitable. And the human rights movement is certainly not one of them. [This] … means that human rights are not so much an inheritance to preserve as an invention to remake – or even leave behind …'.]

By detaching today's international human rights regime from its deep roots and dismissing the relevance of the many historical as well as intellectual struggles to define a shared understanding of the subject, [historical revisionists led by Moyn] are able to present us with a clean sheet from which to begin their own speculations as to both the nature and the origins of the human rights movement. … [One result is that] there is a struggle for the soul of the human rights movement, and it is being waged in large part through the proxy of genealogy.

B. The Road Ahead

Any meaningful history of human rights must disaggregate and address separately the different analytical dimensions of the overall enterprise. The enterprise of "human rights" consists of too many distinct facets to be reduced to one or two variables. The history and power of ideas, the force of grassroots social and political movements, the impact of legal and constitutional traditions, and the influence of institutions at both the domestic and international levels constitute indispensable elements that need to be factored into any effort to understand the origins, nature, and potential significance of the present regime. Several lessons emerge from [recent historiography].

1. The Intrinsic Polycentricity of the Human Rights Enterprise. — Each of the different historiographical approaches has something important to offer, but we should be very wary of any single account that purports to have found the answer to the puzzle and to have invalidated alternative interpretations. The human rights enterprise is intrinsically complex and multifaceted. Its origins are to be found in different and multiple sites, and they cannot usefully be traced back to any single source or through examining the evolution of a single theme, process, or institution.

2. Linear Claims as a Suspect Class. — Histories that rely on strong claims of continuity over a long period of time are inherently questionable. Thus, for example, the history of antislavery alone … has been a remarkably circuitous, uncertain, and often tragic one, even in the limited period from 1807 to the present. Claims of a direct lineage over a century or two will generally imply elements of consistency and perhaps even inevitability that do not resonate with the actual path that history has traced, and this is certainly true of the struggle to abolish slavery. …

… [In the history of human rights] there are crucial continuities as well as discontinuities, and neither should be overlooked or underestimated.

3. The Need for an Analytical Framework. — Given the polycentric nature of the overall enterprise … "human rights" might be thought of as: (a) an idea, including careful consideration of the extent to which vocabularies are interchangeable over time; (b) an elaborated discourse, going beyond basic ideas, but not requiring institutional manifestations; (c) a social movement, including a definition of such a movement and specification of why it is significant; (d) a practice, or an institution, that resembles in at least some respects the elements that we might consider important today; (e) a legal regime, either at the national or international level, or both; or (f) a system that is capable of effectively promoting respect for the rights of individuals and groups. Each of these categories would constitute a plausible focus for analysis, and each is likely to be linked to the other, thus forming elements in the historical genealogy of the system. An isolated focus on one or another will inevitably produce different accounts of the origins, antecedents, precursors, and so on … . The choice of focus will also produce different causal accounts.

4. The Power of Ideas. — At the end of the day, the most compelling reason for the importance of genealogy is to be found in the history of ideas. But human rights does not consist of a single idea. Much of the recent literature seeks to single out one particular element that is then said to have transformed an otherwise amorphous mass of claims and assertions into a suddenly coherent body of "human rights" that had not previously existed. To the extent that [Jenny Martinez, in *The Slave Trade and the Origins of International Human Rights Law* (2012)] seeks to mark out the origins of a regime that consists of the elements that would be most prized by a twenty-first-century international lawyer — treaties, courts, and enforcement — her case is strong. Nor is she oblivious to the broader political and societal contexts in which this regime emerged. But the weakness of the bolder claim that she makes is that she fails to trace the historical evolution of either the basic normative claims of the antislavery movement or the techniques that were pioneered at the time. Even if the case can be made that today's norms and institutions look much like those of yesteryear, any compelling genealogical claim needs to be demonstrated rather than surmised.

For Moyn, the key transformative step is that the claim made by an individual is directed to the international community, rather than to the state of which the individual is a citizen. But this step is just one among many in the long and winding voyage of the concept of human rights, the evolution of which continues. There is no single element, no single idea that enables us to declare that the notion of human rights has reached a definitive threshold that not only marks it off from all that has gone before but also makes it qualitatively and fundamentally different. We are looking at a continuum, albeit not a linear one. …
…
5. The Role of Power. — Power, in both its positive and negative iterations, must be an integral part of any history of human rights. But power comes in many shapes and forms ranging from military force to the soft power of ideas. …

THE PAST AND FUTURE OF HUMAN RIGHTS: SNAPSHOTS

In reading the materials below, keep in mind questions such as the following:

- When we speak of the IHRR, what exactly do we have in mind? Is it necessary to disaggregate the different component parts of the regime (concepts, norms, laws, institutions, social movements, etc.) to arrive at nuanced and meaningful judgments, or is the 'system' sufficiently coherent as to be susceptible to a single overall assessment? How do the authors below conceive of the 'regime', 'movement', or 'system' that they are addressing?

- Given the magnitude, extent, and persistence of the violations that we see worldwide, does it follow that the IHRR has failed? That it is entirely inadequate?

- How much of the authoritarian and populist backlashes against human rights can be attributed to the shortcomings of the regime, or alternatively to its successes?

- How could the IHRR be reformed? Or should it be abandoned/scrapped and replaced with something very different? If so, what form might that take? What alternatives have the critics of the existing system suggested?

- Reflecting back on the many issues and sub-regimes explored in this book, which of the assessments below seems to best capture your own perception?

- To what extent has the overall IHRR been unduly path dependent, or been captured or distorted by one or more political or economic ideologies? How rigid or flexible has it proven to be? How well has it adapted in response to new challenges?

- Are the successes of the regime really significant, or are they largely pyrrhic or marginal?

ABDULLAHI AHMED AN-NAIM, DECOLONIZING HUMAN RIGHTS
(2021) XII

In the absence of verifiable means of evaluating the level or degree of actual protection of human rights, factors such as the ratification of treaties, adoption of laws, and descriptive self-reporting by states or highly selective and arbitrary reporting by international human rights organizations (NGOs) are taken as "evidence" of negative or positive human rights performance by the state. The priorities of so-called donor governments and northern-based NGOs are taken as the sole reliable means of promoting human rights in postcolonial states in Africa and Asia.

Since human rights are by definition universal claims asserted and realized by self-determining human beings, our ability to define and implement these norms is integral to our humanity. The present state-centric international law system and its institutions can provide only limited and contingent protection of human rights norms. Shifting the human rights paradigm from state-centric bureaucratic formalism to people-centered social and political movements will still need states or other forms of large-scale political formations that are subject to total transparency and effective accountability.

... [What is needed is] the mutual linking of being human and human rights, whereby perceptions of what the human is define the scope, content, and methods of the protection of human rights, and the quality of being human is enabled and realized through the protection of those rights. By "human rights," I mean moral and political entitlements that are due to all human beings equally by virtue of their humanity, without any distinction on such grounds as race, sex, religion, or national origin. ... I prefer to present these rights as moral and political – instead of legal – entitlement because the legal dimension is futile without sufficient moral foundation and the political will to implement it.

[Asked by the *UNESCO Courier* in 2019 how respect for human rights can be ensured, An Naim replied that:

> ... human rights should be defined by the people who accept and live by them on the ground, and not imposed by former colonial powers on their former colonies or by delegates of post-colonial states, and international bureaucrats.
>
> Second, human rights norms must be implemented through realistic contextual steps that are suited to the needs and resources of relevant communities, and not by enacting high-sounding legislation to be presented at sanitized meetings of international organizations, and diplomatic or academic conferences.
>
> Third, strategies of implementation must be deeply contextual, and under the control of the human subjects of these rights everywhere.]

UPENDRA BAXI, THE FUTURE OF HUMAN RIGHTS
(3RD ED., 2008) IX[752]

... [W]hile human rights languages provide a striking arena for questioning the barbarity of power and domination, these at the same moment do not exhaust the range of normative politics. Other evaluative ways also exist that are often in conflict with the ethical languages of human rights. ... [There is a] need for constant vigilance against an assumption that human rights norms and standards, and even values and sentiments, instantly justify themselves in terms of the attainment of human/social welfare as distinct from the states of human well-being, or as serving the tasks of just social orderings, nationally, regionally, or globally. The languages of justice remain relatively autonomous of the languages of human rights ... .

... This book explores three distinct but related domains of making, remaking, and unmaking of non-material human rights culture (sentiments, symbols, and values) as well as the material culture of human rights (the infrastructures of power and authority which promote and sustain the articulation of human rights norms and standards).

... Endeavours at making and remaking contemporary human rights norms and standards ... remain more crucial than may be ever fully glimpsed or garnered via the endless (and already sterile) debate about the 'universality' and 'relativity' of human rights.

---

[752] Baxi's work has been described by W. Twining, *General Jurisprudence* (2009), at 430, as 'diffuse, polemical, and difficult to summarise.' Nonetheless, he offers an excellent overview of it, using Baxi's own words. See also W. Twining (ed.), *Human Rights, Southern Voices: Francis Deng, Abdullahi an-Na'im, Yash Ghai and Upendra Baxi* (2009).

...

... [T]he various declarations of human rights since the [UDHR] spawning human rights treaties and related instruments and constitutional enunciations, all in constant interplay, make space for the struggles for the attainment of human rights; these at the same moment also preserve some ultimate or terminal forms and zones of sovereign governmental discretion; in sum, the overall production of human rights free zones of domination and governance. The production constraints thus posed are scarcely amazing. The astonishing feature of the polymorphous production of contemporary human rights norms and standards, at all levels ... is its normative exuberance and excess. The crucial question then is this: How may we read or render legible as well as intelligible these forms of what I name here as the 'carnivalistic' production of human rights exuberances/excesses? Do these speak to us about some new messianic futures of human rights, or even to some future histories of the humankind? Or does all this primarily, and after all, constitute the cunning of instrumental political reason?

[Baxi draws a strong distinction between the 'politics *of* human rights' and 'politics *for* human rights'.]

... It remains rather easy to describe the politics for human rights in the languages of 'transformative', or even as 'redemptive' politics. ... [But in] this genre, the 'transformative'/'redemptive' politics of the State/sovereignty-oriented production of dominant and dominating truths stands constantly exposed as an expedient order of cruel and wounding falsehoods.

The 'best' practices of politics for human rights invoke and use the 'transformative'/'redemptive' imagery differently indeed. In these genera, communities in resistance and suffering (the worst-off) peoples offer the labours of popular and societal resistance to the various forms of the politics of domination and governance. Human rights and social movement activist practices become possible and legible on a register that marshals the power of utterance of the political truths of the suffering peoples and communities in resistance. While the politics of dominance thrives upon the practices of nationalization of truth and the unending nurturance of governmental monopoly over definitions of 'the' public interest or the common good, civil society formations (or more accurately put the ensemble of diverse practices of social and human rights activism) contest this monopoly of a singular and totalizing narrative of official authorial voice. Resistance—the myriad forms of articulation of counter-hegemonic power—thus makes the best narrative sense for the uncertain promise of human rights futures.

I say 'uncertain promise', if only because there exist no easy alternatives to the problematic of representation, that is the activist art and craft of speaking *with*, rather than *for* the suffering or the worst-off peoples. Speaking for (acts/feats of 'political' representation) remains the standard way of dominance/governance; speaking *with* suffering peoples constitutes the 'substance' of politics for human rights. Not all human rights NGOs thus labour to speak *with* the suffering peoples, despite their professed aims and the problem of representation thus becomes acute with some contemporary tendencies towards the conversion of human rights *movements* into human rights *markets*. Many practices of human rights activism fail indeed to restore to suffering peoples, and indeed even claim for themselves the most precious of all human rights—the constantly claimed *human right to interpret human rights*. Nonetheless, I here offer overall some grounds for a belief that in the main various styles of engagement with the politics for human rights aspire at being, and remaining, historically worthy of this designation.

SAMUEL MOYN, THE LAST UTOPIA: HUMAN RIGHTS IN HISTORY
(2010) 212[753]

When the history of human rights is told beyond myths of deep origins, it illustrates the persistence of the nation-state as the aspirational forum for humanity until recently. The state was the incubator for rights claims, both in the rise of the absolutist state, with its well-disciplined interior order and colonialist exterior expansion, then in the creation of the modern nation, in which citizenship and rights, identification and contestation, were always bound up with each other. The relevance of the nation-state was amplified, rather than qualified, in the World War II alliance politics that led to the marginalization in the United Nations of the human rights that some wartime rhetoric had featured. It was geographically dispersed in the anticolonialist imagination, in which

---

[753] For a review, see S. Benhabib, 'Moving beyond False Binarisms: On Samuel Moyn's *The Last Utopia*', 22 *Qui Parle* (2013) 82.

the new human rights were understood as a subversive instrument against imperial rule in the name of liberation and the construction of new states around the world. The perceived crisis of the postcolonial world, however, made the globalization of the nation-state unattractive as the sole formula for the achievement of modern freedom. Accordingly, rights finally lost their long connection with revolution.

. . .

The international human rights movement became so significant, then, neither because it offered a rights-based doctrine alone nor because it forged a truly global vision for the first time. Rather, it was the crisis of other utopias that allowed the very neutrality that had made "human rights" wholly peripheral to the aftermath of World War II—when taking sides in a contest of programmatic visions seemed so pressing—to become the condition of their success. . . .

But the very neutrality that allowed for human rights to survive in the 1970s, and prosper as other utopias died, also left them with a heavy burden later. For even if their breakthrough depended on their antipolitics, human rights were soon affected by two transformative changes. First, the moment that favored pure moral visions passed, not least in American party and electoral politics, as Jimmy Carter's brief presidential career illustrates so vividly. Second, and more important, partisans of the human rights idea were forced to confront the need for political agenda and programmatic vision—the very things whose absence allowed for their utopia to emerge so spectacularly and discontinuously in the first place. If human rights were born in antipolitics, they could not remain wholly noncommittal toward programmatic endeavors, especially as time passed.

. . .

Born of the yearning to transcend politics, human rights have become the core language of a new politics of humanity that has sapped the energy from old ideological contests of left and right. With the advancement of human rights as their standard, a huge number of schemes of transformation, regulation, and "governance" contend with one another across the world. But if in the thirty years since their explosion in the 1970s human rights have followed a path from morality to politics, their advocates have not always forth-rightly acknowledged that fact. Born in the assertion of the "power of the powerless," human rights inevitably became bound up with the power of the powerful. If "human rights" stand for an exploding variety of rival political schemes, however, they still trade on the moral transcendence of politics that their original breakthrough involved. And so it may not be too late to wonder whether the concept of human rights, and the movement around it, should restrict themselves to offering minimal constraints on responsible politics, not a new form of maximal politics of their own. If human rights call to mind a few core values that demand protection, they cannot be all things to all people. Put another way, the last utopia cannot be a moral one. And so whether human rights deserve to define the utopianism of the future is still very far from being decided.

SAMUEL MOYN, NOT ENOUGH: HUMAN RIGHTS IN AN UNEQUAL WORLD
(2018) 216[754]

The real trouble about human rights, when historically correlated with market fundamentalism, is not that they promote it but that they are unambitious in theory and ineffectual in practice in the face of market fundamentalism's success. Neoliberalism has changed the world, while the human rights movement has posed no threat to it. The tragedy of human rights is that they have occupied the global imagination but have so far contributed little of note, merely nipping at the heels of the neoliberal giant whose path goes unaltered and unresisted. And the critical reason that human rights have been a powerless companion of market fundamentalism is that they simply have nothing to say about material inequality. The chief worry about human rights is not that they destroy the very distributive protections they set out to afford, let alone that they abet "disaster capitalism." In too many places, those protections never existed. And global capitalism is hardly the only or even the main source of state abuses. . . .

. . . Precisely because the human rights revolution has focused so intently on state abuses and has, at its most ambitious, dedicated itself to establishing a guarantee of sufficient provision, it has failed to respond to—or even recognize—neoliberalism's obliteration of any constraints on inequality. Human rights have been the signature morality of a neoliberal age because they merely call for it to be more humane. . . .

. . .

---

[754] For a review, see G. de Búrca, [Review of *Not Enough*, by Samuel Moyn], 16 *Int'l J. Con.* L. (2018) 1347.

Could a different form of human rights law or movements correct for their coexistence with a crisis of material inequality? There is reason to doubt that they can do so by changing radically—for example by transforming into socialist movements. There is no contradicting the moral significance and possibly even historical success of human rights when it comes to combating political repression and restraining excessive violence or indeed, although more controversially, in campaigns for economic and social rights. But whenever inequality has been limited, it was never on the sort of individualistic and often antistatist basis that human rights share with their market fundamentalist Doppelgänger. And when it comes to mobilizing support for economic fairness, the chief tools of the human rights movement—playing informational politics to stigmatize the repressions of states or the disasters of war—are simply not fit for use. It is in part because the human rights movement is not up to the challenge that it has been condemned to offer no meaningful alternative, and certainly no serious threat, to market fundamentalism. … The truth is that local and global economic justice requires redesigning markets or at least redistributing from the rich to the rest, something that naming and shaming are never likely to achieve, even when supplemented by novel forms of legal activism.

JOSEPH R. SLAUGHTER, HIJACKING HUMAN RIGHTS: NEOLIBERALISM, THE NEW HISTORIOGRAPHY, AND THE END OF THE THIRD WORLD
40 HUM. RTS Q. (2018) 735, 743

Most of the new historiography comes out of a strain of intellectual history that largely disregards or dismisses ideas that did not occur to or circulate among European and American academic thinkers; more curiously, it does not seem to count history itself as an idea, as something that is mobilized (in the form of historiographic stories that are told and re-told about the origins, identities, and destinies of human rights) on behalf of some interests and not others. Despite dismissing the traditional Western progress narratives of human rights as so much mythmaking, the new historiographers rarely try to account for the political and social power of myth (or historiography, in its academic form)—that is, the particular historical, political, and other "sociofunctionalist" effects that "mythopoeic narratives" themselves produce in the world. To put it most polemically, the new historiography takes neither the Third World (its people and nations) nor the power of historiography (that is, itself) seriously as agents of history in their own right, as agents that affect the character and understanding of human rights and international history. To my mind, then, this new historiography is salutary only insofar as it troubles the potted history of human rights, opens (or re-opens) new windows of opportunity, and amplifies the chorus of skeptics (many from the Global South), who have long maintained, with Malawian historian Zeleza, that "human rights are not organic to or a natural result of a fictive western tradition going back to ancient Greece, a teleological narrative of retrospective appropriation that is fundamentally ahistorical and intellectually flawed." For the most part, however, it fails to engage with those historians, and insofar as the revisionist history displaces and obscures those vital critiques, resubordinating non-Western histories, theories, and accounts of human rights to the new historiographical hegemon, it becomes as much a monolithic part of the problem as any other oversimplified history of the European pedigree of human rights—part of the historical hijacking of human rights described below.

ZACHARY MANFREDI, RADICALIZING HUMAN RIGHTS
THE BOSTON REVIEW (21 JUNE 2022)

Although [the] legacy of left skepticism about human rights retains valuable lessons for advocates, our political moment also provides opportunities for the reconceptualization and radicalization of human rights programs. Contemporary appeals to human rights arguably have the most to offer by developing a more egalitarian dimension to the politics of human rights. The traditional liberal conception of human rights as individual entitlements limits the capacity of the state to regulate private power and mobilizes state authority on behalf of private property and capital accumulation. By contrast, progressive appeals to human rights can link this language to a normative vision for a more just social order and the provision of public welfare. Developing an egalitarian vision requires moving beyond a guarantee of sufficient minimums and instead emphasizing how radical social and economic inequality stifle the realization of a more robust and radical human rights project.

…

… [C]ritics have long observed that a narrow focus on "rights talk" and formal equality can obscure and even ratify substantive inequalities. …

Two contemporary trends in the left criticism of human rights are particularly notable. [Manfredi discusses the work of Samuel Moyn and of anthropologist Talal Asad.] … Critics worry that the legal protections offered by a theory of human rights predicated on a consumerist subject will focus primarily on creation of "free markets" and justify policies that intensify social and economic stratification. Left critics of human rights also observe that different rights regimes encourage and produce particular self-conception among rights holders: if a human right to private property or wealth accumulation is enshrined in law, it helps establish a framework for how people evaluate their life projects.

Recent work by Jessica Whyte and Quinn Slobodian advances this argument and showcases how neoliberal reformers often relied on the language of human rights as part of their own political programs. In *Globalists: The End of Empire and Birth of Neoliberalism* (2018), Slobodian shows how Geneva School neoliberals who were instrumental in the development of postwar international institutions—such as Ludwig von Mises, Fredrich Hayek, and Wilhelm Röpke—framed human rights as "xenos rights," that is, rights of security for foreign capital and protections of private property against state expropriation. In addition, Whyte's 2019 book *The Morals of Market: Human Rights and the Rise of Neoliberalism* shows how "neoliberals developed their own account of human rights as moral and legal supports for a liberal market order." As Whyte documents, neoliberals relied on human rights to advance a consumerist vision of the welfare state subject to means-testing and compatible with international human rights instruments. They appealed to human rights as reason to oppose postcolonial projects of economic redistribution and industry nationalization, including notably opposition to the New International Economic Order. And they turned to human rights as justification for radical programs of reform in Chile and elsewhere that focused on privatization, deregulation of financial markets, and destruction of labor unions.
…
We should not deny the purchase of these critiques, but … the growing contemporary focus on the social and economic dimensions of human rights already helps recast them in ways that depart from neoliberal formulations. …
…
… [I]n some respects, the substantive content of rights claims championed by recent progressive political actors differ dramatically from the rights preferred by neoliberal reformers. Human rights to education, housing, protection from racial discrimination, gender equality, union membership, sustenance, and water all emerged over the course of the twentieth century, and new rights instruments and declarations were often developed in response to the demands of left social movements. … [N]umerous radical thinkers have relied on the language of human rights. In this sense, the progressive turn to a more robust vision of social and economic rights language might be seen as an attempt to resuscitate a more radical tradition of human rights advocacy as an alternative to mainstream liberal and neoliberal formations. This work requires recognizing the plasticity of law and its potential to develop in new directions. This does not mean we should fall prey to what international law scholar Susan Marks has called "false contingency" regarding rights—that is, the assumption that human rights are infinitely malleable and repurposable for left politics. But in the twenty-first century context of extreme economic inequality, claims that there are human rights to food, water, non-discrimination, housing, and labor protections may prove more protean and radical than previously imagined.
…
… [C]ritiques of human rights call our attention to the importance of developing a more radically egalitarian vision of human rights advocacy. Egalitarianism, in this sense, should not be construed as merely a matter of formal equality before the law: the insistence, say, that all members of a polity have "equal rights" in the sense of equal claim to a minimal set of rights claims. Rather, a genuinely egalitarian politics of human rights should underscore the ways that radical social, economic, and political inequality necessarily enable widespread violations of human rights. This is not only because, practically speaking, the concentration of private wealth makes it difficult to achieve even the minimum guarantees of basic economic and social rights. Extreme inequalities in wealth also create disparities in political power and fundamentally undermine democratic control over economic governance. Radical inequality thus undermines human rights because it stifles even the basic right to equal say in the democratic political process that ought to determine what social and economic orders reign.
…

Recent progressive takes on tax policy are particularly interesting examples of how one might develop such an egalitarian account of human rights. As a matter of political rhetoric, progressive politicians have framed their tax proposals specifically as a reaction to both insufficient minimums and to radical economic inequality. Moreover, in a substantial sense these programs have an inherently egalitarian dimension: reducing the holdings of the wealthiest (while either not decreasing or increasing the wealth of those with fewer resources) reduces economic inequality. Framing progressive taxation as a human rights issue then implies an affinity between realizing human rights and securing a more egalitarian social order.

PAUL O'CONNELL, ON THE HUMAN RIGHTS QUESTION
40 HUM. RTS. Q. (2018) 962

Critiques of human rights abound. This is by no means a recent development, but the very ubiquity of the language of human rights in our age, means that a plethora of critiques of human rights have proliferated over the last forty years. While it is true that such critiques arise from various points along the ideological and political spectrum—at times making strange bedfellows of critical theorists and reactionary politicians—what we might, broadly, term "the left" has provided particularly fertile ground for critical accounts of human rights. Notwithstanding these critiques, and a recent spate of declarations about the demise of human rights, social movements around the world continue to frame their struggles and demands, at least partly, through the language of human rights. This can be seen in struggles for housing in Spain and South Africa, land in Brazil, racial equality in the US, or water in Ireland, to name but a few. This presents us with an interesting disjuncture. Throughout the world, millions of people are attempting to confront the misery and injustices heaped upon them by the contemporary global order through, in part, mobilizing the language of human rights to advance and defend their interests. At the same time, many of the putative critics of this extant global order disdain, by implication, such efforts through a sometimes bald, sometimes sophisticated, critique and dismissal of human rights.

This disjuncture—between critical theory and critical practice—raises a number of crucial questions about the relationship between ideas and social movements, law and struggles to bring about social change, and, for present purposes, about the role of human rights in emancipatory politics. It raises, at a critical historical juncture, the fundamental question of how individuals and groups committed to fundamental social change should engage with human rights. The argument developed here, put briefly, is that while many of the critiques of human rights raise important concerns, they fail to meaningfully address the central question of the relationship between human rights and social struggles. In contrast to such critiques, it will be argued here that human rights can and should be deployed in emancipatory political projects today, but that reaching such a conclusion requires us to go beyond narrow, formalistic, and overly juridical concepts of what human rights are, and stress the centrality of social and political struggle in the formulation and defense of human rights.
…

In the contemporary era of austerity and commodification, communities struggling for water, housing, health care, and food find that their immediate struggle also requires thinking about broader, structural issues. The assertion of a human right, in these contexts, becomes, of necessity, a rejection of the logic of the market, of the basic impulse of the capitalist system.

SALLY ENGLE MERRY, THE STATE OF HUMAN RIGHTS CONSCIOUSNESS: NOT YET ENDTIMES
NEHAL BHUTA ET AL. (EDS.), THE STRUGGLE FOR HUMAN RIGHTS (2021) 62

[A]re human rights really on the verge of disappearing? It is certainly the case that many human rights institutions have become more bureaucratic and stodgier; and that human rights organizations in many parts of the world are under threat. Yet the appeal of human rights has always resided in the ideal of justice, fairness, and equality that they represent. These remain appealing ideas globally, even if the institutions designed to promote and enforce human rights are in themselves increasingly unable to do so. …
…

Human rights ... refer to a set of ideals about how governments should treat their citizens and about how all humans should be treated. These ideals, moreover, have the imprimatur of a global consensus. Although there has been a great deal of sophisticated and valuable scholarship about whether human rights are 'effective', measured 'effectiveness' is not the only way to evaluate the importance of human rights. After all, we do not judge the value of national laws because they are effective, but because they articulate goals that we would like to make effective. Most—national and international—laws in fact have an impact in the absence of sanctions, operating instead on the basis of voluntary compliance with a set of rules and ideas that people (or collectives) come to accept. But they are also routinely violated. ...

...

Recognizing the continuing importance and strength of human rights requires looking for them in different places. These places are not simply the HRC or the regular meetings of the [treaty bodies] but also the offices of small NGOs and the streets of poor neighbourhoods. Understanding human rights in practice requires looking at the way the ideas they promote have become part of everyday life for many people around the world.

...

The resilience of some broad conception of human rights in communities around the world rests in part on the universal concern with justice, although it is defined in many ways. Every society has conceptions of justice, although the specific norms and procedures used to produce it are quite variable. Many of these conceptions are grounded in religion while others are based on community standards or state enactments. Human rights differ, however, in that they offer a relatively secular conception of justice rooted not in a particular state but in the consensus of a large majority of states. Thus, they are legitimated by a transnational consensus that gives them a kind of power beyond that of state law. It is far from the only transnational conception of justice, of course. Many religions are transnational and carry these ideas, such as liberation theology, while political ideologies such as Marxism and democracy and the rule of law provide alternative ideas of justice.

This does not mean that there are not problems with human rights as a global model for justice. It offers an over-individualized idea of justice that does not always address the structural causes of inequality. It establishes a platform below which no person or society should fall, but it does not explicitly tackle inequality. Although it covers social and economic rights as well as civil and political ones, the former are often not as well supported and implemented. Human rights as a global justice ideology have not resolved the difficult question of the incompatibility of universal applicability and respect for local cultural practices. States that feel threatened by human rights activism are increasingly shutting down human rights organizations. Yet, human rights ideas remain a major force in global consciousness.

WENDY BROWN, 'THE MOST WE CAN HOPE FOR . . .': HUMAN RIGHTS AND THE POLITICS OF FATALISM
103 S. ATLANTIC Q. (2004) 451

Is the prevention or mitigation of suffering promised by human rights the most that can be hoped for at this point in history? Is this where we are, namely, at a historical juncture in which all more ambitious justice projects seem remote if not utopian by comparison with the task of limiting abuses of individuals? Is the prospect of a more substantive democratization of power so dim that the relief and reduction of human suffering is really all that progressives can hope for? If so, then human rights politics probably deserves the support of everyone who cares about such suffering. But if there are still other historical possibilities, if progressives have not yet arrived at this degree of fatalism, then we would do well to take the measure of whether and how the centrality of human rights discourse might render those other political possibilities more faint.

RATNA KAPUR, GENDER, ALTERITY AND HUMAN RIGHTS
(2018) 1

This book explores the imaginary possibilities of freedom in the aftermath of the critique of human rights. Addressing this issue in relation to gender and alterity, I specifically focus on how, in light of such critique, freedom is to be envisaged once the emancipatory claims of human rights have proven disingenuous, false or simply unrealizable. In the global context, freedom remains defined as a liberal, external pursuit, involving the accumulation of further rights by a rational, finite and individual subject. The critical legal project, including postcolonial and feminist interventions, has successfully dismantled the façade of this claim, exposing the regulatory and governance structures of human rights. The central endeavour of this book is to consciously explore the imaginary possibilities that have emerged in the aftermath of critique by centring and examining articulations of freedom available in non-liberal, alternative epistemologies. I address alternative registers that present radical insights on freedom as based on discrete understandings of the subject which are distinct from/remain beyond the reach of liberal individualism, and posit notions of self-scrutiny, reflection, discernment and the turn inwards as central features.

The focus on non-liberal (as opposed to illiberal) articulations of freedom pushes against the liberal positioning of human rights as indispensable central instruments in struggles for freedom, and further questions their capacity to realize this goal. The discussion not only exposes the parochial, provincialized identity of human rights as liberal, overwhelmingly Western and Eurocentric, but also displays the destructive capacities nestled in the liberal claim to ideological supremacy – one that ultimately seeks to retain its dominance over all others through its coercive formulations of how to be, and be free, in the world. The notion that divergent understandings of freedom have always existed outside of the liberal and neoliberal imaginaries and related market terms is either barely considered by those who shape, support and implement the rights regime, or considered inherently alien and therefore irrelevant to the recursive ideological currents within the fishbowl. ... [F]reedom should be actively delinked from the human rights project as formulated and imposed by the liberal imaginary, and should instead be explored within a range of dynamic and existing alternative philosophical spaces. By exploring whether, and how, non-liberal vocabularies of freedom can address and alleviate the current disillusionment with human rights' capacity to deliver on their emancipatory promise, the book marks a conscious and productive shift in the direction of visualizing the concept of freedom from outside the liberal fishbowl, and exploring considerations of freedom that have always existed beyond the fishbowl.

My analysis is not framed within an either/or binary – that is, between support for the human rights project and a specific intervention (which can have disastrous and unintended consequences), and a refusal to intervene that closes its eyes to the repression and violence experienced by sexual and religious minorities and women (for the most part, it is generally alleged, in rogue, non-Western states). Instead, my starting premise accepts the idea of human rights as a project that is already affected by – and overtly and covertly implicated in – structures of power, laying bare the fallacy of human rights as linked to an external, optimistic pursuit of freedom. ... [E]ven the minimalist claims of human rights advocates – that rights can alleviate human suffering and do not have wider effects – are invariably advancing maximalist projects, such as the need for thriving markets or the embedding of a particular notion of the female subject as unveiled, sexualized and autonomous. ... The trail of disorder, chaos and, at times, unanticipated but irrefutably harmful outcomes produced in and through human rights advocacy ... underscores the urgent need to identify new ways of pursuing freedom. ...

RADHA D'SOUZA, SOCIAL MOVEMENTS, LAW AND LIBERAL IMAGINATIONS
(2018) 6-7

...

Right claims conceal what is entailed in our relationship to land and nature. Indeed, right claims facilitate the transformation of places into properties and homeland into home-market. Yet, even the more radical movements on land such as indigenous peoples' movements that are opposed to the very notion of land, forests and water as property frequently end up supporting the idea of 'human' rights to land.

[In 2009, a speaker] for the radical Mapuche movement in Chile ... relied on the UN Declaration on the Rights of Indigenous People [UNDRIP] as the legal justification for the creation of an autonomous, self-governed Mapuche region. Why do indigenous peoples whose land claims arise from being synonymous with Time's claim to places find the need to invoke an international statute enacted in remote places like the UN headquarters in Geneva as recently as 2005 to make their claims sound 'reasonable'? Social movements sometimes argue that right claims are nothing more than conceptual vehicles that validate ethical and moral claims. The need for legal justifications to validate their land claims invite us to consider why ethical claims are articulated as legal claims in the first place. Further, are right claims strictly ethical claims with no ramifications for law and politics? Right claims as ethical justifications do not lead us to questions why the [UNDRIP] was adopted, who the actors driving the adoption were, and the timing of it coming as it did in the wake of sweeping neoliberal reforms of international order.

…

… Right claims as ethical and moral claims divert attention from the context, the actors and the mechanisms at work … . The powerful indigenous critique of individual property rights in nature ends up reifying the dualism of property and 'human' rights on which liberal rights are founded.

… [T]he rights discourse today is a cacophony of discordant voices. Each actor in coalitions to promote this or that right … has a different understanding of rights, of its history, its philosophical presuppositions, and above all expectations. Each actor canvassing for this or that right is located within a distinct type of institutional setting and carries a particular ideological orientation to rights. Arguments about rights in international coalitions and campaigns take the form of 'my version of rights is better than yours …' . This argument is analogous to the argument 'my god is better than yours', an argument that ultimately relies on faith, a belief that cannot lead a rational engagement about god, yours and mine. …

SYLVIA TAMALE, DECOLONIZATION AND AFRO-FEMINISM
(2020) 207

[The] regime of international human rights protections has indeed proved inadequate to liberate marginalized groups, let alone African women, from the multiple oppressions they suffer. Many commentators have highlighted the limitations of liberally-conceived human rights in securing gender-related liberties to women and sexual minorities. … Neither International NGOs … nor local NGOs are likely to deliver freedom beyond some limited survival. This is because their ideological orientation is largely based in Western liberal individualistic understandings of rights rather than in underscoring the critical vitality of group rights. All of them operate within the universalistic and essentialist norms that undergird the international human rights framework and the concept of gender, respectively. Inevitably, the decolonial project would reject the racism that underlies the ideas of universalism and essentialism.

JACK SNYDER, HUMAN RIGHTS FOR PRAGMATISTS: SOCIAL POWER IN MODERN TIMES [755]
(2022) 239

…

… A top priority on the global human rights agenda should be to lead the way in advocating for reform of the globalized forums of free speech to empower professional journalists and regulate monopoly tech platforms.

…

Finally, the human rights movement needs to be far more circumspect and consequentialist in choosing to intervene in the entrenched cultural practices of societies that are not yet liberal and modern. …

… To organize and mobilize a potent mass movement for the rights cause, three strategic adjustments offer promising avenues.

First, the power of religious zeal and networks should be tapped more assiduously. …

Second, human rights activism needs to focus much more on core rights values that speak to the interests of the majority groups in a society: to the majority ethnic, racial, and religious groups; to the broad middle class and dominant occupational groups; and to local civic leaders in mainstream communities. Instead of addressing mainly the powerless and downtrodden, activists need to emphasize issues in which everyone is in the same boat of exploitation by abusive elites and extractive factions. Emphasize inclusive civic rights such as equality before the law, due process, respect for the right to property and the fruits of one's labor, curtailment of monopoly power in markets and employers' coercion of labor, access to health care and pensions, and systematic checks on arbitrary abuse of official power in dealing with citizens. Activists are of course already in

---

[755] See also J. Snyder, 'Human Rights Pragmatism: Problems of Structure and Agency', 139 *Pol. Sci. Q.* (2024) 21.

favor of these things. What needs to be different is that activism that highlights discrimination against weak or stigmatized groups should always be framed as a message that links abuse of the minority to similar abuse of the majority. …

Third, to get a big, powerful coalition, activists need to mobilize around big, hot-button grievances that unite everybody. One such issue is corruption, which is a top-priority issue for human rights activism because it links to every other kind of human rights abuse: abuse of office, due process, discrimination, torture, atrocities, and every kind of economic, social, and cultural right. …

…

[T]he rhetoric of rights needs to avoid shaming, especially outsiders' explicit or even implicit shaming of widespread, entrenched cultural practices, which only plays into the hands of backlash against rights. Instead, rights persuasion will work better if the conversation is two-way, if vernacular normative ideas of the community are taken into account, and if local notables are fully engaged as intermediaries in packaging global and local concepts in a form that works in local politics. Nonetheless, activists need to find ways to vernacularize rights talk that does not proceed down the slippery slope toward "normalizing deviance": for example, torturing or lynching criminals to protect the "human rights" of the community; "persuading" refugees to agree to go back to an unsafe homeland by making their refuge even worse.

GRÁINNE DE BÚRCA, INTRODUCTION
REFRAMING HUMAN RIGHTS IN A TURBULENT ERA (2021) 1

… [A] growing array of populist and illiberal authoritarian leaders across the world, supported by the continued rise of the far-right …, have overtly contested, distorted, and dismissed the idea of human rights. Domestically they enact and encourage increasingly repressive policies and practices against vulnerable parts of their population and against human rights defenders as well as capturing and controlling independent institutions, and internationally they seek to undermine and weaken human rights institutions and processes. And while many human rights scholars have opted for a business-as-usual approach in the face of rising illiberalism, some of the loudest intellectual voices from both progressive and conservative quarters have expressed deep disenchantment with the human rights enterprise. Prominent scholars and public intellectuals have variously dismissed the language, ideals, practices, and achievements of human rights law and advocacy as flawed, inadequate, hegemonic, confining, overreaching, apolitical, peripheral, or pointless. Human rights approaches have been accused of being tools of Western imperialism, an elitist and bureaucratic legal paradigm, a limiting expert discourse which crowds out emancipatory political alternatives, which limits its ambitions and hides its own 'governmentality', an intellectually 'autistic' culture, an anti-politics, and a companion to neoliberalism.

Yet at the same time that scholars, particularly in the global north, have been outdoing one another with ever more scathing and dismissive critiques, human rights movements, protests, and practices have been abounding and spreading. There may be turbulence in the form of growing political repression and illiberalism, … but there has also been turbulence in recent years in the form of widespread social justice protests and grassroots mobilizations. … The discourse of human rights continues to be used by many progressive social, environmental, indigenous, labour, and other movements and campaigns for justice … .

What is it that explains these two opposite sets of developments? Is the apparently continued vitality of the human rights movement and the conviction of the many actors worldwide who invoke human rights in their quest for social, economic, environmental, and other forms of justice, little more than the remains of a movement approaching its final stages …? Or do the pessimistic and often scathing diagnoses of the human rights sceptics fail to give due credit to the drivers of human rights movements, to the conditions under which and the reasons why they continue to emerge, grow, and flourish?

[T]he human rights movement remains an inherently attractive and appealing one, due to the universally asserted values on which it is based, its continued vitality as one among various languages and tools for challenging injustice, and the adaptability and creative potential of human rights ideas, law, and advocacy to generate legitimacy and help to promote positive change and reform even under turbulent and rapidly changing national and global conditions. … [I]n contrast to accounts that present the human rights movement as elitist, apolitical, top-down, or bureaucratic, the experimentalist account of international human rights law and advocacy …

understands human rights instead as the product of ongoing interaction and contestation between an array of actors, institutions, and norms: between the claims and demands of people affected and concerned, the international norms and institutions which elaborate and monitor their implementation, and the domestic institutions and actors which reinforce and support those claims.

The potency and legitimacy of the human rights project rest on three main foundations. First, it is based on a deeply-rooted and attractive moral discourse that integrates at least three core values: human dignity, human welfare, and human freedom. Second, these values and their more detailed elaboration in various international legal instruments have gained widespread (even if thin and uneven) agreement among states worldwide. Third, the human rights project is a dynamic one which is activated, shaped, and given its meaning and impact through the ongoing mobilization of affected populations, groups, and individuals, and through their iterative engagement with an array of domestic and international institutions and processes over time.

CÉSAR RODRÍGUEZ-GARAVITO, HUMAN RIGHTS 2030: EXISTENTIAL CHALLENGES AND A NEW PARADIGM FOR THE HUMAN RIGHTS FIELD NEHAL BHUTA ET AL. (EDS.), THE STRUGGLE FOR HUMAN RIGHTS (2021) 328

… [W]hile human rights are not in a state of crisis, they are undergoing a moment of transition that raises systemic challenges for the movement. Some challenges come from outside the field, such as technological disruption, populist authoritarianism, the climate crisis, rising inequality, and the end of the Euro-American order. Some others are intrinsic to the architecture and the modus operandi of the traditional paradigm of human rights advocacy, such as strategic stagnation, fragmentation, and competition, insufficient long-term vision, unmanaged complexity, and narrow membership and audiences.

I have argued that, although those challenges create an existential risk for the movement—they are indeed the meteorite in the firmament—, they do not necessarily spell the end of the human rights project. To avoid the collision, however, business as usual will not do. The traditional paradigm of human rights is plainly inadequate to deal with the simultaneity, the speed, and the depth of those challenges.

In order to contribute to a new paradigm of human rights for the next decade, I proposed ways out of the current impasse that draw on lessons from other fields, from journalism to public health to human-centred design, as well as from disciplines that human rights actors have yet to incorporate into their toolkit, from social psychology to geology to social innovation. My aim has been to flesh out an intermediate approach between despair and defensiveness, one that vindicates the rich history and continued value of the human rights project, while searching for and experimenting with new ideas and initiatives capable of disrupting the field's dysfunctionalities and finding solutions to its urgent problems.

To that end, I have suggested that we view the human rights field as an ecosystem, rather than as a hierarchy. In an increasingly complex and interdependent world, human rights strategies need to be informed by biology as much as by law and politics. They need to be more focused on symbiosis and much less on policing the current boundaries of human rights.

I proposed three types of disruptive interventions that could build up a human rights ecosystem: a more collaborative mode of operation, greater sense of time (both long term and short term), and heightened attention to narratives, emotions, and frames capable of connecting with larger constituencies and other social justice movements.

Constructing a human rights ecosystem is easier said than done. For international NGOs, this implies a difficult challenge: transitioning from the vertical and highly autonomous modus operandi that has allowed them to make key contributions, to a more horizontal model that would allow them to work with networks of diverse actors. For domestic organizations, this entails pursuing strategies that allow such organizations to connect to one another and using new leverage points created by increased geopolitical multipolarity, as well as opening up to non-legal professionals, social movements, and online activists. For all actors in the field, this shift implies embracing an experimental approach based on a greater willingness to try new strategies, expand the repertoire of tactics, cultivate new organizational forms and funding models, and develop capabilities for and openness to learning and adjusting to rapidly changing circumstances.

Acknowledgements

Grateful acknowledge is made for the permissions extended by the following publishers and authors to reprint excerpts from the indicated publications. Particular thanks are due to Cambridge University Press and Oxford University Press for their support.

Abi-Saab, Georges, 'The Legal Formulation of A Right to Development', in: Colloques/Workshop Series, The Hague Academy of International Law, 1980.

American Constitution Society Supreme Court Review: Oona A. Hathaway, 'Nestlé USA, Inc. v. Doe and Cargill, Inc. v. Doe: The Twists and Turns of the Alien Tort Statute,' © 2021.

American Journal of International Law and Cambridge University Press: Laurence Helfer, 'Rethinking Derogations from Human Rights Treaties.' © 2021 American Journal of International Law; George Finch, 'Book Review: Sheldon Glueck, The Nuremberg Trial and Aggressive War.' © 1946 American Journal of International Law; Theodor Meron, 'On A Hierarchy of International Human Rights,' © 1986 American Journal of International Law; Beatrice A. Walton, 'Case Note: Nevsun Resources Ltd. v. Araya, Case No. 37919.' © 2021 American Journal of International Law; Benoit Mayer, 'Climate Change Mitigation as an Obligation Under Human Rights Treaties?', © 2021 American Journal of International Law.

American Law Institute: Restatement (Fourth), Foreign Relations Law of the United States section 402, © 2019.

American Political Science Review: Leslie Johns, Máximo Langer, and Margaret E. Peters, in 'Migration and the Demand for Transnational Justice.' © 2022.

American Society of International Law: Tom Ruys, 'Introductory Note to The European Union Global Human Rights Sanctions Regime (EUGHRSR),'International Legal Materials, © 2021.

Annenburg Public Policy Center, University of Pennsylvania: Claire Finkelstein and Harvey Rishikof, 'Beyond Guantánamo: Restoring The Rule of Law to the Law of War.' © 2022.

Bailey Ulbricht et al., 'Digital Eyewitnesses: Using New Technologies to Authenticate Evidence in Human Rights Litigation.' © 2022 Stanford Law Review.

Berlin Institute for Advanced Study and Humboldt University Berlin: Claire O'Brien & Daniel Schönfelder, 'A Defining Moment for the UN Business and Human Rights Treaty Process', from Verfassungsblog, © 2022.

Brill: Andrew Kulick 'Meta's Oversight Board and Beyond – Corporations as Interpreters and Adjudicators of International Human Rights.' from The Law & Practice of International Courts and Tribunals, © 2022 Brill | Nijhoff; Mohammed Bedjaoui, 'The Right to Development', in International Law: Achievements and Prospects, © 1991 Brill; Oscar Schachter, International Law in Theory and Practice, © 1991 Brill.

Business and Human Rights Journal: Nicola Jägers, 'UN Guiding Principles at 10: Permeating Narratives or Yet Another Silo?' © 2021 Business and Human Rights Journal.

Cambridge University Press: Austin Sarat, 'The Death Penalty on The Ballot: American Democracy and the Fate of Capital Punishment,' © 2019 Cambridge University Press; Aziza Ahmed, 'Bandung's Legacy: Solidarity and Contestation in Global Women's Rights', in 'Bandung, Global History, and International Law: Critical Pasts and Pending Futures,' edited by Luis Eslava, Michael Fakhri, and Vasuki Nesiah, © 2017 Cambridge University Press; Zachary Elkins and Tom Ginsburg, 'Imagining a World Without the Universal Declaration of Human Rights', from World Politics, © 2022 Cambridge University Press; Christopher N.J. Roberts, 'The Contentious History of the International Bill of Human Rights,' © 2014 Cambridge University Press; Evan Rosevear, Ran Hirschl and Courtney Jung, 'Justiciable and Aspirational Economic and Social Rights in The Future of Economic and Social Rights, edited by Katharine Young, © 2019 Cambridge University Press; David Landau and Rosalind Dixon, 'Constitutional Non-Transformation?', in The Future of Economic and Social Rights, edited by Katharine Young, © 2019 Cambridge University Press; Alex Cobham, Fariya Mohiuddin and Liz Nelson, 'Global Tax Justice and Human Rights', in Human Rights and Economic Inequalities, edited by Gillian MacNaughton and Diane Frey, © 2021 Cambridge University Press; Kim Lane Scheppele and Arianna Vedaschi, '9/11 and the Rise of Global Anti-Terrorism Law: How the UN Security Council Rules the World,' © 2021 Cambridge University Press; Marko Milanovic, 'The Lost Origins of Lex Specialis: Rethinking the Relationship between Human Rights and International Humanitarian Law', in Theoretical Boundaries of Armed Conflict and Human Rights, edited by Jens Ohlin, © 2016 Cambridge University Press; Anne Peters, Beyond Human Rights: The Legal Status of the Individual in International Law, © 2016 Cambridge University Press; Abdullahi Ahmed An-Na'im, Decolonizing Human Rights, © 2021 Cambridge University Press; Sally

Engle Merry and Peggy Levitt, 'The Vernacularization Of Women's Human Rights' in 'Human Rights Futures,' edited by Stephen Hopgood, Jack Snyder and Leslie Vinjamuri, © 2017 Cambridge University Press; Beth Simmons, Mobilizing for Human Rights: International Law in Domestic Politics, © 2009 Cambridge University Press; A. Getachew and J.Pitts, 'W.E.B. Du Bois: International Thought.' © 2022 Cambridge University Press; Carol Anderson, Eyes Off the Prize: The United Nations and the African American Struggle for Human Rights, 1944–1955, © 2003 Cambridge University Press; Jay Aronson, 'The Utility of User-Generated Content in Human Rights Investigations', in Molly Land and Jay Aronson (eds.) New Technologies for Human Rights law and Practice, © 2018 Cambridge University Press; Jonas Bens, The Sentimental Court: The Affective Life of International Criminal Justice, © 2022 Cambridge University Press; Leila N. Sadat, 'The International Criminal Law of the Future', in Is the International Legal Order Unraveling?, edited by David L. Sloss, © 2022 Cambridge University Press; Monika Nalepa, After Authoritarianism: Transitional Justice and Democratic Stability, © 2022 Cambridge University Press; Ruth Grant and Robert Keohane, 'Accountability and Abuses of Power in World Politics', from American Political Science Review, © 2005 Cambridge University Press; Andrew Byrnes and Gabrielle Simm, Peoples' Tribunals and International Law, ©2017 Cambridge University Press; Ella McPherson, 'Risk and the Pluralism of Digital Human Rights Fact-Finding and Advocacy', in Molly Land and Jay Aronson (eds.) New Technologies for Human Rights law and Practice, © 2018 Cambridge University Press; Gwynne Skinner, Transnational Corporations and Human Rights: Overcoming Barriers to Judicial Remedy, © 2020 Cambridge University Press.

Columbia Law Review, Eric Posner and Adrian Vermeule, 'Reparations for Slavery and Other Historical Injustices,' © 2003.

Congressional Research Service: Michael A. Weber 'The Global Magnitsky Human Rights Accountability Act: Scope, Implementation, and Considerations for Congress Doc. No. R46981.

Constellations: Katarina Pistor, Statehood in the Digital Age, 27 Constellations (2020). By permission of John Wiley & Sons Limited.

Cornell Law Review: Oona A. Hathaway et al., 'Has the Alien Tort Statute Made a Difference?: A Historical, Empirical, and Normative Assessment.' Cornell Law Review, Vol. 107, © 2022 by the Cornell Law Review.

Cornell University Press: The Endtimes of Human Rights, by Stephen Hopgood. Copyright © 2013 Cornell University Press.

Danish Institute for Human Rights: C. O'Brien, R. Jørgensen and B. Hogan, Tech Giants and Human Rights: Investor Expectations. © 2021.

Duke University Press: The Marcus Garvey and Universal Negro Improvement Papers, vol. XII: Reprinted in The Caribbean Diaspora, ed. Robert A. Hill, pp. 32-48. Volume copyright 2014.

Edward Elgar Publishing Gary Clyde Hufbauer and Euijin Jung, in 'Economic sanctions in the twenty-first century', in Peter A.G. van Bergeijk (ed.), Research Handbook on Economic Sanctions, © 2021; Antoine Buyse and Verónica Gómez, 'Human Rights Organizations and Civil Society', in Kees Biekart and Alan Fowler (eds.), A Research Agenda for Civil Society. © Edward Elgar Publishing 2022; Yuval Shany, 'Can Strasbourg be Replicated at a Global Level? A View from Geneva', in Helmut Aust and Esra Demir-Gürsel (eds.), The European Court of Human Rights (2021). Permission of Edward Elgar Publishing Limited.

Emory International Law Review: Mohammad Fadel, 'Muslim Modernism, Islamic Law, and the Universality of Human Rights'.

European Constitutional Law Review: Roger Masterman, 'The United Kingdom's Human Rights Act as a Catalyst of Constitutional Migration: Patterns and Limitations of Rights Importation by Design,' © 2023.

European Foreign Affairs Review: Christina Eckes, 'EU Human Rights Sanctions Regime: Striving for Utopia Backed by Sovereign Power?', © 2021.

European Journal of International Law, and Oxford University Press: G. Neuman, 'Counter-Terrorist Operations and the Rule of Law.' © 2004 European Journal of International Law; W. Abresch, 'A Human Rights Law of Internal Armed Conflict: The European Court of Human Rights in Chechnya.' © 2005 European Journal of International Law; Fionnuala Ní Aoláin, 'Soft Law', Informal Lawmaking and 'New Institutions' in the Global Counter-Terrorism Architecture, Copyright © 2021 Fionnuala Ní Aoláin, 2021. Published by Oxford University Press on behalf of EJIL Ltd; Sejal Parmar, 'The Internationalisation of Black Lives Matter at the Human Rights Council,' EJIL: Talk!, © 2020 European Journal of International Law; Michael Becker and Sarah Nouwen, 'International Commissions of Inquiry: What Difference Do They Make? Taking an Empirical Approach,' © 2019

Global Policy: Excerpts from Robert Howse & Ruti Teitel, Beyond Compliance: Rethinking Why International Law Really Matters, (2010). By permission of John Wiley & Sons Limited.

Global Responsibility to Protect: Anastasia Prokhorova, 'The Special Adviser on the Responsibility to Protect: Performing Norm Leadership,' © 2022.

Harvard Human Rights Journal: Niku Jafarnia, 'The United Nations Security Council's Counterterrorism Resolutions and the Resulting Violations of the Refugee Convention and Broader International Law,' © 2022. S. Knuckey et al., 'Power in Human Rights Advocate and Rightsholder Relationships: Critiques, Reforms, and Challenges,' © 2020.

International & Comparative Law Quarterly: Sandesh Sivakumaran, 'The Influence of Teachings of Publicists on the Development of International Law,' © 2017 International & Comparative Law Quarterly.

International Journal of Constitutional Law: Joseph Weiler, 'State and Nation; Church, Mosque and Synagogue,' © 2010; Gráinne de Búrca, 'Poland and Hungary's EU Membership: On Not Confronting Authoritarian Governments,' © 2022 International Journal of Constitutional Law.

International Law Quarterly: Hans Kelsen, 'Will the Judgment in the Nuremberg Trial Constitute a Precedent in International Law?' ©1947, The International Law Quarterly.

International Peace Institute, Global Observatory: Ben Saul, 'The Legal Black Hole in United Nations Counterterrorism.' © 2021

Johns Hopkins University Press: Joseph R. Slaughter, 'Hijacking Human Rights: Neoliberalism, The New Historiography, and the End of the Third World,' from Human Rights Quarterly, © 2018 Johns Hopkins University Press; Human Rights Quarterly: Suzanne Egan, 'Transforming the UN Human Rights Treaty System: A Realistic Appraisal,' © 2020.

Journal of Contemporary Asia: Amy Doffegnies, and Tamas Wells, 'The Vernacularisation of Human Rights Discourse in Mynamar: Rejection, Hybridisation and Strategic Avoidance.' © 2022.

Journal of International Criminal Justice and Oxford University Press: Wolfgang Kaleck and Patrick Kroker, 'Syrian Torture Investigations in Germany and Beyond: Breathing New Life into Universal Jurisdiction in Europe?' © 2018.

Journal of Law and Religion: Benjamin Lawrence, 'Saffron Suffrage: Buddhist Monks And Constitutional Politics In Cambodia', © Benjamin Lawrence, 2022. Published by Cambridge University Press on behalf of the Center for the Study of Law and Religion at Emory University (CC BY 4.0)

Just Security: Tomaso Falchetta and Anna Oosterlinck, 'UN Counterterrorism and Technology: What Role for Human Rights in Security?; David Kaye, 'A Rejoinder to China's Response to UN Human Rights Experts,' © 2020; Leila Nadya Sadat, 'Why the ICC's Judgment in the al-Bashir Case Wasn't So Surprising.' © 2019; Roger Lu Phillips, 'A Drop in the Ocean: A Preliminary Assessment of the Koblenz Trial on Syrian Torture,' © 2021; Faiza Patel and Mary Pat Dwyer, 'So, What Does Facebook Take Down? The Secret List of 'Dangerous' Individuals and Organizations,' © 2023.

Justice in Conflict: Mark Kersten, Mark Kersten, 'Will Justice catch up with those responsible for Post-Election Violence in Kenya?', Justice in Conflict blog © 2022

Justiceinfo.net: Lena Bjurström, 'Sweden on the Frontline with Syria Cases,' © 2021.

Kanstantsin Dzehtsiaro and Vassilis P Tzevelekos, 'The Aggression Against Ukraine and the Effectiveness of Interstate Cases in Case of War.' © 2022 European Convention on Human Rights Law Review.

Law and Practice of International Courts and Tribunals: Alec Stone Sweet, Wayne Sandholtz, and Mads Andenas, 'The Failure to Destroy the Authority of the European Court of Human Rights: 2010–2018,' © 2022 The Law and Practice of International Courts and Tribunals, published by Brill.

Lieber Institute at West Point: Charles Garraway, 'Fact-Finding in Ukraine: Can Anything Be Learned From Yemen?', © 2022.

LPE Project, Yale Law School: Olúfẹ́mi O. Táíwò, 'Reconsidering Reparations', © 2023

Makerere Institute of Social Research: Mahmood Mamdani, 'Beyond Nuremberg: The Historical Significance of the Post-Apartheid Transition in South Africa,' © 2015.

Melbourne Journal of International Law: Douglas Guilfoyle, 'Lacking Conviction: Is the International Criminal Court Broken? An Organisational Failure Analysis', University of Melbourne, Melbourne Law School © 2019.

Melbourne University Law Review: Keiran Hardy and George Williams, 'Two Decades of Australian Counterterrorism Laws' 2022.

Michigan Journal of International Law: Cora True-Frost, 'Listening to Dissonance at the Intersections of International Human Rights Law', 2022,

N.P. Engel, M. Nowak, UN Covenant on Civil and Political Rights: ICCPR Commentary, © 2005.

Northwestern Journal of International Law: Clara Petch, 'What Remains of the Alien Tort Statute after Nestlé USA, Inc. v. Doe?', © 2022.

Open Society Justice Initiative: 'Restrictions on Muslim Women's Dress in the 27 EU Member States and the United Kingdom: Policy Report, © 2022.

Oxford Journal of Law and Religion: Malcolm Evans, 'State Neutrality and Religion in Europe: What's the Prospect?' © Oxford University Press, 2022; Mukesh Kumar and Garima Yadav, 'Anxieties of the Dominant: Legal, Social, and Religious in the Politics of Religious Conversion in India', (2022) 4 Copyright © Mukesh Kumar and Garima Yadav 2022. Published by Oxford University Press.

Oxford Journal of Legal Studies: Kai Möller, 'Male and Female Genital Cutting: Between the Best Interest of the Child and Genital Mutilation.' © 2020.

Oxford University Press: Erika George, Incorporating Rights: Strategies to Advance Corporate Accountability, © 2021 Oxford University Press; Andrew Clapham, 'Dilemmas Facing Commissions of Inquiry', in The Struggle for Human Rights, © Oxford University Press 2021; A. Pellet and D. Müller, 'Article 38' in Zimmermann and Tams (eds.), The Statute of the International Court of Justice: A Commentary, © 2019 Oxford University Press; Jeremy Waldron, 'Foreign Law and the Modern Ius Gentium', in Courts and Comparative Law, ed. M. Andenas and D. Fairgrieve, Oxford University Press, © 2015; Will Kymlicka, 'Minority Rights', in The Oxford Handbook of International Political Theory, edited by Brown and Eckersley, © 2018 Oxford University Press; Dominic McGoldrick, The Human Rights Committee. © 1991 Oxford University Press; Hugh Thirlway, The Sources of International Law, © 2019 Oxford University Press; José Alvarez, International Organizations as Law Makers,' © 2005 Oxford University Press; Antonio Cassese, Realizing Utopia: The Future of International Law, © 2012 Oxford University Press; L. Volpp, 'Feminist, Sexual, and Queer Citizenship,' in A. Shachar, et al (eds.), The Oxford Handbook of Citizenship, © 2017 Oxford University Press; Martha C. Nussbaum, 'Women's Progress and Women's Human Rights', in The Limits of Human Rights, edited by Bardo Fassbender and Knut Traisbach, © 2020 Oxford University Press; Hilary Charlesworth and Christine Chinkin, in 'Between the Margins and the Mainstream: The Case of Women's Rights,' From The Limits of Human Rights, edited by Bardo Fassbender and Knut Traisbach. © 2019 Oxford University Press; David Kretzmer and Yaël Ronen, 'The Occupation of Justice: The Supreme Court Of Israel And The Occupied Territories,' © 2021 Oxford University Press; Oren Gross, 'The Prohibition on Torture and the Limits of Law', in Sanford Levinson (ed.), Torture: A Collection, © 2004 Oxford University Press; Alan Dershowitz, 'Tortured Reasoning', in ibid.; Nehal Bhuta, 'Recovering Social Rights', in Human Rights in Transition, © 2023 Oxford University Press; Neha Jain, 'The Democratizing Force of International Law: Human Rights Adjudication by the Indian Supreme Court', in Comparative International Law, edited by A. Roberts et al., © 2018 Oxford University Press; Margaret Satterthwaite, 'The Rights to Water and Sanitation,' in The Oxford Handbook on Economic and Social Rights, edited by Malcolm Langford and Katharine Young, © 2023 Oxford University Press; Kent Roach, 'Remedies and Accountability for Economic and Social Rights', in The Oxford Handbook on Economic and Social Rights, edited by Malcolm Langford and Katharine Young, © 2023 Oxford University Press; Amartya Sen, 'Obligations and Economic and Social Rights', in The Oxford Handbook on Economic and Social Rights, edited by Malcolm Langford and Katharine Young, © 2023 Oxford University Press; Marco Duranti, The Conservative Human Rights Revolution: European Identity, Transnational Politics, and the Origins of the European Convention, © 2017 Oxford University Press; Wolfgang Streeck, 'A New Regime', in D. King and P. Le Galès (eds.), Reconfiguring European States in Crisis, © 2017 Oxford University Press; Ka Lok Yip, The Use of Force against Individuals in War under International Law, © 2022 Oxford University Press; David Sloss, The Death of Treaty Supremacy: An Invisible Constitutional Change, © 2016 Oxford University Press; Charles Beitz, The Idea of Human Rights, © 2009 Oxford University Press; Nigel Biggar, What's Wrong with Rights?, © 2020 Oxford University Press; Rachel Murray, The African Charter on Human and Peoples' Rights: A Commentary, © 2019 Oxford University Press; Henry Steiner, 'Some Characteristics of the Liberal Political Tradition,' from 'International Human Rights in Context,' edited by Henry Steiner and Philip Alston, © 1996 Clarendon Press; Dianne Otto, 'Feminist Approaches To International Law', in The Oxford Handbook of the Theory of International Law, edited by Anne Orford and Florian Hoffmann, © 2016 Oxford University Press; Fernando, Mayanthi (2013), 'Cultural Relativism.' Oxford Bibliographies in Anthropology. Editor in Chief, Lee D. Baker; Andrew Clapham in 'The United Nations and Human Rights: A Critical Appraisal,' edited by Frédéric Mégret and Philip Alston, © 2020 Oxford University Press; Ilia Siatitsa, Serious Violations of Human Rights: On the Emergence of a New Special Regime, © 2022 Oxford University Press; Dominic McGoldrick, The Human Rights Committee, © 1994 Oxford University Press; Torkel Opsahl, 'The Human Rights Committee', in Philip Alston (ed.), The United Nations and Human Rights. © 1992 Oxford University Press; Carsten Stahn, Legacies of the International Criminal Tribunal for the Former Yugoslavia. © 2020 Oxford Univeristy Press; Kirsten Campbell and Gorana Mlinarević, Gender and International Criminal Law; © Oxford University Press 2020; Margaret M. deGuzman,

'Punishing for Humanity', in Legacies of the International Criminal Tribunal for the Former Yugoslavia, © Oxford University Press 2020; Rachel López, 'Black Guilt, White Guilt at The International Criminal Court', in Matiangai Sirleaf (ed.), Race and National Security, © Oxford University Press 2023; Kevin Jon Heller et al, The Oxford Handbook of International Criminal Law. © Oxford University Press 2020; Sergey Vasiliev, 'The Crises and Critiques of International Criminal Justice', from The Oxford Handbook of International Criminal Law, © 2020 Oxford University Press; Jacqueline McAllister, 'The Peace versus Justice Debate Revisited', in Legacies of the International Criminal Tribunal for the Former Yugoslavia, © 2020 Oxford Univeristy Press; R. Ashby Wilson and V. Petrović, 'Transitional Justice Histories: Narrating Mass Atrocities', in The Oxford Handbook on Transitional Justice, © Oxford University Press 2023; J. Melvin and A. Pohlman, 'Crimes against Humanity in Indonesia (1965–1966)', in The Oxford Handbook of Atrocity Crimes, © Oxford University Press 2022; Juana Acosta-López and Cindy Espitia-Murcia 'The Transitional Justice Model in Colombia vis-à-vis the Inter-American Human Rights System', in Constitutionalism: New Insights, © Oxford University Press 2021; David Tolbert and Marcela Prieto Rudolphy, 'Transitional Justice in the 21st Century: History, Effectiveness, and Challenges', in The Oxford Handbook of Atrocity Crimes, © Oxford University Press 2022; Nehal Bhuta et al., 'Introduction', in ibid (eds.), The Struggle for Human Rights, © Oxford University Press 2021; Sally Engle Merry, 'The State of Human Rights Consciousness: Not Yet Endtimes', in The Struggle for Human Rights, © Oxford University Press 2021; César Rodríguez-Garavito, 'Human Rights 2030: Existential Challenges and a New Paradigm for the Human Rights Field', in The Struggle for Human Rights, © Oxford University Press 2021; Micah Farfour, 'The Role and Use of Satellite Imagery for Human Rights Investigations', in Digital Witness, Using Open Source Information for Human Rights Investigation, Documentation, and Accountability, edited by Sam Dubberley, Alexa Koenig, and Daragh Murray, © 2019 Oxford University Press; Mohamed El Hachimi and Rachid Touhtou, 'Civil Society, NGOs, and Human Rights in Africa' in The Oxford Handbook of Sociology of Africa, edited by R. Sooryamoorthy and Nene Ernest Khalema, © 2022 Oxford University Press; Beth Van Schaack, Imagining Justice For Syria, © 2020 Oxford University Press.

Pew Research Center: The Future of World Religions: Population Growth Projections, 2010-2050. © 2015.

Princeton University Press: Eric D. Weitz, A World Divided: The Global Struggle for Human Rights in the Age of Nation-States (2019). By permission of Princeton University Press.

Security Council Report: 'The UN Security Council and Climate Change: Tracking the Agenda after the 2021 Veto,' © 2022.

Steven Greer and Lewis Graham, 'Europe', in International Human Rights Law, edited by Daniel Moeckli, Sangeeta Shah, and Sandesh Sivakumaran. © 2022 Oxford University Press.

Taylor and Francis: Timothy Savage, Europe and Islam: Crescent Waxing, Cultures Clashing, 27 The Washington Quarterly No. 3 (2004) copyright © 2004 The Elliott School of International Affairs, reprinted by permission of Informa UK Limited, trading as Taylor & Francis Group, www.tandfonline.com on behalf of 2004 The Elliott School of International Affairs; Sindiso Mnisi and Aninka Claassens, Rural Women Redefining Land Rights in the Context of Living Customary Law, 25 S. Af. J. Hum. Rts. 9 (2009) copyright © 2009 South African Journal on Human Rights, reprinted by permission of Informa UK Limited, trading as Taylor & Francis Group, www.tandfonline.com on behalf of 2009 South African Journal on Human Rights; Roland Burke, Decolonization, Development, and Identity: The Evolution of the Anticolonial Human Rights Critique, 1948-1978, in J. Quataert and L. Wildenthal (eds.), The Routledge History of Human Rights © 2020. Reproduced by permission of Taylor & Francis Group; Frédéric Mégret, The Anthropocentrism of Human Rights, in Vincent Chapaux, Frédéric Mégret and Usha Natarajan (eds.), The Routledge Handbook of International Law and Anthropocentrism © 2023. Reproduced by permission of Taylor & Francis Group.

The International Journal of Press/Politics: Jenifer Whitten-Woodring et al., 'Poison If You Don't Know How to Use It: Facebook, Democracy, and Human Rights in Myanmar.' © 2020.

University of California Press: Harri Englund, Prisoners of Freedom: Human Rights and the African Poor (2006). By permission of University of California Press Books

Virginia Law Review: Francis Biddle, 'The Nurnberg Trial,' © 1947 Virginia Law Review.

Made in the USA
Monee, IL
07 January 2025

76235999R00367